THE WRITINGS OF HERMAN MELVILLE

The Northwestern-Newberry Edition

VOLUME ELEVEN

Published Poems

This volume edited by
ROBERT C. RYAN
HARRISON HAYFORD
ALMA MACDOUGALL REISING
G. THOMAS TANSELLE

Historical Note by
HERSHEL PARKER

Published Poems

Battle-Pieces

John Marr

Timoleon

HERMAN MELVILLE

NORTHWESTERN UNIVERSITY PRESS

and

THE NEWBERRY LIBRARY

Evanston and Chicago

2009

Northwestern University Press
www.nupress.northwestern.edu

PUBLICATION *of this edition of* THE WRITINGS OF HERMAN MELVILLE *has been made possible through the financial support of Northwestern University and its Research Committee and The Newberry Library. The research necessary to establish the text was initially undertaken under the Cooperative Research Program of the U.S. Office of Education. Other acknowledgments appear on pages 325–27. Northwestern University Press produced and published this edition and reserves all rights.*

Printed in the United States of America

10 9 8 7 6 5 4 3 2

ISBN 978-0-8101-2605-3 (cloth)
ISBN 978-0-8101-1112-7 (paper)

Library of Congress Cataloging-in-Publication data
are available from the Library of Congress.

Contents

Timoleon Etc.

FRUIT OF TRAVEL LONG AGO

UNCOLLECTED POEM

EDITORIAL APPENDIX

Battle-Pieces

and

Aspects of the War

THE BATTLE-PIECES

IN THIS VOLUME ARE DEDICATED

TO THE MEMORY OF THE

THREE HUNDRED THOUSAND

WHO IN THE WAR

FOR THE MAINTENANCE OF THE UNION

FELL DEVOTEDLY

UNDER THE FLAG OF THEIR FATHERS

WITH FEW EXCEPTIONS, the Pieces in this volume originated in an impulse imparted by the fall of Richmond. They were composed without reference to collective arrangement, but, being brought together in review, naturally fall into the order assumed.

The events and incidents of the conflict—making up a whole, in varied amplitude, corresponding with the geographical area covered by the war—from these but a few themes have been taken, such as for any cause chanced to imprint themselves upon the mind.

The aspects which the strife as a memory assumes are as manifold as are the moods of involuntary meditation—moods variable, and at times widely at variance. Yielding instinctively, one after another, to feelings not inspired from any one source exclusively, and unmindful, without purposing to be, of consistency, I seem, in most of these verses, to have but placed a harp in a window, and noted the contrasted airs which wayward winds have played upon the strings.

The Portent

(1859)

Hanging from the beam,
    Slowly swaying (such the law),
Gaunt the shadow on your green,
    Shenandoah!
The cut is on the crown   5
(Lo, John Brown),
And the stabs shall heal no more.

Hidden in the cap
    Is the anguish none can draw;
So your future veils its face,   10
    Shenandoah!
But the streaming beard is shown
(Weird John Brown),
The meteor of the war.

Misgivings

(1860)

WHEN ocean-clouds over inland hills
   Sweep storming in late autumn brown,
And horror the sodden valley fills,
   And the spire falls crashing in the town,
I muse upon my country's ills—   5
The tempest bursting from the waste of Time
On the world's fairest hope linked with man's foulest crime.

Nature's dark side is heeded now—
   (Ah! optimist-cheer disheartened flown)—
A child may read the moody brow   10
   Of yon black mountain lone.
With shouts the torrents down the gorges go,
   And storms are formed behind the storm we feel:
The hemlock shakes in the rafter, the oak in the driving keel.

The Conflict of Convictions[a]

(1860–1)

On starry heights
   A bugle wails the long recall;
Derision stirs the deep abyss,
   Heaven's ominous silence over all.
Return, return, O eager Hope,   5
   And face man's latter fall.
Events, they make the dreamers quail;
Satan's old age is strong and hale,
A disciplined captain, gray in skill,
And Raphael a white enthusiast still;   10
Dashed aims, whereat Christ's martyrs pale,
Shall Mammon's slaves fulfill?

        (Dismantle the fort,
        Cut down the fleet—
        Battle no more shall be!   15
        While the fields for fight in æons to come
        Congeal beneath the sea.)

The terrors of truth and dart of death
   To faith alike are vain;
Though comets, gone a thousand years,   20
     Return again,
Patient she stands—she can no more—
And waits, nor heeds she waxes hoar.

8

(At a stony gate,
A statue of stone, 25
Weed overgrown—
Long 'twill wait!)

But God his former mind retains,
    Confirms his old decree;
The generations are inured to pains, 30
    And strong Necessity
Surges, and heaps Time's strand with wrecks.
    The People spread like a weedy grass,
    The thing they will they bring to pass,
And prosper to the apoplex. 35
The rout it herds around the heart,
    The ghost is yielded in the gloom;
Kings wag their heads—Now save thyself
    Who wouldst rebuild the world in bloom.

(Tide-mark 40
And top of the ages' strife,
Verge where they called the world to come,
The last advance of life—
Ha ha, the rust on the Iron Dome!)

Nay, but revere the hid event; 45
    In the cloud a sword is girded on,
I mark a twinkling in the tent
    Of Michael the warrior one.
Senior wisdom suits not now,
The light is on the youthful brow. 50

(Ay, in caves the miner see:
His forehead bears a taper dim;
Darkness so he feebly braves
Which foldeth him!)

But He who rules is old—is old; 55
Ah! faith is warm, but heaven with age is cold.

(Ho ho, ho ho,
The cloistered doubt
Of olden times
Is blurted out!) 60

The Ancient of Days forever is young,
    Forever the scheme of Nature thrives;
I know a wind in purpose strong—
    It spins *against* the way it drives.
What if the gulfs their slimed foundations bare? 65
So deep must the stones be hurled
Whereon the throes of ages rear
The final empire and the happier world.

(The poor old Past,
The Future's slave, 70
She drudged through pain and crime
To bring about the blissful Prime,
Then—perished. There's a grave!)

    Power unanointed may come—
Dominion (unsought by the free) 75
    And the Iron Dome,
Stronger for stress and strain,
Fling her huge shadow athwart the main;
But the Founders' dream shall flee.
Age after age shall be 80
As age after age has been,
(From man's changeless heart their way they win);
And death be busy with all who strive—
Death, with silent negative.

YEA AND NAY— 85
EACH HATH HIS SAY;
BUT GOD HE KEEPS THE MIDDLE WAY.
NONE WAS BY
WHEN HE SPREAD THE SKY;
WISDOM IS VAIN, AND PROPHESY. 90

Apathy and Enthusiasm

(1860–1)

I

O THE clammy cold November,
  And the winter white and dead,
And the terror dumb with stupor,
  And the sky a sheet of lead;
And events that came resounding   5
  With the cry that *All was lost,*
Like the thunder-cracks of massy ice
  In intensity of frost—
Bursting one upon another
  Through the horror of the calm.   10
  The paralysis of arm
In the anguish of the heart;
And the hollowness and dearth.
  The appealings of the mother
  To brother and to brother   15
Not in hatred so to part—
And the fissure in the hearth
  Growing momently more wide.
Then the glances 'tween the Fates,
  And the doubt on every side,   20
And the patience under gloom
In the stoniness that waits
The finality of doom.

II

So the winter died despairing,
   And the weary weeks of Lent;   25
And the ice-bound rivers melted,
   And the tomb of Faith was rent.
O, the rising of the People
   Came with springing of the grass,
They rebounded from dejection   30
   After Easter came to pass.
And the young were all elation
   Hearing Sumter's cannon roar,
And they thought how tame the Nation
   In the age that went before.   35
And Michael seemed gigantical,
   The Arch-fiend but a dwarf;
And at the towers of Erebus
   Our striplings flung the scoff.
But the elders with foreboding   40
   Mourned the days forever o'er,
And recalled the forest proverb,
   The Iroquois' old saw:
Grief to every graybeard
   When young Indians lead the war.   45

The March into Virginia

Ending in the First Manassas

(July, 1861)

DID all the lets and bars appear
  To every just or larger end,
Whence should come the trust and cheer?
  Youth must its ignorant impulse lend—
Age finds place in the rear.   5
  All wars are boyish, and are fought by boys,
The champions and enthusiasts of the state:
  Turbid ardors and vain joys
    Not barrenly abate—
  Stimulants to the power mature,   10
    Preparatives of fate.

Who here forecasteth the event?
What heart but spurns at precedent
And warnings of the wise,
Contemned foreclosures of surprise?   15
The banners play, the bugles call,
The air is blue and prodigal.
  No berrying party, pleasure-wooed,
No picnic party in the May,
Ever went less loth than they   20
  Into that leafy neighborhood.
In Bacchic glee they file toward Fate,
Moloch's uninitiate;
Expectancy, and glad surmise
Of battle's unknown mysteries.   25

All they feel is this: 'tis glory,
A rapture sharp, though transitory,
Yet lasting in belaureled story.
So they gayly go to fight,
Chatting left and laughing right.   30

But some who this blithe mood present,
    As on in lightsome files they fare,
Shall die experienced ere three days are spent—
    Perish, enlightened by the vollied glare;
Or shame survive, and, like to adamant,   35
    Thy after shock, Manassas, share.

Lyon

Battle of Springfield, Missouri

(AUGUST, 1861)

SOME hearts there are of deeper sort,
    Prophetic, sad,
Which yet for cause are trebly clad;
    Known death they fly on:
This wizard-heart and heart-of-oak had Lyon.   5

"They are more than twenty thousand strong,
    We less than five,
Too few with such a host to strive."
    "Such counsel, fie on!
'Tis battle, or 'tis shame;" and firm stood Lyon.   10

"For help at need in vain we wait—
    Retreat or fight:
Retreat the foe would take for flight,
    And each proud scion
Feel more elate; the end must come," said Lyon.   15

By candlelight he wrote the will,
    And left his all
To Her for whom 'twas not enough to fall;
    Loud neighed Orion
Without the tent; drums beat; we marched with Lyon.   20

The night-tramp done, we spied the Vale
    With guard-fires lit;

Day broke, but trooping clouds made gloom of it:
    "A field to die on,"
Presaged in his unfaltering heart, brave Lyon.   25

We fought on the grass, we bled in the corn—
    Fate seemed malign;
His horse the Leader led along the line—
    Star-browed Orion;
Bitterly fearless, he rallied us there, brave Lyon.   30

There came a sound like the slitting of air
    By a swift sharp sword—
A rush of the sound; and the sleek chest broad
    Of black Orion
Heaved, and was fixed; the dead mane waved toward Lyon.   35

"General, you're hurt—this sleet of balls!"
    He seemed half spent;
With moody and bloody brow, he lowly bent:
    "The field to die on;
But not—not yet; the day is long," breathed Lyon.   40

For a time becharmed there fell a lull
    In the heart of the fight;
The tree-tops nod, the slain sleep light;
    Warm noon-winds sigh on,
And thoughts which he never spake had Lyon.   45

Texans and Indians trim for a charge:
    "Stand ready, men!
Let them come close, right up, and then
    After the lead, the iron;
Fire, and charge back!" So strength returned to Lyon.   50

The Iowa men who held the van,
    Half drilled, were new
To battle: "Some one lead us, then we'll do,"
    Said Corporal Tryon:
"Men! *I* will lead," and a light glared in Lyon.   55

On they came: they yelped, and fired;
    His spirit sped;
We leveled right in, and the half-breeds fled,
    Nor stayed the iron,
Nor captured the crimson corse of Lyon.   60

This seer foresaw his soldier-doom,
    Yet willed the fight.
He never turned; his only flight
    Was up to Zion,
Where prophets now and armies greet pale Lyon.   65

Ball's Bluff

A Reverie

(OCTOBER, 1861)

ONE noonday, at my window in the town,
   I saw a sight—saddest that eyes can see—
   Young soldiers marching lustily
       Unto the wars,
With fifes, and flags in mottoed pageantry;   5
    While all the porches, walks, and doors
Were rich with ladies cheering royally.

They moved like Juny morning on the wave,
   Their hearts were fresh as clover in its prime
   (It was the breezy summer time),   10
       Life throbbed so strong,
How should they dream that Death in a rosy clime
    Would come to thin their shining throng?
Youth feels immortal, like the gods sublime.

Weeks passed; and at my window, leaving bed,   15
   By night I mused, of easeful sleep bereft,
   On those brave boys (Ah War! thy theft);
       Some marching feet
Found pause at last by cliffs Potomac cleft;
    Wakeful I mused, while in the street   20
Far footfalls died away till none were left.

Dupont's Round Fight

(November, 1861)

In time and measure perfect moves
    All Art whose aim is sure;
Evolving rhyme and stars divine
    Have rules, and they endure.

Nor less the Fleet that warred for Right,   5
    And, warring so, prevailed,
In geometric beauty curved,
    And in an orbit sailed.

The rebel at Port Royal felt
    The Unity overawe,   10
And rued the spell. A type was here,
    And victory of Law.

The Stone Fleet[b]

An Old Sailor's Lament

(DECEMBER, 1861)

I HAVE a feeling for those ships,
    Each worn and ancient one,
With great bluff bows, and broad in the beam:
    Ay, it was unkindly done.
            But so they serve the Obsolete—   5
            Even so, Stone Fleet!

You'll say I'm doting; do but think
    I scudded round the Horn in one—
The Tenedos, a glorious
    Good old craft as ever run—   10
            Sunk (how all unmeet!)
            With the Old Stone Fleet.

An India ship of fame was she,
    Spices and shawls and fans she bore;
A whaler when her wrinkles came—   15
    Turned off! till, spent and poor,
            Her bones were sold (escheat)!
            Ah! Stone Fleet.

Four were erst patrician keels
    (Names attest what families be),   20
The Kensington, and Richmond too,
    Leonidas, and Lee:
            But now they have their seat
            With the Old Stone Fleet.

To scuttle them—a pirate deed—   25
   Sack them, and dismast;
They sunk so slow, they died so hard,
   But gurgling dropped at last.
         Their ghosts in gales repeat
         Woe's us, Stone Fleet!   30

And all for naught. The waters pass—
   Currents will have their way;
Nature is nobody's ally; 'tis well;
   The harbor is bettered—will stay.
         A failure, and complete,   35
         Was your Old Stone Fleet.

Donelson

(February, 1862)

The bitter cup
  Of that hard countermand
Which gave the Envoys up,
Still was wormwood in the mouth,
  And clouds involved the land, 5
When, pelted by sleet in the icy street,
  About the bulletin-board a band
Of eager, anxious people met,
And every wakeful heart was set
On latest news from West or South. 10
"No seeing here," cries one—"don't crowd"—
"You tall man, pray you, read aloud."

  Important.
        We learn that General Grant,
   Marching from Henry overland, 15
And joined by a force up the Cumberland sent
   (Some thirty thousand the command),
On Wednesday a good position won—
Began the siege of Donelson.

This stronghold crowns a river-bluff, 20
   A good broad mile of leveled top;
Inland the ground rolls off
   Deep-gorged, and rocky, and broken up—

23

A wilderness of trees and brush.
   The spaded summit shows the roods   25
Of fixed intrenchments in their hush;
   Breast-works and rifle-pits in woods
Perplex the base.—
                  The welcome weather
   Is clear and mild; 'tis much like May.   30
The ancient boughs that lace together
Along the stream, and hang far forth,
   Strange with green mistletoe, betray
A dreamy contrast to the North.

Our troops are full of spirits—say   35
   The siege won't prove a creeping one.
They purpose not the lingering stay
Of old beleaguerers; not that way;
   But, full of vim *from Western prairies won,*
   They'll make, ere long, a dash at Donelson.   40

Washed by the storm till the paper grew
Every shade of a streaky blue,
That bulletin stood. The next day brought
A second.

      LATER FROM THE FORT.   45
Grant's investment is complete —
   A semicircular one.
Both wings the Cumberland's margin meet,
Then, backward curving, clasp the rebel seat.
   On Wednesday this good work was done;   50
   But of the doers some lie prone.
Each wood, each hill, each glen was fought for;
The bold inclosing line we wrought for
Flamed with sharpshooters. Each cliff cost
A limb or life. But back we forced   55
Reserves and all; made good our hold;
And so we rest.

      Events unfold.
On Thursday added ground was won,

A long bold steep: we near the Den. 60
Later the foe came shouting down
    In sortie, which was quelled; and then
We stormed them on their left.
A chilly change in the afternoon;
The sky, late clear, is now bereft 65
Of sun. Last night the ground froze hard—
Rings to the enemy as they run
Within their works. A ramrod bites
The lip it meets. The cold incites
To swinging of arms with brisk rebound. 70
Smart blows 'gainst lusty chests resound.

Along the outer line we ward
    A crackle of skirmishing goes on.
Our lads creep round on hand and knee,
    They fight from behind each trunk and stone; 75
    And sometimes, flying for refuge, one
Finds 'tis an enemy shares the tree.
Some scores are maimed by boughs shot off
    In the glades by the Fort's big gun.
    We mourn the loss of Colonel Morrison, 80
    Killed while cheering his regiment on.
Their far sharpshooters try our stuff;
And ours return them puff for puff:
'Tis diamond-cutting-diamond work.
    Woe on the rebel cannoneer 85
Who shows his head. Our fellows lurk
    Like Indians that waylay the deer
By the wild salt-spring.—The sky is dun,
Foredooming the fall of Donelson.
Stern weather is all unwonted here. 90
    The people of the country own
We brought it. Yea, the earnest North
Has elementally issued forth
    To storm this Donelson.

FURTHER. 95
        A yelling rout
Of ragamuffins broke profuse

To-day from out the Fort.
　Sole uniform they wore, a sort
Of patch, or white badge (as you choose)　　　　　　100
　Upon the arm. But leading these,
Or mingling, were men of face
And bearing of patrician race,
Splendid in courage and gold lace—
　The officers. Before the breeze　　　　　　105
Made by their charge, down went our line;
But, rallying, charged back in force,
And broke the sally; yet with loss.
This on the left; upon the right
Meanwhile there was an answering fight;　　　　　　110
　Assailants and assailed reversed.
The charge too upward, and not down—
Up a steep ridge-side, toward its crown,
　A strong redoubt. But they who first
Gained the fort's base, and marked the trees　　　　　　115
Felled, heaped in horned perplexities,
　And shagged with brush; and swarming there
Fierce wasps whose sting was present death—
They faltered, drawing bated breath,
　And felt it was in vain to dare;　　　　　　120
Yet still, perforce, returned the ball,
Firing into the tangled wall
Till ordered to come down. They came;
But left some comrades in their fame,
Red on the ridge in icy wreath　　　　　　125
And hanging gardens of cold Death.
　But not quite unavenged these fell;
Our ranks once out of range, a blast
　Of shrapnel and quick shell
Burst on the rebel horde, still massed,　　　　　　130
　Scattering them pell-mell.
　　　(This fighting—judging what we read—
　　　Both charge and countercharge,
　　　Would seem but Thursday's told at large,
　　　Before in brief reported.—Ed.)　　　　　　135
Night closed in about the Den
　Murky and lowering. Ere long, chill rains.

A night not soon to be forgot,
   Reviving old rheumatic pains
And longings for a cot.   140
   No blankets, overcoats, or tents.
Coats thrown aside on the warm march here—
We looked not then for changeful cheer;
Tents, coats, and blankets too much care.
   No fires; a fire a mark presents;   145
   Near by, the trees show bullet-dents.
Rations were eaten cold and raw.
   The men well soaked, came snow; and more—
A midnight sally. Small sleeping done—
      But such is war;   150
No matter, we'll have Fort Donelson.

      "Ugh! ugh!
'Twill drag along—drag along,"
Growled a cross patriot in the throng,
His battered umbrella like an ambulance-cover   155
Riddled with bullet-holes, spattered all over.
"Hurrah for Grant!" cried a stripling shrill;
Three urchins joined him with a will,
And some of taller stature cheered.
Meantime a Copperhead passed; he sneered.   160
   "Win or lose," he pausing said,
"Caps fly the same; all boys, mere boys;
Any thing to make a noise.
   Like to see the list of the dead;
These *'craven Southerners'* hold out;   165
Ay, ay, they'll give you many a bout."
   "We'll beat in the end, sir,"
Firmly said one in staid rebuke,
A solid merchant, square and stout.
   "And do you think it? that way tend, sir?"   170
Asked the lean Copperhead, with a look
Of splenetic pity. "Yes, I do."
His yellow death's head the croaker shook:
"The country's ruined, that I know."
A shower of broken ice and snow,   175
   In lieu of words, confuted him;

They saw him hustled round the corner go,
　　And each by-stander said—Well suited him.

Next day another crowd was seen
In the dark weather's sleety spleen.   180
Bald-headed to the storm came out
A man, who, 'mid a joyous shout,
Silently posted this brief sheet:

　　Glorious Victory of the Fleet!

　　Friday's great event!   185

　　The enemy's water-batteries beat!

　　We silenced every gun!

　　The old Commodore's compliments sent
　　Plump into Donelson!

"Well, well, go on!" exclaimed the crowd   190
To him who thus much read aloud.
"That's all," he said. "What! nothing more?"
"Enough for a cheer, though—hip, hurrah!"
"But here's old Baldy come again"—
"More news!"—And now a different strain.   195

　　(Our own reporter a dispatch compiles,
　　　As best he may, from varied sources.)

　　Large re-enforcements have arrived—
　　　Munitions, men, and horses—
　　For Grant, and all debarked, with stores.   200

　　　The enemy's field-works extend six miles—
　　The gate still hid; so well contrived.

　　Yesterday stung us; frozen shores
　　　Snow-clad, and through the drear defiles

And over the desolate ridges blew   205
A Lapland wind.
                    The main affair
         Was a good two hours' steady fight
Between our gun-boats and the Fort.
         The Louisville's wheel was smashed outright.   210
A hundred-and-twenty-eight-pound ball
Came planet-like through a starboard port,
Killing three men, and wounding all
The rest of that gun's crew,
(The captain of the gun was cut in two);   215
Then splintering and ripping went—
Nothing could be its continent.
         In the narrow stream the Louisville,
Unhelmed, grew lawless; swung around,
         And would have thumped and drifted, till   220
All the fleet was driven aground,
But for the timely order to retire.

Some damage from our fire, 'tis thought,
Was done the water-batteries of the Fort.

Little else took place that day,   225
         Except the field artillery in line
Would now and then—for love, they say—
         Exchange a valentine.
The old sharpshooting going on.
Some plan afoot as yet unknown;   230
So Friday closed round Donelson.

LATER.
         Great suffering through the night—
A stinging one. Our heedless boys
         Were nipped like blossoms. Some dozen   235
         Hapless wounded men were frozen.
During day being struck down out of sight,
And help-cries drowned in roaring noise,
They were left just where the skirmish shifted—
Left in dense underbrush snow-drifted.   240

Some, seeking to crawl in crippled plight,
So stiffened—perished.
                  Yet in spite
Of pangs for these, no heart is lost.
Hungry, and clothing stiff with frost,   245
Our men declare a nearing sun
Shall see the fall of Donelson.
   And this they say, yet not disown
The dark redoubts round Donelson,
     And ice-glazed corpses, each a stone—   250
       A sacrifice to Donelson;
They swear it, and swerve not, gazing on
A flag, deemed black, flying from Donelson.
Some of the wounded in the wood
   Were cared for by the foe last night,   255
Though he could do them little needed good,
   Himself being all in shivering plight.
The rebel is wrong, but human yet;
He's got a heart, and thrusts a bayonet.
He gives us battle with wondrous will—   260
This bluff's a perverted Bunker Hill.

The stillness stealing through the throng
The silent thought and dismal fear revealed;
        They turned and went,
       Musing on right and wrong   265
       And mysteries dimly sealed—
Breasting the storm in daring discontent;
The storm, whose black flag showed in heaven,
As if to say no quarter there was given
       To wounded men in wood,   270
   Or true hearts yearning for the good—
All fatherless seemed the human soul.
But next day brought a bitterer bowl—
   On the bulletin-board this stood:

Saturday morning at 3 A.M.   275
   A stir within the Fort betrayed
That the rebels were getting under arms;

Some plot these early birds had laid.
But a lancing sleet cut him who stared
Into the storm. After some vague alarms,   280
Which left our lads unscared,
Out sallied the enemy at dim of dawn,
    With cavalry and artillery, and went
    In fury at our environment.
Under cover of shot and shell   285
    Three columns of infantry rolled on,
    Vomited out of Donelson—
Rolled down the slopes like rivers of hell,
    Surged at our line, and swelled and poured
Like breaking surf. But unsubmerged   290
    Our men stood up, except where roared
The enemy through one gap. We urged
Our all of manhood to the stress,
But still showed shattered in our desperateness.
        Back set the tide,   295
But soon afresh rolled in;
    And so it swayed from side to side—
Far batteries joining in the din,
Though sharing in another fray—
    Till all became an Indian fight,   300
Intricate, dusky, stretching far away,
Yet not without spontaneous plan
    However tangled showed the plight:
Duels all over 'tween man and man,
Duels on cliff-side, and down in ravine,   305
    Duels at long range, and bone to bone;
Duels every where flitting and half unseen.
    Only by courage good as their own,
And strength outlasting theirs,
    Did our boys at last drive the rebels off.   310
Yet they went not back to their distant lairs
    In strong-hold, but loud in scoff
Maintained themselves on conquered ground—
Uplands; built works, or stalked around.
Our right wing bore this onset. Noon   315
Brought calm to Donelson.

The reader ceased; the storm beat hard;
  'Twas day, but the office-gas was lit;
  Nature retained her sulking-fit,
    In her hand the shard.   320
Flitting faces took the hue
Of that washed bulletin-board in view,
And seemed to bear the public grief
As private, and uncertain of relief;
Yea, many an earnest heart was won,   325
  As broodingly he plodded on,
To find in himself some bitter thing,
Some hardness in his lot as harrowing
    As Donelson.

That night the board stood barren there,   330
  Oft eyed by wistful people passing,
  Who nothing saw but the rain-beads chasing
Each other down the wafered square,
As down some storm-beat grave-yard stone.
But next day showed—   335

MORE NEWS LAST NIGHT.

STORY OF SATURDAY AFTERNOON.

VICISSITUDES OF THE WAR.

  The damaged gun-boats can't wage fight
For days; so says the Commodore.   340
Thus no diversion can be had.
Under a sunless sky of lead
  Our grim-faced boys in blackened plight
Gaze toward the ground they held before,
And then on Grant. He marks their mood,   345
And hails it, and will turn the same to good.
Spite all that they have undergone,
Their desperate hearts are set upon
This winter fort, this stubborn fort,

This castle of the last resort,   350
    This Donelson.

1 P.M.
        An order given
   Requires withdrawal from the front
    Of regiments that bore the brunt   355
Of morning's fray. Their ranks all riven
Are being replaced by fresh, strong men.
Great vigilance in the foeman's Den;
He snuffs the stormers. Need it is
That for that fell assault of his,   360
That rout inflicted, and self-scorn—
Immoderate in noble natures, torn
By sense of being through slackness overborne—
The rebel be given a quick return:
The kindest face looks now half stern.   365
Balked of their prey in airs that freeze,
Some fierce ones glare like savages.
And yet, and yet, strange moments are—
Well—blood, and tears, and anguished War!
The morning's battle-ground is seen   370
   In lifted glades, like meadows rare;
    The blood-drops on the snow-crust there
Like clover in the white-weed show—
   Flushed fields of death, that call again—
    Call to our men, and not in vain,   375
For that way must the stormers go.

3 P.M.
        The work begins.
Light drifts of men thrown forward, fade
   In skirmish-line along the slope,   380
Where some dislodgments must be made
   Ere the stormer with the strong-hold cope.

Lew Wallace, moving to retake
The heights late lost—
        (Herewith a break.   385

Storms at the West derange the wires.
Doubtless, ere morning, we shall hear
The end; we look for news to cheer—
　　Let Hope fan all her fires.)

Next day in large bold hand was seen　　　　　　390
The closing bulletin:

VICTORY!
　　　　　Our troops have retrieved the day
By one grand surge along the line;
The spirit that urged them was divine.　　　　　395
　　The first works flooded, naught could stay
The stormers: on! still on!
Bayonets for Donelson!
Over the ground that morning lost
Rolled the blue billows, tempest-tossed,　　　　400
　　Following a hat on the point of a sword.
Spite shell and round-shot, grape and canister,
Up they climbed without rail or banister—
　　Up the steep hill-sides long and broad,
Driving the rebel deep within his works.　　　　405
'Tis nightfall; not an enemy lurks
　　In sight. The chafing men
　　　　Fret for more fight:
　　"To-night, to-night let us take the Den!"
But night is treacherous, Grant is wary;　　　　410
Of brave blood be a little chary.
Patience! the Fort is good as won;
To-morrow, and into Donelson.

LATER AND LAST.

　　　　　　THE FORT IS OURS.　　　　　　415

　A flag came out at early morn
Bringing surrender. From their towers
　　Floats out the banner late their scorn.
In Dover, hut and house are full

Of rebels dead or dying.   420
   The National flag is flying
From the crammed court-house pinnacle.
Great boat-loads of our wounded go
To-day to Nashville. The sleet-winds blow;
But all is right: the fight is won,   425
The winter-fight for Donelson.
      Hurrah!
The spell of old defeat is broke,
   The habit of victory begun;
Grant strikes the war's first sounding stroke   430
      At Donelson.

For lists of killed and wounded, see
The morrow's dispatch: to-day 'tis victory.

The man who read this to the crowd
   Shouted as the end he gained;   435
   And though the unflagging tempest rained,
      They answered him aloud.
And hand grasped hand, and glances met
In happy triumph; eyes grew wet.
O, to the punches brewed that night   440
Went little water. Windows bright
Beamed rosy on the sleet without,
And from the cross street came the frequent shout;
While some in prayer, as these in glee,
Blessed heaven for the winter-victory.   445
But others were who wakeful laid
   In midnight beds, and early rose,
   And, feverish in the foggy snows,
Snatched the damp paper—wife and maid.
   The death-list like a river flows   450
      Down the pale sheet,
And there the whelming waters meet.

   Ah God! may Time with happy haste
   Bring wail and triumph to a waste,

     And war be done;   455
The battle flag-staff fall athwart
The curs'd ravine, and wither; naught
     Be left of trench or gun;
The bastion, let it ebb away,
Washed with the river bed; and Day   460
     In vain seek Donelson.

The Cumberland

(March, 1862)

SOME names there are of telling sound,
　　Whose voweled syllables free
Are pledge that they shall ever live renowned;
　　　　Such seems to be
A Frigate's name (by present glory spanned)—　　　　　　5
　　The Cumberland.

　　　　　Sounding name as ere was sung,
　　　　　Flowing, rolling on the tongue—
　　　　　Cumberland! Cumberland!

She warred and sunk. There's no denying　　　　　　10
　　That she was ended—quelled;
And yet her flag above her fate is flying,
　　　　As when it swelled
Unswallowed by the swallowing sea: so grand—
　　The Cumberland.　　　　　　15

　　　　　Goodly name as ere was sung,
　　　　　Roundly rolling on the tongue—
　　　　　Cumberland! Cumberland!

What need to tell how she was fought—
　　The sinking flaming gun—　　　　　　20
The gunner leaping out the port—

Washed back, undone!
Her dead unconquerably manned
The Cumberland.

Noble name as ere was sung,   25
Slowly roll it on the tongue—
Cumberland! Cumberland!

Long as hearts shall share the flame
　Which burned in that brave crew,
Her fame shall live—outlive the victor's name;   30
　For this is due.
Your flag and flag-staff shall in story stand—
　Cumberland!

Sounding name as ere was sung,
Long they'll roll it on the tongue—   35
Cumberland! Cumberland!

In the Turret

(MARCH, 1862)

YOUR honest heart of duty, Worden,
   So helped you that in fame you dwell;
You bore the first iron battle's burden
   Sealed as in a diving-bell.
Alcides, groping into haunted hell   5
To bring forth King Admetus' bride,
Braved naught more vaguely direful and untried.
   What poet shall uplift his charm,
Bold Sailor, to your height of daring,
   And interblend therewith the calm,   10
And build a goodly style upon your bearing.

Escaped the gale of outer ocean—
   Cribbed in a craft which like a log
Was washed by every billow's motion—
   By night you heard of Og   15
The huge; nor felt your courage clog
At tokens of his onset grim:
You marked the sunk ship's flag-staff slim,
   Lit by her burning sister's heart;
You marked, and mused: "Day brings the trial: 20
   Then be it proved if I have part
With men whose manhood never took denial."

A prayer went up—a champion's. Morning
   Beheld you in the Turret walled
By adamant, where a spirit forewarning   25

And all-deriding called:
"Man, darest thou—desperate, unappalled—
Be first to lock thee in the armored tower?
I have thee now; and what the battle-hour
    To me shall bring—heed well—thou'lt share;   30
This plot-work, planned to be the foeman's terror,
    To thee may prove a goblin-snare;
Its very strength and cunning—monstrous error!"

"Stand up, my heart; be strong; what matter
    If here thou seest thy welded tomb?   35
And let huge Og with thunders batter—
    Duty be still my doom,
Though drowning come in liquid gloom;
First duty, duty next, and duty last;
Ay, Turret, rivet me here to duty fast!"—   40
    So nerved, you fought, wisely and well;
And live, twice live in life and story;
    But over your Monitor dirges swell,
In wind and wave that keep the rites of glory.

The Temeraire^c

*(Supposed to have been suggested to an Englishman of the
old order by the fight of the Monitor and Merrimac)*

THE gloomy hulls, in armor grim,
   Like clouds o'er moors have met,
And prove that oak, and iron, and man
   Are tough in fibre yet.

But Splendors wane. The sea-fight yields   5
   No front of old display;
The garniture, emblazonment,
   And heraldry all decay.

Towering afar in parting light,
   The fleets like Albion's forelands shine—   10
The full-sailed fleets, the shrouded show
   Of Ships-of-the-Line.

     The fighting Temeraire,
       Built of a thousand trees,
     Lunging out her lightnings,   15
       And beetling o'er the seas—
     O Ship, how brave and fair,
       That fought so oft and well,
     On open decks you manned the gun
       Armorial.^d   20
     What cheerings did you share,
       Impulsive in the van,
     When down upon leagued France and Spain

41

We English ran—
The freshet at your bowsprit   25
   Like the foam upon the can.
Bickering, your colors
   Licked up the Spanish air,
You flapped with flames of battle-flags—
   Your challenge, Temeraire!   30
The rear ones of our fleet
   They yearned to share your place,
Still vying with the Victory
   Throughout that earnest race—
The Victory, whose Admiral,   35
   With orders nobly won,
Shone in the globe of the battle glow—
   The angel in that sun.
Parallel in story,
   Lo, the stately pair,   40
As late in grapple ranging,
   The foe between them there—
When four great hulls lay tiered,
And the fiery tempest cleared,
And your prizes twain appeared,   45
     Temeraire!

But Trafalgar´ is over now,
   The quarter-deck undone;
The carved and castled navies fire
   Their evening-gun.   50
O, Titan Temeraire,
   Your stern-lights fade away;
Your bulwarks to the years must yield,
   And heart-of-oak decay.
A pigmy steam-tug tows you,   55
   Gigantic, to the shore—
Dismantled of your guns and spars,
   And sweeping wings of war.
The rivets clinch the iron-clads,
   Men learn a deadlier lore;   60

But Fame has nailed your battle-flags—
  Your ghost it sails before:
O, the navies old and oaken,
  O, the Temeraire no more!

A Utilitarian View
of the Monitor's Fight

PLAIN be the phrase, yet apt the verse,
   More ponderous than nimble;
For since grimed War here laid aside
His Orient pomp, 'twould ill befit
     Overmuch to ply   5
   The rhyme's barbaric cymbal.

Hail to victory without the gaud
   Of glory; zeal that needs no fans
Of banners; plain mechanic power
Plied cogently in War now placed—   10
     Where War belongs—
   Among the trades and artisans.

Yet this was battle, and intense—
   Beyond the strife of fleets heroic;
Deadlier, closer, calm 'mid storm;   15
No passion; all went on by crank,
     Pivot, and screw,
   And calculations of caloric.

Needless to dwell; the story's known.
   The ringing of those plates on plates   20
Still ringeth round the world—
The clangor of that blacksmiths' fray.
     The anvil-din
   Resounds this message from the Fates:

War yet shall be, and to the end;   25
   But war-paint shows the streaks of weather;
War yet shall be, but warriors
Are now but operatives; War's made
     Less grand than Peace,
   And a singe runs through lace and feather.   30

Shiloh

A Requiem

(APRIL, 1862)

SKIMMING lightly, wheeling still,
    The swallows fly low
Over the field in clouded days,
    The forest-field of Shiloh—
Over the field where April rain   5
Solaced the parched ones stretched in pain
Through the pause of night
That followed the Sunday fight
    Around the church of Shiloh—
The church so lone, the log-built one,   10
That echoed to many a parting groan
        And natural prayer
    Of dying foemen mingled there—
Foemen at morn, but friends at eve—
    Fame or country least their care: 15
(What like a bullet can undeceive!)
    But now they lie low,
While over them the swallows skim,
    And all is hushed at Shiloh.

The Battle for the Mississippi

(APRIL, 1862)

WHEN Israel camped by Migdol hoar,
    Down at her feet her shawm she threw,
But Moses sung and timbrels rung
    For Pharaoh's stranded crew.
So God appears in apt events—   5
    The Lord is a man of war!
So the strong wing to the muse is given
          In victory's roar.

Deep be the ode that hymns the fleet—
    The fight by night—the fray   10
Which bore our Flag against the powerful stream,
    And led it up to day.
Dully through din of larger strife
    Shall bay that warring gun;
But none the less to us who live   15
    It peals—an echoing one.

The shock of ships, the jar of walls,
    The rush through thick and thin—
The flaring fire-rafts, glare and gloom—
    Eddies, and shells that spin—   20
The boom-chain burst, the hulks dislodged,
    The jam of gun-boats driven,
Or fired, or sunk—made up a war
    Like Michael's waged with leven.

The manned Varuna stemmed and quelled   25
    The odds which hard beset;
The oaken flag-ship, half ablaze,
    Passed on and thundered yet;
While foundering, gloomed in grimy flame,
    The Ram Manassas—hark the yell!—   30
Plunged, and was gone; in joy or fright,
    The River gave a startled swell.

They fought through lurid dark till dawn;
    The war-smoke rolled away
With clouds of night, and showed the fleet   35
    In scarred yet firm array,
Above the forts, above the drift
    Of wrecks which strife had made;
And Farragut sailed up to the town
    And anchored—sheathed the blade.   40

The moody broadsides, brooding deep,
    Hold the lewd mob at bay,
While o'er the armed decks' solemn aisles
    The meek church-pennons play;
By shotted guns the sailors stand,   45
    With foreheads bound or bare;
The captains and the conquering crews
    Humble their pride in prayer.

They pray; and after victory, prayer
    Is meet for men who mourn their slain;   50
The living shall unmoor and sail,
    But Death's dark anchor secret deeps detain.
Yet Glory slants her shaft of rays
    Far through the undisturbed abyss;
There must be other, nobler worlds for them   55
    Who nobly yield their lives in this.

Malvern Hill

(July, 1862)

Ye elms that wave on Malvern Hill
  In prime of morn and May,
Recall ye how McClellan's men
    Here stood at bay?
While deep within yon forest dim   5
  Our rigid comrades lay—
Some with the cartridge in their mouth,
Others with fixed arms lifted South—
    Invoking so
The cypress glades? Ah wilds of woe!   10

The spires of Richmond, late beheld
  Through rifts in musket-haze,
Were closed from view in clouds of dust
    On leaf-walled ways,
Where streamed our wagons in caravan;   15
  And the Seven Nights and Days
Of march and fast, retreat and fight,
Pinched our grimed faces to ghastly plight—
    Does the elm wood
Recall the haggard beards of blood?   20

The battle-smoked flag, with stars eclipsed,
    We followed (it never fell!)—
In silence husbanded our strength—
    Received their yell;
Till on this slope we patient turned   25
    With cannon ordered well;
Reverse we proved was not defeat;
But ah, the sod what thousands meet!—
    Does Malvern Wood
Bethink itself, and muse and brood?   30

        We elms of Malvern Hill
            Remember every thing;
        But sap the twig will fill:
        Wag the world how it will,
            Leaves must be green in Spring.   35

The Victor of Antietam^e

(1862)

WHEN tempest winnowed grain from bran,
And men were looking for a man,
Authority called you to the van,
      McClellan:
Along the line the plaudit ran,   5
As later when Antietam's cheers began.

Through storm-cloud and eclipse must move
Each Cause and Man, dear to the stars and Jove;
Nor always can the wisest tell
Deferred fulfillment from the hopeless knell—   10
The struggler from the floundering ne'er-do-well.
A pall-cloth on the Seven Days fell,
      McClellan—
Unprosperously heroical!
Who could Antietam's wreath foretell?   15

Authority called you; then, in mist
And loom of jeopardy—dismissed.
But staring peril soon appalled;
You, the Discarded, she recalled—
Recalled you, nor endured delay;   20
And forth you rode upon a blasted way,
Arrayed Pope's rout, and routed Lee's array,
      McClellan:

Your tent was choked with captured flags that day,
            McClellan.   25
Antietam was a telling fray.

Recalled you; and she heard your drum
Advancing through the ghastly gloom.
You manned the wall, you propped the Dome,
You stormed the powerful stormer home,   30
            McClellan:
Antietam's cannon long shall boom.

At Alexandria, left alone,
            McClellan—
Your veterans sent from you, and thrown   35
To fields and fortunes all unknown—
What thoughts were yours, revealed to none,
While faithful still you labored on—
Hearing the far Manassas gun!
            McClellan,   40
Only Antietam could atone.

You fought in the front (an evil day,
            McClellan)—
The fore-front of the first assay;
The Cause went sounding, groped its way;   45
The leadsmen quarrelled in the bay;
Quills thwarted swords; divided sway;
The rebel flushed in his lusty May:
You did your best, as in you lay,
            McClellan.   50
Antietam's sun-burst sheds a ray.

Your medalled soldiers love you well,
            McClellan:
Name your name, their true hearts swell;
With you they shook dread Stonewall's spell,[f]   55
With you they braved the blended yell
Of rebel and maligner fell;
With you in shame or fame they dwell,

McClellan:
Antietam-braves a brave can tell.   60

And when your comrades (now so few,
                McClellan—
Such ravage in deep files they rue)
Meet round the board, and sadly view
The empty places; tribute due   65
They render to the dead—and you!
Absent and silent o'er the blue;
The one-armed lift the wine to *you,*
                McClellan,
And great Antietam's cheers renew.   70

Battle of Stone River, Tennessee

A View from Oxford Cloisters

(January, 1863)

WITH Tewksbury and Barnet heath
   In days to come the field shall blend,
The story dim and date obscure;
   In legend all shall end.
Even now, involved in forest shade   5
   A Druid-dream the strife appears,
The fray of yesterday assumes
   The haziness of years.
        In North and South still beats the vein
        Of Yorkist and Lancastrian.   10

Our rival Roses warred for Sway—
   For Sway, but named the name of Right;
And Passion, scorning pain and death,
   Lent sacred fervor to the fight.
Each lifted up a broidered cross,   15
   While crossing blades profaned the sign;
Monks blessed the fratricidal lance,
   And sisters scarfs could twine.
        Do North and South the sin retain
        Of Yorkist and Lancastrian?   20

But Rosecrans in the cedarn glade,
   And, deep in denser cypress gloom,
Dark Breckinridge, shall fade away
    Or thinly loom.
The pale throngs who in forest cowed   25

54

Before the spell of battle's pause,
Forefelt the stillness that shall dwell
  On them and on their wars.
     North and South shall join the train
     Of Yorkist and Lancastrian.   30

But where the sword has plunged so deep,
  And then been turned within the wound
By deadly Hate; where Climes contend
    On vasty ground—
No warning Alps or seas between,   35
  And small the curb of creed or law,
And blood is quick, and quick the brain;
    Shall North and South their rage deplore,
     And reunited thrive amain
     Like Yorkist and Lancastrian?   40

Running the Batteries

As observed from the Anchorage above Vicksburgh

(APRIL, 1863)

A MOONLESS night—a friendly one;
   A haze dimmed the shadowy shore
As the first lampless boat slid silent on;
   Hist! and we spake no more;
We but pointed, and stilly, to what we saw.   5

We felt the dew, and seemed to feel
   The secret like a burden laid.
The first boat melts; and a second keel
   Is blent with the foliaged shade—
Their midnight rounds have the rebel officers made?   10

Unspied as yet. A third—a fourth—
   Gun-boat and transport in Indian file
Upon the war-path, smooth from the North;
   But the watch may they hope to beguile?
The manned river-batteries stretch for mile on mile.   15

A flame leaps out; they are seen;
   Another and another gun roars;
We tell the course of the boats through the screen
   By each further fort that pours,
And we guess how they jump from their beds on those
      shrouded shores.   20

Converging fires. We speak, though low:
   "That blastful furnace can they thread?"

"Why, Shadrach, Meshach, and Abed-nego
   Came out all right, we read;
The Lord, be sure, he helps his people, Ned."   25

How we strain our gaze. On bluffs they shun
   A golden growing flame appears—
Confirms to a silvery steadfast one:
   "The town is afire!" crows Hugh: "three cheers!"
Lot stops his mouth: "Nay, lad, better three tears."   30

A purposed light; it shows our fleet;
   Yet a little late in its searching ray,
So far and strong, that in phantom cheat
   Lank on the deck our shadows lay;
The shining flag-ship stings their guns to furious play.   35

How dread to mark her near the glare
   And glade of death the beacon throws
Athwart the racing waters there;
   One by one each plainer grows,
Then speeds a blazoned target to our gladdened foes.   40

The impartial cresset lights as well
   The fixed forts to the boats that run;
And, plunged from the ports, their answers swell
   Back to each fortress dun:
Ponderous words speaks every monster gun.   45

Fearless they flash through gates of flame,
   The salamanders hard to hit,
Though vivid shows each bulky frame;
   And never the batteries intermit,
Nor the boats' huge guns; they fire and flit.   50

Anon a lull. The beacon dies:
   "Are they out of that strait accurst?"
But other flames now dawning rise,
   Not mellowly brilliant like the first,
But rolled in smoke, whose whitish volumes burst.   55

A baleful brand, a hurrying torch
   Whereby anew the boats are seen—
A burning transport all alurch!
   Breathless we gaze; yet still we glean
Glimpses of beauty as we eager lean.   60

The effulgence takes an amber glow
   Which bathes the hill-side villas far;
Affrighted ladies mark the show
   Painting the pale magnolia—
The fair, false, Circe light of cruel War.   65

The barge drifts doomed, a plague-struck one.
   Shoreward in yawls the sailors fly.
But the gauntlet now is nearly run,
   The spleenful forts by fits reply,
And the burning boat dies down in morning's sky.   70

All out of range. Adieu, Messieurs!
   Jeers, as it speeds, our parting gun.
So burst we through their barriers
   And menaces every one:
So Porter proves himself a brave man's son.[g]   75

Stonewall Jackson

Mortally wounded at Chancellorsville

(May, 1863)

THE Man who fiercest charged in fight,
  Whose sword and prayer were long—
        Stonewall!
  Even him who stoutly stood for Wrong,
How can we praise? Yet coming days   5
  Shall not forget him with this song.

Dead is the Man whose Cause is dead,
  Vainly he died and set his seal—
        Stonewall!
  Earnest in error, as we feel;   10
True to the thing he deemed was due,
  True as John Brown or steel.

Relentlessly he routed us;
  But *we* relent, for he is low—
        Stonewall!   15
  Justly his fame we outlaw; so
We drop a tear on the bold Virginian's bier,
  Because no wreath we owe.

Stonewall Jackson

(Ascribed to a Virginian)

ONE man we claim of wrought renown
  Which not the North shall care to slur;
A Modern lived who sleeps in death,
  Calm as the marble Ancients are:
     'Tis he whose life, though a vapor's wreath,   5
     Was charged with the lightning's burning breath—
     Stonewall, stormer of the war.

But who shall hymn the Roman heart?
  A stoic he, but even more;
The iron will and lion thew   10
  Were strong to inflict as to endure:
     Who like him could stand, or pursue?
     His fate the fatalist followed through;
     In all his great soul found to do
     Stonewall followed his star.   15

He followed his star on the Romney march
  Through the sleet to the wintry war;
And he followed it on when he bowed the grain—
  The Wind of the Shenandoah;
     At Gaines's Mill in the giants' strain—   20
     On the fierce forced stride to Manassas-plain,
     Where his sword with thunder was clothed again,
     Stonewall followed his star.

His star he followed athwart the flood
   To Potomac's Northern shore,   25
When midway wading, his host of braves
   "My Maryland!" loud did roar—
      To red Antietam's field of graves,
      Through mountain-passes, woods and waves,
      They followed their pagod with hymns and glaives,   30
      For Stonewall followed a star.

Back it led him to Marye's slope,
   Where the shock and the fame he bore;
And to green Moss-Neck it guided him—
   Brief respite from throes of war: 35
      To the laurel glade by the Wilderness grim,
      Through climaxed victory naught shall dim,
      Even unto death it piloted him—
      Stonewall followed his star.

Its lead he followed in gentle ways   40
   Which never the valiant mar;
A cap we sent him, bestarred, to replace
   The sun-scorched helm of war:
      A fillet he made of the shining lace
      Childhood's laughing brow to grace—   45
      Not his was a goldsmith's star.

O, much of doubt in after days
   Shall cling, as now, to the war;
Of the right and the wrong they'll still debate,
   Puzzled by Stonewall's star: 50
      "Fortune went with the North elate,"
      "Ay, but the South had Stonewall's weight,
      And he fell in the South's great war."

Gettysburg

The Check

(JULY, 1863)

O PRIDE of the days in prime of the months
   Now trebled in great renown,
When before the ark of our holy cause
     Fell Dagon down—
Dagon foredoomed, who, armed and targed,   5
Never his impious heart enlarged
Beyond that hour; God walled his power,
And there the last invader charged.

He charged, and in that charge condensed
   His all of hate and all of fire;   10
He sought to blast us in his scorn,
     And wither us in his ire.
Before him went the shriek of shells—
Aerial screamings, taunts and yells;
Then the three waves in flashed advance   15
   Surged, but were met, and back they set:
Pride was repelled by sterner pride,
   And Right is a strong-hold yet.

Before our lines it seemed a beach
   Which wild September gales have strown   20
With havoc on wreck, and dashed therewith
     Pale crews unknown—

Men, arms, and steeds. The evening sun
Died on the face of each lifeless one,
And died along the winding marge of fight   25
    And searching-parties lone.

Sloped on the hill the mounds were green,
    Our centre held that place of graves,
And some still hold it in their swoon,
    And over these a glory waves.   30
The warrior-monument, crashed in fight,[h]
Shall soar transfigured in loftier light,
    A meaning ampler bear;
Soldier and priest with hymn and prayer
Have laid the stone, and every bone   35
    Shall rest in honor there.

The House-top

A Night Piece

(JULY, 1863)

No sleep. The sultriness pervades the air
And binds the brain—a dense oppression, such
As tawny tigers feel in matted shades,
Vexing their blood and making apt for ravage.
Beneath the stars the roofy desert spreads   5
Vacant as Libya. All is hushed near by.
Yet fitfully from far breaks a mixed surf
Of muffled sound, the Atheist roar of riot.
Yonder, where parching Sirius set in drought,
Balefully glares red Arson—there—and there.   10
The Town is taken by its rats—ship-rats
And rats of the wharves. All civil charms
And priestly spells which late held hearts in awe—
Fear-bound, subjected to a better sway
Than sway of self; these like a dream dissolve,   15
And man rebounds whole æons back in nature.[i]
Hail to the low dull rumble, dull and dead,
And ponderous drag that shakes the wall.
Wise Draco comes, deep in the midnight roll
Of black artillery; he comes, though late;   20
In code corroborating Calvin's creed
And cynic tyrannies of honest kings;
He comes, nor parlies; and the Town, redeemed,
Gives thanks devout; nor, being thankful, heeds
The grimy slur on the Republic's faith implied,   25
Which holds that Man is naturally good,
And—more—is Nature's Roman, never to be scourged.

Look-out Mountain

The Night Fight

(NOVEMBER, 1863)

WHO inhabiteth the Mountain
   That it shines in lurid light,
And is rolled about with thunders,
   And terrors, and a blight,
Like Kaf the peak of Eblis—   5
   Kaf, the evil height?
Who has gone up with a shouting
   And a trumpet in the night?

There is battle in the Mountain—
   Might assaulteth Might;   10
'Tis the fastness of the Anarch,
   Torrent-torn, an ancient height;
The crags resound the clangor
   Of the war of Wrong and Right;
And the armies in the valley   15
   Watch and pray for dawning light.

Joy, joy, the day is breaking,
   And the cloud is rolled from sight;
There is triumph in the Morning
   For the Anarch's plunging flight;   20
God has glorified the Mountain
   Where a Banner burneth bright,
And the armies in the valley
   They are fortified in right.

Chattanooga

(NOVEMBER, 1863)

A KINDLING impulse seized the host
   Inspired by heaven's elastic air;^j
Their hearts outran their General's plan,
   Though Grant commanded there—
   Grant, who without reserve can dare;   5
And, "Well, go on and do your will,"
   He said, and measured the mountain then:
So master-riders fling the rein—
   But you must know your men.

On yester-morn in grayish mist,   10
   Armies like ghosts on hills had fought,
And rolled from the cloud their thunders loud
   The Cumberlands far had caught:
   To-day the sunlit steeps are sought.
Grant stood on cliffs whence all was plain,   15
   And smoked as one who feels no cares;
But mastered nervousness intense
   Alone such calmness wears.

The summit-cannon plunge their flame
   Sheer down the primal wall,   20
But up and up each linking troop
   In stretching festoons crawl—
   Nor fire a shot. Such men appall
The foe, though brave. He, from the brink,

Looks far along the breadth of slope,   25
And sees two miles of dark dots creep,
    And knows they mean the cope.

He sees them creep. Yet here and there
    Half hid 'mid leafless groves they go;
As men who ply through traceries high   30
    Of turreted marbles show—
    So dwindle these to eyes below.
But fronting shot and flanking shell
    Sliver and rive the inwoven ways;
High tops of oaks and high hearts fall,   35
    But never the climbing stays.

From right to left, from left to right
    They roll the rallying cheer—
Vie with each other, brother with brother,
    Who shall the first appear—   40
    What color-bearer with colors clear
In sharp relief, like sky-drawn Grant,
    Whose cigar must now be near the stump—
While in solicitude his back
    Heaps slowly to a hump.   45

Near and more near; till now the flags
    Run like a catching flame;
And one flares highest, to peril nighest—
    He means to make a name:
    Salvos! they give him his fame.   50
The staff is caught, and next the rush,
    And then the leap where death has led;
Flag answered flag along the crest,
    And swarms of rebels fled.

But some who gained the envied Alp,   55
    And—eager, ardent, earnest there—
Dropped into Death's wide-open arms,
    Quelled on the wing like eagles struck in air—
    Forever they slumber young and fair,

The smile upon them as they died;   60
   Their end attained, that end a height:
Life was to these a dream fulfilled,
   And death a starry night.

The Armies of the Wilderness

(1863–4)

I

LIKE snows the camps on Southern hills
  Lay all the winter long,
Our levies there in patience stood—
  They stood in patience strong.
On fronting slopes gleamed other camps   5
  Where faith as firmly clung:
Ah, froward kin! so brave amiss—
  The zealots of the Wrong.

> *In this strife of brothers*
>   *(God, hear their country call),*   10
> *However it be, whatever betide,*
>   *Let not the just one fall.*

Through the pointed glass our soldiers saw
  The base-ball bounding sent;
They could have joined them in their sport   15
  But for the vale's deep rent.
And others turned the reddish soil,
  Like diggers of graves they bent:
The reddish soil and trenching toil
  Begat presentiment.   20

Did the Fathers feel mistrust?
  Can no final good be wrought?
Over and over, again and again
  Must the fight for the Right be fought?

They lead a Gray-back to the crag: 25
  "Your earth-works yonder—tell us, man!"
"A prisoner—no deserter, I,
  Nor one of the tell-tale clan."
His rags they mark: "True-blue like you
  Should wear the color—your Country's, man!"   30
He grinds his teeth: "However that be,
  Yon earth-works have their plan."

    Such brave ones, foully snared
      By Belial's wily plea,
    Were faithful unto the evil end—   35
      Feudal fidelity.

"Well, then, your camps—come, tell the names!"
  Freely he leveled his finger then:
"Yonder—see—are our Georgians; on the crest,
  The Carolinians; lower, past the glen,   40
Virginians—Alabamians—Mississippians—Kentuckians
  (Follow my finger)—Tennesseeans; and the ten
Camps *there*—ask your grave-pits; they'll tell.
  Halloa! I see the picket-hut, the den
Where I last night lay." "Where's Lee?"   45
  "In the hearts and bayonets of all yon men!"

    The tribes swarm up to war
      As in ages long ago,
    Ere the palm of promise leaved
      And the lily of Christ did blow.   50

Their mounted pickets for miles are spied
  Dotting the lowland plain,
The nearer ones in their veteran-rags—
  Loutish they loll in lazy disdain.
But ours in perilous places bide   55
  With rifles ready and eyes that strain
Deep through the dim suspected wood
  Where the Rapidan rolls amain.

The Indian has passed away,
    But creeping comes another—   60
Deadlier far. Picket,
    Take heed—take heed of thy brother!

From a wood-hung height, an outpost lone,
  Crowned with a woodman's fort,
The sentinel looks on a land of dole,   65
    Like Paran, all amort.
Black chimneys, gigantic in moor-like wastes,
  The scowl of the clouded sky retort;
The hearth is a houseless stone again—
  Ah! where shall the people be sought?   70

Since the venom such blastment deals,
    The South should have paused, and thrice,
Ere with heat of her hate she hatched
    The egg with the cockatrice.

A path down the mountain winds to the glade   75
  Where the dead of the Moonlight Fight lie low;
A hand reaches out of the thin-laid mould
  As begging help which none can bestow.
But the field-mouse small and busy ant
  Heap their hillocks, to hide if they may the woe: 80
By the bubbling spring lies the rusted canteen,
  And the drum which the drummer-boy dying let go.

Dust to dust, and blood for blood—
Passion and pangs! Has Time
Gone back? or is this the Age   85
Of the world's great Prime?

The wagon mired and cannon dragged
    Have trenched their scar; the plain
Tramped like the cindery beach of the damned—
    A site for the city of Cain.   90
And stumps of forests for dreary leagues
    Like a massacre show. The armies have lain
By fires where gums and balms did burn,
    And the seeds of Summer's reign.

Where are the birds and boys?   95
    Who shall go chestnutting when
October returns? The nuts—
    O, long ere they grow again.

They snug their huts with the chapel-pews,
    In court-houses stable their steeds—   100
Kindle their fires with indentures and bonds,
    And old Lord Fairfax's parchment deeds;
And Virginian gentlemen's libraries old—
    Books which only the scholar heeds—
Are flung to his kennel. It is ravage and range, 105
    And gardens are left to weeds.

Turned adrift into war
    Man runs wild on the plain,
Like the jennets let loose
    On the Pampas—zebras again.   110

Like the Pleiads dim, see the tents through the storm—
    Aloft by the hill-side hamlet's graves,
On a head-stone used for a hearth-stone there

The water is bubbling for punch for our braves.
What if the night be drear, and the blast 115
  Ghostly shrieks? their rollicking staves
Make frolic the heart; beating time with their swords,
  What care they if Winter raves?

    Is life but a dream? and so,
      In the dream do men laugh aloud? 120
    So strange seems mirth in a camp,
      So like a white tent to a shroud.

II

The May-weed springs; and comes a Man
  And mounts our Signal Hill;
A quiet Man, and plain in garb— 125
  Briefly he looks his fill,
Then drops his gray eye on the ground,
  Like a loaded mortar he is still:
Meekness and grimness meet in him,—
  The silent General. 130

    Were men but strong and wise,
      Honest as Grant, and calm,
    War would be left to the red and black ants,
      And the happy world disarm.

That eve a stir was in the camps, 135
  Forerunning quiet soon to come
Among the streets of beechen huts
  No more to know the drum.
The weed shall choke the lowly door,
  And foxes peer within the gloom, 140
Till scared perchance by Mosby's prowling men,
  Who ride in the rear of doom.

    Far West, and farther South,
      Wherever the sword has been,

> *Deserted camps are met,*   145
> *And desert graves are seen.*

The livelong night they ford the flood;
   With guns held high they silent press,
Till shimmers the grass in their bayonets' sheen—
   On Morning's banks their ranks they dress;   150
Then by the forests lightly wind,
   Whose waving boughs the pennons seem to bless,
Borne by the cavalry scouting on—
   Sounding the Wilderness.

> *Like shoals of fish in spring*   155
>   *That visit Crusoe's isle,*
> *The host in the lonesome place—*
>   *The hundred thousand file.*

The foe that held his guarded hills
   Must speed to woods afar;   160
For the scheme that was nursed by the Culpepper hearth
   With the slowly-smoked cigar—
The scheme that smouldered through winter long
   Now bursts into act—into war—
The resolute scheme of a heart as calm   165
   As the Cyclone's core.

> *The fight for the city is fought*
>   *In Nature's old domain;*
> *Man goes out to the wilds,*
>   *And Orpheus' charm is vain.*   170

In glades they meet skull after skull
   Where pine-cones lay—the rusted gun,
Green shoes full of bones, the mouldering coat
   And cuddled-up skeleton;
And scores of such. Some start as in dreams,   175

And comrades lost bemoan:
By the edge of those wilds Stonewall had charged—
But the Year and the Man were gone.

At the height of their madness
The night winds pause, 180
Recollecting themselves;
But no lull in these wars.

A gleam!—a volley! And who shall go
Storming the swarmers in jungles dread?
No cannon-ball answers, no proxies are sent— 185
They rush in the shrapnel's stead.
Plume and sash are vanities now—
Let them deck the pall of the dead;
They go where the shade is, perhaps into Hades,
Where the brave of all times have led. 190

There's a dust of hurrying feet,
Bitten lips and bated breath,
And drums that challenge to the grave,
And faces fixed, forefeeling death.

What husky huzzahs in the hazy groves— 195
What flying encounters fell;
Pursuer and pursued like ghosts disappear
In gloomed shade—their end who shall tell?
The crippled, a ragged-barked stick for a crutch,
Limp to some elfin dell— 200
Hobble from the sight of dead faces—white
As pebbles in a well.

Few burial rites shall be;
No priest with book and band
Shall come to the secret place 205
Of the corpse in the foeman's land.

Watch and fast, march and fight—clutch your gun!
   Day-fights and night-fights; sore is the stress;
Look, through the pines what line comes on?
   Longstreet slants through the hauntedness!   210
'Tis charge for charge, and shout for yell:
   Such battles on battles oppress—
But Heaven lent strength, the Right strove well,
   And emerged from the Wilderness.

> *Emerged, for the way was won;*   215
>   *But the Pillar of Smoke that led*
> *Was brand-like with ghosts that went up*
>   *Ashy and red.*

None can narrate that strife in the pines,
   A seal is on it—Sabæan lore!   220
Obscure as the wood, the entangled rhyme
   But hints at the maze of war—
Vivid glimpses or livid through peopled gloom,
   And fires which creep and char—
A riddle of death, of which the slain   225
   Sole solvers are.

> *Long they withhold the roll*
>   *Of the shroudless dead. It is right;*
> *Not yet can we bear the flare*
>   *Of the funeral light.*   230

On the Photograph
of a Corps Commander

Ay, man is manly. Here you see
 The warrior-carriage of the head,
And brave dilation of the frame;
 And lighting all, the soul that led
In Spottsylvania's charge to victory,   5
 Which justifies his fame.

A cheering picture. It is good
 To look upon a Chief like this,
In whom the spirit moulds the form.
 Here favoring Nature, oft remiss,   10
With eagle mien expressive has endued
 A man to kindle strains that warm.

Trace back his lineage, and his sires,
 Yeoman or noble, you shall find
Enrolled with men of Agincourt,   15
 Heroes who shared great Harry's mind.
Down to us come the knightly Norman fires,
 And front the Templars bore.

Nothing can lift the heart of man
 Like manhood in a fellow-man.   20
The thought of heaven's great King afar
 But humbles us—too weak to scan;
But manly greatness men can span,
 And feel the bonds that draw.

The Swamp Angel[k]

THERE is a coal-black Angel
  With a thick Afric lip,
And he dwells (like the hunted and harried)
  In a swamp where the green frogs dip.
But his face is against a City   5
  Which is over a bay of the sea,
And he breathes with a breath that is blastment,
  And dooms by a far decree.

By night there is fear in the City,
  Through the darkness a star soareth on;   10
There's a scream that screams up to the zenith,
  Then the poise of a meteor lone—
Lighting far the pale fright of the faces,
  And downward the coming is seen;
Then the rush, and the burst, and the havoc,   15
  And wails and shrieks between.

It comes like the thief in the gloaming;
  It comes, and none may foretell
The place of the coming—the glaring;
  They live in a sleepless spell   20
That wizens, and withers, and whitens;
  It ages the young, and the bloom
Of the maiden is ashes of roses—
  The Swamp Angel broods in his gloom.

Swift is his messengers' going, 25
    But slowly he saps their halls,
As if by delay deluding.
    They move from their crumbling walls
Farther and farther away;
    But the Angel sends after and after, 30
By night with the flame of his ray—
    By night with the voice of his screaming—
Sends after them, stone by stone,
    And farther walls fall, farther portals,
And weed follows weed through the Town. 35

Is this the proud City? the scorner
    Which never would yield the ground?
Which mocked at the coal-black Angel?
    The cup of despair goes round.
Vainly she calls upon Michael 40
    (The white man's seraph was he),
For Michael has fled from his tower
    To the Angel over the sea.

Who weeps for the woeful City
    Let him weep for our guilty kind; 45
Who joys at her wild despairing—
    Christ, the Forgiver, convert his mind.

The Battle for the Bay

(AUGUST, 1864)

O MYSTERY of noble hearts,
    To whom mysterious seas have been
In midnight watches, lonely calm and storm,
        A stern, sad discipline,
And rooted out the false and vain,   5
    And chastened them to aptness for
    Devotion and the deeds of war,
And death which smiles and cheers in spite of pain.

Beyond the bar the land-wind dies,
    The prows becharmed at anchor swim: 10
A summer night; the stars withdrawn look down—
        Fair eve of battle grim.
The sentries pace, bonetas glide;
    Below, the sleeping sailors swing,
    And in their dreams to quarters spring,   15
Or cheer their flag, or breast a stormy tide.

But drums are beat: *Up anchor all!*
    The triple lines steam slowly on;
Day breaks, and through the sweep of decks each man
        Stands coldly by his gun—   20
As cold as it. But he shall warm—
    Warm with the solemn metal there,
    And all its ordered fury share,
In attitude a gladiatorial form.

The Admiral—yielding to the love   25
   Which held his life and ship so dear—
Sailed second in the long fleet's midmost line;
      Yet thwarted all their care:
He lashed himself aloft, and shone
   Star of the fight, with influence sent   30
   Throughout the dusk embattlement;
And so they neared the strait and walls of stone.

No sprightly fife as in the field,
   The decks were hushed like fanes in prayer;
Behind each man a holy angel stood—   35
      He stood, though none was 'ware.
Out spake the forts on either hand,
   Back speak the ships when spoken to,
   And set their flags in concert true,
And *On and in!* is Farragut's command.   40

But what delays? 'mid wounds above
   Dim buoys give hint of death below—
Sea-ambuscades, where evil art had aped
      Hecla that hides in snow.
The centre-van, entangled, trips;   45
   The starboard leader holds straight on:
   A cheer for the Tecumseh!—nay,
Before their eyes the turreted ship goes down!

The fire redoubles. While the fleet
   Hangs dubious—ere the horror ran—   50
The Admiral rushes to his rightful place—
      Well met! apt hour and man!—
Closes with peril, takes the lead,
   His action is a stirring call;
   He strikes his great heart through them all,   55
And is the genius of their daring deed.

The forts are daunted, slack their fire,
   Confounded by the deadlier aim
And rapid broadsides of the speeding fleet,
      And fierce denouncing flame.   60

Yet shots from four dark hulls embayed
   Come raking through the loyal crews,
   Whom now each dying mate endues
With his last look, anguished yet undismayed.

A flowering time to guilt is given,   65
   And traitors have their glorying hour;
O late, but sure, the righteous Paramount comes—
      Palsy is on their power!
So proved it with the rebel keels,
   The strong-holds past: assailed, they run;   70
   The Selma strikes, and the work is done:
The dropping anchor the achievement seals.

But no, she turns—the Tennessee!
   The solid Ram of iron and oak,
Strong as Evil, and bold as Wrong, though lone—   75
      A pestilence in her smoke.
The flag-ship is her singled mark,
   The wooden Hartford. Let her come;
   She challenges the planet of Doom,
And naught shall save her—not her iron bark.   80

Slip anchor, all! and at her, all!
   Bear down with rushing beaks—and now!
First the Monongahela struck—and reeled;
      The Lackawana's prow
Next crashed—crashed, but not crashing; then   85
   The Admiral rammed, and rasping nigh
   Sloped in a broadside, which glanced by:
The Monitors battered at her adamant den.

The Chickasaw plunged beneath the stern
   And pounded there; a huge wrought orb   90
From the Manhattan pierced one wall, but dropped;
      Others the seas absorb.
Yet stormed on all sides, narrowed in,
   Hampered and cramped, the bad one fought—
   Spat ribald curses from the port   95
Whose shutters, jammed, locked up this Man-of-Sin.

No pause or stay. They made a din
    Like hammers round a boiler forged;
Now straining strength tangled itself with strength,
      Till Hate her will disgorged.   100
The white flag showed, the fight was won—
    Mad shouts went up that shook the Bay;
    But pale on the scarred fleet's decks there lay
A silent man for every silenced gun.

And quiet far below the wave,   105
    Where never cheers shall move their sleep,
Some who did boldly, nobly earn them, lie—
      Charmed children of the deep.
But decks that now are in the seed,
    And cannon yet within the mine,   110
    Shall thrill the deeper, gun and pine,
Because of the Tecumseh's glorious deed.

Sheridan at Cedar Creek

(OCTOBER, 1864)

SHOE the steed with silver
   That bore him to the fray,
When he heard the guns at dawning—
     Miles away;
When he heard them calling, calling—   5
      Mount! nor stay:
        Quick, or all is lost;
        They've surprised and stormed the post,
        They push your routed host—
   Gallop! retrieve the day.   10

House the horse in ermine—
   For the foam-flake blew
White through the red October;
   He thundered into view;
They cheered him in the looming,   15
   Horseman and horse they knew.
        The turn of the tide began,
        The rally of bugles ran,
        He swung his hat in the van;
   The electric hoof-spark flew.   20

Wreathe the steed and lead him—
   For the charge he led
Touched and turned the cypress
   Into amaranths for the head
Of Philip, king of riders,   25

Who raised them from the dead.
       The camp (at dawning lost),
       By eve, recovered—forced,
       Rang with laughter of the host
At belated Early fled.   30

Shroud the horse in sable—
   For the mounds they heap!
There is firing in the Valley,
   And yet no strife they keep;
It is the parting volley,   35
   It is the pathos deep.
       There is glory for the brave
       Who lead, and nobly save,
       But no knowledge in the grave
Where the nameless followers sleep.   40

In the Prison Pen

(1864)

Listless he eyes the palisades
    And sentries in the glare;
'Tis barren as a pelican-beach—
    But his world is ended there.

Nothing to do; and vacant hands   5
    Bring on the idiot-pain;
He tries to think—to recollect,
    But the blur is on his brain.

Around him swarm the plaining ghosts
    Like those on Virgil's shore—   10
A wilderness of faces dim,
    And pale ones gashed and hoar.

A smiting sun. No shed, no tree;
    He totters to his lair—
A' den that sick hands dug in earth   15
    Ere famine wasted there,

Or, dropping in his place, he swoons,
    Walled in by throngs that press,
Till forth from the throngs they bear him dead—
    Dead in his meagreness.   20

The College Colonel

HE rides at their head;
   A crutch by his saddle just slants in view,
One slung arm is in splints, you see,
   Yet he guides his strong steed—how coldly too.

He brings his regiment home—   5
   Not as they filed two years before,
But a remnant half-tattered, and battered, and worn,
Like castaway sailors, who—stunned
      By the surf's loud roar,
   Their mates dragged back and seen no more—   10
Again and again breast the surge,
   And at last crawl, spent, to shore.

A still rigidity and pale—
   An Indian aloofness lones his brow;
He has lived a thousand years   15
Compressed in battle's pains and prayers,
   Marches and watches slow.

There are welcoming shouts, and flags;
   Old men off hat to the Boy,
Wreaths from gay balconies fall at his feet,   20
   But to *him*—there comes alloy.

It is not that a leg is lost,
   It is not that an arm is maimed,

It is not that the fever has racked—
    Self he has long disclaimed.   25

But all through the Seven Days' Fight,
    And deep in the Wilderness grim,
And in the field-hospital tent,
    And Petersburg crater, and dim
Lean brooding in Libby, there came—   30
    Ah heaven!—what *truth* to him.

The Eagle of the Blue[1]

ALOFT he guards the starry folds
   Who is the brother of the star;
The bird whose joy is in the wind
   Exulteth in the war.

No painted plume—a sober hue, 5
   His beauty is his power;
That eager calm of gaze intent
   Foresees the Sibyl's hour.

Austere, he crowns the swaying perch,
   Flapped by the angry flag; 10
The hurricane from the battery sings,
   But his claw has known the crag.

Amid the scream of shells, his scream
   Runs shrilling; and the glare
Of eyes that brave the blinding sun 15
   The vollied flame can bear.

The pride of quenchless strength is his—
   Strength which, though chained, avails;
The very rebel looks and thrills—
   The anchored Emblem hails. 20

Though scarred in many a furious fray,
   No deadly hurt he knew;
Well may we think his years are charmed—
   The Eagle of the Blue.

A Dirge for McPherson^m

Killed in front of Atlanta

(July, 1864)

ARMS reversed and banners craped—
    Muffled drums;
Snowy horses sable–draped—
    McPherson comes.

      But, tell us, shall we know him more,   5
      Lost-Mountain and lone Kenesaw?

Brave the sword upon the pall—
    A gleam in gloom;
So a bright name lighteth all
    McPherson's doom.   10

Bear him through the chapel-door—
    Let priest in stole
Pace before the warrior
    Who led. Bell—toll!

Lay him down within the nave,   15
    The Lesson read—
Man is noble, man is brave,
    But man's—a weed.

Take him up again and wend
    Graveward, nor weep: 20

There's a trumpet that shall rend
   This Soldier's sleep.

Pass the ropes the coffin round,
   And let descend;
Prayer and volley—let it sound   25
   McPherson's end.

True fame is his, for life is o'er—
Sarpedon of the mighty war.

At the Cannon's Mouth

Destruction of the Ram Albemarle by the Torpedo-launch

(OCTOBER, 1864)

PALELY intent, he urged his keel
   Full on the guns, and touched the spring;
Himself involved in the bolt he drove
Timed with the armed hull's shot that stove
His shallop—die or do!   5
Into the flood his life he threw,
   Yet lives—unscathed—a breathing thing
To marvel at.

          He has his fame;
But that mad dash at death, how name?   10

Had Earth no charm to stay in the Boy
   The martyr-passion? Could he dare
Disdain the Paradise of opening joy
   Which beckons the fresh heart every where?
Life has more lures than any girl   15
   For youth and strength; puts forth a share
Of beauty, hinting of yet rarer store;
And ever with unfathomable eyes,
      Which bafflingly entice,
Still strangely does Adonis draw.   20
And life once over, who shall tell the rest?
Life is, of all we know, God's best.
What imps these eagles then, that they

Fling disrespect on life by that proud way
In which they soar above our lower clay.   25

Pretense of wonderment and doubt unblest:
   In Cushing's eager deed was shown
   A spirit which brave poets own—
That scorn of life which earns life's crown;
   Earns, but not always wins; but *he*—   30
   The star ascended in his nativity.

The March to the Sea

(DECEMBER, 1864)

NOT Kenesaw high-arching,
  Nor Allatoona's glen—
Though there the graves lie parching—
  Stayed Sherman's miles of men;
From charred Atlanta marching   5
  They launched the sword again.
      The columns streamed like rivers
        Which in their course agree,
      And they streamed until their flashing
        Met the flashing of the sea: 10
          It was glorious glad marching,
          That marching to the sea.

They brushed the foe before them
  (Shall gnats impede the bull?);
Their own good bridges bore them   15
  Over swamps or torrents full,
And the grand pines waving o'er them
  Bowed to axes keen and cool.
      The columns grooved their channels,
        Enforced their own decree,   20
      And their power met nothing larger
        Until it met the sea:
          It was glorious glad marching,
          A marching glad and free.

Kilpatrick's snare of riders 25
  In zigzags mazed the land,
Perplexed the pale Southsiders
  With feints on every hand;
Vague menace awed the hiders
  In forts beyond command. 30
    To Sherman's shifting problem
      No foeman knew the key;
    But onward went the marching—
      Right onward to the sea:
        It was glorious glad marching, 35
        The swinging step was free.

The flankers ranged like pigeons
  In clouds through field or wood;
The flocks of all those regions,
  The herds and horses good, 40
Poured in and swelled the legions,
  For they caught the marching mood.
    A volley ahead! They hear it;
      And they hear the repartee:
    Fighting was but frolic 45
      In that marching to the sea:
        It was glorious glad marching,
        A marching bold and free.

All nature felt their coming,
  The birds like couriers flew, 50
And the banners brightly blooming
  The slaves by thousands drew,
And they marched beside the drumming,
  And they joined the armies blue.
    The cocks crowed from the cannon 55
      (Pets named from Grant and Lee),
    Plumed fighters and campaigners
      In that marching to the sea:
        It was glorious glad marching,
        For every man was free. 60

The foragers through calm lands
　　Swept in tempest gay,
And they breathed the air of balm-lands
　　Where rolled savannas lay,
And they helped themselves from farm-lands—   65
　　As who should say them nay?
　　　　The regiments uproarious
　　　　　Laughed in Plenty's glee;
　　　　And they marched till their broad laughter
　　　　　Met the laughter of the sea: 70
　　　　　　It was glorious glad marching,
　　　　　　That marching to the sea.

The grain of endless acres
　　Was threshed (as in the East)
By the trampling of the Takers,   75
　　Strong march of man and beast;
The flails of those earth-shakers
　　Left a famine where they ceased.
　　　　The arsenals were yielded;
　　　　　The sword (that was to be),   80
　　　　Arrested in the forging,
　　　　　Rued that marching to the sea:
　　　　　　It was glorious glad marching,
　　　　　　But ah, the stern decree!

For behind they left a wailing,   85
　　A terror and a ban,
And blazing cinders sailing,
　　And houseless households wan,
Wide zones of counties paling,
　　And towns where maniacs ran.   90
　　　　Was the havoc, retribution?
　　　　　But howsoe'er it be,
　　　　They will long remember Sherman
　　　　　And his streaming columns free—
　　　　　　They will long remember Sherman   95
　　　　　　Marching to the sea.

The Frenzy in the Wake[n]

Sherman's advance through the Carolinas

(FEBRUARY, 1865)

So strong to suffer, shall we be
   Weak to contend, and break
The sinews of the Oppressor's knee
   That grinds upon the neck?
      O, the garments rolled in blood   5
        Scorch in cities wrapped in flame,
      And the African—the imp!
        He gibbers, imputing shame.

Shall Time, avenging every woe,
   To us that joy allot   10
Which Israel thrilled when Sisera's brow
   Showed gaunt and showed the clot?
      Curse on their foreheads, cheeks, and eyes—
        The Northern faces—true
      To the flag we hate, the flag whose stars   15
        Like planets strike us through.

From frozen Maine they come,
   Far Minnesota too;
They come to a sun whose rays disown—
   May it wither them as the dew!   20
      The ghosts of our slain appeal:
        "Vain shall our victories be?"
      But back from its ebb the flood recoils—
        Back in a whelming sea.

With burning woods our skies are brass,   25
  The pillars of dust are seen;
The live-long day their cavalry pass—
  No crossing the road between.
    We were sore deceived—an awful host!
    They move like a roaring wind.   30
    Have we gamed and lost? but even despair
    Shall never our hate rescind.

The Fall of Richmond

The tidings received in the Northern Metropolis

(APRIL, 1865)

WHAT mean these peals from every tower,
　　And crowds like seas that sway?
The cannon reply; they speak the heart
　　Of the People impassioned, and say—
A city in flags for a city in flames,　　　　　　　　　5
　　Richmond goes Babylon's way—
　　　　　　Sing and pray.

O weary years and woeful wars,
　　And armies in the grave;
But hearts unquelled at last deter　　　　　　　　　10
The helmed dilated Lucifer—
　　Honor to Grant the brave,
Whose three stars now like Orion's rise
　　When wreck is on the wave—
　　　　　　Bless his glaive.　　　　　　　　　　15

Well that the faith we firmly kept,
　　And never our aim forswore
For the Terrors that trooped from each recess
When fainting we fought in the Wilderness,
　　And Hell made loud hurrah;　　　　　　　　　20
But God is in Heaven, and Grant in the Town,
　　And Right through might is Law—
　　　　　　God's way adore.

The Surrender at Appomattox

(APRIL, 1865)

As billows upon billows roll,
  On victory victory breaks;
Ere yet seven days from Richmond's fall
  And crowning triumph wakes
The loud joy-gun, whose thunders run   5
  By sea-shore, streams, and lakes.
     The hope and great event agree
     In the sword that Grant received from Lee.

The warring eagles fold the wing,
  But not in Cæsar's sway;   10
Not Rome o'ercome by Roman arms we sing,
  As on Pharsalia's day,
But Treason thrown, though a giant grown,
  And Freedom's larger play.
     All human tribes glad token see   15
     In the close of the wars of Grant and Lee.

A Canticle

Significant of the national exaltation of enthusiasm
at the close of the War

O THE precipice Titanic
  Of the congregated Fall,
And the angle oceanic
  Where the deepening thunders call—
    And the Gorge so grim,   5
    And the firmamental rim!
Multitudinously thronging
  The waters all converge,
Then they sweep adown in sloping
  Solidity of surge.   10

      The Nation, in her impulse
        Mysterious as the Tide,
      In emotion like an ocean
        Moves in power, not in pride;
      And is deep in her devotion   15
        As Humanity is wide.

          Thou Lord of hosts victorious,
            The confluence Thou hast twined;
          By a wondrous way and glorious
            A passage Thou dost find—   20
            A passage Thou dost find:
          Hosanna to the Lord of hosts,
            The hosts of human kind.

Stable in its baselessness
    When calm is in the air,   25
The Iris half in tracelessness
    Hovers faintly fair.
Fitfully assailing it
    A wind from heaven blows,
Shivering and paling it   30
    To blankness of the snows;
While, incessant in renewal,
    The Arch rekindled grows,
Till again the gem and jewel
    Whirl in blinding overthrows—   35
Till, prevailing and transcending,
    Lo, the Glory perfect there,
And the contest finds an ending,
    For repose is in the air.

But the foamy Deep unsounded,   40
    And the dim and dizzy ledge,
And the booming roar rebounded,
    And the gull that skims the edge!
        The Giant of the Pool
        Heaves his forehead white as wool—   45
Toward the Iris ever climbing
    From the Cataracts that call—
Irremovable vast arras
    Draping all the Wall.

        The Generations pouring   50
            From times of endless date,
        In their going, in their flowing
            Ever form the steadfast State;
        And Humanity is growing
            Toward the fullness of her fate.   55

            Thou Lord of hosts victorious,
                Fulfill the end designed;
            By a wondrous way and glorious

A passage Thou dost find—
A passage Thou dost find: 60
Hosanna to the Lord of hosts,
The hosts of human kind.

The Martyr

Indicative of the passion of the people on

the 15th of April, 1865

GOOD Friday was the day
   Of the prodigy and crime,
When they killed him in his pity,
   When they killed him in his prime
Of clemency and calm—   5
     When with yearning he was filled
     To redeem the evil-willed,
And, though conqueror, be kind;
   But they killed him in his kindness,
   In their madness and their blindness,   10
And they killed him from behind.

     There is sobbing of the strong,
     And a pall upon the land;
     But the People in their weeping
        Bare the iron hand: 15
     Beware the People weeping
        When they bare the iron hand.

He lieth in his blood—
   The father in his face;
They have killed him, the Forgiver—   20
   The Avenger takes his place,°
The Avenger wisely stern,
     Who in righteousness shall do
     What the heavens call him to,

And the parricides remand;   25
   For they killed him in his kindness,
   In their madness and their blindness,
And his blood is on their hand.

     There is sobbing of the strong,
       And a pall upon the land;   30
     But the People in their weeping
          Bare the iron hand:
     Beware the People weeping
       When they bare the iron hand.

"The Coming Storm"

A Picture by S. R. Gifford, and owned by E. B.
Included in the N. A. Exhibition, April, 1865

ALL feeling hearts must feel for him
    Who felt this picture. Presage dim—
Dim inklings from the shadowy sphere
    Fixed him and fascinated here.

A demon-cloud like the mountain one   5
    Burst on a spirit as mild
As this urned lake, the home of shades.
    But Shakspeare's pensive child

Never the lines had lightly scanned,
    Steeped in fable, steeped in fate;   10
The Hamlet in his heart was 'ware,
    Such hearts can antedate.

No utter surprise can come to him
    Who reaches Shakspeare's core;
That which we seek and shun is there—   15
    Man's final lore.

Rebel Color-bearers at Shiloh[P]

A plea against the vindictive cry raised by civilians shortly

after the surrender at Appomattox

THE color-bearers facing death
White in the whirling sulphurous wreath,
   Stand boldly out before the line;
Right and left their glances go,
Proud of each other, glorying in their show;   5
Their battle-flags about them blow,
   And fold them as in flame divine:
Such living robes are only seen
Round martyrs burning on the green—
And martyrs for the Wrong have been.   10

Perish their Cause! but mark the men—
Mark the planted statues, then
Draw trigger on them if you can.

The leader of a patriot-band
Even so could view rebels who so could stand;   15
   And this when peril pressed him sore,
Left aidless in the shivered front of war—
   Skulkers behind, defiant foes before,
And fighting with a broken brand.
The challenge in that courage rare—   20
Courage defenseless, proudly bare—

Never could tempt him; he could dare
Strike up the leveled rifle there.

Sunday at Shiloh, and the day
When Stonewall charged—McClellan's crimson May,   25
And Chickamauga's wave of death,
And of the Wilderness the cypress wreath—
    All these have passed away.
The life in the veins of Treason lags,
Her daring color-bearers drop their flags,   30
  And yield. *Now* shall we fire?
    Can poor spite be?
  Shall nobleness in victory less aspire
  Than in reverse? Spare Spleen her ire,
    And think how Grant met Lee.   35

The Muster[q]

Suggested by the Two Days' Review at Washington

(MAY, 1865)

THE Abrahamic river—
   Patriarch of floods,
Calls the roll of all his streams
   And watery multitudes:
      Torrent cries to torrent,   5
       The rapids hail the fall;
      With shouts the inland freshets
       Gather to the call.

   The quotas of the Nation,
     Like the water-shed of waves,   10
   Muster into union—
     Eastern warriors, Western braves.

   Martial strains are mingling,
     Though distant far the bands,
   And the wheeling of the squadrons   15
     Is like surf upon the sands.

   The bladed guns are gleaming—
     Drift in lengthened trim,
   Files on files for hazy miles—
     Nebulously dim.   20

   O Milky Way of armies—
     Star rising after star,

New banners of the Commonwealths,
And eagles of the War.

The Abrahamic river   25
To sea-wide fullness fed,
Pouring from the thaw-lands
By the God of floods is led:
His deep enforcing current
The streams of ocean own,   30
And Europe's marge is evened
By rills from Kansas lone.

Aurora-Borealis

Commemorative of the Dissolution of Armies at the Peace

(MAY, 1865)

WHAT power disbands the Northern Lights
  After their steely play?
The lonely watcher feels an awe
  Of Nature's sway,
    As when appearing,   5
    He marked their flashed uprearing
In the cold gloom—
  Retreatings and advancings,
(Like dallyings of doom),
    Transitions and enhancings,   10
    And bloody ray.

The phantom-host has faded quite,
  Splendor and Terror gone—
Portent or promise—and gives way
    To pale, meek Dawn;   15
      The coming, going,
      Alike in wonder showing—
Alike the God,
  Decreeing and commanding
The million blades that glowed,   20
    The muster and disbanding—
    Midnight and Morn.

The Released Rebel Prisoner[t]

(June, 1865)

Armies he's seen—the herds of war,
  But never such swarms of men
As now in the Nineveh of the North—
  How mad the Rebellion then!

And yet but dimly he divines   5
  The depth of that deceit,
And superstition of vast pride
  Humbled to such defeat.

Seductive shone the Chiefs in arms—
  His steel the nearest magnet drew;   10
Wreathed with its kind, the Gulf-weed drives—
  'Tis Nature's wrong they rue.

His face is hidden in his beard,
  But his heart peers out at eye—
And such a heart! like a mountain-pool   15
  Where no man passes by.

He thinks of Hill—a brave soul gone;
  And Ashby dead in pale disdain;
And Stuart with the Rupert-plume,
  Whose blue eye never shall laugh again.   20

He hears the drum; he sees our boys
  From his wasted fields return;

Ladies feast them on strawberries,
   And even to kiss them yearn.

He marks them bronzed, in soldier-trim,   25
   The rifle proudly borne;
They bear it for an heir-loom home,
   And he—disarmed—jail-worn.

Home, home—his heart is full of it;
   But home he never shall see,   30
Even should he stand upon the spot:
   'Tis gone!—where his brothers be.

The cypress-moss from tree to tree
   Hangs in his Southern land;
As wierd, from thought to thought of his   35
   Run memories hand in hand.

And so he lingers—lingers on
   In the City of the Foe—
His cousins and his countrymen
   Who see him listless go.   40

A Grave near Petersburg, Virginia[s]

HEAD-BOARD and foot-board duly placed—
   Grassed is the mound between;
Daniel Drouth is the slumberer's name—
   Long may his grave be green!

Quick was his way—a flash and a blow,   5
   Full of his fire was he—
A fire of hell—'tis burnt out now—
   Green may his grave long be!

May his grave be green, though he
   Was a rebel of iron mould;   10
Many a true heart—true to the Cause,
   Through the blaze of his wrath lies cold.

May his grave be green—still green
   While happy years shall run;
May none come nigh to disinter   15
   The—*Buried Gun.*

"Formerly a Slave"

An idealized Portrait, by E. Vedder, in the Spring
Exhibition of the National Academy, 1865

THE sufferance of her race is shown,
    And retrospect of life,
Which now too late deliverance dawns upon;
    Yet is she not at strife.

Her children's children they shall know   5
    The good withheld from her;
And so her reverie takes prophetic cheer—
    In spirit she sees the stir

Far down the depth of thousand years,
    And marks the revel shine;   10
Her dusky face is lit with sober light,
    Sibylline, yet benign.

The Apparition

(A Retrospect)

CONVULSIONS came; and, where the field
   Long slept in pastoral green,
A goblin-mountain was upheaved
(Sure the scared sense was all deceived),
   Marl-glen and slag-ravine.   5

The unreserve of Ill was there,
   The clinkers in her last retreat;
But, ere the eye could take it in,
Or mind could comprehension win,
   It sunk!—and at our feet.   10

So, then, Solidity's a crust—
   The core of fire below;
All may go well for many a year,
But who can think without a fear
   Of horrors that happen so?   15

Magnanimity Baffled

"SHARP words we had before the fight;
 But—now the fight is done—
Look, here's my hand," said the Victor bold,
 "Take it—an honest one!
What, holding back? I mean you well;   5
 Though worsted, you strove stoutly, man;
The odds were great; I honor you;
 Man honors man.

"Still silent, friend? can grudges be?
 Yet am I held a foe?—   10
Turned to the wall, on his cot he lies—
 Never I'll leave him so!
Brave one! I here implore your hand;
 Dumb still? all fellowship fled?
Nay, then, I'll have this stubborn hand!"   15
 He snatched it—it was dead.

On the Slain Collegians^t

YOUTH is the time when hearts are large,
    And stirring wars
Appeal to the spirit which appeals in turn
    To the blade it draws.
If woman incite, and duty show   5
  (Though made the mask of Cain),
Or whether it be Truth's sacred cause,
    Who can aloof remain
That shares youth's ardor, uncooled by the snow
    Of wisdom or sordid gain?   10

The liberal arts and nurture sweet
Which give his gentleness to man—
  Train him to honor, lend him grace
Through bright examples meet—
That culture which makes never wan   15
With underminings deep, but holds
  The surface still, its fitting place,
  And so gives sunniness to the face
And bravery to the heart; what troops
  Of generous boys in happiness thus bred—   20
  Saturnians through life's Tempe led,
Went from the North and came from the South,
With golden mottoes in the mouth,
  To lie down midway on a bloody bed.

Woe for the homes of the North,   25
And woe for the seats of the South:

118

All who felt life's spring in prime,
And were swept by the wind of their place and time—
   All lavish hearts, on whichever side,
Of birth urbane or courage high,   30
Armed them for the stirring wars—
Armed them—some to die.
            Apollo-like in pride,
Each would slay his Python—caught
The maxims in his temple taught—   35
   Aflame with sympathies whose blaze
Perforce enwrapped him—social laws,
   Friendship and kin, and by-gone days—
Vows, kisses—every heart unmoors,
And launches into the seas of wars.   40
What could they else—North or South?
Each went forth with blessings given
By priests and mothers in the name of Heaven;
        And honor in both was chief.
Warred one for Right, and one for Wrong?   45
So put it; but they both were young—
Each grape to his cluster clung,
All their elegies are sung.

The anguish of maternal hearts
   Must search for balm divine;   50
But well the striplings bore their fated parts
   (The heavens all parts assign)—
Never felt life's care or cloy.
Each bloomed and died an unabated Boy;
Nor dreamed what death was—thought it mere   55
Sliding into some vernal sphere.
They knew the joy, but leaped the grief,
Like plants that flower ere comes the leaf—
Which storms lay low in kindly doom,
And kill them in their flush of bloom.   60

America

I

WHERE the wings of a sunny Dome expand
I saw a Banner in gladsome air—
Starry, like Berenice's Hair—
Afloat in broadened bravery there;
With undulating long-drawn flow,   5
As rolled Brazilian billows go
Voluminously o'er the Line.
The Land reposed in peace below;
   The children in their glee
Were folded to the exulting heart   10
   Of young Maternity.

II

Later, and it streamed in fight
   When tempest mingled with the fray,
And over the spear-point of the shaft
   I saw the ambiguous lightning play.   15
Valor with Valor strove, and died:
Fierce was Despair, and cruel was Pride;
And the lorn Mother speechless stood,
Pale at the fury of her brood.

III

Yet later, and the silk did wind   20
    Her fair cold form;
Little availed the shining shroud,
    Though ruddy in hue, to cheer or warm.
A watcher looked upon her low, and said—
She sleeps, but sleeps, she is not dead.   25
    But in that sleep contortion showed
The terror of the vision there—
    A silent vision unavowed,
Revealing earth's foundation bare,
    And Gorgon in her hidden place.   30
It was a thing of fear to see
    So foul a dream upon so fair a face,
And the dreamer lying in that starry shroud.

IV

But from the trance she sudden broke—
    The trance, or death into promoted life;   35
At her feet a shivered yoke,
And in her aspect turned to heaven
    No trace of passion or of strife—
A clear calm look. It spake of pain,
But such as purifies from stain—   40
Sharp pangs that never come again—
    And triumph repressed by knowledge meet,
Power dedicate, and hope grown wise,
    And youth matured for age's seat—
Law on her brow and empire in her eyes.   45
    So she, with graver air and lifted flag;
While the shadow, chased by light,
Fled along the far-drawn height,
    And left her on the crag.

On the Home Guards

who perished in the Defense of Lexington, Missouri

THE men who here in harness died
   Fell not in vain, though in defeat.
They by their end well fortified
   The Cause, and built retreat
(With memory of their valor tried)   5
For emulous hearts in many an after fray—
Hearts sore beset, which died at bay.

Inscription

for Graves at Pea Ridge, Arkansas

LET none misgive we died amiss
    When here we strove in furious fight:
Furious it was; nathless was this
    Better than tranquil plight,
And tame surrender of the Cause   5
Hallowed by hearts and by the laws.
    We here who warred for Man and Right,
The choice of warring never laid with us.
    There we were ruled by the traitor's choice.
    Nor long we stood to trim and poise,   10
But marched, and fell—victorious!

The Fortitude of the North

under the Disaster of the Second Manassas

No shame they take for dark defeat
   While prizing yet each victory won,
Who fight for the Right through all retreat,
   Nor pause until their work is done.
The Cape-of-Storms is proof to every throe;   5
   Vainly against that foreland beat
Wild winds aloft and wilder waves below:
   The black cliffs gleam through rents in sleet
When the livid Antarctic storm-clouds glow.

On the Men of Maine

killed in the Victory of Baton Rouge, Louisiana

AFAR they fell. It was the zone
   Of fig and orange, cane and lime
(A land how all unlike their own,
With the cold pine-grove overgrown),
   But still their Country's clime.   5
And there in youth they died for her—
        The Volunteers,
For her went up their dying prayers:
   So vast the Nation, yet so strong the tie.
What doubt shall come, then, to deter   10
   The Republic's earnest faith and courage high.

An Epitaph

WHEN Sunday tidings from the front
   Made pale the priest and people,
And heavily the blessing went,
   And bells were dumb in the steeple;
The Soldier's widow (summering sweetly here,   5
   In shade by waving beeches lent)
   Felt deep at heart her faith content,
And priest and people borrowed of her cheer.

Inscription

for Marye's Heights, Fredericksburg

To them who crossed the flood
And climbed the hill, with eyes
   Upon the heavenly flag intent,
   And through the deathful tumult went
Even unto death: to them this Stone—   5
Erect, where they were overthrown—
   Of more than victory the monument.

The Mound by the Lake

THE grass shall never forget this grave.
When homeward footing it in the sun
   After the weary ride by rail,
The stripling soldiers passed her door,
   Wounded perchance, or wan and pale,   5
She left her household work undone—
Duly the wayside table spread,
   With evergreens shaded, to regale
Each travel-spent and grateful one.
So warm her heart—childless—unwed,   10
Who like a mother comforted.

On the Slain at Chickamauga

HAPPY are they and charmed in life
   Who through long wars arrive unscarred
At peace. To such the wreath be given,
If they unfalteringly have striven—
   In honor, as in limb, unmarred.   5
Let cheerful praise be rife,
   And let them live their years at ease,
Musing on brothers who victorious died—
   Loved mates whose memory shall ever please.

And yet mischance is honorable too—   10
   Seeming defeat in conflict justified
Whose end to closing eyes is hid from view.
The will, that never can relent—
The aim, survivor of the bafflement,
      Make this memorial due.   15

An uninscribed Monument

on one of the Battle-fields of the Wilderness

SILENCE and Solitude may hint
  (Whose home is in yon piny wood)
What I, though tableted, could never tell—
The din which here befell,
  And striving of the multitude.   5
The iron cones and spheres of death
  Set round me in their rust,
    These, too, if just,
Shall speak with more than animated breath.
  Thou who beholdest, if thy thought,   10
Not narrowed down to personal cheer,
Take in the import of the quiet here—
  The after-quiet—the calm full fraught;
Thou too wilt silent stand—
Silent as I, and lonesome as the land.   15

On Sherman's Men

who fell in the Assault of Kenesaw Mountain, Georgia

THEY said that Fame her clarion dropped
    Because great deeds were done no more—
That even Duty knew no shining ends,
And Glory—'twas a fallen star!
    But battle can heroes and bards restore.   5
          Nay, look at Kenesaw:
Perils the mailed ones never knew
Are lightly braved by the ragged coats of blue,
And gentler hearts are bared to deadlier war.

On the Grave

of a young Cavalry Officer killed in the Valley of Virginia

BEAUTY and youth, with manners sweet, and friends—
  Gold, yet a mind not unenriched had he
Whom here low violets veil from eyes.
  But all these gifts transcended be:
His happier fortune in this mound you see.   5

A Requiem

for Soldiers lost in Ocean Transports

WHEN, after storms that woodlands rue,
  To valleys comes atoning dawn,
The robins blithe their orchard-sports renew;
  And meadow-larks, no more withdrawn,
Caroling fly in the languid blue;   5
The while, from many a hid recess,
Alert to partake the blessedness,
The pouring mites their airy dance pursue.
  So, after ocean's ghastly gales,
When laughing light of hoyden morning breaks,   10
      Every finny hider wakes—
  From vaults profound swims up with glittering scales;
  Through the delightsome sea he sails,
With shoals of shining tiny things
Frolic on every wave that flings   15
  Against the prow its showery spray;
All creatures joying in the morn,
Save them forever from joyance torn,
  Whose bark was lost where now the dolphins play;
Save them that by the fabled shore,   20
  Down the pale stream are washed away,
Far to the reef of bones are borne;
  And never revisits them the light,
Nor sight of long-sought land and pilot more;
  Nor heed they now the lone bird's flight   25
Round the lone spar where mid-sea surges pour.

On a natural Monument

in a field of Georgia[u]

No trophy this—a Stone unhewn,
   And stands where here the field immures
The nameless brave whose palms are won.
Outcast they sleep; yet fame is nigh—
   Pure fame of deeds, not doers;   5
Nor deeds of men who bleeding die
   In cheer of hymns that round them float:
In happy dreams such close the eye.
But withering famine slowly wore,
   And slowly fell disease did gloat.   10
Even Nature's self did aid deny;
In horror they choked the pensive sigh.
   Yea, off from home sad Memory bore
(Though anguished Yearning heaved that way),
Lest wreck of reason might befall.   15
   As men in gales shun the lee shore,
Though there the homestead be, and call,
And thitherward winds and waters sway—
As such lorn mariners, so fared they.
But naught shall now their peace molest.   20
   Their fame is this: they did endure—
Endure, when fortitude was vain
To kindle any approving strain
Which they might hear. To these who rest,
   This healing sleep alone was sure.   25

Commemorative of a Naval Victory

SAILORS there are of gentlest breed,
    Yet strong, like every goodly thing;
The discipline of arms refines,
    And the wave gives tempering.
    The damasked blade its beam can fling;   5
It lends the last grave grace:
The hawk, the hound, and sworded nobleman
    In Titian's picture for a king,
Are of hunter or warrior race.

In social halls a favored guest   10
    In years that follow victory won,
How sweet to feel your festal fame
    In woman's glance instinctive thrown:
    Repose is yours—your deed is known,
It musks the amber wine;   15
It lives, and sheds a light from storied days
    Rich as October sunsets brown,
Which make the barren place to shine.

But seldom the laurel wreath is seen
    Unmixed with pensive pansies dark;   20
There's a light and a shadow on every man
    Who at last attains his lifted mark—
    Nursing through night the ethereal spark.
Elate he never can be;

He feels that spirits which glad had hailed his worth,   25
   Sleep in oblivion.—The shark
Glides white through the phosphorus sea.

Presentation to the Authorities,

by Privates, of Colors captured in Battles ending in the Surrender of Lee

THESE flags of armies overthrown—
Flags fallen beneath the sovereign one
In end foredoomed which closes war;
We here, the captors, lay before
    The altar which of right claims all—   5
Our Country. And as freely we,
    Revering ever her sacred call,
Could lay our lives down—though life be
Thrice loved and precious to the sense
Of such as reap the recompense   10
    Of life imperiled for just cause—
Imperiled, and yet preserved;
While comrades, whom Duty as strongly nerved,
Whose wives were all as dear, lie low.
But these flags given, glad we go   15
    To waiting homes with vindicated laws.

The Returned Volunteer to his Rifle

Over this hearth—my father's seat—
   Repose, to patriot-memory dear,
Thou tried companion, whom at last I greet
   By steepy banks of Hudson here.
How oft I told thee of this scene—   5
The Highlands blue—the river's narrowing sheen.
Little at Gettysburg we thought
To find such haven; but God kept it green.
Long rest! with belt, and bayonet, and canteen.

The Scout toward Aldie

THE cavalry-camp lies on the slope
  Of what was late a vernal hill,
But now like a pavement bare—
An outpost in the perilous wilds
  Which ever are lone and still;   5
      But Mosby's men are there—
      Of Mosby best beware.

Great trees the troopers felled, and leaned
  In antlered walls about their tents;
Strict watch they kept; 'twas *Hark!* and *Mark!*   10
Unarmed none cared to stir abroad
  For berries beyond their forest-fence:
      As glides in seas the shark,
      Rides Mosby through green dark.

All spake of him, but few had seen   15
  Except the maimed ones or the low;
Yet rumor made him every thing—
A farmer—woodman—refugee—
  The man who crossed the field but now;
      A spell about his life did cling—   20
      Who to the ground shall Mosby bring?

The morning-bugles lonely play,
   Lonely the evening-bugle calls—
Unanswered voices in the wild;
The settled hush of birds in nest   25
   Becharms, and all the wood enthralls:
      Memory's self is so beguiled
      That Mosby seems a satyr's child.

They lived as in the Eerie Land—
   The fire-flies showed with fairy gleam;   30
And yet from pine-tops one might ken
The Capitol Dome—hazy—sublime—
   A vision breaking on a dream:
      So strange it was that Mosby's men
      Should dare to prowl where the Dome was seen.   35

A scout toward Aldie broke the spell.—
   The Leader lies before his tent
Gazing at heaven's all-cheering lamp
Through blandness of a morning rare;
   His thoughts on bitter-sweets are bent: 40
      His sunny bride is in the camp—
      But Mosby—graves are beds of damp!

The trumpet calls; he goes within;
   But none the prayer and sob may know:
Her hero he, but bridegroom too.   45
Ah, love in a tent is a queenly thing,
   And fame, be sure, refines the vow;
      But fame fond wives have lived to rue,
      And Mosby's men fell deeds can do.

Tan-tara! tan-tara! tan-tara!   50
   Mounted and armed he sits a king;
For pride she smiles if now she peep—
Elate he rides at the head of his men;
   He is young, and command is a boyish thing:
      They file out into the forest deep—   55
      Do Mosby and his rangers sleep?

The sun is gold, and the world is green,
  Opal the vapors of morning roll;
The champing horses lightly prance—
Full of caprice, and the riders too   60
    Curving in many a caracole.
        But marshaled soon, by fours advance—
        Mosby had checked that airy dance.

By the hospital-tent the cripples stand—
  Bandage, and crutch, and cane, and sling,   65
And palely eye the brave array;
The froth of the cup is gone for them
    (Caw! caw! the crows through the blueness wing):
        Yet these were late as bold, as gay;
        But Mosby—a clip, and grass is hay.   70

How strong they feel on their horses free,
  Tingles the tendoned thigh with life;
Their cavalry-jackets make boys of all—
With golden breasts like the oriole;
    The chat, the jest, and laugh are rife.   75
        But word is passed from the front—a call
        For order; the wood is Mosby's hall.

To which behest one rider sly
  (Spurred, but unarmed) gave little heed—
Of dexterous fun not slow or spare,   80
He teased his neighbors of touchy mood,
    Into plungings he pricked his steed:
        A black-eyed man on a coal-black mare,
        Alive as Mosby in mountain air.

His limbs were long, and large, and round;   85
  He whispered, winked—did all but shout:
A healthy man for the sick to view;
The taste in his mouth was sweet at morn;
    Little of care he cared about.
        And yet of pains and pangs he knew—   90
        In others, maimed by Mosby's crew.

The Hospital Steward—even he
  (Sacred in person as a priest),
And on his coat-sleeve broidered nice
Wore the caduceus, black and green.   95
    No wonder he sat so light on his beast;
        This cheery man in suit of price
        Not even Mosby dared to slice.

They pass the picket by the pine
  And hollow log—a lonesome place;   100
His horse adroop, and pistol clean;
'Tis cocked—kept leveled toward the wood;
    Strained vigilance ages his childish face.
        Since midnight has that stripling been
        Peering for Mosby through the green.   105

Splashing they cross the freshet-flood,
  And up the muddy bank they strain;
A horse at a spectral white-ash shies—
One of the span of the ambulance,
    Black as a hearse. They give the rein: 110
        Silent speed on a scout were wise,
        Could cunning baffle Mosby's spies.

Rumor had come that a band was lodged
  In green retreats of hills that peer
By Aldie (famed for the swordless charge[v]).   115
Much store they'd heaped of captured arms
    And, peradventure, pilfered cheer;
        For Mosby's lads oft hearts enlarge
        In revelry by some gorge's marge.

"Don't let your sabres rattle and ring;   120
  To his oat-bag let each man give heed—
There now, that fellow's bag's untied,
Sowing the road with the precious grain.
    Your carbines swing at hand—you need!
        Look to yourselves, and your nags beside,   125
        Men who after Mosby ride."

Picked lads and keen went sharp before—
    A guard, though scarce against surprise;
And rearmost rode an answering troop,
But flankers none to right or left.   130
    No bugle peals, no pennon flies:
        Silent they sweep, and fain would swoop
        On Mosby with an Indian whoop.

On, right on through the forest land,
    Nor man, nor maid, nor child was seen—   135
Not even a dog. The air was still;
The blackened hut they turned to see,
    And spied charred benches on the green;
        A squirrel sprang from the rotting mill
        Whence Mosby sallied late, brave blood to spill.   140

By worn-out fields they cantered on—
    Drear fields amid the woodlands wide;
By cross-roads of some olden time,
In which grew groves; by gate-stones down—
    Grassed ruins of secluded pride: 145
        A strange lone land, long past the prime,
        Fit land for Mosby or for crime.

The brook in the dell they pass. One peers
    Between the leaves: "Ay, there's the place—
There, on the oozy ledge—'twas there   150
We found the body (Blake's, you know);
    Such whirlings, gurglings round the face—
        Shot drinking! Well, in war all's fair—
        So Mosby says. The bough—take care!"

Hard by, a chapel. Flower-pot mould   155
    Danked and decayed the shaded roof;
The porch was punk; the clapboards spanned
With ruffled lichens gray or green;
    Red coral-moss was not aloof;
        And mid dry leaves green dead-man's-hand   160
        Groped toward that chapel in Mosby-land.

The road they leave and take the wood,
   And mark the trace of ridges there—
A wood where once had slept the farm—
A wood where once tobacco grew   165
   Drowsily in the hazy air,
      And wrought in all kind things a calm—
      Such influence, Mosby! bids disarm.

To ease even yet the place did woo—
   To ease which pines unstirring share,   170
For ease the weary horses sighed:
Halting, and slackening girths, they feed,
   Their pipes they light, they loiter there;
      Then up, and urging still the Guide,
      On, and after Mosby ride.   175

This Guide in frowzy coat of brown,
   And beard of ancient growth and mould,
Bestrode a bony steed and strong,
As suited well with bulk he bore—
   A wheezy man with depth of hold   180
      Who jouncing went. A staff he swung—
      A wight whom Mosby's wasp had stung.

Burnt out and homeless—hunted long!
   That wheeze he caught in autumn-wood
Crouching (a fat man) for his life,   185
And spied his lean son 'mong the crew
   That probed the covert. Ah! black blood
      Was his 'gainst even child and wife—
      Fast friends to Mosby. Such the strife.

A lad, unhorsed by sliding girths,   190
   Strains hard to readjust his seat
Ere the main body show the gap
'Twixt them and the rear-guard; scrub-oaks near
   He sidelong eyes, while hands move fleet;
      Then mounts and spurs. One drops his cap—   195
      "Let Mosby find!" nor heeds mishap.

A gable time-stained peeps through trees:
  "You mind the fight in the haunted house?
That's it; we clenched them in the room—
An ambuscade of ghosts, we deemed,   200
    But proved sly rebels on a bouse!
      Luke lies in the yard." The chimneys loom:
      Some muse on Mosby—some on doom.

Less nimbly now through brakes they wind,
  And ford wild creeks where men have drowned;   205
The pool they skirt, avoid the fen,
And so till night, when down they lie,
    Their steeds still saddled, in wooded ground:
      Rein in hand they slumber then,
      Dreaming of Mosby's cedarn den.   210

But Colonel and Major friendly sat
  Where boughs deformed low made a seat.
The Young Man talked (all sworded and spurred)
Of the partisan's blade he longed to win,
    And frays in which he meant to beat.   215
      The grizzled Major smoked, and heard:
      "But what's that—Mosby?" "No, a bird."

A contrast here like sire and son,
  Hope and Experience sage did meet;
The Youth was brave, the Senior too;   220
But through the Seven Days one had served,
    And gasped with the rear-guard in retreat:
      So he smoked and smoked, and the wreath he blew—
      "Any *sure* news of Mosby's crew?"

He smoked and smoked, eying the while   225
  A huge tree hydra-like in growth—
Moon-tinged—with crook'd boughs rent or lopped—
Itself a haggard forest. "Come!"
    The Colonel cried, "to talk you're loath;
      D'ye hear? I say he must be stopped,   230
      This Mosby—caged, and hair close cropped."

"Of course; but what's that dangling there?"
  "Where?" "From the tree—that gallows-bough;"
"A bit of frayed bark, is it not?"
"Ay—or a rope; did *we* hang last?—   235
  Don't like my neckerchief any how;"
      He loosened it: "O ay, we'll stop
      This Mosby—but that vile jerk and drop!"ᵂ

By peep of light they feed and ride,
  Gaining a grove's green edge at morn,   240
And mark the Aldie hills uprear
And five gigantic horsemen carved
  Clear-cut against the sky withdrawn;
      Are more behind? an open snare?
      Or Mosby's men but watchmen there?   245

The ravaged land was miles behind,
  And Loudon spread her landscape rare;
Orchards in pleasant lowlands stood,
Cows were feeding, a cock loud crew,
  But not a friend at need was there;   250
      The valley-folk were only good
      To Mosby and his wandering brood.

What best to do? what mean yon men?
  Colonel and Guide their minds compare;
Be sure some looked their Leader through;   255
Dismounted, on his sword he leaned
  As one who feigns an easy air;
      And yet perplexed he was they knew—
      Perplexed by Mosby's mountain-crew.

The Major hemmed as he would speak,   260
  But checked himself, and left the ring
Of cavalrymen about their Chief—
Young courtiers mute who paid their court
  By looking with confidence on their king;
      They knew him brave, foresaw no grief—   265
      But Mosby—the time for thought is brief.

The Surgeon (sashed in sacred green)
   Was glad 'twas not for *him* to say
What next should be; if a trooper bleeds,
Why he will do his best, as wont,   270
   And his partner in black will aid and pray;
      But judgment bides with him who leads,
      And Mosby many a problem breeds.

This Surgeon was the kindliest man
   That ever a callous trade professed;   275
He felt for him, that Leader young,
And offered medicine from his flask:
   The Colonel took it with marvelous zest.
      For such fine medicine good and strong,
      Oft Mosby and his foresters long.   280

A charm of proof. "Ho, Major, come—
   Pounce on yon men! Take half your troop,
Through the thickets wind—pray speedy be—
And gain their rear. And, Captain Morn,
   Picket these roads—all travelers stop;   285
      The rest to the edge of this crest with me,
      That Mosby and his scouts may see."

Commanded and done. Ere the sun stood steep,
   Back came the Blues, with a troop of Grays,
Ten riding double—luckless ten!—   290
Five horses gone, and looped hats lost,
   And love-locks dancing in a maze—
      Certes, but sophomores from the glen
      Of Mosby—not his veteran men.

"Colonel," said the Major, touching his cap,   295
   "We've had our ride, and here they are."
"Well done! how many found you there?"
"As many as I bring you here."
   "And no one hurt?" "There'll be no scar—
      One fool was battered." "Find their lair?"   300
      "Why, Mosby's brood camp every where."

He sighed, and slid down from his horse,
   And limping went to a spring-head nigh.
"Why, bless me, Major, not hurt, I hope?"
"Battered my knee against a bar   305
   When the rush was made; all right by-and-by.—
      Halloa! they gave you too much rope—
      Go back to Mosby, eh? elope?"

Just by the low-hanging skirt of wood
   The guard, remiss, had given a chance   310
For a sudden sally into the cover—
But foiled the intent, nor fired a shot,
   Though the issue was a deadly trance;
      For, hurled 'gainst an oak that humped low over,
      Mosby's man fell, pale as a lover.   315

They pulled some grass his head to ease
   (Lined with blue shreds a ground-nest stirred).
The Surgeon came—"Here's a to-do!"
"Ah!" cried the Major, darting a glance,
   "This fellow's the one that fired and spurred   320
      Down hill, but met reserves below—
      My boys, not Mosby's—so we go!"

The Surgeon—bluff, red, goodly man—
   Kneeled by the hurt one; like a bee
He toiled. The pale young Chaplain too—   325
(Who went to the wars for cure of souls,
   And his own student-ailments)—he
      Bent over likewise; spite the two,
      Mosby's poor man more pallid grew.

Meanwhile the mounted captives near   330
   Jested; and yet they anxious showed;
Virginians; some of family-pride,
And young, and full of fire, and fine
   In open feature and cheek that glowed;
      And here thralled vagabonds now they ride—   335
      But list! one speaks for Mosby's side.

"Why, three to one—your horses strong—
   Revolvers, rifles, and a surprise—
Surrender we account no shame!
We live, are gay, and life is hope;   340
   We'll fight again when fight is wise.
      There are plenty more from where we came;
      But go find Mosby—start the game!"

Yet one there was who looked but glum;
   In middle-age, a father he,   345
And this his first experience too:
"They shot at my heart when my hands were up—
   This fighting's crazy work, I see!"
      But noon is high; what next to do?
      The woods are mute, and Mosby is the foe.   350

"Save what we've got," the Major said;
   "Bad plan to make a scout too long;
The tide may turn, and drag them back,
And more beside. These rides I've been,
   And every time a mine was sprung.   355
      To rescue, mind, they won't be slack—
      Look out for Mosby's rifle-crack."

"We'll welcome it! give crack for crack!
   Peril, old lad, is what I seek."
"O then, there's plenty to be had—   360
By all means on, and have our fill!"
   With that, grotesque, he writhed his neck,
      Showing a scar by buck-shot made—
      Kind Mosby's Christmas gift, he said.

"But, Colonel, my prisoners—let a guard   365
   Make sure of them, and lead to camp.
That done, we're free for a dark-room fight
If so you say." The other laughed;
   "Trust me, Major, nor throw a damp.
      But first to try a little sleight—   370
      Sure news of Mosby would suit me quite."

Herewith he turned—"Reb, have a dram?"
  Holding the Surgeon's flask with a smile
To a young scapegrace from the glen.
"O yes!" he eagerly replied,   375
  "And thank you, Colonel, but—any guile?
    For if you think we'll blab—why, then
    You don't know Mosby or his men."

The Leader's genial air relaxed.
  "Best give it up," a whisperer said.   380
"By heaven, I'll range their rebel den!"
"They'll treat you well," the captive cried;
  "They're all like us—handsome—well bred:
    In wood or town, with sword or pen,
    Polite is Mosby, bland his men."   385

"Where were you, lads, last night?—come, tell!"
  "We?—at a wedding in the Vale—
The bridegroom our comrade; by his side
Belisent, my cousin—O, so proud
  Of her young love with old wounds pale—   390
    A Virginian girl! God bless her pride—
    Of a crippled Mosby-man the bride!"

"Four walls shall mend that saucy mood,
  And moping prisons tame him down,"
Said Captain Cloud. "God help that day,"   395
Cried Captain Morn, "and he so young.
  But hark, he sings—a madcap one!"
    "O we multiply merrily in the May,
    The birds and Mosby's men, they say!"

While echoes ran, a wagon old,   400
  Under stout guard of Corporal Chew
Came up; a lame horse, dingy white,
With clouted harness; ropes in hand,
  Cringed the humped driver, black in hue;
    By him (for Mosby's band a sight)   405
    A sister-rebel sat, her veil held tight.

"I picked them up," the Corporal said,
   "Crunching their way over stick and root,
Through yonder wood. The man here—Cuff—
Says they are going to Leesburg town."   410
   The Colonel's eye took in the group;
      The veiled one's hand he spied—enough!
      Not Mosby's. Spite the gown's poor stuff,

Off went his hat: "Lady, fear not;
   We soldiers do what we deplore—   415
I must detain you till we march."
The stranger nodded. Nettled now,
   He grew politer than before:—
      "'Tis Mosby's fault, this halt and search:"
      The lady stiffened in her starch.   420

"My duty, madam, bids me now
   Ask what may seem a little rude.
Pardon—that veil—withdraw it, please
(Corporal! make every man fall back);
   Pray, now, I do but what I should;   425
      Bethink you, 'tis in masks like these
      That Mosby haunts the villages."

Slowly the stranger drew her veil,
   And looked the Soldier in the eye—
A glance of mingled foul and fair;   430
Sad patience in a proud disdain,
   And more than quietude. A sigh
      She heaved, as if all unaware,
      And far seemed Mosby from her care.

She came from Yewton Place, her home,   435
   So ravaged by the war's wild play—
Campings, and foragings, and fires—
That now she sought an aunt's abode.
   Her kinsmen? In Lee's army, they.
      The black? A servant, late her sire's.   440
      And Mosby? Vainly he inquires.

He gazed, and sad she met his eye;
  "In the wood yonder were you lost?"
No; at the forks they left the road
Because of hoof-prints (thick they were—   445
  Thick as the words in notes thrice crossed),
    And fearful, made that episode.
    In fear of Mosby? None she showed.

Her poor attire again he scanned:
  "Lady, once more; I grieve to jar   450
On all sweet usage, but must plead
To have what peeps there from your dress;
  That letter—'tis justly prize of war."
    She started—gave it—she must need.
    "'Tis not from Mosby? May I read?"   455

And straight such matter he perused
  That with the Guide he went apart.
The Hospital Steward's turn began:
"Must squeeze this darkey; every tap
  Of knowledge we are bound to start."   460
    "Garry," she said, "tell all you can
    Of Colonel Mosby—that brave man."

"Dun know much, sare; and missis here
  Know less dan me. But dis I know—"
"Well, what?" "I dun know what I know."   465
"A knowing answer!" The hump-back coughed,
  Rubbing his yellowish wool like tow.
    "Come—Mosby—tell!" "O dun look so!
    My gal nursed missis—let we go."

"Go where?" demanded Captain Cloud;   470
  "Back into bondage? Man, you're free!"
"Well, *let* we free!" The Captain's brow
Lowered; the Colonel came—had heard:
  "Pooh! pooh! his simple heart I see—
    A faithful servant.—Lady" (a bow),   475
    "Mosby's abroad—with us you'll go.

"Guard! look to your prisoners; back to camp!
    The man in the grass—can he mount and away?
Why, how he groans!" "Bad inward bruise—
Might lug him along in the ambulance."   480
    "Coals to Newcastle! let him stay.
        Boots and saddles!—our pains we lose,
        Nor care I if Mosby hear the news!"

But word was sent to a house at hand,
    And a flask was left by the hurt one's side.   485
They seized in that same house a man,
Neutral by day, by night a foe—
    So charged his neighbor late, the Guide.
        A grudge? Hate will do what it can;
        Along he went for a Mosby-man.   490

No secrets now; the bugle calls;
    The open road they take, nor shun
The hill; retrace the weary way.
But one there was who whispered low,
    "This is a feint—we'll back anon;   495
        Young Hair-Brains don't retreat, they say;
        A brush with Mosby is the play!"

They rode till eve. Then on a farm
    That lay along a hill-side green,
Bivouacked. Fires were made, and then   500
Coffee was boiled; a cow was coaxed
And killed, and savory roasts were seen;
    And under the lee of a cattle-pen
        The guard supped freely with Mosby's men.

The ball was bandied to and fro;   505
    Hits were given and hits were met:
"Chickamauga, Feds—take off your hat!"
"But the Fight in the Clouds repaid you, Rebs!"
    "Forgotten about Manassas yet?"
        Chatting and chaffing, and tit for tat,   510
        Mosby's clan with the troopers sat.

"Here comes the moon!" a captive cried;
  "A song! what say? Archy, my lad!"
Hailing the still one of the clan
(A boyish face with girlish hair),   515
  "Give us that thing poor Pansy made
    Last year." He brightened, and began;
    And this was the song of Mosby's man:

    Spring is come; she shows her pass—
      Wild violets cool!   520
    South of woods a small close grass—
      A vernal wool!
    Leaves are a'bud on the sassafras—
      They'll soon be full:
    Blessings on the friendly screen—   525
    I'm for the South! says the leafage green.

    Robins! fly, and take your fill
      Of out-of-doors—
    Garden, orchard, meadow, hill,
      Barns and bowers;   530
    Take your fill, and have your will—
      Virginia's yours!
    But, bluebirds! keep away, and fear
    The ambuscade in bushes here.

"A green song that," a sergeant said;   535
  "But where's poor Pansy? gone, I fear."
"Ay, mustered out at Ashby's Gap."
"I see; now for a live man's song;
  Ditty for ditty—prepare to cheer.
    My bluebirds, you can fling a cap!   540
    You barehead Mosby-boys—why—clap!"

    Nine Blue-coats went a-nutting
      Slyly in Tennessee—
    Not for chestnuts—better than that—
      Hush, you bumble-bee!   545
      Nutting, nutting—
      All through the year there's nutting!

A tree they spied so yellow,
    Rustling in motion queer;
In they fired, and down they dropped—   550
    Butternuts, my dear!
        Nutting, nutting—
        Who'll 'list to go a-nutting?

Ah! why should good fellows foemen be?
    And who would dream that foes they were—   555
Larking and singing so friendly then—
A family likeness in every face.
    But Captain Cloud made sour demur:
        "Guard! keep your prisoners *in* the pen,
        And let none talk with Mosby's men."   560

That captain was a valorous one
    (No irony, but honest truth),
Yet down from his brain cold drops distilled,
Making stalactites in his heart—
    A conscientious soul, forsooth;   565
        And with a formal hate was filled
        Of Mosby's band; and some he'd killed.

Meantime the lady rueful sat,
    Watching the flicker of a fire
Where the Colonel played the outdoor host   570
In brave old hall of ancient Night.
    But ever the dame grew shyer and shyer,
        Seeming with private grief engrossed—
        Grief far from Mosby, housed or lost.

The ruddy embers showed her pale.   575
    The Soldier did his best devoir:
"Some coffee?—no?—a cracker?—one?"
Cared for her servant—sought to cheer:
    "I know, I know—a cruel war!
        But wait—even Mosby 'll eat his bun;   580
        The Old Hearth—back to it anon!"

But cordial words no balm could bring;
　　She sighed, and kept her inward chafe,
And seemed to hate the voice of glee—
Joyless and tearless. Soon he called   585
　　An escort: "See this lady safe
　　　　In yonder house.—Madam, you're free.
　　　　And now for Mosby.—Guide! with me."

("A night-ride, eh?") "Tighten your girths!
　　But, buglers! not a note from you.   590
Fling more rails on the fires—a blaze!"
("Sergeant, a feint—I told you so—
　　Toward Aldie again. Bivouac, adieu!")
　　　　After the cheery flames they gaze,
　　　　Then back for Mosby through the maze.   595

The moon looked through the trees, and tipped
　　The scabbards with her elfin beam;
The Leader backward cast his glance,
Proud of the cavalcade that came—
　　A hundred horses, bay and cream: 600
　　　　"Major! look how the lads advance—
　　　　Mosby we'll have in the ambulance!"

"No doubt, no doubt:—was that a hare?—
　　First catch, then cook; and cook him brown."
"Trust me to catch," the other cried—   605
"The lady's letter!—a dance, man, dance
　　This night is given in Leesburg town!"
　　　　"He'll be there too!" wheezed out the Guide;
　　　　"That Mosby loves a dance and ride!"

"The lady, ah!—the lady's letter—   610
　　A *lady*, then, is in the case,"
Muttered the Major. "Ay, her aunt
Writes her to come by Friday eve
　　(To-night), for people of the place,
　　　　At Mosby's last fight jubilant,   615
　　　　A party give, though table-cheer be scant."

The Major hemmed. "Then this night-ride
  We owe to her?—One lighted house
In a town else dark.—The moths, begar!
Are not quite yet all dead!" "How? how?"   620
  "A mute, meek, mournful little mouse!—
    Mosby has wiles which subtle are—
    But woman's wiles in wiles of war!"

"Tut, Major! by what craft or guile—"
  "Can't tell! but he'll be found in wait.   625
Softly we enter, say, the town—
Good! pickets post, and all so sure—
  When—crack! the rifles from every gate,
    The Gray-backs fire—dash up and down—
    Each alley unto Mosby known!"   630

"Now, Major, now—you take dark views
  Of a moonlight night." "Well, well, we'll see,"
And smoked as if each whiff were gain.
The other mused; then sudden asked,
  "What would you do in grand decree?"   635
    "I'd beat, if I could, Lee's armies—then
    Send constables after Mosby's men."

"Ay! ay!—you're odd." The moon sailed up;
  On through the shadowy land they went.
"Names must be made and printed be!"   640
Hummed the blithe Colonel. "Doc, your flask!
  Major, I drink to your good content.
    My pipe is out—enough for me!
    One's buttons shine—does Mosby see?

"But what comes here?" A man from the front   645
  Reported a tree athwart the road.
"Go round it, then; no time to bide;
All right—go on! Were one to stay
  For each distrust of a nervous mood,
    Long miles we'd make in this our ride   650
    Through Mosby-land.—On! with the Guide!"

Then sportful to the Surgeon turned:
   "Green sashes hardly serve by night!"
"Nor bullets nor bottles," the Major sighed,
"Against these moccasin-snakes—such foes   655
   As seldom come to solid fight:
      They kill and vanish; through grass they glide;
      Devil take Mosby!"—his horse here shied.

"Hold! look—the tree, like a dragged balloon;
   A globe of leaves—some trickery here;   660
My nag is right—best now be shy."
A movement was made, a hubbub and snarl;
   Little was plain—they blindly steer.
      The Pleiads, as from ambush sly,
      Peep out—Mosby's men in the sky!   665

As restive they turn, how sore they feel,
   And cross, and sleepy, and full of spleen,
And curse the war. "Fools, North and South!"
Said one right out. "O for a bed!
   O now to drop in this woodland green!"   670
      He drops as the syllables leave his mouth—
      Mosby speaks from the undergrowth—

Speaks in a volley! out jets the flame!
   Men fall from their saddles like plums from trees;
Horses take fright, reins tangle and bind;   675
"Steady—dismount—form—and into the wood!"
   They go, but find what scarce can please:
      Their steeds have been tied in the field behind,
      And Mosby's men are off like the wind.

Sound the recall! vain to pursue—   680
   The enemy scatters in wilds he knows,
To reunite in his own good time;
And, to follow, they need divide—
   To come lone and lost on crouching foes:
      Maple and hemlock, beech and lime,   685
      Are Mosby's confederates, share the crime.

"Major," burst in a bugler small,
    "The fellow we left in Loudon grass—
Sir Slyboots with the inward bruise,
His voice I heard—the very same—   690
    Some watchword in the ambush pass;
        Ay, sir, we had him in his shoes—
        We caught him—Mosby—but to lose!"

"Go, go!—these saddle-dreamers! Well,
    And here's another.—Cool, sir, cool!"   695
"Major, I saw them mount and sweep,
And one was humped, or I mistake,
    And in the skurry dropped his wool."
        "A wig! go fetch it:—the lads need sleep;
        They'll next see Mosby in a sheep!   700

"Come, come, fall back! reform your ranks—
    All's jackstraws here! Where's Captain Morn?—
We've parted like boats in a raging tide!
But stay—the Colonel—did he charge?
    And comes he there? 'Tis streak of dawn;   705
        Mosby is off, the woods are wide—
        Hist! there's a groan—this crazy ride!"

As they searched for the fallen, the dawn grew chill;
    They lay in the dew: "Ah! hurt much, Mink?
And—yes—the Colonel!" Dead! but so calm   710
That death seemed nothing—even death,
    The thing we deem every thing heart can think;
        Amid wilding roses that shed their balm,
        Careless of Mosby he lay—in a charm!

The Major took him by the hand—   715
    Into the friendly clasp it bled
(A ball through heart and hand he rued):
"Good-by!" and gazed with humid glance;
    Then in a hollow revery said,
        "The weakest thing is lustihood;   720
        But Mosby"—and he checked his mood.

"Where's the advance?—cut off, by heaven!
    Come, Surgeon, how with your wounded there?"
"The ambulance will carry all."
"Well, get them in; we go to camp.   725
    Seven prisoners gone? for the rest have care."
        Then to himself, "This grief is gall;
        That Mosby!—I'll cast a silver ball!"

"Ho!" turning—"Captain Cloud, you mind
    The place where the escort went—so shady?   730
Go, search every closet low and high,
And barn, and bin, and hidden bower—
    Every covert—find that lady!
        And yet I may misjudge her—ay,
        Women (like Mosby) mystify.   735

"We'll see. Ay, Captain, go—with speed!
    Surround and search; each living thing
Secure; that done, await us where
We last turned off. Stay! fire the cage
    If the birds be flown." By the cross-road spring   740
        The bands rejoined; no words; the glare
        Told all. Had Mosby plotted there?

The weary troop that wended now—
    Hardly it seemed the same that pricked
Forth to the forest from the camp: 745
Foot-sore horses, jaded men;
    Every backbone felt as nicked,
        Each eye dim as a sick-room lamp,
        All faces stamped with Mosby's stamp.

In order due the Major rode—   750
    Chaplain and Surgeon on either hand;
A riderless horse a negro led;
In a wagon the blanketed sleeper went;
    Then the ambulance with the bleeding band;
        And, an emptied oat-bag on each head,   755
        Went Mosby's men, and marked the dead.

What gloomed them? what so cast them down,
   And changed the cheer that late they took,
As double-guarded now they rode
Between the files of moody men?   760
    Some sudden consciousness they brook,
       Or dread the sequel. That night's blood
       Disturbed even Mosby's brotherhood.

The flagging horses stumbled at roots,
   Floundered in mires, or clinked the stones;   765
No rider spake except aside;
But the wounded cramped in the ambulance,
   It was horror to hear their groans—
       Jerked along in the woodland ride,
       While Mosby's clan their revery hide.   770

The Hospital Steward—even he—
   Who on the sleeper kept his glance,
Was changed; late bright-black beard and eye
Looked now hearse-black; his heavy heart,
   Like his fagged mare, no more could dance;   775
       His grape was now a raisin dry:
       'Tis Mosby's homily—*Man must die.*

The amber sunset flushed the camp
   As on the hill their eyes they fed;
The pickets dumb looks at the wagon dart;   780
A handkerchief waves from the bannered tent—
   As white, alas! the face of the dead:
       Who shall the withering news impart?
       The bullet of Mosby goes through heart to heart!

They buried him where the lone ones lie   785
   (Lone sentries shot on midnight post)—
A green-wood grave-yard hid from ken,
Where sweet-fern flings an odor nigh—
   Yet held in fear for the gleaming ghost!
       Though the bride should see threescore and ten,   790
       She will dream of Mosby and his men.

Now halt the verse, and turn aside—
    The cypress falls athwart the way;
No joy remains for bard to sing;
And heaviest dole of all is this,   795
    That other hearts shall be as gay
        As hers that now no more shall spring:
        To Mosby-land the dirges cling.

Lee in the Capitol^x

(April, 1866)

HARD pressed by numbers in his strait,
    Rebellion's soldier-chief no more contends—
Feels that the hour is come of Fate,
    Lays down one sword, and widened warfare ends.
The captain who fierce armies led   5
Becomes a quiet seminary's head—
Poor as his privates, earns his bread.
In studious cares and aims engrossed,
    Strives to forget Stuart and Stonewall dead—
Comrades and cause, station and riches lost,   10
    And all the ills that flock when fortune's fled.
No word he breathes of vain lament,
    Mute to reproach, nor hears applause—
His doom accepts, perforce content,
    And acquiesces in asserted laws;   15
Secluded now would pass his life,
And leave to time the sequel of the strife.
    But missives from the Senators ran;
Not that they now would gaze upon a swordless foe,
And power made powerless and brought low: 20
    Reasons of state, 'tis claimed, require the man.
Demurring not, promptly he comes
By ways which show the blackened homes,
    And—last—the seat no more his own,
But Honor's; patriot grave-yards fill   25
The forfeit slopes of that patrician hill,

And fling a shroud on Arlington.
The oaks ancestral all are low;
No more from the porch his glance shall go
Ranging the varied landscape o'er,   30
Far as the looming Dome—no more.
One look he gives, then turns aside,
Solace he summons from his pride:
"So be it! They await me now
Who wrought this stinging overthrow;   35
They wait me; not as on the day
Of Pope's impelled retreat in disarray—
By me impelled—when toward yon Dome
The clouds of war came rolling home."
The burst, the bitterness was spent,   40
The heart-burst bitterly turbulent,
And on he fared.
                    In nearness now
    He marks the Capitol—a show
Lifted in amplitude, and set   45
With standards flushed with the glow of Richmond yet;
    Trees and green terraces sleep below.
Through the clear air, in sunny light,
The marble dazes—a temple white.

Intrepid soldier! had his blade been drawn   50
For yon starred flag, never as now
Bid to the Senate-house had he gone,
But freely, and in pageant borne,
As when brave numbers without number, massed,
Plumed the broad way, and pouring passed—   55
Bannered, beflowered—between the shores
Of faces, and the dinn'd huzzas,
And balconies kindling at the sabre-flash,
'Mid roar of drums and guns, and cymbal-crash,
While Grant and Sherman shone in blue—   60
Close of the war and victory's long review.

Yet pride at hand still aidful swelled,
And up the hard ascent he held.

The meeting follows. In his mien
The victor and the vanquished both are seen—   65
All that he is, and what he late had been.
Awhile, with curious eyes they scan
The Chief who led invasion's van—
Allied by family to one,
Founder of the Arch the Invader warred upon: 70
Who looks at Lee must think of Washington;
In pain must think, and hide the thought,
So deep with grievous meaning it is fraught.

Secession in her soldier shows
Silent and patient; and they feel   75
   (Developed even in just success)
Dim inklings of a hazy future steal;
   Their thoughts their questions well express:
"Does the sad South still cherish hate?
Freely will Southern men with Northern mate?   80
The blacks—should we our arm withdraw,
Would that betray them? some distrust your law.
And how if foreign fleets should come—
Would the South then drive her wedges home?"
And more hereof. The Virginian sees—   85
Replies to such anxieties.
Discreet his answers run—appear
Briefly straightforward, coldly clear.

"If now," the Senators, closing, say,
"Aught else remain, speak out, we pray."   90
Hereat he paused; his better heart
Strove strongly then; prompted a worthier part
Than coldly to endure his doom.
Speak out? Ay, speak, and for the brave,
Who else no voice or proxy have;   95
Frankly their spokesman here become,
And the flushed North from her own victory save.
That inspiration overrode—
Hardly it quelled the galling load
Of personal ill. The inner feud   100

He, self-contained, a while withstood;
They waiting. In his troubled eye
Shadows from clouds unseen they spy;
They could not mark within his breast
The pang which pleading thought oppressed: 105
He spoke, nor felt the bitterness die.

"My word is given—it ties my sword;
Even were banners still abroad,
Never could I strive in arms again
While you, as fit, that pledge retain.   110
Our cause I followed, stood in field and gate—
All's over now, and now I follow Fate.
But this is naught. A People call—
A desolated land, and all
The brood of ills that press so sore,   115
The natural offspring of this civil war,
Which ending not in fame, such as might rear
Fitly its sculptured trophy here,
Yields harvest large of doubt and dread
To all who have the heart and head   120
To feel and know. How shall I speak?
Thoughts knot with thoughts, and utterance check.
Before my eyes there swims a haze,
Through mists departed comrades gaze—
First to encourage, last that shall upbraid!   125
How shall I speak? The South would fain
Feel peace, have quiet law again—
Replant the trees for homestead-shade.
    You ask if she recants: she yields.
Nay, and would more; would blend anew,   130
As the bones of the slain in her forests do,
Bewailed alike by us and you.
    A voice comes out from those charnel-fields,
A plaintive yet unheeded one:
'Died all in vain? both sides undone?'   135
Push not your triumph; do not urge

Submissiveness beyond the verge.
Intestine rancor would you bide,
Nursing eleven sliding daggers in your side?
Far from my thought to school or threat;   140
I speak the things which hard beset.
Where various hazards meet the eyes,
To elect in magnanimity is wise.
Reap victory's fruit while sound the core;
What sounder fruit than re-established law?   145
I know your partial thoughts do press
Solely on us for war's unhappy stress;
But weigh—consider—look at all,
And broad anathema you'll recall.
The censor's charge I'll not repeat,   150
That meddlers kindled the war's white heat—
Vain intermeddlers and malign,
Both of the palm and of the pine;
I waive the thought—which never can be rife—
Common's the crime in every civil strife: 155
But this I feel, that North and South were driven
By Fate to arms. For *our* unshriven,
What thousands, truest souls, were tried—
    As never may any be again—
All those who stemmed Secession's pride,   160
But at last were swept by the urgent tide
    Into the chasm. I know their pain.
A story here may be applied:
    'In Moorish lands there lived a maid
Brought to confess by vow the creed   165
    Of Christians. Fain would priests persuade
That now she must approve by deed
    The faith she kept. "What deed?" she asked.
"Your old sire leave, nor deem it sin,
    And come with us." Still more they tasked   170
The sad one: "If heaven you'd win—
    Far from the burning pit withdraw,
Then must you learn to hate your kin,

Yea, side against them—such the law,
For Moor and Christian are at war."   175
"Then will I never quit my sire,
But here with him through every trial go,
Nor leave him though in flames below—
God help me in his fire!"'
So in the South; vain every plea   180
'Gainst Nature's strong fidelity;
    True to the home and to the heart,
Throngs cast their lot with kith and kin,
    Foreboding, cleaved to the natural part—
Was this the unforgivable sin?   185
These noble spirits are yet yours to win.
Shall the great North go Sylla's way?
Proscribe? prolong the evil day?
Confirm the curse? infix the hate?
In Union's name forever alienate?   190
From reason who can urge the plea—
Freemen conquerors of the free?
When blood returns to the shrunken vein,
Shall the wound of the Nation bleed again?
Well may the wars wan thought supply,   195
And kill the kindling of the hopeful eye,
Unless you do what even kings have done
In leniency—unless you shun
To copy Europe in her worst estate—
Avoid the tyranny you reprobate."   200

He ceased. His earnestness unforeseen
Moved, but not swayed their former mien;
    And they dismissed him. Forth he went
Through vaulted walks in lengthened line
Like porches erst upon the Palatine: 205
    Historic reveries their lesson lent,
    The Past her shadow through the Future sent.

But no. Brave though the Soldier, grave his plea—
    Catching the light in the future's skies,

Instinct disowns each darkening prophecy: 210
   Faith in America never dies;
Heaven shall the end ordained fulfill,
We march with Providence cheery still.

A Meditation

*Attributed to a Northerner after attending the last of two
funerals from the same homestead—those of a National and a
Confederate officer (brothers), his kinsmen, who had died from
the effects of wounds received in the closing battles*

How often in the years that close,
    When truce had stilled the sieging gun,
The soldiers, mounting on their works,
    With mutual curious glance have run
From face to face along the fronting show,   5
And kinsman spied, or friend—even in a foe.

What thoughts conflicting then were shared,
    While sacred tenderness perforce
Welled from the heart and wet the eye;
    And something of a strange remorse   10
Rebelled against the sanctioned sin of blood,
And Christian wars of natural brotherhood.

Then stirred the god within the breast—
    The witness that is man's at birth;
A deep misgiving undermined   15
    Each plea and subterfuge of earth;
They felt in that rapt pause, with warning rife,
Horror and anguish for the civil strife.

Of North or South they recked not then,
    Warm passion cursed the cause of war: 20
Can Africa pay back this blood

Spilt on Potomac's shore?
Yet doubts, as pangs, were vain the strife to stay,
And hands that fain had clasped again could slay.

How frequent in the camp was seen   25
   The herald from the hostile one,
A guest and frank companion there
   When the proud formal talk was done;
The pipe of peace was smoked even 'mid the war,
And fields in Mexico again fought o'er.   30

In Western battle long they lay
   So near opposed in trench or pit,
That foeman unto foeman called
   As men who screened in tavern sit:
"You bravely fight" each to the other said—   35
"Toss us a biscuit!" o'er the wall it sped.

And pale on those same slopes, a boy—
   A stormer, bled in noon-day glare;
No aid the Blue-coats then could bring,
   He cried to them who nearest were,   40
And out there came 'mid howling shot and shell
A daring foe who him befriended well.

Mark the great Captains on both sides,
   The soldiers with the broad renown—
They all were messmates on the Hudson's marge,   45
   Beneath one roof they laid them down;
And, free from hate in many an after pass,
Strove as in school-boy rivalry of the class.

A darker side there is; but doubt
   In Nature's charity hovers there: 50
If men for new agreement yearn,
   Then old upbraiding best forbear:
"The South's the sinner!" Well, so let it be;
But shall the North sin worse, and stand the Pharisee?

O, now that brave men yield the sword,   55
   Mine be the manful soldier-view;
By how much more they boldly warred,
   By so much more is mercy due:
When Vicksburg fell, and the moody files marched out,
Silent the victors stood, scorning to raise a shout.   60

NOTES

Notes

Note^a, *page 8*

The gloomy lull of the early part of the winter of 1860–1, seeming big with final disaster to our institutions, affected some minds that believed them to constitute one of the great hopes of mankind, much as the eclipse which came over the promise of the first French Revolution affected kindred natures, throwing them for the time into doubts and misgivings universal.

Note^b, *page 21*

"The terrible Stone Fleet, on a mission as pitiless as the granite that freights it, sailed this morning from Port Royal, and before two days are past will have made Charleston an inland city. The ships are all old whalers, and cost the government from $2500 to $5000 each. Some of them were once famous ships." —(From Newspaper Correspondence of the day.)

Sixteen vessels were accordingly sunk on the bar at the river entrance. Their names were as follows:

Amazon,	Leonidas,
America,	Maria Theresa,
American,	Potomac,
Archer,	Rebecca Simms,
Courier,	L. C. Richmond,
Fortune,	Robin Hood,
Herald,	Tenedos,
Kensington,	William Lee.

All accounts seem to agree that the object proposed was not accomplished. The channel is even said to have become ultimately benefited by the means employed to obstruct it.

NOTE^c, *page 41*

The *Temeraire,* that storied ship of the old English fleet, and the subject of the well-known painting by Turner, commends itself to the mind seeking for some one craft to stand for the poetic ideal of those great historic wooden war-ships, whose gradual displacement is lamented by none more than by regularly educated navy officers, and of all nations.

NOTE^d, *page 41*

Some of the cannon of old times, especially the brass ones, unlike the more effective ordnance of the present day, were cast in shapes which Cellini might have designed, were gracefully enchased, generally with the arms of the country. A few of them—field-pieces—captured in our earlier wars, are preserved in arsenals and navy-yards.

NOTE^e, *page 51*

Whatever just military criticism, favorable or otherwise, has at any time been made upon General McClellan's campaigns, will stand. But if, during the excitement of the conflict, aught was spread abroad tending to unmerited disparagement of the man, it must necessarily die out, though not perhaps without leaving some traces, which may or may not prove enduring. Some there are whose votes aided in the re-election of Abraham Lincoln, who yet believed, and retain the belief, that General McClellan, to say the least, always proved himself a patriotic and honorable soldier. The feeling which surviving comrades entertain for their late commander is one which, from its passion, is susceptible of versified representation, and such it receives.

NOTE^f, *page 52*

At Antietam Stonewall Jackson led one wing of Lee's army, consequently sharing that day in whatever may be deemed to have been the fortunes of his superior.

NOTE^g, *page 58*

Admiral Porter is a son of the late Commodore Porter, commander of the frigate Essex on that Pacific cruise which ended in the desperate fight off Valparaiso with the English frigates Cherub and Phœbe, in the year 1814.

Note[h], *page 63*

Among numerous head-stones or monuments on Cemetery Hill, marred or destroyed by the enemy's concentrated fire, was one, somewhat conspicuous, of a Federal officer killed before Richmond in 1862.

On the 4th of July, 1865, the Gettysburg National Cemetery, on the same height with the original burial-ground, was consecrated, and the corner-stone laid of a commemorative pile.

Note[i], *page 64*

"I dare not write the horrible and inconceivable atrocities committed," says Froissart, in alluding to the remarkable sedition in France during his time. The like may be hinted of some proceedings of the draft-rioters.

Note[j], *page 66*

Although the month was November, the day was in character an October one—cool, clear, bright, intoxicatingly invigorating; one of those days peculiar to the ripest hours of our American autumn. This weather must have had much to do with the spontaneous enthusiasm which seized the troops—an enthusiasm aided, doubtless, by glad thoughts of the victory of Look-out Mountain won the day previous, and also by the elation attending the capture, after a fierce struggle, of the long ranges of rifle-pits at the mountain's base, where orders for the time should have stopped the advance. But there and then it was that the army took the bit between its teeth, and ran away with the generals to the victory commemorated. General Grant, at Culpepper, a few weeks prior to crossing the Rapidan for the Wilderness, expressed to a visitor his impression of the impulse and the spectacle: Said he, "I never saw any thing like it:" language which seems curiously undertoned, considering its application; but from the taciturn Commander it was equivalent to a superlative or hyperbole from the talkative.

The height of the Ridge, according to the account at hand, varies along its length from six to seven hundred feet above the plain; it slopes at an angle of about forty-five degrees.

Note[k], *page 78*

The great Parrott gun, planted in the marshes of James Island, and employed in the prolonged, though at times intermitted bombardment of Charleston, was known among our soldiers as the Swamp Angel.

St. Michael's, characterized by its venerable tower, was the historic and aristocratic church of the town.

Note[l], *page 89*

Among the Northwestern regiments there would seem to have been more than one which carried a living eagle as an added ensign. The bird commemorated here was, according to the account, borne aloft on a perch beside the standard; went through successive battles and campaigns; was more than once under the surgeon's hands; and at the close of the contest found honorable repose in the capital of Wisconsin, from which state he had gone to the wars.

Note[m], *page 90*

The late Major General McPherson, commanding the Army of the Tennessee, a native of Ohio and a West Pointer, was one of the foremost spirits of the war. Young, though a veteran; hardy, intrepid, sensitive in honor, full of engaging qualities, with manly beauty; possessed of genius, a favorite with the army, and with Grant and Sherman. Both Generals have generously acknowledged their professional obligations to the able engineer and admirable soldier, their subordinate and junior.

In an informal account written by the Achilles to this Sarpedon, he says:

"On that day we avenged his death. Near twenty-two hundred of the enemy's dead remained on the ground when night closed upon the scene of action."

It is significant of the scale on which the war was waged, that the engagement thus written of goes solely (so far as can be learned) under the vague designation of one of the battles before Atlanta.

Note[n], *page 97*

This piece was written while yet the reports were coming North of Sherman's homeward advance from Savannah. It is needless to point out its purely dramatic character.

Though the sentiment ascribed in the beginning of the second stanza must, in the present reading, suggest the historic tragedy of the 14th of April, nevertheless, as intimated, it was written prior to that event, and without any distinct application in the writer's mind. After consideration, it is allowed to remain.

Few need be reminded that, by the less intelligent classes of the South, Abraham Lincoln, by nature the most kindly of men, was regarded as a monster wantonly warring upon liberty. He stood for the personification of tyrannic power. Each Union soldier was called a Lincolnite.

Undoubtedly Sherman, in the desolation he inflicted after leaving Atlanta, acted not in contravention of orders; and all, in a military point of view, is by military judges deemed to have been expedient, and nothing can abate General Sherman's shining renown; his claims to it rest on no single campaign. Still, there are those who can not but contrast some of the scenes enacted in Georgia and the

Carolinas, and also in the Shenandoah, with a circumstance in a great Civil War of heathen antiquity. Plutarch relates that in a military council held by Pompey and the chiefs of that party which stood for the Commonwealth, it was decided that under no plea should any city be sacked that was subject to the people of Rome. There was this difference, however, between the Roman civil conflict and the American one. The war of Pompey and Cæsar divided the Roman people promiscuously; that of the North and South ran a frontier line between what for the time were distinct communities or nations. In this circumstance, possibly, and some others, may be found both the cause and the justification of some of the sweeping measures adopted.

Note°, *page 104*

At this period of excitement the thought was by some passionately welcomed that the Presidential successor had been raised up by heaven to wreak vengeance on the South. The idea originated in the remembrance that Andrew Johnson by birth belonged to that class of Southern whites who never cherished love for the dominant one; that he was a citizen of Tennessee, where the contest at times and in places had been close and bitter as a Middle-Age feud; that himself and family had been hardly treated by the Secessionists.

But the expectations built hereon (if, indeed, ever soberly entertained), happily for the country, have not been verified.

Likewise the feeling which would have held the entire South chargeable with the crime of one exceptional assassin, this too has died away with the natural excitement of the hour.

Note^P, *page 107*

The incident on which this piece is based is narrated in a newspaper account of the battle to be found in the "Rebellion Record." During the disaster to the national forces on the first day, a brigade on the extreme left found itself isolated. The perils it encountered are given in detail. Among others, the following sentences occur:

"Under cover of the fire from the bluffs, the rebels rushed down, crossed the ford, and in a moment were seen forming this side the creek in open fields, and within close musket-range. Their color-bearers stepped defiantly to the front as the engagement opened furiously; the rebels pouring in sharp, quick volleys of musketry, and their batteries above continuing to support them with a destructive fire. Our sharpshooters wanted to pick off the audacious rebel color-bearers, but Colonel Stuart interposed: 'No, no, they're too brave fellows to be killed.'"

NOTE^q, *page 109*

According to a report of the Secretary of War, there were on the first day of March, 1865, 965,000 men on the army pay-rolls. Of these, some 200,000—artillery, cavalry, and infantry—made up from the larger portion of the veterans of Grant and Sherman, marched by the President. The total number of Union troops enlisted during the war was 2,668,000.

NOTE^r, *page 112*

For a month or two after the completion of peace, some thousands of released captives from the military prisons of the North, natives of all parts of the South, passed through the city of New York, sometimes waiting farther transportation for days, during which interval they wandered penniless about the streets, or lay in their worn and patched gray uniforms under the trees of the Battery, near the barracks where they were lodged and fed. They were transported and provided for at the charge of government.

NOTE^s, *page 114*

Shortly prior to the evacuation of Petersburg, the enemy, with a view to ultimate repossession, interred some of his heavy guns in the same field with his dead, and with every circumstance calculated to deceive. Subsequently the negroes exposed the stratagem.

NOTE^t, *page 118*

The records of Northern colleges attest what numbers of our noblest youth went from them to the battle-field. Southern members of the same classes arrayed themselves on the side of Secession; while Southern seminaries contributed large quotas. Of all these, what numbers marched who never returned except on the shield.

NOTE^u, *page 134*

Written prior to the founding of the National Cemetery at Andersonville, where 15,000 of the reinterred captives now sleep, each beneath his personal head-board, inscribed from records found in the prison-hospital. Some hundreds rest apart and without name. A glance at the published pamphlet containing the list of the buried at Andersonville conveys a feeling mournfully impressive. Seventy-four large double-columned pages in fine print. Looking through them is like getting lost among the old turbaned head-stones and cypresses in the interminable Black Forest of Scutari, over against Constantinople.

Note^V, *page 142*

In one of Kilpatrick's earlier cavalry fights near Aldie, a Colonel who, being under arrest, had been temporarily deprived of his sword, nevertheless, unarmed, insisted upon charging at the head of his men, which he did, and the onset proved victorious.

Note^W, *page 146*

Certain of Mosby's followers, on the charge of being unlicensed foragers or fighters, being hung by order of a Union cavalry commander, the Partisan promptly retaliated in the woods. In turn, this also was retaliated, it is said. To what extent such deplorable proceedings were carried, it is not easy to learn.

South of the Potomac in Virginia, and within a gallop of the Long Bridge at Washington, is the confine of a country, in some places wild, which through-out the war it was unsafe for a Union man to traverse except with an armed escort. This was the chase of Mosby, the scene of many of his exploits or those of his men. In the heart of this region at least one fortified camp was main-tained by our cavalry, and from time to time expeditions were made therefrom. Owing to the nature of the country and the embittered feeling of its inhabitants, many of these expeditions ended disastrously. Such results were helped by the exceeding cunning of the enemy, born of his wood-craft, and, in some instances, by undue confidence on the part of our men. A body of cavalry, starting from camp with the view of breaking up a nest of rangers, and absent say three days, would return with a number of their own forces killed and wounded (ambushed), without having been able to retaliate farther than by foraging on the country, destroying a house or two reported to be haunts of the guerrillas, or capturing non-combatants accused of being secretly active in their behalf.

In the verse the name of Mosby is invested with some of those associations with which the popular mind is familiar. But facts do not warrant the belief that every clandestine attack of men who passed for Mosby's was made under his eye, or even by his knowledge.

In partisan warfare he proved himself shrewd, able, and enterprising, and always a wary fighter. He stood well in the confidence of his superior officers, and was employed by them at times in furtherance of important movements. To our wounded on more than one occasion he showed considerate kindness. Officers and civilians captured by forces under his immediate command were, so long as remaining under his orders, treated with civility. These things are well known to those personally familiar with the irregular fighting in Virginia.

NOTE^x, *page 163*

Among those summoned during the spring just passed to appear before the Reconstruction Committee of Congress was Robert E. Lee. His testimony is deeply interesting, both in itself and as coming from him. After various questions had been put and briefly answered, these words were addressed to him:

"If there be any other matter about which you wish to speak on this occasion, do so freely." Waiving this invitation, he responded by a short personal explanation of some point in a previous answer, and, after a few more brief questions and replies, the interview closed.

In the verse a poetical liberty has been ventured. Lee is not only represented as responding to the invitation, but also as at last renouncing his cold reserve, doubtless the cloak to feelings more or less poignant. If for such freedom warrant be necessary, the speeches in ancient histories, not to speak of those in Shakspeare's historic plays, may not unfitly perhaps be cited.

The character of the original measures proposed about this time in the National Legislature for the treatment of the (as yet) Congressionally excluded South, and the spirit in which those measures were advocated—these are circumstances which it is fairly supposable would have deeply influenced the thoughts, whether spoken or withheld, of a Southerner placed in the position of Lee before the Reconstruction Committee.

Supplement

WERE I fastidiously anxious for the symmetry of this book, it would close with the notes. But the times are such that patriotism—not free from solicitude—urges a claim overriding all literary scruples.

It is more than a year since the memorable surrender, but events have not yet rounded themselves into completion. Not justly can we complain of this. There has been an upheaval affecting the basis of things; to altered circumstances complicated adaptations are to be made; there are difficulties great and novel. But is Reason still waiting for Passion to spend itself? We have sung of the soldiers and sailors, but who shall hymn the politicians?

In view of the infinite desirableness of Re-establishment, and considering that, so far as feeling is concerned, it depends not mainly on the temper in which the South regards the North, but rather conversely; one who never was a blind adherent feels constrained to submit some thoughts, counting on the indulgence of his countrymen.

And, first, it may be said that, if among the feelings and opinions growing immediately out of a great civil convulsion, there are any which time shall modify or do away, they are presumably those of a less temperate and charitable cast.

There seems no reason why patriotism and narrowness should go together, or why intellectual impartiality should be confounded with political trimming, or why serviceable truth should keep cloistered because not partisan. Yet the work of Reconstruction, if admitted to be feasible at all, demands little but common sense and Christian charity. Little but these? These are much.

Some of us are concerned because as yet the South shows no penitence. But what exactly do we mean by this? Since down to the close of the war she never confessed any for braving it, the only penitence now left her is that which springs solely from the sense of discomfiture; and since this evidently would be a contrition hypocritical, it would be unworthy in us to demand it. Certain it is that penitence, in the sense of voluntary humiliation, will never be displayed. Nor does this afford just ground for unreserved condemnation. It is enough, for all practical purposes, if the South have been taught by the terrors of civil war to feel that Secession, like Slavery, is against Destiny; that both now lie buried in one grave; that her fate is linked with ours; and that together we comprise the Nation.

The clouds of heroes who battled for the Union it is needless to eulogize here. But how of the soldiers on the other side? And when of a free community we name the soldiers, we thereby name the people. It was in subserviency to the slave-interest that Secession was plotted; but it was under the plea, plausibly urged, that certain inestimable rights guaranteed by the Constitution were directly menaced, that the people of the South were cajoled into revolution. Through the arts of the conspirators and the perversity of fortune, the most sensitive love of liberty was entrapped into the support of a war whose implied end was the erecting in our advanced century of an Anglo-American empire based upon the systematic degradation of man.

Spite this clinging reproach, however, signal military virtues and achievements have conferred upon the Confederate arms historic fame, and upon certain of the commanders a renown extending beyond the sea—a renown which we of the North could not suppress, even if we would. In personal character, also, not a few of the military leaders of the South enforce forbearance; the memory of others the North refrains from disparaging; and some, with more or less of reluctance, she can respect. Posterity, sympathizing with our convictions, but removed from our passions, may perhaps go farther here. If George IV. could raise an honorable monument in the great fane of Christendom over the remains of the enemy of his dynasty, Charles Edward, the invader of England and victor in the rout at Preston Pans—upon whose head the king's ancestor but one reign removed had set a price—is it probable that the grandchildren of General Grant will pursue with rancor, or slur by sour neglect, the memory of Stonewall Jackson?

But the South herself is not wanting in recent histories and biographies which record the deeds of her chieftains—writings freely published at the North by loyal houses, widely read here, and with a deep though saddened interest. By students of the war such works are hailed as welcome accessories, and tending to the completeness of the record.

Supposing a happy issue out of present perplexities, then, in the generation next to come, Southerners there will be yielding allegiance to the Union, feeling all their interests bound up in it, and yet cherishing unrebuked that kind of feeling for the memory of the soldiers of the fallen Confederacy that Burns, Scott, and the Ettrick Shepherd felt for the memory of the gallant clansmen ruined through their fidelity to the Stuarts—a feeling whose passion was tempered by the poetry imbuing it, and which in no wise affected their loyalty to the Georges, and which, it may be added, indirectly contributed excellent things to literature. But, setting this view aside, dishonorable would it be in the South were she willing to abandon to shame the memory of brave men who with signal personal disinterestedness warred in her behalf, though from motives, as we believe, so deplorably astray.

Patriotism is not baseness, neither is it inhumanity. The mourners who this summer bear flowers to the mounds of the Virginian and Georgian dead are, in their domestic bereavement and proud affection, as sacred in the eye of Heaven as are those who go with similar offerings of tender grief and love into the cemeteries of our Northern martyrs. And yet, in one aspect, how needless to point the contrast.

Cherishing such sentiments, it will hardly occasion surprise that, in looking over the battle-pieces in the foregoing collection, I have been tempted to withdraw or modify some of them, fearful lest in presenting, though but dramatically and by way of a poetic record, the passions and epithets of civil war, I might be contributing to a bitterness which every sensible American must wish at an end. So, too, with the emotion of victory as reproduced on some pages, and particularly toward the close. It should not be construed into an exultation misapplied—an exultation as ungenerous as unwise, and made to minister, however indirectly, to that kind of censoriousness too apt to be produced in certain natures by success after trying reverses. Zeal is not of necessity religion, neither is it always of the same essence with poetry or patriotism.

There were excesses which marked the conflict, most of which are perhaps inseparable from a civil strife so intense and prolonged, and involving warfare in some border countries new and imperfectly civilized. Barbarities also there were, for which the Southern people collectively can hardly be held responsible, though perpetrated by ruffians in their name. But surely other qualities—exalted ones—courage and fortitude matchless, were likewise displayed, and largely; and justly may these be held the characteristic traits, and not the former.

In this view, what Northern writer, however patriotic, but must revolt from acting on paper a part any way akin to that of the live dog to the dead lion; and yet it is right to rejoice for our triumph, so far as it may justly imply an advance for our whole country and for humanity.

Let it be held no reproach to any one that he pleads for reasonable consideration for our late enemies, now stricken down and unavoidably debarred, for the time, from speaking through authorized agencies for themselves. Nothing has been urged here in the foolish hope of conciliating those men—few in number, we trust—who have resolved never to be reconciled to the Union. On such hearts every thing is thrown away except it be religious commiseration, and the sincerest. Yet let them call to mind that unhappy Secessionist, not a military man, who with impious alacrity fired the first shot of the Civil War at Sumter, and a little more than four years afterward fired the last one into his own heart at Richmond.

Noble was the gesture into which patriotic passion surprised the people in a utilitarian time and country; yet the glory of the war falls short of its pathos—a pathos which now at last ought to disarm all animosity.

How many and earnest thoughts still rise, and how hard to repress them. We feel what past years have been, and years, unretarded years, shall come. May we all have moderation; may we all show candor. Though, perhaps, nothing could ultimately have averted the strife, and though to treat of human actions is to deal wholly with second causes, nevertheless, let us not cover up or try to extenuate what, humanly speaking, is the truth—namely, that those unfraternal denunciations, continued through years, and which at last inflamed to deeds that ended in bloodshed, were reciprocal; and that, had the preponderating strength and the prospect of its unlimited increase lain on the other side, on ours might have lain those actions which now in our late opponents we stigmatize under the name of Rebellion. As frankly let us own—what it would be unbecoming to parade were foreigners concerned—that our triumph was won not more by skill and bravery than by superior resources and crushing numbers; that it was a triumph, too, over a people for years politically misled by designing men, and also by some honestly-erring men, who from their position could not have been otherwise than broadly influential; a people who, though, indeed, they sought to perpetuate the curse of slavery, and even extend it, were not the authors of it, but (less fortunate, not less righteous than we) were the fated inheritors; a people who, having a like origin with ourselves, share essentially in whatever worthy qualities we may possess. No one can add to the lasting reproach which hopeless defeat has now cast upon Secession by withholding the recognition of these verities.

Surely we ought to take it to heart that that kind of pacification, based upon principles operating equally all over the land, which lovers of their country yearn for, and which our arms, though signally triumphant, did not bring about, and which law-making, however anxious, or energetic, or repressive, never by itself can achieve, may yet be largely aided by generosity of sentiment public and private. Some revisionary legislation and adaptive is indispensable; but with this should harmoniously work another kind of prudence, not unallied with entire magnanimity. Benevolence and policy—Christianity and Machiavelli—dissuade from penal severities toward the subdued. Abstinence here is as obligatory as considerate care for our unfortunate fellow-men late in bonds, and, if observed, would equally prove to be wise forecast. The great qualities of the South, those attested in the War, we can perilously alienate, or we may make them nationally available at need.

The blacks, in their infant pupilage to freedom, appeal to the sympathies of every humane mind. The paternal guardianship which for the interval government exercises over them was prompted equally by duty and benevolence. Yet such kindliness should not be allowed to exclude kindliness to communities who stand nearer to us in nature. For the future of the freed slaves we may well be concerned; but the future of the whole country, involving the future of the blacks, urges a paramount claim upon our anxiety. Effective benignity, like the Nile, is not narrow in its bounty, and true policy is always broad. To be sure, it is vain to seek to glide, with moulded words, over the difficulties of the situation. And for them who are neither partisans, nor enthusiasts, nor theorists, nor cynics, there are some doubts not readily to be solved. And there are fears. Why is not the cessation of war now at length attended with the settled calm of peace? Wherefore in a clear sky do we still turn our eyes toward the South, as the Neapolitan, months after the eruption, turns his toward Vesuvius? Do we dread lest the repose may be deceptive? In the recent convulsion has the crater but shifted? Let us revere that sacred uncertainty which forever impends over men and nations. Those of us who always abhorred slavery as an atheistical iniquity, gladly we join in the exulting chorus of humanity over its downfall. But we should remember that emancipation was accomplished not by deliberate legislation; only through agonized violence could so mighty a result be effected. In our natural solicitude to confirm the benefit of liberty to the blacks, let us forbear from measures of dubious constitutional rightfulness toward our white countrymen—measures of a nature to provoke, among other of the last evils, exterminating hatred of race toward race. In imagination let us place ourselves in the unprecedented position of the Southerners—their position as regards the millions of igno-rant manumitted slaves in their midst, for whom some of us now claim the suffrage. Let us be Christians toward our fellow-whites, as well as philan-thropists toward the blacks, our fellow-men. In all things, and toward all, we are enjoined to do as we would be done by. Nor should we forget that benevolent desires, after passing a certain point, can not undertake their own fulfillment without incurring the risk of evils beyond those sought to be remedied. Something may well be left to the graduated care of future legislation, and to heaven. In one point of view the co-existence of the two races in the South—whether the negro be bond or free—seems (even as it did to Abraham Lincoln) a grave evil. Emancipation has ridded the country of the reproach, but not wholly of the calamity. Especially in the present transition period for both races in the South, more or less of trouble may not unreasonably be anticipated; but let us not hereafter be too swift to charge the blame exclusively in any one quarter. With certain evils men must be more or less patient. Our institutions have a potent digestion, and may in time convert and assimilate to good all elements thrown in, however originally alien.

But, so far as immediate measures looking toward permanent Re-establishment are concerned, no consideration should tempt us to pervert the national victory into oppression for the vanquished. Should plausible promise of eventual good, or a deceptive or spurious sense of duty, lead us to essay this, count we must on serious consequences, not the least of which would be divisions among the Northern adherents of the Union. Assuredly, if any honest Catos there be who thus far have gone with us, no longer will they do so, but oppose us, and as resolutely as hitherto they have supported. But this path of thought leads toward those waters of bitterness from which one can only turn aside and be silent.

But supposing Re-establishment so far advanced that the Southern seats in Congress are occupied, and by men qualified in accordance with those cardinal principles of representative government which hitherto have prevailed in the land—what then? Why, the Congressmen elected by the people of the South will—represent the people of the South. This may seem a flat conclusion; but, in view of the last five years, may there not be latent significance in it? What will be the temper of those Southern members? and, confronted by them, what will be the mood of our own representa-tives? In private life true reconciliation seldom follows a violent quarrel; but, if subsequent intercourse be unavoidable, nice observances and mutual are indispensable to the prevention of a new rupture. Amity itself can only be maintained by reciprocal respect, and true friends are punctilious equals. On

the floor of Congress North and South are to come together after a passion-
ate duel, in which the South, though proving her valor, has been made to
bite the dust. Upon differences in debate shall acrimonious recriminations
be exchanged? shall censorious superiority assumed by one section provoke
defiant self-assertion on the other? shall Manassas and Chickamauga be
retorted for Chattanooga and Richmond? Under the supposition that the
full Congress will be composed of gentlemen, all this is impossible. Yet, if
otherwise, it needs no prophet of Israel to foretell the end. The maintenance
of Congressional decency in the future will rest mainly with the North.
Rightly will more forbearance be required from the North than the South,
for the North is victor.

But some there are who may deem these latter thoughts inapplicable,
and for this reason: Since the test-oath operatively excludes from Congress
all who in any way participated in Secession, therefore none but Southern-
ers wholly in harmony with the North are eligible to seats. This is true for
the time being. But the oath is alterable; and in the wonted fluctuations of
parties not improbably it will undergo alteration, assuming such a form,
perhaps, as not to bar the admission into the National Legislature of men
who represent the populations lately in revolt. Such a result would involve
no violation of the principles of democratic government. Not readily can
one perceive how the political existence of the millions of late Secessionists
can permanently be ignored by this Republic. The years of the war tried
our devotion to the Union; the time of peace may test the sincerity of our
faith in democracy.

In no spirit of opposition, not by way of challenge, is any thing here
thrown out. These thoughts are sincere ones; they seem natural—inevitable.
Here and there they must have suggested themselves to many thoughtful
patriots. And, if they be just thoughts, ere long they must have that weight
with the public which already they have had with individuals.

For that heroic band—those children of the furnace who, in regions like
Texas and Tennessee, maintained their fidelity through terrible trials—we
of the North felt for them, and profoundly we honor them. Yet passionate
sympathy, with resentments so close as to be almost domestic in their bitter-
ness, would hardly in the present juncture tend to discreet legislation. Were
the Unionists and Secessionists but as Guelphs and Ghibellines? If not, then
far be it from a great nation now to act in the spirit that animated a trium-
phant town-faction in the Middle Ages. But crowding thoughts must at last
be checked; and, in times like the present, one who desires to be impartially
just in the expression of his views, moves as among sword-points presented
on every side.

Let us pray that the terrible historic tragedy of our time may not have been enacted without instructing our whole beloved country through terror and pity; and may fulfillment verify in the end those expectations which kindle the bards of Progress and Humanity.

John Marr

and

Other Sailors

with

Some Sea-Pieces

Inscription Epistolary
to
W. C. R.

Health and content.

Hilary, my companionable acquaintance, during an afternoon stroll under the trees along the higher bluffs of our Riverside Park last June, entertained me with one of those clever little theories, for the originating and formulating whereof he has a singular aptitude. He had but recently generalised it—so at least I inferred—from certain subtler particulars which in the instances of sundry individuals he flattered himself his perspicacity had enabled him to discern.

Let me communicate to you this theory; not that I imagine you will hail it as a rare intellectual acquisition; hardly that; but because I am much mistaken if it do not attract your personal interest, however little it may otherwise and with other people win consideration or regard.

Briefly put, it is this. Letting alone less familiar nationalities, an American born in England or an Englishman born in America, each in his natural make-up retains through life, and will some way evince, an intangible something imbibed with his mother's milk from the soil of his nativity.

But for a signal illustration hereof whom, think you, he cites? Well, look into any mirror at hand, and you will see the gentleman. Yes, Hilary thinks he perceives in the nautical novels of W. C. R. an occasional flavor as if the honest mid-sea brine, their main constituent, were impregnated with a dash of the New World's alluvium,—such, say, as is discharged by our Father of Waters into the Gulf of Mexico. "Natural enough," he observes; "for though a countryman of the Queen—his parentage, home, and allegiance all English—this writer, I am credibly informed, is in his birth-place

A New-Worlder; ay, first looked out upon life from a window here of our island of Manhattan, nor very far from the site of my place in Broadway, by Jove!"

Now Hilary is that rare bird, a man at once genial and acute. Genial, I mean, without sharing much in mere gregariousness, which with some passes for a sort of geniality; and acute, though lacking more or less in cautionary self-skepticism. No wonder then that however pleasing and instructive be Hilary's companionship, and much as I value the man, yet as touching more than one of his shrewder speculations I have been reluctantly led to distrust a little that penetrative perspicacity of his, a quality immoderately developed in him; and, perhaps (who knows?) developed by his business; for he is an optician, daily having to do with the microscope, telescope, and other inventions for sharpening and extending our natural sight, thus enabling us mortals (as I once heard an eccentric put it) liberally to enlarge the field of our original and essential ignorance.

In a word, my excellent friend's private little theory, while, like many a big and bruited one, not without a fancifully plausible aspect commending it to the easy of belief, is yet, in my humble judgment—though I would not hint as much to him for the world—made up in no small part of one element inadmissible in sound philosophy, namely, moonshine.

As to his claim of finding signal evidence for it in the novels aforementioned, that is another matter. That, I am inclined to think is little else than the amiable illusion of a zealous patriot eager to appropriate anything that in any department may tend to reflect added lustre upon his beloved country.

But, dismissing theory, let me come to a fact, and put it fact-wise; that is to say, a bit bluntly: By the suffrages of seamen and landsmen alike, *The Wreck of the Grosvenor* entitles the author to the naval crown in current literature. That book led the series of kindred ones by the same hand; it is the flag-ship; and to name it, implies the fleet.

Upon the *Grosvenor's* first appearance—in these waters, I was going to say—all competent judges exclaimed, each after his own fashion, something to this effect: The very spit of the brine in our faces! What writer so thoroughly as this one, knows the sea, and the blue water of it; the sailor and the heart of him; the ship, too, and the sailing and handling of a ship. Besides, to his knowledge he adds invention. And, withal, in his broader humane quality he shares the spirit of Richard H. Dana, a true poet's son, our own admirable *"Man-before-the-Mast."*

Well, in view of those unanimous verdicts summed up in the foregoing condensed delivery, with what conscientious satisfaction did I but just now in the heading of this Inscription, salute you, W. C. R., by running up your colors at my fore. Would that the craft thus embraved were one of some tonnage, so that the flag might be carried on a loftier spar, commanding an ampler horizon of your recognising friends.

But the pleasure I take in penning these lines is such, that did a literary Inscription imply aught akin to any bestowment, say, or benefit—which it is so very far indeed from implying—then, sinner though I am, I should be tempted to repeat that divine apothegm, which, were it repeated forever, would never stale—"It is more blessed to give than to receive." And though by the world at large so unworldly a maxim receives a more hospitable welcome at the ear than in the heart—and no wonder, considering the persistent deceptiveness of so many things mundane—nevertheless, in one province—and I mean no other one than literature, not every individual, I think, at least not every one whose years ought to discharge him from the minor illusions, will dispute it, who has had experience alike in receiving and giving, in one suggestive form or other, sincere contemporary praise. And what, essentially, is such praise? Little else indeed than a less ineloquent form of recognition.

That these thoughts are no spurious ones, never mind from whomsoever proceeding, one naturally appeals to the author of *The Wreck of the Grosvenor,* who in his duality as a commended novelist and liberal critic in his more especial department, may rightly be deemed an authority well qualified to determine.

Thus far as to matters which may be put into type. For personal feeling—the printed page is hardly the place for reiterating that. So I close here as I began, wishing you from my heart the most precious things I know of in this world—Health and Content.

John Marr

JOHN MARR, toward the close of the last century born in America of a mother unknown, and from boyhood up to maturity a sailor under divers flags, disabled at last from further maritime life by a crippling wound received at close quarters with pirates of the Keys, eventually betakes himself for a livelihood to less active employment ashore. There, too, he transfers his rambling disposition acquired as a seafarer.

After a variety of removals, at first as a sail-maker from sea-port to sea-port, then adventurously inland as a rough bench-carpenter, he, finally, in the last-named capacity, settles down about the year 1838 upon what was then a frontier-prairie sparsely sprinkled with small oak-groves and yet fewer log-houses of a little colony but recently from one of our elder inland States. Here, putting a period to his rovings, he marries.

Ere long a fever, the bane of new settlements on teeming loam, and whose sallow livery was certain to show itself, after an interval, in the complexions of too many of these people, carries off his young wife and infant child. In one coffin put together by his own hands they are committed with meagre rites to the earth:—another mound, though a small one, in the wide prairie, nor far from where the Mound-Builders of a race only conjecturable had left their pottery and bones, one common clay, under a strange terrace serpentine in form.

With an honest stillness in his general mien; swarthy, and black-browed; with eyes that could soften or flash, but never harden, yet disclosing at times a melancholy depth, this kinless man had affections which, once placed, not readily could be dislodged, or resigned to a substituted object. Being now arrived at middle life he resolves never to quit the soil that holds the only

195

beings ever connected with him by love in the family-tie. His log-house he lets to a new-comer, one glad enough to get it, and dwells with the household.

While the acuter sense of his bereavement becomes mollified by time, the void at heart abides. Fain, if possible, would he fill that void by culti-vating social relations yet nearer than before, with a people whose lot he purposes sharing to the end—relations superadded to that mere work-a-day bond arising from participation in the same outward hardships making reciprocal helpfulness a matter of course. But here, and nobody to blame, he is obstructed.

More familiarly to consort, men of a practical turn must sympathetically converse, and upon topics of real life. But, whether as to persons or events, one can not always be talking about the present; much less, speculating about the future; one must needs recur to the past; which, with the mass of men, where the past is in any personal way a common inheritance, supplies, to most practical natures, the basis of sympathetic communion.

But the past of John Marr was not the past of these pioneers. Their hands had rested on the plough-tail; his upon the ship's helm. They knew but their own kind and their own usages; to him had been revealed something of the checkered globe. So limited unavoidably was the mental reach, and by consequence the range of sympathy, in this particular band of domestic emigrants, hereditary tillers of the soil, that the ocean, but a hearsay to their fathers, had now, through yet deeper inland removal, become to themselves little more than a rumor traditional and vague.

They were a staid people; staid through habituation to monotonous hardship; ascetics by necessity not less than through moral bias; nearly all of them sincerely, however narrowly, religious. They were kindly at need, after their fashion. But to a man wonted—as John Marr in his previous homeless sojournings could not but have been—to the free-and-easy tavern-clubs affording cheap recreation of an evening in certain old and comfortable sea-port towns of that time, and yet more familiar with the companion-ship afloat of the sailors of the same period, something was lacking. That something was geniality, the flower of life springing from some sense of joy in it, more or less. This their lot could not give to these hard-working endurers of the dispiriting malaria, men to whom a holiday never came; and they had too much of uprightness and no art at all or desire to affect what they did not really feel. At a corn-husking, their least grave of gather-ings, did the lone-hearted mariner seek to divert his own thoughts from sadness, and in some degree interest theirs, by adverting to aught removed from the crosses and trials of their personal surroundings, naturally enough he would slide into some marine story or picture; but would soon recoil upon himself, and be silent; finding no encouragement to proceed. Upon one such occasion an elderly man—a blacksmith, and at Sunday gatherings an earnest exhorter, honestly said to him, "Friend, we know nothing of that here."

Such unresponsiveness in one's fellow creatures set apart from factitious life, and by their vocation—in those days little helped by machinery—standing, as it were, next of kin to Nature; this, to John Marr, seemed of a piece with the apathy of Nature herself as envisaged to him here on a prairie where none but the perished Mound-Builders had as yet left a durable mark.

The remnant of Indians thereabout—all but exterminated in their recent and final war with regular white troops, a war waged by the Red Men for their native soil and natural rights, had been coerced into the occupancy of wilds not very far beyond the Mississippi;—wilds *then,* but now the seats of municipalities and states. Prior to that, the bisons, once streaming countless in processional herds, or browsing as in an endless battle-line over these vast aboriginal pastures, had retreated, dwindled in number, before the hunters, in main a race distinct from the agricultural pioneers, though generally their advance-guard. Such a double exodus of man and beast left the plain a desert, green or blossoming indeed, but almost as forsaken as the Siberian Obi. Save the prairie-hen, sometimes startled from its lurking-place in the rank grass; and, in their migratory season, pigeons, high overhead on the wing, in dense multitudes eclipsing the day like a passing storm-cloud; save these—there being no wide woods with their underwood—birds were strangely few.

Blank stillness would for hours reign unbroken on this prairie. "It is the bed of a dried-up sea" said the companionless sailor—no geologist—to himself, musing at twilight upon the fixed undulations of that immense alluvial expanse bounded only by the horizon, and missing there the stir that, to alert eyes and ears, animates at all times the apparent solitudes of the deep.

But a scene quite at variance with one's antecedents may yet prove suggestive of them. Hooped round by a level rim, the prairie was to John Marr a reminder of ocean.

With some of his former shipmates, *chums* on certain cruises, he had contrived, prior to this last and more remote removal, to keep up a little correspondence at odd intervals. But from tidings of anybody or any sort, he, in common with the other settlers, was now cut off; quite cut off except from such news as might be conveyed over the grassy billows by the

last-arrived prairie-schooner; the vernacular term in those parts and times
for the emigrant-wagon arched high over with sail-cloth, and voyaging
across the vast champaign. There was no reachable post-office; as yet, not
even the rude little receptive box with lid and leathern hinges set up at
convenient intervals, on a stout stake along some solitary green way, afford-
ing a perch for birds; and which, later in the unintermitting advance of
the frontier, would perhaps decay into a mossy monument, attesting yet
another successive overleaped limit of civilized life; a life which in America
can to-day hardly be said to have any western bound but the ocean that
washes Asia. Throughout these plains, now in places over-populous with
towns over-opulent; sweeping plains, elsewhere fenced off in every direc-
tion into flourishing farms—pale townsmen and hale farmers alike, in part,
the descendants of the first sallow settlers; a region that half a century ago
produced little for the sustenance of man, but to-day launching its super-
abundant wheat-harvest on the world; of this prairie, now everywhere
intersected with wire and rail, hardly can it be said that at the period here
written of there was so much as a traceable road. To the long-distance trav-
eller, the oak groves, wide apart and varying in compass and form; these,
with recent settlements, yet more widely separate, offered some landmarks;
but otherwise he steered by the sun. In early midsummer, even going but
from one log-encampment to the next—a journey, it might be, of hours
or good part of a day—travel was much like navigation. In some more
enriched depressions between the long green graduated swells, smooth as
those of ocean becalmed receiving and subduing to its own tranquility the
voluminous surge raised by some far-off hurricane of days previous; here
one would catch the first indication of advancing strangers, either in the
distance, as a far sail at sea, by the glistening white canvas of the wagon,—
the wagon itself wading through the rank vegetation, and hidden by it,—or,
failing that, when near to, in the ears of the team, peaking, if not above the
tall tiger-lilies, yet above the yet taller grass.

   Luxuriant this wilderness. But to its denizen, a friend left behind
anywhere in the world, seemed not alone absent to sight, but an absentee
from existence.

   Though John Marr's shipmates could not all have departed life, yet as
subjects of meditation they were like phantoms of the dead. As the grow-
ing sense of his environment threw him more and more upon retrospective
musings, these phantoms, next to those of his wife and child, became spiri-
tual companions, losing something of their first indistinctness and putting
on at last a dim semblance of mute life. And they were lit by that aureola

circling over any object of the affections in the past for reunion with which an imaginative heart passionately yearns.

He invokes these visionary ones, striving, as it were, to get into verbal communion with them; or, under yet stronger illusion, reproaching them for their silence:—

> Since as in night's deck-watch ye show,
> Why, lads, so silent here to me,
> Your watchmate of times long ago?
>
> Once, for all the darkling sea,
> You your voices raised how clearly,   5
> Striking in when tempest sung;
> Hoisting up the storm-sail cheerly,
> *Life is storm:—let storm!* you rung.
> Taking things as fated merely,
> Child-like though the world ye spanned;   10
> Nor holding unto life too dearly,
> Ye who held your lives in hand:
> Skimmers, who on oceans four
> Petrels were, and larks ashore.
>
> O, not from memory lightly flung,   15
> Forgot, like strains no more availing,
> The heart to music haughtier strung;
> Nay, frequent near me, never staling,
> Whose good feeling kept ye young.
> Like tides that enter creek or stream,   20
> Ye come, ye visit me; or seem
> Swimming out from seas of faces,
> Alien myriads memory traces,
> To enfold me in a dream!
>
> I yearn as ye. But rafts that strain,   25
> Parted, shall they lock again?
> Twined we were, entwined, then riven,
> Ever to new embracements driven,

Shifting gulf-weed of the main!
And how if one here shift no more,   30
Lodged by the flinging surge ashore?

Nor less, as now, in eve's decline,
Your shadowy fellowship is mine.
Ye float around me, form and feature:—
Tattooings, ear-rings, love-locks curled;   35
Barbarians of man's simpler nature,
Unworldly servers of the world.
Yea, present all, and dear to me,
Though shades, or scouring China's sea.

Whither, whither, merchant-sailors,   40
Whitherward now in roaring gales?
Competing still, ye huntsman-whalers,
In leviathan's wake what boat prevails?
And man-of-war's men, whereaway?
If now no dinned drum beat to quarters   45
On the wilds of midnight waters—
Foemen looming through the spray;
Do yet your gangway lanterns, streaming,
Vainly strive to pierce below,
When, tilted from the slant plank gleaming,   50
A brother you see to darkness go?

But, gunmates lashed in shotted canvas,
If where long watch-below ye keep,
Never the shrill *"All hands up hammocks!"*
Breaks the spell that charms your sleep;   55
And summoning trumps might vainly call,
And booming guns implore—
A beat, a heart-beat musters all,
One heart-beat at heart-core.
It musters. But to clasp, retain;   60
To see you at the halyards main—
To hear your chorus once again!

Bridegroom Dick

(1876)

SUNNING ourselves in October on a day
Balmy as Spring though the year was in decay,
I lading my pipe, she stirring her tea,
My old woman she says to me,
"Feel ye, old man, how the season mellows?"   5
And why should I not, blessed heart alive,
Here mellowing myself, past sixty-five,
To think o' the May-time o' pennoned young fellows
This stripped old hulk here for years may survive.

Ere yet, long ago, we were spliced, Bonny Blue,   10
(Silvery it gleams down the moon-glade o' time;
Ah, sugar in the bowl and berries in the prime!)
Coxswain I o' the Commodore's crew,—
Under me the fellows that manned his fine gig,
Spinning him ashore, a king in full fig.   15
Chirrupy even when crosses rubbed me,
Bridegroom-Dick lieutenants dubbed me.
Pleasant at a yarn, Bob o' Linkum in a song,
Diligent in duty and nattily arrayed,
Favored I was, wife, and *fleeted* right along;   20
And though but a tot for such a tall grade,
A high quarter-master at last I was made.

All this, old lassie, you have heard before,
But you listen again for the sake e'en o' me;

No babble stales o' the good times o' yore   25
To Joan, if Darby the babbler be.

Babbler?—o' what? Addled brains they forget!
O—quarter-master I; yes, the signals set,
Hoisted the ensign, mended it when frayed;
Polished up the binnacle—minded the helm;   30
And prompt every order blithely obeyed.
To me would the officers say a word cheery—
Break through the starch o' the quarter-deck realm;
His coxswain late, so the Commodore's pet.
Ay, and in night-watches long and weary,   35
Bored nigh to death with the naval etiquette,
Yearning, too, for fun, some younker, a cadet,
Dropping for time each vain bumptious trick,
Boy-like would unbend to Bridegroom Dick.
But a limit there was—a check, d'ye see: 40
Those fine young aristocrats knew their degree.

Well, stationed aft where their lordships keep,
Seldom going forward excepting to sleep—
I, boozing now on by-gone years,
My betters recall along with my peers.   45
Recall them? Wife, but I see them plain:
Alive, alert, every man stirs again.
Ay, and again on the lee-side pacing,
My spy-glass carrying, a truncheon in show,
Turning at the taffrail, my footsteps retracing,   50
Proud in my duty, again methinks I go.
And Dave, Dainty Dave, I mark where he stands,
Our trim sailing-master, to time the high-noon,
That thingumbob sextant perplexing eyes and hands,
Squinting at the sun, or twigging o' the moon;   55
Then, touching his cap to Old Chock-a-Block
Commanding the quarter-deck—"Sir, twelve o'clock."

Where sails he now, that trim sailing-master,
Slender, yes, as the ship's sky-s'l pole?
Dimly I mind me of some sad disaster:—   60
Dainty Dave was dropped from the navy-roll!

And ah, for old Lieutenant Chock-a-Block—
Fast, wife, chock-fast to death's black dock!
Buffeted about the obstreperous ocean,
Fleeted his life, if lagged his promotion.   65
Little girl, they are all, all gone, I think,
Leaving Bridegroom Dick here with lids that wink.

Where is Ap Catesby?—The fights fought of yore
Famed him, and laced him with epaulets, and more.
But fame is a wake that after-wakes cross,   70
And the waters wallow all, and laugh *Where's the loss?*
But John Bull's bullet in his shoulder bearing
Ballasted Ap in his long seafaring.
The middies they ducked to the man who had messed
With Decatur in the gun-room, or forward pressed   75
Fighting beside Perry, Hull, Porter and the rest.

Humped veteran o' the Heart-o'-Oak War,
Moored long in haven where the old heroes are,
Never on *you* did the iron-clads jar!
Your open deck when the boarder assailed,   80
The frank old heroic hand-to-hand then availed.

But where's Guert Gan? Still heads he the van?
As before Vera-Cruz, when he dashed splashing through
The blue rollers sunned, in his brave gold-and-blue,
And, ere his cutter in keel took the strand,   85
Aloft waved his sword on the hostile land!
Went up the cheering, the quick chanticleering;
All hands vying—all colors flying:
"Cock-a-doodle-do!" and "Row, boys, row!"
"Hey, Starry Banner!" "Hi, Santa Anna!"—   90
Old Scott's young dash at Mexico.

Fine forces o' the land, fine forces o' the sea,
Fleet, army, and flotilla—tell, heart o' me,
Tell, if you can, whereaway now they be!
But, ah, how to speak of the hurricane unchained—   95
The Union's strands parted in the hawser over-strained;

Our Flag blown to shreds, anchors gone altogether—
The dashed fleet o' States in Secession's foul weather.

Lost in the smother o' that wide public stress,
In hearts, private hearts, what ties there were snapped!   100
Tell, Hal—vouch, Will, o' the ward-room mess,
On you how the riving thunder-bolt clapped.
With a bead in your eye and beads in your glass
And a grip o' the flipper, it was part and pass:
"Hal, must it be? Well, if come indeed the shock,   105
To North or to South let the victory cleave,
Vaunt it he may on his dung-hill the cock,
But *Uncle Sam's* eagle never crow will, believe."

Sentiment: ay, while suspended hung all,
Ere the guns against Sumter opened there the ball,   110
And partners were taken, and the red dance began,
War's red dance o' death!—Well, we, to a man,
We sailors o' the North, wife, how could we lag?—
Strike with your kin, and you stick to the Flag!
But to sailors o' the South that easy way was barred.   115
To some, dame, believe, (and I speak o' what I know)
Wormwood the trial and the Uzzite's black shard;
And the faithfuller the heart, the crueller the throe.
Duty? it pulled with more than one string,
This way and that, and anyhow a sting.   120
The Flag and your kin, how be true unto both?
If either plight ye keep, then ye break the other troth.
But elect here they must, though the casuists were out:
Decide—hurry up—and throttle every doubt.

Of all these thrills thrilled at kelson, and throes,   125
Little felt the shoddyites a'toasting o' their toes;
In mart and bazar Lucre chuckled the huzza,
Coining the dollars in the bloody mint o' war.
But in men, gray knights o' the Order o' Scars,
And brave boys bound by vows unto Mars,   130
Nature grappled Honor, intertwisting in the strife:—
But some cut the knot with a thoroughgoing knife.

For how when the drums beat? how in the fray
In Hampton Roads on the fine balmy day?

There a lull, wife, befell—drop o' silence in the din.   135
Let us enter that silence ere the belchings rebegin.—
Through a ragged rift aslant in the cannonade's smoke
An iron-clad reveals her repellent broadside
Bodily intact. But a frigate, all oak,
Shows honeycombed by shot, and her deck crimson-dyed.   140
And a trumpet from port of the iron-clad hails
Summoning the other whose flag never trails:—
"Surrender that frigate, Will! Surrender,
Or I will sink her—*ram,* and end her!"
'Twas Hal. And Will, from the naked heart-o'-oak,   145
Will, the old messmate, minus trumpet, spoke,
Informally intrepid—"Sink her and be damned."*
Enough. Gathering way, the iron-clad *rammed.*
The frigate, heeling over, on the wave threw a dusk.
Not sharing in the slant, the clapper of her bell   150
The fixed metal struck—uninvoked struck the knell
Of the *Cumberland* stilettoed by the *Merrimac's* tusk;
While, broken in the wound underneath the gun-deck,
Like a sword-fish's blade in leviathan waylaid
The tusk was left infixed in the fast-foundering wreck.   155
There, dungeoned in the cockpit, the wounded go down,
And the Chaplain with them. But the surges uplift
The prone dead from deck, and for moment they drift
Washed with the swimmers, and the spent swimmers drown.
Nine fathom did she sink,—erect, though hid from light   160
Save her colors unsurrendered and spars that kept the height.

Nay, pardon, old aunty!—Wife, never let it fall,
That big started tear that hovers on the brim;
I forgot about your nephew and the *Merrimac's* ball;
No more then of her since it summons up him.   165

But talk o' fellows' hearts in the wine's genial cup:—
Trap them in the fate, jam them in the strait,

*Note. Historic.

Guns speak their hearts then, and speak right up.
The troublous colic o' intestine war
It sets the bowels o' affection ajar.   170
But, lord, old dame, so spins the whizzing world,
A humming-top, ay, for the little boy-gods
Flogging it well with their smart little rods,
Tittering at time and the coil uncurled.

Now, now, Sweetheart, you sidle away,   175
No, never you like *that* kind o' *gay:*
But sour if I get, giving truth her due,
Honey-sweet forever, wife, will Dick be to *you!*

But avast with the War! Why recall racking days
Since set up anew are the ship's started stays?   180
Nor less, though the gale we have left behind,
Well may the heave o' the sea remind.
It irks me now, as it troubled me then,
To think o' the fate in the madness o' men.
If Dick was with Farragut on the night-river   185
When the boom-chain we burst in the fire-raft's glare
That blood-dyed the visage as red as the liver;
In the *Battle for the Bay* too if Dick had a share,
And saw one aloft a'piloting the war—
Trumpet in the whirlwind, a Providence in place—   190
Our Admiral old whom the Captains huzza,
Dick joys in the man nor brags about the race.

But better, wife, I like to booze on the days
Ere the Old Order foundered in these very frays,
And tradition was lost and we learned strange ways.   195
Often I think on the brave cruises then;
Re-sailing them in memory, I hail the press o' men
On the gunned promenade where rolling they go
Ere the dog-watch expire and break up the show.
The Laced Caps I see between forward guns: 200
Away from the powder-room they puff the cigar:
"Three days more, hey, the donnas and the dons!"—
"Your Xeres widow, will you hunt her up, Starr?"

The Laced Caps laugh, and the bright waves too;
Very jolly, very wicked both sea and crew.   205
Nor heaven looks sour on either, I guess,
Nor Pecksniff he bosses the gods' high mess.

Wistful ye peer, wife, concerned for my head,
And how best to get me betimes to my bed.

But, king o' the club, the gayest golden spark,   210
Sailor o' sailors, what sailor do I mark?
Tom Tight, Tom Tight, no fine fellow finer,
A cutwater-nose, ay, a spirited soul;
But, bowsing away at the well-brewed bowl,
He never bowled back from that last voyage to China.   215

Tom was lieutenant in the brig-o'-war famed
When an officer was hung for an arch mutineer,
But a mystery cleaved, and the captain was blamed,
And a rumpus, too, raised, though his honor it was clear.
And Tom he would say, when the mousers would try him   220
And with cup after cup o' Burgundy ply him—
"Gentlemen, in vain with your wassail you beset,
For the more I tipple, the tighter do I get."
No blabber, no, not even with the can—
True to himself and loyal to his clan.   225

Tom blessed us starboard and d——d us larboard,
Right down from rail to the streak o' the garboard.
Nor less, wife, we liked him.—Tom was a man
In contrast queer with Chaplain Le Fan,
Who blessed us at morn, and at night yet again,   230
D—ning us only in decorous strain;
Preaching 'tween the guns—each cutlass in its place—
From text that averred Old Adam, a hard case.

I see him—Tom—on *horse-block* standing,
Trumpet at mouth, thrown up all amain,   235

An elephant's bugle, vociferous demanding
Of topmen aloft in the hurricane of rain,
"Letting that sail there your faces flog?
Manhandle it, men, and you'll get the good grog!"
O Tom but he knew a blue-jacket's ways,   240
And how a lieutenant may genially haze:
Only a sailor sailors heartily praise.

Wife, where be all these chaps, I wonder?
Trumpets in the tempest, terrors in the fray,
Boomed their commands along the deck like thunder;   245
But silent is the sod, and thunder dies away.

But Captain Turret, *"Old Hemlock"* tall
(A leaning tower when his tank brimmed all)
Manœuvre out alive from the War did he?
Or, too old for that, drift under the lee?   250
Kentuckian colossal, who touching at Madeira
The huge puncheon shipped o' prime *Santa Clara;*
Then rocked along the deck so solemnly!
No whit the less though judicious was enough
In dealing with the Finn who made the great huff:—   255
Our three-decker's giant; a grand boatswain's mate,
Manliest of men in his own natural senses;
But, driven stark mad by the Devil's drugged stuff,
Storming all aboard from his run-ashore late,
Challenging to battle, vouchsafing no pretences.   260
A reeling King Og, delirious in power,
The quarter-deck carronades he seemed to make cower.
"Put him in *brig* there," said Lieutenant Marrot.
"Put him in *brig!*" back he mocked like a parrot;
"Try it then!" swaying a fist like Thor's sledge   265
And making the pigmy constables hedge—
Ship's-corporals and the Master-at-Arms.
"In *brig* there, I say!"—They dally no more.
Like hounds let slip on a desperate boar
Together they pounce on the formidable Finn,   270

Pinion and cripple and hustle him in.
Anon, under sentry, between twin guns,
He slides off in drowse, and the long night runs.

Morning brings a summons. Whistling it calls,
Shrilled through the pipes of the Boatswain's four aids—   275
Thrilled down the hatchways along the dusk halls:
Muster to the Scourge!—Dawn of doom, and its blast!
As from cemeteries raised, sailors swarm before the mast,
Tumbling up the ladders from the ship's nether shades.

Keeping in the background and taking small part,   280
Lounging at their ease, indifferent in face,
Behold the trim marines, uncompromised in heart.
Their Major, buttoned up, near the staff finds room—
The staff o' Lieutenants standing grouped in their place.
All the Laced Caps o' the ward-room come,   285
The Chaplain among them, disciplined and dumb.
The blue-nosed Boatswain, complexioned like slag,
Like a Blue Monday lours—his implements in bag.
Executioners, his aids, a couple by him stand,
At a nod there the thongs to receive from his hand.   290
Never venturing a caveat whatever may betide,
Though functionally here on humanity's side,
The grave Surgeon shows like the formal physician
Attending the rack o' the Spanish Inquisition.

The Angel o' the "brig" brings his prisoner up.   295
Then, steadied by his old *Santa Clara,* a sup,
Heading, all erect, the ranged assizes there,
Lo, Captain Turret, and under starred bunting
(A florid full face and fine silvered hair)
Gigantic the yet greater giant confronting.   300

Now the culprit he liked, as a tall Captain can
A Titan subordinate and true *sailor-man;*
And frequent he'd shown it: no worded advance,

But flattering the Finn with a well-timed glance.
But what of that now? In the martinet-mien   305
Read the *Articles of War,* heed the naval routine;
While, cut to the heart a dishonor there to win,
Restored to his senses, stood the Anak Finn;
In racked self-control the squeezed tears peeping
Scalding the eye with repressed inkeeping.   310
Discipline must be; the scourge is deemed due.
But, ah for the sickening and strange heart-benumbing,
Compassionate abasement in shipmates that view:
Such a grand champion shamed there succumbing!

"Brown, tie him up."—The cord he brooked: 315
How else?—his arms spread apart—never threaping;
No, never he flinched, never sideways he looked,
Peeled to the waistband, the marble flesh creeping,
Lashed by the sleet the officious winds urge.
In function his fellows their fellowship merge—   320
The twain standing nigh—the two boatswain's-mates,
Sailors of his grade, ay, and brothers of his mess.
With sharp thongs adroop, the junior one awaits
The word to uplift.

       "Untie him:—so!   325
Submission is enough.—Man, you may go."
Then, promenading aft, brushing fat Purser Smart,
"Flog? never meant it—had'nt any heart.
Degrade that tall fellow?"—Such, wife, was he,
Old Captain Turret who the brave wine could stow.   330
Magnanimous, you think?—But what does Dick see?
Apron to your eye! Why, never fell a blow:
Cheer up, old wifie, 'twas a long time ago.

But where's that sore one, crabbed and severe,
Lieutenant Don Lumbago, an arch scrutineer?   335
Call the roll to-day, would he answer—*Here!*
When the *Blixum's* fellows to quarters mustered
How he'd lurch along the lane of gun-crews clustered,

Testy as touchwood, to pry and to peer.
Jerking his sword underneath larboard arm   340
He ground his worn grinders to keep himself calm.
Composed in his nerves, from the fidgets set free,
Tell, Sweet Wrinkles, alive now is he
In Paradise a parlor where the even tempers be?

Where's Commander All-a-Tanto?   345
Where's Orlop Bob singing up from below?
Where's Rhyming Ned? has he spun his last canto?
Where's Jewsharp Jim? Where's Rigadoon Joe?
Ah, for the music over and done,
The band all dismissed save the droned trombone!   350
Where's Glen o' the gun-room who loved Hot-Scotch—
Glen, prompt and cool in a perilous watch?
Where's flaxen-haired Phil?—a gray lieutenant?
Or, rubicund, flying a dignified pennant?
But where sleeps his brother?—The cruise it was o'er,   355
But ah for Death's grip that welcomed him ashore!
Where's Sid the cadet so frank in his brag,
Whose toast was audacious—*"Here's Sid, and Sid's flag!"*
Like holiday-craft that have sunk unknown,
May a lark of a lad go lonely down?   360
Who takes the census under the sea?
Can others like old ensigns be,
Bunting I hoisted to flutter at the gaff—
Rags in end that once were flags
Gallant streaming from the staff?   365
Such scurvy doom could the chances deal
To Top-Gallant Harry and Jack Genteel?

Lo, Genteel Jack in hurricane weather
Shagged like a bear, like a red lion roaring;
But, O, so fine in his chapeau and feather,   370
In port to the ladies never once *jawing.*
All bland *politesse,* how urbane was he:—
"Oui, Mademoiselle"—*"Ma chere amie!"*
'Twas Jack got up the ball at Naples,

Gay in the old *Ohio* glorious;   375
His hair was curled by the berth-deck barber,
Never you'd deemed him a cub of rude Boreas;
In tight little pumps, with the grand dames in rout,
A'flinging his shapely foot all about;
His watch-chain with love's jewelled tokens abounding,   380
Curls ambrosial shaking out odors,
Waltzing along the batteries, astounding
The Gunner glum and the grim-visaged loaders.

Wife, where be all these blades, I wonder,
Pennoned fine fellows so strong, so gay?   385
Never their colors with a dip dived under:
Have they hauled them down in a lack-lustre day,
Or beached their boats in the Far Far Away?

Hither and thither, blown wide asunder,
Where's this fleet, I wonder and wonder.   390
Slipt their cables, rattled their adieu
(Whereaway pointing? to what rendezvous?)
Out of sight, out of mind, like the crack *Constitution,*
And many a keel Time never shall renew—
Bon Homme Dick o' the buff Revolution,   395
The *Black Cockade* and the staunch *True-Blue.*

Doff hats to Decatur! But where is his blazon?
Must merited fame endure time's wrong—
Glory's ripe grape wizen up to a raisin?
Yes! for Nature teems, and the years are strong,   400
And who can keep the tally o' the names that fleet along!

But his frigate, wife, his bride? Would blacksmiths brown
Into smithereens smite the solid old renown?

Rivetting the bolts in the iron-clad's shell,
Hark to the hammers with a *rat-tat-tat:*   405
"Handier a *derby* than a laced cocked hat!

The *Monitor* was ugly, but she served us right well,
Better than the *Cumberland,* a beauty and the belle."

Better than the Cumberland!—Heart alive in me!
That battlemented hull, Tantallon o' the sea,   410
Kicked in, as at Boston the taxed chests o' tea!
Ay, spurned by the *ram,* once a tall shapely craft
But lopped by the *Rebs* to an iron-beaked raft—
A blacksmith's unicorn in armor *cap-a-pie.*

Under the water-line a *ram's* blow is dealt: 415
And foul fall the knuckles that strike below the belt.
Nor brave the inventions that serve to replace
The openness of valor while dismantling the grace.

Aloof from all this, and the never-ending game,
Tantamount to teetering, plot and counterplot: 420
Impenetrable armor—all-perforating shot;
Aloof, bless God, ride the war-ships of old,
A grand fleet moored in the roadstead of fame;
Not submarine sneaks with *them* are enrolled;
Their long shadows dwarf us, their flags are as flame.   425

Do'nt fidget so, wife; an old man's passion
Amounts to no more than this smoke that I puff;
There, there now, buss me in good old fashion;
A died-down candle will flicker in the snuff.

But one last thing let your old babbler say,   430
What Decatur's coxswain said who was long ago hearsed,
"Take in your flying-kites, for there comes a lubber's day
When gallant things will go, and the three-deckers first."

My pipe is smoked out, and the grog runs slack;
But bowse away, wife, at your blessed Bohea: 435
This empty can here must needs solace me.
Nay, Sweetheart, nay; I take that back:
Dick drinks from your eyes and he finds no lack!

Tom Deadlight

(1810)

DURING a tempest encountered homeward-bound from the Mediterranean, a grizzled petty-officer, one of the two captains of the forecastle, dying at night in his hammock, swung in the *sick-bay* under the tiered gun-decks of the British *Dreadnaught,* 98, wandering in his mind, though with glimpses of sanity, and starting up at whiles, sings by snatches his good-bye and last injunctions to two messmates his watchers, one of whom fans the fevered tar with the flap of his old sou'-wester.

Some names and phrases, with here and there a line, or part of one; these, in his aberration wrested into incoherency from their original connection and import, he involuntarily derives, as he does the measure, from a famous old sea-ditty, whose cadences, long rife, and now humming in the collapsing brain, attune the last flutterings of distempered thought:—

Farewell and adieu to you noble hearties,—
  Farewell and adieu to you ladies of Spain,
For I've received orders for to sail for the Deadman,
  But hope with the grand fleet to see you again.

I have hove my ship to, with main-top-sail aback, boys;   5
  I have hove my ship to, for to strike soundings clear—
The black scud a'flying; but by God's blessing, dam'me,
  Right up the Channel for the Deadman I'll steer.

I have worried through the waters that are callèd the Doldrums,
    And growled at Sargasso that clogs while ye grope—   10
Blast my eyes, but the light-ship is hid by the mist, lads:—
    Flying-Dutchman—oddsbobbs—off the Cape of Good Hope!

But what's this I feel that is fanning my cheek, Matt?
    The white goney's wing?—how she rolls!—'tis the Cape!—
Give my kit to the mess, Jock, for kin none is mine, none;   15
    And tell *Holy Joe* to avast with the crape.

Dead-reckoning, says *Joe,* it w'ont do to go by;
    But they doused all the glims, Matt, in sky t'other night.
Dead-reckoning is good for to sail for the Deadman;
    And Tom Deadlight he thinks it may reckon near right.   20

The signal!—it streams for the grand fleet to anchor.
    The Captains—the trumpets—the hullabaloo!
Stand by for blue-blazes, and mind your shank-painters,
    For the Lord High Admiral he's squinting at you!

But give me my *tot,* Matt, before I roll over;   25
    Jock, let's have your flipper, it's good for to feel;
And do'nt sew me up without *baccy* in mouth, boys,
    And do'nt blubber like lubbers when I turn up my keel.

Jack Roy

KEPT up by relays of generations young
Never dies at halyards the blithe chorus sung;
While in sands, sounds, and seas where the storm-petrels cry,
Dropped mute around the globe, these halyard-singers lie.
Short-lived the clippers for racing-cups that run,   5
And speeds in life's career many a lavish mother's-son.

But thou, manly king o' the old *Splendid's* crew,
The ribbons o' thy hat still a'fluttering should fly—
A challenge, and forever, nor the bravery should rue.
Only in a tussle for the Starry Flag high   10
When 'tis piety to do, and privilege to die,
Then, only then would heaven think to lop
Such a cedar as the Captain o' the *Splendid's* main-top:
A belted sea-gentleman; a gallant, off-hand
Mercutio indifferent in life's gay command.   15
Magnanimous in humor: when the splintering shot fell,
"Tooth-picks a'plenty, lads; thank 'em with a shell!"

Sang Larry o' the Cannakin, smuggler o' the wine,
At mess between guns, lad in jovial recline:
"In Limbo our Jack he would chirrup up a cheer,   20

The martinet there find a chaffing mutineer;
From a thousand fathoms down under hatches o' your Hades,
He'd ascend in love-ditty, kissing fingers to your ladies!"

Never relishing the knave though allowing for the menial,
Nor overmuch the king, Jack, nor prodigally genial.   25
Ashore on liberty, he flashed in escapade,
Vaulting over life in its levelness of grade,
Like the dolphin off Africa in rainbow a'sweeping—
Arch irridescent shot from seas languid sleeping.

Larking with thy life, if a joy but a toy,   30
Heroic in thy levity wert thou, Jack Roy.

The Haglets

By chapel bare, with walls sea-beat,
The lichened urns in wilds are lost
About a carved memorial stone
That shows, decayed and coral-mossed,
A form recumbent, swords at feet,   5
Trophies at head, and kelp for a winding sheet.

I invoke thy ghost, neglected fane,
Washed by the waters' long lament;
I adjure the recumbent effigy
To tell the cenotaph's intent—   10
Reveal why fagotted swords are at feet,
Why trophies appear and weeds are the winding sheet.

By open ports the Admiral sits,
And shares repose with guns that tell
Of power that smote the arm'd Plate Fleet   15
Whose sinking flag-ship's colors fell;
But over the Admiral floats in light

His squadron's flag, the red-cross Flag of the White.
  The eddying waters whirl astern,
The prow, a seedsman, sows the spray;   20
With bellying sails and buckling spars
The black hull leaves a Milky Way:
Her timbers thrill, her batteries roll,
She revelling speeds exulting with pennon at pole.
  But ah, for standards captive trailed   25
For all their scutcheoned castles' pride—
Castilian towers that dominate Spain,
Naples, and either Ind beside;
Those haughty towers, armorial ones,
Rue the salute from the Admiral's dens of guns.   30

Ensigns and arms in trophy brave—
Braver for many a rent and scar,
The captor's naval hall bedeck,
Spoil that insures an earldom's star—
Toledoes great, grand draperies too,   35
Spain's steel and silk, and splendors from Peru.
  But crippled part in splintering fight,
The vanquished flying the victor's flags,
With prize-crews, under convoy-guns,
Heavy the fleet from Opher drags—   40
The Admiral crowding sail ahead,
Foremost with news who foremost in conflict sped.
  But out from cloistral gallery dim,
In early night his glance is thrown;
He marks the vague reserve of heaven,   45
He feels the touch of ocean lone;
Then turns, in frame part undermined,
Nor notes the shadowing wings that fan behind.

There, peaked and gray, three haglets fly,
And follow, follow fast in wake   50
Where slides the cabin-lustre shy,
And sharks from man a glamour take,

Seething along the line of light
In lane that endless rules the war-ship's flight.
   The sea-fowl here whose hearts none know,   55
They followed late the flag-ship quelled
(As now the victor one) and long
Above her gurgling grave, shrill held
With screams their wheeling rites—then sped
Direct in silence where the victor led.   60
   Now winds less fleet, but fairer, blow,
A ripple laps the coppered side,
While phosphor sparks make ocean gleam
Like camps lit up in triumph wide;
With lights and tinkling cymbals meet   65
Acclaiming seas the advancing conqueror greet.

But who a flattering tide may trust,
Or favoring breeze, or aught in end?—
Careening under startling blasts
The sheeted towers of sails impend;   70
While, gathering bale, behind is bred
A livid storm-bow, like a rainbow dead.
   At trumpet-call the topmen spring;
And, urged by after-call in stress,
Yet other tribes of tars ascend   75
The rigging's howling wilderness;
But ere yard-ends alert they win,
Hell rules in heaven with hurricane-fire and din.
   The spars, athwart at spiry height,
Like quaking Lima's crosses rock;   80
Like bees the clustering sailors cling
Against the shrouds, or take the shock
Flat on the swept yard-arms aslant
Dipped like the wheeling condor's pinions gaunt.

A lull! and tongues of languid flame   85
Lick every boom and lambent show
Electric 'gainst each face aloft;
The herds of clouds with bellowings go:

The black ship rears—beset—harassed,
Then plunges far with luminous antlers vast.   90
  In trim betimes they turn from land,
Some shivered sails and spars they stow:
One watch, dismissed, they troll the can,
While loud the billow thumps the bow—
Vies with the fist that smites the board   95
Obstreperous at each reveller's jovial word.
  Of royal oak by storms confirmed,
The tested hull her lineage shows;
Vainly the plungings whelm her prow—
She rallies, rears, she sturdier grows;   100
Each shot-hole plugged, each storm-sail home,
With batteries housed she rams the watery dome.

Dim seen adrift through driving scud,
The wan moon shows in plight forlorn;
Then, pinched in visage, fades and fades   105
Like to the faces drowned at morn,
When deeps engulfed the flag-ship's crew
And, shrilling round, the inscrutable haglets flew.
  And still they fly, nor now they cry,
But constant fan a second wake,   110
Unflagging pinions ply and ply,
Abreast their course intent they take;
Their silence marks a stable mood,
They patient keep their eager neighborhood.
  Plumed with a smoke, a confluent sea,   115
Heaved in a combing pyramid full,
Spent at its climax, in collapse
Down headlong thundering stuns the hull:
The trophy drops; but, reared again,
Shows Mars' high-altar and contemns the main.   120

Rebuilt it stands, the brag of arms,
Transferred in site—no thought of where
The sensitive needle keeps its place.
And starts, disturbed, a quiverer there;

The helmsman rubs the clouded glass—   125
Peers in, but lets the trembling portent pass.
   Let pass as well his shipmates do
(Whose dream of power no tremors jar)
Fears for the fleet convoyed astern:
"Our flag they fly, they share our star;   130
Spain's galleons great in hull are stout:
Manned by our men—like us they'll ride it out."
   To-night's the night that ends the week—
Ends day and week and month and year:
A four-fold imminent flickering time,   135
For now the midnight draws anear:
Eight bells! and passing-bells they be—
The Old Year fades, the Old Year dies at sea.

He launched them well. But shall the New
Redeem the pledge the Old Year made,   140
Or prove a self-asserting heir?
But healthy hearts few qualms invade:
By shot-chests grouped in bays 'tween guns
The gossips chat, the grizzled, sea-beat ones.
   And boyish dreams some graybeards blab: 145
"To sea, my lads, we go no more
Who share the Acapulco prize;
We'll all night in, and bang the door;
Our ingots red shall yield us bliss:
Lads, golden years begin to-night with this!"   150
   Released from deck, yet waiting call,
Glazed caps and coats baptized in storm,
A watch of Laced Sleeves round the board
Draw near in heart to keep them warm:
"Sweethearts and wives!" clink, clink, they meet,   155
And, quaffing, dip in wine their beards of sleet.

"Ay, let the star-light stay withdrawn,
So here her hearth-light memory fling,
So in this wine-light cheer be born,
And honor's fellowship weld our ring—   160

Honor! our Admiral's aim foretold:
A tomb or a trophy, and lo, 'tis a trophy and gold!"
 But he, a unit, sole in rank,
Apart needs keep his lonely state,
The sentry at his guarded door   165
Mute as by vault the sculptured Fate;
Belted he sits in drowsy light,
And, hatted, nods—the Admiral of the White.
 He dozes, aged with watches passed—
Years, years of pacing to and fro;   170
He dozes, nor attends the stir
In bullioned standards rustling low,
Nor minds the blades whose secret thrill
Perverts overhead the magnet's Polar will;—

Less heeds the shadowing three that ply   175
And follow, follow fast in wake,
Untiring wing and lidless eye—
Abreast their course intent they take;
Or sigh or sing, they hold for good
The unvarying flight and fixed inveterate mood. 180
 In dream at last his dozings merge,
In dream he reaps his victory's fruit:
The Flags-o'-the-Blue, the Flags-o'-the-Red,
Dipped flags of his country's fleets salute
His Flag-o'-the-White in harbor proud— 185
But why should it blench? Why turn to a painted shroud?
 The hungry seas they hound the hull,
The sharks they dog the haglets' flight;
With one consent the winds, the waves
In hunt with fins and wings unite,   190
While drear the harps in cordage sound
Remindful wails for old Armadas drowned.

Ha—yonder! are they Northern Lights?
Or signals flashed to warn or ward?
Yea, signals lanced in breakers high;   195
But doom on warning follows hard:

While yet they veer in hope to shun,
They strike! and thumps of hull and heart are one.
    But beating hearts a drum-beat calls,
And prompt the men to quarters go;   200
Discipline, curbing nature, rules—
Heroic makes who duty know:
They execute the trump's command,
Or in peremptory places wait and stand.
    Yet cast about in blind amaze—   205
As through their watery shroud they peer:
"We tacked from land: then how betrayed?
Have currents swerved us—snared us here?"
None heed the blades that clash in place
Under lamps dashed down that lit the magnet's case.   210

Ah, what may live, who mighty swim,
Or boat-crew reach that shore forbid,
Or cable span? Must victors drown—
Perish, even as the vanquished did?
Man keeps from man the stifled moan;   215
They shouldering stand, yet each in heart how lone.
    Some heaven invoke; but rings of reefs
Prayer and despair alike deride
In dance of breakers forked or peaked,
Pale maniacs of the maddened tide;   220
While, strenuous yet some end to earn,
The haglets spin, though now no more astern.
    Like shuttles hurrying in the looms
Aloft through rigging frayed they ply—
Cross and recross—weave and inweave,   225
Then lock the web with clinching cry
Over the seas on seas that clasp
The weltering wreck where gurgling ends the gasp.

Ah, for the Plate-Fleet trophy now,
The victor's voucher, flags and arms;   230
Never they'll hang in Abbey old

And take Time's dust with holier palms;
Nor less content, in liquid night,
Their captor sleeps—the Admiral of the White.

Imbedded deep with shells   235
And drifted treasure deep,
Forever he sinks deeper in
Unfathomable sleep—
His cannon round him thrown,
His sailors at his feet,   240
The wizard sea enchanting them
Where never haglets beat.

On nights when meteors play,
And light the breakers' dance,
The Oreads from the caves   245
With silvery elves advance;
And up from ocean stream,
And down from heaven far,
The rays that blend in dream
The abysm and the star.   250

The Æolian Harp
At the Surf Inn

LIST the harp in window wailing
  Stirred by fitful gales from sea:
Shrieking up in mad crescendo—
  Dying down in plaintive key!

Listen: Less a strain ideal   5
  Than Ariel's rendering of the Real.
What that Real is, let hint
  A picture stamped in memory's mint.—

Braced well up, with beams aslant,
Betwixt the continents sails the *Phocion*   10
For Baltimore bound from Alicant.
Blue breezy skies white fleeces fleck
Over the chill blue white-capped ocean:
From yard-arm comes—"Wreck ho, a wreck!"

    Dismasted and adrift,   15
    Long time a thing forsaken;
    Overwashed by every wave
    Like the slumbering kraken;
    Heedless if the billow roar,
    Oblivious of the lull,   20

Leagues and leagues from shoal or shore,
It swims—a levelled hull:
Bulwarks gone—a shaven wreck,
Nameless, and a grass-green deck.
A lumberman: perchance, in hold　　　　25
Prostrate pines with hemlocks rolled.

It has drifted, waterlogged,
Till by trailing weeds beclogged:
　Drifted, drifted, day by day,
　Pilotless on pathless way.　　　　　　30
It has drifted till each plank
Is oozy as the oyster-bank:
　Drifted, drifted, night by night,
　Craft that never shows a light;
Nor ever, to prevent worse knell,　　　　35
Tolls in fog the warning bell.
From collision never shrinking,
Drive what may through darksome smother;
Saturate, but never sinking,
Fatal only to the *other!*　　　　　　40
　Deadlier than the sunken reef
Since still the snare it shifteth,
　Torpid in dumb ambuscade
Waylayingly it drifteth.

　O the sailors—O the sails!　　　　　45
　O the lost crews never heard of!
　Well the harp of Ariel wails
　Thoughts that tongue can tell no word of!

To the Master of
the Meteor

LONESOME on earth's loneliest deep,
Sailor! who dost thy vigil keep—
Off the Cape of Storms dost musing sweep
Over monstrous waves that curl and comb;
Of thee we think when here from brink   5
We blow the mead in bubbling foam.

Of thee we think, in a ring we link;
To the shearer of ocean's fleece we drink,
And the *Meteor* rolling home.

Far Off-Shore

Look, the raft, a signal flying,
    Thin—a shred;
None upon the lashed spars lying,
    Quick or dead.

Cries the sea-fowl, hovering over,   5
    "Crew, the crew?"
And the billow, reckless rover,
    Sweeps anew!

The Man-of-War Hawk

Yon black man-of-war hawk that wheels in the light
O'er the black ship's white sky-s'l, sunned cloud to the sight,
Have we low-flyers wings to ascend to his height?

No arrow can reach him; nor thought can attain
To the placid supreme in the sweep of his reign.   5

The Figure-Head

THE *Charles-and-Emma* seaward sped,
(Named from the carven pair at prow)
He so smart, and a curly head,
She tricked forth as a bride knows how:
   Pretty stem for the port, I trow!   5

But iron-rust and alum-spray
And chafing gear, and sun and dew
Vexed this lad and lassie gay,
Tears in their eyes, salt tears nor few;
   And the hug relaxed with the failing glue.   10

But came in end a dismal night
With creaking beams and ribs that groan,
A black lee-shore and waters white:
Dropped on the reef, the pair lie prone:
   O, the breakers dance, but the winds they moan!   15

The Good Craft Snow-Bird

STRENUOUS need that head-wind be
From purposed voyage that drives at last
The ship sharp-braced and dogged still
Beating up against the blast.

Brigs that figs for market gather,   5
Homeward-bound upon the stretch,
Encounter oft this uglier weather,
Yet in end their port they fetch.

Mark yon craft from sunny Smyrna
Glazed with ice in Boston Bay;   10
Out they toss the fig-drums cheerly,
Livelier for the frosty ray.

What if sleet off-shore assailed her,
What though ice yet plate her yards:
In wintry port not less she renders   15
Summer's gift with warm regards!

And, look, the underwriters' man,
Timely, when the stevedore's done,
Puts on his *specs* to pry and scan,
And sets her down—*A, No. 1.*   20

Bravo, master! brava, brig!
　　For slanting snows out of the west
Never the *Snow-Bird* cares one fig;
　　And foul winds steady her, though a pest.

Old Counsel
Of the young Master
Of a wrecked California clipper

COME out of the Golden Gate,
Go round the Horn with streamers,
Carry royals early and late;
But, brother, be not over-elate—
All hands save ship! has startled dreamers. 5

The Tuft of Kelp

ALL dripping in tangles green,
  Cast up by a lonely sea,
If purer for that, O Weed,
  Bitterer, too, are ye?

The Maldive Shark

ABOUT the Shark, phlegmatical one,
Pale sot of the Maldive sea,
The sleek little pilot-fish, azure and slim,
How alert in attendance be.
From his saw-pit of mouth, from his charnel of maw   5
They have nothing of harm to dread,
But liquidly glide on his ghastly flank
Or before his Gorgonian head;
Or lurk in the port of serrated teeth
In white triple tiers of glittering gates,   10
And there find a haven when peril's abroad,
An asylum in jaws of the Fates!

They are friends; and friendly they guide him to prey,
Yet never partake of the treat—
Eyes and brains to the dotard lethargic and dull,   15
Pale ravener of horrible meat.

To Ned

Where is the world we roved, Ned Bunn?
   Hollows thereof lay rich in shade
By voyagers old inviolate thrown
   Ere Paul Pry cruised with Pelf and Trade.
To us old lads some thoughts come home   5
Who roamed a world young lads no more shall roam.

Nor less the satiate year impends
   When, wearying of routine-resorts,
The pleasure-hunter shall break loose,
   Ned, for our Pantheistic ports:—   10
Marquesas and glenned isles that be
Authentic Edens in a Pagan sea.

The charm of scenes untried shall lure,
   And, Ned, a legend urge the flight—
The Typee-truants under stars   15
   Unknown to Shakespere's *Midsummer-Night;*
And man, if lost to Saturn's Age,
Yet feeling life no Syrian pilgrimage.

But, tell, shall he the tourist find
   Our isles the same in violet-glow   20
Enamoring us what years and years—

Ah, Ned, what years and years ago!
Well, Adam advances, smart in pace,
But scarce by violets that advance you trace.

But we, in anchor-watches calm,   25
   The Indian Psyche's languor won,
And, musing, breathed primeval balm
   From Edens ere yet over-run;
Marvelling mild if mortal twice,
Here and hereafter, touch a Paradise.   30

Crossing the Tropics

(*From* The Saya-y-Manto)

WHILE now the Pole Star sinks from sight
  The Southern Cross it climbs the sky;
But losing thee, my love, my light,
O bride but for one bridal night,
  The loss no rising joys supply.   5

Love, love, the Trade-Winds urge abaft,
And thee, from thee, they steadfast waft.

By day the blue-and-silver sea
  And chime of waters blandly fanned—
Nor these, nor Gama's stars to me   10
May yield delight since still for thee
  I long as Gama longed for land.

I yearn, I yearn, reverting turn,
My heart it streams in wake astern.

When, cut by slanting sleet, we swoop   15
  Where raves the world's inverted year,
If roses all your porch shall loop,
Not less your heart for me will droop
  Doubling the world's last outpost drear.

O love, O love, these oceans vast: 20
Love, love, it is as death were past!

The Berg

(A Dream)

I SAW a Ship of martial build
(Her standards set, her brave apparel on)
Directed as by madness mere
Against a stolid Iceberg steer,
Nor budge it, though the infatuate Ship went down.   5
The impact made huge ice-cubes fall
Sullen, in tons that crashed the deck;
But that one avalanche was all—
No other movement save the foundering wreck.

Along the spurs of ridges pale   10
Not any slenderest shaft and frail,
A prism over glass-green gorges lone,
Toppled; nor lace of traceries fine,
Nor pendant drops in grot or mine
Were jarred, when the stunned Ship went down.   15

Nor sole the gulls in cloud that wheeled
Circling one snow-flanked peak afar,
But nearer fowl the floes that skimmed
And crystal beaches, felt no jar.
No thrill transmitted stirred the lock   20
Of jack-straw needle-ice at base;
Towers undermined by waves—the block

Atilt impending—kept their place.
Seals, dozing sleek on sliddery ledges
Slipt never, when by loftier edges,   25
Through very inertia overthrown,
The impetuous Ship in bafflement went down.

Hard Berg (methought) so cold, so vast,
With mortal damps self-overcast;
Exhaling still thy dankish breath—   30
Adrift dissolving, bound for death;
Though lumpish thou, a lumbering one—
A lumbering lubbard loitering slow,
Impingers rue thee and go down,
Sounding thy precipice below,   35
Nor stir the slimy slug that sprawls
Along thy dense stolidity of walls.

The Enviable Isles

(From Rammon)

THROUGH storms you reach them and from storms are free.
　　Afar descried, the foremost drear in hue,
But, nearer, green; and, on the marge, the sea
　　Makes thunder low and mist of rainbowed dew.

But, inland, where the sleep that folds the hills　　　　5
A dreamier sleep, the trance of God, instills—
　　On uplands hazed, in wandering airs aswoon,
Slow-swaying palms salute love's cypress tree
　　Adown in vale where pebbly runlets croon
A song to lull all sorrow and all glee.　　　　10

Sweet-fern and moss in many a glade are here,
　　Where, strown in flocks, what cheek-flushed myriads lie
Dimpling in dream—unconscious slumberers mere,
　　While billows endless round the beaches die.

PEBBLES

I

THOUGH the Clerk of the Weather insist,
    And lay down the weather-law,
Pintado and gannet they wist
That the winds blow whither they list
    In tempest or flaw.   5

II

Old are the creeds, but stale the schools
   Revamped as the mode may veer.
But Orm from the schools to the beaches strays,
And, finding a Conch hoar with time, he delays
   And reverent lifts it to ear.   5
That Voice, pitched in far monotone,
   Shall it swerve? shall it deviate ever?
The Seas have inspired it, and Truth—
   Truth, varying from sameness never.

III

In hollows of the liquid hills
   Where the long Blue Ridges run,
The flattery of no echo thrills,
   For echo the seas have none;
Nor aught that gives man back man's strain—   5
The hope of his heart, the dream in his brain.

IV

On ocean where the embattled fleets repair,
Man, suffering inflictor, sails on sufferance there.

V

IMPLACABLE I, the old implacable Sea:
  Implacable most when most I smile serene—
Pleased, not appeased, by myriad wrecks in me.

VI

CURLED in the comb of yon billow Andean,
   Is it the Dragon's heaven-challenging crest?
Elemental mad ramping of ravening waters—
   Yet Christ on the Mount, and the dove in her nest!

VII

Healed of my hurt, I laud the inhuman Sea—
Yea, bless the Angels Four that there convene;
For healed I am even by their pitiless breath
Distilled in wholesome dew named rosmarine.

Timoleon

Etc.

TO

MY COUNTRYMAN

ELIHU VEDDER

Timoleon

(394 B.C.)

I

If more than once, as annals tell,
Through blood without compunction spilt,
An egotist arch rule has snatched,
And stamped the seizure with his sabre's hilt,
   And, legalised by lawyers, stood;   5
Shall the good heart whose patriot fire
Leaps to a deed of startling note,
Do it, then flinch? Shall good in weak expire?
   Needs goodness lack the evil grit
That stares down censorship and ban,   10
And dumfounds saintlier ones with this—
God's will's avouched in each successful man?
   Or, put it, where dread stress inspires
A virtue beyond man's standard rate,
Seems virtue there a strain forbid—   15
Transcendence such as shares transgression's fate?
   If so, and wan eclipse ensue,
Yet glory await emergence won,
Is that high Providence, or Chance?
And proved it which with thee, Timoleon?   20
   O, crowned with laurel twined with thorn,
Not rash thy life's cross-tide I stem,

But reck the problem rolled in pang
And reach and dare to touch thy garment's hem.

II

When Argos and Cleone strove   25
Against free Corinth's claim or right,
Two brothers battled for her well:
A footman one, and one a mounted knight.
    Apart in place, each braved the brunt
Till the rash cavalryman, alone,   30
Was wrecked against the enemy's files,
His bayard crippled, and he maimed and thrown.
    Timoleon, at Timophanes' need,
Makes for the rescue through the fray,
Covers him with his shield, and takes   35
The darts and furious odds and fights at bay;
    Till, wrought to pallor of passion dumb,
Stark terrors of death around he throws,
Warding his brother from the field
Spite failing friends dispersed and rallying foes.   40
    Here might he rest, in claim rest here,
Rest, and a Phidian form remain;
But life halts never, life must on,
And take with term prolonged some scar or stain.
    Yes, life must on. And latent germs   45
Time's seasons wake in mead and man;
And brothers, playfellows in youth,
Develop into variance wide in span.

III

Timophanes was his mother's pride—
Her pride, her pet, even all to her   50
Who slackly on Timoleon looked.
Scarce *he* (she mused) may proud affection stir.
    He saved my darling, gossips tell:

If so, 'twas service, yea, and fair;
But instinct ruled, and duty bade,   55
In service such, a henchman e'en might share.
  When boys they were I helped the bent;
I made the junior feel his place,
Subserve the senior, love him, too;
And sooth he does, and that's his saving grace.   60
  But me the meek one never can serve,
Not he, he lacks the quality keen
To make the mother through the son
An envied dame of power, a social queen.
  But thou, my first-born, thou art I   65
In sex translated; joyed, I scan
My features, mine, expressed in thee;
Thou art what I would be were I a man.
  My brave Timophanes, 'tis thou
Who yet the world's fore-front shalt win,   70
For thine the urgent resolute way,
Self pushing panoplied self through thick and thin.
  Nor here maternal insight erred:
Forsworn, with heart that did not wince
At slaying men who kept their vows,   75
Her darling strides to power, and reigns—a Prince.

IV

  Because of just heart and humane,
Profound the hate Timoleon knew
For crimes of pride and men-of-prey
And impious deeds that perjurous upstarts do;   80
  And Corinth loved he, and in way
Old Scotia's clansman loved his clan,
Devotion one with ties how dear,
And passion that late to make the rescue ran.
  But crime and kin—the terrorised town,   85
The silent, acquiescent mother—
Revulsion racks the filial heart,
The loyal son, the patriot true, the brother.

In evil visions of the night
He sees the lictors of the gods,   90
Giant ministers of righteousness,
Their *fasces* threatened by the Furies' rods.
    But undeterred he wills to act,
Resolved thereon though Ate rise;
He heeds the voice whose mandate calls,   95
Or seems to call, peremptory from the skies.

                              V

    Nor less but by approaches mild,
And trying each prudential art,
The just one first advances him
In parley with a flushed intemperate heart.   100
    The brother first he seeks—alone,
And pleads; but is with laughter met;
Then comes he, in accord with two,
And these adjure the tyrant and beset;
    Whose merriment gives place to rage: 105
"Go," stamping, "what to me is Right?
I am the Wrong, and lo, I reign,
And testily intolerant too in might";
    And glooms on his mute brother pale,
Who goes aside; with muffled face   110
He sobs the predetermined word,
And Right in Corinth reassumes its place.

                             VI

    But on his robe, ah, whose the blood?
And craven ones their eyes avert,
And heavy is a mother's ban,   115
And dismal faces of the fools can hurt.
    The whispering-gallery of the world,
Where each breathed slur runs wheeling wide,
Eddies a false perverted truth,

Inveterate turning still on fratricide.   120
    The time was Plato's. Wandering lights
Confirmed the atheist's standing star;
As now, no sanction Virtue knew
For deeds that on prescriptive morals jar.
    Reaction took misgiving's tone,   125
Infecting conscience, till betrayed
To doubt the irrevocable doom
Herself had authorised when undismayed.
    Within perturbed Timoleon here
Such deeps were bared as when the sea   130
Convulsed, vacates its shoreward bed,
And Nature's last reserves show nakedly.
    He falters. And from Hades' glens
By night insidious tones implore—
Why suffer? hither come, and be   135
What Phocion is who feeleth man no more.
    But, won from that, his mood elects
To live—to live in wilding place;
For years self-outcast, he but meets
In shades his playfellow's reproachful face.   140
    Estranged through one transcendent deed
From common membership in mart,
In severance he is like a head
Pale after battle trunkless found apart.

VII

    But flood-tide comes though long the ebb,   145
Nor patience bides with passion long;
Like sightless orbs his thoughts are rolled
Arraigning heaven as compromised in wrong:
    "To second causes why appeal?
Vain parleying here with fellow-clods.   150
To *you,* Arch Principals, I rear
My quarrel, for this quarrel is with gods.
    "Shall just men long to quit your world?
It is aspersion of your reign;

Your marbles in the temple stand—   155
Yourselves as stony, and invoked in vain?"
    Ah, bear with *one* quite overborne,
Olympians, if he chide ye now;
Magnanimous be even though he rail
And hard against ye set the bleaching brow.—   160
    "If conscience doubt, she'll next recant.
What basis then? O, tell at last,
Are earnest natures staggering here
But fatherless shadows from no substance cast?
    "Yea, *are* ye, gods? Then ye, 'tis ye   165
Should show what touch of tie ye may,
Since ye too, if not wrung, are wronged
By grievous misconceptions of your sway.
    "But deign, some little sign be given—
Low thunder in your tranquil skies;   170
Me reassure, nor let me be
Like a lone dog that for a master cries."

                            VIII

    Men's moods, as frames, must yield to years,
And turns the world in fickle ways:
Corinth recalls Timoleon—ay,   175
And plumes him forth, but yet with schooling phrase.
    On Sicily's fields, through arduous wars,
A peace he won whose rainbow spanned
The isle redeemed; and he was hailed
Deliverer of that fair colonial land.   180
    And Corinth clapt: Absolved, and more!
Justice in long arrears is thine:
Not slayer of thy brother, no,
But saviour of the state, Jove's soldier, man divine.
    Eager for thee thy City waits: 185
Return! with bays we dress your door.
But he, the Isle's loved guest, reposed,
And never for Corinth left the adopted shore.

After the Pleasure Party

LINES TRACED
UNDER AN IMAGE OF
AMOR THREATENING

Fear me, virgin whosoever
Taking pride from love exempt,
Fear me, slighted. Never, never
Brave me, nor my fury tempt:
Downy wings, but wroth they beat
Tempest even in reason's seat.

BEHIND the house the upland falls
With many an odorous tree—
White marbles gleaming through green halls—
Terrace by terrace, down and down,
And meets the star-lit Mediterranean Sea.   5

'Tis Paradise. In such an hour
Some pangs that rend might take release.
Nor less perturbed who keeps this bower
Of balm, nor finds balsamic peace?
From whom the passionate words in vent   10
After long revery's discontent?

"Tired of the homeless deep,
Look how their flight yon hurrying billows urge
  Hitherward but to reap
Passive repulse from the iron-bound verge!   15
Insensate, can they never know
'Tis mad to wreck the impulsion so?

  "An art of memory is, they tell:
But to forget! forget the glade
Wherein Fate sprung Love's ambuscade,   20
To flout pale years of cloistral life
And flush me in this sensuous strife.
'Tis Vesta struck with Sappho's smart.
No fable her delirious leap:
With more of cause in desperate heart,   25
Myself could take it—but to sleep!

  "Now first I feel, what all may ween,
That soon or late, if faded e'en,
One's sex asserts itself. Desire,
The dear desire through love to sway,   30
Is like the Geysers that aspire—
Through cold obstruction win their fervid way.
But baffled here—to take disdain,
To feel rule's instinct, yet not reign;
To dote; to come to this drear shame—   35
Hence the winged blaze that sweeps my soul
Like prairie-fires that spurn control,
Where withering weeds incense the flame.

  "And kept I long heaven's watch for this,
Contemning love, for this, even this?   40
O terrace chill in Northern air,
O reaching ranging tube I placed
Against yon skies, and fable chased
Till, fool, I hailed for sister there

Starred Cassiopea in Golden Chair.   45
In dream I throned me, nor I saw
In cell the idiot crowned with straw.

  "And yet, ah yet, scarce ill I reigned,
Through self-illusion self-sustained,
When now—enlightened, undeceived—   50
What gain I, barrenly bereaved!
Than this can be yet lower decline—
Envy and spleen, can these be mine?

  "The peasant-girl demure that trod
Beside our wheels that climbed the way,   55
And bore along a blossoming rod
That looked the sceptre of May-Day—
On her—to fire this petty hell,
His softened glance how moistly fell!
The cheat! on briers her buds were strung;   60
And wiles peeped forth from mien how meek.
The innocent bare-foot! young, so young!
To girls, strong man's a novice weak.
To tell such beads! And more remain,
Sad rosary of belittling pain.   65

  "When after lunch and sallies gay
Like the Decameron folk we lay
In sylvan groups; and I——let be!
O, dreams he, can he dream that one
Because not roseate feels no sun?   70
The plain lone bramble thrills with Spring
As much as vines that grapes shall bring.

  "Me now fair studies charm no more.
Shall great thoughts writ, or high themes sung
Damask wan cheeks—unlock his arm   75
About some radiant ninny flung?

How glad, with all my starry lore,
I'd buy the veriest wanton's rose
Would but my bee therein repose.

"Could I remake me! or set free   80
This sexless bound in sex, then plunge
Deeper than Sappho, in a lunge
Piercing Pan's paramount mystery!
For, Nature, in no shallow surge
Against thee either sex may urge,   85
Why hast thou made us but in halves—
Co-relatives? This makes us slaves.
If these co-relatives never meet
Selfhood itself seems incomplete.
And such the dicing of blind fate   90
Few matching halves here meet and mate.
What Cosmic jest or Anarch blunder
The human integral clove asunder
And shied the fractions through life's gate?

"Ye stars that long your votary knew   95
Rapt in her vigil, see me here!
Whither is gone the spell ye threw
When rose before me Cassiopea?
Usurped on by love's stronger reign—
But, lo, your very selves do wane: 100
Light breaks—truth breaks! Silvered no more,
But chilled by dawn that brings the gale
Shivers yon bramble above the vale,
And disillusion opens all the shore."

One knows not if Urania yet   105
The pleasure-party may forget;
Or whether she lived down the strain
Of turbulent heart and rebel brain;
For Amor so resents a slight,
And hers had been such haught disdain,   110

He long may wreak his boyish spite,
And boy-like, little reck the pain.

   One knows not, no. But late in Rome
(For queens discrowned a congruous home)
Entering Albani's porch she stood   115
Fixed by an antique pagan stone
Colossal carved. No anchorite seer,
Not Thomas a'Kempis, monk austere,
Religious more are in their tone;
Yet far, how far from Christian heart   120
That form august of heathen Art.
Swayed by its influence, long she stood,
Till surged emotion seething down,
She rallied and this mood she won:

   "Languid in frame for me,   125
To-day by Mary's convent-shrine,
Touched by her picture's moving plea
In that poor nerveless hour of mine,
I mused—A wanderer still must grieve.
Half I resolved to kneel and believe,   130
Believe and submit, the veil take on.
But thee, arm'd Virgin! less benign,
Thee now I invoke, thou mightier one.
Helmeted woman—if such term
Befit thee, far from strife   135
Of that which makes the sexual feud
And clogs the aspirant life—
O self-reliant, strong and free,
Thou in whom power and peace unite,
Transcender! raise me up to thee,   140
Raise me and arm me!"

                Fond appeal.
For never passion peace shall bring,
Nor Art inanimate for long
Inspire. Nothing may help or heal   145

While Amor incensed remembers wrong.
Vindictive, not himself he'll spare;
For scope to give his vengeance play
Himself he'll blaspheme and betray.

    Then for Urania, virgins everywhere,   150
O pray! Example take too, and have care.

The Night-March

With banners furled, and clarions mute,
　An army passes in the night;
And beaming spears and helms salute
　The dark with bright.

In silence deep the legions stream,　　　　　　　　　5
　With open ranks, in order true;
Over boundless plains they stream and gleam—
　No Chief in view!

Afar, in twinkling distance lost,
　(So legends tell) he lonely wends　　　　　　　　10
And back through all that shining host
　His mandate sends.

The Ravaged Villa

In shards the sylvan vases lie,
   Their links of dance undone,
And brambles wither by thy brim,
   Choked Fountain of the Sun!
The spider in the laurel spins,   5
   The weed exiles the flower:
And, flung to kiln, Apollo's bust
   Makes lime for Mammon's tower.

The Margrave's Birth Night

Up from many a sheeted valley,
From white woods as well,
Down too from each fleecy upland
Jingles many a bell,

Jovial on the work-sad horses   5
Hitched to runners old
Of the toil-worn peasants sledging
Under sheepskins in the cold,

Till from every quarter gathered
Meet they on one ledge,   10
There from hoods they brush the snow off
Lighting from each sledge

Full before the Margrave's castle,
Summoned there to cheer
On his birth-night, in midwinter,   15
Kept year after year.

O the hall, and O the holly!
Tables line each wall;
Guests as holly-berries plenty,
But—no host withal!   20

May his people feast contented
While at head of board
Empty throne and vacant cover
Speak the absent lord?

Minstrels enter. And the stewards   25
Serve the guests; and when,
Passing there the vacant cover,
Functionally then

Old observance grave they offer;
But no Margrave fair,   30
In his living aspect gracious,
Sits responsive there;

No, and never guest once marvels,
None the good lord name,
Scarce they mark void throne and cover—   35
Dust upon the same.

Mindless as to what importeth
Absence such in hall;
Tacit as the plough-horse feeding
In the palfrey's stall.   40

Ah, enough for toil and travail,
If but for a night
Into wine is turned the water,
Black bread into white.

Magian Wine

AMULETS gemmed, to Miriam dear,
Adown in liquid mirage gleam;
Solomon's Syrian charms appear,
   Opal and ring supreme.
The rays that light this Magian Wine   5
Thrill up from semblances divine.

And, seething through the rapturous wave,
What low Elysian anthems rise:
Sybilline inklings blending rave,
   Then lap the verge with sighs.   10
Delirious here the oracles swim
Ambiguous in the beading hymn.

The Garden of Metrodorus

THE Athenians mark the moss-grown gate
And hedge untrimmed that hides the haven green:
   And who keeps here his quiet state?
   And shares he sad or happy fate
Where never foot-path to the gate is seen?   5

Here none come forth, here none go in,
Here silence strange, and dumb seclusion dwell:
   Content from loneness who may win?
   And is this stillness peace or sin
Which noteless thus apart can keep its dell?   10

The New Zealot to the Sun

PERSIAN, you rise
Aflame from climes of sacrifice
   Where adulators sue,
And prostrate man, with brow abased,
Adheres to rites whose tenor traced   5
   All worship hitherto.

   Arch type of sway,
Meetly your overruling ray
   You fling from Asia's plain,
Whence flashed the javelins abroad   10
Of many a wild incursive horde
   Led by some shepherd Cain.

   Mid terrors dinned
Gods too came conquerors from your Ind,
   The brood of Brahma throve;   15
They came like to the scythèd car,
Westward they rolled their empire far,
   Of night their purple wove.

   Chymist, you breed
In orient climes each sorcerous weed   20
   That energises dream—

Transmitted, spread in myths and creeds,
Houris and hells, delirious screeds—
　　And Calvin's last extreme.

　　What though your light   25
In time's first dawn compelled the flight
　　Of Chaos' startled clan,
Shall never all your darted spears
Disperse worse Anarchs, frauds and fears,
　　Sprung from these weeds to man?   30

　　But Science yet
An effluence ampler shall beget,
　　And power beyond your play—
Shall quell the shades you fail to rout,
Yea, searching every secret out,   35
　　Elucidate your ray.

The Weaver

For years, within a mud–built room
For Arva's shrine he weaves the Shawl,
Lone wight, and at a lonely loom,
His busy shadow on the wall.

The face is pinched, the form is bent,   5
No pastime knows he nor the wine,
Recluse he lives and abstinent
Who weaves for Arva's shrine.

Lamia's Song

DESCEND, descend!
Pleasant the downward way—
From your lonely Alp
With the wintry scalp
To our myrtles in valleys of May.   5
    Wend, then, wend:
Mountaineer, descend!
And more than a wreath shall repay.
    Come, ah, come!
With the cataracts come,   10
That hymn as they roam—
How pleasant the downward way!

In a Garret

Gems and jewels let them heap—
　Wax sumptuous as the Sophi:
For me, to grapple from Art's deep
　One dripping trophy!

Monody

To have known him, to have loved him,
   After loneness long;
And then to be estranged in life,
   And neither in the wrong;
And now for death to set his seal—   5
   Ease me, a little ease, my song!

By wintry hills his hermit-mound
   The sheeted snow-drifts drape,
And houseless there the snow-bird flits
   Beneath the fir-tree's crape: 10
Glazed now with ice the cloistral vine
   That hid the shyest grape.

Lone Founts

THOUGH fast youth's glorious fable flies,
View not the world with worldlings' eyes;
Nor turn with weather of the time.
Foreclose the coming of surprise:
Stand where Posterity shall stand;   5
Stand where the Ancients stood before,
And, dipping in lone founts thy hand,
Drink of the never-varying lore:
Wise once, and wise thence evermore.

The Bench of Boors

In bed I muse on Teniers' boors,
Embrowned and beery losels all:
    A wakeful brain
    Elaborates pain:
Within low doors the slugs of boors   5
Laze and yawn, and doze again.

In dreams they doze, the drowsy boors,
Their hazy hovel warm and small:
    Thought's ampler bound
    But chill is found: 10
Within low doors the basking boors
Snugly hug the ember-mound.

Sleepless, I see the slumberous boors
Their blurred eyes blink, their eyelids fall:
    Thought's eager sight   15
    Aches—overbright!
Within low doors the boozy boors
Cat-naps take in pipe-bowl light.

The Enthusiast

"Though He slay me
yet will I trust in Him."

SHALL hearts that beat no base retreat
    In youth's magnanimous years—
Ignoble hold it if discreet
    When interest tames to fears;
Shall spirits that worship light   5
    Perfidious deem its sacred glow,
    Recant, and trudge where worldlings go,
Conform, and own them right?

Shall Time with creeping influence cold
    Unnerve and cow? the heart   10
Pine for the heartless ones enrolled
    With palterers of the mart?
Shall Faith abjure her skies,
    Or pale probation blench her down
    To shrink from Truth so still, so lone   15
Mid loud gregarious lies?

Each burning boat in Cæsar's rear
    Flames—No return through me!
So put the torch to ties though dear,
    If ties but tempters be.   20
Nor cringe if come the night:
    Walk through the cloud to meet the pall,
    Though light forsake thee, never fall
From fealty to light.

Art

In placid hours well pleased we dream
Of many a brave unbodied scheme.
But form to lend, pulsed life create,
What unlike things must meet and mate:
A flame to melt—a wind to freeze;   5
Sad patience—joyous energies;
Humility—yet pride and scorn;
Instinct and study; love and hate;
Audacity—reverence. These must mate,
And fuse with Jacob's mystic heart,   10
To wrestle with the angel—Art.

Buddha

"For what is your life? It is
even a vapor that appeareth for a
little time and then vanisheth away."

SWOONING swim to less and less,
    Aspirant to nothingness!
Sobs of the worlds, and dole of kinds
    That dumb endurers be—
Nirvana! absorb us in your skies,   5
    Annul us into Thee.

C——'s Lament

How lovely was the light of heaven,
What angels leaned from out the sky
In years when youth was more than wine
And man and nature seemed divine
Ere yet I felt that youth must die.   5

Ere yet I felt that youth must die
How insubstantial looked the earth,
Aladdin-land! in each advance,
Or here or there, a new romance;
I never dreamed would come a dearth.   10

And nothing then but had its worth,
Even pain. Yes, pleasure still and pain
In quick reaction made of life
A lovers' quarrel, happy strife
In youth that never comes again.   15

But will youth never come again?
Even to his grave-bed has he gone,
And left me lone, to wake by night
With heavy heart that erst was light?
O, lay it at his head—a stone!   20

Shelley's Vision

WANDERING late by morning seas
When my heart with pain was low—
Hate the censor pelted me—
Deject I saw my shadow go.

In elf-caprice of bitter tone   5
I too would pelt the pelted one:
At my shadow I cast a stone.

When lo, upon that sun-lit ground
I saw the quivering phantom take
The likeness of Saint Stephen crowned: 10
Then did self-reverence awake.

Fragments of a Lost Gnostic Poem of the 12th Century

* * * *

FOUND a family, build a state,
The pledged event is still the same:
Matter in end will never abate
His ancient brutal claim.

* * * *

Indolence is heaven's ally here,   5
And energy the child of hell:
The Good Man pouring from his pitcher clear
But brims the poisoned well.

The Marchioness of Brinvilliers

He toned the sprightly beam of morning
With twilight meek of tender eve,
Brightness interfused with softness,
   Light and shade did weave:
And gave to candor equal place   5
With mystery starred in open skies;
And, floating all in sweetness, made
   Her fathomless mild eyes.

The Age of the Antonines

WHILE faith forecasts Millennial years
Spite Europe's embattled lines,
Back to the Past one glance be cast—
    The Age of the Antonines!
O summit of fate, O zenith of time   5
When a pagan gentleman reigned,
And the olive was nailed to the inn of the world
Nor the peace of the just was feigned.
    A halcyon Age, afar it shines,
Solstice of Man and the Antonines.   10

Hymns to the nations' friendly gods
Went up from the fellowly shrines,
No demagogue beat the pulpit-drum
    In the Age of the Antonines!
The sting was not dreamed to be taken from death,   15
No Paradise pledged or sought,
But they reasoned of fate at the flowing feast
Nor stifled the fluent thought.
    We sham, we shuffle while faith declines—
They were frank in the Age of the Antonines.   20

Orders and ranks they kept degree,
Few felt how the parvenu pines,
No lawmaker took the lawless one's fee

In the Age of the Antonines!
Under law made will the world reposed   25
And the ruler's right confessed,
For the heavens elected the Emperor then,
The foremost of men the best.
Ah, might we read in America's signs
The Age restored of the Antonines.   30

Herba Santa

I

AFTER long wars when comes release
Not olive wands proclaiming peace
    An import dearer share
Than stems of Herba Santa hazed
    In autumn's Indian air.   5
Of moods they breathe that care disarm,
They pledge us lenitive and calm.

II

Shall code or creed a lure afford
To win all selves to Love's accord?
When Love ordained a supper divine   10
    For the wide world of man,
What bickerings o'er his gracious wine!
    Then strange new feuds began.

Effectual more, in lowlier way,
    Pacific Herb, thy sensuous plea   15
The bristling clans of Adam sway
    At least to fellowship in thee!
Before thine altar tribal flags are furled,
Fain wouldst thou make one hearthstone of the world.

III

To scythe, to sceptre, pen and hod—   20
    Yea, sodden laborers dumb;
To brains overplied, to feet that plod,
In solace of the *Truce of God*
    The Calumet has come!

IV

Ah for the world ere Raleigh's find   25
    Never that knew this suasive balm
That helps when Gilead's fails to heal,
    Helps by an interserted charm.

Insinuous, thou, that through the nerve
    Windest the soul, and so canst win   30
    Some from repinings, some from sin,
The Church's aim thou dost subserve.

The ruffled fag foredone with care,
    And brooding, Gold would ease this pain:
Him soothest thou, and smoothest down   35
    Till some content return again.

Even ruffians feel thy influence breed
    Saint Martin's summer in the mind,
They feel this last evangel plead,
As did the first, apart from creed,   40
    Be peaceful, man—be kind!

V

Rejected once on higher plain,
O Love supreme, to come again
    Can this be thine?
Again to come, and win us too   45
    In likeness of a weed
That as a god didst vainly woo,
    As man more vainly bleed?

VI

Forbear, my soul! and in thine Eastern chamber
  Rehearse the dream that brings the long release: 50
Through jasmine sweet and talismanic amber
  Inhaling Herba Santa in the passive Pipe of Peace.

Venice

WITH Pantheist energy of will
The little craftsman of the Coral Sea
Strenuous in the blue abyss,
Up-builds his marvellous gallery
   And long arcade,   5
Erections freaked with many a fringe
   Of marble garlandry,
Evincing what a worm can do.

Laborious in a shallower wave,
   Advanced in kindred art,   10
A prouder agent proved Pan's might
When Venice rose in reefs of palaces.

In a Bye-Canal

A SWOON of noon, a trance of tide,
The hushed siesta brooding wide
   Like calms far off Peru;
No floating wayfarer in sight,
Dumb noon, and haunted like the night   5
   When Jael the wiled one slew.

A languid impulse from the oar
Plied by my indolent gondolier
Tinkles against a palace hoar,
   And, hark, response I hear!   10
A lattice clicks; and, lo, I see,
Between the slats, mute summoning me,
What loveliest eyes of scintillation,
What basilisk glance of conjuration!

   Fronted I have, part taken the span   15
Of portents in nature and peril in man.
I have swum—I have been
'Twixt the whale's black flukes and the white shark's fin;
The enemy's desert have wandered in,
And there have turned, have turned and scanned,   20
Following me how noiselessly,
Envy and Slander, lepers hand in hand.
All this. But at the latticed eye—

"Hey! Gondolier, you sleep, my man;
Wake up!" And, shooting by, we ran;   25
The while I mused, This, surely, now,
Confutes the Naturalists, allow!
Sirens, true sirens verily be,
Sirens, waylayers in the sea.

Well, wooed by these same deadly misses,   30
   Is it shame to run?
No! flee them did divine Ulysses,
   Brave, wise, and Venus' son.

Pisa's Leaning Tower

THE Tower in tiers of architraves,
    Fair circle over cirque,
A trunk of rounded colonades,
The maker's master-work,
Impends with all its pillared tribes,   5
And, poising them, debates:
It thinks to plunge—but hesitates;
Shrinks back—yet fain would slide;
Withholds itself—itself would urge;
Hovering, shivering on the verge,   10
    A would-be suicide!

In a Church of Padua

IN vaulted place where shadows flit,
An upright sombre box you see:
A door, but fast, and lattice none.
But punctured holes minutely small
In lateral silver panel square   5
Above a kneeling-board without,
Suggest an aim if not declare.

Who bendeth here the tremulous knee
No glimpse may get of him within,
And he immured may hardly see   10
The soul confessing there the sin;
Nor yields the low-sieved voice a tone
Whereby the murmurer may be known.

Dread diving-bell! In thee inurned
What hollows the priest must sound,   15
   Descending into consciences
Where more is hid than found.

Milan Cathedral

THROUGH light green haze, a rolling sea
Over gardens where redundance flows,
   The fat old plain of Lombardy,
The White Cathedral shows.

   Of Art the miracles   5
   Its tribes of pinnacles
Gleam like to ice-peaks snowed; and higher,
Erect upon each airy spire
   In concourse without end,
Statues of saints over saints ascend   10
Like multitudinous forks of fire.

What motive was the master-builder's here?
Why these synodic hierarchies given,
Sublimely ranked in marble sessions clear,
Except to signify the host of heaven.   15

Pausilippo

(In the time of Bomba)

A HILL there is that laves its feet
In Naples' bay and lifts its head
In jovial season, curled with vines.
Its name, in pristine years conferred
By settling Greeks, imports that none   5
Who take the prospect thence can pine,
For such the charm of beauty shown
Even sorrow's self they cheerful weened
Surcease might find and thank good Pan.

Toward that Hill my landau drew;   10
And there, hard by the verge, was seen
Two faces with such meaning fraught
One scarce could mark and straight pass on:
I bade my charioteer rein up.

A man it was less hoar with time   15
Than bleached through strange immurement long,
Retaining still, by doom depressed,
Dim trace of some aspiring prime.
Seated, he tuned a homely harp
Watched by a girl, whose filial mien   20
Toward one almost a child again,
Took on a staid maternal tone.
Nor might one question that the locks

Which in smoothed natural silvery curls
Fell on the bowed one's thread-bare coat   25
Betrayed her ministering hand.

   Anon, among some ramblers drawn
A murmur rose, "'Tis Silvio, Silvio!"
With inklings more in tone suppressed
Touching his story, part recalled: 30
Clandestine arrest abrupt by night;
The sole conjecturable cause
The yearning in a patriot ode
Construed as treason; trial none;
Prolonged captivity profound;   35
Vain liberation late. All this,
With pity for impoverishment
And blight forestalling age's wane.

   Hillward the quelled enthusiast turned,
Unmanned, made meek through strenuous wrong,   40
Preluding, faltering; then began,
But only thrilled the wire—no more,
The constant maid supplying voice,
Hinting by no ineloquent sign
That she was but his mouth-piece mere,   45
Himself too spiritless and spent.

   Pausilippo, Pausilippo,
Pledging easement unto pain,
   Shall your beauty even solace
If one's sense of beauty wane?   50

Could light airs that round ye play
Waft heart-heaviness away
Or memory lull to sleep,
   Then, then indeed your balm

Might Silvio becharm,   55
And life in fount would leap,
    Pausilippo!

Did not your spell invite,
    In moods that slip between,
    A dream of years serene,   60
And wake, to dash, delight—
    Evoking here in vision
    Fulfillment and fruition—
Nor mine, nor meant for man!
    Did hope not frequent share   65
    The mirage when despair
Overtakes the caravan,
    Me then your scene might move
    To break from sorrow's snare,
    And apt your name would prove,   70
    Pausilippo!

But I've looked upon your revel—
    It unravels not the pain:
Pausilippo, Pausilippo,
    Named benignly if in vain!   75

It ceased. In low and languid tone
The tideless ripple lapped the passive shore.
As listlessly the bland untroubled heaven
Looked down, as silver doled was silent given
In pity—futile as the ore!   80

The Attic Landscape

Tourist, spare the avid glance
   That greedy roves the sights to see:
Little here of "Old Romance",
   Or Picturesque of Tivoli.

No flushful tint the sense to warm—   5
Pure outline pale, a linear charm.
The clear-cut hills carved temples face,
Respond, and share their sculptural grace.

'Tis Art and Nature lodged together,
   Sister by sister, cheek to cheek;   10
Such Art, such Nature, and such weather
   The All-in-All seems here a Greek.

The Same

A CIRCUMAMBIENT spell it is,
    Pellucid on these scenes that waits,
Repose that does of Plato tell—
    Charm that his style authenticates.

The Parthenon

I

Seen aloft from afar

ESTRANGED in site,
Aerial gleaming, warmly white,
You look a sun-cloud motionless
In noon of day divine;
Your beauty charmed enhancement takes   5
In Art's long after-shine.

II

Nearer viewed

Like Lais, fairest of her kind,
In subtlety your form's defined—
The cornice curved, each shaft inclined,
While yet, to eyes that do but revel   10
   And take the sweeping view,
Erect this seems, and that a level,
   To line and plummet true.

Spinoza gazes; and in mind
Dreams that one architect designed   15
   Lais—and you!

III

The Frieze

What happy musings genial went
With airiest touch the chisel lent
  To frisk and curvet light
Of horses gay—their riders grave—   20
Contrasting so in action brave
  With virgins meekly bright,
Clear filing on in even tone
With pitcher each, one after one
  Like water-fowl in flight.   25

IV

The Last Tile

  When the last marble tile was laid
The winds died down on all the seas;
  Hushed were the birds, and swooned the glade;
  Ictinus sat; Aspasia said
"Hist!—Art's meridian, Pericles!"   30

Greek Masonry

Joints were none that mortar sealed:
Together, scarce with line revealed,
The blocks in symmetry congealed.

Greek Architecture

Not magnitude, not lavishness,
   But Form—the Site;
Not innovating wilfulness,
But reverence for the Archetype.

Off Cape Colonna

ALOOF they crown the foreland lone,
   From aloft they loftier rise—
Fair columns, in the aureola rolled
   From sunned Greek seas and skies.
They wax, sublimed to fancy's view,   5
A god-like group against the blue.

Overmuch like gods! Serene they saw
   The wolf-waves board the deck,
And headlong hull of Falconer,
   And many a deadlier wreck.   10

The Archipelago

SAIL before the morning breeze
The Sporads through and Cyclades,
They look like isles of absentees—
      Gone whither?

You bless Apollo's cheering ray,   5
But Delos, his own isle, to-day
Not e'en a Selkirk there to pray
      God friend me!

Scarce lone these groups, scarce lone and bare,
When Theseus roved a Raleigh there,   10
Each isle a small Virginia fair—
      Unravished.

Nor less, though havoc fell they rue,
They still retain, in outline true,
Their grace of form when earth was new   15
      And primal.

But beauty clear, the frame's as yet,
Never shall make one quite forget
Thy picture, Pan, therein once set—
      Life's revel!   20

'Tis Polynesia reft of palms,
Seaward no valley breathes her balms—
Not such as musk thy rings of calms,
               Marquesas!

Syra

(A Transmitted Reminiscence)

FLEEING from Scio's smouldering vines
(Where when the sword its work had done
The Turk applied the torch) the Greek
Came here, a fugitive stript of goods,
Here to an all but tenantless isle,   5
Nor here in footing gained at first,
Felt safe. Still from the turbaned foe
Dreading the doom of shipwrecked men
Whom feline seas permit to land
Then pounce upon and drag them back,   10
For height they made, and prudent won
A cone-shaped fastness on whose flanks
With pains they pitched their eyrie camp,
Stone huts, whereto they wary clung;
But, reassured in end, come down—   15
Multiplied through compatriots now,
Refugees like themselves forlorn—
And building along the water's verge
Begin to thrive; and thriving more
When Greece at last flung off the Turk,   20
Make of the haven mere a mart.

I saw it in its earlier day—
Primitive, such an isled resort
As heartless Homer might have known

309

Wandering about the Ægean here.   25
Sheds ribbed with wreck-stuff faced the sea
Where goods in transit shelter found.
And here and there a shanty-shop
Where Fez-caps, swords, tobacco, shawls,
Pistols, and orient finery, Eve's—   30
(The spangles dimmed by hands profane)
Like plunder on a pirate's deck
Lay orderless in such loose way
As to suggest things ravished or gone astray.

    Above a tented inn with fluttering flag   35
A sunburnt board announced Greek wine
In selfsame text Anacreon knew,
Dispensed by one named "Pericles."
Got up as for the opera's scene,
Armed strangers, various, lounged or lazed,   40
Lithe fellows tall, with gold-shot eyes,
Sunning themselves as leopards may.

    Off-shore lay xebecs trim and light,
And some but dubious in repute.
But on the strand, for docks were none,   45
What busy bees! no testy fry;
Frolickers, picturesquely odd,
With bales and oil-jars lading boats,
Lighters that served an anchored craft,
Each in his tasseled Phrygian cap,   50
Blue Eastern drawers and braided vest;
And some with features cleanly cut
As Proserpine's upon the coin.
Such chatterers all! like children gay
Who make believe to work, but play.   55

    I saw, and how help musing too.
Here traffic's immature as yet:
Forever this juvenile fun hold out

And these light hearts? Their garb, their glee,
Alike profuse in flowing measure,   60
Alike inapt for serious work,
Blab of grandfather Saturn's prime
When trade was not, nor toil nor stress,
But life was leisure, merriment, peace,
And lucre none, and love was righteousness.   65

Disinterment of the Hermes

WHAT forms divine in adamant fair—
Carven demigod and god,
And hero-marbles rivalling these,
Bide under Latium's sod,
Or lost in sediment and drift   5
Alluvial which the Grecian rivers sift.

To dig for these, O better far
Than raking arid sands
For gold more barren, meetly theirs
Sterile, with brimming hands.   10

The Apparition

(The Parthenon uplifted on its rock first challenging the view
on the approach to Athens)

Abrupt the supernatural Cross,
   Vivid in startled air,
Smote the Emperor Constantine
And turned his soul's allegiance there.

With other power appealing down,   5
   Trophy of Adam's best!
If cynic minds you scarce convert,
You try them, shake them, or molest.

Diogenes, that honest heart,
   Lived ere your date began;   10
Thee had he seen, he might have swerved
In mood nor barked so much at Man.

In the Desert

NEVER Pharoah's Night,
Whereof the Hebrew wizards croon,
Did so the Theban flamens try
As me this veritable Noon.

Like blank ocean in blue calm   5
Undulates the ethereal frame;
In one flowing oriflamme
God flings his fiery standard out.

Battling with the Emirs fierce,
Napoleon a great victory won,   10
Through and through his sword did pierce;
But, bayonetted by this sun,
His gunners drop beneath the gun.

Holy, holy, holy Light!
Immaterial incandescence,   15
Of God the effluence of the essence,
Shekinah, intolerably bright!

The Great Pyramid

YOUR masonry—and is it man's?
More like some Cosmic artizan's.
Your courses as in strata rise,
Beget you do a blind surmise
            Like Grampians.   5

Far slanting up your sweeping flank
Arabs with Alpine goats may rank,
And there they find a choice of passes
Even like to dwarfs that climb the masses
            Of glaciers blank.   10

Shall lichen in your crevice fit?
Nay, sterile all and granite-knit:
Weather nor weather-stain ye rue,
But aridly you cleave the blue
            As lording it.   15

Morn's vapor floats beneath your peak,
Kites skim your side with pinion weak;
To sand-storms, battering, blow on blow,
Raging to work your overthrow,
            You—turn the cheek.   20

All elements unmoved you stem,
Foursquare you stand and suffer them:
Time's future infinite you dare,
While, for the Past, 'tis you that wear
        Eld's diadem.   25

Slant from your inmost lead the caves
And labyrinths rumored. These who braves
And penetrates (old palmers said)
Comes out afar on deserts dead
        And, dying, raves.   30

Craftsmen, in dateless quarries dim,
Stones formless into form did trim,
Usurped on Nature's self with Art,
And bade this dumb I AM to start,
        Imposing Him.   35

The Return
of the Sire de Nesle
A.D. 16—

My towers at last! These rovings end,
Their thirst is slaked in larger dearth:
The yearning infinite recoils,
  For terrible is earth.

Kaf thrusts his snouted crags through fog: 5
Araxes swells beyond his span,
And knowledge poured by pilgrimage
  Overflows the banks of man.

But thou, my stay, thy lasting love
One lonely good, let this but be!   10
Weary to view the wide world's swarm,
  But blest to fold but thee.

Uncollected Poem

Inscription
For the Dead
At Fredericksburgh

A DREADFUL glory lights an earnest end;
In jubilee the patriot ghosts ascend;
Transfigured at the rapturous height
   Of their passionate feat of arms,
Death to the brave's a starry night,—   5
   Strewn their vale of death with palms.

Editorial Appendix

For
HARRISON HAYFORD

THE FIRST of the six parts of this APPENDIX is a HISTORICAL NOTE by Hershel Parker on the place of poetry, criticism of poetry, and aesthetics in the life of Herman Melville from his early childhood through the composition of Battle-Pieces. It was published in a slightly different form as Melville: The Making of the Poet (Evanston: Northwestern University Press, 2008). Following the HISTORICAL NOTE is a postscript on the critical reception of Melville's published poems; it includes a section on Battle-Pieces—reprinted (and slightly enlarged) from Parker's biography of Melville—and the single known review of John Marr.

The second part, by G. Thomas Tanselle, is an essay on the printing and publishing history of Battle-Pieces, John Marr, and Timoleon, the three books by Melville included in Published Poems.

The third part, the TEXTUAL RECORD, consists of two sections. The first is an essay on textual matters, outlining the textual history of Melville's published poems, identifying the copy-texts for the present edition, stating the general editorial principles followed, and explaining the apparatus employed for recording textual information. This essay was originally drafted by Robert C. Ryan, following the plan used in other Northwestern-Newberry volumes, with the collaboration of Alma MacDougall Reising and G. Thomas Tanselle; since then it has been extensively revised and rewritten by Tanselle. The other section of the TEXTUAL RECORD presents notes on individual poems; for each poem there may be one or more of three kinds of notes. The discursive notes were initially drafted by Ryan, in collaboration with Reising and Tanselle, then revised by Harrison Hayford; more recently these notes were reviewed by Robert D. Madison and Hershel Parker before being heavily revised by Tanselle. The lists of emendations result from textual decisions made by Ryan, Hayford, and Tanselle. The textual notes, recording variant readings and manuscript and proof alterations, were prepared by Ryan, checked by Hayford, and revised by Reising and Tanselle.

The fourth part of the APPENDIX presents three RELATED DOCUMENTS: "Melville's Dated Reading in Poetry and Poetics: A Chronological Short-Title List," prepared by Robert D. Madison; "Melville's Marginalia on Poetry and Poetics," prepared by Dennis Berthold; and "The Sources of Melville's Notes (1849–51) in a Shakespeare Volume," with illustrations of those notes, prepared by Hershel Parker. All of the editors and contributing scholars and associates assisted in preparing one or more parts of the three sections just mentioned. The final documents in this section are illustrations showing Melville's marginalia in his copy of Hazlitt's Lectures and in his copy of Vasari's Lives of the Artists.

The fifth section is a list of WORKS CITED in the HISTORICAL NOTE and all other sections of the APPENDIX, and the sixth section is an INDEX OF TITLES AND FIRST LINES.

To insure uniform textual policy in all volumes of the Edition the same three editors, Harrison Hayford, Hershel Parker, and G. Thomas Tanselle, participated in the planning and establishment of textual policy for all volumes, except as otherwise noted; even when other editors are specifically named (as in the case of certain writings edited from manuscript) the final decisions still rest with one or more of these editors, as noted in individual volumes. The texts of Melville's poems included in Published Poems are edited by Robert C. Ryan, Harrison Hayford, Alma MacDougall Reising, and G. Thomas Tanselle. Final responsibility for all aspects of every volume before this one has been exercised by the general editor, Harrison Hayford, who supervised this volume up to a very late stage in its completion. In this volume, the first to be issued after Hayford's death, the responsibility for supervision of the textual sections has been taken on by Tanselle, while the final responsibility for the volume as a whole has devolved on Parker, the successor to Hayford as general editor.

Alma MacDougall Reising, as a joint editor of this volume and as executive editor of the Edition, contributed to every aspect of this volume. In addition to the editorial work cited above, she supervised the production of the volume and provided copyediting and proofreading. JoAnn Casey provided valuable assistance to Hayford in the course of his work on this volume.

Authorization to edit manuscripts and permission to publish material from their collections has been granted by Houghton Library, Harvard University, the New York Public Library, the Rare Book and Manuscript Library of Columbia University, the Harry Ransom Humanities Research Center of the University of Texas at Austin, the Library of Congress, the University of Virginia Library, and William S. Reese. The Battle-Pieces section of the postscript to the HISTORICAL NOTE is reprinted with the permission of The Johns Hopkins University Press.

Robert C. Ryan's work was partly supported by grants of money and released time from The Defiance College, Boston University, The Newberry Library, the National Endowment for the Humanities, and Northwestern University. Ryan is also grateful to the library staffs at Harvard, the New York Public Library, the Berkshire Athenaeum, the American Antiquarian Society, Boston University, Brown University, Columbia University, the University of Florida, Georgetown University, Lehigh University, Princeton University, the University of Texas, the United States Naval Academy, the University of Virginia, and Yale University. He was also aided by Susan R. Horton, Abigael MacGibeny, William S. Reese, Joan Reddy, and Heather, Kevin, and Brittany Ryan.

Renewed acknowledgment is made here to those whose assistance was recorded by Hershel Parker in Melville: The Making of the Poet, among them the late

Jay Leyda, Harrison Hayford, Merton M. Sealts Jr., and Wilson Heflin. Parker particularly thanks Dennis C. Marnon and Scott Norsworthy, Joyce Deveau Kennedy, Robert D. Madison, Alma MacDougall Reising, and Heddy-Ann Richter, as well as Priscilla Osborne Ambrose, William S. Reese, and Ruth Degenhardt and Kathleen Reilly. On behalf of Dennis Marnon, Parker also thanks Ellen Gamache and Jim Tobin of the Albany Public Library. Parker thanks all the editorial associates and contributing scholars on the Northwestern-Newberry edition of Melville's Published Poems as well as Lottie Cain Honea, Chris Coughlin, Mary K Bercaw Edwards, Athel Eugene Gibson, Thomas F. Heffernan, James A. Hime, Stephen D. Hoy, Frederick J. Kennedy, Deborah Norsworthy, Gary Scharnhorst, Benton Tindall, Richard E. Winslow III, and Mark Wojnar. For assistance with his essay on the printing and publishing history, Tanselle acknowledges Richard Bucci, Christian Dupont, Jill Gage, Jennifer Lee, and Irene Tichenor, as well as the bibliographical associate Dennis Marnon. Parker, Tanselle, and Reising all thank the director and staff at Northwestern University Press for exemplary help and cooperation.

Herman Melville, 1861. Carte de visite by R. H. Dewey.
Courtesy of Berkshire Athenaeum, Pittsfield, Massachusetts.

Historical Note

*P*UBLISHED POEMS presents the three collections of short poetry and the single uncollected poem published during Herman Melville's lifetime—*Battle-Pieces* (Harper, 1866), *John Marr and Other Sailors* (De Vinne Press, 1888), *Timoleon Etc.* (Caxton Press, 1891), and "Inscription For the Dead At Fredericksburgh" (1864). Melville's long poem *Clarel* (1876) appears separately as volume 12 and other poems and prose left uncompleted at his death as volume 13. Publication of the poems in the present volume spanned a quarter century during which Melville wrote *Clarel* and wrote or revised many short poems and worked on *Billy Budd, Sailor* and other prose. The total span may be more than three decades since some of the poems in the 1891 collection may have been written in the late 1850s or 1860 (and may in some form have been in the lost volume called *Poems* which Melville tried to publish in 1860).[1] For this reason, instead of presenting an account of the composition, publication, reception, and later critical history of a single book as in other volumes, this HISTORICAL NOTE focuses on how Melville became a poet after a

---

1. For more on the volume of poetry Melville prepared for publication in 1860, see section 7.

329

career initially focused on prose.[2] The composition and publication of the three books and of individual poems in them are treated mainly in the NOTE ON PRINTING AND PUBLISHING HISTORY and the NOTES ON INDI-VIDUAL POEMS. The reception of *Battle-Pieces* is told in a postscript to this NOTE,[3] which also prints the single known newspaper review of *John Marr* (no reviews of *Timoleon* are known). No survey of twentieth- and early twenty-first-century commentary is offered in this NOTE, although some scholarship is cited in notes on particular poems.

Despite the attention lavished on Melville by critics, relatively little has been known about his familiarity with poetry of his own time and of previous centuries. Pioneering specialized studies such as Henry F. Pom-mer's on the influence of Milton on Melville (1950)[4] and Edward Fiess's on the influence of Byron (1951) have not been followed by books that examine the place of poetry in the successive milieux of Melville's life, from schoolboy through his sea-going years, through the renewed inter-est in poetry near the end of his work on his third book, *Mardi,* and his rigorous study of poets and of aesthetics from early 1849 onward. Crucial evidence for such a general study has sometimes been ignored but more often has not been available. Melville's copy of Wordsworth's poems came to light in the late 1970s, for example, his Milton and Dante in the 1980s, his Vasari, Hazlitt (*Lectures*), and Spenser in the 1990s, his Warton in the first decade of the twenty-first century (all six heavily annotated). There is now high interest in Melville's poetry, but not yet a comprehensive study of Melville's reading of English, Continental, and American poets. There have been studies of Melville and the visual arts, but not a study of Melville as a student of aesthetics through his reading of poetry, of critical books such as *Modern British Essayists,* and of histories of art and poetry. The present HISTORICAL NOTE aims to open up these areas for further study.

2. A slightly revised form of *Melville: The Making of the Poet* (Northwestern University Press, 2008), this is the only HISTORICAL NOTE to have been previously published as a separate book.

3. The postscript is taken from the second volume of my *Herman Melville: A Biography* and slightly augmented by recent discoveries.

4. Full bibliographical information for any sources not provided in this HISTORICAL NOTE appears in a comprehensive list of WORKS CITED at the end of the volume.

I

A POET IN PROSE: HOW CRITICS PREPARED MELVILLE TO THINK OF HIMSELF AS A POET

WHEN HE TOOK up his pen in Manhattan late in 1844, Melville would never have considered poetry as a medium for telling the once-in-a-lifetime story of his experiences with natives in the interior of one of the Marquesas Islands. He had been a published writer of competent amateurish prose as early as 1839, and prose was faster and easier to write than poetry. Besides that, he had been telling his story on shore and on ship for two years by then, a period when he had the ideal audience for perfecting his ambiguous sexual teasing or bragging—men (many of them young) who at times had long been deprived of sex with women. The more or less autobiographical part of the book would be comparatively easy to put down on paper in acceptable (and for the most part conventional) prose. Yet from the first, beginning at the publication of *Typee* in 1846, two decades before Melville surprised the American reading public by re-emerging into literary life as a poet with *Battle-Pieces*, some reviewers resorted to "poetic" and its cognates in referring to his books. In some minds "poetic" prose was opposed to moral prose. Low-church Protestants in religious newspapers and magazines called Melville's style in *Typee,* and later in the sequel, *Omoo* (1847), "poetic" in the sense of false, misleading, and even dangerously alluring. This outraged passage is from "*Typee:* The Traducer of Missions," in the New York *Christian Parlor Magazine* (July 1846): "We do not look at the history of the missionary work from the merely enthusiastic or poetic point of view. . . . We shall probably give Typee a glance among the authorities [on Polynesia], as a specimen of that genus of writers whose poetry and poetic feelings lead them to admire only what is savage, and condemn, under assumed pretexts, the ripening fruit of the gospel of Christ."⁵ The most vicious of Melville's reviewers, George Washington Peck, in the New York *American Whig Review* for July 1847 stressed the insidious effects of Melville's style: "Omoo is a book one may read once with interest and pleasure, but with *a perpetual recoil*. It is poetically written, but yet carelessly, and in a

---

5. Reviews are quoted from Higgins and Parker, *Herman Melville: The Contemporary Reviews* (1995), which preserves any unusual spelling and punctuation. The exception is the review of *Mardi* in the New Bedford *Mercury* (see note 10), a more recent discovery communicated to me by Mark Wojnar.

bad spirit." On July 5, 1849, reviewing the Harper reissue of *Typee,* the New York *Evangelist,* a Presbyterian organ, declared that the book "exhibits a spirit and grace irresistible to most readers, and depicts the loveliest scenery in the world with true poetic genius." The problem was that these graces were put to the service of a "degraded moral tone," in which Melville slanderously attacked "missionary labors and character," so that his writing constituted "unquestionable falsehood from beginning to end." Reviewers in such denominational papers were uneasily sure that Melville through his delightful style was seducing his readers into sinful delights and perhaps even corrupt opinions. Earnest and even vicious as they were, these reviewers constituted a minority, and became almost quiescent during the reception of Melville's next books, *Mardi* (1849), *Redburn* (1849), and *White-Jacket* (1850), but rose up, freshly empowered, to attack *Moby-Dick* brutally late in 1851 and early in 1852.

In some British and American reviews in the secular press, the style of *Typee* and then of *Omoo* was also, and more often, declared "poetic" in the sense that the descriptions were fanciful, highly imaginative, and idealized, as when the Edinburgh *Weekly Register and General Advertiser* for April 14, 1847, called *Omoo* a "work very exquisitely written on an exquisite subject; bursts of what is almost brilliant poetry alternating with the raciest drollery" or when the Boston *Bee* on May 5, 1847, said *Omoo* had "all the attractiveness of a book of travels, abounding in passages of wit, humor, romance and poetry." In a similar spirit the London *Times* (September 24, 1847) came late but happily to *Omoo:* "A better material has not for years fallen into the way of the creator and the poet; a more skilful workman it has been seldom our lot to welcome." This praise of Melville as creator and poet was given very wide circulation in the "Supplement" to the New York *Tribune* of October 30, 1847, in the form of a letter (dated October 4) from its London correspondent, "P." Still later, on November 13, 1847, the *Times* review was touted by Melville's friend Nathaniel Parker Willis in his very popular weekly, the New York *Home Journal,* where Willis reprinted the tribute to Melville as "the creator and the poet."

In keeping with this dominant public opinion was an article by Sarah Jane Clarke, writing as "Grace Greenwood." Her spoof in the Philadelphia *Saturday Evening Post* (October 9, 1847) purported to be a "Letter from the Author of 'Typee.'" Here "H.M." asserted his belief that "*poets are not properly esteemed and recompensed in our country,*" as contrasted with the Typee valley, where the "veritable Polynesian Tom Moore," "Clingy Lingy," the finest poet on the island, was indulged in every way, including the granting of sexual privileges: "He was allowed to choose for his bride the prettiest maiden in the valley, and to change his wife every new moon, if so inclined. *The* place of all the world for your Shelleys and Byrons were Typee. . . . I also ascertained that no man was allowed to play critic in Typee, unless himself a poet. The body-servant of the bard was pointed out to me, a poor devil of a fellow, who though of most aristocratic connections, had been degraded to his present position for an impromptu but cutting review, produced upon one of Clingy Lingy's improvisations." After this, Clarke added a fanciful last note from "H.M.": "I should have included this account in my work [*Typee*], but for the fear that on hearing of such a Paradisean state of things, our entire squad of poets would immediately emigrate to Typee." Melville could not have missed this charming supplement to *Typee* on poetry, a subject in which his interest was burgeoning. After his return from England in early February 1850, he would also have been shown the reprinting of this piece in Clarke's *Greenwood Leaves,* published in late November 1849, dated 1850.[6]

In early March 1848 Melville's friend Evert A. Duyckinck, a New York City editor, wrote to his brother George: "Melville the other night brought me a few chapters of his new book, which in the poetry and wildness of the thing will be ahead of Typee & Omoo" (*Log,* p. 273).[7] Melville himself was thinking in just those terms, and may have so expressed himself to Duyckinck. Melville's earliest letters to John Murray, the London publisher of his first two books, focus on the charges in the press that *Typee* was not authentic—not written by the real man named "Herman Melville" and not based on a real experience of that Herman Melville. Still concerned to be believed as a truth-teller, on March 25, 1848, in a letter to Murray he had called his manuscript in progress "authentic" then replaced that assertion with "it shall have the right stuff in it."[8] (The manuscript of *Mardi* then presumably stood without any chapters on the contemporary European and American political situation, news of revolution in Paris

6. The publisher was Ticknor, Reed, & Fields, who were already promising a new work by Nathaniel Hawthorne, one not yet named as *The Scarlet Letter.*

7. *Log* is used throughout to refer to Jay Leyda's *The Melville Log* (1951; reprinted with a Supplement, 1969), which is arranged chronologically. *New Log* refers to my ongoing version of *The New Melville Log.*

8. Unless otherwise specified, all quotations of letters to or from Melville are from the Northwestern-Newberry *Correspondence* volume, where they can be located by date. References to dates, events, or documents that are not otherwise documented here are based on my biography (1996 and 2002), my ongoing *The New Melville Log* (the revised and greatly expanded edition of Jay Leyda's *The Melville Log*), the various published volumes of the Northwestern-Newberry Edition of the writings of Herman Melville (hereafter NN), and the publications listed in the WORKS CITED.

having arrived in New York only the week before.) Melville explained that his new book was not, as previously described, "a bona-fide narrative of my adventures in the Pacific, continued from 'Omoo.'" Instead, he was writing "a 'Romance of Polynisian Adventure.'" Partly, he said, he was writing in reaction to "the reiterated imputation of being a romancer in disguise," but also for other reasons, including this: "I have long thought that Polynisia furnished a great deal of rich poetical material that has never been employed hitherto in works of fancy; and which to bring out suitably, required only that play of freedom & invention accorded only to the Romancer & poet." Unexpectedly, he said, he had begun to feel "an invincible distaste" for factual adventure and gone "to work heart & soul at a romance which is now in fair progress." He promised: "It opens like a true narrative like Omoo for example, on ship board & the romance & poetry of the thing thence grow continuously, till it becomes a story wild enough I assure you & with a meaning too." In Melville's usages, the "poet" and the "poetic" are not associated with the metrical activity of verse-making but evoke the Romantic writer's liberated consciousness in bold pursuit of the wild, the strange, the exotic. Romance and poetry were synonymous—they were imaginative, not factual and not common-place, and they were associated in Melville's mind with a higher form of literature than factual (and partially fictionalized) travel and adventure narrative. In this dodgy, bragging, defensive, confessional letter, Melville proclaimed the supremacy of his literary instincts over fiscal practicality and exulted in the superiority of his new work as a literary achievement. He seriously misapprehended the tastes of his correspondent. Murray had no use for novels, poems, or fictions of any kind. Melville quickly recovered from the rebuff by selling *Mardi* to the British publisher Richard Bentley, who had made overtures to him earlier.

Into the manuscript of *Mardi,* by this time, Melville had introduced companions for his two voyagers, among them "Yoomy, or the Warbler," whose role is to provide songs when songs are needed or when he needs to sing them (chap. 65 in the American edition).[9] "Grace Greenwood" (Sarah Clarke) had presented her account of the treatment of poets in the Typee valley as if it were a passage Melville had omitted from *Typee* for fear

---

9. Unless otherwise noted, all quotations of Melville's works follow the NN edition. Because the chapters in Melville's works are short, citations to prose works are by chapter to allow location in other editions. Citations to the present volume are by page and line, with a "o" line number used to refer to any line(s) preceding the first line of text, such as titles and subtitles. (For pages of prose, line numbering is separate for each page; for pages of verse, line numbering proceeds continuously through each poem, as the printed line numbers indicate.)

that it would cause a mass exodus of American poets for the Pacific. Her article may have been an unwitting gift to *Mardi,* for Melville may have recognized her depiction of "Clingy Lingy" as too good not to make use of. The name Melville chose for his poet, Yoomy, may be his respelling of Umi, a character in Hawaiian legends whom he may have encountered in William Ellis's 1826 or 1827 *Narrative.* Yoomy is anything but a self-portrait of a successful young author suddenly aspiring to poetic greatness:

> A youthful, long-haired, blue-eyed minstrel; all fits and starts; at times, absent of mind, and wan of cheek; but always very neat and pretty in his apparel; wearing the most becoming of turbans, a Bird of Paradise feather its plume, and sporting the gayest of sashes. Most given was Yoomy to amorous melodies, and rondos, and roundelays, very witching to hear. But at times disdaining the oaten reed, like a clarion he burst forth with lusty lays of arms and battle; or, in mournful strains, sounded elegies for departed bards and heroes.

The reference to "oaten reed" shows that Melville was familiar with Virgil (or with his English followers), who in the first *Eclogue* described Pan's gift to shepherds, a pipe made from a reed. He may have known the song in Shakespeare's *Love's Labor's Lost* in which shepherds pipe on oaten straws. He probably knew, already, Edmund Spenser's "Astrophel," the pastoral elegy on Sir Philip Sidney, where Spenser's conceit is that the shepherds who pipe their poetic "plaints" on oaten reeds will accept his plaint among their own, as well as the beginning of *The Faerie Queene,* where Spenser abandons his "Oaten reeds" for a stern trumpet—abandons the pastoral form for the epic. Thanks to his invention of "Yoomy," Melville could introduce into his genuinely poetic prose some rhymes of his own composing, the verses safely placed in the mouth of a minor poetaster, whom Melville's friend Duyckinck characterized as "a fair type of the class, all sensibility and expression" (in his New York *Literary World* review, April 21, 1849). Yoomy allowed Melville to try his hand at verse uninhibited by the perils of exposing himself as attempting in his own person to write good poetry.

In 1849 most reviewers of *Mardi* acknowledged that Melville, for good or ill, had indeed poured romance and poetry into this book, and his prose was sometimes seen as aspiring, however ineptly, to the status of poetry. On April 19, the Hartford *Republican* decided that the book was written "in a pleasant, but somewhat exaggerated style, abounds in fine description, and passages of great poetic beauty, and is scarcely more romantic in its incidents than the veritable narrative of 'Typee.'" Two days later the Boston *Daily Times* denied that Melville had great poetic qualities: "His previous works and the first part of 'Mardi,' are founded on facts; or rather they relate to facts altogether, but because these facts happened to be out of the common course of life, and are given in a graceful and animated style, some critics jumped to the conclusion that Mr. Melville had that quality which renders men great as novelists and poets." *Mardi* would be "saved from oblivion only by the life-like character of its earlier chapters." In its May 1849 issue the New York *Merchants' Magazine* announced: "The matter is truly poetical—philosophical as Plato, yet beautifully imaginative as Moore; the treatment thoroughly dramatic. As a whole, it is a master stroke of genius." In the May 3 New Orleans *Commercial Bulletin* "Croton," the young New York City correspondent A. Oakey Hall (later district attorney and mayor) made a higher claim while punning for his Crescent City readers: *Mardi* was "a regular Mardi-gras of a novel, to judge from the richness of its prose. Prose! It is a poem; and you can pencil out of its pages blank verse enough to set up an hundred newspaper poets, for the balls of bowling critics to roll at." Hall, a protégé of Evert A. Duyckinck, was the first to make such an extravagant claim for Melville as poet. On May 10 in the New York *Tribune,* where Horace Greeley himself had expressed his moral scruples about Melville's first books in 1847, George Ripley defined, even as he deplored, a quality of Melville's new writing: "Even the language of this work is a hybrid between poetry and prose.—Every page abounds in lines which might be dovetailed into a regular poem without any change in the rhythm. It can easily be read aloud so that the nicest ear could not distinguish it from heroic verse." The hybrid was not a success: "Let the author return to the transparent narration of his own adventures, in the pure, imaginative prose, which he handles with such graceful facility, and he will be everywhere welcomed as one of the most delightful of American writers." Yet on the same day the Boston *Daily Chronotype* declared: "There is at times a majestic poetry in this book that reminds us of the old prophets, Isaiah and others."

The reviewer in the London *Sun* (May 29, 1849) called attention to a flaw in the "mixture of the prose and poetic" in *Mardi:* "In this concoction of his literary repast, however, Mr. Melville when he least wishes it makes the intended prose poetical, and the intended poetry prose." The youthful Yoomy, to whom the poetry was ascribed, was "rather a bit of a bore." The reviewer in the *Sun* recognized the quality Oakey Hall responded to, the poetic prose, but mentioned several of the verses given to Yoomy, finding the chorus about the discovery of gold in California so much like "Thomas Hood's memorable chaunt about the leg of Miss Kilmansegge" as to suggest Melville had plagiarized it. The New Bedford *Mercury* of June 8 published a remarkable triple review of *Mardi,* Henry

W. Longfellow's prose *Kavanagh: A Romance,* and Arthur Hugh Clough's *The Bothie of Toper na Vuolich,* offering this disclaimer: "We are not sure but that we ought to have entitled this notice—Three new *poems.* They seem to stand on the debateable land between the two realms of poetry and prose, outlaws from the stricter jurisdiction of either. The first, being thickly strewn with little lyrical fragments some of which are exceedingly graceful, is written in that flowing metrical prose which bears the same relation to actual verse that Mr. Melville's previous records of his Polynesian adventures bear to fiction."[10] *Mardi* was "a prose poem in style." The New York *United States Magazine and Democratic Review* (July 1849) began with an elaborate defense:

> We do not despise criticism, nor do we believe that there is much for sale that a man would care to buy; but there are honest men who are petty in their strictures upon works of genius. They do not believe in poetry unless it is fettered with feet, or with rhymes. Like the old lady, they know that "poetry begins with capital letters, and has the lines of a length" and an author who should write a book full of poetic fire, without regard to their rules, is an insubordinate officer, who must be disciplined, or broke, but most likely the latter. To them genius is irregular. It does not curvet according to their patterns, which they assure us are highly ornamental, and very proper. These men would pluck the eagle's quills, and sell them at "a penny a piece," and reduce the royal bird to a respectable barn-yard fowl.

The *Democratic Review* continued with this remarkable tribute to Melville as a man inspired: "We have small respect for authors who are wilful, and cannot be advised; but we reverence a man when God's *must* is upon him, and he does his work in his own and other's spite. Portions of Mardi are written with this divine impulse, and they thrill through every fibre of the reader with an electric force."

On September 29, 1849, the New York *Saroni's Musical Times* declared that style was the "sole redeeming feature" of *Mardi:* "Mr. Melville possesses many of the essentials of poetry—a store of images, a readiness at perceiving analogies and felicitous expressions. Poetic thoughts and turns of phrase occur at every page. Nevertheless, although so poetic in his prose, he is remarkably unfortunate in his verse." The verses in *Mardi* were "not worth quoting." The reviewer launched into a theory that several would-be American versifiers, "who strive for originality of metre, and whose unsaleable works throng the shelves of their publishers," should

10. This review was discovered and communicated to me by Mark Wojnar.

stop trying to reach poetry: "The English tongue no longer admits of such experiments; its genius has reached its culminating point; it has nothing to do but to remain at its level or descend. To climb higher is impracticable. After the great works of any language have made their appearance, a certain standard is obtained, from which to depart is to sink." The great poetry in English had already been written. The reviewer did not circle back to Melville, but left unelaborated the assertion that he possessed many of the essentials of poetry. For all the contempt showered upon its last two-thirds, *Mardi* apprised British and American readers that Melville was manifesting remarkable if undisciplined literary talents—that he possessed "many of the essentials of poetry."

Early in 1849 Melville found himself prepared to go beyond what had seemed "poetical" to him in 1848, but, after the failure of *Mardi* with most critics and book-buyers, he knew he had to forgo "rich poetical material" for a time. At an astonishing pace he wrote the deliberately more realistic *Redburn* in two months (June–July 1849). Subsequently (in August–September 1849) Melville wrote *White-Jacket,* which also abounds in realism, although the narrator is prone to sudden, intensely rhetorical excursions of the "poetic" sort displayed so prominently in *Mardi*. Reviewers of *Redburn* found nothing poetic, just as Melville had intended when he began the book. In *White-Jacket* Melville gave extended descriptions of the importance of poetry in day-to-day life on an American man-of-war, and reviewers commented not just on the topic of poetry but also on Melville's employment of poetic prose. The London *Athenæum* (February 2, 1850) declared: "Mr. Melville stands as far apart from any past or present marine painter in pen and ink as Turner does from the magnificent artist vilipended by Mr. Ruskin for Turner's sake—Vandervelde. We cannot recall another novelist or sketcher who has given the poetry of the Ship— her voyages and her crew—in a manner at all resembling his." The March 1850 London *Bentley's Miscellany* (Melville's publisher's magazine, granted, but also Cooper's) drew a contrast between him and other sea-writers: "The difference between them may be not inaccurately expressed, as the difference between prose and poetry. The great charm of the marine story in the hands of such writers as Cooper, Marryatt, and [Basil] Hall, is literal truthfulness, shown through just a sufficient haze of imagination, caught from the wide expanse of sky and water, to render it picturesque and effective. But Mr. Melville bathes the scene in the hues of a fanciful and reflective spirit, which gives it the interest of a creation of genius. He is everywhere original, suggestive, and individual. We follow him as if we were passing through an exciting dream." Perhaps taking his cue from the *Athenæum,* Evert A. Duyckinck in the New York *Literary World* on March 16, 1850, contrasted Melville to most other writers: "Your men of choice literature and of educated fancy, your Sternes, Jean Pauls, Southeys, and Longfellows, are not likely to acquire the practical experiences of the tar bucket. The sea of course attracts them with its materials for poetic illustration, but they copy from the descriptions of others. To have the fancy and the fact united is rare in any walk, almost unknown on the sea. Hence to Herman Melville, whose mind swarms with tender, poetic, or humorous fancies, the ship is a new world, now first conquered. No one has so occupied it. . . . We have intimated Herman Melville is a poet, and such he is, though, perhaps, 'lacking the accomplishment of verse.'" What Duyckinck quoted to "prove it" was two paragraphs from chapter 68, the description of the main-mast-man of the *Neversink,* which ended by describing the man's look as "the fadeless, ever infantile immortality within"—phrasing which was a foretaste of passages Melville was to write the next year or two. On March 30, the New York *Two Worlds: A Weekly Journal of American and European Literature, News, Science and the Fine Arts* declared that "a poetic glow" was often thrown over Melville's writings, imparting additional charm to his "flowing and pointed style." By the time the reviews of *White-Jacket* had accumulated, Melville was acknowledged in major papers on both sides of the Atlantic as an extraordinary talent. All this was vague, as *Saroni's* had been the year before, but reviewers were responding to the new "poetic" qualities in the prose—here without the distraction of banal interpolated verses. The praise Melville had wanted to receive for *Mardi* he sometimes received, all unexpectedly, for *White-Jacket.* The praise put him at last where he had longed to be when he wrote Murray that what he was writing had the "right stuff" in it.

After his voyage to England to sell *White-Jacket* and his tentative, frugal excursion onto the Continent, Melville next began a whaling book in which he could be comically realistic yet could reach deeper into the poetical veins he had mined in portions of *Mardi.* Impractical as he had been in following his Romantic and poetical instincts in *Mardi,* he was not so irresponsible as a husband and father as to attempt to write an epic of whaling in poetry. He was ready, in the great burgeoning of his genius, to attempt extraordinary experiments in literary styles, in 1850 and the next years, but in prose, now genuinely poetic, and at times expressed in lines closely akin to Shakespearean blank verse. The British reviewers of *The Whale* recognized this genuinely poetic prose, as when the London *Morning Advertiser* (October 24, 1851) cited "the chapter on the 'whiteness of the whale,' and the scene where Ahab nails the doubloon to the mast" as proof that "we have not overrated his dramatic ability for producing a prose poem." The *Athenæum* (October 25, 1851) in a review fiercely hostile (largely because the "Epilogue" had been left out of the English edition), nevertheless acknowledged "a wild humorous poetry in some of his terrors which distinguishes him from the vulgar herd of fustian-weavers. For instance, his interchapter on 'The Whiteness of the Whale' is full of ghostly suggestions for which a Maturin or a Monk Lewis would have been thankful." This was printed and reprinted in Boston, so Melville and his family could not have escaped it. The London *John Bull* (October 25, 1851) exclaimed at the extraordinary qualities of the book: "Who would have looked for philosophy in whales, or for poetry in blubber? Yet few books which professedly deal in metaphysics, or claim the parentage of the muses, contain as much true philosophy and as much genuine poetry as the tale of the *Pequod*'s whaling expedition." The London *Atlas* (November 1, 1851) acknowledged "that there are fine poetic elements" in the conception of Captain Ahab. The London *Leader* (November 8, 1851) called *The Whale* "a strange, wild, weird book, full of poetry and full of interest."

Melville saw this review, for portions of it were quoted in *Harper's New Monthly Magazine,* and his brother Allan had the whole review, from which he copied other parts into his copy of *Moby-Dick*. Melville probably saw almost no other London reviews, many of which, like that in the London *Weekly News and Chronicle* (November 29, 1851), were filled with extraordinary praise: "This is a wild, weird book, full of strange power and irresistible fascination for those who love to read of the wonders of the deep. The poetry of the great South Seas, the rude lawless adventure of the rough mariners who for years of continuous voyaging peril themselves on its waters; the excitement and the danger of the fishery for the sperm whale, the fiercest and hugest monster 'of all who swim the ocean stream,' combine to make these pages attractive and interesting to many different classes of readers." He may not even have seen his publisher's magazine, *Bentley's Miscellany* (January 31, 1852): "There are descriptions in this book of almost unrivalled force, coloured and warmed as they are, by the light and heat of a most poetical imagination, and many passages might be cited of vigorous thought, of earnest and tender sentiment, and of glowing fancy, which would at once suffice to show—contest or dispute about the matter being out of the question—that Herman Melville is a man of the truest and most original genius." Melville never had any idea how many London reviewers had recognized in him a "most poetical imagination."

In the United States few reviewers commented on poetical qualities in *Moby-Dick* directly. The New York *Parker's Journal* (November 22, 1851) came near to high praise before retracting: "If any writer of the present day could play with his subject, after this fashion, with impunity, it would be Melville; for his style is a rare mixture of power and sweetness, and, indeed, under the influence of the least excitement becomes as truly poetry as if every line were measured for verse, and the fine madness of his soul poured out in lyric flow instead of straightened into prose. But, even his power of expression, and elegance of style, will not redeem a book from being prosy after the natural interest of its subject has been exhausted. More than five acts of the best tragedy would be too much for mere mortals to bear." Duyckinck in the *Literary World* (November 22, 1851) and William Allen Butler in the *Washington Intelligencer* (December 16) compared Melville's characters to Shakespeare's, and Butler pronounced the book "a prose Epic on Whaling" and liked his formulation so much that he elaborated it: "a sort of prose epic on whales, whalers, and whaling."

In the fury that greeted *Pierre* in 1852 the rare mentions of anything poetic were contemptuous, as when the Boston *Post* (August 4) professed not to know what the book meant: "To save it from almost utter worthlessness, it must be called a prose poem, and even then, it might be supposed to emanate from a lunatic hospital rather than from the quiet retreats of Berkshire." The New York *Evening Mirror* (August 27) said that *Pierre* contained "a good deal of fine writing and poetic feeling," but that the metaphysics were "abominable." Still, the reviewer lingered: "And yet we concede that the book is marked by great intellectual ability; while some of the descriptive portions are transcendently beautiful. It reminds one of a summer day that opens sweetly, glittering with dew-drops, redolent of rose-odors, and melodious with the singing of birds; but early clouded with *artificial smoke,* and ending in a terrific display of melo-dramatic lightnings and earthquakes."

Not until *The Piazza Tales* (1856) did reviewers feel comfortable again with Melville's poetic prose. The scoundrel-journalist Thomas Powell in the New York *News* (May 26, 1856) was rhapsodic:

> The series of beautifully written sketches embraced under the title of the Enchanted Isles exert an indefinable but irresistable sway over the imagination and may be read and dwelt upon again and again, like [the most] gorgeous poem. In fact, if we may use such a comparison and be understood, Mr. Melville's prose, particularly in his magnificent descriptions of scenery, sea and cloud-land, resembles the Tennysonian verse. It possesses all the glowing richness, exquisite coloring and rapid, unexpected turn of phrase that distinguishes the Poet Laureate of our day—Marianna of the Piazza, "the lonely girl, sewing at a lonely window; the pale-cheeked girl and fly-specked window, with wasps about the mended upper panes"—has a distinct and yet not traceable relationship to "Marianna in the Moated Grange."

The "very cadence of the thought—the same heart melody," filled both. In the final paragraph, Powell urged: "Buy this Book, and take it into the country with you, where its hearty, healthy vivacity will gratify and excite as much as its deep undertone of native poetry, inspired by the rural scenes will soothe."[11] The *Republican* of Springfield, Massachusetts (July 9, 1856), praised especially the introductory essay, "The Piazza": "It is a poem—essentially a poem—lacking only rhythm and form." Other reviewers did not use the words *poem* or *poetic,* but the consensus was that Melville had regained his powers as an alluring imaginative writer. Melville would have been inattentive to his critics if he had not, years before, begun to think what it would be like to write poetry instead of only writing poetic prose.

II

MELVILLE AS HEARER AND RECITER OF POETRY

MELVILLE EXPERIENCED POETRY in the unbroken continuity between nursery rhymes and songs and rhymes for older children. As the third in a family of eight children, Herman heard not only nursery rhymes from his mother but more complicated poems and songs from his older brother and sister, Gansevoort and Helen. From infancy Herman heard what Gansevoort and Helen were memorizing, as they spoke lines aloud, even if he did not wholly understand the meanings, and from the time he was three or four there were always babies in the house learning the same songs and poems he had already learned, as well as different ones. Poetry was not a passive art for the Melville children: they heard, but as soon as they were able to speak they imitated what they heard, both words and rhythms. As the primary medium for recitation, poetry involved the whole body, since children were trained to fit posture, gesture, and tone of voice to a piece of poetry when "declaiming" it.

As the children grew older they understood that popular songs were considered to be poetry. After all, highly ranked poets from Shakespeare to Lord Byron to Thomas Moore and Joseph Rodman Drake were

11. Since the only known copy of the *Daily News* is defective, the quotation beginning "Buy this Book" is eked out from the passage as quoted in the advertisement in the New York *Tribune* for May 31, 1856.

acknowledged as great songwriters. In the surviving draft manuscript for chapter 14 of *Typee*,[12] Melville declares: "With Captain Macheath in the opera I could have sung 'Thus I lay like a Turk with my doxies around.'" He knew John Gay's *Beggar's Opera*—perhaps from the 1830s, when he may well have derived part of his early image of himself from the song if not from the portrayal of the character onstage. He knew Richard Brinsley Sheridan's "Here's to the maiden of bashful fifteen," a song from *School for Scandal* (3.1), and remembered it in 1862 when he read Abraham Cowley's "The Inconstant," Sheridan's source.[13] The words to popular hymns were often composed by notable religious poets such as Isaac Watts and William Cowper. Melville makes his lank Bildad, for example, sing Watts's "A Prospect of Heaven Makes Death Easy" as he pilots the *Pequod* out of Nantucket in chapter 22 of *Moby-Dick*. Many hymns by Cowper appeared in the 1779 *Olney Hymns* along with some by his friend John Newton, including the one now known as "Amazing Grace," from the poem entitled "Of Faith's Review and Expectation." David H. Battenfeld showed that Melville adapted the hymn in Father Mapple's sermon in *Moby-Dick* from an edition of *The Psalms and Hymns . . . of the Reformed Protestant Dutch Church in North America.* Memorized songs and other poetry were portable, retrievable for private delectation or commiseration and for making a contribution to sociality even in ships or islands at the ends of the earth.

At the time Melville was born and for as long as he lived, spoken poetry was part of people's everyday lives. Even illiterate people memorized poems and songs, and people with even a restricted education memorized long tracts of poetry, which they were often able to retrieve from memory all through their lives. Given the fact that he had a brilliant literary-minded older brother in Gansevoort, and a brilliant older sister in Helen (who rivaled or surpassed Gansevoort in verbal originality), Melville must have heard his parents reading poetry to him and to the two older children long before he could read himself. He probably memorized his first poems by listening to Gansevoort and Helen read and recite. At seven, in 1826, he would have heard Gansevoort memorizing Fitz-Greene Halleck's "Marco Bozzaris" before reciting it at the High School in New York City. After that recitation (which Herman did not witness), Gansevoort was chosen

---

12. The sixteen known surviving manuscript leaves from the first draft of *Typee* are in the Gansevoort-Lansing Collection, Rare Books and Manuscript Division, The New York Public Library, Astor, Lenox, and Tilden Foundations (hereafter NYPL-GL); the transcription is mine, as printed in Parker 1996, p. 365.

13. For Melville's reading of Cowley in 1862, see section 10 below.

to hold Sir Walter Scott's *The Lady of the Lake* so he could prompt two older lads enacting the scene between Roderick Dhu and Fitz-James—a scene that his mother, Maria Melville, on December 28, 1826, identified so knowingly in a letter to her mother as to show that all the family knew the poem well (*New Log*). At school Herman recited poetry and listened as others recited poetry. After being taken out of the Albany Academy at twelve and a half, he must have memorized some poetry even during his years as a bank clerk and store clerk as well as during his attendance again at the Classical School in Albany around 1835 and at the Albany Academy from September 1836 through February 1837. In 1835 and 1836 he heard Simeon De Witt Bloodgood read or recite many lines from British and American poems (as detailed in the next section). At the Lansingburgh Academy during November 1838 through March 1839 he "declaimed" (presumably poetry as well as prose) every two weeks as part of the curriculum, and listened to other students declaim.

Boylike, Herman used some of the poetry he memorized as a weapon for teasing his decorous sisters. On November 27, 1843, when he was in the Pacific, his sister Helen, then in Boston visiting Elizabeth Shaw (later Herman's wife), wrote her sister Augusta of seeing "Macready the tragedian" play Macbeth twice, adding: "The witch scenes were admirably got up, and when, dancing about the 'cauldron of hell-broth,' one of the horrid creatures, puts in some terrible contribution; and enjoins it 'to make the gruel thick & slab,' I *could* not help thinking of poor Herman, who made it a favorite quotation, and talked about the 'pilot's thumb, wrecked as homeward he did come,' 'eye of newt, toe of frog,' &c." (Parker 1996, p. 107). If the young Herman had made "a favorite quotation" from *Macbeth,* then he also had memorized a good number of other "favorite" quotations with which to regale the family or to delight himself. In 1849 Melville made his young Redburn while away tedious hours at sea by "repeating Lord Byron's Address to the Ocean" (from *Childe Harold's Pilgrimage*), which he "had often spouted on the stage at the High School at home" (chap. 26). Herman probably declaimed poetry of Lord Byron to himself during his checkered early career—farmhand, youthful school-teacher (near Pittsfield, Massachusetts, and at schools roundabout Albany and Lansingburgh), merchant sailor (on a voyage to Liverpool), whaleman (to the Pacific), and Ordinary Sailor (in the Pacific and on the voyage home). There was a rock south of his uncle Thomas's house where (he told Evert Duyckinck on August 8, 1851) he "used to linger" (probably in 1837) "overlooking the fair plateau on which Pittsfield rears its homes and steeples"—a place that seemed to be created by Nature for reciting Byron. Melville probably satirized himself in chapter 35 of *Moby-Dick:*

"Childe Harold not unfrequently perches himself upon the mast-head of some luckless disappointed whale-ship, and in moody phrase ejaculates:—/ 'Roll on, thou deep and dark blue ocean, roll! / Ten thousand blubber-hunters sweep over thee in vain.'" In Melville's early prose narratives the recitation of verse became, as in these examples, a recurrent recreational activity, usually in the form of a sailor giving vent to a sometimes incongruously romanticized poetic temperament. This depiction was based on the reality of Melville's own and other men's recitations.

In the Marquesas in 1842, aboard the *Lucy Ann,* Melville met John Troy, the original of Long Ghost in *Omoo,* and was much in his company at sea and then ashore at Tahiti and Eimeo. Troy may, like Long Ghost, have quoted Virgil and recited poetry by the canto, especially Samuel Butler's *Hudibras.* Whatever Troy recited, Herman heard. In one of Melville's source-books for *White-Jacket,* a "Fore-Top-Man" described a scene on *"Old Ironsides"* in which sailors read aloud novels, mainly, but also poetry: "[J]ust glance your eye along our ships' decks when lying in port; under the break of the poop you may observe a group of mizen-topmen, eagerly listening to some more talented shipmate, who, with voice and effect worthy the subject, is reading aloud passages from one of the splendid and romantic poems of the celebrated Byron."[14] In 1843 and 1844 Melville himself had discovered that some of the sailors on the man-of-war *United States* joyfully read poetry aloud and recited poetry. He made literary friends there, friends selected because they were literary-minded. In particular he admired the Englishman Jack Chase, who "had read all the verses of Byron, and all the romances of Scott" (*White-Jacket,* chap. 4). (In the custom of the time, even those romances by Scott were stuffed with quotations from poetry.) Above all things, White-Jacket says, Chase "was an ardent admirer of Camoens" (chap. 4) and could recite in the original Portuguese parts of the *Lusiad,* the national epic of commerce which anticipated the nineteenth century's obsession with the riches to be gained from what we call the Pacific Rim. Edifying Melville and others with stories of his following "the very track that Camoens sailed" and visiting spots which Camoëns described and where parts of the *Lusiad* were written (chap. 65), Chase was fond of quoting passages from William Julius Mickle's translation (chap. 74), judging from *White-Jacket* (where the accuracy of the quotation may be a testament to Melville's memory but more likely a fair indication that he owned Mickle's translation in 1849).

14. *Life in a Man-of-War or Scenes in "Old Ironsides" During her Cruise in the Pacific. By a Fore-Top-Man* (Philadelphia: Lydia R. Bailey, Printer, 1841).

Among the literary sailors in *White-Jacket* who displayed, like Chase, a taste for the epic form was a poet Melville calls Lemsford. He was based on a seaman named E. Curtiss Hine, who after his return published *The Haunted Barque, and Other Poems* (reviewed February 1848 in the *American Whig Review*), as well as a novel called *Orlando Melville or Victims of the Press-Gang* (1848). According to the narrator of *White-Jacket,* Lemsford knew "the truth of the saying, that *poetry is its own exceeding great reward*," and dashed off "whole epics, sonnets, ballads, and acrostics," some of which he read to the narrator (chap. 11, "The Pursuit of Poetry under Difficulties"). The "saying," more than a little blasphemous since it echoed Genesis 15:1, was from Coleridge's preface to the 1797 *Poems*. Melville may have read the whole preface, but the saying was widely quoted, and identified as Coleridge's, in, for example, the *Southern Literary Messenger* (November 1834), the *United States Democratic Review* (October 1848), and the *American Whig Review* (February 1852). Literary dicta were available in the popular press, and might even be quoted by a literary-minded companion who had not gained access to the original source.

The following passage from *White-Jacket* (chap. 11) may be greatly fictionalized, but it suggests the kind of literary society Melville experienced while he was in the navy, when Chase acted as a patron to Lemsford:

> My noble Captain, Jack Chase, rather patronized Lemsford, and he would stoutly take his part against scores of adversaries. Frequently, inviting him up aloft into his top, he would beg him to recite some of his verses; to which he would pay the most heedful attention, like Mecænas listening to Virgil, with a book of the Æneid in his hand. Taking the liberty of a well-wisher, he would sometimes gently criticise the piece, suggesting a few immaterial alterations. And upon my word, noble Jack, with his native-born good sense, taste, and humanity, was not ill qualified to play the true part of a *Quarterly Review;*—which is, to give quarter at last, however severe the critique.

A whaleship may have been Melville's Yale College and his Harvard, as Ishmael says in *Moby-Dick* (chap. 24, "The Advocate"), but a frigate was his Scriblerus Club and his Ambrose's Tavern. In the intervals between his watches Melville was a member of an ongoing symposium in which poetry was its own exceeding great reward. From then onward throughout Melville's lifetime, poetry was an essential part of the lives of men and women in all the social classes he lived among, whether they were his brothers in New York City and his mother and sisters in Lansingburgh, literary New Yorkers he met through Evert and George Duyckinck, fellow breakfasters in the poet-banker Samuel Rogers's house in London, intellectuals in

Dr. John W. Francis's Bond Street house in New York, or fellow customs-officers in New York City (one of whom was the poet Richard H. Stoddard). In Melville's time, no confirmation was needed that it was manly to love poetry. If any such confirmation had been needed, Jack Chase had supplied it bountifully.

Given his admiration for the art of recitation as practiced by Jack Chase and other proficients, Melville had much to endure when poetry was read by someone lacking "voice and effect." During an excursion to Monument Mountain on August 5, 1850, Melville and Hawthorne, both excited about meeting each other and eager to continue their conversation, were forced to listen to Cornelius Mathews read aloud all of the poem he had brought with him, William Cullen Bryant's "Monument Mountain" (*Log*, p. 384). In an expansive mood Melville may have attended the dedication of the new Pittsfield Cemetery on September 9, 1850, where original odes "by John C. Hoadley, Mrs. Emily P. Dodge and Mrs. J. R. Morewood were sung by a choir" (*Log*, p. 394). (Both Hoadley and Sarah Morewood later became important in Melville's life, and he gave them both volumes of poetry—Chatterton to Hoadley, Dryden to Sarah Morewood.) On September 20, 1850, Hoadley, a Pittsfield manufacturer, wrote (or copied out) a poem on the vulgar saying, "A man should never weep." It began, "It may be manliness to boast / Thy cheek was never wet / With tears of sorrow or remorse, / Of pity or regret," and culminated in the shortest verse in the Bible: "[W]hen thou call'st it manliness, / Remember, JESUS WEPT!" Augusta Melville copied out that poem on October 7, 1850, just as the Melvilles moved into Arrowhead (*New Log*). Is it possible that Herman Melville was never favored with a recital of it by its author? In 1851 Hoadley read his own poetry aloud in Pittsfield at the Fourth of July celebration (again with Melville's neighbor, Sarah Morewood); and later, in 1854, in Lawrence, after he had become Melville's brother-in-law, he read aloud to his family all of Longfellow's *The Golden Legend*. Eloquent reading of dreary poetry could be hilarious, as Melville showed on August 7, 1851, when he read aloud "On Onota's Graceful Shore / A Ballad of the Times that Tried Men's Souls," in the presence of the author, J. E. A. Smith—"the mad poet," Evert Duyckinck called him. Deftly managing not to let Smith gain an inkling that he was being satirized, Melville read the patriotic lines "with emphasis" and interrupted his performance "with such phrases as 'great glorious' 'By Jove that's tremendous &c.' "[15] Melville's tolerance had limits. In early October 1852, while crushed by the

---

15. Evert A. Duyckinck to his wife, August 9, 1851 (*New Log*). From an 1896 text we know at least roughly what Melville read aloud.

reviews of *Pierre,* he went to hear the Albany poet Alfred Billings Street (a neighbor of his uncle Peter Gansevoort) read at the Pittsfield Young Ladies' Institute ("And then the loved one changes to the wife. / Home is a bower of roses to his life") but afterward could not bring himself to speak to Street and invite him out to Arrowhead. His rudeness greatly distressed the poet, who complained to Peter Gansevoort when he returned to Albany (*Log,* p. 461). (Hoadley, always diplomatic as well as less burdened by discriminating taste, on occasion exchanged poems with Street [*Log,* p. 477].)

Melville at Arrowhead, even as he had done as a youth, continued to go about the house and grounds reciting bits of poetry. We know because in 1854 one of his sisters mentioned his repeating his favorite lines about "little breezes" and "little zephyrs"—lines still unidentified (Parker 2002, p. 215). In his first lecture, in 1857, Melville quoted both Burns's "To a Mountain Daisy, On turning one down with the plough, in April 1786" and Byron's *Childe Harold's Pilgrimage.*[16] At the funeral of his Unitarian father-in-law in 1861 Melville listened to the Unitarian Orville Dewey (whose account of his visit to Wordsworth had been famous for many years) recite the ending of "Thanatopsis" by the Unitarian William Cullen Bryant. During the composition of *Clarel* Melville tried out lines in his house in New York within hearing of his younger daughter, Frances, who well into the twentieth century "derided" his performance, perhaps seeing it as too stagy, perhaps simply as immodest and self-indulgent, since she had long known from the newspapers that his poetry was very bad.

Melville's last, and sympathetic, audience was his wife, Lizzie, after they were living in New York City alone except for their unmarried daughter, Bessie. Poetry, at the end, drew Melville and his wife closer together as she helped him prepare his poetic manuscripts for publication. At this time, even though his energies were failing, Melville would probably have read some of his poems aloud to Lizzie as they prepared for the press *John Marr and Other Sailors* and *Timoleon and Other Ventures in Minor Verse.* And surely he read aloud to Lizzie some of the poems left unpublished at his death that were to become part of *Weeds and Wildings,* a volume designed specifically to honor her. He would have especially enjoyed reading to her the poems he wrote to commemorate shared memories of their years at Arrowhead. In the dedication addressed to her, "To Winnefred," he summons thoughts, memories, and feelings about a

---

16. Reconstructed texts of the lectures Melville delivered in 1857–58 ("Statues in Rome"), 1858–59 ("The South Seas"), and 1859–60 ("Travel") are included in *"The Piazza Tales" and Other Prose Pieces, 1839–1860,* volume 9 of the NN edition, pp. 398–423.

flower that was, to them both, "one of the dearest of the flowers of the field"—the red clover.[17] Writing of this flower, he was reminded of their "bridal month" more than forty-four years past, as well as one October afternoon when he had brought into her warm "chamber" a red clover bouquet. "Tears of the happy," she had said, seeing the melting snowflakes roll off the flower petals. Many of these poems, especially those of "Part I – The Year," are simple yet vivid evocations of rural, family-centered scenes and events from the Melvilles' years at Arrowhead: "Butterfly Ditty," "The Blue-Bird," "A Way-side Weed," and "Stockings in the Farm-house Chimney." At the end of his life as at the beginning, Melville lived nourished and blessed by the sound of poetry spoken aloud, even if he himself was the speaker he most often heard.

III
THE OMNIPRESENCE OF
POETRY, 1820s–1848

AS A MEMBER of a highly literate Boston society, Melville's father, Allan Melvill, frequently quoted poetry or alluded to poems.[18] On May 28, 1804, in a letter to Lemuel Shaw (later Herman's father-in-law) Allan elaborately proclaimed that he held himself aloof from partisan politics (just then emerging in the new republic), then broke into blank verse: "*I was a Politician once, but late I've lost the relish for the work, discovering that fair play is seldom used, to effect the end desired, leaving the path of honest argument, & shunning truth, patriots of modern days, 'WHO LOVE GOOD PLACES, AT THEIR HEARTS,' yet give the tongue a licence, descend to scurrilous abuse, and deal out loathsome ribaldry, till Falsehood foul coadjutor, is fairly tired*—this much for blank verse—blank indeed you will say, & perhaps exclaim with the

17. Quotations here from *Weeds and Wildings Chiefly, With a Rose or Two*, follow the text in Robert C. Ryan's 1967 Northwestern University dissertation. The near-final *Weeds and Wildings Chiefly*, along with other poetic and prose manuscripts preserved by his widow after Melville's death, including "House of the Tragic Poet," *Billy Budd, Sailor*, and the variously titled "Naples" and "At the Hostelry," are in the Houghton Library of Harvard University and are published in volume 13 of the NN edition.

18. The family surname was usually spelled Melvill in Allan's lifetime; after his death in 1832 Maria Gansevoort Melvill and her children normally used the spelling Melville. Allan's letter to Shaw is in the Houghton Library of Harvard University, bMS Am 188 (68); it is quoted here with permission.

Irishman, behold the *footsteps* of a Dabbler's *hand*." (Characteristically, he embodied in his poetry a quotation from a poem, Cowper's *Table Talk*, clearly assuming that Shaw would recognize it and relish it.) Books of poetry that Allan owned were auctioned off in the late 1820s, so Herman Melville was denied the complex experience of reading many of the great English poets in books owned by his father. Melville did in fact read Spenser in the eight-in-four edition his father had owned (but not marked) since January 1803.[19] Melville's first reading of *The Faerie Queene* may have occurred as early as in the "cholera summer" of 1832, when, after work at the New York State Bank, his long evenings were his own for the first time in his life, with his mother and her other children in Pittsfield. That timing would fit an autobiographical reading of the description (written late in 1851) of Pierre's reading his own dead father's copy of *The Faerie Queene,* when aesthetic responses to lusciously sensual passages occur simultaneously with and hardly distinguishable from pubescent stirrings, creating an intense, bewildering confusion.

In the Melville house also was the copy of William Tennant's *Anster Fair* (Edinburgh: Cockburn, 1812; Sealts, no. 500a) that the Reverend Robert Swan had inscribed to Allan Melvill on May 20, 1818, at St. Monans, during Allan's visit to Scotland. This mock-heroic poem in ottava rima was commonly said to have influenced John Hookham Frere's 1817 *The Monks and the Giants* (published as by William and Robert Whistlecraft), then, directly or indirectly, Byron's *Beppo* (1818) and *Don Juan* (which started publication in 1819). The Melville brothers may have delighted in Tennant's account of the revenge the lovelorn and temporarily noseless Charlie Melvil took on his tormenters, but that passage is unmarked. Apparently as late as 1875 Melville noted across from the title page: "This poem gave the hint of style to Frere in the 'Monks & Giants' (Whistlecraft) which suggested to Lord Byron the style and stanza of Don Juan—acknowledged by the last named poet."[20] In the invocation to the god of poetry he checked

19. Books Melville is known to have owned or consulted are identified by the number assigned by Merton M. Sealts Jr. in his *Melville's Reading* and its supplements (including Sealts 1990 and Olsen-Smith and Sealts 2004). The Spenser owned by Allan Melvill and later Herman Melville was *The Poetical Works of Edmund Spenser* (London: J. Bell, 1787–88), 8 v. in 4; Sealts, no. 483a. It was a New Year's gift to Allan from his friend Obadiah Rich Jr. (1783–1850—born in Truro, Massachusetts, and later the great London dealer in Americana). It is now in the Melville Collection of the Houghton Library of Harvard University, donated by Melville's great-granddaughter Priscilla Osborne Ambrose and her children Will and Catherine.

20. Jay Leyda included much of Melville's marginalia in *The Melville Log,* in remarkably reliable transcriptions, and Walker Cowen put more in his dissertation and book,

"Why scorch me ev'n to death with fiery inspiration?"—the poet's plea to Phoebus to give him a more moderate spark of poetic fire. Just possibly, the book was so precious a reminder of her husband that Maria Melville kept it away from the children.

From childhood Melville knew Sir Walter Scott as a poet before he knew him as a novelist, and in the 1830s he became fascinated by the younger Scottish poet George Gordon, Lord Byron. In 1834 Herman's older brother, Gansevoort, perforce the man of the family at nineteen, the proprietor of a cap and fur store, and too poor to seek a bride of his own, was delighted by a sensuous description in Byron:

> Slept in the store, before going to bed read part of the bride of Abydos, and was particularly pleased with the 10th. 11th. 12th. & 13th stanzas especially the lines immediately following "My love thou surely knewest before" in the 13th the character of Zuleika as pourtrayed by Byron in the bride of Abydos, is the most sweetly beautiful female character that I have ever met with in Poetry, so gentle, affectionate, amiable, & ingenuous in disposition, so simply beautiful in her ideas, and so happy in expressing them, and appearing to possess every quality of heart and mind, calculated to make those around her happy, joined with a person, which would realize all the ideas that the Mahometan has of the beauty of the Houris, those dark eyed girls of Paradise, all conspire to make a woman as near perfection, as it is possible for her to attain. (Parker 1996, p. 92)

Tellingly, Gansevoort expected to meet characters in poetry, which often meant in the narrative poems of Scott and Byron, not lyric poetry. On November 9, 1843, the year before Herman returned from the Pacific, Gansevoort cried out to "the Friends of Ireland" at Washington Hall in New York City that the "enemies of Ireland and of Liberty shall be taught that 'Freedom's battle once begun, / Bequeathed from bleeding sire to son, / Though baffled oft, is ever won'" (New York *Tribune,* November 10, 1843). He counted on his audience to know its Byron and to recognize in the quotation from *The Giaour* a parallel between still-oppressed Ireland and formerly enslaved Greece. Gansevoort's specific responses to

---

Melville's Marginalia, in sometimes shaky transcriptions. Many books containing important marginalia (for example, the Wordsworth, the Milton, the Dante, Hazlitt's *Lectures,* the Vasari, and the Spenser) surfaced too late for Cowen to see them. Transcriptions throughout of Melville's markings and marginalia in his books are mine unless otherwise noted. Among the RELATED DOCUMENTS in the present volume, see "Melville's Marginalia on Poetry and Poetics" and "The Sources of Melville's Notes (1849–51) in a Shakespeare Volume," where for the first time all three sources for these notes are identified.

poetry are not an invariable indicator of Herman's, but in the 1830s both brothers read all the Byron they could get hands on—satires, love poetry, plays, and certainly the great narrative poems. Before Herman could have dared to aspire to a literary life, Gansevoort, his notes show, was thinking of authorship as an ultimate career choice, alone or in conjunction with the law.

Scornful of conventional values, self-dramatizing, world-wandering, startlingly beautiful, uninhibited in sensuality, unrestrainable in poetic output, self-involved yet heroically self-sacrificial in the cause of freedom, Lord Byron became the embodiment of the ideal poet for Herman, not least because he was himself a Scot of noble blood. Probably by the mid-1830s, Melville was especially familiar with *Manfred* and *Childe Harold's Pilgrimage,* if not *Don Juan.* For Herman, *Childe Harold's Pilgrimage* was eminently quotable from lofty vantage points on land and sea—and as late as 1857 and 1858 he quoted it from the moderate elevation of lecture stages. Before and just after his years at sea Herman could not have missed, nor could he have failed to admire, the Byronic aspects of his brother's own character and the infused, poetic energy of the rhetorical declamations that in 1844 led one admirer to call Gansevoort (as the third Melville brother, Allan, wrote Herman in October 1844), "the orator of the human race." After his death at the age of thirty in 1846, Gansevoort seemed to Herman more Byronic than ever—heroically burnt out by his both fervored and painstaking pursuit of impossible goals. And Herman just at that time saw himself as Byronic when he self-consciously echoed the poet's declaration that he had awakened to find himself famous (in his letter to William B. Sprague, July 24, 1846). In his fiction Melville seized on Byron's life and poetry as embodying quintessentially poetic qualities, all that was inherently antipathetic to commonplace conventionalities, all the profoundly reckless and irrepressibly creative powers that would lead the unimaginative, uncomprehending lawyer-narrator of "Bartleby" (1853) to try to tame Byron patronizingly as merely a "mettlesome poet." Byron was an alter ego whose example proclaimed that a great poet could live triumphantly, if tragically, during Melville's own lifetime. In his hints about the earlier life of one of the most alluring characters in *Clarel,* the mysterious Vine, Melville evoked the mythic story of Admetus, the king of Thessaly, whom the god Apollo had served, for a time, as his humble shepherd (pt. 1, canto 29). Melville had himself been Apollo laboring as a shepherd to Francis Bloodgood, the Admetus of the New York State Bank, or laboring for Gansevoort Melville, the Admetus of the cap and fur store, or whaling under the command of Captain Valentine Pease, the Admetus of the *Acushnet*—an unrecognized poetic genius held as hireling to a succession of masters until his discharge from the navy in October 1844. Melville by the 1850s knew Percy Bysshe Shelley's *Prometheus Unbound,* the modern drama of a freed Greek god; Lord Byron, in the 1830s and 1840s, had been a poetic god, alive in Melville's own lifetime, an Apollo Unbound.

In the 1830s even for impoverished young men and youths like Gansevoort and Herman Melville, for whom captivating recent poetry was as near as a copy of Scott or Byron, Albany itself was far from a backwoods or backwater outpost, literarily speaking. Never the equal of New York City for literary publishing, Albany as the political capital was the home of expert printers of the state documents. For local readers (Albanians, they sometimes called themselves) and for politicians from the rest of the state in temporary residence, Albany printers competently supplied, a few weeks late, the most recent quarterlies and monthlies from Scotland and England, in full or in selections chosen for their readers. Then, as all through Melville's life, in the absence of an international copyright law, reprints of even the best British magazines and books could be purchased cheaply—although often in wretchedly small type—because American printers paid no royalties and turned a profit as soon as they recouped their printing costs. Albany bookstores also stocked foreign and domestic periodicals shipped up from New York City and, less often, Philadelphia or Boston. The British magazines that reviewed volumes of poetry invariably printed long quotations, carefully selected, whether to capture the best of the verse or to illustrate some challenging argument of the reviewer. Local printers sometimes offered cheap reprints of British poetry, and booksellers stocked poetry reprinted in New York City and elsewhere. A printer in any upstate New York or inland New England town might publish hundreds of copies of a rhetoric or elocution textbook that contained advice on reading poetry aloud. The Erie Canal made it easy to ship such books to Albany from Utica, for instance, and textbooks from Andover, Massachusetts, reached Albany even before a railroad linked the Hudson River valley and Boston in the early 1840s.

Albany had literary people of its own, notable among whom was Francis Bloodgood's son, Simeon De Witt Bloodgood (1799–1866), whose wife was a Van Schaick, a fourth cousin of Gansevoort and Herman Melville (whose Gansevoort grandmother had been a Van Schaick), and who were connected in other ways, as were all the old Dutch families. As Janette Currie and Scott Norsworthy have shown, Simeon De Witt Bloodgood played a remarkable role in bringing contemporary British writings to Albany. After Sir Walter Scott's death in 1832 Americans were avid for anecdotes about the great poet and novelist. Knowing that James Hogg, world-famous as "the Ettrick Shepherd," had anticipated this appetite with his "First Interview with Sir Walter Scott" in 1829, Bloodgood wrote directly to Hogg requesting "something original or anecdotes about Sir Walter," as Hogg explained to Scott's son-in-law, John Gibson Lockhart, in 1833 (Currie, p. 1). Lockhart was then trying to block the publication of Hogg's *Anecdotes of Scott* in Great Britain, so Hogg sent Bloodgood "Familiar Anecdotes of Sir Walter Scott," which Bloodgood placed with the Harpers (1834), prefaced with his own "A Sketch of the Life of the Shepherd." For all his hardships at this period, Hogg was proud, as he wrote in 1833, to hear from different parts of the United States that he was "more read there, and oftener reprinted, than any other living author" (Currie, p. 2). Janette Currie found in the Albany *Daily Advertiser* of April 27, 1833, this item headed "THE ETTRICK SHEPHERD":

> We had the pleasure to receive a few days since, a long letter from James Hogg, the Ettrick Shepherd, in relation to the publication of some of his works in the United States. He is about writing a series of ten or twelve volumes. We regret to learn from his own pen, that though "a poor shepherd half a century ago," he is, notwithstanding a life of industry, "a poor shepherd to this day." He writes that he has heard of the "splendid city of Albany on the Hudson," "at his own cottage in Yarrow," and that his poems have been extensively read in the United States. The fame and fate of Burns seem almost that of Hogg. When he is no more, we shall probably hear of anniversary dinners on his birthday, and a monument to his memory "in Edinboro' town", but it would be much more honorable to the British public to place him in comfort and independence at once, rather than expend their tardy benevolence in building him a grave.

The *Advertiser* was printed and published by yet another family connection of the Melvilles, J. B. Van Schaick & Company, who also printed and published the Albany *Gazette*.

Although his earliest known reference to the poems of the "Ettrick Shepherd" comes as late as 1866, in the "Supplement" to *Battle-Pieces,* Melville knew James Hogg's poetry in his youth, when the Shepherd was almost as popular a Scottish poet as Robert Burns and Sir Walter Scott. Much of Hogg's work printed in the United States was prose, but some of his poems were reprinted as well, and his prose anecdotes sent readers back both to Scott's poetry and Hogg's own. In Philadelphia Adam Waldie rivaled Bloodgood in reprinting Hogg's prose, and Waldie also reprinted some of Hogg's poetry in the *Port Folio, and Companion to the Circulating Library* and the *Museum of Foreign Literature, Science and Art.* (Gansevoort Melville pored over the volumes of the *Circulating Library* in

1837, making notes from them in his *Index Rerum,* a popular device for the instant retrieval of useful information, described below.) In January 1834 Hogg promised Bloodgood that he would send a tale or one or two ballads for a new eclectic Albany magazine called *The Zodiac: A Monthly Periodical Devoted to Science, Literature and the Arts.* Several remarkably intimate pieces of prose by and about Hogg were printed there between July 1835 and June 1836, including (in August 1835) "A Letter from Professor Wilson" written to Hogg in September 1815, in which John Wilson commented sardonically on Wordsworth's *White Doe of Rylstone,* Robert Southey's "Roderick, the Last of the Goths," and Scott's "Field of Waterloo." The *Zodiac* was treating Albanians to rich gossip sure to appeal to literary-minded youths hungry for news of the great contemporary British writers, in this case gossip printed in Albany almost three decades, it seems, before it was printed in Edinburgh in 1862. In October 1835 the *Zodiac* printed Hogg's "The Moon was A-Wanin' "; in February 1836 "Verses to the Comet"; and in March 1836 "A Father's Lament." The *Zodiac* regularly acknowledged its sources in British periodicals available in Albany: "Walter the Witless" was from the London *Athenæum;* "Literary Remunerations" from *Chambers' Edinburgh Journal;* Thomas Carlyle's "State of German Literature" from the *Edinburgh Review;* the Reverend J. Moultrie's "Stanzas" from the *Etonian* ("In many a strain of grief and joy, / My youthful spirit sang to thee; / But I am now no more a boy, / And there's a gulf 'twixt thee and me"); "To A Sleeping Child. From the French of Victor Hugo" from the *Foreign Quarterly Review;* and from the same magazine "To Luigia Pallavicini, On her Recovery from Sickness. From the Italian of *Ugo Foscolo."* The *Zodiac* printed Coleridge's "An Ode to the Rain" in November 1836 and quoted that poet in "Literary Fashions" from *Chambers' Edinburgh Journal.*

The *Zodiac* of July 1836 reprinted from Park Benjamin's *American Monthly Magazine* an editorial on German literature (not specifically on poetry) that seems to have made a lasting impression on Melville. The writer rejoiced that growing interest in German literature would be beneficial in counterpoising the American emphasis on materialism, on "internal improvements" (like canals) that are purely external: "Let us not forget that there are internal improvements of another sort very proper to immortal beings; and beware, lest in a contented ignorance we turn our backs upon what is elegant, refined, and imaginative, because it will do nothing either for steamboat or rail-road, and is therefore stigmatized as not being 'practical.' " In Melville's own criticism of the United States at the end of his lecture on "Statues in Rome" (1857) he calls the locomotive a symbol of modernity in contrast to the Apollo Belvedere and immediately thereafter complains that the "world has taken a practical turn." Besides this editorial, the *Zodiac* printed some translations from German, including in October 1836 an unsigned translation of Johann Christoph Friedrich von Schiller's "The Song of the Bell." The lines "When with the strong, the delicate, / When with the bold, the mild we mate, / Then melodious is the song" (as Norsworthy pointed out to me privately in 2005) may have stuck in Herman Melville's head for many years before it informed the imagery and rhythms of his poem "Art" (in *Timoleon*).

Gansevoort and Herman were not the only members of the family eager to read the latest *Zodiac*. One of Augusta Melville's teachers at the Albany Female Academy, A. D. Woodbridge, whose family home was in Stockbridge, Massachusetts, was a frequent contributor of poetry to that paper. The September 1835 *Zodiac* contained a poem by Woodbridge to Catharine Sedgwick, "To the author of 'Redwood,' 'Hope Leslie,' etc. on her return to this her native village, July, 1835" (at a time when Helen Melville was a student at Elizabeth Dwight Sedgwick's school, conducted in the house in Lenox where the novelist summered). Of special interest to Augusta would have been the September 1836 issue, with Woodbridge's "My Parting Gift" ("Lines addressed by a teacher, at the close of a term, to different members of her class, who at the commencement of a new term were to enter a higher department"); Woodbridge copied out this all-purpose memento for Augusta, who retained it all her life.[21] Poetry was something that students wrote about in their composition classes: on January 15, 1837, Augusta submitted an appreciative essay at the Albany Female Academy on Felicia Hemans's poetry.

---

21. Woodbridge's other pieces in the *Zodiac* are indicative of the allusive poetry of the time. "The Last Day of Summer" (August 1835) was subtitled "Imitated from Moore" (whose "The Last Rose of Summer" was already world famous). Billed as expressly written "For the Zodiac" were "To My Little Nephew Willy" and "Genius" (both December 1835); "The New-Year's Book" (January 1836); and "Scenes on the Ocean" (February 1836), with the epigraph "Likeness of heaven! / Agent of power, / Man is thy victim, / Shipwreck thy dower." Also "for the *Zodiac*" (April 1836) was an untitled poem by Woodbridge introduced as "written for and sung at the opening of a Literary Institution" as well as an "Impromptu—to Eliza." For the May 1836 magazine she contributed "Not All a Dream," with an epigraph from Byron: "I had a dream, which was not all a dream" (the opening of "Darkness"), followed below by "My Brain!" Others were "The Gentle Nurse" and "I've Strung my Lyre" (June 1836); "The Ocean Dirge" (September 1836); and "Gertrude" (November 1836). The January 1837 issue contained "Night Scene Upon Kirauea," the epigraph of which reads: "Péle abode in Kirauea, / In the pit, ever feeding the fires," footnoted to *"Polynesian Researches"* as "Goddess of Volcanoes"—that is, William Ellis's *Polynesian Researches,* later a source for Herman Melville.

Gansevoort had the advantage of extra years of schooling, and was therefore better equipped to make up for gaps in his education, but Herman also did the best he could. Out of school since October 1831, Herman attended the Albany Classical Institute for a time in 1835–36, where his teacher, Charles E. West, had been a Union College classmate of Gansevoort's friend and mentor, Alexander W. Bradford. Then Herman attended the Albany Academy from September 1, 1836, to March 1, 1837. At both schools he probably encountered much poetry, but the textbooks have not been identified. A splendid Albany resource was the Young Men's Association for Mutual Improvement, a quintessentially American institution designed for ambitious young men, most often those denied higher education but eager to improve their minds. It was anything but a boys' club. In the Albany YMA members could develop skills ranging from polite conversation to formal debating to delivering public orations. On March 9, 1837, the Albany *Evening Journal* published a report on the association and its 736 members. In the reading room were 1,400 volumes, 26 daily newspapers, 5 triweekly papers, 7 semiweekly papers, 41 weekly papers, and some 30 monthly and quarterly reviews (magazines). Most of the magazines were Scottish or English—not imported sets, for the most part, but volumes reprinted in Albany or New York City or Philadelphia. Eager to garner and retain full runs of periodicals, the YMA in the Albany *Argus* on January 1, 1835, requested all readers to check any of their "broken sets" of *Brewster's Edinburgh Encyclopedia* to see if they could spare one of the numbers the YMA listed as needed to complete its set. The YMA library nurtured Herman's lifelong love of the older British quarterlies and monthlies—volumes that almost invariably contained much poetry. The earliest catalogue of the YMA library yet discovered, published in 1837, contains all the books available to Herman except perhaps some of the most recent acquisitions; an 1843 catalogue shows that the YMA continued to make regular additions to its library. In 1837 the YMA possessed, mostly in the form of American publications printed well after the War of 1812 but before Herman became a member, an enormous library of British and American poetry, some classical poetry, many books on the lives of poets, and many volumes containing shrewd, knowledgeable literary criticism on the greatest British poetry of the previous decades.

When Herman joined the Albany Young Men's Association for Mutual Improvement in January 1835, Gansevoort was already flourishing as a member. On September 21, 1835, Gansevoort was elected to the Executive Committee of the YMA. The next year, on January 23, 1836, Gansevoort was elected president of the Debating Society of the YMA, and that Fourth of July he read aloud the Declaration of Independence as part of the YMA's procession and celebration. Herman managed to keep paying his membership dues for two and a half years. He joined in time to hear Westerlo Woodworth speak on "American Poetry" on March 6, 1835 (a lecture announced in the Albany *Argus*). More important, he was in time to benefit from a pioneering series of lectures on American literature given at the YMA by their cousin-by-marriage Simeon De Witt Bloodgood, beginning on February 10, 1835. Documentation proving Gansevoort Melville's association with Bloodgood survives fortuitously from a decade later when, as Secretary to the American Legation in London, Gansevoort regularly sent newspapers home to Bloodgood. Given his character, his prominence in the YMA, and the family connection, it is possible that Gansevoort had something to do with a "request"—that Bloodgood give "A Series of Lectures on American Literature, Delivered by Request before the Young Men's Association, in the City of Albany, New York, by S. De Witt Bloodgood." Reaching a wider audience, and allowing the young men of the association to ponder them in type, Bloodgood's lectures were printed in the monthly Albany *Zodiac* beginning in the August 1835 issue. The *Zodiac* for July 1836 (the month Gansevoort read Jefferson's Declaration aloud) contained the lecture by Bloodgood devoted to the third president. The publication of the lectures, if not Bloodgood's delivery of them, terminated abruptly in October 1836. Herman remained a member of the YMA into 1837. On April 26, 1837, after failing in business during the financial panic of that year, Gansevoort resigned from the Executive Committee and soon left for New York City, in the hope of starting a career as a lawyer, and in June Herman went off to Pittsfield to work his uncle Thomas's farm for a few months before teaching school in the hills nearby.

A safe assumption, given the Melville brothers' connection to Bloodgood and to the YMA, and given their zeal for learning, is that both of them attended all or most of his lectures and that they read them all in the *Zodiac*. Bloodgood began his "Introductory Remarks" (printed in August 1835) with a tribute to earnest, ambitious young men denied a formal higher education, the men who had created the Young Men's Association for Mutual Improvement: "Felicitous in its design, and successful in its progress, this Association may become illustrious in its career. Who can say what noble traits of character, what heaven born energies may not yet be developed through its influence? Who can tell what pre[e]minence may not be obtained through its means by some who hitherto were unaided in their efforts, solitary in their reflections, and diffident of themselves, though conscious of something within them 'struggling to be free'" (*Hamlet*, 3.3). That "Who can say" ranks as one of the most prophetic questions young

Herman Melville heard or read. What Bloodgood said in the lecture was already conventional but nevertheless inspiring: "[T]he history of a nation is inseparably connected with, if not absolutely dependent upon its cultivation of literature." He cited Timothy Dwight's asking how long there had been an England before England had a well-written book—a rejoinder to the British who had scoffed at the meagerness of American literary productions. Bloodgood declared that England owed "her fame to three individuals more than any others" including its kings and queens—three poets, Spenser, Shakespeare, and Milton. He named three later British poets as of particular interest because they wrote about the American colonies or the new country: James Thomson (in "Liberty," 5.2.638–46); Thomas Campbell (in *Gertrude of Wyoming*); and Thomas Moore (in "The Lake of the Dismal Swamp" and other poems), although he chastised Moore for mingling "ridicule of the country with his praise."

In his survey of American literature from the Pilgrims to the present Bloodgood quoted many British poems. He quoted nine lines from Byron's *Childe Harold's Pilgrimage* (2.88) on Greece as a "shrine of departed greatness" and twelve lines from Byron's "By the Rivers of Babylon We Sat Down and Wept," one of the "Hebrew Melodies." Bloodgood warned that great writers may die in poverty: "Antiquity is full of impressive examples, but even in modern times we see Cervantes begging his bread, Camoens perishing in a hospital, Tasso borrowing a crown from a companion to save himself from starvation, Corneille dying of hunger, the author of the Fairy Queen perishing of hope deferred,—he who knew, by sad experience, what it was, in spite of his genius, 'To fawn, to crouch, to wait, to ride, to run, / To speed, to give, to want, to be undone.'" These lines were familiar, Bloodgood assumed, from the passage on suitors at court in Spenser's *Mother Hubbard's Tale,* especially since the passage only recently had been brought to the attention of the English-reading world in Sir Walter Scott's *The Fortunes of Nigel* (chap. 9). Bloodgood quoted a line on Bishop Berkeley from Pope's *Essay on Man,* the "Epilogue to the Satires, Dialogue 2." He quoted ten satirical lines from Cowper's *The Task* (bk. 4, "The Winter Evening") about the arrival of the newspaper and its perusal ("Cat'racts of declamation thunder there, / There, forests of no meaning spread the page, / In which all comprehension wanders lost"). He quoted a long passage from Sir William Jones's "Ode in Imitation of Alcaeus" ("What constitutes a state?"). Jones the poet was also the great linguist whom Melville cited in chapter 79 of *Moby-Dick.*

In the course of describing and quoting many American poems Bloodgood took for granted that his auditors all knew at least a few of them. One was Timothy Dwight's "Columbia, Columbia, to glory Arise!" of which he quoted the two last stanzas as "familiar to every American school boy." He quoted sixteen lines from John Pierpont's "The Pilgrim Fathers." He quoted an American version of one of the Psalms, which he acknowledged was wretched in comparison with Byron's. He quoted Henry Ware Jr.'s "The Vision of Liberty" ("let the blessings thou [great Heaven] hast freely given, / Freely on all men shine, / Till equal rights be equally enjoyed, / And human power for human good employed"). He quoted some lines from Mrs. Warren, whom he identified as the daughter of James Otis (Mercy Otis Warren, really the sister of the patriot James Otis). He elaborately introduced a long passage from near the end of canto 3 of John Trumbull's *M'Fingal: A Modern Epic Poem* (first published in full in 1782),[22] dually inspired by Butler's *Hudibras* and James Macpherson's *Fingal,* and quoted lengthy passages from Trumbull's "Destruction of Babylon." Bloodgood quoted a kinswoman of Mrs. Bloodgood's, Eliza Bleecker, apologizing a little: "We have been more minute perhaps, than we should have been, had not a peculiar interest attached to the circumstance of her former residence in our vicinity."[23] Bloodgood ran together passages from James Gates Percival's "The Graves of the Patriots" before paying tribute to Samuel Adams, an intimate friend of the Melville brothers' Boston grandfather. He quoted Charles Sprague's "The Centennial Ode," a tribute to the Pilgrims, as recited in September 1830 in Boston.

In treating Joel Barlow in the fourth lecture Bloodgood dismissed the ambitious efforts at writing an American epic and praised a trifling work: "He is principally remarkable in his literary career for his Columbiad, which nobody reads, and his poem of Hasty Pudding, which every one reads." In the fifth lecture Bloodgood quoted eighteen lines from the opening of "Hasty Pudding" ("I sing the sweets I know, the charms I feel, / My morning incense, and my evening meal! / The sweets of Hasty Pudding!"), declaring that the "whole poem is kept up with equal spirit, and a humor not to be found in any other of his poems." Bloodgood liked the early *Vision of Columbus* (1787) no better than the later *Columbiad* (1807): "His longer poems can not be expected to retain a lasting place in our literature." In fairness he quoted thirty lines from the *Vision of Columbus,* a "contrast between a northern and southern climate," as being

22. *M'Fingal* (in the 1782 or the 1826 edition) may have been in the Boston house on Green Street during Herman and Gansevoort's visits to their Melvill grandparents because it depicted an event in which Major Thomas Melvill had participated—as one of those who "In shape of Indians, drown'd the tea."

23. In his 1837 *Index Rerum* (see note 25 below), Gansevoort noted under "Bleecker": "some notice of Mrs. Ann Eliza, one of our early poets—her Memoirs & works were published but are now not to be found—see Stone's Life of Brant vi, c9. p206-207—note."

in Barlow's "graver manner" and as having been "selected by competent judges as a fair specimen of his poetic talent." Bloodgood took occasion to inveigh against the *Quarterly Review* for scorning American literature ("There is, or was, a Mr. Dwight, who wrote some poems, his baptismal name was Timothy"). He meant Sydney Smith's notorious article in the 1818 *Edinburgh Review,* but some of what he quotes suggests that he may also have been thinking about a slur by Southey that the first plaything given to an American child was a rattlesnake tail. From "Greenfield Hill" Bloodgood cited enough to vindicate his (Dwight's) "poetic powers" against any foreign criticism. As evidence that Dwight was entitled to "a place in the front rank of letters" Bloodgood quoted eighteen lines from "The Destruction of the Pequods" ("And soon man's Demon Chiefs from memory fade"). Bloodgood in his sixth lecture quoted from Francis Hopkinson a song to "fair Rosina" and some twenty satirical lines addressed to medical students in Philadelphia. He noted that Colonel David Humphreys (spelled Humphrey in the *Zodiac*), a friend of Dwight and Trumbull, wrote the well-received "An Address to the Armies of America," and he mentioned also Humphreys's "The Happiness of America" and "American Industry." Deciding that Humphreys's "poetic powers" never "soar to any uncommon height" but rarely "fall below mediocrity," Bloodgood acknowledged that "great popularity" had attended Humphreys's efforts, and quoted from the "Address to the Armies of America" three stanzas on the departure of the British fleet from American shores ("E'en now from half the threaten'd horrors freed, / See from our shores the lessening sails recede").

Superficial as they were, Bloodgood's lectures, read from the stage and later printed, gave Herman Melville what was then a rarity, a course in American literature, one he could supplement with knowledge acquired elsewhere. For instance, from his youth Herman must have known from his uncle Thomas Melvill something of Joel Barlow the man because his father and uncle were Americans in Paris when Barlow was. According to a letter from Melville's uncle Thomas to Lemuel Shaw on February 3, 1834 (Parker 1963, p. 54), Barlow had recommended him to Thomas Jefferson as the best-qualified American in Paris to take over the American consulate when the incumbent, Fulwar Skipwith, resigned—possibly in 1796, when Skipwith resigned as consul general, but perhaps in 1808, when he resigned as commercial agent. Although Bloodgood dismissed the importance of Barlow's *The Vision of Columbus* and *The Columbiad,* Melville at the start of *The Confidence-Man* (1857) may have drawn on one or both of them for his mention of Manco Capac. Bloodgood seems not to have mentioned either William Emmons or Richard Emmons, poetical brothers. In the late 1820s during visits to Boston Melville would have seen the poet-orator William Emmons on the Common. From a booth there, Emmons alternately sold copies of his orations and cups of a delicious beverage, egg-pop, the source of the sobriquet "Pop" Emmons. Given his grandfather's role in the raising of the monument across the Charles River, Melville may have encountered *The Battle of Bunker Hill, or The Temple of Liberty; an Historical Poem in Four Cantos* (1839), identified on the title page as by "Col. William Emmons." The poem, in which several of Melville's family names appear as heroic colonists, concludes with the address "forwarded by those patriots who composed the Continental Congress, 10th May, 1775, to the oppressed people of Ireland," to whom the Congress offered "a safe asylum from poverty, and in time from oppression also," an asylum, the address continued, already sought by thousands of Irishmen. In his oration "An Address Commemorative of the Battle of Bunker Hill, June 17, 1775," William Emmons quoted extensively from his yet-unpublished poem on that subject; the epic poet and former president John Quincy Adams paid for the publication of this oration.[24]

During the 1820s and 1840s, and afterward, writers (novelists, essayists, orators who printed their speeches, as Ralph Waldo Emerson sometimes did) punctuated their prose pages with tags from poetry, the conventions of the time allowing them to strew phrases from Shakespeare and other writers with or often without much regard to their original context. But readers recognized contexts that are now quite elusive. On November 25, 1851, the Edinburgh *Evening Courant* in its review of *The Whale* assessed Ahab's resolve: "The interests of his employers, the safety of his crew, and every other consideration gave way to this. 'No love-lorn swain, in lady's bower, / E'er panted for the appointed hour' as did Captain Ahab to fall in with Moby Dick." Many readers in 1851 would instantly have recognized the martial nature of the wished-for confrontation in Scott's *The Lady of the Lake*. To read a novel was often to encounter dozens of passages of poetry. Many popular novelists besides Scott (James Fenimore Cooper was one) quoted lines of poetry as mottoes to chapters. Gansevoort

24. Melville's awareness of the Boston Common concessionaire and his Bunker Hill speeches (there was one in 1827 and perhaps others) and poem might explain how he formed the false impression (recorded in his 1850 essay on Hawthorne) that "Pop" Emmons was also the epic poet, the author of *The Fredoniad* (which in fact was by his brother Richard Emmons). Melville, however, was not alone in this confusion; Park Benjamin in the New York *New World* of July 18, 1840, wrote: "The Fredoniad is an epic poem—a great epic in five books or cantos, by the illustrious Emmons, some times called 'Pop'—a monosyllable worthy of his genius."

owned the edition of Scott published in Boston by Parker, and he and Herman were reading Cooper in 1837. Growing up when he did, Melville saw many bits of poetry, couplets, stanzas, in many prose books that he encountered, very often before seeing the whole poems. Any literate American in books, magazines, and newspapers had ready access to lavish quotations from old poetry and new poetry without necessarily being put to the expense of buying a recent book; for example, as explained below, Melville apparently knew something about an imaginary dialogue between Petrarch and Boccaccio, a discussion of Dante, in Walter Savage Landor's *Pentameron and Pentalogia* (1837) before the book was published in the United States. The convention of interspersing poetry into prose may well have influenced Melville's practice in *Mardi* of interrupting the narrator's prose with pieces of Yoomy's light verse.

In America in the 1830s and 1840s many studious young men availed themselves of John Todd's invention, the *Index Rerum,* already referred to, which transformed the venerable commonplace book into an instant retrieval system, the poor man's self-made index to "things," the equivalent of a personalized Internet browser. Henry David Thoreau used an *Index Rerum* at Harvard. More often, the *Index Rerum* was used by young men looking to improve themselves without the benefits of enrolling in a college, and often without the benefits of a mutual improvement association. The purpose was to guarantee that striking passages (on authorship, say) which one encountered in reading would not be lost but would be instantly available thereafter for use in public speeches or in any sort of writing. Just how dedicated Gansevoort was to self-improvement (and to making best use of his reading) is manifest in his surviving volumes of the *Index Rerum* for 1837 and 1840 (both of which contain notes made in other years).[25] No such evidence as an *Index Rerum* remains for Herman's self-improvement efforts. Some indications suggest that he was never as devotedly systematic as Gansevoort, but he may have made up in intensity of focus and capaciousness of memory what he seemed to lack in drudging application. We know from letters Gansevoort wrote the next younger brother, Allan, and the youngest, Tom, that he considered himself very much in the place of a father in recommending courses of study, so he undoubtedly encouraged Herman by passing him books as well as (something we have record of) newspapers: Gansevoort demonstrably sent Herman newspapers from New York when Herman was in or

25. Gansevoort Melville's surviving volumes of the *Index Rerum,* along with his letters and other documents quoted in this section, are in the Melville Collection of the Berkshire Athenaeum.

around Lansingburgh. Even though the strongest evidence for Herman's education and self-education in poetry comes in literary allusions in his writings, beginning in 1839, much can be learned by mustering evidence like that of Bloodgood's lectures.

Much can also be learned by examining Gansevoort's surviving volumes of his *Index Rerum*. In the course of 1837, at the start of which he and Herman were in the same house in Albany, and during the rest of which he was in New York while Herman was in Pittsfield, Gansevoort filled thirty-seven pages of the "Appendix" of his *Index Rerum* with quotations from his reading, including poetry in novels by Sir Water Scott. Pretty clearly, most of the books Gansevoort took notes on were borrowed from the Young Men's Association. He noted a passage on German language and poetry in Basil Hall's *Schloss Hainfield;* three stanzas of "Life" by "the Hon: R. H. Wilde, of Georgia"; and two lines on weariness ("And weary day, and weary week / And wearier month went lagging by—"). From Lord Chesterfield's *Letters to his Son* (which Herman also read about the same time), he copied down (on the topic of "Stooping to Conquer") two vulgarly applied lines from Dryden: "The prostrate lover, when he lowest lies, / But stoops to conquer & but kneels to rise." He also copied Chesterfield's two lines from Congreve on critics: "Rules for good writing, they with pains indite / Then show us what is bad, by what they write." Perhaps from Scott's *Fair Maid of Perth,* Gansevoort took a quotation from Dryden on country girls ("A country lip may have the velvet touch / Though she's no lady, she may please as much"); and from some unlocated source a quotation from Coleridge's "Genevieve" on "Woman's feelings" ("Hopes, and fears that kindle hope"). (He meant the poem about Genevieve called "Love.")

For many weeks in 1837 Gansevoort was enthralled by Washington Irving's *The Sketch-Book,* at least one copy of which was in the YMA library. Irving's book was exceptionally peppered with poetry, for he not only used poetic mottoes for chapters but also quoted poetry within many of the articles. He was such an open and enthusiastic quoter that at one point he thought in print about crowding some of his pages "with extracts from the older British poets" on one particular topic, burial customs. Irving gave poetic passages from Thomson; William Roscoe (the Liverpool poet whom Allan Melvill had met in 1818); Thomas Middleton (one on "the concealed comforts of a man / Lock'd up in woman's love"); William Cartwright; Cowper; Thomas Moore; John Fletcher; Roger L'Estrange; James I of Scotland; Henry Howard, Earl of Surrey; Marlowe; Drummond of Hawthornden; Shakespeare (*Cymbeline, Hamlet, As You Like It,* and *The Winter's Tale*); Robert Herrick (quoted half a dozen times);

Beaumont and Fletcher's *The Maid's Tragedy* (quoted more than once); "Corydon's Doleful Knell"; Thomas Stanley; and Christolero's Epigrams, by "T. B." (i.e., *Chrestolero: Seven Bookes of Epigrams,* by Thomas Bastard). He quoted from songs in *Poor Robin's Almanack* (1684), from Cartwright, George Withers, Sir John Suckling, Garrick on the Avon, Shakespeare's epitaph, Sir H. Wooton, and Chaucer ("Belle Dame sans Mercie"). Irving referred to the "monumental bronze" tint of Outalissi in Campbell's *Gertrude of Wyoming,* the "good Indian" to whom Melville casually alluded in his 1849 review of *The Oregon and California Trail,* "Mr Parkman's Tour." ("Wyoming" then applied only to a part of northeast Pennsylvania, the site of Campbell's poem, and another area in western New York State.) Irving's quotations from Herrick were substantial enough to work as a little anthology, and he quoted in full one famous Moore poem, "She is far from the land where her young hero sleeps." Strewing poetic tags through a work could be merely pedantic bragging, but writers like the antiquarian Irving intended the quoted passages to open remote periods of literature to their readers so that their awareness of their poetic heritage might be expanded. Gansevoort was impressed enough to write down in his *Index Rerum* some of the poetry quoted in *The Sketch-Book,* "The Wife" from Middleton and a passage from Cowper on the pleasures of rural domestic life. Gansevoort very likely passed *The Sketch-Book* on to Herman. Whenever he got hold of it, Herman fell under its spell. This fact has been obscured by the vehemence of his essay on Hawthorne's *Mosses from an Old Manse,* written in August 1850, where he scorned Irving as merely imitative, content to be the "American Goldsmith."[26] By that time Melville had already plundered *The Sketch-Book* for *Redburn;* in the mid-1850s he paid it the high homage of loving imitation in "The Paradise of Bachelors and the Tartarus of Maids" (1855); and later in life he wrote a poem, "Rip Van Winkle's Lilac," on the long-classic piece in *The Sketch-Book.* Irving helped teach Melville to write prose, but he also exposed him to dozens of lines of poetry, and probably from a wider range of English poets than he had yet encountered elsewhere.

In 1837, probably using the copy listed in the Young Men's Association catalogue of that year, Gansevoort worked through the second edition of J. H. Dwyer's *An Essay on Elocution; with Elucidatory Passages from Various Authors to which are added Remarks on Reading Prose and Verse, with Suggestions to Instructors of the Art* (New York: G. & C. Carville, & E. Bliss, 1828). Gansevoort made notes on the "Character of a Libertine," on Lord Chatham, on Charles Phillips's praise of his late friend John Philpot Curran in a

---

26. The *Mosses* essay is collected in the NN *Piazza Tales* volume, pp. 239–53.

speech at Cheltenham in 1819 to the Gloucester Missionary Society, and on Phillips's after-dinner remarks on Irish gratitude toward the United States. Already, long before 1843, when he became famous as a Repealer (demanding the repeal of the 1800 Act of Union between England—and Scotland—and Ireland, as the United Kingdom), Gansevoort was saturating himself in stories of heroic Irishmen who had resisted Union. Herman would have found in Dwyer some useful advice as a reader of poetry and as a teacher. In "Remarks on Reading Prose and Verse" (that is, on reading aloud) Dwyer offered the sensible advice that "reading and speaking are precisely the same thing, save that in reciting we have a greater intimacy with the subject, and are enabled to give a little more energy and action. The tones, emphasis, accent, and sense, are the same, whether we speak or read." Far from inculcating artificial techniques of declamation, Dwyer coolly advised: "The material difference between reading prose and rhyming verse, rests in giving more time between each word and sentence in verse than in prose; reading with very little reference to the jingle, or rhyme, but with great attention to the sense; using the same inflections as in prose, and rather avoiding than encouraging that measured tone, improperly called musical; for if the harmony of that author's verse, to whose sense we do justice, do not distinctly speak for itself, his claims to poetry must rest on a very slight foundation indeed."

Breaking down his topic for the benefit of teachers as much as for students, Dwyer listed these aspects of elocution: *Articulation; Accent; Emphasis* (a topic he exemplified by poetic passages from Joseph Addison's *Cato* and Portia's "quality of mercy" speech from *The Merchant of Venice*); *Pronunciation; Climax* (exemplified by passages from *The Tempest*, James Thomson, W. W. Dimond, and *Hamlet*); *Suspension* (a bit of Edward Young's *The Revenge*, and Portia on mercy); *Parenthesis* (John Home's *Douglas*, Addison's *Cato*, and the "long farewell to all my greatness!" from the collaborative *Henry VIII*); *Antithesis; Monotony*, or *Monotone* (the "to be or not to be" soliloquy from *Hamlet*, but commencing late, at "For who would bear the whips and scorns o' the time" [*sic*], and "Satan exalted sat" from the opening of book 2 of Milton's *Paradise Lost*—the passage illustrated in Melville's print that hung in the dining room at Arrowhead during his occupancy and for decades afterward); *Modulation* (two pages from book 4 of *Paradise Lost*, more than three pages from Dryden's *Alexander's Feast*, a page from Campbell's "Hohenlinden," and almost three pages from William Collins's *The Passions*); *Enumeration* or *Amplification* (four lines from Thomson's *The Seasons* and Othello's "Farewell" speech); *Pauses* (bits from *King Lear* and *Othello*); *Irony* (bits from *Othello* and *The Merchant of Venice*); *Alliteration* (snippets from Byron's *Childe Harold's Pilgrimage*, cantos 2 and 3);

Interrogation; Iteration or *Repetition*, by some called *Echo* (a line from *Othello* and the "With thee conversing" passage from book 4 of *Paradise Lost*); *Personation* (defined as "the representation by a single reader or speaker of the words, manner, and actions of one person, or of many individuals, as if he or they were themselves reading or speaking; in effect 'giving form to fancy, and embodying thought'" and exemplified by a long passage from canto 6 of Scott's *Marmion,* Hotspur's popinjay speech from *Henry IV, Part 1,* Mercutio's Queen Mab speech from *Romeo and Juliet* [cautiously stopping short of the lines about teaching maids good carriage], Jaques' "seven ages" speech from *As You Like It,* and Campbell's "Lochiel's Warning"); *Metaphor* (a passage from John Home, newly famous for being quoted in chapter 28 of Scott's *Woodstock,* and a line from Campbell's *Pleasures of Hope,* part 1); *Comparison* (bits from Goldsmith's *The Deserted Village* and book 3 of *Fingal*); *Personification* or *Prosopopoeia* (book 5 of *Paradise Lost* ["These are thy glorious works"]); *Apostrophe;* and *Action.* Dwyer also quoted several prose passages in exemplifying these topics.

Dwyer thus included several soliloquies and other extended purple passages suitable for memorizing, though he did not describe them that way. Curiously, he did not instruct teachers or students as to the best ways of using the "Poetic Pieces" he appended at the end of the book, following the samples of oratory that caught Gansevoort's eye. These poems included S. Osborne's "Time"; Charles Woolf's "The Burial of Sir John Moore" (listed in the table of contents as by "Anonymous"); Ambrose Philips's "Winter at Copenhagen"; and Scott's "The Interview between Fitzjames and the Lady of the Lake." Then followed several selections from Campbell: "The Sacking of Prague," "The Pilot," "The Soldier of Hope," "On Woman," "The Sceptic," "The Rose of the Wilderness," "The Last Man," and "The Rainbow." From N. P. Willis (who was to become a friend of Gansevoort's, and then of Herman's) he included "The Sacrifice of Abraham." Several pieces from Lord Byron followed: "Night before and Battle of Waterloo," "Venice," "Rome," "The Ocean," "Greece," and "The Corse." Then came Moore's "Paradise and the Peri" and an exercise in maudlinity, Dimond's "The Sailor Boy's Dream." The author identifications, notably, were made only in a "Contents" page at the back of the book, not along with each of the "Poetic Pieces." The function of the selections in teaching elocution was valued over acknowledgment of authorship; what counted was not who wrote a passage but what a teacher could do with it. So far, it has not been proven that Herman ever held Dwyer's book, but Gansevoort used it, and chances are that in 1837 or later Herman had occasion to read it as a student, even if an autodidact, and as a teacher. Evidence that the family knew poems quoted by Dwyer may survive fortuitously, as in Melville's reference to Thomson's *The Seasons* in *Redburn* or Augusta's quotation from it in her record of 1852 excursions discovered in 1983.

Herman, like Gansevoort, earnestly worked to improve his skill in elocution by becoming a debater. Evidence is strong that young men's debates were laced with quotations from poetry, as were surviving orations from this time when oratory was an integral part of belles lettres. During his term at the Albany Academy between September 1836 and March 1837 Herman joined the Ciceronian Debating Society. His behavior there and in the successor organization, the Philo Logos Society, earned him a public reprimand by "R." in the Albany *Microscope* on April 15, 1837, two months before he left Albany to manage his uncle's farm near Pittsfield. Returning early in 1838, after teaching in the Berkshires in the fall, Melville convened the inactive Philo Logos Society at a meeting in which he was elected president. Controversy over the validity of the election and his behavior in the previous year was played out in the *Microscope* in what is now known as the "Philo Logos Letters."[27] How serious these letters were, how much they are exercises in vituperation, in imitation of British political philippics, is not clear. However, they demonstrate that as a debater and as a polemicist Melville did indeed gain additional exposure to poetry, even though no poetic tags have been identified in his own letters to the *Microscope*. In his letter in April 1837 "R." had lamented the difficulty of getting "rid" of Melville: "He, like a wary pettifogger, never considers 'this side right, and that stark naught,' or in other words, has no fixed principles." The allusion is to a popular poem (printed in the Quebec *Gazette* of November 9, 1775, for example, and sometimes casually attributed to Benjamin Franklin) on "Paper," built on the analogy of blank paper and tabula rasa, where these lines occur: "The retail Politician's anxious thought / Deems *this* side always right, and *that* stark naught." On March 10, 1838, Charles Van Loon, the deposed president of the Philo Logos Society, repeated R.'s epithet "Ciceronian baboon" and accused Melville of playing "fantastic tricks" (words from *Measure for Measure,* a passage from which was on Gansevoort's mind as he was dying in London in 1846). Van Loon called Herman's "abusive language" in a February 28 letter to the *Microscope* "the raving of an unmasked hypocrite, the 'wincing, of a gall'd jade'" (*Hamlet*) and announced himself ready to punish Melville by lashing the "rascal naked through the world" (*Othello*). "To Herman Melville—Sir,—," Van Loon continued in the March 31 *Microscope,* "the sensible Hudibras has well observed, that, there is no kind

27. See *Correspondence,* pp. 10–19 and 551–64.

of argument like matter of fact" (*Hudibras,* 2.3.192). On April 7, attacking Melville for convening the special meeting at which Melville was elected president, Van Loon declared (carelessly, if we are to believe "Americus" in the same issue of the *Microscope*), "there is something rotten about Denmark." In the April 14 *Microscope* Van Loon had the last word: "[A]lthough silly prejudice may condemn me for publishing in the Microscope, I shall enjoy my 'exceeding great reward'"—the phrase from Genesis 15:1 given new currency by Coleridge's assertion in the 1797 preface that poetry is its own exceeding great reward. All Melville's early life poetry was, as the "Philo Logos Letters" show, inescapable in public speech, especially formal speech, and inescapable in print—not just in magazines and newspapers and in books of poetry but in many other sorts of books, including the newly popular literary gift-books or annuals.

While he taught school near Pittsfield in late 1837 and the first weeks of 1838, Herman would have used poetry as a tool for teaching elocution and literary devices, even if he did not "teach" poetry in the modern sense. From mid-November 1838 through the first few days of April 1839 Herman was back in school, enrolled at the Lansingburgh Academy, his mother having moved her family to Lansingburgh, on the east side of the Hudson, just north of Troy, in May 1838. While Herman was at the Lansingburgh Academy, Gansevoort was also there (after a period in New York City), bedridden, so that Herman had to carry him from bed to fireplace, but surrounded by books which he read and abstracted into the first, second, and then third volumes of his *Index Rerum.* Herman was casually or purposefully exposed to all the books Gansevoort was reading and many he had been reading. There in February 1839, and probably earlier in Albany, Herman was expected to write verse for Valentine's Day, for a youth of either sex was required to strive for proficiency if not high originality in the composition of light verse. The recorded family comment comes late but applies to earlier years: on February 15, 1847, in Lansingburgh Helen wrote to her younger sister Augusta, who was away in Albany: "We received Fanny's letter yesterday, and also Kate's Valentine written by the same hand & Pen. What geese, Cuyler [Van Vechten, an Albany cousin] & Fanny [the youngest of the Melville sisters] were to send note paper with his own initials stamped thereon, and then get it written in such a well-known hand.—We opened one directed to Herman [away on a trip to Washington], quite a pretty one, from some fair lady in the village" (NYPL-GL). A young man would not only write facile, flirtatious poetry but would also read aloud seductive new poems from England. William H. Gilman (p. 104) recorded an unconfirmed report that Herman used poems by Tennyson in a youthful courtship on the riverbank at Lansingburgh—in the summer of 1838, possibly, or the spring of 1839 or 1840.

Even though he was taking the course that was to prepare him as a surveyor on the Erie Canal, Herman was required to write an original composition and to "declaim" every two weeks, a stipulation spelled out in the 1839 Catalogue of the Lansingburgh Academy (discovered by Dennis Marnon in 2005). He may have been able to consult a copy of Dwyer's *Elocution,* although the copy Gansevoort had read in 1837 may have been the YMA's. In the Catalogue of the Lansingburgh Academy the textbooks for rhetoric are Lord Kames's *Elements of Criticism,* Hugh Blair's *Lectures on Rhetoric and Belles Lettres,* and Samuel P. Newman's *A Practical System of Rhetorick, or The Principles and Rules of Style, Inferred from Examples of Writing; to which is added a Historical Dissertation on English Style,* all three in unspecified American reprints. The text by Newman, a professor of rhetoric at Bowdoin College, was pedestrian in comparison to the two by the Scots, and Herman would not willingly have settled for using it if there was a choice, despite the passages of literature by Byron, Goldsmith, Hemans, Irving, Scott, Butler, Milton, Mark Akenside, Thomson, Cowper, Shakespeare, and extensive use of *The Sketch-Book.* (Newman also quoted Daniel Webster's Bunker Hill address more than once—probably an oration already familiar to Herman.) Blair in his *Lectures* was very much a "D.D." ("One of the Ministers of the High Church," said the title page on the 1817 edition published in New York City by Evert Duyckinck, the father of Melville's editorial friend of the same name) and a fervent Scottish nationalist. Blair was particularly good in providing an introduction to pastoral poetry, quoting English translations of Virgil's "Eclogues" (by Thomas Warton, in particular). Blair's judgments were self-assured: he seconded Dr. Johnson's praise of Thomson; Blair himself praised Thomas Parnell's "The Hermit" (a poem whose popularity requires a readjustment of values in the twenty-first century, being singularly apt to disturb modern sensibilities); he praised Milton's "Il Penseroso"; but his religious and grammarian's scruples spoiled Shakespeare for him. His lectures on epic poetry made a good guide to classic epics as well as later examples, among them Tasso's *Jerusalem,* Camoëns's *Lusiad,* Fénelon's *Telemachus,* Voltaire's *Henriade,* and Milton's *Paradise Lost.* Blair had already published his *A Critical Dissertation on the Poems of Ossian, the Son of Fingal* (1763), and spoke here of the works of Ossian as abounding "with examples of the sublime" and as manifesting the mastery of poetic description.

The great textbook at the Lansingburgh Academy was Lord Kames's *Elements of Criticism,* a remarkable introduction to aesthetic issues that

relied for illustrations upon hundreds of brief quotations mainly from clas-
sical and from British poetry. Since his literary illustrations were chosen to
make specific rhetorical points, attention was directed to them sharply—
out of context, but in such a way that they would be remembered when
encountered again in context. These passages from literature were used
to exemplify both lofty aesthetic concepts and rough-and-ready problems
in such matters as personification, hyperbole, metaphor, and other figures
of speech, as well as practical advice on how to order material effectively.
Anyone using this text was introduced to many characters of Shakespeare
(notably Othello and Hotspur) in specific problematical situations; to
much praise of *Fingal* (including an endorsement of Blair's "delicious mor-
sel of criticism," his book on Ossian); to much Pope, particularly *The Rape
of the Lock* (often mined for bad examples); Butler's *Hudibras;* Edmund
Waller; Cowley; Milton's *Paradise Lost;* Battista Guarini's *Pastor Fido* (*The
Faithful Shepherd,* which Melville bought long afterward in the 1647 Rich-
ard Fanshawe translation); Thomson's *Seasons;* and many quotations from
Congreve's *The Mourning Bride.* Kames offered serious disquisitions on
many topics, including versification, and in a chapter on "Narration and
Description" gave wise advice about starting an epic modestly (as Melville
was to do in *Clarel*). Kames's *Elements of Criticism* was a very great intro-
duction to poetry. To read Kames was to take a master's class in theoretical
poetics and the practical reading of poetry. The exposure to such critical
strictures, while it did not make Melville a poet in his teens and twenties,
may have provided materials for the foundation on which he was later to
construct his poetics and his artistic credo.

One slight reason for thinking that Melville had Kames as a text rather
than Newman or Blair is his own quoting from *The Mourning Bride* just after
he left the academy. In his "Fragments from a Writing Desk" (printed in
the Lansingburgh *Democratic Press* in May 1839) Melville wrote allusively,
just as his models did. In the "Fragments" Melville quoted Chesterfield's
Letters, which he and Gansevoort had shared, as well as poetic passages
from Campbell's "The Pleasures of Hope" (ten lines!), from Shakespeare's
Hamlet and *Romeo and Juliet,* from Congreve's *The Mourning Bride,* Byron's
Childe Harold's Pilgrimage, Milton's "L'Allegro," Akenside's *The Pleasures of
Imagination,* and the "gentle" Coleridge's "Genevieve." (Melville would
have seen in the March 1836 *Zodiac* John Wilson's praise of "Genevieve" as
a poem "known to all readers of poetry.") In his own voice (or Ishmael's)
Melville claims in *Moby-Dick* (chap. 42) that he had not read "The Rime
of the Ancient Mariner" when he first experienced a profound mystical
thrill at the sight of an albatross: "For neither had I then read the Rhyme,
nor knew the bird to be an albatross. Yet, in saying this, I do but indirectly

burnish a little brighter the noble merit of the poem and the poet." He certainly knew some of Coleridge's poetry early in life. Failing to gain a job on the Erie Canal, Melville left on June 1, 1839, for New York City and Liverpool. After his voyage to Liverpool, Melville would have taught with poetry again in the fall at Greenbush, across the river from Albany, then again in the spring of 1840 at Brunswick, near Lansingburgh, and somewhere near Lansingburgh, yet again, for a short time in the late summer and early fall of 1840, before he left for New York City.

Together or apart, Gansevoort shared poems with his younger brothers.[28] In a letter from Lansingburgh on June 26, 1841, to Allan in New York City, Gansevoort quoted Burns's "Elegy on Captain Matthew Henderson," with "Robin" instead of the usual "Matthew": "If thou art staunch without a stain, / Like the unchanging blue, man, / He was a kinsman o' thy ain / For Robin was *a true man*." From Bridgeport on September 2, 1842, Gansevoort wrote Allan, identifying himself with "Old Ironsides," the ship in the most famous poem by Oliver Wendell Holmes, who had satirized their heroic paternal grandfather in "The Last Leaf": "As for your amiable brother, his old hulk seems to be so much shattered that it will not bear refitting—and yet the governing spirit of that old hulk is determined as ever to 'Set every threadbare sail, and give her / To the GOD of storms, the battle and the gale.'" Gansevoort must have sent similar messages to Herman when he sent newspapers from New York City to Herman in or around Lansingburgh, probably including some of the papers he made note of in his *Index Rerum*.

It is clear from his notes that throughout 1840 while Gansevoort Melville was pursuing his legal studies (despite being tempted by the possibilities of becoming a political orator) he was also still weighing an alternative route to fame, a literary career. Some of his entries recorded poetry and popular songs. In 1840 he cross-referenced his now lost *Index Rerum* (3.106): "Anacreon, rivalled by Willis." In March or later he noted an article on "The English Language" in that month's *Knickerbocker Magazine*. On April 9 or later he copied a sonnet, "A poetical fragment—N Yk Courier & Enquirer April 9, 1840, being a satire on Benj F. Butler, now District Attorney of the Southern District of N Yk occasioned by his conspicuous opposition to the registry law lately passed." Perhaps in early September he copied part of a poem addressed to "Nat Willis" by "Straws," in the New Orleans *Picayune*:

---

28. Gansevoort Melville's letters and other documents quoted in this paragraph and the following one are transcribed from the originals in the Melville Collection of the Berkshire Athenaeum.

"The curse of Genus"
Oh, Nat! it's true vot people says
About "the curse of genus?",
For me I'm cursin' all the time,
In a vay vot's wery heinous! . . .
For ev'ry pop'lar genus now
Is of the genus loafer.

On the last two lines Gansevoort commented: "Popular geniuses nowa-days." Perhaps in September he copied from that month's *Ladies Companion* lines from Rufus Dawes's poem "Lift Your Hearts &c." (Dawes [1803–59] was a justice on the Massachusetts Supreme Court, under Lemuel Shaw, and a novelist and a poet—a model as a man with a legal and a literary career.) Around September Gansevoort copied lines by Mrs. Lydia H. Sigourney, "On Parting with a Pupil." From *Brother Jonathan* of September 12, 1840, Gansevoort copied part of a poem on "The Deluge" (possibly Mary Ann Carter's 1838 *The Deluge, the General Resurrection, and Other Poems*). While at Galway, New York, after September 19 Gansevoort Melville copied "The Schwitzers War Song" from *Brother Jonathan*. Perhaps this was "War-Song of the Royal Edinburgh Light Dragoons," in which Sir Walter Scott bitterly criticized the Swiss for not avenging the Swiss Guards slaughtered in the August 1792 attack on the Tuileries ("Switzers," however spelled, being the term familiar from *Hamlet*). Gansevoort also copied part of a song, "The Next Presidency," from the New York *Herald* of September 22. On September 25 from Galway he wrote his brother Allan: "The news from Maine looks rather lowering, & seems to discourage our friends in this part of the country: 'But shall we go mourn for that, my dear / But shall we go mourn for that?' "—a line Sir Walter Scott copied into his journal from Joanna Baillie's *Orra*.

Once he sailed on a whaler in 1841, Herman Melville found that almost all sailors knew many hymns (which could be sung straight or parodied) and many popular songs (in this era, it bears repeating, when honored poets often wrote popular songs). His casual quoting of Allan Cunningham's "A Wet Sheet and a Flowing Sea" in *The Confidence-Man* (chap. 22), for instance, may indicate a long knowledge of this and other pieces in *Poems of Scotland*. Probably many sailors had left home knowing poems which they could recite. Perhaps a few carried printed poetry they could read, memorize, and lend to any other sailors they found to be literary-minded, but whale-ship libraries (in those ships that had libraries at all) were not stocked with poetry, judging from the inventory of the books taken aboard the *Charles and Henry*, Melville's third whaler

(Heflin, pp. 11–17). The library on the *United States* did contain poetry, notably William Cullen Bryant's 1840 *Selections from American Poets,* where more than seventy-five poets were sampled, including the compiler. Of the seventy-eight poets represented in Bryant's anthology, only a few are poets Melville is known to have read. The library on the *United States* may well have contained poetic dramas, judging from the books Melville gives the *Neversink* in *White-Jacket* (chap. 41): "some odd volumes of plays, each of which was a precious casket of jewels of good things, shaming the trash nowadays passed off for dramas, containing 'The Jew of Malta,' 'Old Fortunatus,' 'The City Madam,' 'Volpone,' 'The Alchymist,' and other glorious old dramas of the age of Marlow and Johnson, and that literary Damon and Pythias, the magnificent, mellow old Beaumont and Fletcher."

While at sea Melville may well have read some of Richard Emmons's American epic, *The Fredoniad.* In the South Pacific on November 27, 1843, the *United States,* with Melville aboard, hoisted its colors at half mast in memory of "the late Commodore Porter," only recently dead, and at noon fired thirteen minute guns in tribute to his memory. This would have been the time for someone to produce the four-volume *The Fredoniad: or, Independence Preserved. An Epick Poem of the Late War of 1812,* and turn to canto 11, "Cruise of Captain Porter," and especially the exalted conclusion of canto 12, "Porter's Defence of the Essex." Set there, in the stretch of the Pacific the *United States* was then sailing, this passage depicts Fredonia herself streaming down the heavens and calling bright angels down with her trumpet as she cries: "Earth! list to the decree! Porter shall live, / Whilst Fame immortal, has a breath to give!" In the right mood, driven to a temporary rhetorical excess of patriotism, a literary nationalist among the tars might have sounded much like the Virginian vacationing in Vermont in Melville's essay on Hawthorne's *Mosses from an Old Manse.* There the "Virginian" declares that Americans should "first praise mediocrity even," in her own poets, before praising merit in foreigners: "I was much pleased with a hot-headed Carolina cousin of mine, who once said,—'If there were no other American to stand by, in Literature,— why, then, I would stand by Pop Emmons and his 'Fredoniad,' and till a better epic came along, swear it was not very far behind the Iliad.' Take away the words, and in spirit he was sound." Melville did not often praise mediocrity, but his chauvinism was at its most intense point because of the grandeur of what he was writing, *Moby-Dick,* and the war which guaranteed the independence of the United States was still very close. Others could rise in at least tongue-in-cheek praise of Emmons, among them Park Benjamin, quoted earlier.

William Falconer's *The Shipwreck* (1762) might have been circulated aboard the *United States,* for in chapter 65 of *White-Jacket* Melville has Jack Chase declare that the "'Shipwreck' will never founder, though he himself [the author], poor fellow, was lost at sea in the Aurora frigate." Melville quotes a bit of it in "Extracts" in *Moby-Dick,* and recalls it in "Off Cape Colonna," first published in *Timoleon.* Melville's continuing interest in Falconer, after 1862 if not much earlier, was heightened by a passage in Thomas Moore's biography in which Byron explained his own preferences among sea-poets: "In what does the infinite superiority of 'Falconer's Shipwreck' over all other shipwrecks consist? In his admirable application of the terms of his art; in a poet-sailor's description of the sailor's fate." In *White-Jacket* Melville casually alludes to Byron's verses on his cousin Peter Parker, the ruthless raider of the Chesapeake: "There is a tear for all who die, / A mourner o'er the humblest grave" (chap. 52). By the time he returned from the Pacific in 1844 Melville knew many poems by Scott, Byron, and others that only the most learned Romantic specialist knows today. *Hudibras* had figured in a Philo Logos letter, and in 1846 as he wrote *Omoo,* he recalled the sound of *Hudibras* being recited in the South Seas. Into chapter 46 of *Omoo* Melville worked two provocatively appropriate lines from Pope's epistle "To a Lady," in the wrong order: "A sad good Christian at the heart— / A very heathen in the carnal part." In chapter 65 of *White-Jacket,* Jack Chase, the idolator of Camoëns, honors the translator Mickle as himself a poet, deducing from one of Scott's own footnotes that Mickle's ballad of Cumnor Hall "gave Sir Walter Scott the hint of Kenilworth." Few admirers of Camoëns were devoted enough to make pilgrimages to remote waters and shores he described in the *Lusiad,* but by the 1840s several poets, including Felicia Hemans, had addressed poems of praise to Camoëns. Many of the British critics of the previous century (such as Hugh Blair) and poets of Melville's youth became ardent admirers of Camoëns through Mickle's translation or in the original Portuguese. (In Melville's time neoclassic treatment still governed epic discourse, as is clear in the translations selected for Melville's Harper's Classical Library, which he purchased early in 1849 [Sealts, no. 147]. The Renaissance era of translation that had begun with Chapman and merged into the neoclassical translations of Dryden, Pope, and others was still highly regarded among professional critics and poets throughout the first half of the nineteenth century.)

Home from the Pacific, Melville was exposed again to a great deal of poetry in the newspapers and magazines as well as books of poetry and anthologies. His brother Allan had saved many newspapers containing Gansevoort's speeches, so Melville may have seen the great Jackson Day speech of March 15, 1844, in which Gansevoort had quoted Halleck's "Alnwick Castle" ("And died, the sword in his red hand, / On the holiest spot of that blessed land" ["mailed hand," he may have said]). Gansevoort also quoted Joseph Rodman Drake's "The American Flag" ("Flag of the free heart's only home, / By angel hands to valor given, / Thy stars have lit the welkin dome, / And all thy hues were born in Heaven"). He quoted Halleck's "beautiful lines to the memory of Burns," followed by two passages from Byron's *Marino Faliero*.[29] Winding up his speech, Gansevoort appealed for unity in words from Whittier's "Ritner" on "Forgetting the feuds and the strife of past time" and "Counting coldness, injustice, and silence a crime." All of these passages were probably equally familiar to both Gansevoort and Herman.

After late 1847, when the Melvilles moved to New York City (mother, four daughters, Herman and his bride, Elizabeth Shaw, and Allan and his bride, Sophia Thurston), Melville began to have access to private and public libraries, but he still could encounter poetry in the household, for at any time two, three, or more of the young women kept commonplace books into which they copied poems. Particular poems available in the Melville household, known by others in the family if not Melville himself, are cited here to show the pervasive availability of poetry—whether great, good, indifferent, or downright wretched. As elsewhere in this section, the listing of poems is at times minute, but even the poems his late brother Gansevoort had noted in his *Index Rerum* or his sister Augusta now copied into her commonplace book, *Orient Pearls at Random Strung,* are only representative. Some of Gansevoort's volumes of *Index Rerum* are lost, as are the commonplace books of Melville's wife and his sister Catherine, and probably of his other sisters as well. Probably around 1842, after eight or nine years of writing weekly compositions, Frances (Fanny) Melville, the youngest sister, wrote in "Myself" that "nothing as the poet truly says, 'is so bad as getting familiar with sorrow'"—the poet being the English songwriter Thomas Haynes Bayly (1797–1839) and the poem the look-on-the-bright-side "Never Look Sad," not Melville's own view of life. In early 1848 the first poem that his sister Augusta copied into her *Orient Pearls* was from "A Persian Song of Hafiz,"[30] by the linguist admired

29. See Parker 1996, pp. 320–21, where I had not identified this poetry as by Byron.

30. Fanny Melville's "Myself" and Augusta Melville's *Orient Pearls* are among the "Augusta Papers" discovered in 1983—those of Melville's sister Augusta, now in NYPL-GL. Other poems Augusta entered into her book include "The Rights of Women" (1849, by Mrs. E. Little—"'The rights of women,' what are they? / The right to labor and to pray; / The right to watch while others sleep, / The right o'er others' woes to weep; / The right to succor in distress"); "When I am Old" ("Copied from Fanny's book"); "The

by Melville, Sir William Jones (1746–94); Herman learned enough about Hafiz to feel certain that William Davenant had caught "a fine Persian tone" in a "Song" ("The Lark Now Leaves").[31]

In late 1847 and 1848 Melville was working too hard on *Mardi* to pay full attention to the mutual admiration society of American literary chauvinists constituted by Evert Duyckinck and Cornelius Mathews and a few others. A problem for chest-beating nationalists like Mathews was that they were hopelessly Anglophiliac, would-be literary chauvinists trapped as hapless idolators of almost all things British and poetic. Mathews and Duyckinck had been devoted advocates of the poetry of Elizabeth Barrett since one or the other of them reviewed her *The Seraphim, and Other Poems* (1838) in the February 1841 issue of their magazine, *Arcturus*. In December of that year Cornelius Mathews began a correspondence with her with a fan letter along with the February magazine. She replied in kind, with letters and copies of her works, some in her own hand, and hid her amusement in 1842 after the egregious Mathews appointed himself to what she called "the office of *trustee for the further extension of my reputation in America*." Year by year Barrett and Mathews both adeptly played the half-cynical, half-sincere game of reciprocity, here scratching a shoulder, there massaging a neck. Mathews was privileged early in 1847 to have a

---

Love of Later Years" (1849, "Copied from Lizzie's book"); "We are Growing Old" (1849, by the blind poet of Stranolar, Ireland, Frances Browne, 1816–79); "I Think of Thee in the Night" (1850, by T. K. Hervey, 1799–1859); "The Virgin's Grave" (1850, by William Gilmore Simms); "The Crown of Amaranth" (1851, by "L. S."—Lydia Sigourney); "Lines Written on Leaving New Rochelle" (1851, by Joseph Rodman Drake—just as Allan Melville's brother-in-law Richard Lathers was building an Italianate villa there); "And his victor crown of amaranth, / Shall never fade away" (1851, a reference to 1 Peter 5:4); "Jesus of Nazareth passeth by" (1851, by Lydia H. Sigourney, a reference to Luke 18:37); "Woman's Faith" (1851; probably Sir Walter Scott's "The Truth of Woman," which begins "Woman's faith, and woman's trust"); "Sadly we Mourn Each Vanished Grace" (1851, by Barry Cornwall); "My Last Resting Place" (1851, by A. D. V. S.); "Yield Not to Despair" (1851, by the English physician Nathaniel Cotton, 1705–88, from "The Fireside"); and "To be Resigned when Ills Betide" (1852, also by Cotton). Inside the front cover of her commonplace book Augusta pasted a newspaper printing of Longfellow's "Endymion," which she dated September 19, 1853, the day of George Griggs's engagement to her sister Helen. The women in his household may have shared very few of their favorite poems with the author in their midst, but into the house came the sources of the poems they copied into their "books," and the commonplace books themselves were cherished for many years.

31. Melville commented that this poem was "Hafiz Englished," and added: "Ah, Will was a trump." I examined Melville's copy of Davenant's *Works* (London: Printed by T. N. for Henry Herringman, 1673; Sealts, no. 176) at the Howard S. Mott Bookstore in Sheffield, Massachusetts, on June 8, 1990.

letter from Pisa in which the poet informed him of her marriage and her change "from the long seclusion in one room, to liberty and Italy's sun-shine"; duped by Anglophilia, he imprudently shared it with an English confidence man two years later (Powell, p. 150).

It is not known when Melville first became friends with Henry T. Tuckerman, the essayist and poet, but it was probably well before they both attended Anne Lynch's Valentine's Day party in 1848. They may have met at the house on Bond Street of the great obstetrician and genial repository of all there was to know about Manhattan, Dr. John W. Francis. Melville had been on good terms with Dr. Francis since September 22, 1847, at the latest, when the doctor was a guest at Allan Melville's wedding to a Bond Street girl, Sophia Thurston. Melville considered Dr. Francis an intimate friend all through the 1850s, a time when Dr. Francis in public addresses and writing spoke admiringly of Melville and Tuckerman in the same breath. Both men were regulars at Dr. Francis's Sunday evenings, whenever Melville and Tuckerman were in New York. By January 1850 and again in 1852 Tuckerman praised Melville's narrative powers in *Typee*. Tuckerman in person showed toughness of mind that rarely manifested itself in his prose, so Melville may well have read Tuckerman's essays, and even some of his poems, in a way more kindly than some of them merited. A man who longed to see Italy himself, Melville seems to have read Tuck-erman's *Sicily* in the 1839 text (*Isabel, or Sicily a Pilgrimage*), for the section on Syracuse is the only source yet identified for his treatment of the Are-thusa fountain in *Moby-Dick*. In all likelihood Melville looked through Tuckerman's *Thoughts on the Poets* (1846)—more than two dozen poets, several of the eighteenth-century British poets Melville had known since childhood, all of the great Romantic poets as well as Campbell, Samuel Rogers, Hemans, two Italians (Petrarch and Alfieri), the younger English poets Tennyson and Elizabeth Barrett, and two Americans (Joseph Rod-man Drake and Bryant). For the most part, Tuckerman was a friendly guide over familiar poetic territory, but it was perhaps through him that Melville developed an intense interest in Alfieri. (Melville had a nodding personal acquaintance with William Cullen Bryant, who had fiercely resented Gansevoort Melville because he had helped gain the nomination for Polk in 1844; later Melville's wife, like Bryant a member of the Uni-tarian All Souls Church, felt entirely free to call at the Bryant house to see the Bryants' visitor, Orville Dewey.)

Poetry was not just something that eminent foreigners and eminent American citizens wrote. Many people the Melvilles knew wrote and published—and not just Augusta's Miss Woodbridge. Everyone might write valentines and have valentines addressed to them in youth, and poetry about people they knew, and even about family members, could be printed. In 1848 Anne Lynch assigned young Bayard Taylor the task of writing a public valentine to Herman Melville as well as to several other celebrities, and N. P. Willis (that "rival of Anacreon," as Gansevoort had noted) promptly published the results in his *Home Journal*. Herman, unlike most people, became the subject of poetry other than valentines. On February 8, 1847, Maria Melville relayed to Augusta news from Washington: "Herman writes that he was shewn a very pretty volume of Poetry by Mr W E Chan[n]ing of Boston they are now published for the first time, one is called the 'The Island of Nukeheva.' It is poetically descriptive of Tipee and is very pretty" (Parker 1996, p. 487). This poem (written after Ellery Channing and Henry David Thoreau had shared their ideas about *Typee,* if not sharing a single copy) begins:

> It is upon the far-off deep South Seas,
> The island Nukuheva, its degrees
> In vain—I may not reckon, but the bold
> Adventurous Melville there by chance was rolled,
> And for four months in its delights did dwell,
> And of this Island writ what I may tell.
> So far away, it is a Paradise.

In July 1850 the London *Town and Country Miscellany* printed this stanza of Albert Smith's "A Dream of the Grand Exposition": "Quite hard at work, Herman (I don't mean the German / Who conjures, but Melville the sailor—the sailor) / Was showing a few how a Typee ragout / Could be made from the crew of a whaler—a whaler." In the November 16, 1850, *Literary World* the Duyckincks reprinted H. W. Parker's "Berkshire Valley, Mass." from the Dansville, New York, *Herald,* dated September 1850. The poem pays tribute to summer visitors in the Berkshires, comparing them to migratory birds. After Holmes ("Here he has built his summer nest") comes Melville: "And he is here whose plumage smiles / With every changing rainbow hue, / And who has brought from tropic isles / The spiciest fruits that ever grew." The next stanzas describe Hawthorne, Fanny Kemble Butler, and Catharine Sedgwick. Until the white whale began to wash her aside, Fayaway was the character who long dominated the imagination of poets, as in book II of *The Vestics,* by "Eurymachus" (the London *Le Follet,* September 1, 1859), where "Hermann Melville's pretty Fayaway, / Au naturelle" is described as disporting herself "upon the green, / Devoid of corset, skirts, or crinoline." Later poems inspired by Melville or written directly to him range from Robert Buchanan's high tribute to both Fayaway and the white whale in his poem on Whitman, "Socrates in Camden" (1885), to W. Henry Canoll's earnest "Melville" (1886), and Buchanan's expanded tribute, *The Outcast* (1891).

Melville knew many poems written by his personal friends such as Nathaniel Parker Willis as well as poems in which some of his acquaintances figured, notably James Russell Lowell's *A Fable for Critics* (1848), which satirized Evert Duyckinck and Cornelius Mathews. Despite Melville's growing popularity as a subject for poetry, all through the century the most famous poem anyone ever wrote about anyone in the family was Holmes's "The Last Leaf" (1831), a cheeky caricature of the old Major Melvill.

Some of what Melville learned about poetry and poets was gossip. Americans heard and read stories of famous poets from American travelers, and not only literary people, who had made pilgrimages to British authors, casually intruding themselves upon poets. James Hogg was pestered in his last years by dozens of callers a day. Orville Dewey, who preached Melville's father-in-law Judge Shaw's funeral service in 1861 and baptized three of Melville's children in 1863, had published in 1836 an account, quickly famous, of the way Wordsworth had received him at Rydal Mount in 1833. The tendency of British poets to gossip to travelers is clear in *Haps and Mishaps of a Tour in Europe* (1853), by "Grace Greenwood" (Sarah Jane Clarke), the admirer of Melville, who recalled her encounter with "Barry Cornwall,—born Procter," the songwriter Melville had met at Samuel Rogers's in 1849. She wrote: "It gave me quite a new sensation to hear personal recollections of such men as Byron, Moore, Wordsworth, Keats, Coleridge, and Charles Lamb. Of the latter, Mr. Procter related some new anecdotes, giving his peculiar delicious drolleries in a manner surely not unworthy of Elia himself." Melville too contributed to the spread of such anecdotes when he regaled his brother Allan by mail with a description of dining with the poet-novelist Sir Walter Scott's cold fish son-in-law, John Gibson Lockhart, himself a poet, in London in 1849, for Allan promptly put the gossip into further circulation so that it quickly reached as far as Long Island.[32]

The hard evidence that Melville read a particular poet may consist of a single known comment in his marginalia or his literary works, and sometimes that evidence may not be as hard as it looks. Into a copy of Dante, Melville copied this from Landor's *Pentameron and Pentalogia*:

---

32. George L. Duyckinck repeated the story about Lockhart as a cold fish to Joann Miller in his letter of December 11, 1849 (in the Duyckinck Collection, Rare Books and Manuscript Division, The New York Public Library, Astor, Lenox, and Tilden Foundations [hereafter NYPL-D]).

"What execrations! What hatred against the human race! What exultation and merriment at eternal sufferings!"[33] Melville may have taken these words secondhand from Leigh Hunt's *Stories from the Italian Poets* (1846) or another source. Similarly, Melville may well have known poems by Jonathan Swift (as he definitely knew poems by Swift's friends), but his few known references to "the Dean" do not indicate a specific knowledge of his poetry (nor for that matter of *Gulliver's Travels,* commonly available in expurgated texts). Often, only a reference or two strongly suggests or actually proves that Melville knew the poetry of a famous contemporary, Robert Browning being the most conspicuous example. In the manuscript of his essay on Hawthorne's *Mosses* Melville held up for national pride N. P. Willis's "The Belfry Pigeon," yet this is his only known reference to Willis's poems. (A further twist in the fortuitous survival of evidence is that if Willis had not published a passage from a letter Melville wrote to him from London in 1849 we would not know for sure that the two men had ever been on confidential terms.[34])

But the pervasiveness of poetry in Melville's time is further manifest in its common function as an acceptable award or gift. A courtship gift from Melville's father to his mother was a New York 1813 Akenside's *The Pleasures of Imagination.* In 1831 the Albany Academy awarded young Herman *The London Carcanet. Containing Select Passages from the Most Distinguished Writers,* which included poems by Scott, Moore, and Byron (Sealts, no. 331). Herman is said to have given an early (1830 or so) edition of Tennyson's *Poems* to Mary Parmalee, at Lansingburgh, around 1838 or 1839 (Gilman, p. 104). At some time (1840?) the *London Carcanet* passed out of Herman's possession (to Mary L. Day? Harriet M. Day, Harriet Fly?—all names that are now in the volume), but not before he had inscribed in three very different samples of penmanship three sensual stanzas from Gay's *The Beggar's Opera,* where young Melville identified himself with Macheath. On December 19, 1844, Mrs. R. M. Blatchford gave Augusta the 1842 two-volume Ticknor edition of Tennyson's *Poems,* which Augusta surely shared with her newly returned brother Herman during his visits to Lansingburgh and later, when they lived in the same house. In this edition was a poem that caught Herman's imagination, "Will Waterproof's Lyrical Monologue" (as evidenced by his sightseeing in London in late 1849; see sect. 4 below). A gift from Gansevoort to their sister Fanny in 1845, as he left for London, was Longfellow's *Voices of the Night.* Oliver Wendell

33. Melville's Dante was the Cary translation entitled *The Vision; or Hell, Purgatory, and Paradise* (London: Bohn, 1847; Sealts, no. 174).

34. See *Piazza Tales,* p. 669, and *Correspondence,* pp. 150–51.

Holmes gave his *Urania* (1846) to Judge Lemuel Shaw, whose daughter Elizabeth married Melville the next year. Melville's mother-in-law, Hope Savage Shaw, in 1848 gave him Longfellow's *Evangeline, a Tale of Acadie.* In April 1849 Evert A. Duyckinck gave Augusta Melville (when she was in Melville's New York City household) a "most acceptable gift," Leigh Hunt's new two-volume *A Book for a Corner; or, Selections in Prose and Verse.* On Wednesday the eleventh in 1849 (either April or July), Augusta thanked Evert Duyckinck for "volumes" on (meaning by?) Leigh Hunt— perhaps including one already mentioned, *Stories from the Italian Poets.* (In October 1861 Melville acquired Hunt's *Rimini and Other Poems* [Boston: Ticknor & Fields, 1844; Sealts, no. 290a], the title poem of which was a treatment of Dante's story of Paolo and Francesca so important in Landor's *Pentameron* and in Melville's own *Pierre.*) The first volume of *A Book for a Corner* contained William Shenstone's "The Schoolmistress" and Pope's "Ode on Solitude." The second volume contained Thomson's "The Enchantments of the Wizard" and "Indolence" from *The Castle of Indo- lence;* Parnell's "The Hermit"; Thomas Gray's "Ode on a Distant Prospect of Eton College" and "A Long Story"; Cowley's "Thoughts on a Garden, from a letter to Evelyn" (mostly verse); Lady Winchilsea's "Petition for an Absolute Retreat"; Warton's "Two Sonnets" and "Inscription over a Calm and Clear Spring"; and Gray's "Elegy in a Country Churchyard."[35]

---

35. In July 1850 Evert Duyckinck sent Augusta the prose *The Vale of Cedars,* by Grace Aguilar, and *In Memoriam* (see also sect. 4 below). In November 1852 Duyckinck sent Augusta the Reverend R. A. Willmott's *Summer Time in the Country,* a sort of summer diary of Willmott's promiscuous reading and outings and thoughts about literary and artistic subjects in which the pages are strewn with carefully selected quotations from poetry relevant to esoteric topics, descriptions of birds, then of bird calls, or descrip- tions of gardens—real ones and ones in poems. One entry is a disquisition on how lucky Waller has been in his critics; another gives a snippet of Cowley's verse letter to Evelyn, quoted at length in Leigh Hunt's *Book for a Corner,* which Duyckinck had given Augusta earlier. Among the poets repeatedly cited by Willmott are Spenser, Shakespeare, Milton, Thomson, Shenstone, Cowper, on through Wordsworth, Coleridge, Byron, and some Keats. The Willmott book displays a mind so saturated with British poetry that it could be retrieved topically. *Summer Time in the Country* was at Arrowhead for several years, available to Melville, whose own mind was equally saturated with the same poetry. (In 1853 John C. Hoadley, engaged to Melville's sister Catherine, gave their sister Helen the new volume by Whittier, *The Chapel of the Hermits.*) As a more special gift than a mere book, Cornelius Mathews in the summer of 1850 sent Elizabeth Shaw Melville "The Cry of the Human" in Elizabeth Barrett Browning's own hand, a gift to him from the poet years before (*Log,* pp. 388–89). In January 1854, under pressure to welcome his new brother-in-law into the family, Melville gave Hoadley the volumes of Chatterton he had bought in London in 1849 (Sealts, no. 137). In 1859 Melville's brother-in-law Sam Shaw gave him the new (1858) volume of *Poems* by Judge Shaw's old acquaintance Ralph

As far as we know, Melville bought few volumes of poetry before 1849, one being Philip Pendleton Cooke's *Froissart Ballads, and Other Poems,* which he bought on December 2, 1847 (Philadelphia: Carey & Hart, 1847; Sealts, no. 158), another important one being Macpherson's *Fingal, an Ancient Epic Poem,* in 1848 (London: Becket & De Hondt, 1762; Sealts, no. 343). In his middle and later years the proportion of books Melville purchased shifted from prose to poetry. From 1849 on, and especially from the late 1850s on, he bought more and more poetry or books about poetry and art books that dealt with issues in aesthetics. In the late 1860s and 1870s he continued to buy prose books by and about Hawthorne and research books for *Clarel,* for instance, but fewer miscellaneous prose volumes.

It is clear that from his childhood and his youth Melville was steeped in English poetry of the Renaissance, Restoration, and eighteenth century, and of the great generation of Scottish and English poets born around 1770. By his young manhood he knew poetry by Edmund Spenser (c.1552–99), William Shakespeare (1564–1616), Ben Jonson (1572–1637), Edmund Waller (1606–87), John Milton (1608–74), Samuel Butler (1613–80), Abraham Cowley (1618–67), Andrew Marvell (1621–78), John Dryden (1631–1700), Matthew Prior (1664–1721), Alexander Pope (1688–1744), and John Gay (1685–1732), among others. He knew especially well the poets of his grandparents' and parents' childhoods and early lives, among them James Thomson (1700–1748), Samuel Johnson (1709–84), William Shenstone (1714–63), Thomas Gray (1716–71), William Collins (1721–59), Mark Akenside (1721–70), Oliver Goldsmith (?1730–74), William Cowper (1731–1800), James Macpherson (1736–96), Thomas Chatterton (1752–70), George Crabbe (1754–1832), Robert Burns (1759–96), Samuel Rogers (1763–1855), and the more recent poets such as William Wordsworth (1770–1850), James Hogg (1770–1835), Sir Walter Scott (1771–1832), Samuel Taylor Coleridge (1772–1834), Robert Southey (1774–1843), Walter Savage Landor (1775–1864), Thomas Campbell (1777–1844), Thomas Moore (1779–1852), Leigh Hunt (1784–1859), Barry Cornwall (the pseudonym of Bryan Waller Procter, 1787–1874), and Lord Byron (1788–1824).

Waldo Emerson. Melville gave many of his books of poetry to his sisters (books that he did not feel he needed any more, but also books that he felt he had no exclusive claim to, such as his father's set of Spenser); to his daughters, including some that he seems to have wanted to have around the house); and to his wife (for instance, his copy of Poe's poems, and, late in life, an occasion-specific gift—the poems of Thomas Bailey Aldrich, bestowed because Aldrich had bought a house on Mount Vernon Street near the Shaw house on Beacon Hill).

William H. Gilman (p. 104) recorded the Lansingburgh rumor that Melville in his youth knew poetry by Alfred Tennyson (1809–92). It is possible, however, that Melville knew little or nothing of Tennyson or, for that matter, of Percy Bysshe Shelley (1792–1822) and John Keats (1795–1821) until after his return from the Pacific in 1844. The early catalogs of the Albany Young Men's Association list no separate volume under the name of Shelley, Keats, or Tennyson. Exigencies of publishing (such as Tennyson's silence through much of the 1830s) and of American republishing seem to have retarded the American reputations of all three poets.

From childhood Melville also knew some American poems and in his youth heard and read lectures that focused on specifically American literature, including poetry. By youth or early manhood he had at least sampled several ambitious American poems. The YMA had a fine collection of classical literature in translation. In adult life Melville's purchase of the thirty-seven-volume Classical Library from Harpers in 1849 provided him with translations of Virgil, Horace, Ovid, Homer, and Pindar. Earlier, he knew something of Italian poets of the Renaissance. Melville bought the Cary translation of Dante in the 1847 Bohn edition entitled *The Vision; or Hell, Purgatory, and Paradise* on June 22, 1848 (Sealts, no. 174), and, as Merrell R. Davis suggested (p. 85), soon wrote "Babbalanja relates to them a Vision" (*Mardi,* chap. 188). The next year, 1849, may be when Melville wrote Ariosto's and Tasso's names beside Milton's invocation at the beginning of *Paradise Lost*—clear evidence that he knew something about their own invocations.[36] He knew some of Virgil's *Eclogues* in translation, and probably by this time knew the *Aeneid,* in Dryden's translation. Early in life, he knew some poetry of Goethe and Schiller, in translation, and had, before his later reading of Heine and Staël, at least a general sense of recent German poetry, what one could learn from Carlyle's essays in magazines and the remarkable essay in the *Zodiac* taken from the *American Monthly Magazine.* Long before he manifested any longing to become a poet himself, Herman Melville was familiar with many thousands of lines of poetry and could probably quote hundreds of them at will. In this he was not greatly unlike many of his contemporaries, but in this he was quite unlike most educated persons of the twentieth or twenty-first century including even most academic specialists in British and American poetry.

---

36. Melville's copy of *The Poetical Works of John Milton* (2 vols., Boston: Hilliard, Gray, 1836; Sealts, no. 358b) first surfaced in 1983.

IV
THE RENEWED POWER OF POETRY
IN MELVILLE'S LIFE, 1849–1856

A T SEA, ESPECIALLY on whalers, where books were scarce, vulnerable, and the supply rarely replenished, any man whose head was stuffed with poetry, as Melville's was when he went to sea, was in demand. (By the end of 1842 Melville was also in demand as a man who had stories to tell—or teasingly to withhold—about his and others' sexual adventures in whaleships and on Pacific islands.) At home, while he was writing *Typee* and *Omoo*, Melville read mainly prose works by voyagers which he could plunder for his own narrative. *Mardi* (1849) was the book in which Melville declared his literary independence, although he was not to win it until *White-Jacket* (1850) or, arguably, not until *Moby-Dick* (1851). When he began *Mardi* in May 1847, Melville turned to nautical books for sources, then as he underwent sudden intellectual growth from late 1847 through 1848 he turned to books by philosophical and psychological writers— Robert Burton, Rabelais, Sir Thomas Browne, Bishop Berkeley, Lord Chesterfield, Dr. Johnson, Edmund Burke, and many other prose writers. For the most part, he read poetry when it impinged on his daily life, as Channing's "The Island of Nukuheva" did early in 1847 and Longfellow's *Evangeline* did later, or as *A Fable for Critics* did late in 1848, when Evert Duyckinck and Cornelius Mathews were stung by Lowell's satire. Chances are that not until early 1849 did poetry again mean more to Melville than prose, as it had in his youth and early manhood when he had been under the spell of Lord Byron.

Most of Melville's allusions to poetry in *Mardi* are casual. Early he calls Dante "grim" (chap. 3), echoing Lord Byron (*Don Juan*, 10.27), but perhaps also knowing that "grim Dante" was in the 1833 text of Tennyson's "The Palace of Art." In *Mardi* are references to "Manfred-like" behavior (chap. 4); borrowings from the marginal glosses of "The Ancient Mariner" (as in the title of chap. 16); echoes from Tennyson's "Mariana at the Moated Grange" (chap. 31); references to two of Shakespeare's more gnarled characters (Richard III, chap. 84, and Timon of Athens, chap. 174); a reference (chap. 174) to the impossibility of disentangling collaborative passages by Beaumont from those by Fletcher; and (in chap. 177) a portrayal as Marko of Fitz-Greene Halleck (the writer of the 1820s international war cry, "Marco Bozzaris," who had descended from shining poet to prosaic clerk for John Jacob Astor). The book also contains some spoof titles of typical books of poetry: "Suffusions of a Lily in a Shower," "Sonnet on the last

Breath of an Ephemera," and "The Gad-fly, and Other Poems" (chap. 123).[37]

Melville's interest in putative Norse or Gaelic heroic poems is manifest in his buying, in 1848, the *Froissart Ballads* (Sealts, no. 158), which consisted of "versified transcripts from Froissart" as well as new imitations of Froissart; in borrowing *Frithiof's Saga* from Evert A. Duyckinck early that year (London: Hookham, 1838; Sealts, no. 500); and in buying sometime that year James Macpherson's *Fingal, an Ancient Epic Poem, in Six Books: Together with Several Other Poems, Composed by Ossian the Son of Fingal* (Sealts, no. 343). From his months at the Lansingburgh Academy, Melville probably remembered that Lord Kames, respectful of Hugh Blair's "dissertation," had drawn repeatedly on *Fingal* for illustrations in *Elements of Criticism*. Technically *Fingal* was in prose, purportedly translated from the Gaelic poet, but admirers thought of the language as if it were like that of the book of Job and other Hebrew poetry in the King James translation. The Dantean title of chapter 185 of *Mardi* (from *Purgatory*) showed he was freshly and powerfully influenced by the edition he bought in 1848, and in chapter 188 he borrowed Babbalanja's vision from *Paradise*. The most important poetic influences on *Mardi* seem to be Ossian and, in some late-written chapters, Dante.

In *Mardi* Melville (as far as we know) first tried his hand at writing poems he was willing to publish, but the verses were not as ambitious and powerful as many of the sections of prose. Indeed, by putting verses into the mouth of Yoomy, the warbler, Melville defined them as examples of a lower order of verse. Chapter 119 sets forth Melville's rankings: "Like a grand, ground swell, Homer's old organ rolls its vast volumes under the light frothy wave-crests of Anacreon and Hafiz; and high over my ocean, sweet Shakespeare soars, like all the larks of the spring. Throned on my sea-side, like Canute, bearded Ossian smites his hoar harp, wreathed with wild-flowers, in which warble my Wallers; blind Milton sings bass to my Petrarchs and Priors, and laureats crown me with bays." (The laureates in Melville's time were Southey, until 1843, then Wordsworth until 1850, then Tennyson.) Seeing the world of poetry as capacious, Melville

---

37. "Gad-fly" as a mock title for a literary magazine was used by Poe in the "Thingum Bob" skit printed in the *Southern Literary Messenger* in December 1844 and reprinted in the *Broadway Journal* in July 1845; that piece begins by facetiously naming two great poets, Shakespeare and Emmons, a collocation that hints at a humorous contemporary context for Melville's pairing of Emmons and Homer in his 1850 essay on Hawthorne's *Mosses,* where Shakespeare figures largely, though not in the short passage about Pop Emmons.

acknowledged the grandeur of Homer while being protective of the lesser and more vulnerable poets such as Anacreon and Hafiz. Ossian looms over poets like Petrarch and Matthew Prior, but the Petrarchs and Priors are also true poets. In his comments in book 17 of *Pierre* on poets of the first, second, and third degree, Melville made much the same distinctions when he asserted that, as a reader, his young hero Pierre had "freely and comprehendingly ranged" among "the beautiful imaginings of the second and third degree of poets"—not the first degree—not Homer, Shakespeare, Ossian, Milton, and (judging from some passages late in *Mardi,* then in *Moby-Dick, Pierre,* and elsewhere) not Dante. Yoomy was, at best, a Waller.

At the beginning of 1849 Melville was open for profound new experiences—fatherhood, first of all, but also intellectual and aesthetic growth. He had finished the ambitious book by which he hoped to win a high general literary reputation, not just additional fame as a writer of South Sea adventure; he had completed an intense self-education in the profound thinkers (as he would have said) of Western civilization, including classical writers and modern foreign writers in translation. He had realized that it was time for him not only to engage weighty ideas involving history, religion, philosophy, psychology, and political theory, but also to clarify in his own mind the terms in which the best critics of his time had been talking about literature. His attempts to temporize about *Mardi* to John Murray may have been enough to make him confront serious deficiencies in his own aesthetic vocabulary. He found literary criticism in his *Penny Cyclopædia,* enough to make him discontented with the casual criticism he had seen accompanying poetry in magazines or newspapers, or introducing poetry in any of the new annual gift-books, or criticism quoted in or promulgated in books on poets, such as his friend Tuckerman's *Thoughts on the Poets.*

The best literary criticism, Melville knew, was to be found in the great British quarterlies. From his father, long before he could read the quarterlies for himself, he knew the name of Francis Jeffrey, who had entertained Allan Melvill in 1818 and from whose garden in Edinburgh Allan had plucked a rose as a keepsake for his wife. Melville would have known that Byron had castigated Jeffrey in "English Bards and Scotch Reviewers," even to the point of comparing him to another Jeffrey, the George Jeffrey of the Bloody Assizes in James II's time, a period familiar from Macaulay's history, and Melville would have understood the basis for Byron's attacks on Southey and Wordsworth, in particular. A high point in his erratic education had been the time he was free to read the British periodicals in the library of the Young Men's Association in Albany.

At the end of 1848 or the first weeks of 1849 Melville ordered *The Modern British Essayists* (Philadelphia: Carey & Hart, 1847–48; Sealts, no. 359), a widely advertised new compendium which dealt with religion, history, philosophy, political science, and other subjects but which in most volumes gave much space to poetry. On February 16, 1849, the New York City publisher and bookseller John Wiley charged Melville's account $18 for the set. No scholar has reported seeing it, but it presumably consisted of eight volumes, as Merton M. Sealts Jr. explained in his *Melville's Reading* (no. 359):

> The "set" . . . included eight numbered volumes: v. 1 (1847 *or* 1849): Thomas Babington Macaulay, 1st Baron Macaulay. Essays, Critical and Miscellaneous . . . v. 2 (1847): Sir Archibald Alison, Bart. Miscellaneous Essays . . . v. 3 (1848): Sydney Smith. The Works . . . v. 4 (1848): John Wilson. The Recreations of Christopher North [pseud.] . . . v. 5 (1848): Thomas Carlyle. Critical and Miscellaneous Essays . . . v. 6 (1848): Francis Jeffrey, Lord Jeffrey. Contributions to the Edinburgh Review . . . v. 7 (1848): Sir James Stephen. Critical and Miscellaneous Essays . . . Sir Thomas Noon Talfourd. Critical and Miscellaneous Writings . . . With Additional Articles Never Before Published in This Country . . . v. 8 (1848): Sir James Mackintosh. The Miscellaneous Works . . . In addition, an unnumbered volume published by Carey & Hart in 1841 was advertised in some catalogues as part of the set: Sir Walter Scott, Bart. Critical and Miscellaneous Essays . . . Collected by Himself . . .[38]

The 1841 Scott volume cited by Sealts may well have been (or have been *intended as*) the source for the Scott volume advertised as "in press" under its new title *The Critical Writings of Sir Walter Scott* about the time Melville would have ordered his set. The book advertised with this title may never have been printed. One three-volume set of Scott has been located with the series title *Modern British Essayists* on the spine, in what seems to be the publisher's binding, but unlike the other volumes just named the Scott is not in double columns, and is printed on better paper. What came into Melville's hands are probably the eight volumes enumerated by Sealts (and not a Scott volume, although some of Scott's critical writings may have been in the Melville house already).

---

38. The present Houghton Library number for this account statement from Wiley is bMS Am 188 (524). (Sealts's location of the document as in Harvard College Library–Wiley Collection was erroneous: it is in what Sealts referred to elsewhere as HCL-M, the Melville family papers at Harvard.)

However ready Melville was for a profound shift in his life as a literary man, a shift in which he would ponder the great British reviewers of the previous half century, chance had a featuring blow at events. In Boston in February 1849, awaiting the birth of his and Lizzie's first child, and then staying on during her recovery, Melville found a seven-volume set of Shakespeare, locally printed by Hilliard, Gray (1837; Sealts, no. 460) in what he called "glorious great type," easy enough for him to read with his already weak eyes. On February 24, 1849, a week after Malcolm was born, Melville wrote to Evert A. Duyckinck:

> I have been passing my time very pleasurably here. But chiefly in loung-
> ing on a sofa (a la the poet Grey) & reading Shakspeare. It is an edition in
> glorious great type, every letter whereof is a soldier, & the top of every "t"
> like a musket barrel. Dolt & ass that I am I have lived more than 29 years,
> & until a few days ago, never made close acquaintance with the divine
> William. Ah, he's full of sermons-on-the-mount, and gentle, aye, almost
> as Jesus. I take such men to be inspired. I fancy that this moment Shak-
> speare in heaven ranks with Gabriel Raphael and Michael. And if another
> Messiah ever comes twill be in Shakespere's person.——I am mad to think
> how minute a cause has prevented me hitherto from reading Shakspeare.
> But until now, every copy that was come-atable to me, happened to be in
> a vile small print unendurable to my eyes which are tender as young spar-
> rows. But chancing to fall in with this glorious edition, I now exult over
> it, page after page.——

What Duyckinck wrote in response was designed to dash this irreverent exuberance, particularly any linking of Shakespeare with the archangels (toward whom Duyckinck felt fiercely protective). On March 3, Melville rejected any implication that he was ready to join the bard-idolators, the snobs (in the now obsolete sense of sycophants) "who burn their tuns of rancid fat at his shrine." Melville would instead "stand afar off & alone, & burn some pure Palm oil, the product of some overtopping trunk." And he would look to Shakespeare, at first, for ideas, not for "poetical" qualities such as diction and sound. His theory now was that in Elizabeth's time all men wore muzzles on their souls, even Shakespeare: "For I hold it a verity, that even Shakspeare, was not a frank man to the uttermost. And, indeed, who in this intolerant Universe is, or can be? But the Declaration of Inde-pendence makes a difference." Melville fondly hoped at this moment that he might be frank in the books he would write. Duyckinck's own review of *Moby-Dick* less than three years later (*Literary World,* November 22, 1851), where he protested at Melville's dislodging "from heaven, with contumely, 'long-pampered Gabriel, Michael and Raphael,'" would have

served, all alone, to disillusion him. Whatever specifically aesthetic quali-
ties he recognized in Shakespeare then or later, Melville first articulated
his awe of Shakespeare as thinker ("Here is forcibly shown the great Mon-
taignism of Hamlet"), a man with profound ideas.[39] That he did not single
out for comment anything about Shakespeare's astonishing language may
simply indicate that he felt ill-equipped to talk in such terms, though
within two years he was able to imitate that language magnificently in
Moby-Dick.

It was while Melville was reveling in Shakespeare in Boston that the
set of *Modern British Essayists* arrived in New York. Some of the volumes
(likely the Macaulay, Wilson, and Jeffrey) included a bound-in aggres-
sively worded late 1848 Carey & Hart advertisement declaring this "a new,
revised, and very cheap edition." Carey & Hart confidently promised:
"The series will contain all the most able papers that have ever appeared
in *The Edinburgh Review, The London Quarterly Review,* and *Blackwood's
Magazine,* and may indeed be called the cream of those publications." It
announced volumes by Robert Southey, J. G. Lockhart, William Gifford,
and J. Wilson Crocker (i.e., Croker) that apparently were never printed.
Carey & Hart then itemized potential customers: heads of families (want-
ing models of style for their children); managers of book societies and book
clubs; school inspectors, schoolmasters, and tutors (wanting suitable prizes
or additions to school libraries); travelers (the publishers thinking the hefty
volumes suitable "to fill a corner in a portmanteau or carpet-bag"); pas-
sengers on board a ship; officers in the army and navy, and all "Economists
in space or pocket," who need to lay up "a *concentrated Library,* at a moder-
ate cost"; and those who need to send gifts to friends in distant countries.
Judging from his letter to Richard Bentley on July 20, 1851 ("This coun-
try & nearly all its affairs are governed by sturdy backwoodsmen—noble
fellows enough, but not at all literary"), Melville would particularly have
delighted in the next paragraph of the Carey & Hart ad: "The Modern
Essayists will yield to the Settler in the Backwoods of America, the most
valuable and interesting writings of all the most distinguished authors of
our time, at less than one quarter the price they could be obtained in any
other form." The last buyer was envisioned as the "Student and Lover of
Literature at Home, who has hitherto been compelled to wade through
volumes of Reviews for a single article," who "may now become pos-
sessed of *every article worth reading* for little more than *the cost of the Annual
subscription*" (presumably not a subscription to a British periodical but to
an American reprint).

39. For this annotation in Melville's copy of Shakespeare see *Log,* p. 291.

Here in one set, as advertised, were hundreds of articles from the great British quarterlies that enlightened the age, especially the Whig *Edinburgh Review,* founded in 1802 by Sydney Smith (1771–1845), Francis Jeffrey (1773–1850), and Henry Peter Brougham (1778–1868). Here also were an abundance of articles from the great magazine's two Tory rivals, the London *Quarterly Review* (founded in 1809) and *Blackwood's Edinburgh Magazine* (founded in 1817), as well as others. In the preface of his volume, Smith itemized his and his friends' Whig grievances against the state and church:

> To appreciate the value of the Edinburgh Review, the state of England at the period when that journal began should be had in remembrance. The Catholics were not emancipated—the Corporation and Test Acts were unrepealed—the Game Laws were horribly oppressive—Steel Traps and Spring Guns were set all over the country—Prisoners tried for their Lives could have no Counsel—Lord Eldon and the Court of Chancery pressed heavily upon mankind—Libel was punished by the most cruel and vindictive imprisonments—the principles of Political Economy were little understood—the Law of Debt and of Conspiracy were upon the worst possible footing—the enormous wickedness of the Slave Trade was tolerated—a thousand evils were in existence, which the talents of good and able men have since lessened or removed; and these effects have been not a little assisted by the honest boldness of the Edinburgh Review.

The Tory *Quarterly Review,* stoutly defending Church and Crown, was founded by William Gifford (1756–1826), the first editor; among the contributors were George Canning (1770–1827), John Hookham Frere (1769–1846), Sir Walter Scott (1771–1832), and Robert Southey (1774–1843). William Hazlitt (1778–1830) chastised Gifford in *The Spirit of the Age* (1825) for his hostile recasting of Charles Lamb's essay on Wordsworth's *The Excursion* and for his publishing the virulent attack by John Wilson Croker (1780–1857) on Keats's *Endymion*. The *Quarterly Review* was no friend to the followers of the Romantics, either, particularly Tennyson, whose 1832 book Croker had savaged in what became a notorious review, said to have kept the poet from publishing for a decade. The Tory *Blackwood's Edinburgh Magazine* soon after its founding came into the hands of John Gibson Lockhart (1794–1854), John Wilson (1785–1854), and James Hogg (1770–1835), the poet known to Melville as the "Ettrick Shepherd."

Melville may have picked up his *Modern British Essayists* as early as March 3, when he made a brief trip back home to Manhattan. If so, being a man who traveled light, he would have left the volumes off at his house on Fourth Avenue rather than hauling them to Boston. The insides of the volumes were never handsome, despite the Carey & Hart claims. The paper used was of inferior quality, and the texts were in double columns, with tight gutters and skimpy margins, even when the edges had not been cut in rebinding. Worst of all, the tiny print was torturous even to eyes not "as tender as young sparrows," although Melville could read small print when he needed to, at least in the daylight, if he paced himself. These were bulky volumes, but with the series title "THE / MODERN / BRITISH / ESSAYISTS" and the volume author's name (or probably in one instance two authors' names) in gold stamping on the spine, Melville's set would have looked handsome enough ranged on a shelf. There would be scant authority for thinking of volumes sold together by Carey & Hart as constituting a "set," bibliographically speaking, but presumably any shipping clerk would have put together Melville's set in one color of cloth, either red or brown. One modern assemblage of these volumes, variously bound, stretches to some thirteen linear inches on the shelf and stands roughly nine and a half inches tall by six inches deep. *Modern British Essayists* may have remained in Melville's library for the rest of his life, but, perhaps because no one has found in his writings a specific reference to the set or to a volume in it by title, his use of *Modern British Essayists* has gone virtually unexplored, except for brief references in my two-volume biography of Melville. *Modern British Essayists* played a significant role in Melville's self-education, particularly about British poetry. Pretty clearly, he looked through the set right away, for his next book, *Redburn,* bears marks of familiarity with at least the Smith and the Wilson volumes.

For Melville the volumes were all valuable but far from equally so as far as poetry was concerned. The Stephen volume did not contain essays on poetry. The essays by Sir James Mackintosh (1765–1832) for the most part had been published in the *Edinburgh Review*. In an "Advertisement to the London Edition" the editor explained that he has in general arranged the pieces in order, moving from the "more purely Philosophical, and proceeding through Literature to Politics." Melville might have been attracted to a review of Samuel Rogers's *Poems* (especially after meeting the author late in 1849) and Staël's *De L'Allemagne*. In the Carlyle volume Melville had the review of Lockhart's biographies of Burns and of Scott along with a great deal on contemporary German writers, including a review of a biography of Jean Paul Friedrich Richter, and a good deal on Goethe, but this volume did not contain the great Carlyle, with whom Melville became acquainted elsewhere. The bulk of the Macaulay volume consisted of essays from the *Edinburgh Review* in roughly their order of publication, beginning with an essay on Milton (1825), one on

Machiavelli (1827), and one on Dryden (1828). The volume contained several other essays likely to attract Melville's eye, such as one from 1831 on "Moore's Life of Lord Byron" and an undated essay on "Cowley and Milton" (following an 1840 essay). In Melville's volume the 1847 additions to an earlier Carey & Hart volume began with an "Appendix" on page 569, two poems, "Pompeii" (source not identified) and "The Battle of Ivry," from *Knight's Quarterly Magazine* (1824), followed by ten essays from the *Edinburgh Review* (these out of chronological order). Melville quickly would have tired of Macaulay's pomposity, pedantry, and vacuity, as in this definition in an essay on an inherently fascinating topic, "Milton": "By poetry we mean, the art of employing words in such a manner as to produce an illusion on the imagination: the art of doing by means of words what the painter does by means of colour." The other volumes were more to the purpose when Melville began studying poetry again, now as a famous prose writer himself.

Archibald Alison (1792–1867) was the son of the Archibald Alison (1757–1839) famous for *Essays on the Nature and Principles of Taste* (1790). (In the sixth volume of the set Melville could read Francis Jeffrey's extensive review of the father's book, "Alison on Taste.") The term "master-spirits," which Melville used in his essay on Hawthorne, derived ultimately from *Julius Caesar,* but his use of it may have been suggested by the younger Alison's applying it in "The Copyright Question" to great geniuses who are too profound to be appreciated by their own times. All profound writers experienced the pressure "to exchange deep writing for agreeable writing," Alison said. No "metaphysics, no conic-sections, nothing but cakes & ale," Melville reassured Richard Bentley on June 5, 1849, about his work in progress, *Redburn;* "nothing weighty," he reassured George P. Putnam on June 7, 1854, about *Israel Potter* (1855). The last essay in the Alison volume, "Homer, Dante, and Michael Angelo," from the January 1845 *Blackwood's,* concluded that great subjects remain untreated: "Nature is inexhaustible; the events of men are unceasing, their variety is endless. . . . Rely upon it, subjects for genius are not wanting; genius itself, steadily and perseveringly directed, is the thing required. But genius and energy alone are not sufficient; COURAGE and disinterestedness are needed more than all." All this would have been heartening to Melville.

The volume by Sydney Smith consisted of contributions to the *Edinburgh Review* followed by some speeches. From his citation of it in his essay on Hawthorne, we know that Smith's 1820 query in "America" rankled in Melville, as in many Americans: "In the four quarters of the globe, who reads an American book? or goes to an American play? or looks at an American picture or statue?" In his 1818 essay on "America" (also reprinted in the *Modern British Essayists* volume) Smith had been more particular:

> Literature the Americans have none—no native literature, we mean. It is all imported. They had a Franklin, indeed; and may afford to live for half a century on his fame. There is, or was a Mr. Dwight, who wrote some poems; and his baptismal name was Timothy. There is also a small account of Virginia by Jefferson, and an epic by Joel Barlow; and some pieces of pleasantry by Mr. Irving. But why should the Americans write books, when a six weeks' passage brings them, in their own tongue, our sense, science and genius, in bales and hogsheads? Prairies, steam-boats, grist-mills, are their natural objects for centuries to come. Then, when they have got to the Pacific Ocean—epic poems, plays, pleasures of memory and all the elegant gratifications of an ancient people who have tamed the wild earth, and set down to amuse themselves.—This is the natural march of human affairs.

Smith was incendiary, as Melville remembered from one of Simeon De Witt Bloodgood's lectures at the Albany Young Men's Association for Mutual Improvement. But you never knew what would catch Melville's eye. The 1821 essay on "Man Traps and Spring Guns" (pp. 227–32) seems a likely source for the "frightful announcement" the young hero encounters in chapter 43 of *Redburn,* the book Melville wrote the summer after buying the collection.

The volume by T. Noon Talfourd (1795–1854) is made up primarily of essays from the *New Monthly Magazine,* the *Retrospective Review,* and the *London Magazine.* Several public addresses conclude the volume, the most interesting to literary people being the one delivered "in the Court of Queen's Bench, June 23, 1841," where Talfourd defends Moxon, the publisher of Shelley's works. This was Edward Moxon (1801–58), the cold, stiff man Melville managed to thaw during his interview late in 1849. One of the literary essays, "On the Genius and Writings of Wordsworth," reprinted from the *New Monthly Magazine,* was just the sort of loving guide to poems that Melville could benefit from. Toward the end of it, Talfourd appealed to his readers to take up Wordsworth for themselves rather than being kept away by "base or ignorant criticism":

> Not only Coleridge, Lloyd, Southey, Wilson, and Lamb—with whom his name has been usually connected—but almost all the living poets have paid eloquent homage to his genius. He is loved by Montgomery, Cornwall, and Rogers—revered by the author of Waverley—ridiculed and pillaged by Lord Byron! Jeffrey, if he begins an article on his greatest work with the pithy sentence *"this will never do,"* glows even while he criticises, and

before he closes, though he came like Balaam to curse, like him "blesses
altogether."

Here was exemplified the riches of the *Modern British Essayists,* for Tal-
fourd was referring to the November 1815 article on *The Excursion; being
a Portion of the Recluse, a Poem,* which began: "This will never do!"—an
essay Melville now possessed in the Jeffrey volume of the same set.

John Wilson (1785–1854), the author of the volume entitled in this
Carey & Hart set *The Recreations of Christopher North,* was a glamorous
figure in Melville's early life, famous not only for his writing but for his
striking physique and long blond hair and for his exploits as a sportsman.
Melville remembered him from the Albany *Zodiac.* In his twenties, after
graduation from Oxford, Wilson had bought an estate at Windermere
called Elleray, and while there became a friend of Wordsworth, Coleridge,
Southey, and De Quincey. Melville found in the Wilson volume primarily
reprints from *Blackwood's Magazine* (later *Blackwood's Edinburgh Magazine*),
original publication dates not given, but all dating from before or during
1842, when the collection was first published. This volume was immedi-
ately useful at the end of May or early June 1849, for Redburn's shooting
jacket may have derived from the frontispiece illustration. Scanning the
"Christopher North" volume, Melville would have remembered his read-
ing of Wilson's letter to Hogg in the *Zodiac* long before. Wilson himself
then became the renewed object of interest for his comments on *Mardi*
in the August 1849 *Blackwood's* review of Mayo's *Kaloolah.* (On August
21, 1849, the Boston *Evening Transcript* spread the news that in North's
review *Mardi* was "spoken of as having been 'closed with a yawn, a day
or two after its publication!'") In early September 1849, Thomas Powell
(discussed later in this section) wrote Evert Duyckinck about "that old
humbug Christopher North" in relation to this review (*Log,* pp. 311–12).
Knowing that the curmudgeonly John Wilson had deigned to pontificate
about him may well have heightened Melville's interest in the volume
over the next years. He would have found challenging Wilson's question
of whether there was a great English poem (answer: only *Paradise Lost*). In
the volume Melville found many comments on Wordsworth, and could
read, with hostility, Wilson's praise of doctrinally correct sacred poetry.
The long-term importance of the *Recreations* for Melville is that it afforded
him intimate glimpses into the Wordsworthian milieu of the Lake Dis-
trict through several of the pieces: "A Day at Windemere [*sic*]," "Stroll to
Grassmere" ("First Saunter" and "Second Saunter"), in particular. Words-
worth is quoted and expounded in other essays, including "Morning
Monologue," "An Hour's Talk about Poetry," "Sacred Poetry" (which

contained Wilson's conclusions about religion in Wordsworth's poetry), and "A Few Words on Thomson." "Go, read the EXCURSION," Christopher North commanded in the prologue to "The Moors." Melville did read it, and other poems by Wordsworth, carefully, aided by Wilson's sympathetic, intimate guidance. In this volume Melville probably experienced his first encounter with many passages by Wordsworth which would strike him sharply when he read them later, in their contexts.

The volume by Francis Jeffrey (1773–1850) was probably even more important to Melville than the Wilson, beginning with the preface, which contained this explicit statement: "The Edinburgh Review, it is well known, aimed high from the beginning:—And, refusing to confine itself to the humble task of pronouncing on the mere literary merits of the works that came before it, professed to go deeply into *the Principles* on which its judgments were to be rested; as well as to take large and original views of all the important questions to which those works might relate." In modern terminology, the quarterly, from the first, aspired to address theoretical issues, issues involving aesthetic principles. What would have caught Melville's attention in this volume, after the preface, were reviews of the great Romantic poems that Jeffrey had published in the *Edinburgh Review* as the poems were appearing. *Lyrical Ballads* predated the establishment of the magazine, but the poetry section of the volume contained Jeffrey's reviews of Campbell's *Specimens of the British Poets;* Byron's *Sardanapalus* and *Manfred;* R. H. Cromek's *Reliques of Robert Burns;* Campbell's *Gertrude of Wyoming* and *Theodoric;* Scott's *The Lay of the Last Minstrel* and *The Lady of the Lake;* Crabbe's *Poems, The Borough, Tales,* and *Tales of the Hall;* Keats's *Endymion, Lamia, Isabella,* and *The Eve of St. Agnes;* Rogers's *Human Life;* Southey's *Roderick: The Last of the Goths;* Byron's *Childe Harold's Pilgrimage* and *The Prisoner of Chillon;* Moore's *Lalla Rookh;* Wordsworth's *The Excursion* and *The White Doe of Rylstone;* and Hemans's *Records of Women* and *The Forest Sanctuary.* However little of this poetry we ourselves are familiar with, we would be wise to assume that Melville knew almost all of it, even if the best evidence for his knowing, say, *Gertrude of Wyoming,* is the offhand reference to the "good Indian" Outalissi in his 1849 review of Francis Parkman's *The Oregon and California Trail.* Here Melville possessed an extraordinary cache of classic practical criticism, Jeffrey's brilliant tutorials in how to read *The Excursion* or *White Doe of Rylstone,* for two examples. These reviews embodied Jeffrey's determination to write criticism from aesthetic principles, so that, self-taught in the theory of literature, Melville found in Jeffrey, no matter how belatedly, one of his best teachers. As late as 1862 he copied out aesthetic hints from Jeffrey's essay on the Italian dramatist Victor Alfieri.

Having passed 1848 frugally by borrowing books from Evert Duyckinck (the Dante he purchased in June was an exception), Melville had embarked on a satisfying buying spree on the strength of his expectations for *Mardi*. Besides the seven-volume edition of Shakespeare (bought very early in February) and *Modern British Essayists,* Melville's other purchases early in 1849 included the two-volume *Poetical Works of John Milton* (Boston: Hilliard, Gray, 1836; Sealts, no. 358b), in typography a companion to the Shakespeare. He dated the set New York 1849, but the "N.Y." was probably his notation of his home city, not the place of purchase, and he may have bought it late in February or in March, for early in the summer he showed that he had been re-reading Milton. For many years critics tended not to consider poetical influences on Melville if they did not have his own marked copies, thereby sometimes slighting his knowledge of Spenser, Milton, Wordsworth, Tennyson, Elizabeth Barrett Browning, Robert Browning, and others. (An exception is an acute early book on Melville and Milton by Henry Pommer, based largely on verbal echoes of Milton in Melville—a study vindicated by Melville's markings when his two-volume set of Milton's poems came to light.) Melville's copy of Wordsworth first turned up in the 1970s, his Milton in the 1980s, his Spenser in the 1990s. Melville may have bought his *The Complete Poetical Works of William Wordsworth* (Philadelphia, 1839 [Sealts, no. 563a]) soon after seeing how largely the poet figured in *Modern British Essayists* and before he realized how little money *Mardi* would bring in.

On March 19 Melville bought the thirty-seven-volume Harper's Classical Library (Sealts, no. 147), which included in translation the major Greek and Roman historians and orators, the Greek tragedians and Roman satirists, and abundant classical poetry: Anacreon and Pindar (who gave their names to forms of verse, Anacreontics and Pindarics), Virgil's *Eclogues* (translated by Francis Wrangham) and *Georgics* (translated by William Sotheby), Dryden's translation of the *Aeneid,* Pope's translation of Homer, Philip Francis's of Horace, and Ovid translated by Dryden, Pope, Congreve, Addison, and others. Cicero and Demosthenes were included in the set as "orators." In Boston, in late March or the first day or so of April, he bought the four-volume (or more) Pierre Bayle's *An Historical and Critical Dictionary* (London: Harper, 1710; Sealts, no. 51). Melville looked forward, he wrote to Duyckinck on April 5, to continuing his course of reading, when he could lay his "great old folios side by side & go to sleep on them thro' the summer, with the Phaedon in one hand & Tom Brown in the other." The *Phaedrus* he possessed in the Classical Library (not a folio set), but his *Phaedon* is unlocated. *Plato's Phaedrus: A Dialogue*

Concerning Beauty and Love was in fact available in a thin London folio (Edward Jeffrey, 1792), and Sir Thomas Browne could be found in more than one folio edition, including the one he had borrowed from Duyckinck in 1848. It was December before Melville bought his known folio of Sir Thomas Browne. The folio *Phaedon* may have been a flight of wish-fulfillment, named as an evocative companion for the tangible volumes of the Bayle dictionary.

Melville's intense encounter with Shakespeare alone seems enough to call 1849 the year Melville became a serious student of poetry. But that year he also re-encountered Milton. He was of course sensitive to aesthetic qualities, as shown by his copying out Cowper's tribute to the music of *Paradise Lost* and, still more clearly, by his astonishing recall of Milton's vivid words when he came across echoes of them in later English poetry. Yet Melville seems to have read Milton in large part for poetic expression of ideas, particularly theological doctrine. Before long he began paying attention to Wordsworth, if only, for a time, through the lavish quotations in his *Modern British Essayists,* from which he could have fashioned his comment that August or September, in *White-Jacket,* on the "gentle and sequestered Wordsworth" at "placid Rydal Mount" (chap. 11). He also started reading the poetry in the Harper's Classical Library. In 1849 he bought Schiller's *Poems* in the Tauchnitz edition (Leipzig, 1844; Sealts, no. 439), probably picking it up at the Astor House in the shop of Rudolph Garrigue, "Foreign Bookseller," for thirty-seven and a half cents. (The Tauchnitz Burns, Byron, Moore, Ossian, Pope, and others were for sale at the same price.) In London in December he bought Thomas Chatterton's *Poetical Works* (Cambridge: Grant, 1842; Sealts, no. 137).

Melville's fantasy about a summer's luxuriant reading (which surely would have included poetry) collapsed as it became clear that *Mardi* would be a commercial and critical failure both in England and the United States. Guilty, and making amends, Melville wrote *Redburn* in June and July; then he wrote *White-Jacket* in August and September. Late that spring Melville had ill-advisedly meddled in the explosive matter of the warring actors, William Charles Macready and Edwin Forrest (perhaps without seeing either production of *Macbeth*), thereby playing a small part in the Astor Place riots, from which he could conclude that literary people were better off reading Shakespeare in the closet than seeing him mangled on the "tricky stage" (as Melville said in August 1850 in his essay on Hawthorne). Then even as he absorbed himself in writing *Redburn* he was drawn into the edges of another British-American sensation, the eruption into the Duyckinck literary circle of Thomas Powell, a genuine London literary man as well as a forger of commercial and literary documents. Powell came bearing British poetry and intimate tales of the living British poets and other literary people.

In London, Powell had used one poet as the means to approach another, and he sealed his new intimacies in two ways: by gifts (the more ready since Powell paid for them with stolen money, which also subsidized the publication of his own plays and poems from year to year) and by flattering comments on his new acquaintances' literary productions. He had made the acquaintance of Wordsworth by 1836. By 1839 his dear friend Southwood Smith had introduced him to Leigh Hunt, to whom he gave financial advice. By the winter of 1839–40 Powell had some hand in *The Poems of Geoffrey Chaucer, Modernized* (1841), being "edited" by R. H. Horne in loose collaboration with Wordsworth, Hunt, Elizabeth Barrett, and Powell's brother-in-law, Leonahard Schmitz (Dickens, 3:578). On July 18, 1841, Elizabeth Barrett cited Powell to Mary Russell Mitford as not only a friend of R. H. Horne but "a very dear friend also of Wordsworth's." She went on: "Mr Powell has written to me two or three times, & sent me his poems, which are marked by poetical sentiment & pure devotional feeling, but by no remarkable power. You know we had him with us in the Chaucer" (Kelley and Hudson, 5:81–82). Through Thomas Talfourd, Powell met Robert Browning and soon became "a constant visitor" at his house at Peckham; in 1842 Browning "took pity on him and helped his verses into a little grammar and sense" (Dickens, 3:578) and gave him his manuscript of act 1 of *Colombe's Birthday* (Dickens, 3:578). As Elvan Kinter says, "Browning was completely taken in; he introduced Powell to the 'Colloquials,' and, most telling of all, apparently confided to him the secret of *Pauline,* which was carefully withheld from everyone else where possible" (Kinter, p. 1097). In 1843 Powell dedicated a play, *The Blind Wife,* to Browning (Dickens, 3:578), and proved so charming that Browning's father violated his son's privacy by giving Powell some of Robert's juvenilia (unless Powell forged these documents). Powell added Charles Dickens to his list of friends, and by April 16, 1844, Dickens was inviting him to dinner.

In 1846 Powell's London literary career unraveled. Robert Browning on January 11, 1846, denounced him to Elizabeth Barrett in a letter that testifies to Powell's extraordinary power of insinuating himself into the good graces of writers much superior to himself and testifies even more clearly to Powell's genius for producing complicated states of outrage in people who had found him out. Browning continued to sputter out his outrage to Barrett, as in the letter of June 8, 1846, denouncing Powell's "impudence and brazen insensibility" (Kinter, p. 766). Powell was annoy-ing and persistent, "dreadful to encounter beyond all belief," a gnat-like Nemesis all the rest of Browning's life. Impudence and brazen insensibil-ity in literary and social matters were one thing, embezzlement another. The story of Powell's defrauding Thomas Chapman broke in June or July 1846. From Lausanne, Dickens wrote, "It is terrible to think of his wife and children." Shortly after this, Powell took laudanum in what passed as a suicide attempt. For the sake of his family, Chapman did not prosecute him (Dickens, 4:575 n. 2). By late in 1848, Powell was again in trouble with the law, accused of "obtaining money by means of false checks" (*Times* [London], January 10, 1849) and was arrested and committed to an insane asylum, Miles's Lunatic Asylum, at Hoxton. The magistrates were highly indignant, according to the same reprint, suspecting that Pow-ell's insanity "had been produced by artificial means—by the excessive use of opium, and resorting to the expedient of igniting charcoal in his bedroom—the object being to produce a temporary state of delirium, in the expectation by that means to evade justice." Early in 1849 Powell fled with his wife and children to the New World.

Powell arrived in Manhattan, forty years old (Poe's age), a few months before the term "Confidence Man" was coined in that city to identify the modus operandi of a kindred spirit, a native rogue. Already a portly embodiment of John Bull, Powell lightly resumed his career of crime, finding it good to be shifty on a new island. He cashed forged letters of credit at a local banking house even as he burst into the Anglophiliac New York literary world with a brilliantly contrived gift to the chief editor of the weekly *Literary World,* Evert A. Duyckinck (co-owner of the maga-zine with his brother George)—not a forged Browning association copy this time but something his American recipient would value more highly: "You take such good care of a book that I feel a double pleasure in begging your acceptance of the accompanying copy of 'Tennyson'—it contains some alterations in his own hand—Tho' trifling I thought you would prize it—."[40] It would not have occurred to the enthralled Anglophile Duyckinck to wonder whether the alterations were in Tennyson's hand or Powell's own. At least Powell truthfully claimed to be (or once to have been) on friendly terms with almost anybody who was anybody in the London literary milieu. His intimate anecdotes of literary London con-tinued for many weeks to charm Evert and George Duyckinck and their friend Cornelius Mathews (in effect a co-editor of the *Literary World*); and their hard-writing associate Herman Melville was impressed enough with

40. Powell's May(?) 1849 letter to Evert A. Duyckinck (Parker 1996, p. 646).

Powell to give him a copy of his new book, *Mardi*. On September 8, 1849, the *Literary World* under the heading "Unique Poems" printed as its lead article Powell's headnote to a recent poem by Robert Browning, there entitled "The Duke's Interview with the Envoy," then the poem itself, the text marred by Powell's italicizing many of its "characteristic" lines. His headnote began: "The genius of Browning is as peculiar and *provoking,* as it is *undoubted:* he enjoys the singular merit of being the most wilful and impracticable poet of the present time. He delights in putting the reader into the difficult position of either believing himself or the poet to be at fault. . . . He is the antithesis to Common-place—but while he avoids the old route he often gets shipwrecked on the rocks of the unintelligible; he compresses everything; as in some system of shorthand, he begins by leaving out the musical vowels, and then cuts down the consonants, till a few letters alone remain, which he insists upon doing the work of the whole Alphabet." Busy as he was with *White-Jacket,* Melville surely read this poem and Powell's literary criticism on it, only the first of the poems by Browning that Powell would soon help bring to Melville's attention.

With Duyckinck having boosted him into the pages of the *Literary World,* Powell soon gained a contract with G. P. Putnam (the eminent publisher of the greatest American writers, Cooper and Irving) for a two-volume survey of contemporary English and American writers. Sensing danger somehow, Putnam broke the contract, but by September (despite being arrested early in the month for forgery) Powell had a book in press at the respectable house of Appleton's—the scurrilously gossipy anecdotal *Living Authors of England,* which he had produced by copying out lengthy quotations from literary works of his quondam acquaintances and preceding them or tagging onto them magisterial-sounding off-the-cuff commentary. Powell's method of rushing his book-making along (all the while bemoaning the heat and humidity of a Manhattan summer) meant that Americans got a good sampling of British poetry (and prose passages) along with their gossip. Two features of *Living Authors of England* proved explosive. First, Powell gratuitously dragged Washington Irving into discussion only to slur him, an act of irreverence which evoked ferocious hostility, notably a denunciation from the Transcendentalist George Ripley in Horace Greeley's influential New York *Tribune.* Anyone who wants to comprehend the depth and intensity of American reverence for Irving at mid-century need only read these documents. Second, Powell included an impudent chapter on Dickens's personal habits in which he flattered Cornelius Mathews with an extended comparison between the New York novelist (who liked to be known as "the American Dickens") and the London novelist—just possibly a devious strategy for setting

Mathews up as a comic butt. The comparisons were so absurd that William Cullen Bryant's *Evening Post* omitted all mention of Mathews when it offered a prepublication sample from the Dickens chapter in September. A copy of the *Post* article reached Dickens fast. All afroth with outrage, Dickens exposed Powell in a letter to a New York acquaintance who had given a dinner for him in February 1842, Lewis Gaylord Clark, the editor of the *Knickerbocker.* Since Dickens wrote on the basis of the excerpt in the *Evening Post,* he had no idea that Powell had compared him to Mathews. Dickens probably did not know (and wouldn't have cared if he had known), but Clark was the bitterest enemy of the Duyckinck-Mathews clique. In writing to a literary man who had befriended him Dickens was innocently blundering into the hornets' nests of the publishing world of lower Manhattan. This storm broke while Melville was away.

Before, during, and after Melville's voyage to England in 1849–50 Tennyson was the contemporary British poet he was most aware of. Tennyson had not been famous enough to be collected by the Young Men's Association of Albany, judging from the catalogues of 1837 and 1843. If Melville really possessed a volume of Tennyson's poetry and gave it away in the late 1830s, as William H. Gilman was told (p. 104), he gave away an uncommon book. A few years later, in 1842, the Ticknor reprint of the new London two-volume edition became widely available. Augusta's friend Mary Blatchford's mother gave Augusta this set just before Christmas, 1844, so Melville could have seen it during his stays at Lansingburgh, where he finished *Typee* in 1845. Among the poems in it were "Mariana," which Melville may have alluded to in *Mardi,* and a poem that caught his fancy, the boozy tribute to the Cock Tavern, "Will Waterproof's Lyrical Monologue." In the next years after his return from the Pacific, Melville saw Tennyson commented upon in the press as a good second-rate poet, a delicate lyricist, but not serious, not hefty like Wordsworth, even (as Edward Bulwer-Lytton notoriously charged in 1846 in the first edition of his poem *The New Timon*) effeminate, the "School-miss Alfred." Too full of eccentric compound words said another, listing them scornfully the way G. W. Peck later listed Melville's coinages in *Pierre.* Melville at this time would have formed a long-lived view of Tennyson as a thin substitute for the too-early-lost Shelley and Keats—softly sensuous like Keats but lacking Keats's acute powers of observation, and aspiring like Shelley but lacking Shelley's fearless outspokenness on specific political abuses and remedies. Aside from aesthetic and intellectual qualities, Tennyson may already have struck Melville as too melancholy a poet to be endured in sustained doses. Nevertheless, it was flattering to be compared to him, as in this 1846 piece on *Typee* in the London *New Quarterly Review:* "There is something very striking in Mr. Melville's account of the approach of the vessel to the land of promise. The mild influence of the climate spread a 'delightful lazy languor' over the ship's company. We are reminded of the fine passage in Tennyson's 'Lotos Eaters': 'In the afternoon they came unto a land, / In which it seemed always afternoon; / All round the coast the languid air did swoon, / Breathing like one that hath a weary dream.'" In his attack on *Omoo* in the July 1847 *Whig Review* (a long review characterized by unintended revelation of his own weird sexual twists), Peck linked Melville and Tennyson as objects of disdain: "The manliness of our light literature is curdling into licentiousness on the one hand and imbecility on the other; witness such books as Omoo, and the namby-pamby Tennysonian poetry we have of late so much of." Melville was licentious, Tennyson imbecilic.

The Duyckinck circle followed Tennyson's career more tolerantly than Peck and others, especially after Powell arrived bearing that veritable volume by Tennyson that purported to contain a few changes in the poet's own hand. On September 22, 1849, just before Melville sailed for England, the *Literary World* in its review of Lieutenant Frederick Walpole's *Four Years in the Pacific* pointed out "coincidences" between that book and *Typee,* quoting as authority the London *Examiner.* The *Literary World* elaborated on "other coincidences still more remarkable": "Like Melville in Typee, Lieut. Walpole became lame and disabled in the Sandwich Islands, and found similar careful nurture in a domestic household with a gentle Fayaway in the person of the graceful little Elekeke." Then the *Literary World* printed a poem it entitled "Lieut. Walpole's 'Fayaway'": "So innocent-arch, so cunning-simple. / From beneath her gathered wimple. / Glancing with black beaded eyes, / Till the lightning laughters dimple, / The baby-roses in her cheeks; / Then away she flies." This was signed "Tennyson"—and indeed the lines were Tennyson's, but from the early poem "Lilian." Melville sailed for England with many readers of the *Literary World* duped into thinking that Tennyson had written about the heroine of *Typee,* Fayaway, as young Channing had in fact done. On the voyage Melville may have anticipated some literary tavern-crawling, and a week and a half later he went to "'the Dr Johnson Tavern'" (November 16).[41] Having steeped himself in "Will Waterproof's Lyrical Monologue," Melville the same day made his way to the "Cock Tavern," identifying it as "Tennyson's." The poet was nowhere near as great as Byron, say,

---

41. This quotation and ones later in this paragraph are from the journals Melville kept during his trips, printed in the NN *Journals* volume; citations are to the date of the entry.

but the man Tennyson, saturated with tobacco and steeped in port, was well worth following about in London. Two days later Melville made his way "to the Rainbow tavern—(Tennyson's)," no matter that the Cock, celebrated by the boozy Will, was by far Tennyson's favorite haunt. (On his return visit at the end of April 1857 Melville recorded: "Lay a sort of waterlogged in London.—Reverie at the 'Cock'"—in a Tennysonian mood, he meant, but no longer waterproofed, no longer proof against typhoons or mere spring rains.)

On his voyage home from England in January 1850 Melville may have sampled some of the poetic Elizabethan and Jacobean dramas he had purchased, but his longing to saturate himself in the poetic dramatists contemporary with Shakespeare was lifelong and probably never wholly satisfied because other interests intruded—in 1850 his starting *Moby-Dick* (after he asked to borrow a set of Elizabethan dramatists from Duyckinck in 1862, he was deflected into many weeks of reading books that helped him articulate an aesthetic credo). On New Year's Day, 1850, early in the voyage home, he read in his copy of Davenant's *Works* (London: Printed by T. N. for Henry Herringman, 1673; Sealts, no. 176), marking this passage in the preface to *Gondibert:* "For a wise Poet, like a wise General, will not show his strengths till they are in exact Government and order; which are not the postures of chance, but proceed from Vigilance and labor." Melville had been cagey enough in *Mardi* when he published poems appropriate to his young Yoomy, but not to a writer as ambitious as Melville had himself been in 1848. His "strengths," although he may not have recognized them, had been in the poetic prose of some of the earlier chapters such as 19, "Who Goes There?" Perhaps he also looked through his new volume of Chatterton's poems. Bridling at the editor's bland confidence in the introduction that "Shakspere must ever remain unapproachable," Melville called this "Cant" and retorted that no man "must ever remain unapproachable," an opinion that would break out a few months later in his essay on Hawthorne's *Mosses from an Old Manse.*

The Powell scandal had followed Melville to London in November 1849, for Allan sent newspapers to him; "the Powell Papers," Melville called them (in a December 13 journal entry). Even while Melville was still in England, sympathizing with the "poor devel" (December 17), Powell in a new manuscript treacherously linked Melville with Irving as the two worst enemies of the American mind (for allegedly hogging the money British publishers paid to Americans), and thereafter pursued his attack on Melville with information from a November 14 letter of Melville's from London that N. P. Willis had incautiously quoted in his

Home Journal on January 12. Upon his arrival in New York on the last day of January 1850 Melville was confronted by some of the damage Powell had done already, particularly the ugly charge in *Living Authors of America* that the Duyckincks quoted in the *Literary World* two days later, on February 2—that Melville and Irving were the worst enemies of the American mind. (Powell had dropped this calumny into his chapter on Edgar Allan Poe, who had died just at the time Melville was leaving for England.) Then Melville was assaulted by Powell's new diatribe against him and Irving in the *Herald* on the sixth. By good fortune, he never, even during the most vituperative stages of the Powell scandal or the ongoing slinging match between N. P. Willis and the *Literary World* group, became tarred by Lewis Gaylord Clark or others as a mere member of the Duyckinck-Mathews "Mutual Admiration Society," and Powell's personal attacks on him faded away.

Nevertheless, in February 1850 Melville must have looked through both *Living Authors of England* (published in late October, while he was bound for England) and *Living Authors of America* (published while he was on his long voyage home). The furor had died down by the time Melville saw *Living Authors of England,* so he could focus on any value the lengthy quotations from poetry might have for him—verse by Wordsworth, Landor, Rogers, Barry Cornwall, Moore, Hunt, Tennyson, Robert Browning, Arthur A. Clough, R. H. Horne, Elizabeth Barrett Browning, Henry Taylor, Coventry Patmore, Alfred Domett, and others. The quotations from poems were so extensive as to form little anthologies—of Tennyson, in particular, where lines were quoted about many women: Claribel, Lilian, Madeline, Adeline, Oriana (the name Melville had adopted for his Lizzie), and Eleanore. Powell intermixed quotations from "The Two Voices" (Tennyson's "greatest poem") with lengthy explication. He quoted "The Sisters," "Margaret," the "opening to 'Oenone [printed as Æone],'" "Locksley Hall," "The Lotos-Eaters," and "Choric Song." He ended with an economical introduction to the recent "The Princess: A Medley" as "a pleasing banter on the rights of women."

Mathews had imprudently entrusted Powell with his letters from Elizabeth Barrett written before and after her marriage, and Powell had stuffed them into the end of his chapter on her in *Living Authors of England.* Here in this tawdry setting she was made to hope that Mathews's *Wakondah* "may attain his full 'bulk' as a worthy national poem, and be recognised as such on either side of the Atlantic," then she was exposed as continuing with a cliché borrowed from American chauvinists, the notion that grandeur of natural scenery produces great poetry:

When American poets write, as they too often do, English poems, must not the sad reason be that they draw their inspiration from the English poets, rather than from the grand omnipresence of nature; must not both cause and result partake of a certain wrongness? I fear so. And all should be hope, and nothing fear, in America! You have room there for whole choruses of poets—Autochthones—singing out of the ground. *You,* with your Niagara for a Hippocrene, and your silent cities of the woods, too old for ruins, and your present liberties, and your aspirations filling the future.

Entrusting Powell with Barrett's letters was an act of insolent vainglory on Mathews's part. Now they were published, and however specious they were as literary theory, her ideas had gone into Melville's thinking before he burst out in August 1850 with his own rhapsodic literary nationalism, apparently soon after he had borrowed from Evert Duyckinck "Miss Barrett's Poems" in the 1844 two-volume London edition (*Log,* p. 376).

Powell's second hasty book, *Living Authors of America,* which had no chapter on Melville, contained a number of quotations from poems by Emerson; Willis; Poe; Longfellow; Bryant; Halleck (with due attention to "Marco Bozzaris"); Richard Henry Dana (the elder, the "Idle Man," where Powell used space to quote from Crabbe, Goldsmith, and Wordsworth); and Frances Sargent Osgood. Powell stuck all of "The World is too much with us" into his Poe chapter, where he also buried his attack on Irving and Melville.

In his figurative or actual basket (Allan had saved articles for Gansevoort during 1844 in an actual bushel basket) Melville found the January 26, 1850, issue of the *Literary World* with Elizabeth Barrett Browning's "The Child's Grave at Florence" from the London *Athenæum.* The paper continued to promote her, even more than her husband. Cornelius Mathews, most likely, on September 14, 1850, denounced the two-volume *Poems* (New York: C. S. Francis) as "discreditable," notably in its dropping of two notes "complimentary to Mr. Mathews, her own chosen medium of communication with the American public." The reviewer took further swipes at the Francis edition in the February 1, 1851, second notice of it along with the Chapman & Hall *Poems* (London, 1850). From the new poems in the London edition ("not to be found in the Francis edition") the reviewer quoted "Hiram Powers's Greek Slave" as Elizabeth Barrett Browning's tribute to "our country," the "West" whose grief was reflected in the face of the statue. The poem was a quarter century belated as an addition to the poems about Greek slavery; really, it was about the power of Art to effect political changes, to "break up ere long / The serfdom of this world!" (which would include American slavery as well as Italian domination by foreign tyrants). The reviewer reproached the poet for including "The Runaway Slave." She had failed to grasp that slavery was "purely a local institution": "The plan of the American Federation, which hereby proves itself essentially original, seems difficult of apprehension to the foreign mind; and statesmen and practical men have committed the confusion in which our respected poet is involved." In any case, the subject of a runaway slave was not "truly poetical." Mrs. Browning should not meddle with American institutions.

On June 21, 1851, the *Literary World* printed a review of the Francis & Company *"Casa Guidi Windows"* (as the heading read)—*Prometheus Bound, and other Poems; including Sonnets from the Portuguese, Casa Guidi Windows, etc.* The reviewer, a friend of Margaret Fuller, was presumably Mathews, whose poetic achievements she had praised in her essay on "American Literature," collected in the 1846 *Papers on Literature and Art.* As he read the part about the death of Garibaldi's wife and child, he remembered Fuller's fate off Fire Island and insisted that she deserved praise along with Mrs. Browning for "her devotion at Rome" and her (possibly factitious) "lost history of the time." America through Margaret Fuller had a claim on the Italian struggle for freedom. On July 5, 1851, the *Literary World* printed the second notice of "Mrs. Browning's Italian Poem," with ecstatic praise prefacing long quotations. On March 13, 1852, before Melville (angry since January) had succeeded in getting the Duyckincks to stop sending him their paper, the *Literary World* reviewed the new Francis edition of "Mrs. Browning's Poems," which more closely followed "the text of the author's copy," the London editions. There the reviewer concluded with a modern ranking: "The genius of Mrs. Browning, with the poems of her husband and Alfred Tennyson, and a few others, redeem the age succeeding that of Coleridge, Shelley, Wordsworth, and Keats, from the fear of abandonment by the Muses." Melville had the authority of the *Literary World* for thinking of the two Brownings and the new laureate as the greatest living poets.

In the sixteen months following the publication of *Mardi* in April 1849 Melville had his fill of seeing himself and his friends in the news, and particularly of dreading to see himself flecked with mud merely because he had been standing too close to reckless assailants in the petty New York literary feuds. In the early summer, his whaling book far along, he went off to the Berkshires for a vacation, and his buying a house in the Berkshires in September cannot have been wholly unrelated to his desire to escape from the cannibal island of Manhattan. He may have taken some contemporary poetry with him. The new poem of the early summer of 1850 was *In Memoriam;* the news in poetry was Tennyson's becoming poet laureate on Wordsworth's death. When *In Memoriam* appeared anonymously, at first some American reviewers did not know it was by Tennyson, though others did, right away. Melville borrowed it from Duyckinck somewhere about the time when Duyckinck gave a copy to Augusta. She wrote the donor on July 20: "Many thanks for 'The Vale of Cedars' [by Grace Aguilar] & Tennyson's new poem—I had been sighing for both of them. What a treat I shall have—the very titles breathe sadness!" (*New Log;* NYPL-D). Aguilar used poetic mottoes for her title page and all the chapters of her novel, some of them from a manuscript of her own, and the others from more or less conventional sources: Byron ("Hebrew Melodies" twice; *The Corsair,* "Well! Art thou happy," and *Parisina*); Mrs. Hemans eleven times; Shakespeare (*Richard II,* three times, *Othello, Measure for Measure* twice, *The Winter's Tale, The Merchant of Venice*); Sir Walter Scott (*The Lady of the Lake, Rokeby,* and the l'envoy from *Marmion*); Bulwer twice; Joanna Baillie twice; Charles Swain; James Grahame; and several from Grace Aguilar herself, identified as "MS." Chances are that Augusta and members of the household recognized quotations from Hemans almost as readily as quotations from Scott and Byron. Augusta, known as "the sad one," was a special lover of the sentimental and melancholy, and therefore of Tennyson. Melville, himself capable of writing a prose hymn to sadness, in chapter 188 of *Mardi* ("Sadness makes the silence throughout the realms of space"), particularly associated Tennyson with sadness. But just as Tennyson was never as interesting as his two early models, Keats and Shelley, he was never as important to Melville as the less likable Wordsworth. He was too much the melancholiac, too unable or unwilling to grapple for long with strenuous thoughts. In his longer works he was guilty of appalling aesthetic-intellectual lapses. On theological issues that mattered to Melville, he was far too willing to collapse into blind faith and wishful thinking.

In 1850 and 1851 Melville had been skimming and plundering source-books for the whaling narrative and reading his new friend Hawthorne's books, reading poetry quoted in books and reviews rather than reading whole volumes of recent poetry such as Wordsworth's *Poetical Works.* That changed. He turned to Wordsworth, probably as early as the fall of 1851, as passages in *Pierre* show. He had not been able to look at *The Prelude* the summer before (when Duyckinck had Appleton proof sheets at Pittsfield), but he had scanned a number of reviews and posthumous reassessments in 1850, from one of which he probably took a hint for the way he used the cathedral of Cologne in *Moby-Dick.* Melville was always alert for coincidences between his circumstances and those of other great writers, so he would have paid special attention to one topic he repeatedly encountered in comments on Wordsworth.[42] The *Literary World* in reviewing *The Excursion* (December 1, 1849) had quoted Wordsworth on retiring "to his native mountains, with the hope of being able to construct a literary work that might live." Although this review was published when Melville was abroad, he may well have skimmed the issues he missed, including this part of the first paragraph:

> It is a fine thing to think of a man, in a moral solitude, swung away into a quiet eddy beside the rushing current of the world's life, with mind full of imagery, and drinking in new draughts from its loving contact with this beautiful earth; full of profound and consoling thoughts upon human life and destiny, the harvest of a serene and blameless spirit; with heart blessed in its love of nature, and busy in active sympathies for the miseries of humankind; addressing himself to the labor of unfolding his inner mind, of sending forth his meditations, clad in the melody, and with all the adornments of noble verse, for the profit and comfort of mankind.

Melville was not a Berkshire "native," but his "first love" had been his uncle's Berkshire farm, and late in 1850 he "retired" (that is to say, withdrew) to his beloved American Lake District with the hope of being able to complete a literary work that might live. The Berkshires in topography constituted America's Lake District, the terrains so similar that lofty configurations were known as "Saddleback" in both regions.[43] In "Glimpses

---

42. After printing extracts in two earlier August 1850 issues, the Duyckincks on August 31 printed a review of *The Prelude* by Professor Henry Reed, the editor of Melville's edition of Wordsworth, and on September 14 a second paper by Reed, dated Philadelphia, September 6, which began with a letter from the late American artist Henry Inman to Reed describing the circumstances of his painting a much-admired portrait of the poet at Rydal Mount. The September 28 issue contained "Visit to Wordsworth's Grave" by "R. F.," reprinted from the London *Literary Gazette,* and two poems by E. A. W., "Wordsworth" ("He laid him down beside the murmuring streams") and "Keats" (followed by a poem by Tuckerman, "To Jenny Lind"). On October 12 the *Literary World* printed J. J. R.'s "In Memory of Wordsworth," and on November 23 the Reverend J. A. Spencer's "A Visit to Wordsworth." In the first year and a half after Wordsworth's death, however busy Melville was with *Moby-Dick* and *Pierre,* such tributes were inescapable.

43. Ironically, late in 1851, after the excursion to Mount Saddleback (or Greylock), George Duyckinck and surely Evert Duyckinck (from whom his brother kept no secrets) were distressingly reminded that poetry in America could embody dangerous impulses. Augusta Melville as a confidante of Sarah Morewood was entrusted with the "heart poetry" she had written in August on Greylock in the first frenzy of her infatuation with George, to whom she recklessly sent copies of the verses. Sarah Morewood's letters to George Duyckinck are in NYPL-D, carefully preserved by Evert Duyckinck. Augusta's consoling letter (see Parker 2002, p. 46) exists in a draft in NYPL-GL.

of Berkshire Scenery" (*Literary World,* September 27) Evert Duyckinck made the comparison explicit: "The mountains here are very closely grouped, descending rapidly in sharp outlines, and leaving narrow valley intervals, as the once beautiful valley of the Hoosac, which has the same elegance of a level floor, from which the hills rise at a well defined angle, which Wordsworth has noticed among the mountains of Westmoreland." He continued the comparison in regard to Stockbridge Bowl, below the Hawthorne cottage: "It has the cool freshness and life of some of our larger waters, with a more delicate sylvan beauty. The view partakes of the general breadth and expansiveness of American scenery, aided by the cold dry atmosphere, qualities which separate the landscape from the more limited, but softer lake country in England." Melville would quite naturally have associated his place as a writer in the Berkshires with Wordsworth's as a poet domiciled not in London but at Rydal Mount, as he had emphasized in chapter 11 of *White-Jacket.* In their 1855 *Cyclopedia* the Duyckincks declared that in the "comparative retirement" of Melville in the Berkshires was to be found "the secret of much of the speculative character engrafted upon his writings." Melville had been aware, all along, of similarities in his new "sequestered" situation and that of Wordsworth.

As Melville read Wordsworth he felt a growing diffidence toward the man along with admiration for much of the poetry. Many Americans had gained their sense of the poet as political reactionary from the Unitarian minister Orville Dewey's account of his visit to Wordsworth at Rydal Mount in 1833, as published in *Old World and the New* (New York: Harper & Brothers, 1836). Dewey, a Berkshire man, a native of Sheffield, Massachusetts, and a close friend of Lemuel Shaw, had by his own account lectured Wordsworth pompously but had enjoyed with him a memorable sunset at "Grassmere Lake." By contrast, John Wilson had made the Lake District a walkable guide to Wordsworth, endearing the man as he memorialized the landscape. Probably before he read Wilson, Melville had seen Wordsworth through the eyes of Lord Byron's *English Bards and Scotch Reviewers* and the introduction to *Don Juan,* as well as through Lord Jeffrey's skeptical essays in the *Edinburgh Review*—ironically, given Jeffrey's status as the chief of the "Scotch reviewers." Byron told him the man was a dullard author of a ridiculous theory and that his poetry was prosaic; and Jeffrey told him at the start of his review of *The Excursion* that Wordsworth's "peculiar system" (his literary theory) was deplorable. "Theory" was an accusation in the air. O. W. Wight, the reviewer of *The Prelude* in the May 1851 *American Whig Review,* wrote that Wordsworth's name, "on account of his real merit," had begun to be associated with Cowper and

Goldsmith, despite "his theory." News of Wordsworth's death on April 23 arrived before the same reviewer recorded this in the July issue: "A theory, vicious in some respects, has led him, in many places, to use unpoetic language and imagery." Chances are that Melville fixed on the association of Wordsworth with theory from reading his friend Tuckerman's *Thoughts on the Poets.* Tuckerman declared that Crabbe had no "elevated theory of his own, like that of Wordsworth," and he treated Wordsworth as an important figure in "an intellectual history of our age," perhaps more important that way than as a poet. Melville may well have responded powerfully to Tuckerman's description of Wordsworth as choosing to "voluntarily remain secluded amid the mountains, the uncompromising advocate of a theory."[44] In Italy in 1857 on viewing Leonardo's Last Supper, damaged by his experimenting with paints, Melville thought of another great man, Wordsworth, and his theory—one with deleterious effects on the permanent value of at least some of his poetry. Furthermore, Melville came to resent Wordsworth's sense of superiority toward other writers.[45]

Advocating a theory was undesirable but there was much to be said, as far as Melville was concerned, for choosing to remain secluded amid mountains. By the first years of the 1850s Melville was absorbing some works now seldom read, notably *The Excursion. The Prelude* likely came at too awkward a time (the summer of 1850) for it to become important to him, except for portions that had been published before 1850, such as "Vaudracour and Julia" (a separate poem in his edition of Wordsworth, and just possibly an influence on *Pierre,* in the story of Isabel). *Pierre* begins with an evocation of Spenser's power to arouse a young reader sexually and aesthetically, but it progresses with passages that echo particular Wordsworth poems and show "active sympathies for the miseries of humankind" as well as for the unfolding of the inner mind in majestic natural settings. In *Pierre,* and in works written in the next

44. The chapter on Wordsworth had been printed as early as February 1841, in the *Southern Literary Messenger* of February 1841, long before Tuckerman collected it in *Thoughts on the Poets.* Tuckerman reused this essay again as the introduction for *Poems of William Wordsworth* (New York: C. S. Francis, 1849). This was one of several editions of British poetry Tuckerman introduced, among them one of Felicity Hemans's *Poems* (Philadelphia: Sorin & Ball, 1845), edited by Rufus Griswold; Coleridge's *Poems* (New York: C. S. Francis, 1848); and the two-volume *Poems* by Elizabeth Barrett Browning (New York: C. S. Francis, 1854). Inevitably, given their close association over many years, Melville would have handled some of these volumes and others introduced by Tuckerman, although he is not known to have owned any of them.

45. In section 9 below, see Melville's 1862 annotation in Hazlitt's *Lectures on the English Poets* about "that contemptable man" Wordsworth.

years, Melville often described landscapes which derive a haunting part of
their power from human associations with them—a familiar Wordswor-
thian situation. Furthermore, humble, resolute, suffering Wordsworthian
cottagers appear in Melville's Berkshire writings, notably "Poor Man's
Pudding and Rich Man's Crumbs" (1854). Wordsworth helped human-
ize the Berkshires for Melville, helped teach him "To look on nature,
not as in the hour / Of thoughtless youth; but hearing oftentimes / The
still, sad music of humanity" ("Lines Written a few Miles above Tintern
Abbey").

Spenser, on Melville's mind as he wrote *Pierre,* was demonstrably off
his shelf and in his hands by the end of 1853 or the beginning of 1854,
when he used his father's copy of Spenser for mottoes in "The Encan-
tadas" (first published serially in *Putnam's Monthly Magazine* beginning
in March 1854).[46] Facing the title page he copied out: "'Spencer to me
(is dear) / whose deep conceit is such / As passing all conceit needs no
defence' / Shakspeare." Now he recognized passages that later writers had
echoed—Shakespeare (several times), Milton (several times), Pope (twice),
Wordsworth, even Poe ("Ulalume"). Melville recognized a Milton bor-
rowing in "The Ruins of Rome" (stanza 25: "To build with level of my
lofty stile"), and annotated: "Build the lofty rhyme / Milton." Melville
commented on a Wordsworth borrowing from "Vergil's Gnat," stanza 10,
underlining "Now in the valleys wandring at their wills" and identifying
a borrowing: "'The river wanders at its own secret will' Wordsworth."
He added, "How W. W. must have delighted in this stanza." Almost
surely reading Spenser for the first time as a grown man, he saw the poet
in the light of his own failing career as a writer. At 1.9.40 of *The Faerie
Queene* he marked: "Sleepe after toyle, port after stormie seas, / Ease after
warre, death after life, does greatly please." He marked the description
of Scudamour (4.1.45) after Blandamour has denounced him: "He little
answer'd, but in manly heart / His mightie indignation did forbeare."
Then Melville turned the little volume around so the spine was facing
him and wrote across the back flyleaf: "He little answered, but in manly
heart / His mighty indignation did forbear." He had made no effort to
influence or rebut any reviewer, or any treatment in the press, since he
first defended the authenticity of *Typee.* At 4.6.1 he drew a line along the
left margin and checked line 5: "What medicine can any leaches art" and
annotated it: "Macbeth to the doctor." That passage dealt with a theme
powerful in Melville's imagination, that of inward feeding:

46. For Allan Melvill's copy of Spenser, see note 19 above.

What equall torment to the griefe of mind,
And pyning anguish hid in gentle hart,
That inly feeds itself with thoughts unkind,
And nourisheth her owne consuming smart?
What medicine can any leaches art
Yeeld such a sore.

Much later he recalled this passage in portraying a Spenserean character, Mortmain, who lies "with one arm wedged under cheek, / Mumbling by starts the other hand, / As the wolf-hound the bone" (*Clarel,* 3.15.18–20). At 7.7.30 Melville did not bother to note "Autumne coming by" as a source for Keats's "To Autumn," but he marked lines 4–5: "And the dull drops that from his purpled bill / As from a limbeck did adown distill," and footnoted: "Keats—the monk in the chapel." In "Colin Clout's Come Home Again" Melville bracketed these lines: "Who life doth loath, and longs death to behold / Before he die, already dead with fear, / And yet would live with heart half stony cold, / Let him to sea, and he shall see it there." He annotated: "Absolute coincidence here between Spenser's conceit and another person's, in connection with a very singular thought." Melville knew his equals (he similarly noted a "singular coincidence" between his views on personal religion and Milton's). Melville took the Spenser volumes with him on his voyage on the *Meteor* in 1860 and, although he gave them to Augusta in August 1864, he retained a fresh memory of the poems all his life, as his annotations in other books show.

Melville's reading of Robert Browning is not well documented.[47] Melville had seen some poems early, notably "My Last Duchess" in 1849,

47. The line "But God is in Heaven, and Grant in the Town" in "The Fall of Richmond" (*Battle-Pieces,* 99.21 above) seems to be an allusion to the already famous lines from Robert Browning's *Pippa Passes* (1841): "God's in his Heaven— / All's right with the world" (1.227–28). When he read "The Unknown Masterpiece" (about a monk who paints anonymously) in *The Works of Eminent Masters,* apparently in 1871 or later, Melville noted "'Pictor Ignotus' by Browning," recalling a poem first published in 1845 in *Dramatic Romances and Lyrics* as "Pictor Ignotus. (Florence, 15–.)." The poem was included in the two-volume *Poems by Robert Browning* (London: Chapman & Hall, 1849), which was reprinted in 1850 by Ticknor, Reed, & Fields (Boston) and subsequently under the Ticknor & Fields imprint. "Pippa Passes" is in volume 1 of the Boston edition and "Pictor Ignotus" in volume 2. In 1864 Ticknor & Fields marketed these two volumes along with a third, *Men and Women,* as a three-volume set.

No one has reported seeing a volume of Robert Browning's poetry owned by Melville. Given the present ignorance, Melville's casual but specific allusion to "Pictor Ignotus" is almost as tantalizing as E. C. Stedman's comment to Melville on February 1, 1888: "as you said so much of Whitman" (see the next note).

and some reviews. On December 8, 1849, while Melville was away but Allan or Lizzie was saving issues for him, the *Literary World* reviewed the new two-volume *Poems* by Robert Browning (Boston: Ticknor, Reed, & Fields). For "the poetic faculty" and poems "suggestive of thought" the reviewer ranked Browning second only to Tennyson among the poets of "the present generation," the next after the aged poet laureate. There was "too much of the metaphysical element" in Mr. Browning's poems, but he "everywhere shows that he possesses a mind of great originality, a strong and fervid imagination, a moderate fancy, a clear insight into character, and no ordinary skill in its delineation." The reviewer carefully explained that Browning's "poems are cast in a dramatic form, but they are dramatic poems rather than regular dramas. A few only can be considered as dramas, yet all have the dramatic element in a greater or less degree." Delineation of character, particularly feminine character, exhibited his creative powers to the best advantage. Perhaps most striking to Melville was the reviewer's quoting Landor's extraordinary praise (even while dissenting from it): "Since Chaucer was alive and hale / No man hath walkt along our roads with step / So active, so inquiring eye, or tongue / So varied in discourse."

By the mid-1850s Melville had grounds for taking Robert Browning seriously. He could not have missed high praise of Browning in the December 1855 issue of *Putnam's* along with the third installment of his "Benito Cereno." Then in the April 1856 *Putnam's* appeared an article on Browning which constituted an excellent guided tour of several poems (here using the titles given by the magazine): "Soliloquy of the Spanish Cloister," "In a Year," "Marching Along," "A Toccata of Galuppi's," part of "Master Hugues of Saxe-Gotha," bits of "Sordello" ("as hard reading as anything we know"), and a lurid section from "Pippa Passes." Toward the end the writer acknowledged that Browning "is called obscure, because he is not particularly easy reading; and immoral, because he recognizes every great fact of human development, but is never for a moment warped from the true vision of what is essentially true." For Melville the better defense had come earlier: "The fact of occasional obscurity is not to be denied. Upon the whole, Browning's poetry is harder to follow than that of any other great English poet. But the chief reason is, that he boldly aims to express what is, in its nature, so evanescent and shadowy—to put into words processes of thought and feeling, so delicately inwrought and fluctuating, that only sharp self-observers and students of human character can pursue them." What Melville had done in *Pierre* (where he pervasively used words like *evanescence, evanescent, shadowy, process, transient thought, feeling, feelings, fluctuate,* and *fluctuations*), Browning was credited with doing in poetry. Melville could not have missed this reminder of his own achievement in prose and the possibility of his pursuing his psychological investigations in poetry.

Two other contemporary poets, one a principal inspiration to the other, stand out as possible models, the Englishman Martin Farquhar Tupper, whose long pop-philosophic pseudo-biblical poems had been astonishingly successful during Melville's early career, and the American Walt Whitman. Melville carried Tupper's address with him to London, but did not call on him. (In the early 1850s Melville's mother idolized the Englishman as the Christian writer her son was not.) When he read *Clarel* Melville's brother-in-law John Hoadley identified one line as taken from "The Moon," a poem in a minor Tupper volume, *A Thousand Lines* (1848), not the book everyone knew, *Proverbial Philosophy* (published in Wiley & Putnam's Library of Choice Reading in 1846, the year *Typee* appeared in another Wiley & Putnam series, the Library of American Books). The New Yorker Walt Whitman (away in New Orleans during much of Melville's own early New York career) had taken strong hints for his poetic form, subject, and even his hope of wild popular success from Tupper, and Melville may have heard in 1855 or 1856 about the poet whose ambition to incorporate the country into his poetry was still more recklessly daring than Melville's own ambitions at the time of *Moby-Dick* and *Pierre*. A copy of the first edition of *Leaves of Grass* had been in Hoadley's library since soon after it was published in 1855, but apparently years passed before Melville sat down with *Leaves of Grass*. Late in his life, Whitman apparently meant much to Melville, judging by his responses to "Socrates in Camden," Robert Buchanan's tribute to Whitman with incidental exalted praise of Melville, and especially judging by Edmund Clarence Stedman's reference to Melville's having said "so much" about Whitman that Stedman felt justified in sending him what he had written on the poet.[48] In the early and mid-1850s, however, Melville did not take Tupper seriously and did not take any American poet seriously.

In the mid-1850s Melville continued to allude to poetry in his prose. Into the manuscript of *The Confidence-Man* in late 1855 or in 1856, to give a few examples, he made allusions to several of Shakespeare's plays (including a song from *The Winter's Tale*) as well as to William Makepeace Thackeray's parody of Goethe, "The Sorrows of Werther"; Wordsworth's "Immortality" ode and, later, "My Heart Leaps Up When I Behold"; John Ruskin's "Mount Blanc Revisited"; Dryden's translation of Virgil's *Aeneid;* Allan Cunningham (a line from *Songs of Scotland, Ancient and*

---

48. *Log,* p. 806; see also the preceding note.

Modern); Pope's "Elegy to the Memory of an Unfortunate Lady"; Hunt's "Bacchus in Tuscany"; Pope again (drawing the title of chap. 31 from the last two stanzas of "Sandys' Ghost; Or, A Proper New Ballad on the New Ovid's Metamorphosis: As it was Intended to be Translated by Persons of Quality"); and Burns's "Tam o'Shanter." Melville may have been reading much of Dryden besides the translation of the *Aeneid*. While he was at Arrowhead Melville owned the 1854 London edition (Sealts, no. 191) of Dryden's *Poetical Works* published by George Routledge, who had pirated *Israel Potter,* although an 1854 Little, Brown edition was available in Boston. Melville may have picked his Dryden up in England in 1857. He did not mark the poems at the front, possibly because he already knew them. Toward the back he marked passages in *Tales from Chaucer,* "Palamon and Arcite," book 3. In Dryden's translations from Boccaccio he marked "Sigismonda and Guiscardo" and "Cymon and Iphigenia." Melville gave the book to Sarah Morewood, most likely in the late 1850s. In his customary way, he exhausted the book before giving it away.

In the 1850s, as throughout his life, Melville enjoyed many British poets even while harboring no illusions that they were great poets. This is clear in the passage from *Mardi* quoted early in this section, clear also in his 1862 marginalia on Hazlitt's dismissal (in *Lectures on the English Poets*) of Samuel Rogers as "a very lady-like poet," an "elegant, but feeble writer."[49] Melville offered a reasonable defense: "Rogers, tho' no genius, was a painstaking man of talent who has written some good things. 'Italy' is an interesting book to every person of taste." A poet of genius would be in the first rank, but "a painstaking man of talent" might well earn a place in the third or even second rank of poets. By contrast, in the same passage Melville read with apparent approval Hazlitt's indictment of Campbell's "Pleasures of Hope" for paying "a painful attention" when "there is little to express." When Hazlitt labeled *Gertrude of Wyoming* as "a kind of historical paraphrase of Mr. Wordsworth's poem of Ruth," showing "little power, or power enervated by extreme fastidiousness," Melville marked with a bow the continuation of the indictment, which included the accusation that Campbell is "so afraid of doing wrong, of making the smallest mistake, that he does little or nothing." Melville checked the line "The poet, as well as the woman, that deliberates, is undone." Melville marked Hazlitt's declaration that Thomas Moore lacks "intensity, strength, and grandeur," shows no "feeling of continued identity." "Lalla Rookh" was a mistake: "Fortitude of mind is the first requisite of a tragic or epic writer,"

---

49. For Melville's copy of Hazlitt (New York: Derby & Jackson, 1859), see Olsen-Smith and Sealts, no. 263b, and pp. 917–19 below.

Hazlitt declared, and Melville underlined the sentence and triple-checked it. Melville was an elitist, but not to the point of letting his sense of a poet's ultimate rank (as long it was in the top three) interfere with his enjoyment of "beautiful imaginings." He could learn something from minor British poets.

In the satirical "Young America in Literature" (bk. 17), which he recklessly interpolated into his completed manuscript of *Pierre* early in January 1852,[50] Melville all belatedly asserted that his hero "possessed every whit of the imaginative wealth which he so admired" in poetry when it was "by vast pains-takings, and all manner of unrecompensed agonies, systematized on the printed page." Melville was careful to say that Pierre had not really become a true poet himself: "Not that as yet his young and immature soul had been accosted by the Wonderful Mutes, and through the vast halls of Silent Truth, had been ushered into the full, secret, eternally inviolable Sanhedrim, where the Poetic Magi discuss, in glorious gibberish, the Alpha and Omega of the Universe. But among the beautiful imaginings of the second and third degree of poets, he freely and comprehendingly ranged." If Spenser, Milton, and Shakespeare were poets of the first degree of greatness, then Wordsworth, Coleridge, Byron, Shelley, and Keats might be ranked in the second degree, while a hoard of genuinely competent eighteenth-century poets and moderns like Cowper, Rogers, Crabbe, and Campbell might have helped populate the third degree, if not the lower reaches of the second. Tennyson, successor to Wordsworth as poet laureate, and younger poets like Elizabeth Barrett Browning and Robert Browning would already be recognized as newcomers, in the third rank but perhaps already earning their way into the second.

In the Berkshires Melville saw his career falter with *Moby-Dick*, his popularity all but lost with *Pierre* to the point that he could not publish his next book, *The Isle of the Cross*, his telling of the story of the long-suffering Agatha Hatch which he had heard in Nantucket in 1852.[51] For three years he wrote short stories or serials—wrote almost unremittingly except during the worst of the illnesses that began to strike him. Being so ambitious ever since he had worked his way into *Mardi*, Melville would naturally have thought of what it might be like to emulate on their own grounds the greatest writers, the poets, with whom he knew he stood on equal footing, recognizing, more than once, singular coincidings between

50. See *Reading Melville's "Pierre; or, The Ambiguities,"* by Brian Higgins and Hershel Parker.

51. For *The Isle of the Cross* see section 12 below, Parker 2002, pp. 136–61, and Parker 2007.

his thoughts and experiences and theirs. But there is no evidence that Melville in the mid-1850s was suffering any tension between having to continue to write prose while hoping to write poetry. Until after 1856, he was simply struggling against horrific odds to hang onto his career as a prose writer.

V

THE STATUS OF POETRY AND THE TEMPTATION OF FLUNKEYISM

UP FOR DEBATE all through the nineteenth century had been the question of whether there was a great modern poem and great modern poet in English. Francis Jeffrey in the *Edinburgh Review* had weighed candidate after candidate without discovering one. In May 1851, the month Melville left the manuscript of *The Whale* with the stereotyper Craighead, the New York *International Magazine* featured an excerpt from the London *Eclectic Review* focused not on poem but poet: "Has There Been a Great Poet in the Nineteenth Century?" The *Eclectic Review* listed twenty-three renowned British poets of the first half of the century: "Bloomfield, Wordsworth, Coleridge, Southey, Campbell, Moore, Byron, Shelley, Keats, Professor Wilson, Hogg, Croly, Maturin, Hunt, Scott, James Montgomery, Pollok, Tennyson, Aird, Mrs. Browning, Mrs. Hemans, Joanna Baillie, and the author of 'Festus'" (that is, Philip James Bailey). None of them, according to the *Eclectic,* had "produced a work uniquely and incontestably, or even, save in one or two instances, professedly GREAT." Then the *International Magazine* grouched patriotically: "The critic appears never to have heard of our Bryant, Dana [that is, the elder Dana, "the Idle Man"], Halleck, Poe, Longfellow, or Maria Brooks, any one of whom is certainly superior to some of the poets mentioned in the above paragraph; and his doctrine that a great poem must necessarily be a long one—that poetry, like butter and cheese, is to be sold by the pound—does not altogether commend itself to our most favorable judgment." The debate over who might or might not be a great modern poet could rage year after year, but everyone agreed that a great poet was needed and a great poem was to be looked for. No serious critic said the day of poetry was over.

A misconception conspicuously promulgated by John P. McWilliams in *The American Epic: Transforming a Genre, 1770–1860,* holds that by the time Melville wrote *Moby-Dick* he and his contemporaries would have seen the "prose epic" as the highest literary form for his time, not epic poetry. Analysis of hundreds of contemporary reviews of poetry (including dozens of reviews of particular poems such as *Evangeline* and *Hiawatha*) indicates that, to the contrary, most literary people in Great Britain and the United States looked upon poetry as the highest literary form and assumed that the great writers of a country would be its poets, not its prose writers. All during his early career in New York City Melville saw evidence that most critics who hoped for the emergence of great American literature were looking for it to come in the form of poetry, not prose. Late in 1847 and early in 1848, the months he was working his way deep into the manuscript of *Mardi,* Melville knew that some critics were hailing Longfellow's *Evangeline* as the great literary work they had been looking for. In the Washington *National Era* of November 25, 1847, had not Whittier cried out, "EUREKA!—Here, then, we have it at last! An American poem, with the lack of which British reviewers have so long reproached us"? However poetic his own prose was sometimes called in 1849 in reviews of *Mardi,* Melville could still see on every hand that the great American literary work was expected to come as a real poem, not as a poetic prose work.

The idea that impelled Whittier's enthusiasm for *Evangeline* flourished in the consciousness of many literary people: since a great national literature must come in the form of poetry, America, highly desirous of achieving literary independence from Great Britain, was on the lookout for a great national poem. The Washington *National Intelligencer* (November 23, 1855) opened the review of *Hiawatha* this way: "We have in this newest Poem of Mr. Longfellow perhaps the only American Epic. . . . What the greatest Poets have done for their lands Longfellow has done for his." Through the 1850s poems such as Longfellow's *The Golden Legend* and then *Hiawatha* (an adaptation of a Finnish epic) received far more extensive and admiring journalistic coverage than Melville's books (even allowing that much of the writing on *Hiawatha* dealt with charges that the metrics and subject were plagiarized). The bias toward poetry is clear in the fate of two works by Charles Kingsley. In the spring of 1855 his novel *Westward Ho!* tended to receive only slightly longer reviews in the United States than Melville's *Israel Potter.* The next year, while *The Piazza Tales* was receiving mainly short polite notices, Kingsley's *Poems* had five columns lavished on it in the New York *Tribune* of May 10, 1856.

To be sure, some critics complained that would-be epics were too long. As early as his review of Joel Barlow's *The Columbiad* in the *Edinburgh Review* (October 1809), Francis Jeffrey had acknowledged that "men certainly bore" (that is, endured) "long stories" (epic poems) "with more patience of old than they do now." (This review Melville owned in *Modern British Essayists*.) By the late 1850s ordinary British and American readers were seldom inclined to spend their evenings reading long poems by Spenser or Milton, and still less likely to read or reread lengthy poems by long-popular eighteenth-century writers like Thomson, whose *The Seasons* had been familiar to the Melvilles from the 1830s (so that as late as 1852 Augusta could casually apply a line from it to Melville's youthful schoolteaching). Scott's beloved *The Lady of the Lake* and other long poems and even Byron's long narrative poems were read less frequently. Nevertheless, educated readers were still willing, and eager, to devote many hours to new poems. Melville's brother-in-law John Hoadley was far from the only man in the country who read Longfellow's *The Golden Legend* aloud to his assembled family nightly until he had finished it, and who expected to find in poetry a higher reward than in prose. All through the 1860s, the status of poetry remained higher than that of prose. The phrase "the great American novel" (famous now as the title of a January 1868 article by J. W. DeForest in the *Nation*) pre-dates by a decade or so the time when working critics stopped looking for great American literature to come in the form of an epic poem. Throughout the 1860s and even the early 1870s (when Melville was writing *Clarel*), the status of poetry, especially epic poetry, remained high. At some yet-to-be-established point toward the end of Melville's life, perhaps before the 1870s were over, a majority of influential literary critics ceased looking for great new literary works to come in the form of the long poem and began looking for such a great work to come as prose fiction.

That shift was too late to affect Melville. All his life he had heard the poets and critics say that the surest way to achieve ultimate immortality in literature was to write great poetry, and he believed them. If Apollo and the Muses inspired anything, it was poetry, not prose. When he read Milton's appeal to Urania at the start of book 7 of *Paradise Lost,* Melville noted, "Tasso's invocation," remembering the address to an explicitly Christian (not Hellenic) muse in *Jerusalem Delivered*. (He also marked heavily Wordsworth's obviously Miltonic "Preface" to *The Excursion,* where Wordsworth also invokes Urania.) Therefore "Why poetry?" was not a question Melville would have thought to ask after his prose career floundered. If he wanted to keep writing, and ultimately to publish again, the supremely challenging alternative was poetry. Melville came to see, after 1857, that his own most prolonged mature wrestling with the "angel—Art" (a struggle memorialized in his short poem "Art," in *Timoleon*) would thereafter be in poetry, whether short poem or poetic epic.

Without believing that Apollo or Urania had descended upon New York or Pittsfield and swept him to the top of Trinity Church or Greylock, Melville knew that he had the true "godlike gift" depicted by Collins in the "Ode on the Poetical Character," where God the Creator imagines the universe into existence, and, in Collins's daring analogy, the poet imagines a new literary world into existence. Becoming a great poet in the New World, however, was more problematical.

From the mid-1830s, at the latest, Melville had pondered Sydney Smith's infamous observations on what passed as poetry (and literature in general) in the United States. Even that early, from Simeon De Witt Bloodgood's lectures, if nowhere else, Melville caught reverberations from patriotic demands that America have its own national literature, and he knew from Bloodgood's comments on Joel Barlow that patriotism without poetic power would not win discerning and enduring praise. During his whaling years and his year in the navy, Melville missed some of the furor over the dubious merits of American poetry, notably the pyrotechnics of early 1844 when the *Foreign Quarterly Review* disdainfully reviewed the qualifications of most of the candidates Rufus Griswold had brought forth in his *Poets and Poetry of America*. The opening set the tone: " 'AMERICAN Poetry' always reminds us of the advertisements in the newspapers, headed 'The best Substitute for Silver': if it be not the genuine thing, it 'looks just as handsome, and is miles out of sight cheaper.' " The reviewer was gentle with Peter Gansevoort's neighbor and friend, the Albany versifier Alfred B. Street, and considered a few to be competent poets—chiefly Bryant and Poe (although the latter was an imitator of Tennyson). The best American poet, Longfellow, could not really be considered "an indigenous specimen" of a poet because his mind had been "educated in Europe." Poe was sure Dickens was the writer of the article, and in fact Dickens may have had a hand in it, although John Forster, later his biographer, all but confessed to the chuffed Longfellow that he had written it himself (Moss, p. 158).

American critics and some American versifiers of the young Republic had brought the scorn of the *Foreign Quarterly Review* on themselves. Rather than taking the risk of claiming high originality and power, these Americans had resorted to justifying and ennobling their poets by billing them as equivalents of established British poets, following the classical precedent whereby Romans exalted the creators of its fledging literature by comparing them to Greek masters. Just as Virgil had been called the Roman Homer and Plautus the Roman Aristophanes, now in the modern updating Washington Irving was the American Goldsmith, William C. Bryant the American Wordsworth, James Fenimore Cooper the American Scott, and Fitz-Greene Halleck the American Byron. Below these loftiest claimants was a range of other poets claiming equivalence or inviting favorable comparisons with British poets—including some British poets whose reputations did not long outlive those of their American imitators. In the *Foreign Quarterly Review* Forster was merciless, beginning with Lydia H. Sigourney, who was "usually advertised, as if it were something to boast of, as the American Hemans." Charles Sprague imitated Pope badly; Wilcox imitated Thomson badly (a compounded folly, since he should have imitated the Spenser of *The Faerie Queene* directly instead of imitating an imitator); Trumbull imitated Butler's *Hudibras;* Dwight imitated Pope; Robert Paine was "esteemed by his countrymen as a copier of Dryden's" (but he copied him "so badly" that Forster was "inclined to let him off as a worse original"); Pierpont imitated Burns; Poe was "a capital artist after the manner of Tennyson"; Hill toiled "hopelessly after the bounding lyrics of Barry Cornwall"; and Fairfield plagiarized Byron's *Don Juan* ("Ave Maria! 'tis the hour of prayer"). Charles Fenno Hoffman distanced "all plagiarists of ancient and modern times in the enormity and openness of his thefts," being merely Thomas Moore "hocused for the American market." There was no end to Hoffman's thievery: "The turns of the melody, the flooding of the images, the scintillating conceits—are all Moore. Sometimes he steals his very words." Hoffman's songs were "monkeyana," as in "monkey-see, monkey-do."

The next to last paragraph in the *Foreign Quarterly Review* was devastating:

> The result upon the whole examination may be thus briefly summed up: that American poetry is deficient in originality; that it is not even based upon the best examples; that it is wanting in strength of thought, in grace and refinement; and errs largely on the side of false taste and frothy exuberance. The classical acquirements of the American poets are loudly insisted upon by their critics: but no such influence is visible in their works— Longfellow and three or four more excepted. It might rather be predicated that they are utterly ignorant of the principles of art, or that they hold all principles in contempt. The qualifications of the poet are lowered in them to the meanest and scantiest elements. They are on a level with the versifiers who fill up the corners of our provincial journals, into which all sorts of platitudes are admitted by the indiscriminate courtesy of the printer. . . . Numerous anecdotes are related, even by themselves, of their velocity in composition. We can readily believe them. But they will find out in the long run, that the go-ahead system is as fallacious in literature as they have already, to their cost, found it to be in more substantial affairs.

This issue of *Foreign Quarterly Review* was reprinted in the United States, as usual, probably in various cities, and the entire review was reprinted separately in Park Benjamin's *The New World* on January 27 and February 3, 1844, where it was cringingly read by everyone except Longfellow and his circle. Some of the other Cambridge-Boston poets were outraged at how Forster had dismissed the verse of the elder Richard Henry Dana. The only thing worse than being held up for worldwide contempt was being left out of Griswold's collection altogether, as young James Russell Lowell had been. A few months later, in July, the Boston *North American Review* printed a ferocious and at points downright Swiftian rebuttal exposing the social evils of contemporary England. Echoes of the barrage from the *Foreign Quarterly Review* and the retort from the *North American Review* were reverberating still in New York circles when Melville returned at the end of October 1844 and soon settled down to writing *Typee* in lower Manhattan. (There at the end of January 1845 he witnessed the hoopla over Poe's new American poem, "The Raven.")

From mid-1846 through 1851 Melville was on close terms with American literary nationalists associated with Evert Duyckinck, after 1847 joint editor of the *Literary World* (in a format blatantly copied from the London *Athenæum*). Rather than abandoning their self-glorifying comparisons to British writers after the contempt shown by the *Foreign Quarterly Review,* American critics and poets shamelessly persisted in applying these comparisons. Given the competitive climate, when Melville was hailed (mercifully, in London) as the modern Crusoe or the new DeFoe, that seemed about as high a status as he could attain as a writer. Only after declaring his intellectual independence and lofty ambition in *Mardi* had Melville read Shakespeare and found him titanic but approachable. Indeed, the common assertion that Shakespeare was unapproachable was "Cant," according to Melville.[52] In his essay on Hawthorne (written at Pittsfield in early August 1850, with Duyckinck and Mathews at hand, and carried by Duyckinck back to New York to rush into the next two issues of the *Literary World*) Melville proclaimed that we needed no American Goldsmith, and, by implication, no American Dickens. As he wrote his way into this fervent essay, Melville adopted the persona of a hyperbolic Virginian summering in Vermont, an extravagant man who pleaded with America

52. Melville made this comment in annotating his copy of Chatterton; see section 4 above.

to "prize and cherish her writers." Melville as the Virginian says that even "were there no Hawthorne, no Emerson, no Whittier, no Irving, no Bryant, no Dana, no Cooper, no Willis (not the author of the 'Dashes', but the author of the 'Belfry Pigeon')—were there none of these, and others of like calibre among us, nevertheless, let America first praise mediocrity even, in her own children, before she praises . . . the best excellence in the children of any other land. Let her own authors, I say, have the priority of appreciation." The "I say," as always with Melville, was the sign that he was stem-winding his oratory. Since his Virginian was not sufficiently passionate, he invented an even more "hot-headed Carolina cousin" who on the fiery topic of American Literature once said, "If there were no other American to stand by, in Literature,—why, then, I would stand by Pop Emmons and his 'Fredoniad,' and till a better epic came along, swear it was not very far behind the Iliad." "Take away the words," says the Virginian, "and in spirit he was sound." In this manuscript version, before Duyckinck censored what he wrote, Melville was thinking of Emerson not as poet but as an essay writer; Dana was the younger Dana, the author of *Two Years Before the Mast,* not his poet father. Melville had praised only three poets, Whittier, Bryant, and Willis, but he had learned nothing he wanted to know from any American poets he had yet encountered, and none of these three meant much to him, once his rhetorical point had been made.

Once wound up in his argument, Melville went on with a personal criticism of Washington Irving (which somehow escaped Duyckinck's censorship but which outraged the old man and for many years rankled Pierre Irving, his nephew and biographer). That "graceful writer," he said, not needing to name Irving, "who perhaps of all Americans has received the most plaudits from his own country for his productions,— that very popular and amiable writer, however good, and self-reliant in many things, perhaps owes his chief reputation to the self-acknowledged imitation of a foreign model, and to the studied avoidance of all topics but smooth ones." Melville as the Virginian declared, "it is better to fail in originality, than to succeed in imitation." We "want no American Goldsmiths; nay, we want no American Miltons." Perhaps because Longfellow had received so much praise from British critics, Melville identified the Boston (or Boston-Cambridge) poets and critics as the most subservient: "Let us away with this Bostonian leaven of literary flunkeyism towards England. If either must play the flunkey in this thing, let England do it, not us."

"Hawthorne and his Mosses" caught the eye of literary people (Longfellow called it to Hawthorne's attention), but its fervent nationalism did nothing to stop the search for American equivalents of British poets. By the late 1850s E. C. Stedman, because he was a banker who wrote poetry, was called the American Rogers. Melville had been entertained by Rogers in London and had read much of Rogers's poetry, and Stedman was no Rogers. (Decades later, he became a decent, respectful admirer of Melville.) Richard Henry Stoddard, whom Hawthorne had thought of hiring to work at the consulate in Liverpool but instead went into the New York Custom House, brazenly set himself up as the American Keats. The Duyckincks in their *Cyclopedia* at the end of 1855 validated Stoddard's claims by printing in its entirety his ode called "Autumn": "Divinest Autumn! who may sketch thee best, / For ever changeful o'er the changeful globe? / Who guess thy certain crown, thy favorite crest, / The fashion of thy many-colored robe? / Sometimes we see thee stretched upon the ground, / In fading woods where acorns patter fast." Rowland Morewood signed his copy of Stoddard's *Songs of Summer* (Boston: Ticknor & Fields, 1857) "Broadhall / 1858," so over the hill from Arrowhead Melville could easily have sampled some of the poems by Stoddard in his later Browningesque phase.

When Melville's half-brother-in-law Sam Shaw came to visit in the summer of 1859, he brought a gift, Emerson's *Poems* (Boston: Phillips, Sampson, 1858; Sealts, no. 206), which Melville may not have read before, although chances are that he had sampled some Emerson poems in his promiscuous reading of his countrymen's and countrywomen's poetry. Emerson, by contrast with the others, was a poet to be taken seriously in the late 1850s, the way Melville took Robert Herrick, a copy of whose poetry he acquired late that summer of 1859 (*Hesperides: or The Works Both Humane and Divine* [Boston: Little, Brown, 1856; Sealts, no. 271])—all the more so because Melville had begun writing short poems as a way of learning the craft, and Emerson had never been visited by the epic muse. In Emerson's "Merlin" Melville scored the injunction that a poet should not try to write poetry in "weak, unhappy times" but should wait "his returning strength" (after which his rhymes might again be "efficacious") and the injunction not to force poetry into existence through the use of mere "meddling wit" but, again, to wait until the mind is "propitious," for the mind of the poet will publish, produce, only when it is inclined to do so. It might have been better for Melville to read advice less in accord with his own early vaunting of the certain something unmanageable in a writer, but at least he got from Emerson's poem confirmation that elsewhere in the United States, and in fact in his own Massachusetts, someone had been grappling with some of his own "poet-problems" (the term he used in a verse-epistle to Daniel Shepherd, dated July 6, 1859).

Melville may have recognized as a poet-problem the difficulty of connecting his admiration of the classical past with genres he might imitate in his own poetry, but he had little guidance. He had read the vague address to the "Genius of Ancient Greece!" by Akenside, which ends with the poet's pointing the high example of the Greek poets to his "compatriot youth" and urging that the British lyre be tuned to Attic themes: could he derive anything suggestive for tuning his American lyre to Attic themes? Whether he was defining himself in relation to his contemporaries or in opposition to them, as a writer of some poetic prose he had ample reason for thinking that he might make a new career as a poet. The Melville who made confident judgments as to the first, second, and third degree of poets would never have started to write poetry with the thought that he would be one more American mediocrity. Having experienced what being called the American DeFoe amounted to, Melville felt no urge as a poet to become the American Alfred Tennyson or the American Robert Browning. He would not have become a poet at all unless he thought he could become as good a poet as they were. After all, even Shakespeare was approachable.

VI
A NONPARTISAN BECOMING A POET DURING THE RISORGIMENTO

FROM HIS YOUTH Melville knew poetry that dealt with immediate political issues and more ambitious poetry that dealt with the destiny of nations. In their ways the American *The Columbiad* and *The Fredoniad* (and even the less sweeping *M'Fingal*) had been, like Virgil's *Aeneid,* attempts to celebrate the founding of a nation. Melville may not have known that Spenser had been an ultra-partisan in *The Present State of Ireland.* His annotations in *The Faerie Queene* do not suggest that he knew that Duessa was sometimes thought to be a portrait of the beheaded Mary Queen of Scots, yet in "Prothalamion" he queried "Essex?" as the man alluded to as the "noble peer" (one "Whose dreadfull name late thro' all Spain did thunder"). The editors of *The Life and Death of King Richard the Second* in Melville's Hilliard, Gray Shakespeare had taught him that the name of Essex was politically explosive in the mid-1590s. From *Richard II,* Melville also knew the "this England" passage, perhaps the greatest patriotic tribute to the isle (never mind that the island did not consist only of England). He knew, and probably did not admire without reservations, Milton's "To the Lord General Fairfax" and "To the Lord General Cromwell." Milton's sonnet "On the late Massacher in Piemont" (1655) would have appeared, by Melville's time, to be the first great English denunciation of Catholic Italy, the "triple tyrant" accused of the murder of the Waldenseans being the pope, from the bejeweled three-tiered papal tiara. Melville knew Samuel Butler's *Hudibras* (London: Baker, 1710; Sealts, no. 104), in which part 3, canto 2 (1678) is a partisan political history of the period between the death of Oliver Cromwell and the Restoration, scathing toward both Presbyterians and Jesuits, and singling out for contempt the slippery side-switching Earl of Shaftesbury. (He knew that Butler, for his own epic adventures of knight and squire, had revived Spenser's Hudibras, a minor character in *The Faerie Queene*.) Melville almost surely knew Dryden's "Absalom and Achitophel" (1681), in which Achitophel was a portrait of Anthony Ashley Cooper, the Earl of Shaftesbury, whose most recent schemings were to exclude any Catholic from succession to the throne, particularly the king's brother James. Melville had seen Thomson's five-part *Liberty,* the first part a comparison of ancient and modern Italy and the fourth a consideration of the advantages of modern Britain, and he would have known Thomson's inescapable lyrics to "Rule Britannia" ("Rule Britannia, rule the waves; / Britons never will be slaves").

One of the standard poems of Melville's childhood, Campbell's "The Pleasures of Hope" (1799), had a section on the evils of Negro slavery (written before Britain's abolition of the slave trade) and a section on the sufferings of the Polish people after the first and second partitions. Tadeusz Kościuszko, the Colonel of Engineers in the Continental Army, who led a revolt against the Russian army in 1794, after his capture and release from prison, had spent a year in Philadelphia, 1797–98, time enough to confer with many of his old friends like Thomas Jefferson and confirm his position as a hero of the world, not merely of the former colonies. His residence in the United States helped to make the sufferings of Poland real for many Americans. The Partitions of Poland constituted an early international cause about which the young American Republic could express the sort of polite sympathy that made them feel better about themselves as an altruistic people but cost them little or nothing and did no practical good for the Poles. Melville reflected this general knowledge in *Moby-Dick* when he referred offhand to the three pirate powers, Russia, Prussia, and Austria, who had dismembered Poland while England and France had stood by without helping the Poles.

Melville's first ideas about the French Revolution came from appalled comments he heard from his Melvill grandfather and other elderly relatives.

The issues all his life were embodied by two mighty opposites, Edmund Burke and Thomas Paine. In his maturity the image that stuck in his mind was derived from Carlyle's history of the revolution, Anacharsis Cloots addressing the first French Assembly as a representative of all mankind. Apparently none of his main ideas about the French Revolution came from poetry. Wordsworth's "Vaudracour and Julia" in Melville's edition was extracted from its context in *The Prelude* in such a way that it was not obviously a poem about the French Revolution. Melville did know some poetry of the Napoleonic era, and respected Napoleon profoundly all his life despite the hostile tenor of some of that poetry. Melville probably knew from early life Campbell's tribute to Horatio Nelson's victory, "The Battle of the Baltic" (1801), though his surviving reference to it is in the late *Billy Budd, Sailor* manuscript.[53] (Later he knew Tennyson's 1852 tribute to Nelson in the poem on the death of the Duke of Wellington, and recalled it in *Billy Budd,* also.) Melville probably read but did not mark Wordsworth's "Sonnets Dedicated to Liberty" or the following 1816 "Thanksgiving Ode." From his comment in Hazlitt's *Lectures* we know that he was offended by Wordsworth's repeated criticisms of Napoleon, such as Wordsworth's hostile interpretation of B. R. Haydon's painting of Napoleon on St. Helena (a sonnet which Melville did not mark).

Felicia Hemans in "Modern Greece" (1817) was sure that modern Greeks were so slavishly docile to their Muslim rulers that they did not deserve to look at the great marbles on the Parthenon. Some of those marbles, thanks to Lord Elgin, now served a higher purpose in London, she thought, where they could inspire new generations of British artists to great achievements. (Others in the family possessed Hemans's poetry, but Melville's own copy of *The Poetical Works* [Boston: Phillips, 1859; Sealts, no. 269] was purchased late, 1859.) Given the classical training some women and all educated men still received, it was natural that other British poets soon found in the efforts of the Greeks to free themselves from Turkish oppression a political cause more appealing than the plight of Poland, whatever their varying views on the Elgin marbles. Most of the poets of the time, British and American, championed the cause of Greek liberty. Lord Byron, Melville knew, had joined Greek fighters for independence and died on the field, albeit from medical mistreatment rather than wounds. Melville knew Byron's poems celebrating the Greek struggle for independence from the Turks, a theme in *The Giaour,* from

---

53. The Campbell allusion ("the deadly space between"), first identified by Stanton Garner (1977), occurs in chapter 11; the Tennyson allusion is in chapter 4 (see also sect. 8 below). Citations for *Billy Budd, Sailor,* are to the text by Hayford and Sealts (1962).

the opening invocation to the tomb supposed to be that of the Greek hero Themistocles. Judging from his allusion in 1846 to Byron's waking one morning to find himself famous, Melville knew Thomas Moore's *Life of Lord Byron* (which details the importance of Greece to Byron) long before he bought the surviving set (Boston: Little, Brown, 1853[?]; Sealts, no. 369), probably in 1862. Shelley celebrated the Greek spirit in *Hellas* (1822), which he hoped would sway British public opinion in favor of the Greek revolt against the Turks. In the United States, William Cullen Bryant by speeches and poems in the early 1820s and Fitz-Greene Halleck by the great popularity of "Marco Bozzaris" (a celebration of a great hero of the war) stirred high feelings for the Greek cause. Melville, of course, knew from childhood that "Marco Bozzaris" had affected a national mood, if not national policy. As it turned out, this great European political cause of the 1820s ended with Greek freedom from the Turks, whether or not British and American good will facilitated that result at all. Allowing for a few exceptions (Shelley, Whittier), the political poetry Melville encountered tended to focus attention on foreign injustices while disguising or glossing over the fissures in the society at home, whether that was Great Britain or the United States.

Avidly following news reports of the European revolutions of 1848, Melville had eagerly engorged the manuscript of *Mardi* with international and national political allegory. His own response, like that of most Americans, was intense but brief. The uprisings in Europe were widespread and quickly suppressed, so that Americans turned their attention back to the consequences of their own just-ended war against Mexico, the discovery of gold in California, and the perturbing new focus on slavery in the national political campaign, especially in upstate New York. Melville's impulse to make himself a national and international political commentator, to record "the peculiar thoughts & fancies of a Yankee upon politics & other matters" (as he called it on June 5, 1849), was further dashed by the reception of *Mardi*. Any residual impulse to meddle with local political controversies died in the days after May 8, 1849, when he incautiously put his name to the petition urging the English actor Macready to play Macbeth at the Astor Place Opera House despite the intimidation of Bowery ruffians, champions of the Macbeth of the American actor Forrest. By encouraging Macready without protecting him, he had played a small part in bringing on the Astor Place riots, and he never again let anyone else vote his proxy. The evidence is that he did not vote at all during his years at Pittsfield, and perhaps never.

Late in 1851, when all good Whigs and Democrats were still telling themselves they had set the slavery issue to rest for their generation by the Compromise of 1850, which included the Fugitive Slave Law, Americans gave Lajos Kossuth a triumphal tour of the country on behalf of the liberation of Hungary from Austria. Pretty clearly, in this national obsession with Hungary at a time when the United States should have been confronting its own political crisis, there was an element of hysterical displacement, a feel-good ineffectual celebration which required no national outlay of money and no commitment of American troops. Melville would have read in the *Literary World* of December 6, 1851, the "Lines Addressed by Walter Savage Landor to Kossuth on his departure for America," an appeal to the north wind Boreas to spare him so that the United States might arm him for a return to his home: "Hungary! no more / Thy saddest loss [Kossuth] deplore; / Look to the star-crowned Genius of the West, / Sole guardian of the opprest. / Oh! that one only nation dared to save / Kossuth the true and brave!" Melville heard firsthand reports of Kossuth's triumphant address in New York City. His attitude, expressed in a grim pun as he was completing the short version of *Pierre,* was that if he left home to look after Hungary (that is, to join in the feting of Kossuth) the cause of supporting his family "in hunger would suffer" (Parker 2002, 49). After Kossuth's departure, Americans, already manifesting a short national memory, turned their attention elsewhere, although for a while people remembered Kossuth whenever they saw an ostrich plume on a man's hat. The fad he created outlived his cause.

After the preoccupation with the liberation of Greece in the late 1810s and 1820s it was the dream of Italian liberty and unity, not the freedom of Hungary or any other country, that enlisted the passionate attention of English poets of Melville's time. Through his friend Henry T. Tuckerman's *Thoughts on the Poets* (New York: C. S. Francis & Co., 1846) Melville may have known that Felicia Hemans, having celebrated the presence of the Elgin marbles in London, had shifted her ground on national thievery of another nation's art. In "The Restoration of the Works of Art to Italy" (1816) she exposed the French under Napoleon as looters and spoilers and celebrated the return of treasures to Italy. Melville may have known her "Sonnet—To Italy," where she celebrates Italy as luxuriant, genial, fragrant, and lightly concludes with one caveat: "Yet far from thee inspiring freedom flies, / To Albion's coast and ever-varying skies." By 1862, and probably long before that, Melville knew at least one version of Samuel Rogers's *Italy,* in which his host of 1849 contrasted the beauty of the country with its present status, foreseeing a time when it would be both liberated and unified. In Melville's copy of Wordsworth was "On the Extinction of the Venetian Republic" as well as "On the Departure of Sir Walter Scott from Abbotsford, for Naples," where Wordsworth wished the brave, sick

Scotsman safe passage to "soft Parthenope" (Naples). (That was, Melville knew, a precedent for the Landor poem on Kossuth.) Melville knew how important Italy had been to the poets of his childhood—Byron, who had lived there, and Shelley and Keats, who had perished there. Byron and Shelley had been scornful of the Congress of Vienna's sorting out the governing of northern Italy so high-handedly that the Austrians were still in charge in 1857, during Melville's visit there. He knew Shelley's "Lines Written Among the Euganean Hills," where the "Sun-girt City," Venice, now with her "conquest-branded brow," stooped "to the slave of slaves." Before visiting the Baths of Caracalla in 1857, Melville knew that Shelley had written part of *Prometheus Bound* there. When he said that from the Baths he was led, by a natural process, down twisting streets to the Protestant Cemetery, he did not have to specify that he was following poetical associations, thinking of Shelley, then of the cemetery. He was so steeped in the poetry and the biographical accounts of the poets of his youth that his going from locale to locale in a foreign city was altogether natural, even though the previously unknown way down to the cemetery turned out to be torturous. Byron and Shelley were not remote figures. At least one member of Dr. Francis's circle in Bond Street, the painter William E. West, had painted Byron (and Felicia Hemans) and had met Shelley. A gondolier in Venice had regaled Melville with personal tales of witnessing Byron en route to sexual adventures.[54] These poets had been approachable men, and in making his notes in the 1857 journal, in Venice, say, Melville would naturally have been thinking of what Byron or Shelley might have done had they been with him on an excursion or experienced such an event as he had just experienced. They were, after all, no older than many living men he knew, and both in his mind were as much associated with Italy as England. How could he think of the Coliseum without thinking of Byron or the Baths of Caracalla without thinking of Shelley? Or the Baths of Caracalla without thinking of the Protestant Cemetery and not only Shelley but Keats and his heartbreaking tombstone?

Yet Melville had been no faster than most Americans to interest himself in the liberation and unification of Italy. In *Mardi*, chapter 145, written in 1848 well after the European revolts early in the year, Melville glided over any problems in Italy. There were "many chiefs of sunny Latianna; minstrel monarchs, full of song and sentiment; fiercer in love than war; glorious bards of freedom: but rendering tribute while they sang;—the priest-king of Vatikanna; his chest marked over with antique tatooings;

54. See Melville's journal entry for April 5, 1857 (*Journals*, p. 120).

his crown, a cowl; his rusted scepter swaying over falling towers, and crumbling mounds; full of the superstitious past." The ruler-bards might sing gloriously even while paying tribute to Austria, the pope, or the Bourbons imposed upon the two Sicilies (Sicily and Naples), recently or long ago, by outside powers. Melville may have learned a different attitude in Robert Browning's "Italian in England" after he returned from England, for that Hamlet-like dithering of a patriot in exile was in the late 1849 *Poems* (Boston: Ticknor, Reed, & Fields, dated 1850). Browning had made the subject of Italian resistance to Austrian rule a fit subject for poetry long before Melville looked askance at the Austrian soldiers in northern Italy in 1857. The year before, in April 1856, Melville had surely seen in *Putnam's Monthly* (where he had published the month before and the month after) an essay on five books by Robert Browning—the Ticknor & Fields (so it said) *Poems* (1848) and *Men and Women* (1856) and the London *Sordello* (1840), *Christmas Eve, and Easter Day* (1850), and *Strafford, an Historical Tragedy* (1837). This ten-page article, which celebrated Browning as "the most purely dramatic genius in English literature since the great dramatic days," identified him with Italy: "The secret sympathy of Browning's genius with everything Italian, is one of the most remarkable peculiarities of his poetry. It is the key, also, to the character of his genius. Many of the recent English poets have had the same fondness for Italy. Byron was never so much Byron as in Italy; Shelley lived there; Keats died there [as of course did Shelley]. But none of them has so completely and dramatically reproduced the romance and tragedy of the Italian nature as Browning."

Melville's friend Tuckerman owned a great run of American editions of both Brownings and had included a chapter on "Miss Barrett" in his *Thoughts on the Poets*. Elizabeth Barrett Browning was an even stronger partisan for Italian freedom and unity than her husband, and her "Casa Guidi Windows" had been available in the United States since 1851 in the C. W. Francis edition, where Melville would have learned of it from the June 21 *Literary World* article headed "Casa Guidi Windows," a review of *Prometheus Bound, and other Poems; including Sonnets from the Portuguese, Casa Guidi Windows, etc.,* published by Francis & Company. It consisted mainly of long quotations: "Freedom's Hopeful Day," "The Return of the Grand Duke," passages on Michelangelo, on Cimabue, on the wife of Garibaldi (martyred in the lost cause of Italian independence), and a sequel on "Charles Albert," the king of Piedmont-Sardinia. The second part of the review (July 5, 1851) celebrated the poet's "great thought threading the history of a great people. Liberty and Rome!" The section "What's Italy?" took the poet's own question, which she answered by naming great men of the remote past through the Renaissance but expressed her hope that "one quick breath would draw an avalanche / Of living sons around her, to succeed / The vanished generations" in creating a new heroic Italy. The reviewer devoted almost all his space to other quotations under the section-titles "Vallombrosa" and "Our Italy." Unable to let go, the *Literary World* printed almost another column on September 6, 1851, titled "A Poet's Sight of the Exhibition" (the new Crystal Palace in London). Altogether the *Literary World* gave more than four full three-column pages to the poem. Since the first installment arrived in Pittsfield when Melville was about to become a "disengaged" man,[55] he gained from it and the following pieces a good working knowledge of what the reviewer called "the fair and active morning of 1848 sinking into the heavy lethargic noon of 1851." On March 13, 1852 (during the time Melville was trying to get the Duyckinck brothers to stop mailing the paper to him), the *Literary World* printed a favorable review of the new edition of "Mrs. Browning's Poems" by Francis & Company, who made amends for textual errors in its earlier edition.

Melville knew that in "Casa Guidi Windows" Elizabeth Barrett Browning had identified the first part as written during the initial success of the Risorgimento, in 1848, and the second part in 1851. Beginning with "Italy enchained," she traced the course of hopes as she witnessed the lighting of the "first torch of Italian freedom," and then wrote resolutely: "Will, therefore, to be strong, thou Italy! / Will to be noble! Austrian Metternich / Can fix no yoke unless the neck agree." Yet despite Mazzini and Garibaldi there was not a hero strong enough, so that she resorted to hoping indefinitely for "Whatever hand shall grasp this oriflamme" and "insphere / These wills into a unity of will, / And make of Italy a nation." Then as the revolution collapsed she cried: "Help, lands of Europe!" Part 2 began with the betrayal of Florence by the Grand Duke, who returned supported by Austrian troops, so that she beheld "the armament of Austria flow / Into the drowning heart of Tuscany." In 1851 she called on Giuseppe Mazzini to persevere and record the fate of Giuseppe Garibaldi's wife (dead in 1849 while following his troops, she and the baby were so hastily buried that dogs dug up their bodies). Mazzini and other revolutionists had proclaimed Rome a Republic late in 1848 but the pope called in French troops to restore him to power, and in early July the troops took Rome and the Republic was dead. Some of Elizabeth Barrett Browning's most scathing passages dealt with the Catholic hierarchy and in particular the pope. She praised King Charles Albert of Piedmont-Sardinia, who

---

55. See Melville's letter to Hawthorne, July 22, 1851 (*Correspondence*, p. 199).

supported the revolt in Milan and struggled to repel the Austrians until in 1849 he abdicated in favor of his son and went into exile and speedy death. She evoked Romans of classical times and Renaissance writers and artists to shame modern Italians, those "oil-eaters," their mouths "Agape for maccaroni," who shouted for freedom then submitted to tyranny. Looking a little back in the history of resistance to tyranny, she mentioned "Pellico's Venetian dungeon" and the Neopolitan Masaniello, who dried his nets in haste when the sky was blue—two heroes recalled also by Melville in his unpublished poem on Naples.[56] Insofar as Melville was moved by contemporary political writings, it was probably the poetry of English poets who had been protesting the oppression of parts of Italy under the Austrians in the north and the Bourbon Ferdinand II in the Kingdom of the Two Sicilies.

Melville's travels in the Mediterranean in 1856 and 1857 made him more sensitive than ever to the tradition of the English poem written in or about a famous location in Italy. Some of this poetry he probably knew before he visited Italy; he read and reread this poetry with quickened interest after being on the scene, especially since Italy was little short of an obsession of his friend Tuckerman. A year or two after Melville met him, Tuckerman heard the exiled Garibaldi at a meeting called to deal with the funds raised in the Italian cause in 1850, the cause familiar to New Yorkers from Margaret Fuller's letters to Greeley's *Tribune*. Tuckerman then, in 1850, at the time of his early acquaintance with Melville, a sailor like Garibaldi, had been reminded "of some masterly portraits of mediaeval celebrities which haunted our memory, almost alive with courage, adventure, and loyalty,—whose effigies hint a stern romance and a chivalric history."[57] Tuckerman idolized Garibaldi as "one of Nature's noblemen," his complexion "bronzed by exposure to the elements; his gait rather that of a sailor than of a soldier; but through, within, and above all these traits was distinctly visible the hero." Tuckerman's intimacy with Melville was still flourishing in the mid-1850s. During the war, when he was working on an introduction to a reissue of Dr. Francis's *Old New York*, Tuckerman misdated to 1850 an important document of his friendship with Melville, but he had in his hands, in the 1860s, both an article he had saved from

56. Variously titled, this poem, probably dating from the late 1850s or early 1860s, was incorporated by Melville in the late 1870s into his so-called "Burgundy Club Sketches." Pellico was in a passage Melville removed from the poem to publish in *Timoleon* as "Pausilippo." The Naples poem is discussed in more detail in section 8 below.

57. These comments are from Tuckerman's January 1861 article in the *North American Review*.

the New Orleans *Commercial Bulletin* in November 1854 and its reprinting in the New York *Times* in January 1855, for he drew on both of them (and perhaps the originals, for he was probably the author). This was the tribute to Dr. Francis which identified four men as habitual intimate guests at the Bond Street house of the great old man—Tuckerman, Griswold, Duyckinck, and Melville (on his visits to town from Pittsfield).

Melville could have found a powerful theme in the Crimean War, which during 1854–56 had astonished Americans with the magnitude of the arrayed forces, like nothing since the Napoleonic era—Russia poised to take Constantinople from Turkey, Great Britain and France sending forth a great combined fleet to fight the Russians. In the late 1850s, having passed through waters which warships had sailed just about the time he was deciding to become a poet, Melville might understandably have chosen a topic from that war for a theme. Other international topics were available, not least the Great Revolt in India in 1857. Alternatively, he might have found robust current subjects from the American Northern Hemisphere in the filibustering in Nicaragua, where William Walker had captured Granada in 1855 and made himself president, only to be driven out by the British in mid-1857, after Melville's return home from Europe. During the years Melville became a poet, Walker remained in the news, repeatedly trying to control a route across the isthmus until the British captured him in Honduras and turned him over to local forces who executed him by a firing squad in 1860. Through family news of Samuel Savage, a cousin of his wife's half brothers, Melville had intermittent news from Central America. In 1855 he bought Ephraim George Squier's *Waikna: or, Adventures on the Mosquito Shore* (New York: Harper, 1855; Sealts, no. 485). Squier, Melville probably knew, had also written *Nicaragua: Its People, Scenery, Monuments, and the Proposed Interoceanic Canal* (New York: D. Appleton, 1852), a two-volume work with evocative foldout maps. He knew accounts of the horrendous sufferings of the Strain expedition (Parker 2002, 375). His awareness of Walker's filibustering and the construction of the railroad across Panama are topics in his second lecture, "The South Seas" (1858–59). Melville could have written with some confidence about the epic construction of the Panama Railroad with its uncountable sacrifice of human life, since he could have relied on his copy of the chronicle of that achievement written by his old friend Robert Tomes and published by the Harpers, *Panama in 1855: An Account of the Panama Railroad, of the Cities of Panama and Aspinwall, with Sketches of Life and Character on the Isthmus* (New York: Harper, 1855; Sealts, no. 528).

After finishing his book on Panama, Tomes had become the recording author on the great expedition led by Matthew Perry that opened Japan to Western commerce. No one in the Melville family could have forgotten the report of Gansevoort Melville's impromptu speech in Cambridge, England, in March 1846, as reported in American papers after his death, a description of Gansevoort's "walking up to an immense terrestrial globe suspended in the centre of one of the rooms, and placing his hand upon it," then declaring:

"Look here, gentlemen, and see if any American can carefully examine the map of our globe, and not feel a gratitude and just pride at seeing the geographical position our country holds upon its face. Here lies Asia and the whole East, with its immense wealth. There is the mouth of the Columbia River, almost as near Canton as London is to New York. Now here is a little speck called Europe, upon the Eastern shores of the Atlantic, and a smaller speck on its Western shore called New England, including New York city, which have ever held the trade of this immense region, at the expense of passing Cape Horn, or the Cape of Good Hope, the South Atlantic, Indian Ocean, &c. &c. . . . Look here," said he, "and tell me if any American can give up, or barter away the valley of the Columbia, and not, Esau like, sell his birth-right?" (Parker 1966, p. 51)

Knowing as he did that Camoëns's *Lusiad* celebrated the Portuguese establishing of trade with India and the Far East, Melville would have seen a theme for a modern epic in the ongoing conflict between the British, French, and Americans for military and commercial control of the Pacific (a conflict to which he had been an eyewitness). His second lecture, "The South Seas," sufficiently confirms his well-informed interest in current Pacific affairs, but judging by what survives, he rejected Central America and the Pacific as a theme for poetry, although, as we will see later, he tried for a time to work up, presumably into poetry, a Hawaiian legend.

At home the slavery issue, supposedly laid to rest in 1850, had erupted the next year, when his father-in-law had been party to one of the most dramatic scenes involving the enforcement of the Fugitive Slave Law (see Parker 1996, p. 831). In the mid-1850s, when slavery was dividing Democrats from the dying Whig Party and the emerging Republicans, Melville could have made high tragic use of stories fully reported from Kansas, or only briefly publicized and then suppressed for years, like news from Pottawattamie. But rather than brooding over the slavery crisis or over the broader topic of what had happened to the American national character (as he had done in *The Confidence-Man* in 1856) Melville seems to have started with Italy, following, in his way, the Brownings. At least, Melville's first known poem of the late 1850s, "To Daniel Shepherd"

(July 6, 1859),[58] begins with an allusion to the current military and political situation in Italy. This verse-epistle to his and his brother Allan's friend Daniel Shepherd is far from amateurish, especially when one considers that it served a mundane purpose, to invite the friend to Arrowhead. In the nature of things Melville would not have spent much time on it—an hour or two? Therefore it testifies to Melville's facility as well as his competence in writing verse. Characteristically, Melville plays on the name of his friend and that of the Hebrew prophet, making Shepherd the fit expounder of his dream:

> Come, Daniel, come and visit me:
> I'm lost in many a quandary:
> I've dreamed, like Bab'lon's Majesty:
> Prophet, come expound for me.
> —I dreamed I saw a laurel grove,
> Claimed for his by the bird of Jove,
> Who, elate with such dominion,
> Oft cuffed the boughs with haughty pinion.
> Indignantly the trees complain,
> Accusing his afflictive reign.
> Their plaints the chivalry excite
> Of chanticleers, a plucky host:
> They battle with the bird of light.
> Beaten, he wings his Northward flight,
> No more his laurel realm to boast,
> Where now, to crow, the cocks alight,
> And—break down all the branches quite!
> Such a weight of friendship pure
> The grateful trees could not endure.
> This dream, it still disturbeth me;
> Seer, foreshows it Italy?

The Austrian eagle had been "afflictive" but the plucky troop of roosters who drove it back home may do more destruction than the eagle: disintegration of the whole Italian fabric might follow such success, particularly if the "friendship pure" (presumably of France) might prove an ironic illusion. He had long ago acknowledged the danger of trying to promulgate his political opinions, but it was hard not to be drawn into commentary on bloody battles in the Holy Land of Art.

---

58. Because it was written as a letter inviting Shepherd to visit, the poem appears in the NN *Correspondence* volume (pp. 337–39).

As *The Confidence-Man* had demonstrated, Melville had even recently been willing to venture into national criticism, but after writing *Mardi* he never again assumed the role of partisan. Partisanship, he decided, was always inappropriate for poetry, commenting on lines 115–31 in Milton's "Lycidas": "Mark the deforming effect of the intrusion of partizan topics & feelings of the day, however serious in import, into a poem otherwise of the first order of merit." Aware of and influenced by the English poetry of the Risorgimento, Melville kept to his own preoccupations rather than merely echoing the political stances of other poets or his acquaintances, even those of his friend Tuckerman. Without becoming a partisan, Melville might, in the spirit of Akenside, see what of value he might derive by tuning his new American lyre to Attic themes, or Roman themes, drawing on his recent experiences and observations in the Mediterranean.

VII
MELVILLE'S PROGRESS AS POET, 1857(?) TO MAY 1860

IN LATE MAY 1857 in Boston upon his return from his trip to the Mediterranean Melville reportedly said that he was not going to write any more at present (*Log,* p. 580). This was good news to the man who told the story, Elizabeth Melville's half brother Lemuel Shaw Jr., who had been convinced ever since *Mardi* that Melville had written too many books. Whatever Melville actually said, he probably meant he was not going to write any more fiction right away, for he may have decided already to write a lecture during the summer. As it turned out, he wrote the lecture "Statues in Rome" and delivered it from November 23, 1857, to February 23, 1858; he wrote "The South Seas" and delivered it from December 6, 1858, to March 16, 1859; and wrote "Travel" and delivered it between November 7, 1859, and February 21, 1860. Howard Horsford, the editor of Melville's *Journals,* calls attention to memoranda Melville added on the pages following the last dated entry for his 1856–57 travel journal. Whether these were made on his voyage home or later is not certain, but they include titles: "Frescoes of Travel" and "Subjects for Roman Frescoes." These may have been titles for a lecture, but they may have been titles for poetry (or even fiction, despite Melville's demurral). The full entry on the first title consists of "Frescoes of Travel / by / Three Brothers / Poet,

Painter, and Scholar" (later he changed "Scholar" to "Idler"). Adjacent
to these lines were four names of men followed by an open bracket and
four more names, three of places and one of a man: Rosseau [*sic*], Cicero,
Byron, and Haydon in one column facing Venice, Olympus, Parthenon,
and Leonardo on the other side of the bracket. These eight words have
not been satisfactorily accounted for, not even to the point that we can say
whether Rousseau was meant to be associated with Venice, Cicero with
Olympus, Byron with the Parthenon, and Haydon with Leonardo.

Horsford makes clear that Melville did plunder his recent journal for
his first lecture, as his marks on the pages show and as the lecture itself
reveals. Horsford cautiously comments on the possibility that Melville
also consulted his journal as he wrote some of his early poetry:

> Melville began writing poetry seriously in those years [starting in 1857],
> seriously enough and extensively enough that he had a book of poems
> ready in 1860 for publication, though it found no publisher; and he con-
> tinued writing poems for the rest of his life. Most of them are difficult or
> impossible to date very precisely. But whenever written, many of them
> make direct and repeated levy on the experiences recorded in the journal.
> Still, as with the lectures, there is very little in the way of supplementary
> marking of the journal related to them. Quite possibly in reading it over
> for other purposes Melville was prompted, incidentally as it were, to ren-
> der his imaginative impressions in poetic form. But even the passages on
> the Egyptian desert and the heavily reworked ones on the Pyramids . . .
> only indirectly foreshadow his two published poems on these subjects, "In
> the Desert" and "The Great Pyramid." Both were among eighteen poems
> in a section titled "Fruit of Travel Long Ago" in *Timoleon* (1891), all of
> which relate to experiences recorded in the journal in passages without
> later markings suggesting such use; their dates of composition are conjec-
> tural. (pp. 191–93)

As Horsford indicates, if Melville did consult his journal as he wrote these
short poems, he did not work directly from it, in contrast to the way he
worked on the unpublished Naples poem and parts of *Clarel*.

Already in May 1857 Melville may have been planning to write poetry
as well as a lecture. In the next months after his return from his travels,
within a year or so at the latest, perhaps even while he was traveling with
his first lecture in 1857 and 1858, Melville set about making himself a poet.
We know that he had a volume of poetry entitled simply *Poems* ready for
publication in May 1860. Two years or so for the composition of *Poems* fits
with Melville's letting George Duyckinck know in July 1858 that he was

"busy on" what George understood to be "a new book."[59] In his report George seems to have taken for granted that Melville was writing prose, but this may be the first known reference to the book of poetry Melville completed early in 1860. The second possible reference is a letter apparently to the Harpers on May 18, 1859: "Here are two Pieces, which, if you find them suited to your Magazine I should be happy to see them appear there.—In case of publication, you may, if you please, send me what you think they are worth." Since he knew what the Harpers were likely to pay for prose pieces, the likelihood is that these were unlike what he had sold to *Harper's Monthly* in the mid-1850s. The use of the term "piece" may or may not be significant. In Melville's known letters about the stories he published in *Harper's* and in *Putnam's New Monthly Magazine* from 1853 to 1856, he calls them "pages" or a "parcel" or an "article" (lowercase or capital) and only once refers to a short prose work as a "piece"—when he identifies "The Piazza" as the "accompanying piece." In his instructions to his brother Allan about the publication of his book of poems, printed below, he uses a form of the word "piece" three times to mean "poem." These pieces were not published in *Harper's New Monthly Magazine,* and their rejection may be one reason Melville ruled out offering the Harpers his full book of poems when it was ready the next year: there was no point trying them for the whole book when they had rejected two poems already. *Putnam's Monthly* folded with the September 1857 issue, but on August 19 of that year, in response to an invitation from the publishers, Melville expressed willingness to write for the new *Atlantic Monthly.* A reason for not sending the two rejected pieces to the *Atlantic* or another magazine may have been that by mid-1859, after the rejection by the Harpers, he thought himself far enough along that he could wait for exposure and criticism until he could publish his book of poetry.

Whenever Melville began writing poetry, it was in the profoundest secrecy possible in the Melville-Shaw family, which on scandalous matters could be cautiously reticent but normally was briskly communicative. You "know how such things spread," Elizabeth Melville wrote to her stepmother in 1875 (*Log,* p. 741), in the act of violating Herman's wish that she keep it secret that he had been writing poetry again, as he had asked her to keep it secret in the late 1850s. On June 23, 1860, when she was trying to think of a likely publisher for the volume of poems, Lizzie commented to Evert Duyckinck that Melville's writing poetry had "been

59. George Duyckinck to Rosalie Baker, July 26, 1858 (see *Log,* p. 594; Parker 2002, p. 379).

such a profound secret" between the two of them "for so long" that she was glad now to talk openly about it, and to solicit an objective opinion about it (*Log,* p. 620). "For so long" is indefinite—probably more than a year, possibly two years or more, up until around May of 1860, when two of the sisters were told: Helen, who was with Elizabeth the second time she wrote Evert A. Duyckinck about Melville's volume of poems, and probably Fanny, who had been released as caretaker of Allan's motherless children upon his remarriage and who had probably stopped at Arrowhead before going to Boston, where she saw Herman and Tom off on the *Meteor* on the voyage around Cape Horn.

After the letter to the Harpers on May 18, 1859, the next evidence about Melville's poetry is from July of that year, when he wrote the verse-epistle directed to Daniel Shepherd, whom Allan had known since 1850 at the latest. It survives as a draft, found in Allan's papers, but it was a letter to be copied out and mailed, not a poem to go into a growing stack of poems that would become a book. Judging from its competence as an impromptu composition, it was far from his first poem (whether or not the two "pieces" mentioned in May were poems). No other poem of Melville's (not counting effusions such as those in *Mardi*) can be assigned an earlier date. The first known reference to the poems as a collection to be published is Melville's letter to Duyckinck, May 21, 1860, although this letter does not itself specify that the subject is poetry, not prose. There Melville begins with a reference to his brother Allan, who had taken his second wife only the month before: "If you have met Allan lately he has perhaps informed you that in a few days I go with my brother Tom a voyage round Cape Horn. It was only determined upon a short time since; and I am at present busy, as you may imagine in getting ready for a somewhat long absence, and likewise in prepareing for type certain M.S.S." Then followed a request for Duyckinck's editorial services in Melville's absence: "Now may I with propriety ask of you, conditionally, a favor? Will you, upon the arrival of the M.S.S. in New York—that is, in the course of two weeks, or less—look over them and if they seem of a sort that you care to be any way concerned with, advice [advise] with Allan as to a publisher, and form of volume, &c. . . . In short, may I, seeming too confident, ask you, as a veteran & expert in these matters, and as an old acquaintance, to lend something of an overseeing eye to the launching of this craft—the committing of it to the elements?" Evert's response, which Melville on May 28 referred to as "a very welcome one—quite a wind from the feilds of old times," included an agreement to help see the volume into print.

On May 22, the next day after he wrote Duyckinck, Melville "jotted down" for his wife's copying a set of "Memoranda for Allan concerning the publication of my verses." These "Memoranda for Allan" (known in his wife's transcription) constitute the fullest instructions he had ever given for the publication of one of his works, as far as we know:

Memoranda for Allan
concerning the publication of my verses.

1—Don't stand on terms much with the publisher—half-profits after expenses are paid will content me— —not that I expect much "profits"— but that will be a fair nominal arrangement—They should also give me 1 doz. copies of the book—

2—Don't have the Harpers.—I should like the Appletons or Scribner—But Duyckinck's advice will be good here.

3—The sooner the thing is printed and published, the better— The "season" will make little or no difference, I fancy, in this case.

4—After printing, dont let the book hang back—but publish & have done.

5—For God's sake don't have *By the author of "Typee" "Piddledee" &c* on the title-page.

6—Let the title-page be simply,

Poems
by
Herman Melville.

7—Dont have any clap-trap announcements and "sensation" puffs—nor any extracts published previous to publication of book—Have a decent publisher, in short.

8—Don't take any measures, or make inquiries as to expediency of an English edition simultaneous with the American—as in case of "Confidence-Man".

9—In the M.S.S. each piece is on a page by itself, however small the piece. This was done merely for convenience in the final classification; and should be no guide for the printer—Of course in printing two or more pieces will sometimes appear on the same page—according to length of pieces &c. You understand—

10—The poems are divided into books as you will see; but the divisions are not *called* books—they are only numbered—Thus it is in the M.S.S., and should be the same in print. There should be a page with the number between every division.

11—Anything not perfectly plain in the M.S.S. can be referred to Lizzie— also have the M.S.S. returned to her after printing.

12—Lizzie should by all means see the printed sheets *before* being bound, in order to detect any gross errors consequent upon misconstruing the M.S.S.—

These are the thoughts which hurriedly occur to me at this moment. Pardon the abruptness of their expression, but time is precious.—

—Of all human events, perhaps, the publication of a first volume of verses is the most insignificant; but though a matter of no moment to the world, it is still of some concern to the author,—as these *Mem.* show—Pray therefore, don't laugh at my *Mem.* but give heed to them, and so oblige

Your brother
Herman—

Aware of the insignificance of a volume of American poetry in a glutted market ("Of all human events, perhaps, the publication of a first volume of verses is the most insignificant"), Melville nevertheless admitted that it was "still of some concern to the author,—as these *Mem.* show," and left Lizzie, Allan, and Evert Duyckinck all aware of their responsibilities toward him and his poems. The twelve points reveal the seriousness with which Melville took the poetry he had been writing during the past two years or more. No one preserved a table of contents, however, so we are left to what deductions we can make about such matters as the numbered sections—not "called" books, the way the sections of, say, *Paradise Lost* are called books, but nevertheless constituting books in the sense of separate and presumably unrelated sections.

The twelve points are almost all self-explanatory. Melville gave no reason for not having the Harpers, natural enough if what they rejected in 1859 had been two poems. The one problematic point, the ninth, seems to say flatly that every poem was so short that it was contained on a single page. However, Melville is saying he knows that the printer will need to put two or possibly more short poems on a single page, even though in the manuscript short poems are not put on the same page. We know from Mrs. Melville's June 4 letter to Duyckinck (quoted below) that the manuscript ran to 111 pages, at the least, and presumably beyond that. Taking the ninth memorandum literally would mean that *Poems* consisted of a great many very short poems, perhaps many more than a hundred, even allowing for pages left blank except for section numbers. Melville's haste in jotting down the notes (or Lizzie's difficulty in making a perfect copy of them) may account for the imprecision, for Melville most likely meant to say that in the manuscript every poem *started* on a separate page. Points 11

and 12 constitute the earliest evidence that Lizzie was so intimately famil-
iar with the poems that she could explain anything that was confusing and
would have to be the one to exercise final judgment over the proofs.

In the letter Melville wrote to Evert Duyckinck on board the *Meteor*
in Boston Harbor on May 28, he explained that his wife would send
"the parcel" of poems "in the course of a week or so—there remaining
something to be finished in copying the M.S.S." His wife, he explained,
had "interested herself a good deal in this matter," to the point that she
seemed "to know more about it" than he did, "at least about the *merits* of
the performance." George Duyckinck, he hoped, would also look over his
"scribblings"—this he added before breaking off his "egotistic" requests.
Constitutionally Melville loathed asking favors of anyone, as his mother
had observed long before, so his "egotistic" placing of his poetry in the
capable editorial hands of the Duyckincks reveals how momentous to him
the publication of his *Poems* was.

The memorandum to Allan left out any consideration of physical aspects
of the book such as binding and typeface, although it mentioned some
internal features such as the numbered page Melville wanted before each
section. Melville may have been taking for granted that his book would
be in black or brown cloth, in octavo or twelvemo. Once in Boston, Mel-
ville must have looked sharply at the appearance of poetry books he came
across in the publishers' houses and bookstores. Ticknor & Fields may have
been displaying *Lucile* by "Owen Meredith" (the novelist Bulwer-Lytton's
son), officially published on May 24, 1860, although advertisements have
not been found. *Lucile* was in Ticknor & Fields's "blue and gold" poetry
series—blue cloth, stamped blind, gold title and cartouche on spine, gilt
edges, brown glazed endpapers. There in Boston Melville seems to have
reacted strongly to this or another "blue and gold" book. Overgilt would
be bad enough, but the fussy preciousness of Ticknor & Fields's "blue and
gold" was egregious and not to be endured. Realizing that he had to head
off Duyckinck from putting his own volume in blue and gold, he took the
trouble to write Lizzie immediately to ask her to add another item to his
dozen points in the memorandum to Allan.

Accordingly, on June 1, Elizabeth Melville wrote to Evert Duyckinck:

On Monday or Tuesday of next week I shall forward to you by Express,
the manuscript of which Herman wrote you—and with this I enclose a
copy of the memoranda which he jotted down for Allan,—according to
his request—

To this also should have been added an item which Herman omitted in
his haste—and that is, that the book should be plainly bound, that is, not

over-gilt—and to "blue and gold" I know he has a decided aversion—He may have mentioned it in his letter to you, from Boston—[60]

On June 4, Elizabeth Melville sent Evert Duyckinck the manuscript of the whole volume, accompanied by a letter:

> I send you the manuscript and hope the printers will find no difficulty in reading it—though it has been (the greater part of it) necessarily copied in great haste—If anything in it should be obscure, please enclose the page to me and I will compare it with the original draught—
>
> In making up the table of "contents," I am not sure I have always used capitals in the right place—will you have the kindness to overlook it, and right it, if wrong—In the printed book, the titles of the verses are all in capitals, I believe—so of course the printer will arrange that—and I see that in the manuscript they are sometimes underscored which is accidental—
>
> One question more occurs to me about titles—which is this—When the first line is quoted at the heading (as on page 111) what punctuation should be used about it? quotation marks and *period,* or with whatever punctuation immediately follows in the verse?—With this the contents should also correspond—
>
> I am sorry to trouble you about these little matters, Mr Duyckinck, but Herman was obliged to leave much in an unfinished state, and I should feel much easier, as I know he would, if you would overlook the sheets for these little inaccuracies—
>
> When you have read the manuscript, I should be very glad to have your opinion of it, as a whole, and you need not be afraid to say *exactly* what you think,—I am the more desirous of this, because as yet, no one has seen the sheets, excepting two of Herman's sisters, who are now with me—and I want to know how they would strike an unprejudiced person—If your brother also would add his impressions, so much the better—[61]

The reference to "unfinished state" meant that the poems were not fully arranged in final order with proper divisions, not that poems themselves were not completed.

Melville had suggested Scribner as a "decent" publisher. Long afterward, Richard Henry Stoddard wrote a chapter on Edmund Clarence Stedman in *Poets' Homes: Pen and Pencil Sketches of American Poets and Their Homes,* by "R. H. Stoddard and Others" (Boston: D. Lothrop & Co., 1877). Before June 19, 1860, Charles Scribner had obliged Stoddard:

---

60. The letter is in NYPL-D (Box 12); most of it is transcribed in *Log,* p. 618.
61. The letter is in NYPL-D (Box 12); it is partially transcribed in *Log,* p. 618.

My good friend Bayard Taylor and I were living together in the same
house when these poems [by E. C. Stedman] appeared [in the *Tribune*], and
I remember his coming home one afternoon and telling me that he had
that day, or the day before, met their author in the editorial rooms of the
Tribune, and had had a talk with him, and that he liked him very much.
A few evenings afterwards this likable young poet came to see me, and I
was charmed with him. . . . I asked him to show me his poems printed
and unprinted, for he told me that he had enough to make a small vol-
ume, and he did so. I read them with great care; I corrected them where I
thought they needed it, and I tried to get a publisher for him. I think that
my opinion was not without weight with the gentleman who became his
publisher—the late Mr. Charles Scribner.—(p. 255)

The weight of that opinion is clear. Scribner returned Melville's manu-
script to Duyckinck, writing him on June 19: "I have looked over Melville's
Poems. I have no doubt they are excellent, they seem so to me, and I have
confidence in your judgement—But I have not got the heart to publish
them—I doubt whether they would more than pay expenses, and as I have
issued two vols of Poems [by E. C. Stedman and G. P. Morris] this season
and the prospect is that neither of them will pay I don't feel like making
another venture in that line" (*Log,* pp. 619–20). Upon the refusal from
Scribner, Duyckinck sent the manuscript to Rudd & Carleton, and wrote
to Elizabeth Melville. Her reply is dated June 23:

I received yours of the 19th yesterday, and hasten to thank you for your
kind endeavors about the manuscript, regretting that its course does not
run smoothly, thus far—For myself, I am willing to wait patiently for the
result, so that the publication is eventually accomplished—and do not con-
sider its rejection by the publishers as any test of its merit in a literary point
of view—well-knowing, as Herman does also, that *poetry* is a compara-
tively uncalled-for article in the publishing market—I suppose that if John
Milton were to offer "Paradise Lost" to the Harpers tomorrow, it would be
promptly rejected as "unsuitable" not to say, denounced as dull—
    I think infinitely more of yours and your brother's opinion of it, and
feel more confidence in its worth, since it has been looked at by persons of
judgment and taste, than ever before—it has been such a profound secret
between Herman and myself for so long, that I rejoice to have my own
prejudice in its favor confirmed by some one in whose appreciation we
can feel confidence—for I do not believe you would speak favorably of it,
unless you could do so sincerely—so for that, your letter gives me great
satisfaction—
    The name of one publishing firm in New York occurs to me who might
possibly take a personal interest in the matter—that of "Derby and Jackson"

the first named being a brother-in-law of "Toby" of Typee memory—if he is the same that I think he is—"C.L. Derby"—former "Actuary of Cosmopolitan Art Association"—I do not know of what standing the firm may be, but I merely offer the hint, in case "Rudd and Carleton" should decline to publish—

I feel that you and Allan will do everything that is suitable and proper about it and am deeply sensible of your kindly efforts to further its success—indeed I feel that it is in better hands than even with Herman's own management for he might be disheartened at the outset, by its rejection, and perhaps withhold it altogether, which would be a great disappointment to me—

I am prepared to be very patient in any delay that may ensue, even when the book shall have been accepted for publication—bearing in mind the "midsummer" "stagnation in trade"—"season"—and all that—though I shall count on your promised report of progress in good time.[62]

What Lizzie says about Milton offering *Paradise Lost* to the Harpers tomorrow is a secularized version of Melville's comment to Hawthorne about what would happen if he wrote the Gospels in his century. She may have been echoing him, if he had said much the same thing to her as he had written to Hawthorne.

Rudd & Carleton must have declined the volume, leaving Duyckinck with only Lizzie's somewhat imprecise suggestion about Derby & Jackson. Of the four Derby brothers—James, George, Henry, and Chauncey— active in publishing and bookselling, the one who had a link to Toby, Thomas F. Heffernan explains,[63] was Chauncey, whose marriage to Charlotte Flower, sister of the widowed Mary Jane Flower Stone (Toby's wife), made him and Toby brothers-in-law, by common American usage. The Derby who was a partner in Derby & Jackson was James Derby, not Toby's brother-in-law Chauncey. As far as we know, Duyckinck did not follow up on this hint, and the Rudd & Carleton rejection marked the end of anyone's efforts to publish *Poems* by Herman Melville in 1860. Naturally Melville expected to find a copy of his *Poems* waiting for him in San Francisco, sent by way of the celebrated new Panama Railroad. Instead of the book he found one or more letters from his wife telling him the fate of his verses.

62. The letter is in NYPL-D (Box 12); it is partially transcribed in *Log,* p. 620.
63. In a private communication to me, February 21, 2003.

VIII
POSSIBLE CONTENTS OF *POEMS* (1860)

WHAT WE KNOW about the dating of Melville's poems is rudi-
mentary and may remain so unless new documentary evidence is
discovered.[64] We know, to display the level of current ignorance, that the
poems in *Battle-Pieces* (1866) were written during and just after the Civil
War and that certain ones could not have been written before battles and
other datable events took place. It is now almost certain that Melville wrote
Clarel (1876) between early 1870 and the first half of 1875. Of the poems in
John Marr we know only that they were written before the publication of
that little book in 1888, just as we know only that the poems in *Timoleon*
were written before the publication of that little book in 1891. We strongly
suspect, but cannot now prove, that many of the poems in *Timoleon* ante-
date some if not most of the poems in *John Marr*. Of the many poems that
Melville left unpublished (some in provisionally titled collections), few
have been dated at all closely. Only one poem by Melville seems absolutely
certain to date from the late 1850s, the July 1859 verse-epistle, "To Daniel
Shepherd." Not a single poem of Melville's can be identified as one indis-
putably included in the 1860 collection Melville called *Poems*. It is possible,
although not likely, that not one poem survives from all those that were
in *Poems*. Yet despite all this uncertainty we need to try to speculate rea-
sonably about the possible contents of *Poems* and about the possibility that
some poems Melville published late in life or left unpublished might (per-
haps in an earlier form) have stood in the 1860 collection.

Our imperfect knowledge about Melville's poetry got off to a gro-
tesque start in 1921 when Raymond Weaver in the first full-length
biography (p. 360) put the date 1859 on a confidential letter from Mel-
ville's wife to her stepmother about his writing poetry (a letter written
in 1875), then said nothing more of Melville's writing poetry in the late
1850s and did not mention *Poems*. Meade Minnigerode in 1922 became
the first modern researcher to know that Melville had written a volume
he called *Poems*.[65] The name "Duyckinck" is not in Weaver's index, but

---

64. Facts about the dates of composition of Melville's poetry are based on the second
volume of my biography (2002), Robert Sandberg's 1989 Northwestern University dis-
sertation, and on work reported elsewhere in this volume.

65. After 1922, the documents Minnigerode discovered were quoted by Willard
Thorp (1938) and many others, particularly Jay Leyda, who in 1951 printed a supple-
mentary document, Charles Scribner's rejection of *Poems*. Melville's memorandum to
Allan Melville on the publication of his verses was reprinted in full in *Letters* (1960) and

Minnigerode located many Melville items in the Duyckinck Collection of the New York Public Library, among them the letters written in 1860 by Melville and his wife to Evert Duyckinck about the volume of poems and Melville's memorandum of instructions to his brother Allan. Rushing the information into his bibliography, Minnigerode guessed that this 1860 poetry might be *Clarel* (p. 77). By reading more carefully the memorandum to Allan which Minnigerode printed, Lewis Mumford (1929) realized that *Poems* must have consisted of shorter poems, not *Clarel*. In 1938 Willard Thorp ventured to speculate about the contents of *Poems:* "There is reason to suppose the book contained some if not all of that little group of poems which were printed in *Timoleon* (1891) under the caption 'Fruit of Travel Long Ago.' The themes treated in these poems can all be traced to impressions of the 1856–1857 journey and many of them are foreshadowed in the diary which he kept at that time" (p. lxxxv). Here Thorp was more cautious ("some if not all") than some later commentators have been.

Correspondence (1993) and quoted in many other publications. Strangely, the existence of the lost *Poems* was challenged repeatedly in 2002 by reviewers of the second volume of my biography, Richard H. Brodhead in the *New York Times,* Andrew Delbanco in the *New Republic,* and Elizabeth Schultz in *Common Review.* Confusion in subsequent commentary shows that this baseless but conspicuous skepticism has distracted public awareness from the abundant documentary evidence for *Poems.*

The damage done by these reviews (exacerbated by their all having prolonged afterlives on the Internet) is further compounded because the same three also expressed doubt as to Melville's completion in 1853 of another real but now-lost book, *The Isle of the Cross* (the title of which was discovered only in 1987). The 1853 book has yet been treated in relation to Melville's whole career only in the second volume of my biography. Because knowledge of *The Isle of the Cross* has not yet been absorbed by all Melville critics and because prominent critics have cast doubt on the existence of *Poems,* general knowledge of the trajectory of Melville's career stands as thwarted and obscured.

Even aside from the damage caused by errors published in conspicuous places, the failure of *Poems* to be published in 1860 has created or contributed to other prevalent misconceptions in criticism about Melville's poems, particularly about which poems were indubitably written "late" in his life. In this HISTORICAL NOTE, the subtitle of section 11 is designed to guide the reader to think of *Battle-Pieces* historically—as the second volume of poetry Melville completed, although the earliest one which we possess.

My 2007 *Nineteenth-Century Literature* article and the introduction to *Melville: The Making of the Poet* lay out the known facts about *The Isle of the Cross* (1853) and *Poems* (1860). Both also acknowledge a related problem, the difficulty any critic has in taking account of these two books even when fully aware that they existed—a difficulty resulting from the universal psychological inhibition against treating as real something which is no longer tangible.

Demonstrably, Melville worked up portions from his early 1857 journal as he wrote his first lecture, "Statues in Rome," for the 1857–58 season, the topic being ancient statues, not Renaissance or modern statues. Therefore Thorp reasonably assumed that in the two or three years after his return from the Mediterranean, when he seems to have begun his career as a poet, Melville had also made much use of his recent impressions and had refreshed his memory by looking over pages of his journal. For all we know, some poems in the 1860 volume could have been grouped under the title (or at least the idea) listed in his journal, "Frescoes of Travel / by / Three Brothers / Poet, Painter, and Idler" ("Idler" replacing what he first wrote, "Scholar"). When a number of poems associated with long-ago travel are published late in life, some of them in a section called "Fruit of Travel Long Ago," as part of a grand erratic campaign aimed at cleaning accumulations out of a writing desk and getting poems into print one little self-subsidized volume at a time, the sensible thing is to assume, as Thorp did, that some of the pieces may have languished in the desk for a very long time. The foliation of surviving pages of Melville's poetry does not suggest that any pages survive from *Poems,* but some of the poems in *Poems* may survive after having been recopied (and presumably revised) during the years or even decades after 1860. The eighteen poems of "Fruit of Travel Long Ago" (Weaver counted twenty-one), all set in the Mediterranean regions Melville had visited from December 1856 through early April 1857, are "Venice," "In a Bye-Canal," "Pisa's Leaning Tower," "In a Church of Padua," "Milan Cathedral," "Pausilippo" (written as part of the much longer "Naples in the Time of Bomba," which Melville did not live to publish), "The Attic Landscape," "The Same," "The Parthenon," "Greek Masonry," "Greek Architecture," "Off Cape Colonna," "The Archipelago," "Syra," "Disinterment of the Hermes," "The Apparition," "In the Desert," and "The Great Pyramid." At least one of them, "Disinterment of the Hermes," was occasioned by a widely reported discovery in 1877, but as Melville arranged poems for *Timoleon* he could have thought of it as fairly recent fruit of travel long ago, since in Rome he had been powerfully moved by what he learned of the excavation of colossal horses from the ruins of the Baths of Caracalla ("like finding the bones of the mastadon," he noted in his journal on February 28, 1857). The other seventeen may have been poems written long ago, soon after the long-past travels. No one has suggested any other plausible reason for Melville's segregating these poems (even allowing for his putting at least one late poem into the group). "Fruit of Travel Long Ago," without the "Hermes" poem, could not have constituted the entire *Poems* (1860); many more pages of poetry were included in that lost manuscript.

Disgusted with the late 1850s' worship of technology, Melville for many months after the summer of 1857 found an intellectual home in ancient Greece and Rome. In the 1857–58 lecture Melville announced his preference for classical values in a passage contrasting the Vatican as the index of the ancient world with the Washington Patent Office as the index of the modern, then contrasting the Apollo Belvedere with a locomotive and the Coliseum with the Crystal Palace. He concluded with a quotation from Byron's *Childe Harold's Pilgrimage* that everyone knew: "While stands the Coliseum, Rome shall stand; / When falls the Coliseum, Rome shall fall; / And when Rome falls, the world." The statuary and architecture of Rome would outlast the institutions, inventions, and buildings of the progressive modern world. Two lads from Williams College, Titus Munson Coan and John Thomas Gulick, who made a literary pilgrimage to Arrowhead in late April 1859, testified that Melville harangued them on the superiority of classical times to the present, just the position he had taken in his first lecture a year and a half earlier.[66] Influenced by Edward Gibbon's *Decline and Fall of the Roman Empire,* he idealized the reigns of Antoninus Pius, Marcus Aurelius, and Lucius Verus (A.D. 138–69). A family report suggests that Melville left a set of Gibbon behind at Arrowhead when he left at the end of 1863 (see Sealts, no. 223b), so the poem praising that golden era, "The Age of the Antonines," may have dated to his first years as a poet although it was not printed until *Timoleon* (1891). Retreating into an idealized Golden Age of politics and literature could not, of course, be complete, however much Melville wanted to avert his eyes from the political realities of the late 1850s. Having already written an exhaustive anatomy of American overconfidence in 1855 and 1856, it was understandable that now (like many other Americans) he would turn to contemporary Mediterranean politics rather than the crisis in the United States. His verse-epistle "To Daniel Shepherd" (July 1859) begins with an allusion to the current military and political situation in Italy. Surely not his first poem, it probably followed other poems set in Italy and elsewhere in the Mediterranean. In the late 1850s, when memories of his travels were sharpest and when Italy was more and more in the news, Melville very likely wrote some, most, or perhaps even all of his poems that drew on his journals and his memories of the Mediterranean. Besides such poems as those on the Parthenon and the Great Pyramid in "Fruit of Travel Long Ago," Melville might also have tried his hand at poems based on classical history, such as the story of Timoleon and his brother.

66. For the pilgrimage by Coan and Gulick, see Parker 2002, pp. 397–400. Melville referred to the superiority of classical times at the end of "Statues in Rome" (*Piazza Tales,* pp. 408–9).

Melville could have written "In a Bye-Canal" without reading Browning's lurid "In a Gondola," but it seems unlikely that he would not have known that poem. Before he wrote "After the Pleasure Party" Melville almost surely knew some of the striking examples of dramatic monologues or soliloquies in Browning's *Poems* (Boston: Ticknor, Reed, & Fields, 1850) and Browning's *Men and Women* (Boston: Ticknor & Fields, 1856). "After the Pleasure Party" may show the influence of Tennyson. Melville kept up with Tennyson's poetry, and continued to do so for decades, reading new poems probably as late as the 1882 tribute on the nineteen-hundredth anniversary of Virgil's death. Very late in life, in the manuscript of *Billy Budd, Sailor,* Melville had, as previously noted, recalled the tribute to Lord Nelson from the 1852 "Ode on the Death of the Duke of Wellington": "Alfred in his funeral ode on the victor of Waterloo ventures not to call him the greatest soldier of all time, though in the same ode he invokes Nelson as 'the greatest sailor since our world began'" (chap. 4). Already by the late 1850s Melville had gone far beyond his "Will Waterproof" phase of reading Tennyson. At some point Melville bought Ticknor & Fields's 1855 *Maud, and Other Poems.* In "The Piazza," written early in 1856, he probably echoed Tennyson's weary "Mariana" as well as *Measure for Measure;* he had known it a long time. In August 1861 Melville bought *The Poetical Works of Alfred Tennyson* (Boston: Ticknor & Fields, 1861; Sealts, no. 508), in two volumes. Later, pasting in a newspaper clipping which disparaged "The Charge of the Light Brigade," Melville defended the poet, labeling the criticism "stuff by a Small Man" ("small man" being a phrase from Carlyle employed by Melville in "Hawthorne and his Mosses" and in *The Confidence-Man,* chap. 22).[67]

On the grounds that one is usually more likely to write about something when it is fresh in mind, and on the basis of echoes of words and themes from Tennyson's *The Princess,* one could suspect that the 1860 volume may have included the second poem in *Timoleon,* "After the Pleasure Party." Much of that poem consists of a strong, self-revealing dramatic monologue by a female astronomer presumably suggested by Maria Mitchell, who had impressed Melville in 1852 during the evening he and his father-in-law spent "with Mr. Mitchell the astronomer, & his celebrated daughter, the discoverer of comets" (see *Log,* p. 452). Although using an Italian setting for the poem, Melville may have adapted some

67. When I found the description in the *Log* (p. 642) unclear, Deborah Norsworthy kindly examined the clipping as Melville had placed it in his edition of Tennyson's poetry and showed that in his contemptuous comment Melville was defending Tennyson against the writer of the piece he had pasted in. The "stuff" was not Tennyson's.

details from Tennyson's *The Princess,* which is set in England. Melville knew about it, at least, from Powell's description of it, and probably from the 1848 William D. Ticknor edition or the 1855 Ticknor & Fields "New Edition" (lacking some lines criticized by the first reviewers). Here Tennyson, poet laureate since 1850, explored the topic of female education, specifically the challenge that "with equal husbandry / The woman were an equal to the man" (1.129–30), and the proposition that men hate "learned women" (1.442). Some of the names and images in *The Princess* and "After the Pleasure Party" are suggestive even though they do not prove that Melville drew them from Tennyson. The words "terrace" and "balm," not extremely common words, occur six lines apart in Tennyson and five lines apart in "After the Pleasure Party." Tennyson has Cupid and Uranian Venus: "The seal was Cupid bent above a scroll, / And o'er his head Uranian Venus hung" (1.238–39). Melville's poem begins with "Lines Traced Under an Image of Amor Threatening," Cupid warning virgins not to slight him. In Melville the name of the female astronomer is "Urania," but she is not Milton's or Wordsworth's muse. She is a woman tormented by Amor, who "boy-like" (263.112) wreaks his boyish spite on her. Melville's Urania prays to an "arm'd Virgin," the "Helmeted woman" Athena (263.132, 134), and there is a bust of Pallas (Athena) in Tennyson's poem (1.219). (In *The Princess,* 1.131, is a woman "that arm'd / Her own fair head.") This is *The Princess,* 3.283–85: "either sex alone / Is half itself, and in true marriage lies / Nor equal, nor unequal." This is Melville: "For, Nature, in no shallow surge / Against thee either sex may urge, / Why hast thou made us but in halves— / Co-relatives?" (262.84–87). Finally, *The Princess* deals with the topic of "After the Pleasure Party"—the repressed sexuality of educated women, particularly the idea that "One's sex asserts itself" (260.29).

Two others of Melville's surviving longer poems, unpublished in his lifetime, may well have been written in the late 1850s and may have been in *Poems,* in some form. Both are set in the Mediterranean (or at least involve old Italian artists and recent Italian history). One at an early stage was entitled "A Morning in Naples" and later retitled in various ways, including "An Afternoon in Naples" and "Naples in the Time of Bomba" ("Bomba" being the contemptuous name Ferdinando II earned by bombarding Messina into submission in 1848 and Palermo in 1849). The other is "At the Hostelry," in which a symposium of artists, mainly Italian and Dutch, discuss art (their own and their fellows'). Fairly soon after *Clarel* was published, Melville took one or both of these two poems out of his desk and attempted to salvage them by prefacing them with newly composed prose headnotes and supplementary sketches which introduced dramatic characters to speak the poems as well as (later) an editor who transcribes and prepares them for publication. Melville worked on the headnotes intermittently even during the later years when he was also engaged in writing or salvaging other poems and when he was, also intermittently, engaged in elaborating a burgeoning time-and-energy-consuming prose headnote to a poem, the manuscript, left nearly finished at his death, about a sailor named Billy Budd. There is as of now no way of saying which of the two poems was written first, but the lines about Garibaldi in "At the Hostelry" seem to have begun as an (early 1860s?) updating or continuation of the Naples poem and then been moved over into the poem about a symposium of artists (Italian and Dutch) discussing the idea of the picturesque. The topic of discussion in "At the Hostelry," the picturesque, is a theme that Melville recurred to several times in the 1850s. It is also present in poetry that may have been composed much later, particularly in the prose headnote to the poem about Rip Van Winkle, but, as Dennis Berthold has shown, it constitutes a significant motif in *Pierre* and some stories of the mid-1850s. The chapters on literary theory in *The Confidence-Man* are not aesthetically complicated, and Melville in his first lecture, on "Statues in Rome," reveals himself as still lacking a vocabulary of aesthetic terminology and as not having worked through some basic aesthetic problems. In "At the Hostelry" Melville amuses himself by vividly describing some low Dutch scenes but he does not grapple with aesthetic issues there beyond what he had done in *The Confidence-Man*.

On the admittedly weak grounds of Melville's rather unsophisticated treatment of the topic, the picturesque, it is tempting to argue that the initial composition of "At the Hostelry" belongs in the late 1850s. (Revisions made later include references to more recent Italian events, the substitution of a ship name famous in the Civil War for an earlier name, and possibly a reference to an engraving of Dürer that Melville may not have seen before it appeared in *Harper's Magazine* in 1870.) Melville's interest in art antedates the 1850s, but his known study of art and artists dates from 1859, when he borrowed from Evert Duyckinck four volumes of a five-volume set of Giorgio Vasari's *Lives of the Most Eminent Painters, Sculptors, and Architects* (London: Bohn, 1850–52; Sealts, no. 534a) and a three-volume set of Luigi Lanzi's *The History of Painting in Italy* (London: Bohn, 1847; Sealts, no. 320). When he wrote *Poems,* Melville surely had at hand not only poems by both Brownings about political turmoil in Italy but also poems by Robert Browning about Renaissance artists in Italy. (He would have devoured a poem like Browning's "Fra Lippo Lippi" in the 1856 Boston edition.)

Much of "A Morning in Naples" is directly based on Melville's own experiences. On February 19, 1857, Melville had pushed into the vast crowded Neapolitan streets that reminded him of Broadway, at least until there was a most un-American show of armed force: "Palace—soldiers—music—clang of arms all over city. Burst of troops from archway. Cannon posted inwards." Two days later he himself experienced the small adventure he recorded in his journal. The long poem he wrote based on his own drive through Naples examines the speaker's desire to avert his eyes from a political reality that intermittently imposes itself on him, however unwilling he is to face it. This continues Melville's moral scrutiny of the picturesque, for in *Pierre* and afterward he had been distrustful of aesthetic appreciation of the picturesque that came at the cost of ignoring economic injustices. The speaker of the poem, Melville, or a tourist seeking guilt-free enjoyment of the picturesque, is pulled in two directions—toward a denunciation of the displays of military power and an amelioristic acceptance that vineyards glow even if bayonets flash, that Nature's beauty makes living in Naples possible and even agreeable, even under an oppressive dictatorship. The speaker broods over Virgil, "here inurned / On Pausilippo, legend tells—/ Here on the slope that pledges ease to pain" (Pausilippo meaning freedom from pain). This leads into a passage on the world as two poet laureates knew it, Virgil and now Tennyson, a "Melancholy sphere" set in motion by some Deistic force ("Ruled by the primary impulse given—/ Forever revolving on"). In this sphere "Opinion and vogue" are "recurring still," although some things wait long before recurring: "life's too brief to note some long returns." In this melancholy sphere wise unconsciousness is lord, and "reason, that gladdens not the wise," alarms the fool. (That seems to be the sense, but so far the passage is imperfectly transcribed.[68]) In this world there is more to fear from life than there is from death; and in this world "truth takes falsehood graft, and hence / Equivocal fruit—." Beginning with a meditation on Virgil and Tennyson's both having "known" the world as a "melancholy sphere," the speaker has worked himself into a state of depressed brooding which is broken not by anything within but by a cheery distraction from without, the sight and fancied speech of the flower in his lapel.[69]

68. This transcription is mine, with the assistance of Dennis Marnon, from the manuscript in the Houghton Library of Harvard University (HCL-M), but I consulted Robert A. Sandberg's dissertation, as I did regularly in working with the "Naples" poem and "At the Hostelry."

69. Presumably by the late 1850s Virgil was linked with Tennyson in Melville's mind not only as melancholy laureates but also as fellow imitators. In 1862, reading in his set of Vasari, Melville marked a passage on Raphael's imitating Michelangelo (3.23) and commented: "The inimitable imitator. Good deal of the Virgil about Raphael—." In the *Mosses* essay Melville had cried, "Let us boldly contemn all imitation, though it comes to us graceful and fragrant as the morning."

The narrator of the Naples poem is unable to suppress his historical memory any more than he can suppress awareness of present military displays. A "flash of thought" carries him back to Queen Joanna, the cool murderer of her husband, then that scene is replaced by an older one, Agrippina, the granddaughter of Augustus, who starved herself to death when "In cruel craft exiled from Rome / To gaze on Naples' sunny bay." Pulled as he is by the rose, the symbol of present beauty of life, the speaker is haunted by fearful images from history, "Spectres of Naples under Spain"; an "incensed Revolt" in the seventeenth century, led by Tomaso Aniello (Masaniello); and the Terror imported from France, so that beautiful and bountiful Naples became "Hell's cornucopia crammed with crime!" As Melville wrote this part, he included the lines on Silvio Pellico (1789–1854), seized from his house, at night, never tried, imprisoned for many years and kept at hard labor, all because he wrote a "patriot ode / Construed as treason." He was internationally famous as a political prisoner, as shown by Felicia Hemans's honoring him with "To Silvio Pellico, on Reading his 'Prigione.'" This section, however revised, was published as "Pausilippo (In the time of Bomba)," sixth in the "Fruit of Travel Long Ago." The whole of the "Naples" poem in an early version, one including this section on Silvio but lacking a reference to Garibaldi, may well have been part of the 1860 *Poems*. The surviving manuscript, which Melville never published, shows that the ascription of the poem to the character Jack Gentian was an addition of the mid-1870s, and nothing prevents one's taking the speaker as "Melville" or an invented character reenacting Melville's own adventures and elaborating his own thought processes as he went about Naples, looking from superb palaces to smoking Vesuvius, visible from the main square. Very possibly Melville completed "Naples in the Time of Bomba" in the late 1850s and later added a few lines on the conquest of Bomba's son by Garibaldi's Red Shirts. The poem does not exist in an early, complete form but only as revised for inclusion in a volume which was also to contain prose introductory sketches and prefaces, and another long poem, "At the Hostelry"—perhaps written after it but placed before it.

Robert Milder has objected that "a fledgling poet seems unlikely to write a poem so thematically and technically accomplished" as "After the Pleasure Party" (2005, p. 57 n. 43). But Melville was a fast learner. He went from *Typee* to *Moby-Dick* in five or six years and had been a great prose writer for several years by 1857 or 1858, when he began writing serious poetry. For the best part of a decade, he had also been an extraordinarily sensitive reader of poetry, including some of the greatest poetry in the language. It is almost certain that Melville offered poems for publication early in 1859 and there is hard evidence of his facility as a poet in July 1859. *Poems* (1860) was Melville's first book of poetry, but it did not consist of the amateurish verse of a "fledgling poet."

IX
ON THE *METEOR:* MELVILLE WHEN HE THOUGHT HE WAS A PUBLISHED POET

WHEN HE DEPARTED on the *Glasgow* for Europe in 1856 Melville had left his brother Allan to see that *The Confidence-Man* would be published in New York and London. When he sailed on the *Meteor* in 1860 Melville was equally sure that his *Poems* would be published, guided not only by Allan but also by Evert Duyckinck, while Lizzie, after relaying his last-minute instructions, would make herself available to answer any questions that might arise about his intentions. With his secret apprenticeship and early mastery of poetry behind him, soon to be enshrined within covers, Melville was free to think about taking the next ambitious step. He had heard of Krakens, he said (perhaps from a recent reading of Tennyson), just after *Moby-Dick* was published.[70] He may not have regarded *Poems* as having reached in poetry the level of *Moby-Dick* in prose, but he was ready to propel himself from the company of Tennyson and the Brownings, small or smallish poets of his own time, into the company of Spenser and Milton, ready to think about writing not just a long poem like *The Excursion* but a still more ambitious poem like *The Faerie Queene,* whether it was technically a tragic dramatic poem or an epic. The evidence for thinking so is in his selection of reading material for his voyage and in his annotations in books he took.

Captain Thomas Melville had sailed the *Meteor* to Manila as early as 1855. When the family last heard from him, in 1859, he had been in Manila prepared to sail with his cargo to Calcutta before returning home. Now, the captain's brother had packed carefully, thinking that he would sail to Manila and thence he hardly knew where, he told Duyckinck—perhaps onward around the world. Indeed, the *Berkshire County Eagle* announced that the *Meteor* "sails direct for San Francisco, and thence across the

---

70. The reference to Krakens occurs in Melville's letter to Hawthorne, November [17?], 1851.

Pacific," making a year-long "voyage round the world." Always packing light, like his Ishmael, Melville could arrive at Southport in 1856 with a nightshirt and a toothbrush and then abandon his trunk to a storeroom in Liverpool.[71] Now able to indulge himself, since his brother could see to the stowing and retrieving of luggage and since he intended to stay in the same cabin for many months without transferring to another ship or to a shore lodging, Melville packed heavier yet managed to practice the *multum in parvo* principle, which always appealed to him, whether in tomahawks, Sheffield knives, or books. Freshly in the habit of borrowing old British magazines from Duyckinck for winter reading, on April 10, 1860, he consulted three of the 1834 volumes of the London *Quarterly Review* in the Astor Library (Olsen-Smith and Sealts, no. 414a). Now he packed some old quarterlies—"lazy reading for lazy latitudes," he called it in his May 28 letter to Duyckinck, by which he meant thought-provoking reading. More directly to his purpose as a poet, he packed a small (or perhaps a middling large) library of great poetry—classical epic poetry in English translation, early modern European poetry in translation, and much English poetry, with an emphasis on the epic or very long poem.

On the *Meteor* he did not read much, apparently, until sailing up the western coast of South America. Then, acutely conscious of the grandeur of this episode in his life, which might include a circumnavigation of the globe, he began locating himself as he read—"Cape Horn," "Pacific Ocean," by convention designating this voyage "Cape Horn 2" although he was rounding the cape for the third time. In his Spenser he wrote "C. H. 2." He wrote "C. H. 2" in Thomas Duer Broughton's *Selections from the Popular Poetry of the Hindoos* (London: Martin, 1814; Sealts, no. 87a)—an appropriate book to carry to Manila and perhaps on to Calcutta. Some of the surviving annotations establish at least a rough sequence of his reading. In Béranger's *Songs* (Philadelphia: Carey & Hart, 1844; Sealts, no. 58) he wrote: "Pacific Ocean / Sep 4th 1860 / 19 S.L." In his Wordsworth he wrote, "Pacific Ocean, Sep. 14th 1860 / 5° 60" N.L." In his Milton he wrote "C. Horn 1860" and "Pacific Ocean / N. L. 15° / Sep. 21th 1860." In his Dante he wrote "Pacific Ocean / Sunday Afternoon / Sep 22 1860." In Schiller's *Poems and Ballads* beside the last stanza of "To Emma," he wrote: "Sept 25th 1860 / North Pacific." In George Chapman's translation of excerpts from Homer, Hesiod, Musaeus, and Juvenal (London: Smith, 1858; Sealts, no. 276), he wrote "C. H. 2."; in Chapman's two volumes of the *Iliads* in the same set (London: Smith, 1857; Sealts, no. 277) he inscribed "C. H. 2." in the first and "Cape Horn 2." in the second (along

71. See *Journals,* pp. 628, 633.

with an annotation indicating that he was near San Francisco). In Chapman's *Odysseys* (London: Smith, 1857; Sealts, no. 278) he wrote "Pacific Ocean / Oct 3d 1860 / 700 miles from San Francisco / C H 2." On October 15, while he was in San Francisco, he wrote the date in his copy of *Songs of England. The Book of English Songs* (London: Houlston & Wright, 1857; Sealts, no. 342), edited by Charles Mackay (which he may have brought with him or may have acquired there). Returning to his copy of Wordsworth's poems on his way home, he annotated it "Gulf of Mexico Nov 6th 1860 / Steamer 'North Star.' " He carried a blank-book in which he wrote a few journal entries or else he wrote a few entries onto pages previously torn from a blank-book. There is no indication that he carried with him any of the four notebooks which he had used for his longer journals in 1849–50 and 1856–57.

All these books carrying Cape Horn notations are books of poetry— strong indication that he carried with him (besides the old periodicals) mainly a library of poetry (although he took a going-away present from Sarah Morewood, Hawthorne's new *The Marble Faun*). Of the books known to survive with 1860 Cape Horn annotations, Melville gave two away (one of which, the Spenser, later went out of the family for about a century). Others, the Wordsworth and the Dante, were apparently dispersed after his death. The particular books we know of cannot be the only volumes of poetry he took with him. Others may have been destroyed, some may survive with no record that they went round the Horn, and others with Cape Horn designations may yet show up. One clue to additional books Melville carried is that he repeatedly made cross-references between writers we know he had with him, comparing Spenser and Milton, Spenser and Wordsworth. Melville may have packed Pope's Homer in the Harper's Classical Library; a second translation of Dante, by John Carlyle; his Classical Library copy of Dryden's translation of Virgil's *Aeneid;* perhaps translations of Tasso and Ariosto; Chaucer (perhaps in the 1835 expurgated, modernized edition he picked up at some time). He refers to all of these in his annotations in some of the volumes he demonstrably took (though it cannot be proved that he made all the annotations on this voyage). In other marginalia possibly dating from this voyage, Melville referred to Byron, Keats, and Poe. Broughton was pleasant to carry to the Far East, but on a great clipper ship commanded by his brother, a veteran of several mercantile voyages to the Orient, Melville would have been in the mood to appreciate more than ever Camoëns's epic poem about Vasco da Gama's 1497–98 voyage around Africa to India, a celebration of the birth of modern commerce. (The purchase date Melville put in his only known copy of Camoëns, 1867 [Sealts, no. 116], makes it too late for this voyage.) Melville may have brought along his copy of Ossian, James Macpherson's *Fingal, An Ancient Epic Poem,* which he had bought in 1848 and still remembered well in March 1862, as he showed in markings in Hazlitt's *Lectures on the English Comic Writers* and *Lectures on the English Poets.* There he underlined Hazlitt's remark that Ossian "is even without God in the world" and wrote in the top margin: "True: no gods, I think, are mentioned in Ossian," and applauded a passage in which Hazlitt praised Ossian: "I am rejoiced to see Hazlitt speak for Ossian. There is nothing more contemptible in that contemptible man (tho' good poet, in his department) Wordsworth, than this contempt for Ossian. And nothing that more raises my idea of Napoleon than his great admiration for him.— The loneliness of the spirit of Ossian harmonized with the loneliness of the greatness of Napoleon."[72]

Planning to think about the shape a long serious American poem might take, Melville may have brought along some American epics, perhaps even the plodding *Fredoniad* that he mentioned in his essay on Hawthorne, or Barlow's *The Vision of Columbus* (1787) or *The Columbiad* (1807). Even more likely, he may have had with him John Quincy Adams's *Dermot MacMorrogh, or, The Conquest of Ireland: an historical tale of the 12th century: in four cantos* (Boston: Carter & Hendee, 1832). He knew that the four cantos of *Dermot MacMorrogh* might have been six, for the *Literary World* of March 18, 1848, had announced that among the unpublished works of the late former president were poems, "including two new cantos of Dermot MacMorrough," cantos which seem to have disappeared. Reading Milton's justification "Of that Sort of Dramatic Poem which is Called Tragedy," his preface to *Samson Agonistes,* Melville was struck by the passage on how men in the highest dignity had labored "not a little to be thought able to compose a tragedy," even Augustus Caesar having abandoned his tragedy of Ajax after being displeased with what he had written. Melville groused: "J. Q. A. might have followed his example," evidence enough that he was familiar with the former president's *Dermot MacMorrogh.* Adams seems to have been on his mind, for he copied out into his Dante a passage from *Dermot MacMorrogh* (or something else, now erased, which he identified by Adams's initials). It looks as if Melville was optimistically weighing his prospects for succeeding in composing the highest form of verse (that sort of dramatic poem which is called a tragedy) against the former president's chances.

72. Transcriptions of Melville's marginalia in his edition of Hazlitt's *Lectures* (New York: Derby & Jackson, 1859; Olsen-Smith and Sealts, no. 263b) are mine throughout.

In September and early October of 1860, by the time the *Meteor* reached the Pacific, Melville had every reason to assume that *Poems* had already been published and was being reviewed. A powerful consequence of his certainty that *Poems* then existed as a printed and bound book was that when he read poets in the Pacific, even more than in the first weeks of the voyage, he thought of himself as a poet reading *other* poets, Spenser, Milton, Wordsworth. Melville was not merely deluded in thinking that his next step, the way of achieving the greatest prestige as a poet, lay in writing a long, ambitious poem. He had, by now, thought about how to do it. George Chapman, according to Michael Drayton's poetic praise, by his translation of the *Georgics* of Hesiod and other classical works had brought ancient treasures to England (very much, the language implied, as Drake and other great Elizabethan seamen had brought home new wealth). Reading this, Melville marked Drayton's assertion that by his toil Chapman had strongly expressed the "large dimensions of the English tongue." He was identifying a hope for himself as a poet, though he could never be a translator. Melville was also impressed by Richard Hooper's praise of Chapman in the introduction to the *Iliads,* especially this sentence: "When we consider the subtle influence of poetry upon the rising spirits of the age, it tempts me to hazard the speculation that, if Chapman's noble paraphrase had been read instead of Pope's enervating monotony, and as extensively, the present class of general readers would not only have been a more poetical class—as the fountain-head from the rock is above the artificial cascade in a pleasure-ground—but a finer order of human beings in respect of energy, love of nature at first-hand, and faith in their own impulses and aspirations." Melville drew three vertical lines along "subtle influence of poetry upon the rising spirits of the age" and underlined those words, and he underlined from "but a finer order" on through the rest of the sentence. Far from remaining in his state of alienation from the contemporary world, Melville was now thinking of how through poetry he might arouse "a finer order of human beings," at least among the English-reading world. It was in this ambitious mood that he checked and underlined "To build with level of my lofty stile" in Spenser's "The Ruins of Rome" and wrote at the foot of the page one of his characteristic notations of literary borrowing, "Build the lofty rhyme / Milton."

As they sailed up the coast of South America Melville was either luxuriating in remembering some pieces that would be in the book waiting for him in San Francisco, or else writing new poetry. He jocularly reminded Tom on May 25, 1862, of the time he had overflowed with his own poetry: "I cant help thinking what a luckless chap you were that voyage you had a poetaster with you. You remember the romantic moonlight

night, when the conceited donkey repeated to you about three cables'
length of his verses." He may have been writing a work—presumably a
poem—based on a Hawaiian legend, for at some time between the late
1850s and 1862 he tried and felt he had "bungled" the attempt. Gorham
D. Gilman, a Boston businessman who had been in Hawaii, in 1858 or
earlier sent Melville some of his manuscripts of Hawaiian tales, thinking
Melville might appreciate the literary material. Among these was "Umi:
A Tale of Hawaii as Narrated by King Kamehameha III." In returning the
material on November 29, 1862, Melville said he had been charmed by the
traditional Hawaiian tale of Umi, in which an illegitimate son of the king
ultimately inherits the throne, and had found it "graceful & Greekish." He
may have been bemused as well as charmed, for the name "Umi" would
have had complicated associations for him, since long before, he may have
responded to Grace Greenwood's irresistible portrait of Clingy Lingy by
introducing a poetaster named Yoomy into the manuscript of *Mardi*. The
fun of writing Yoomy's verses in 1848 or so had helped prepare him to
write real poetry, a decade later. In his 1858–59 lecture on the South Seas
Melville alluded to a "traditional Polynesian legend" that might particu-
larly appeal to the ladies in his audience, since it was a "love legend of
Kamekamehaha, Tahiti, and Otaheite, that was told by a king of one of
these islands, and which has much of the grace, strangeness, and audacity
of the Grecian fables." This was an allusion to Gilman's material, for the
editor of the Milwaukee *Daily Wisconsin,* William Cramer, a family friend
of the Melvilles, specified that Melville had mentioned "a manuscript tra-
dition he had seen that was told by a King of one of those Islands."[73] When
Melville at last returned the documents to Gilman on November 29, 1862,
he said that he had taken Gilman's suggestion seriously: "Some time ago
I tried my hand at elaborating it, but found I bungled, and gave it up." A
reasonable guess is that Melville tried to elaborate the Hawaiian legend on
the *Meteor,* when he was expecting to sail across the Pacific.

In San Francisco in mid-October there was weighty news to catch
up on about the momentous American election, the partial unification
of Italy—everything but "a bloody battle in Affghanistan" (*Moby-Dick,*
chap. 1). None of that meant much to Melville at the moment, for at the
Harbormaster's there was no book-sized package for him, arrived ahead
of him by the Panama route, and the letters awaiting him confirmed that
his poems had not been published. Tom also received startling news at
the Harbormaster's—that he was to return around the Horn after an

73. See *Piazza Tales,* pp. 779–80.

indefinite wait in San Francisco. His self-image as a published poet shattered, Melville immediately decided to go home—by ship to the isthmus, then across on the Panama Railroad to another ship. On October 20, Tom had his brother's gear transferred onto the steamship *Cortes*. Without porters, Herman could not easily transport his old periodicals and books of poetry off the ship, onto the train, and onto a ship again for the voyage to New York, but his annotations show that he kept at least the Wordsworth and the Schiller, which he read in the Caribbean. He may have left some of the bulkier and heavier volumes for Tom to carry home on his ship, for his need to have Homer and Milton and other epic volumes at hand would have evaporated when *Poems* was not awaiting him in San Francisco. A year and a half later Melville recalled the voyage as the time Captain Melville had "a poetaster" as passenger. The hard truth is that what distinguishes a real poet (even an Alfred Street) from an amateur is that his verses get published. Even an author of many published prose books cannot call himself a poet if he cannot publish his poetry. Melville had thought himself a published poet while on the *Meteor* in the Pacific, but he returned to New York City in November 1860 as a stalled poetaster, not the triumphant author of *Poems* and the author and planner of new, even more ambitious poetry.

If what he had written had been printed, we would know Melville as the man who published these volumes between 1846 and 1860: *Typee, Omoo, Mardi, Redburn, White-Jacket, Moby-Dick, Pierre, The Isle of the Cross, Israel Potter, The Piazza Tales, The Confidence-Man,* and *Poems.* We might now think of "Morning in Naples"—or "Afternoon in Naples"—in relation to "Benito Cereno" and to Melville's then-recent 1857 European observations rather than as a waif from Melville's last decade and a half, twinned with another waif, "At the Hostelry." The loss of *Poems,* like the loss of *The Isle of the Cross* (not to mention slighter losses like some of the prose tortoise pages[74] and the bungled attempt at writing a Hawaiian legend) has meant that we cannot see Melville's working life as a whole and cannot see the interrelationships of his works, between *The Isle of the Cross* and "Bartleby," for instance, or between anything in *Poems* and anything in *Battle-Pieces* (1866).

---

74. In 1854 Melville supplied the Harpers with now lost sections of a "tortoise-hunting" book that did not duplicate anything in "The Encantadas" (Parker 2002, pp. 216–23).

X

HIS VERSE STILL UNPUBLISHED, MELVILLE DEFINES HIMSELF AS POET, 1861–1862

MELVILLE SET FOOT in Manhattan on November 13, 1860, a week after the election of Abraham Lincoln. The autumn was bleak as winter in his memory. In *Clarel* he recalled the next months of 1860–61: "That evil day, / Black in the New World's calendar— / The dolorous winter ere the war; / True Bridge of Sighs—so yet 'twill be / Esteemed in riper history— / Sad arch between contrasted eras" (4.5.74–79). A little surprisingly, not all his family and friends had been focused on the present American crisis. Some had preferred, as he phrased it at an agitated time in 1851, to look after Hungary—now to look after Italy, to take sides in a foreign struggle. His brother-in-law John C. Hoadley and his old friend Henry T. Tuckerman had been championing Garibaldi's campaign to unify Italy, Hoadley out of his passionate, erratic enthusiasm for a cause, Tuckerman on the basis of long close knowledge of Italy, Italian literature, and Garibaldi the man. American agitation for Greek freedom in the 1820s and the hysteria over Kossuth and Hungarian freedom late in 1851 had set a recognizable pattern: Americans tended to fixate on foreign crises during greater crises at home. What Tuckerman called "the sacred cause of Italian nationality" had come home to the educated classes in the northern United States as a feel-good liberal topic easier to talk about at the dinner table than, say, John Brown's raid on Harper's Ferry in October 1859. At a meeting in Newport (as reported in the Boston *Daily Transcript* on August 1, 1860), Tuckerman had offered the resolution that it was the "sacred duty" of Americans, "as citizens of a prosperous republic," to contribute money "to furnish arms and ammunition to Garibaldi in his holy crusade to free the oppressed and establish Italian independence." No one mentioned any impropriety in arming revolutionaries in a foreign land—certainly not in the Holy Land of Art. Early in 1861 in Lawrence, Massachusetts, Hoadley, chairman of a committee charged with congratulating Italy upon its unification, wrote resolutions out "most beautifully" in the French language for the Secretary of State to forward to their destination. By then, Tuckerman had published the definitive American article on Garibaldi in the January 1861 *North American Review*.

For months many members of Melville's family and their friends had been attempting to prevent an American war, doing all they could to placate the South in the face of a likely Republican victory. Before the election, Melville's father-in-law, Lemuel Shaw, retired as Chief Justice of the Commonwealth of Massachusetts, had been importuned to become an elector of the Constitutional Union Party, whose members hoped to prevent secession, and, failing that, to prevent war between the states. At Thanksgiving, while Melville was in the Shaw house, Shaw joined with Massachusetts unionists who urged conciliation toward the South. In December in New York City Melville's brother Allan's first wife's brother-in-law, Richard Lathers (treated as a brother-in-law of Herman's still), was working with John A. Dix and other men Melville knew, trying to stave off secession through a breathtakingly tardy plan for black colonization to Africa. In February 1861 Lathers attended a Peace Convention in Washington presided over by former president John Tyler (who had boarded at the Melvill house in Pittsfield in 1848), then set out with his wife, the aunt of Melville's brother Allan's daughters, on a quixotic, heroic mission to the South. Bewildered by unreal hopes and unpredictable realities after months away, Melville may have felt he had not grasped the subtleties of people's positions, and years later decided he needed to perform a little historical research if he were to grasp some of the issues. On June 30, 1866, at the Astor Library in New York he consulted the 626-page *A Report of the Debates and Proceedings in the Secret Sessions of the Conference Convention, for Proposing Amendments to the Constitution of the United States, held at Washington, D.C., in February, A.D. 1861* (New York: D. Appleton & Co., 1864), compiled by L. E. Chittenden (Olsen-Smith and Sealts, no. 143.2). He wanted to have the history freshly in mind as he worked on the "Supplement" to his volume of Civil War poetry.

Despite the momentousness of the national crisis and despite his own uncharacteristic visits to his now-scattered family, Melville may have laid in some of his habitually weighty reading for that winter, one which proved brutally harsh as well as historically dolorous. Although he was humiliated that *Poems* was not on his work table (bound any way but blue and gold), he may have kept on writing poetry: it was now what he did. The year 1860 is the most likely for his composing a little poem for the captain of the *Meteor,* who was keeping his Christmas "Lonesome on the torrid deep":

> Thou that, duty-led, dost roam
> Far from thy shepherd-brother's home—
> Shearer of the ocean-foam!
> To whom one Christmas may not come,—
>   Of thee I think
>   Till on its brink
> The glass shows tears, beloved Tom!

This compliment to Tom looks like a poem for the specific occasion, a poetical toast offered amid other thoughtfully constructed Christmas toasts traditionally given by the males of the family (see *Log*, p. 631). The next week, in the Dutch tradition of New Year's Day gift-giving, he inscribed to Lizzie his now-lost copy of *The Works of the Late Edgar Allan Poe* (New York: Blakeman & Mason, 1859; Sealts, no. 404a). He had bought it in 1860, perhaps to carry round Cape Horn, and now had absorbed it to the point that it could be given away, though not to the point that he was willing to send it out of the house.

With his hopes dashed that he could become accepted at home as an American poet, Melville took seriously the possibility of becoming the American consul at Florence. In late March 1861, himself "duty-led," he agreed to go to Washington to seek the assistance of Thurlow Weed and Charles Sumner, a friend of Hoadley's. Called back urgently by word of Shaw's illness, Melville arrived in Boston too late to see his father-in-law alive but in time to participate in the momentous public mourning and state funeral. With her inheritance coming, Lizzie and Herman could more easily give up the idea of uprooting themselves as the Hawthornes had done and instead could consider how to keep their capital (the first they had possessed) from dwindling away before Herman was able to find some new way of making money. Even without a job, Herman felt he could afford to begin buying books again, for, a week after Shaw's funeral, he put the date April 9 in the two-volume *The Poetical Works of Shelley* (Boston: Little, Brown, 1857; Sealts, no. 469) and a recent set of *The Poetical Works of Edmund Spenser* in five volumes (Boston: Little, Brown, 1855; Sealts, no. 483). Presumably he bought them in Boston, where there were real bookstores, although he wrote "Pittsfield" after the date each time. Odd memories of the dead were at work in the purchase of each of these books, the Shelley reminding him of the artist William Edward West, who had told vivid stories of the living Shelley and Byron at Dr. Francis's house in Bond Street, the Spenser inevitably reminding him of his poring over his father's set, which he may already have promised to give to Augusta once he had found a suitable replacement.

Going to a bookstore on April 9, 1861, was a persistence of the quotidian amid extraordinary circumstances. The state funeral for Judge Shaw on April 2 had been followed four days later by news that Lincoln was sending a relief expedition to Fort Sumter, in the harbor of Charleston, since February in the Confederate state of South Carolina. Melville's life did not change immediately because of the war. He continued to visit scattered members of the family, and he continued to buy poetry. On July 3 he bought *The Poetical Works of James Thomson* (Boston: Little, Brown,

1854; Sealts, no. 516), which contained poems familiar to him from his youth, perhaps picking up the volume on his way to New Rochelle, which he visited that day. On August 14 during a layover in Albany after visiting his mother in Gansevoort, he bought the two-volume *The Poetical Works of Alfred Tennyson* (Boston: Ticknor & Fields, 1861; Sealts, no. 508). Later, in 1864 or afterward, he pasted in a newspaper clipping in which an anonymous critic expressed disdain for "The Charge of the Light Brigade," citing Tennyson's plagiarism of Drayton's "The Battle of Agincourt" as exposed in William Brighty Rands's *Tangled Talk: An Essayist's Holiday* (London: A. Strahan & Co., 1864). Defending Tennyson, as mentioned earlier, Melville wrote "Stuff by a small man," drawing his version of a printer's fist pointing at the clipping. In October in New York near Central Park, at a yet-unidentified "Cedar Home," Melville bought Leigh Hunt's *Rimini and Other Poems* (Boston: Ticknor & Fields, 1844; Sealts, no. 290a), much of which he must have been familiar with already.

On October 27, 1861, Melville made a momentous purchase, as far as we know the most important purchase of the year: Henry Taylor's *Notes from Life in Seven Essays* (Boston: Ticknor, Reed, & Fields, 1853; Sealts, no. 290a). In Taylor he found a kindred spirit—a man equally familiar with the wisdom of Solomon as recorded in Ecclesiastes and the wisdom of Jesus the Son of Sirach as recorded in Ecclesiasticus. Another point of kinship for the erratically educated Melville was that Taylor, unlike many British writers, was not fluent in foreign languages. Yet Taylor was an intensely literary man, steeped like Melville in centuries of English poetry, so that his field of reading was near Melville's own. Throughout his book Taylor quoted much poetry, some of it his own, some of it yet unidentified. He quoted George Herbert's "The Church Porch"; Chaucer's "Clerke's Tale"; Francis Quarles's lines on prodigality beginning "Thrice happy he whose nobler thoughts despise / To make an object of so easy gains" (from *Emblems, Divine and Moral,* 1.4); lines from his own *A Sicilian Summer* ("In many a vigil of her last sick bed"); *Hamlet; As You Like It; Coriolanus; As You Like It,* again; *Othello.* He quoted from Aubrey De Vere's *Waldenses, and Other Poems; Twelfth Night;* Crabbe's "The Parish Register"; *Julius Caesar;* Sir Walter Raleigh; Milton (*Paradise Lost); Southey (Oliver Newman);* Christopher Hervie (*The Synagogue);* the book of Job; *Hamlet,* again; John Fletcher ("Melancholy"); *Othello,* again; Cowley ("Ode upon Liberty"); Tennyson's "The Gardener's Daughter"; Coleridge's "The Night-Scene: A Dramatic Fragment"; William Wordsworth's "Malham Cove"; Shakespeare's sonnet 111; Southey's "My days among the dead are past"; Milton's sonnet "How soon hath Time"; Wordsworth's sonnet to B. R. Haydon; *Paradise Lost,* again; *King Lear;* Walter Savage Landor; *Coriolanus,* again ("a

most inherent baseness"); Goethe's *Faust;* and Landor's "Imaginary Con-
versations." Of the quotations listed above, those from Fletcher to the last
one by Milton were in the long essay "The Life Poetic," which Melville
read meticulously, most likely late in 1861.

According to Taylor in "The Life Poetic," the "man of genius" (the
poet) should lean "towards retirement," meaning removal from the bustle
of cities. (The Duyckincks had referred to Melville's life at Arrowhead as
"comparative retirement." In 1862, in his set of Cowley [discussed later in
this section], Melville marked T. Sprat's reproach of Cowley for showing
a too earnest "Affection for Obscurity and Retirement.") Still, for culti-
vation of "the highest order of poetry" the poet should "be conversant
with life and nature at large," should be "to a moderate extent, mixed up
with the affairs of life." Melville marked this sentence: "He is but a child
in knowledge, however versed in meditation, who has not to act, to suf-
fer, and to teach, as well as to inquire and to learn." Taylor recognized
the difficulty of achieving balance between the "contemplative life" and
"the inordinate activities of the age." How a poet was to earn money
was always a problem. The professions were too demanding for a poet
to undertake; commercial life forced men into competition unsuited to a
poet; political life was "too violent a diversion from poetic pursuits." If a
poet failed to find a field for "external activity, which would admit also
of leisure and retirement," he nevertheless needed to lead a disciplined
life. He needed the "regimen of external circumstances and of obligations
contracted to others"—the sort of regimen Melville finally achieved at
the end of 1866 in the Custom House. A poet with no occupation might
find himself "prey to many demands for small services, attentions, and
civilities, such as will neither exercise his faculties, add to his knowledge,
nor leave him to his thoughts." Cousin Elizabeth Gansevoort long ago, in
1840, had identified Herman as the brother who had nothing to do and
therefore could escort Augusta across the width of the Empire State to
Bath, New York. Melville had done an inordinate amount of visiting after
his return from San Francisco. If the family learned that he was no longer
farming Arrowhead, what demands would be made on him, now that he
was plainly not publishing anything regularly? Melville marked this pas-
sage on the dangers of being imposed on, and checked the conclusion that
a poet in the midst of the "bustling crowds of this present world" would
find himself "in a position of oppugnancy to those around him," so that
he "must struggle in order to stand still."

The ideal life of the poet was one of "semi-seclusion" such as Ten-
nyson described, Taylor said. Thinking of Samuel Rogers, probably, and
the excitement of city life, Melville marked this passage in Taylor: "In

London, in the present times, an eminent man is beset with a multiplic-
ity of social enjoyments and excitements, the very waste-pipes of genial
sensibility; and the poet's imagination, instead of forming a fund to be
continually deepened and widened by influx from secret sources, is dif-
fused and spread abroad and speedily dried up." Melville marked other
passages on the poet's need for "an adequate unpopularity" to constitute
self-protection, and a line on "the perils of social popularity." He boxed a
line Taylor quoted from Coleridge's "The Night-Scene: A Dramatic Frag-
ment": "Deep self-possession, an intense repose"—part of the argument
that a poet is by temperament so excitable that he should avoid stimula-
tion. Melville underlined this assertion: "To the poet, solitude itself is an
excitement." The poet should look to the future for his reward, cherishing
"some more or less conscious anticipation of sympathy to come," Taylor
advised, and, agreeing, Melville marked the passage on the poet's not
being granted "contemporaneous and immediate admiration." Taylor said
bluntly, "I doubt whether any high endeavor of poetic art ever has been
or ever will be promoted by the stimulation of popular applause." Even
the greatest poets had found that their popularity during most if not all of
their lives was "still a popularity which extends only to the cultivated, as
distinguished from the merely educated classes, and does not bring with
it any very profitable sale." Brooding on this, Melville underlined the dis-
tinction between the merely educated and the cultivated.

Acknowledging that poets cannot subsist by writing poetry, Taylor
asked if they might "subsist by the aid of prose." But prose, Taylor real-
ized, "will fail to return a profit, unless it be written for the market."
(Melville marked all this.) Taylor held up Southey as a poet who wrote
prose for the market ("marketable literature," a phrase Melville under-
lined) and wrote with "unrivalled industry, infinite stores of knowledge,
extraordinary talents, and a delightful style," and yet merely subsisted in
the most frugal manner and died leaving planned poetic works unfinished
for lack of time. The last "marketable literature" Melville had published
was *Israel Potter;* apparently unlike Southey, he had felt pulled apart by the
need to write what he wanted to write and the conflicting need to write
what would sell. In 1861 writing marketable prose was not an option
to be considered. Illustrating the poignancy of Southey's leaving works
unfinished, Taylor printed three lines from "Wordsworth": "Things
incomplete, and purposes betrayed, / Make sadder transits o'er Truth's
mystic glass, / Than noblest objects utterly decayed." (Melville may have
remembered the words from the sonnet "Malham Cove," unmarked in
his copy of Wordsworth's *Complete Poetical Works,* where it occurs a few
pages after the sonnet to Haydon, which he annotated.) From 1876 until

his death Melville would struggle to salvage old works and to complete new ones, and fail, notably in the biggest thing he left unfinished, the manuscript of *Billy Budd*. Taylor had no patience with a "spendthrift poet" or "one who is incompetent to the management of his affairs," words that may have stung Melville, whom the entire family in 1856 had recognized to be incapable of making financial decisions. Ideally, poets should not have to earn all the money they need for living, for "pecuniary difficulties" almost always impair men of "character and content." Ideally, there would be some "needful protection" for men of genius. His wife's inheritance had relieved Melville of the obligation to earn money, at the moment. What allowed Melville the leisure to read about the poetic life and to prepare to write more poetry rather than to go out looking for work seems to have been a sense of the entitlements due to genius, especially now that his long struggle to write marketable prose had ended in failure. Melville underlined Taylor's observation that poetry "is the fruit of the whole moral, spiritual, intellectual, and practical being" and would be weakened if the poet lacked a frugal competence. At the end of this almost page-long sentence, Melville underlined and marked a passage on the gifts of the poet which were too often dimmed by imperfections of humanity. At best, on a poet with "a pure and unspotted life" God might bestow the "gifts of high reason, ardent imagination, efflorescence of fancy and intrepidity of impulse," so that he might write great poetry. "Out of the heart are the issues of life, and out of the life are the issues of poetry," Taylor declared. Melville underlined "intrepidity of impulse" and drew a line along the remaining part of the passage. Coolly as he expressed himself, Taylor allowed all along for the boldness of true genius.

Turning to how poets train themselves, Taylor recommended (in a passage Melville marked) "*select* reading," chiefly the literature of the seventeenth century because "the diction and the movement of that literature," both prose and poetry, is best fitted "to be used for the training of the mind for poetry." The complexity of that century's prose and poetry detained the reader "over what was pregnant and profound" and trained "the ear and utterance" of a would-be poet. This rang true to Melville, the lover of Robert Burton, Jeremy Taylor, Abraham Cowley, and John Dryden. Taylor celebrated a style difficult enough that a reader would be forced to suspend in mind complex thought as it was embodied in many phrases and clauses and then, at the end of the sentence, would comprehend in its entirety the whole of the complex meaning. Taylor continued: "For if we look at the long-suspended sentences of those days, with all their convolutions and intertextures—the many parts waiting for the ultimate wholeness—we shall perceive that without distinctive movement and <u>rhythmical significance of a very high order</u>, it would be impossible that they could be sustained in any sort of clearness" (Melville did the underlining). Under discussion was prose such as Melville had mastered in *Moby-Dick*, even more so in *Pierre*, and yet more so, to the detriment of popularity, in *The Confidence-Man*.

Taylor advised that the poet abstain from reading books plainly directed at the current popular reading audience, the sort of books which one may read on the run, and instead become familiar with "elder models in the matter of diction." (Melville marked the part on avoiding books "written *in* these times and *for* these times, to catch the fugacious or stimulate the sluggish reader.") Then, Taylor said, the poet would be able to employ as his own "that slightly archaistic coloring of language" (underlined and marked by Melville) which Spenser and others had thought "the best costume in which poetry can be clothed, combining what is common to other ages with what is characteristic of its own." Yet the true poet would be "choice and chary, as well as moderate, in the use of archaisms," shunning old forms which deserve to be forgotten while acting as a conservator of language. By "observing with a keener insight the latent metaphorical fitness or unfitness by which all language is pervaded," the poet would find himself "remanding to their more derivative significations, words which are beginning to go astray." Melville marked the passage on the precision of language required of the poet: "And though this peculiar aptitude will escape many of the poet's readers, (if he have many,) and much of it will not be recognised at once even by the more skilful few, yet in this, as in other matters of art, it is what can be fully appreciated only by continual study, that will lay the strongest foundations of fame." Alerted here, in the next months Melville marked many passages about poets' continual study and painstaking effort.

Melville marked Taylor's long footnote on Crabbe Robinson's testifying that Schiller had told him he read foreign writers in German lest he "lose his nicer perceptions" of what belonged to his own language. As a poet who knew only English, Melville could take consolation from Taylor's conclusion that Milton, whose "store of poetical images and material" was "greatly enriched" by his knowledge of the Latin and Greek classics and by Italian, yet had been damaged by letting Latin pervert his diction away from English. Melville marked Taylor's claim that a poet should not "deem himself to be prepared for the exercise of his vocation on a large scale" until he had reached middle age. (Milton himself had thought that he was maturing slowly, at twenty-three; and Melville in his Milton marked the section on Milton's age when he wrote *Paradise Lost* and his seasonal and daily working habits.) Melville marked "sixty-seventh year"—the age at which, according to Taylor, Dryden wrote "Alexander's Feast." Even the best "amorous poetry," Taylor thought, was apt to be the product of the "richer vein" available to a man well past his youth. More important, Taylor reflected: "The sense of proportion, which is required equally in the lighter as in the graver kinds of poetry, is naturally imperfect in youth, through undue ardor in particulars; and no very young poet will be content to sacrifice special felicities to general effect" (Melville's underlining). Taylor continued on the difficulty of attaining proper equilibrium in youth: "Nor can there well exist, at an early period of life, that rare and peculiar balance of all the faculties, which, even more perhaps than a peculiar force in any, constitutes a great poet:—the balance of reason with imagination, passion with self-possession, abundance with reserve, and inventive conception with executive ability" (that last meaning the ability to execute, to carry out). Melville underlined "peculiar balance of all the faculties" and sidelined all the rest of the sentence. That balance was something he could look for in himself now, long past his youth, when he could acknowledge that during the completion of *Moby-Dick* he had possessed everything Taylor described except a balanced judgment in matters financial.

Taylor advised that a youthful poet publish at once, freeing himself to move on to a work with "an ambition sufficiently long-sighted" (words Melville underlined). Taylor said that "early failure in those in whom there is genuine poetic genius, and what commonly accompanies it—'Faith in the whispers of the lonely Muse'—acts as a sort of narcotic stimulant, allaying impatience, but quickening the deeper mind." Melville underlined "Faith" through "Muse," which (even without the footnoted "Wordsworth") he may have identified as from Wordsworth's "Sonnet to B. R. Haydon." Melville also carefully read Taylor's advice that poets should stop writing new poetry at seventy or so and set themselves to putting their earlier work in order, but not revising it obsessively, since by that time the poet might have lost his "clearness and decisiveness of choice" (words Melville underlined). The presumption, Taylor insisted, "should be in favor of the first draft." All in all, Melville found *Notes from Life* exceptionally thought-provoking, Taylor confirming much that he had already experienced and justifying him in courses he was prepared to continue. The essay "The Life Poetic," judging by his markings, came as a momentous help in Melville's defining his present condition as an unrecognized poet living on his wife's money and projecting cautiously how the rest of his life as a poet might work itself out. Nothing Taylor described was alien to his experience.

On April 11, 1860, while he was finishing *Poems,* Melville had visited the Astor Library in Lafayette Place to consult the two volumes of Moore's biography of Byron, a book long familiar to him (Olsen-Smith and Sealts, no. 369a). In December 1861, probably a few weeks after he read *Notes from Life,* Melville put the address 103 East Tenth Street in a set of Byron (Boston: Little, Brown, 1853; Sealts, no. 112). Beside *Don Juan,* canto 11, stanzas 5 and 6 (an ironic passage on growing more orthodox with every new push of an illness), Melville wrote: "this is excellent—the practical abandonment of good-humored devil-may-care. Byron is a better man in Don Juan than in his serious poems." He reminded himself to "learn by heart" ten lines of section 3 of the third canto of *The Island: or Christian and His Comrades:*

> A little stream came tumbling from the height,
> And straggling into ocean as it might,
> Its bounding crystal frolick'd in the ray,
> And gush'd from cliff to crag with saltless spray;
> Close on the wild, wide ocean, yet as pure
> And fresh as innocence, and more secure,
> Its silver torrent glitter'd o'er the deep,
> As the shy chamois' eye o'erlooks the steep,
> While far below the vast and sullen swell
> Of ocean's alpine azure rose and fell.

He may have wanted to get these particular lines by heart because they reminded him of the Marquesas or Tahiti, but, whatever his motive, this "learn by heart" shows that in his forties Melville was still memorizing poetry, and not merely purple passages or commonly quoted passages. From his instant recognition of poetic echoes, even in books where he could hardly have been prompted by critical commentaries or editorial footnotes, we have to conclude that he knew many hundreds, probably thousands of lines of poetry "by heart." When he encountered allusions, borrowings, and echoes as he read poems, he took pleasure in footnoting the interdebtedness of poets, putting an X by the passage and another X at the foot of the page, typically, along with the line borrowed from an earlier poet or influencing a later poet. Part of the pleasure of reading, for Melville, was recognizing and appreciating the debts that poets, especially great poets, owed to their predecessors.

While living in that rented space on East Tenth Street Melville walked a few steps over to call on Henry T. Tuckerman at 15 West Tenth Street, the Tenth Street Studio Building where many artists set up their studios.

He missed his man, and Tuckerman could not return his call because he was laid up "with a severe neuralgic attack" (Parker 2002, p. 484). Talk had to wait into the next year. In late January 1862 Melville was back in New York, renting at 150 East Eighteenth Street. Tuckerman got his address through Evert Duyckinck, and they met as valetudinarians after their slightly farcical failures to connect. Melville had experienced many failures to connect, perhaps most recently when he reported ruefully to his uncle Peter on March 21, 1861, that one political bird he tried to find, Thurlow Weed, had flown "back to its perch—Albany." Given Melville's intense interest in Italy and especially given the likelihood that he had already written his "Naples" poem in 1858 or 1859, Garibaldi must have been a topic of conversation between Melville and Tuckerman early in 1862, however large the American war loomed in their thoughts. As Melville had prepared to sail with Tom on the *Meteor,* Garibaldi had been preparing to sail from Genoa with his thousand Red Shirts. At the end of May 1860, just as Melville sailed, Garibaldi took Palermo, and in August he crossed the Strait of Messina. In early September he entered Naples, claiming Sicily and Naples for Victor Emmanuel II of Savoia. In early 1861 Italy was united, except what the Austrians held in the north and, most rankling, except for Rome. Melville could have seen many old articles printed during his absence at sea, for he caught up with some of the news in San Francisco, but Tuckerman's long essay in the *North American Review* of January 1861 by itself contained most of the details he used when he wrote a new hundred lines or so devoted to Garibaldi's liberation of Sicily and his crossing the strait to free Naples from "King Fanny, Bomba's heir." He may have written the new lines thinking he could fit them into the end of his poem about a drive through Naples, even though the poem was about what one form of the title stressed, Naples in the time of Bomba, before the brief reign of "King Fanny" (Francis II). Later he updated some of the lines (such as those that refer to Venice and Rome as both liberated and as part of Italy, which happened to Venice in 1866 and Rome in 1871). Whenever Melville gave renewed attention to Garibaldi, very possibly in 1861–62, he echoed Tuckerman's language. Much later, probably in the late 1870s, Melville revised the lines on Garibaldi and attached them to "At the Hostelry," but he never revised out of them some references that must have been put there in the early 1860s, such as the allusion to Turin as the capital of the new kingdom of Italy, which was true only until 1865.

On the first of February 1862, ready to make up a deficiency in his reading, Melville asked Evert Duyckinck for some volumes by dramatists contemporary with Shakespeare. Marlowe he knew, but he was ready to read Thomas Dekker and John Webster if Duyckinck had their plays. Either Melville borrowed the books and read them quickly or else he postponed that reading until very late in his life, when volumes in the Mermaid series became available. Instead of pursuing the Elizabethan dramatists and instead of writing more poetry, in the middle of February 1862 Melville embarked on what became an intense course of reading. With some of Lizzie's money in hand, he began buying books, week after week or even day after day, apparently pretty much for immediate sampling or thorough reading. After his purchases in London at the end of 1849 Melville never again bought books in bulk knowing that for the most part his delectation would be postponed. During his work on *Moby-Dick* (starting early in 1850) and his work on *Clarel* (starting early in 1870) he bought several books as source material, but never in such bulk in the long interval between those two projects. The single intense period of book-buying we know of, after his acquisitions in London, is that of early 1862. These books were not bought as source material for a projected book or a work in progress. Melville may not have started with a clear purpose in mind, but his book-buying rather quickly became focused. He bought volumes of poetry, usually by neglected or not-yet-established poets (he already owned most standard poets, though he added Cowley on March 21, 1862). He also bought books of literary history and criticism, and, toward the end, one major multivolume art history, the Vasari, which he had read in 1859 in Evert Duyckinck's copy (read carefully enough that he remembered a slight detail on shipboard in 1860). In all likelihood, in these months, February through April, Melville also bought books we know nothing about, for two of the most important, the Vasari and the Hazlitt, described below, were discovered late in the twentieth century. Furthermore, he was almost certainly borrowing some books, from Duyckinck or Tuckerman, most likely, for it was probably at this time that he took notes in his new Hazlitt from an article in the *Edinburgh Review* and took notes in his new Vasari from the third volume of Ruskin's *Modern Painters,* a book Melville did not yet own.

The following account of Melville's reading in early 1862 proceeds roughly in the sequence of his book-buying, skewed by his sometimes writing down only the month of purchase, not the day. The sequence in which Melville read his new books did not, of course, correspond precisely with the order in which he bought them, but most of his markings and annotations in them seem to have dated from this February through April period. To a great extent he was reading or at least looking over what he bought soon after buying it. Melville's annotations as well as his underlinings, marginal scorings, and other symbols in the texts and in the margins are obvious evidence of his engagement with what he read, but he did not always make any mark by passages that struck him powerfully. Building this section on some of Melville's markings in his books is not meant to foreclose the study of other markings and of these markings in relation to the whole texts.

At the outset of this extraordinary period of book-buying and reading, Melville was freshly prompted by his study of Taylor's *Notes from Life* to refine his efforts to place his own experience as prose writer and as poet in relation to what he could learn of other poets, particularly British poets of the previous three hundred years, both the long-famous and the obscure. He was alert to compare his sense of his own abilities and achievements with what others defined as the qualities that constituted literary greatness. Rather quickly he began actively marking recurrent topics, as when he focused repeatedly on the "pains" that writers had taken in their composition, on how "painstaking" they had been (even if others thought they had dashed their poems off). What he marked in writer after writer confirmed his own conviction that he too had taken infinite pains, even if his books had been "botches,"[75] and would always take such pains with his more ambitious poetry. Writing good poetry, in particular, took painstaking labor which often went unrewarded in the poet's lifetime, as it conspicuously had done in his own life, in 1860. Melville was enthralled by accounts of other writer's work habits in general. He became fascinated by the question of how much of poetic genius is innate and how much can be developed. He developed a rueful sense of himself as a perfectly ordinary genius, acting according to the well-established peculiarities of the class, not the unreasonably demanding fellow he had sometimes seemed to members of his family. Geniuses really were different from normal people although sometimes surprisingly like each other. After scanning some of his purchases he found himself wanting to study rhetoric in literature, to pick up, very likely, from about where he had dropped the great textbooks in 1839, when he left the Lansingburgh Academy. Now he took conscientious notes on literary techniques, most elaborately from Francis Jeffrey's review-essay on the Italian dramatist Victor Alfieri (writing down the notes in Hazlitt's *Lectures*). By the end of

---

75. See Parker 1996, pp. 840–42, for my redating of the letter to Hawthorne dated [June 1?], 1851, in *Correspondence* (p. 191), on evidence in a letter from Augusta Melville to Allan Melville dated May 16, 1851, and deposited at Arrowhead by Anna Morewood in the early 1990s. The *Correspondence* volume was already in print when I made the redating. When I went over the evidence with him, Hayford approved the redating.

his course of reading and notetaking the autodidact was ready to articulate an aesthetic credo of his own.

On February 14, 1862, Melville bought *The Poetical Works of Thomas Hood* (Boston: Little, Brown, 1860; Sealts, no. 279). In Richard Monckton Milnes's memoir Melville marked a section on the poet's excessive facility: "[I]f Mr. Hood had been able to place under some restraint the curious and complex machinery of words and syllables which his fancy was incessantly producing, his style would have been a great gainer." Among many other poems, Melville marked the entirety of "The Poet's Fate" ("What is a modern Poet's fate? / To write his thoughts upon a slate;— / The Critic spits on what is done,— / Gives it a wipe,—and all is gone"). In the first volume he did not bother to mark "The Haunted House," but he apparently noticed Hood's saying, in quotation marks, that wild birds fed near the deserted mansion with "shocking tameness." Melville knew this as an allusion to Cowper's "The Solitude of Alexander Selkirk," a poem he had quoted from memory in his journal in London, in late November 1849 ("Oh Solitude! where are thy charms"). As will become clear below, Melville had paid close attention to this passage even though he did not mark it.

On February 15, 1862, Melville bought *Poems of James Clarence Mangan* (New York: Haverty, 1859; Sealts, no. 347). As he frequently did, Melville jotted down an essential biographical date: "Died about 1848." The introduction by John Mitchel began with something sure to arouse an ironic smile in Melville, an apology for daring to call the attention of the literary world to a poet not included in *Poets of the Nineteenth Century*, edited by the Reverend Robert Aris Willmot and (in its American edition) Evert A. Duyckinck. The volume was divided into four sections: "German Anthology," "Irish Anthology," "Apocrypha," and "Miscellaneous." Many pages in the first section consisted of translations from Schiller, who had long been of interest to Melville. One of the many poems by Schiller that Melville triple-checked was "The Words of Delusion" (Triumph, Treasure, and Truth), where the delusion is the hope that worth will be rewarded by "Triumph and Treasure" and the dream that the "noonbeams of Truth" will ever shine on human clay. Early in the introduction Melville marked the account of Mangan's being an outsider: "Mangan was not only an Irishman,—not only an Irish papist,—not only an Irish papist rebel;—but throughout his whole literary life of twenty years, he never deigned to attorn to English criticism," never "seemed to be aware that there was a British public to please." (Melville did not query "attorn," which meant "to pay homage to.") This description defined some of Mangan's appeal beyond his translating German poets. He was an obscure outsider, theologically suspect, oblivious to the judgments of the literary elite. On back flyleaves Melville noted (from p. 156) "at whiles" (which he underlined in the text), "aneath," the foreign word "Franquis-tán," the rhymes "e'ening – meaning," "sternest – earnest" (these two in reverse order of occurrence), and "lonely – only." Then he noted: "shorn & cowled" (also on 156). Melville plainly found a highly self-conscious use of "archaisms" in form and diction to be attractive in Mangan, as a little later he did in the Pre-Raphaelites.

Also on February 15, 1862, Melville bought *The Poetical Works of Thomas Moore* (Boston: Little, Brown, 1856 [1854?]; Sealts, no. 370). He may have read in this book at once, in mid-February, but if so he returned to it in October 1862. Probably he knew already many of the "Poems Relating to America." Certainly he already knew many of Moore's songs and Moore's life of Byron. He knew *Lalla Rookh* (dedicated to Samuel Rogers), and he knew enough of literary history to identify the people referred to in "The 'Living Dog' and 'The Dead Lion'" as Leigh Hunt and Byron. Now he was struck by Moore's portrayal of himself as being, "at all times, a far more slow and pains-taking workman than would ever be guessed, I fear, from the result." In the preface to *Lalla Rookh* Moore went farther, in words Melville partially underlined: "Having thus laid open the secrets of the workshop to account for the time expended in writing this work, I must also, in justice to my own industry, notice the pains I took in long and laboriously reading for it" (that is, historical research for *Lalla Rookh*). Whatever pains in "time and trouble" Moore took in his "preparatory process," he felt repaid by the result. Moore's account of beginning verse tales and progressing hundreds of lines into them before abandoning them would have struck home to Melville, who had apparently tried to write the tale of Umi, very likely in verse, in the late 1850s or 1860.

On February 17, 1862, Melville bought *The Works of Robert Fergusson* (London: Fullarton, 1857; Sealts, no. 215). Melville was interested in some passages that had nothing to do with poetry (on seagoing, on men disap-pearing). In all likelihood he saw poignant parallels from his own life. In Gansevoort's vein is the letter from Robert Fergusson's brother Henry requesting him to take more care with his verses: "I desire it as a favour, [that] you would often examine your poetical pieces before you commit them to the press: this advice I hope you'll the more readily take, as most young authors are apt to be more criticized than those who have had a little experience. Pope himself was one of the most careful in this respect, and none yet has ever surpass'd him." Melville marked a contrast of a "poor, down-crushed lad" with the rich man who writes "as a recreation" in his study, "surrounded with all the delicacies, and comforts, and securities of life." He was struck by dialect words (though he did not mark the Scottish glossary) and by the stated influence of Fergusson's "Farmer's Ingle" on Burns's "The Cotter's Saturday Night."

On February 26, 1862, Melville bought four volumes by Isaac Disraeli. *Amenities of Literature, Consisting of Sketches and Characters of English Literature* (London: Routledge, 1859; Sealts, no. 184) was a very solid literary history, scholarship packaged for the educated general reader. Melville was interested in what Disraeli said about "many beautiful archaisms, scattered remnants of our language, which explain those obscurities of our more ancient writers, singularities of phrase, or lingual peculiarities, which have so often bewildered the most acute of our commentators." Disraeli went on to say that modern editors have corrected in error, not knowing the original provincial idiom. The second volume was Disraeli's *The Calamities and Quarrels of Authors, with Some Inquiries Respecting their Moral and Literary Characters, and Memoirs for our Literary History* (London: Routledge, 1860; Sealts, no. 185). Melville found himself justified as he read on. He heavily marked and underlined this: "No man is the wiser for his learning: it may administer matter to work in, or objects to work upon; but wit and wisdom are born with a man." Isaac Disraeli's *Curiosities of Literature* (London: Routledge, 1859; Sealts, no. 186) proved to be a richly gossipy three-volume work containing many items on poetry, including Plato's description of the feelings of the poet in the *Phaedon*. Melville found confirmation for one of his deep convictions in a passage he marked and partly underlined: "Faultless mediocrity industry can preserve in one continued degree; but excellence, the daring and the happy, can only be attained, by human faculties, by starts." He found stories that may have aroused ugly memories or else have given him precedent for future actions, conspicuously an account of the poet Baron Haller's burning his manuscripts. The last Disraeli purchase from February 26, 1862, was *The Literary Character; or, The History of Men of Genius, Drawn from Their own Feelings and Confessions* (London: Routledge, 1859; Sealts, no. 187). This richly anecdotal book, perhaps more than any other, confirmed for Melville that he was not an abnormal genius at all but on the contrary a perfectly normal literary genius. His reclusiveness was normal, for geniuses, because "prolonged solitary work" was necessary if great literary works were to be produced. Even his unbroken industry in writing *Redburn, White-Jacket,* and the short version of *Pierre* was normal, he found, in a passage he marked heavily: "If there are not periods when they shall allow their days to melt harmoniously into each other, if they do not pass whole weeks together in their study, without intervening absences, they will not be admitted into the last recess of the Muses. Whether their glory come from researches, or from enthusiasm, time, with not a feather ruffled on his wings, time alone opens discoveries and kindles meditation. This desert of solitude, so vast and so dreary to the man of the world, to the man of genius is the magical garden of Armida, whose enchantments arose amidst solitude, while solitude was everywhere among those enchantments." Melville found here an anatomy of genius and a palliation of every domestic offense he had committed, including his neglecting "family affairs." The Disraeli volumes provided massive, infinitely varied histories of creative writers both obscure and famous, all of whom Melville could identify with one way or another. These Disraeli volumes, perhaps more than any others he ever read, allowed him to situate himself confidently in a thick context of writers. His volume of poetry had gone unpublished and unread, but he was not alone.

On March 1, 1862, Melville bought Giorgio Vasari's *Lives of the Most Eminent Painters, Sculptors, and Architects* in five volumes (London: Bohn, 1849–52; Sealts, no. 534a). He had read Vasari earlier, in a set borrowed from Evert Duyckinck, but reread this five-volume set. Melville's notes throughout the volumes of Vasari do not reveal much about poetry directly, given Vasari's subject matter, but indirectly they reveal much, for at times he quickly applied to the art of poetry what he read about painting and sculpture. Notably, Vasari helped clarify for him the distinction between expression and form, or design. Melville was struck by Leonardo da Vinci's deliberately not manifesting the greatest "clearness of forms" but emphasizing "the great foundation of all, design" (5:385); clarity of design he saw as more important than coloring (the painterly equivalent of literary "expression"). In the third volume (p. 23) Melville marked a passage on Raphael's imitating Michelangelo and commented: "The inimitable imitator. Good deal of the Virgil about Raphael." He may already have made the association of Virgil and Tennyson as imitators, and of course may have taken note of this passage already in 1859 in Duyckinck's copy. That is, Vasari may have influenced the passage he wrote on Tennyson and Virgil as part of the Naples poem, even if he wrote it in 1859 or early 1860. In his lives of working artists, or the working lives of artists, Vasari was fascinated by the proportion of genius to industry and of genius and industry in contrast to laziness and self-indulgence and also alert when an artist was content with less than the highest art. There was no substitute for genius, for an artist (4:65) could work "with infinite difficulty and most laborious pains-taking" without ever having the facility with which Nature and study sometimes reward those who labor and who have genius. (Reading notes Melville made in the first volume of the Vasari are discussed below.)

On March 4, 1862, Melville bought Anne Louise Germaine (Necker), Baronne de Staël's *Germany* (New York: Derby & Jackson, 1859; Sealts, no. 487), annotating the first volume with that date but annotating the second April 1862, presumably when he got round to it. The first volume had two parts: "Of Germany, and the Manners of Germans" and "Of Literature and the Arts" (which dealt with particular writers and salient works, including separate essays on Goethe and on different works by him). The second volume concluded the section "On Literature and the Arts" and included a section on "Philosophy and Ethics" and another on "Religion and Enthusiasm." Melville read and marked parts of all four sections. Staël interested him and challenged him on philosophical and particularly on ethical issues, but she also challenged him about literary techniques and on distinctions among literary genres. Staël confirmed again what he had recognized in Disraeli, ways of accounting for his role in his family, where his legitimate artistic demands were or were not recognized and where his writerly crotchets might not be cheerfully tolerated. Like Disraeli, she helped him see his own place as a working writer. Throughout the volumes he marked sections on writers (the importance of having one's mind "developed in solitude"); on men of genius; on style; on attitudes toward art (particularly the importance of taking talent seriously and working at art painstakingly). He underlined the assertion that rhyme "is the image of hope and of memory" (the earlier sound making one hope for another, the latter making one remember the earlier). In the chapter "Of Poetry" Melville boxed this sentence: "Poetic genius is an internal disposition, of the same nature with that which renders us capable of a generous sacrifice." Staël saw Schiller's earliest works as over-fervid: "The education of life depraves the frivolous, but perfects the reflecting mind," a judgment which confirmed what Melville had read in Taylor's *Notes from Life*. In the chapter on "Wallenstein and Mary Stuart" Melville paid attention to this assertion about achieving unity: "Nothing is so easy as to compose what are called brilliant verses; there are moulds ready made for the purpose; but what is very difficult, is to render every detail subordinate to the whole, and to find every part united in the whole, as well as the reflection of the whole in every part." In "Of Style, and of Versification in the German Language" he triple-lined and checked her statement that "the effects of poetry depend still more on the melody of words than on the ideas which they serve to express," and commented: "This is measurably true of all but dramatic poetry and, perhaps, narrative verse." Melville was profoundly sympathetic with Staël's "Of Ignorance and Frivolity of Spirit in Their

Relation to Ethics," where he marked this passage: "The ignorance of our days is contemptuous, and endeavors to turn into ridicule the labors and the meditations of enlightened men. The philosophical spirit has spread over almost all classes a facility of reasoning, which is used to depreciate every thing that is great and serious in human nature, and we are at that epoch of civilization in which all the beauties of the soul are mouldering into dust." He took balm from her denunciation of "our civilized barbarians" who "only instruct themselves just enough to ridicule, by a few set phrases, the meditations of a whole life." At some time Melville put these closing lines to his "Hostelry" poem: "But sprinkle, do, some drops of grace, / Nor polish us all into commonplace."[76] In *Clarel* Melville would similarly inveigh against culture debased into commonplace (e.g., at 1.34 and 4.21).

Interested throughout in generic distinctions, Melville focused on this formulation by Staël: "Lyric poetry is expressed in the name of the author himself; he no longer assumes a character, but experiences in his own person, the various emotions he describes." This presumably was what Melville had done in his "Naples" poem. Melville followed with great interest Staël's distinction between Epic and Romance. "Events like those of the Iliad interest of themselves, and the less the author's own sentiments are brought forward, the greater is the impression made by the picture; but if we set ourselves to describe romantic situations with the impartial calmness of Homer, the result would not be very alluring." Melville commented: "Admirable distinction. In the 'Idylls of the King' (Tennyson) we see the Homeric, or rather Odyssean manner pervading *romantic* stories, and the result is a kind of 'shocking tameness.'" Melville saw in Tennyson's attempt at the epic a startling, almost ludicrous sentimentalizing, romanticizing, and trivializing of characters that ought to have been mighty pageant creatures. Tennyson in his *Idylls* was building in an aesthetic and intellectual anomaly that would shock and ultimately repel the wiser readers. (Here Melville's writing down "shocking tameness" rather than Cowper's "Their tameness is shocking to me" suggests that he was remembering Thomas Hood's rewording of Cowper in "The Haunted House" from his reading a few weeks earlier.)

Sometime in March 1862 Melville bought William Hazlitt's *Lectures on the English Comic Writers* and *Lectures on the English Poets,* the two volumes bound as one. The first volume contained these lectures: "On Shakespeare and Ben Jonson," "On Cowley, Butler, Suckling, Etherege, &c.," "On Wycherley, Congreve, Vanbrugh, and Farquhar," "On the Periodical

---

76. This is Sandberg's transcription from the surviving manuscript in HCL-M.

Essayists," "On the English Novelists," "On the Works of Hogarth," and "On the Comic Writers of the Last Century." Melville made annotations about poetry even in the first volume, for some of the comic writers Hazlitt treated there were poets and Hazlitt at times expatiated explicitly on poetry. In the first lecture, "On Wit and Humour," Melville read a passage on "the intrinsic superiority of poetry or imagination to wit" and both marked and checked the culmination of the discussion about how easy it is to mar an effect: "The slightest want of unity of impression is an infallible ground to rest the ludicrous upon. But in serious poetry, which aims at rivetting our affections, every blow must tell home. The missing a single time is fatal, and undoes the spell." In the second lecture Melville marked quotations from John Donne and some of Hazlitt's judgments ("His satires are too clerical. He shows, if I may so speak, too much disgust, and, at the same time, too much contempt for vice"). Melville marked the quotation from Cowley's "The Grasshopper" as well as this judgment: "Cowley's Essays are among the most agreeable prose compositions in our language, being equally recommended by sense, wit, learning, and interesting personal history, and written in a style quite free from the faults of his poetry." In the lecture on the English novelists Melville marked long sections on the *"instinct of the imagination"* which Hazlitt said was what "stamps the character of genius on the productions of art more than any other circumstance: for it works unconsciously, like nature, and receives its impressions from a kind of inspiration."

   Lectures on the English Poets consisted of eight lectures: "Introductory.— On Poetry in general," "On Chaucer and Spenser," "On Shakspeare and Milton," "On Dryden and Pope," "On Thomson and Cowper," "On Swift, Young, Gray, Collins, &c.," "On Burns, and the old English Ballads," "On the Living Poets"; and four appendices: "On Milton's Lycidas," "On the Character of Milton's Eve," "On Mr. Wordsworth's Poem, 'The Excursion,'" and "Pope, Lord Byron, and Mr. Bowles" (the Reverend W. L. Bowles, author of *Strictures on the Life and Writings of Pope*). In the introductory essay Hazlitt recurred to the lecture "On Wit and Humour" to emphasize that he was concerned with "serious" poetry. Melville marked this: "It [poetry] is not a mere frivolous accomplishment (as some persons have been led to imagine,) the trifling amusement of a few idle readers or leisure hours—it has been the study and delight of mankind in all ages." He bracketed what Hazlitt called Milton's idea of poetry, "Thoughts that voluntary move / Harmonious numbers," and underlined the word "voluntary." He checked and underlined the assertion that "Nothing is a subject for poetry that admits of a dispute." In an excursus by Hazlitt in "On Shakspeare and Milton," Melville marked this:

The great fault of a modern school of poetry is that it is an experiment to reduce poetry to a mere effusion of natural sensibility; or, what is worse, to divest it both of imaginary splendour and human passion, to surround the meanest objects with the morbid feelings and devouring egotism of the writers' own minds. Milton and Shakspeare did not so understand poetry. They gave a more liberal interpretation both to nature and art. They did not do all they could to get rid of the one and the other, to fill up the dreary void with the Moods of their own Minds. . . . But to the men I speak of there is nothing interesting, nothing heroical, but themselves. To them the fall of gods or of great men is the same. They do not enter into the feeling. . . . They are even debarred from the last poor, paltry consolation of an unmanly triumph over fallen greatness; for their minds reject, with a convulsive effort and intolerable loathing, the very idea that there ever was, or was thought to be, anything superior to themselves.

Melville marked the whole passage, but at this point he noted: "Wordsworth was in the writer's mind here, very likely." He was beginning to define himself as a poet against Wordsworth, not against any of his younger, lesser contemporaries such as Tennyson.

Later in this third lecture Hazlitt, without identifying his source, quoted at length from "Reason of Church Government Urged Against Prelaty" Milton's early hope that he "might perhaps leave something so written to after-times as they should not willingly let it die." Melville marked the whole of Milton's magnificent passage, perhaps the greatest statement of literary ambition by any writer in the English language, and marked the subsequent quotation from Spenser on the same topic: "The noble heart that harbours virtuous thought, / And is with child of glorious great intent, / Can never rest until it forth have brought / The eternal brood of glory excellent." Milton, Hazlitt said in comment on these lines, "did not write from casual impulse, but after a severe examination of his own strength, and with a resolution to leave nothing undone which it was in his power to do. He always labours, and almost always succeeds." Shakespeare was greater: "In Milton, there is always an appearance of effort: in Shakspeare, scarcely any." Melville marked, without comment, what Hazlitt said about Milton's "spirit of partisanship" and Donne's also being "a political partisan." Melville's own firm rejection of partisanship in poetry (in his note on "Lycidas") may have been written before or after he read this passage.

In the chapter "On Thomson and Cowper" Melville triple-lined the following passage, which follows a discussion of the pleasing but humble efforts of the poet Robert Bloomfield: "It should seem from this and other instances that have occurred within the last century, that we cannot expect

from original genius alone, without education, in modern and more arti-
ficial periods, the same bold and independent results as in former periods."
He marked the lengthy discussion of the difficulty a modern writer, even a
writer marked by original genius, has in achieving the highest excellence.
In "On Swift, Young, Gray, Collins, &c.," Melville marked the passage
where Hazlitt quoted someone's mockery of *Candide* (a book Melville
had admiringly alluded to in *The Confidence-Man* and casually referred to
in "At the Hostelry") as "the dull product of a scoffer's pen." Recogniz-
ing the source, the pugnacious passage disparaging *Candide* in the second
book of *The Excursion,* Melville noted: "Wordsworth so called it." In the
seventh lecture, "On Burns, and the Old English Ballads," Hazlitt con-
demned Wordsworth for muffing his great chance to defend the "moral
character" of Burns and "the moral tendency of his writings." In "On the
Living Poets," as mentioned in section 4 above, Melville took exception
to Hazlitt's characterization of Rogers in *Pleasures of Memory* as "a very
lady-like poet," elegant but feeble, and reflected on the source: "In Hazlitt
you have at times to allow for indigestion." Melville was ready to make
allowances, particularly when he approved Hazlitt's judgments on Words-
worth, such as his saying that the poem of Ruth "shows little power, or
power enervated by extreme fastidiousness." He approvingly underlined
and triple-checked this conclusion about the weakness of Thomas Moore:
"Fortitude of mind is the first requisite of a tragic or epic writer." He
marked Hazlitt's characterization of Wordsworth: "the only person from
whom I ever learnt anything." Melville heavily marked the last half of
the stanza Hazlitt quoted from the "Ode—Intimations of Immortality"
("I do not grieve, but rather find / Strength in what remains behind; / In
the primal sympathy, / Which having been, must ever be; / In the sooth-
ing thoughts that spring / Out of human suffering; / In years that bring
the philosophic mind!"). For the lines "In the soothing thoughts that
spring / Out of human suffering" Melville had recourse to an unusual
symbol instead of his simple X in the margin—an X with each space dot-
ted, and he wrote this note at the foot of the page: "A rigid analysis would
make this sentiment appear in a different light from the one in which it
is, probably, generally received. Its vagueness makes it susceptible of many
interpretations; but Truth is susceptible of but one." Its vagueness made it
easy for the superficial to use in sentimental and pious reassurances, made
it especially useful to some of the Unitarians of Melville's acquaintance
who did not take other people's suffering very seriously. Having probed
deeper into the nature of human suffering than most, Melville may have
felt skeptical that deeply soothing thoughts were likely to spring out of
profound human suffering.

Melville may or may not have read much in this two-in-one book before making revealing notations that had nothing to do with Hazlitt.[77] Starting on the page opposite the beginning of the text in *Lectures on the English Comic Writers,* Melville entered notes on Francis Jeffrey's January 1810 *Edinburgh Review* essay on Victor Alfieri. Profoundly interested in what Jeffrey said about how Alfieri conceived a literary work, developed it, versified it, then polished, corrected, and revised it, Melville filled the page with notes from Jeffrey, then added three lines on the top of the next page, above the start of the first lecture.[78] In his notes, reminders to himself, not exact quotations, Melville was not intent on improving his knowledge of Alfieri so much as using Jeffrey's comments to fix in his mind what he might eschew and what he might employ in his own style.

In his review-essay Jeffrey had written:

As they [Alfieri's dramas] have not adopted the choral songs of the Greek stage . . . they are, on the whole, less poetical than those ancient compositions; although they are worked throughout with a fine and careful hand, and diligently purified from every thing ignoble or feeble in the expression. The author's anxiety to keep clear of figures of mere ostentation, and to exclude all showpieces of fine writing in a dialogue of deep interest or impetuous passion, has betrayed him, on some occasions, into too sententious and strained a diction, and given an air of labour and heaviness to many parts of his composition. He has felt, perhaps a little too constantly, that the cardinal virtue of a dramatic writer is to keep his personages to the business and the concerns that lye before them; and by no means to let them turn to moral philosophers, or rhetorical describers of their own emotions. But, in his zealous adherence to this good maxim, he seems sometime to have forgotten, that certain passions are declamatory in nature as well as on the stage; and that, at any rate, they do not all vent themselves in concise and pithy sayings, but run occasionally into hyperbole and amplification. As it is the great excellence, so it is occasionally the chief fault of Alfieri's dialogue, that every word is honestly employed to help forward the action of the play, in serious argument, necessary narrative, or the direct expression of natural emotion. There are no excursions or digressions,—no episodical conversations,—and none but the most brief moralizings. This gives a certain air of solidity to the whole structure of

---

77. We know little about Melville's note-taking. Blank-books were available at stationers and he used them for journals but we do not yet have evidence for his using them for note-taking while we do have evidence for his using library slips and for his using pages in other books which he was sure he would keep.

78. The pages are reproduced in "Melville's Notes in a Hazlitt Volume," in the RELATED DOCUMENTS section of this volume, pp. 917–19 below.

the piece, that is apt to prove oppressive to an ordinary reader, and reduces the entire drama to too great uniformity.

Glancing back and forth at Jeffrey, perhaps struggling with small type, Melville made these summary notes in his Hazlitt: "Worked throughout with a fine and careful hand. Figures of mere ostentation. Show-pieces of fine writing. Nature is not confined to conciseness, but at times amplifies. Too sententious & strained a diction. The solidity of the structure is apt to prove oppressive to the *ordinary* reader. Too great uniformity."

Jeffrey had said this about Alfieri's dramas:

> With regard to the diction of these pieces, it is not for *tramontane* critics to presume to offer any opinion. They are considered, in Italy, we believe, as the purest specimens of the *favella Toscana* that late ages have produced. To us they certainly seem to want something of that flow and sweetness to which we have been accustomed in Italian poetry, and to be formed rather upon the model of Dante than of Petrarca. At all events, it is obvious that the style is highly elaborate and artificial; and that the author is constantly striving to give it a sort of factitious force and energy, by the use of condensed and emphatic expressions, interrogatories, antitheses, and short and inverted sentences. In all these respects, as well as in the chastized gravity of the sentiments, and the temperance and propriety of all the delineations of passion, these pieces are exactly the reverse of what we should have expected from the fiery, fickle and impatient character of the author. From all that Alfieri has told us of himself, we should have expected to find in his plays great vehemence and irregular eloquence—sublime and extravagant sentiments—passions rising to frenzy—and poetry swelling into bombast. Instead of this, we have a subdued and concise representation of energetic discourses—passions, not loud but deep—and a style so severely correct and scrupulously pure, as to indicate, even to unskilful eyes, the great labour which must have been bestowed on its purification.

Melville extracted from that passage these notes: "Wanting flow & sweetness. Strives to give a fictitious force & energy by condensation & emphasis & inversion. Chastised quality. Temperance and propriety of delineation of the passions."[79] The use of "fictitious" is bothersome. Perhaps it was only a slip in copying, but perhaps Melville's eyes were so weak that they

---

79. The spelling in the *Edinburgh Review* was "chastized" and in *Modern British Essayists* "chastised." Melville's word may be read either as "Chastised" or as "Chastized." If he had unmistakably used a "z", that might be an indication that he was taking notes from the 1810 *Edinburgh Review;* however, the spelling may have varied according to whatever American reprint of the *Review* he was using.

did not read the word right (particularly if the text he was reading was in small print, as *Modern British Essayists* was and American reprints of the *Edinburgh Review* typically were). We have to assume that he knew the word "factitious."

Over on the next page, Melville made another note not from "<u>Jeffrey on Alfieri</u>" (as he jotted down to identify his longer plunder) but from "Alfieri himself," meaning, as Scott Norsworthy first noticed, from *The Autobiography of Vittorio Alfieri, The Tragic Poet,* as translated by C. Edwards Lester (New York: Paine & Burgess, 1843). Melville, perhaps characteristically, was taking notes with at least two different works at hand, not just Jeffrey's classic article in the *Edinburgh Review* (reprinted in his set of *Modern British Essayists*) but Alfieri's autobiography in a more recent and American translation than the one Jeffrey was reviewing. Copying and condensing from Lester, Melville wrote this down: "Discerning, with <u>a mind that has reposed from the subject</u> the best thoughts & rejecting the dross."

In this passage from the *Autobiography* Alfieri explains three words he uses in describing his composition process. Lester renders the words with his best English equivalents: "*ideare* (idiate), *stendere* (extend), and *versiggiare* (versify).￼" To idiate, Lester has Alfieri explain, is "to distribute the subject into acts and scenes, to establish and fix the number of persons, and in two leaves of prose draw a plan, scene by scene, of all the characters are to say and do." To extend, Alfieri continues in Lester's translation, is to take up "that first sheet" and "fill up the scenes in prose dialogue," all the way to the end, writing as powerfully as he can, not pausing to criticize himself. The third stage of the composition process was the one which caught Melville's attention most strongly: "By versifying I mean not only the rendering of the prose into verse, but discerning with a mind that has reposed from the subject, the best thoughts, and rejecting the false matter of the first hurried effort. Then follows, as in every other composition, the necessary filing, pruning, and changing." Although he summarized toward the end of his note, Melville faithfully copied "reposed" from Lester, no doubt struggling to get past the awkward translation to precisely what Alfieri was trying to convey. As it happens, Jeffrey quoted this full passage in his review, including these sentences: "By versifying, in short, must be understood, not only converting this prose into verse, but also curtailing the exuberances of the style, selecting the best thoughts, and clothing them in poetic language. After these three operations, I proceed, like other authors, to polish, correct, and amend." The uncredited translator had used much more colloquial English than Lester was to do, as in saying "*conceive*" where Lester used the impossible "idiate."

Nothing survives to show Melville ever took Alfieri's advice to the point of writing out prose drafts in preparation of versifying his material, but in the long run, in the composition of *Clarel,* memory of this passage from Alfieri may have helped Melville "distribute the subject into acts and scenes, to establish and fix the number of persons."

Perhaps examination of the books Melville was reading or perhaps the emergence of other documentary evidence will yet identify the point, presumably early in 1862, when Melville was reminded of Jeffrey's essay on Alfieri and when he got access to Lester's edition of Alfieri's *Autobiography.* If he had brought his Jeffrey volume in *Modern British Essayists* to New York City, Melville would probably have made his notes in the Alfieri essay in that volume, despite its intimidatingly small margins. Melville could easily have borrowed the Jeffrey essay in a collection or in a reprint of the *Edinburgh Review.* The American authority on Alfieri was Henry T. Tuckerman, whom Melville had called on late in 1861, who had been trying to get hold of him early in the year, and who in all likelihood found his way to Melville early in 1862, soon after Melville settled into the rented house. For parallel examples of Melville's making notes on one volume in another volume, see his notes in the seventh volume of his Shakespeare, which are from three separate sources.[80] Another close parallel is Melville's taking detailed notes from the third volume of Ruskin's *Modern Painters* in his Vasari (see below).

On March 17, 1862, Melville bought Heinrich Heine's *The Poems of Heine* (London: Bohn, 1861; Sealts, no. 268). Later, apparently, perhaps after he read Swinburne's *Mary Stuart* (1881), Melville made a note on Heine's "Clarissa": "Swinburne's inspiration is tracable distantly in some of these things,—Especially in Queen Mary."

Reminded of Abraham Cowley by Taylor, Hazlitt, and other writers, on March 21, 1862, Melville bought an early three-volume set of Cowley (London: Tonson, 1707, and Charles Harper, 1711; Sealts, no. 160a). In the preface to the first volume he marked a passage on men becoming poets for life and on the times (civil war or peace), moods, conditions, in which men may write poetry. Melville triple-checked "On the Death of Mr. Crashaw," the "Poet and Saint," and marked the tolerant passage on how Richard Crashaw (who became a Catholic) may harmlessly have diverged from Cowley's *"Mother Church":* "His *Faith* perhaps in some nice Tenets might / Be wrong; his *Life,* I'm sure, was *in the right"* (1:44). Melville footnoted: " 'He can't be wrong whose life is in the right.' Pope," recognizing

---

80. The notes are reproduced in "The Sources of Melville's Notes (1849–51) in a Shakespeare Volume," in the RELATED DOCUMENTS section of this volume.

that Pope had borrowed from Cowley in the *Essay on Man,* epistle 3, section 6, where Pope had decried religious partisanship and concluded that one's particular modes of faith "can't be wrong whose life is in the right." In *The Mistress,* the subsection on "The Prophet" (1:113), Melville marked what Cowley boasted that he would teach the God of Love: "I'll teach him things he never knew before; / I'll teach him a *Receipt* to make / *Words* that *weep,* and *Tears* that *speak.*" Melville noted: "Thoughts that breathe and words that burn," having recognized Thomas Gray's borrowing in "The Progress of Poesy." Melville regularly paid close attention to English poets when they wrote about poems about poetry. By "The Inconstant" (1:153) Melville wrote "Sheridan's Song," meaning "Here's to the maiden of bashful fifteen," a song from *School for Scandal* (3.1) plainly suggested by this Cowley poem. In stanza 6 of the "Second Olympique Ode of Pindar" (1:189), Melville marked a passage on a topic he was brooding about: "Greatness of *Mind* and *Fortune* too / Th' *Olympique Trophies* shew. / Both their several Parts must do / In the noble *Chase* of *Fame,* / This without that is *blind,* that without this is *lame.*" In "Destiny" (1:228) he marked the Muse's injunction to Cowley that he should be content "with the small *barren Praise* / That neglected *Verse* does raise." In the ode "To Dr. Scarborough" (1:237) he triple-checked "When all's done, *Life is an Incurable Disease*" and wrote "Pope"—reminded of "long disease, my life" in "An Epistle to Dr. Arbuthnot." (Later, in the prose discourse "Of Liberty" [2:682], Melville marked Cowley's "the Epidemical Disease of Life" without mentioning Pope.) In the long "Davideis, A Sacred Poem of the Troubles of David," taking music as involving song, or poetry, Melville marked a passage in the first book (1:305–6) on the power of music to soothe Saul. As in Collins's later ode, the singer of verses was a creator imitating God the Creator: "As first a various unform'd *Hint* we find / Rise in some god-like *Poet's* fertile *Mind,* / 'Till all the Parts and Words their Places take, / And with just Marches *Verse* and *Musick* make; / Such was *God's Poem,* this *World's* new *Essay;* / So wild and rude in its first Draught it lay; / Th'ungovern'd Parts no *Correspondence* knew, / An artless *War* from thwarting *Motions* grew; / 'Till they to *Number* and fixt Rules were brought / By the *eternal Mind's Poetick Thought.*" In the discourse "Of Agriculture" (2:714) Cowley described Virgil's portrayal of Evander's welcoming Aeneas into his "rustick Court." Recognizing the passage, Melville noted: "'Dare to be poor' Dryden's Æneid." (The reference is in book 8 of the *Aeneid.*) In the essay "Of My Self" (2:782) Melville double-checked passages about the importance of Cowley's reading Spenser early—reading all of Spenser's poetry before he was twelve years old. Twelve, as it happens, may have been Herman's age when he first read Spenser (see Parker 1996, pp. 72–73). Melville marked much of the last portion of the preface to "Cutter of Coleman-Street." At the end (2:[800]) he drew a box around this assertion of Cowley's: *"That from all which I have written I never receiv'd the least Benefit, or the least Advantage, but, on the contrary, have felt sometimes the Effects of Malice and Misfortune."* He footnoted: "How few will credit this; nevertheless how true, one doubts not, said by a man like Cowley."

On March 22, 1862, Melville bought Ralph Waldo Emerson's *Essays, Second Series* (Boston: Munroe, 1844; Sealts, no. 205). He already knew some of Emerson's essays from his reading at the Hawthorne cottage in 1850, and his young brother-in-law Sam Shaw on a visit to Arrowhead in the summer of 1859 had brought him a copy of the 1858 edition of Emerson's *Poems*. Now in 1862 in reading Emerson's essays Melville raged against the Unitarian coldness toward human suffering which he recognized in the Transcendentalist, the former Unitarian minister. When he came upon Emerson's assertion that the poet "disposes very easily of the most disagreeable facts," Melville retorted sarcastically, "So it would seem. In this sense Mr E. is a great poet." Melville could never relax for long with Emerson: some dunderheaded blindness to human suffering would jolt him out of his admiration. He marked the passage in "The Poet" where Emerson described the low and plain way in which the poet should live ("the air should suffice for his inspiration, and he should be tipsy with water") and footnoted his partial agreement: "This makes the Wordsworthian poet—not the Shakespearian." As he read during these weeks in New York City, Wordsworth was more and more the great modern poet against whom he was steadily defining himself.

In April 1862 Melville bought Charles Churchill's *The Poetical Works . . . With Copious Notes and a Life of the Author* (Boston: Little, Brown, 1854; Sealts, no. 144). In Churchill's "Gotham" he could have seen many mentions of the pains poets must take, a recurrent subject in this season's reading. In "The Author" Melville marked these bitter lines: "Much are the precious hours of youth misspent / In climbing learning's rugged steep ascent; / When to the top the bold adventurer's got, / He reigns vain monarch o'er a barren spot, / Whilst in the vale of ignorance below / Folly and vice to rank luxuriance grow; / Honours and wealth pour in on every side, / And proud preferment rolls her golden tide." Melville wrote: "Wordsworth."

During all the time he read in these early months of 1862, Wordsworth was the poet most prominent in Melville's mind as his modern predecessor, the one he envied for his tenure as poet laureate and other honors and was contemptuous of for Wordsworth's own contempt for ordinary people (ironic in view of the subject matter of much of his poetry). Chances are that Melville, as surmised above, knew the interview with Wordsworth in 1833 which Orville Dewey had recorded in his *Old World and the New* (New York: Harper & Brothers, 1836). Dewey had lectured the poet, but allowed him a few phrases: "He thought there could be no independence in legislators who were dependant for their places upon the ever wavering breath of popular opinion." Acknowledging Dewey's declaration that there was no stopping "political liberty," that in the civilized world "the course of opinion was irresistibly setting towards universal education and popular forms of government," Wordsworth had seen "nothing but darkness, disorder, and misery in the immediate prospect," so that "all he could do was to cast himself on Providence." Melville himself could be ironically contemptuous of the "independent electors" in the infant United States, but he was repulsed by the disdain shown by the elderly Wordsworth. Melville's introduction to criticism on Wordsworth had come in the massive Carey & Hart compendium, *Modern British Essayists,* and he had kept on reading about Wordsworth, if not often rereading the poems in his volume of Wordsworth or seeking out late-published volumes. At some time he read the prose supplements in his Wordsworth with some care, and in 1869 or later he marked lines quoted from *The Prelude* in Matthew Arnold's *Essays in Criticism* (Boston: Ticknor & Fields, 1865; Sealts, no. 17): "The marble index of a mind forever / Voyaging through strange seas of Thought, alone." Even in 1862, Melville never failed to acknowledge the grandeur of Wordsworth's early achievements, but he never warmed to the man as he did to so many other poets.

On April 3, 1862, Melville bought Henry Kirke White's *The Poetical Works and Remains* (New York: Appleton, 1857; Sealts, no. 556). Melville marked a passage in "Warton: Remarks on the English Poets" on the damage Pope and his imitators had done by introducing

> a species of refinement into our language, which has banished that nerve and pathos for which Milton had rendered it eminent. Harmonious modulations, and unvarying exactness of measure, totally precluding sublimity and fire, have reduced our fashionable poetry to mere singsong. But Thomas Warton, whose taste was unvitiated by the frivolities of the day, immediately saw the intrinsic worth of what the world then slighted. He saw that the ancient poets contained a fund of strength, and beauty of imagery as well as diction, which in the hands of genius would shine forth with redoubled lustre. Entirely rejecting, therefore, modern niceties, he extracted the honied sweets from these beautiful, though neglected flowers. Every grace of sentiment, every poetical term, which a false taste had rendered obsolete, was by him revived and made to grace his own ideas; and though many will condemn him as guilty of plagiarism, yet few will be able to withhold the tribute of their praise.

Once again Melville was rejecting mere excellence of technique, mere
polish. Nothing he attempted would preclude "sublimity and fire" any
more than it would eschew what Henry Taylor called "intrepidity of
impulse."

According to Merton M. Sealts Jr. (1988, p. 168), Raymond Weaver
reported seeing Melville's copy of *The Poetical Works of William Collins*
(dated April 1862), in the 1854 Boston: Little, Brown edition (Sealts, no.
156). On May 19, 1862, Melville gave a copy of Collins's poetry, bound
with some Shakespeare (London: Cooke, 17——; Sealts, no. 464), to his
sister Fanny, along with the Cooke edition of Shenstone and Thomson.
He must have known, long before 1862, the odes, including the "Ode on
the Poetical Character" with its echo of Cowley on God and the poet as
creators.

On April 6, 1862, Melville made one of the most important of his
1862 purchases, Matthew Arnold's *Poems* (Boston: Ticknor & Fields,
1856; Sealts, no. 21). Reading Arnold, like reading Hazlitt, helped focus
Melville's feelings about Wordsworth. He read Arnold's "Obermann" in
the light of Wordsworth and Goethe. Asking if Obermann is unpopu-
lar because of a pain too sharp that underlies his calm, Arnold looks at
the two greatest poets of his time—Wordsworth still living as he writes,
Goethe buried at Weimar—and identifies their failures: "Wordsworth's
eyes avert their ken / From half of human fate; / And Goethe's course few
sons of men / May think to emulate." Melville noted: "True as to Words-
worth. Of Goethe it might also be said that he averted his eyes from
everything except Nature, Intellect, & Beauty." Having read enough of
"The Youth of Nature" to understand what the subject was, Melville
rejoiced at the aptness of Arnold's opening, "Rais'd are the dripping
oars— / Silent the boat." The oars are raised above the waters of Win-
dermere (unnamed) in tribute to Wordsworth. Melville at once saw the
literary allusions. In "Ode on the Death of Thomson. The Scene on the
Thames near Richmond" (1749), Collins had written words that Melville
now wrote down: "and oft suspend the dashing oar / to bid his gentle
spirit rest." This poem had been particularly mentioned on page xiv of
the 1854 edition of Collins Melville owned, in the "Memoir" composed
from the researches of Alexander Dyce. Then Wordsworth in "Remem-
brance of Collins. Composed upon the Thames near Richmond" (1798),
a poem unmarked in Melville's copy of Wordsworth's *Poetical Works,* had
returned the compliment: "Now let us, as we float along / For *him* suspend
the dashing oar." Melville commented: "How beautifully appropriate
therefor this reminiscent prelude of Arnold concerning Wordsworth,"
a clear example of Melville's alertness to literary echoes and re-echoes.

By now he was about as close as one could get to being an ideal reader of poetry.

Arnold's preface, which had first appeared in the 1853 edition, as an aesthetic document was taken seriously by Arnold's and Melville's contemporaries, and within a generation was ranked with some of Dryden's and Wordsworth's theoretical treatises. Among Victorian aesthetic documents, it was almost on a par with the third, 1856 volume of Ruskin's *Modern Painters,* which may have been indebted to it, although what is similar in them may be their mutual indebtedness to Aristotle. Whatever Melville thought of Arnold's poems, he recognized the writer of the "Preface" as a thinker worth grappling with, although at moments showing an ameliorative spirit too near to Emerson's. When Arnold quoted Schiller as saying that all Art is " 'dedicated to Joy'," Melville retorted: "The 'Laocoon' is not dedicated to Joy, neither is 'Hamlet.' Yet there is a degree of truth in this, only it don't imply that the subjects of true Art must be joyful subjects.—Schiller was at once helped & hurt by Goethe. This saying is a Schillerized Goethecism." Melville marked and underlined Arnold's insistence on "the all-importance of the choice of a subject," scored what Arnold said about "one moral impression left by a great action treated as a whole," marked the qualities Arnold praised in classical works ("their intense significance, their noble simplicity, and their calm pathos"), underlined the warning against "the jargon of modern criticism," and heavily checked and marked this sentence: "If they are endeavoring to practise any art, they remember the plain and simple proceedings of the old artists, who attained their grand results by penetrating themselves with some noble and significant action, not by inflating themselves with a belief in the preëminent importance and greatness of their own times." Melville also marked a passage quoting Goethe on two kinds of dilettanti in poetry: "he who neglects the indispensable mechanical part, and thinks he has done enough if he show spirituality and feeling; and he who seeks to arrive at poetry merely by mechanism . . . without soul and matter."

Melville took Arnold as a friendly interpreter of Greek theories of tragedy, paying attention to what Arnold said about greater actions and nobler personages, as in this passage: "For what reason was the Greek tragic poet confined to so limited a range of subjects? Because there are so few actions which unite in themselves, in the highest degree, the conditions of excellence. . . . A few actions, therefore, eminently adapted for tragedy, maintained almost exclusive possession of the Greek tragic stage." Arnold quoted from Aristotle, "All depends upon the subject." The ancients had subordinated expression to action; the moderns did the reverse, to the detriment of their art. Throughout the essay Melville also focused upon Arnold's allusions to "expression"—"a certain baldness of expression in Greek tragedy"; Shakespeare's "wonderful gift of expression," particularly in a summation of three things for a modern writer to learn from the ancients: "the all-importance of the choice of a subject; the necessity of accurate construction; and the subordinate character of expression." Melville responded profoundly to the peroration, in which Arnold discounted modern chauvinism and argued that serious poets, steeped in the past, will not "talk of their mission, nor of interpreting their age, nor of the coming Poet."

Reading Arnold's "Preface" brought Melville toward the end of his prolonged phase of gathering and testing ideas on aesthetics and particularly on what constitutes literary greatness. At last he was ready to begin distilling what he had been learning for months and to integrate those ideas with his own long-held convictions based on his own experience as a reader and writer. The sequence is in doubt, as with so much of Melville's reading and annotating during early 1862, but at some time, probably while he was in New York City, away from his own bookshelves so that he had to buy or borrow books or consult them in a library (the Astor Library shows no use by him for this period), he got hands on Ruskin's *Modern Painters.* The likelihood is that Melville used a borrowed copy of Ruskin rather than the set which he acquired no earlier than 1865, since he made notes on it in the Vasari he had acquired on March 1 (see below). In the later set which he is known to have owned he did not mark the passages he took notes on in the Vasari, having, it may be, already absorbed those passages. Quite possibly Melville had found Arnold's ideas stimulating enough to be discussed with his friend Tuckerman, who then loaned him the Ruskin. Tuckerman in 1862 had a good run of Ruskin. Four volumes of the 1856–60 edition of *Modern Painters,* including the third volume published in 1856, were auctioned from his estate in June 1872 along with these volumes: *Unto This Last; Four Essays on the First Principles of Political Economy* (1866); *Sesame and Lilies* (1866); *The Stones of Venice, with Illustrations on Wood* (1860); *The Mystery of Life and Its Arts* (1869); *Lectures on Architecture and Painting* (1854?); *The Political Economy of Art* (1858); *The Queen of the Air; Being a Study of the Greek Myths of Cloud and Storm* (1869); *The Two Paths; Being Lectures on Art, and Its Application to Decoration and Manufacture* (1859); and *The Ethics of the Dust* (1866).[81]

81. See Parker 2002, p. 745. The sale of Tuckerman's books is documented in the Leavitt auction catalogue in the American Antiquarian Society; most of the books were sold on the first day of the auction, June 10, 1872.

It would seem likely that Melville read Arnold before Ruskin because if he had read Ruskin first he would have marked similar phrasing when he found it in the Arnold, his 1862 copy of which survives. There could be other reasons for Melville's making his notes from Ruskin in his Vasari, and nothing ties the notes to 1862 except the fact that the subject matter of the earlier notes is very close to the subject matter of the Arnold preface and the topics in the latter notes in the Vasari are quite close to other topics Melville was reading and annotating in this intense session of reading in early 1862.

As Scott Norsworthy discovered in 2006, most of Melville's notes on the flyleaf of his Vasari are from Ruskin's *Modern Painters* (mainly in the 1856 third volume).[82] Wanting to make notes on literary greatness where he could consult them over and over again, Melville turned to a work he had bought in March. On the recto of the front flyleaf of the first volume of his set of Vasari he wrote: "Attain the highest result.—" He was quoting verbatim from a footnote in Ruskin's second volume of *Modern Painters*. The next note is verbatim from the third volume of *Modern Painters*, "A quality of Grasp.—" After reading Ruskin's section on "Choice of Noble Subject" (where he wrote of "the habitual choice of subjects" and the "habitual choice of sacred subjects"), Melville jotted down in the Vasari: "The habitual choice of noble subjects.—" In the fourth line of his notes in the Vasari Melville simply wrote "The Expression," probably having in mind Ruskin's emphasis on the "perfect unison of expression" with "the full and natural exertion" of a painter's pictorial power in the details of a work. He apparently was not referring to "expression" as Arnold used it, as a weaker quality than action. Some of Arnold's 1853 phrases may have suggested some of Ruskin's 1856 phrases: "great human action"; "a noble action"; "the all-importance of the choice of a subject"; the fact that the old artists "attained their grand results by penetrating themselves with some noble and significant action." In any case, phrases Melville read (and sometimes marked) in Arnold were close to phrases he copied down from Ruskin—close enough to suggest that there was some connection between his buying and reading Arnold and his getting hold of a copy of Ruskin.

After "Expression" Melville wrote: "Get in as much as you can.—/ Finish is completeness, fulness, not polish.—" There is "a meritorious finish," Ruskin had said, "but that finish does not consist in smoothing or polishing,

---

82. The notes are reproduced in "Melville's Notes in a Vasari Volume," in the RELATED DOCUMENTS section of this volume, pp. 920–21 below.

but in the *completeness of the expression of ideas*." Melville continued, draw-
ing on Ruskin's "On the Real Nature of Greatness of Style," section 18:
"Greatness is a matter of scale.—/ Clearness & firmness.—/ The greatest
number of the greatest ideas.—" Next Melville focused on Ruskin's saying
that "the greatness or smallness of a man is, in the most conclusive sense,
determined for him at his birth." Education, Ruskin said, and "favourable
circumstances, resolution, and industry can do much," but could never
make "great man out of small." The idea that aesthetic finish was fullness
and not polish had been held by Melville for many years (witness in chap.
32 of *Moby-Dick* his tribute to the builders of the cathedral of Cologne). At
this point Melville stopped making verbatim or near-verbatim notes and
began paraphrasing more loosely and elaborating what he had been learn-
ing, and not only from Ruskin: "Greatness is determined for a man at his
birth. There is no *making* oneself great, in any act or art. But there is such a
thing as the development of greatness—prolonged, painful, and painstak-
ing." Earlier Melville had marked in Disraeli's *Calumnies and Quarrels* that
learning made no man wiser: "[W]it and wisdom are born with a man."
Greatness was determined at birth. Melville had also, for months now,
been marking terms like *pains* and *painstaking* as he tried to weigh the
significance of hard application in the production of art, such as Thomas
Moore's self-description, and was using such terms, as in his defense of
Samuel Rogers against William Hazlitt as "a painstaking man of talent."
In the Vasari itself Melville may already have noticed passages such as one
he marked in the fourth volume on Sebastiano's performing "all that he
did with infinite difficulty and most laborious pains-taking." Now at last
Melville was summing up the disparate injunctions and admonitions he
had been absorbing (and had been testing against his own experience)
and was able to jot down, in a place where he could keep it, an integrated
aesthetic credo.

If indeed he made his notes from Jeffrey in his Hazlitt and his notes
from Ruskin in his Vasari during his session of study in New York City
in 1862, then Melville's aesthetic investigations of the previous months
came to a satisfying conclusion: he had done his winter's research and
reflection, and was ready to go home to Arrowhead. In "At the Hostelry"
he said that Claude Lorraine wisely refused to waver in aesthetic theory's
"wildering maze"; instead, he haunted the hazy Arcadian woods, pursu-
ing Beauty. This winter Melville was not wavering in theory's wildering
maze: he had distilled practical advice from people who had thought seri-
ously about aesthetic issues, and at the end of his quest he had defined his
own aesthetic credo.

XI
BATTLE-PIECES AND ASPECTS OF THE WAR: MELVILLE'S SECOND VOLUME OF POEMS

AFTER HE RETURNED to Arrowhead in the last week of April 1862, laden with his fresh plunder from the New York booksellers, Melville gave away some of his books of poetry. On May 15 he inscribed to his sister Helen the five-volume set of Spenser he had procured only a year earlier. Uniquely, she took the trouble to start copying into it his marginalia from their father's eight-in-four set of Spenser, which Melville at some point gave Augusta.[83] On May 19 Melville gave his sister Fanny his Cooke editions of Shakespeare and Collins (bound together) and of Shenstone and of Thomson. He was not depriving himself: he kept his beloved 1849 set of Shakespeare and his newly purchased edition of Collins; he kept the Thomson he purchased in 1861; and in various collections he probably had all the Shenstone he needed. Now that he had found a satisfying aesthetic credo and had identified historical precedents for his status as a literary genius living in obscurity, Melville's giving away some duplicate books of poetry may have been a way of clearing the deck for a new stage in his creative life.

Judging from a letter he wrote his brother Tom on May 25, 1862, Melville was not only giving away books of poetry but also putting away some of his own poetic manuscripts. Counting on Tom to know the difference between Byron's *Don Juan* and the Bible, he humorously advised corporal punishment for hapless lads on the *Meteor:* "Strap them, I beseech you. You remember what the Bible says: 'Oh ye who teach the children of the nations, / Holland, France, England, Germany or Spain, / I pray ye *strap* them upon all occasions, / It mends their morals; never mind the pain.'" Melville went on, in a passage mentioned earlier:

Since I have quoted poetry above, it puts me in mind of my own dog-gerel. You will be pleased to learn that I have disposed of a lot of it at a great bargain. In fact, a trunk-maker took the whole stock off my hands at ten cents the pound. So, when you buy a new trunk again, just peep at the lining & perhaps you may be rewarded by some glorious stanza

83. In the twentieth century the annotations Helen transcribed into the 1855 Little, Brown set were known decades before the eight-in-four set surfaced, and her handwriting was mistaken for Melville's own.

stareing you in the face & claiming admiration. If you were not such a devel of a ways off, I would send you a trunk, by way of presentation-copy. I cant help thinking what a luckless chap you were that voyage you had a poetaster with you. You remember the romantic moonlight night, when the conceited donkey repeated to you about three cables' length of his verses. But you bore it like a hero. I cant in fact recall so much as a single *wince*. [Melville was punning on a sailor-pronunciation of *wince,* or wind-lass, which could make light work of long cables.] To be sure, you went to bed immediately upon the conclusion of the entertainment; but this much I am sure of, whatever were your sufferings, you never gave them utterance. Tom, my boy, I admire you. I say again, you are a hero.—By the way, I hope in God's name, that rumor which reached your owners (C & P.) a few weeks since—that dreadful rumor is not true. They heard that you had begun to take to——drink?—Oh no, but worse— —to sonnet-writing. That off Cape Horn instead of being on deck about your business, you devoted your time to writing a sonnet on your mistress' eyebrow, & another upon her "tournure".—"I'll be damned" says Curtis (he was very profane) "if I'll have a sonneteer among my Captains."—"Well, if he has taken to poetizing," says Peabody—["]God help the ship!"—I have written them contradicting the rumor in your name. What villian & secret enemy of yours set this cursed report afloat, I cant imagine.

After this loving self-mockery and teasing, Melville posed a new question—"Do you want to hear about the war?"—and followed it with a few lines of ironic extravaganza similar to what he wrote to Gansevoort in 1846, at the outbreak of the war against Mexico. In the tall tale of his selling his manuscripts to a trunk-maker Melville was putting an end to the first phase of his career as a poet, but giving no sign that his next poetry would be about the war.

No one familiar with literary conventions would take this letter to Tom as a literal announcement that Melville had sold his poetic manuscripts to a trunk-maker, but it may be an oblique fashion of announcing that he was destroying some of his poetic manuscripts. More likely, he was putting away manuscripts, including the poems that had been in the rejected volume and any he had written on the voyage with Tom or later, such as the lines on Garibaldi that he added to the Naples poem and later moved to "At the Hostelry." Melville may simply have put his poetic manuscripts so far out of sight that he did not begin to sort through them again until a decade and a half later. Early in 1877 he sent "The Age of the Antonines" (published in *Timoleon*) to Hoadley with the disclaimer "I send you something I found the other day—came across it—in a lot of papers. I remember that the lines were suggested by a passage in Gibbon

(Decline & Fall)." (In this usage a "lot" is a discrete batch, like an auc-
tioneer's lot, not necessarily a large batch.) When he wrote Hoadley,
months after the humiliating failure of *Clarel,* Melville was pulling him-
self together to continue his career as a poet. Within a few more weeks,
he published some poetry which has never been identified and is known
only by his sister Fanny's query to their cousin Kate Gansevoort Lansing
(Mrs. Abraham Lansing): "Ever so much love for Abe. Did he receive the
paper containing those lines by Herman?" (Parker 2002, p. 816). (In the
family correspondence, "lines" meant lines of poetry and, as used here,
"paper" meant a newspaper, postal regulations and cheap rates allowing
one member of the family to send an issue of a newspaper to another when
it contained something of special interest.) Recently retrieved from a pile
of old manuscripts, and then recently copied out once already for Hoad-
ley, the poetry Melville published in 1877 could well have been "The
Age of the Antonines." It may yet be found in a newspaper, printed there
perhaps around two decades after it was written and a decade and a half
before it appeared in *Timoleon.*

In the middle of 1862, when the war was continuing far longer than
anyone had predicted, Melville seems to have hesitated before moving on
to the next phase of his career as a poet. Fanny on April 1, 1862, had writ-
ten their cousin Kate Gansevoort about Kate's younger brother, Henry,
wanting to know what company he was in so she could follow him in the
papers as he moved about.[84] Nothing suggests that Melville followed the
fortunes of his friends and kinsmen as assiduously as Fanny was prepared
to do with Cousin Henry, but the war was inescapable. His brother-in-
law Sam Shaw described his and Melville's driving and walking in the
Berkshires as being interspersed with much news of the war. Later in 1862,
when Melville's first cousin Guert Gansevoort was court-martialed for
being drunk and wrecking his ship, Allan was one of Guert's comforters,
so everyone in the family must have had private information to supple-
ment what they read in the papers. The other Gansevoort cousin, Henry,
was not taking a role in the war comparable to those the Hero of the Tea
Party (Herman's Melvill grandfather) and the Hero of Fort Stanwix (Her-
man and Henry's Gansevoort grandfather) had taken in the Revolutionary
War. If no grandson of the Heroes would equal or surpass their military
exploits, might their quieter cousin record the war in poetry? Arnold had
insisted on the importance of a poet's choosing a great action and Ruskin
had directed him to noble subjects, but Melville may not have been ready

---

84. Fanny's letter is in NYPL-GL (Box 215).

to take up the present "noble and significant action" in his own time and his own country.

A bit of evidence that Melville may have been thinking of writing war poetry is his possible purchase of a book hastily written and hastily published by an old acquaintance, Richard Grant White: *National Hymns. How They Are Written and How They are Not Written: A Lyric and National Study for the Times.* White dated the preface September 16, 1861, just before the book was printed, so Melville could have bought it during his stay in New York City later that year or his longer stay in 1862. In 1922, when forging a Melville item was hardly worthwhile (although forgers had been at work on Melville even earlier), the reputable Anderson Galleries sold what purported to be a presentation copy of *National Hymns* from him to the musician Fanny M. Raymond (Sealts, no. 556.1b). No one has reported seeing this book since 1922, and there is no other record of Melville's knowing this woman, who moved, as far as we know, in Manhattan circles that did not overlap with his own narrow circuit. If Melville in fact bought this book, he may have been misled by the title, for it was about what White, in curmudgeonly mode, saw as the necessity, after the outbreak of war, to choose a national song because, according to White's prolonged, contradictory rant, the extremely popular "Star-Spangled Banner" had proved "almost useless" as "a patriotic song for the people at large." The book was not about putting the war into poetry.

People Melville knew were writing about the war very early, in prose. One of his closest literary friends, Henry T. Tuckerman, put the date July 1861 on the introduction to his *The Rebellion: Its Latent Causes and True Significance. In Letters to a Friend Abroad* (New York: James G. Gregory, 1861). A few months later, Tuckerman was seeking Melville out; and Melville, given a look at the *Rebellion* pamphlet, would have found much to stir him, not least the reference to an event that transpired while he was in Pittsfield—New Yorkers' hearing "the bugle charge which proclaimed Garibaldi's invincible forays under the walls of Rome, wake the peaceful echoes of the Astor Library." Garibaldi's own flag, fresh from the siege of Rome, had been "presented to the Garibaldi Guard, in Lafayette Place, New York, when the regiment marched to the bugle charge of their Italian hero." Situated on Lafayette Place, the Astor Library, visited by Melville and members of his family before, during, and after the war, had reverberated with martial music. Melville would have found many of Tuckerman's arguments worth pondering and discussing, and the wide-ranging pamphlet gives a good idea of some topics of their conversations, although, always, art and literature would have been on both their minds. Still, his imperfect health and stressful family life would have postponed any literary response to his friend's pamphlet.

After mid-fall of 1862 any thought Melville had of putting the war into a book (whether consisting of "doggerel" or lofty new poetry) would have been hampered if not thwarted by domestic disruptions. Tacitly admitting that he was now unable to run the farm successfully, Melville moved his family into a rented house on South Street in Pittsfield, all but emptying Arrowhead. His severe injury in a carriage accident in November 1862, at the end of the move, put a halt to his creative life for a considerable duration. Over the next months he made a slow recovery but his body was never again as strong as it had been. Weak or not, Melville in 1863 witnessed war preparations in Pittsfield and in visits to New York City, and went out at night to witness one great public demonstration, the celebration of the victories at Gettysburg and Vicksburg. Besides enduring physical pain from the accident and confusion in his living space, Melville experienced a series of private traumas, great or small. Negotiating the sale of Arrowhead to Allan in May 1863, on terms distinctly in Allan's favor, may have been severely traumatic, for Melville was raiding Lizzie's inheritance to purchase Allan's now-shabby Twenty-sixth Street house. In 1863, also, his friends David Davidson and George L. Duyckinck died a day apart in March, and throughout the early fall Sarah Morewood fought to stay active but at last collapsed and died. Late in the year, in October, Melville himself was uncharacteristically "busy with his house" (Allan's former house on Twenty-sixth Street) while his wife was living in the chaos of South Street.[85]

Another writer might not necessarily have needed access to his library for planning a book of war poems, but Melville liked to have his books around him and needed a writing desk (to the point of wiping off one speckled with chicken droppings, so he could dash off an essay on Hawthorne). From late 1862, when he moved to South Street, Melville most likely did not have anything like normal access to his library. Late in 1863 the Melvilles not only moved to New York but moved again in New York, after their possessions had to be left temporarily at Allan's new house before being moved to Twenty-sixth Street, where most of the Civil War poems were presumably written. When Duyckinck sent him a book to review in December 1863, just as the family was becoming settled, Melville replied (December 31): "As for scribbling anything about it, tho' I

85. The phrase is Allan's, writing to Augusta on October 12, 1863 (Parker 2002, p. 552).

would like to please you, I have not spirit enough." The successive moves had been traumatic, not having all his books at hand had been disrupting and frustrating, and Melville was damaged physically and psychologically all through 1863. Tempting as it is to think that he must have been writing war poems all along, there is no hard evidence that Melville wrote any of his Civil War poems in 1861, 1862, or 1863.

Yet by early 1864, at the latest, Melville was writing about the war, even if he had still not set himself the grander role of putting the war into a book of poetry. The evidence comes only several weeks after his refusing to scribble anything for Duyckinck. In a printed circular dated February 5, 1864, Alexander Bliss and John P. Kennedy asked many writers to contribute a manuscript for a volume benefiting union hospital work, *Autograph Leaves of Our Country's Authors*. It is not known if Melville received the invitation in February or not until several weeks later, so it is impossible to tell how soon he acted on the request. Presumably following directions in a lost personal note accompanying the printed request, Melville around mid-March submitted to Bliss a poetic manuscript, "Inscription / For the Slain / At Fredericksburgh." On March 22 he wrote again, apologizing for having blundered "the other day" by sending "an uncorrected draught—in fact, the *wrong sheet*." Copies of the book, printed from the "uncorrected draught," were available by April 9, 1864. Except for the verses in *Mardi* and perhaps some verses in other prose works, this was Melville's first appearance in print as a poet.

In *Battle-Pieces* Melville did not republish the poem from *Autograph Leaves,* in any version, although he recast a line ("Death to the brave's a starry night") for the last lines of "Chattanooga" ("Life was to these a dream fulfilled, / And death a starry night," 68.62–63). He did include in the book sixteen other "Verses Inscriptive and Memorial." Several of these memorialize the slain and battlefields of 1861–63, so by early 1864 Melville may have already composed a number of such "Inscriptions." Being brief by their nature and taking only a matter of minutes or hours to compose after reading newspaper or magazine accounts, the inscriptions might naturally have been among those written while Melville's living situation was unsettled and before he had a fuller sense of what kinds of war poems he might write. His placing the group to the back of *Battle-Pieces* ("relegating" may be more appropriate than "placing") could reflect his awareness that some of them were somewhat older than poems in the body of the book.

By April 8, 1864, Allan Melville, at least, was behaving as if he thought Herman would write about the war. Seeking a pass for him and Herman to visit their cousin Henry Gansevoort in camp in Virginia, Allan asked

Richard Lathers to write Secretary of War Edwin M. Stanton "introduc-
ing Herman & stating his wish, as a literary man he might be favored."
Allan specified, "such men should have opportunities to see that they may
describe" (Parker 2002, pp. 562–63). Stanton issued the pass, and Melville
made his visit, during which he took part in a raid against the great guer-
rilla fighter John S. Mosby. Overtired and overexposed to the cold nights,
Melville did not write about his experience immediately, but within a few
weeks or months he may have made the best of his opportunity by writing
his longest war poem, "The Scout toward Aldie."

   In the prefatory note to *Battle-Pieces* Melville made this flat statement
about when he wrote the poems: "With few exceptions, the Pieces in this
volume originated in an impulse imparted by the fall of Richmond"—
which occurred on April 3, 1865. By December 1865 or January 1866
Melville had enough poems in hand for him to arrange for their publica-
tion in a book, if in fact the anonymous publication of "The March to
the Sea" on two full pages of the February issue of *Harper's New Monthly
Magazine* (out in mid-January) means that Melville had already arranged
that poems be published in the magazine before the book was brought
out. In the March issue the Harpers published "The Cumberland"; in the
April issue, "Philip"; in the June issue, "Chattanooga"; and in the July
issue "Gettysburg." At least one poem, "Lee in the Capitol," had not been
thought of when Melville arranged for book publication. It is based on
Robert E. Lee's testimony before the Reconstruction Committee of Con-
gress on February 17, 1866. Publication of the testimony was long delayed,
and only after the Washington *National Intelligencer* printed it on March 28
was it rapidly picked up by New York papers. Two or three months after
finishing the Lee poem, by early summer of 1866, appalled at the fury of
Radical Republicans intent on punishing the South, Melville decided he
had to add a prose "Supplement." On June 30, 1866, at the Astor Library
he consulted a book identified by a staff member in the library's "Daily
Record" as "Secret Debate" (that is, Chittenden's *A Report of . . . the Secret
Sessions,* mentioned earlier) to get back in mind some of the arguments
used by people he knew and others who hoped to appease the South
(Olsen-Smith and Sealts, no. 143.2). In August 1865 *Harper's* had reviewed
John W. Draper's *Thoughts on the Future Civil Policy of America* (New York:
Harper, [1865]; Sealts, no. 190), but Melville waited a year, until July 11,
1866, to buy it. Going by the title, or perhaps attracted by Draper's men-
tion of Machiavelli, who was on his own mind, Melville may have hoped
it would help him with the "Supplement," but much of it had been deliv-
ered as lectures early in 1865, before Reconstruction was under way, and
he probably found little use for it.

So far, what we know of Melville's printed sources for poems in *Battle-Pieces* tells us very little about the order in which he wrote the poems. All through the war, we know, Melville had access to *Harper's Weekly: A Journal of Civilization*, at first (1859–61) through a subscription in the name of his mother, who was living in Gansevoort, New York. Melville subscribed for himself from 1861 through 1863, and probably through the rest of the war, for in 1864 his mother commented on a cartoon in an issue he had sent to her, in that era when it was cheap to mail newspapers back and forth (Sealts 1988, p. 182). In late June 1863 Melville's wife bore up patiently under her mistreatment by Allan's new wife until (explaining that she felt like "Greel[e]y & the nigger") she exploded: "I *must* relieve my feelings—*Great fool!*—say it—or 'bust.'" Lizzie was referring to a cartoon in the April 5, 1862, *Harper's Weekly,* where "Old Mother Greeley," in female garb, on "the rampage" after General McClellan for not emancipating slaves on his own authority, stands behind the seated general, shouting, "SAY NIGGER OR I'LL BUST!!!" (In the second volume of my biography, p. 538, I had not yet identified the source of Lizzie's allusion.) Since in mid-1863 Lizzie assumed that Augusta would remember a particular cartoon from April 1862, it seems likely that all during the war the whole family discussed items in many issues of *Harper's Weekly.* Late in 1865 Melville gave five bound volumes, volumes 5 (1861) through 9 (1865), as Christmas gifts to his wife and children. That meant, of course, that he could have access to them at a need.

Harper's Weekly included elaborate prose reports from battlefields, printed rarely more than a week or two after the events described, and excellent engravings, often made from photographs by Mathew Brady and other skillful men. The weekly paper brought home to the Melvilles not only scenes of camp and battle but also detailed maps of embattled areas and meticulous diagrams and depictions of such novelties as a revolving turret on an ironclad ship. In addition, hardly a battle described in Melville's book had not promptly been commemorated in verse in the weekly newspaper. Walt Whitman's "Beat! Beat! Drums!" was there (September 28, 1861) along with many conventional verses as good as Alfred Street's or John C. Hoadley's. Melville very likely saw issues of *Frank Leslie's Illustrated Newspaper,* which also printed many reports from the seat of war as well as many engravings, and he may have seen issues of the *New York Illustrated News* and the *London Illustrated News.* Many other monthly and weekly periodicals contained prose descriptions and visual depictions of events he memorialized in his battle poems.

Although Melville had *Harper's Weekly* at hand during the composition of *Battle-Pieces* and undoubtedly saw other illustrated periodicals during the war, and although he deliberately consulted some books toward the end (at least for work on the "Supplement"), it was daily newspaper reports, most often as reprinted in collections, that provided details Melville used in some of the poems in *Battle-Pieces*. Through much of 1861, the second half of 1862, and almost all of 1863 Melville had only irregular access to a range of daily New York and Boston papers, mainly during his stays in New York and his briefer visits to Allan. Throughout the war Allan subscribed to several newspapers, but nothing indicates that Melville ever borrowed any of them. Surviving stacks of Allan's Civil War–era papers which surfaced in the 1990s were not mutilated, as might have happened if sources for *Battle-Pieces* poems had been cut out. Whenever he was in New York, however, Melville could visit reading rooms where current and back files of many newspapers were available. Toward the end of the war, while living in New York City, Melville seems indeed to have clipped some newspaper items for use in his poetry, judging from his notes to "The Stone Fleet" and "The Frenzy in the Wake." Still, lack of access to his own library or other libraries and to big city newspapers early in the war would not necessarily have kept Melville from writing poems that went into *Battle-Pieces*, for compilations of war reporting were available for sale starting late in 1861.

Melville's old friend Robert Tomes, who had made himself into an American military historian, issued three volumes on *The War with the South: A History of the Great American Rebellion,* the last ready in 1865; some of the many engravings were from drawings that Melville's illustrator friend Felix Darley had made for the volume. During the war years Melville stayed in contact with Evert A. Duyckinck, who was collecting documents for what turned out to be another three-volume *National History of the War for the Union, Civil, Military and Naval, Founded on Official and Other Authentic Documents* (copyrighted in 1861 by Johnson, Fry & Co. of 27 Beekman Street, published beginning in 1862). That first volume (1862) ends in November 1861; the second (dated 1865) covers October 1861 to November 1862; and the third (also dated 1865) covers December 1862 to April 1865. As Duyckinck's title pages explained, the volumes were illustrated with highly finished steel engravings, including battle scenes by sea and land, and full-length portraits of naval and military heroes, engraved from original paintings by Alonzo Chappel (a phenomenally speedy brushman) and by the young Thomas Nast, not yet known as a political satirist. Melville may never have owned a set, although John C. Hoadley bought the three volumes and had them bound in half calf, gilt. Still, Melville might have had access at need to documents that went into the *National History of the War* as well as the rest of the massive array of documents which Duyckinck gathered before ultimately rejecting many of them from the compilation. Nothing has been adduced to show that anything in Duyckinck's volumes was irrefutably the *specific* source for anything in *Battle-Pieces,* but supplementary information was available to Melville, in abundance, in Duyckinck's working files. Whether Melville knew the volumes or not is not known, but in his search for documents he would naturally have consulted works his friends had compiled. As noted above, Melville also had access all through the war to *Harper's Weekly,* that lavish source of news and engravings made from on-the-scene photographs and sketches. Once he began writing, Melville could find in compilations documenting the war anything he had missed in current newspapers.

The greatest compilation, the volumes of the *Rebellion Record* (consisting of, as the subtitle said, *A Diary of American Events, with Documents, Narratives, Illustrative Incidents, Poetry, Etc.*), became Melville's source for many newspaper reports of battles. Separate numbers of the *Record* were issued roughly every month, before being collected into the folio volumes, the first of which was published late in 1861. In engaging to publish the *Rebellion Record* George P. Putnam had expected the documentary history to be completed in a single volume or at most two, according to *Putnam's Monthly Magazine* (January 1868), when the eleventh volume was published, before the series was cut short at twelve volumes. Even if scholars were to establish the precise chronology of the publication of volumes and individual numbers of the *Rebellion Record,* that information might not tell much about the sequence of Melville's composing in relation to the reporting of military events. In view of all the uncertainties, it is no wonder that Stanton Garner in his *Civil War World of Herman Melville* decided the simple and elegant strategy was to discuss the poems in *Battle-Pieces* in the chronology of the events they depict, whenever that was possible.

When Melville wrote the prefatory note to *Battle-Pieces* has not been established—perhaps after writing all but the "Supplement." This note consists of three paragraphs:

> With few exceptions, the Pieces in this volume originated in an impulse imparted by the fall of Richmond. They were composed without reference to collective arrangement, but, being brought together in review, naturally fall into the order assumed.
>
> The events and incidents of the conflict—making up a whole, in varied amplitude, corresponding with the geographical area covered by the war—from these but a few themes have been taken, such as for any cause chanced to imprint themselves upon the mind.
>
> The aspects which the strife as a memory assumes are as manifold as are the moods of involuntary meditation—moods variable, and at times

widely at variance. Yielding instinctively, one after another, to feelings not inspired from any one source exclusively, and unmindful, without purposing to be, of consistency, I seem, in most of these verses, to have but placed a harp in a window, and noted the contrasted airs which wayward winds have played upon the strings.

This note plainly was written after the basic order of the book had been created, even if the body of the book had not yet been set in type.

In the second sentence, Melville may have been commenting about two phases, of separate composition and subsequent ordering. By saying "collective arrangement" he could have meant collection into a book of poems, as opposed to some other publication, but the subsequent phrasing seems to indicate that he meant arrangement in particular order *within* his book of war poems. Aware that his prefatory notes are seldom notable for strictest clarity and veracity, critics have tended to discount the possibility that Melville may have composed many of the poems without intending to put them into a book of war poems. As far as the rapidity of composition is concerned, critics have also been skeptical, but, allowing some leeway for the phrase "few exceptions," Melville may have been speaking accurately. It is not necessary to assume that for some occult reason he was misrepresenting himself when he denied what his readers might otherwise have taken for granted, that he had been writing poems all through the war, as events portrayed in the poems occurred. Melville was a practiced poet, author of a complete book of poems that should have been published in 1860, and he was, after all, the man who had written *Redburn* in two months, then in the next two months wrote *White-Jacket*. Without further evidence, dates of composition of individual poems remain speculative, limited mainly by the dates of the events described, starting with the stated initiatory date (for most of the poems) of April 1865, and ending with the date assigned to "Lee in the Capitol" (April 1866), and the publication of *Battle-Pieces* in mid-August 1866.

The main title, *Battle-Pieces,* Melville expected his readers to know, was borrowed from the sister art of painting, particular Dutch and English paintings which depicted sea-battles, but also from the sister art of music, where popular battle-pieces included the bagpipers' favorite, "The Battle of Waterloo." Set-pieces in poems by Scott and others were known in Melville's time as "battle-pieces." The subtitle, *Aspects of the War,* allowed for poems that did not deal specifically with battles. Melville made it clear that the prose "Supplement" was written after the poems and the notes: "Were I fastidiously anxious for the symmetry of this book, it would close with the notes. But the times are such that patriotism—not free from solicitude—urges a claim overriding all literary scruple." He dated his writing as "more than a year since the memorable surrender," and further dated it by alluding to recent histories and biographies written by Southerners and already "freely published at the North by loyal houses," and widely read. He also alluded to the "mourners who this summer bear flowers to the mounds of the Virginian and Georgian dead"—a strong indication that he wrote the "Supplement" some weeks after the actual anniversary of the surrender, and in response to the excessively punitive mood of the Radical Republicans.

As far as we know, Melville seems not to have been influenced by any of the war poems which peppered collections like the *Rebellion Record* and appeared in newspapers and magazines (such as *Harper's Weekly,* to which he subscribed). There is no evidence that he paid attention to other poets' volumes of Civil War poems such as Henry Howard Brownell's *Lyrics of a Day; or, Newspaper-Poetry* (New York: Carleton, 1864). Nor, with the possible but unlikely exception of "Donelson," does he show the influence of the recent war poets of Britain such as Sydney Dobell, whose poems in *England in Time of War* (1856) focus on a home front rather than distant battles. As we have seen, Melville knew Tennyson's "The Charge of the Light Brigade," which anticipated *Battle-Pieces* in its newspaper origins, but he seems not to have been influenced by the poet laureate's major response to the Crimean War, in *Maud.* Older British poets such as Milton, Scott, and Wordsworth demonstrably did influence Melville in *Battle-Pieces.* For all of his self-conscious violation of "literary scruples" as to "the symmetry of this book" (by including the "Supplement"), *Battle-Pieces* was very much in British literary traditions, very obviously the product of a man steeped not only in British poetry of the previous three and a half centuries but also in their writings about that poetry in "supplementary" essays.

The poem sent to Bliss, like the sixteen poems printed in the back of *Battle-Pieces* under the subtitle "Verses Inscriptive and Memorial" (for example, "Inscription for Graves at Pea Ridge, Arkansas"), demonstrates how closely Melville was working in a British literary tradition. At least one of the poems in this group, "A Requiem for Soldiers lost in Ocean Transports," reflected his painstaking metrical analysis of "Lycidas," but the inspiration for using the genre of "Inscriptions" was mainly eighteenth century and modern. Such "inscriptions" were familiar to Melville from Southey's *The Doctor,* where he had found the idea of "extracts" for *Moby-Dick.* He also knew the group of "Inscriptions" in his edition of Wordsworth, the appendix called "Essay Upon Epitaphs," and the end of the fifth book of *The Excursion.* He was familiar with at least some of these: Shenstone's "Inscription: On a Tablet Against a Root-House,"

Burns's "Inscription on a Goblet," Coleridge's "Inscription for a Fountain on a Heath," and Bryant's "Inscription for the Entrance to a Wood."

Melville had marked and taken to heart this passage in Wordsworth's "Essay Supplementary to the Preface":

> The appropriate business of poetry, (which, nevertheless, if genuine, is as permanent as pure science,) her appropriate employment, her privilege and her *duty,* is to treat of things not as they *are,* but as they *appear;* not as they exist in themselves, but as they *seem* to exist to the *senses* and to the *passions.* What a world of delusion does this acknowledged principle prepare for the inexperienced! what temptations to go astray are here held forth for them whose thoughts have been little disciplined by the understanding, and whose feelings revolt from the sway of reason!

Melville had made it his business to witness war at first hand, but he emphasized in the prefatory note that he was capturing in the poems the aspects which episodes of the strife took on in his informed memory, his variable moods coloring the way he recalled the battles. Like Wordsworth, he was attempting to do the proper business of poetry by treating of things as they appeared to him, as they *seemed* to exist to his senses and passions. Melville's decision in many of his poems not to aim for what was then being called Dutch realism or Pre-Raphaelite realism was not designed to win him the widest audience, but it was a conscious literary choice made under the influence of the former poet laureate, dead only a decade and a half.

As one would expect, Melville's poetic strategies in *Battle-Pieces* reflect his note-taking in 1862, particularly his summary of what Jeffrey said of Alfieri; now he too would avoid "Figures of mere ostentation.—Show-pieces of fine writing." Like Alfieri, Melville was prepared in some poems to sacrifice "flow & sweetness" in striving to give "force & energy by condensation & emphasis & inversion." Alfieri had achieved, Jeffrey said, a chastised gravity, and had displayed "Temperance and propriety of delineation of the passions." Ruskin's aesthetic tenets which Melville had written down in his Vasari were also in his mind as he wrote his war poems. He would value "completeness, fullness," even in a short poem, over "fine writing" and high polish. *Battle-Pieces* was a more literary book than the reviewers realized—in his immersion in the genre of inscriptions; in his choice of Wordsworth for authority on poetic distance from subject; in his choice of Milton (along with Alfieri as interpreted by Jeffrey) as authority for a spareness in rhyme and diction; and in his choice of Arnold and Ruskin for contemporary applications of Aristotelian principles involving the choice of noble actions.

Earnestly trying not to idealize military glory, especially in this modern war where impersonal mechanical power often seemed to overwhelm any personal heroism, Melville recollected one of Milton's pronouncements. These opening lines from "A Utilitarian View of the Monitor's Fight" (44.1–6) are fitted to its speaker, who is not to be identified with the poet:

> Plain be the phrase, yet apt the verse,
>   More ponderous than nimble;
> For since grimed War here laid aside
> His Orient pomp, 'twould ill befit
>   Overmuch to ply
> The rhyme's barbaric cymbal.

Here Melville was acknowledging "The Verse" section preceding *Paradise Lost,* where Milton declared that "Rime" was "no necessary Adjunct or true Ornament of Poem or good Verse, <u>in longer Works especially,</u> but the Invention of a barbarous Age, to set off wretched matter and lame Meeter" (see Mathieu; the underlining is Melville's in his copy of Milton). True "musical delight," Milton declared, "<u>consists only in apt Numbers, fit quantity of Syllables, and the sense variously drawn out from one verse into another,</u> not in the jingling sound of like endings" (Melville's underlining). In *The Poetical Works and Remains of Henry Kirke White,* which Melville bought during his quest for an aesthetic credo in 1862, he had read the comment that "Harmonious modulations, and <u>unvarying exactness of measure,</u> totally precluding sublimity and fire, have reduced our fashionable poetry to mere sing-song"—and he underlined the indicated words as a good modern affirmation of Milton's principles. Melville was not abjuring rhyme for his war poems but moving toward flexible rhyme schemes such as those in battle-pieces by Thomas Campbell and Sir Walter Scott.

Basing "Lee in the Capitol" on newspaper articles, Melville mythologized the man who had endured a public renunciation of military glory—something parallel to the grandeur of his own renunciation, for years now, of literary glory: informing the poem is Melville's profound though covert identification with Lee. Even his depiction of Lee's choosing not "coldly to endure his doom" (165.93) is infused with the determination he mustered in order to write and publish *Battle-Pieces.* In its form, an imaginary oration by a real historical figure, "Lee in the Capitol" follows hallowed rhetorical precedent, classical and Shakespearean, as well as American classroom exercises.

Just as the "Inscriptions" were conventional, however odd-looking to twenty-first-century readers without a grounding in eighteenth-century British poetry, so was the "Supplement" part of a literary convention as honorable, almost, as a "l'envoy." In particular, Melville had pored over Wordsworth's "Essay Supplementary to the Preface" from the 1815 edition of *Poems* (which he possessed in his 1839 *Poetical Works* along with the more famous preface to the second edition of *Lyrical Ballads*). His own "Supplement" shows that Melville was brooding over British parallels, not over the unresolved issues of the War of the Roses and Cromwell's regime but over the more recent Stuart-Hanoverian parallels, especially George IV's rearing a monument "over the remains of the enemy of his dynasty, Charles Edward, the invader of England and victor in the rout at Preston Pans"—a gesture that mitigated against the ugly possibility that Grant's descendants might "pursue with rancor, or slur by sour neglect, the memory of Stonewall Jackson" (182.29–31, 33–34). The course of events was controlled by Northern politicians who had not yet learned to act like statesmen, but Melville dared to hope that the South could be defeated without being shamed:

> Supposing a happy issue out of present perplexities, then, in the generation next to come, Southerners there will be yielding allegiance to the Union, feeling all their interests bound up in it, and yet cherishing unrebuked that kind of feeling for the memory of the soldiers of the fallen Confederacy that Burns, Scott, and the Ettrick Shepherd felt for the memory of the gallant clansmen ruined through their fidelity to the Stuarts—a feeling whose passion was tempered by the poetry imbuing it, and which in no wise affected their loyalty to the Georges, and which, it may be added, indirectly contributed excellent things to literature. (183.1–9)

Melville saw himself like Robert Burns, like Sir Walter Scott, and like James Hogg (the Ettrick Shepherd, that powerful presence in the Albany of Melville's youth)—a poet daring to be fair to defeated rebels while contributing to the poetic record of the victors. As he looked over the accumulating postwar histories and biographies, Melville recognized his own battle-pieces as constituting a parallel "poetic record" of the war.

XII
THE TRAJECTORY OF MELVILLE'S LITERARY CAREER

IN THE TWENTY-FIRST century, after many (but far from all) old gaps in basic knowledge about Melville's life have been filled and after many often-repeated errors have long been corrected, misconceptions persist about the period from late 1851 up through Melville's finishing his first book of poetry in 1860 and writing *Battle-Pieces*. One of the hoariest canards is that Melville renounced writing after the reception of *Moby-Dick* (or, in a variation, of *Pierre*). In 1946 Harrison Hayford showed that Melville had started work on a new book at the end of 1852, half a year after the publication of *Pierre,* and in 1960 Merrell R. Davis and William H. Gilman showed that he had completed it in the spring of 1853, evidence that William Charvat later confirmed. Disregarding the evidence produced by these scholars, Nina Baym by a 1979 article with an arresting title, "Melville's Quarrel with Fiction," gave fresh life to the idea that Melville had renounced writing after *Pierre*. In fact, Melville had no quarrel at all with fiction: his quarrels were with his publishers and his reviewers. Rather than renouncing writing with *Pierre,* in less than a year after its publication he had completed a book, as Davis and Gilman said in 1960. In 1987 I discovered the title, *The Isle of the Cross.*

Critics have also found it hard to accept that Melville finished yet another now-lost book seven years after *The Isle of the Cross.* Raymond Weaver had not known about *Poems* in time to mention it in his 1921 biography, but the next year Meade Minnigerode published an array of documents about the volume which Melville himself called "Poems." The documents have been printed many times, notably in the 1960 *Letters* and the 1993 *Correspondence*. There simply is no doubt that when he sailed for the Pacific in 1860 Melville left behind a volume of poems he expected his wife and his brother Allan to publish with the assistance of Evert and George Duyckinck. Yet in 2002 influential reviewers of *Herman Melville: A Biography, 1851–1891*, Richard Brodhead, Andrew Delbanco, and Elizabeth Schultz, all expressed skepticism or outright disbelief that Melville had finished *The Isle of the Cross* in 1853 and another book called *Poems* in 1860. According to these critics, I had merely "surmised" the existence of these two books. My biography was to "be used with caution" (as Delbanco put it) since I presented "inferences" about these lost books "as facts." With their misplaced skepticism these critics muddied waters which were already far from clean.

In the 2007 "*The Isle of the Cross* and *Poems:* Lost Melville Books and the Indefinite Afterlife of Error," I show just how groundless is the skepticism about these two books, and how damaging, for the recent allegations were published in prominent places and have remained alive on the Internet. Because ignorance about *The Isle of the Cross* and *Poems* has grossly distorted the verifiable stages in Melville's development as a writer, particularly as a poet, further discussion is required here.

Even when they acknowledge that *The Isle of the Cross* and *Poems* existed, many critics remain partially blind to the trajectory of Melville's career because they do not take active account of the reality of those two lost books. In the second volume of my biography of Melville I suggested that in the future critics can speculate responsibly about how Melville might have changed (in style, psychology, intellect) in the process of writing the lost *The Isle of the Cross* from mid–December 1852 till late May 1853. A responsible critic will also take account of how Melville might have developed as a poet in the process of writing the lost *Poems* from 1857 or 1858 until May 1860. The failure to take account of these two books stems not just from neglect of scholarship but from something basic about human cognitive psychology, the difficulty anyone has in taking active account of something that does not exist in a form that can be held in the hand the way *Battle-Pieces, John Marr,* or *Timoleon* can be held. It is hard for any human being, no matter how fine a critic or even how competent a scholar, to visualize something that does not exist and then to make complicated allowances for it. In the 1950s, for instance, the great scholar-critic Walter E. Bezanson thought that Melville's failure to publish a book between *The Confidence-Man* and *Battle-Pieces* showed a "contraction" of his "creative powers" (1954, p. 375). Bezanson could not have been certain that Melville had finished a book in 1853 (Melville's eighth, if it had been published), but he could have cited *Poems* as evidence that Melville's publishing outlets had contracted, not his creative powers. Hard as it is, any responsible critic now must begin to rethink the trajectory of Melville's career in the light of the only partially tangible *The Isle of the Cross* and *Poems.* No one can think responsibly about *Battle-Pieces* (1866), *Clarel* (1876), *John Marr* (1888), and *Timoleon* (1891) without taking into account the fact that Melville completed a book of poetry in 1860.

It will take self-conscious determination if we are to avoid common pitfalls of Melville critics who, for instance, write as if *Battle-Pieces* followed *The Confidence-Man* (1857) without any intermediate literary work, or, at best, as if it followed next after the composition of Melville's three lectures in the late 1850s. We can vow not to ascribe anything poetically "unconventional" in *Battle-Pieces* to Melville's turning directly, however belatedly, from prose to his Civil War poetry. We can stop referring to *Battle-Pieces* as Melville's "first book of poetry" instead of his first *published* book of poetry. We can stop calling Melville "a novice poet" in *Battle-Pieces*. We can avoid statements such as Lawrence Buell's 1998 comment that "Melville published poetry long before turning intensively to it" (p. 138). A more precise statement might be that "Melville turned intensively to poetry (in the late 1850s) long before publishing any of the ambitious poetry he wrote then." The latter formulation would allow us to remember that Melville wrote poetry with high intensity in 1858 through early 1860, perhaps again during intervals in the next two years or so, and again around 1864 or after the fall of Richmond in 1865, whenever he began serious work on *Battle-Pieces,* the first book of poems he was able to publish (1866). Buell also observes that the "unfinished Grandvin-Gentian sketches comprise two major poetic sequences interspersed with prose commentary, a hybrid genre Melville often favored in his late work" (p. 151). Yet the two poems referred to, the variously titled "Naples" poem and "At the Hostelry," are not late, certainly not from Melville's last decade. One or both of them may well have been in *Poems* (1860), although parts of "At the Hostelry" seem to date from the next year or two, or a little later. The prose pieces written to introduce them, the sketches involving Gentian and Grandvin, date (in their first versions) from the late 1870s. In his last years Melville continued to rework some of the prose parts (and perhaps some of the poetry) and added the new prefatory essay "The House of the Tragic Poet." A pervasive and powerful misconception is that any poetry that Melville published in *John Marr* (1888) or *Timoleon* (1891) and any poetry he left unpublished at his death (such as the poems in a "near-final" collection to be called *Weeds and Wildings*) is exclusively "late" poetry, composed late in his life. This misconception has proved almost unshakable because it is so seemingly commonsensical. In fact, a yet-undetermined amount of that poetry must be late, or must have been revised late, while a yet-undetermined amount of it may have been written much earlier. As Thorp suggested in 1938, some early (1857–60) poetry, however much it was later revised, almost surely survives from the lost *Poems* (1860). The upshot is that we need to keep the reality of the lost *Poems* in mind whenever we set out to talk about Melville's later poetry.

In what is less a misconception than an example of hasty misjudgment, the still-influential early twentieth-century biographers were contemptuous of Melville's poetry and assumed that he never took it very seriously. Raymond Weaver in 1921 said "the inspiration flags throughout" *John Marr* and *Timoleon,* the volumes Melville printed at the end of his life (p. 365). Lewis Mumford in 1929 was sure that "Melville rarely achieved form as a poet" in *Battle-Pieces,* and that in *Clarel* Melville "was too frequently the victim of his uncertain taste," so that the "clumsiness in detail adds to the clumsiness of conception: what might have been vivid prose became dull verse" (p. 321). This old disdain survives in Delbanco's assertion in 2005 that reading the poems gathered in "Fruit of Travel Long Ago" "is like overhearing a musician who no longer expects to play in public recitals but who still practices in private in order to keep his fingers limber" (p. 267). According to this still-prevalent misconception, after the failure of his career as a prose writer Melville took up versifying as a hobby, not caring enough about the hobby to study the poetry by older British poets or his British contemporaries. Self-indulgent and inefficient, Melville did not trouble to analyze poetic techniques and did not struggle to master poetic principles. The misconception that poetry was merely a harmless hobby for Melville was most succinctly, if brusquely, stated by Alfred Kazin in a 1997 forum on Melville at the Barnes & Noble bookstore in Union Square, New York City, where the other participants were Paul Metcalf (one of Melville's great-grandsons) and me. Kazin cautioned: "You have to remember that poetry was just a sideline with Melville; it was never important to him and he was never good at it" (Parker 2002, p. xiii).

Melville's shrewd annotations in dozens of volumes of poetry and books on poetry demonstrate the falseness of this Weaver-Kazin-Delbanco theory. Poetry was anything but a sideline for Melville. He became a poet when he was thirty-nine or forty and remained a poet until he died at seventy-two. He had been a regular writer of prose for publication only for a dozen years, from the end of 1844, when he started *Typee,* until the summer of 1856, when he completed *The Confidence-Man.* He wrote very little prose after that—a lecture in 1857, another in 1858, and a third in 1859, none of which he published. After April 1857 (when *The Confidence-Man* was published), the prose he published, aside from a few letters to newspaper editors, consisted mainly of the notes and the "Supplement" in *Battle-Pieces;* a brief memoir of his uncle Thomas Melvill Jr., which his friend Joseph Smith prevailed upon him to write (after 1872, Smith said) for the 1876 *History of Pittsfield;*[86] and prose headnotes to poems. The Jack Gentian and Marquis de Grandvin prose sketches were from the start attempts to introduce and thereby salvage two longish poems written long before. The story of Billy Budd, which Melville was working on at his death, began as a prose headnote to the ballad of "Billy in the Darbies" and then greatly outgrew its initial purpose. With only a few exceptions,

---

86. The memoir was published in Smith, *History of Pittsfield* (1876). See *Log,* pp. 63–64 and, for a reprint of the full text, Sealts, "Thomas Melvill, Jr." (1987).

what Melville wrote for publication from around 1858 until his death in September 1891 was poetry. The cyclopedias, Melville warned in 1886,[87] were no more infallible than the pope, and some encyclopedias printed and bound in the twenty-first century as well as some Internet encyclopedias assert, among other errors, that Melville did not write any substantial amount of poetry until late in his life and that only toward the end of his life did he concentrate on writing poetry. The facts need to be repeated for emphasis: Herman Melville was a practicing poet (1857 or 1858 through 1891) for three times as long as he was a professional, publishing writer of prose (1846–57). Poetry was not just a sideline for Melville: it was what he wrote for a third of a century. It was important to him; indeed, it was, for many years of his life, certainly from 1870 into 1875, when he was working on *Clarel* (1876), obsessively important.

Yet much of what we know about Melville and poetry has come to light only in recent decades, mainly from belated study of the "Augusta Papers" discovered in 1983[88] or from books newly recovered from Melville's library (notably his copies of Wordsworth, Milton, Dante, and Spenser, and his copies of Hazlitt's *Lectures on the English Poets* and Thomas Warton's *History of English Poetry*). With some exceptions, such as Thomas F. Heffernan's 1977 article on Melville's copy of Wordsworth and my biography, the new information was slow in being made public. In this HISTORICAL NOTE previously published evidence has been brought together with new evidence about basic topics such as Melville's hearing and reading poetry, his buying books of poetry and books containing poetry, his habit of spotting and annotating poetic echoes, his standards for ranking poets, his conscious study of poetic techniques, and his quest for satisfying aesthetic principles. A challenge for the writers of the HISTORICAL NOTE for the last Northwestern-Newberry volume—Melville's uncompleted writings— will be to clarify the trajectory of Melville's career as a poet as well as the full trajectory of his whole literary career.

87. Melville made the comment in a letter to Leonard G. Sanford, June 22, 1886.
88. See note 30 above.

POSTSCRIPT ON RECEPTION

*B*ATTLE-PIECES.[89] On August 12, 1866, a note in the New York *Herald* commented on one of the new books from Harper's, *Battle-Pieces:* "[F]or ten years the public has wondered what has become of Melville." The public was to learn from a good number of reviews what Melville had recently done, if not what had become of him. Much of the commentary in the still highly politicized months of the reviewing dealt with the "Supplement." The Boston *Daily Advertiser* (August 24) did not recall a literary precedent, despite Wordsworth's famous essay: "Rather a novel feature, for a volume of poems appears in a political essay inserted at the close under the head of 'Supplement.'" Henry Raymond, the editor of the New York *Times* (no longer merely a juvenile intruder in the newspaper world), had been campaigning for a policy of non-punitive reconciliation toward white Southerners, so on August 27 it may have been Raymond himself who seized on the "Supplement" as showing that Melville did not have "the fear of the Radicals before his eyes" in advocating a position like Raymond's own. Barely mentioning the "poems themselves" (a "succession of lyrics, many of them vivid battle pictures, which were dashed off from time to time during the war"), the *Times* managed to praise them particularly for their political stance: "They make all the more pleasant a contribution to the literature of the war, because they are not marked by those extravagances in which nearly all our bellicose poets have so freely indulged."

In his summary of the "Supplement" the reviewer in the *Times* played ironically with Melville's authority as an anthropological political philosopher:

> Mr. Melville ventures to advise that we should "be Christians toward our fellow whites, as well as philanthropists toward the blacks, our fellow men;" that "something may well be left to the graduated care of future legislation, and to heaven;" and, he adds, that "in all things, and toward all, we are enjoined to do as we would be done by." The use of such treasonable language as this shows a singular hardihood on the part of one who has studied and written about the ferocious inhabitants of the South Sea Islands, who were accustomed, as we all know, to keep cold missionary on their

---

89. The *Battle-Pieces* section of this postscript is reprinted with the permission of the Johns Hopkins University Press from my *Herman Melville: A Biography*, vol. 2 (Baltimore, 2002), pp. 615–23. I have interpolated quotations from reviews Richard Winslow III discovered in the Worcester *Spy*, the Philadelphia *Press*, the Bath (Maine) *Sentinel*, the San Francisco *Alta California*, and the Providence *Journal*.

sideboards, and it is perhaps unkind to Mr. Melville to draw down upon his devoted head Radical wrath by calling attention thus publicly to his views.

In warning the Radicals about the "Supplement" the *Times* claimed to be acting with "the most benevolent intentions," to keep the followers of Thaddeus Stevens and Charles Sumner from "pitching the book out the window." The warning, however, was ambidexter, as Melville would have said, and may have kept such Radicals from picking up the book at all.

On August 31 the Augusta (Maine) *Kennebec Journal* decided that Melville "did not help his reputation any by his prosy supplement, which is a sort of apology for some of the sentiments in his poetry which, less than some others required any apology and a rather discursive and uncalled-for essay on the present situation." The reviewer added that one "hardly knows after reading it what opinions the author holds." The Worcester *Spy* on September 1 recognized "The March to the Sea" from the *Harper's* printing and praised all the poems as "spirited and musical expressions of the feeling inspired by leading military events." The poems, however, were "followed by a half apologetic supplement in which Mr. Melville deprecates any farther manifestation of the spirit toward the defeated section which the appearance of his poems at this time is calculated to strengthen." The *Spy* went on: "There is certainly an inconsistency between the author's poetical impulses and his prosaic caution. But inasmuch as there is a greater danger the people will forget there has ever been a rebellion than that they will treat the rebels themselves harshly, we can afford to welcome the poems even with the prose addition, because they will help keep alive a little longer the memory of the great wrong that has been done." On September 3 the New York *Herald* directed "special attention" to the "Supplement," insisting that "far from spoiling the symmetry of the book, this supplement completes it, and converts it into what is better than a good book—into a good and patriotic action." Writing under the threat of Radical triumph, the *Herald* welcomed Melville's "'words in season,' not only as the deliberate, impartial testimony of a highly cultivated individual mind, but as hopeful signs of a change in public opinion and sentiment." (On September 14 the Baltimore *Sun* coolly plagiarized this excellent passage to deck out a brief notice.) The extract in the *Herald* was from the prose "Supplement," not the poetry. On September 5 the New York *Commercial Advertiser* also excerpted the "Supplement," "in which the author ventilates his political philosophy." For the Radical taste of the Boston *Traveller* (September 8) there was "too much said about generosity to the vanquished" in the "Supplement." The Bath (Maine) *Sentinel* on September 10 said the "Supplement" was written "in a calm, reflective, charitable manner,—showing it to be the author's sincere desire to conciliate the brothers of the North, with those of the South; there is much of sound philosophy in it as well, which commends it to all that are interested in the advancement of RIGHT." On October 6 the Portland (Maine) *Transcript: An Independent Family Journal of Literature, Science, News &c.* was harsh on Melville: "[H]e so far violates literary taste as to add a 'Supplement' in which, in somewhat stilted prose, he urges the duty of moderation and magnanimity to a fallen foe on the part of the victor. All will agree that a generous forbearance should be exercised towards the South, but the nation will not forget that it is bound to be just as well as generous."

The "Supplement" outraged the Radical New York *Independent* (January 10, 1867), which called Melville "this happy optimist" for saying Northern whites were "bound to be Christians toward our fellow-whites as well as philanthropist toward the blacks" and declaring that something "may well be left to the graduated care of future legislation and of Heaven." A portion of the denunciation shows just how dangerous the ground was on which Melville had so cautiously trodden:

> Does Mr. Melville really believe that, if William Lloyd Garrison had not called the Constitution "a Covenant with Death and Agreement with Hell," or if Robert Toombs had never hoped to call the roll of his slaves on Bunker Hill, red Wrong would not one day have arraigned Right for being Right, and been compelled to hear her terrible justification! Almost a century the North labored with the dull mechanic oar, to find at last, through a fearful awakening, that "the strong wind is blowing, and the strong current flowing, right onward to the Eternal Shore." We speak at this length because gentlemen of Mr. Melville's class are mischievous men in these troublous times. Only absolute justice is safe. Peaceable, by all means peaceable, in God's name; but *first pure,* in God's name, also.

(Robert Augustus Toombs was the fiery Georgian, first Confederate secretary of state, notorious for defiling the hallowed monument at Bunker Hill by exercising his constitutional rights to enumerate his slaves.) This was hard reading for the family from the paper that had warned Melville and the Harpers of hell-fire, hard reading for Melville as he went about his daily rounds in the district office and the docks.

One small decision about rhyme made Melville a laughingstock among the reviewers. The Philadelphia *American Literary Gazette and Publishers' Circular* (September 1) decried the rhymes as "fearful": "The first one [poem] in his book makes 'law' and 'Shenandoah' rhyme," then Melville went from bad to worse, making "'war' and 'Shenandoah' rhyme." On

September 8 the Cincinnati *Enquirer* condemned some of the rhymes as "hardly canonical" and some of the lines "would be prose but for the typography." Still, some of the pieces had "more than mere spasmodic force; and some have hardly as much"—a two-sided reference to the British Spasmodic poets of the previous decade. On September 15 the New York *Round Table* called some of the rhymes "positively barbarous": "In his first poem, *The Portent,* 'Shenandoah' rhymes with 'law,' and 'John Brown' with 'shown.'" The reviewer in the New York *World* (October 19), possibly Richard Henry Stoddard, declined to enumerate "such technical blemishes as the rhyming of 'law' and 'Shenandoah,' 'more' and 'Keneshaw,'" lest he should seem to be "carping at a book which, without having one poem of entire artistic *ensemble* in it, possesses numerous passages of beauty and power." The *Independent* had no such scruples, and enumerated the various words Melville had rhymed with "Shenandoah," "regardless of incompatibility," then added that "Shenandoah" made "another Mormon marriage with half-a-dozen unfit terminations, of which 'star' is the least unlike." Only a handful of reviewers got far past their contempt for the rhymes to "Shenandoah." Melville was renouncing rhyme's barbaric cymbal—but was he also carrying into his middle years some pronunciation derived from his Boston-born father and wife, just as he wrote "Happar" to identify the Marquesan tribe others called "Happa"?

On August 27 the Philadelphia *Press* was ambivalent: "These poems are of various degrees of merit—some are little more than rhymed paraphrases of war-items from newspapers; others have the true ring of the good metal, and among these we would particularly mention the pieces entitled 'Running the Batteries,' 'The Armies of the Wilderness,' 'The Scout Toward Aldie,' and 'Lee in the Capitol.' The writer is loyal, true, and very earnest." The Springfield *Republican* (August 29) decided that none of the poems was "absolutely bad, but many of them cannot be called good." The Boston *Post* (August 30) judged that the verse was "pregnant, but not artistic," and that the volume was "likely to fall into its place among the subordinate depositories of war verse, which the time has been so prolific in." Melville wrote verse much as Bulwer did, "understandingly, scholarly, but not imaginatively in the fine poetic sense of that word." One of the terser comments was in the August 31 Boston *Christian Witness and Church Advocate:* "This is a series of descriptive and lyrical poems, on subjects and incidents fresh in the memory of us all. It is full of a certain offhand heartiness but will not bear severe criticism." The *Kennebec Journal* said Melville's poems were "inspired by particular events" which followed "each other so rapidly as to demand of the writer a fresh poem every few days," so they could not be meritorious; however, some were "musical in their rhythm" and showed "some poetical talent," particularly "the descriptive pieces, such as 'Donelson' and 'The Scout towards Aldie.'" The New York *National Quarterly Review* (September 1866) was blunt: "Had this really been a book of poetry, as it purports to be, it would have had a different imprint; it would have reached us, not from New York, but from Boston." The reviewer in the New York *Nation* (September 6) read the book "with a certain melancholy," finding proof that Nature did not make Melville a poet. In Taunton, Massachusetts, the *Daily Gazette* (September 8) thought that probably not one poem in the collection would be remembered, since the poems lacked "that free and musical flow of fine words and fervid fancies which give verses a place in all newspapers." The Boston *Traveller* asserted that the war had given birth to "little poetry that is worth preserving, but Mr. Melville's poems are an exception to the rule, for they have both vigor and sweetness, and often rise to the element of grandeur."

The New York *Albion* (September 15) elaborated with a good memory the "few short 'swallow-flights'" in *Mardi* which were "not so poetical as the prose" in which they were set. The writer had thought about the subject: "Mr. Melville's prose, indeed, was less prose than poetry in the rough, resembling, we take it, the spirited but careless memoranda which poets throw together in their moments of inspiration as the skeleton of future poems. It was rich in diction, full of colour, and, after its fashion, imaginative." The "interval of silence" on Melville's part was now broken, and not agreeably, for the volume showed that his mind, "while lying fallow," had "changed in many respects, and not to his advantage in a poetical point of view." The merit in the poems was intermixed with much that was "worthless," for Melville was "less an artist now than ever": "His conceptions are frequently obscure, and his style uncouth and harsh. Of verse as verse—meaning thereby the falling together of words in rhythmical order—he knows but little, seldom writing a stanza that is melodious throughout. Some of his discords are fine, but music has other and higher qualities than mere discords." On September 29 the San Francisco *Evening Bulletin* thought some of the pieces were "spirited and full of poetic fire; but taken as a collection" they were "rather mediocre": "They are cast in unfamiliar metre, and the versification is at times harsh and limping." The San Francisco *Alta California* on October 1 found very little to praise Melville for: "He has attempted to turn the war into rhyme, and although there are forcible passages, and well-turned lines here and there, the book as a whole is a decided failure; but perhaps no worse than a hundred other books of verse published every year. The principal events of the war are each made the subject of a piece of verse, so that there is no continuity of story, or unity of execution; nor is there a uniform measure." The Providence *Journal* on October 3 was no happier: "This volume of poems will not add to the reputation Mr. Melville has gained by his prose. With occasional gleams of poetic inspiration, his verses are generally uncouth in form, rambling in measure, and rough and discordant in their rhyme. We have no fancy for poetry which runs on eccentricities and zigzags. We would rather read one chapter of Typee than all the patriotic and pathetic battle-pieces in this curious volume." The reviewer in the New York *Evening Post* (October 10) mentioned *Pierre* twice—highly unusual—and offered a cautious praise: "These war-lyrics are full of martial fire, and sometimes are really artistic in form, but often the thought of the author is too vaguely expressed." Melville's "style in verse" was "as unfettered by ordinary precedents as in such of his prose works as 'Pierre.'" The long review in the New York *World* cautiously observed that "the poetic nature and the technical faculty of poetry writing are not identical": "Whole pages of Mr. Melville's prose are, in the highest sense, poetic, and nearly all the battle-pieces would be much more poetic if they were thrown into the external prose form."

Reviewers often singled out for comment the longest poem of the first section, "Donelson." The New York *Evening Express* (August 25) said the book's "principal 'piece'" appears to be a versification and attempted idealization of the bulletin board of some daily newspaper office during the Fort Donelson excitement." The September *National Quarterly Review* resisted taking many of the pieces, including this one, as poetry: "Mr. Melville has great faith in difference of type; sometimes he prints whole pages in *Italics,* as if he thought he could render them more poetical by the process. Thus, for example, the poem entitled Donelson is chiefly in that type; but the amount of poetry it contains may be pretty safely inferred from the first stanza"—which it then quoted in full. On September 3 the Philadelphia *Inquirer* complained that "Donelson" exemplified the "fault of needless and commonplace detail," a fault Melville had "generally" avoided. The New York *Round Table* enumerated defects, and found counterbalancing virtues, "nervous phrases and energetic passages, and fine bits of description, now of landscapes and now of battle movements," such as in "Donelson," which was "in some respects the most original poem of the collection." The *Albion* called it one of the most "sustained" poems, "the execution of which is fantastic enough, the effect depending upon the reading on a city bulletin of the daily telegraphic reports of the battle." The New York *Evening Post* offered an example of Melville's style as unconventional: "His account of the impressions produced by the various reports from Fort Donelson—about the time of its surrender—is a specimen of this, yet it presents a faithful picture of the times, and recalls them vividly to the mind of the reader."

Several reviewers praised one of the most conventional poems, one comfortingly in the genre of Browning's "How they Brought the Good News"—"Sheridan at Cedar Creek" ("Shoe the steed with silver / That bore him to the fray," 84.1–2). The *Albion* described it as best of all the poems and advised "Mr. Melville's readers to turn to it first, since it ought to cover the multitude of his poetic sins." The *Round Table* called it "the best thing in the volume" and pronounced that it far surpassed "Mr. Buchanan Read's poem on the same theme," being imaginative and having "the true lyrical ring." It was often reprinted, in the Boston *Commonwealth* for October 6, for example, and in the New York *Leader* for December 8. This is the poem Melville copied for Stoddard, by request.

Other poets of the war had done better. The reviewer in the New York *Nation* had thought the matter through and decided that Melville did not compare with the true war poet, James Russell Lowell, whose "Commemoration Ode" "takes its place securely, not only among the finest works of our generation, but among the noblest poems of all time." Granted, even lesser poets are inspired by great events, but not to worthy achievement: "the same storm that piles up the waves of the sea sets all the duck-ponds in ineffectual commotion." Melville's duck-pond had been ruffled, as *Battle-Pieces* bore witness, and the reviewer, having responded to Lowell's mastery, confessed to feeling "a little impatience and weariness with the common handiwork of the journeymen and apprentices, however much he may approve their industry or sympathize with the emotion which, in their degree, they experienced and attempt to express." Melville, to be blunt, "must take his place with the herd of recent versifiers." Furthermore, it "was Melville's bad luck that his 'Shiloh: A Requiem' would almost inevitably suggest, by contrast, the very striking poem of Mr. Forceythe Wilson's, of which a great part of the scene is laid on the battle-field of Shiloh, called 'The Old Sergeant.'" The reviewer could hardly stop praising this great poem, which, if his memory served, had first appeared in mid-war in the Louisville *Journal*. The Philadelphia *Inquirer* concluded that as "a singer of soldierly deeds" Melville was "preferable even to Brownell; possessing all the vivid powers of that warrior poet, without his fault of detailing minutely all the accessories of an action." This was Henry Howard Brownell, whose *Lyrics of a Day* (1864) had been followed by *War-Lyrics and Other Poems* (1866). On September 8 the Boston *Commercial Bulletin* elaborated a contrast: "Some of the battle-pieces remind one of Brownell, but the resemblance goes not beyond the quality of brusqueness. With more polish and less freedom than Brownell, Mr. Melville writes what he thinks rather than what he feels."

The New York *National Quarterly Review* looked abroad for cruelly limited comparisons: "Lee in the Capitol" was "nearly, if not quite, as long as Campbell's 'Hohenlinden,' or Goldsmith's 'Traveller;' but we cannot point out any further resemblance." The *Albion* also made comparisons: "We read his [Melville's] songs, if we may call them such, and wonder while we read, first, that the events should have presented themselves to his mind in the shape that they did; and, second, that, with his genius, he has not succeeded in placing us more *en rapport* with them. Mr. Brownell has this last power in many of his patriotic pieces, while Mr. Walter Whitman, the most shapeless of all our versifiers, possesses it in a remarkable degree. We fail, however, to sympathize with the mass of Mr. Melville's poems, which are scarcely intelligible, as he has handled them." The "Yea and Nay" of the end of "The Conflict of Convictions" was "Emerson at second-hand." The San Francisco *Evening Bulletin* knew Melville's worth as a poet: "The author delights in grotesque metaphors and strained similes, and uses strange phrases to express the most simple ideas. We can pardon barbarism of style in men like Carlyle or Emerson, who are original thinkers; but when Herman Melville affects the obscurely-profound and dislocates the parts of speech from sheer contempt of good English, we confess it makes our gorge rise." Greeley's *Tribune* ignored *Battle-Pieces* (except for a Harper publication notice ["this day," August 24] and a later advertisement), but on October 4 it lavished more than two columns on James A. Dorgan's *Studies* under the heading "A New Poet": "Of all the so-called young poets of America, we are much mistaken if he is not quite the best that has appeared since the death of Poe." The Portland *Transcript* made a comparison to the writer who may most have warranted Melville in some of his stylistic experiments: "Though the lines have not a very melodious flow, they are not lacking in spirit and vigor, and some of the descriptive pieces remind one of Browning in his more intelligible mood."

The New York *Independent* was vicious, not least in seeming to praise the early works it had condemned when they were published: "The odorous South winds which blew through Mr. Herman Melville's earlier books might have filled the sails of his graceful bark, and wafted him to Cathay, for all the world has known of him of late. It seems, however, that he has been coquetting with the Muse—and we say advisedly, coquetting—for the majestic presence has not possessed and enthralled him. It is rather as if he were the humble 'meejum' alternately influenced by the overmastering personalities of Walt. Whitman, Dante, Emerson, Brownell, and Mother Goose." (The odd "meejum" is an archly contemptuous spelling of

"medium," the conduit of spirits, from the current excitement over "spir-
itualism.") The *Independent* continued scathingly: "He coins words and
phrases with the prodigality of Elizabeth Browning, and without her fine
fitness." Even "Sheridan at Cedar Creek," which had received some praise
when printed in *Harper's,* seemed "founded on the two familiar poems of
an earlier writer: one beginning 'Ride a black horse to Banbury Cross, to
see an old woman,' etc., etc.; the other 'Shoe the old horse, and shoe the old
mare, but let the little colt go bare.'" Melville may have ruined the subject
of "Sheridan's Ride" for any real poet, and it was certain that he had "*not*
written" the poem the subject deserved. "'A Canticle significant of the
national exaltation of enthusiasm at the close of the war' out-Whitmans
Whitman," the *Independent* continued, before offering strange mitigation,
recognizing "the real power which underlies his vagaries, and careless-
nesses, and crudities." There were "poetic hints enough" "to set up half
a dozen popular poets in life-long business," and there were even "lines
strong as Robert Browning, pictures vivid as life, phrases clear-cut as
Emerson." The conclusion was downright charitable: "when a man needs
to eliminate, rather than to strengthen, there is hope for him."

The privilege of driving the last nail into the coffin devolved upon
young William Dean Howells, in the February 1867 *Atlantic Monthly*
(as the most respected American monthly, the worst possible place for
a grudging review). Howells had kept well informed of the actualities
of the war from his charming villa in Venice, suffering there only from
the occasional severe affront to his aesthetic sensibilities, as when he sur-
veyed disdainfully the green drapery marble in the Jesuit church which
Melville had so admired. Now, home in a peacetime United States, he
pronounced the events and characters in Melville's poems ghostlike rather
than realistic:

> Mr. Melville's work possesses the negative virtues of originality in such
> degree that it not only reminds you of no poetry you have read, but of no
> life you have known. Is it possible—you ask yourself, after running over
> all these celebrative, inscriptive, and memorial verses—that there has really
> been a great war, with battles fought by men and bewailed by women? Or
> is it only that Mr. Melville's inner consciousness has been perturbed, and
> filled with the phantasms of enlistments, marches, fights in the air, paren-
> thetic bulletin-boards, and tortured humanity shedding, not words and
> blood, but words alone?

With "certain moods or abstractions of the common mind during the
war," Melville's faculty was "well fitted to deal," but even when he treated
events "realistically" the events "seem to have presented themselves as

dreams," and "at last they remain vagaries, and are none the more substantial because they have a modern speech and motion." Melville's "quality of remoteness" was heroic but it separated "our weak human feelings" from his subjects "by trackless distances"; the description of the death of General Nathaniel Lyon's horse was undeniably noble but the passage was "as far off from us" as any of the poetry of Ossian's. The curious aspect to this specific criticism is that Howells identified quite precisely what Melville, following Wordsworth's dictum, had attempted to do, but never thought that he might have intended doing it. One passage he praised without reservation: "We have never seen anywhere so true and beautiful a picture as the following of that sublime and thrilling sight,—a great body of soldiers marching:—'The bladed guns are gleaming—/Drift in lengthened trim,/Files on files for hazy miles/Nebulously dim.'" By late January 1867, these words were read not just by Bostonians but New Yorkers and literate people all over the country.

JOHN MARR. Of the other books and poems in the present volume, only one review is known—of *John Marr* in the New York *Mail and Express,* November 20, 1888.

> The reputation of no American writer stood higher forty years ago than that of Herman Melville. Like his predecessor, Richard Henry Dana Jr., he went to sea before the mast, starting, if we have not forgotten, from Nantucket or New Bedford on a whaler. Familiar from boyhood with such eminent writers of sea stories as Smollett and Marryat, he adventured into strange seas in "Omoo" and "Typee," which were speedily followed by "Mardi," a not very skillful allegory, and "Moby Dick," which is probably his greatest work. He was the peer of Hawthorne in popular estimation, and was by many considered his superior. His later writings were not up to the same high level. With all his defects, however, Mr. Melville is a man of unquestionable talent, and of considerable genius. He is a poet also, but his verse is marked by the same untrained imagination which distinguishes his prose. He is the author of the second best cavalry poem in the English language, the first being Browning's "How They Brought the Good News from Ghent to Aix." His prose is characterized by a vein of true poetical feeling, as elemental as the objects to which it is directed. Nothing finer than his unrhymed poems exists outside of the sea lyrics of Campbell. The present text of these observations is to be found in the little volume, "John Marr, and Other Sailors," of which only a limited edition is published, and which contains about twenty poems of varying degrees of merit, but all with the briny flavor that should belong to songs of the sea.

The passage has been attributed to Richard H. Stoddard, the "literary editor" of the *Mail and Express* (Sealts 1971).

Note on Printing and
Publishing History

THE STORY OF the production of Melville's three printed collections of short poems cannot be told in the detail one would wish because crucial archival documents from the printing and publishing firms involved are not known to have survived. No contract for *Battle-Pieces* has been discovered, for example, and no printing bills for *John Marr* and *Timoleon* have surfaced. But even if such documents were known, or become available in the future, the account would probably not be very different in its general outline from what can now be constructed: for *Battle-Pieces,* the contractual arrangements can be inferred from the publisher's statements of account to Melville; for the other two books, since in those cases Melville simply paid a printer to produce a small edition for private distribution, there were no contractual details to be settled regarding payment, review copies, and the like. And although no manuscripts or proofs are known for *Battle-Pieces,* there are more production documents available for the other two books (in the form of printer's-copy manuscripts for both and proofs for *John Marr*) than for any other of Melville's books. (The only comparable survivals are the printer's-copy manuscripts of his contributions to the *Literary World.*) *John Marr,* in fact, offers a demonstration, in a detail impossible for Melville's other books, of precisely how his manuscript was handled in the printing shop and how he and the printer dealt with the proofs.

BATTLE-PIECES

THE REASONS BEHIND Melville's choice of Harper & Brothers for *Battle-Pieces* are not known; indeed, that choice seems surprising. Although the Harpers published Melville's first seven books,[1] the next three to be published were brought out by other firms (*Israel Potter* by Putnam, *The Piazza Tales* and *The Confidence-Man* by Dix & Edwards). Thus the Harpers had not been Melville's publisher since 1852; and in 1860, when Melville hoped to publish a collection of his poems, he explicitly told his brother Allan not to select the Harpers.[2] By late 1865 his attitude had clearly changed, presumably for reasons other than a growing nostalgia for his "old imprint" (as his wife called it in 1891).[3] In the second volume of his *Herman Melville* (p. 592), Hershel Parker has suggested two possibilities: that Melville's finally being free of debt to the Harpers, for the first time in seventeen years, might have made him feel less awkward about approaching them; or that perhaps Melville had come to be well disposed toward the firm as a result of friendly treatment by William H. Demarest, the Harpers' cashier-bookkeeper, or Alfred Hudson Guernsey, the editor of *Harper's New Monthly Magazine*.[4]

1. They took over the American publication of *Typee* from Wiley & Putnam in 1849 and were the original American publishers of his next six books (from *Omoo* through *Pierre*).

2. In his "Memoranda for Allan concerning the publication of my verses" (May 22, 1860, a few days before beginning his voyage on the *Meteor* with his brother Thomas), the second item stated, "Don't have the Harpers. — I should like the Appletons or Scribner". (The proposed volume, to be called simply "Poems," was indeed offered to Scribner and also to Rudd & Carleton, both of which rejected it.) In the first item of his "Memoranda," concerning financial arrangements, he said, "half-profits after expenses are paid will content me"—which was the system under which *Battle-Pieces* was later to be published by the Harpers. See the Northwestern-Newberry *Correspondence* volume, p. 343. Unless otherwise specified, all quotations of letters to or from Melville are from this volume; citations are by date.

3. In her letter of December 14, 1891, to Harper & Brothers, consenting to the cancellation of all Harper contracts for Melville's works (Contract Book 7, p. 309, in the Harper archives at the Columbia University Rare Book and Manuscript Library). Referring to her arrangements for new editions of some of Melville's works, she said, "I have already expressed to you in my letters and through Mr. Phelps, my regret that your house was not to bring out the volumes, and that the old imprint was not to be upon them." This nostalgic comment, coming a quarter-century after Melville's renewed association with the Harpers for *Battle-Pieces,* may perhaps reflect Melville's changed feelings toward the firm in his later years.

4. Full bibliographical information for any source not provided with it in this NOTE is given in the comprehensive list of WORKS CITED at the end of the volume.

There is no doubt that Melville had dealings with Guernsey, for five of his Civil War poems were published in *Harper's* between February and July 1866 ("The March to the Sea" in February, "The Cumberland" in March, "Philip"—later entitled "Sheridan at Cedar Creek"—in April, "Chattanooga" in June, and "Gettysburg" in July). And Guernsey was indeed well disposed toward Melville, as is indicated by a memorandum that he addressed to the Harper management in late May, a copy of which was forwarded to Melville on May 31: "From Mr. Melville's Volume, besides 'The March to the Sea,' settled for, have been used in the Magazine. / 'The Cumberland' / 'Philip' / 'Chattanooga' / 'Gettysburg' (to appear in the July No.) / I think you ought to agree with Mr Melville what should be paid for these poems for this use in the Magazine, apart from their use in the volume. They will make, one with another, a half page each of the Magazine."[5] Melville wrote on this memorandum, "I never got." The Harper firm's unwillingness to pay for any of the poems except the first one may reflect the view that the publication of these poems in the magazine would serve to stimulate sales of *Battle-Pieces* and that there was no obligation to compensate Melville for them in any other way (perhaps a reasonable position, given the magazine's circulation of 112,000, except that the poems were published anonymously in the magazine).

But the fact that the first poem was paid for raises the question whether it was accepted for the magazine before an agreement to publish the book had been reached. If Guernsey's cordiality did in fact play a role in causing Melville to settle on offering the book to the Harpers, then at least the first poem for the magazine would have been submitted before a book proposal (and perhaps Guernsey even suggested that the book be sent to his firm). The production schedule of the magazine is made clear in a long article on "Making the Magazine" that appeared in the December 1865 issue—that is, at nearly the time when Melville's renewed contact with the Harpers was beginning. This article stated that it took a month to print each issue and that each one had to be ready for mailing to California (the most distant American destination) by the 15th of the month preceding the month stated on the issue.[6] Because the first of Melville's poems in *Harper's* appeared in the February 1866 issue, it had to be in

5. This memorandum survives among Melville's papers at Harvard. The "half page each" refers to the poems not yet paid for; the one that had been "settled" covered a two-page spread in the magazine.

6. "Making the Magazine," *Harper's New Monthly Magazine* 32 (1865–66): 1–31. Comments on the length of time taken for printing appear on pp. 15 and 23; those on the date of mailing to California are on p. 21.

Guernsey's hands by December 15, 1865, at the latest. But it was probably there several weeks earlier, since Guernsey would have been assembling the contents for the February issue during that time.

Whether the idea of publishing some Civil War poems in *Harper's* was Melville's (before or after proposing a book to the same firm) or whether the magazine publication was a by-product of a book agreement is not known. Conceivably Melville could have sent a book proposal or manuscript to the Harpers in October or November 1865, and the publication of poems in the magazine followed from that, beginning about as promptly as could be managed. If the payment for the February poem and the nonpayment for the March poem are significant, it is possible that a book agreement was reached in January or February (whether the submission of the book proposal or manuscript came before or after Guernsey's acceptance of the first poem). Six years earlier, one of Melville's instructions to Allan regarding his proposed volume of poems had been, "Don't have . . . any extracts published previous to publication of book" (May 22, 1860). This attitude toward advance excerpts, if Melville still held it in 1866,[7] could be used to argue that he did not send a book proposal prior to submitting the poems (or the first one, at least) to the magazine. But it is hard to believe that the nonpayment for the last four magazine pieces was not in some way connected to the book publication; perhaps some months elapsed between the submission of a book proposal or manuscript and a publication contract, and payment was withheld pending the outcome, on the grounds that no payment was to follow if the book was to be published. At any rate, a contract had been signed before the end of May, as Guernsey's memorandum makes clear. It may well have been signed long before that, but one is bound to wonder whether the memorandum might have been prompted by the completion of the agreement (though other explanations for the timing of it are possible, such as the imminent publication of the last poem or an inquiry from Melville).

---

7. An indication that he might still have held it is the fact that he did not include in *Battle-Pieces* a Civil War poem that he had published in April 1864: "Inscription For the Slain At Fredericksburgh" was reproduced in facsimile from his manuscript in *Autograph Leaves of Our Country's Authors,* ed. John Pendleton Kennedy and Alexander Bliss (Baltimore: Cushings & Bailey, 1864). (If Melville had included it in *Battle-Pieces,* he would have had the opportunity to print his intended version—with "Dead" for "Slain" in the title and a few other small differences—rather than the "uncorrected draught" that got published because he had mistakenly sent it to Bliss, as he explained in his letter to Bliss on March 22, 1864, enclosing the correct version.) On the other hand, he may have left this poem out of *Battle-Pieces* because it is echoed in the last stanza of "Chattanooga."

Whatever the date of the contract, the chief provision of that now missing document[8] is clear: *Battle-Pieces* was to be published on the half-profits-after-expenses system, like all of Melville's Harper books except *Typee* and *Pierre* (which were published on a per-copy royalty—"copyright"—basis). This fact is evident from the Harpers' periodic statements of account rendered to Melville, which place *Battle-Pieces* with Melville's other half-profits books, in an expense-and-income tally that was separate from his personal cash account, where any royalties from *Typee* and *Pierre* were reported. The way this double system worked was that all production expenses incurred in a given accounting period for any of the half-profits books were added together; then that total was subtracted from the total of all income received from the sale of the half-profits books (less a 5 percent "guaranty" for the publisher). If the result was positive, the profits were divided in half, and the half-profit figure was moved to Melville's personal current cash (or "copyright") account. There it joined any royalties from *Typee* and *Pierre*, and from that total were deducted any debits for books purchased by Melville or money borrowed by him; the result, if positive, was due Melville,[9] or, if negative, was owed by him. If, however, the half-profits account showed a deficit, that figure would simply be carried forward to the next accounting period and had no bearing on the figures in the personal cash account, since the author was not expected to cover deficits but only to share in profits.

The statement of February 13, 1868—the first one after the production costs of *Battle-Pieces* had been incurred—shows that those costs, plus the expenses of a new printing of *White-Jacket* and of binding some of the unbound sheets of *Omoo* and *Moby-Dick,* amounted to $1,012.14, whereas the income from sales of *Omoo, Redburn, White-Jacket, Moby-Dick,* and *Battle-Pieces* came only to $708.64. After the 5 percent guaranty was deducted from the sales figure, the deficit was $338.93. (This figure did not affect Melville's personal account, which showed that the cost of the books he had purchased—eleven copies of *Battle-Pieces*—almost precisely equaled his royalty from *Typee* and *Pierre* during that period.) By the time

8. It is not only missing from Melville's own set of his contracts (now at Harvard), but it is also not present in the Harper archive at Columbia University, either as an original or as a copy in Contract Book 1, where the contracts for Melville's other seven Harper books are copied. This coincidence makes one wonder whether it ever existed; yet one cannot conceive of the Harpers' publishing a book on the half-profits system without some kind of written agreement, and one must assume that there was a contract.

9. Money due Melville on the copyright account was not paid immediately if there was a deficit in the half-profits account; instead it was carried forward to the next statement. But it was never applied to the reduction of the deficit.

of the next statement, on November 2, 1870, the deficit had been reduced to $187.71. The next account, on June 17, 1872, showed a larger deficit, $210.55, as a result of new printing and binding costs for some of Melville's other books. The deficits continued—$52.38 on February 12, 1875, and $84.12 on August 1, 1876—until the account of February 9, 1878, which showed a positive figure of $11.83. From that statement on, through the three remaining statements (the last being March 4, 1887), the half-profits account showed a profit, and Melville was duly paid his share.[10]

Although the sales of *Battle-Pieces* never came close to covering the expenses of its production (as shown by the figures to be discussed below), the deficit thus created was eventually offset by the sales of Melville's other books. Even if it had not been, Melville would not have been expected to pay. Of course, there was an obvious advantage to the publisher in pooling the cost and sales figures for all the half-profits books, since revenue that would otherwise have gone to Melville (from sales of earlier books that had passed their break-even point) could be used to defray the cost of *Battle-Pieces*. In that sense, Melville was helping to pay for *Battle-Pieces,* through forgone income, but only up to half the cost—since total sales income (less the 5 percent guaranty) was applied to the manufacturing costs, whereas only half of it would have come to Melville in any case. There was nothing unusual in this arrangement: it was the way all of Melville's half-profits books had been reported in the Harpers' statements since the sixth one on April 29, 1851.[11]

10. Figures in the Harper statements of account to Melville, now at Harvard, catalogued as MS Am 188 (456) through 188 (497), are summarized in G. Thomas Tanselle's "The Sales of Melville's Books"—where the figures are recalculated to reflect income and expense for each title individually rather than as the pooled results presented in the actual statements.

11. Eugene Exman, speaking of *Battle-Pieces* in *The House of Harper,* states, "Melville underwrote the costs of a 1,260-copy edition, of which 300 copies went to reviewers" (p. 98). This statement has sometimes been given more credence than it deserves, on the assumption that Exman, who served as an executive in the Harper firm from 1928 to 1965, had access to documents that have not become generally available. And of course it was not uncommon in the nineteenth century for major publishers to publish books on behalf of authors who were prepared to pay the production costs. (*Clarel* is itself an example, published by Putnam, a major firm, and largely paid for by Melville's uncle Peter Gansevoort.) Exman's source for his statement is unknown, despite his effort to record his sources. In his "Acknowledgments and Credits" (p. 303), he says that he is placing annotated copies of his book in the Pierpont Morgan Library and the library of the R. R. Bowker Company. The Morgan copy has laid into it a typewritten set of notes for specific statements, but the note on the sentence in question says only "Letter from Demarest to Melville, *Houghton.*" The Demarest letter in Houghton Library at Harvard (quoted below) does indeed give the figures Exman cites, but it says nothing about

Besides the provision for half-profits, Melville's Harper contracts normally specified the number of review copies to be sent out. The *Battle-Pieces* contract may have named 300, the number Demarest gave as an approximate figure in late 1866, though the number actually sent was 263 (according to the Harper statement of February 13, 1868)—a considerably larger number than for any of Melville's earlier Harper books (the highest being 169 for *Moby-Dick,* but Dix & Edwards gave away 260 for *The Piazza Tales*). Another standard element of Melville's Harper contracts was to specify that the type would be plated and that after seven years Melville was free to buy the plates at a discount; there is no reason to think that this provision would not also have been present in the *Battle-Pieces* contract, since there is no doubt that the book was indeed plated (as the Harper account shows). The publisher was also free to end the agreement after seven years and to dispose of any copies of the book remaining on hand. And the contract probably stated, as was usual, that the copyright was to be Melville's and that the Harpers had exclusive rights to publication in the United States. Among the other items sometimes covered in the contracts was a provision for agreeing on the retail prices of copies bound in cloth and in paper; *Battle-Pieces* was bound only in cloth, and this point, as well as the price of $1.75, may have been specified in the contract. The number of copies to be printed was not usually mentioned, but possibly the figure of 1,260 copies was there (a figure much smaller than the printing size of Melville's other Harper books, which—except for *Pierre,* at 2,310—ranged from 3,000 to 4,500). One item that would not have been present was a reference to an extra set of proofs for dispatch to England, since there was no thought of publication abroad (Melville's memorandum to Allan about his proposed 1860 volume of poems had said, "Don't take any measures, or make inquiries as to expediency of an English edition simultaneous with the American").

With a contract for *Battle-Pieces* signed by late May 1866 (if not considerably earlier), the Harper firm was free to begin typesetting, assuming there was an appropriate manuscript in hand. No doubt Melville had sent the Harpers a substantial manuscript (containing more than the five poems for the magazine) at some point before a contract was signed; but

---

financial arrangements. If Exman meant only that Melville contributed toward the cost of *Battle-Pieces* through forgone income from the sales of his books, his statement would not be wrong. But the meaning that most people would take from it—that Melville laid out cash to cover the cost of producing *Battle-Pieces*—is unquestionably incorrect. (The other book of Exman's on the history of the firm—*The Brothers Harper* [New York: Harper, 1965]—contains nothing relevant to the present point.)

a near-final manuscript, in the form of his wife's transcription, may not have reached the publisher until July,[12] and the typesetting may not have begun until mid-July or later.[13] (No production documents that might shed light on the date—such as the printer's-copy manuscript or proofs— are known to survive.)[14] Whenever typesetting began, the whole process of bookmaking—including proofreading, correcting the type, electro- typing, printing the sheets, and binding the sewn gatherings—was not completed until sometime after July 24 because the Harpers' statement of that date to Melville reported no manufacturing costs. (The proofread- ing stage may have been completed before Melville went to Gansevoort, New York, on July 21, but it is also possible that he took the proofs, or some of them, with him.) A printed title-page was deposited for copyright purposes at the District Court for the Southern District of New York on

12. See Amy Puett, "Melville's Wife," pp. 126–27. The fair copy that went to the pub- lisher may or may not have included revised magazine clippings of the poems published in *Harper's* rather than transcriptions of them. (But the tear-leaves from *Harper's* now at Harvard, *AC85.M4977.Lz99, sewn in two packets and annotated in pencil by Melville's wife—with the publication month and year of each, Melville's name, and the fact that they were included in *Battle-Pieces*—but not marked in any other way, clearly were not part of a printer's-copy manuscript but rather part of her assemblage of tear-leaves of most of Melville's periodical publications, neatly laid into a commercially produced binder manu- factured in Pittsfield, with an added gold title on the front: "MAGAZINE STORIES/ BY/HERMAN MELVILLE.")

13. Allan Melville's letter of July 20 to his cousin Henry Gansevoort (in the Gan- sevoort-Lansing Collection of the New York Public Library) says that the book is "in press shortly to appear"; but of course the phrase "in press" was then (and is now) com- monly used to mean "going through the publishing process" and not literally "being printed."

14. The red-buckram custom-bound copy of *Battle-Pieces* at Harvard (Copy C)— *AC85.M4977.866b(C)—has the following note in Melville's wife's hand, on the blank binder's leaf following the front free endpaper: "'Revised' sheets—with Herman's cor- rections—". These "sheets" are clearly not proofs, for the leaves are printed on both sides, and they seem identical to the published book (though the leaf height is slightly less, to be accounted for by the binder's trimming). Obviously they came from the regular print run and were simply a set of unbound sheets, either sent by the publisher in advance of binding or ordered by Melville (from the large stock of unbound sheets the publisher had on hand) for his use in recording revisions (he did in fact enter many post-publication revisions on them). That Melville's wife called them "'Revised' sheets" is not surprising, since they were in the form of "sheets" (as the printer would have called the unbound gatherings), and they were "revised" because they incorporated the revisions that had been made on the proofs. (Melville's wife had earlier written, on the recto of the next binder's leaf, a note—now erased but visible—to the binder: "New Fly leaves may be put/on here—and two added at/the end—/Muslin or Buckram binding—/Edges to be trimmed". Obviously the binder did not supply new leaves.)

July 28, but that fact tells one nothing about what stage the bookmaking process had reached by then. The law required only that a title page be deposited before publication; but the existence of a printed title page does not necessarily mean that typesetting of the text of a book was under way, for publishers often set a title page earlier for copyright purposes. One can be sure, however, that the production of *Battle-Pieces* was completed before August 17, the date on which a copyright-deposit copy was received at the District Court. (The other required deposit copy, for the Library of Congress, was received there on August 20.) The official publication date, as set by the publisher, was August 23.[15]

If the production process took place during the last part of July and the first half of August, there was probably time for Melville to make additions to the book through late July, and possibly even early August. At least one poem, "Lee in the Capitol," was probably added after a proposed book manuscript was originally sent to the publisher: the poem was based on Lee's Congressional testimony of February 17, which was not published in the newspapers until the end of March, and the poem is dated in print "April, 1866." If it had been sent to the Harpers in April or May (or even June or early July), it would have created no production problem because it would have become part of the book manuscript before any typesetting had begun. (Possibly "A Meditation," the poem that follows it as the last poem in the published volume, was also sent at this time.) Two other parts of the book, however, may have been added still later: the short untitled preface and the prose "Supplement" that ends the book. The preface, which seems obviously to have been written after the arrangement of the poems had been determined (they "naturally fall into the order assumed," he says), could nevertheless have been a part of the book manuscript as first submitted; but it could equally well have come later, if Melville had subsequently decided that the book, especially with a prose essay at the end, needed some sort of introductory comment.

As for the "Supplement," Melville dates it as "more than a year since the memorable surrender"—thus later than April 9, 1866. He is known to have consulted two books in the summer of 1866 that he may have expected to find useful in writing it. On June 30 he visited the Astor

---

15. So noted by Demarest on p. 287 of his handwritten record of Harper publications (the "Demarest Catalogue"), now in the Columbia University Rare Book and Manuscript Library. The two copyright deposit copies were clearly sent in very promptly, since the law required only that one copy go to the Library of Congress within one month of publication and that another copy go to the District Court within three months of publication.

Library to use L. E. Chittenden's *A Report of the Debates and Proceedings in the Secret Sessions of the Conference Convention, for Proposing Amendments to the Constitution of the United States* (New York: Appleton, 1864), and on July 11 he bought from the Harpers a copy of John W. Draper's *Thoughts on the Future Civil Policy of America* (New York: Harper, 1865). Stanton Garner, in *The Civil War World of Herman Melville* (pp. 433–39), speculates that Melville may not have formed the idea of writing the "Supplement" until during his visit with his mother at the family place in Gansevoort, New York, beginning on July 21, when he would have heard his brother-in-law John Hoadley's strong opinions about punishing the South. If this encounter caused him to feel the necessity of a prose essay to emphasize his tolerationist views (already implicit in the last two poems), he could have written it, Garner argues, during his stay in Gansevoort (for he did not accompany the others on an excursion to Lake George on July 23–25); and he could have delivered it to the Harper office when he went to New York on August 6–7.

The physical evidence in the book as published gives no obvious indication that either the preface or the "Supplement" was, or might easily have been, added in the latest stages of bookmaking, after the rest of the book had been printed. The preface is not on a leaf that is stuck in (either as an additional leaf or as a replacement for an excised one), and the "Supplement" does not constitute a separate gathering. The preface leaf is an integral part of the first gathering, which consists of a sheet of paper folded to form twelve leaves that include, besides the preliminaries, the texts of the first five poems. Similarly, the beginning of the "Supplement" (its section-title leaf and first six pages of text) forms the last four leaves of the twelve-leaf gathering L, the first eight leaves of which contain the last poem of the volume, "A Meditation," and the section of "Notes"; and the remaining eight pages of the "Supplement" form a four-leaf gathering M. Without the "Supplement," gathering L would have consisted of eight leaves, and if the "Supplement" had been added after L was printed, it would have formed its own eight-leaf gathering M. What this evidence allows one to say with certainty is that the preface was on the press at the same time as the first five poems (because they were all printed on the same sheet of paper) and that part of the "Supplement" was on the press at the same time as "A Meditation" and the "Notes" (because they, too, shared the same sheet of paper).

The possibility nevertheless remains that either the preface or the "Supplement," or both, was set in type at a late stage—just not so late as to leave evidence in the finished book. The preface could even have been set in type after everything else, as long as the printing of sheet A had not begun. But because the preface as published uses a whole leaf (with the text on the recto and with a blank verso), this possibility would seem to depend on the prior existence of another planned leaf (such as a half-title preceding the title leaf, or a fly-title or section-title preceding the first poem) that could be replaced by the preface leaf; if there had been, it would have been no problem to rearrange the type-pages in the forme to accommodate a leaf that was to go in a different position. The fact that there is no irregularity in the pagination of the preliminaries in *Battle-Pieces*—that is, the unnumbered pages (excluding the binder's leaves) total the proper number to fit with the first numbered page—is significant here, for the pagination would have been established earlier (at this period printers did not send galley proofs to authors but instead divided the type into pages immediately after setting it or after an in-house proofreading).[16]

The "Supplement," coming at the end of the book, would have been the last part of the text to be set in any event. But it might have been a separate typesetting job (not continuous with the rest) if it had been sent or delivered to the publisher so late that the typesetting of the rest of the text had been completed. In that case, it could have been set during the time when Melville was proofreading the body of the text (and the entry for the "Supplement" in the table of contents could have been added at the proof stage). Alternatively, he might have had the proofs in hand before he wrote it and might have given the manuscript of it to the publisher when he returned the proofs. It is possible to read the opening paragraph as reflecting some constraint as to where the essay could be placed and a rationalization for its position at the end: "Were I fastidiously anxious for the symmetry of this book, it would close with the notes. But the times are such that patriotism—not free from solicitude—urges a claim overriding all literary scruples." If the essay had been written after the typesetting of the rest of the book was under way, or finished, the essay could not

---

16. At the time of *Battle-Pieces,* galley proofs, which had not been used for book work earlier, began to be used by some American printers for in-house proofreading, before dividing the composed type into pages and sending page proofs to authors. It was not until a decade or so later that galley proofs for authors came into use in book work, and they did not become routine until late in the century. That the Harper firm in 1855 took proofs only after type was made up in pages is indicated in Jacob Abbott's *The Harper Establishment,* pp. 67, 69–71. See also John Bush Jones, "Galley Proofs in America: A Historical Survey." Galley proofs were used for newspaper and magazine work earlier than for book work; the 1865 article on "Making the Magazine" (see note 6 above) mentions the use of galley proofs both for in-house proofs and for author's proofs, but it also says, "Quite as often the proof is not taken until the matter has been 'made up' into pages" (p. 9).

have been made to fit into the already established pagination at the begin-
ning of the book.[17] A date as late as August 7 or 8 for the completion of
the typesetting and proofreading of the "Supplement" would have left (if
everything else had already been proofread) ten days at most for electro-
typing, printing, and binding—a short time, but perhaps not impossibly
short.[18] These observations obviously do not prove that the preface or the
"Supplement" was set in type at an unusually late stage, but they show
that either could have been.

The finished book, as published under the title *Battle-Pieces and Aspects
of the War* on August 23 at $1.75, consists of 272 pages (containing 72
poems plus the notes and "Supplement"), printed on white wove paper,
with a leaf size of 7⁷⁄₁₆ by 4⅞ inches; it is made up of eleven gatherings of
twelve leaves each and a final four-leaf gathering. The book begins (after
a title page that prints the two parts of the title in equally large capitals)
with an eight-line dedication to the memory of the war dead, followed by
the preface and the table of contents. The structure of the book's contents,
as reflected in the typographic layout (both of the text and of the table
of contents), is worth noting because of Melville's interest in such mat-
ters, as demonstrated by his comments and markings on the documents
that survive for *John Marr* and *Timoleon* (and in his 1860 memorandum,

17. The arabic numbering could have been made to start with "1" rather than con-
tinuing from the roman sequence used in the table of contents, but only ten pages would
have been available; and the "Supplement," which occupies fourteen as printed, could not
have fit without being set in smaller type. In any case, Melville would not have known
how many pages the essay would fill in type and probably would not have imagined that
a position at the beginning was possible, even if that had been his preference.

18. If the proofs had been sent in batches and the electrotyping performed as the
correction of each batch was completed, the time would seem less tight; but in that case
Melville would have had to know that he was going to add the "Supplement" at the time
the first batch went back in order to get the "Supplement" listed in the table of con-
tents (or else the publisher would have had the expense of making a second plate). (The
assumption here is that the electrotyping would have begun with the beginning of the
book, for there would have been no reason in this case, as there was with some books, to
leave the preliminaries for later.)

If there were evidence of bound copies having been available much before August 17
(when the deposit copy was received at the District Court), the possibility of such a late
date for the "Supplement" would be weakened; but the presumably early presentation
copies so far examined are either undated (as is the copy Melville inscribed to his mother,
now in the Barrett Collection at the University of Virginia) or are dated only as "Aug." or
"August", without a specific date (as in the copy sent by the publisher to Evert Duyckinck
or in Melville's presentation copy to his sister Helen, now in the Duyckinck Collection
and the Berg Collection, respectively, of the New York Public Library, or in the copies
Melville presented to his wife and his mother-in-law, now at Harvard).

asking Allan among other things to make sure that the numbered sections of his proposed book of poems were separated in print by leaves bearing the section numbers). There is no way to know what instructions about section-titles, indicating major divisions of *Battle-Pieces*, were present in the printer's-copy manuscript, or how he wished them to be reflected in the table of contents. But the results as published are inconsistent, perhaps because it was impractical to make changes in proof that would affect pagination—though there was no reason that the table of contents could not have been made to match.

The first oddity is that the opening poem, "The Portent," is not listed in the table of contents, and the poem itself is on a leaf with a blank verso, whereas elsewhere in the book versos contain text, except when they precede section-titles—raising the possibility that the poem was a late addition, replacing a fly-title, which might have been expected here in the absence of the book title at the head of the first page of text (though the blank verso—like the italics in which the whole poem is printed—does serve to set the poem off as introductory and perhaps thus furthers Melville's intention, whenever the poem was put in place). Next, the only centered and capitalized subheading in the table of contents is for "Verses Inscriptive and Memorial," which in the text forms a section-title leaf with a blank verso. But in the text there are five other section-titles not so treated in the table of contents (that is, they have the same left margin as all the other titles and are followed at the right margin with page numbers): "The Scout toward Aldie," "Lee in the Capitol," "A Meditation," "Notes," and "Supplement." Of these, the first, fourth, and fifth are printed in large and small italic capitals, rather than ordinary upper- and lower-case italics like all the other titles. If the section-titles reflect Melville's wishes, as seems probable, the table of contents obscures the organization thus established by making "The Scout toward Aldie" appear to be parallel with "Notes" and "Supplement" and the two intervening poems to be subordinate to it.[19]

These typographical anomalies in the table of contents—as well as the omission in it of the last word of "Battle of Stone River, Tennessee" and the few places in it where the punctuation and capitalization do not agree with those in the titles at the heads of the poems—could be indica-

---

19. The fact that the last three section-titles are set with more widely spaced capitals than the others does not necessarily imply anything about timing and may only mean that a different compositor set them. But of course it could also mean that "A Meditation" and "Notes" had not been set at the time the "Supplement" arrived (if indeed it was later) and that all three were set at the same time.

tions that the compositor was setting from a manuscript table of contents (whether supplied by Melville or not), but they could also be oversights in making up the table of contents directly from the titles at the heads of the poems in the proofs. One feature of the printed table of contents, however, that seems more likely to reflect authorial instruction than compositorial decision is the inclusion of full titles (including subtitles) for the poems in the section of "Verses Inscriptive and Memorial" but not for the other poems (except the second "Stonewall Jackson" poem, presumably to distinguish it from the first).

Following the usual practice, the book was bound in various cloths and colors, so that customers in bookstores had a choice: it was available in smooth or pebbly cloth, and in dark green, brown, purple, purplish blue, or reddish orange. The spine is stamped in gold with the title, Melville's name, a decoration, and the publisher's name; the covers have beveled edges and a blind-stamped circular Harper monogram ("HB") in their centers; and the endpapers are of brown coated paper. The cost of producing the book amounted to $893.65: setting and electrotyping came to $411.60; the paper for an edition of 1,260 copies cost $220.80; the printing of that number of copies was another $60; and the binding of 805 copies was $201.25 (it was customary not to bind a whole edition at once, in case demand never reached that level).

The Harpers included *Battle-Pieces* in their announcement of new publications sent to newspapers and magazines: it was mentioned with other Harper books in "The Book World" column of the New York *Herald* on August 12, where the columnist could not refrain from saying that "for ten years the public has wondered what has become of Melville." And the publisher gave the book a display advertisement in the September 15 issue of *Harper's Weekly,* calling attention to its "Beveled Edges" and quoting favorable comments from the New York *Times.* The Harpers also included it for several months in the notices of the firm's "New Books" printed on the inside back cover of issues of *Harper's New Monthly Magazine.* That some copies had been exported for sale in England is shown by *Trübner's American and Oriental Literary Record* for October 1, where the book was listed at nine shillings, and by Trübner's advertisement in the *Bookseller* for October 31. Most of the reviews, beginning immediately after publication, were not encouraging;[20] and Melville apparently wrote Demarest in October or November to inquire about sales, for Demarest's report on December 7 implies earlier correspondence: "According to promise I beg

---

20. For a summary of the reviews, see the "Postscript on Reception" section of the HISTORICAL NOTE (pp. 518–27 above).

to report that there were printed of the 'Battle Pieces,' 1260 copies: there have been given to Editors, say in round numbers, 300: there were on hand yesterday 409. So there were sold or in hands of booksellers on sale, up to yesterday, say 551 copies."

Fourteen months later, the Harpers' next account to Melville (dated February 13, 1868) reported total sales of *Battle-Pieces* as 486 copies, somewhat less than Demarest had stated (no doubt because of copies returned by booksellers). Over the next twenty-one months (to November 2, 1870) only 11 more copies were sold, though during this period 299 more copies were bound[21] (since the number of bound copies on hand had fallen to fewer than 50). No sales at all occurred during the next twenty months (to June 17, 1872); and by the time the next account was rendered (February 12, 1875), so many copies had been returned by bookstores that the sales figure was a negative 76, reducing the total number sold by that point to 421. Although a small sales spurt of 28 copies occurred by August 1, 1876 (perhaps because of the Centennial), the next decade (through the last Harper account on March 4, 1887) saw only 22 more copies sold. Thus the book's total sales over a twenty-year period came to 471 copies, only about 200 more than the number of review copies sent out, leaving the publisher with over 500 copies on hand (or more than half of the edition, after the review copies are taken out). The total income from sales amounted to about $537 (before the 5 percent deduction for figuring half-profits), not much more than half of the production costs (about $969, including the cost of the second-batch binding). Of the 500 copies unsold in 1887, those still unbound were surely destroyed, and the 360 or so that were bound either went to a publisher's trade sale for remaindering or were also destroyed.

JOHN MARR

BY EARLY 1888 Melville, having considered various possibilities for grouping his poems into books (such as a gathering to be called something like "Meadows and Seas, with a Rose or Two"), was concentrating on a collection of his poems about sailors and the sea. In late March or early April he apparently wrote to W. Clark Russell (the American-born British sea novelist who in an 1884 essay had expressed admiration for

---

21. The number is given as 399 in the account, but the error was noted, and the necessary adjustments made, in the account of February 9, 1878.

Melville's work), asking permission to dedicate the book to him. Russell's reply, expressing pleasure in the idea, was dated April 10. Melville had given up the idea of commercial publication of his poetry, in light of the small sales of *Battle-Pieces* and the fact that *Clarel* (1876) had to be underwritten by his uncle and received little attention. In July 1888, after settling on twenty-five poems to make up the contents, he was ready to hire a printer to produce a small number of copies to be presented to family and friends. He turned to Theodore Low De Vinne, now regarded as one of the great figures in the history of American printing.[22] De Vinne (1828–1914), who was partially of Dutch ancestry like Melville, had learned the printing trade as a teenager and by the time he was thirty had become a partner in a New York printing firm. In 1877, after his partner's death, he took over the business, and for the next thirty years his firm (first Theodore L. De Vinne & Co. and then The De Vinne Press) was one of the dominant American printing firms, producing widely admired work for prominent publishers and leading cultural institutions (such as the Grolier Club, of which he was one of the founders). De Vinne also attracted notice by being active in printing-trade organizations, representing employers in labor disputes, and he wrote influential books on the practice and history of printing, such as *The Printers' Price List* (1869) and *The Invention of Printing* (1876).

Just two years before *John Marr,* De Vinne published his *Historic Printing Types* and oversaw the building of his great Romanesque printing plant and office at the northeast corner of Lafayette Place and Fourth Street (12 Lafayette Place, later changed to 393–99 Lafayette Street), about a mile south of Melville's house and only a few steps south of the Astor Library, which Melville knew well. Melville may have noticed that De Vinne was the printer of the *Century Illustrated Magazine* (formerly, until 1881, *Scribner's Monthly*), where De Vinne's artistry and expertise were particularly evident. Among the books his firm was engaged on just before and during 1888 were George Parsons Lathrop's *Gettysburg: A Battle Ode* (New York: Charles Scribner's Sons, 1888), Brander Matthews's *Pen and Ink* (New York and London: Longmans, Green, 1888), and De Vinne's own *Christopher Plantin* (New York: Grolier Club, 1888). Among the privately printed books besides *John Marr* that came from the De Vinne Press in 1888 were Alice A. Holmes's *Lost Vision* (which, like *John Marr,* had the De Vinne

---

22. Indeed, Nicolas Barker in a 1989 lecture called him "the most accomplished printer in the Western Hemisphere" in his time (*The Future of Typographical Studies,* p. 13). (De Vinne's middle name is pronounced to rhyme with "how"; his last name has three syllables.)

Press imprint on the title page) and William Reed Huntington's *Quinquaginta* (which had "New York: Privately Printed" on the title page). But there is no point speculating about how De Vinne came to Melville's attention, for De Vinne's renown was so great that Melville could have come across his name and his work in any number of ways.

No correspondence between Melville and De Vinne is known to survive, nor have any of De Vinne's office records relating to the production of *John Marr* been found in the few collections of his papers.[23] The only known surviving documentary evidence of the production process consists of the printer's-copy manuscript largely in Melville's hand, along with a set of galley and page proofs for "John Marr," a set of galley proofs for the rest of the book, and a complete set of page proofs (including "John Marr"), each with Melville's and the printer's markings.[24] One may be surprised that this much is extant, given the De Vinne Press's policy for disposing of material. According to Frank Hopkins, who began working for De Vinne in the fall of 1888 and who wrote about him in 1936, there was a standard routine for destroying all manuscripts and papers relating to each job, once they were no longer needed; the material was tied into bundles once a month, to be stuffed into burlap bags in due course for sale to waste-paper merchants. Perhaps the *John Marr* documents survive because Melville asked to have them returned; Hopkins states that papers specifically asked for by customers were faithfully sent back.[25]

The surviving manuscript consists of 147 leaves[26] (averaging about 7 by 5⅝ inches), of primarily two off-white paper stocks, one somewhat lighter

23. Acknowledgment is made to Irene Tichenor, author of *No Art Without Craft: The Life of Theodore Low De Vinne,* for information about the collections of De Vinne's papers at the American Antiquarian Society, Columbia University, and Choate Rosemary Hall.

24. This material is preserved among Melville's papers at Houghton Library, Harvard University, with the following call numbers: MS Am 188 (370) (the printer's-copy manuscript); *fAC85.M4977.888ja (galley proofs for "John Marr," July 23, 1888, and for the rest of the book, July 31, 1888); *fAC85.M4977.888jaa (page proofs for "John Marr," July 26, 1888); and *fAC85.M4977.888jab (page proofs for the whole volume, August 16, 1888).

25. Whatever caused the materials to be returned, they would have joined one batch of proofs, the first page proofs for the "John Marr" section, that Melville had never returned and that had thus remained in his possession all along (the evidence is summarized below). Hopkins's account appears in *The De Vinne and Marion Presses,* pp. 40–41.

26. In the numbering that Melville blue-penciled at the upper left corners of the manuscript leaves, the last leaf is numbered 141; but there is also an unnumbered leaf with text for the title page (labeled "Title Page" by Melville in blue pencil) and a leaf between leaves 99 and 100 with a note "To the Printer", and each of the numbers 18, 32, 33, and 34 is used twice.

in color and thinner than the other, though various other papers were also used. Forty-five of the leaves have one or more part-leaves attached to them (with paste and originally with pins at some places as well).[27] The handwriting, in several inks and occasionally in pencil, is mostly Melville's, but the leaves containing "The Haglets" (leaves 100–108) consist of pasted-on clippings from the New York *Tribune* (where an abridgment of this poem, under the title "The Admiral of the White," had appeared on May 17, 1885), interspersed with passages mainly in Melville's wife's hand (to fill in the omitted stanzas, which had in fact been included in the full version printed with the same title in the Boston *Herald* the same day).

This manuscript, despite the messiness of its construction and the many textual revisions and erasures it contains, is the one that Melville prepared for the printer, as shown by the instructions to the printer that he inserted at ten places. Three of them deal with spacing and the others with indention, and together they reflect Melville's concern with the visual appearance of his poems. On leaf 92, at the beginning of "Tom Dead-light," Melville penciled, "To the Printer: Leave something of a space between the prose & verse." And in "The Haglets" he wrote two inked notes to make clear that the first two and last two stanzas were to be set off from the body of the poem: at the first of these points (on leaf 100) he wrote "Leave more of a space between", and at the second (on leaf 108) he wrote, "Widen the space between these two lines." His first note on indention appears in ink on a separate leaf between leaves 99 and 100: "To the Printer The greater part of this Piece, 'The Haglets,' is marked off (in blue pencil) into stanzas of eighteen lines each. I think their seventh and thirteenth lines should be indented." Then at the top of leaf 109, where "The Æolian Harp" begins, there is this inked note: "To the Printer: Where the line has a red cross in margin—indent. And so in other Pieces similarly marked." Despite this blanket instruction, he repeated it (in the form "To the Printer: Indent." in ink and circled) at the beginnings of "Far-Off Shore" (leaf 115), "The Good Craft *Snow-Bird*" (leaf 119), "To Ned" (leaf 125), "Crossing the Tropics" (leaf 128), and "The Enviable Isles" (leaf 134). He also marked stanza and paragraph beginnings with a blue-penciled bracket.

That this manuscript was in fact used by the printer is indicated by the presence on it of De Vinne's job number and the names of the compositors who set the type, along with their notations of where each galley began.

---

27. The manuscript has received full conservation treatment, and the pins have been removed and saved (with notations of their previous positioning); the pinholes are of course still visible.

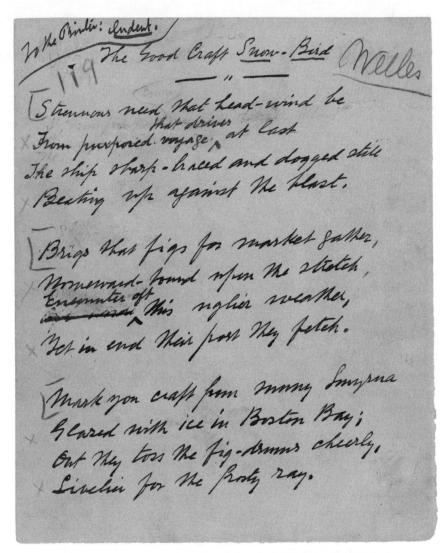

Figure 1. Leaf 119 of Melville's manuscript of *John Marr and Other Sailors*, containing the first twelve lines of "The Good Craft *Snow-Bird*" and showing two revisions, a note to the printer, brackets indicating indention, and the signature of the compositor ("Welles"). Size of original: 7" × 5⅜". Courtesy of Houghton Library, Harvard University: MS Am 188 (370).

The job number, 2457, is penciled at the top right of the first leaf (Melville's title page), and a red gummed label, bearing this number in printed form, is affixed at the top right of the second of the two leaves numbered 18 (containing the beginning of "John Marr"). The names of two of De Vinne's compositors, Hughes and Welles (occasionally spelled "Wells"), are written in various pencils and inks at the tops of the leaves where each of their "takes" began (and are sometimes repeated, within what would seem to be a single take, at the beginnings of poems). Hughes set 82 of the manuscript text pages, Welles 63 (or in terms of text pages in type, as finally made up from the galleys, Hughes set 47 pages and Welles 35).[28]

Melville had sent or delivered this manuscript (or at least the "John Marr" part of it) to De Vinne at some point in the summer of 1888 prior to July 23, for that is the date of De Vinne's blue-inked stamp at the head of the galley proofs of the "John Marr" section. Melville's handwritten

---

28. The figure for Hughes includes the four pages of additional manuscript text for "Bridegroom Dick" (about two pages in type) that Melville sent back with the galley proofs and that Hughes set in type when he made the other corrections on these proofs. (The figures for the number of type-pages set by Hughes and Welles add up to 82; the other 26 pages in the final book consist of blanks, section-titles, and the preliminaries.) The two compositors marked their takes on the manuscript at the points noted in the following list. The first number in each set, preceding the parentheses, is the manuscript leaf number; the second number, in parentheses, is the page-line number in the current Northwestern-Newberry (NN) volume corresponding to the first line of text on that manuscript leaf ("0" refers to the title line or lines, and for pages with poetry the printed line numbers are used). Hughes—1 (191.0), 18[2] (195.0), 29 (197.12), 42 (201.0), 90 (214.0), 96 (216.0), 104 (220.85), 108 (223.193), 114 (228.0), 115 (229.0), 116 (230.0), 117 (231.0), 123 (236.0), 137 (243.0); Welles—11 (192.31), 59 (206.173), 99 (217.24), 101 (219.25), 107 (222.133), 109 (226.0), 119 (232.0), 128 (239.0), 134 (242.0). In other words, the eight segments of text set by Hughes, expressed in NN page-line numbers, are as follows: 191.0–192.30, 195.0–206.172, 214.0–217.23, 220.85–222.132, 223.193–225.250, 228.0–231.15, 236.0–238.30, 243.0–249.4; and Welles's seven segments are as follows: 192.31–193.27, 206.173–213.438, 217.24–220.84, 222.133–223.192, 226.0–227.48, 232.0–235.4, 239.0–242.14.

The compositors also noted on the manuscript the points at which each galley began (except in three instances), usually by writing "Gal." followed by a number and the compositor's name. The following list shows the beginning point of each galley, in terms first of page-line references to the manuscript and then (in parentheses) of NN page-line references: galley 1—18(2).0 (195.0); 2—29.1 (197.12); 3—36.6 (199.1 [of poem]); 4—42.0 (201.0); 5—52.5 (203.94); 6—63.2 (207.206); 7—74.2 (209.298); 8—84.3 (212.391); 9—93.6 (215.14); 10—101.1 (219.25); 11—106.19 (222.127); 12—108.32 (224.224); 13—115.7 (229.7); 14—124.6 (236.15); 15—133.3 (241.29); galley 1 of "Inscription Epistolary"—1.0 (191.0); 2 of "Inscription"—13.12 (193.5). The three instances in which the compositors did not note beginning points of galleys (presumably because they were the beginning points of separate units of the job, as explained below) are galleys 1 and 4 and the first galley of the "Inscription Epistolary."

title page originally had the date "July 1888" at the foot, but in pencil he changed "July" to "Aug.", either before sending the manuscript to De Vinne (recognizing that "July" was already too optimistic) or when the manuscript was returned to him at the end of the month with the galley proofs for the bulk of the book. The July 23 galley proofs of the "John Marr" section, which Melville's wife marked "First Proof", consist of three long sheets (about twenty-four inches long, containing printed text not yet divided into page units). "First Proof" means only that these were the first proofs Melville received; normal shop routine would have dictated an earlier set of galley proofs (or more than one) for proofreading in the shop, so that the proofs as sent out would already have benefited from proofreading.[29] At the top left of each galley proof is written "W./2457/ Rev.GK.", meaning that Welles (presumably) was the compositor who had corrected any errors discovered in the office proofreading and that G.K. was the proofreader who gave this "revise" a final review before sending it out. He found three errors in this process and noted them in ink (a mistake in dividing a word at line-end, a misspelling, and a misplaced dash). At the top right of each proof is a penciled number (A–5, 215, 219), indicating the position where the composed type was stored in the galley racks.

Exactly why the "John Marr" poem and its prose preface were set in type and sent to Melville before the rest of the book is not entirely clear from the surviving materials; but perhaps this section, containing both prose and verse, was meant to serve as a typographic sample, whether or not Melville had supplied the whole manuscript by this time. The idea that the preface (the "Inscription Epistolary")—the only text preceding "John Marr" in the completed book—had not yet been sent to De Vinne can be supported by some evidence, but not conclusively so. Melville's blue-penciled leaf numbering begins at the beginning of the "Inscription" and reaches "18" by its last leaf; but the first leaf of "John Marr" is

---

29. One of the standard accounts of printing-shop practices at about this time was written by De Vinne himself and published in 1904 as *Modern Methods of Book Composition* (New York: Century Co.), part of his four-volume series on "The Practice of Typography" (1900–1904). The relevant section for present purposes is "Customary Routines on Books," pp. 76–85 (supplemented by p. 260 in the "Making Up" chapter and pp. 323–25 in the "Taking Proofs" section). At the time of *John Marr,* author's galley proofs had become fairly widely used in book work (see note 16 above); but apparently De Vinne had only recently begun to employ them, for in his 1883 *Manual of Printing Office Practice,* he had recognized galley proofs only for magazine work (pp. 31, 39). By the time of the 1904 book, however, he strongly recommended author's galley proofs for any text set from manuscript copy (p. 84).

also numbered "18". Since there are erased leaf numbers on the last sev-
eral leaves of the "Inscription" indicating a sequence ending with "17",
it is possible that Melville, expecting the "Inscription" to have seventeen
leaves, began numbering "John Marr" with "18" and sent it (with or with-
out the following poems) to De Vinne.[30] The "18" on the first leaf of "John
Marr" has a small circled "2" in black ink following it, to indicate that
this is the second leaf numbered "18", though the first one does not have
a circled "1". But in the other three instances of duplicated numbers (32,
33, 34), both a circled "1" and a circled "2" are used, and those numbers
are in blue pencil, like the main numbers; they occur in the prose part of
"John Marr" and clearly result from additions that Melville made after the
numbering had been done but before the manuscript was sent off (since
the full text is present in the galley proofs). Thus it is conceivable that the
addition of "2" to the second "18" (unlike these other duplications) was
not a part of readying the manuscript for De Vinne because at that time
this "18" would not have been a duplicate, and the "2" was added at a later
point when the "Inscription" leaves were put in place at the beginning.[31]

30. The blue-penciled numbering appears to have been done before sending the man-
uscript to De Vinne: although there are many erased numbers on the manuscript (some
simply indicating the sequence within a given poem, others reflecting different orderings
of the poems), there are none that would have served as a safeguard against the leaves of
the entire manuscript becoming disarranged in the printing-shop. In two instances where
the text at the top of a leaf is on an affixed part-leaf and where a compositor's name, as
well as the blue-penciled number, are also written on that part-leaf, the part-leaf appears
to have been trimmed after the compositor's name was written ("Welles" on leaves 11 and
59). It is not reasonable, however, to suppose that the manuscript was differently pieced
together when the compositors used it and that its present combination of leaves and part-
leaves was created and numbered later; such an inference is not supported by the other
evidence adduced below (such as the duplicated leaf numbers) or by common sense. A
more likely explanation would be that these two part-leaves were originally attached only
by pins (the pinholes are visible) and that when (sometime after the compositor wrote his
name) the decision was made to paste the pieces on, the top edges were trimmed, cutting
off a minuscule bit of the name in each case. (On leaf 59 Welles wrote his name a second
time on the part-leaf, possibly as a result of the trimming, though trimming did not make
his other signature difficult to read in the slightest.) Many other part-leaves, it should be
noted, show signs of having been pinned before they were pasted.

31. Another piece of evidence, which occurs in the July 31 galley proofs for the rest
of the book, is the inked notation "p. 14" at the top left of the proof-sheet numbered "4",
where "Bridegroom Dick" begins. This notation was apparently meant to tell the com-
positor who would later make up the pages that the previous poem ("John Marr") had
already been paged and that it ended with page 13. Since the pagination of "John Marr"
was later changed to accommodate the "Inscription," it is possible that the "Inscription"
had not yet arrived at the time the galley proof containing the opening of "Bride-
groom Dick" was pulled and proofread. (But the "p. 14" could also be explained by the

This interpretation of the evidence is of course not the only defensible one and does not entirely rule out the possibility that the whole manuscript, including the "Inscription," was sent at one time, though it makes that possibility seem less likely.

In any case, whatever the reason for beginning the typesetting with "John Marr," the compositors' indications, on the manuscript, of the starting points of each galley proceed steadily from "John Marr" onward to the end: that is, galleys 2 and 3 are noted within the "John Marr" section; and, although no galley number is given at the beginning of "Bridegroom Dick" (because it came at the top of the first galley of a new batch), galley 5 is duly noted at the appropriate point in that poem, and all the other galley numbers, from 6 through 15, continue the numerical sequence. The manuscript leaves for the "Inscription Epistolary," on the other hand, contain one galley notation, written at the point where its second (and last) galley began, and that notation reads "Gal. 14 Welles". Why Welles used the number "14" is unclear, but the anomaly suggests that the "Inscription Epistolary" was set as a separate operation, possibly after much of the rest of the typesetting had been completed;[32] and the galleys for it did in fact form a separate sequence, as the printed numbering of the proofs shows.[33]

Melville must have gone over the three "John Marr" galley proofs immediately, since only three days separate the date stamps on them (July 23) from those on the "John Marr" page proofs (July 26). He marked ten revisions on these galley proofs: four of them were restorations of manuscript readings (three in wording, one in punctuation), and the other six were new revisions (four in wording, two in punctuation). In the process he missed several errors of single letters; and he failed to, or decided not to, restore his manuscript spelling, capitalization, and punctuation at some seven dozen places where Hughes had made alterations on his own. General printing-shop procedure, as codified by De Vinne in his *Correct Composition* (New York: Century, 1901), called for compositors to follow

---

compositor's or proofreader's assumption that the "Inscription" would have a separate roman-numeral pagination sequence.) See also note 32 below.

32. If the manuscript of the "Inscription" was sent late, as suggested above, conceivably the typesetting had reached galley 12, and Welles may have thought that galley numbers 13 and 14 could be allocated to the "Inscription." Although he did some setting for galley 12, the end of that galley fell within one of Hughes's takes. If Welles did his work on the "Inscription" during an interval when Hughes was working on another job and had not yet completed galley 12, Welles might have thought he could use 13 and 14.

33. The second of the two galley-proof sheets containing the "Inscription Epistolary" was headed "marr inscrip 2" in type, to distinguish it from "marr 2", the second of the "John Marr" galley proofs sent to Melville earlier.

a house rule in these matters except when the author gives "particular directions" (p. 10). In regard to punctuation, for example, although he insists that the compositor is "enjoined strictly to follow the copy and never to change the punctuation of any author who is precise and systematic," the compositor is "also required to punctuate the writings of all authors who are not careful, and to make written expression intelligible in the proof" (p. 241). It was De Vinne's belief that readers "will find more fault with the printer than with the author if the text is confused by bad punctuation, for it is generally understood that punctuation is the duty of the printer"; and thus "the printer has to conform for the sake of his reputation and has to require the compositor to give his aid when the copy has been hastily prepared" (p. 243). De Vinne summarizes, "In all printing houses it is the duty of the compositor to try to make composition intelligible, so far as it can be done, by the proper use of points" (p. 244). Hughes, the compositor who set the type for the "John Marr" section, did not stint in his application of these guidelines. Melville's only other marking on the "John Marr" galley proofs was a note about spacing. At the foot of the second galley proof, where the prose introduction ended, he wrote in pencil, "To the Printer: Some space should be left between the prose & verse."

Near the top of the first of the "John Marr" galley proofs, someone in De Vinne's office (probably G.K.) wrote in the right margin, "show revise in pages", meaning that the next proof stage would not be a second galley proof but would display the text divided (or "made up") into pages, complete with running-titles and page numbers. A compositor named Tully, whose name is penciled at the lower right corners of the first two galley proofs, made all of Melville's corrections, and the "maker-up" (perhaps Tully also) divided the text into pages and set the running-titles.[34] There is in fact an additional revision (not marked by Melville on the galley proofs) that is incorporated into the page proofs—"enfold" for "embrace" on page 11 (199.24). This revision is unquestionably Melville's, for no one in De Vinne's shop would change a customer's text in this way; but the presence of the revision cannot be taken to mean that there was a second, now lost, stage of galley proof—not only because of the note explicitly ordering the revise to be "in pages" but also because the whole set of

34. He also marked the location of each page break on the galley proofs, something that was not done on the galley proofs for the rest of the book—perhaps another indication that the "John Marr" section was being used to develop the typography and layout (or perhaps only a sign of the different habits of two different makers-up). There is no initial on the "John Marr" page proofs to indicate the maker-up, as there is on the later page proofs for the rest of the book.

alterations was not complicated enough to call for second galley proofs in any case. This one revision therefore must have been communicated to De Vinne's office in some other way, such as by means of a note sent by mail or messenger.[35]

The page proofs of the "John Marr" section, bearing De Vinne's blue-inked date-stamp of July 26, 1888, at the upper left and the word "Revise" in Melville's wife's hand penciled at the upper right of the first one,[36] consist of five galley-length sheets, each of which has space for three text pages; the first four do contain three pages each, and the fifth has one page on it. Of these thirteen pages, all except the first have running-titles and page numbers, from 2 through 13—a fact again suggesting the possibility that at this time "John Marr" was the beginning of the manuscript in the printer's hands—although as a typographic sample in pages these proofs would presumably have needed to show page numbers of some kind, even if they were not the final ones. (These pages correspond to the pages numbered 12 to 23 in the final book, and the opening page of "John Marr," 11, also has a number.) In the upper left corner of each of the galley-length sheets is written "2457/muGK." in ink, showing that G.K. was the proof-reader who went over the proofs of the "made-up" pages. The revision from "embrace" to "enfold" that Melville had sent separately from the galley proofs evidently arrived after the page proofs had been prepared: the proof sheet containing pages 10, 11, and 12 was cut apart, page 11 was removed, and a substitute page 11 was pinned in its place, containing the new reading and the notation (at the upper left below the job number) "Au.Rev.GK", signifying that this page incorporated authorial revision.

Melville marked three changes on these page proofs, two of them corrections of compositorial misreadings of the manuscript that he had not caught on the galley proofs (he corrected "not" to "nor" at 195.18 and "nature" to "Nature" at 197.8) and the other one a new revision ("by"

35. If Melville had received two duplicate sets of galley proofs, the revision could theoretically have been sent in the form of the relevant portion of the retained duplicate proof. But De Vinne's *Modern Methods of Book Composition* makes no mention of sending authors two sets of galley proofs; and although the absence of duplicate proofs among the surviving papers does not mean that they never existed, the likelihood of their having existed is somewhat lessened by the fact that the first "John Marr" page proofs, which (as explained below) were retained by Melville and never sent back to De Vinne, do survive.

36. Her use of the word "revise" was not quite the same as the printer's: she merely meant that this was the second proof Melville received, incorporating the corrections and revisions marked on the first one; but to the printer "revise" was any proof that incorporated corrections from the previous stage, and thus even the first author's proof was a "revise" because it included corrections made on the original in-house proof (and possibly a second in-house proof).

for "with" at 198.16). He did not, however, send these proofs back to De Vinne's office, a fact made obvious by several pieces of evidence. First, there is no compositor's name written at the lower right corners, as there would have been if the proof had been used in De Vinne's office by a compositor, who would have placed his name there after making the corrections in the type. Second, the complete page proofs that came later (to be commented on further below) have a handwritten note on page 11 reading "No proof of pp. 11–23 to revise by." Third, Melville's three alterations are not incorporated into the text of those later page proofs.

Five days after the date on the "John Marr" page proofs, the galley proofs for all the rest of the book were ready. They consist of fourteen galley-proof sheets, in two sequences: first are the two sheets containing the "Inscription Epistolary," with the second one headed in type "marr inscrip 2"; then come the remaining twelve sheets, containing all the text that follows "John Marr" and continuing the sequence begun with the three earlier "John Marr" galley proofs—the headings in type thus running from "marr 4" through "marr 15". De Vinne's blue-inked date-stamp of July 31, 1888, appears at the top left of all fourteen proofs, and a penciled galley-rack number is at the top right of each; at the top center of the first one (that is, the one that begins the "Inscription"), "First proof" is penciled in Melville's wife's hand. At the upper left of each galley proof is also the three-line notation "H./2457/Rev.GK.": thus Hughes (presumably) corrected the errors found in the in-house proofreading, and G.K. again was the proofreader who went over this "revise" before it was sent to Melville (adding neatly—in the right margin usually—a few alterations still needed and, in one case, a question regarding spelling).[37] Although the two compositors who set the text (Hughes and Welles) made several hundred alterations in punctuation and capitalization,[38] as they were authorized to do by De Vinne's rules, they generally did a good job of deciphering the many difficult spots in the manuscript. Sometimes, however, Melville's handwriting defeated them, especially in the case of uncommon words, as when Hughes read "bruited" as "trusted" (192.17) and "thingumbob" as "thin-gonsbot" (202.54).

37. He queried "Tantallon" in line 410 of "Bridegroom Dick"; Melville, when going over the proofs later, replied with a circled "All right."

38. In the text as a whole (including "John Marr"), Hughes departed from copy some 240 times, and Welles (who set about twenty fewer manuscript pages) departed from copy about 200 times. They both made fewer alterations when setting from the printed copy in "The Haglets."

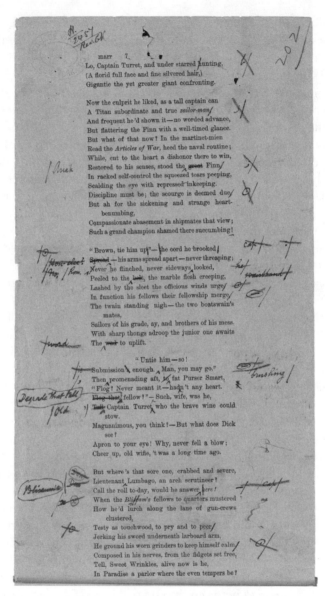

Figure 2. The upper portion of galley proof 7 for *John Marr and Other Sailors,*
containing lines 298–344 of "Bridegroom Dick" and showing Melville's
corrections and revisions (most of them marked through in blue pencil by the
compositor who carried out the alterations), along with the notation of a
De Vinne Press employee who checked the proofs (upper left) and an
indication of the galley-rack number where the type for this proof was
stored (upper right). Size of original: 11¹³⁄₁₆″ (portion shown) × 5½″.
Courtesy of Houghton Library, Harvard University: *fAC85.M4977.888ja.

Melville marked numerous alterations on the galley proofs, not only correcting such errors as these but also making new revisions, the most extensive of which was thirty-four lines (written on four small sheets of paper, the same size as those used for the manuscript, with verse-paragraph openings marked by blue-penciled brackets) to be inserted in "Bridegroom Dick" (205.135–206.168) as a replacement for eighteen lines marked out on galley proof 5. At the top left corner of these leaves Melville placed the numbers 1 through 4 in blue pencil, and at the top right of the first leaf he wrote in black pencil, "To be inserted in 'Bridegroom Dick' after the line on p. 5—'In Hampton Roads &c". (The second of the leaves was itself made up of two pieces of paper.) Then on galley proof 5, to the left of the line beginning "In Hampton Roads" (205.134), he wrote in a greenish pencil, "Insert here the M.S. pages affixed."

He also made five penciled notes to show where he wished to have section-title leaves (leaves bearing only titles on their rectos and with blank versos). At the top of galley proof 4, for example, where "Bridegroom Dick" begins, he wrote, "A page should precede this Piece—a page bearing its title." (For clarity, he marked out "its" and added "The Piece's" in a circle, with an arrow pointing to "its".) He made similar notes at the beginning of "Tom Deadlight" (galley proof 8), "Jack Roy" (galley proof 9), and "Pebbles" (galley proof 15). But at the beginning of "The Haglets" (galley proof 9) the note was slightly different in that it called for a different title: "A Page should precede 'The Haglets,' bearing the Title Sea-Pieces." (He had earlier penciled, and then erased, a note to the same effect—"extra page / Sea-Pieces"—at the beginning of "The Æolian Harp.") Thus the structure he apparently envisioned for the book at this time, as reflected in the placement of section-title leaves, was that the three poems dealing with the "other sailors" (referred to in "John Marr and Other Sailors") would have their own title-leaves, whereas the rest of the poems would be grouped under two section headings: "Sea-Pieces" for the poems from "The Haglets" through "The Enviable Isles," and "Pebbles" for the seven short poems collectively entitled "Pebbles."

A division within the "Sea-Pieces" group was suggested by Melville's note on galley proof 12 between the end of "The Haglets" and the beginning of "The Æolian Harp": "A liberal space, or, perhaps, a page should be left between these two Pieces." Within "The Æolian Harp," he wrote (in ink in the left margin) "Leave more space here" between the third and fourth stanzas and again between the fifth and sixth, and he penciled vertically in the right margin beside the fourth and fifth stanzas, "The whole of this should be placed more to the right." On galley proof 9, after the first two short stanzas of "The Haglets," he wrote two circled notes in ink to correct the compositors' failure to follow his manuscript instructions: "Leave more space here"; and "The stanza of eighteen lines here begins." (He clarified the latter point by writing beside the top six lines of the next galley proof, "This belongs to the first stanza of eighteen lines.") Two other notes regarding spacing further show Melville's interest in the visual effect of the finished book. On galley proof 13 beside "Old Counsel" and "The Tuft of Kelp," he penciled, "These two Pieces might occupy, if it is manageable, a page by themselves." And at the beginning of the "Inscription Epistolary," to the left of the three lines following the title ("TO / W. C. R. / HEALTH AND CONTENT."), which the compositor had centered, Melville placed this instruction: "This salutation should be in Roman, and placed more to the left—pretty much as if it were '<u>My dear Sir</u>' at the opening of any other epistle."

Once these galley proofs went back to De Vinne's office, Hughes was the compositor who incorporated Melville's alterations into the standing type, as the presence of his penciled name at the lower right corner of each proof attests.[39] After he had finished, the word "Makeup" was written with a heavy orange crayon vertically in the right margin of the first sheet (the beginning of the "Inscription"), signifying that the next step was to make up the type into page units and that no revised galley proof was to be sent to the author.[40] The type was duly divided into pages, and the running-titles and page numbers, as well as the section-titles, were set and placed.

39. He is probably the person who marked out most of the marginal corrections in blue pencil, indicating that he had made the corrections (those not marked out were also made and do not seem to fall into a pattern). To accommodate the long insertion in "Bridegroom Dick," which replaced eighteen lines but resulted in sixteen more lines than were present before (more than the galley tray would hold), Hughes moved the standing type for the thirty-seven lines following the revision point (206.169–207.205)—that is, the rest of the text originally in galley 5—into a new galley; and he cut off the lower part of the galley proof, corresponding to those lines, and labeled it "5 1/2 MARR". He was then able to set Melville's new text and place the type in galley 5, where there was now room for it. Before Melville's marked galley proofs were sent back to him to accompany the page proofs, the two separated pieces of galley 5 were pinned together, with the bottom piece overlapping the last four marked-out lines of the upper piece. (The office set of revised galley proofs, which would have been pulled for the office proofreading, does not survive, as the other office proofs do not; Melville would have first seen his new passage in type in the page proofs.)

40. Another reference to the makeup stage occurs on galley proof 12, where Melville indicated that there should be more space before the fourth and after the fifth stanzas of "The Æolian Harp" and that both stanzas should be moved to the right: at this point Hughes wrote "Makeup attend to this." Melville's other notes on spacing dealt with matters that would clearly have to be handled in the makeup stage; this one involved spacing within a poem, and Hughes wanted to make sure that the maker-up did not miss it.

The resulting page proofs for the entire book (including "John Marr") were ready to send to Melville on August 16, 1888, the date of De Vinne's blue-inked stamp on pages 1 and 103 (the last page). For these proofs, each text page was provided on a separate piece of paper (unlike the earlier "John Marr" page proofs, where groups of three pages were printed on galley-size sheets). In their present form, these proofs are bound as a hard-cover volume; the leaves measure 8¾ by 6 inches, but they were cut down in binding from their original page-proof size. The first leaf is a proof for the front cover, marked by a De Vinne employee with the penciled word "Cover" at the top, and annotated by Melville's wife in pencil with Melville's name below the main part of the title and with the words "Revise Proof (complete)" in the space between the subtitle and the imprint. In the upper left corner, a De Vinne proofreader, "E.", having examined this "revise," wrote the job number, 2457, and "Rev.E." in ink. The leaf may or may not have originally been the first leaf of the page proofs: possibly Melville's wife placed it on top of the stack of page proofs as a cover on which to write "Revise Proof (complete)". One would expect that the title page, copyright page, and table of contents would have been part of these proofs, but they are not present now.[41]

The next leaf, which carries the date stamp, contains the first page of the "Inscription Epistolary," and the page proofs are complete from there on. At the upper left corner of all these leaves the job number, 2457, is written in ink; above that on the first one is an "H", presumably referring to Hughes as the corrector of the standing type and maker-up of the pages; and below that on all the pages except those containing "John Marr" (pp. 11–23) appear the letters "M.U.E.", designating that "E." was the proofreader who reviewed the proofs of the made-up pages before sending them out. He did not put his initial on the "John Marr" pages

41. A title-page proof that was probably part of these proofs does exist, now housed with the galley proofs (see note 45 below). In addition to the cover proof bound with these complete page proofs, there are two proofs of the cover now housed with the page proofs of the "John Marr" section—one on paper measuring 6½ by 4½ inches, with the job number inked in red at the top left corner, and the other on the first recto of a piece of tan cover stock folded in half to form a trim size of 6⅝ by 4½ inches. These two proofs did not necessarily accompany the "John Marr" page proofs originally, especially since they presumably represent two different stages in the development of the cover: the paper proof lacks the phrase "25 Copies" that appears on the cover as finally used, and the proof on cover stock has it. But if the early setting of "John Marr" was to provide a sample of the typography, it is possible that the cover design was worked out at the same time and that at least the paper proof of the cover did accompany the "John Marr" page proofs. The cover proof that is now bound with the complete page proofs is a "revise" because it does include the "25 Copies" line.

because the earlier page proofs for those pages had not been returned, and instead (as noted above) he merely indicated on page 11 that there was "No proof of pp. 11–23 to revise by."

The presence of this note should not be taken to imply that there was an earlier (and now missing) set of page proofs for all the other pages. A comparison of the galley proofs with the page proofs does not suggest that there was an intervening proof stage; if there had been, neither Melville nor the proofreader would, for example, have had to mark so many changes in running-titles at this stage, and Melville's wife would probably not have written "Revise Proof" on the cover leaf but "Second Revise Proof." The reason for E.'s note was simply that, since he knew an earlier set of page proofs for these pages had been sent to Melville, he was aware that he did not have access to the latest stage of possible alterations. (There would have been no point in his comparing the page-proof text of these pages against the marked galley proofs because G.K. had already done that before sending the earlier page proofs to Melville.)

These page proofs as delivered to Melville contained a number of notes by De Vinne's proofreader, "E.", such as "wf" for wrong-font types (three times), "x" for badly inked or damaged types (six times), marginal lines to call attention to poor alignment, lineation, or spacing (five times), an instruction on page 32 (after line 93 of "Bridegroom Dick") to delete the "lead," a note on page 89 (after "Old Counsel") stating "Page 2 lines short," and marginal corrections of typographical errors in running-titles (27 times, almost all of them to correct an upside-down "S" to a "J" in "John").[42] Because Melville had not seen the running-titles before, he needed to change their wording on seventeen verso pages, mainly in order to make them match his current thinking about a tripartite structure for the volume, as reflected in his notes on the galley proofs and as shown in the final table of contents. (The running-titles on rectos correspond to the individual pieces on those pages.) Whereas De Vinne's maker-up had used *"John Marr and Other Sailors"* as the verso running-title throughout the entire volume, Melville changed it to *"Sea-Pieces"* beginning with "The Haglets" and continuing through "The Enviable Isles,"[43] and he changed it to *"Pebbles"* on the one verso in the "Pebbles" section. (He also changed it to *"Inscription Epistolary"* in that section, even though the "Inscription

---

42. A De Vinne employee also penciled page numbers on some of the pages that were to carry no number in print, but Melville's wife added others, along with the notation of preceding blank pages.

43. He also penciled and then erased, on the section-title page preceding "The Haglets," a note specifying "Sea-Pieces" as the running-title.

Epistolary" is not separated in the table of contents from the four poems that follow it.)

Melville also altered four of the section-titles in these page proofs, and in the process he made their function less consistent. This result may in part have been induced by printer's errors, though it is conceivable that what seem to be printer's errors were changes that Melville communicated to the printer after the galley proofs were returned. In the page proofs, the section-title preceding "The Haglets" reads "The Haglets," despite Melville's explicit galley-proof note calling for "Sea-Pieces" at this point; and "Sea-Pieces" appears as a section-title preceding "To the Master of the *Meteor*," where Melville had not specified a section-title at all. On the page proofs, Melville duly corrected the first to "Sea-Pieces"; but instead of deleting the second (which would have entailed changing the pagination of the eighteen pages that followed), he added "Minor" to it, thus accepting the presence of a section-title here (if only to accommodate a printer's error) and creating a new category. Another section-title not specifically requested on the galley proofs is the one preceding "The Æolian Harp." But in this case the printer had no choice but to create it: since Melville's galley-proof note asked for "perhaps" a blank page here and since the preceding poem ended on a verso, it would have been unacceptable to have the next leaf consist of a blank recto and the beginning of "The Æolian Harp" on the verso. The fact that Melville added "At the Surf Inn" to this section-title shows that he was willing to accept the printer's typographical decision to have a section-title at this point. His other change to the section-titles in the page proofs was to add "And other Sailors" to the one preceding "John Marr."[44]

---

44. Melville had not specifically called for a section-title here on the galley proofs; its presence signifies either (1) that Melville communicated in another way his desire to have it, in order to give "John Marr" the same treatment he had given the next three poems on the galley proofs, or (2) that the printer inserted it here as a matter of course, since a fly-title leaf was sometimes used following the preliminaries and preceding the main text (though in that case the full title would be expected).

Since the presence of a section-title for "The Haglets" and the placement of the one for "Sea-Pieces" might seem unlikely printer's errors, some speculation may be in order. One purely hypothetical sequence of events would go as follows: after receiving Melville's marked galley proofs, the printer may have informed him about the necessity for a section-title preceding "The Æolian Harp," if any break at all was to be observed there. Accepting this idea, Melville may then have decided that the preceding poem, "The Haglets," should have a section-title reading "The Haglets," not "Sea-Pieces" (as called for in his note on the galley proofs), and that "Sea-Pieces" should be moved to a position preceding "To the Master of the *Meteor*." But when reviewing the result in the page proofs, he may have felt that the structure of the book had become obscured, and he then

As a consequence of these changes, two of the section-titles that seem to announce a group of poems are in fact announcements of single poems: "John Marr and Other Sailors" introduces only "John Marr," since each of the next three poems, on the "other sailors," has its own section-title (as specified by Melville on the galley proofs); and "Sea-Pieces" introduces only "The Haglets," since the next poem after it, "The Æolian Harp," has a section-title of its own. "Minor Sea-Pieces" is left as the only section-title introducing a group of differently titled poems. Although these changes produced inconsistencies that did not exist in the page proofs as printed (where all the longer poems had their own section-titles, and only the shorter poems were gathered under the collective headings "Sea-Pieces" and "Pebbles"), the changes may represent Melville's attempt to emphasize, as best he could at this stage, the structure implied in the title "John Marr and Other Sailors with Some Sea-Pieces," supplemented by the envoi of "Pebbles." His changes to the running-titles clearly were intended to serve this function, and the table of contents as printed also falls into three parts, with centered subheadings for the last two—"Sea-Pieces" (preceding "The Haglets") and "Pebbles." In the absence of manuscripts or proofs of the table of contents, the stages of its evolution, if any, and the timing of its submission to De Vinne cannot be known. But its printed form, designating a three-part structure, is of a piece with the thinking underlying Melville's alterations to the running-titles and the section-titles on the page proofs.

In the body of the text, Melville made corrections or revisions on thirty of the pages in the page proofs. Except for those in "Bridegroom Dick," the changes were usually small adjustments to spelling, capitalization, punctuation, and spacing (a few of them correcting compositors' errors not caught earlier, and two repeating corrections made on the unreturned "John Marr" page proofs), with only an occasional revision of wording. But in "Bridegroom Dick" he made substantive revisions on eight of its pages, including a replacement of two lines on page 32 (203.95–96) and a concentration of ten revisions on page 35 (205.145–58). In the former case, he penciled a note to the printer: "If this can not be got into two lines, then occupy the space between the paragraphs." One other note shows his concern with spacing: on page 81, after marking a bracket and asterisk to the left of the last stanza of "The Æolian Harp" (227.45–48), he wrote in ink, "Leave more space between these and the preceding lines;

---

made the alterations that survive on the page proofs. Other speculations are obviously possible.

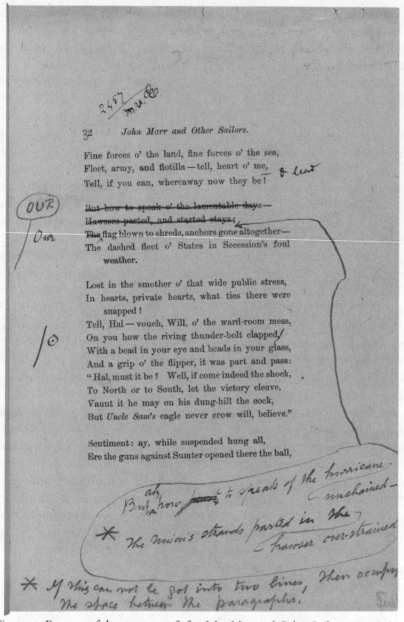

Figure 3. Page 32 of the page proofs for *John Marr and Other Sailors,* containing
lines 92–110 of "Bridegroom Dick" and showing Melville's corrections
and revisions, his note to the printer (at the foot), and two notations by the
De Vinne Press proofreader (at upper left and to the right of the second and
third lines). Size of original: 8¾" × 6" (as trimmed in binding). Courtesy
of Houghton Library, Harvard University: *fAC85.M4977.888jab.

and set to the right a little". (This note, like some of the others, had been provisionally written in pencil first, then erased and rewritten in ink.)[45]

After Melville returned these page proofs, his alterations were incorporated into the standing type by Tully and possibly another compositor: Tully's penciled name shows up at the lower right corners of the first two-thirds of the page proofs as they presently exist.[46] The printing of the sheets for the final product could then begin. Production of the book was completed sometime before September 7, when the two copyright deposit copies were received at the Library of Congress. Thus probably no more than about two weeks intervened between Melville's return of the page proofs and De Vinne's mailing of the deposit copies; Melville might have received his copies any time between about August 24 and September 4.[47] The book contains 108 pages printed on paper with a laid pattern, the leaf size being 6¾ by 4½ inches; its structure consists of thirteen four-leaf gatherings, preceded by a preliminary two-leaf gathering. The sheets are enclosed in a cover of light creamy tan stiff paper, printed on the front

45. It was possibly during the reading of the page proofs that Melville wrote in blue pencil at the top of the title-page proof now housed with the galley proofs, "Correction", followed by three page numbers (67, 101, 32), for those are three of the proof pages on which he marked changes that restored his manuscript readings. This title-page proof was marked by the printer only with the penciled job number at the top left and the name of the compositor, "Bothwell," vertically at the lower right. (James W. Bothwell, then in his early twenties, was an experienced compositor who had worked in the shop since he was a boy and who in 1919 became the head of the firm.) It is likely that this proof was not originally a part of the galley proofs and was rather part of the page proofs (it is wider than the galley proofs, and its dimensions, 9⅜ by 6⅞ inches, could have been the size of all the page proofs before they were cut down for binding). Melville's wife may have decided to use this proof as a cover-sheet for the galley proofs—she wrote "First Proof (complete)" on it—at the time when she used the proof of the cover to serve the same function for the page proofs and wrote "Revise Proof (complete)" on it.

46. As a result of the trimming of the page proofs for binding, Tully's name is partially cut off in some cases. No name appears from page 66 onward; his name might once have been written on those pages, but conceivably the name of another compositor, who wrote his name nearer the edge of the paper than Tully did, could have been present there.

47. At this time the copyright requirements were that a title page be deposited (or mailed for deposit) at the Library of Congress before publication and that two completed copies be deposited (or mailed) within ten days after publication. A "publication" date for a book intended for private circulation has no meaning, and one could perhaps regard it as the date on which the printer sent copies to the author. If De Vinne followed the letter of the law, one would have to consider the date on which he made his shipment to the Library of Congress (a few days prior to September 7) as the "publication" date, since he sent the title page as well as finished copies at the same time. But of course the book may in fact have been finished, and copies sent to Melville, earlier—though not plausibly before about August 24 (which would allow only about a week for Melville to read page proofs and for De Vinne's office to receive them and perform the rest of the work).

with the full title (incorporating a decorative band), a small fleuron centered below, the De Vinne Press imprint (dated 1888) at the foot, and—at the upper left—the phrase "*25 Copies*" with a wavy underlining. Melville's name does not appear anywhere—not on the cover, or the title page,[48] or the copyright page (the copyright is in the name of "Theodore L. De Vinne & Co.").[49] The well-proportioned text pages reflect De Vinne's typographic taste: with twenty-four lines to the page (plus the running-title) and a text width of three inches, the remaining space is divided to produce precisely the relationship among the four margins that De Vinne specified as "most acceptable to publisher and book-buyer."[50] The presence of eight section-title pages with blank versos adds to the spaciousness of the layout (even if it does not reflect Melville's final intention regarding the structure of the contents).

Melville must have dispatched a copy promptly to the dedicatee, for Russell expressed his appreciation in a letter dated September 18. Although no reviews would be expected for a book intended for private distribution, a review did appear in the New York *Mail and Express* on November 20. Possibly by Richard Henry Stoddard, it called Melville "the author of the second best cavalry poem in the English language ["Sheridan at Cedar Creek" in *Battle-Pieces*], the first being Browning's 'How They Brought the Good News from Ghent to Aix' "; the reviewer also said, "Nothing finer than his unrhymed poems exist outside of the sea lyrics of Campbell."[51] Melville gave copies of the book away during the remaining three years of his life, and he continued to revise the poems. Eleven such revisions are known from surviving copies, some of which contain handwritten alterations in Melville's or (more often) his wife's hand.

48. The title page and the cover have the same layout, with the title in three lines, the first in larger capitals than the other two ("JOHN MARR / AND OTHER SAILORS / WITH SOME SEA-PIECES"), and the imprint at the foot in three lines ("NEW-YORK / THE DE VINNE PRESS / 1888"). But the title page does not have the "*25 Copies*" line, nor does it have a decorative band to the right of the first line of the title and to the left of the second, or a long J in "JOHN"; and it has a different ornament in the space between the title and the imprint. (The full title as printed is the same one that was on Melville's handwritten title page, though not with the same lineation; Melville wrote, "John Marr / and / Other Sailors / with / Some Sea-Pieces".)

49. The copyright was transferred to Melville's wife, at her request, on December 23, 1891, three months after Melville's death.

50. *Modern Methods of Book Composition,* p. 300. His recommended proportions of 4:5:7:8 (inner margin, top margin, outer margin, bottom margin) match those in *John Marr.*

51. The full review appears in the "Postscript on Reception" section of the HISTORICAL NOTE (p. 527).

TIMOLEON

IN THE YEARS after *John Marr,* Melville, despite illness and family distractions, worked on new and old manuscripts, concentrating in early 1890 on a collection of poems to be called "As They Fell" (comprising two groups, "A Rose or Two" and "Weeds & Wildings"). By the spring of 1891, however, he felt that a different collection of poems, finally entitled *Timoleon Etc.* and containing forty-two poems, was the one he wished to send to a printer. This time he chose a New York firm called the Caxton Press—not a distinguished or famous printer like De Vinne, but simply one of the many job-printing businesses in the city that could handle book work. No information has come to light that would suggest why Melville switched to this firm. It was located at 171 Macdougall Street, only slightly farther from his house than the De Vinne Press, though to the southwest rather than straight south. Since he may well have dealt with the firm by mail or messenger, its proximity to him was not particularly relevant, but it does suggest one way he may have known about the firm, since he did a great deal of walking in the city. He may of course have seen its name in published books, for unlike some job printers the Caxton Press was capable of printing substantial books and did so for several publishers, including Fleming H. Revell, Dodd Mead, Scribner, and the New York branch of George Routledge. For example, the Routledge edition of Lamb's *Tales from Shakespeare* (undated, but probably from the late 1880s) lists the Caxton Press as printer; the Press's name, however, would not necessarily have appeared in all the books it printed on behalf of trade publishers. But sometimes books undertaken for individuals or institutions carried the Press's name on the title page; an example from 1891, besides *Timoleon,* is Charles H. Winfield's ninety-seven-page *Monograph on the Founding of Jersey City.*

The only documentary evidence of the production process for *Timoleon* known to exist is a pair of manuscripts at Harvard (MS Am 188 [387]), one a much-revised manuscript in Melville's hand and the other a transcription for the printer largely in Melville's wife's hand.[52] The holograph in its present form consists of 112 leaves,[53] generally of an off-white or cream paper

---

52. There are four unbound, unsewn gatherings of printed sheets at Harvard—*AC85. M4977.891t(B)—but they are not annotated and are not proofs (the paper is printed on both sides); they are simply folded sheets from the regular press run (gatherings 2 through 5).

53. The last leaf is numbered "111," but the total comes to 112 when the following adjustments are made: an extra unnumbered leaf follows leaf 70 (and contains a superseded

with a laid pattern and averaging 7⅛ by 5¾ inches; 3 leaves (17, 18, 24) are of brighter yellow paper, the first 2 with handwriting in blue ink, as opposed to the predominant black ink (though other inks and pencils were also used). This manuscript would not have been suitable for the printer because of its extensive and complex revisions, and 27 leaves have part-leaves attached to them.[54] The complexity of the document, however, reveals a wealth of information about Melville's processes of revision (among the poems for which the record is especially rich are "Art," "Milan Cathedral," and "The Return of the Sire de Nesle," as the textual notes below make clear).

Melville's wife's transcript of the poems, copied from his manuscript, consists of 104 leaves of generally the same off-white or cream paper as the holograph (with 12 leaves of the same brighter yellow paper that appears three times in the holograph), inscribed mostly in a gray-black ink.[55] The transcript is neatly written and revised; although four dozen leaves contain revisions or clarifications of wording (both in Melville's and in his wife's hand), nearly all of them relate to single words, and the few that are more involved are equally clear and easy to follow.[56] It is obvious that this manuscript was prepared for the printer's use because Melville's wife wrote on it seven notes to the printer, and Melville added one more; six of them deal with spacing between stanzas and two (including Melville's) with indention. On leaf 12, Melville placed a bracket and asterisk at the beginning of the eighth line from the end of section VII of "Timoleon"

version of "Venice"); leaf 78 is missing ("Milan Cathedral," now at the University of Virginia); and a second leaf numbered "103" comes between leaves 110 and 111 (and contains a superseded version of "The Return of the Sire de Nesle"). (Leaf 18, a smaller piece of yellowish paper, containing the text—but not the title—of "The Ravaged Villa," is not numbered but is allowed for in the numbering.) Many leaves have earlier numbers marked out.

54. They are leaves 6–11 (11 has two notes added to the back), 16, 31, 33–36, 39, 46–48, 54 (three slips added to the front), 58, 60, 74, 82, 84, 85, 92–94, 103. This manuscript has been given conservation treatment (see note 27 above).

55. The last leaf is numbered "103," but there are two leaves numbered "91" (containing lines 13–34 of "Syra"). Leaves 53 ("Fragments of a Lost Gnostic Poem of the 12th Century"), 70 (the last six lines of "In a Church of Padua"), 72–78 (the last four lines of "Milan Cathedral" and all of "Pausilippo"), and 95–97 ("The Apparition" and the first eight lines of "In the Desert") are the ones on the brighter yellow paper.

56. Some of the leaves were probably copied from earlier transcribed leaves. The fact that the extant transcript sometimes has different wording from Melville's manuscript suggests that he had made the changes on earlier transcript leaves, which became untidy enough to require recopying. This situation probably occurred with some of the leaves of "Timoleon," "The Apparition," "In the Desert," "The Great Pyramid," and "The Return of the Sire de Nesle" (see the textual notes below).

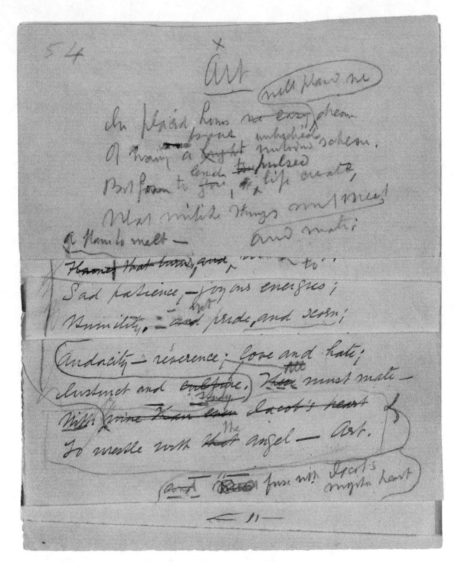

Figure 4. Leaf 54 of Melville's manuscript of *Timoleon Etc.* in its final
state, containing the heavily revised text of "Art" and consisting of four
pieces of paper that were originally pinned together: Stage Be patch at
the top (lines 1–4); Stage Bc mount (line 5, the only part of the
underlying main leaf that shows); Stage Bb clip (lines 6–7, the first two
lines of the text on this clip); Stage Bd patch (lines 8–11, covering all
but the first two lines of Stage Bb clip). (For further detail, see
pp. 797–800 below.) Size of original: 7⅛" × 5¾". Courtesy of
Houghton Library, Harvard University: MS Am 188 (387).

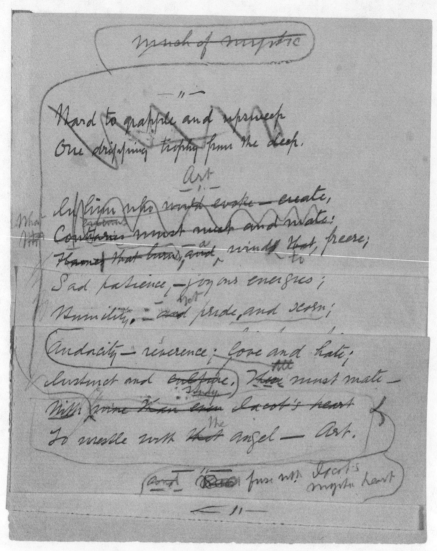

Figure 5. Leaf 54 of Melville's manuscript of *Timoleon Etc.,* with Stage
Be patch removed at the top and Stage Bd patch removed at the bottom,
leaving Stage Bc text at the top and Stage Bb clip at the bottom. (For further
detail, see pp. 797–800 below.) Size of original: 7⅛" × 5¾". Courtesy of
Houghton Library, Harvard University: MS Am 188 (387).

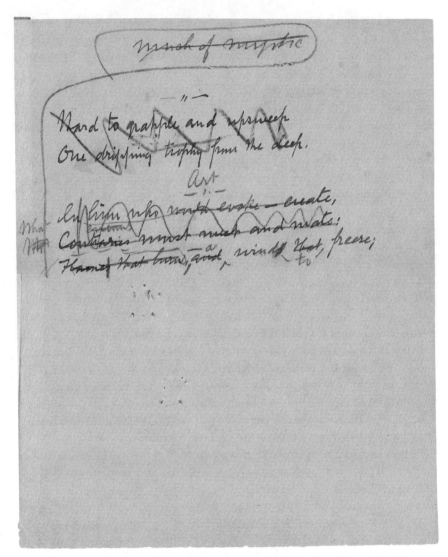

Figure 6. Leaf 54 of Melville's manuscript of *Timoleon Etc.*, with all
patches and clips removed, showing Stage Bc text on the main leaf.
(For further detail, see pp. 797–800 below.) Size of original: 7⅛" × 5¾".
Courtesy of Houghton Library, Harvard University: MS Am 188 (387).

(258.165) and then penciled a note in a circle, with a corresponding aster-isk, at the end of that section: "Indent,—to correspond with the rest." On leaf 19, his wife wrote the circled instruction "Double space" at the end of "The Margrave's Birth Night," with an arrow pointing to the space preceding the last stanza. At the top of leaf 27, she left a considerable space and wrote in it this circled note: "Double space—between this and the preceding italicized lines" (the preceding lines were the epigraph to "After the Pleasure Party," at the bottom of the previous leaf). Similarly, she left the top half of leaf 35 blank, a location that precedes the last forty-six lines of the same poem (beginning with 262.105), and her circled note reads "Double space between this and the foregoing." At the top of leaf 76 (preceding the forty-sixth line of "Pausilippo") and the top of leaf 78 (preceding its last five lines), she wrote "Leave double space here".[57] At the top of leaf 90, preceding "Syra," her circled note says, "Indent first line of paragraphs". Finally, preceding the last stanza of "The Great Pyra-mid" on leaf 101, she inserted in a circle, "Leave double space here". In four of these instances—the last two and the two in "After the Pleasure Party"—she called attention to the instructions with a jagged line meant to suggest a pointing finger. (There are also occasional brackets at the left margin to designate indention.) Another indication that this manuscript was intended for the printer is Melville's triple underlining of the title of every poem, which to the printer would signal that the titles were to be set in full capitals, and his double-underlining of the title of the epigraph to "After the Pleasure Party," indicating that it was to be set in small capi-tals (notations that were followed by the compositors).[58]

The manuscript, thus marked, was indeed used by the printer, a fact made clear by the presence of two compositors' names penciled on it at the beginnings of their takes. On leaf 1 (where "Timoleon" begins) is written the name "Steed". At the top left of leaf 21, where "The Garden of Metrodorus" begins, there is the name "Cullen". Apparently Cullen set most of the rest of the book, though in several separate takes, for Steed's name does not occur again. Cullen's name is penciled at the tops of leaves 39 (where "Lamia's Song" begins), 49 (where "Buddha" begins), and 90 (where "Syra" begins). At the top of leaf 97 (where "In the Desert" begins)

---

57. The second time "double" was capitalized, and the note was not circled.

58. He also marked the end of every poem, for clarity, with his characteristic divi-sional or ending mark—a horizontal line followed by two short vertical lines and another horizontal line—without meaning for the printer to translate it into a typographic ornament. (His consistency in marking titles for the printer here is in contrast with the holograph printer's copy for *John Marr,* where the titles are variously double-underlined, single-underlined, or followed by his divisional mark.)

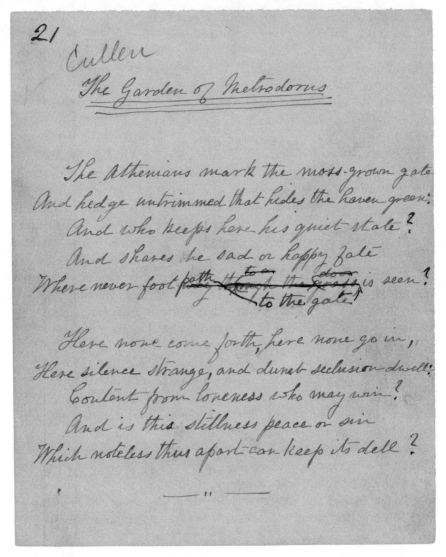

Figure 7. Leaf 21 of Elizabeth Shaw Melville's transcript of *Timoleon Etc.*, containing the text of "The Garden of Metrodorus" and showing Melville's revision, his triple-underlining of the title, and the signature of the Caxton Press compositor ("Cullen"). Size of original: 7⅛" × 5¾". Courtesy of Houghton Library, Harvard University: MS Am 188 (387).

appears the word "office", the significance of which is not clear.[59] There are no other markings made in the printing office: unlike De Vinne's compositors, Steed and Cullen did not indicate on the manuscript the beginning points of each galley. They were like De Vinne's workmen, however, in making numerous changes in punctuation, though they apparently did not make nearly as many.

In the absence of any proofs, there is no way in most cases to reconstruct what happened at the galley-proof stage as opposed to the page-proof stage.[60] All one can do is look at the differences between the final printed text and the printer's-copy manuscript and take those differences to represent a combination of changes made at the two stages, plus any uncorrected compositors' errors or alterations—recognizing that any restorations Melville made of compositors' alterations in punctuation and capitalization would not be observable. How often he made such restorations cannot be determined, but it is known that in reading the *John Marr* proofs he did not make a large number of them, and certainly *Timoleon* as printed contains over a hundred instances of compositorial punctuation. Melville made some three dozen substantive alterations in proof, sometimes correcting errors present in his wife's transcript (such as the omission of the fourteenth line of "Pausilippo") and sometimes making new revisions.

One change that was more likely to have been made at the galley-proof than at the page-proof stage was the shift in the location of "After the Pleasure Party" from its place in the printer's copy, following "The Weaver," to a position as the second poem in the book, following "Timoleon." In the galley proofs that poem must have followed "The Weaver," because the compositor would have made some notation on the manuscript (to explain his order of setting and alert the in-house proofreader to it) if Melville had communicated instructions about the move after sending the manuscript and before receiving the galley proofs. Such a change marked on galley proofs would have been easier (and less expensive) to

59. Since the typesetting was so nearly finished at the end of Cullen's last take, conceivably the shop foreman decided to set the three remaining short poems himself and indicated that the "office" was responsible.

60. Throughout this discussion it is assumed, first, that there were author's galley proofs as well as page proofs, for by this time author's galley proofs were in regular use by printers (see note 16 above)—and of course De Vinne used them for *John Marr*. It is also assumed that there were only one stage of galley proof and one of page proof—a reasonable assumption given the clean state of the printer's copy and the uncomplicated nature of the later revisions, and given De Vinne's practice in handling *John Marr,* where the printer's copy was not as clean and the later revisions were more extensive.

accommodate than if it had been marked on page proofs. But of course that point does not eliminate the possibility that Melville failed to settle on the new position of the poem in time and that he marked it on the page proofs, despite the shifting of fourteen page numbers that would have been involved.

Further support for the idea that it was entered on the galley proofs is afforded by the six leaves that are presently housed at the beginning of the printer's-copy manuscript. The first leaf, unnumbered, is a title page in Melville's hand; the next four leaves, numbered "1" through "4", contain a table of contents almost entirely in Melville's wife's hand; and the final leaf, numbered "5", contains (in Melville's hand) a dedication to Elihu Vedder, the expatriate American painter whose work Melville admired, especially the painting that Melville celebrated in "'Formerly a Slave'" (in *Battle-Pieces*) and the illustrated and hand-lettered 1886 edition of the *Rubáiyát,* which Melville owned. That these leaves were intended as printer's copy is shown, first, by Melville's circled "Title Page" in the upper right corner of the first leaf and his circled "Dedication" in that position on the last one (both circled to show that these words were not to be printed). Then, on the first leaf of the table of contents, Melville added "Table of" to his wife's "Contents." and double-underlined the whole rather than circling it (to show that it was to be printed in small capitals).[61] His use of the blank lower part of the second leaf to write "Fruit of Travel Long Ago" (triple-underlined) and the first two titles in that section (marking out those titles at the top of the next leaf) was obviously intended to make clear to the printer (as it would not have been otherwise) that "Fruit of Travel Long Ago" was to be a centered section-title in the table of contents, set in full capitals. The titles listed on the four table-of-contents leaves, after a few alterations by Melville, correspond exactly in order and wording with the table of contents as finally printed, except for the accidental omission of "Monody."[62] Although there are no printer's markings on the six leaves

61. In connection with this alteration, he marked out her other leaf-headings: "Timoleon &c" in parentheses on the first two, "Fruit of Travel Long Ago" in parentheses on the second two, and "Contents" on all after the first.

62. Besides the details relating to "After the Pleasure Party" (discussed below), there are three places that reflect an effort to make this table of contents display the final text: the title "C——s Lament" appears in that form, though on leaf 50, at the head of the poem, the title is "Coleridge's Lament" (which was later changed to "C——'s", presumably on the galley proofs); the title "Pisa's Leaning Tower" appears in that form without any revisions, though on leaf 68 "Pisa's" is a revision in Melville's hand of "The" in his wife's transcription; "Syra" was originally written in the table of contents as "Syra

(unless the unidentified hand that penciled "The Caxton Press" at the foot of the title page, marked to occupy a line between Melville's "May" and "1891", belonged to a Caxton employee),[63] it is possible that they did go to the printer.[64] If so, it also seems likely that they were not sent with

---

long Ago", and the last two words are marked out to make the title conform with the one on leaf 90, at the head of the poem, where those two words are also marked out. It seems clear, therefore, that pains were taken to make this table of contents correct for the printer.

But just when it was first written out is a separate matter and is not as clear: the "Pisa" instance would suggest a time after Melville had gone over the printer's copy, whereas the "Syra" one would suggest an earlier time; and the "Coleridge" instance would suggest a time close to the reading of galley proofs. Possibly the basic list is an early one, for which Melville's wife drew on manuscripts no longer extant (but late enough to include in its basic inscription the title "Pausilippo," a poem added to the manuscript after the initial foliation had been completed). Certainly the basic inscription of the title "After the Pleasure Party," as explained below, seems to represent the first of three recoverable stages in the evolution of the title of that poem. A relatively early date is also suggested by the fact that (probably on Melville's instruction) his wife wrote the titles in the "Fruit of Travel Long Ago" section on two separate pieces of paper (so labeled), which could be placed before or after the two leaves of "Timoleon &c" poems (so labeled), and all four leaves show signs of having been differently numbered. Thus the basic list was made at a time before Melville had finally decided which group of poems was to come first. The two "Timoleon &c" leaves were first numbered "1" and "2" in ink; then they were changed to "3" and "4" in pencil when Melville inked "1" and "2" on the leaves of "Fruit of Travel Long Ago"; and finally they became "1" and "2" again when he inked "3" and "4" on the "Fruit" leaves.

63. Who was following Melville's instruction, for it could not be assumed that a customer wished to have the printer's name on the title page. The fact that the manuscript title page, even with the addition of the printer's name, still does not match the imprint as printed (since it lacks "New York" and includes "May") is probably of no consequence: once the compositor knew that the printer's name was to be used, he would no doubt have proceeded to make a conventional imprint (adding the city and deleting the month), even without explicit copy—as De Vinne's compositor had apparently also done. (On the later change in the book's title, see below.)

64. That they might have been used by the printer as setting copy is suggested by two instances in which the printed table of contents follows them in leaving out hyphens (in "Night March" and "Bye Canal"), even though hyphens are present in those titles at the heads of the poems in the body of the text. There is, however, some strong contrary evidence: the printed table of contents departs from the manuscript leaves in spelling "Colonna" with one "l". "Colonna" is also spelled with one "l" at the head of the poem in the printed text, suggesting that the printed table of contents may have been made up from the titles in the printed text (regardless of when the printer's-copy spelling "Collona" was corrected). The printed table of contents also departs from the manuscript table of contents in capitalizing "A", "Lost", and "Century" in "Fragments of A Lost Gnostic Poem of the 12th Century" and the second "the" in "The Age of The Antonines." Since

the manuscript of the poems themselves but rather with the galley proofs, when Melville returned those proofs with his markings.

Support for this conjecture (aside from the separate numbering of these leaves) comes from clues offered by the multi-stage treatment of "After the Pleasure Party" on the first leaf of the table of contents. Melville's wife originally listed that title following "The Weaver," corresponding to its position in her transcript of the texts of the poems (and in Melville's manuscript). Next Melville (reverting to an earlier title in his manuscript) penciled "A Boy's Revenge" to the right of it, perhaps near the time when he squeezed "A Boys Revenge / or /" in above "After the Pleasure Party" at the head of the poem on leaf 26. Then, after deciding to move the poem, he marked out the original entry for "After the Pleasure Party" and wrote "A Boy's Revenge" at the upper right, with a line connecting it to the space between "Timoleon" and "The Night-March." Finally, he marked out "A Boy's Revenge" and wrote "After the Pleasure Party" below it, still making clear that it was to follow "Timoleon."

If this leaf, so marked, along with the other five leaves of preliminaries, had accompanied the manuscript of the poems, the change in position and title of "After the Pleasure Party" would also have been marked on that manuscript. And if the leaves of preliminaries had indeed been sent later than the texts of the poems, the likely moment would have been when the galley proofs were returned, since ideally the text for the preliminaries was needed in time to be made part of the page proofs (especially given the printer's decision to paginate them continuously with the body of the text). It thus seems plausible that Melville marked the change in position and the final change in title of "After the Pleasure Party" on the galley proofs and on the manuscript of the table of contents at about the same time. And presumably he also took this occasion to indicate that he wished to have a section-title leaf preceding "After the Pleasure Party," with the poem's title on the recto and the epigraph (with its own title) on the verso—an effective way to make absolutely clear that "Lines Traced

-----

all the poem titles are set in full capitals at the heads of poems in the printed book, a compositor who was making up the table of contents from the printed text would have no way of knowing (other than by convention) which words were to be capitalized. His unconventional capitalizing of "A" and "The" may have reflected his judgment that "A Lost Gnostic Poem" and "The Antonines" were units that needed to begin with capital letters. (That the printed table of contents spells "Birthnight" as one word and "L'Envoi" with an "i" is irrelevant to the present question, since they are also spelled that way in the printed text and the printer's copy, despite Melville's manuscript spelling of "Birth Night" and "L'Envoy.")

Under an Image of Amor Threatening" was the title of the epigraph, not the subtitle of the whole poem.[65]

The manuscript leaves of preliminaries, if they did go to the Caxton office along with the marked galley proofs, allow one to infer a few changes that were made at the page-proof stage. For example, Melville's wife inadvertently omitted "Monody" from the table of contents (though she had copied the poem itself at its proper place in her transcript, on leaf 41), and this omission was not corrected by Melville when he went over her table of contents. Since "Monody" does appear in the table of contents of the finished book, the error was rectified either by the compositor who set the page proofs of the preliminaries (in the course of supplying the page numbers for each poem) or else by Melville when reading the page proofs (which would have lacked "Monody" in the table of contents if the compositor had strictly followed the manuscript table of contents). The manuscript title leaf and dedication leaf also suggest page-proof alterations on Melville's part. The manuscript title reads "Timoleon / And Other Ventures / in / Minor Verse." And the manuscript dedication says simply "To / Elihu Vedder". Thus if these manuscript leaves accompanied the marked galley proof, these wordings would have been the ones in the page proofs. But since both are different in the finished book ("Timoleon / Etc." and "To / My Countryman / Elihu Vedder"), Melville would have made the changes on the page proofs.

Evidence for the timing of the Caxton Press's work on *Timoleon* comes from Melville's handwritten title page, where he wrote "May 1891", and from the copyright records. A printed title page was received at the Library of Congress on May 15, 1891, and the deposit copies of the finished book were received on June 16. The requirements of the law had changed slightly since the time of *John Marr:* the title page was still to be deposited in (or mailed to) the Library of Congress sometime before publication, but the deposit copies were now to be deposited (or mailed) no later than the day of publication. Since the concept of a publication day is meaningless for *Timoleon,* all the second deposit date tells us is that finished copies of *Timoleon* were available, at the latest, a few days before June 16. Probably they were available earlier, since the Caxton Press would have been under

---

65. This section-title leaf in the finished book does, however, produce some awkwardness, as far as the overall organization of the collection is concerned. The only two subdivisions indicated in the table of contents are "Fruit of Travel Long Ago" and "L'Envoi"; yet the section-title for "After the Pleasure Party" suggests that it, too, is a similar subdivision, since no other individual poem (including "Timoleon") has its own section-title.

no pressure to deposit copies promptly, given that there was no official publication date. Similarly, all the title-page deposit date tells us is that sometime before May 15 the Caxton Press had been engaged by Melville to do the printing. There is no way to know how much time had elapsed after Melville's initial approach to the Caxton Press; his date of "May 1891" on the manuscript title-page, even if that page were (improbably) written as early as when his wife's transcript was receiving its final touches as a printer's copy, does not rule out the possibility that he approached the printer in April and assumed that the book could not be completed until May. Nor can one know whether the typesetting for *Timoleon* was actually under way by May 15, since title pages for deposit purposes were often set up in advance of other work on a book. But because the deposited title page carried the title "Timoleon / (Etc.)" and because, as suggested above, that title may not have been reported to the Caxton office until page-proof stage, there is a possibility that the typesetting had been completed by May 15. If the Caxton Press handled *Timoleon* as expeditiously as De Vinne produced *John Marr,* it is conceivable that Melville could have received finished copies before the end of May. But the early part of June may seem more likely in light of an inscription to Melville's wife, dated "June 1891", laid into one of the Harvard copies of *Timoleon* (see pp. 593–94).

In physical form, the book is a companion piece to *John Marr.* The leaf size is nearly identical (7 by 4⅝ inches—that is, a quarter of an inch taller); the text paper again has a laid pattern; and the structure is again four-leaf gatherings, though this time there are only nine of them, and the external thickness of the book is an eighth of an inch less. But the desire to keep the text within nine gatherings cannot excuse the amateurishly crowded makeup. The section-title for "Fruit of Travel Long Ago" has the first poem in that section and the beginning of the second one on its verso, even though there is a blank leaf at the end—meaning that there was space to have a blank verso for this section-title. Alternatively, the other major division in the table of contents, "L'Envoi," could have had its own section-title with a blank verso; but "L'Envoi." appears above the title of the last poem, rather than on a separate page. Similarly, the cramped feel of this volume is enforced by many places where two poems appear on the same page. An example of unprofessional layout that would not have been tolerated by De Vinne is the two-page spread at pages 26–27, where two short poems fill the left-hand page, and on the right the beginning of another poem, "The Margrave's Birth Night," starts about an inch and a half lower, more than the usual drop-down space for the longer poems. And there are a number of other openings where the lack of balance calls attention to itself.

As with *John Marr*, Melville's name appears nowhere; the copyright notice gives "The Caxton Press" as the copyright holder.[66] The paper cover is different from that on *John Marr* only in being somewhat less stiff and of a slightly grayer shade of tan.[67] Unlike *John Marr*, however, the front cover does not declare the number of copies printed; but *Timoleon* is now equally scarce, and one can be reasonably safe in assuming that Melville followed the pattern of *John Marr* and again had only twenty-five copies printed. But he did not have much time to distribute them, because within four months of the completion of the production of *Timoleon*, he was dead. His work with the Caxton Press was thus the last in his forty-five-year series of experiences with the printers and publishers of his books.

66. Three months after Melville's death, his wife had the copyright assigned to her (the transfer date, December 22, 1891, was one day prior to the transfer date for *John Marr*).

67. A copy is known in a contemporary cloth binding—white, with "TIMO-LEON / ETC. / HERMAN MELVILLE" stamped in gold on the front cover. But no information has come to light regarding the circumstances surrounding the production of this binding, and thus there is no way to know whether it has any connection with Melville, his wife, or his family. The copy bears no inscription, but a clipped signature of Melville is pasted on its title page. It is now in the collection of William S. Reese, who bought it at the sale of H. Bradley Martin's collection at Sotheby's, New York, on January 30, 1990.

General Note on the Text

THIS EDITION OF Melville's published short poems presents an unmodernized critical text, prepared according to the theory of copy-text formulated by W. W. Greg.[1] Central to that theory is the distinction between substantives (the words of a text) and accidentals (spelling and punctuation). Persons involved in the printing and publishing of texts have often taken it on themselves to alter accidentals; and authors, when examining or revising printed forms of their work, have often been relatively unconcerned with accidentals.[2] An author's failure to change

---

1. In "The Rationale of Copy-Text" (1950–51). For the application of this method to the period of Melville, see the Center for Editions of American Authors, *Statement of Editorial Principles and Procedures* (1972). G. Thomas Tanselle's *Textual Criticism Since Greg: A Chronicle, 1950–2000* provides a survey of the influence of, and responses to, Greg's rationale; a comprehensive listing of writings on textual criticism, both before and after Greg, is in Tanselle's *Introduction to Scholarly Editing* (pp. 61–142). Full bibliographical information for any source not provided with it in this NOTE is given in the comprehensive list of WORKS CITED at the end of the volume. Unless otherwise specified, all quotations of letters to or from Melville are from the Northwestern-Newberry *Correspondence* volume, where they can be located by date.

2. Accidentals can affect the meaning (or substance) of a text, and Greg's distinction is not meant to suggest otherwise; rather, its purpose is to emphasize the fact that persons involved in the transmission of texts have habitually behaved differently in regard to the two categories.

certain accidentals altered by a copyist, compositor, or publisher does not amount to an endorsement of those accidentals. When the aim of a critical edition, as here, is to establish a text that represents as nearly as possible the author's final intentions, it follows that—in the absence of contrary evidence—the formal texture of the work will be more accurately reproduced by adopting as copy-text[3] either the fair-copy manuscript or the first printing based on it. The printed form is chosen if the manuscript does not survive or if the author worked in such a way that corrected proof became in effect the final form of the manuscript. This basic text may then be emended with any later authorial alterations (whether in substantives or accidentals) and with other obvious corrections. Following this procedure maximizes the probability of keeping authorial readings when evidence is inconclusive as to the source of an alteration in a later authorized text. The resulting text is the product of critical judgment and does not correspond exactly to that of any single surviving document; but its aim is to come closer to the author's intentions—insofar as they are recoverable—than any such document.

The Harper edition of *Battle-Pieces* (1866), the only edition of this collection published during Melville's lifetime, was set directly from the manuscript he furnished the printer; and, since that manuscript is not known to have survived, the text of the Harper edition becomes the copy-text for the present edition.[4] For the De Vinne Press edition of *John Marr and Other Sailors* (1888) and the Caxton Press edition of *Timoleon Etc.* (1891), Melville's manuscripts do survive at Harvard, and in each case the manuscript becomes the copy-text. For the one uncollected poem, "Inscription For the Dead At Fredericksburgh," published in facsimile in *Autograph Leaves of Our Country's Authors* (1864), Melville's manuscript with his preferred text survives at the Library of Congress, and it becomes the copy-text.[5]

3. "Copy-text" is the text accepted as the basis for an edition.

4. Five of the poems were published earlier in *Harper's New Monthly Magazine*; for the decision not to designate these magazine printings as copy-texts, see pp. 583–84 below.

5. The particular copy of *Battle-Pieces* that served (in the form of a marked xerographic reproduction) to furnish the text to the publisher of the present edition was Newberry Library Case Y274.56. The copies of *John Marr* and *Timoleon* used for this purpose were xerographic reproductions of the printed editions, altered to match the readings in the manuscripts (except when emendation was necessary): the particular copies were Brown University (Harris Collection) 76.M531j and 76.M531t. For the uncollected poem, a typewritten transcript prepared by the present editors was used. The possibility that there are other uncollected published poems by Melville has occasionally been raised by scholars who have proposed that certain unsigned or pseudonymous periodical poems be attributed to him. But the present editors have not found the arguments for these attributions,

In addition to the editors' close reading of the texts, the principal sources for possible emendation of the copy-texts in this volume are a number of documents with varying degrees of authority. Newspaper, magazine, and anthology printings of some of the poems in Melville's lifetime, or possibly overseen before his death, were examined for variants conceivably authorized by him. A holograph manuscript of "Philip" (later entitled "Sheridan at Cedar Creek") of undetermined date in the New York Public Library is a possible source for emendations. More clearly authoritative sources for emendation are several documents in which Melville can be seen considering, rejecting, and adopting particular revisions: two copies of *Battle-Pieces* at Houghton Library (Harvard), one of which Melville's wife labeled " 'Revised' sheets—with Herman's corrections"; the *John Marr* manuscript, galley proof, page proof, and finished book, all of which contain revisions in his hand; and his manuscript and his wife's transcript (the printer's copy) of *Timoleon,* which display many reworkings. In addition, collations between the surviving stages of *John Marr* and *Timoleon* reveal more variants, some of which can be judged to be Melville's revisions made at stages for which no documentary evidence survives.[6] Finally, collations were performed to test for variants among copies of the first editions.[7]

---

or the nature of the poems themselves, sufficiently convincing to warrant the inclusion of the proposed poems in the present edition. On the other hand, at least one poem that Melville printed has not yet been located, the "lines" (possibly "The Age of the Antonines") that Melville's sister Frances referred to on June 17, 1877 (see Parker 2002, p. 816).

6. The following documents were collated: (1) for *John Marr,* the manuscript (MS Am 188 [370]) versus the galley proofs (*fAC85.M4977.888ja), the galley proofs versus the page proofs (*AC85.M4977.888jab), and the page proofs versus the first edition (photocopy of Brown University 76.M531j); (2) for *Timoleon,* Melville's manuscript (MS Am 188 [387]) versus his wife's transcript (same call number), and his wife's transcript versus the first edition (photocopy of Brown University 76.M531t). In addition, routine procedures in the process of compiling, checking, and preparing the textual information for publication have resulted in a larger total number of collations.

7. In fact, multiple collations by sight and by the Hinman Collator have revealed nothing but negligible type wear and faulty inking. (By superimposing page images, the Hinman Collator enables the human collator's eye to see differences, including minute changes not otherwise easily detected, such as resettings and type damage.) The copies of each book collated for the record are here reported by identification number (for those in the Melville Collection of The Newberry Library) or by library name and call number (for any copy not in the Melville Collection). The number of collations that must be performed in order to detect all significant variations in printed editions can never be prescribed with certainty, since chance determines, at least to some extent, the particular copies available for collation. Regardless of the number of copies collated, there is always

From all these sources, the present edition incorporates 1,017 emendations into the specified copy-texts—the 1866 *Battle-Pieces* and Melville's manuscripts for *John Marr, Timoleon,* and the uncollected published poem. In order to make clear the evidence and rationale on which these decisions rest, a summary account of the relevant documentary evidence is given below (with sketches of the subsequent textual histories of the works), followed by a brief description of Melville's method of preparing printer's copy, a discussion of the treatment in this edition of substantives and accidentals, and an explanation of the editorial apparatus through which the evidence is presented.

THE TEXTS

*B*ATTLE-*PIECES.* No holograph manuscript of *Battle-Pieces,* or any of the poems in it, is known to survive, except for the transcript of "Philip" ("Sheridan at Cedar Creek") that is now in the New York Public Library.[8]

---

the chance that one or more variant states are missing. To reduce the element of chance somewhat, the editors have selectively examined copies in addition to those listed here.

For *Battle-Pieces,* five copies were collated on a Hinman Collator: copy 1 = photocopy of Newberry Library Case Y274.56; copy 2 = Gift 70-27 (Leyda/Howard); copy 3 = 67-1299-2; copy 4 = 67-722-79; copy 5 = 67-1790-2. The collations were of copies 1 vs. 2; 2 vs. 3; 3 vs. 4; 4 vs. 5.

For *John Marr,* seven copies were collated, four by Hinman Collator and three by sight: copy 1 = photocopy of Brown University 76.M531j (Harris); copy 2 = photocopy of Library of Congress PS2384.J6.1888; copy 3 = photocopy of British Library C.95.a.7; copy 4 = photocopy of University of Texas AX.M497.888j; copy 5 = Harvard *AC85. M4977.888j(A); copy 6 = New York Public Library *KL(Melville) [Melville's presentation copy to his wife]; copy 7 = New York Public Library *KL(Melville) [Kate Gansevoort Lansing's copy]. The Hinman collations were of copies 1 vs. 2 and 3; 3 vs. 4. The sight collations were of copy 1 vs. 5, 6, and 7.

For *Timoleon,* six copies were collated, four by Hinman Collator and two by sight: copy 1 = photocopy of Brown University 76.M531t (Harris); copy 2 = photocopy of University of Texas AX.M497.891t; copy 3 = photocopy of Columbia University PS2384. TS.1891; copy 4 = photocopy of American Antiquarian Society Melville 69-1610; copy 5 = Harvard *AC85.M4977.891t(C); copy 6 = New York Public Library *KL(Melville). The Hinman collations were of copies 1 vs. 2 and 4; 2 vs. 3. The sight collations were of copy 1 vs. 4, 5, and 6.

8. In the Alfred Williams Anthony Collection, Box 21, Folder 1. How soon Melville wrote the poem after October 19, 1864, the day of Sheridan's famous ride, is not known, nor is it known when he made the transcription and when he gave it to Richard Henry Stoddard. Stoddard did not use this text in his 1873 revision of R. M. Griswold's *Poets and Poetry of America* (see below), but he did publish a photofacsimile of the second page of the

This document consists of a sheet of blue laid writing paper, folded to form two leaves (each 8 by 5 inches) and carrying the embossed device of "Carson's Congress" brand in the upper left corner of each leaf (the same paper that Melville used sporadically from at least 1861 to 1868). Melville transcribed the poem on the two recto pages at an undetermined time (he signed the transcript "H.M." but did not date it). The text seems intermediate between that of the magazine printing (the *Harpers' New Monthly Magazine* for April 1866) and the book publication: it has the same title as the magazine ("Philip" rather than "Sheridan at Cedar Creek"), but the wording of lines 17–18 agrees with the book rather than the magazine. In other respects its variants (aside from those in indention) are at points where the magazine and the book agree with each other, and they are mostly insignificant differences in punctuation (there is one indifferent substantive variant, "with" for "in" in line 11). Regardless of when Melville wrote out this copy, there is no evidence to suggest that its variants should be preferred to the readings in the book version.

Other potential sources for emendation of the book texts are the printings of five poems in *Harpers' New Monthly Magazine* prior to the publication of the book in late August 1866.[9] The relative timing of the magazine publications and the submission of the whole book manuscript is discussed in the NOTE ON PRINTING AND PUBLISHING HISTORY, along with an account of the publication and physical appearance of the book. Surviving evidence does not make clear whether or not Melville used copies of the magazine printings of those five poems—instead of his own transcript—to prepare printer's copy of them for *Battle-Pieces*. In "Chattanooga," the *Battle-Pieces* text has much lighter, less formal pointing; but in "Sheridan at Cedar Creek," where Melville changed the wording of lines 17–18, the pointing is heavier or more formal in both the magazine and book versions than it is in Melville's "Philip" transcript. In the other three, Melville seems to have purposefully revised the punctuation along with the wording. There are grounds, therefore, for believing that the chances of obtaining Melville's finally intended punctuation are somewhat greater by adopting the *Battle-Pieces* versions, rather than the magazine ones, as

---

transcript (containing the last two stanzas of the poem) in the illustrated limited edition of his *Recollections, Personal and Literary* (New York: A. S. Barnes, 1903), facing page 143. In the accompanying text (pp. 142–44), Stoddard offers no indication as to when or how he acquired the transcript.

9. "The March to the Sea" appeared in the February 1866 issue (32:366–67), "The Cumberland" in March (32:474), "Philip" ("Sheridan at Cedar Creek") in April (32:640), "Chattanooga" in June (33:44), and "Gettysburg" in July (33:209).

copy-text. And certainly the substantive differences in the *Battle-Pieces* texts are more likely to be the work of Melville than of a house editor.

If there is no justification for emending the book text with any variants in the magazine printings, there does exist an important source for possible emendation, in the form of two copies of *Battle-Pieces,* now at Harvard, with annotations in Melville's hand. One of them, Copy A (*AC85. M4977.866b(A)), carries, on the recto of the first leaf following the front free endpaper, Elizabeth Shaw Melville's penciled inscription, "Mrs. Herman Melville / 105 East 18ᵗʰ st" (her residence at the Florence Apartments after Melville's death).[10] On the verso of the front free endpaper Melville penciled "27" and "129", the numbers of two of the pages (the other is 23) on which he entered alternative readings—in "The March into Virginia," "Lyon," and "The March to the Sea." In the table of contents, he also penciled a check mark at the left of the title "The Battle of the Bay" and at the right of the entries for "Shiloh," "The Battle for the Mississippi," and "Running the Batteries," although he did not enter any alterations on the pages where those poems appear.

The other copy, Copy C, is a custom-bound set of " 'Revised' sheets—with / Herman's corrections", in the words of the note his wife penciled on the recto of the binder's leaf following the front free endpaper. As explained above (p. 536), these sheets are simply from the regular press run, presumably sent to Melville in unbound form. In this copy Melville penciled alternative readings at 49 points, only one of which coincides with an alteration marked in Copy A. The basis for using some of the annotations in Copies A and C to emend the copy-text is set forth below, in the section on "Treatment of Substantives," where the precise locations of all the annotations are listed. Since no variants have been discovered in the printed text among copies of the first printings of *Battle-Pieces,* and no new printings or editions of *Battle-Pieces* appeared during Melville's lifetime, the copy-text for the present edition can be defined simply as the text of the 1866 Harper edition.

There are no other sources for emending the first-edition copy-text except theoretically the few reprintings of poems from *Battle-Pieces* that appeared during Melville's lifetime. Seven poems were included in R. H.

---

10. There is another Harvard copy, Copy F, containing the same penciled inscription by Melville's wife on the recto of the first leaf following the front free endpaper: it is the copy presented to her by Melville, with his inked inscription on the next recto, "Lizzie / from / Herman. / August, 1866 / New York." It does not, like Copies A and C, contain any textual alterations in Melville's hand, though his wife penciled on page 132 the two-line revision of "The March to the Sea" (lines 91–92) that Melville penciled into Copy C.

Stoddard's edition of Rufus M. Griswold's *Poets and Poetry of America* (New York: James Miller, 1873), on pages 630–31: "Shiloh," "The Victor of Antietam," "Battle of Stone River," "Philip" ("Sheridan at Cedar Creek"), "The Mound by the Lake," "An uninscribed Monument," and "The Returned Volunteer to his Rifle"). It is conceivable that Melville did more than merely agree to Stoddard's request to reprint these poems, and for that reason the variants in this anthology are recorded in the textual apparatus below (there are none in two of the poems, "The Mound by the Lake" and "The Returned Volunteer to his Rifle"). But the evidence is insufficient to justify the adoption of any of the variants, which in any case are mostly insignificant differences in accidentals and the omission of the date lines. Any variants that appear in other printings seem either indifferent or wrong, the result of the sort of compositorial or editorial carelessness that in George Cary Eggleston's *American War Ballads and Lyrics* (New York: G. P. Putnam's Sons, 1889) turned Melville's "for" into "far" in line 15 of "Running the Batteries" and "Virginian's" into "Virginia's" in line 17 of "Stonewall Jackson Mortally wounded at Chancellorsville." Other known printings are in Edmund Clarence Stedman and Ellen Mackay Hutchinson's anthology *A Library of American Literature* (New York: Webster, 1888–90), 7:476–78, where the only variants are accidentals in "The Stone Fleet," "Sheridan at Cedar Creek," and "In the Prison Pen." Any reprintings in newspapers can be assumed to have no direct authority from Melville.

Since Melville's death, there have been five new editions of the whole book and four facsimiles of the original edition, as well as several selective editions of Melville's work that include poems from *Battle-Pieces.* The Constable edition of *Battle-Pieces,* anonymously edited by Raymond Weaver,[11] appears in volume 16, *Poems* (London, 1924; reprinted in New York in 1963 by Russell & Russell and in Tokyo in 1983 by Meicho Fukyu

---

11. Weaver's editorship is beyond question, though the amount of control he finally had over the text transmitted may not ever be determinable. Not much beyond the fact of his editorship, for example, is inferable from such fragments as a carbon copy of the first page of a letter he wrote to Michael Sadleir (a devotee of Melville and a director of the Constable firm), dated "22-May-23" from "Livingston Hall / Columbia University": "I am, on the morrow, sending off to you most of the Melville material. It seems to me that there is stuff for three volumes. . . . In the other volume I would include *Battle-Pieces, John Marr, Timoleon,* and the unpublished verse. The copy for this volume is almost complete—I have on it not more than two more days work to do" (Box 2, Raymond Weaver Collection, Rare Book and Manuscript Library, Columbia University). For some background on the Constable texts, see Philip Durham, "Prelude to the Constable Edition of Melville."

Kai), and is significant because it was the first edition after Melville's death as well as because it is part of the only complete set of Melville's works that has been available to scholars in the past and that has therefore often been cited as standard. Though it offers no comment on its text, it generally follows the 1866 edition, departing only occasionally in punctuation and spelling (especially through the substitution of British forms). *Battle-Pieces* was less fortunate in its next edition, Howard P. Vincent's *Collected Poems of Herman Melville* (Chicago: Packard & Co., Hendricks House, 1947), which was made available both as an independent volume and as volume 14 of the *Complete Works of Herman Melville,* the latter providing some textual notes. Flaws are frequent in the text (an errata sheet included in some copies lists less than 20 percent of the errors). Vincent's "Preface" announces that his text "faithfully follows" that of the 1866 edition; only a note in the *Complete Works* volume reveals that his text incorporates "the corrections made by Melville in his own copy" (p. 492), meaning Harvard Copy C. Vincent adopts most of the revisions penciled into that copy, including instances where Melville did not line out the printed readings, but he ignores Melville's markings and annotations in Harvard Copy A.[12]

The 1866 Harper edition was reprinted in 1960 by Scholars' Facsimiles and Reprints (Gainesville, Fla.) in the form of a facsimile with commentary by Sidney Kaplan. His "A Note on the Text" states erroneously (p. xxiii) that all the pencilings in Copy A are in Elizabeth Shaw Melville's hand; and in "Melville's Revisions" (pp. xxv–xxviii), he lists all the variants Melville penciled into Harvard Copies A and C, but he does not distinguish between instances where the printed readings are lined out and those where they are not.[13]

Three new editions appeared in the 1960s and 1970s. Norman Jarrard's "Poems by Herman Melville: A Critical Edition of the Published Verse" (Ph.D. diss., University of Texas, 1960) presents a text of *Battle-Pieces* in which all of Melville's post-publication penciled variants are adopted, whether or not the printed readings were lined out. Jarrard makes the questionable decision of adopting the "Philip" transcript as his copy-text for "Sheridan at Cedar Creek," assuming that its accidentals are closer to those Melville intended, though he does not show that the transcript

---

12. Vincent's edition is included in Chadwyck-Healey's *American Poetry: The American Poetry Full-Text Database* (1996), available on CD-ROM and the World Wide Web.

13. This facsimile was reprinted in 1972 by the University of Massachusetts (Amherst). Other facsimiles appeared in 1995 (New York: Da Capo Press, with introduction by Lee Rust Brown), 2000 (Edison, N.J.: Castle Books), and 2001 (Amherst, N.Y.: Prometheus Books, with essays edited by Richard H. Cox and Paul M. Dowling).

dates from either before or after the publication of *Battle-Pieces*. Hennig Cohen's edition, *The Battle-Pieces of Herman Melville* (New York: Thomas Yoseloff, 1964), is generally reliable in following the 1866 edition; even though he characterizes all of Melville's markings in Harvard Copies A and C as "revisions" (sometimes definite, as on p. 209, in the reproduction of p. 16 of Copy C), he does not adopt them. In *Poems of Herman Melville* (New Haven, Conn.: College & University Press, 1976), Douglas Robillard's aim is to print "the complete contents of the three volumes of short poems that Melville saw through the press" (p. 11); but he silently adopts fourteen of the more than forty variants in Copy C of *Battle-Pieces* (and his text has some serious typographical errors in lines 90–91 of "The March to the Sea" on p. 97). The text remains the same in his revised edition of 2000 (Kent, Ohio: Kent State University Press).

Of the various selections from Melville's poetry that have been published, a few may be mentioned for their textual interest. Robert Penn Warren's *Selected Poems of Herman Melville* (New York: Random House, 1970; rpt. Jaffrey, N.H.: David R. Godine, 2004) includes fewer than half the poems in *Battle-Pieces,* but they are most of the longer ones, along with the "Supplement." His edition is worth consideration because he carefully examined Harvard Copies A and C. Though he follows the 1866 text, he comments in his notes (e.g., pp. 363, 365, 367, 369, 375, 376, 381–82, 384) on the penciled variants in those copies; he recognizes that some are "not definite" (p. 363), only "possible" (p. 365) or "tentative" (p. 375), as well as that others are definite revisions (though he misinterprets Melville's revisions of lines 35–36 of "The March into Virginia" on p. 355). In 2001 John Bryant edited for the Modern Library a substantial collection entitled *Tales, Poems, and Other Writings,* which contains eighteen poems from *Battle-Pieces* (plus the "Supplement"). His text (as he points out in "A Note on the Text," p. li) is that of the Northwestern-Newberry Edition, published by advance arrangement with Northwestern University Press; and in his notes he makes occasional reference to Melville's revisions in the Harvard copies. Five years later Robert Faggen edited a *Selected Poems* volume (New York: Penguin Books, 2006) that includes forty-two poems from *Battle-Pieces* (plus the "Supplement"). He states (p. xlv) that his texts of *Battle-Pieces, John Marr,* and *Timoleon* come from "facsimiles of the first editions that have been compared with Melville's own corrected copies" (though no such copy exists for *Timoleon*). He does not say what the comparison led to; but none of Melville's definite revisions in Harvard Copy C of *Battle-Pieces* are incorporated into his text.

Melville's poems have of course appeared in many multi-author anthologies in the past seventy-five years, most of them aimed for college-course adoptions. But of those intended for a more general audience, the one that has been the most widely circulated and received the most attention is perhaps the Library of America volume, *American Poetry: The Nineteenth Century,* volume 2, edited by John Hollander (New York, 1993); it devotes eighty-six pages to Melville's poetry, including fourteen poems from *Battle-Pieces,* and takes its text, by advance arrangement, from the present Northwestern-Newberry volume.

JOHN MARR. The surviving fair-copy manuscript, mostly in Melville's hand—Harvard MS Am 188 (370)—is the source of the copy-text for the present edition;[14] it is described in detail in the NOTE ON PRINTING AND PUBLISHING HISTORY. *John Marr and Other Sailors with Some Sea-Pieces* was set from it in late July 1888 by the De Vinne Press, whose compositors left their marks on it. Since some revisions and clarifications in the manuscript are in Elizabeth Shaw Melville's hand, it is worth making explicit that Melville's further revisions and his sending the result on to the printer indicate that his authority is behind her alterations. It is also behind the section of the manuscript not in his hand—the leaves containing "The Haglets," which consist of a combination of clippings of printed text and handwritten passages in Melville's wife's hand (further revised by Melville). It is not clear why the Melvilles took the printed text from the abridged version of the poem that appeared under the title "The Admiral of the White"[15] in the New York *Tribune* on Sunday, May 17, 1885, rather than from the full text that was published in the Boston *Herald* the same day. Transcribing the sixty-five lines (eleven stanzas) left out of the *Tribune* text obviously took more time than would have been taken to insert into a clipping of the *Herald* text the dozen words and small group of accidentals that Melville ended up changing between the *Herald* text and the *John Marr* manuscript version. The *Herald* text was apparently not available to them; in any case, the kind of attention Melville gave to these leaves makes the text they contain (and not the *Herald* text) the appropriate choice for copy-text, as is the text of the rest of the printer's-copy manuscript they are a part of.[16]

---

14. For more on the definition of copy-text for the pieces based on manuscripts in the present volume, see p. 598 below.

15. There is a different poem, also entitled "The Admiral of the White," that survives in manuscript at Harvard, in MS Am 188 (361); see the introductory note to "The Haglets" below (pp. 725–27).

16. It is possible that there was a transcription of the whole manuscript (or much of it) in Melville's wife's hand—a transcription kept at home when Melville's manuscript was sent to the printing shop. A clue that such a transcript once existed is afforded by a leaf in the *Billy Budd* slipcase at Harvard—MS Am 188 (363). This now disjunct leaf

Because the De Vinne Press galley proofs (completed on July 31, 1888), which were set from this manuscript, and the page proofs (completed on August 16, 1888) both survive at Harvard, it is possible to follow the progress of Melville's text through the printing process in considerable detail. This story is told (and the proofs and printed book are described) above in the Note on Printing and Publishing History. These documents are a basic source for emending the manuscript copy-text, for they show Melville's proofreading corrections and revisions (along with some markings by the printing-shop proofreaders) and explain most of the differences between the text of Melville's manuscript and that of the final printed text. The other source for emendations comprises the eighteen located copies of the finished book in which Melville or his wife entered revisions. The basis for using these annotations to emend the copy-text is set forth below, in the section on "Treatment of Substantives," where there is a listing of which revisions were marked in each copy.

No further printings of *John Marr,* and no other editions of either the whole collection or the individual poems in it, appeared in Melville's lifetime. Since then, there have been five comprehensive editions (not all of them complete), as well as two printed facsimiles of the original edition, one electronic "facsimile," and several printings of selected poems that are of some textual interest. The first, Henry Chapin's edition of *John Marr and Other Poems* (Princeton, N.J.: Princeton University Press, 1922), omits the "Inscription Epistolary to W. C. R." and the prose portion of "John Marr," and it silently adopts all eleven of the post-publication revisions that Melville or his wife inked into some of the copies of the first edition.

(362B) is from a sheet Melville later used as the front cover for what he labeled "Nelson at Trafalgar". Earlier he had used the cover for something called in large blue pencil letters "Sea-Weed". Canceling "Sea-Weed", he inserted above, also in blue pencil and with a continuous double underlining, "John Marr". Below these titles he penciled a list of page numbers: "See P. 25 'little' / See P. 25 / See p. 21 / See p. 23 [*the 23 erased immediately, with* 32 *substituted*] / For " " 34¹ P.M. / Lizzie " " 34² To Correct / (From 321 P.21 / to 35 inclusive) " 34". (All this is circled in blue pencil, and the whole leaf is canceled with two large green pencil Xs.) The page numbers Melville penciled on this cover do not refer to anything his wife corrected or revised in the surviving manuscript. For example, though the word "little" does appear on page 25 of the manuscript, her hand does not appear in the inscription of the word there. One possible conclusion is that Melville was here directing her to amend her own transcript of at least this one piece, "John Marr"—indicating the page in his manuscript where she could find the word that she had either queried or mistranscribed. (The canceled "Sea-Weed" title suggests that the earlier contents of the folder may have been material for the volume Melville earlier had in mind, the one perhaps provisionally called "Meadows and Seas," featuring both weeds, as in "Weeds and Wildings," and seaweed.)

Chapin may have had access to the copy given by the Melvilles' daughter Elizabeth ("Bessie") to Frank Jewett Mather before her death in 1908;[17] Mather taught at Princeton and gave his copies of *John Marr* and *Timoleon* to the university library.

In the Constable *Poems* volume, two years after Chapin's edition, Raymond Weaver offers a "few varieties of phrasing from Melville's MS. . . . as foot-notes" and a "prefatory paragraph [actually two paragraphs as presented] . . . printed from a MS. note in Melville's handwriting inserted in his copy of *John Marr* and marked as referring to that book" (p. 192):

> Touching certain expletives in the verse, it should be borne in mind that with sailors their profane language is essentially without profane purpose. Doubtless the originator of an exclamative oath passionately intends for the moment whatever etymological meaning it may have, but in generations of parroted repetition the ejaculation becomes a mechanical habit less of the utterer than of his organ of utterance; and, ethically viewed, is but a percussion of the air.
>
> Hence, however reprehensible with the polite a sailor's habitual swearing may be, it is yet reverently to be presumed that the Recording Angel makes no note of it in that book wherein transgressions of the proprieties are never entered; the discriminating scribe setting down not the trespass of the tongue but the sins of the heart.

This "Author's Note" does not seem to have come into public view since 1924.[18] Although it sounds authentic, Weaver's claim cannot be confirmed, and the present edition does not adopt the note as part of the text of *John Marr*. In his rendering of the *John Marr* pieces, Weaver silently adopts Melville's post-publication revisions in eight of eleven instances (printed in British spelling in two cases, as generally throughout); but without explanation he places the other three revisions (in "The Æolian Harp," "The Figure-Head," and "The Berg") in footnotes.

In Howard P. Vincent's *Collected Poems of Herman Melville* (1947), the *John Marr* pieces, intended to replicate the 1888 text, contain many errors, the most serious of which renders the first nine lines of "To Ned" as the last nine of "The Maldive Shark" (p. 200). Otherwise, Vincent adopts some of Melville's revisions—silently in the independent volume, but

17. Not, that is, in 1920, the year Mather mistakenly wrote in the copies of *John Marr* and *Timoleon* that Bessie gave him at some point in the course of "many talks."

18. Weaver's marked-up copy of *John Marr,* now at the University of Texas, contains revisions in Melville's wife's hand and could be the copy Weaver called "Melville's own copy"; but the "Author's Note" is not present in it. (This copy possibly served as printer's copy for the Constable edition.)

in the textual notes of the *Complete Works* volume (14) he mentions six out of seven and claims to have adopted one that he has not. The next edition, Jarrard's "Poems by Herman Melville" (1960), takes the manuscript of *John Marr* as copy-text, transmits a usually reliable final text, and describes variants much more thoroughly than do Weaver and Vincent. Like Vincent, however, he is limited by what he can understand from photocopies (as when he cannot tell that punctuation has been added in a different color of ink). Jarrard also makes a decision that illustrates the hazards of regularizing accidentals: thinking that for Melville the difference between "bowsing" and "boozing" was only one of spelling (p. 340), he substitutes "bowsing" every time "boozing" appears, unaware of the distinction Melville intended, both in his manuscript and in his revisions in the printed book (see the discussion at 207.214).[19]

Charles Haberstroh's facsimile of *John Marr* (Folcroft, Pa.: Folcroft Library Editions; Norwood, Pa.: Norwood Editions, 1975) offers a nearly complete census of known copies of the first edition and a list of Melville's revisions entered into them—revisions that Haberstroh feels are "slight," not affecting "the substance of the poems in which they appear" (p. 135). Douglas Robillard's *Poems of Herman Melville* (1976) silently adopts three of Melville's post-publication revisions in *John Marr* and rejects eight others. In his section of "Additional Poems," he prints the two different poems called "The Admiral of the White": the one that remains in manuscript (pp. 251–53) and the one "that Melville published in newspapers in 1885," the latter in the abridged text from the New York *Tribune* (pp. 253–58) rather than the complete one from the Boston *Herald*. (Robillard's revised edition in 2000 retains the same text of the *John Marr* poems but omits the "Additional Poems" and suggests on p. 29 that Melville expanded "The Admiral of the White"—"The Haglets"—in his *John Marr* manuscript rather than restoring what had been left out of the *Tribune* version.) In 2006, Robillard produced a facsimile of the first edition, *John Marr and Other Sailors with Some Sea-Pieces: A Facsimile Edition* (Kent, Ohio: Kent State University Press), which includes reproductions of a few selected pages from the manuscript and proofs;[20] his accompanying commentary

19. References to page and line of the present edition take this form, with a "o" line number used to refer to any line(s) preceding the first line of text, such as titles and subtitles. (For pages of prose, line numbering is separate for each page; for pages of verse, line numbering proceeds continuously through each poem, as the printed line numbers indicate.) In the few cases where prose and verse appear on the same page, the type of text is indicated in brackets.

20. He shows the manuscript title page and leaves 18(2)–41 ("John Marr"), 90–95 ("Tom Deadlight"), 100–108 ("The Haglets," along with the unnumbered leaf preceding

does not distinguish Melville's and his wife's handwriting and is not always accurate in reporting proof revisions (as when, on p. 212, he says that the galley proofs do not show Melville's change in the seventh line of "Pebbles II"). The previous year Paul Royster produced a rekeyboarded "facsimile" of *John Marr* (Lincoln: Libraries at University of Nebraska–Lincoln, 2005), with notes, a publication history, and the 1924 Constable text.

Of the selective editions, Hennig Cohen's *Selected Poems of Herman Melville* (Garden City, N.Y.: Doubleday Anchor, 1964; reprinted with revisions, Carbondale: Southern Illinois University Press, 1968; New York: Fordham University Press, 1991) and Robert Penn Warren's 1970 *Selected Poems* are of some textual interest, since they deal somewhat differently with Melville's post-publication revisions in copies of *John Marr*. Cohen silently adopts two of the revisions (one each in "John Marr" and "The Æolian Harp") and silently declines to adopt the other one that falls in one of his selected poems ("The Berg"). Warren adopts only the two that he apparently regards as corrections of typographical errors (those in line 12 of "John Marr" and line 167 of "Bridegroom Dick"), but he cites the others in his notes, rejecting one of them (in line 37 of "The Berg") in forceful terms: "In the book 'dead indifference' is disastrously corrected to 'dense stolidity'" (p. 430). John Bryant's Modern Library edition of *Tales, Poems, and Other Writings* (2001) includes twelve poems from *John Marr* (counting the seven "Pebbles" separately) in the Northwestern-Newberry text (by advance arrangement) and refers in notes to some of Melville's handwritten revisions in printed copies of the book. Robert Faggen, in the Penguin edition of *Selected Poems* (2006), states that he used the New York Public Library copy with revisions in Melville's hand; but of the two such revisions made in poems that he includes, he incorporates one (in line 12 of "John Marr") and not the other (in line 37 of "The Berg"). John Hollander's Library of America anthology of nineteenth-century American poetry (1993) includes eight poems from *John Marr* in the Northwestern-Newberry text.[21]

TIMOLEON ETC. Melville's surviving fair-copy manuscript—Harvard MS Am 188 (387)—is adopted as copy-text for the present edition. Eliza-

---

100), 115 ("Far Off-Shore"), 123–24 ("The Maldive Shark"), 128–30 ("Crossing the Tropics"), 131–33 ("The Berg"), and 137–41 ("Pebbles"). From the galley proofs, he shows lower 8 and upper 9 ("Tom Deadlight"), lower 9 ("The Haglets"), middle 12 ("The Æolian Harp"), lower 13 ("The Maldive Shark"), and middle 15 ("Pebbles"). From the page proofs, he shows pages 32, 35, 48 ("Bridegroom Dick"), 70 ("The Haglets"), 79–81 ("The Æolian Harp"), and 101–3 ("Pebbles").

21. The poem "John Marr" was printed in an edition of thirty-three copies in 1980 by the Menhaden Press of Vermilion, S.D.

beth Shaw Melville's transcript—also in MS Am 188 (387)—was made from Melville's manuscript, was much revised by him, and became the printer's copy at the Caxton Press, as described in the NOTE ON PRINT-ING AND PUBLISHING HISTORY. Her transcript, therefore, is a major source of authoritative emendations. No galley or page proofs for this book are known to survive, and the only record of what Melville may have altered in proof is the printed book itself, which is therefore another source of emendations, though in using it one must attempt to distinguish Mel-ville's changes from those made by someone on the Caxton Press staff.

There is, however, one other document that must be considered as a possible source for emending the dedication, though in the end the evidence does not justify doing so. The dedication in the printed book ("TO / MY COUNTRYMAN / ELIHU VEDDER") must have been approved by Melville in proof (and is an expansion of the form—"To / Elihu Vedder"—that appears in Melville's hand on the first of the six leaves of preliminaries now housed with the manuscript and transcript). The question is whether that dedication was superseded by a tribute to his wife written on a piece of paper (with a fleur-de-lys watermark and cut to the size of the printed book) laid into one of the Harvard copies of *Timoleon*—*AC85.M4977.891t(C): "To Her—without whose / assistance both manual / and literary Timoleon &c / could not have passed / through the press—with her / name I gratefully and / affectionately inscribe / this volume. / Herman Melville / New York / June 1891".[22]

This leaf is puzzling in several ways. The inscription, in ink, is in Eliza-beth Shaw Melville's hand; but from all we know about her habits as an amanuensis, it is unthinkable that she would create such a document on her own. We may safely infer that she wrote out these words either from Melville's dictation or from a now missing document in his hand. The question, then, is whether the words were meant as a public dedication of the book or as a private presentation inscription. Several considerations argue against the latter possibility. First, there are two pinholes at the top

---

22. A typewritten transcription of these words is tipped inside the front cover of a copy of *Timoleon* in the New York Public Library. It is accompanied by an undated note (but between 1928 and 1933) on the stationery of the dealer Arthur Swann (598 Madison Avenue, New York): "Of high association interest being a presentation copy from the author to his wife, being the dedication copy to his wife with the unpublished dedication written on the typewriter by Melville's own hand, according to his daughter from whose collection it comes. This work comes directly from the family. It has never been out of the family until now." The daughter referred to has to be Frances Melville Thomas, but Swann may have gotten the book and information from her daughter, Frances Cuthbert Thomas Osborne, Melville's granddaughter.

of the leaf, showing that it (like many others in Melville's manuscripts) was once attached to another leaf; but the holes are not matched by holes anywhere in the copy of *Timoleon* into which it is laid. Second, the word "inscribe" recalls the dedications of *Typee, Omoo, Redburn, Moby-Dick,* and *John Marr* (the last with its "Inscription Epistolary" to W. Clark Russell). Third, the impersonal formality of the wording (without the "Her" being named) is unlike Melville's inscriptions in copies of other books that he gave her[23] and is more suggestive of a public dedication. Nevertheless, there is no evidence that it was meant to supplant the dedication to Elihu Vedder in future editions of the book, and it is not adopted in the present edition.

There were no further editions or printings of *Timoleon Etc.,* or of individual poems from it, in Melville's lifetime. Since then, four new editions, two printed facsimiles of the original edition, and an electronic "facsimile" have appeared, as well as a few selective editions of textual interest. In putting together the 1924 Constable *Poems* volume, Raymond Weaver perhaps sent off his personal copy of the first edition of *Timoleon* (now at the University of Texas) to be used as printer's copy. The *Poems* text of the *Timoleon* poems displays only a half-dozen outright errors, though a few are such notable failures of the British compositor to follow copy that one may wonder how Weaver—if he ever saw proofs—could have missed them. For the 1947 *Collected Poems of Herman Melville,* Howard P. Vincent did not read proofs. The "Errata" leaf that may be found in some copies catches a handful of the instances in which this edition fails to follow the 1891 *Timoleon* text; Vincent also provided fifteen pages of brief textual notes that appear only in the *Complete Works* version of this edition (vol. 14). And Douglas Robillard's *Poems of Herman Melville* (1976) also aims to transmit the first-edition text of *Timoleon;* his revision in 2000 corrects an error in his earlier edition (the repetition of line 49 of "Timoleon").

The only more thorough editor of the *Timoleon* poems has been Norman Jarrard in his 1960 University of Texas dissertation. Jarrard takes Melville's manuscript as copy-text and is clear about where he emends and why. At crucial points, he recovers and transmits the readings in Melville's manuscript (in line 12 of "Timoleon," for example, and line 14 of "Pausilippo"), and his final text is accordingly more authoritative than Weaver's or Vincent's. Though working from photocopies, he does a

---

23. For example, he inscribed on the front free endpaper of a copy of *Clarel*—Harvard *AC85.M4977.876c(D): "This copy is specially presented to my wife, without whose assistance in manifold ways I hardly know how I could have got the book (under the circumstances) into shape, and finally through the press." And a copy of *John Marr* in the New York Public Library is inscribed simply "To Lizzie / N.Y. Nov. 5, 1888."

much better job than Vincent of reporting variants in the transcripts, but what he cannot see in the photocopies mars his account with errors.

Of the two printed facsimiles, one presents an enlarged and the other a reduced reproduction. The one from Literature House / Gregg Press (Upper Saddle River, N.J., 1970) gives something like a 110 percent enlargement and contains no editorial commentary; the one from Folcroft Library Editions and Norwood Editions in 1976 (also University Microfilms International, 1976; Richard West, 1977; Arden Library, 1978) provides text pages reduced to about 90 percent and includes an introduction and census of copies by Charles Haberstroh. In 2005 Paul Royster made available an electronic rekeyboarded "facsimile" of *Timoleon* (Lincoln: Libraries at University of Nebraska–Lincoln), accompanied by the text of the 1924 Constable volume.

The largest, most continuously available, selection of *Timoleon* poems in the past forty years has been Hennig Cohen's *Selected Poems* (1964; rev. 1968, 1991), with useful notes. Robert Penn Warren (1970) selected only eight of the *Timoleon* poems for his "Reader's Edition" but offered a thoughtful note on "After the Pleasure Party" (pp. 430–37). The 2001 Modern Library edition of *Tales, Poems, and Other Writings,* edited by John Bryant, includes nineteen poems from *Timoleon* in the Northwestern-Newberry text; he presents six versions of "Art" (pp. 537–41) based on the manuscript evidence and accompanied by "revision narratives," representing "a good guess at what Melville might have done as he revised his poem." Northwestern-Newberry texts are also used for the twelve poems from *Timoleon* that John Hollander includes in the Library of America anthology of nineteenth-century American poetry (1993).

"INSCRIPTION FOR THE DEAD AT FREDERICKSBURGH." For this poem (not collected into a volume by Melville), the manuscript that was published in facsimile in Melville's lifetime—in *Autograph Leaves of Our Country's Authors* (Baltimore: Cushings & Bailey, 1864), entitled "Inscription For the Slain at Fredericksburgh"—survives at the University of Texas. A revised version, with "Dead" instead of "Slain" in the title, also survives, in the Bancroft-Bliss Collection at the Library of Congress. On March 22, 1864, Melville sent this revised version to the co-compiler of the volume, Alexander Bliss, along with a letter urging him to "suppress" the earlier version, but it was too late for Bliss to do so. With this clear indication of Melville's preference, his revised version is the obvious choice of copy-text for the present edition.

No further printings or editions of *Autograph Leaves* and no other printings of this poem appeared during Melville's lifetime. Since then the poem has been published at least six times. In his 1960 dissertation,

Norman Jarrard prints the *Autograph Leaves* version as part of *Battle-Pieces* (pp. 109–10, 311, 315) and reports no variants. Sidney Kaplan reproduces the facsimile from *Autograph Leaves* in his facsimile of *Battle-Pieces* (1960, 1972). Merrell R. Davis and William H. Gilman in *The Letters of Herman Melville* (New Haven: Yale University Press, 1963) provide an accurate text and record of variants (pp. 223–24, 364). Hennig Cohen uses their text among the notes in his edition of *Battle-Pieces* (1964) but prints "Slain" in the title and substitutes "that" for "the" in line 2 (p. 224). Lynn Horth in the Northwestern-Newberry *Correspondence* volume (1993) extends the Davis-Gilman account and records variants (pp. 389–91). And Stanton Garner prints the poem accurately in *The Civil War World of Herman Melville* (Lawrence: University Press of Kansas, 1993) and supplies useful commentary (pp. 207, 215, 284, 291).

THE MANUSCRIPTS

I N ADDITION TO the characteristics of the manuscripts described in the NOTE ON PRINTING AND PUBLISHING HISTORY, some further general features of the manuscripts need to be commented on. The copy-text manuscripts of *John Marr* and *Timoleon* are not clear straightforward documents; like Melville's other surviving manuscripts, they display the results of complex revision, and his hand is sometimes not easy to decipher. Although what survives for these poems is more often fair-copy transcription than a full record of composition and revision, the manuscripts nevertheless provide a great many pre- and post-copy-text variants. Thus they are a major source both for emendation and for evidence as to whether later differences in printed forms are possibly authorial and whether anomalous readings are the result of errors made during revision. An understanding of Melville's method of preparing printer's copy is therefore essential for establishing the critical texts in the present edition. The following general account introduces and defines a few special terms (italicized) that will be used in the detailed accounts of revisions in the NOTES ON INDIVIDUAL POEMS below.[24]

---

24. For the fullest account of the characteristics of Melville's manuscripts, see the "Genetic Text" in *Billy Budd, Sailor,* ed. Harrison Hayford and Merton M. Sealts Jr. Other useful analyses appear in the Northwestern-Newberry editions of *The Confidence-Man* (pp. 401–99), *Clarel* (pp. 883–93), and *Correspondence* (pp. 847–51), and in Eleanor M. Tilton's "Melville's 'Rammon': A Text and Commentary."

Evidence from surviving manuscripts demonstrates that, in creating most of his later works, Melville habitually used pencil for his first draft, and often for his first fair copy from it, a practice that facilitated the rapid and often manifold revisions he typically made in the process of composition, before he was satisfied enough with the text to venture a fair copy in ink. But pencil is not a sure sign that a Melville manuscript is a first or second draft. For example, he used pencil for his late-stage fair copies of "Art" and "Venice." On the other hand, his using ink generally does indicate that he thought the text was close to final. But since Melville was an inveterate reviser, many fair copies he made in ink turned out not to be final. Here, too, the manuscript evidence shows that Melville went on revising many of his ink fair copies until he was at least temporarily satisfied with the text and then made a new fair copy in ink.

In doing so, he might copy the whole page, but he had two ways of getting around that labor. Often, if a passage was not much revised or obscured by revision, he would scissor it from the leaf (or from an earlier fair copy) and then carry the *clip* forward into his next fair-copy sequence by mounting it—with a straight pin or sealing wax—on a new full-sized *main leaf.* On that new leaf he might also add later-stage text. Any such leaf that Melville used in this way as a *mount* signals that the text on it is from a later inscription stage than the text on any *clip* he attached to it. The other way Melville often avoided copying a whole page of revised text was the one he used when much of the text was still quite clear and only a passage was obscured. He would copy just that passage (perhaps with some rewording) on a part-leaf and then pin or stick the resulting *patch* to the old leaf, covering up the superseded earlier version. The text of a *patch,* therefore, is from a later inscription stage than the text on any whole- or part-leaf to which it is attached.

Melville habitually canceled the text on a superseded fair-copy leaf (or portion thereof) by X-ing it through with blue, green, orange, brown, red, or black pencil or crayon, and he then saved the leaf so that he could use its uninscribed verso for future drafting or copying. The canceled sides of many such thriftily reused leaves offer further insight into Melville's revision practices. Some leaves were reused for poems in the same volume: a canceled version of the first eight lines of "The Margrave's Birth Night" appears on the verso of the first leaf of "The Return of the Sire de Nesle," and six canceled lines of "In a Bye-Canal" appear on the verso of leaf 4 of "The Parthenon." Many leaves were reused in other works, especially *Billy Budd, Sailor,* which carries on the versos of its leaves matter from, among others, "Pebble VII" in *John Marr* and "After the Pleasure Party" and "Syra" in *Timoleon.* Difficult as these canceled versos can be to decipher, especially their tangles of composition in pencil, they can reveal something more about the development, for example, of "Bridegroom Dick," "Venice," "Art," and *Billy Budd, Sailor.*

On the basis of such physical evidence and that of verbal interrelations, the present edition assigns alphabetical inscription stage labels to each leaf and part-leaf of manuscript. So, too, the evidence of a distinctive pencil, pen, or color of ink allows the assignment of stage labels to most variants. As the account just given implies, it is also possible to make out revision stages by the presence of and relations among clips, patches, or other physical and contextual evidence. Furthermore, Melville's page numbers assist in this process by showing that a given leaf either stood or did not stand in a particular fair-copy sequence.[25] Two warnings are needed here. First, the alphabetical designations of Melville's stages of *inscription* and *revision* do not necessarily or even usually also designate or define his stages of *composition.* Only in rare cases does enough evidence survive to support more than a beginning on a reliable account of how Melville at first or in later stages conceived a work.[26] Second, alphabetical stage labels should be understood as defining only relations within each individual poem.

Eventually Melville came to a point in his own copying at which he thought the text close enough to completion that he then passed it along to his wife, either to tidy it up for printer's copy or to make a wholly new printer's copy from it. For the present edition, that earliest surviving finished state (that is, before it was passed along to his wife) is defined as the copy-text for each manuscript piece (with a few exceptions—such as in the case of "The Haglets"—that are specified in the NOTES ON INDIVIDUAL POEMS). Later markings on that document as it now exists are considered post-copy-text readings. For *John Marr,* Elizabeth Shaw Melville's hand appears here and there on Melville's manuscript, clarifying certain readings, changing spellings, and expanding abbreviations. For *Timoleon,* she presumably did the same things while making the separate printer's copy that exists in her hand. Then, after Melville had made further revisions

25. Foliation evidence also supplies a major clue that Melville seriously considered printing his projected collection entitled "Meadows and Seas" before he changed his mind and instead printed many of the same pieces in *John Marr* and put others into his projected collection "Weeds and Wildings." For another example of the use of foliation to determine compositional stages, see Hayford and Sealts's *Billy Budd, Sailor,* pp. 228–69.

26. The poem "Art" is, though only in part, one of those rare cases. See the notes to "Art" on pp. 797–800 below and the essay by Robert C. Ryan cited there. Cf. the textual notes to "Milan Cathedral" (pp. 826–28) and "The Return of the Sire de Nesle" (pp. 864–66).

in that printer's copy, her hand appears in Melville's manuscript copy-
ing these revisions into it (usually without punctuation), apparently in an
effort to have a close to final copy at hand while the other went to the
printer. She also copied revisions into his manuscript from a nonextant
source, presumably revised leaves of her transcript that were discarded
after being recopied (see p. 606 below).

Melville's long-established procedure for preparing printer's copy was
to have his copyists transcribe without punctuation, so that he could attend
to the final pointing of his text.[27] Elizabeth Shaw Melville's transcript of
the *Timoleon* poems generally shows Melville penciling in punctuation
that she subsequently inks in, though occasionally he inks it in himself.
Often, however, their hands are not distinguishable in the making of such
small marks as periods and commas; and in such cases, though Melville
is reasonably inferable as the one initiating or directing the pointing of
her transcript, an editor's most prudent course is simply to indicate the
transcript as the source of many variant readings in accidentals—and thus
also of emendations. Despite such uncertain cases, Melville's manuscript
and his wife's transcript taken together constitute an extended display of
Melville's habits in revising and punctuating his poetry.

TREATMENT OF SUBSTANTIVES

THE COPY-TEXTS AS defined above—the 1866 Harper edition of
Battle-Pieces and Melville's fair-copy manuscripts for *John Marr* and
Timoleon—require substantive emendation when it is likely that later
variants are Melville's intended revisions. The surviving galley and page
proofs of *John Marr,* with revisions and corrections in Melville's hand,
provide ample evidence for making such emendations, supplemented by
his holograph revisions in copies of the printed book. He also entered
revisions into two copies of the published *Battle-Pieces.* For *Timoleon,* there
is Melville's wife's transcript that served as printer's copy, but there is no
documentary evidence to support editorial judgment as to which post-
printer's-copy variants in *Timoleon* as finally printed reflect Melville's
alterations rather than a compositor's.

BATTLE-PIECES. The major sources of possible substantive emendation
in the verse and prose of *Battle-Pieces* are Melville's penciled markings in

27. See the Northwestern-Newberry *Piazza Tales* volume (pp. 549–50, 558, 660–63,
665–67).

Harvard Copies A and C (see pp. 536, 584 above), which show him considering various revisions (almost all substantive) that he might make in the printed text. Although markings appear on only three pages in Copy A, the set of custom-bound sheets identified as Copy C is marked extensively with "Herman's corrections" (as Elizabeth Shaw Melville annotated it). There is no reason, however, to believe that his revisions in Copy A are tacitly superseded by his having revised Copy C more thoroughly, and there is no evidence as to which may have been marked first. It is possible, however, that Copy A might have been first: one revision appears in both Copies A and C—"pale" for "brave" in "Lyon" (18.65)—and Melville may have neglected to transfer the other two revisions from Copy A rather than implicitly rejecting them. More significant is the fact that, in both copies, not all revisions are marked in the same way. Although all the markings are in pencil, there are signs that some were erased, and some were first erased and then replaced by other revisions; the printed text is lined through in some instances, but in others the words are only underlined or not marked at all; and some revisions are accompanied by virgules—the proofreader's diagonal line to mark insertions—but others are not.

Though it is obvious that the erased revisions were rejected, the differences in Melville's ways of marking the other revisions make the question of which ones (if any) represent his final intentions more complicated. An editor must take the following matters into account. The two numbers that Melville penciled on the recto of the first leaf following the front free endpaper of Copy A ("27/129") refer to pages on which he made revisions and lined through the printed text (the revision in "Lyon" noted above and "marching—/Right onward" for "marching/Unpausing" in "The March to the Sea" at 95.33–34). He did not, however, pencil on that leaf the third page number (23) where he had marked a revision, and it was a place where he did not line through the text (in "The March into Virginia" at 15.35). In Copy C, he first underlined but did not line through the last line of the same poem—"The throe of Second Manassas share."—and penciled a question mark in the right margin. Next he lined through the printed line and penciled, then canceled, two variant readings—"Manassas' second throe and deadlier share" and "Thy second shock, Manassas, share."—before finally settling upon "Thy after shock, Manassas, share."

Such examples suggest that readings for which the printed text is not lined through may be more provisional than those for which a line does mark through the printed wording. Melville's markings of "The Scout toward Aldie" in Copy C provide a further example. On the section-title page (185) and first page (187) of the poem, he penciled "Ride" above the second word, but he did not line through or underline "Scout"; he then lined through and erased his penciled "Ride". He also penciled "ride" above "scout" in the first line of the sixth stanza (line 36), and again "scout" was not lined through or underlined; in context, the likelihood seems small that, having rejected the substitution in his title, he would finally have intended "ride" here. With these examples in mind, an editor must be less sure about revisions for which the printed text is not lined through; the most conservative course is to treat all such revisions as provisional and not to adopt them.[28]

Therefore the present edition adopts the handwritten revisions at points where Melville also lined through the printed text.[29] For example, only one of two revisions in "On the Slain Collegians" (Copy C, p. 159) is adopted: the one in line 44 (119.44), where Melville penciled "all" (with a virgule) in the right margin but only underlined (without lining through) "both" in the printed line, is not accepted; but the one in line 46, where he lined through "he", penciled a caret to its right, and entered "put" in the right margin, is adopted as clearly intended.[30] Altogether twenty-five of Melville's revisions are adopted in the present edition, while twenty-seven possibly provisional ones are not. The emendations from Copy A are recorded in the lists of emendations below at 18.65, 95.33, and 95.34; for the one not adopted, see the discussion at 15.35. The emendations from Copy C are at 8.11, 9.52, 9.53, 9.54, 15.36, 18.65 (the one also entered in Copy A), 35.443, 45.25, 61.53, 92.11, 92.12, 96.91, 96.92, 119.46, 124.1, 134.12, 144.162, 145.200, 145.206, 146.266, 166.133, 179.23, and 182.28; for the ones not adopted, see the discussions at 15.33, 30.275, 41.17, 44.4, 64.18, 67.54, 69.8, 69.14, 80.19, 104.0, 111.3, 113.35, 119.44, 140.36 (three

28. However, in marking Harvard Copy B of *Clarel*—*AC85.M4977.876c(B)—published ten years later, Melville only underlined printed text, and did not line through any of it, including text obviously needing correction of compositorial error; it is reasonable to conclude that all his revisions of the 1876 poem are definite (see the Northwestern-Newberry edition, pp. 681–83, 849–63). Twelve years after that, in 1888, his methods of marking the *John Marr* proofs and copies of the printed book vary in ways similar to those in Copies A and C of *Battle-Pieces* (see pp. 602–5 below).

29. And at a few other places where Melville's intention seems clear, such as where he inserted a transposition line in the text to show that he wanted to reverse the order of two words or phrases (45.25, 124.1, 134.12, 144.162, 145.206).

30. Melville's use of virgules with some revisions (as in the line 44 revision noted here) but not others does not seem to indicate definiteness. Seven of the revisions adopted here are accompanied by virgules (at 35.443, 45.25, 92.11, 92.12, 167.133, 179.23, and 182.28), as are six of those not followed here (at 30.275, 111.3, 113.35, 119.44, 167.152, and 168.200). On the other hand, Melville's use of carets to show where an insertion is to be made (as in the line 46 revision noted here) is associated with lined-out words (8.11, 9.52, 18.65, 61.53, 96.91, 119.46, 146.266)—except of course where the insertion does not involve a deletion (92.11, 179.23)—but carets do not always accompany lined-out words.

instances), 142.100, 143.146, 154.540, 157.644, 158.684, 167.152, 168.200, 181.19, 181.20, and 188.1.

Aside from these emendations based on Melville's post-publication markings, the present edition makes only one further substantive emendation: correcting "boats" to possessive at 57.50.

JOHN MARR. The many surviving states of the texts in *John Marr* provide much evidence for Melville's process of inscription and revision, but their many substantive variants present few emendational problems. Melville's final manuscript, which—with some clarifications and changes in Elizabeth Shaw Melville's hand—became printer's copy for the book, is so readily decipherable that compositorial misreadings are easily found; and Melville's intentions in proof revisions are clear even when they were incorrectly carried out in the printing shop. Similarly straightforward are his intentions when he made revisions in the printed book.

Elizabeth Shaw Melville's substantive changes in Melville's manuscript are adopted as representing his intention; these are especially extensive in "The Haglets" (three other substantive changes are in her hand: see the emendations at 198.35, 207.220, and 213.416). A clearly authorial substantive variant in the "John Marr" page proofs (199.24) shows that Melville communicated with the printer in some fashion after the galley proofs had been returned, but the communication resulted in no other substantive variants. In proofreading the galley and page proofs, Melville corrected all but two of their substantive errors: the galley proof's "leather" for "leathern" (at 198.4) is a compositorial error, and its substitution of "hold" for "held" at 199.12 is confirmed as an error by the fact that Melville or his wife corrected it in all of the known copies of *John Marr* that contain handwritten revisions. The only other substantive variant in the galley proofs, "coxswain" for "coxswain's" at 213.431, is a correction of Melville's error. At one point the present edition does not follow Melville's own change in the proofs because it was possibly his accommodation of a printer's error: his addition of "Minor" to "Sea-Pieces" on the section-title page that precedes "To the Master of the *Meteor*" in the page proofs (see pp. 560–61 above).

In eighteen of the located copies of *John Marr*, either Melville or his wife inscribed marginal revisions in ink; the eleven revisions thus entered can be judged authoritative, and they are adopted in the present text. Not all eleven appear in each revised copy, however, as the two lists below make clear (the first identifying the copies, the second the revisions). The eighteen copies are as follows (with the revisions keyed by letter to the second list below):

1. American Antiquarian Society (Reserve 1888). Inscribed by Melville at the top of the title page: "Edmund Clarence Stedman / from Herman

Melville"; and penciled below the subtitle, "Herman Melville". Penciled queries (not necessarily Melville's) appear at lines 133 and 234 of "The Haglets" ("To-night's", 222.133; "White", 225.234) and lines 5 and 6 of "The Enviable Isles" ("sleep that folds the hills", 242.5; "the trance of God", 242.6). Revisions in Melville's hand in ink: A–D, F, H, K.

2. Berkshire Athenaeum (V.811.M49.4, copy 1). On the title page, Melville's wife wrote "by" below the subtitle and pasted Melville's signature; on the verso she wrote "For the Berkshire / Atheneum Library / from Mrs. Melville / Aug. 1892". Revisions in Melville's wife's hand in ink: A, B, D–K.

3. Berkshire Athenaeum (V.811.M49.4, copy 2). Inscribed by Melville at the top of the title page: "To / W. Clark Russell"; and below the subtitle, "by Herman Melville". Penciled revisions by Melville: "mute" (216.4) in "Jack Roy" lined through and "pale" written in right margin; and "truants under" (237.15) in "To Ned" revised to "truants, and strange". Revisions in Melville's hand in ink: A–I, K.

4. British Library (C.95.a.7). Inscribed by J. W. Barrs at the top of the title page: "J. W. Barrs / 1888 / from the Author / New York"; and below the subtitle, "(by Herman Melville)". Revisions in Melville's wife's hand in ink: A–I, K.

5. Brown University (Harris 76.M531j). Inscribed below the subtitle on the title page (perhaps by Eleanor Melville Metcalf, Melville's granddaughter): "by Herman Melville". Revisions by Melville in ink: A, B, D–F, H, K. Revisions in Melville's wife's hand in ink: C[?], G, I.

6. Columbia University (Engel Collection). Inscribed by Melville at the top of the title page: "James Billson / from Herman Melville". Revisions in Melville's hand in ink: A–D, F, H, K.

7. University of Florida (Parkman D. Howe Collection). Below the subtitle on the title page a clipping of Melville's signature is pasted. A penciled double check mark by Melville appears at left of lines 26–27 in "The Berg" (241.26–27). Next to line 288 of "Bridegroom Dick" (209.288) Melville penciled "stands" (not explicitly a revision of "shows", which was changed in ink to "lours" in other copies). Revision by Melville in pencil: A (in the form of "e/" in right margin).

8. Harvard University (Houghton *AC85.M4977.888j(A)). Inscribed by Melville's wife on title page: "E. Melville". Revisions in Melville's wife's hand in ink: A–I, K.

9. Harvard University (Houghton *AC85.M4977.888j(B)). Inscribed by Melville at the top of the title page: "To / W. Clark Russell"; and below the subtitle "by / Herman Melville". Revisions in Melville's hand in ink: A–I, K.

10. Lehigh University (818.4.M497j.1888.T). Inscribed by Melville on a piece of paper pasted to the title page: "To my Niece / Maria G. Mackintosh / Herman Melville". Revisions in Melville's wife's hand in ink: A–I, K.

11. Navy Department Library (Naval History Center LF.1546.1). Inscribed in an unidentified hand at the top of the title page: "Presented to, Admiral / Franklin by the widow / of the author"; below the subtitle is pasted a clipping of Melville's signature. Revisions in Melville's wife's hand in ink: A–K.

12. New York Public Library (*KL(Melville)). Inscribed by Melville's wife on a dark piece of paper pasted inside the front cover: "Mrs. Abraham Lansing / 115 Washington Ave. / Albany / N.Y." Revisions in Melville's wife's hand in ink: A–K.

13. New York Public Library (*KL(Melville)). Inscribed by Melville at the top of the title page: "To Lizzie / N.Y. Nov. 5, 1888." Revisions in Melville's hand in ink: A–I, K.

14. Newberry Library (Case Y285.M511). Revisions in Melville's wife's hand in ink: A–I, K.

15. Princeton University (Ex.3854.9.35.11). Below the subtitle on the title page is pasted a clipping of Melville's signature. (This copy was given to Frank Jewett Mather Jr. by Melville's daughter Elizabeth.) Revision in Melville's hand in pencil: A (in the form of "e/" in right margin). Revisions in Melville's wife's hand in ink: B–K.

16. University of Texas (AX.M497.888j). Below the subtitle on the title page is pasted a clipping of Melville's signature. The signature of Raymond Weaver appears on the front free endpaper of this rebound copy. Revisions in Melville's wife's hand in ink: A–K.

17. University of Virginia (Barrett *PS2384.J6.1888). Inscribed by Melville's wife on the inside front cover: "Francis W. Hoadley / from his Aunt / E.S.M." Below the subtitle on the title page is pasted a clipping of Melville's signature. Revisions in Melville's wife's hand in ink: A–K.

18. Yale University (Beinecke Za.M497.888). Inscribed by Melville below the subtitle on the title page: "by Herman Melville"; and on a piece of paper tipped to the margin of the title page, "To / Richard Henry Stoddard / from Herman Melville / Nov. 1888". Revisions in Melville's wife's hand in ink: A–I, K.

The eleven revisions are as follows (cited by page and line of the present edition, with the printed readings of the first edition first and the handwritten revisions second, followed by copy numbers referring to the list above):

A. 199.12 hold] held *Copies* 1–18

B. 204.122 one] either *Copies* 1–6, 8–18

C. 205.167 jamb] jam *Copies* 1, 3–6, 8–18

D. 207.214 boozing] bowsing *Copies* 1–6, 8–18

E. 207.215 that voyage] that last voyage *Copies* 2–5, 8–18

F. 209.288 shows] lours *Copies* 1–6, 8–18; stands *Copy* 7

G. 213.414 armed] in armor *Copies* 2–5, 8–18

H. 213.435 booze] bowse *Copies* 1–6, 8–18

I. 226.11 To] For *Copies* 2–5, 8–18

J. 231.14 Wrecked] Dropped *Copies* 2, 11, 12, 15–17

K. 241.37 dead indifference] dense stolidity *Copies* 1–6, 8–18

The only one of these revisions that lacks the authority of Melville's hand in at least one located copy is the substitution of "Dropped" for "Wrecked" in "The Figure-Head" (231.14), which is made in his wife's hand in six of the copies. But that revision in his own hand was undoubtedly present in some copy: to anyone who has studied Elizabeth Shaw Melville's role in preparing Melville's works for publication, it is inconceivable that she would have made that substitution on her own.

A pair of further variants, in pencil, does not pose a difficult problem. For some reason, Melville inscribed two copies to the dedicatee, W. Clark Russell, one now at the Berkshire Athenaeum, the other at Harvard. There are ten revisions that he made identically in both copies, and all ten of them are adopted here. But in the Berkshire Athenaeum copy he penciled two more variants, which are not adopted in the present edition. What seems likely to have happened is that Melville prepared that copy for Russell first, entered the ten revisions in ink, inscribed it, and only then discovered that he had earlier marked it up in pencil: he had lined out "mute" in line 4 of "Jack Roy" (216.4) and written "pale" in the right margin; and he had lined out "under" in line 15 of "To Ned" (237.15) and turned the phrase into "truants, and strange". After noticing its marked-up state, he set that copy aside as not appropriate for the dedicatee and inscribed another copy, now at Harvard, sending it off to Russell after entering in it the same ten inked revisions as those in the first copy, but not the two penciled ones. Melville's omitting those two penciled variants strongly suggests that he had finally rejected them (and they do not appear in any other of the marked copies).[31] Similarly, it is plausible to regard as tentative Melville's penciling into the University of Florida copy (on

31. The alternative possibility, that the copy Melville sent to Russell was the Berkshire Athenaeum copy, with the two penciled variants added as his last-minute intended revisions, is not at all probable. It leaves unexplained why he entered them in pencil, why he did not enter them also in the retained second copy (or any of the other known copies), and why he inscribed that second copy at all.

p. 42) the word "stands" as a possible alternative for "shows" in "Bridegroom Dick" (209.288). The tentativeness of that alternative, aside from its being penciled, is clear from the fact that "shows" is neither underlined nor lined out and that "lours" is the revision of "shows" inked into seventeen other known copies. Thus only the ink-inscribed variants in the marked copies of *John Marr* are adopted in this edition.

TIMOLEON. *Timoleon* offers few difficult questions about emending substantively. As indicated above, Melville's manuscript is adopted as copy-text, and his wife's transcript—made from his manuscript and then revised by him before being sent to the Caxton Press as printer's copy—is clearly a major source of emendation. No galley or page proofs are known to survive. Thus hardly any additional decisions are necessary about Melville's finally intended wording once one realizes that, when his wife's final reading differs substantively from the reading in his manuscript, her final reading may normally be taken as authoritative because it was directed by him, even though the visible evidence of his direction does not survive. What probably happened in these cases is that he revised certain leaves of her transcript so extensively that she made a new fair copy of them and discarded the earlier ones. (See the emendations at 253.1,12,13,15,20; 258.163–68,173; and pp. 313–17 passim.) In general, therefore, since his wife did not make changes on her own authority (pp. 598–99 above), the substantive variants in her surviving transcript generally seem less likely to be transcription errors than deliberate changes reflecting Melville's latest intention. In only five instances do they seem to be transcription errors (253.12, 255.74, 277.2, 297.14, and 307.13), and these are the only places where the latest substantive variants in her transcript are not adopted in this edition.

Of the forty-one substantive changes that occurred after the printer's copy was sent to the Caxton Press, thirty-eight are adopted here. Nine are judged authorial because they restore the final readings in Melville's manuscript (and therefore are not listed as emendations). All but three of the remaining variants are adopted on the grounds that they probably represent Melville's revising hand at some stage in the proofs. Nine of them are the same as pre-copy-text versions in Melville's manuscript: see, for instance, "demure" at 261.54, "And" at 269.7, and "quelled" at 298.39.[32] Others, from the addition of "My Countryman" in the dedication to "friendly" and "fellowly" in lines 11 and 12 of "The Age of the

---

32. For a special case, see the discussion of "ease" in "Herba Santa" at 289.34; this reading also occurs in the same phrase Melville penciled at the foot of the first leaf of "The Marchioness of Brinvilliers," possibly as he was reading proofs.

Antonines" (p. 286) to the major changes in lines 80–83 of "After the Pleasure Party" (p. 262), are not likely to have been introduced by anyone but the author. The three that are judged as not reflecting Melville's intentions are "fir-trees" for "fir-tree's" at 276.10, "fordone" for "foredone" at 289.33, and "sight" for "sights" at 300.2. Although the book text restores line 14 of "Pausilippo," which Melville's wife omitted, it repeats her misreadings at 253.12, 255.74, 277.2, and 307.13. There are no authoritative revisions inscribed in any of the located copies of the 1891 first edition.

"INSCRIPTION FOR THE DEAD AT FREDERICKSBURGH." Although the manuscript used for the facsimile published in 1864 contains three substantive variants from the later manuscript used as copy-text here (see pp. 595 and 866–67), none is adopted because Melville's letter accompanying the later manuscript states his clear preference for the later version.

TREATMENT OF ACCIDENTALS

EVEN WHEN A final manuscript survives, an editor can have difficulty settling conclusively whether the author is responsible, at particular points, for a printed text's accidentals—its spelling, punctuation, and such formal features as indention and line-spacing. Recovering the author's final intention is facilitated when revised proofs also survive, as two sets do for *John Marr*. Thus the editor will adopt the revisions clearly made by the author and consider whether other variants in the final printed text could have been sanctioned by the author. The compositors of *John Marr* altered much of Melville's punctuation when setting the manuscript, and other changes in the proofs after the galley-proof stage are clearly the work of someone in the printer's office. Nevertheless, since some of the changes restore the manuscript readings, each variant has been examined to determine the possibility of authorial intervention, whether or not the change is recorded in a surviving document. When no proofs survive, as with *Timoleon,* the odds are still strong that variants in accidentals in the published form are attributable to the compositors, even though the author may have made some changes in proof. The 1891 first printing of *Timoleon* contains abundant evidence that the Caxton staff felt as licensed as their 1888 De Vinne counterparts to intervene in the formal details of the text. Thus the present edition follows the accidentals in Melville's manuscript (or his repointing in his wife's transcript) and scrutinizes the printed variants for the possibility of their being authorial (but adopts them sparingly).

When neither manuscript nor proofs survive, and just a few later authoritative revisions are known—as with *Battle-Pieces*—an editor has no choice but to adopt most of the accidentals of the first edition, recognizing that the text may have nonauthorial features.[33] As indicated above, the transcript of "Philip" that Melville gave to Richard Henry Stoddard at an unknown time is of no help in determining the finally intended pointing of "Sheridan at Cedar Creek" (pp. 84–85). Similarly unhelpful are the versions of five *Battle-Pieces* poems published earlier in 1866 by *Harper's New Monthly Magazine*—versions that were apparently superseded by the book texts, since Melville seems to have paid attention to the accidentals as well as the substantives in preparing those book texts. (On the choice of the book texts as copy-text, see also pp. 583–84 above.)

Decisions to emend accidentals are made conservatively; no attempt is made to impose a general consistency on spelling, punctuation, or other formal features.[34] Any changes have been made according to guidelines specified in the paragraphs that follow.

SPELLING. The general rule adopted here is to retain any spellings (even when inconsistent) that were acceptable by the standards of 1860–91, as well as any obsolete variants that may have been intended by Melville or reflect his reading in earlier material; spellings are corrected only when they do not fall into these categories. One available guide for decisions about spelling is the 1847 revision of Webster's *American Dictionary of the English Language* (Springfield, Mass., 1848). Webster's was the dictionary

---

33. Melville's habits in the extant manuscripts are not definite enough to offer grounds for emendation (with the few exceptions discussed in note 37 below). Neither is enough known about Harper house styling to be helpful in determining precisely what elements of the spelling and punctuation of *Battle-Pieces* resulted from it.

34. Except when there is evidence in the manuscripts that Melville was working toward a consistency not observed in his time in some matters (see note 37 below). No emendations are made to secure consistency, for example, in the use of capital letters; the insertion of hyphens in compounds; the use (or nonuse) of apostrophes in inflected second-person forms of verbs (e.g., "wouldst" at 288.19) or their placement in contractions (such as "do'nt" or "wo'nt") and in verb forms prefixed with "a" (e.g., "a'toasting" at 204.126); the punctuation of penultimate items in series; and the placement of punctuation before or after closing quotation marks (for further discussion of quotation marks, see pp. 612–13 below). Thus while "birth-night" appears in line 15 of "The Margrave's Birth Night" (p. 267), the hyphen is not added to the title; similarly, a hyphen appears in a late stage of manuscript in one of the occurrences of the compound "Bridegroom Dick" (201.17), but since there is no evidence in either the manuscript or the proofs that Melville was attempting consistency in this matter, the present edition does not emend to add hyphens in the other instances (201.0, 202.39, 203.67). Likewise "pleasure party" appears in both open and hyphenated versions (259.0, 262.106).

used by Harper & Brothers, American publishers of most of Melville's earlier books, as well as of *Battle-Pieces*. Melville remarked, in his letter to John Murray, his first English publisher, on January 28, 1849, that "my printers here 'go for' Webster." The Harper accounts show that Melville ordered at least three copies of Webster's (on April 10 and November 15, 1847, and on November 16, 1848), the third of which could have been the 1848 edition. Recourse to it and to other nineteenth-century dictionaries, such as Worcester's *A Universal and Critical Dictionary of the English Language* (Boston, 1847), to editions of American poetry and other works published from 1860 through 1891, and to such sources for the historical study of spelling as the *Oxford English Dictionary* and the *Dictionary of American English* has supplied sufficient contexts to justify the retention of some anomalous-appearing copy-text forms. In *Battle-Pieces,* for instance, the use of "prophesy" as a noun is allowed to stand (11.90), as is "bonetas" for the mid-size tuna usually spelled "bonitos" (80.13). In the *John Marr* and *Timoleon* pieces, Melville's manuscript spelling is retained whenever it follows this general rule—e.g., "chymist" (271.19), "colonades" (294.3), and "artizan's" (315.2). The rule normally applies whether or not a copyist or compositor later changed a spelling[35] and whether or not it is consistent with other pieces in this volume. Thus "Sybilline" at 269.9 and "Pharoah's" at 314.1 are retained even though Elizabeth Shaw Melville altered them in copying *Timoleon* and even though "Sibylline" (115.12) and "pharaoh" (47.4) appear in *Battle-Pieces*.

The present edition follows Melville's own post-copy-text spelling changes[36] and corrects obvious slips of the pen in the manuscript copy-texts, most of which were also changed by the copyist or compositor. Further, like the copyist or compositor, the present edition corrects a few other copy-text forms not found in reliable parallels in contemporary sources: e.g., "avalanch" (240.8), "beleive" (a common Melville misspelling, occurring here at 204.108,116, and 263.130–31), "dieing" (214.2), and "bazalisk" (292.14). Other forms corrected in this edition include "caricole" (for "caracole" at 141.61), "staleing" (199.18), "palor"

35. In changing various spellings in *John Marr,* however, Melville's wife was apparently sometimes acting on Melville's instruction to check certain spellings (a penciled underline and check mark accompanying his "maneuver" at 208.249 evidently indicated that the spelling needed to be checked; his wife changed the first "e" to the "œ" ligature). In these cases, her spelling is followed even when Melville's spelling was an acceptable form (208.249, 209.273, 216.4). For an analogous instance, see the discussion of "d——d" at 207.226.

36. In many copies of *John Marr,* for example, Melville changed "jamb" to "jam" (205.167), "boozing" to "bowsing" (207.214), and "booze" to "bowse" (213.435).

(254.37), and "Witholds" (294.9). Nevertheless, any changes to bring spelling into conformity with a late-nineteenth-century standard have been made cautiously so as to preserve the wide latitude then allowed, especially for proper names. Both "Shakspeare" (106.8) and "Shakespere's" (237.16) are retained, as are "Opher" for "Ophir" (219.40) and "Xeres" for "Jerez" (206.203). Especially open to variation are the spellings of Civil War sites; "Culpepper" (74.161), "Spottsylvania" (77.5), "Lackawana's" (82.84), "Loudon" (159.688), and "Fredericksburgh" (321.0) are retained on the basis of the *Rebellion Record* and other contemporary sources. Other proper names have been corrected, when no contemporary source has been located to support the variant: e.g., "Mirriam" (269.1), "Bramha" (271.15), and "Collonna" (for "Colonna" at 306.0).

Since contemporary practice did not demand accuracy in the use of diacritical marks and accents on foreign words (indeed, contemporary dictionaries sometimes listed them without accents), "chere" (211.373) and "a'Kempis" (263.118) are retained as they appear in the copy-text. And the otherwise anomalous use of an accent mark with "Trafalgar'" in "The Temeraire" (42.47) is probably authorial, to indicate the Spanish pronunciation and poetic emphasis.

Editorial decisions regarding capitalization sometimes have to be made, as when in *Timoleon* a reading in the printed book does not match that in the printer's copy. Such a reading could possibly be a change entered by Melville on the proofs; it could also be a compositorial change not corrected by Melville (and his failure to do so cannot automatically be taken to signify his agreement). Melville's changes in his wife's transcript go in both directions: he sometimes reduced capital letters to lowercase (as at 258.179) and apparently directed her to do so (as at 263.121, 284.6, and 292.16); but he also changed lowercase letters to capitals (as at 281.6, 314.4, and 316.35) and apparently directed her to do the same (as at 279.18). Compositorial changes, on the other hand, are likely to be from uppercase to lowercase. In the proofs of *John Marr,* where the compositors made such changes at dozens of places without Melville's authorization, he changed them back six times. Thus when there is no contextual or other evidence for the reduction in *Timoleon* of capital letters to lowercase, Melville's original intention (even if in some cases possibly not his final intention) is honored by retaining the capital letters. (Examples are at 265.8, 266.4, 273.2, 279.13, 286.1, and 316.24.)

PUNCTUATION. Melville was not as erratic or unknowledgeable about punctuation as he has occasionally been portrayed—and at least once even represented himself (in a March 24, 1856, letter to one of his publishers). The manuscripts for *John Marr* and *Timoleon* show that he kept trying out different possibilities to the very end; the reader who tracks his changes by consulting the textual notes in the present volume will see how seriously Melville regarded his punctuation. (The very fact that he wanted to insert the punctuation in his wife's transcripts is a clear reflection of this attitude.) Therefore emendations in punctuation are made in this edition only to correct obvious slips of the pen in manuscripts and clearly incorrect pointing; but when punctuation is not manifestly wrong, no alterations are made to bring it into conformity with some presumed standard, except when consistency is obviously intended.[37] Melville's punctuation generally conforms to the rhetorical style of punctuation common in the nineteenth century, rather than to the syntactical style that has now become standard. Some of Melville's punctuation that appears strange to twenty-first-century readers, particularly his use of semicolons, may seem more intrusive in the poems than in the prose works; but any alteration of the punctuation to make it more syntactical would conflict with the aim of presenting an unmodernized text. Neither is it normally feasible to consider questioning the choice of rhetorical punctuation at particular places, because the basis for rhetorical punctuation is too subjective to allow one to determine conclusively that the copy-text punctuation could not have been intended by Melville.

Under these guidelines, then, the present edition makes no emendations in the punctuation of *Battle-Pieces* aside from following Melville's own deletion of a dash in Harvard Copy C (at 9.53) and his addition of one in Copy A (at 95.33) and correcting four errors in the use of quotation

---

37. For instance, the evidence is clear, in these manuscripts and others, that Melville used hyphens in compound numbers; therefore, like the *John Marr* compositor, the present edition adds a hyphen to "sixty-five" at 201.7. The *John Marr* manuscripts and proofs also show Melville carefully standardizing the treatment of book titles and ship names from quotation marks and italics to just italics—see, for example, the book title *The Wreck of the Grosvenor* (193.20–21) and the ship names *Monitor, Meteor, Charles-and-Emma,* and *Snow-Bird* (213.407, 228.0, 231.1, 232.0, and 233.23). Thus in cases where he did not follow through on this intention in his manuscripts or his proof corrections, the present edition deletes the quotation marks (as at 192.27–28, 212.375, 239.0, and 242.0).

There is also evidence that Melville intended to expand some (but not all) abbreviations: in the *John Marr* and *Timoleon* manuscripts Melville spelled out "though" and "through" in fifty-six of the eighty instances; he expanded them from the shortened forms in three cases; and his wife expanded them in twenty cases (expansions that are followed in the present edition on the assumption that Melville directed her to check his spellings). In the one remaining case (193.9), the present edition also expands "tho'" to "though." (Likewise, Elizabeth Shaw Melville's expansion of "&" to "and" is followed, and one remaining ampersand is emended here; nevertheless, other short forms such as "o'" for "of" are not expanded, since such forms are common in poetry.)

marks (see below). In addition to emendations based on Melville's own changes in the *John Marr* pieces, the present edition emends at several places where Melville's revisions apparently led him to lose track of the punctuation (e.g., 193.1, 193.14, and 211.372) or where a compositorial change caused Melville to make further changes connected to it. His galley-proof revision of the punctuation at 222.131, for example, seems prompted by the compositor's use of a dash instead of a comma in line 132 (see also the comma in 211.358 and the lowercase "nor" in 240.13). For *Timoleon,* the present edition generally adopts the punctuation variants in Elizabeth Shaw Melville's transcript since they are likely to carry Melville's authority (see p. 599 above). When the punctuation in that transcript is not followed here, it is normally because (1) some confusion, error, or omission evidently occurred in the process of adding the punctuation or in revision (e.g., 278.6, 291.3–4, 299.55, 310.29); (2) some punctuation is clearly called for, but Melville delayed making a decision until a later stage (257.150, 258.184); (3) the book reading is unlikely to have been introduced by anyone other than the author (261.53,58, 263.111, 119,132, 275.1, 289.20); or (4) the book punctuation is judged authorial since it restores the copy-text reading (260.34–35, 269.2,8, 276.4, 317.10) or an earlier version of the punctuation (258.168, 262.80, 268.36, 309.15–17). The first edition's erroneously added comma after "clear" at 284.7, evidently the result of a compositor's or proofreader's misunderstanding of the meaning of "But" in the succeeding line, is further confirmation that the pointing in the book is not necessarily Melville's.

The only other category of punctuation that calls for particular discussion is quotation marks. The manuscript copy-texts make clear that, though Melville was occasionally inconsistent, he intended to employ consistently three conventions in the use of quotation marks: (1) that quotation marks, if they are used at all, must mark both the beginning and the ending of the quoted matter; (2) that each paragraph-opening within a quotation should be provided with an opening quotation mark to signal the continuation of the quotation (which does not end until a closing quotation mark appears); and (3) that quotation marks should regularly take the form of double superscript commas (or "inverted commas," as they are often called, though only the opening set is inverted), with the exception that those used to indicate a quotation within a quotation should take the form of single superscript commas (the next level of quotation reverting to double ones, and so on). The present edition incorporates the few emendations required to produce consistency in these practices, on the ground that Melville intended, even when he did not always achieve, such consistency.[38] No other inconsistencies, or seeming inconsistencies, in the copy-text treatment of quoted matter are regularized here, since they may reflect nuances of meaning and since, even if they do not, they point to no single standard and reflect no concern for consistency.[39]

Another question regarding quotation marks is whether or not Melville wished to use them in connection with unspoken thoughts. The inconsistency of the manuscripts in this regard could result simply from Melville's own lack of concern or from oversight. But there are grounds for believing that he came to favor using quotation marks only for spoken words, not unspoken ones. Examples of the absence of quotation marks around "musings" are at 254.52, 255.72, 278.3–4,9–10,15–16, and 293.26–33; "brooding" is treated the same way at 289.34. Furthermore, Melville's final deletion of a quotation mark seems clearly deliberate at one of these places (293.26) in both his manuscript and his wife's transcript. And the omission of quotation marks in the printed book at four points where they were present in his wife's transcript (257.149, 258.156,161,172) is possibly the result of changes made by Melville on the proofs.[40] In the present edition, therefore, unspoken thoughts are generally not enclosed in quotation marks. But the lack of quotation marks around two such "speeches" in "Timoleon" and two in "After the Pleasure Party" has caused so much confusion among critics and other readers that the present edition retains at these places the quotation marks in Melville's manuscript (and in four cases in his wife's transcript) and adds eight more to complete the pattern. Melville's indecision here is shown by his first leaving some of them out of his manuscript and then inserting some of them; and there is no way to be certain that those omitted from his wife's transcript (and thus from the printed book) were left out deliberately. Although the general policy in the present edition is to follow the punctuation of his wife's transcript, there is enough uncertainty here to warrant adopting the punctuation that adds significant clarity to these two poems—and that was intended by Melville at one stage, whether or not the last. (For the specific locations of the resulting quotation marks, see the discussions at 257.149 and 260.12.)

38. On this basis, quotation marks are incorporated into *Battle-Pieces* at 28.193, 146.238, and 177.36 and into *John Marr* at 201.5 and 208.265. They are omitted from *Timoleon* at 298.47–299.75, as explained in the discussion at 298.47.

39. Thus the present edition retains several copy-text readings with punctuation outside quotation marks, as in British practice, and does not insert punctuation to separate direct quotations from phrases before or after them.

40. The elimination of italics for unspoken thoughts at five places is part of the same pattern (263.129, 278.3–4,9–10,15–16, 279.18).

Spacing is often a textual matter in poetry, not just a matter of graphic design. Indention and line-spacing must be regarded among the accidentals, as a kind of punctuation. Melville's manuscripts and revisions in his wife's transcript and in proofs demonstrate repeatedly that he was thinking carefully about these matters. In the *John Marr* galley proofs, for example, he called for more space between the prose and verse in "Tom Deadlight" (p. 214); and in the printer's copy for *Timoleon,* he specified, "Leave double space here", after line 30 of "The Great Pyramid" (p. 316). As a result of many such markings, his intentions in these two books are fairly easy to ascertain. In *John Marr* only a few cases require editorial decision. Of the four sets of indention and spacing changes in the proofs not explicitly called for by Melville, one is adopted as following through on his original intention (215.10) and another as representing the intention implied by the manuscript context (199.1,4), while two line-spaces that appear in the proofs (after 199.2 and 206.168) are rejected. In the second "Pebble" poem Melville did not employ his usual methods to mark indention and spacing; in their absence the present edition conservatively indents but leaves no space. For *Timoleon,* the indention and spacing in Elizabeth Shaw Melville's transcript are followed except in two situations: (1) when there is some possibility of error (compare, for example, the decision to follow her transcript in not indenting and leaving a space before 263.134 with the decision to reject her reversal of Melville's indention at 295.16–17); (2) when it is possible that the book reading is authorial (compare the decisions to follow the book's restoration of earlier readings at 263.142 and 306.5–6 with the rejection of the book's treatment of indention at 270.6 and 299.57).

With *John Marr* and *Timoleon,* the manuscripts and proofs thus make clear some spacing matters that were obscured in the first editions (as at 218.12 and 226.14); but there is no such material for *Battle-Pieces* to help in determining whether any intended line-spaces or double line-spaces coincide with page-breaks in the first edition.[41] In most cases the stanzaic pattern, the indention and spacing pattern, or a change in typography makes clear whether a space of some kind is intended. In some of these places, however, the amount of space is at issue. Indeed, the question of how much space should come between stanzas or verse-paragraphs, whether at page-breaks or not, is raised by the fact that in the first edition of *Battle-Pieces* there is no consistency, from one poem to the next, in the

---

41. As for indention, anomalies in the first edition of *Battle-Pieces* are easily recognized and are emended at 5.8–14, 23.13–17, 83.100, and 167.164–65. (Unlike *Timoleon,* where display capitals obscure first-line indentions, there are no display capitals in *Battle-Pieces.*)

amount of space at such points. The decision here is consistently to use a single line-space whenever the spacing within a poem is uniform and to use two different amounts of spacing when there is reason to believe that an intended pattern of variable spacing exists within a given poem. Thus in "The Conflict of Convictions" (pp. 8–11), where the indented stanzas consistently have less space preceding than following them, a single line-space is used here to separate each of those stanzas from the preceding stanza, and double line-spaces are placed after those stanzas. It follows, then, that the page-breaks after lines 17 and 60 coincide with double line-spaces, and the one after line 39 coincides with a single line-space. Three other poems have indented stanzas that are spaced in the same manner in the first edition ("The Cumberland," pp. 37–38; "The Armies of the Wilderness," pp. 69–76; "A Dirge for McPherson," pp. 90–91), and that spacing is followed here.[42]

Similarly, the wide spaces in the first edition following the first and second stanzas of "Malvern Hill" (pp. 49–50) are retained here (as double line-spaces) because the last stanza of the poem is an indented stanza with a single line-space preceding it. And the page-break after line 17 of "The Martyr" (pp. 104–5) is here judged (in light of the pattern of these other poems) to coincide with a double line-space, since the poem contains two indented stanzas preceded by single line-spaces. Two other stanza-breaks that coincide with page-breaks in the first edition are also considered to require double line-spaces as a result of stanzaic patterns: those following line 12 of "The Temeraire" (pp. 41–43) and line 39 of "A Canticle" (pp. 101–3). And the wide spaces in the first edition after lines 8 and 24 of "The Muster" (pp. 109–10) are retained in order to maintain the separation of the opening and closing stanzas from the differently structured middle four stanzas, which have single line-spaces before them. In "The Scout toward Aldie" (pp. 139–62), on the other hand, the spaces after the two indented italicized songs (after lines 518 and 541) are not made larger here than the spaces after the regular stanzas because no distinction is made in the first edition. And the variable spacing within "Donelson" (pp. 23–36) in the first edition is taken to reflect typographical adjustment to balance the page-length rather than intended variation.

---

42. Therefore the page-breaks after line 15 of "The Cumberland," lines 58 and 226 of "The Armies of the Wilderness," and line 14 of "The Dirge for McPherson" coincide with single line-spaces; and the page-breaks after lines 36, 98, and 182 of "The Armies of the Wilderness" coincide with double line-spaces. (In the printing of "The Cumberland" in *Harper's*, there was no line-space after the sixth line of each stanza and only a single line-space between stanzas.)

In all these cases there is no question that stanza-breaks are present; the only issue is how much space there should be at those points. But in twenty-six instances where a sentence ends at the foot of a page, the need for a space after it is not immediately obvious, and an editorial decision is required at each place. On the basis of rhyme scheme, analogous spacing within the poem and similar poems, and narrative time-sequence within the poem, the present edition incorporates single line-spaces after the following lines: 32.329, 33.351,376 ("Donelson"); 51.15, 53.60 ("The Victor of Antietam"); 87.17 ("The College Colonel"); and 109.12 ("The Muster"). The spaces in the present text at these points (and the page-break instances discussed above) are not emendations to the copy-text but the result of editorial interpretation of page-breaks in the first edition.[43]

One further category requires editorial interpretation: whether certain line-end hyphens in the copy-texts are to be retained. The issue does not come up in *John Marr* and *Timoleon* since in inscribing and transcribing Melville and his wife did not break any words at the end of a line; and in *Battle-Pieces* the question is essentially limited to the prose sections—the dedication, notes, and supplement—since only four verse lines run on to a second line of type and only one of those breaks a word, which should obviously be printed as a single word ("driv-/ing" at 7.14). Likewise the decision whether to retain line-end hyphens in the prose is obvious in all but four instances: "war-/ships" (174.4, retained here), "never-/theless" (176.27, not retained), "Common-wealth" (177.3, not retained), and "Some-/thing" (186.8, not retained).[44]

The present edition avoids line-spaces at page-breaks as much as possible, especially when the verse-paragraphing is irregular. Intended spaces coincide with the ends of the following pages in the present edition (in most of these cases the stanzaic pattern or typography makes the spacing

---

43. Line-spaces are judged as not present after the following lines: 14.15, 25.89, 27.140, 29.228, 30.253, 31.278, 34.398, 35.422,445, 42.38, 64.16, 79.39, 84.16, 134.19, 163.17, 164.42, 165.66,90, 167.139, 168.190. For the record, the page-breaks in the first edition that coincide with obvious single-line stanza-breaks (and thus where no editorial judgment is involved) occur after the following lines: 16.15, 17.35,55, 19.14, 24.40, 28.186, 37.15, 47.16, 56.15, 57.35,55, 59.12, 60.15, 61.39, 65.16, 66.18, 78.16, 80.16, 82.80, 86.16, 89.16, 95.60, 96.84, 97.16, 99.15, 101.16, 113.32, 135.18, 139.14, 140.35,56, 141.77, 142.98,119, 143.140,161, 144.182, 145.203,224, 146.245,266, 147.287, 148.308,329, 149.350,371, 150.392, 151.413,434, 152.455,476, 153.497, 154.518,541, 155.560,581, 156.602, 157.623,644, 158.665,686, 159.707, 160.728,749, 161.770,791, 170.18, 171.42.

44. Though "war-ships" does not appear elsewhere in the copy-text for *Battle-Pieces*, Melville hyphenates it in the *John Marr* manuscript at 213.422 and 220.54. The other three words all appear as one word elsewhere in *Battle-Pieces*.

clear anyway): 8, 9 (double line-space), 10, 12, 17, 21, 31, 44, 47, 49 (double line-space), 57, 60, 69, 70 (double line-space), 71, 78, 80, 82, 94, 95, 97, 101, 120, 139–61, 171, 214, 232, 259, 288, 289, 302, 307, and 315. Of the words that are hyphenated at the ends of lines in the present edition, the following should retain the hyphen when copied: "non-combatants" (179.24–25), "Re-establishment" (186.19–20), "sea-port" (195.7–8), and "work-a-day" (196.7–8). These lists involve no editorial decisions but are essential for reconstructing the copy-texts and making exact quotations from the present edition.

EDITORIAL APPARATUS

FOLLOWING THIS NOTE is a series of NOTES ON INDIVIDUAL POEMS. Not every poem requires annotation; but for those that do, there may be, first, an introductory note on the composition and sources of the piece, followed by one or more of the following sections, providing basic evidence for textual decisions:

DISCUSSIONS. These discussions are of particular readings and include explanations of decisions to emend or not to emend, selective identifications of allusions and sources, and occasional references to published commentary.

EMENDATIONS. These lists record every change made from the copy-texts, in accidentals as well as in substantives. The first item in each entry (after the page-line citation) is the Northwestern-Newberry reading (followed by a bracket and an abbreviation designating the source of the reading);[45] the second is the rejected copy-text reading (with an abbreviation denoting that copy-text). The abbreviations and symbols employed are identified below, on pp. 622–23. Emendations marked with an asterisk are commented on in the preceding section of discussions of individual readings. No textual emendations of any sort have been made silently. Using the lists of emendations, as well as the information on page-end

---

45. When the source is given as the Northwestern-Newberry Edition itself, the designation NN signifies only that the reading does not occur in the copy-text; it does not imply that no one has ever thought of it before. Also the presence of the JMg symbol merely records the fact that the reading appears in the *John Marr* galley proofs and does not imply that the authority of the reading derives from its presence there; the readings so labeled are obvious ones that would have had to be made whether or not they occurred in the galley proofs.

line-spaces and line-end hyphens (pp. 616–17), one can reconstruct the copy-texts in every detail.[46]

VARIANTS AND TEXTUAL NOTES. For *Battle-Pieces,* whenever more than one authorized printed text is involved, these lists record all variant readings, in both substantives and accidentals. For *John Marr* and *Timoleon,* the textual notes set forth not only variants among the final readings of the manuscript texts and the printed texts but also alterations within the manuscripts. Each entry begins with the reading of the present edition and then reports successive changes in readings (words, phrases, passages, or punctuation), indicating (1) the order in which they were made (signi-fied by arabic figures), (2) the document in which the change occurred (identified by an abbreviation), (3) the person by whom the change was made (specified by a left-slanting slash and initials, as when "HM\EM" refers to Elizabeth Shaw Melville's alteration of Melville's manuscript),[47] and, when possible, (4) the inscription-revision stage at which the change occurred (designated by letters).[48]

For example, the following entry lists a series of substantive changes in "John Marr" (in line 24 of page 196 in the present edition):

46. Nontextual physical features of the documents containing the copy-texts are of course not recoverable from the lists. Examples of such nontextual features in the first-edition copy-text for *Battle-Pieces* are the following: the typography and layout throughout (including the typographic treatment of poem titles, their end-punctuation in main titles and subtitles, and the opening words of poems, but not including patterns of indention and line-spacing in poems); the content of running-titles and of the preliminaries (title page, copyright page, and table of contents, but not the prefatory note and dedication); and the placement and end-punctuation of the dedication and section-titles. The same features (some of which are applicable to manuscripts) are also considered nontextual for *John Marr* and *Timoleon,* whether they appear in the copy-text manuscripts or the first editions. Marginal line numbers for the poems are supplied by the present edition and do not appear in any of the first editions.

47. For alterations in manuscripts, the person is identified only when different from the main inscriber; for alterations entered on printed documents, the person making the alterations is always identified. It is also important to note that, in the textual notes for *Timoleon,* hundreds of accidentals are labeled "EM", not "EM\HM" (Elizabeth Melville's transcript, Herman Melville's hand), because, although the inference is almost always safe that his hand (or voice) directed her inscription (as explained above), the physical evi-dence is not sufficient to determine for sure either that a penciled mark is distinguishably his or that any penciled mark at all precedes and is concealed by her inked punctuation.

48. The stage labels for a given piece do not apply to other pieces. That is, stage Bc of poem X is not stage Bc of poem Y, or of any other piece. Though the alphabetical stage labels sometimes point toward certain compositional possibilities, they should not be mistaken for more than they are: indications of the order of fair-copy stages.

196.24 a] HM2,JMg\HM; an unheeded HM1; an idle HM3

This entry shows that Melville in his manuscript (HM) first wrote "an unheeded" (HM1), then "a" (HM2), then "an idle" (HM3, the copy-text reading, which is the HM reading with the highest arabic number). The compositor followed his copy in printing "an idle";[49] but in reading the galley proofs (JMg) Melville changed (JMg\HM) the reading back to "a" (a change followed as an emendation in the present edition).

The following entry from "Art" provides an example from *Timoleon:*

280.3 form] HM,T; forms EM\HM[*not copied back into HM*]

This entry specifies that Melville began with "form" in his manuscript (HM, the copy-text) and then altered it in his wife's transcript (EM) to "forms" (EM\HM); but she did not copy it back into his manuscript, as would otherwise be assumed. In *Timoleon* (T), however, the word becomes "form" again and presumably represents Melville's returning to his earlier reading when marking the proofs. (Such instances do not appear in the lists of emendations since the copy-text reading is in the present text.)

Changes in substantives (and associated accidentals) are listed first, grouped by page in the present edition; changes in accidentals (not connected with substantive changes) follow.[50] Though most of the changes are local enough to be listed simply in the form of successive readings, some more complex revisions, such as the matter on superseded leaves, are

49. This example and the one below display a convention followed throughout these textual notes: unless otherwise indicated, the copyist or compositor is assumed to have followed accurately the document being copied or set in type. Thus, in this example, the compositor printed "an idle" in the galley proof, but that fact is here, as in most entries, left implicit. Similarly, the subsequent documents are assumed to follow the latest reading in the sequence; for this entry, then, it can be assumed that the *John Marr* page proofs (JMp—or, in the case of the "John Marr" piece, where there were two stages of page proofs, JMp1 and JMp2) and the printed book (JM) read "a", following Melville's galley-proof change (JMg\HM). In the example just below, for "Art," the entry supplies no explicit indication that the word "form" appeared in Elizabeth Shaw Melville's transcript (EM), just as it did in his manuscript (HM). Thus for the *Timoleon* poems, the convention is not to report explicitly all the instances when Melville's wife copied accurately but only those instances in which the absence of any indication of what she transcribed might seriously impair a reader's understanding of the nature, agents, and/or sequence of the variants. And the reading in the book text is not listed unless it differs from hers. The sequence, therefore, is: HM, EM, EM\HM, HM\EM[copying back], T.

50. Such variants as "can not"/"cannot", "kelson"/"keelson", and "dozing"/"dosing" are considered accidentals whenever contemporary dictionaries indicate that they were interchangeable forms of the same word.

described by means of a genetic text (in which all words in roman type are authorial, and all words in italics are editorial).

To allow readers to correlate the present text with the leaves of the manuscripts, the textual notes also include, in the sections for substantives, notations specifying the first and last uncanceled words of each leaf or part-leaf and the stage at which it was inscribed or revised. Preceding the textual notes are reported in brief summary the inscription-revision stages that have been identified in surviving manuscripts by the study of such evidence as physical and verbal interrelations among main- and part-leaves, the position of writing on them, and their foliations, as well as of such further clues as color of ink and pencil, kind of pen, and color and/or thickness of paper. In the twenty-six final leaves of "John Marr," for example, four stages—B, Ca, Cb, and D—can be distinguished. Entries such as the following pair indicate stage designations for leaves and particular words:

> 196.1–9 His . . . helpfulness] [*leaf 5(Cb)*]
> 196.2 dwells] HM3(D); boards HM1; lives HM2

Leaf 5, encompassing the words from "His" to "helpfulness" in lines 1–9 of page 196 in the present edition, was inscribed at stage Cb. At this stage, Melville in line 2 originally wrote "boards" (HM1), then "lives" (HM2). At a later stage (D), he revised the leaf again, substituting "dwells" (HM3, the copy-text reading). (See also the list of symbols below, pp. 622–23.)

In the notes for each poem, readers will thus find all the copy-text readings that have been emended in this critical text and any alterations and variants in manuscripts, proofs, or authorized printed texts. With these lists they can reconsider for themselves the textual decisions for the present edition and in the process see more clearly the relationship between the authoritative manuscripts or the printed texts that were published in Melville's lifetime and the text that is offered here as a more faithful representation of his intentions.

Notes on Individual Poems

UNLESS OTHERWISE SPECIFIED, all quotations from Melville's writings (and page references cited) follow the Northwestern-Newberry (NN) Edition (e.g., volume 15, *Journals*); quotations of letters to or from Melville are from the NN *Correspondence* volume, where they can be located by date. Citations to the present volume are by page and line, with a "o" line number used to refer to any line(s) preceding the first line of text, such as titles and subtitles. (For pages of prose, line numbering is separate for each page; for pages of verse, line numbering proceeds continuously through each poem, as the printed line numbers indicate.)

Biblical quotations follow the King James Version—the version Melville owned. Books Melville owned or borrowed are identified by the number assigned by Merton M. Sealts Jr. in *Melville's Reading* and its supplements (including Sealts 1990 and Olsen-Smith and Sealts 2004); books he used as sources are identified by the number assigned by Mary K Bercaw in *Melville's Sources*. Any variation between a document as transcribed in cited secondary works and as printed here is based on an examination of the original. Full citations for sources referred to in short form appear in the comprehensive list of WORKS CITED.

SYMBOLS, ABBREVIATIONS,
AND TERMS

BH	Boston *Herald* printing of "The Haglets"
BP	*Battle-Pieces and Aspects of the War* (1866)
clip	a leaf or part-leaf of manuscript inscribed at an earlier stage than that of the leaf to which it is attached (cf. "patch")
———"———	a mark (———"———) used by Melville to indicate the beginning, ending, or major division of a verse or prose work
EM	Elizabeth Shaw Melville or a transcript in her hand
EM\HM	Elizabeth Shaw Melville's transcript, Herman Melville's inscription
HM	Herman Melville or a transcript in his hand
HM\EM	Herman Melville's transcript, Elizabeth Shaw Melville's inscription
JM	*John Marr and Other Sailors with Some Sea-Pieces* (1888)
JM\EM	*John Marr,* Elizabeth Shaw Melville's inscription
JM\HM	*John Marr,* Herman Melville's inscription
JMg	*John Marr* galley proof
JMg\HM	*John Marr* galley proof, Herman Melville's inscription
JMg\r	*John Marr* galley proof, reviser/proofreader's inscription
JMp	*John Marr* page proof
JMp\HM	*John Marr* page proof, Herman Melville's inscription
JMp\r	*John Marr* page proof, reviser/proofreader's inscription
line-space	one text-line of blank space
NN	Northwestern-Newberry Edition
NYT	New York *Tribune* printing of "The Haglets"
NYT\HM	New York *Tribune* printing of "The Haglets," Herman Melville's inscription
patch	a leaf or part-leaf of manuscript inscribed at a later stage than that of the leaf to which it is attached (cf. "clip")
T	*Timoleon Etc.* (1891)
v	verso
x	undeciphered inscription (number of x's approximates number of letters involved; e.g., "Mxxxer")

1...	arabic numerals indicate order of variants; these variant numbers follow the symbol(s) that indicate location and/or inscriber of each variant (e.g., "HM2" means the second reading Herman Melville inscribed in his own manuscript; "EM\HM3" means the third reading he inscribed in Elizabeth Shaw Melville's transcript)
¹word	a superscript numeral prefixed to a word specifies which occurrence of that word in the NN line
?	prefixed italic question mark indicates conjectural report
→	an arrow before the variant number (e.g., "HM→2") means that the variant was immediately superseded; an arrow before the word *"then"* ("→*then*") means "then immediately"
*	asterisk marks a reading (in the emendations lists or in the textual notes) for which a separate discussion is provided
[ ]	brackets enclose editorial matter, such as descriptions of superseded leaves and part-leaves
{ }	braces enclose descriptions of variants within variants
^	caret indicates the absence of a punctuation mark
/	slash indicates end of line
=	an equals sign at the end of a line in the textual notes indicates a hyphen in the document being cited
~	wavy dash stands for the word(s) previously cited in the entry and signals that only the accompanying punctuation (or lack of it) is at issue

Battle-Pieces (pp. 1–188)

NN copy-text is the first printing, *Battle-Pieces* [BP] (New York: Harper & Brothers, 1866). There was no later printing of the book in Melville's lifetime, and no manuscript (other than a transcript of one poem) is known. In total, BP is here emended at 40 points: at 25 points from Melville's revisions in Harvard Copies A and C of BP [BP\HM]; at 15 points by NN. Substantives are emended at 26 points, accidentals at 14 points.

The HISTORICAL NOTE above outlines the historical and biographical background of *Battle-Pieces,* and a postscript summarizes the book's reception (pp. 518–27). The NOTE ON PRINTING AND PUBLISHING HISTORY, pp. 530–43 above, describes the preparation of the book for publication, the separate publication of some of its poems in *Harper's New Monthly Magazine,* its physical appearance, and its meager sales. The GENERAL NOTE ON THE TEXT above supplies information on the copies used for collation and on the printer's copy for NN (pp. 580–82); comments on the sources for assessing the text, including Harvard Copies A and C and the transcript of "Philip" (pp. 582–85); sets forth the principles for emendation of the copy-text (pp. 599–602, 607–17); and explains the makeup of this textual apparatus (pp. 617–18).

The notes below do not comment on line-end hyphens or on spacing between stanzas or verse-paragraphs. These matters are discussed on pp. 614–17 above (reporting NN treatment of the copy-text in these respects and also specifying which line-end hyphens in NN should be retained in quoting and which NN page-breaks coincide with stanza-breaks).

[TABLE OF CONTENTS] (pp. vii–x)

DISCUSSION. vii.2 *The Portent*] This title is not present in the table of contents of the first edition; the omission is conceivably a sign that "The Portent" was a late addition (see p. 541 above), but it could simply have been the result of an oversight. The NN table of contents is made up from the titles that appear at the heads of the poems in NN, which are the same as those at the heads of the poems in the first edition (except for end-punctuation). The titles in the first-edition table of contents differ at nine places—once in wording, five times in capitalization, and three times in punctuation. Even if these differences reflect the text of a manuscript table of contents in Melville's or his wife's hand (and they may not), the readings at the heads of the poems are more likely to have received his close attention (both in his manuscript of the poems and in the proofs) than those in a table of contents. The first-edition table of contents does not include "Tennessee" and its preceding comma (viii.4); it uses lowercase initial letters in "Utilitarian" (vii.15), "Ascribed" (viii.7), "Released" (viii.32), and "Returned" (ix.28), and it capitalizes the initial letter of "field" (ix.24); it has no hyphen in "Aurora-Borealis" (viii.31); and it has no commas following "Authorities" and "Privates" (ix.26). NN also departs from the first-edition table of contents in making the last five entries typographically consistent to reflect their status as section-titles. But NN follows the first-edition table of contents in using full titles (including subtitles) only for the poems in the section of "Verses Inscriptive and Memorial" and for the second "Stonewall Jackson" poem. For further discussion of these matters, see pp. 541–42 above.

EMENDATION. *vii.2 *The Portent*] NN; [*not present*] BP

[PREFACE] (p. 3)

DISCUSSION. 3.13 a harp in a window] Here, as in "The Æolian Harp At the *Surf Inn*" in *John Marr* (pp. 226–27 above), the instrument is one whose strings are played upon not by a human agent but by the wind (identified by Pierre in an Æolian harp passage in *Pierre* as "God's breath!" [bk. 2, sect. vii]). Elsewhere, Melville refers to the Æolian harp in *White-Jacket* (chap. 12). Melville had an Æolian harp on his back porch on East 26th Street (Parker 2002, p. 908).

THE PORTENT (p. 5)

On October 16, 1859, the abolitionist John Brown and his followers attacked the Federal arsenal at Harper's Ferry, Virginia, and occupied it for two and a half days until forced to surrender by U.S. Marines under the command of army colonel Robert E. Lee. Brown was found guilty of treason and hanged six weeks later. The first edition distinguishes "The Portent" typographically from the rest of the poems: it appears in italic type and is followed by a blank verso page. NN retains this typography.

DISCUSSIONS. 5.12–14 *streaming beard . . . meteor*] A contemporary meteor sighting is reported by Kent Ljungquist in "'Meteor of the War': Melville, Thoreau, and Whitman Respond to John Brown." On the morning of November 15, 1859, not quite a month after the assault on Harper's Ferry, a meteor "with a body as large as a house, and a tail about 40 feet long" appeared with a "luminous whiteness" over New York City (p. 675). While Melville may not have seen the meteor in Pittsfield, the *Berkshire County Eagle* of November 17 paraphrased the New York newspaper reports about it under the headline "A Meteoric Ball in New York."

5.14 *war*] As William H. Shurr remarks, "It is likely that *law, draw, Shenandoah, war,* and *more* are all meant to rhyme, in accordance with Melville's regional pronunciation" (p. 16). (See Harrison Hayford's long note on Melville's spelling of Polynesian words, influenced by his New England pronunciation, in the Hendricks House edition of *Omoo*, pp. 343–47.)

EMENDATION. 5.8–14 *Hidden . . . war*] [*left margin and indention same as first stanza*] NN; [*left margin and indention to the left of corresponding lines in first stanza*] BP

THE CONFLICT OF CONVICTIONS (pp. 8–11)

DISCUSSIONS. 8.12 Shall Mammon's slaves fulfill?] Jesus' words in Matthew 6:24: "No man can serve two masters: for either he will hate the one, and love the other; or else he will hold to the one, and despise the other. Ye cannot serve God and mammon." Melville marked Matthew 6:25–26 in the New Testament he took with him round Cape Horn in 1860 (New York: American Bible Soc.,

1844; Sealts, no. 65). Cf. "Mammon's tower" in "The Ravaged Villa" (in *Timoleon,* 266.8 above).

8.22–23 Patient . . . waits] An echo of "They also serve who only stand and wait," the last line in Milton's sonnet "On His Blindness" (as titled in Melville's edition of *The Poetical Works* [Boston: Hilliard, Gray, 1836], 2:357–58; Sealts, no. 358b, Bercaw, no. 499).

9.37 The ghost is yielded in the gloom] A possible echo of Matthew 27:50: "Jesus, when he had cried again with a loud voice, yielded up the ghost."

9.44 *rust on the Iron Dome*] Seeking a consular position in early 1861, Melville went to Washington, where he saw the incomplete new Capitol dome, "not carved of stone, as was the rest of the building, but manufactured of iron and painted white to give the appearance of stone" (Garner 1993, p. 77). In *Battle-Pieces,* the dome also appears in "The Victor of Antietam" (52.29), "The Scout toward Aldie" (140.32–35), and "Lee in the Capitol" (164.31,38).

9.54 *Which foldeth him!*] In replacing BP's "A meagre wight" with Melville's revision in Harvard Copy C of BP, NN retains the exclamation point and italics of BP: while Melville lined out the exclamation point along with the italicized words, he substituted no other pointing and presumably meant for the exclamation point to remain along with the italics.

10.61 The Ancient of Days] Daniel 7:9: "I beheld till the thrones were cast down, and the Ancient of days did sit, whose garment was white as snow, and the hair of his head like the pure wool: his throne was like the fiery flame, and his wheels as burning fire." In "A Canticle" (pp. 101–3 above), "The Giant of the Pool / Heaves his forehead white as wool—" (lines 44–45).

11.90 PROPHESY] A variant spelling (with the final vowel pronounced as in "multiply") for the noun now spelled "prophecy"; the *Oxford English Dictionary* (*s.v.* "prophesy") explains that the "modern differentiation of *prophesy* [verb] and *prophecy* [noun] was not established till after 1700, and has no etymological basis, *prophesy* being at first a mere spelling variant in both [noun and verb]."

EMENDATIONS. 8.11 whereat] BP\HM; at which BP 9.52 *taper dim*] BP\HM; *blinking light* BP 9.53 braves^] BP\HM; ~— BP *9.54 *Which foldeth him!*] BP\HM; *A meagre wight!* BP

APATHY AND ENTHUSIASM (pp. 12–13)

DISCUSSIONS. 13.27–28 And the tomb of Faith was rent . . . the People] Matthew 27:51–53: "And behold, the vail of the temple was rent in twain from the top to the bottom: and the earth did quake, and the rocks rent; And the graves were opened, and many bodies of the saints which slept, arose, And came out of the graves after his resurrection, and went into the holy city, and appeared unto many."

13.31 came to pass] The biblical phrasing may imply not only "happened" but also "occurred as a predictable or prophesied event."

THE MARCH INTO VIRGINIA (pp. 14–15)

The poem glosses the first major engagement of the Civil War—called both the First Battle of Bull Run and First Manassas, July 18–21, 1861.

DISCUSSIONS. 14.16–15.30 The banners . . . right] Frank L. Day (1959, pp. 11–12) thinks that Melville probably relied on a narrative in the July 23, 1861, New York *World* (*Rebellion Record,* 2:81–89, doc. 5) for its account of the weather and the high spirits of the troops marching to slaughter.

14.23 Moloch's uninitiate] 2 Kings 23:10: "And he defiled Topheth, which is in the valley of the children of Hinnom, that no man might make his son or his daughter to pass through the fire to Molech." David McAuley finds a source for the poem in "Slaughter of the Innocents," a July 22, 1861, editorial in the New York *Times* (p. 4) that deplores how Southern forces are using "boys, or mere children," and claims "the Confederate leaders, as remorseless as Moloch, cause such sinless and gentle beings to 'pass through the fire' of their treason and perish in the cruel havoc of war." William Pommer in *Milton and Melville* (p. 80) and Hennig Cohen in his edition of *Battle-Pieces* (p. 213) cite *Paradise Lost,* 1.392–98, for its passage on Moloch.

15.33 three days] Having arrived at Bull Run in the afternoon of July 18, the Union forces were withdrawing three days later, July 21.

15.33 are] In Harvard Copy C of BP, Melville penciled "be" in the right margin as a possible alternative, but NN does not emend since he neither underlined nor lined out "are" (see pp. 600–602 above).

15.35 shame] In Harvard Copy A of BP, Melville penciled "some" in the left margin as a possible alternative, but NN does not emend since he only pencil-underlined, but did not line out, "shame" (see pp. 600–602 above).

15.36 Thy . . . share] In Harvard Copy C of BP, Melville first underlined but did not line-through the printed last line—"The throe of Second Manassas share."—and penciled a question mark in the right margin. Then he explicitly lined through the printed line and penciled, then lined through, "Manassas' second throe and deadlier share"; then he penciled, below, "Thy second shock, Manassas, share", and finally he substituted "after" for "second".

EMENDATION. *15.36 Thy after shock, Manassas,] BP\HM; The throe of Second Manassas BP

LYON (pp. 16–18)

On August 10, 1861, at Wilson's Creek, near Springfield, Missouri, Brigadier General Nathaniel Lyon was killed in the first major battle in the western theater of operations. Willard Thorp (pp. lxxxviii, 425), Frank L. Day (1959, pp. 4–5), and Hennig Cohen in his edition of *Battle-Pieces* (pp.

214–15) indicate some of Melville's possible sources in accounts from the Missouri *Democrat* and New York *Tribune* collected in the *Rebellion Record* (2:511–19, doc. 175; 3:20–21, "Poetry and Incidents").

DISCUSSION. 17.24,39 field to die on] Day (1959, p. 12) takes note of a poem entitled "Lyon," by "H. P." (*Rebellion Record*, 3:20–21, "Poetry and Incidents"), but finds "no strong echoes of word or phrase" from it in Melville's poem. In his edition of *Battle-Pieces* (pp. 214–15), Cohen, however, surmises that the last four lines in the third stanza of the earlier "Lyon" "may have given Melville the phrase *a field to die on* . . . as well as his unfortunate refrain and the title itself":

> They feared not death—men bless the field
> That patriot soldiers die on—
> Fair Freedom's cause was sword and shield,
> And at their head was Lyon.

EMENDATION. 18.65 pale] BP\HM; brave BP

BALL'S BLUFF (p. 19)

Though this poem is not explicitly concerned with the Ball's Bluff disaster of October 21, 1861, Melville could be sure his contemporary reader would recognize the name as that of another Union debacle, this one mainly caused by the bad judgments of senior officers, especially of Colonel Edward D. Baker, a brigade commander who had given over being senator from Oregon in order to serve his country more generally. Another poem titled "Ball's Bluff" (*Rebellion Record*, 3:32, "Poetry and Incidents") begins: "Big Bethel, Bull Run, and Ball's Bluff—/ Oh, alliteration of blunders!"

DUPONT'S ROUND FIGHT (p. 20)

On November 7, 1861, Commodore Samuel Francis Du Pont conducted a devastating assault on Forts Beauregard and Walker, at the mouth of Port Royal Sound, South Carolina, the deep-water port that thereafter became a strategically indispensable base for the Union's South Atlantic Blockading Squadron. Turning their line of battle counterclockwise in a sort of ellipse, the Union ships fired first on Beauregard, to the north, as they went upriver, then on Walker to the south, as they came downriver. Frank L. Day (1959, p. 6) and Hennig Cohen (*Battle-Pieces*, p. 216) reproduce the illustrated battle plan that the *Rebellion Record* (3:106, doc. 36) took from the New York *Tribune.*

DISCUSSION. 20.1 In time and measure perfect] Sister Lucy Marie Freibert (p. 79) points out the parallel between this first line and line 50 of Emerson's "Merlin II"—"In perfect time and measure they" (*Poems* [7th ed., Boston: Phillips, Sampson, 1858], pp. 185–87; Sealts, no. 206).

THE STONE FLEET (pp. 21–22)

See Melville's note b (p. 173 above). Melville may have felt some special connection to a few of the old whalers he lists in his note (copying their names off the list in the *Rebellion Record* (3:504, doc. 235) from a New York *Tribune* account dated December 17, 1861—also the source of the quotation that begins the note. The *William Lee* and the *Herald* were spoken by Melville's first whaler, the *Acushnet*, while he was aboard (Leyda, *Log*, pp. 121, 128). His cousin Thomas W. Melville (1806–44) shipped twice on the *Amazon* (*Log*, pp. 91, 121). In 1854, the *Rebecca Sims* took the whale that stove the *Ann Alexander* in 1851, the latter an actual event that seemed to validate Moby Dick's sinking the *Pequod* (*Log*, p. 487). And the *Potomac* of Nantucket was in Nukahiva Harbor when Melville jumped ship there (see Molloy, p. 634, and Bercaw Edwards, pp. 57–71).

DONELSON (pp. 23–36)

On Sunday, February 16, 1862, "after three days of the most desperate fighting ever witnessed on this continent," Fort Donelson fell (Richmond *Dispatch* account, *Rebellion Record,* 4:187, doc. 46). The fort, on the Cumberland River near Dover in northwest Tennessee, had been under siege by General Ulysses S. Grant as part of a campaign to open up the rivers to Federal shipping.

DISCUSSIONS. 23.1–3 The bitter cup . . . Envoys up] Confederate commissioners James M. Mason and John Slidell, on a diplomatic mission to seek aid from Great Britain, were seized from the British mail steamer *Trent* on November 8, 1861, and held at Fort Warren in Boston Harbor until British efforts brought about the State Department "countermand" (line 2) that caused them to be surrendered to the British, at Provincetown, on January 1, 1862.

23.14–17 *General Grant, . . . command)*] On Saturday, February 15, 1862, the New York *Times* correspondent reported from camp near Fort Donelson this news from Wednesday the twelfth: "The column which thus reached here, by way of the Cumberland, numbered not far from ten thousand men, who were conveyed in fourteen transport steamers; the column which came from Fort Henry, across the country, under Gen. Grant in person, was composed, in round numbers, of twenty thousand men" (*Rebellion Record,* 4:171, doc. 46).

23.20–24.24 *This . . . brush*] Frank L. Day (1959, p. 9) indicates the *Times* account as a probable source, most evidently in the sentence: "To the rear the bluff has been to some extent levelled for the distance of a mile" (*Rebellion Record,* 4:171, doc. 46).

24.39 vim] Day (1959, p. 9) points out the use of this word in the *Times* account (*Rebellion Record,* 4:171, doc. 46).

24.46–50 *Grant's . . . done*] Day (1959, p. 9) compares Melville's phrasing to "the Fort is completely invested" in the *Times* (*Rebellion Record,* 4:173, doc. 46) and its description of the Federal forces as deployed "up and down a line parallel with the river . . . enclosing the Fort in a semi-circular line" (4:171).

25.72–88 *Along . . . salt-spring*] As possible sources for some of these lines Day (1959, p. 14) indicates two passages from the *Times* report: (1) "A large number of the wounds were caused by falling limbs, which were wrenched off by the fiery showers of grape sent from the rebel batteries" (*Rebellion Record,* 4:172, doc. 46); (2) a description of the operations of a regiment of sharpshooters (each of whom wears "a gray felt cap, whose top is rigged 'fore-and-aft' with squirrel-tails dyed black"): "Lying flat behind a stump, one would watch with finger on trigger for rebel game with all the excitement of a hunter waylaying deer at a 'salt-lick.' Woe to rebel caput that was lifted ever so quickly above the parapet for a glance at Yankee operations. Fifty eyes instantly sighted it, and fifty fingers drew trigger on it, and thereafter it was seen no more" (4:171–72). The report in the Missouri *Democrat* of the sharpshooters uses similar wording: "[W]oe to the unwary rebel who dared to show his head above the entrenchments" (4:178; quoted in Day, p. 14). Both the *Times* and the *Democrat,* as Day notes (p. 15), report the "loss of Colonel Morrison" (line 80).

25.92–94 *earnest North . . . storm*] Day (1959, p. 17) traces these lines to the report in the Missouri *Democrat:* "But, cold and hungry, and with garments stiff with frost, the soldiers were still hopeful and firm. . . . and it is this self-same spirit of dogged determination, and steady, long-enduring courage, peculiar to the Anglo-Saxon of the North, that at last outwore the perhaps more impetuous bravery of the opposing force" (*Rebellion Record,* 4:179, doc. 46).

26.99–100 *Sole uniform . . . white badge*] Day points out (1959, p. 23) that both the Charleston *Courier* and Richmond *Dispatch* describe the white armband which Confederate troops wore to distinguish friend from foe (*Rebellion Record,* 4:184, 186, doc. 46).

26.104 *gold lace*] Day notes (1959, p. 23) the *Times* correspondent's report that Confederate officers wear uniforms both "regular gray" and "army blue, the only difference from the United States style being in the great profusion of gold lace" (*Rebellion Record,* 4:176, doc. 46).

26.115–18 *trees . . . wasps*] Day (1959, p. 24) cites this passage in the *Democrat* account: "But it was not in the power of man to scale the abatis before them. Brush piled upon brush, with sharp points fronting them everywhere, met them wherever they turned; and so, after a few interchanges of musketry with the swarming regiments which had been concentrated here, the order for retiring was given" (*Rebellion Record*, 4:179, doc. 46). Day adds that "the swarming regiments" (also called "swarming rebel masses") may have suggested Melville's "Fierce wasps."

28.188 COMMODORE's] Belonging to Flag Officer Andrew H. Foote, commander of the flotilla of naval craft supporting Grant's land assault.

29.210 *Louisville's*] The *Louisville* was one of the ironclad gunboats badly damaged in the action at Donelson. Day (1959, p. 19) points to the *Times* passage (*Rebellion Record*, 4:172, doc. 46) that Melville draws upon in lines 210–22: "[A] shot disabled the steering apparatus of the Louisville, by carrying off the top of the wheelhouse, and knocking the wheel itself into fragments. . . . Of course the boat became instantly unmanageable, and swung around, receiving a shot in the woodwork towards the stern, which . . . wounded several seamen. Under these circumstances, it was thought best to retire, and accordingly the whole fleet fell back to the position it had occupied in the morning. The most serious damage sustained during the action was from one of those monster one hundred and twenty-eight-pound shots, which passed through a bow-port of the Louisville and dismounted the second gun on the starboard quarter, killing three men and wounding six others. A captain of one of the guns was cut completely in two."

29.227–28 *Would . . . valentine*] Day (1959, p. 20) quotes the Missouri *Democrat* (*Rebellion Record*, 4:179–80, doc. 46): "Cavender, Taylor, Woods . . . and Swartz [artillery commanders] would occasionally exchange a valentine, as they were playfully called," given the mid-February timing of the battle.

30.253 *flag, deemed black*] Day (1959, p. 21) quotes the *Times:* "The rebels have a flag flying from the Fort which is thought to be a black one" (*Rebellion Record*, 4:173, doc. 46).

30.254–55 *Some . . . night*] Day (1959, p. 21) points out Melville's source in this *Times* sentence: "In some cases, a few of our wounded were cared for by the rebels, although they were without fire, and could give them but little valuable assistance" (*Rebellion Record*, 4:173, doc. 46).

30.261 *a perverted Bunker Hill*] The book edition of Melville's *Israel Potter* (1855) is dedicated "To His Highness the Bunker-Hill Monument."

30.275 *A.M.*] In Harvard Copy C of BP, Melville pencil-underlined these italicized letters, penciled and erased an interlocked triple check mark in the left margin, and penciled over the erased check mark what is either a virgule (to indicate a revision) or a marginal mark (to indicate a passage needing revision). His final intention may have been to change the italic letters to roman; but since his intention is ambiguous, NN retains the reading in BP.

32.349–33.351 *This . . . Donelson*] Hennig Cohen (*Battle-Pieces*, p. 221) cites comparable lines in Shakespeare's *Richard II* (2.1.40–50). Melville's edition reads:

"This royal throne of kings, this scept'red isle . . . This blessed plot, this earth, this realm, this England" (Boston: Hilliard, Gray, 1837; Sealts, no. 460).

33.383 *Lew Wallace*] General Lewis ("Lew") Wallace (1827–1905), later (1880) the author of *Ben Hur,* commanded a division at Donelson. He was also at Shiloh; see the introductory note to Melville's poem of that name, p. 637 below.

34.419–35.420 *In Dover . . . dying*] Day (1959, p. 26) quotes the *Times* report that after the surrender: "Every house in Dover was filled with dead and wounded" (*Rebellion Record,* 4:176, doc. 46).

EMENDATIONS. 23.13–17 IMPORTANT . . . *command),*] *[each line moved to the right so that the leftmost ones (13, 16) have the same left margin as those in the following italic lines*] NN; *[each line begins to the left of the positions established by the following italic lines*] BP 28.193 Hurrah!"] NN; ~!^ BP 28.194 again"—] NN; ~^— BP 35.443 cross] BP\HM; deep BP

THE CUMBERLAND (pp. 37–38)

On Saturday, March 8, 1862, in Hampton Roads, off Newport News, Virginia, the Confederate ironclad *Virginia* (the reconstructed and rechristened *Merrimac*) sank the Union wooden sloop-of-war *Cumberland* by ramming and raking it with devastating fire. After visiting the site a few days later, Nathaniel Hawthorne concluded that "the Minnesota belongs to a class of vessels that will be built no more, nor ever fight another battle,—being as much a thing of the past as any of the ships of Queen Elizabeth's time" (p. 57 in "Chiefly about War-Matters," by "A Peaceable Man," *Atlantic Monthly* 10 [July 1862]: 43–61). Also, after claiming "that last gun from the Cumberland . . . sounded the requiem of many sinking ships" and foreseeing a future wherein "human strife is to be transferred from the heart and personality of man into cunning contrivances of machinery," Hawthorne issued a call: "[I]n the mean while, so long as manhood retains any part of its pristine value, no country can afford to let gallantry like that of Morris and his crew [of the *Cumberland*], any more than that of the brave Worden [commander of the *Monitor*], pass unhonored and unrewarded. . . . Let poets brood upon the theme, and make themselves sensible how much of the past and future is contained within its compass, till its spirit shall flash forth in the lightning of a song!" (p. 59). Melville may have responded to this call in "The Cumberland" and in the following three poems in *Battle-Pieces,* all about this clash.

In "Hawthorne, Melville, and the *Monitor,*" Leo B. Levy pointed out the relevance of Hawthorne's essay to "The Cumberland," "In the Turret," "The Temeraire," and "A Utilitarian View of the Monitor's Fight."

These poems in *Battle-Pieces,* a much-expanded section of "Bridegroom Dick" in *John Marr* (205.135–61 above), and passages in *Billy Budd, Sailor* (e.g., Hayford-Sealts opening paragraph, end of chap. 3, p. 56, and chap. 4, pp. 56–57) show Melville brooding on the theme and exploring a few possible responses to the increasing powers of iron and steam at sea, as well as to the obsolescence of wooden sailing vessels for military and commercial purposes.

"The Cumberland" was first printed in *Harper's New Monthly Magazine* [H] 32 (March 1866): 474; the variant readings in that printing are listed below for the historical record, but none is adopted as an emendation (see pp. 583–84 above).

DISCUSSIONS. 37.12–14 her flag . . . sea] The pilot on board the *Cumberland* reported that "after about three fourths of an hour of the most severe fighting, our vessel sank, the Stars and Stripes still waving. That flag was finally submerged, but after the hull grounded on the sands, fifty-four feet below the surface of the water, our pennant was still flying from the topmast above the waves" (*Rebellion Record,* 4:272–73, doc. 82). This would be enough to suggest that the Baltimore *American* account in the *Rebellion Record* is in error or referring just to the pennant when it reports, "She went down with her *flag still flying,* and it still flies from the mast above the water" (4:274). But we also have Hawthorne's independent firsthand testimony to "the masts of the Cumberland rising midway out of the water, with a tattered rag of a pennant fluttering from one of them. . . . The flag (which never was struck, thank Heaven!) is entirely hidden under the waters of the bay, but is still doubtless waving in its old place, although it floats to and fro with the swell and reflux of the tide" (p. 59 in the *Atlantic Monthly* piece cited in the introductory note). And Melville himself may have seen that "tattered rag" if he visited Hampton Roads in April 1864, as Stanton Garner speculates (1993, pp. 302–3).

37.20–38.22 The sinking . . . undone!] Frank L. Day (1959, pp. 35–36) identifies the Baltimore *American* passage that provided Melville his detail of the intrepid but doomed gunner: "This last shot was fired by an active little fellow named Matthew Tenney, whose courage had been conspicuous throughout the action. As his port was left open by the recoil of the gun, he jumped to scramble out, but the water rushed in with so much force that he was washed back and drowned" (*Rebellion Record,* 4:274, doc. 82).

VARIANTS (EXCEPT IN INDENTION). 37.0 (MARCH, 1862)] BP; [*not present*] H 37.16 Goodly] BP; Proud a H 37.20 sinking^] BP; ~, H 38.29 crew,] BP; ~^ H 38.30 live—] BP; ~; H

VARIANTS (IN INDENTION). 37.4,13; 38.22, 31] [*H indents like line 2*] 37.6,15; 38.24,33] [*H does not indent*]

IN THE TURRET (pp. 39–40)

The ironclad *Monitor* (the Ericsson steam-battery with a revolving tur-
ret) arrived at Hampton Roads about nine in the evening of Saturday,
March 8, 1862, and some five hours later was alongside the *Minnesota,* a
dozen hours too late to prevent the destruction visited that day by the *Vir-
ginia* (formerly the *Merrimac*) upon the *Cumberland,* the *Congress,* and other
Union ships. The duel the *Monitor* joined with the *Virginia* on Sunday
was immediately understood as historically significant. Neither ironclad
totally vanquished the other in their four-hour clanging fight, though
the *Virginia* (persistently called the *Merrimac* by its former owners and
eventual re-possessors) withdrew precipitously after receiving the last of
three telling shots, and the *Monitor* did not keep up a hot pursuit, partly
because in the fight its commander, Lieutenant John Lorimer Worden,
had his sight seriously impaired when he was looking through a slit in
the armor as his boat took a hit from a *Virginia* round shot, "causing some
scalings from the iron, and fragments of the paint to fly with great force
against his eyes" (Baltimore *American* account, in *Rebellion Record,* 4:276,
doc. 82). The revolving turret was nine feet high, had an internal diameter
of twenty feet, and was armored all around with eight layers of vertically
overlapped wrought-iron slabs nine feet long by two feet wide by one
inch thick, plus an additional two-inch thick shield on the fighting side
(*Rebellion Record,* 4:58–59, doc. 23).

DISCUSSIONS. 39.1 heart of duty, Worden] Frank L. Day (1959, pp. 36–37) indi-
cates two passages in the *Rebellion Record* that could have suggested the poem's
central notion that the *Monitor's* commander was duty-driven. Learning of the
rebel ironclad's destruction of the *Cumberland* and other Union ships, "though his
crew were suffering from exposure and loss of rest from a stormy voyage around
from New-York, he [Worden] at once made preparations for taking part in what-
ever might occur next day" (Baltimore *American* account, *Rebellion Record,* 4:275,
doc. 82). Captain G. J. Van Brunt of the *Minnesota* officially reported, "At two
A.M. the iron battery Monitor, Com. John L. Worden . . . came alongside and
reported for duty, and then all on board felt that we had a friend that would stand
by us in our hour of trial" (4:267).

   39.4 diving-bell] For another diving-bell metaphor, see line 14 in "A Church
of Padua" (p. 295 above).

   39.7–11 direful and untried. . . . bearing] Compare the Baltimore *American*
account (*Rebellion Record,* 4:276, doc. 82): "Once the Merrimac struck her near
midships, but only to prove that the battery could not be run down nor shot
down. She spun round like a top, and as she got her bearing again, sent one of her
formidable missiles into her huge opponent. . . . The fight then assumed its most
interesting aspects. The Monitor ran round the Merrimac repeatedly, probing

her sides, seeking for weak points, and reserving her fire with coolness, until she had the right spot and the exact range, and made her experiments accordingly. In this way the Merrimac received three shots, which must have seriously damaged her." More of this passage is quoted in the discussion at 44.13–18 below.

39.15–16 of Og/The huge] The reference is to the *Virginia,* which by all accounts was much larger than the *Monitor.* See Deuteronomy 3:11: "For only Og king of Bashan remained of the remnant of giants; behold, his bedstead was a bedstead of iron." (See also the discussion at 208.261 below.)

40.42–43 live, . . . swell] In the early hours of December 31, 1862, as it was being towed to the Carolina coast, the *Monitor* foundered in heavy seas off Cape Hatteras.

THE TEMERAIRE (pp. 41–43)

Melville's title, poem, and two notes (c and d, p. 174 above) refer a reader to historic events. First is the 1805 Battle of Trafalgar, in which the *Temeraire* fought alongside Horatio Nelson's *Victory* (named in lines 33 and 35), and in which Nelson was killed, though the combined fleets of France and Spain were defeated (line 23). On September 6, 1838, the painter J. M. W. Turner witnessed "the event he would memorialize the following May as *The Fighting 'Temeraire', tugged to her Last Berth to be broken up, 1838*" (Wallace 1992, p. 53). The fight of the *Monitor* and *Merrimac* occurred on March 9, 1862.

Turner painted the *Temeraire* on her way to the scrapper's dock, being towed there by a black double-sidewheeler steam-tug belching black smoke back at the doomed sailing craft's twilight-whited bare masts and spars, only the tops of its masts and its crosstrees still tinted by the setting sun. Melville had seen the painting. In the week before he left England on May 6, 1857, he visited the National Gallery on Trafalgar Square, and saw there, as he later recorded, "Sunset scenes of Turner. 'Burial of Wilkie.' The Shipwreck. 'The Fighting ——— taken to her last birth'" (*Journals,* p. 128). Later, he also owned a black and white engraving of *The Fighting Temeraire* by J. T. Willmore after Turner's painting (reproduced in Wallace 1992, p. 54).

DISCUSSIONS. 41.17 fair] In Harvard Copy C of BP, Melville penciled "rare" in the margin as a possible alternative, but NN does not emend since he only pencil-underlined, but did not line out, "fair" (see pp. 600–602 above).

42.38 The angel in that sun] Hennig Cohen (*Battle-Pieces,* p. 226) cites Revelation 10:1: "And I saw another mighty angel come down from heaven . . . and his face was as it were the sun." He also invites a comparison of *Paradise Lost,* 3.622–23: "Saw within ken a glorious angel stand, / The same whom John saw also in the sun." In his copy of Milton (Boston: Hilliard, Gray, 1836; Sealts, no. 358b) Melville sidelined these two lines, and noted in the margin, "The Italian paintin[gs] he saw in Rome."

42.47 Trafalgar′] The otherwise anomalous accent mark was apparently supplied by Melville, to indicate that he intends the Spanish pronunciation and emphasis here.

A UTILITARIAN VIEW OF THE MONITOR'S FIGHT (pp. 44–45)

Describing his first view of the *Monitor,* Nathaniel Hawthorne said it was

> the strangest-looking craft I ever saw. . . . It could not be called a vessel at all; it was a machine, . . . it looked like a gigantic rat-trap. It was ugly, questionable, suspicious, evidently mischievous,—nay, I will allow myself to call it devilish; for this was the new war-fiend, destined, along with others of the same breed, to annihilate whole navies and batter down old supremacies. The wooden walls of Old England cease to exist, and a whole history of naval renown reaches its period, now that the Monitor comes smoking into view. . . . There will be other battles, but no more such tests of seamanship and manhood as the battles of the past; and, moreover, the Millennium is certainly approaching, because human strife is to be transferred from the heart and personality of man into cunning contrivances of machinery, which by-and-by will fight out our wars with only the clank and smash of iron, strewing the field with broken engines, but damaging nobody's little finger except by accident. (pp. 58–59)

This passage is from "Chiefly about War-Matters," by "A Peaceable Man," *Atlantic Monthly* 10 (July 1862): 43–61; quoted in Levy.

DISCUSSIONS. 44.4 Orient] In Harvard Copy C of BP, Melville penciled "painted" in the left margin as a possible alternative, but NN does not emend since he only pencil-underlined, but did not line out, "Orient" (see pp. 600–602 above).

44.13–18 Yet . . . caloric] Frank L. Day (1959, pp. 38–39) points to a passage in the Baltimore *American* account of the *Monitor-Merrimac* battle (*Rebellion Record,* 4:276, doc. 82) as a predecessor of lines 13–18, if not a source for the poem's concepts of "intense," "closer," "calm," "No passion": "[T]his distance was subsequently reduced to fifty yards, and at no time during the furious cannonading that ensued, were the vessels more than two hundred yards apart. . . . The officers of the Monitor, at this time, had gained such confidence in the impregnability of their battery, that they no longer fired at random nor hastily. The fight then assumed its most interesting aspects. The Monitor ran round the Merrimac repeatedly, probing her sides, seeking for weak points, and reserving her fire with coolness, until she had the right spot and the exact range, and made her experiments accordingly." Cf. the discussion at 39.7–11.

44.20–21 The ringing . . . world] Hennig Cohen (*Battle-Pieces,* p. 228) notes the echo of line 4 of Emerson's "Concord Hymn" (1837): "And fired the shot heard round the world."

44.22 blacksmiths' fray] Cf. "Bridegroom Dick" in *John Marr,* where the old sailor describes the *Merrimac* (i.e., the *Virginia,* the ironclad ram reconstructed from the *Merrimac*) as "A blacksmith's unicorn in armor *cap-a-pie*" (213.414 above).

EMENDATION. 45.25 yet shall] BP\HM; shall yet BP

SHILOH (p. 46)

The two-day fight that raged around "the little log-cabin called Shiloh church" (*Rebellion Record,* 4:387, doc. 114) on Sunday and Monday, April 6 and 7, 1862, is also known as the Battle of Pittsburg Landing. Frank L. Day (1959, pp. 39–41) concludes that of the sixty pages of *Rebellion Record* documents about the battle available to Melville, he relied most on the long Cincinnati *Gazette* narrative (4:385–400, doc. 114). This passage describing the first half of the night following the first day's battle contributed to the poem's "mood" and last line:

> Then his wearied men [under General Lew Wallace; see the discussion at 33.383 above] lay down to snatch a few hours of sleep before entering into the valley of the Shadow of Death on the morrow.
>
> By nine o'clock all was hushed near the Landing. The host of combatants that three hours before had been deep in the work of human destruction had all sunk silently to the earth, "the wearied to sleep, the wounded to die." The stars looked out upon the scene, and all breathed the natural quiet and calm of a Sabbath evening. (4:395)

For lines 5–6, Melville drew on the following description of the second half of Sunday night:

> A heavy thunder-storm had come up about midnight, and though we were all shivering over the ducking, the surgeons assured us that a better thing could not have happened. The ground, they said, was covered with wounded not yet found, or whom we were unable to bring from the field. The moisture would to some extent, cool the burning, parching thirst, which is one of the chief terrors of lying wounded and helpless on the battle-field, and the falling water was the best dressing for the wounds. (4:396)

"Shiloh" was reprinted in R. H. Stoddard's edition of Rufus M. Gris-wold's *Poets and Poetry of America* [PPA] (New York: James Miller, 1873), p. 631; the variants in that printing are listed below for the historical record, but none is adopted as an emendation (see pp. 584–85 above).

DISCUSSION. 46.0 *Shiloh*] Hennig Cohen (*Battle-Pieces,* p. 230) cites Melville's "The Bell-Tower": "A silence, as of the expectation of some Shiloh, pervaded the swarming plain" (NN *Piazza Tales* volume, p. 181). In "Hawthorne and his Mosses" Melville calls Hawthorne "the literary Shiloh of America" (NN *Piazza Tales* volume, p. 252).

VARIANTS. 46.0 (APRIL, 1862)] BP; [*not present*] PPA 46.3 Over] BP; O'er PPA 46.6 pain^] BP; ~, PPA 46.7 pause] BP; pauses PPA 46.7 night^] BP; ~— PPA

THE BATTLE FOR THE MISSISSIPPI (pp. 47–48)

On April 18, 1862, Captain David Glasgow Farragut, commander of the Union's Western Gulf Blockading Squadron, began his assault on New Orleans from the south by moving Commander David D. Porter up the Mississippi with twenty-six mortar boats to begin shelling Forts Jackson and St. Philip. The horrendous fire continued, according to Porter's account in the *Rebellion Record* (4:511–12, doc. 149), "without intermission" for six days and nights, but the forts did not surrender despite being virtually demolished. The night of April 20, Farragut's gunboats managed to cut a passage through what Melville in *John Marr* called the "boom-chain" ("Bridegroom Dick," 206.186 above) attached to hulks extending across the river from Jackson; and between three-thirty and five in the morning on the twenty-fourth, as Porter wrote, his flotilla "passed the forts under a most terrific fire, which they returned with interest." Porter went on, "The sight of this night attack was awfully grand. The river was lit up with rafts filled with pine-knots, and the ships seemed to be fighting literally amidst flames and smoke." Having passed through the fire, Farragut took New Orleans on the twenty-fifth.

Frank L. Day (1959, pp. 41–44) points to the several reports on the capture of New Orleans in the *Rebellion Record* (4:510–25, doc. 149), many of which may have supplied information Melville uses in the poem. Porter's report of what happened to the Confederate ram *Manassas* is plausibly the source of lines 29–32: "Her only gun went off, and emitting flames through her bow-port, like some huge animal, she gave a plunge and disappeared under the water" (4:511). Also lines 33–38 seem indebted to Farragut's report: "At length the fire slackened, the smoke cleared off, and we saw to our surprise that we were above the Forts, and here and there a rebel gun-boat on fire" (4:522). Stanton Garner (1993, p. 144) points to Henry Howard Brownell's firsthand account, "The River Fight." Melville could have read the poem in a newspaper; Brownell's *Lyrics of a Day* (New York: Carleton, 1864), which includes it, is subtitled *Newspaper-Poetry*.

DISCUSSIONS. 47.3 But Moses sung and timbrels] See Exodus 15:1, 20.

47.4 For Pharaoh's stranded crew] See Exodus 15:19. Melville marked Exodus 14:18 in his copy of the King James Version (Philadelphia: Butler, 1846; Sealts, no. 62): "And the Egyptians shall know that I am the LORD, when I have gotten me honour upon Pharaoh, upon his chariots, and upon his horsemen."

47.6 The Lord is a man of war] Melville marked Exodus 15.3 in his copy of the King James Version (see the discussion just above): "The LORD is a man of war: the LORD is his name."

47.23–24 made . . . leven] See Revelation 12:7–8.

MALVERN HILL (pp. 49–50)

In late June of 1862, having failed to take Richmond, and realizing he was not going to be reinforced as he had requested, General George B. McClellan began to move his Army of the Potomac south toward Harrison's Landing on the James River, in order to secure his supply lines, to keep General Robert E. Lee's Army of Northern Virginia from carving up his regiments one by one, and to join forces with the navy in a renewed assault on the Confederate capital.

One of Melville's more graphic sources, especially for line 8, may be the account of the battle in the Richmond *Examiner*: "The different postures of the dead always strike a spectator as he passes over the battle-field. One lay on his back, with his arms stretched upward at length" (*Rebellion Record*, 5:268, doc. 78). Frank L. Day (1959, p. 44) suggests that Melville found the prototypes for his elms in the account of the battle in the Grenada (Mississippi) *Appeal* (a Memphis newspaper which published in various places as it dodged battle zones during the war; *Rebellion Record*, 5:266, doc. 78): "The house at Malvern Hill is a quaint old structure. . . . A fine grove of ancient elms embowers the lawn in a grateful shade, affording numberless vistas of far-off wheat-fields and little gleaming brooks of water, with the dark blue fringe of the primitive pines on the horizon. It seemed a bitter satire on the wickedness of man, this peaceful, serene, harmonious aspect of nature, and I turned from the joyous and quiet landscape to the mutilated victims around me with something very like a malediction upon Seward and Lincoln and their participants in the crime of bringing on this accursed war."

THE VICTOR OF ANTIETAM (pp. 51–53)

After the Peninsular campaign (see the preceding introductory note), General George B. McClellan was relieved as general in chief of the Army of the Potomac, then recalled to command after his replacement, General John Pope, failed at the Battle of Second Manassas and Lee invaded Maryland. The Federal forces stopped Lee's at South Mountain, Turner's Gap, and Crampton's Gap on September 14, 1862, and on the seventeenth, "the bloodiest single day of the war" (Boatner, p. 21), occurred the massive Battle of Antietam around Sharpsburg, near Antietam Creek.

"The Victor of Antietam" was reprinted in R. H. Stoddard's edition of Rufus M. Griswold's *Poets and Poetry of America* [PPA] (New York: James Miller, 1873), p. 631; the variants in that printing are listed below for the historical record, but none is adopted as an emendation (see pp. 584–85 above).

DISCUSSION. 51.12 Seven Days] The June 25–July 1, 1862, series of battles in the Peninsular campaign, ending in the Battle of Malvern Hill.

VARIANTS. 51.0 (1862)] BP; [*not present*] PPA 51.2 man,] BP; ~^ PPA 51.16 then,] BP; ~^ PPA

BATTLE OF STONE RIVER, TENNESSEE (pp. 54–55)

Wednesday, December 31, 1862, and Friday, January 2, 1863, saw the heaviest action of the Battle of Stone River, around Murfreesboro. By Saturday, said the account in the Louisville *Journal* (*Rebellion Record,* 6:160, doc. 26), "the rebel fire was visibly feebler and less in both volume and extent." On Sunday, General William S. Rosecrans "felt too sacred a regard for the Sabbath to attack," and "when Monday came, the rebels were gone." From one point of view, the battle "was like most engagements of the war—there was nothing decisive in the result, and the enemy carrying what he would, withdrew unmolested" ("General Rosecrans's Great Battle," *Rebellion Record,* 4:156, doc. 26).

"Battle of Stone River" was reprinted in R. H. Stoddard's edition of Rufus M. Griswold's *Poets and Poetry of America* [PPA] (New York: James Miller, 1873), p. 630; the variant in that printing is listed below for the historical record, but it is not adopted as an emendation (see pp. 584–85 above).

DISCUSSIONS. 54.0 *A View from Oxford Cloisters*] Melville had visited Oxford cloisters in May 1857, when he noted that the town "Has beheld unstirred all the violence of revolutions" (*Journals*, pp. 128–29, 156).

54.1 Tewksbury and Barnet heath] In the Wars of the Roses, the battles of Barnet (Easter, April 17, 1471) and Tewksbury (May 3, 1471) established the dominance of the Yorkists over the Lancastrians.

VARIANT. 54.0 (JANUARY, 1863)] BP; [*not present*] PPA

RUNNING THE BATTERIES (pp. 56–58)

During the night of April 16, 1863, Admiral David D. Porter ran a flotilla of "eight gunboats, three transports, and various barges and flat-boats" down the Mississippi through a "gauntlet of some eight miles of batteries, past the stronghold of Vicksburgh," in order to furnish naval firepower, troop carriers, and supplies to Grant's army waiting to cross the river south of the city, at New Carthage ("The Siege of Vicksburgh, Mississippi," in the New York *Tribune; Rebellion Record,* 6:546–47, doc. 169). The transports were protected with cotton bales in lieu of armor, but one of them, the *Henry Clay,* was destroyed when she "was set on fire by a shell exploding among the cotton with which her engines were protected" (6:548; see lines 53–58). Her "crew got safely to shore," though, and the only casualties reported were one killed and two wounded on Porter's flagship, the *Benton.*

DISCUSSION. 58.75 brave man's] Since Melville also devotes a note to identifying him (note g, p. 174 above), he may again be acknowledging a debt to the elder Porter's *Journal of a Cruise Made to the Pacific Ocean, in the U.S. Frigate Essex* (Philadelphia, 1815; 2d ed., New York, 1822), which he used in writing *Typee* (see the NN edition, p. 291) and "The Encantadas" (see the NN *Piazza Tales* volume, p. 603).

EMENDATION. 57.50 boats'] NN; ~^ BP

STONEWALL JACKSON (p. 59)

In the early evening of May 2, 1863, General Thomas J. ("Stonewall") Jackson was shot by at least two Confederate skirmishers as he and his staff returned to their own lines from forward observations of Federal positions in the Wilderness area near Chancellorsville, Virginia, just west of Fredericksburg. He died on May 10 from the complications of an arm amputation and pneumonia.

DISCUSSION. 59.12 True as John Brown] Jackson had been present at John Brown's hanging, December 2, 1859, in his capacity as commander of cadets at the Virginia Military Institute.

STONEWALL JACKSON (ASCRIBED TO A VIRGINIAN) (pp. 60–61)

Melville would have known the details of Jackson's life and career through newspaper accounts. Several biographies of Jackson had been published in the North before the appearance of *Battle-Pieces,* notably one subtitled "by a Virginian" (John Esten Cooke, *The Life of Stonewall Jackson* [New York: Richardson, 1863]); for other contemporary biographies, see the discussion at 182.35 below.

DISCUSSIONS. 60.5 life, though a vapor's wreath] The allusion is to the same passage (James 4:14) that Melville uses as an epigraph for "Buddha" in *Timoleon* (p. 281 above): "For what is your life? It is even a vapor that appeareth for a little time and then vanisheth away."

60.9 A stoic he] Cf. the Stoic in *Clarel* (3.21.253); stoicism is "the great school begun by Zeno about 310 B.C., in which a severe philosophy of wisdom, virtue, and self-control takes the place of religion" (*Clarel,* p. 811).

61.53 great] In revising from "vain" to "great" in Harvard Copy C of BP, Melville presumably noticed that the second of the two debating speakers quoted in lines 51–53—evidently a Southerner—would not be likely to characterize the war as "vain."

EMENDATION. *61.53 great] BP\HM; vain BP

GETTYSBURG (pp. 62–63)

Following his failure at Antietam in September 1862, General Robert E. Lee made a second and last attempt to invade the North, in June 1863, which began with initial successes. Federal forces wheeled into action, and the two armies converged upon Gettysburg, Pennsylvania, and met in the battles of July 1–3 that ended with the disaster of "Pickett's Charge" and a final check (as noted in Melville's subtitle) to Confederate ambitions north of the Potomac.

"Gettysburg" was first printed in *Harper's New Monthly Magazine* [H] 33 (July 1866): 209; the variants in that printing are listed below for the historical record, but none is adopted as an emendation (see pp. 583–84 above).

Discussions. 63.31 the warrior-monument] The *Rebellion Record* documents make no mention of this particular headstone which "crashed in fight," specified by Melville in note h (p. 175 above) as belonging to the grave of "a Federal officer killed before Richmond in 1862." Nevertheless the scene was noted in a dispatch in the New York *Herald* (July 6), and was likely part of other accounts: "In one of the [iron-railed burial places] a marble slab marked the resting place of an orderly sergeant killed at Fair Oaks [May 31–June 1, 1862, in the Peninsular campaign]. Alas! how little did his mother think . . . that his comrades would ever do battle above him, and crimson with their blood the myrtle on his grave."

63.35 Have laid the stone] Melville's note h (p. 175 above) explains his reference to an Independence Day celebration in 1865, at which, according to the New York *Tribune* (July 6), "the corner-stone of the Soldier's Monument was laid with imposing ceremonies."

Variants. 62.0 *Gettysburg.*] BP; ~:— H 62.0 *The Check*] BP; [*not present*] H 62.0 (July, 1863)] BP; [*no parentheses*] H 62.14 taunts^] BP; ~, H

THE HOUSE-TOP (p. 64)

In the worst of the violence of the New York City draft riots of July 13–16, 1863, mobs made up of Irish immigrants and other whites hanged blacks. The riots were occasioned mainly by two provisions in the new Enrollment Act—both of which plainly discriminated in favor of those with access to money: a draftee could pay a substitute to serve in his stead, or he could avoid serving by paying a commutation fee of three hundred dollars. Blacks were exempt from the draft.

Discussions. 64.0 *House-top*] In his King James Version of the Bible (Philadelphia: Butler, 1846; Sealts, no. 62), Melville underlined and sidelined verse 7 in Psalm 102 ("The psalmist's prayer in the midst of great trouble"): "I watch, and am as a sparrow alone upon the house top." The poem may echo the opening section of Robert Southey's *The Curse of Kehama* (1810):

Midnight, and yet no eye
Through all the Imperial City closed in sleep!
Behold her streets a-blaze
With light that seems to kindle the red sky,
Her myriads swarming through the crowded ways!
Master and slave, old age and infancy,
All, all abroad to gaze;

House-top and balcony
Clustered with women, who throw back their veils
    With unimpeded and insatiate sight
To view the funeral pomp which passes by,
    As if the mournful rite
Were but to them a scene of joyance and delight.

64.16 nature] Hennig Cohen (*Battle-Pieces,* p. 240) points out that Melville, in his note to this line (note i, p. 175 above), quotes from Lord Berners's translation of Jean Froissart's *Chronicles of England, France and Spain* (New York, 1854; Bercaw, no. 282) the passage that details the excesses of the Jacquerie, a peasant uprising in 1358.

64.18 shakes] In Harvard Copy C of BP, Melville penciled "jars" in the right margin as a possible alternative, but NN does not emend since he only pencil-underlined, but did not line out, "shakes" (see pp. 600–602 above).

64.19 Draco] Stanton Garner (1993, pp. 254, 277) says that the specific reference here is to General John A. Dix, whom Lincoln assigned, July 18, 1863, to the command of the military Department of the East, headquartered in New York City. Dix was a personal friend of Melville's uncle Peter Gansevoort; Melville had enlisted Dix's support when he was seeking a government position in February 1847 (see NN *Correspondence* volume, pp. 81, 586–87). Melville presented Dix with a copy of *Battle-Pieces* (now in the collection of William S. Reese).

64.27 Roman, never to be scourged] Acts 16:37–38: "But Paul said unto them, They have beaten us openly uncondemned, being Romans, and have cast us into prison. . . . And the sergeants told these words unto the magistrates: and they feared when they heard that they were Romans." Also Acts 22:25–29: "And as they bound him with thongs, Paul said unto the centurion that stood by, Is it lawful for you to scourge a man that is a Roman, and uncondemned? . . . and the chief captain also was afraid, after he knew that he was a Roman, and because he had bound him." The same passages are invoked in chapter 34 of *White-Jacket,* in a polemic against the flogging of American sailors.

LOOK-OUT MOUNTAIN (p. 65)

On November 24, 1863, occurred what would soon be called the "Battle above the Clouds," as General Joseph ("Fighting Joe") Hooker's troops did not stop when they reached a high plateau on Lookout Mountain, south of Chattanooga overlooking the Tennessee River. Their next objective was to have been Craven's Farm, heavily reinforced and fortified by the Confederates; instead of pausing, Hooker reported that "fired by success, with a flying, panic-stricken force before them, they pressed impetuously forward" till "the enemy, with his reënforcements, driven from the walls and pits around Craven's house, . . . all broken and destroyed, were hurled in great numbers over the rocks and precipices into the valley" (*Rebellion Record,* 8:212, doc. 14).

Hooker's word "hurled" may have inspired Melville's image of "the Anarch's plunging flight" (line 20). Frank L. Day (1959, pp. 48–50) finds a handful of passages in the Cincinnati *Gazette* account of the battle (*Rebellion Record,* 8:228–36, doc. 14) that may have influenced Melville. One is this sentence in the *Gazette* (8:231), "Seen from Chattanooga, it was the realization of olden traditions; and supernatural armies contended in the air!"

DISCUSSIONS. 65.5 Like Kaf the peak of Eblis—] Eblis is the prince of apostate angels in Mohammedanism, referred to also in *Clarel* ("A land of Eblis burned with fire," 2.10.108; see the NN edition, p. 767) and in *White-Jacket* (chap. 73). See also "The Return of the Sire de Nesle" in *Timoleon:* "Kaf thrusts his snouted crags through fog" (317.5).

65.7–8 Who . . . night?] Psalms 47:5: "God is gone up with a shout, the LORD with the sound of a trumpet."

65.11 Anarch] Hennig Cohen (*Battle-Pieces,* p. 242) points to *Paradise Lost,* 2.988, where "the Anarch is identified with Chaos as lord of misrule," but Melville may have in mind the Gnostic Anarch or some other of his own manufacture. Cf. "What Cosmic jest or Anarch blunder" in "After the Pleasure Party" (*Timoleon,* 262.92 above).

65.15–16 armies . . . pray] Day (1959, p. 50) notices a poem Melville may have drawn on, "The Storming of Lookout Mountain," by Captain Thomas H. Elliott (*Rebellion Record,* 8:1–2, "Poetry and Incidents"), in which Union troops similarly watch and pray.

CHATTANOOGA (pp. 66–68)

On Wednesday, November 25, 1863, following the capture of Lookout Mountain the day before (see the preceding introductory note), Federal forces took Missionary Ridge and the remaining high ground around Chattanooga: "[T]he shout of triumph rousing the blood to a very frenzy of enthusiasm. . . . Cheering each other forward, the three divisions began to climb the ridge" (p. 233 in the Cincinnati *Gazette* account; *Rebellion Record,* 8:228–36, doc. 14).

Frank L. Day (1959, pp. 50–52) advances several parallels in the Cincinnati *Gazette* account, two of which seem most plausible as sources: for lines 19–20, "despite a plunging fire from the enemy's artillery upon the crest, they entered the timbered portion near the summit" (8:233); and for lines 60–63, this passage:

The expression upon the faces of our own men who had fallen here, was most touching and remarkable, for not all the pains of dissolution had been able to drive from their features the smile of victory, or the placid look of contentment which always rests upon the countenance of him who feels his work well done. . . . it was plain as the sun at noonday, that these men had died, not only without mental agony, but that their last earthly feeling was one of calm contentment or triumphant joy. True this was death—but it was death without its hideousness—death robbed of all its terrors—death whose grandeur made it preferable to life. (8:235)

When "Chattanooga" appeared in *Harper's New Monthly Magazine* (see below), it lacked present lines 55–63, whether by design or accident or because they did not yet exist. Norman E. Jarrard (in his 1960 edition of Melville's "Published Verse," p. 306), assuming they existed earlier, guesses they were "not included" in the magazine printing "possibly because an even number of stanzas was needed to fill out the double-columned page." Stanton Garner (1993, p. 284) makes explicit what Hennig Cohen (*Battle-Pieces,* p. 244) left tacit—that Melville "adapted" the last stanza of "Chattanooga" from the six lines of "Inscription For the Dead At Fredericksburgh" (p. 321 above), published in 1864, which is also about a "height" (Marye's Heights near Fredericksburg). The concept of an "earnest end" (in line 1 of that poem) appears in lines 56 and 61 here, and the last line of "Chattanooga" closely echoes that poem's "Death to the brave's a starry night" (line 5).

"Chattanooga" was first printed in *Harper's New Monthly Magazine* [H] 33 (June 1866): 44; the variants in that printing are listed below for the historical record, but none is adopted as an emendation (see pp. 583–84 above).

DISCUSSIONS. 66.2 elastic air] The Cincinnati *Gazette* account reports that on November 25 "the sun shone brilliantly from a cloudless sky." In the only substantive difference from BP, the reading in H is "October air"; the first sentence in Melville's note j in BP (p. 175 above) seems to refer to the reading in H, since it explains that "Although the month was November, the day was in character an October one."

66.7 measured the mountain] Melville's note j (p. 175 above) supplies, from an "account at hand" (not the Cincinnati *Gazette* or other accounts in the *Rebellion Record*), the height and angle of Missionary Ridge.

67.54 rebels] In Harvard Copy C of BP, Melville penciled "foemen" in the left margin as a possible alternative, but NN does not emend since he neither underlined nor lined out "rebels" (see pp. 600–602 above).

VARIANTS. 66.0 (NOVEMBER, 1863)] BP; [*not present*] H *66.2 elastic] BP; October H 66.2 air;] BP; ~, H 66.6 on^] BP; ~, H 66.7 mountain] BP; Mountain H 66.10 yester-morn^] BP; yestermorn, H 66.11 Armies^] BP; ~, H 66.11 ghosts^] BP; ~, H 66.11 fought,] BP; ~; H 66.12 And^] BP; ~, H 66.12 cloud^] BP; ~, H 66.13 caught:] BP; ~; H 66.20 wall,] BP; ~; H 66.24 He,] BP; ~^ H 66.24 brink,] BP; ~^ H 67.28 Yet^] BP; ~, H 67.28 there^] BP; ~, H 67.31 show—] BP; ~, H 67.41 color-bearer^] BP; ~, H 67.42 Grant,] BP; ~— H 67.43 stump—] BP; ~, H 67.44 While^] BP; ~, H 67.44 solicitude^] BP; ~, H 67.49 name:] BP; ~. H 67.51 caught,] BP; ~; H 67.52 death] BP; Death H 67.52 led;] BP; ~ [*punctuation unclear: faulty type or inking*] H 67.55–68.63 But . . . night.] BP; [*not present*] H

THE ARMIES OF THE WILDERNESS (pp. 69–76)

The Battle of the Wilderness, May 5 and 6, 1864, was fought in the same obscuring wasteland of second-growth timber and underbrush south of the Rapidan River as battles the previous May around Chancellorsville (for Melville's further thoughts on this area, see "An uninscribed Monument on one of the Battle-fields of the Wilderness," p. 130 above).

A problem related to this poem is whether Melville ever actually met Grant in this area before the 1864 battle. In an undated memorandum, Elizabeth Shaw Melville recalled that when her husband visited his cousin Henry Gansevoort in camp at Vienna, Virginia, in April 1864 (see p. 668 below), he also visited "various battle-fields & called on Gen. Grant" (Sealts 1974, p. 172). In his 1951 biography (p. 276), Leon Howard is guarded but speculates, "If Elizabeth's later recollection that the brothers 'called on General Grant' may be trusted, they visited the headquarters of the commanding general at Culpepper, Virginia, on Monday or Tuesday [April 11 or 12] and looked over the Wilderness battle line." Stanton Garner (1993, p. 301), however, points out that railroad bridges and some tracks had become impassable because of flooding rains, and so casts some doubt on whether Melville could have visited Grant on the eleventh or twelfth—or, perhaps, any other time (unless he, like his brother Allan's wife, saw Grant not at the front, but at Willard's hotel in Washington [p. 303]). While Garner, too, wants to believe that Melville met Grant (p. 326), his inferred calendar leaves too little time for a visit at the front following the scout toward Aldie but before Melville's departure for New York; he also admits that "Herman's further travels are almost completely undocumented" (p. 323) and offers no more direct evidence than Mrs. Melville's recollections. Garner further surmises, like Howard, that in his note to "Chattanooga" (note j, p. 175 above) Melville himself was the "visitor" in this passage: "General Grant, at Culpepper, a few weeks prior to crossing the Rapidan for the Wilderness, expressed to a visitor his impression . . . ." Still, Garner evidently cannot believe Allan Melville's wife when she writes to her stepdaughter Florence, on Wednesday, April 13, 1864, that Allan went "with Uncle Herman to the *front* of the Army of the Potomac on Sunday last" (Leyda, *Log,* p. 667), because he is convinced that, with the railroads partly under water, the Melville brothers could not have found other means of transport to Culpeper Court House. Hershel Parker (2002, p. 573) declared that Mrs. Melville's "record for veracity is unimpeachable on any matter so important as whether or not Melville visited Grant. . . . The daughter of Chief Justice Shaw would never have claimed her husband had met a famous general if he had not done so."

DISCUSSIONS. 69.8 zealots] In Harvard Copy C of BP, Melville penciled "bravos" in the right margin as a possible alternative, but NN does not emend since he only pencil-underlined, but did not line out, "zealots" (see pp. 600–602 above).

69.14 base-ball] In Harvard Copy C of BP, Melville penciled "foot" in the margin as a possible alternative for "base", but NN does not emend since he only pencil-underlined, but did not line out, "base" (see pp. 600–602 above).

70.34 *Belial's*] As indicated by Henry F. Pommer in *Milton and Melville* (p. 152 n. 82), Melville probably here alludes to the Belial of Milton's *Paradise Lost* (2.108–15, 226), who "could make the worse appear / The better reason."

70.49 *Ere the palm of promise leaved*] The biblical reference is presumably to John 12:13, in which the crowd "Took branches of palm-trees, and went forth to meet him, and cried, Hosanna; Blessed is the King of Israel that cometh in the name of the Lord."

71.66 Paran] In Genesis 21:21, Ishmael "dwelt in the wilderness of Paran," words that Melville underlined in one of his Bibles (the King James Version, Philadelphia: Butler, 1846; Sealts, no. 62).

71.77–80 A hand reaches out . . . the woe] Melville alludes to the dirge from John Webster's *The White Devil* (5.4.95–104), the first line of which he later checkmarked in his copy of Robert Bell's *Songs from the Dramatists* (London: Parker, 1854; acquired in 1873; Sealts, no. 56):

> Call for the robin-redbreast and the wren,
> Since o'er shady groves they hover,
> And with leaves and flowers do cover
> The friendless bodies of unburied men.
> Call unto his funeral dole
> The ant, the field-mouse, and the mole,
> To rear him hillocks that shall keep him warm,
> And (when gay tombs are robbed) sustain no harm;
> But keep the wolf far thence, that's foe to men,
> For with his nails he'll dig them up again.

72.83 *Dust to dust*] Genesis 3:19: "In the sweat of thy face shalt thou eat bread, till thou return unto the ground; for out of it wast thou taken: for dust thou art, and unto dust shalt thou return."

73.133 *War would be left to the red and black ants*] Toward the end of his vivid account of a red- and black-ant struggle, in "Brute Neighbors," chapter 12 of *Walden* (1854), Thoreau cites William Kirby and William Spence's *An Introduction to Entomology* (6th ed., Philadelphia: Lea & Blanchard, 1846) as authority for saying that "the battles of ants have long been celebrated and the date of them recorded." He proceeds to recount a few, then ends by saying, "The battle which I witnessed took place in the Presidency of Polk, five years before the passage of Webster's Fugitive-Slave Bill." Merton M. Sealts Jr. (1988, p. 116) first cited the *Walden* parallel passage.

73.141 Mosby's] Mosby and his "prowling men" figure significantly in "The Scout toward Aldie" (pp. 139–62 above); see the introductory note to that poem.

74.161 Culpepper] Melville could have found this common variant spelling of "Culpeper" in the *Rebellion Record* (e.g., 9:329, "Documents") or elsewhere. The spelling appears also in Melville's note to line 2 of "Chattanooga" (note j, p. 175 above).

74.170 *And Orpheus' charm is vain*] Melville also invokes Orpheus in *White-Jacket* (chap. 2) and in *Billy Budd, Sailor* (Hayford and Sealts, chap. 27, p. 128).

76.216 *Pillar of Smoke*] See Exodus 13:21.

76.220 Sabæan lore!] "Sabæan lore" has not been satisfactorily glossed; "Hadean lore" occurs in *Clarel*, 4.5.98.

76.227–28 *Long . . . dead.*] The *National Republican* dispatch dated Sunday, May 8, and printed in the New York *Times* on May 9 commented: "The list of killed and wounded have not reached the city [Washington, D.C.] yet, and probably will not before to-morrow or next day, as the time of every one is employed in rendering relief to the unfortunates."

ON THE PHOTOGRAPH OF A
CORPS COMMANDER (p. 77)

Whether or not an actual photograph is the subject here, the figure that the poem ostensibly celebrates may be presumed to be General Winfield Scott Hancock; commander of the Second Corps of the Army of the Potomac, he was severely wounded at Gettysburg. Hennig Cohen (*Battle-Pieces*, p. 248) points to the cover of *Harper's Weekly*, May 28, 1864, which shows "a heroic three-quarter-length portrait of Hancock."

DISCUSSIONS. 77.14 Yeoman or noble] Shakespeare (*Henry V*, 4.3) has his "great Harry" "gentle" the condition of every soldier after this battle. The note in Melville's Hilliard-Gray edition (1836) explains that veterans of the Battle of

Agincourt could bear coats of arms and occupy chief seats at feasts and public meetings all their lives.

77.18 Templars] In his 1856–57 journal Melville characterizes the Knights Templar as a "mixture of monk & soldier" (*Journals,* p. 129; see also p. 156 and pp. 281–82) and in *Clarel* (2.1.31) as "cavalier and monk in one." See also the first part of his "The Paradise of Bachelors and the Tartarus of Maids" (NN *Piazza Tales* volume, pp. 316–23) for intimations of lost Templar consecrations.

THE SWAMP ANGEL (pp. 78–79)

On August 22, 1863, from a Morris Island marsh, a Parrott rifled gun began throwing two-hundred-pound explosive and incendiary shells four and a half miles into Charleston. This great Parrott lasted only a day before bursting on the thirty-sixth round (see Melville's note k, p. 175 above). If the poem were to follow the chronological sequence of the main body of *Battle-Pieces,* it would come after "The House-top" (p. 64 above), as Stanton Garner notes (1993, p. 261).

Frank L. Day (1959, p. 53) points to a poem by "T. N. J." entitled "The Swamp Angel" in the *Rebellion Record* (8:3, "Poetry and Incidents"). Day assumes that Melville adopted the title and much of T.N.J.'s epigraph ("'The large Parrott gun used in bombarding Charleston from the marshes of James Island is called the Swamp Angel.'—*Soldier's Letter*"). This poem is also apparently the source for Melville's placing the gun on James Island rather than Morris Island; both Union and Confederate batteries were stationed on these two islands.

DISCUSSIONS. 78.17–19 It comes . . . glaring] Hennig Cohen (*Battle-Pieces,* pp. 250–51) points to 1 Thessalonians 5:2–3: "For yourselves know perfectly, that the day of the Lord so cometh as a thief in the night. For when they shall say, Peace and safety; then sudden destruction cometh upon them, as travail upon a woman with child; and they shall not escape."

79.39 The cup of despair goes round] Cohen (*Battle-Pieces,* p. 250) suggests that Melville may have been remembering "the cup of his fury" and "desolation, and destruction, and the famine, and the sword" from Isaiah 51:17–22.

79.40 Michael] Cf. "Michael the warrior one" in "The Conflict of Convictions" (9.48 above).

THE BATTLE FOR THE BAY (pp. 80–83)

Admiral David Farragut, with fourteen wooden warships, four monitors (generic term for shallow-draught ironclads designed for bombarding), and supporting gunboats of the Western Gulf Blockading Squadron, captured the port of Mobile, Alabama, in something under six hours on the morning of August 5, 1864. Farragut's and subordinate officers' reports of the action are in the *Rebellion Record* (8:98–144, doc. 3). Frank L. Day (1959, pp. 53–56) points to Farragut's longest report (8:100–106) as Melville's probable source of information for at least stanzas six, seven, and ten through thirteen (lines 41–56 and 73–104). Melville may have noticed in Farragut's long report (8:105) that on board his flagship was "Acting Ensign H. H. Brownell . . . on the poop . . . taking notes of the action, a duty which he performed with coolness and accuracy." This was Henry Howard Brownell, whose popular "The Bay Fight" (*Harper's*, December 1864), Stanton Garner thinks, "justifies his selection as the admiral's poet laureate" (1993, p. 349).

DISCUSSIONS. 80.13 bonetas] Mid-sized tunas, here spelled in a nineteenth-century variant (according to the *Oxford English Dictionary*) of the word usually rendered "bonitos." The spelling "bonetas" also appears in *Typee* (chap. 4), "bonettas" is the spelling in *Omoo* (chap. 3), and "Boneetas" occurs in *Mardi* (chap. 48). In Melville's 1860 journal, his spelling is "bonetoes" (*Journals*, p. 132).

80.19 breaks, and through] In Harvard Copy C of BP, Melville penciled in the margin a semicolon and "along" (to make a possible reading of "breaks; along"), but NN does not emend since he only pencil-underlined, but did not line out, "and through" (see pp. 600–602 above).

81.44 Hecla that hides in snow] Melville refers to the Icelandic volcano also in *Moby-Dick* (chap. 3); for this spelling, see the NN edition of *Moby-Dick*, p. 833.

82.96 Man-of-Sin] Hennig Cohen (*Battle-Pieces*, p. 251) cites as a possible biblical source of the allusion 2 Thessalonians 2:3: "Let no man deceive you by any means: for that day shall not come, except there come a falling away first, and that man of sin be revealed, the son of perdition."

EMENDATION. 83.100 Till] [*this line indented to correspond with the fourth lines of the other stanzas*] NN; [*indented like line 98*] BP

SHERIDAN AT CEDAR CREEK (pp. 84-85)

As General Philip Sheridan recalled the morning of October 19, 1864 (*Rebellion Record*, 11:726, doc. 117), he was "unconscious of the true condition of affairs until about nine o'clock, when, having ridden through the town of Winchester, the sound of the artillery made a battle unmistakable, and . . . fugitives appeared in sight, trains and men coming to the rear with appalling rapidity." Previously head of the Cavalry Corps and at this point in command of the Middle Military Division, Sheridan was returning up the Shenandoah from a weekend conference in Washington; the fugitives were coming down the valley from Cedar Creek, some twelve miles away, where at daybreak the forces of General Jubal Early (see line 30) had surprised and routed a large number of the Union troops camped there. Sheridan "immediately . . . ordered the brigade at Winchester to stretch across the country and stop all stragglers." He continued: "Taking twenty men from my escort, I pushed on to the front." Sheridan's dramatic return to Cedar Creek transformed a near disaster into victory, as he explained (11:727): "This battle practically ended the campaign in the Shenandoah valley." Some—like the brilliant Colonel Charles Russell Lowell, whom Melville had met and talked with in April during his visit to Vienna, Virginia—did not survive that glorious day.

"Sheridan at Cedar Creek" was first printed as "Philip," in *Harper's New Monthly Magazine* [H] 32 (April 1866): 640. Melville also transcribed the poem as "Philip" [P] at some undetermined time and apparently gave the transcript (now in the New York Public Library) to Richard Henry Stoddard. Stoddard included the poem in his edition of Rufus M. Griswold's *Poets and Poetry of America* [PPA] (New York: James Miller, 1873), p. 630. The H, P, and PPA variant readings are listed below for the historical record, but none is adopted as an emendation (see pp. 582–85 above).

DISCUSSIONS. 84.25 Philip, king of riders] As noted by Gail Coffler (p. 121), in Greek "Philip" means "lover of horses."

85.26 Who raised them from the dead] Hennig Cohen (*Battle-Pieces*, p. 253) cites John 11:1–43, in which Jesus raises Lazarus from the dead.

VARIANTS (EXCEPT IN INDENTION). 84.0 *Sheridan at Cedar Creek*] BP,PPA; Philip H,P 84.0 (OCTOBER, 1864)] BP; [*not present*] H,P,PPA 84.3 dawning—] H,BP,PPA; ~, P 84.4 away;] H,BP,PPA; ~— P 84.5 calling, calling—] H,BP,PPA; ~, ~, P 84.6 Mount!] H,P(HM2),BP,PPA; ~^ P(HM1) 84.6 stay:] H,BP; ~; PPA; ~— P 84.7 lost;] H,BP,PPA; ~, P 84.10 retrieve] H,BP,PPA; retreive P 84.11 in] H,BP,PPA; with P 84.11 ermine—] H,BP,PPA; ~^ P 84.13 through] H,BP,PPA; thrugh P 84.13 October;] H,BP,PPA; ~— P 84.14 view;] H,BP,PPA; ~, P 84.17–18 The turn . . . ran,] P,BP,PPA; They faced about, each man; / Faint hearts were strong again; H 84.19 van;] H,BP,PPA; ~, P 84.21 him—] H,BP,PPA; ~, P 85.27 camp^ (at . . . lost),] BP,PPA; ~, (~ . . . ~)^ H; ~, ^~ . . . ~^, P 85.31 horse] H,BP,PPA; hose P 85.31 sable—] H,BP,PPA; ~, P 85.32 heap!] H,BP,PPA; ~, P 85.33 Valley,] H,BP,PPA; ~^ P 85.34 keep;] H,BP,PPA; ~, P 85.35 volley,] H,BP,PPA; ~^ P 85.38 lead,] H,BP,PPA; ~^ P

VARIANTS (IN INDENTION). *NN indention follows BP; variants in H, P, and PPA are stated in relation to BP:* 84.4,6] [*H and P indent like line 2; PPA indents line 4 farther than line 6 but in both cases less far than BP]* 84.7–9,17–19; 85.27–29,37–39] [*H and P indent less far than BP; PPA indents slightly farther than H and P but less far than BP]* 84.10,20; 85.30, 40] [*H and P indent like BP; PPA does not indent*]

IN THE PRISON PEN (p. 86)

Some reports and transcripts of congressional hearings concerning prison conditions and treatment were published in the *Rebellion Record*. Document 2 in volume 8, for example, runs for eighteen chilling pages (80–98), and immediately precedes the account of Farragut's taking of Mobile Bay that Melville certainly read and used (see the introductory note to "The Battle for the Bay," pp. 650–51 above). Document 1 in that volume (pp. 1–80) is filled with eyewitness accounts of the treatment of soldiers captured at Fort Pillow. Melville also comments on prison conditions in "On a natural Monument in a field of Georgia" (p. 134 above), for those who died in the notorious Andersonville prison.

DISCUSSIONS. 86.3 barren as a pelican-beach] Psalm 102: "I am like a pelican of the wilderness: I am like an owl of the desert." Melville marked the next verse ("I watch, and am as a sparrow alone upon the house top") in one of his Bibles (see the discussion at 64.0 above).

86.9–10 ghosts . . . shore—] Hennig Cohen (*Battle-Pieces*, p. 253) cites Virgil's *Aeneid*, 6.297–316, and adds, "the passage concerns the unsanctified dead who plead with Charon to be carried across the River Styx."

THE COLLEGE COLONEL (pp. 87–88)

The model for Melville's partly fictionalized figure is Colonel (later Brigadier General) William Francis Bartlett. As captain, Bartlett commanded a company of the Twentieth Massachusetts Volunteer Infantry (the "Harvard Regiment") in the October 1861 disaster at Ball's Bluff; lost a leg on April 24, 1862, in the Peninsular campaign; returned briefly to Harvard to complete his degree; then was recalled on September 20, 1862, to command Fort Briggs, the training camp of the Forty-ninth Massachusetts, in Pittsfield. As colonel, he commanded the Forty-ninth and was wounded in the left arm at the siege of Port Hudson, Louisiana, in the early summer of 1863. On August 22, 1863, the soldiers of the Forty-ninth, their ranks reduced by a third, returned in their best uniforms for a triumphal Pittsfield parade, Bartlett at their head, "mounted on the horse he had ridden at Port Hudson, his left fore arm still in [a box] sling, his crutch visible by his saddle" (Garner 1993, p. 267).

DISCUSSION. 88.29 Petersburg crater] See the introductory note to "The Apparition (A Retrospect)" (pp. 662–63 below).

THE EAGLE OF THE BLUE (p. 89)

Frank L. Day (1959, pp. 56–57) points out the source that Melville's note (l, p. 176 above) half-acknowledges without naming: an anonymous poem, "The Eagle of the Eighth Wisconsin" (*Rebellion Record,* 8:59–60, "Poetry and Incidents"). Day finds in the *Rebellion Record* "no evidence that more than one regiment maintained an eagle ensign," but Hennig Cohen (*Battle-Pieces,* p. 255) points to "The Eagle of Corinth" by "H. H. B." (6: 28–29, "Poetry and Incidents") as confirming "Melville's statement that other regiments had eagles as mascots"; the poem (by Henry Howard Brownell, also published in his *Lyrics of a Day* [New York: Carleton, 1864], pp. 30–34) is about an eagle carried by the Eighth Iowa. Cohen also reproduces a "sketch of emblematic eagles used as a tailpiece" in George Ward Nichols's *The Story of the Great March* (New York: Harper, 1865) and surmises that it "may have suggested details which Melville used in his poem"; but in "Melville's Sherman Poems: A Problem in Source Study," R. D. Madison disagrees: "The details do not seem to me to coincide at all" (p. 11 n. 9).

DISCUSSIONS. 89.8 Sibyl's hour] In " 'Formerly a Slave' " the subject of the painting is described as "Sibylline" (115.12 above).

89.12 But his claw has known the crag] Cohen (*Battle-Pieces,* p. 256) cites Job 39:27–30: "Doth the eagle mount up at thy command, and make her nest on high? She dwelleth and abideth on the rock, upon the crag of the rock, and the strong place. . . . Her young ones also suck up blood: and where the slain are, there is she."

89.15 eyes that brave the blinding sun] In *Mardi,* Melville refers twice to this notion (chaps. 85 and 135), but also has Babbalanja suppose, "Few grand poets have good eyes; for they needs blind must be, who ever gaze upon the sun" (chap. 180). Among Melville's penciled notes in volume 7 of his copy of Shakespeare's *Dramatic Works* (Boston: Hilliard, Gray, 1837; Sealts, no. 460, Bercaw, no. 634) is the question, in quotation marks: " 'do eagles wear spectacles?' " See "The Sources of Melville's Notes (1849–51) in a Shakespeare Volume," in the RELATED DOCUMENTS below.

A DIRGE FOR MCPHERSON (pp. 90–91)

Major General James B. McPherson, thirty-five years old, was killed in the early afternoon of July 22, 1864, in one of the counterattacks that John

B. Hood mounted when he succeeded Joseph E. Johnston as defender of Atlanta in the face of Sherman's advance.

DISCUSSION. 91.28 *Sarpedon*] This reference to Sarpedon, combined with the one in Melville's note m (p. 176 above), suggests that Melville could casually mix his Greeks and Trojans. Hennig Cohen (*Battle-Pieces,* p. 256) summarizes the difficulty: "Melville seems to have confused Sarpedon with Patroclus or Achilles with Hector. According to the *Iliad,* Sarpedon, son of Jupiter and Europa, fought on the side of Troy. He was slain by the Greek warrior, Patroclus, friend of Achilles. Hector, the Trojan hero, avenged Sarpedon's death by killing Patroclus." First reported here is Scott Norsworthy's identification of Melville's avenging "Achilles" as General William T. Sherman, whose "informal account," "The Late Major-General J. B. McPherson," in *Hours at Home* 2, no. 6 (April 1866): 485–93, was for sale in late March 1866 and quoted in newspapers. According to Sherman (p. 491), on his death day McPherson's name became a battle-cry: "On that day we avenged his death, for the slaughter of the enemy exceeded any thing I have seen during the war. Near twenty-two hundred of the enemy's dead remained on the ground when night closed upon the scene of action."

Melville's final couplet and his introduction of Sarpedon may be a reworking of Pope's translation, where the final couplet of Sarpedon's speech to Glaucus reads, "The life which others pay, let us bestow, / And give to fame what we to nature owe." Melville owned the Pope translation in his set of Harper's Classical Library (Sealts, no. 147); he also owned Matthew Arnold's *Essays in Criticism* (Boston: Ticknor & Fields, 1895; Sealts, no. 17), where the couplet is quoted on pp. 298 and 299.

AT THE CANNON'S MOUTH (pp. 92–93)

Navy Lieutenant William B. Cushing seized the public imagination with acts of daring. At the age of nineteen he made off with two Confederate schooners and escaped on one of them after running his own craft aground. He went on to perform other feats of reconnaissance and harassment behind enemy lines. Then, at the age of twenty-one, on the night of October 27, 1864, he and a crew of fifteen (thirteen according to his own report) took a shallow-draft steam launch, a "David" (that is, a small boat rigged with a spring-loaded torpedo at the end of a long boom), over Hatteras Bar and up Albemarle Sound to Plymouth, North Carolina, where lay a great threat to Union shipping, the mighty Confederate ram *Albemarle*. Subjected to withering small-arms fire, Cushing drove his craft up over the *Albemarle*'s protective log perimeter (designed to defend against just such a "David," a weapon the Confederates had first designed). Just as the reputed Goliath's sizable cannon blew his tiny steamer out of the water, Cushing touched off his torpedo and sent the ram to the bottom. Only Cushing and one crew member escaped to tell the tale. The November 3 New York *Daily Times* carried the story of the "Bold, Daring and Romantic Feat," printing Cushing's own report of the action. An editorial in the same issue extolled Cushing's "gallantry, presence of mind, coolness and daring" that "have few parallels in our own or any other time."

DISCUSSIONS. 92.0 *Cannon's Mouth*] In "Melville's Examination of Heroism in 'At the Cannon's Mouth,'" Robert E. Hogan notes an echo of the soldier in Jaques' "seven ages of man" speech in *As You Like It* (2.7), who seeks "the bubble reputation / Even in the cannon's mouth." In Melville's brother Allan's copy of John Evans's *Shakespeare's Seven Ages* (New York: Charles P. Fessenden, 1831; Sealts, no. 209), the lines are illustrated by a woodcut (facing p. [160]).

92.12 The] In Harvard Copy C of BP, Melville indicated that he wished to delete "From" by lining it out and entering a delete symbol in the left margin; NN supplies the capital "T" in "The", which now begins the line.

EMENDATIONS. 92.11 stay in] BP\HM; stay BP *92.12 The] BP\HM [*capital supplied by NN*]; From the BP

THE MARCH TO THE SEA (pp. 94–96)

Having leveled Atlanta by mid-November of 1864, Sherman moved on Savannah, concealing his true objective with complex flanking maneuvers by troops under Generals Oliver Otis Howard and Hugh Judson Kilpatrick (line 25). Both Frank L. Day (1959, pp. 70–75; 1964, pp. 134–36) and Hennig Cohen (*Battle-Pieces*, pp. 258–59) see George Ward Nichols's *The Story of the Great March* (New York: Harper, 1865) as a source, though Cohen acknowledges that "Melville could have obtained information about Sherman's march to the sea from any number of contemporary sources," and that only in lines 55–56, where the Union soldiers' pet gamecocks are described, is he "almost certainly" drawing upon Nichols (pp. 76–77). R. D. Madison makes explicit what Cohen leaves tacit—that Nichols's demonstrable contribution to the poem is "significant but nevertheless small" (p. 11). Among other possible sources Cohen instances two paintings—Thomas Nast's *General Sherman's March through Georgia*—his *Advance arriving at a Plantation* and F. O. C. Darley's *Foraging Party*—both of which were on display at the National Academy of Design in New York in the spring of 1865 (*Catalogue of the Fortieth Annual Exhibition* [New York, 1865], nos. 86 and 35), along with two others Melville presumably saw there (see the introductory notes to " 'The Coming Storm' " and " 'Formerly a Slave' " [pp. 659–60 and 662 below]).

"The March to the Sea" was first printed in *Harper's New Monthly Magazine* [H] 32 (February 1866): 366–67; the variant readings in that printing are listed here for the historical record, but none is adopted as an emendation (see pp. 583–84 above).

DISCUSSIONS. 96.77–78 The flails . . . ceased] Cohen (*Battle-Pieces,* p. 260) cites Matthew 24:7: "For nation shall rise against nation, and kingdom against kingdom: and there shall be famines, and pestilences, and earthquakes, in divers places."

96.91–92 Was the havoc . . . be] As revised by Melville in Harvard Copy C of BP. (Before inscribing his final revision of these lines, Melville penciled and erased at least two text-lines of undeciphered words; his wife also penciled his final revision into her copy of BP, Copy F at Harvard, leaving out the commas.) For the unrevised version of line 92—"Necessity the plea?"—Cohen (*Battle-Pieces,* p. 260) cites as source or analogue *Paradise Lost,* 4.393–94: "So spake the Fiend, and with necessity, / The Tyrant's plea, excus'd his devilish deeds."

EMENDATIONS. 95.33 marching—] BP\HM; ~^ BP 95.34 Right onward] BP\ HM; Unpausing BP *96.91 the havoc, retribution?] BP\HM; it Treason's retribution— BP *96.92 But howsoe'er it be,] BP\HM; Necessity the plea? BP

VARIANTS. 95.0 (DECEMBER, 1864)] BP; [*not present*] H 94.1 high-arching] BP; ~^~ H 96.86 terror^] BP; ~, H 96.91 Was the] BP\HM; It was H; Was it BP 96.91 retribution?] BP\HM; ~^ H; ~— BP 96.92 But howsoe'er it be,] BP\HM; (Necessity the plea); H; Necessity the plea? BP

THE FRENZY IN THE WAKE (pp. 97–98)

Since Melville names the Roman biographer in his note to the poem, Hennig Cohen (*Battle-Pieces,* p. 261) cites some other Plutarch references in Melville's works (*Redburn,* chap. 14; *White-Jacket,* chap. 41; "At the Hostelry," line 43 [to be published in the NN volume *"Billy Budd, Sailor" and Other Uncompleted Writings*]) and notes both the source (Judg. 4.2–23) and other uses of the Jael and Sisera story ("In a Bye-Canal" [in *Timoleon,* 292.5–6 above]; "The Bell-Tower" [in the NN *Piazza Tales* volume, pp. 180, 182]) that Melville here has his frenzied Southern speaker invoke in lines 11–12. R. D. Madison suggests that Sisera may refer to "the 'commander of the army' (Judges 4:2), Sherman himself" (p. 10). Madison further claims (1) that "The Frenzy in the Wake" draws upon

George Ward Nichols's *The Story of the Great March* (New York: Harper, 1865; Sealts, no. 384a; acquired August 18, 1865) and (2) that Melville's use of this book, which he did not acquire until August 1865, belies his assertion, in his note (n, pp. 176–77 above), that the poem was written before Lincoln's assassination in April of that year. Stanton Garner (1993, p. 376) speculates that Melville may have written the poem, in part, out of "respect for Richard Lathers," a close family friend from South Carolina (see NN *Correspondence,* pp. 259–60) who, before the war, had tried hard to persuade influential Southerners to preserve the Union.

DISCUSSION. 98.31–32 Have . . . rescind] Echoed here is one of the first self-characterizing speeches of another unrepentant and unseeing rebel, Satan, in *Paradise Lost,* 1.105–8:

> What though the field be lost?
> All is not lost; th'unconquerable will,
> And study of revenge, immortal hate
> And courage never to submit or yield.

THE FALL OF RICHMOND (p. 99)

Convinced that his remaining forces could no longer defend the Confederate capital, General Robert E. Lee withdrew them from Richmond during the night of April 2, 1865.

DISCUSSIONS. 99.11 helmed dilated Lucifer] Henry F. Pommer (p. 79 n. 81) points out the allusion to *Paradise Lost,* 4.985–86: "On th'other side Satan alarm'd, / Collecting all his might, dilated stood."

99.16 the faith we firmly kept] Hennig Cohen (*Battle-Pieces,* p. 262) cites 2 Timothy 4:7: "I have fought a good fight, I have finished my course, I have kept the faith."

99.21 But God is in Heaven, and Grant in the Town] An allusion to the already famous lines from Robert Browning's *Pippa Passes* (1841): "God's in his Heaven — / All's right with the world" (1.227–28).

THE SURRENDER AT APPOMATTOX (p. 100)

At dawn on Palm Sunday, April 9, 1865, Lee tried one last time to break out at Appomattox Station, but was outnumbered. That afternoon he arranged the terms with Grant at Appomattox Court House, and formally surrendered the Army of Northern Virginia.

A CANTICLE (pp. 101–3)

DISCUSSIONS. 101.1 Titanic] No particular Titan appears to be invoked here; see also "Titan" in "The Temeraire" (42.51 above). In the context of the Poesque meter, the word "Titanic" may recall "Ulalume," which Melville cited in annotating his edition of Spenser.

102.26 The Iris] The rainbow. Genesis 9:16: "And the bow shall be in the cloud; and I will look upon it, that I may remember the everlasting covenant between God and every living creature of all flesh that is upon the earth."

102.44–45 Giant of the Pool . . . white as wool] Presumably this Giant of the Pool was suggested by the splash and foam at the foot of a waterfall, which, when it ascends as mist, creates some of the conditions for a rainbow. The appearance of the foam would also suggest a "forehead white as wool." But the phrase also alludes to the passage where Daniel tells that in one of his dreams "the Ancient of days did sit, whose garment was white as snow, and the hair of his head like the pure wool" (Dan. 7.9; also referred to in line 61 of "The Conflict of Convictions," pp. 8–11 above).

THE MARTYR (pp. 104–5)

April 14, 1865, when John Wilkes Booth shot President Lincoln, was in fact Good Friday.

DISCUSSION. 104.0 *The Martyr*] In Harvard Copy C of BP, Melville lined out this title, but he supplied no alternative.

"THE COMING STORM" (p. 106)

Dan Vogel straightens out an earlier confusion of Robert Swain Gifford with Sandford Robinson Gifford. Both were established portrayers of landscapes and had paintings in the 1865 Annual Exhibition of the National Academy of Design (see *Catalogue of the Fortieth Annual Exhibition* [New York, 1865]), but as Melville's subtitle states, S. R. Gifford is the painter to whose *The Coming Storm* the poem refers. Melville presumably saw this painting at the exhibition (catalogued as no. 85 and listed as owned by Edwin Booth) as well as Elihu Vedder's *Jane Jackson,* the subject of "'Formerly a Slave'" (p. 115 above). According to the records of the academy, the exhibition opened in a new building on April 27 of that year and ran through July 1; Melville's sister-in-law Jennie (Allan's wife) was a "Fellow for Life" (catalogue, p. 52). Hennig Cohen notes that "the subject . . . was not an unusual one for the period. George Inness, for example, painted at least six such landscapes, including one dated 1878 which bears the same title" (*Battle-Pieces,* p. 268).

As shown by the poem's association of the picture with Shakespeare and his Hamlet, the "him" in lines 1 and 13 refers primarily to "E. B.," the painting's owner—that is, to Edwin Booth, the well-known actor of Shakespearean tragedy, as well as brother of John Wilkes Booth, Lincoln's assassin. It may also be understood as indicating S. R. Gifford as the painting's creator. As Cohen notes (p. 268), on March 24, 1865, Edwin Booth had completed "an unprecedented New York run of one hundred nights" as Hamlet, and returned to the part on January 3, 1866, after a temporary retirement. A portrait entitled *Edwin Booth as Hamlet* by John Pope was also on exhibition at the National Academy of Design (no. 450). Stanton Garner (1981, pp. 10–12; 1993, p. 386) adduces a possible more personal connection to S. R. Gifford: the painter was born near Gansevoort, New York, grew up in Hudson, and served with Melville's cousin Henry Gansevoort in New York City's Seventh Regiment. Melville's veneration of Shakespeare's "flashings-forth of the intuitive Truth" (expressed here as "Man's final lore," line 16) is most explicit in his essay "Hawthorne and his Mosses" (NN *Piazza Tales* volume, p. 244).

REBEL COLOR-BEARERS AT SHILOH (pp. 107–8)

In his note p (p. 177 above) Melville acknowledges, "The incident on which this piece is based is narrated in a newspaper account of the battle to be found in the 'Rebellion Record.'" Frank L. Day (1959, p. 57) points out the specific passage "that inspired the poem": the Cincinnati *Gazette* account of the action at Shiloh in April 1862 (*Rebellion Record*, 4:391, doc. 114). Melville's note alters the passage only very slightly, changing one word from "this" to "the" and omitting an "also," in addition to spelling out Stuart's rank and omitting two commas (cf. Cohen, *Battle-Pieces,* p. 270).

THE MUSTER (pp. 109–10)

On May 23, 1865, as the Army of the Potomac passed in review through the capital, flags flew at full staff for the first time since Lincoln's assassination. Then on May 24, Sherman's men of the West paraded by President Andrew Johnson and members of his cabinet.

DISCUSSION. 109.1–4 Abrahamic river . . . multitudes] In the "River" passage rejected from *The Confidence-Man* (see the NN edition, p. 497), Melville begins:

"As the word Abraham means the father of a great multitude of men so the word Mississippi means the father of a great multitude of waters. His tribes stream in from east & west, exceeding fruitful the lands they enrich." Thus the poem's epithet "Abrahamic" invokes both the Father of Waters and the late Father of his newly reuniting country, Abraham Lincoln.

AURORA-BOREALIS (p. 111)

References to "Northern Lights" in connection with armor appear also in *Moby-Dick,* chap. 56 ("at Versailles . . . every sword seems a flash of Northern Lights"), and *Mardi,* chap. 32 ("But true warriors polish their good blades by the bright beams of the morning . . . keep their metal lustrous and keen, as the spears of the Northern Lights charging over Greenland"). Melville saw newspaper articles such as the Cincinnati *Gazette* story of Chattanooga (*Rebellion Record,* 8:228, doc. 14): "The rays of the sun, reflected from ten thousand bayonets, dazzled the beholder's eyes."

DISCUSSION. 111.3 The . . . awe] In Harvard Copy C of BP, Melville underlined these words and wrote at the top of the page "The watcher feels a creeping awe"; but NN does not emend since he did not line out the printed words (see pp. 600–602 above).

THE RELEASED REBEL PRISONER (pp. 112–13)

Melville's note r (p. 178 above) sets the scene of this poem as New York City ("the Nineveh of the North" in line 3) and further describes the circumstances and activities of the released Southern captives awaiting transport there.

DISCUSSIONS. 112.3 Nineveh] For other lessons or associations Melville may have in mind here, see the brief book of Jonah, and Father Mapple's Jonah sermon in *Moby-Dick* (chap. 9).

112.10 His steel the nearest magnet drew] Most prominent of Melville's uses of the personal magnet figure is in his excited November [17?], 1851, letter to Hawthorne: "The divine magnet is in you, and my magnet responds. Which is the biggest? A foolish question—they are *One.*"

113.35 wierd] In Harvard Copy C of BP, Melville penciled "drear" and a virgule in the left margin to indicate a possible alternative, but NN does not emend since he only pencil-underlined, but did not line out, "wierd" (see pp. 600–602 above). While the now-standard spelling "Weird" appears at 5.13 above, "wierd" is retained here as an acceptable nineteenth-century variant.

"FORMERLY A SLAVE" (p. 115)

As title and subtitle indicate, this poem is not directly about a black woman, but a response to "an idealized Portrait" by Elihu Vedder of an actual ex-slave named Jane Jackson. Melville apparently saw the portrait at the Fortieth Annual Exhibition of the National Academy of Design in the spring of 1865 (see also the introductory note to " 'The Coming Storm,' " pp. 659–60 above); the exhibition catalogue (New York, 1865; no. 589) describes it as a "Drawing in Oil-Color."

During the Civil War, Vedder later recalled, he frequently passed a corner near his Broadway studio "where an old negro woman sold peanuts. Her meekly bowed head and a look of patient endurance and resignation" touched his heart (*The Digressions of V.,* p. 236). Vedder later turned his Jane Jackson images into many further-idealized Sibyls (p. 237). Melville's 1891 dedication of *Timoleon* to Vedder (see the discussion at 252.2 below) was based on this "sympathy with the artist," as Elizabeth Shaw Melville described it in a letter to Vedder (see Jaffe, " 'Sympathy with the Artist': Elizabeth Melville and Elihu Vedder").

DISCUSSION. 115.1 The sufferance of her race is shown] Here, long-endured suffering. Hennig Cohen (*Battle-Pieces,* p. 276) cites as analogue for this use Shakespeare's *Merchant of Venice,* 1.3.111: "For sufferance is the badge of all our tribe."

THE APPARITION (p. 116)

In his article about this poem, David Cody aptly cites particular passages in Carlyle's *Sartor Resartus* and *The French Revolution* as influential analogues of and bases for understanding the extra-physical implications of "The Apparition." He also offers (p. 6) as the physical sources of Melville's "volcanic" imagery in the poem Alfred R. Waud's illustration and verbal account of the Petersburg mine explosion in the August 20, 1864, issue of *Harper's Weekly,* pp. 537–38, 542. The incident was also covered in newspapers, such as the New York *Times,* August 1–3. A regiment of Pennsylvania miners had tunneled under and on July 30 set off a huge explosion intended to breach a fortified salient in the Confederate line at Petersburg, Virginia. Waud wrote: "With a muffled roar it came, and as from the eruption of a volcano—which it much resembled—upward shot masses of earth, momentarily illuminated from beneath by the lurid flare. . . . then the . . . smoke . . . enveloped all, like a shadowy pall for the two hundred souls thus rushed into eternity. As if for breath there was a short pause, the rebels regarding the great apparition as though spell-bound. . . . when the smoke lifted the attacking column . . . became visible in the crater of the explosion." See the "Supplement" to *Battle-Pieces:* "Wherefore in a clear sky do we still turn our eyes toward the South, as the Neapolitan, months after the eruption, turns his toward Vesuvius? Do we dread lest the repose may be deceptive? In the recent convulsion has the crater but shifted?" (p. 185 above).

ON THE SLAIN COLLEGIANS (pp. 118–19)

Gail Coffler (p. 4) indexes Melville's many invokings of Apollo, from his first work to his last. Robert K. Wallace (1992, p. 27) reproduces Melville's print of an engraving by L. Stock, *Apollo killing the Python,* based on J. M. W. Turner's 1811 oil painting *Apollo and the Python.* In his 1857–58 lecture, "Statues in Rome," Melville reportedly said of the Apollo Belvedere: "If one were to try to convey some adequate notion, other than artistic, of a statue which so signally lifts the imaginations of men, he might hint that it gives a kind of visible response to that class of human aspirations of beauty and perfection that, according to Faith, cannot be truly gratified except in another world" (NN *Piazza Tales* volume, p. 402).

DISCUSSION. 119.44 both] In Harvard Copy C of BP, Melville penciled "all" and a virgule in the margin to indicate a possible alternative, but NN does not emend since he only pencil-underlined, but did not line out, "both" (see pp. 600–602 above).

EMENDATION. 119.46 put] BP\HM; be BP

AMERICA (pp. 120–21)

DISCUSSIONS. 120.17–19 Fierce . . . brood] Hennig Cohen (*Battle-Pieces,* p. 279) cites *Paradise Lost,* 2.44–45 ("Stood up, the strongest and fiercest spirit / That fought in heaven, now fiercer by despair") and 4.115 ("Thrice chang'd with pale, ire, envy, and despair"). At one point, Melville titled chapter 12 of *Billy Budd, Sailor* "Pale ire, envy and despair" (Hayford and Sealts, p. 165).

121.25 She sleeps . . . dead] Cohen (*Battle-Pieces,* p. 279) notes a poem in *Harper's Weekly,* May 25, 1861, titled "Not Dead," a response to a New York regiment's adopting "The Union is not dead but sleeping" as motto to be displayed on its flag.

121.29 Revealing earth's foundation bare] Cf. "The Conflict of Convictions" (10.65 above): "What if the gulfs their slimed foundations bare?"

ON THE HOME GUARDS (p. 122)

During the nine-day siege of Lexington, Missouri, September 12–20, 1861, the Federal forces of Colonel James Mulligan were outnumbered five to one by the Secessionist Missourians under General Sterling Price. Mulligan expected reinforcements via the Missouri River, from General John Charles Frémont in Saint Louis, or from General John Pope at Jefferson City, but none came.

DISCUSSION. 122.0 VERSES INSCRIPTIVE AND MEMORIAL] "Inscriptions" constituted a well-established genre in British and American poetry. Melville apparently got the idea for "Extracts" in *Moby-Dick* from Robert Southey's *The Doctor,* which contains a sections of poetic inscriptions, mainly quite short. Melville's copy of Wordsworth (Sealts, no. 563a) also contains a section of "Inscriptions," pp. 331–34. (See pp. 509–10 above.)

INSCRIPTION FOR GRAVES AT PEA RIDGE, ARKANSAS (p. 123)

General Sterling Price led Confederate troops at both Lexington, Missouri (see the previous poem), and at Pea Ridge, just over the border into Arkansas.

THE FORTITUDE OF THE NORTH (p. 124)

The disaster of Second Manassas, August 29–30, 1862, was precipitated by the strategic blunders of Lincoln, his military adviser Henry W. Halleck, and General John Pope. Melville's figure in lines 5–9 derives from the impression he had recorded in his August 8, 1860, journal entry: "Just before sunset, in a squall, the mist lifted & showed, within 12 or fifteen miles the horrid sight of Cape Horn — (the Cape proper) — a black, bare steep cliff, the face of it facing the South Pole" (*Journals,* p. 134).

DISCUSSION. 124.1 No shame they take] For similar transpositions by Melville in Harvard Copy C of BP, see the discussion at 144.162 below.

EMENDATION. *124.1 No shame they take] BP\HM; They take no shame BP

ON THE MEN OF MAINE (p. 125)

On August 5, 1862, as part of an attempt to recapture New Orleans, former vice president and senator, now Major General John C. Breckinridge, led some twenty-six hundred Confederate troops against twenty-five hundred Federals, including the Fourteenth Maine Infantry, at Baton Rouge.

INSCRIPTION FOR MARYE'S HEIGHTS, FREDERICKSBURG (p. 127)

Melville published another Fredericksburg "Inscription" in 1864 in *Autograph Leaves of Our Country's Authors* (see p. 321 above and the corresponding introductory note to that poem, pp. 866–67 below).

ON THE SLAIN AT CHICKAMAUGA (p. 129)

Despite the successful day-long defensive battle fought at Snodgrass Hill, on September 20, 1863, by Federal troops under General George Henry Thomas—nicknamed thereafter the "Rock of Chickamauga"—the September 19–20 Battle of Chickamauga was a tactical Federal defeat in the larger struggle for control of Chattanooga.

AN UNINSCRIBED MONUMENT (p. 130)

"An uninscribed Monument" was reprinted in R. H. Stoddard's edition of Rufus M. Griswold's *Poets and Poetry of America* [PPA] (New York: James Miller, 1873), p. 630; the variant readings in that printing are listed below for the historical record, but none is adopted as an emendation (see pp. 584–85 above).

VARIANTS. 130.0 *on*] BP; *On* PPA 130.2 piny] BP; piney PPA 130.9 breath.] BP; ~^ PPA

ON SHERMAN'S MEN (p. 131)

DISCUSSION. 131.5 But . . . restore] Stephen Hoy points to "Gods are we, Bards, Saints, Heroes, if we will.—/ Dumb judges, answer, truth or mockery?" in Matthew Arnold's "Written in Emerson's Essays," contained in an edition of Arnold's *Poems* that Melville owned (Sealts, no. 21).

ON THE GRAVE OF A YOUNG CAVALRY OFFICER (p. 132)

The probable model for this brief epitaph is Colonel Charles Russell Lowell (1835–64; a nephew of James Russell Lowell), the cavalry officer with whom Melville talked and went on a scout when he visited the front at Vienna, Virginia, in April 1864. Lowell was in part a model for the newly married young officer who leads the foray in "The Scout toward Aldie" (see the introductory note to that poem, pp. 668–69 below). Leading his troops with selfless gallantry, he was mortally wounded in the Shenandoah Valley at the Battle of Cedar Creek, October 19, 1864, and died the next day. (For further accounts of Lowell, see Garner 1982 and 1993.)

A REQUIEM (p. 133)

DISCUSSIONS. 133.15 Frolic] Assuming that this word is a verb, Norman E. Jarrard (p. 312) suggests "Frolics" as an emendation. Robert Penn Warren (p. 377) points out, however, that "Frolic" here "is an adjective, a form derived from Melville's reading in seventeenth-century poetry (as in Herrick's 'Out-did the meat, out-did the frolic wine')." It is, moreover, probably a deliberately chosen adjective substitute for the present participle "Frolicking" (cf. line 17's "joying").

133.19–23 Whose bark . . . the light] Henry F. Pommer (p. 25) compares Melville's lines 20–23 to Milton's "Lycidas," lines 62–63: "His goary visage down the stream was sent, / Down the swift Hebrus to the Lesbian shore," also lines 154–60:

> Ay me! Whilst thee the shores, and sounding seas
> Wash far away, where'er thy bones are hurl'd,
> Whether beyond the stormy Hebrides,
> Where thou perhaps under the whelming tide
> Visit'st the bottom of the monstrous world;
> Or whether thou to our moist vows denied,
> Sleep'st by the fable of Bellerus old.

Hennig Cohen (*Battle-Pieces,* p. 282) adds that Melville's line 19 may be compared to "Lycidas," line 164: "And, O ye dolphins, waft the hapless youth." He further suggests that in line 23 "Melville may have been thinking of Milton's Invocation to Light, with which Book III of *Paradise Lost* begins" (including the passage "thee I revisit safe, / . . . but thou / Revisit'st not these eyes"); but he notices that both God and Milton's "holy light" are absent from Melville's poem.

ON A NATURAL MONUMENT (p. 134)

Visiting Constantinople in December 1856, Melville had noted in his journal "Forrests of cemeteries" (December 13) and, at Scutari, "Cemeteries like Black Forrest" (December 18)—forests as a result of the Muslim custom of planting a cypress at each grave (*Journals,* pp. 58, 68, 397). (Cf. his note u, p. 178 above.) On the fourteenth (p. 62), he recorded witnessing in a cemetery at Pera a newly bereaved woman, head close to the ground, who cried out to the departed "as if calling down a hatchway or cellar; besought — 'Why dont you speak to me? My God! — It is I! — Ah, speak — but one word!['] — All deaf. — So much for consolation. — This woman & her cries haunt me horribly."

DISCUSSION. 134.12 In horror they choked] For similar transpositions by Melville in Harvard Copy C of BP, see the discussion at 144.162 below.

EMENDATION. *134.12 In horror they choked] BP\HM; They choked in horror BP

COMMEMORATIVE OF A NAVAL VICTORY (pp. 135–36)

Stanton Garner (1993, p. 394) suggests that Melville's model for the naval victor is Admiral David Farragut (celebrated in "The Battle for the Mississippi" and "The Battle for the Bay," pp. 47–48, 80–83 above). Farragut was "In social halls a favored guest / In years that follow victory won" (lines 10–11); in failing health, he returned to New York City in December 1864 to a hero's welcome at a public reception, at which he was given money to purchase a home.

DISCUSSIONS. 135.7–8 The hawk . . . king] As the picture that "best fits Melville's description," Hennig Cohen (*Battle-Pieces,* pp. 284–85) identifies and reproduces Titian's *The Man with a Falcon.* The "king," says Cohen, probably refers to Charles V, to whom Titian's gift of another painting is recorded in the chapter on Titian in Melville's edition of Vasari's *Lives of the Painters,* 5:391 (London: Bohn, 1849–52; acquired March 1862; Sealts, no. 534a). Melville did not mark page 391, but he did mark other passages in the chapter.

136.26 The shark] The white shark is one of Melville's major cautionary emblems, as in "The Maldive Shark" ("Pale ravener of horrible meat," 236.16 above). In an elaborated footnote in *Moby-Dick* (chap. 42, "The Whiteness of the Whale") Ishmael claims that, in part, the white shark generates "intensified terror" because its "white gliding ghostliness of repose" signals "the white, silent stillness of death" (cf. the word "Repose" in line 14 here). In "The Scout toward Aldie" a simile (139.13–14 above) evoking the legendary guerrilla raider has it that "As glides in seas the shark, / Rides Mosby through green dark."

PRESENTATION TO THE AUTHORITIES (p. 137)

Stanton Garner (1993, pp. 397–98) hypothesizes that Melville may have created the poem's presentation of captured colors out of what he heard or read of a July 4, 1865, Albany presentation by New York State volunteer regiments of about two hundred of their own flags to Governor Reuben E. Fenton.

THE RETURNED VOLUNTEER
TO HIS RIFLE (p. 138)

Melville need not have had a particular Hudson River veteran's rifle and homestead in mind in this poem, though he may well have. Hennig Cohen (*Battle-Pieces,* p. 286) calls attention to an instance in line 26–27 of "The Released Rebel Prisoner" (p. 113 above). Other examples of such displayed battle weapons and trophies come up in *Typee* (chaps. 25 and 32), *Moby-Dick* (chap. 3), and *Pierre* (bk. 1, sect. iv).

THE SCOUT TOWARD ALDIE (pp. 139–62)

In the spring of 1864 Melville traveled with his brother Allan to the front; in gaining permission to do so, Allan on April 8 wrote to his first wife's brother-in-law, Richard Lathers, describing Herman as "very anxious to go to the front, but it appears that it is difficult to get a pass," and suggesting that "perhaps you might address a line to Secretary [of War] Stanton introducing Herman and stating his wish, as a literary man he might be favored. As such men should have opportunities to see that they may describe" (Library of Congress–Lathers Collection). The two brothers apparently set out soon afterward to visit their cousin Lieutenant Colonel Henry Gansevoort, commander of the Thirteenth New York Cavalry, in camp at Vienna, Virginia. It was in the course of this visit that Melville went on an actual "scout" toward Aldie, Virginia.

In "Melville's Scout Toward Aldie" (1982) and *The Civil War World of Herman Melville* (1993, pp. 299–323) Stanton Garner alters earlier accounts of when this scout occurred—not April 14, but April 18–20, 1864—and provides considerable detail relevant to an understanding of how the poet likely blended factual with legendary elements. Not finding Henry in camp on Saturday and Sunday, April 16 and 17 (he was away in Washington on ordnance business), Melville and Allan were probably entertained by other officers of the cavalry brigade of General Robert O. Tyler's division of the Washington defenses—including the young brigade commander, Colonel Charles Russell Lowell (accompanied by his wife, Josephine Shaw Lowell, a tireless attender to the needs of the sick and wounded); the brigade surgeon, a former neighbor in Pittsfield, Doctor Oscar C. DeWolf; the new regimental surgeon of the Thirteenth New York Cavalry, Doctor Benjamin Rush Taylor; and the regimental chaplain of the Second Massachusetts Cavalry, the Reverend Charles A. Humphreys (who later wrote a book that gives an account of the ensuing scout, *Field, Camp, Hospital and Prison in the Civil War, 1863–1865* [Boston: Geo. H. Ellis, 1918]). By the time he published his Aldie poem, Melville would have known that Lowell, conducting himself with conspicuous bravery, insisting on leading though repeatedly wounded, had died on October 20, 1864, of wounds received the day before at the critical Battle of Cedar Creek (see the introductory note to "Sheridan at Cedar Creek," pp. 651–52 above). He was posthumously promoted to brigadier general, and one month later Josephine Shaw Lowell gave birth to a daughter.

From people in the camp Melville may have heard (during the visit or later) stories of varying reliability but certain literary usefulness about Colonel John Singleton Mosby, commander of the Forty-third Battalion of Virginia Cavalry. Mosby's Partisan Rangers, as they were called, and their guerrilla tactics of surprise hit and strategic run kept a disproportionately large force of Federal troops pinned down to the defense of Washington between January 1863 and April 1865. (For a fuller account of Mosby and his battalion's operations, see Jeffry D. Wert's *Mosby's Rangers*.)

While he was in the camp, Melville, but not his brother, decided to accompany a scout, in the course of which upwards of a dozen prisoners were taken, three Federal troopers were wounded, and one trooper was killed. The casualties occurred during a night skirmish in Leesburg, where Lowell had sent a contingent of seventy-five dismounted troopers after hearing that many of Mosby's men would be gathered there celebrating the wedding of one of their number (not a victory, as in the poem [line 607], although the ten captured earlier in the poem were at a wedding the night before [line 387]). Garner suggests that the characterizations in the poem may tell us more than the factual record otherwise reveals about the civilian guide and informer from Aldie, Alexander F. ("Yankee") Davis, as well as about prototypes of surgeon and chaplain, Doctor Taylor and the Reverend Mr. Humphreys.

DISCUSSIONS. 139.13–14 As glides . . . dark] For other gliding sharks, see the discussion at 136.26 above.

140.32–35 Capitol Dome . . . seen] The new iron dome of the Capitol build-
ing in Washington, D.C., could be seen from "Mosby's Confederacy" in nearby
northern Virginia. See also the discussion at 9.44 above.

140.36 scout] In Harvard Copy C of BP, Melville penciled "ride" above this
word as a possible alternative, but NN does not emend since he did not line out
or even underline "scout" (see pp. 600–602 above). He also canceled and erased
the same penciled alternative wording in the poem title, both on the first page of
the poem and on the separate section-title page preceding it.

140.38 all-cheering lamp] Though the phrasing might be taken as formulaic,
Hennig Cohen's citation (*Battle-Pieces*, p. 288) of Shakespeare's *Romeo and Juliet*,
1.1.141 ("so soon as the all-cheering sun") seems relevant in a context where the
"Leader" is about to be portrayed as Romeo-like.

140.53 Elate] Cf. "Elate he never can be" in "Commemorative of a Naval
Victory" (135.24 above).

142.100 lonesome] In Harvard Copy C of BP, Melville penciled "dreary" in
the left margin as a possible alternative, but NN does not emend since he only
pencil-underlined, but did not line out, "lonesome" (see pp. 600–602 above).
(Cf. the discussions at 143.146 and 158.684.)

143.146 strange lone] In Harvard Copy C of BP, Melville penciled "spell-
bound" in the margin as a possible alternative, but NN does not emend since
he only pencil-underlined, but did not line out, "strange lone" (see pp. 600–602
above).

144.162 The road they leave] Melville's inversion of "They leave the road" in
Harvard Copy C of BP is part of a series of such revisions (see also the emenda-
tions at 124.1, 134.12, and 145.206). Inverted phrasings like this are typical of the
poem as it appeared in BP; cf. lines 173 and 492.

145.206 The pool they skirt] See the discussion just above.

145.221 Seven Days] Melville's cousin Henry Gansevoort was a reserve artil-
lerist in the Seven Days of marching and battling that ended with Malvern Hill
on July 1, 1862, as McClellan moved his army across Lee's front to Harrison's
Landing. See the introductory note to "Malvern Hill," p. 639 above.

146.238 vile jerk and drop] The first paragraph of Melville's note w (p. 179
above) appended to this line makes clear the general outlines of the hangings and
counter-hangings that actually occurred after his visit to Henry Gansevoort's
camp in April 1864. (For more on this episode, see Garner 1993, pp. 363–67.)

146.247 Loudon] Melville's spelling also occurs in the "Poetry and Incidents"
section of the *Rebellion Record* (8:62).

148.325–27 The pale . . . student-ailments] This character may be drawn by
Melville from the Reverend Charles A. Humphreys, just out of divinity school,
who did go on the actual scout, and later wrote a book that gives an account of
it, *Field, Camp, Hospital and Prison in the Civil War, 1863–1865* (Boston: Geo. H.
Ellis, 1918).

150.389 Belisent] Among the extracts and modernized paraphrases in George
Ellis's *Specimens of Early English Metrical Romances* (3 vols., 1805; edited by J. O.

Halliwell and published in London by Bohn in 1848), Melville could learn from "Merlin. Part II" that Belicent (with a "c" or with an "s": both forms are in Ellis, pp. 103, 115) was the half sister of Arthur, the second daughter of Arthur's mother, Igerna, and her husband, Hoel; she was the wife of King Lot, and the mother of Gawain, Guerehas, Agravain, and Gaeriet (p. 103).

151.430 A glance of mingled foul and fair] Shakespeare's *Macbeth*, 1.1.11 ("Fair is foul, and foul is fair").

151.431 Sad patience] In "Art" (*Timoleon*, p. 280 above) one of the qualities the artist needs is "Sad patience" (line 6).

154.540 My bluebirds] In Harvard Copy C of BP, Melville penciled "Comrades" in the margin as a possible alternative, but NN does not emend since he only pencil-underlined, but did not line out, "My bluebirds" (see pp. 600–602 above). Perhaps Melville had noticed this line's repetition of "bluebirds" in line 533.

157.644 One's buttons shine] In Harvard Copy C of BP, Melville penciled "This gold-lace gleams" at the bottom of the page as a possible alternative, but NN does not emend since he only pencil-underlined, but did not line out, "One's buttons shine" (see pp. 600–602 above).

158.684 come lone and lost] In Harvard Copy C of BP, Melville penciled a comma following "come" and, in the left margin, "astray" as a possible alternative for "lone and lost", but NN does not emend since he only pencil-underlined, but did not line out, "lone and lost" (see pp. 600–602 above).

EMENDATIONS. 141.61 caracole] NN; caricole BP *144.162 The road they leave] BP\HM; They leave the road BP 145.200 deemed] BP\HM; thought BP *145.206 The pool they skirt] BP\HM; They skirt the pool BP 146.238 drop!"ᵂ] NN; ~!^ᵂ BP 146.266 for thought] BP\HM; to think BP

LEE IN THE CAPITOL (pp. 163–69)

In the HISTORICAL NOTE (p. 511 above), Parker points out that the poem is "an imaginary oration by a real historical figure," a genre familiar to Melville from classical and Shakespearean precedents as well as American classroom exercises. The historical Lee was questioned by the Joint Committee on Reconstruction on February 17, 1866. The proceedings are recorded in the *Reports of the Committees of the House of Representatives, made during the . . . Thirty-Ninth Congress, 1865–'66* (2:129–36). While the New York *Daily Tribune* for February 19, 1866, did report on the hearing, it was not sufficiently detailed that it could have formed the basis for what Melville represents as the facts of the hearing. On March 28, 1866, both the New York *Times* and the *Daily Tribune* published Lee's testimony in its entirety; it covered, for instance, the questions Lee was asked about the

South's loyalty and the status of the Negroes that appear in lines 79–88 of Melville's poem.

DISCUSSIONS. 163.0 (APRIL, 1866)] Since February, not April, was the month of Lee's appearance before the Joint Committee on Reconstruction, this month (presumably not an error by Melville) seems to refer not to that event but to the time of the poem's composition, probably after the March 28 publication of the testimony (see above).

164.31 looming Dome] See the discussion at 9.44 above.

167.152 and] In Harvard Copy C of BP, Melville penciled "or" and a virgule in the right margin to indicate a possible alternative, but NN does not emend since he only pencil-underlined, but did not line out, "and" (see pp. 600–602 above).

168.200 Avoid . . . reprobate."] In Harvard Copy C of BP, Melville penciled a virgule in the right margin, and, at the top of the page, as a possible revision, "Forbear to wreak the ill you reprobate"; but NN does not emend since he did not line out or even underline "Avoid the tyranny you reprobate" (see pp. 600–602 above).

EMENDATIONS. 166.133 those] BP\HM; these BP 167.164 'In] [indented] NN; [not indented] BP 167.165 Brought] [not indented] NN; [indented] BP

A MEDITATION (pp. 170–72)

DISCUSSIONS. 170.0 Attributed . . . battles] In BP the subtitle is printed below the title only on the preceding section-title page; NN places it below the head-title as a matter of design.

171.54 the Pharisee] See, e.g., Luke 18.10–14, one of many references to Pharisaical activities and attitudes in the Gospels.

NOTES (pp. 173–80)

DISCUSSIONS. 175.22–23 General Grant . . . to a visitor] For the likelihood that the visitor was Melville himself, see the introductory note to "The Armies of the Wilderness," pp. 647–48 above.

179.23 having been] Melville, detecting the grammatical irregularity in this sentence (which read "being able" at this point), penciled "having" in the right margin of Harvard Copy C of BP and penciled a caret at the left of "being"; but he neglected to alter "being" to "been". NN completes the intended correction.

EMENDATIONS. 177.36 'No] NN; ^~ BP 177.36 killed.' "] NN; ~.^" BP *179.23 having] BP\HM; being BP *179.23 been] NN; [not present] BP

SUPPLEMENT (pp. 181–88)

The New York *Herald* for September 3, 1866, carried one of the more favorable reviews of *Battle-Pieces,* a review probably influenced by that paper's approval of what it took to be Melville's political stance in the "Supplement," from which it proceeded to reprint large passages. Noticing in passing that Melville's "patriotism—not free from solicitude—urges a claim overriding all literary scruples" (181.2–3), the *Herald* hastened to add: "So far from spoiling the symmetry of the book, this supplement completes it, and converts it into what is better than a good book—into a good and patriotic action."

DISCUSSIONS. 181.19 narrowness] In Harvard Copy C of BP, Melville underlined this word and penciled "narrowmindedness" in the left margin but then erased both his underlining and the word.

181.20 impartiality] In Harvard Copy C of BP, Melville penciled an "x" in the margin and, at the top of the page, another "x" and "fairmindedness" as a possible alternative, but NN does not emend since he only pencil-underlined, but did not line out, "impartiality" (see pp. 600–602 above).

182.28–31 If George IV. could raise . . . Preston Pans] In Rome, on Sunday, March 8, 1857, Melville visited St. Peter's and saw the monument to the Stuarts—James II and his sons Charles and Henry—commissioned in 1819 by George IV when he was prince regent. (See *Journals,* pp. 110, 481.)

182.35 recent histories and biographies] Some of these volumes published "at the North by loyal houses" included *The Life of Stonewall Jackson . . . by a Virginian* [John Esten Cooke] (New York: Richardson, 1863), Addey Markinfield, *The Life and Military Career of Thomas Jonathan Jackson* (New York: Evans, 1863), and *Southern Generals, Who They Are and What They Have Done* (New York: Richardson, 1865; reissued in 1867 as *Lee and His Generals,* by William Parker Snow). According to Douglas Southall Freeman, in *The South to Posterity,* the books on Jackson "were published in New York and were distributed without protest on the part of the Federal Government" (p. 16).

183.5 the Ettrick Shepherd] The established epithet for the Scottish writer James Hogg (1770–1835); the reference may imply that Melville read such poems as Hogg's *The Queen's Wake* (1813). See the HISTORICAL NOTE for Hogg's fame in Albany in the 1830s (pp. 353–55 above).

183.36–37 But surely other . . . fortitude matchless] Henry F. Pommer (p. 120 n. 18) notes the echo of Milton's "To the Lord General Cromwell," line 3—"Guided by faith and matchless fortitude"—and notes further that "Melville out-Miltons Milton by using a postpositional adjective."

186.25 honest Catos] Presumably those like Cato the Elder (234–149 B.C.) who tried to restore by legislation the virtues and simple values he found in the early republic. But Cato the Younger (95–46 B.C.) had a reputation for incorruptibility and dedication—his dedication to Pompey, for example, may lie behind the comment in the first paragraph of *Moby-Dick* that "with a philosophical flourish" he threw "himself upon his sword" (when he heard of Caesar's final defeat of the Pompeiian army at Thapsus).

188.1 terrible] In Harvard Copy C of BP, Melville penciled "great" in the margin as a possible alternative, but NN does not emend since he only pencil-underlined, but did not line out, "terrible" (see pp. 600–602 above).

EMENDATION. 182.28 could] BP\HM; could, out of the grateful instinct of a gentleman, BP

John Marr and Other Sailors (pp. 189–249)

NN copy-text is Melville's manuscript [HM], "John Marr and Other Sailors," in Harvard MS Am 188 (370). The first and only printing in Melville's lifetime, set from this manuscript, was *John Marr and Other Sailors* [JM] (New York: De Vinne Press, 1888). In total, HM is emended at 261 points: at 25 points from Elizabeth Shaw Melville's inscription in HM [HM\EM]; at 49 points from printed variants in JM galley [JMg] and page [JMp] proof; at 1 point from the De Vinne reviewer's alteration of the galley proof [JMg\r]; at 169 points from Melville's revisions in JM galley and page proof [JMg\HM, JMp\HM]; at 9 points from Melville's revision of JM [JM\HM]; at 1 point from Elizabeth Shaw Melville's revision in JM [JM\EM]; at 7 points by the present edition [NN]. Substantives are emended at 102 points, accidentals at 159 points.

The HISTORICAL NOTE provides background relating to Melville's poetic development. The NOTE ON PRINTING AND PUBLISHING HISTORY, pp. 543–64 above, describes the printer's-copy manuscript, the galley and page proofs, and the finished book; and it recounts, on the basis of these documents, the course of Melville's text through the printing process. The GENERAL NOTE ON THE TEXT supplies information on the copies used for collation and on the printer's copy for NN (pp. 580–82); comments on the sources for assessing the text, including the manuscript, the galley and page proofs, and copies of the finished book (pp. 588–89); outlines Melville's methods of preparing and revising manuscripts (pp. 596–99); sets forth the principles for emendation of the copy-text (pp. 602–17); and explains the makeup of the textual apparatus, including the system employed for recording manuscript revisions (pp. 617–20).

NN uses three section-titles ("John Marr and Other Sailors" on p. 195, "Sea-Pieces" on p. 218, and "Pebbles" on p. 243) in conformity with Melville's alterations of running-titles on the page proofs—which reflect the arrangement implied by his holograph title page ("John Marr and

Other Sailors with Some Sea-Pieces") taken together with the printed table of contents (where "Sea-Pieces" and "Pebbles" are centered section headings). The alternative plans for marking sections that emerged at the galley- and page-proof stages are discussed above (pp. 556, 560–61). NN page-breaks that coincide with stanza-breaks, as well as NN line-end hyphens that should be retained in quoting, are listed on pp. 616–17.

[TABLE OF CONTENTS] (p. x)

DISCUSSION. x.6 JOHN MARR AND OTHER SAILORS] NN places this section-title in the table of contents to correspond with Melville's designation of it as one of three section-titles in his alterations of running-titles on the page proofs. It does not appear in the table of contents of the first edition, though the other two section-titles ("Sea-Pieces" and "Pebbles") do. No manuscript or proof for the table of contents is known to survive, and the poem titles in the NN table of contents are those that appear at the heads of the poems in NN, which reflect Melville's intention as it emerges from the surviving documents. In fact, the only substantive differences between the poem titles in the NN table of contents and those of the first edition are the presence in NN of the full titles of "Inscription Epistolary to W. C. R.," "The Æolian Harp At the *Surf Inn*," and "Old Counsel Of the young Master Of a wrecked California clipper" (shortened in the first edition to "Inscription Epistolary," "The Æolian Harp," and "Old Counsel").

INSCRIPTION EPISTOLARY
TO W. C. R. (pp. 191–93)

W. Clark Russell was born in New York City on February 22, 1844, and died in Bath, England, on November 8, 1911. Mostly resident in England, he served from the ages of fourteen to twenty-two in the British merchant marine, then became a writer of both fiction and nonfiction—many sea-tales, articles with a sea slant (a long series for the London *Daily Telegraph*, 1882–89), and biographies (of Dampier in 1889, Nelson in 1890, and Collingwood in 1891).

Just when Melville became acquainted with Russell's work is not known, but possibly not earlier than 1875, when *John Holdsworth, Chief Mate* appeared, or 1877, when *The Wreck of the Grosvenor* was published. These books "led the series of kindred ones" (192.29)—among them, *My Watch Below* (1882), *Round the Galley Fire* (1883), and *The Frozen Pirate* (1887). Perhaps Melville's attention was first drawn by Russell's "Sea Stories," an article in the September 1884 London *Contemporary Review* in which Russell rated Melville highest among such other "poets of the deep" as Richard Henry Dana Jr., Michael Scott, and Captain George Cupples. (While in New York City in March 1885, Melville's cousin Kate Gansevoort Lansing went to Brentano's, accompanied by Melville's wife, and ordered a copy of this issue.)

By July 1885, at any rate, Melville recommended Russell's sea-tales to a probable admirer of his own work, and by April 1886 Melville and Russell were in communication, agreeing, as Russell put it, that "Dana is indeed great," and Russell characterizing Melville as "so admirable a genius" (*Correspondence*, pp. 486–87, 498–500, 731–32). Such genial enthusiasm and recognition from a fellow writer probably touched Melville enough that he decided, in late 1887 or early 1888, to address if not exactly dedicate his group of sea-poems to Russell (*Correspondence,* pp. 742–43; see also Ryan 1967, pp. 142–47). Russell was deeply grateful, and the literary relationship flourished further when he again praised Melville highly in "The Honour of the Flag," an article in the January 24, 1889, issue of *America,* a Chicago weekly, and dedicated *An Ocean Tragedy* to him in 1890 (the dedication did not appear in the Harpers 1889 publication of the book; *Correspondence,* pp. 744–46, 754–56). Their "mutual generosity of recognition . . . profound in its sincerity," as Russell's son put it, persisted for at least six or seven years ("When the Sea Came into Literature," *Literary Digest International Book Review* 3 [May 1925]: 373; cited in *Correspondence,* p. 524).

DISCUSSIONS. 191.1 Health and content.] When these words appeared in JMg set in small capitals and centered, Melville wrote on the galley proof, "This salutation [*written over an undeciphered erased word*] should be in Roman, and placed more to the left—pretty much as if it were 'My dear Sir' at the opening of any other epistle." By "Roman" Melville meant "lower-case roman except where explicitly upper-case"—that is, he wished to restore the reading in HM, the one retained here. Presumably he also wished to restore the non-indented position of the salutation in HM (since "My dear Sir" would normally be placed flush left), though the blue bracket he had added in the manuscript may (but need not) mean "indent." In any case his direction in JMg ("more to the left") is ambiguous, but the compositor evidently assumed that no indention was intended; in JMp and JM these words appear flush left, though still in large and small capitals and followed by a colon rather than a period.

191.21 alluvium,—] In revising his manuscript at stage C (see the textual notes below), Melville may have intended the dash to supersede the comma (as the JMg compositor apparently assumed), but he did not cancel the comma, and the comma-dash combination is not at all unusual in the manuscripts.

192.22 think] The comma following this word in JMg clarifies the sense; but it is clearly a compositorial insertion and is not adopted here, since there is no evidence that Melville regarded it as necessary.

192.27–28 *The . . . Grosvenor*] JMg omits the quotation marks that appear around this title (also underlined) in HM. Melville penciled, then erased, what seems to be "[*check mark*] use" beside this line in JMg, possibly to indicate that he considered restoring the manuscript's quotation marks, then decided not to. Because Melville seems to have considered the matter, and because in JMg he explicitly canceled the quotation marks around the same italicized title at 193.20– 21, NN adopts the reading in JMg here. (Cf. the discussion of ship names at 212.375.)

193.14 think,] The copy-text semicolon, which was appropriate punctuation in an earlier version of this complicated and much-revised sentence, obscures Melville's final meaning; NN adopts the comma in JMg (which was also the first manuscript reading) on the assumption that it coincides with Melville's final intention.

EMENDATIONS. 191.21 of . . . World's] JMg\HM; of HM 192.1 ay, first] JMg\HM; first HM 192.11 immoderately] JMg; immoderatly HM 192.14 enabling] JMg; ennabling HM 192.16 while] JMg\HM; tho' HM 192.17 plausible] HM\EM; plausable HM 192.20 inadmissible] JMg; inadmissable HM *192.27–28 ^*The . . . Grosvenor*^] JMg; "<u>The . . . Grosvenor</u>" HM 192.31 *Grosvenor's*] JMg; <u>Grosvonor's</u> HM 192.38 *"Man-before-the-Mast"*] NN; "<u>Man-before-the-^Mast</u>" HM 192.38 *Mast."*] JMg\HM; [*see textual notes for the complex passage that Melville revised and finally canceled*] HM 193.1 R.,] JMg; R.^ HM 193.5 penning] JMg\HM; inscrib- ing HM 193.6 any bestowment, say, or benefit] JMp\HM; the bestowment of a decoration HM 193.9 though] NN; tho' HM *193.14 think,] JMg; ~; HM 193.16 contemporary] JMg; contemproary HM 193.17 And] [*no paragraph*] JMg\HM; [*paragraph*] HM 193.17–18 And . . . recognition] JMg\HM; [*see textual notes for Melville's earlier inscription and revision*] HM 193.20–21 ^*The . . . Grosvenor*^] JMg\ HM; "<u>The Wreck of the Grosvonor</u>" HM 193.24 type] JMg\HM; type subject to any chance reader's eye HM 193.27 Health and Content] JMg\HM; health and content HM

TEXTUAL NOTES: INSCRIPTION STAGES. At least four stages of inscription-revision: A (nonextant pre-fair-copy stage); B (brown ink on thicker paper; leaf foliated in upper middle pencil sequence); Ca (tan-gray ink on thicker paper); Cb (tan-gray ink on leaves introduced after the upper middle pencil foliation sequence had been abandoned). The "praise" passage draft stage represented on superseded leaf 12 ("Orme" 7.verso) may be inferred to have occurred between stage Cb and Melville's galley-proof revision of that passage, but it could have occurred earlier.

TEXTUAL NOTES: SUBSTANTIVES. 191.0–5 *Inscription . . . and*] [*leaf 1(B)*] 191.0 *Inscription . . . W. C. R.*] HM2(C); Inscription Epistolary / to / W. Clark Russell HM1 191.1 Health and content] HM4(C); Health and well-being HM1; Health and [*undeciphered scratched-out word* {?happiness}] HM2; [*seven or more undeciphered*

erased words, with a stylized finger pointing to them, seem to be an alternative salutation]
HM3 191.2 stroll] HM2(C); stroll we took HM1 191.5–6 formulating . . . from]
[*leaf 2(Cab)*] 191.5 singular] HM2; peculiar HM1 191.6–10 certain . . . because]
[*leaf 2.patch(Caa)*] 191.7 his] HM1,HM3; his peculiar HM2 191.8 enabled . . . dis-
cern] HM2; discerned HM1 191.10 rare] HM4; precious bo [*?beginning of* boon]
HM→1; precious HM2; valuable HM3 191.10 hardly that;] HM2; no, HM1
191.10–14 I . . . his] [*leaf 3(B)*] 191.11 not] HM1,HM3; not at least [*?instinc-
tively*] HM2 191.12 and] HM1,HM3; or HM2 191.12 people] HM2; persons
HM1 191.12 consideration or regard] HM3(C); regard HM1; especial regard
HM2 191.14–16 natural . . . nativity] [*leaf 4.clip(B)*] 191.15 evince] HM1,HM3;
evince to the amiable HM2 191.17–20 But . . . if the] [*leaf 4(Ca)*] 191.17–20
But . . . if the] HM2(?C); [*as revision of text once following* milk . . . nativity *but
now scissored away, HM pencil-inscribed, partly lined-through, then erased* previously
known to {?many} {*then added, (without canceling* previously known to [?many]*)*,
to the [*undeciphered erased word*]} {*two undeciphered erased words, the second of which
is also lined-through*}, *but by* {?people *canceled and replaced by an undeciphered erased
word*} {?reputed}] HM1 191.18 any] HM2; the nearest HM1 191.18 the gentle-
man] HM2; him HM1 191.20–22 honest . . . observes] [*leaf 5(Bb)*] 191.20 mid-sea
brine] HM1,HM6; blue water [*?brine*] HM2; mid-sea [*?brine*] HM3; Blue Water
[*?brine*] HM4; [*?mid-sea Blue Water*] HM5 191.21 of . . . World's] JMg\HM;
of HM 191.21 alluvium,—such, say, as is] HM3(C); the alluvial[?,] discharged
HM1; alluvium, discharged, say, HM2(C) 191.22 observes;] HM2(C); says,
HM1 191.23–192.3 for . . . Jove] [*leaf 5.clip (Ba)*] 191.23 his parentage,] HM3(C);
and with a HM1; [*?and with his parentage,*] HM2 191.24 all] HM2(C); that
are HM1

192.1 ay, first] JMg\HM; in fact first HM1; first HM2(C) 192.1 life] HM3(?C);
this transitory sphere HM1; life and this transitory sphere HM2 192.1 here of]
HM2; of HM1 192.2 place] HM2,HM4; [*one or two undeciphered erased words—or
a compound word {?ending -shop}*] HM1; [*undeciphered variant for second undeciphered
erased word or second half of compound word*] HM3 192.4–8 Now . . . value] [*leaf
6(Ca)*] 192.6 for a sort of] HM1,HM3; for HM2 192.6 lacking more or less] HM4;
lacking HM1; a little lacking HM2; [*?more or less lacking*] HM?3 192.8 be]
HM2; upon the whole be HM1 192.8–10 the . . . little] [*leaf 6.clip(B)*] 192.8 the
man] [*along the top edge of the clip on leaf 6 are the undeciphered, erased vestiges of one
or more scissored-away words*] 192.10 a little] HM2(C); more or less HM1 192.10–11
that . . . in] [*leaf 7.clip 1(Ca)*] 192.11 in] [*along the bottom edge of the first clip on leaf 7
are the remains of two or more scissored-away words*] 192.11–13 him . . . our] [*leaf 7(Ca)*]
192.13 sharpening and] HM2; sharpening our HM→1 192.13 our] HM2(C); the
HM1 192.13–17 natural . . . big] [*leaf 7.clip 2(B)*] 192.13 natural] [*along the top edge
of the second clip on leaf 7 are the canceled, erased, undeciphered remains of two or three
mostly-scissored-away words*] 192.14 as . . . liberally] HM4(C); liberally HM1; by
the way liberally HM2; as [*eight or nine undeciphered erased words, some of which were
further revised*] HM3 192.16 while] JMg\HM; the one just broached, tho' HM1;
tho' HM2(C) 192.17–23 and . . . illusion] [*leaf 8(B)*] 192.17 bruited] HM,JMg\

HM; trusted JMg[*misreading*] 192.17 without] HM,JMg\HM2; [*undeciphered erased word*] JMg\HM1 192.17 fancifully plausible] HM3; certain taking HM1; plausible HM2 192.18 easy of belief] HM2; prodigals HM→1 [prodigals easy of belief *seems only a marginally possible reading*] 192.21 finding] [*above finding but perhaps having to do with* moonshine *in the preceding sentence is an undeciphered erased word or two* {?discovering}] 192.21 it] HM1,HM3; his theory HM2 192.23–28 of . . . Wreck] [*leaf 9(Cab)* {*no inscription except erased foliation*} *leaf 9.clip(Caa) of . . . Wreck*] 192.23 anything] HM2; everything HM1 192.24 that] HM2; and HM→1 192.24 his] HM1,HM3,HM5,HM7; our HM2,HM4; the HM?6 192.24–25 beloved country] HM1,HM8; [*from a mass of erased words the following probable and possible readings may be derived, some evidently entertained more than once, their sequence often problematic:*] America HM2,HM?6; beloved America HM?3; Great [*undeciphered erased word*] HM?4; Great Republic HM?5,HM?7 192.26 theory] HM4; theory in general, HM1; theory[,] my [?friend] HM2; theory here, HM3 192.27 a bit bluntly] HM3, bluntly HM1; a little bluntly HM2 192.27 The] HM3[*see also accidentals*]; your HM2; [?the] HM1 192.28–30 of . . . fleet] [*leaf 10(Bb)*] 192.28 crown] HM1,HM3; crown (if any such there be in reserve for the earner thereof HM2 [*the parenthetical phrase might otherwise be construed as having been considered to follow* literature *since HM only begins the phrase above* crown *but does not explicitly caret it in anywhere*] 192.30 flag-ship] HM2(C); flag-ship of the squadron, so to speak HM1 192.30 the fleet] HM2; all HM1 192.31–33 Upon . . . brine] [*leaf 11.clip(B)*] 192.31 Upon] [*to the left of line 31, at the top edge of the clip, circled for insertion in now-scissored-away text, is what seems to be either* leadership *or* leader *and one undeciphered erased word*] 192.31 first] HM1,HM3[*marked for restoration, but without having been explicitly canceled*]; [*scissored-away word*] HM2 192.33 brine] HM2(C); sea HM1 192.33–37 in . . . spirit] [*leaf 11(C)*] 192.36 ¹his] HM,JMg\HM; the JMg[*misreading*] 192.37–38 of . . . Mast] [*leaf 12(Bb) of . . . comprehend*] 192.38 Mast."] JMg\HM2; [*before finally canceling the passage, HM inscribed and revised as follows:*] On the part of the critics my countrymen this [*then an then* this] allusion to Dana closing their commendation of a foreign nautical author [*then* writer] by way, very likely, of putting what one may call <u>a crown on the</u> [*then* putting a <u>crown</u> on the *then(C)* <u>crowning</u> the] <u>wall-knot</u> of their praise. A rather venturesome [*then* A] figure of speech, but the significance whereof [*then* speech. But its significance speech whose significance *then* speech the significance whereof] the author of "<u>Forecastle Yarns</u>" will practically [*then* fully *then* practically] comprehend if not every yachtsman. [*then* <u>Yarns</u>," if not every yachtsman, will practically comprehend.] HM; [*the compositor followed copy, except in adding commas after* critics, countrymen, Dana, writer, *and* speech] JMg; [*the De Vinne reviewer inscribed a vertical wavy line in the right margin of the galley proof, a line accompanied by a circled question mark*] JMg\r; [*in the left and right margins of the galley, HM pencil-inscribed, then erased two dozen or more undeciphered words as possible revisions, before ink-canceling the passage*] JMg\HM1 192.38 Mast."] HM2 [*see following description of superseded inscription probably connected to matter on leaf 12; it is a reasonable though not necessary surmise that at an indeterminate point in the composing or revising of the "praise" passage—see the immediately preceding entry, but*

also cf. the variants described, below, for 193.17–18—HM pencil-inscribed, revised, then
canceled the following (for alternative surmises and transcriptions, see Freeman 1948, pp.
369–70; Leyda, Log, p. 799; Davis and Gilman, pp. 284, 378; NN Correspondence,
p. 500)] [?Superseded leaf 12 {"Orme" leaf 7 verso} Praise . . . countrymen &c]

Praise when merited is not a boon; [*or* boon:] yet to a generous nature, it is
pleasant to utter it. This pleasure have you [*then* you {?distinctly}] taken in
some [?magazine ?recent] articles [→*then* contributions] citing various [*then*
certain] marine authors of the past; [*or* past, *then* past;] and [*then* past—most
of them dead. *then* past— nearly all of them dead. *then* past—one or two
{*then* past—two} of them, I think, still living {*then* still surviving}][.] now
[*then, tacitly,* Now], have you bestowed in one [*then* an] instance that comes
a little near to me [*then* instance that touches near to me *then (though without*
canceling near to me) instance that touches me somewhat nearly].

You: You have [?esteemed ?estimated] [*then* have {?rendered}] at his
[?exceptional] worth, [*?then* have {?rendered}] as a [?serious] [?delineator]
of [*then* ?serious] and [?admirable] [?delineator] of the sea & the seaman
[→*then* {?admirable} {?maritime ?marine} {?delineator}], R H Dn, Jun
[*then* {?delineator} and made {*then* offered} a tribute &c {*then* a warm trib-
ute not less the [*then* none the less]} just, to R.H.D]

It is his countrymen [*or* countryman] &c

[both instances of &c implying one or more passages previously inscribed and into which
this present draft may be inserted as revision; the whole leaf is then canceled with an orange
X, and its other side used for "Orme"] HM1 192.39–40 Well . . . satisfaction] [*leaf*
12.clip(Ba)] 192.40 with what] HM2; with HM1 192.40–193.6 did . . . Inscription]
[*leaf 13(Ca)*] 192.40 did I] HM2; I HM1

193.1 W. C. R.] HM?2,HM7; W. Clark Russell HM1,HM?3,HM?5; [*?deco-*
rating plus at least two undeciphered erased words, though these words may be variants
of those described in the following entry for 193.2 colors] HM?4; [*two or more undeci-*
phered erased words, constituting at least one further variant reading] HM?6 193.2 colors]
HM1,HM4; colors in those [?letters] HM2; colors in those initials HM3 193.2
my] HM1,HM3; the HM2 193.2 fore.] HM5; fore—the mast of honor HM1;
[?mast— *or* ?foremast—][?the mast of honor] HM2,HM?4; [?foremast *or* ?mast]
here, the mast of honor HM3 193.2 embravened] HM2; adorned HM1 193.3 the
. . . spar] HM3; on a loftier spar the flag might be carried the higher HM1; on a
taller spar the flag more aloft might be carried HM2 193.5 penning] JMg\HM;
inscribing HM 193.6–8 imply . . . tempted] [*leaf 14.clip(?Ca)*] 193.6 any bestow-
ment, say, or benefit] JMp\HM3; the bestowment of a decoration HM,JMg\
HM3; the bestowment of a [*undeciphered erased word* {?largess}] JMg\HM?1; [*in the*
left margin of the galley are eight or nine words, constituting at least one variant reading]
JMg\HM2; [*fifteen or so undeciphered erased words at the bottom and five or so undeci-*
phered erased words at the top of page 5 of JMp constitute at least two and probably more
variant readings; the only readily decipherable words at the bottom of that page are any

(twice) and benefit] JMp\HM1,JMp\HM2 193.7 then, . . . should] HM2; then^
should I, sinner though I am, HM1 193.8–12 to repeat . . . nevertheless, in] [*leaf
14(Cb)*] 193.8 that divine apothegm,] HM2; a saying^ HM1 193.8 which, . . .
forever,] HM4; that^ HM1; that[?,] though it were repeated endlessly[?,] HM2;
which, though it were repeated forever, HM3 193.9 would] HM2,HM4; can
HM1; could HM3 193.9 stale—] HM5; stale, HM1; stale: namely, HM2,HM4;
stale[:] [*undeciphered erased word {?defined}*] HM3; stale: JMg 193.11–12 and . . .
nevertheless] HM2; nevertheless HM→1 193.12–16 one . . . contemporary praise]
[*leaf 15(Cab) {no substantive inscription preceding clip} leaf 15.clip(Caa)*] one . . . con-
temporary praise] 193.12 one] HM2; at least one HM1 193.13 province—and . . .
literature,] HM3; province, literature— HM1; province, that is to say, literature
HM2 193.14 ought] HM2; aught HM→1 193.14–15 the minor illusions,] HM6[*in
the area on leaf 15 where HM ink-inscribed* minor illusions *are also at least two unde-
ciphered erased words which may not constitute variants of this reading*]; the vanities^
HM1; the petty and the vain, HM2[*however, another and earlier possible reading might
be* the petty *(or pettier)* vanities^]; [?the] pettier delusions HM?3; [?the] illusions
HM?4; what prove minor illusions HM5 193.15 experience^] HM2; experience,
in his day, HM1 193.15 in] HM2; of HM1 193.17–18 And . . . recognition] [*leaf
16(Cbb)*] 193.17–20 And . . . recognition] JMg\HM3[*HM's* Strike out.*plus at least
eight undeciphered erased words in the right margin of the galley signal his intention to
delete the paragraph described here, below, and incorporate two new sentences into the pre-
ceding paragraph; the undeciphered erased words could be, in part, early versions of those
two sentences*]; [*the following paragraph (with revisions described) stands in the manuscript
and galley*] And such [*then* Such *then* And in general it may be said, {*JMg omits
the comma*} that such] praise, in however high a [*JMg omits* a] degree merited,
and coming from a competent source, though in the recipient it were a touch of
Malvolio [*JMg has* malvolio *which HM changes back to* Malvolio] loftily to regard
it as but his rightful due; yet in him from whom it [→*then* whom the praise]
proceeds, however generous the man [→*then cancel and reinscribe* man, *then (?later)
cancel* however . . . man,] it is no largess or gratuity, nor intended to be, but simply
a more eloquent form of recognition.] HM,JMg; And in JMg\HM→1[*probably
the beginning of an uncompleted variant reading begun by HM before he decided not to do
initial drafting of his paragraph's replacement sentence(s) on the galley proof itself*]; And
what, essentially, is such praise? Little else indeed than a more eloquent form of
recognition. JMg\HM2[*cf. also variants described, above, for 192.38*] 193.19–23 That
. . . determine] [*leaf 17(Cba)*] 193.24–27 Thus . . . Content] [*leaf 18 (Cba)* Thus
. . . content] 193.24 type] JMg\HM; type subject to any chance reader's eye HM
193.26–27 heart . . . world—] HM2; heart, HM→1

<small>TEXTUAL NOTES: ACCIDENTALS.</small> 191.0 *Inscription*] [*EM pencil-reinscribed the word
for clarity*] *191.1 Health and content.] HM; <small>HEALTH AND CONTENT.</small> [*small capitals
centered*] JMg; [*in JMg, HM penciled an asterisk above* <small>CONTENT</small> *and keyed to it the
instruction* This salutation should be in Roman, and placed more to the left—
pretty much as if it were "<u>My dear Sir</u>" at the opening of any other epistle] JMg\

HM; HEALTH AND CONTENT: [*larger and smaller capitals at the left margin*] JMp
191.2 Hilary] [*in galley proof, a display capital "H" takes up almost two line-spaces
vertically and as many letter-spaces as "along" in line 2; in page proof, the "H" becomes a
normal capital, "Hilary" is indented, and the first three lines of type are realigned*] 191.5
formulating] HM; formula-/ting JMp; formulat-/ing JM 191.6 generalised] HM;
generalized JMg 191.6 so^ . . . least^] HM; ~, . . . ~. JMg; ~, . . . ~, JMg\r 191.6–7
which^ . . . individuals^] HM; ~, . . . ~, JMg 191.9 Let] [*paragraph*] HM2; [*no
paragraph*] HM1 191.10 intellectual] HM2; intelectual HM1 191.10 that;] HM[*and
see substantives*]; ~, JMg 191.12 otherwise^ . . . people^] HM; ~, . . . ~, JMg 191.13
put,] HM,JMg\r; ~^ JMg 191.13 this.] HM2; ~: HM1 191.13 alone^] HM,JMg\r;
~, JMg 191.14 England^] HM; ~, JMg 191.15 through] HM\EM; thro' HM
191.15 evince,] HM2; ~^ HM1 191.15–16 something] HM2; something HM1
191.17 But] [*paragraph*] HM2; [*no paragraph*] HM1 191.17 hereof^] HM; ~, JMg
191.18 hand,] HM; ~^ JMg 191.19 W. C. R.] [*in JMp, HM called attention to the ini-
tials because poor inking made each period look like two dots*] 191.20 mid-sea brine] [*see
substantives*] 191.20 constituent,] HM2; ~^ HM1 *191.21 alluvium,—] HM; ~^—
JMg 191.21 alluvium . . . is] [*see substantives*] 191.22 Father of Waters] HM1,HM3;
Father of Waters HM2 191.22 observes;] [*see substantives*] 191.23 for^] HM; ~, JMg
191.23 Queen^—] HM; ~,— JM 191.23 home,] HM2[*accompanies substantive revi-
sion*]; ~^ HM1 191.24 English—] HM2; ~, HM1; ~,— JM 191.24 am] [*reinscribed
for clarity*] 191.24 birth-place] HM; birthplace JM

192.1 A] HM; a JMg 192.1 ay, first] [*see substantives*] 192.3 Jove!"] HM2; ~.^
HM1 192.4 Now] [*paragraph*] HM2; [*no paragraph*] HM1 192.4 Now^] HM; ~,
JM 192.4 bird,] HM,JMg\HM; ~^ JMg 192.5 sharing] HM2; shareing HM1
192.5 which^ with some^] HM; ~, ~ ~, JMg 192.7 that^] HM; ~, JMg 192.11
immoderately] JMg; immoderatly HM 192.11 him;] HM; ~, JM 192.11 knows?)^]
HM; ~?), JMg 192.12 business;] HM,JM; ~, JMg 192.14 enabling] JMg; enna-
bling HM[*but see enabled at 191.8*] 192.14 mortals (as . . . it)] HM4; ~, ~ . . . ~,
HM1,HM3; ~——~ . . . ~—— HM2 192.16 while,] JMg\HM; tho'^ HM1; tho',
HM2; though, HM\EM[*also see substantives*] 192.17 one,] HM2; ~^ HM1 192.17
plausible] HM\EM; plausable HM 192.18 belief] HM2; beleif HM→1 192.18
judgment] HM2[?EM]; judgement HM1 192.18–19 judgment^— . . . world^—]
HM; ~,— . . . ~,— JMg 192.18 though] HM\EM; tho HM 192.20 inadmis-
sible] JMg; inadmissable HM 192.20 philosophy,] HM; ~— JMg[*in JMg the De
Vinne reviewer also calls for the redivision of the word at the end of the line—from* phil-/
osophy *to* phi-/losophy] *192.22 think^] HM; ~, JMg 192.23 illusion] [*on leaf
9.clip, HM repeated his last word on leaf 8, then canceled the repetition*] 192.24 lus-
tre] HM; luster JMg\r 192.26 But, . . . theory,] HM2; ~^ . . . ~^ HM1[*also see
substantives*] 192.26 fact-wise;] HM2; ~^ HM1 192.27 alike,] HM2; ~^ HM?1
*192.27–28 ^The . . . Grosvenor^] JMg; "The . . . Grosvenor" HM 192.27 The]
HM2[*mending or altering*]; the HM?1[?*and not, at first, underlined*] 192.28 ^naval
crown^] HM1,HM3; "naval crown" HM2[*HM may also have considered single quo-
tation marks*] 192.29 hand;] HM2; ~, HM1 192.30 flag-ship;] HM; ~, JMg 192.30
name it,] HM2; ~ ~^ HM1,JMg 192.31 Grosvenor's] JMg; Grosvonor's HM 192.31

waters] HM1,HM3; <u>waters</u> HM2 192.33 effect:] HM2; ~[?.] HM?1 192.33 ^spit]
HM1,HM3; "~ HM2[*at the same time, HM may have underlined* spit *of the sea as well
as any further, now-scissored-away words; cf., below, 192.38* "Man-before-the-Mast"]
192.33 writer^] HM; ~, JMg 192.35 ²ship.] HM; ~? JMg 192.36 withal] HM2;
withall HM1 192.38 *"Man-before-the-Mast"*] NN; "<u>Man-before-the^Mast</u>" HM;
"*man^before^the^mast*" JMg; "*Man^before^the^Mast*" JMg\HM 192.38 *Mast."*] [*see
substantives*] 192.40 now^] HM; ~, JM

    193.1 Inscription] HM; inscription JMg 193.1 R.,] HM1,JMg; R.^ HM2[*HM
inadvertently omits the comma in ink-reinscribing his penciled revision*] 193.2 Would]
[*no paragraph*] HM2(C); [*paragraph*] HM1 193.4 recognising] HM; recognizing
JMg 193.5 such, that^] HM2; ~^ ~, HM1,JMg 193.6 Inscription] HM; inscription
JMg 193.7–8 benefit^— . . . implying^—] HM; ~,— . . . ~,— JMg 193.7 then,
. . . should] [*see substantives*] 193.8 apothegm,] [*see substantives*] 193.8 which, . . .
forever,] [*see substantives*] 193.9 stale—] [*see substantives*] 193.9 "It . . . receive."]
HM2[*see also next entry*]; ^It . . . receive.^ HM1 193.9 receive." And] JMp; ~".
And HM,JMg\HM; ~": and JMg 193.11–12 heart—and . . . mundane—] HM3;
~; ~ . . . ~; HM1; ~^ (~ . . . ~)— HM2; ~,—~ . . . ~,— JMg 193.13 province^—]
HM; ~,— JMg[*also see substantives*] 193.13 literature,] HM2; ~— HM1; ~,— JMg
*193.14 think,] HM1,JMg; ~— HM2; ~; HM3 193.15 illusions,] [*see substantives*]
193.15 experience^] [*see substantives*] 193.16 contemporary] JMg; contemporary
HM 193.17 And] [*no paragraph*] HM1,JMg\HM; [*paragraph*] HM2 193.17–18
And . . . recognition] [*see substantives*] 193.17 essentially] JMg\HM2; essentialy
JMg\HM→1 193.20–21 ^The . . . Grosvenor,^] JMg\HM; "<u>The Wreck of the
Grosvonor</u>", HM; "*The Wreck of the Grosvenor,*" JMg 193.21 who^] HM; ~, JM
193.26–27 heart . . . world—] [*see substantives*] 193.27 Health and Content] JMg\
HM; health and content HM

JOHN MARR (pp. 195–200)

DISCUSSIONS. 195.17 earth:—another] In his manuscript, Melville revised the
punctuation after "earth" from a period to the colon-dash. Though he did not
explicitly indicate the corresponding change of the capitalized "Another" into
lowercase, NN follows JMg in assuming that the change is tacitly directed.

    197.22 Siberian Obi] From mountains in the vicinity of Ust'-Kamenogorsk,
the Ob (or Obi) River curves northward some fifteen hundred miles, much
of it through Siberian swampy wasteland, before emptying into the Kara Sea
just east of Novaja Zemla. In *Clarel* (2.15.72–73), Mortmain invokes the Obi as
a wasteland. In his first version of this sentence, Melville had written "Sahara"
here.

    198.18 oak^groves] NN retains the unhyphenated copy-text reading, though
"oak-groves" appears in JMg at this point and the hyphen appears at 195.10 in
HM (and in JMg). It is not NN policy to impose consistency on hyphenation
(see p. 611 above).

198.30 above the yet taller grass] This phrase is unclear, since, if the grass is taller than the "ears of the team" they could not be seen above the grass. Something may have gone astray in the revision process, but no emendation is feasible.

199.1[*verse*] Since] In the manuscript, this line and lines 4 and 20 are indented; this line and line 4 are also marked with the blue bracket that Melville generally used to indicate the beginning of a stanza or verse-paragraph, but line 20 is not so marked. Because none of the other opening lines of verse-paragraphs in this poem is indented in the manuscript and because Melville did not alter the flush-left placement of lines 1, 4, and 20 in JMg, NN does not indent these lines.

199.24[*verse*] enfold] This word appears in JMp in place of "embrace" in HM and JMg. It seems clearly authorial, perhaps to avoid the repetition with "embracements" in line 28, and its presence suggests that Melville communicated with the printer after the galley proofs were returned.

EMENDATIONS. 195.0[*section-title*] JOHN MARR AND OTHER SAILORS] JMp2\HM; [*no section-title*] HM *195.17 another] JMg; Another HM 195.17 though] HM\EM; tho' HM 196.24 a] JMg\HM; an idle HM 196.26 ascetics . . . bias] JMg\HM; where inclination did not dictate it, ascetics by necessity HM 197.6 unresponsiveness] JMg; unresponsiness HM 197.19 though] HM\EM; tho' HM 197.30 expanse] JMg; expance HM 198.13 descendants] JMg; ?descendents HM 198.14 little] JMg\HM; nothing HM 198.25 voluminous] JMg\HM; narrower mad HM 198.26 first] JMg; frist HM 198.31 Luxuriant] JMg; Lururiant HM 198.34 Though] HM\EM; Tho' HM 198.35 'the] HM\EM; he HM 198.39 semblance] HM\EM; semblence HM 198.39 mute] HM\EM; muti HM [*Prose:*] 199.2 passionately] JMg; passionatly HM 199.5 silence:—] JMg\HM; ~.— HM [*Verse:*] *199.1,4,20 Since/Once/Like] [*no indent*] JMg; [*indent*] HM 199.18 staling] NN; staleing HM *199.24 enfold] JMp; embrace HM 200.53 where^] JMg\HM; ~, HM

TEXTUAL NOTES: INSCRIPTION STAGES. At least five stages of inscription-revision: A (nonextant pre-fair-copy stage); B (blue ink on thicker leaves foliated in upper middle pencil sequence); Ca (brown ink on thicker, darker paper); Cb (brown ink on generally thinner, lighter paper); D (gray ink).

TEXTUAL NOTES: SUBSTANTIVES. 195.0[*section-title*] JOHN MARR AND OTHER SAILORS] JMp2\HM[*to JMp2's all-capitals* JOHN MARR *HM adds and double-underlines* And other Sailors]; [*no section-title or section-title page*] HM,JMg,JMp1; JOHN MARR. [*on section-title page*] JMp2; JOHN MARR [*large capitals*] / AND OTHER SAILORS [*small capitals*] [*on section-title page, but not included as section-title in table of contents*] JM 195.0–6 John . . . seafarer] [*leaf 1(Cb)*] 195.0 *John Marr*] [*no subtitle present*] HM1,HM4; (Introductory to [?the sketch following].) HM2; (A sketch introductory to the Piece next following) HM3 195.2 sailor] HM1,HM3; sailor in various services HM2(D) 195.3 flags] HM1,HM3;

flags and in various services HM2 195.3 from] HM1,HM3; for HM2 195.3 life by a crippling] HM4; service by a HM1; service by a crippling HM2; activity by a crippling HM3 195.7–10 After . . . oak-groves] [*leaf 2.clip(Ca)*] 195.9 settles down] HM1,HM3; settles HM2 195.9 1838] HM1,HM3; 1835 HM2 195.10–12 and . . . marries] [*leaf 2(Cb)*] 195.11 one] HM2; an HM→1 195.11 our] HM2; the HM1 195.12 putting . . . to] HM2; ending HM1 195.13–20 Ere . . . form] [*leaf 3(Ca)*] 195.14 sallow] HM2; yellow HM1 195.14 was . . . in] HM4; was shown in HM1; was shown after a certain interval in HM2; was [*undeciphered scratched-out word or beginning of word*] HM→3 195.15 too many] HM?2,HM5(D); most HM1,HM?4; many HM?3 195.16 hands] HM2; hands for the occasion HM1 195.16 they are committed] HM1,HM3,HM5; he commits them HM2,HM4 195.16 with] HM2; back with HM1 195.17 to the] HM1,HM3; to HM2 195.17 small] HM2; little HM1 195.18 nor] HM,JMp\HM; not JMg[*misreading*] 195.21–24 With . . . be] [*leaf 4.clip(Ca)*] 195.21 swarthy, and] HM2(D); swarthy, HM1 195.22 with] HM1,HM3; and HM2 195.23 man] HM1,HM3,HM5; [?wight] HM2,HM4 195.23 had] HM1,HM3; has HM2 195.24 could] HM1,HM3; can HM2 195.24–196.1 dislodged . . . family-tie] [*leaf 4(Cb)*] 195.24 dislodged . . . object] HM1,HM5; ?dislodged HM?2; ?dislodged or transferred HM?3; ?dislodged or transferred to a substituted object HM?4 195.25 resolves] HM1,HM4(D); silently resolves HM2(D); resolves in his undivulged heart HM3(D)

196.1 beings . . . family-tie] HM7(D); beings he had ever known connected [*then (?immediately) add* with] him by family-tie HM?→1,HM2; beings he had ever known connected with him [*or* beings ever connected with him] by [*then* by sacxxx {?sacred} *then* by true *then* by] love and the family-tie HM3(D),HM4(D),HM5(D),HM6(D) 196.1–9 His . . . helpfulness] [*leaf 5(Cb)*] 196.2 new-comer, one . . . it,] HM2(D); new-comer^ HM1 196.2 dwells] HM3(D); boards HM1; lives HM2 196.5–6 Fain . . . social] HM3(D),HM7(D); Fain would the widower cultivate HM1; Fain would he cultivate HM2; Fain, if possible, in the isolation that now [?was] his would he fill that void by cultivating social HM?4(D); Fain in the [*then* this] spiritual isolation now his would he fill that void by cultivating social HM?5(D),HM?6(D) 196.6 yet nearer] HM2(D); nearer HM1 196.8 hardships] HM2(D); condition HM1 196.9 reciprocal] HM2(D); mutual HM1 196.9 helpfulness] HM2; help HM→1 196.9–16 a matter . . . communion] [*leaf 6(D)*] 196.10 is] HM2; was HM1 196.12 real] HM2; common HM1 196.12 But, whether] HM?2[*perhaps* whether *was inadvertently omitted at first*]; But HM?→1 196.16 to . . . communion.] HM4,HM6; for the most part the basis of sympathetic communion with men of the p [→*then* with practical men. {→*then* with practical natures.}] HM→1,HM→2,HM3; at least to most practical natures, the basis of sympathetic communion HM5 196.17–19 But . . . kind] [*leaf 7(D)*] 196.17 these] HM,JMg\HM; those JMg[*misreading*] 196.17–18 Their . . . helm] HM3; <u>They</u> had ploughed the land; <u>he</u> had furrowed the waters [*then* sea]. HM1,HM2 196.19–20 and . . . globe] [*leaf 7.clip 1(Cb)*] 196.20–22 So . . . hereditary] [*leaf 7.clip 2(Ca)*] 196.22–27 tillers . . . religious] [*leaf 8(D)*] 196.22 hearsay]

HM3; here HM→1; hear HM→2[*inscribed over* here] 196.23 through . . . to them-
selves] HM2; to themselves [*uncompleted; immediately canceled*] HM→1 196.24 a]
HM2,JMg\HM; an unheeded HM1; an idle HM3 196.26 ascetics . . . bias] JMg\
HM; where inclination did not dictate it, ascetics by necessity HM 196.27–30
They . . . cheap] [*leaf 8.clip(Ca)*] 196.28 a man] HM2(D); one HM1 196.30–38
recreation . . . mariner] [*leaf 9(Ca)*] 196.32–33 That something] HM2(D); It HM1
196.33 geniality] HM1,HM3; cordiality HM2 196.33 life] HM1,HM3; the heart
HM2 196.33–34 some . . . less] HM4; [*undeciphered scratched-out word {?taking}*] joy
in it HM1; some vital sense of joy in it HM2; more or less of vital joy in it HM3
196.34 This] HM1,HM3; This geniality HM2 196.35 malaria . . . came] HM2;
malaria HM1 196.38 lone-hearted mariner] HM2(D); mariner HM1 196.38–40
seek . . . enough] [*leaf 10(D)*] 196.38–39 seek . . . theirs] HM2; try to interest them
HM1(Ca) 196.40 from] HM2; from their HM→1[*?a transcriptional slip*]

197.1–3 he . . . elderly] [*leaf 10.clip 1(Ca)*] 197.2 proceed] HM2; go on HM→1
197.3–5 man . . . here] [*leaf 10.clip 2(Cb)*] 197.3 man—a blacksmith] HM6(Cb);
man HM1(Ca); ?and most respectable man HM?2(Cab)[*and yet another reading may
have intervened between the ones here designated as occurring at stages Ca and Cab*]; [?and
most respectable] man, a blacksmith, HM?3(Cb),HM5(Cb); [?and most respect-
able] man, a farmer HM4(Cb) 197.3 Sunday] HM2; some Sunday HM1 197.4
earnest] HM2[*if* religious *was immediately canceled*],HM5(D); earnest religious
HM?→1; strict [?religious] HM3; staid [?religious] HM4 197.6–10 Such . . . prai-
rie] [*leaf 11.clip(Ca)*] 197.6 one's fellow creatures] HM2; men HM1 197.7 vocation]
HM3; primitive p HM→1; primitive vocation HM2 197.7 little helped] HM3;
not facilitated HM→1; not helped HM2 197.9 the . . . Nature] HM2,HM4;
Nature HM1; the strange apathy of Nature HM3 197.9 on a] HM2,HM5; in a
HM→1; [*three or four undeciphered erased words, constituting at least two variant read-
ings*] HM3,HM4 197.9–10 prairie] HM1,HM3; soil HM2 197.10–11 where . . .
mark] [*leaf 11(Cb)*] 197.11 mark.] HM3(D); mark, and that not distinguishable
at a glance. HM1; mark,[*and, perhaps, at this time an opening parenthesis was sub-
stituted for the comma*] and that not distinguishable at HM→2[*uncompleted revision*]
197.12–19 The . . . main] [*leaf 12(Ca)*] 197.12 all but exterminated] HM3; among
the last organised defenders upon principle of their native soil—all but exter-
minated HM1; inated HM→2[*result of inadvertently excessive cancellation*] 197.13
recent and final war] HM5(D); x HM→1[*undeciphered scratched-out letter(s)*]; final
war HM2,HM?4(D); war HM3(D) 197.13–14 troops . . . rights] HM2(D); troops
HM1 197.18 these . . . pastures] HM4(D); the great natural pasture HM1; [?the
?these] [?great] natural pastures HM2; [?the ?these] [?great] aboriginal pastures
HM3 197.19–22 a race . . . prairie-hen] [*leaf 13(Cb)*] 197.19 distinct] HM2(D); par-
tially distinct HM1 197.20 advance-guard] HM2; advanced HM→1 197.21–22
the Siberian Obi] HM5(D); Sahara HM1; Obi HM2; the sands of Obi HM3; the
wastes of Obi HM4[*and two circled, undeciphered erased words may constitute an earlier
variant reading for this passage*] 197.22–26 sometimes . . . few] [*leaf 13.clip(Ca)*] 197.22
startled] HM2(D); startled into visibility [*earlier spelled* visability] HM1 197.23
rank] HM5; jungles of tall HM1; [*at least five undeciphered erased words, constituting*

perhaps more than one reading] HM2; [*undeciphered scratched-out word*] HM3; jungles of [?rank] HM4 197.25 these . . . underwood] HM3; these HM1; these[,] there being no woods—[*undeciphered erased word {?woods}*] with underwood HM2 197.27–33 Blank . . . scene] [*leaf 14.clip(Ca)*] 197.27 unbroken . . . prairie] HM2; unbroken HM1 197.28 a] HM1,HM3; some HM2 197.28 companionless] HM2; lonely HM1 197.29 immense] HM2(D); vast HM1 197.30 bounded . . . and] HM2(D); and HM1 197.31 alert . . . ears,] HM3(D); eyes and ears like his HM1; eyes and ears, like his, HM2(D) 197.31 at all] HM2,HM4; all HM→1; [*one or two undeciphered erased words*] HM3 197.33–35 quite . . . ocean] [*leaf 14(Cb)*] 197.33 quite at] HM2; wholly x[*undeciphered beginning of uncompleted word*] HM→1 197.34 rim] HM2(D); horizon HM1 197.34 Marr] HM2(D); Marr—as has just been intimated— HM1 197.36–198.1 With . . . prairie-schooner] [*leaf 15.clip(Da)*] 197.36 some] HM2; certain HM1 197.37 last . . . removal] HM5; last removal HM→1; last and distant removal HM2; last and remotest removal HM3; last and remoter removal HM4 197.39 other settlers] HM2; the rest HM1 197.39–40 quite . . . from] HM3; excepting, indeed, HM1; [?quite cut off] except[?,] indeed[?,] from HM2 197.40 grassy billows] HM2; billows of grass HM1

198.1–3 the vernacular . . . champaign] [*leaf 15(Db)*] 198.2 arched] HM2; [?lo*(uncompleted word)*] HM→1 198.2–3 sail-cloth . . . champaign] HM4(Dc); sail-cloth HM1; sail-cloth, and voyaging across the [*two undeciphered erased words, successive variants*] champaign HM2(Dc),HM3(Dc) 198.3–6 There . . . advance] [*leaf 16(Dc)*] 198.4 receptive box] HM2; box HM1 198.4 leathern] HM; leather JMg 198.4–5 at . . . stake] HM2; on a stout stake at con[*uncompleted variant reading*] HM→1 198.5–6 affording . . . which] HM2; and which affording a perch for birds HM→1 198.6–9 of the . . . but the] [*leaf 17.clip(Ca)*] 198.7 monument] HM2(D); land-mark HM1 198.9 but the] HM2; for HM→1 198.9–12 ocean . . . and] [*leaf 17(D)*] 198.11 over-opulent;] HM4; over-rich^ HM→1; over-affluent[?^] and HM→2; over-affluent; HM3 198.11 sweeping plains] HM3; plains HM1; wide plains HM2 198.11 fenced off] HM2; fenced all ove[*uncompleted variant reading*] HM→1 198.12 pale] HM3; both HM1; luxurious HM2 198.12–17 hale . . . road] [*leaf 18(D)*] 198.12 hale farmers] HM2; farmers HM1 198.14 little] JMg\HM; nothing HM 198.15 of this] HM2[*HM did not ink in of when he initially inscribed leaf 18, but (?soon) toward the bottom of that leaf penciled and erased of this prairie and two or three undeciphered words*]; this HM1 198.16 with] HM,JMp2\HM2; by JMp1\HM,JMp2\HM1 198.16 said] HM1,HM3; said of it HM2 198.17–23 To . . . as] [*leaf 19(Da)*] 198.18 oak groves] HM3; wx[*uncompleted word*] HM→1; groves HM2 198.19 recent] HM2; the HM1 198.20 In early] HM2; At HM1 198.20 even going but] HM4; even in but going HM1; even going HM2; ?going but HM?3 198.21 log-encampment] HM2; encampment HM1 198.21 a] HM2; in instances a HM1 198.21 journey, . . . be,] HM2; journey^ HM1; journey^ . . . be^ JMg 198.23 graduated swells] HM2; swells HM1 198.24–26 those . . . advancing] [*leaf 19.patch(Db)*] 198.24–26 those . . . either] HM2(Db); [*see following description of stage Da text superseded and covered over by stage Db patch*] those of ocean becalmed after a West Indian hurricane [*then* after gales *then* after a prolonged West Indian hurricane *or* after prolonged gales *then* after a West Indian hurricane], one would catch the first indication of advancing strangers, either [*then cancel with blue pencil and cover over with stage Db patch*] HM1 198.25 voluminous] JMg\HM; narrower mad HM 198.26–29 strangers . . . that] [*leaf 20(Db)*] 198.27 of] HM2; arch over HM1 198.28 the wagon itself] HM2; itself HM1 198.28 wading through] HM3; hidden by HM1; hidden [*plus one or two undeciphered erased words*] HM2 198.28 vegetation . . . it] HM2; vegetation HM1 198.29–31 when . . . its] [*leaf 20.clip 1(Da)*] 198.29 team] HM2; horses HM→1 198.31–34 denizen . . . Marr's] [*leaf 20.clip 2(Ca)*] 198.34–199.2 shipmates . . . yearns] [*leaf 21(Ca)*] 198.34 have departed life,] HM2(D); be gone^ HM1 198.35 like] HM2(D); as HM1 198.35 'the] HM\ EM; he HM[*pen slip*] 198.35 As] HM1,HM3; And, as HM2 198.36 environment] HM1,HM3(D); alien environment HM2(D) 198.39 dim] HM2(D); pale HM1 198.39 lit] HM4; irradiated HM1; lighted HM2; illumed HM3

[*Prose:*] 199.3–5 He . . . silence] [*leaf 22(Da)*] 199.3 these] HM,JMg\HM; those JMg[*misreading*] 199.5 silence:—] [*no following prose; see also accidentals*] HM2; [*see following description of superseded text:*] [*indent*] But enough; this outlined sketch being [*then* this sketch] sufficiently indicates the ground of the Piece next following. [*then cancel with pencil, blue pencil, and by covering over with patch*] HM1

[*Verse:*] 199.1–8 Since . . . rung] [*leaf 22.patch(Db)*] 199.6 Striking] HM3; Singing HM1; [*undeciphered erased word—perhaps* Striking] HM2 199.9–19 Taking . . . young] [*leaf 23(B)*] 199.10 world] HM4(C); [*undeciphered scratched-out word {?sphere}*] HM1; [*undeciphered erased word {?globe}*] HM2; [*undeciphered erased word*] HM3 199.12 held] HM,JM\HM; hold JMg[*misreading*] 199.17 strung] HM2; [?flung ?sprung] HM→1[*?inadvertent mistranscription*] 199.20–200.31 Like . . . ashore] [*leaf 24(B)*] 199.20 tides] HM,JMg\HM; tide JMg[*misreading*] 199.21 or] HM1,HM3; ye HM2 *199.24 enfold] JMp; embrace HM 199.28 embracements] HM2; ?embracement HM?1

200.31 Lodged] HM3(D); Flung HM1; [*undeciphered erased word*] HM2 200.31 flinging] HM5(D); fateful HM1; [*undeciphered erased word {?flying}*] HM2; [*undeciphered erased word*] HM3; [*undeciphered erased word*] HM4 200.32–39 Nor . . . sea] [*leaf 25.clip(B)*] 200.32 in eve's decline] HM5(D); [*three undeciphered scratched-out words*] HM1,HM3; in [?time] [?benign] HM2; at eve's decline HM4 200.33 Your shadowy fellowship] HM3(D); Your mute companionship HM1; What sea-companionship HM2 200.34 Ye float] HM2(D); Float HM1 200.36 man's] HM2(D); the HM1 200.38 dear] HM3(D); clear HM1; near HM2 200.39 China's] HM1,HM4; Java's HM?2; yet the HM?3 200.40–43 Whither . . . prevails] [*leaf 25(D)*] 200.42 Competing still, ye] HM4; Striving vieing HM1; Striving= vieing HM2; Competing [*one or two undeciphered erased words*], ye HM3 200.42 huntsman-whalers] [*along the right edge of the clip above appears HM's penciled and erased* n whalers *the rest scissored away*] 200.44–55 And . . . sleep] [*leaf 26(D)*] 200.47 Foemen] HM2; The foeman HM1 200.53 where long watch-below] JMg\HM; where, deep down, your watch HM1; where, long watch-below HM2 200.56–62 And . . . again] [*leaf 27(B)*] 200.56 trumps] HM1,HM3; drums HM2 200.61 To . . . main] HM6(D); [*no text-line present*] HM1; To hear you at the halyards main

HM2(C); [*now or before stage C, as possible ink inscription of the variant just described* (*To* hear you at the halyards main*) or as revision of line 61 or line 62, HM tried at least three readings, many of the words of which are hard to decipher with any certainty; in one of these three readings probably stand the words* in the halyards *and another ends with* halyards again *followed by a parenthetical question mark, presumably querying it as a possible revision; the word* shroud{s} *may also appear in one or both of these readings; a third reading would have ended* in the flesh again] HM?3,HM?4,HM?5 200.62 chorus] HM2(D); voices HM1

TEXTUAL NOTES: ACCIDENTALS 195.0[*section-title*] JOHN MARR AND OTHER SAILORS] [*see substantives*] 195.1 century] HM; cen-/tury JMg; cent-/ury JM 195.5 There, too,] HM2; ~^ ~^ HM1 195.6 seafarer] HM; sea=farer JMg 195.7 After] [*paragraph*] HM2; [*no paragraph*] HM1 195.8 he, finally,] HM2; ~^ ~^ HM1 195.9 capacity,] HM2; ~^ HM1 195.10 frontier-prairie^] HM; ~, JMg 195.12 Here,] HM2; ~^ HM1 195.16 coffin^ . . . hands^] HM; ~, . . . ~, JMg 195.17 meagre] HM; meager JMg 195.17 earth:—] HM2; ~.^ HM1; ~^— JMg *195.17 another] JMg; Another HM 195.17 though] HM\ EM; tho' HM 195.18 Mound-Builders] HM; mound-builders JMg 195.21 mien;^] HM3(?D); ~:— HM1; ?~—: HM2; ~^— JMg 195.21 swarthy,] HM; ~^ JMg 195.21 black-browed;] HM2; ~, HM1,JMg 195.22 flash,] HM2; ~^ HM1 195.23 melancholy] HM2; melancholly HM1 195.23 depth,] HM1,HM3; ~— HM2,JMg 195.24 dislodged,] HM2; ~^ HM1,JMg 195.25 middle^life^] HM; ~-~, JMg

196.1 family-tie] HM; ~^~ JMg 196.2 new-comer, one . . . it,] [*see substantives*] 196.4 While] [*paragraph*] HM2; [*no paragraph*] HM1 196.6 before,] HM; ~^ JMg 196.7 sharing] HM2; shareing HM1 196.7 end—] HM2; ~?. HM?→1 196.8 hardships^] HM; ~, JMg 196.13 can not] HM; cannot JMg 196.13 present; much less,] HM; ~, ~ ~^ JMg 196.14 past;] HM; ~, JMg 196.15–16 supplies, . . . natures,] HM; ~^ . . . ~^ JMg 196.18 plough-tail,] HM; plow-tail, JMg 196.19 kind^] HM2; ~; HM1 196.20 checkered] HM2,[?HM\EM]; checcquered HM1 196.21 sympathy,] HM2; ~^ HM1 196.23 now, . . . removal,] HM; ~^ . . . ~^ JMg 196.24 rumor^] HM,JMg\HM; ~, JMg 196.28 fashion. But] HM; fashion; but JMg 196.29 but] HM[*EM reinscribed for clarity*] 196.29 to] HM2; x [*beginning of undeciphered letter*] HM→1 196.34 it,] HM2[*see substantives*]; ~. HM1 196.35 malaria,] HM2[*accompanies substantive revision*]; ~; HM1; ~— JMg; ~,— JM 196.35 came;] HM; ~— JMg; ~,— JM

197.1 picture;] HM; ~, JMg 197.2 himself,] HM2; ~^ HM?1,JMg 197.2 silent;] HM2; ~, HM?1,JMg 197.3 man—] [*see substantives*] 197.4 exhorter,] HM1,HM3; ~— HM2,JMg 197.6 unresponsiveness] JMg; unresponsiness HM 197.6 fellow^creatures] HM; ~-~ JMg 197.7 vocation— . . . machinery—] HM2; ~, . . . ~, HM1 197.8–9 Nature . . . Nature] HM,JMp\HM; nature . . . nature JMg 197.10 Mound-Builders] HM; mound-builders JMg 197.11 mark.] [*see substantives*] 197.12 The] [*paragraph*] HM2; [*no paragraph*] HM1 197.14 rights,] HM; ~— JMg 197.15 Mississippi;—] HM2 ~;^ HM1; ~^— JMg 197.15 then] HM2(D);

[*not underlined*] HM1 197.16 states] HM2; States HM1,JMg 197.17 herds,] HM2; ~^ HM1 197.19 though] HM\EM; tho HM 197.22 startled] [*see substantives*] 197.25 these— . . . underwood—] HM2; ~, . . . ~, HM?1 197.26 few.] HM2; ~^ HM1 197.27 Blank] [*paragraph*] HM2; [*no paragraph*] HM1 197.28 sea^] HM; ~, JMg 197.28 sailor—no geologist—] HM2; ~, ~ ~, HM1 197.30 expanse] JMg; expance HM 197.31 that,] HM2(D); ~^ HM1 197.31 alert . . . ears,] [*see substantives*] 197.33 But] [*paragraph*] HM2; [*no paragraph*] HM1 197.34 Marr^] [*see substantives*] 197.38 correspondence] HM; corres-/pondence JMg; corre-/spondence JMG/r 197.39 sort,] HM; ~^ JMg 197.39–40 quite . . . from] [*see substantives*] 197.39 ²off^] HM; ~, JMg

198.1 prairie-schooner;] HM3; ~, HM?1; ~—[*or comma-dash*] HM2; ~— JMg 198.1 term^ . . . times^] HM; ~, . . . ~, JMg 198.2 sail-cloth,] HM; ~^ JMg 198.3 post-office; as yet,] HM; ~^ ~ ~; JMg 198.4 hinges^] HM; ~, JMg 198.5 intervals,] HM; ~^ JMg 198.6 birds;] HM; ~, JMg 198.7 monument,] HM3; land-mark^ HM1; land-mark, HM2 198.8 civilized] HM2; civilised HM1 198.10 Throughout] [*no paragraph*] HM2; [*paragraph*] HM1 198.10 plains,] HM2; ~^ HM1 198.10–11 over-populous . . . over-opulent] HM; overpopulous . . . overopulent JMg; [*in the left margin of JMg, HM penciled two check marks with a hyphen between them*] JMg\HM 198.11 over-opulent;] [*see substantives*] 198.11 plains,] HM2; ~^ HM1 198.12 farms—] HM2; ~^ HM1[*HM left a large space for future punctuation when he inscribed the leaf*] 198.12 alike, in part,] HM2; ~^ ~ ~^ HM1 198.13 descendants] JMg; ?descendents HM 198.14 man,] HM2; ~^ HM1 198.15 world;^] HM; ~;— JMg 198.17–18 traveller,] HM; traveler^ JMg *198.18 oak^groves] HM; ~-~ JMg 198.18 apart^] HM; ~, JMg 198.18 varying] HM,JMg\r; varrying JMg 198.18 compass] HM2; compas HM1 198.19 separate,^] HM,JM; ~,— JMg 198.21–22 next— . . . day—] HM; ~, . . . ~, JMg 198.21 journey, . . . be,] [*see substantives*] 198.23 long^ green^] HM; ~, ~, JMg 198.24 subduing] HM2[?\EM]; subdueing HM1 198.24 tranquility] HM; tranquillity JM 198.25 voluminous] HM; vol-/uminous JMg; vo-/luminous JM 198.25 previous;] HM; ~, JMg 198.26 first] JMg; frist HM 198.26 strangers,] HM; ~^ JMg 198.27–28 wagon,— . . . it,—] HM2[*the comma in the second comma-dash gets covered over by a caret as HM inserts his substantive revision*]; ~,^ . . . ~,^ HM1,JMg 198.28 vegetation,] HM; ~^ JMg 198.28 or,] [*in both states of page proof, HM drew attention to the looseness of the comma in the forme*] 198.30 tiger-lilies] HM2; Tiger-lilies HM1 198.31 Luxuriant] [*paragraph*] HM2; [*no paragraph*] HM1 198.31 Luxuriant] JMg; Lururiant HM 198.31 Luxuriant^] HM; ~, JMg 198.31 wilderness. But^] HM; wilderness; but, JMg 198.32 world, . . . sight,] HM2(D); ~^ . . . ~^ HM1; ~^ . . . ~, JMg 198.34 Though] [*paragraph*] HM2; [*no paragraph*] HM1 198.34 Though] HM\EM; Tho HM 198.34 life,] [*see substantives*] 198.35 As] [*see substantives*] 198.37 next] HM[*EM reinscribed for clarity*] 198.38 losing] HM2; loseing HM1 198.39 semblance] HM\EM; semblence HM 198.39 mute] HM\EM; muti HM[*pen slip*] 198.39 life. And] HM; life; and JMg

[*Prose:*] 199.2 passionately] JMg; passionatly HM 199.3 He] [*no line-space precedes*] HM; [*line-space*] JMp 199.3 ones,^ striving,] HM; ~,^ ~— JMg; ~,—~^ JMg\r; ~,—~, JM 199.4 ¹them;] HM; ~, JMg 199.5 silence:—] JMg\HM; ~.^ HM1,JMg; ~.— HM2[*also see substantives*]

[*Verse:*] 199.1 Since] [*HM penciled, then erased two check marks and a parenthetical* Use {*undeciphered erased word*} type here *just preceding the first manuscript verse-line; then, in galley proof, following the end of the prose introduction, he penciled* To the Printer: Some space should be left between the prose & verse] *199.1,4,20 Since/Once/Like] [*no indent*] JMg; [*indent*] HM 199.3 ago?] HM2; ~. HM1 199.7 cheerly,] [*an inky fingerprint has smudged HM's comma and any revisions he may have made of it*] 199.8 ¹storm:—] HM3; ~,^ HM1; ~^— HM2,JMg 199.8 ²storm!] HM2; ~, HM1 199.8 rung.] HM2; ~; HM1 199.9 merely,^] HM1,HM3; ~,— HM2 199.10 Child-like^] HM2; ~, HM1 199.10 spanned;] HM2; ~. HM1 199.12 hand:] HM3; ~. HM1; ~:— HM2; ~— JMg 199.20 Like] [*no line-space precedes*] HM2; [*line-space; at first tacit, perhaps, concealed by line 20 beginning on a new leaf; then penciled in by bracketed direction*] HM1 199.21 me;] HM2; ~, HM1,JMg 199.24 dream!] HM2; ~. HM1

200.29 gulf-weed] HM?2,HM4; Gulf-Weed HM1,HM?3 200.30 more,] HM2; ~^ HM1 200.31 ashore?] HM2; ~. HM1 200.34 me,] HM2; ~^ HM1 200.34 feature:—] HM3; ~^^ HM?1; ~,^ HM2 200.35 curled;] HM3; ~[?,] HM1; ~— HM2 200.42 Competing still, ye] [*see substantives*] 200.53 where long watch= below] [*see substantives*] 200.55 sleep;] HM; ~, JMg 200.56 call,] HM2; ~^ HM1 200.60 It] [*no line-space precedes*] HM2; [*line-space*] HM1 200.60 retain;] HM3; ~— HM1; ~! HM2

BRIDEGROOM DICK (pp. 201-13)

Dick's feelings are similar to those expressed by the supposed "Englishman of the old order" in "The Temeraire" (pp. 41–43 above) and the speaker in "The Cumberland" (pp. 37–38 above). The historical events that prompt each of these poems are mainly those of March 8 and 9, 1862—the *Virginia/Merrimac* easily destroying the *Cumberland* and the *Congress* on the eighth, then battling the *Monitor* to an inconclusive but epoch-marking draw on the ninth. In "Bridegroom Dick," Melville refers not only to well-known American naval heroes of the "Heart-o'-Oak" days (line 77), but also, partly disguising them, to some less well known heroic figures from his personal experience of the U.S. Navy—officers and men on board the *United States* during his enlistment in 1843–44 and his naval officer–cousin Guert Gansevoort (1812–68). (The galley and page proofs of this poem are illustrated on pp. 555 and 562 above.)

DISCUSSIONS. 201.0 *Bridegroom Dick*] In the manuscript, Melville did not hyphenate this name here and in lines 39 and 67, but he did use a hyphen at a later inscription-revision stage (D) in line 17. Though JMg imposed consistency by omitting the hyphen in line 17, it is not NN policy to do so, since there is no evidence that Melville was attempting to achieve some consistency in his treatment of the name.

201.5 "Feel] NN follows JMg in supplying the opening quotation marks. Though Melville scratched out the opening quotation marks in the manuscript, he did not delete the closing quotation marks at the end of the line, and his final intention seems indistinguishable from that in line 265, where his omission of opening quotation marks was clearly inadvertent.

201.7 sixty-five] NN follows JMg in adding a hyphen, since Melville's usual practice was to hyphenate spelled-out numbers.

201.18 Bob o' Linkum] The *Dictionary of American English* lists this form among the variants of "bobolink."

202.26 Joan, if Darby] "The Happy Old Couple" in an eighteenth-century ballad attributed by some to Matthew Prior, but usually to Henry Woodfall, who served an apprenticeship to printer John Darby, of Bartholomew Close. Melville also refers to this couple in *Omoo* (chap. 67) and *Mardi* (chap. 23).

202.56 Chock-a-Block] Lieutenant Chock-a-Block is one of the figures in the poem who may possess, at least vaguely, some of the aspects of the life of Guert Gansevoort, Melville's cousin, whose promotion to captain, for example, also "lagged" (line 65) till at the age of fifty he was assigned to command the brand new *Adirondack* in 1862 (and in six more years he would be "chock-fast to death's black dock" [line 63]). (See also the discussions at 202.61, 203.82, and 207.212 below.)

202.61 Dainty Dave . . . navy-roll] Howard P. Vincent (1947, p. 470) claims, "Dainty Dave is apparently a reference to Lieutenant Guert Gansevoort." The historical circumstances make a more obvious fit between Gansevoort and Tom Tight (lines 210–42; see the discussion at 207.212 below). And "Guert Gan" is specifically named in the poem, appearing in lines 82–91 (see the discussion at 203.82 below), which focus on his heroic role in the war with Mexico. But a connection might be made between Dainty Dave's unspecified "sad disaster" (line 60) and the one that befell Gansevoort on August 18, 1856, when he was found drunk aboard the ship he was commanding, the *Decatur,* at the Navy Yard, Mare Island, California. The future hero of Civil War naval operations, Commodore David G. Farragut (see the discussion at 206.185–91 below), was the yard commandant who found him thus and sent him home to await orders. For three and a half years he languished, though not officially "dropped from the navy-roll," and he bought a house and furnishings in preparation for permanent retirement. Only in February 1860 was he recalled to active service as ordnance officer at the Brooklyn Navy Yard. (See Garner 1993, pp. 12–14, 48; also the discussion at 202.56 above.)

203.68 Ap Catesby] Commodore Thomas ap Catesby Jones (1790–1858) was commander of the Pacific Squadron, with the frigate *United States* as his flagship, while Melville was aboard in 1843–44. In 1842, thinking war had broken out with Mexico, he captured Monterey, then had to give it back when his suspicions proved unfounded. He was temporarily relieved of his command as a gesture of conciliation to Mexico by the U.S. government (which was not, in fact, displeased at his vigilance and enterprise). Line 72 refers to the wound he had received from "John Bull's bullet" in the War of 1812. As lines 75–76 relate, Jones did, in fact, begin his career under Stephen Decatur (1779–1820) and Isaac Hull (1773–1843) at Norfolk, and served under David Porter (1780–1843) at New Orleans (see "Running the Batteries," pp. 56–58 above). He may also have served—and "messed" if not "forward pressed"—with Oliver Hazard Perry (1785–1819).

203.76 Perry, Hull, Porter and the rest] See the preceding discussion.

203.82 Guert Gan] Guert Gansevoort, Melville's cousin, became the "only living hero of the family" (Garner 1993, p. 12) by leading a landing party in the assault on Vera Cruz, Mexico, March 9, 1846. He thus partly "redeemed himself" (Garner, p. 13) from the shame attached to his name by those who continued to blame him for his part, as second officer of the brig *Somers,* in the 1842 summary hanging of Philip Spencer and two others as mutineers. For this controversial episode, see Hayford 1959 and the discussion at 207.212 below. Here, celebrating one of his cousin's more heroic episodes, Melville uses his actual name, and briefly characterizes what he did, including planting a U.S. flag on the beach.

203.90–91 "Hi, Santa Anna!"— . . . dash at Mexico] In 1846 and 1847, the forces of General Winfield Scott (1786–1866) defeated those of General Antonio Lopez de Santa Anna (1795?–1876) at Vera Cruz, Buena Vista, Cerro Gordo, Puebla, and Mexico City.

203.96–205.161 The Union's . . . height] Frank L. Day (1959, pp. 60–63) plausibly speculates that Melville's representation here of the encounter (in Hampton Roads, Virginia [line 134]) of the Confederate ironclad *Merrimac* and Union wooden warship *Cumberland* may derive, in part, from his remembering or re-reading three versions of it that were printed in volume 4 of the *Rebellion Record*. In the first, "Reception of the Heroes of the Congress and Cumberland, At New-York, April 10, 1862" (doc. 128, pp. 465–68), a *Cumberland* survivor recounts an exchange in which the commander of a rammed ship vows never to surrender (a possible basis for the interaction between Hal and Will in lines 143–47); the document also includes a statement from a veteran man-of-warsman named Willard on how old friends were divided by the war (cf. lines 96–100). The second document (doc. 82, pp. 273–76) is the Baltimore *American* account of the sinking of the *Cumberland* that Melville also used for "The Cumberland" in *Battle-Pieces* (pp. 37–38 above). Third is George Henry Boker's poem "On Board the Cumberland" (in "Poetry and Incidents," pp. 79–80), which contains this stanza: "Alas! alas! my Cumberland, / That ne'er knew grief before, / To be so gored, to feel so deep / The tusk of that sea-boar!" The names Hal and Will do not come from these sources, nor do such details as the *Cumberland*'s bell striking its knell (lines 150–51) and the chaplain going down with the dungeoned wounded (lines 156–57).

204.116 believe,] Retained here, as elsewhere, is Melville's comma preceding rather than following parenthetical matter. That the usage is deliberate is shown by the fact that Melville inscribed the comma here at a later stage than the parentheses.

204.117 the Uzzite's black shard] When Satan "smote Job with sore boils from the sole of his foot unto his crown," that "man in the land of Uz" "took him a potsherd to scrape himself withal; and he sat down among the ashes" (Job 1:1, 2:7–8).

204.126 a'toasting] While JMg usually substitutes a hyphen in these constructions, the unvarying apostrophe of the copy-text is retained here and at 206.189 ("a'piloting"), 212.379 ("A'flinging"), 214.7[*verse*] ("a'flying"; here JMg reads "a' flying"), 216.8 ("a'fluttering"), and 217.28 ("a'sweeping"), as well as, in an analogous usage, at 216.17 ("a'plenty").

205.147 damned.] In his extensive revision in JMg of this section of the poem, Melville spelled out this word (rendered as "d——d!" in HM) and followed it with a period. The exclamation point in JMp may indicate that he restored the exclamation mark in an intervening communication, but it is just as likely that the compositor ignored the period, which Melville presumably intended to reflect the change in tone of Will's response from "Very impolitely" to "Informally intrepid." See also the discussion at 207.226,231 below.

206.185–91 Farragut . . . Admiral old] Rear Admiral David Glasgow Farragut (1801–1870), who turned sixty at the beginning of the Civil War, captured New Orleans on April 25, 1862, after braving, the night before, the guns of Forts Jackson and St. Philip and breaking the Confederate's "boom-chain" (line 186) blocking the Mississippi south of the city. On August 5, 1864, he won the Battle of Mobile Bay and thus shut down a major port of Confederate resupply. In *Battle-Pieces,* "The Battle for the Mississippi" is a response to the night-fight on the river; "The Battle for the Bay" evokes the Mobile operation. Here, the "one aloft" (line 189) is Farragut, who lashed himself in the rigging near the top so that he could better see the whole battle scene and not be dislodged by a mere wound.

206.194 Old Order] That is, the Old Order of wooden warships under sail, before the advent of steam engines, metal armor, and revolving gun-turrets.

206.203 Xeres] An older spelling of Jerez, in Spain.

207.207 Pecksniff] In Dickens's *Martin Chuzzlewit* (1843), Pecksniff is a "sleek, smiling," moralizing hypocrite.

207.212 Tom Tight] The name "Tight" and the entire passage about Tom Tight (lines 210–42) are based on the part played by Guert Gansevoort in the *Somers* mutiny affair of 1842. Gansevoort, then a thirty-year-old lieutenant and second in command of the training brig *Somers,* was the first to inform his superior officer, Alexander Slidell Mackenzie, that, in Mackenzie's words, "a conspiracy existed on board of the brig, to capture her, murder the commander, the officers, and most of the crew, and convert her into a pirate, and that Acting-Midshipman Philip Spencer was at the head of it" (*Proceedings of the Naval Court Martial in the Case of Alexander Slidell Mackenzie* [New York: Henry C. Langley, 1844], p. 194; quoted in Hayford 1959, p. 30). After initially ridiculing his executive officer's report, Mackenzie regarded it very gravely, and appointed Gansevoort to preside over an officers' council (not a court martial) to advise him, even though, as he later admitted in an unguarded moment, he had already made up his mind that the leading mutineers must die as a monitory example. Also, as Thurlow Weed later reported in his *Autobiography* (it had been revealed to him by another of Gansevoort's cousins, Hunn Gansevoort), Mackenzie repeatedly pressed Guert and the rest of the advisory council to reverse their findings of a lack of sufficient evidence, and finally succeeded in getting them to recommend that Spencer and two crew members who had been close to him be summarily hanged (1:516; quoted in Hayford 1959, p. 205). They were indeed hanged, despite the fact that Philip Spencer was the son of the Secretary of War. Predictably, a naval court of inquiry and court martial followed, and though both Mackenzie and Gansevoort were acquitted, major questions remained—and persist. Melville evidently wanted to believe that both Mackenzie's and Gansevoort's "honor . . . was clear" (line 219), though passages in chapters 70 and 72 of *White-Jacket* (1850) show that he had doubts, which still may have tinged *Billy Budd, Sailor*.

The besieged Lieutenant Gansevoort declined to talk—even to kindly disposed relatives—about the *Somers* affair, especially after he discovered from Weed in 1843 that cousin Hunn had told Weed all he had been told by Guert. Responding to that discovery, writes Weed, Guert "looked thoughtfully a moment, then drank off his champagne, seized or raised the bottle, again filled his glass and emptied it, and, without further remark, left the table" (1:518–19; quoted in Hayford 1959, p. 206). Robert Penn Warren (pp. 417–21) analyzes the characters and motives of those involved and then summarizes the covert significance of Melville's choice of fictional name for the barely disguised cousin: "Tom Tight may be taken to suggest not only that Guert was tight-lipped, but was apt to get 'tight' from drink."

207.214 bowsing] In HM, Melville used "bouseing" here and "bouse" at 213.435 below; though JMg and JMp both follow HM, in JM "boozing" and "booze" appear. That the use of "booze" was not a change by Melville is indicated by his changing these words to "bowsing" and "bowse" in six copies of *John Marr* (and his wife made the changes in other copies). Melville's correction indicates that he intended a distinction between "bouse" or "bowse" (both acceptable spellings), used interchangeably to mean literal drinking (as here and at 213.435) or carousing (as in "The Scout toward Aldie," 145.201 above: "But proved sly rebels on a bouse!"), and "booze", used only when his meaning is figurative, as at 202.44 ("I, boozing now on by-gone years") and 206.193 ("But better, wife, I like to booze on the days").

207.226,231 d——d. . . . D—ning] That the substitution of dashes for letters in these words was made in Melville's wife's hand in HM may suggest that she influenced him to make the revision. But he let the bowdlerization stand, possibly to make a distinction between a quoted voice that did "historically" curse (see line 147, where Melville spelled out "damned" at galley-proof stage) and the voice of old Bridegroom Dick, who might be concerned not to offend his wife.

See also the purported "Author's Note" quoted above (p. 590), which explains the appropriateness of quoting the "habitual swearing" of sailors

207.234 *horse-block*] Ashore, this is a raised stand used for more easily mounting a horse; on shipboard a "horse-block" is a grating or platform that elevates and identifies the "vociferous demanding" one (line 236) as an officer of the deck.

208.247 Captain Turret, *"Old Hemlock"* tall] On May 1, 1950, soon after the publication of *White-Jacket,* Melville wrote Richard Henry Dana Jr. that he shrank from recording on paper any personal identification of the officers of the frigate *United States,* on which he had sailed in 1843–44, with characters in that book. Nevertheless, many scholars have drawn parallels both for that book and for the characters in this poem. The consensus, beginning with Howard P. Vincent in his edition of the *Collected Poems* (p. 470), is that Captain Turret was based on James Armstrong, captain of the *United States* during Melville's first ten months aboard. S. R. Franklin's 1898 *Memories of a Rear-Admiral* (p. 64) specifies Armstrong as the main model for Captain Claret in *White-Jacket;* Franklin also provides the physical description that supports Vincent's claim. A green midshipman aboard the *United States* on the cruise that Melville joined in Hawaii, Franklin recalls Armstrong as "a stalwart Kentuckian [cf. line 251], about six feet tall and large in proportion. I remember he wore a sort of leather cap adorned with a gold band with ragged edges. . . . the grotesqueness of his whole appearance made an impression upon my youthful mind which has never been effaced" (p. 18).

208.254 less though] In HM, commas enclose "though". In JMg the second one does not appear, and Melville then deleted the first one. Since he as easily could have added as deleted a comma, there is no need to restore the manuscript reading on grounds that Melville was forced into making the galley change. He interchangeably used either two commas or none in constructions like the present one.

208.261 King Og] See Deuteronomy 3:11: "only Og king of Bashan remained of the remnant of giants." Since no source has been discovered with Melville's copy-text spelling of the king's name, "Ogg," NN emends to the conventional spelling. "Og/The huge" is a figure for the *Virginia/Merrimac* that was much larger than the *Monitor* in "In the Turret" (*Battle-Pieces,* 39.15 and 40.36 above). In *Clarel,* a giant Albanian is twice called "Og" (3.11.189; 3.27.166).

209.288 lours] In seventeen of the twenty-one located copies of *John Marr,* either Melville or his wife inked in "lours" as a revision of "shows". In the University of Florida (Howe Collection) copy, Melville did not line out "shows" but in the left margin penciled "stands", which seems to be a tentative earlier revision that was supplanted by "lours".

209.295 Angel o' the "brig"] The master-at-arms, chief police officer of the warship, hence warden of its jail.

210.306 Read the *Articles of War*] As Melville notes in chapter 35 of *White-Jacket,* "the article that, above all others, puts the scourge into the hands of the

Captain" is 32—"All crimes committed by persons belonging to the Navy, which are not specified in the foregoing articles, shall be punished according to the laws and customs in such cases at sea." The treatment of the Articles of War is mainly concentrated in chapters 70–72.

210.308 Anak] One of the aboriginal giants who lived in southern Palestine before the Hebrews annihilated them, as in Numbers 13:33, here used adjectivally. The name appears in *Mardi* (chap. 159), *Moby-Dick* (chap. 59), "The Bell-Tower" and "Hawthorne and his Mosses" (in the NN *Piazza Tales* volume, pp. 174, 253), and *Clarel*, 3.14.66 and 4.3.55.

210.328 had'nt] Melville's copy-text placement of the apostrophe is retained here and in four other instances in *John Marr* (213.426; 215.17,27,28) because in such negative contractions Melville consistently did not put the apostrophe between the "n" and "t", and because, in his earlier books, this placement of the apostrophe was common.

210.335–211.367 Lieutenant Don Lumbago . . . Top-Gallant Harry] Although no specific identifications have been proposed for the characters named in these lines, the adjectives are suggestive. "All-a-Tanto" (line 345) means "completely in order (shipshape)"; the orlop deck (line 346) is the lowest deck in a ship; and a rigadoon (line 348) is a lively dance performed with a jumping step, popular in the seventeenth and eighteenth centuries.

211.367 Jack Genteel] Robert Penn Warren (p. 422) implies that Jack Genteel is another version (like "Jack Roy," pp. 216–17 above) of Jack Chase, who is celebrated in *White-Jacket* and to whom Melville dedicated *Billy Budd, Sailor.*

211.372 *politesse,*] NN follows JMg in supplying the comma here. In his manuscript, Melville converted an earlier comma into a caret as he made substantive revisions in the line, and probably inadvertently did not add another comma to replace it. It is highly uncharacteristic of him to omit a comma in this construction.

212.375 *Ohio*] In the aftermath of the *Somers* affair (see the discussion at 207.212 above), Guert Gansevoort served on the *Ohio* while it was a receiving ship in the Charlestown Navy Yard in 1843 and 1844 (see Weed, 1:519; quoted in Hayford 1959, p. 206, and *Correspondence*, p. 570).

NN follows JMg in dropping the quotation marks that enclosed this ship name in HM. While it is not normally NN policy to impose consistency in such matters, it is clear in this case that Melville's intention was to achieve consistency in the treatment of ship names. Although his initial treatment of these names, both in this poem and in the entire book, was inconsistent—sometimes with just quotation marks, sometimes with italics, sometimes both—he then, at stages B (see the textual notes at 228.0, 231.1, 232.0, and 233.23) and D (see the textual note at 213.407) and in JMg (see the textual note at 212.396), revised to make these ship names consistently italic.

212.393 *Constitution*] For a brief overview of the long and illustrious history of "Old Ironsides," launched on October 21, 1797, see *Dictionary of American Naval Fighting Ships,* 2:173–77.

212.395 *Bon Homme Dick*] On February 4, 1779, the French king placed the *Bonhomme Richard* (then the *Duc du Duras*) at the disposal of John Paul Jones. Jones renamed it in honor of both its French donors and Benjamin Franklin ("Poor Richard"). Despite efforts to save it, the *Bonhomme Richard* sank on September 25, 1779, after Jones and his men had battered the *Serapis* into submission late on the 23rd. Melville's Israel Potter sails with Jones and participates in this battle in *Israel Potter,* chaps. 14–19.

212.396 *Black Cockade . . . True-Blue*] In HM, these words, so far not identified as either ship names or nicknames, are not underlined; in JMg, they are italicized. In marking the galley proof, Melville first directed, with a fist pointing to the direction, "Restore Black Cockade and True-Blue", then erased the direction and indicated the same change by "Rom" (i.e., roman), then decided (by lining this instruction out) to accept the compositor's italics. That Melville italicized nicknames as well as ships' names is evident in line 247, where Captain Turret is "'*Old Hemlock*'". The context suggests that the names refer to ships that, along with the *Bonhomme Richard,* make up a list of "many a keel Time never shall renew" (line 394). According to quotations in the *Dictionary of American English,* "black cockade" referred to the Federalist party of the late 1800s, while "true-blue," meaning "dependable, sound," had already acquired the connotation of patriotism.

212.397 Decatur] See the discussions at 202.61 and 203.68 above.

213.407 *Monitor*] For the Union ironclad *Monitor,* see the discussions of "In the Turret" and "A Utilitarian View of the Monitor's Fight" in *Battle-Pieces* (pp. 634–35, 636–37 above).

213.408 *Cumberland*] For the *Cumberland,* see the discussion at 203.96–205.161 above, as well as the discussions for "The Cumberland" in *Battle-Pieces* (pp. 632–33 above).

213.410–13 battlemented hull, Tantallon . . . iron-beaked raft] Robert Penn Warren (p. 422) identifies Castle Tantallon in East Lothian, Scotland, as the "old seat of the Douglas clan, long since in ruins." Here, Dick compares the *Cumberland's* "kicked in" condition after being rammed by the *Virginia/Merrimac* to both the ruined state of Castle Tantallon and the underwater fate of the Boston tea. In lines 412–13, he laments what the Confederates did in turning the burned-out hull of the formerly "tall shapely" steam frigate *Merrimac* into the ironclad *Virginia.* Though the fifteen-hundred-pound iron beak of the *Virginia* broke off in sending the *Cumberland* to the bottom, the loss was fortunate because the *Virginia,* if impaled on the *Cumberland,* could easily have gone down with its prey.

213.411 Boston the taxed chests o' tea!] Melville's paternal grandfather, Major Thomas Melvill, participated in the Boston Tea Party, December 16, 1773. A vial of the tea brought home in his boots was proudly preserved in the family and is now at the Bostonian Society.

213.426 Do'nt] See the discussion at 210.328 above.

213.431 Decatur's coxswain] No source has been located for Melville's attributing such a piece of advice to any one of Decatur's coxswains. Flying kites are the highest sails of a ship, set only in light winds—skysails, royal studding sails, and any above them.

213.435 bowse] See the discussion at 207.214 above.

213.435 Bohea] This name of a region in China was used to refer to the best China black tea.

EMENDATIONS. 201.2 though] HM\EM; tho' HM *201.5 "Feel] JMg; ^~ HM *201.7 sixty-five] JMg; ~^~ HM 201.23 before,] JMg\HM; ~; HM 201.24 e'en o'] JMp\HM; o' HM 202.29 mended] JMg\HM; darned HM 202.36 naval^etiquette] JMp\HM; sea-etiquette HM 202.50 footsteps] JMg; foosteps HM 202.55 sun, . . . moon;] JMg\HM; ~^ . . . ~. HM 203.95–96 But, . . . over-strained] JMp\HM; But^ how to speak o' the lamentable days— / Hawsers parted, and started stays HM 204.97 Our] JMp\HM; The HM 204.108 believe] JMg; beleive HM 204.110 there the] JMg\HM; the HM 204.112 death!—] JMg\HM; ~.— HM 204.113 how could we] JMg\HM; hardly could HM 204.113 lag?—] JMg\HM; ~:— HM 204.116 believe] JMg; beleive HM 204.122 either] JM\HM; one HM 204.126 toes;] JMg\HM; ~. HM 204.127 bazar^] JMg\HM; ~, HM 204.127 Lucre] JMg\HM; who HM 204.128 war.] JMg\HM; ~; HM 204.129 But] JMg\HM; While HM 205.135–206.168 There . . . up] JMg\HM; [see textual notes for Melville's extensive revision of this passage] HM 205.150 Not sharing] JMp\HM; Shareing JMg\HM 205.151 The . . . struck—] JMp\HM; Smiting there the metal, JMg\HM 205.156 dungeoned] JMp\HM; helpless JMg\HM 205.156 down,] JMp\HM; ~; JMg\HM 205.157 And . . . them.] JMp\HM; Them the billows submerge, JMg\HM 205.157 But] JMp\HM; but JMg\HM 205.157 surges] JMp\HM; dead they JMg\HM 205.158 The . . . from] JMp\HM; From proneness on the JMg\HM 205.161 colors unsurrendered] JMp\HM; unsurrendered colors JMg\HM 205.161 and] JMp\HM; and some JMg\HM 205.162 Nay, pardon] JMp\HM; But wherefore JMg\HM 205.162 aunty!—] JMp\HM; ~?— JMg\HM 205.162 Wife] JMp\HM; ah JMg\HM 205.167 jam] JM\HM; jamb JMg\HM 206.176 No, never] JMp\HM; Never HM 206.178 forever, wife,] JMg\HM; forever HM 206.179 War! . . . days^] JMp\HM; war, its stress and maze: HM 206.180 Since set] JMp\HM; Set HM 206.180 the ship's] JMp\HM; the HM 206.180 stays?] JMp\HM; ~. HM 206.189 war—] JMg\HM; ~, HM 206.190 place—] JMg\HM; ~, HM *207.214 bowsing] JM\HM; bouseing HM 207.215 that last] JM\HM; that HM 207.218 cleaved,] JMg\HM; ~^ HM 207.219 though] HM\EM; tho' HM 207.220 he would] HM\EM; he'd HM *207.226 d——d] HM\EM; damned HM *207.231 D—ning] HM\EM; Damned HM 207.233 averred] JMg\HM; condemned HM 208.243 chaps] HM\EM; blades HM 208.249 Manœuvre] HM\EM; Maneuver HM *208.254 less^ though^] JMg\HM; ~, ~, HM 208.254 though] HM\EM; tho' HM 208.259 Storming all] JMg\HM; Storming HM 208.260 Challenging to battle,] JMg\HM; Primed for murder^ HM *208.261 Og] NN; Ogg HM 208.264 brig!] JMg\HM; ~, HM 208.264 back he mocked] JMg\HM; mocking back HM 208.265 "Try] JMg; ^~ HM 208.265 it then!" swaying] JMg\HM; it!" lifting HM 208.268 dally] JMg\

HM; hedge there HM 208.269 let slip on] JMg\HM; upon HM 208.270 for-
midable] JMg\HM; Anak HM 209.273 drowse] HM\EM; drouze HM 209.275
Shrilled] JMg\HM; Thrilled HM 209.276 Thrilled] JMg\HM; Shrilled HM
*209.288 lours] JM\HM; shows HM 209.293 grave Surgeon shows] JMg\HM;
Surgeon behold HM 209.293 physician] JMg; physcian HM 209.302 *sailor-man;*]
JMg\HM; ~. HM 210.308 Anak] JMg\HM; great HM 210.308 Finn;] JMg\
HM; ~. HM 210.311 scourge] JMg; scouge HM 210.315 brooked:] JMg\HM; ~;
HM 210.316 How else?] JMg\HM; Spread^ HM 210.317 No, never] JMg\HM;
Never HM 210.317 sideways he] JMg\HM; sideways HM 210.318 waistband]
JMg\HM; belt HM 210.320 merge—] JMg\HM; ~, HM 210.326 Submission
is] JMg\HM; Submission's HM 210.327 brushing] JMg\HM; to HM 210.329
Degrade that tall] JMg\HM; Flog that HM 210.330 Old] JMg\HM; Tall HM
210.335 Don Lumbago] JMg\HM; Lumbago HM 211.347 Ned?] JMg\HM; ~,
HM 211.351 Hot-Scotch—] JMg\HM; ~, HM 211.352 Glen] JMg\HM; But cool
HM 211.355 cruise it] JMg\HM; cruise HM 211.358 Sid,] JMg; ~— HM 211.358
and Sid's] JMg\HM; his HM 211.362 others like old] JMg\HM; other fellows
like to HM 211.363 Bunting] JMg\HM; Flags HM 211.363 to flutter at the] JMg\
HM; up to HM 211.369 ²like] JMp\HM; and HM *211.372 *politesse,*] JMg; ~^
HM 211.373 *Mademoiselle*] NN; Madamoiselle HM 211.373 *Oui . . . amie*] HM\
EM; [*not underlined*] HM *212.375 ^*Ohio*^] JMg; "Ohio" HM 212.376 barber,]
JMg\HM; ~; HM 212.393 crack] JMg\HM; flagged HM 212.395 *Homme*] JMg\
HM; Hom HM 212.395 *Dick*] HM\EM; [*not underlined*] HM *212.396 *Black
Cockade . . . True-Blue*] JMg\HM; [*neither* Black Cockade *nor* True-Blue *indi-
cated for italic*] HM 212.400 Yes! for Nature] JMp\HM; Yes, Nature she HM
212.403 solid] JMg\HM; grand HM 213.409 *Cumberland!*—] JMg\HM; ~:—
HM 213.411 in, as at Boston] JMg\HM; right in, like HM 213.412 Ay, spurned]
JMg\HM; Spurned HM 213.412 tall shapely] JMg\HM; true tall HM 213.414 in
armor] JM\HM; armed HM 213.416 knuckles that strike] HM\EM; knuckles,
foul fall HM 213.431 coxswain] JMg; coxswain's HM *213.435 bowse] JM\HM;
bouse HM

TEXTUAL NOTES: INSCRIPTION STAGES. At least seven stages of inscription-revision:
A (nonextant pre-fair-copy stage); Ba (blue ink on thicker paper; superseded
leaf 16–17 ["Orme" 17.clip.verso]); Bb (blue ink on thicker leaves foliated in
upper middle pencil sequence); B–C (pencil; superseded leaf 16 ["Orme" 10.clip.
verso]); C (brown ink on both thicker and thinner leaves, many foliated in upper
middle pencil sequence); D (gray ink); E (extensive galley proof revisions in gray
ink). Other Harvard manuscripts are also occasionally cited in the textual notes
below, such as "Rammon" (see 204.112, 206.196) and the "Naples" Trial Lines
(see 208.264–68); on "Rammon," which has Melville's notation "Bridegroom
Dick Dec 4, 1887" on leaf 11 verso, see also the introductory note to "The Envi-
able Isles," p. 745 below.

TEXTUAL NOTES: SUBSTANTIVES. 201.0–4 *Bridegroom Dick . . . me*] [*leaf 1(C)*] 201.0 *Bridegroom Dick*] HM1,HM3; [*three or four undeciphered erased words following HM's penciled* Bridegroom Dick *may be an extended variant of that title, a different title, or a notation concerning it*] HM2 201.0[*subtitle*] (1876)] HM4(D); [*no subtitle*] HM1; 18xx [*HM penciled, canceled, and subsequently erased at least two undeciphered ending numerals before settling upon* 76] HM2–3 201.1 Sunning] [*below the title and above the first text-line in the manuscript appear five or six undeciphered erased words that seem to constitute HM's querying something*] 201.2 as] HM1,HM3; as the HM2 201.3 lading] HM,JMp\HM; loding JMg[*misreading*]; loading JMg\r[*misreading*] 201.3 she] HM1,HM3; she [*undeciphered scratched-out word*] HM2 201.5–12 Feel . . . prime] [*leaf 2(D)*] 201.9 This . . . survive] HM4; [*when originally ink-inscribing leaf 2, HM only penciled in the text of line 9; his initial version on this stage D leaf was* This stripped old hulk, *plus two or three undeciphered erased words (?and a comma) and* survive] HM1; A stripped old hulk here may long [*?time ?years*] survive HM2; [*three or four undeciphered erased words below line 9 may be variants for text in either line 9 or line 10*] HM?3 201.10 yet, . . . spliced,] HM4; yet^ [*two or three undeciphered scratched-out words, careted in above the last of which, as substitute for or addition to it, is one more undeciphered erased word*] HM1,HM2; yet, long ago, we were [*at least one undeciphered erased word, as variant of the final* spliced] HM3 201.13–23 Coxswain . . . before] [*leaf 3(C)* Coxswain . . . rubbed me *followed by stage D inscription on the stage C leaf (inscription that replaces text on an evidently nonextant earlier-stage clip):* Bridegroom-Dick . . . before] 201.13 Coxswain I o'] HM1,HM3; [*penciled, circled, then erased above is the query* Captain of ———? *which HM may temporarily have considered as a revision of either line 13 or of line 22's* A high quarter-master] HM?2 201.14 Under . . . fellows] HM4(D); Picked fellows dapper HM1; Dapper young fellows HM2; Under me the [*undeciphered erased word*] HM3 201.18 Pleasant at a] HM4; Reeler of the HM1; [*at least five or six undeciphered erased words, constituting at least two variant readings*] HM2,HM3 201.18 Bob . . . a] HM2; and warbler of the HM1 201.21 And . . . grade] HM6; Ay, though a <u>tot</u> for such a tall grade HM1; And though but a [*?youngster* →*then* young one] to [*undeciphered erased word, then* hop] it [*?the ?*→*then ?high* →*then* the] grade HM2,HM3; And tho' but a gay one [→*then supply the inadvertently omitted* for] graver [*then* serious] grade HM4,HM5 201.22 A high] HM1,HM3; A HM2 201.22 quarter-master^ at last] HM1,HM4; quarter-master, yes HM2; quarter-master, next, HM3; quartermaster^ at last JMg 201.24 e'en o'] JMp\HM; o' HM 201.24–202.33 But . . . realm] [*leaf 4(B)*] 202.25 No babble] HM3(D); No story HM1; Never babble HM2(D) 202.25 good times] HM2,HM4(D); times HM1,HM3 202.26 babbler] HM3(D); teller HM1; teller but HM2 202.27 Babbler] HM2(D); Teller HM1 202.28 yes] HM1,HM3; ay HM2 202.29 Hoisted . . . frayed] JMg\HM; Darned the old ensign when torn or frayed [*above this earlier text of line 29 on leaf 4 are six or seven undeciphered erased words, which may or may not be the same as the ones ink-inscribed over (thus covering and further obscuring) them at stage D (for which see description below)*] HM1; Darned them when torn, [*?and*] [*?the ensign*] when frayed HM2; Darned them when torn, [?and] [*one or two undeciphered erased words*] when frayed HM3; Hoisted the ensign, darned it when frayed HM4(D); Hoisted the ensign, darned it when it frayed JMg 202.34–43 His . . . sleep] [*leaf 5(B)*] 202.35 long] HM2(D); lone HM1 202.36 naval^etiquette] JMp\HM; sea-etiquette HM 202.37 Yearning, too,] HM4(D); And yearning^ HM1,HM3; Ay, yearning^ HM2 202.38 Dropping for time each] HM3(C),HM5; Laying aside each HM1; Dropping for the time HM2,HM4 202.40–41 But . . . degree] HM1,HM3(C); [*after penciling and rejecting a number of revisions of line 41 (see following two entries), but before deciding upon his stage C changes, HM considered canceling lines 40–41*] HM2 202.40 limit] HM1,HM3; limit [?wife] HM2 202.41 Those fine] HM5(C); [*one or two undeciphered scratched-out words*] HM1; Those [?so] HM2,HM4; Those [?ripe] HM3 202.41 aristocrats^ . . . degree] HM?3,HM?5,HM8(C); aristocrats, credit me HM1; [?aristocrats] [*three or four undeciphered erased words*] HM2; [?aristocrats] [*two or three undeciphered erased words*] o' me HM4; [?aristocrats] ran in their glee HM6; [*at some point before deciding to make his stage C changes, HM considered canceling lines 40–41*] HM?7 202.43 Seldom] HM2; And seldom HM1 202.43 excepting] HM3(D); except HM1; except for HM2(C) 202.44–53 I . . . high-noon] [*leaf 6(C)*] 202.48 Ay] HM2(D); Yes HM1 202.49 My spy-glass carrying] HM4(D); Carrying my spy-glass HM1; Armed with my spy-glass HM2(D); Spy-glass carrying HM3(D[*pencil*]) 202.52 Dave, Dainty Dave] [*not underlined*] HM4(D); <u>Dave, Dandy Dave</u> HM1; <u>Dave, Dainty Dave</u> HM2(D); <u>Dainty Davy</u> HM3(D[*pencil*]) 202.54–203.64 That . . . ocean] [*leaf 7(C)*] 202.54 That] HM2,HM4(D); With HM1; This HM3 202.56 touching his cap] HM?3,HM5(D); touching cap HM1; a'touching [?his] cap HM?2; cap-front touching HM?4 202.57 quarter-deck] HM2(D); deck HM1 202.58 that trim] HM2(D); that HM1 202.59 ship's sky-s'l pole] HM3(D)[*the penciled version tries* skys'l *or* sky s'l]; [*three or four undeciphered scratched-out words {?ship's sky-sail pole}*] HM1; sky-s'l pole HM2 202.61 Dainty Dave] [*not underlined*] HM6(D); His name HM1; [*six or more undeciphered erased words, constituting at least two variant readings*] HM2,HM3; <u>Dandy Dave</u> HM4; <u>Dainty Dave</u> HM5(D)

  203.62 And] HM1,HM3; But HM?2[But *could be part of a variant for the beginning of line 61 (see preceding entry)*] 203.65–72 Fleeted . . . bearing] [*leaf 8(B)*] 203.65 Fleeted] HM2(C); Speeded HM1 203.65 lagged his] HM2(D); lagged HM1 203.66 are all, all] HM3(D); all are HM1; all, all are HM2(D) 203.67 here with] HM2(D); with HM1 203.68 Where is] HM2(D); Where's HM1 203.68 fought of] HM3(D); of HM1; [?o'] HM?2 203.69 and . . . epaulets] HM2(D); made him a Captain HM1 203.72 in his] HM2(D); in HM1 203.73–81 Ballasted . . . availed] [*leaf 9(B)*] 203.75 With . . . pressed] HM3(C); [*no text-line present*] HM1; With Decatur in the ward-room, or forward pressed HM2(C) 203.76 Fighting] HM2(C); [*undeciphered scratched-out word*] HM1 203.76 Perry, Hull, Porter] HM2(C); Porter, Hull, Perry HM1 203.79 did] HM2(D); shall HM1 203.80 Your] HM1,HM3(D); But your HM2(D) 203.82–89 But . . . row] [*leaf 10(B)*] 203.83 before] HM2(C); at old HM1 203.84 sunned] HM1,HM5[*and EM reinscribed for clarity*]; playing HM2,HM4; [*undeciphered erased word*] HM3 203.85 strand] HM2(D); sand HM1 203.87 quick] HM3(C); high HM1; brave HM2 203.90–94 Hey . . . be] [*leaf 11.clip(B)*] 203.93 tell, heart o'] HM2(D); tell^ it HM1 203.94 Tell . . . can] HM5(D); [*three or four undeciphered scratched-out words*] HM1; [*two or three stage C undeciphered scratched-out words, followed by the third or fourth of the stage B undeciphered scratched-out words; these stage C undeciphered scratched-out words may have been inked transcriptions of one or more of the penciled variants that possibly preceded but may have succeeded stage C inking-in of* Pray *?then* Speak *?then* Tell *plus one or two undeciphered erased words, ?then* {*?Speak*} *plus one or more other partly scissored-away undeciphered erased words*] HM?2,HM?3,HM4(C) 203.95–98 But . . . weather] [*leaf 11(D)*] 203.95–96 But . . . over-strained] JMp\HM2; But how to speak o' the lamentable days— / Hawsers parted, and started stays HM; But how, heart, to speak of the hurricane unchained— / The Union's strands parted in the hawser over-strained JMp\HM1

204.97 Our] JMp\HM; The HM 204.98 dashed fleet o'] HM2; fleet o' the HM1 204.99–108 Lost . . . believe] [*leaf 12(D)* Lost . . . beleive] 204.106 or] HM,JMg\HM; as JMg[*misreading*] 204.107 Vaunt it] HM2; Vaunt HM1 204.109–13 Sentiment . . . lag] [*leaf 13(B)*] 204.110 there the] JMg\HM; the HM 204.111 red dance] HM2(D); dance HM1 204.112 War's . . . death] HM3(Db); The red dance of death HM1; The red dance of War HM2(Daa)[*this version appears, canceled, on the verso of "Rammon," leaf 16 (upper left corner blue); see following two entries for line 112*] 204.112 War's red] HM3(Db); The red HM1; The mad HM2 204.112 death] HM1,HM3(Db); war HM2(Dab) 204.112 Well, we] HM2,HM4(D); [*undeciphered scratched-out word* {*?We,*}] HM1,HM3 204.113 We] HM1,HM3; Common HM2 204.113 how could we] JMg\HM; hardly could HM 204.114–20 Strike . . . sting] [*leaf 14.clip(B)*] 204.116 some, dame, believe,] HM3(D)[*see also accidentals*]; some^ at least— HM1; some, beleive,— HM2(C) 204.116 o' what] HM2(D); what HM1 204.117 the Uzzite's] HM2(D); Job's HM1 204.119 string] [*to the right of line 119 in JMg, there is at least one undeciphered erased word*] 204.121–23 The . . . out] [*leaf 14(D)*] 204.122 either] JM\HM; one HM 204.124–32 Decide . . . knife] [*leaf 15(B)*] 204.125 these] HM,JMg\HM; those JMg[*misreading*] 204.125 thrills thrilled at] HM2,HM4(D); throbs at the HM1; throbs thrilled at HM3 *204.126 a'toasting o'] HM2(D); toasting HM1; a-toasting of JMg; a-toasting o' JMg\HM 204.127 mart] HM,JMg\r; mast JMg[*misreading*] 204.127 Lucre] JMg\HM2; who HM; they JMg\HM1 204.129 But] JMg\HM; While HM 204.130 And] HM2(C); And in HM1 204.130 unto] HM2(C); to HM1 204.132 a thoroughgoing] HM9(D); [*one or two undeciphered scratched-out words*] HM1; a fratricide HM2(?C); remorseless HM3; [*undeciphered scratched-out word* {*?remorseless*}] HM4(?C) [*at least three undeciphered erased words, each a variant reading*] HM?5,HM?6,HM?7; peremptory HM?8

205.133–34 For . . . day] [*leaf 16(C)* For . . . Historic] 205.133–52 For . . . tusk] HM2(E); [*see following description of superseded stage Ba inscription*] [*Superseded leaf 16–17(Ba)*] {*"Orme" leaf 17.clip verso*} From . . . <u>Merrimack</u>]

From such another devel's clinker
As that in Hampton Roads:—"Surrender
That friggate, Hal, or I will sink her."
And Will, his old chum, shouted back,
Ferocious, "Sink her and be d....d!"

[*then at least these five text-lines (From . . . d....d!") canceled with pencil and perhaps replaced with nonextant revision patch*]

And straight the iron [*then* metal *then* adamant *then* blacksmiths'] uni-
    corn rammed,
And O the havock, wreck, [*then* wreck^] and rack—
The <u>Cumberland</u> sunk [*then* gored] by the <u>Merrimack</u>!

[*then cancel whole leaf with orange X and replace with nonextant stage Bb leaf*] HM1(Ba) 205.134 balmy] HM2; Spring HM1 205.135–39 There . . . oak] HM2(E); [*see following description of superseded stage B–C inscription*] [*Superseded leaf 16(B–C) {"Orme" leaf 10.clip verso}*]

Hark! tis the voice [*then* Hark! a bellow *then one or more undeciphered erased words (mostly scissored away when the "Orme" clip was made)*] from
    the ship in mail,
[*one or more undeciphered erased words, indented, probably erased and written over immediately by the unindented:*] Thro' the iron port the trumpet's
    hail—
[*then* The brass {*then (?indented)* Brass thrust *then* Brass poked} thro' the
    iron port in hail: *then (?indented)* Brass poked thro' the iron port in
    hail—
Hark! {*one or more mostly-scissored-away undeciphered erased words*} from
    the ship in mail,
then
Hark! {*one or more mostly-scissored-away undeciphered erased words*} from
    the ship in mail,
Poked thro' the iron port in hail:*]
"Surrender that friggate, Hal; surrender,
Or I will sink her; [*insert dash above, but without canceling semicolon*] she's
    but slender."
Whereto from the [*then* the faithful *?then* the (loyal) *HM's parentheses indicating, perhaps, tentativeness; then* the gamecock] port of sturdy
    [*?then* of (loyal) *then* of Perry's *?then* of everglade *then* of] oak
[*two or more mostly-scissored-away undeciphered erased words*] [*?messmate's*]
    answer broke,

[*then cancel* answer broke *before canceling whole leaf with orange pencil and replacing with nonextant pre–stage C leaf*] HM1(B–C) 205.135–206.172 There . . . boy-gods] [*leaf 16–17a(E)* There . . . trails *leaf 16–17b.patch(Eb)* Surrender . . . dusk *leaf 16–17b(Ea)* Shareing . . . knell *leaf 16–17c(E)* Of . . . light *leaf 16–17d(E)* Save . . . up *leaf 17.clip(Bb)* The . . . him *leaf 17(C)* But . . . boy-gods] 205.135–206.168 There . . . up] JMg\HM2(E); [*at stage E, subsequent to making the galley-proof changes described in this entry, HM further revised and expanded 17 stage D lines into the 33 he directed be substituted for them in page proof; these 33 lines he inscribed on four new leaves (here designated 16–17a–d), and are accordingly identified (where there are page-proof and later variants from them) as JMg\HM manuscript readings in NN entries for lines 135–68 that follow the description below of their superseded stage B, C, D, and galley-proof variants; following immediately here, then, is a genetic account of the superseded text as it appears on leaves 16 (*For. . . Historic*), 17.clip (*The <u>Cumberland</u> . . . him*), and 17 (*But . . . boy-gods*), and indicating all changes made by HM and the compositor in the 17 lines as they stand in the galley proof, before they were further revised and superseded at stage E*]

 Listen.—[*then(JMg), and without leaving a space following the dash* Lis-
  ten!—]A trump from the iron-clad calls [*then(JMg)* calls,]
 Summoning the war-ship [*then* battle-ship *then(JMg—a misreading)*
  battle-ships *then(JMg\HM1)* battle-ship] with wooden [*then* wooden=
  built] walls: [*then(JMg)* walls; *then(JMg\r)* walls. *then(JMg\HM1)*
  walls—]
 "Surrender that frigate [*then* friggate *then* frigate], Will [*then* Hal *then*
  Will]! surrender; [*then two undeciphered erased words in parentheses* {*?*he
  warned} *then* Surrender!] Or I will <u>ram</u>, and that will end her."
 'Twas [*then(JMg)* 'T was] Hal [*then* Will *then* Hal]. And Will [*then* Hal
  then Will], from the unclad [*for clarity, HM (in pencil) and EM (in ink)
  reinscribe* unclad] oak,
 Will, the old [*?then* Hal, the old *then* That old time *then* Will, the old]
  messmate, minus trumpet [*then(D)* trump *then(D)* trumpet], spoke,
  [*then(JMg)* spoke,—]
 Defiant—[*?then undeciphered erased word* {*?*defiant} *then(D)* Promptly
  defiant— *then(D)* Very impolitely,—]"Sink [*then* "Do!—Sink *then*
  "Do{*?*,}—Sink *then* "Sink] her, [*then* her, then *then* her,] and be
  damned!" [*then(D)* d——d!"* *plus, at the bottom of leaf 16, a penciled*
  (Historical.) *succeeded by a D inked* *<u>Note</u>. Historic. *translated by JMg
  into* *Note.—Historic. {*in smaller type*}]
 Enough. And, [*then (penciled by HM, inked in by EM)* No more. But
  then (JMg\HM1) Enough. And^] gathering way, Hal [*then* Will *then*
  Hal] <u>rammed</u>, [*then* rammed; *then (JMg)* rammed,]
 And O [*in JMg* And, O,] the havock [*in JMg* havoc], wreck and [*then*
  havock, O the wreck, the *then(D)* havock—the wreck—the] rack—
  [*then(D)* rack:]

The <u>Cumberland</u> sunk [*then* rammed *then* sunk] by the <u>Merrimac</u>!—
   [*in JMg no dash and the exclamation mark is italic*]
[*line-space*]
Pardon, old mother [*then(JMg\HM1)* aunty], and do'nt [*in JMg* don't] let
   it fall,
That started tear that hovers on the brim;
I forgot about [*undeciphered scratched-out word followed by a comma, ?then*
   one or two undeciphered erased words as alternative names, then(D) Tommy
   then (inked in by EM) Billy *then(JMg\HM1)* your nephew] and the
   <u>Merrimac</u>'s ball;
No more then of her [*then* her,] since it summons up him.
[*add line-space*]
But talk o' truth [*then(JMg\HM1)* o' man's heart] in the genial [*then*
   wine's genial] cup, [*then* cup! *then* cup;]
[*before stage C inking, HM probably considered beginning this text-line with*
   the penciled words on the clip above Well, truth speaks in guns, too, says
   but erased those words and instead inked in an undeciphered scratched-out
   word (?followed by a dash), then Ha, ha! *then(JMg\HM1.1)* Man's heart
   then(JMg\HM1.2) Some hearts *then(JMg\HM1.3—an uncompleted read-*
   ing) hearts] hobnob [*then(JMg\HM1)* hobnobs] with Herr Von Krupp:
   [*then* Krupp! *then(JMg)* Krupp. *then(JMg\HM1)* Krupp:]
Truth speaks in the guns [*then(JMg\HM1)* His guns speak his heart],
   and they speak right up! [*then* up.]

[*then(JMg\HM2) cancel* Listen . . . up *and direct insertion of 33 stage E lines (205.135–*
206.168) on four new leaves of manuscript (leaves 16–17a–d) attached to the galley; in the
entries here following, all the variants described for lines 135–68 are from these four stage E
leaves and later page-proof revision] HM1 205.142 Summoning . . . trails] JMg\HM2;
Summoning the other, whose colors know the nails JMg\HM1[*this version appears*
not only on leaf 16–17a, but also at the top of leaf 16–17b, where it has been canceled with
orange pencil and covered over by leaf 16–17b.patch] 205.148 iron-clad *rammed*] JMg\
HM4; ironclad <u>rammed</u> JMg\HM1; Merrimac <u>rammed</u> JMg\HM2; Merrimac
<u>rams</u> JMg\HM3 205.149 heeling] JMg\HM2; hexxx JMg\HM1[*?only a transcrip-*
tional error] 205.150 Not sharing] JMp\HM; Shareing JMg\HM; Sharing JMp
205.151 The . . . uninvoked] JMp\HM2; Smiting there the metal, uninvoked
JMg\HM; The fixed metal struck—inw[*the rest of the word cut away in the trimming*
and binding of the page proofs] JMp\HM1 205.156 dungeoned] JMp\HM; helpless
JMg\HM 205.157 And . . . them.] JMp\HM; Them the billows submerge, JMg\
HM 205.157 But] JMp\HM2; but JMg\HM; And JMp\HM1 205.157 surges]
JMp\HM; dead they JMg\HM 205.158 The . . . from] JMp\HM2,JMp\HM4;
From proneness on the JMg\HM; The prone from [*?the*] JMp\HM→1[*?an*
uncompleted reading immediately altered]; The dead from the JMp\HM3 205.161
colors unsurrendered] JMg\HM1,JMp\HM; unsurrendered colors JMg\HM2
205.161 and spars] JMp\HM; and the poles JMg\HM1; on poles JMg\HM2; ?on

some spars JMg\HM?3; and some spars JMg\HM4 205.162 Nay, pardon,] JMp\
HM4; Pardon, JMg\HM1; But wherefore, JMg\HM2; But, wherefore, JMp; [*two
undeciphered erased words*] JMp\HM1; [*undeciphered erased word*], pardon [*for this and
the following variant, any further punctuation once present has been cut away in trim-
ming and binding the page proofs*] JMp\HM2; Wife, [?pardon] JMp\HM?3 205.162
Wife,] JMp\HM2; and^ JMg\HM1; ah, JMg\HM2; wife, JMp\HM1 205.164
Merrimac's] [*underlined*] JMg\HM2; iron-clad's JMg\HM1[*with an a added for clar-
ity*] 205.167[*footnote*] *Note. Historic.] HM; [*on the stage E leaf 16–17b HM did not
inscribe the asterisked footnote that accompanies line 147, though he did inscribe the asterisk
in line 147; when JMp picked up the footnote from the galley version, it dropped the word
NOTE. (underlined in HM)*]

    206.171 the whizzing] HM4(D); the HM1; the [*undeciphered scratched-out word*]
HM2; the round HM3 206.173–77 Flogging . . . due] [*leaf 18.clip(B)*] 206.176 No,
never] JMp\HM; Never HM 206.176 kind] HM1,HM3; sort HM2 206.176 gay]
HM2(C); xay[?say] [*not underlined*] HM1 206.178–82 Honey-sweet . . . remind]
[*leaf 18(C)*] 206.178 Honey-sweet . . . you!] JMg\HM; Sweet, wife, forever shall
I be to you: [*then* you!] HM1[*and a partially scissored-away undeciphered erased word
at the bottom edge of the clip above may be part of a pre–stage C revision of line 178*];
Honey-sweet forever will Dick be to you! HM2(D) 206.179 War! . . . days^]
JMp\HM5; war^ and the fleet in a maze: HM1; war^ and [?its] stress and maze
HM?2; war^ and [*three or four undeciphered erased words*] HM?3; war^ and its stress
and maze: HM4; ?war^ and its stress and [?its] maze HM?5; war, and its stress
and the maze: HM6(D); war, its stress and maze: HM7(D); war, and its dolorous
says: JMg\HM,JMp\HM1; war, and its dolorous days: JMp[*misreading*]; war, and
[*three undeciphered erased words*] JMp\HM2; war, let it take time's haze^[?*but tacitly*
haze:] JMp\HM3; War! why recall stormy days^ JMp\HM4 206.180 Since set]
JMp\HM; Set HM 206.180 the ship's] JMp\HM2; the HM; [*six or more undeci-
phered erased words may constitute one or more variant readings for this passage*] JMp\
HM?1 206.182 sea] HM1,HM4; sea [*undeciphered {?beginning of a} word*] HM?2;
sea yet HM3 206.183–90 It . . . place] [*leaf 19(B)*] 206.183 as it] HM2(D); it HM1
206.189 a'piloting] HM2(D); directing HM1 206.191–97 Our . . . men] [*leaf
20(B)*] 206.191 Captains] HM1,HM3; admirals HM2 206.196 Often . . . cruises]
HM6(Db)[*along the right edge of the verso of "Rammon" leaf 20 (foliated 16 in upper
left corner blue pencil) appear penciled versions (canceled with green pencil) of portions of
line 196—?first (i.e., at the left) the rare cruises ?then (at right) Often I think of the
cruises versions conjecturable as fitting into the revisionary process as follows, though other
sequences and readings are possible, especially if one assumes the Often I change to have
been made before HM began trying different modifiers in the latter part of the line*]; I like
to think on the cruises HM1; I like to think on the fine cruises HM?2; I like
to think on the rare cruises HM?3[*from "Rammon" leaf*]; I like to think on the
brave cruises HM?4; Often I think of the cruises HM?5[*from "Rammon" leaf*]
206.197 memory, . . . o'] HM3(D); memory, I see the HM1; dream^ I hail the
press o' HM2(D) 206.198–207.204 On . . . too] [*leaf 21(B)*] 206.201 puff] HM2(D);
smoke HM1 206.203 Xeres widow] HM6; [*undeciphered scratched-out word*] widow

HM1; [*undeciphered erased word* {?Seville}] widow HM?2; [*undeciphered erased word* {?Malaga}] widow HM?3; widow of [*undeciphered erased word* {?Malaga}] HM?4; widow of Xeres HM?5

207.204 bright] HM3(C); [*undeciphered scratched-out word*] HM1; sunned HM2 207.205–15 Very . . . China] [*leaf 22(B)*] 207.211 what sailor do] HM5(D); [*two or three undeciphered scratched-out words*] HM1; [*two or three undeciphered erased words*] HM2; sea-man [*?underlined*] [?do] HM3; who there do HM4(C) 207.213 ay, a] HM1,HM3; a HM2 *207.214 bowsing] JM\HM; bxxxxing HM1; bouseing HM2(C); boozing JM 207.215 that last] JM\HM; that HM 207.216–22 Tom . . . beset] [*leaf 23(B)*] 207.217 an arch] HM2; a HM1 207.218 cleaved] HM,JMg\ HM,JMp\HM; cleaned JMg[*misreading*]; cleared JMp[*misreading*] 207.219 rum-pus, too,] HM2(D); rumpus^ HM1 207.219 honor it] HM2,HM4(D); honor HM1,HM3 207.220 he would] HM\EM[*?also penciled in by EM*]; he'd HM1; he [*undeciphered erased word* {?did}] HM2[*?penciled in by EM*] 207.221 o' Burgundy] HM2; of [*beginning of undeciphered erased word*] HM→1 207.223–27 For . . . gar-board] [*leaf 24.clip(Ba)*] 207.223 do I] HM?2,HM4(D); I HM1,HM3 207.224 no] HM1,HM3; wife HM2 *207.226 d———d] HM\EM2; <u>blanked</u> HM1; damned HM2,HM\EM1[*that is, inked in by EM*] 207.226 larboard] HM1,HM3; [*no variant inscribed*] HM→2 207.227 rail] HM2(D); gunnel HM1 207.227 o' the] HM1,HM3; o' HM2 207.228–31 Nor . . . strain] [*leaf 24(Bb)*] 207.230 at morn] HM2; [*one or two (or the beginning of the second of two) undeciphered scratched-out words*] HM→1 *207.231 D—ning] HM\EM; <u>Blanking</u> HM1; Damning HM2; Damned HM3 207.232–34 Preaching . . . standing] [*leaf 25.clip(B)*] 207.232 each . . . place] HM3; [*four or more undeciphered scratched-out words*] HM1; [*three or more undeciphered erased words, constituting perhaps another variant reading*] HM?2 207.233 From] HM2; From a HM1 207.233 averred] HM1,HM?4,JMg\HM; [*undeciphered erased word* {?declared}] HM2; averring HM3; condemned HM5(D) 207.235–208.240 Trum-pet . . . ways] [*leaf 25(C)*]

208.236 An elephant's bugle] HM3(D); [*two undeciphered scratched-out words, the first of which may be* Like] bugle HM1; [?Like] the elephant's trunk HM2 208.241–49 And . . . he] [*leaf 26(C)*] 208.241 lieutenant] HM3(D); <u>Luff</u> too HM1; [*one or two undeciphered erased words*] HM?2 208.243 chaps] HM1,HM\EM[*the res-toration marks were made by EM*]; [*undeciphered erased word* {?blades}] HM2; blades HM?3(D)[*at left, above* be *in HM, appear, successively, one undeciphered erased word and the numeral 105; 105 is the penciled upper middle foliation number on the clip on leaf 42 of "Bridegroom Dick," on which clip, in line 384, HM made the wording change rejected here*] 208.245 Boomed] HM2(D); Pealed HM1 208.248 tower] HM2(D); turret HM1 208.250–55 Or . . . huff] [*leaf 27(Cb)*] 208.250 drift] HM2(D); drive HM1 208.252 The . . . shipped] HM3(D); Laid in the huge puncheon HM1; Laid in the puncheon [*or* The puncheon shipped] HM2[*and below line 252 are four to six undeciphered erased words, these possibly HM's response to EM's query* indent here? (*a query elicited by the apparently indented position of the revised line), but more probably his penciled trial phrasings for some other line than 252*] 208.254 No] HM2; [?Nor {*or only an earlier-(?mis-)inscribed* No *that needed to be clarified*}] HM1 208.255 who . . . great]

HM2; and his [*undeciphered scratched-out word that may end* fied] HM1 208.256–60
Our . . . pretences] [*leaf 27.clip(Ca)*] 208.256 Our three-decker's] HM4(D); The
<u>Old Waggon's</u> HM1; The "<u>Old Wagon's</u>" HM2[*a vaguely horizontal stage D ink
mark above and to the right of the s seems to be neither an apostrophe nor any other sig-
nificant mark of punctuation, but intended rather as a cancellation of the ending quotation
mark*]; The three-decker's HM3(D) 208.259 Storming all] JMg\HM; Storming
HM 208.260 Challenging to battle,] JMg\HM; Primed for murder HM[*JMg
has* murder,] 208.261–68 A . . . more] [*leaf 28(Cb)*] 208.264–68 Put . . . more]
HM2(Cb); [*see following description of superseded stage Ca inscription*] [*Superseded leaf
28(Ca) {"Naples" Trial Lines.clip verso* [*in Harvard MS Am 188 (386.C.1)*]}] Put . . .
more {*a leaf unfoliated, inscribed in brownish ink, and revised in pencil*}]

> Ay, put me [*then* "Put him] in <u>brig</u>, [*then, without lining-out the comma,*
>   <u>brig</u>!] backed [*then* back] he mocked like a parrot,
> Try it then!" swaying a fist like Thor's sledge,
> Making the poor [*then* the] pigmies of constables hedge—
> Ship's corporals and the master-at-arms.
> [*the first three or four words in the following text-line have been mostly scissored
>   away; but the double quotation mark following the last of these is visible, and
>   they correspond to the final* In <u>brig</u> there I say]" Irresolute [*then* They
>   dally *then* They shrink] no more,

[*then cancel whole leaf with orange X and replace with stage Cab leaf*] HM1(Ca) 208.264
back he mocked] JMg\HM; mocking back HM 208.265 it then!" swaying] JMg\
HM2; it!" lifting HM; it then!" lifting JMg\HM1 208.265 a] HM2; [?his] HM1
208.266 constables] HM2; constable HM1 208.268 In . . . say] HM1,HM3; Put
him in brig HM2 209.268 dally] JMg\HM; hedge HM1; hedge there HM2(D)
208.269–71 Like . . . in] [*leaf 29.clip(C)*] 208.269 let slip on] JMg\HM; upon
HM 208.270 formidable] JMg\HM; Anak HM 208.272–73 Anon . . . runs] [*leaf
29(D)*]

209.272 Anon, under] HM2,HM4; Under armed HM1,HM?3 209.272
twin] HM2; two HM1 209.273 He] HM4; The sinner HM1; The giant HM2;
Ogg HM3 209.273 slides] HM2,HM4; falls HM1,HM3 209.273 off in] HM2;
into HM1 209.274–80 Morning . . . part] [*leaf 30(D)*] 209.275 Shrilled] JMg\
HM; Thrilled HM 209.275 'the] HM2; a HM→1 209.276 Thrilled] JMg\
HM; Shrilled HM 209.281–87 Lounging . . . slag] [*leaf 31(D)*] 209.285 Laced
Caps] HM3; high gents HM1; [?high] [*undeciphered erased word*] HM2 209.287
slag] HM,JMg\HM; slog JMg[*misreading*] 209.288–96 Like . . . sup] [*leaf 32(D)*]
*209.288 lours] JM\HM; shows HM[*in the Howe Library, University of Florida
copy, HM does not line out* shows *but in the left margin pencils* stands] 209.288 bag]
HM,JMg\HM; bog JMg[*misreading*] 209.291 Never venturing a caveat^] HM3;
Not so rash as to protest, HM1; Not so [?mad] as to protest, HM2 209.293
grave Surgeon shows^] JMg\HM2; Surgeon you see, HM1; Surgeon behold^
HM2; surgeon behold, JMg; grave Surgeon see^ JMg\HM1 209.297–210.304

Heading . . . glance] [*leaf 33(C)*] 209.297 all erect] HM2; erect HM1 209.297 ranged assizes] HM4(D); assizes HM1; ?[*?undeciphered erased word*] assizes HM?2; grim assizes HM3(D) 209.298 Lo,] HM1,HM4; Behold^ HM2; [?See]^ HM3 209.298 Turret, and] HM2(D); Turret^ HM1 209.298 bunting] HM,JMg\HM; hunting JMg[*misreading*] 209.300 yet greater giant] HM3(D); greater giant HM1; ?great son o' Anak HM2[*only* giant *in the HM1 reading is explicitly pencil-canceled; then* great *is penciled in above* giant *and* son o' Anak *below*] 209.302 subordinate] HM2(D); subaltern HM1 209.303 worded] HM2(D); verbal HM1

210.304 well-timed] HM1,HM3(D); timely HM2(D) 210.305–14 But . . . succumbing] [*leaf 34(C)*] 210.305 now] HM2(D); <u>here</u> HM1 210.306 heed] HM5(D); note HM1,HM?3(D); mark HM2(D); read HM4(D) 210.307 there to] HM2(D); to HM1 210.308 Anak] JMg\HM; sad HM1; strong HM2(D); great HM3(D) 210.310 repressed] HM2(D); their red HM1 210.313 Compassionate] HM2(D); Sympathetic HM1 210.313 abasement] HM2; disquietude HM1[*canceled and erased at the top of leaf 35.clip*] 210.315 Brown] [*at the top edge of leaf 35.clip are* A *and two undeciphered erased words, the second of these canceled before erasure, all three words indicated for insertion in a pre–stage D version of the line (now scissored away) that preceded final line 315*] 210.315–19 Brown . . . urge] [*leaf 35.clip(B)*] 210.316 How else?] JMg\HM; Spread^ HM 210.316 spread apart] HM3(D); apart HM1; wide apart HM2 210.316 never] HM2(D); [*undeciphered scratched-out word* {?nor} *or perhaps an unusually squeezed* never *that caused EM first to query, then to pencil in* never *before HM inscribed the word over the scratched-out letters of its predecessor*] 210.317 No, never he] HM?2,JMg\HM; Never he HM1,HM4; [?No,] he never HM3 210.317 sideways he] JMg\HM; sideways HM,HM\EM?2; [*undeciphered erased word* {?never ?ever ?nor}] HM\EM1 210.318 waistband] JMg\HM; [*undeciphered scratched-out word* {?waist}] HM1; belt HM2(D) 210.318 marble] HM2(D); white HM1 210.319 Lashed] HM2(D); Cut HM1 210.319 'the] HM,JMg\HM2; [*undeciphered erased word* {?slant}] JMg\HM1 210.320–28 In . . . heart] [*leaf 35(D)*] 210.323 adroop] HM2; droop HM→1 210.323 the junior one] HM4; one of them HM1; one now HM2; one of them now HM?3 210.324 word] HM,JMg\HM; wad JMg[*misreading*] 210.325 him] HM,JMg\HM3; him [?there ?then] [*plus a comma or semicolon and four or more undeciphered erased words, constituting perhaps more than one variant reading, and maybe accompanied by a provisional direction to delete the half-line spacing of at least line 325*] JMg\HM1,JMg\HM?2 210.326 Submission is] JMg\HM; Submission's HM 210.327 promenading] HM2; rolling along HM1 210.327 brushing] JMg\HM; to HM 210.328 Flog . . . heart] HM,JMg\HM3; [*as a revision of part or all of line 328, HM penciled in* Never meant to flog *plus two undeciphered erased words, the second of which he canceled and supplanted with another undeciphered erased word*] JMg\HM1,JMg\HM2 210.328 any] HM2; the HM1 210.328–35 Flog . . . scrutineer] [*leaf 36(Db)*] 210.329 Degrade that tall fellow] JMg\HM3; Flog that fellow HM; [?Degrade that tall] man JMg\HM1; [?Usurp ?Wrong] a true man JMg\HM2 210.330 Old] HM1,JMg\HM2; Tall HM2; Brave JMg\HM1 210.331 does Dick] HM2; is this I HM1 210.333 wifie] HM2; lady HM1 210.334–35 But . . . scrutineer?] HM2(Db); [*stage Db lines 334 and 335 (at the bottom of leaf 36) seem*

*to have been expanded from one stage Da text-line inscribed at the top of leaf 37; this line
first read* Where's First Lieutenant Scrutineer? *the line was subsequently revised to read*
Where's Lieutenant Scrutineer? *?then* Where's Lieutenant {*?Don ?and, successively,
one or more other proper nouns*} Scrutineer? *if not earlier, HM then penciled in above and
successively erased* But tell me {*?is*} *plus perhaps three or more undeciphered erased words,
or the ending words of the earlier line (?as revised), ?then* But where's {*?that irritable*}
Scrutineer? *or some other combination of decipherable and undeciphered words in the
area*}, *then* But where is that irritable Seer? *so that just before he erased all his penciled
versions and both in pencil and blue pencil canceled his earlier inked version (as revised),
the resulting two lines probably read* But where is that irritable Seer? / Where's Lieu-
tenant {*?Don*} Scrutineer?] HM1(Da) 210.334 sore one] HM2; officer HM1(Db)
210.335 Don Lumbago] JMg\HM; Lumbago HM(Db) 210.336–211.344 Call . . .
be] [*leaf 37(Da)*] 210.336 Call the roll] HM1,HM3; Were the roll called HM2
210.338 How] HM2; H[?e] HM1[*perhaps a pen slip*]

211.341 himself] HM2; him HM1 211.343 Tell] HM2; Tell us HM1 211.343
alive now is he] HM3,HM\EM[*EM reinscribed for clarity*]; at home now is he?
HM1; alive is he HM2 211.345–50 Where's . . . trombone] [*leaf 38.clip(Ba)*] 211.350
save] HM2(C); [*undeciphered scratched-out word* {*?but*}] HM1 211.351–52 Where's
. . . watch] [*leaf 38(Bb)*] 211.352 Glen] JMg\HM; But cool HM 211.353–60 Where's
. . . down] [*leaf 39(B)*] 211.355 cruise it] JMg\HM; cruise HM 211.356 Death's
grip] HM2(D),HM4; the host HM1; Death's hand HM3 211.357 Sid] HM1,HM3;
Larry HM2 211.358 was audacious] HM3(C); gayly was HM1; [*two or three unde-
ciphered erased words*] HM2 211.358 Sid] HM1,HM3; Larry HM2 211.358 *and
Sid's*] JMg\HM; his HM 211.359 holiday-craft] HM4(D),HM6; thousand ships
HM1,HM3; holiday-[*undeciphered scratched-out word* {*?yachts*}] HM2; holiday=
ships HM5 211.360 lark of a lad] HM3; larking lad HM1; larking lad wife, HM2
211.361–68 Who . . . weather] [*leaf 40(B)*] 211.361 under] HM,JMg\HM2; under-
neath JMg\HM1 211.362 others like old] JMg\HM2; others like to HM1; other
fellows like to HM2(D); [*two or more undeciphered erased words may be a preliminary
revision of this passage*] JMg\HM?1 211.363 Bunting] JMg\HM; Flags HM 211.363
to . . . the] JMg\HM2; to HM1; up to HM2; [*two or more undeciphered erased words
may be a preliminary version of this passage*] JMg\HM?1 211.366 doom] HM2; f[?
beginning of fate] HM→1 211.367 Top-Gallant Harry and] HM4(C),JMg\HM;
my streamer o' streamers, brave HM1; that streamer o' streamers, brave HM2;
Top-Gallant Harry [*undeciphered erased word* {*?or*}] HM3; Top-Gallant Harry and
the JMg[*misreading*] 211.368 Lo,] HM2(C); So^ HM1 211.368 hurricane] HM2(D);
stormy HM1 211.369–212.379 Shagged . . . about] [*leaf 41(C)*] 211.369 ²like] JMp\
HM; and HM 211.369 red lion] HM4(D); lion HM1; [*undeciphered erased word*]
HM2; roused lion HM3(D) 211.370 in his] HM2(D); in HM1 211.370 chapeau]
HM1,HM3; chapeau laced [*or* laced chapeau *perhaps; cf. line 406's* laced cocked
hat] HM2 211.371 ladies never once] HM3(D); ladies never HM1; ladies, [?no,]
never HM2 211.372 All . . . urbane] HM5(D); All politesse, how sweet HM1; In
politesse sweet how urbane HM2(D); ?In politesse bland how urbane HM?3; ?In

politesse bland how sweet HM?4 211.374 at Naples] HM3(D); in harbor HM1; at [*undeciphered erased word*] HM2

212.377 Never . . . him] HM3(D); [*three or four undeciphered scratched-out words*] HM1; Never you'd thought him HM2 212.377 of rude] HM4(D); of HM1; of [*undeciphered erased word*] HM2; of [*?undeciphered erased word*] HM?3 212.378 In . . . the] HM5(D); In tight [*undeciphered scratched-out word—or beginning of a word*] with the HM1; [*two or three undeciphered erased words*] [*?plus* with the] HM2; In tight [*?pumps* with the] HM3; In tight little pumps, with HM4 212.378 grand dames] HM5(D); dames HM1,HM3; [*undeciphered erased word* {*?high*}] dames HM2,HM4 212.379 A'flinging] HM2; Flinging HM1 212.379 foot all] HM2(D); foot HM1 212.380–84 His . . . wonder] [*leaf 42.clip(Ca)*] 212.380 with . . . tokens] HM(D); hung with trinkets HM1; with love's jewelled [*undeciphered erased word*] HM2; with ladies jewels HM3 212.380 abounding] HM2; [*undeciphered scratched-out word*] HM1 212.381 shaking out] HM2(D); shaking HM1 212.382 astounding] HM2; [*undeciphered scratched-out word*] HM1 212.383 glum] HM1,HM3; [*undeciphered erased word* {*?grimly*}] glum HM2 212.383 grim-visaged] HM3(D); grim old HM1; [*?grim*] growling HM2 212.384 blades] HM2(D) [*at the left, HM inscribed the upper middle pencil foliation of leaf 26, on which leaf, in line 243, he rejected the change made here*]; chaps HM1 212.385–88 Pennoned . . . Away] [*leaf 42(Cb)*] 212.385 fine fellows] HM2(D); fellows HM1 212.389–96 Hither . . . *True-Blue*] [*leaf 43(D)* Hither . . . *True-Blue*] 212.391 adieu] HM,JMg\HM; adieux JMg 212.392 pointing] HM2; sailing HM1 212.393 crack] JMg\HM2; flagged HM,JMg\HM1; flogged JMg[*misreading*] 212.395 *Homme*] JMg\HM,JMp\HM; Hom HM[*the compositor followed copy; the reviewer queried the result in JMg*]; Homer JMp[*misreading*] 212.397–402 Doff . . . brown] [*leaf 44 {no substantive inscription} leaf 44.clip(C)* Doff . . . brown] 212.400 Yes! for Nature] JMp\HM; Nature she HM1; Yes, Nature she HM2,HM4; Yes, nature she HM3,JMg 212.400 years] HM1,HM3; years they HM2 212.402 But . . . Would] HM4; But how with his frigate? Would HM1; But his frigate [*then (when inked in)* friggate *then* frigate], wife, his bride? [*one (?or two successive) undeciphered erased word(s)*] HM2,HM?3 212.403–213.407 Into . . . us] [*leaf 45.clip(?Ca)*] 212.403 Into . . . renown] HM2(Cb)[*HM squeezed line 403 in at the top of the clip; line 402 was probably inserted at the same time at the bottom of leaf 44.clip*]; [*no text-line present*] HM1 212.403 the solid] JMg\HM; [*?an*] HM1; the old HM2; the grand HM3(D)

213.407–14 right . . . *cap-a-pie*] [*leaf 45(D)*] 213.411 in, . . . taxed] JMg\HM; in^ as at Boston the taxed HM1; in! as at Boston the taxed HM2; right in^ like the taxed HM3; right in, like the taxed HM4; right in^ like the tossed JMg 213.412 Ay, spurned] HM1,JMg\HM[*three to five undeciphered erased words, in the margin of the galley, may constitute variant readings HM considered for line 412*]; Spurned HM2 213.412 tall shapely] HM1,JMg\HM; true tall HM2 213.414 in armor] JM\HM; armed HM 213.415–23 Under . . . fame] [*leaf 46(C)*] 213.415 a] HM2(D); the HM1 213.416 knuckles that strike] HM?2,HM\EM; knuckles, foul fall HM1 213.417 replace] HM1,HM3; [*undeciphered erased word*] HM2 213.418 openness] HM,JMg\HM2; virtue JMg\HM1 213.424–31 Not . . . hearsed] [*leaf 47(C)*] 213.424 Not

. . . them] HM7(D); [*six or seven undeciphered scratched-out words, the third or fourth of which is* in] HM1; [*six or seven scissored-away words, the last of which was underlined*] HM2; Torpedo-boats, sneaks, not with <u>them</u> HM3,HM5; [*one or two undeciphered erased words*] sneaks, not with <u>them</u> HM4; Not [*one or two undeciphered erased words*] [?sneaks, not with] them HM6 213.424 enrolled] HM2; [*undeciphered scratched-out prefix {?in} or word*] rolled HM1 213.431 Decatur's coxswain said] HM4,JMg; [*two or three undeciphered scratched-out words*] crowed HM1,HM3; Decatur's coxswain sang HM2; Decatur's coxswain's[*transcriptional slip*] crowed HM5; Decatur's coxswain's said HM6(D) 213.432–38 Take . . . lack] [*leaf 48 {no substantive inscription}* leaf 48.clip 1(I.C) Take . . . first *leaf 48.clip 2(...II.C)* My . . . lack] 213.434 My . . . slack] HM4; [*an earlier version of this text-line was scissored away*] HM1; My pipe is out, and the grog runs slack HM2; My pipe is [*undeciphered erased word*] out, and the grog runs slack HM3 *213.435 bowse away, wife,] JM\HM; bouse away^ HM1; bouse away, wife, HM2,HM4; wife, bouse away, HM3; booze away, wife, JM 213.436 here^ must needs] HM4(D); here^ must HM1; it must HM2; here, let it HM3[*the comma was not erased when the final revision was made*] 213.437 Sweetheart] HM3(D); sweeting HM1; Sweeting HM2

TEXTUAL NOTES: ACCIDENTALS. 201.0 *Bridegroom Dick*] [*title not repeated as a section-title*] HM; [*in JMg, HM directs* A page should precede this Piece, {*then add a dash*} a page bearing its {*then one undeciphered erased word [?sea] then the Piece's*} title.] JMg\HM; BRIDEGROOM DICK [*on section-title page as well as at beginning of poem*] JMp 201.2 Spring^] HM; spring, JMg 201.2 though the] HM\EM [*EM reinscribed the words for clarity*]; tho' the HM *201.5 "Feel] HM1,JMg; ^~ HM2 *201.7 sixty-five] JMg; ~^~ HM 201.9 This . . . survive] [*see substantives*] 201.10 yet, . . . spliced,] [*see substantives*] 201.11 time;] HM2; ~— HM1; ~, JMg 201.13 crew,—] HM2; ~,^ HM1 201.14 Under me] HM1,HM3; <u>Under me</u> HM2 201.14 gig] HM1,HM3; <u>gig</u> HM2 201.15 full fig] HM1,HM3; <u>full fig</u> HM2 201.17 Bridegroom-Dick] HM1,HM3; <u>Bridegroom-Dick</u> HM2; Bridegroom^Dick JMg 201.18 yarn,] HM2; ~^ HM1 201.19 Diligent] HM2; Dilligent HM1 201.21 And . . . grade] [*see substantives*] 201.22 quarter-master^] [*see substantives*] 201.23 before,] JMg\HM; ~: HM1; ~; HM2

202.27 o'] HM2(D); o^ HM1; O' JMg 202.27 brains^] HM; ~, JMg 202.27 forget!] HM2(D); ~^ HM1 202.28 quarter-master] HM; quartermaster JMg 202.28 I;] HM3(D); ~— HM1; ~: HM?2(D) 202.28 set,] HM2(D); ~— HM1 202.29 ensign,] HM2(D); ~^ HM1[*also see substantives for 202.29*] 202.29 frayed;] HM2(D); ~— HM1; ~. JMg; ~, JMg\r 202.30 binnacle—] HM; ~, JMg 202.30 helm;] HM?2(D); ~, HM?1,JMg 202.35 long^] HM2; ~, HM1 202.36 naval^etiquette] [*see substantives*] 202.37 Yearning, too,] [*see substantives*] 202.39 unbend] HM[*EM reinscribed for clarity*] 202.39 Bridegroom Dick] HM2,JMg,JMg\ HM2; <u>Bridegroom Dick</u> HM1,JMg\HM1 202.40 was—] HM2(C); ~, HM1 202.40 d'ye] HM; d 'ye JMg; d' ye JM 202.40 see:] HM3(C); ~, HM1; ~?; HM?2 202.41 aristocrats^ . . . degree] [*see substantives*] 202.42–43 keep,^ . . . sleep^—] HM; ~,— . . . ~,— JMg 202.44 I,] HM2; ~^ HM1 202.44 on] [*reinscribed for clarity*]

202.44 by-gone] HM2; bye-gone HM1 202.44 years,] HM2; ~^ HM1 202.48
pacing,] HM2; ~^ HM1 202.50 footsteps] JMg; foosteps HM 202.50 retracing,]
HM2(D); retraceing^ HM1 202.51 duty,] HM2; ~^ HM1 202.52 Dave, Dainty
Dave] [*see substantives*] 202.54 thingumbob] HM,JMg\HM; thin gonsbot JMg
202.55 Squinting] HM2; Squintin HM 202.55 sun, . . . moon;] JMg\HM,JMp\
HM; ~^ . . . ~. HM; ~, . . . ~. JMp 202.56 Old Chock-a-Block] HM2; <u>Old Chock
a' Block</u> HM1 202.57 quarter-deck^—] HM; ~,— JMg 202.57 twelve] HM,JMg\
HM; 12 JMg 202.59 ship's sky-s'l pole] [*see substantives*] 202.60 disaster:—] HM3;
~.^ HM1; ~:^ HM2; ~^— JMg 202.61 Dainty Dave] [*see substantives*] 202.61 navy=
roll!] HM2; ~. HM1

    203.62 ah,] HM3; Ah^ HM1; ah^ HM2 203.62 Lieutenant] HM2(D); lieuten-
ant HM1[*in inscribing at stage C, HM seems also to have misspelled the word at first,
then to have corrected himself immediately*] 203.62 Chock-a-Block—] HM2; <u>Chock=
a-Block</u> ^ HM1 203.67 Bridegroom Dick] HM2; <u>Bridegroom Dick</u> HM1 203.68
Catesby?—] HM; ~?^ JMg 203.69 epaulets] HM2; epauletts HM1 203.69 epau-
lets,] HM2(D); ~^ HM1(D) 203.71 *Where's*] HM; *Where 's* JMg 203.73 seafaring]
HM2(C); seafareing HM1; sea-faring JMg 203.76 Porter^] HM; ~, JMg 203.77
Humped] HM2; Humpt HM1 203.77 War,] HM1,HM3; War! HM2; war, JMg
203.79 jar!] HM2; ~. HM1 203.80 assailed,] HM2; ~^ HM1 203.82 where's] HM;
where 's JMg 203.82 Guert] HM,JMg\HM; Gnert JMg 203.82 van?] HM2; ~,
HM1[*HM did not explicitly cancel the comma*] 203.84 rollers^] HM,JMg\HM; ~,
JMg[*the compositor mistook part of a caret for a comma*] 203.85 And, . . . strand,] HM2;
And^ . . . sand^ HM1[*and see substantives*] 203.86 land!] HM2(C); ~^ HM1 203.87
chanticleering;] HM2[*the semicolon is almost indistinguishable from the colon at the end
of the following text-line in the manuscript*],JMg\r; chantercleering, HM1; chanti-
ceering; JMg 203.88 vying—] HM2(D); ~, HM1 203.89 "Cock-a-doodle-do"!]
HM2(D); "<u>Cock-a-doodle-do</u>"^ HM1; "Cock-a-doodle-doo!" JMg 203.89
"Row, boys, row"!] HM2(D); "<u>Row, boys, row</u>." HM1; "Row, boys, row!" JMg
203.90 "Hey, Starry Banner"!] HM2(D); "<u>Hey, Starry Banner</u>", HM1[*in adding the
exclamation mark, HM did not explicitly cancel the second comma*]; "Hey, Starry Ban-
ner!" JMg 203.90 "Hi, Santa Anna"!—] HM2(D); "<u>Hi, Santa Anna</u>"^— HM1;
"Hi, Santa Anna!"— JMg 203.92 Fine] [*line-space precedes*] HM2; [*?no line-space*]
HM?1 203.93 tell, heart o'] [*see substantives*] 203.93 me,] HM1,HM3(D); ~! HM2
203.94 Tell] [*on leaf 11, a penciled bracket left of* Tell *indicates where text on galley 5
begins*] 203.95 But] [*line-space precedes*] HM2; [*?no line-space*] HM1 203.95–96 But
. . . over-strained] JMp[*in JMp, regarding his substantive revisions there, HM directed*
If this can not be got into two lines, then occupy the space between the para-
graphs.] 203.95 But,] JMp\HM; ~^ HM[*see substantives*],JM 203.96 over-strained;]
JM; [*the earlier version of line 96 ended with a semicolon; the line-end punctuation in
HM's JMp revision has been scissored away in the process of trimming and binding the
proof pages*] JMp

    204.97 Flag] HM; flag JMg 204.97 gone] HM2; gome HM→1[*transcriptional
slip*] 204.98 Secession's] HM,JMg\HM; secession's JMg 204.102 clapped.]
HM,JMp\HM; ~, JMg 204.103 glass^] HM; ~, JMg 204.106 South^] HM; ~, JMg

204.108 believe] JMg; beleive HM 204.109 all,] HM2; ~^ HM1 204.112 death!—]
JMg\HM; ~.— HM; ~^— JMg 204.112 Well] HM,JMg\HM; well JMg 204.113
lag?—] JMg\HM[*see substantives, the second entry for line 113; in substituting* lag? *HM
did not explicitly cancel the JMg* lag:—]; ~:— HM 204.114 Strike . . . Flag] HM2;
[*underlined*] HM1 204.114 Flag] HM; flag JMg 204.115 barred.] HM,JMg\HM;
~, JMg 204.116 believe] JMg; beleive HM *204.116 believe,] HM; ~^ JMg[*and
see substantives, the first entry for line 116*] 204.116 (and . . . know)] HM2(D); —~
. . . ~— HM1; (~ . . . ~), JMg 204.118 throe.] HM1,HM3; ~! HM2 204.119
Duty?] HM,JMg\HM; ~! JMg 204.119 it] HM; It JMg 204.120 that,] HM2(D);
~^ HM1 204.121 Flag] HM; flag JMg 204.123 out:] HM3; ~— HM1; ~. HM2;
~; JMg 204.125 Of] [*line-space precedes*] HM2; [*no line-space*] HM1 204.125 kelson]
HM; keelson JM 204.126 shoddyites] HM1,HM3; [*underlined*] HM2 *204.126
a'toasting o'] [*see substantives*] 204.126 toes;] JMg\HM; ~. HM; ~, JMg 204.127
bazar^] HM1,JMg\HM; ~, HM2 204.127 huzza] HM2(D); huzzah HM1 204.128
o'] HM; of JMg[*misreading*] 204.128 war.] JMg\HM; ~; HM1,HM3; ~? HM2
204.129 Order] HM2; order HM→1 204.131 Honor] HM; honor JMg

205.133 ²how] HM; How JMg 205.135–206.168 There . . . up] [*see substan-
tives*] 205.140 crimson-dyed.] JMg\HM,JMp\HM; ~, JMp 205.141 hails^] JMg\
HM; ~, JMp 205.142 other^] JMg\HM2; ~, JMg\HM1,JMp 205.142 trails:—]
JMg\HM2; ~,^ JMg\HM1; ~:^ JMp[*and* nails *(the substantive predecessor of* trails*)
was first followed by a period (in the superseded version on leaf 16–17b), and then by a
comma-dash*] 205.145 'Twas] JMg\HM; 'T was JMp 205.147 intrepid^—] JMg\
HM; ~,— JMp 205.147 her^] JMg\HM; ~, JMp *205.147 damned.] JMg\HM2; ~!
JMg\HM1,JMp[*see also substantives*] 205.148 iron-clad] JMg\HM2; ironclad JMg\
HM1[iron-clad *was also pencil-underlined twice, possibly to indicate attention needed to
be paid to its hyphenation, but perhaps as a not-finally-carried-through emphasis of its status
as a new word*] 205.148 rammed.] JMg\HM,JMp\HM; ~, JMp 205.149 over,] [*comma
mended for clarity*] 205.149 dusk.] JMg\HM3; ~, JMg\HM1; ~; JMg\HM2 205.150
sharing] [*see substantives*] 205.150 bell^] JMg\HM,JMp\HM; ~, JMp 205.151 The
. . . uninvoked] [*see substantives*] 205.152 tusk;] JMg\HM2; ~. JMg\HM1 205.153
While, . . . gun-deck,] JMg\HM2; ~^ . . . ~^ JMg\HM1 205.154 waylaid^] JMg\
HM; ~, JMp 205.156 down,] JMp\HM; ~; JMg\HM 205.157 And . . . them.] [*see
substantives*] 205.157 But] [*see substantives*] 205.157 Chaplain] JMp\HM; chaplain
JM 205.162 Nay, pardon,] [*see substantives*] 205.162 aunty!—] JMp\HM; ~,^ JMg\
HM1; ~?— JMg\HM2 205.162 Wife,] [*see substantives*] 205.164 Merrimac's] JMg\
HM2; [*not underlined*] JMg\HM1 205.164 ball;^] JMg\HM2; ~;— JMg\HM1
205.165 her^] JMg\HM; ~, JMp 205.167 jam] JM\HM; jamb JMg\HM

206.169 The] [*no line-space precedes*] HM; [*line-space*] JMp[*line-space introduced
when, as part of the extensive galley revisions in lines 135–68, HM scissored galley 5 apart
just before line 169, thus seeming to indicate a new paragraph should begin there*] 206.171
whizzing] HM,JMg\r; whizing JMg 206.175 Sweetheart] HM; sweetheart JMg
206.176 that] HM2; [*not underlined*] HM1 206.176 gay] [*see substantives*] 206.176 gay:]
HM2; ~. HM1; ~; JMg 206.178 Honey-sweet . . . you!] [*see substantives*] 206.179
War! . . . days^] [*see substantives*] 206.180 stays?] JMp\HM; ~. HM; ~, JMg; ~;

JMg\HM 206.183 It] [*no line-space precedes*] HM1,HM3; [*line-space*] HM2 206.183 now,] HM,JMg\HM; ~^ JMg 206.183 then,] HM2; ~^ HM1 206.184 men.] HM,JMg\HM; ~, JMg 206.185 night-river] HM,JMg\HM; ~^~ JMg 206.185 night-river^] HM; ~, JMg 206.186 glare^] HM; ~, JMg 206.189 a'piloting] HM; a–piloting JMg 206.189 war—] JMg\HM; ~, HM 206.190 place—] JMg\HM; ~, HM 206.191 Captains] HM; captains JMg 206.191 huzza] HM2,JMg\HM; huzzah HM1,JMg 206.193 But] [*line-space precedes*] HM2; [*no line-space*] HM1 206.195 ways.] HM,JMg\HM; ~; JMg; ~: JMg\r 206.196 then;] HM2; ~. HM1; ~, JMg 206.197 memory, . . . o'] [*see substantives*] 206.197 memory,] HM,JM; ~^ JMg 206.197 men^] HM,JMg\HM; ~, JMg 206.198 gunned] HM2; gunnd HM1 206.198 go^] HM; ~, JMg 206.200 guns:] HM; ~; JMg 206.201 cigar:] HM; ~; JMg 206.202 dons!"—] HM; ~!"^ JMg

207.204 too;] HM2; ~, HM1 207.205 wicked^ . . . crew.] HM; ~, . . . ~, JMg 207.206 Nor] [*on leaf 22, a penciled bracket left of* Nor *indicates where text on galley 6 begins*] 207.206 either,] HM,JMg\HM; ~^ JMg 207.207 mess.^] HM1,HM3; ~.— HM2 207.208,210 Wistful/But] [*line-space precedes*] HM2; [*?no line-space*] HM1 207.210 But,] HM; ~^ JMg 207.211 sailors,] HM1,HM3(C); ~^ HM2[*see substantives*] 207.211 what sailor] [*see substantives*] 207.214 bowsing] [*see substantives*] 207.216 lieutenant] HM2(C); lxxtenant HM1 207.217 arch^mutineer] HM1,HM3; ~-~ HM2,JMg 207.218 cleaved,] JMg\HM; ~^ HM 207.219 rumpus, too,] HM; ~^ ~, JMg; ~^ ~^ JM[*also see substantives*] 207.219 though] HM\EM; tho' HM 207.220 him^] HM; ~, JMg 207.221 him—] HM; ~: JMg 207.223 tipple,] HM2; ~^ HM1 207.226 d——d] [*see substantives*] 207.227 garboard] HM2; [*underlined*] HM1 207.227 garboard.] HM,JMg\HM; ~, JMg 207.228 him.—] HM,JMg\HM; ~^— JMg 207.229 Le^Fan] HM2; ~-~ HM1 207.231 D—ning] [*see substantives*] 207.232 cutlass] HM2; cutlas HM1 207.233 Old Adam, a hard case] HM2; <u>Old Adam—a hard case</u> HM1; old Adam^ a hard case JMg 207.233 Adam,] HM2; ~ [*undeciphered scratched-out punctuation*] HM1 207.234 horse-block] HM2(D); [*not underlined*] HM1

208.239 you'll] HM; you 'll JM 208.240 Tom^] HM; ~, JMg 208.241 haze:] HM2 <u>haze</u>: HM1; haze; JMg 208.247 But] [*line-space precedes*] HM2; [*no line-space*] HM1 208.247 tall^] HM; ~, JMg 208.248 leaning] HM2; [*underlined*] HM1 208.248 all^)] HM; ~,) JMg 208.249 Manœuvre] HM\EM; Maneuver HM[Maneuver *pencil-underlined and a penciled check mark put in left margin to indicate the word's spelling needs to be checked*] 208.249 War] HM; war JMg 208.251 who^ . . . Madeira^] HM; ~, . . . ~, JMg 208.252 Santa^Clara;] HM2; ~^~, HM1; ~-~; JMg *208.254 less^ though^] JMg\HM; ~, ~, HM; ~, ~^ JMg 208.254 though] HM\EM; tho' HM 208.255 huff:—] HM2; ~:^ HM1; ~;^ JMg 208.256 Our three–decker's] [*see substantives*] 208.256 giant;] HM; ~, JMg 208.258 But,] HM; ~^ JMg 208.258 Devil's] HM2; Devel's HM1; devil's JMg 208.260 Challenging to battle,] [*see substantives*] 208.260 pretences] HM; pretenses JMg 208.260 pretences.] HM,JMg\HM; ~, JMg 208.263 there,] HM; ~! JMg 208.263 Marrot] HM2; [*?Marret*] HM1 208.264 brig!] JMg\HM; ~, HM 208.265 "Try] JMg; ^~ HM 208.265 it^] JMg\HM; ~! HM[*see substantives*]; ~, JMp 208.265 sledge^]

HM; ~, JMg 208.267 Ship's-corporals] HM2,JMg\HM; ~^~ HM1,JMg 208.267 Master-at-Arms] HM; master-at-arms JMg 208.268 They] HM,JMg\HM; they JMg 208.268 more.] HM; ~; JMg 208.269 boar^] HM; ~, JMg

209.273 drowse,] HM\EM,JMg\HM; drouse, HM1; drouze, HM2; drowse^ JMg 209.274 summons. Whistling] HM,JMg\HM; summons, whistling JMg 209.275 Boatswain's] HM; boatswain's JMg 209.275 aids—] HM; ~; JMg 209.276 halls:] HM,JM; ~; JMg 209.277 Dawn] HM,JMg\HM; dawn JMg 209.277 doom,] HM; ~^ JMg 209.282 marines,] HM; ~^ JMg 209.282 heart.] HM; ~; JMg 209.283 Major] HM,JMg\HM; major JMg 209.284 Lieutenants] HM; lieutenants JMg 209.284 place.] HM,JMg\HM; ~, JMg 209.286 dumb.] HM,JMg\HM; ~, JMg 209.287 The blue-nosed] [*no line-space precedes*] HM2; [*line-space*] HM1 209.287 Boatswain] HM; boatswain JMg 209.287 slag,] HM2; ~^ HM1 209.288 Blue Monday] HM3(D); blue Monday HM1,JMg; <u>Blue Monday</u> HM2 209.288 lours—] JM\HM[*see substantives*]; shows, HM; shows^ JMg; shows— JMg\HM 209.291 Never venturing a caveat^] [*see substantives*] 209.293 shows^] JMg\HM; ~, JMp[*also see substantives*] 209.293 physician] JMg; physcian HM 209.294 Spanish] HM2; spanish HM→1 209.295 Angel] HM; angel JMg 209.295 up.] HM; ~; JM 209.296 *Santa^Clara*] HM; ~-~ JMg 209.297 Heading,] HM; ~^ HM\EM[*in reinscribing for clarity, EM did not repeat HM's uncanceled comma*],JMg 209.298 Lo,] [*see substantives*] 209.298 Turret, and] [*see substantives*] 209.299 hair^)] HM; ~,) JMg 209.301 Captain] HM; captain JMg 209.302 *sailor-man;*] JMg\HM; ~. HM; ~, JMg 209.303 it: no] HM2; it. No HM1; it—no JMg

210.305 now] [*see substantives*] 210.308 senses,] HM2; ~^ HM1 210.308 Finn;] JMg\HM; ~. HM; ~, JMg 210.309 peeping^] HM; ~, JMg 210.311 scourge] JMg; scouge HM 210.311 due.] HM,JMg\HM; ~, JMg 210.312 But, ah] HM2; But, Ah HM1; But^ ah JMg 210.313 view:] HM2(D); ~— HM1; ~; JMg 210.315 up."— The] HM,JMg\HM; ~,"—the JMg 210.315 brooked:] JMg\HM; ~— HM1; ~; HM2 210.316 How else?] [*see substantives*] 210.316 threaping] HM2; [*underlined*] HM1 210.317 No,] [*see substantives*] 210.318 Peeled] HM2; pexled HM1[*the word's third letter is later clarified or altered*] 210.319 urge.] HM,JMg\HM; ~, JMg 210.320 merge—] JMg\HM; ~, HM 210.321 boatswain's-mates] HM; ~^~ JMg 210.323 adroop,] HM; ~^ JMg 210.325 Untie] [*line-space precedes*] HM2; [*no line-space*] HM1 210.325 him:—] HM; ~^— JMg 210.326 enough.—] HM2,JMg\HM; ~.^ HM1,JMg 210.327 Then,] HM,JMg\HM; ~^ JMg 210.328 never] HM; Never JMg *210.328 had'nt] HM; hadn't JMg; had n't JMg\r 210.330 Turret^] HM; ~, JMg\r 210.330 stow.^] HM2; ~.— HM1 210.332 blow:] HM; ~; JMg 210.333 'twas] HM; 't was JMg 210.334 where's] HM; where 's JMg 210.335 Lieutenant] HM2; Liutenant HM1 210.336 answer—Here] HM,JMg\HM; answer^here JMg 210.336 *Here!*] HM2; ~? HM1 210.337 *Blixum's*] HM,JMg\HM; *Bliscum's* JMg 210.338 he'd] HM; he 'd JM

211.339 peer.] HM,JMg\HM; ~, JMg 211.340 arm^] HM; ~, JMg 211.341 calm.] HM,JMg\HM; ~, JMg 211.342 Composed] [*no line-space precedes*] HM1,HM3; [*line-space*] HM2 211.343 he^] HM; ~, JMg[*also see substantives*] 211.345 Where's] [*line-space precedes*] HM2; [*no line-space? leaf division makes any*]

previous spacing indeterminable] HM*?*1 211.345 Where's] HM; Where 's JMg 211.345
All-a-Tanto] HM2,HM4; All-a-tanto HM1; <u>All-a-Tanto</u> HM2 211.346 Where's]
HM; Where 's JMg 211.346 Orlop Bob] HM1,HM3; [*underlined*] HM2 211.347
Where's] HM; Where 's JMg 211.347 Ned?] JMg\HM; ~, HM; ~; JMg 211.348
Where's] HM; Where 's JMg 211.348 Where's] HM; Where 's JM 211.349 Ah,]
HM2; ~^ HM1 211.351 Where's] [*no line-space precedes*] HM1,HM3; [*line-space*]
HM2 211.351 Where's] HM; Where 's JMg 211.351 gun-room^] HM; ~-~,
JMg 211.351 Hot-Scotch—] JMg\HM; Hot-Scotch, HM1,HM3; <u>Hot-Scotch,</u>
HM2; hot^Scotch, JMg 211.352 cool^] HM,JMg\HM; ~, JMg 211.353 Where's]
HM; Where 's JMg 211.353 Phil?—] HM2; ~?^ HM1,JMg 211.353 lieutenant]
HM2(C); liutenant HM1 211.354 Or,] HM; ~^ JMg 211.355 brother?—] HM2;
~?^ HM1 211.355 The] HM; the JMg 211.356 ah^] HM2; Ah^ HM1; ah, JMg
211.356 Death's] HM; death's JMg 211.357 Where's] HM; Where 's JMg 211.357
Sid^ the cadet^] HM; ~, ~ ~, JMg 211.357 brag] HM1,HM3; [*underlined*] HM2
211.357 brag,] HM2; ~^ HM1[*and when EM reinscribed the word for clarity, she omit-
ted the comma*] 211.358 "Here's . . . flag!"] JMp; ^~ . . . ~!^ HM1; "~ . . . ~"! HM2;
"~ . . . ~!^ JMg 211.358 Here's] HM; Here 's JMg\r 211.358 Sid,] JMg; ~— HM
211.359 holiday-craft] [*see substantives*] 211.360 lad] [*see substantives*] 211.362 be,]
HM2; ~^ HM1 211.363 gaff—] HM3; ~. HM*?*1; ~: HM2 211.366 scurvy] HM2;
scury HM—>1 211.367 Top-Gallant Harry] HM2; [*underlined*] HM1(C) 211.367
Jack Genteel] HM1,HM3; [*underlined*] HM2 211.368 Lo,] [*see substantives*] 211.368
hurricane^weather] HM; [*EM queried hyphen here? with a pointer aimed at the
space between* hurricane *and* weather] HM\EM 211.368 weather^] HM; ~, JMg
211.369 bear,] HM,JMg\HM; ~^ JMg 211.369 roaring;] HM2; ~, HM1 211.370
But,] HM; ~^ JMg 211.370 feather,] HM2; ~^ HM1 211.371 ladies never once] [*see
substantives; there seems to be no other particular point to the one and a half penciled under-
lines below* ladies *than to draw attention to the portion of the text-line in need of metrical
attention*] 211.371 ladies^] HM1,HM3; ~, HM2[*perhaps the comma was inadvertently
erased*] 211.371 jawing.] HM3(D); jawing; [*not underlined*] HM1; <u>jawing</u> HM2,JMg;
jawing; JMp *211.372 politesse,] JMg; politesse, [*not underlined*] HM1; politesse^ [*not
underlined*] HM2(D)[*the previous comma is turned into a caret*]; <u>politesse</u>^ HM3[*also
see substantives*] 211.372 he:—] HM; ~^— JMg 211.373 Oui . . . amie] HM1,HM\
EM; [*underlining scratched out*] HM2 211.373 Mademoiselle] NN; <u>Madamxxxxxxx</u>
[*undeciphered misspelling*] HM1; <u>Madamoiselle</u> HM\EM,HM2; madamoiselle JMg;
mademoiselle JMp 211.373 Ma] HM,JMg\HM; <u>ma</u> JMg 211.373 chere] HM; chère JM
211.373 amie!] HM2; ~^ HM1 211.374 'Twas] HM; 'T was JMg\r
*212.375 ^Ohio^] JMg; "Ohio" HM 212.376 berth-deck] HM2; birth-deck
HM1 212.376 barber,] HM1,JMg\HM; ~; HM2 212.377 you'd] HM; you 'd JMg
212.377 Boreas;] HM2; ~, HM1 212.379 A'flinging] HM; A-flinging JMg 212.380
jewelled] HM; jeweled JMg 212.380 abounding,] HM2[*the undeciphered scratched-
out word which* abounding *replaced was followed by a comma*]; ~^ HM1 212.383
Gunner] HM; gunner JMg 212.384 wonder,] HM1,HM3; ~? HM2 212.385 fel-
lows^] HM; ~, JMg 212.386 under:] HM; ~; JMg 212.387 day,] HM1,HM3; ~?
HM2[*but without explicitly canceling the comma*] 212.388 Far^ Far] HM; ~, ~ JMg

212.390 Where's] HM; Where 's JMp 212.391 adieu^] HM; adieux, JMg 212.394
Time] HM; time JMg 212.395 *Homme*] [*see substantives*] 212.395 *Dick*] HM1,HM\
EM; [*not underlined*] HM2 212.395 Revolution,] HM,JMg\HM,JM; *Revolution,*
JMg; Revolution^ JMp *212.396 *Black Cockade . . . True-Blue*] JMg,JMg\HM2;
[*neither* Black Cockade *nor* True-Blue *indicated for italic*] HM; [*in JMg, HM first
penciled in* Restore Black Cockade & True-Blue *with a finger pointing at his penciled
direction; he then indicated the restoration to non-italic type by inking in* Rom *twice; then
he decided the italic type was appropriate after all by lining out his previous instruction*]
JMg\HM1 212.397 Doff] [*line-space precedes*] HM,JMg\HM; [*no line-space*] JMg
212.397 Decatur!] HM2; ~. HM1 212.399 wizen] HM2; wizzen HM1 212.400
Yes! for Nature] [*see substantives*] 212.401 o'] HM2(D); of HM1 212.402 But] [*line-
space precedes*] HM2; [*no line-space*] HM1 212.402 But . . . Would] [*see substantives*]
212.402 Would] HM1,HM3; would HM2 212.404 shell,] HM2; ~^ HM1 212.405
rat-tat-tat:] HM2; ~— HM1; ~; JMg 212.406 *derby*] HM2; [*not underlined*] HM1
     213.407 ^*Monitor*^] HM2; "Monitor" [*not underlined*] HM1 213.409 *Better*]
[*line-space precedes*] HM2; [*?no line-space*] HM1 213.409 *Better than the Cumberland*]
HM2; [*not underlined*] HM1 213.409 Cumberland!—] JMg\HM; ~:— HM; ~^—
JMg 213.409 Heart] HM,JMg\HM; heart JMg 213.410 Tantallon] [*in JMg, the
De Vinne reviewer queries, and HM responds that the word is* All right.] 213.411 in,
. . . taxed] [*see substantives*] 213.411 o'] HM2; of HM1 213.411 tea!] HM2; ~[*unde-
ciphered erased punctuation*] HM1 213.412 Ay, spurned] [*see substantives*] 213.412
tall^] HM; ~, JMp\r 213.412 craft^] HM; ~, JMg 213.414 *cap-a-pie*] HM2,JM; [*not
underlined*] HM1,JMg 213.415 dealt:] HM2,JMg\HM2; ~, HM1,JMg; ~; JMg\
HM1 213.416 knuckles^] [*see substantives*] 213.419 Aloof] [*line-space precedes*] HM2;
[*?no line-space*] HM1 213.419 this,] HM2; ~^ HM1,JMg 213.419 never-ending]
HM,JMg\HM; ~^~ JMg 213.420 teetering,] HM2; ~— HM→1 213.420 coun-
terplot:] HM; ~; JMg 213.421 shot;] HM2(D); ~— HM1 213.424 Not . . . them]
[*see substantives*] 213.424 enrolled;] HM2; ~, HM1 *213.426 Do'nt] HM; Don't
JMg 213.428 there^] HM; ~, JMg 213.430 But] [*line-space precedes*] HM2; [*?no
line-space*] HM1 213.432 "Take] HM1,HM3(D); ^~ HM2 213.432 flying-kites,]
HM2; ~^ HM1 213.433 first."] HM2; ~.^ HM?1 213.434 My] [*line-space precedes*]
HM2; [*?no line-space*] HM1 213.434 slack;] HM2; ~^ HM1 *213.435 bowse away,
wife] [*see substantives*] 213.435 Bohea:] HM; ~; JMg 213.436 here^ must needs] [*see
substantives*] 213.436 me.] HM; ~— JMg 213.437 Sweetheart] HM; sweetheart
JMg[*also see substantives*] 213.437 nay;] HM2; ~, HM1 213.437 back:] HM2; ~[?; ?,]
HM1; ~; JMg 213.438 lack!] HM2; ~. HM1

TOM DEADLIGHT (pp. 214–15)

Nautically, a deadlight is either a cover to keep water from coming in
cabin windows or portholes or a thick piece of glass set into the deck to
let light into a hold. The "famous old sea-ditty" from which this poem's
song "derives" (214.10–11) is "Spanish Ladies," which Joan Tyler Mead, in

discussing the songs in chapter 40 of *Moby-Dick,* describes as "usually considered to be a leisure song but also used as a shanty to weigh anchor when a ship began its homeward voyage." She points out that in that chapter this song is stopped by a protesting Nantucket sailor because it is "sentimental" (p. 3). Other relationships between versions of the traditional song and Melville's variations are noted by Hennig Cohen (p. 212) and Robert Penn Warren (pp. 422–23) in their respective *Selected Poems.* Cohen also cites Jack Chase in *White-Jacket* as often singing "Spanish Ladies"— the song called there "a favorite thing with British man-of-war's-men" (chap. 74).

DISCUSSIONS. 214.12[*prose*] thought:—] In revising JMg, Melville used pencil to change a period to the colon-dash. Since the period appears in JMp and JM, the De Vinne compositor perhaps concluded that Melville's revision was tentative rather than definite, because only penciled, not inked in. NN accepts Melville's revision, however, judging that to Melville's eye the revision was already dark and definite enough.

214.3[*verse*] Deadman] Hennig Cohen (*Selected Poems,* p. 212) says the literal reference here and in lines 8 and 19 is to Dodman's Point; also called Dodman Point, or simply the Dodman, it is a prominent headland on the Cornish coast near Plymouth, England.

215.10 And] For the last three stanzas of the poem (on leaves 4–6), Melville did not explicitly mark the second and fourth lines of each stanza for indention as on the first leaf of the verse (leaf 3). With the exception of line 22, these lines are indented in JMg. That Melville's intention was for the succeeding even-numbered lines to be indented is corroborated by his correcting the galley's failure to indent line 22.

215.9–10 Doldrums . . . Sargasso] The Doldrums are equatorial waters which abound with calms, squalls, and light baffling winds; the Sargasso Sea is a great mass of floating seaweed in the North Atlantic (see also *Clarel,* 2.17.33).

215.12 *Flying-Dutchman*] As differing legends have it, the *Flying Dutchman,* a spectral ship that haunts the waters around the Cape of Good Hope, is an omen of disaster; those who see it will also never again be able to make port. See also *Omoo,* chap. 26, p. 100.

215.14 white goney's] In *Moby-Dick,* chapter 42, "The Whiteness of the Whale," Ishmael reports learning "that goney was some seaman's name for albatross."

215.17 w'ont] See the discussion at 210.328 above.

215.23 blue-blazes] Robert Penn Warren says that this refers "to a blue pyrotechnic torch, called Bengal light, used to signal at night" (p. 423).

215.23 shank-painters] An anchor secured by its ring and crown with a stopper at the cathead also requires a shank-painter—a short length of chain or rope—to keep its shank and flukes from swinging and damaging the bows. Here, "mind your shank-painters" is a preparatory command to get ready for the order to let go the shank-painter so that the anchor may be dropped (see line 21).

215.27,28 do'nt] See the discussion at 210.328 above.

EMENDATIONS. [*Prose:*] 214.0[*subtitle*] (1810)] JMg\HM; ^1810^ HM 214.2 dying] HM\EM; dieing HM 214.4 though] HM\EM; tho' HM 214.9 aberration] HM\ EM; aberation HM *214.12 thought:—] JMg\HM; ~.^ HM [*Verse:*] 214.5 main= top-sail aback] JMg\HM; the wind at sou'-west HM 214.6 clear—] JMg\HM; ~, HM 215.9 through] HM\EM; thro' HM *215.10–28 [*even-numbered lines indented*] JMg[*HM had to correct JMg, however, in line 22 where the compositor did not follow the indention pattern tacitly established as governing the whole poem in its first eight lines*]; [*no indent*] HM 215.11 lads:—] JMg\HM; ~.— HM 215.17 Joe] JMg\HM; [*not underlined*] HM 215.18 night.] JMg\HM; ~; HM 215.21 anchor.^] JMg\HM; ~:— HM

TEXTUAL NOTES: INSCRIPTION STAGES. At least four stages of inscription-revision: A (nonextant pre-fair-copy stage); B (blue ink on thicker paper; foliated in upper middle pencil sequence); C (brown ink on thicker paper); D (gray ink; substage Da leaf 6 is foliated in upper middle pencil).

TEXTUAL NOTES: SUBSTANTIVES [*Prose:*] 214.0–7 Tom . . . tar] [*leaf 1(B)*] 214.0[*subtitle*] 1810] HM1,HM3; (His Death-song) / 1810 HM2[*this parenthetical subtitle penciled in above* 1810] 214.1 tempest] HM2; tempest in the Channel HM1 214.1 homeward-bound^ . . . Mediterranean,] HM3(C); homeward-bound, HM1; homeward-bound^ from the Straits, HM2 214.2 petty-officer . . . forecastle] HM2(D); Captain-of-the Forecastle HM1 214.4 the British] HM2(D); the HM1 214.4–5 mind, . . . sanity,] HM2(D); mind^ HM1 214.5–6 good-bye . . . injunctions] HM3[*inked in by EM*]; death-song HM1; [?farewell] [?ramblings] [*plus two or more undeciphered erased words*] HM2 214.7–9 with . . . aberration] [*leaf 2(Dbb)*] 214.8 Some] HM2; The measure, with some HM→1 214.8 with] HM2; and HM1 214.9–12 wrested . . . thought] [*leaf 2.clip(Dba)*] 214.9 wrested into incoherency] HM2(Dbb); wrested HM1 214.10 import] HM1,HM3; import in HM2[*an uncompleted revision; or this* in *could be an immediately abandoned penciled beginning of the revision in line 9*] 214.10 derives, . . . measure,] HM2; derives^ HM1

[*Verse:*] 214.1–8 Farewell . . . steer] [*leaf 3(Db)*] 214.4 But hope^ . . . fleet^] HM7; But [*undeciphered scratched-out word* {?hope}]—[*three undeciphered scratched-out words*] HM1; But [*undeciphered pencil revisions of or in the space earlier occupied by the undeciphered scratched-out words*] HM?2; But [*above the first undeciphered scratched-out word, EM penciled with* and *above the third, HM penciled, in no determinable order, a* G *and a* g *as well as, above the fourth, an* F] HM\EM?1,HM?3; But I hope in [*undeciphered erased word* {?due}] time HM?4; But I hope in good time HM?5; Where I hope in good time HM\EM2; There [*then insert* ?I] hope to drop anchor HM\EM3,HM\EM4; But hope—with the grand fleet— HM6 214.4 to see]

HM1,HM2; & meet HM\EM 214.5 main-top-sail aback] JMg\HM; the wind at sou'-west HM

215.9–16 I . . . crape] [*leaf 4(C)*] 215.9 I have] HM1,HM2; I've HM\EM 215.9 waters] HM?2,HM6(D); weather HM1,HM?3; [*undeciphered erased word*] HM?4; seas HM?5 215.9 are] HM2(D); is HM1 215.11 mist] HM1,HM3; storm HM2 215.11 lads] HM5(D); [*one or two undeciphered scratched-out words*] HM1; [*at least two successive undeciphered erased words*] HM?2,HM?3; here[?.] HM4(D) 215.13 Matt] HM2(D); [*undeciphered scratched-out word {?lads}*] HM1 215.15 Jock] HM5(D); mind HM1; [*undeciphered scratched-out word {?Ned}*] HM2; Dan HM?3; Ben HM?4 215.15 for kin . . . ²none] HM6; [*five or six undeciphered scratched-out words*] HM1; [*at least four variant readings, each consisting of five or six mainly undeciphered erased words; for begins one of these readings; two end with* none *and another two with* Ned] HM2,HM3,HM4,HM5 215.17–24 Dead-reckoning . . . you] [*leaf 5(C)*] 215.18 Matt] HM4(D); [*undeciphered scratched-out word*] HM1; ?Ned HM2; ?Ben HM3 215.19 Dead-reckoning is] HM2; Dead-reckoning's HM→1 215.20 may reckon] HM2(D); reckons HM1 215.20 near right] HM1,HM3; aright HM2 215.24 Admiral he's] HM2; Admiral's HM1 215.25–28 But . . . keel] [*leaf 6(Da)*] 215.25 give me] HM2; give HM1[*inadvertent omission*] 215.25 Matt] HM2; [*undeciphered scratched-out word {?Ned}*] HM1 215.26 Jock] HM2; Matt HM1 215.28 blubber like lubbers] HM,JMg\HM; blabber like blubbers JMg

TEXTUAL NOTES: ACCIDENTALS. [*Prose:*] 214.0 *Tom Deadlight*] [*title not repeated on a separate section-title page*] HM; [*in JMg, HM directed* A page should precede "Tom Deadlight" bearing that title] JMg\HM; TOM DEADLIGHT [*on section-title page as well as at beginning of poem*] JMp 214.0[*subtitle*] (1810)] JMg\HM; ^1810^ HM 214.1–12 During . . . thought] HM1,HM3; [*bracketed*] HM2 214.1 home-ward-bound . . . Mediterranean] [*see substantives*] 214.1 Mediterranean,] HM3(D); Medeterranean^ HM1(C); Mediterranean^ HM2 214.2 petty-officer . . . fore-castle] [*see substantives*] 214.2 dying] HM\EM; dieing HM 214.4 though] HM\EM; tho' HM 214.4–5 mind, . . . sanity,] [*see substantives*] 214.6 messmates^] HM; ~, JMg 214.7 flap] [*EM queried, HM pencil-reinscribed the word, and EM retraced* p *for clarity*] 214.8 Some] [*paragraph*] HM; [*no paragraph*] JMg 214.8 Some] [*see substantives*] 214.9 aberration^] HM\EM; aberation^ HM; aberration, JMg 214.10 derives, . . . measure,] [*see substantives*] 214.12 brain,] HM2; ~^ HM1 *214.12 thought:—] JMg\HM; ~.^ HM,JMg,JMp

[*Verse:*] 214.1 During] [*after scratching out a beginning device that earlier preceded the verse, HM directed* To the Printer: / Leave something of a space between the prose & verse. *and in galley proof, where less space appeared between the prose and verse than between the verse stanzas, he directed* Leave more space here. *but the problem was solved when JMp put a page-break between the prose and verse*] 214.1 you^] HM,JMg\HM; ~, JMg 214.1 hearties,—] HM2; ~,^ HM1 214.2 you^] HM,JMg\HM; ~, JMg 214.3 I've] HM; I 've JMg 214.4 But hope^ . . . fleet^] [*see substantives*] 214.6 'to,] HM,JMg\HM; ~^ JMg 214.6 clear—] JMg\HM; ~, HM 214.7 a'flying] HM;

a' flying JMg 214.7 but^] HM; ~, JMg 214.7 dam'me] HM; dam' me JMg 214.8
Channel] HM,JMp\HM; channel JMg 214.8 I'll] HM; I' ll JM
    215.9 through] HM\EM; thro' HM 215.9 callèd] HM,JMg\HM; called JMg
215.9 Doldrums] HM?1,HM3; [*underlined*] HM?2 *215.10–28 [*even-numbered lines
indented*] JMg[*HM had to correct JMg, however, in line 22 where the compositor did not
follow the indention pattern tacitly established as governing the whole poem in its first eight
lines*]; [*no indent*] HM 215.10 at Sargasso] HM?1,HM3(D); <u>at Sargassx</u> HM2 [*pen-
cil-underlined—to draw attention to misspelling or to clarify final (here undeciphered) letter
(later scratched out)*] 215.11 eyes,] HM?1,HM3(D); ~^ HM?2 215.11 lads:—] JMg\
HM; ~.— HM; ~, JMg[*also see substantives*] 215.12 *Flying-Dutchman*] HM1; ~^~
HM?2,JMg 215.12 oddsbobbs] HM; odd bobbs JMg; odds bobbs JMg\r 215.13
But^] HM,JMg\HM; ~, JMg 215.13 what's] HM; what 's JMg 215.14 wing?—]
HM2(D); ~^— HM1 215.14 rolls!—] HM2; ~^— HM1 215.14 'tis] HM; 't is
JMg 215.14 Cape!—] HM2(D); ~:— HM1 215.15 ²none;] HM2; ~. HM1 215:16
Holy Joe] HM2(D); [*not underlined*] HM1 215.17 Dead-reckoning] HM2(D);
Dead-reackoning HM1; Dead^reckoning JMg 215.17 Joe] HM2,JMg\HM; Joe
HM1,HM3,JMg *215.17 w'ont] HM; won't JMg 215.17 by;] HM2; ~, HM1
215.18 doused all the glims] HM1,HM3; <u>doused</u> all the <u>glims</u> HM2 [*the penciled
underlinings may be querying marks*] 215.18 t'other] HM; t' other JMg 215.18 night.]
JMg,JMg\HM2; ~; HM1,HM3,JMg\HM1; ~^ HM→2 215.19 Dead-reckoning]
HM3(D); Dexx-reackoning HM1; Dexx-reckoning HM2; Dead^reckoning JMg
215.19 Dead-reckoning . . . Deadman] [*in JMp, the line was respaced so that the
word is divided as* Dead-/man] 215.19 Deadman;] HM2; <u>Deadman</u>^ HM1 215.20
reckon] HM3(D); reackons HM1[*see substantives*]; reackon HM2 215.21 anchor.^]
JMg,JMg\HM2; ~:— HM; [*undeciphered revision; M erased whatever punctuation (a
dash?) he at first intended to insert instead of or in addition to the JMg period*] JMg\HM1
215.22 Captains] HM; captains JMg 215.24 Admiral^ he's] HM; Admiral, he 's
JMg 215.24 you!] HM2; ~[?.] HM?1 215.26 let's] HM; let 's JMg 215.26 it's] HM;
it 's JMg *215.27,28 do'nt] HM; don't JMg 215.27 baccy] HM,JMg\r; *bacy* JMg

JACK ROY (pp. 216–17)

In their editions of *Selected Poems,* Hennig Cohen (p. 213) and Robert
Penn Warren (pp. 423–24) have connected Jack Roy with Jack Chase,
captain of the maintop in the *Neversink,* whom Melville celebrates in
White-Jacket, especially in chapter 4, and they explore the poem's king/
knave/jack associations. For the historical Jack Chase, Melville's shipmate
aboard the frigate *United States* in 1843–44, see Howard P. Vincent, *The
Tailoring of Melville's "White-Jacket,"* pp. 33–47.

DISCUSSIONS. 216.4 mute] Though Melville pencil-altered "mute" to "pale" in
one of the Berkshire Athenaeum copies of *John Marr* (V.811.M49.4), that vari-
ant reading does not appear in any other of the twenty-one located copies, in

eighteen of which Melville and his wife inked in eleven other revisions. A further indication that this tentative revision was rejected is the fact that it occurs in one of two copies inscribed to the dedicatee, W. Clark Russell. The existence of two copies (the other is at Harvard) is explainable as resulting from Melville's discovery, when inscribing the copy now at the Berkshire Athenaeum, that he had previously penciled revisions to "Jack Roy" and "To Ned" (237.15) in it; he then had to inscribe another presentation copy not marred by pencilings or erasures of revisions that he did not ultimately mean to make permanent in ink.

216.18 Larry o' the Cannakin] This character has not been identified with any specific person in Melville's nautical travels. "Cannakin" is a variant of "cannikin," a small can or drinking vessel.

EMENDATIONS. 216.2 blithe] JMp\HM; glad HM 216.2 sung;] JMg\HM; ~, HM 216.4 Dropped] HM\EM; Dropt HM 217.21 martinet] JMg\HM; Martinet HM 217.21 mutineer;] JMg\HM; ~. HM 217.28 a'sweeping—] JMg\HM; ~, HM

TEXTUAL NOTES: INSCRIPTION STAGES. At least three stages of inscription-revision: A (nonextant pre-fair-copy stage); B (brown ink); C (gray ink).

TEXTUAL NOTES: SUBSTANTIVES. 216.0–6 *Jack . . . mother's-son*] [*leaf 1(C)*] 216.0 *Jack Roy*] HM1,HM3[*inked in by EM*]; [*undeciphered erased word*] Roy HM2 216.2 blithe] JMp\HM; glad HM *216.4 mute*] HM; pale JM\HM[*HM penciled this variant into the Berkshire Athenaeum copy (V811.M49.4) of* John Marr *inscribed to but probably not sent to W. Clark Russell*] 216.4 halyard-singers] HM2[*there may also be one undeciphered erased word above* singers]; chorus-singers HM1 216.7–15 But . . . command] [*leaf 2(Ca)*] 216.7 king] HM1,HM3; trump HM2[*though* king *was never explicitly canceled*] 216.8 a'fluttering] HM2; fluttering HM1 216.16–17 Magnanimous . . . shell] [*leaf 3(I.B)*] 216.18–20 Sang . . . cheer] [*leaf 3.patch(Cb)*] 216.18–20 Sang . . . cheer] HM2(Cb); [*see following description of superseded stage B matter later covered by stage Cb revision patch*]

> Sang Larry o' the Cannakin [*then(C)* Larry o' the Cannakin], in jovial
>   recline[?,]
> At mess between broadside[*then add hyphen*]guns in long line. [*?then
>   ?*line— *then* line^]
> [*then(?Ca) transpose to read*]
> At mess between broadside-guns in long line
> Sang Larry o' the Cannakin, in jovial recline{?,}
> *then(Cb) cancel the transposition line and revise the text-lines to read*
> Sang Larry o' the Cannakin, smuggler o' the wine,
> At mess between guns, lad in jovial recline]
> In Limbo [*then* To {*undeciphered scratched-out word*} *?then ?*In {*undeciphered scratched-out word*} *then(C)* In Limbo] our Jack he will [*then(C)*
>   would] chirrup up a cheer,

[*then pencil-cancel* Sang . . . cheer *and cover over with revision patch*] HM1

217.21–23 The martinet . . . ladies] [*leaf 3(...II.B)* The Martinet . . . ladies] 217.23 He'd] HM2(C); He'll HM1 217.24–31 Never . . . Roy] [*leaf 4(C)*] 217.28 dolphin] HM2; dolphins HM1 217.29 Arch irridescent] HM1,HM3; Irridescent arch HM2[*HM imagined this as a possible reading by underlining each word and putting a 2 below* Arch *and a 1 below* irridescent] 217.30 thy life] HM1,HM3; life HM2

TEXTUAL NOTES: ACCIDENTALS. 216.0 *Jack Roy*] [*title not repeated on separate section-title page*] HM; [*in JMg, HM directed* A page should preceed "Jack Roy," {*then add* a page} *bearing that title.*] JMg\HM; JACK ROY [*on section-title page as well as at beginning of poem*] JMp 216.2 sung;] JMg\HM[*also, in JMp, HM called attention to how the semicolon seemed loose in the forme*]; ~^ HM1; ~, HM2 216.3 sands,] HM2[*and EM reinscribed the word for clarity*]; ~^ HM1 216.3 sounds,] HM?1[*the comma seems not to have been omitted at the time of original ink inscription, but rather penciled larger than customary when HM did the final pointing of the line*],HM2 216.3 seas^] HM,JMg\HM; ~, JMg 216.3 storm-petrels] HM2; ~^~ HM1 216.3 cry,] HM2; ~^ HM1 216.4 Dropped] HM\EM; Dropt HM 216.4 globe,] HM2; ~^ HM1 216.4 halyard-singers] HM; ~^~ JMg 216.4 lie.] HM2,JMg\r; ~^ HM1; ~, JMg 216.6 mother's-son] HM,JMg\HM; ~^~ JMg 216.7 But] [*line-space precedes*] HM2; [*?no line-space {leaf division makes the line-space problematic}*] HM1 216.7 thou,] HM2; ~^ HM1 216.8 a'fluttering^] HM; a-fluttering, JMg 216.8 fly—] HM2; ~, HM1 216.9 challenge, and forever,] HM2; ~^ ~ ~^ HM1 216.9 rue.] HM,JMg\HM; ~, JMg 216.10 Starry Flag] HM; starry flag JMg 216.10 high^] HM; ~, JMg 216.11 'tis] HM; 't is JMg 216.11 do,] HM2; ~^ HM1 216.11 privilege] HM2; privelege HM1 216.11 die,] HM,JMg\HM; ~. JMg 216.12 then^] HM; ~, JMg 216.13 Captain] HM; captain JMg 216.15 Mercutio^] HM,JMg\HM; ~, JMg 216.16 humor:] HM; ~; JMg 216.16 when] HM2; When HM1 216.16 fell,] HM2; ~— HM1 216.17 a'plenty] HM; a^plenty JMg; a–plenty JM 216.17 lads;] HM2; ~! HM1 216.17 shell!] HM2; ~. HM1

217.21 martinet] JMg\HM; Martinet HM; Martinot JMg 217.21 mutineer;] JMg\HM; ~. HM 217.23 He'd] HM; He 'd JMg 217.24 Never] [*line-space precedes*] HM2; [*?no line-space (leaf division makes the line-space problematic)*] HM1 217.24 knave^] HM; ~, JMg 217.28 a'sweeping] HM; a-sweeping JMg; a-sweep-/ing JM 217.28 a'sweeping—] JMp\HM[*see preceding entry; HM changes only the comma to a dash*]; ~, HM 217.29 irridescent] HM; iridescent JMg 217.31 Heroic . . . Roy] [*with a question mark in the left margin, HM queried something about the text-line*]

THE HAGLETS (pp. 218–25)

This poem was first printed under the title "The Admiral of the White" in the Boston *Herald* [BH] on Sunday, May 17, 1885, and (in abridged form) in the New York *Tribune* [NYT] the same day. Although the rest of the printer's copy for the *John Marr* volume consists of manuscript in Melville's hand, this poem was submitted in the form of scissored-apart and ink-revised (by both Melvilles) printed sections of the *Tribune* publication. These cuttings were pasted onto leaves the same size as those for other pieces in *John Marr;* Elizabeth Shaw Melville then ink-inscribed between the pasted printed sections the lines left out of the *Tribune* abridgment [EM], and Melville further revised her inscription [EM\HM]. (It is not clear why the Melvilles did not revise a copy of the complete Boston *Herald* printing.) Presumably earlier, Melville wrote a different poem that he left in manuscript, also titled "The Admiral of the White," a poem that describes captured French swords swaying the compass of a victorious British ship and driving it on the rocks. In the upper left-hand corner of the first page of this three-page manuscript poem (Harvard MS Am 188 [361]), Elizabeth Melville penciled "Herman gave this to Tom—" (that is, Thomas Melville, his younger brother). There is no evidence to suggest when, prior to 1884 (when Thomas died in March), Melville wrote this version of "The Admiral of the White." (A transcription of the manuscript poem will be printed in NN volume 13, *"Billy Budd, Sailor" and Other Uncompleted Writings.*)

The manuscript poem and the published poem finally titled "The Haglets," as well as the Timoneer's story in *Clarel* (3.12.56–128), have something of their beginnings in what Melville recorded in a journal entry for December 7, 1856: "Captain [Robert Taitt, of the *Egyptian*] told a story about the heap of arms affecting the compass" (previous transcriptions have rendered "heap" as "heat"). The next day, in the middle of another subject, he added, "Arms all taken down into the cabin after being discharged," explaining this sentence with a marginal notation: "Cap. T's story of arms" (*Journals*, pp. 56, 389, and 553).

The bird that fits the characteristics attributed to the birds in this poem is the greater shearwater (of the genus *Puffinus*), also called the haglet or gray hag. Melville would have been familiar with this Atlantic Ocean wanderer, which goes on prolonged glides (cf. lines 111 and 177) on a wingspan of some three feet and has gray on its head and back (cf. line 49). Its flight characteristics also conform to Melville's "Cross and recross— weave and inweave" (line 225). Whether these specific birds actually look ominously fateful may not matter so much as that their name, meaning "little hags," reminds us of "hag-ridden" (as in nightmares and depression) and the greater Hags, the Fates as they are conventionally figured in Greek religion. There are no ominous birds in the manuscript poem, but three gulls appear in the Timoneer's story (*Clarel,* 3.12.96 and 115), plying continually in the snakelike wake of *The Peace of God* and screaming around its mast when that vessel goes on the rocks because the Moor's smuggled-aboard arms have affected the compass and made the old Greek pilot, Agath, lose his bearings.

DISCUSSIONS. 218.13–15 By open ports . . . arm'd Plate Fleet] Here presumably the invoked ghost of the "neglected fane" (line 7) begins to tell the tale of the British admiral of the White Fleet (conventionally considered foremost of the fleets of the British navy), who has conquered the well-armed Spanish Plate Fleet and has taken not only the gold and silver it was transporting from the Americas to Spain but also "Ensigns and arms in trophy brave" (lines 31–36).

219.40 Opher] A variant spelling of Ophir, which appears in the King James Version of 1 Kings 9:26–28, the account of a naval expedition to remove gold from Ophir and take it to Solomon. Melville placed a check mark by verse 26 and double-sidelined verse 28 in one of his Bibles (Philadelphia: Butler, 1846; Sealts, no. 62).

220.80 Like quaking Lima's crosses] Melville refers often to the effects of the Lima, Peru, earthquake of 1746. When he was a member of the crew of the *United States,* he saw the portion of the old city that was then under water, and he went ashore as well, around January 1, 1844, and saw the remaining devastation there. For other Lima references, see, for example, *Moby-Dick,* chap. 54, and *Clarel,* 1.31.161–79.

221.101 storm-sail] NN adopts this hyphenated reading (in BH and JMg) as more likely representative of Melville's intentions than the unhyphenated word in the copy-text (EM), because he ordinarily hyphenated words like this one and could easily have overlooked his wife's unhyphenated word (its elements, as usual, only slightly separated).

222.132 men—] That Melville accepted the dash (substituted in JMg for the comma of the manuscript) is suggested by his ensuing revision in JMg of the punctuation in the previous line (from a comma to a colon after "stout").

EMENDATIONS. 218.0[*section-title*] SEA-PIECES] [*on section-title page*] JMg\HM; [*no section-title*] HM 218.8 lament;] JMg\HM; ~, NYT 219.21 and] JMg; & EM 220.79 spars,] JMg\HM; ~^ EM 220.79 height,] JMg; ~^ EM 221.95 Vies . . . smites] JMg\HM;' Vying with fists that smite EM\HM *221.101 storm-sail] JMg; stormsail EM 222.128 dream . . . jar] JMp\HM; tremors sole the cannon's are EM\HM 222.131 Spain's] JMp\HM; The EM 222.131 stout:] JMg\HM; ~, EM *222.132 men—] JMg; ~, EM 222.132 out."] JMg\HM; ~.^ EM 222.149 bliss:] JMg\HM; ~, NYT 223.161 Honor!] JMg\HM; ~, NYT 223.168 nods—] JMg\HM; ~, NYT 223.174 will;—] JMp\HM; ~.^ NYT 223.183 the-Blue] JMg; ~^~ NYT 223.183 Flags-o'-the-Red] JMg; ~-~^-~-~ NYT 223.195 Yea] JMg\HM; Yes NYT 224.215 moan;] JMg\HM; ~, NYT 224.228 gasp.] [*wide line-space follows*] JMg\HM; [*line-space*] NYT 225.233 content, . . . night,] JMg\HM; ~^ . . . ~^ NYT 225.234 Their] JMp\HM; The NYT 225.234 sleeps—] JMg\HM; ~, NYT

TEXTUAL NOTES: SUBSTANTIVES. 218.0[*section-title*] SEA-PIECES] [*in JMg, after erasing his penciled* Sea-Pieces *and* page *between* HM *directed that* A Page should precede "The Haglets," *bearing the title {then add* <u>Sea-Pieces</u> *double-underlined}*] JMg\HM1,JMg\HM2; [*no section-title*] HM; THE HAGLETS [*on section-title page as well as at the beginning of the poem*] JMp; <u>Sea-Pieces</u> [*on section-title page, double-underlined; in JMp, HM also revises the verso running heads from this point through "The Enviable Isles" to read* Sea-Pieces *instead of* John Marr and Other Sailors] JMp\HM 218.0–219.18 The . . . White] [*EM leaf 1.clip(NYT)*] 218.0 The Haglets] NYT\HM2; The Admiral of the White BH,NYT; The Fates NYT\HM1 218.0 Haglets] [*no comparable following words present*] NYT\HM; By the Author of "Omoo," "Typee," "Moby Dick," Etc. [*in very small capitals*] / Copyright, 1885 [*in smaller italic type*] NYT; Copyright, 1885. [*bracketed*] BH

219.19–24 The eddying . . . pole] [*EM leaf 1*] 219.19–30 The . . . guns] BH,EM; [*not present*] NYT 219.25–30 But . . . guns] [*EM leaf 2*] 219.31–220.54 Ensigns . . . flight] [*EM leaf 2.clip(NYT)*]

220.54 endless^ rules the] NYT,JMg\r; endless, JMg[*misreading*] 220.55–66 The . . . greet] [*EM leaf 3*] 220.55–66 The . . . greet] BH,EM; [*not present*] NYT 220.60 victor] EM; admiral BH 220.67–78 But . . . din] [*EM leaf 4.clip(NYT)*] 220.79–84 The . . . gaunt] [*EM leaf 4*] 220.79–221.114 The . . . neighborhood] BH,EM; [*not present*] NYT 220.84 Dipped] EM; Slipped BH 220.84 wheeling] EM2; [?whiling] EM1[*mistranscription*] 220.85–221.96 A . . . word] [*EM leaf 5*] 220.88 bellowings] EM\HM; billowings EM[*misreading*]

221.91 In . . . turn] EM\HM2; [*in originally transcribing this passage, EM left a blank space for at least the last three words of it; perhaps she had already misconstrued its first two or three words, or HM decided to alter them; whatever the case, those first two or three words (here undeciphered) were later scratched out and replaced by EM with* In trim betimes] EM1,EM\HM?1,EM2 221.95 Vies . . . smites] BH,EM,JMg\HM; Vying with fists that smite EM\HM 221.97–108 Of . . . flew] [*EM leaf 6*] 221.101 home] EM\HM; [*undeciphered scratched-out word—perhaps a mistranscription*] EM 221.103 driving] EM\HM; spooming BH,EM 221.109–14 And still . . . neighborhood] [*EM leaf 7(I)*] 221.109 And . . . nor] EM4; [*in originally transcribing, EM left blank the space now occupied by line 109's first five words*] EM1; ?And yet they fly EM?2; And yet they fly nor EM3 221.110 But . . . wake] EM3; [*in originally transcribing, EM left blank the space for line 110*] EM1; But [*one or two undeciphered erased words, perhaps* fan and] follow in the wake EM2 221.115–222.126 Plumed . . . pass] [*EM leaf 7.clip(NYT)*]

222.127–32 Let . . . out] [*EM leaf 7(II)*] 222.127–32 Let . . . out] BH,EM; [*not present*] NYT 222.128 (Whose . . . jar)] JMp\HM3; ^Whose tremors sole the cannon's are, BH; ^Whose tremors sole the cannon's are^ EM; (Whose tremors sole the cannon's are) EM\HM,JMg\HM; (Whose tremors sole the cannons are) JMg; [*De Vinne's reviewer's query is pencil-canceled, then the cancellation mark is erased*] JMp\r; (Whose dream of [*undeciphered erased word*] no tremors jar) JMp\HM1; (Whose dream of life no tremors jar) JMp\HM2 222.129 Fears] EM,JMg\HM; Tears JMg 222.131 Spain's] JMp\HM; The BH,EM 222.133–223.192 To-night's

. . . drowned] [*EM leaf 8* {*no substantive inscription*} *EM leaf 8.clip(NYT)* To-night's
. . . drowned] 222.153 Laced] NYT; Lace BH

223.168 hatted] NYT; hated BH 223.193–225.250 Ha . . . star] [*EM leaf 9* {*no
substantive inscription*} *EM leaf 9.clip(NYT)* Ha . . . star] 223.195 Yea] JMg\HM; Yes
BH,NYT 223.196 follows] NYT,JMg\r; fellows JMg[*misreading*]

224.199 drum-beat] NYT,JMg\HM; heart-beat JMg[*misreading*] 224.209
clash] NYT; dash BH[*?misreading*]

225.234 Their] JMp\HM; The NYT 225.239 His] NYT,JMp\HM2; The
JMp\HM1

TEXTUAL NOTES: ACCIDENTALS. 218–25[*indention and stanzaic division*] [*in the
upper-left corner of EM leaf 1, HM penciled a reminder to himself consisting of one or two
undeciphered erased words plus* Indent &c *then on a separate leaf (foliated* 99² *and pre-
ceding "The Haglets") he directed* To the Printer / [*indent for paragraph*] The greater
part of this Piece {*then* Piece, "The Haglets,"} is marked off (in blue pencil) into
stanzas of eighteen lines each. I think the {*then their*} seventh and thirteenth
lines should be indented. *The compositor followed directions, except in line 19, where
(in both JMg and JMp) HM again had to ask for indention (and in JMg, HM directs to
close up space between lines 18 and 19). Since the compositor had set lines 13–30 in three
six-line stanzas (the BH, NYT, and EM versions of the poem are divided into six-line
stanzas except for the two concluding stanzas of eight lines each), HM had to re-specify
(above line 13, in JMg)* The stanza of eighteen lines here begins. *and (at the top of a
new galley, at the left of lines 25–30)* This belongs to the first stanza of eighteen lines
{*then to the stanza of eighteen lines coming first*}.] 218.6 winding^sheet] NYT;
~-~ JM 218.8 lament;] JMg\HM; ~, BH,NYT 218.12 winding^sheet] NYT;
wind-/ing-sheet JM 218.12 sheet.] [*wide line-space follows*] NYT\HM,JMg\HM;
[*line-space followed by rule*] NYT,JMg; [*line-space concealed by page division; rule omit-
ted*] JMp 218.13,17 Admiral] NYT; admiral BH 218.15 Plate Fleet] NYT; plate
fleet BH 218.16 flag-ship's] NYT; flagship's BH

219.18 red-cross] NYT; ~^~ BH 219.18 Flag] NYT; flag BH 219.19 The] [*indent*]
NYT,JMg\HM,JMp\HM; [*no indent*] JMg,JMp[*see above, the entry for 218–25* {*inden-
tion and stanzaic division*}] 219.21 and] JMg; & EM 219.22 Milky Way] EM,JMg\
HM; milky way BH,JMg 219.22 Way:] EM\HM2; ~; BH,EM\HM1,JMg 219.23
thrill, . . . roll,] EM\HM; ~^ . . . ~^ EM 219.24 pole.] EM\HM; ~^ EM 219.25
ah,] EM\HM; ~^ BH,EM 219.26 scutcheoned] EM2; scx[*undeciphered pen slip*]
EM→1 219.26 castles'] EM\HM1,EM\HM3; ~^ EM,EM\HM2 219.27 Spain,]
EM\HM; ~^ EM 219.28 Naples,] EM\HM; ~^ BH,EM 219.28 beside;] EM\HM;
~^ EM 219.29 towers,] EM\HM; ~^ EM 219.30 Admiral's] EM; admiral's BH
219.31 brave—] BH,NYT; ~, JM 219.34 star—] NYT\HM2; ~; BH,NYT; ~?:
NYT\HM?1 219.35 draperies^] NYT; ~, BH 219.39 prize-crews,] NYT; ~^~^
BH 219.39 convoy-guns] NYT; ~^~ BH 219.41 Admiral] NYT; admiral BH
219.42 sped.] BH,NYT\HM[*period mended*],JMp\HM; ~^ JMp[*faint in JMg, the
period vanishes in JMp*] 219.42 sped.] [*following line 42, the NYT text is half-scissored
apart, perhaps inadvertently, perhaps as part of a temporary plan to insert more text-lines*]
219.51 cabin-lustre] NYT,JM; cabin^lustre BH; cabin-luster JMg

220.54 endless] [*see substantives*] 220.54 war-ship's] NYT; ~^~ BH 220.55
sea-fowl] EM\HM; ~^~ BH,EM 220.55 here^] EM,EM\HM2; ~, BH,EM\
HM1,JMg 220.55 know,] EM\HM; ~^ EM 220.56 flag-ship] EM\HM; flagship
BH; flag^ship EM 220.56 quelled^] BH,EM; ~, JMg 220.57 (As . . . one)^] EM\
HM; (~ . . . ~), BH; ^~ . . . ~^^ EM 220.58 grave,] EM\HM; ~^ EM 220.58 shrill]
EM\HM; shirll EM[*mistranscription*] 220.59 rites—] EM\HM; ~^ EM 220.60 led.]
EM\HM; ~^ EM 220.61 fleet, but fairer, blow,] EM\HM; ~^ ~ ~^ ~^ EM 220.62
side,] EM\HM; ~^ EM 220.63 gleam^] BH,EM; ~, JMg 220.64 wide;] EM\HM;
~^ EM 220.65 and] EM\HM; & EM 220.65 tinkling] EM\HM; tin kling EM
220.66 greet.] EM\HM; ~^ EM 220.68 end?—] NYT; ~?^ BH 220.69 blasts^]
NYT; ~, BH 220.72 storm-bow] NYT; ~^~ BH 220.78 din.] BH,NYT\HM;
~^ NYT 220.79 spars,] JMg\HM; ~^ BH,EM 220.79 height,] BH,JMg; ~^ EM
220.80 rock;] EM\HM; ~^ EM 220.82 shrouds,] EM\HM; ~^ EM 220.83 yard=
arms] EM\HM; ~^~ EM 220.83 aslant^] BH,EM; ~, JMg 220.84 condor's] EM\
HM; condon's EM[*misreading*] 220.84 gaunt.] EM\HM; ~^ EM 220.85 lull!] EM\
HM; ~^ EM 220.86 boom^] BH,EM; ~, JMg 220.87 Electric] EM; Eectric BH
220.87 aloft;] EM\HM3; ~^ EM; ~— EM\HM1; ~: EM\HM?2

221.88 go:] EM\HM; ~^ EM 221.89 rears—beset—] [*HM mended, so that
EM's dashes (abbreviated by her having to squeeze much into the physical line) would not
be mistaken for hyphens*] EM\HM 221.89 harassed,] EM\HM; ~^ EM 221.91 land,]
EM\HM; ~^ EM 221.92 shivered] EM[*penciled before inked in*] 221.92 stow:] EM\
HM; ~^ EM; ~; BH,JMg 221.93 watch, dismissed, . . . can,] EM\HM; ~^ ~^
. . . ~, BH; ~^ ~^ . . . ~^ EM 221.94 bow—] EM\HM; ~^ EM 221.95 board^]
BH,EM,JMg\HM; ~, JMg,JMp 221.96 word.] EM\HM; ~^ EM 221.97 Of royal
oak] EM2[*penciled before inked in*]; [*EM at first left blank space, presumably to query or
wait upon HM's final intention*] EM1 221.97 confirmed,] EM\HM; ~^ EM 221.98
shows;] BH,EM\HM2; ~^ EM; ~: EM\HM1,JMg 221.99 prow—] EM\HM;
~^ EM 221.100 rallies, rears,] EM\HM; ~^ ~^ EM 221.100 grows;] EM\HM2;
~^ EM; ~?: EM\HM?1 221.101 plugged,] EM\HM; ~^ EM *221.101 storm-sail]
BH,JMg; stormsail EM 221.101 home,] EM\HM2; ~^ EM\HM1[*see substantives*]
221.102 watery] EM2; xatery EM1[*undeciphered misreading*] 221.102 dome.] EM\
HM; ~^ EM 221.103 Dim seen adrift] EM2; [*EM originally left blank space, pre-
sumably to query or wait upon HM's final intention*] EM1 221.103 scud,] EM\HM2;
~^ BH; ~[?^] ?EM; ~— EM\HM1 221.104 forlorn;] EM\HM3; ~[?.] ?EM; ~—
EM\HM1; ~: EM\HM2 221.105 Then, . . . visage,] EM\HM; ~^ . . . ~^ EM
221.105 ²fades] EM; ~, BH 221.106 morn,] EM\HM; ~^ EM 221.107 engulfed]
EM; ingulfed BH 221.107 flag-ship's] EM\HM; flagship's BH; flag^ship's EM
221.107 crew^] EM; ~, BH,JMg 221.108 And, . . . round, . . . flew.] EM\HM; ~^
. . . ~^ . . . ~^ EM 221.109 fly, . . . cry,] EM\HM; ~^ . . . ~^ EM 221.110 wake,]
EM\HM; ~^ EM 221.111 ²ply] EM\HM; ~^ EM 221.112 take;] EM\HM2; ~^
EM; ~[?,] EM\HM?1 221.113 mood,] EM\HM; ~^ EM 221.118 hull:] NYT; ~;
BH 221.120 high-altar] NYT; ~^~ BH 221.123 place.] NYT,BH; ~, JMg

222.127 do^] EM; ~, BH 222.128 (Whose . . . jar)] [*see substantives*] 222.129
astern:] EM; ~; BH 222.130 star;] EM; ~, BH 222.131 stout:] JMg\HM; ~, BH,EM
*222.132 men—] JMg; ~, BH,EM 222.132 they'll] BH,EM; they 'll JMg 222.132

out."] BH,JMg\HM; ~.^ EM 222.133 To-night's] NYT; Tonight's BH 222.134 year:] NYT; ~; BH 222.135 four-fold] BH,NYT; fourfold JM 222.136 anear:] NYT; ~; BH 222.137 passing-bells] NYT; ~^~ BH 222.138 ²Year] NYT; year BH 222.143 shot-chests] NYT; ~^~ BH 222.148 We'll] NYT; We 'll JMg 222.149 ingots] NYT,JMg\HM; Ingots JMg 222.149 bliss:] JMg\HM; ~, NYT,BH; ~. JMg 222.150 to-night] NYT; tonight BH 222.157 Ay,] NYT\HM; Aye, BH; Ay^ NYT 222.157 star-light] NYT; starlight BH 222.158 hearth-light] NYT; ~^~ BH 222.159 wine-light] NYT; ~^~ BH

223.161 Honor!] JMg\HM; ~, BH,NYT 223.161 foretold:] NYT\HM; ~; BH,NYT 223.162 'tis] BH,NYT; 't is JMg 223.168 And, hatted,] NYT\HM; ~^ ~^ BH[*see also substantives*],NYT 223.168 nods—] JMg\HM; ~, BH,NYT 223.170 fro;] NYT; ~[?:] BH 223.174 will;—] JMp\HM; ~.^ BH,NYT 223.182 fruit:] NYT; ~; BH 223.183 the-Blue] BH,JMg; ~^~ NYT 223.183 Flags-o'-the-Red] JMg; ~-~'-~^~ BH; ~-~^-~-~ NYT

224.199 calls,] BH,NYT; ~^ JM 224.202 know:] NYT; ~; BH 224.206 peer:] NYT; ~; BH 224.207-8 "We . . . here?"] NYT\HM; ^~ . . . ~?^ BH,NYT 224.207 land:] NYT; ~; BH 224.215 moan;] JMg\HM; ~, BH,NYT 224.222 though] NYT\EM; tho' BH,NYT 224.224 through] NYT\HM; thro' BH,NYT 224.228 wreck where] [*the words are pencil-underlined in the NYT portion of the printer's copy, then the underlining is erased*] NYT\HM?1,NYT\HM?2 224.228 gasp.] [*wide line-space follows*] JMg\HM[*HM calls for* More space *but his penciled, then erased* x *and short rule, between lines 228 and 229, in his printer's copy, indicate he had considered such a revision earlier*]; [*line-space*] NYT 224.231 they'll] BH,NYT; they 'll JMg

225.233 content, . . . night,] JMg\HM; ~^ . . . ~^ BH,NYT 225.234 sleeps—] JMg\HM; ~, BH,NYT 225.234 White.] [*wide line-space follows*] NYT\HM[*HM directs* Widen the space between these two lines]; [*line-space*] NYT 225.243 play,] BH,NYT; ~^ JMg 225.250 star.] [*NYT's* HERMAN MELVILLE {*in small and smaller caps*} *is canceled*] NYT\?HM; [*BH closes with* HERMAN MELVILLE {*in small and smaller caps*} *followed by* Author of "Omoo," "Typee; or, Life in the Marquesas," "Moby Dick," etc.] BH

THE ÆOLIAN HARP AT THE
SURF INN (pp. 226–27)

DISCUSSIONS. 226.1 harp] See the discussion at 3.13 above.

226.10 *Phocion*] This Athenian general and statesman is also mentioned in "Timoleon" (257.136 above).

226.11 Alicant] Alicante, the Spanish port on the Mediterranean.

226.14 wreck] In his 1947 *Collected Poems* Howard P. Vincent (p. 471) cites a similar wreck in *Redburn* (chap. 22); Hennig Cohen in his *Selected Poems* (p. 217) cites another in a book Melville reviewed in 1847, John Codman's *Sailors' Life and Sailors' Yarns* (see the NN *Piazza Tales* volume, pp. 210–11, 627).

226.18 kraken] Melville also refers to this fabulous Scandinavian sea monster in his November [17?], 1851, letter to Hawthorne and in *Moby-Dick,* chap. 59.

EMENDATIONS. 226.11 For] JM\HM; To HM 226.14 wreck!"] [*double line-space follows*] JMg\HM; [*single line-space*] HM 226.16 forsaken;] JMg\HM; ~, HM 227.45–48 O the sailors. . . . word of] [*double line-space precedes and these lines indented*] JMp\HM; [*wide line-space; HM inscribed lines 45–48 with a margin to the left of the one formed by the four preceding lines (the only other lines on this leaf)*] HM 227.45 sailors—] JMg\HM; ~, HM 227.45 sails!] JMg\HM; ~, HM

TEXTUAL NOTES: INSCRIPTION STAGES. At least five stages of inscription-revision: A (nonextant pre-fair-copy stage); B (gray ink on thicker, darker paper; stage B precedes the upper middle pencil foliation sequence); C (blue ink on thicker, darker paper; leaves foliated in upper middle pencil sequence); D (gray ink on thicker, darker paper; leaf foliated in upper middle pencil sequence); E (gray ink on thinner, lighter paper; leaves lack upper middle pencil foliation numbers).

TEXTUAL NOTES: SUBSTANTIVES. 226.0 *The Æolian Harp*] [*no section-title*] HM1,JMg\HM2; [*see accidentals; in the galley proofs, HM considered starting the "Sea-Pieces" section here*] JMg\HM1 226.0–8 The . . . mint] [*leaf 1(C)*] 226.0 The . . . Inn] [*perhaps related to the poem's title are at least two undeciphered erased words in the upper-right corner of leaf 1 and one or more at the left of the final title*] 226.9–14 Braced . . . wreck] [*leaf 2(E)*] 226.9 well] HM2; sharp HM1 226.10 Betwixt] HM2; Between HM1 226.10 continents] HM,JMg\HM; continent's JMg 226.10 sails] HM3; drives HM1; speeds HM2 226.11 For] JM\HM; To HM 226.14 From yard-arm comes] HM3; When from yard-arm HM1; And, from yard-arm HM2 226.15–227.21 Dismasted . . . shore] [*leaf 2.clip(C)*] 226.18–227.29 Like . . . by day] HM2; [*see following description of superseded stage B leaf 2*] [*Superseded leaf 2(B) {"Orme" leaf 9 verso} Like . . . by day*]

> Like the slumbering kraken;
> Heedless if the tempest roar,
> Oblivious of the lull,
> Leagues and leagues from any shore,
> She drifts—[*then* She xxxxx *then* She xxxxx *then* It float →*then* It
>   swims,] a lifeless hull.
> Bulwarks gone, [*then* gone;] a nameless wreck, [*then* at times, {*then*
>   times^} a speck; *then* a level wreck,]
> Exposing but [*then* Nameless, and] a grass-green deck.
> A lumberman; and, lodged [*then* lumberman; perchance,] in hold,
> Prostrate pines with hemlocks rolled.
> [*line-space*]
> She [*then* It *then* That hull *then* That xxxx *then* It] has drifted,
>   waterlogged,
> Till by trailing weeds beclogged;
> Drifted, drifted, day by day,

[*then cancel whole leaf with orange pencil, and replace with nonextant stage C leaf*] HM1(B)

227.22 It] HM2; [*at the bottom edge of leaf 2.clip are the top portions of eight or nine inked and penciled letters now mostly scissored away*] HM1 227.22–26 It . . . rolled] [*leaf 3(E)*] 227.27–40 It . . . other] [*leaf 4(D)*] 227.27 It] HM1,HM3; She HM2 227.35 prevent worse] HM4(E); avert the HM1; avert worse HM2; [*undeciphered erased word*] worse HM3 227.39 Saturate] HM,JMg\HM; Satinate JMg 227.41–48 Deadlier . . . of] [*leaf 5(B)*] 227.43 dumb] HM2(D); deep HM1

Textual Notes: Accidentals. 226.0 The . . . Inn] [*title at beginning of poem, but not on section-title page*] HM2(E)[*title underlined in stage E ink; NN sets* Surf Inn *in roman type to contrast with the italic design of the rest of the title*]; The Æolian Harp / At the Surf Inn [*title at beginning of poem, but not on section-title page*] HM1; THE ÆOLIAN HARP / at the surf inn [*title at beginning of poem, but not on section-title page*] JMg; [*in revising JMg, after entertaining the possibility of beginning the "Sea-Pieces" section with this poem instead of "The Haglets" (he penciled into the galley's left margin, then erased a check mark and* extra page / Sea-Pieces)*, HM next penciled into the galley and erased a dozen or so undeciphered erased words, then penciled over these, with a lateral caret pointing at the space between "The Haglets" and this poem* A liberal space, or, perhaps, a page should be left between these two Pieces.] JMg\HM; THE ÆOLIAL HARP [*on section-title page in addition to full title at beginning of poem*] JMp; [*HM added to JMp's section-title (on a line below)* At the Surf Inn *and the JMp reviewer corrected the misspelled* ÆOLIAL] JMp\HM,JMp\r; THE ÆOLIAN HARP / at the surf inn [*on half-title page in addition to the full title at the beginning of the poem*] JM 226.0 Harp^] HM,JMg\HM; ~. JMg 226.1–8 [*indention*] [*at the top of leaf 1, HM wrote* To the Printer: Where the line has a red cross in margin—indent. *then added* An {*corrected to* And} *so in other pieces similarly marked. In earlier inscribing the leaf, HM had indented lines 1 and (faintly) 3. Using red crosses in the left margin to mark indention, HM next indicated for indention lines 1, 3, 5, and 7, then, changing his mind, lines 2, 4, 6, and 8*] 226.1 wailing^] HM2; ~, HM1 226.2 sea:] HM2(D–E); ~, HM1 226.3 crescendo—] HM2(D–E); ~, HM1 226.4 Dying] [*the word is underlined to query its spelling; below the word HM penciled* right *and then* right *and the underlining of* Dying *were erased*] 226.4 plaintive] HM2; plantive HM1 226.4 key!] HM2(D–E); ~. HM1 226.5 Listen:] HM2,JMg\HM; ~. HM1; ~, JMg 226.5 Less] HM; less JMg 226.8 mint.—] HM; ~.^ JMg 226.9 up,] HM,JMg\HM; ~^ JMg 226.10 Phocion^] HM; ~, JMg 226.13 ocean:] HM2; ~, HM1 226.14 From yard-arm comes] [*see substantives*] 226.14 wreck!"] [*wide line-space follows*] JMg\HM[*HM directs, with a lateral caret,* Leave more space here *but his intention is concealed by page division in JMp and JM*]; [*line-space*] HM 226.15–227.44 [*indented*] HM; [*not indented*] JMg; [*indicating lines 15–44, in JMg, HM directed* The whole of this should be placed more to the right. *and the De Vinne proofreader in turn directed* Makeup attend to this:— *and in page proof the lines are indented*] JMg\HM 226.16 forsaken;] JMg\HM; ~, HM

227.22 hull:] HM2; ~[*undeciphered punctuation*] HM1 227.23 gone—] HM2;
~; HM1 227.23 wreck,] HM1,HM3; ~^ HM2 227.27 waterlogged,] HM,JMg\
HM; ~^ JMg 227.28 beclogged:] HM2; ~. HM1 227.29,30,33,34,41,43 [*indent*]
HM2; [*no indent*] HM1 227.32 oyster-bank:] HM2; ~. HM1 227.35 ever,] HM2;
~^ HM1 227.40 *other*!] HM2; ~. HM1 227.42,44 Since/Waylayingly] [*no indent*]
HM1,HM3; [*indent*] HM2 227.45–48 [*double line-space preceding, and these lines
indented farther than lines 15–44*] JMp\HM[*penciling and erasing* More space between
these & the preceding lines & set to the right a little *HM next inked in (with an
asterisk keying to another asterisk left of the now braced lines 45–48)* Leave more space
between these and the preceding lines; and set to the right a little]; [*wide line-
space, no indent (HM inscribed lines 45–48 with a margin to the left of the one formed by
the preceding four lines (the only other lines on this leaf)*] HM,JMg; [*wider line-space, no
indent*] JMg\HM[*HM directed (with a lateral caret pointing at the space before line 45)*
Leave more space here]; [*wide line-space, indented same as lines 15–44*] JMp; [*JM fol-
lows HM's instructions to leave a wider space, but lines 37–44 (at the top of the page) are
at the left margin (not indented as in JMp)*] JM 227.45–46 O^ . . . O^ . . . O^] HM;
~, . . . ~, . . . ~, JMg 227.45 sailors—] JMg\HM; ~, HM 227.45 sails!] JMg\HM;
~, HM 227.46 never] HM2; nea[*uncompleted; final version written over the misspelling*]
HM→1 227.47 Ariel] HM,JMg\HM; Oriel JMg 227.48 of!] HM2; ~. HM1

TO THE MASTER OF THE *METEOR* (p. 228)

Thomas Melville (1830–84), Melville's younger brother, was captain of
the clipper ship *Meteor* from sometime in 1857 or 1858 until late in 1861,
when he sold the vessel in Calcutta. For Christmas in one of those years,
perhaps 1860 or 1861, Melville (who had shipped with Tom on the *Meteor*
from late May to early October 1860), wrote "To Tom," an earlier and
more personal version of the present poem. It survives in manuscript and
is printed below (and in *Correspondence,* p. 646):

> To Tom
> Thou that dost thy Christmas keep
> Lonesome on the torrid deep,
> But in thy "Meteor" proudly sweep
> O'er the waves that vainly comb—
>   Of thee we think,
>   To thee we drink,
> And drain the glass, my gallant Tom!
>
> Thou that, duty-led, dost roam
> Far from thy shepherd-brother's home—
> Shearer of the ocean-foam!
> To whom one Christmas may not come,—

> Of thee I think
> Till on its brink
> The glass shows tears, beloved Tom!

For "The Admiral of the White" manuscript, on which Elizabeth Shaw Melville penciled, "Herman sent this to Tom—", see the introductory note to "The Haglets," pp. 725–27 above.

TEXTUAL NOTES: INSCRIPTION STAGES. At least two stages of inscription-revision: A (nonextant pre-fair-copy stage); B (brown ink on thicker paper; leaf foliated in upper middle pencil sequence).

TEXTUAL NOTES: SUBSTANTIVES. 228.0 [*no section-title*] HM; SEA-PIECES [*on section-title page*] JMp; Minor SEA-PIECES JMp\HM1,JMp\HM3,JM[*on section-title page but not repeated in table of contents as a section-title*]; Yet Other SEA-PIECES JMp\HM2 228.0–9 To . . . home] [*leaf 1(B)*] 228.0 Meteor] [*no subtitle follows*] HM1,HM3; 1856 HM2 228.1 on] HM1,HM3; upon HM2 228.1 earth's] HM2; the HM1; earth JMg 228.1 loneliest] HM2(C); lonelier HM1 228.3 dost musing] HM3; [*?do*] musing HM1; in musings HM2

TEXTUAL NOTES: ACCIDENTALS 228.0 ^*the* ^Meteor^] [*Meteor underlined, without quotation marks*] HM3 [*NN sets the word in roman type to contrast with the italic design of the titles*]; "The ^Meteor" HM1; ^the "<u>Meteor</u>" HM2 228.0 [*in JMp, someone— perhaps EM—asked that of be placed on the first title line, and the whole title be centered; the compositor had followed the spacing of the title as it appeared in HM's manuscript*] 228.1 earth's^] HM,JMg\HM; earth, JMg 228.2 Sailor!] HM2; ~, HM1 228.2 dost] HM1,HM3(C); [*HM underlines and further queries the word with a question mark in the margin; see also substantives for 228.3*] HM2 228.2 keep—] HM2; ~, HM1 228.7 Of] [*line-space precedes*] HM2; [*no line-space*] 228.7 link;] HM2; ~[?,] HM?1 228.8 drink,] HM2; ~^ HM1 228.9 the] HM2; <u>The</u> HM1 228.9 home.] HM2; ~! HM1

FAR OFF-SHORE (p. 229)

TEXTUAL NOTES: INSCRIPTION STAGES. At least three stages of inscription-revision: A (nonextant pre-fair-copy stage); B (blue ink on thicker paper; leaf foliated in upper middle pencil sequence); C (tan-gray ink).

TEXTUAL NOTES: SUBSTANTIVES. 229.0–8 *Far* . . . anew] [*leaf 1(B)*] 229.1 Look] HM?3,HM5(C); [*undeciphered scratched-out word {?Lo}*] HM1; [*undeciphered erased word {?See}*] HM2; [*one or more undeciphered erased words (if more, then successive variants)*] HM4 229.5 Cries the sea-fowl] HM1,HM6; Cry the curlews HM2; Cries a sea-bird HM?3,HM?5; Calls a sea-bird HM4

TEXTUAL NOTES: ACCIDENTALS. 229.0 *Far^Off-Shore*] HM,JMg\HM; ~-~^~ JMg 229.1 Look,] HM1,HM4(C); [Look *and substantive variants of it are fol-lowed, in no easily determinable order, by comma, exclamation mark, and perhaps dash*] HM?2,HM?3 229.1 the] HM1,HM3; The HM2[*see preceding entry*] 229.1 flying,] HM2(C); ~— HM1 229.2,4,6,8 Thin/Quick/"Crew/Sweeps] [*indent*] HM2[*at the top of the leaf, HM directed (with an x keyed to both a stage C and a red x at the left of each line he wanted indented)* To the Printer: Indent]; [*no indent*] HM1 229.2 Thin—] HM2(C); ~, HM1 229.5 sea-fowl,] HM2(?C); ?~^ HM?1 229.7 billow,] HM1,HM3; ~— HM2

THE MAN-OF-WAR HAWK (p. 230)

This bird, also called the frigate bird (of the family *Fregatidae*), is strong-winged and rapacious. The "sky-hawk" in chapter 135 of *Moby-Dick* is possibly the same bird.

EMENDATION. 230.3 we] JMp\HM; the HM

TEXTUAL NOTES: INSCRIPTION STAGES. At least two stages of inscription-revision: A (nonextant pre-fair-copy stage); B (gray ink on thinner paper).

TEXTUAL NOTES: SUBSTANTIVES. 230.0–5 The . . . reign] [*leaf 1(B)*] 230.0 The . . . Hawk] HM2; [*no title inscribed*] HM1 230.3 Have] HM,JMg\HM; Wave JMg 230.3 we] JMp\HM; the HM

TEXTUAL NOTES: ACCIDENTALS. 230.0 The] [*before inking in his title, HM penciled, at the top right of the leaf, then erased* The Man-of-War hawk / to follow "Shark" &c] 230.2 sky-s'l] HM2; sky-sl HM1

THE FIGURE-HEAD (p. 231)

DISCUSSION. 231.14 Dropped] NN adopts this revision of "Wrecked", inscribed by Elizabeth Shaw Melville in six of the twenty-one located copies of JM. Though "Dropped" does not appear in Melville's hand in any of the known copies, presumably his wife was transcribing from a copy revised by him that has not been located.

EMENDATION. *231.14 Dropped] JM\EM; Wrecked HM

TEXTUAL NOTES: INSCRIPTION STAGES. At least three stages of inscription-revision: A (nonextant pre-fair-copy stage); B (brown ink on thicker paper; foliated in upper middle pencil sequence); C (gray ink).

TEXTUAL NOTES: SUBSTANTIVES. 231.0–5 *The* . . . trow] [*leaf 1(C)* {*no substantive inscription*} *leaf 1.clip(B)* The Figure-Head . . . trow] 231.0 *The Figure-Head*] HM2(C); [*no title, though one probably appeared (as also may have another beginning stanza) on the top half now scissored away from the leaf*] HM1 231.6–15 But . . . moan] [*leaf 2(B)*] 231.8 Vexed] HM1,HM3; Plagued HM2 231.8 lassie] HM1,HM3(C); lady HM2 231.11 But] HM1,HM3; And HM2 231.11 dismal] HM1,HM3; gruesome HM2 *231.14 Dropped] JM\EM; Dashed HM1; Wrecked HM2(C)

TEXTUAL NOTES: ACCIDENTALS. 231.1 ^*Charles-and-Emma*^] HM2; "~^~^~" HM1 231.2 (Named . . . prow)] HM2(C); ^~ . . . ~ HM1[*the stage C closing parenthesis may cover an earlier comma*]; (~ . . . ~,) JMg 231.6 alum-spray] HM,JMp\HM; ~^~ JMp[*a hyphen faint in JMg fades completely away in JMp*] 231.7 gear,] HM2; ~^ HM1 231.10 glue.] HM2(C); ~, HM1[*also, whether to clarify which word he intended or its spelling, HM twice penciled in* glue] 231.11 night^] HM; ~, JMg 231.13 black^lee= shore^] HM,JMp\HM; ~-~^~^ JMg,JMg\HM2; ~-~^~, JMg\HM1

THE GOOD CRAFT *SNOW-BIRD* (pp. 232–33)

The snow-bird for which this good craft is named is possibly the "ice-loving" ivory gull, *Pagophilia eburnea.* The common snow-bird of the nineteenth century, however, was not white but gray: a species of finch, *Fringilla hudsonia,* now called the slate-colored junco, with habits matching Melville's theme. (The manuscript is reproduced on p. 547.)

DISCUSSION. 232.9 Smyrna] During his tour of the Levant in 1856–57, Melville touched twice at Smyrna, the first time going ashore daily on December 20, 21, and 22 (see *Journals,* pp. 69–71, 98, and 409); the day before entering the harbor, he "bought olives & figs"—the figs (lines 5, 11, 23) for which Smyrna was famous.

EMENDATION. 233.24 though] HM\EM; tho' HM

TEXTUAL NOTES: INSCRIPTION STAGES. At least three stages of inscription-revision: A (nonextant pre-fair-copy stage); B (brown ink on thicker paper; foliated in upper middle pencil sequence); C (gray ink).

TEXTUAL NOTES: SUBSTANTIVES. 232.0–12 *The* . . . ray] [*leaf 1(B)*] 232.0 *The Good Craft*] HM1,HM3; The [?*undeciphered erased word(s)*] HM2 232.2 From . . . drives] HM5(C),HM7; [*three undeciphered scratched-out words*] HM1; It [*two undeciphered scratched-out words*] HM2; From purposed [*undeciphered erased word*] [?*that*] [?*takes*] HM3; From purposed course [?*that*] [?*takes*] HM4; From purposed voyage that [?*takes*] HM?6 232.2 at last] HM1,HM3; [*whatever alternative words—if any—HM inscribed or intended here are not readily decipherable; before restoring* at last *he rein-scribed those two words in pencil, above*] HM2 232.3 The] HM2(C); [*?*A] HM1 232.5 Brigs] HM1,HM4; Ships HM2; [*undeciphered erased word*] HM*?*3[*the undeciphered erased word may tentatively have been considered as an alternative to the following word, that*] 232.7 Encounter oft] HM3(C); Oft [*undeciphered scratched-out word*] HM1; [*one or two undeciphered erased words*] HM2 232.13–233.24 What . . . pest] [*leaf 2(B)*] 232.14 though . . . plate] HM2(C); if ice still plates HM1 232.16 gift] HM1,HM3; boon HM2

233.21 brava] HM; Bravo JMg; Brava JMg\HM 233.22 slanting] HM3(C); [*undeciphered scratched-out word*] HM1; blizzard HM2(C) 233.22 snows] HM1,HM3; sleet HM2 233.24 steady] HM*?*3,HM*?*5,HM7(C); serve HM1; [*undeciphered erased word*] HM2; [*undeciphered erased word*] HM4,HM*?*6

TEXTUAL NOTES: ACCIDENTALS. 232.0 ^Snow-Bird^] [*underlined, without quota-tion marks*] HM2(C) [*NN sets in roman type to contrast with the italic design of the titles*]; "Snow-Bird" [*not underlined*] HM1; "SNOW-BIRD" JMg 232.1 be^] HM3; ~, HM*?*1; ~— HM*?*2 232.2–233.24 [*indent all even-numbered lines*] HM2; [*no indent*] HM1 232.3 ship^] HM; ~, JM 232.3 still^] HM; ~, JMg 232.5 gather,] HM2; ~^ HM1 232.6 Homeward-bound] HM,JMp\HM; ~^~ JMg 232.6 stretch,] HM2; ~^ HM1 232.14 yards:] HM; ~; JMg 232.16 regards!] HM2(C); ~[?:] HM*?*1 232.18 stevedore's] HM; stevedore 's JMg 232.20 1] HM; [*not in italic type*] JMg

233.21 master!] HM2(C); ~; HM1 233.21 brava] [*see substantives*] 233.22 west] HM; West JMg 233.23 ^Snow-Bird^] HM2; "~" HM1 233.24 her,] HM2; ~^ HM1 233.24 though] HM\EM; tho' HM

OLD COUNSEL OF THE YOUNG MASTER OF A WRECKED CALIFORNIA CLIPPER (p. 234)

EMENDATION. 234.4 over-elate] JMg\HM; too elate HM

TEXTUAL NOTES: INSCRIPTION STAGES. At least three stages of inscription-revision: A (nonextant pre-fair-copy stage); B (blue ink on thicker paper; foliated in upper middle pencil sequence); C (gray ink).

TEXTUAL NOTES: SUBSTANTIVES. 234.0–5 Old . . . dreamers] [*leaf 1(B)*] 234.0 wrecked California] HM3(C); shi[*uncompleted* {*?*shipwrecked}] HM→1; wrecked HM2 234.0 clipper] [*no subtitle follows*] HM1,HM3; 1856 HM2 234.4 over-elate] JMg\HM; too elate HM

TEXTUAL NOTES: ACCIDENTALS. 234.[*paging request*] [*in JMg, with a brace enclos-ing "Old Counsel" and "The Tuft of Kelp," and after erasing a brief EM query that was presumably to the same point* {*?*These on one page?} *HM specified* These two

Pieces might occupy, if it is manageable, a page by {*then* to} themselves *but the imagined scheme evidently proved unmanageable*] JMg\HM 234.0 Old . . . *clipper*] [*double-underlined, except for the stage C inserted* California *with no distinction of* Of the . . . clipper *as a subtitle*] HM; [Old Counsel *in large capitals, the remaining words in small capitals, that is, as a subtitle; in JM only* Old Counsel *appears in the table of contents*] JMg; [*someone—?HM—pencil-indicated that* California *should be moved to the last line of the title and that the result be recentered*] JMp\?HM,JM 234.0 Counsel] HM1,HM3; [*above the* s HM *queried his spelling with a* c] HM2 234.2 streamers,] HM2; ~; HM1

THE TUFT OF KELP (p. 235)

TEXTUAL NOTES: INSCRIPTION STAGES. At least two stages of inscription-revision: A (nonextant pre-fair-copy stage); B (gray ink on thinner paper).

TEXTUAL NOTES: SUBSTANTIVES. 235.0–4 *The . . . ye*] [*leaf 1(B)*)] 235.1 All^] HM2; O, HM1 235.4 Bitterer] HM1,HM3; The bitterer HM2

TEXTUAL NOTES: ACCIDENTALS. 235.1 All^] [*see substantives*] 235.3 If] [*aligned with line 1*] HM; [*indented more than line 1, but not as much as lines 2 and 4*] JMg

THE MALDIVE SHARK (p. 236)

The shark of this poem hunts tropical waters around the Maldives, a group of coral islands southwest of India at 3°15' N., 73° E. Of Melville's references to sharks, those most relevant to this poem occur in *Mardi*, chapter 18, "My Lord Shark and his Pages," where the lethargic shovel-nose is attended by "little sparks, hardly fourteen inches long"; almost the whole of chapter 18 anticipates this poem and its attitude. A different shark "Glides white through the phosphorus sea" of "Commemorative of a Naval Victory" in *Battle-Pieces* (136.27 above) and is instanced in "In a Bye-Canal" in *Timoleon* as one extreme of danger: "'Twixt the whale's black flukes and the white shark's fin" (292.18 above). Hennig Cohen (*Selected Poems*, p. 218) cites a "parallel to the symbiotic relation of the shark and pilot fish" in a passage from Montaigne's "Apology for Raimond Sebond" that Melville used for one of the "Extracts" that preface *Moby-Dick* (modified there from p. 219 in William Hazlitt's *The Complete Works of Michel Eyquem de Montaigne* [London, 1842; Sealts, no. 366, Bercaw, no. 502]): "And whereas all the other things, whether beast or vessel, that enter into the dreadful gulf of this monster's (whale's) mouth, are immediately lost and swallowed up, the sea-gudgeon retires into it in great security, and there sleeps" (see *Moby-Dick*, pp. xix, 817).

DISCUSSION. 236.8 Gorgonian] A passage in chapter 18 of *Mardi* makes clear what Melville has in mind here: Taji notices that "clinging to the back of the shark, were four or five Remoras, or sucking-fish; snaky parasites," which make the sluggish swimmer appear to be "ever and anon shaking his Medusa locks, writhing and curling with horrible life."

EMENDATIONS. 236.4 attendance] JMg; attendaence HM 236.5 maw^] JMg\HM; ~, HM

TEXTUAL NOTES: INSCRIPTION STAGES. At least four stages of inscription-revision: A (nonextant pre-fair-copy stage); B (brown ink on thicker paper; foliated in upper middle pencil sequence); C (blue ink on thicker paper; foliated in upper middle pencil sequence); D (gray ink).

TEXTUAL NOTES: SUBSTANTIVES. 236.0 *The Maldive Shark*] [*leaf 1(D)*] 236.0 *Maldive*] HM2,HM6; Pale HM1,HM3; White HM4; [*?Ravener* {*?and perhaps not intended to be followed by* Shark}] HM5 236.1–9 About . . . teeth] [*leaf 1.clip(C)*] 236.1 phlegmatical] HM1,HM3; phlegmatic HM2 236.3 sleek] HM,JMg\HM; sleet JMg 236.4 How . . . attendance] HM2(D); Alert attendants HM1 236.4 be] HM,JMg\HM; he JMg 236.5 from his] HM2(D); and HM1 236.9 lurk in] HM3; sport in HM1; enter HM2 236.10–16 In . . . meat] [*leaf 2(B)*] 236.10 In . . . gates] HM6; In tripple [*revised to* triple] tiers of glittering gates HM1,HM5; [*one or two undeciphered erased words*] and tripple [*?rows*] [*two undeciphered erased words*] [*?of* gates] HM2; [*one or two undeciphered erased words*] and tripple [*?rows*] [*three or four undeciphered erased words, which are then replaced by another three or four undeciphered erased words, among these, perhaps,* show *and* lines] [*?ending gates*] HM3,HM4 236.11 haven] HM2,HM4; refuge HM1; harbor HM3 236.14 never] HM1,HM3; never they HM2 236.16 Pale] HM2(C); [*undeciphered scratched-out word*] HM1 236.16 ravener] HM3(D+); mumbler HM1; gorger HM2(D)

TEXTUAL NOTES: ACCIDENTALS. 236.0 *Maldive*] HM,JMg\r; Madlive JMg 236.1 About] [*indent*] HM; [*indention obscured by display capital*] JMg 236.1 Shark] HM2(D); shark HM1 236.4 attendance] JMg; attendaence HM 236.5 mouth,] HM2(D)[*see substantives*]; ~^ HM1 236.5 maw^] HM1,JMg\HM; ~, HM2 236.8 head;] HM?1,HM4; ~, HM2; ~— HM?3[*HM may also have tried here a comma-dash, period, and/or colon*] 236.9 teeth^] HM3; ~; HM1; ~— HM2 236.10 In . . . gates] [*see substantives*] 236.11 peril's] HM; peril 's JMg 236.12 of] HM1,HM3; o' HM2 236.13 They] [*line-space precedes*] HM2; [*no line-space*] HM1

TO NED (pp. 237–38)

The Ned Bunn of this poem is possibly another version of Richard Tobias Greene, Melville's ship-jumping companion at Nukahiva, portrayed as his fellow-truant Toby in *Typee*.

DISCUSSIONS. 237.4 Paul Pry] A type of the meddler, from the curious, intrusive protagonist in John Poole's *Paul Pry* (1825), whose repeated self-introducing line is, "I hope I don't intrude."

237.11 Marquesas] For a further indication of what the Marquesas mean in Melville's iconography, cf. lines 21–24 of "The Archipelago" in *Timoleon* (pp. 307–8 above).

237.15 Typee-truants under] Though Melville pencil-altered "Typee-truants under" to "Typee-truants, and strange" in one of the Berkshire Athenaeum copies of *John Marr* (V.811.M49.4), NN does not adopt this revision because it does not appear in any other of the twenty-one known surviving copies of *John Marr,* in eighteen of which Melville and his wife inked in eleven other revisions. For a comment on the significance of that copy, see the discussion at 216.4 above.

238.23–24 Adam advances . . . trace] William H. Shurr's explanation (p. 142) of these lines seems plausible: "When Zeus changed Io into a white heifer in an attempt to evade Juno's jealous eye, he caused violets to spring up wherever she went, compensating her at least with sweet food. The advance of modern man is not similarly favored." (Cf. "violet-glow" in line 20.)

238.26 Indian Psyche's] The most likely candidate from the Hindu pantheon is probably the goddess Đakti.

EMENDATIONS. 237.4 Trade.] JMg\HM; ~? HM 238.23 pace,] JMg\HM; ~: HM

TEXTUAL NOTES: INSCRIPTION STAGES. At least four stages of inscription-revision: A (nonextant pre-fair-copy stage); B (blue ink on thicker paper; foliated in upper middle pencil sequence); C (brown ink on thicker paper); D (gray ink).

TEXTUAL NOTES: SUBSTANTIVES. 237.0–12 *To . . . sea*] [*leaf 1(C)*] 237.0 *To*] HM2;[*undeciphered scratched-out word* {*?Hymn*}] to HM1 237.2 Hollows] HM1,HM3; The hollows HM2 237.2 thereof] HM2,HM4; whereof HM1,HM3 237.6 roamed] HM2; roam HM1 237.8 wearying of routine-resorts] HM5(D); [*three undeciphered scratched-out words*] resorts HM1; wearying quite of [*undeciphered erased word* {*?staid*}] resorts HM2; wearying of routined resorts HM3; [*?wearying of*] [*?gilt*] [*?resorts*] HM4 237.13–238.24 *The . . . trace*] [*leaf 2(C)*] 237.13 scenes] HM1,HM5(D); things HM2; joys HM?3; lands HM4(D) *237.15 Typee-truants under] HM2(D); xx[*then the undeciphered letters immediately scratched out and replaced with ?truant then* truants] in Typee [*then* Typee], and HM1; Typee-truants, and JM\HM1; Typee-truants, and strange JM\HM2 [*HM penciled the last two variants here into the Berkshire Athenaeum copy* of John Marr *(V811.M49.4) inscribed to but probably not sent to W. Clark Russell; see discussion at 216.4*] 237.21 Enamoring] HM1,HM3; Enrapturing and enamoring HM2 237.21 what years and years] HM4(D); in bloom of life HM1; of life HM2; [*three or four undeciphered erased words*] HM3

238.22 years and] HM1,HM3; long long HM2 238.23 smart in pace] HM3(D); and apace HM1; [*undeciphered scratched-out word* {*?quick*}] in pace HM2(D) 238.25–30 *But . . . Paradise*] [*leaf 3(B)*] 238.27 musing] HM,JMg\HM; nursing JMg

TEXTUAL NOTES: ACCIDENTALS. 237.0 *To*] [*see substantives*] 237.1 Bunn?] HM2; ~, HM1 237.2,4,8,10,14,16,20 [*indent*] HM2; [*no indent*] HM1 237.4 Trade.] JMg\ HM; ~? HM 237.5,11,17 To/Marquesas/And] [*no line-space precedes*] HM1,HM3; [*line-space*] HM2 237.8 routine-resorts,] HM1,HM3; ~^ HM2[*see substantives*] 237.11 Marquesas] HM1,HM3,JMg\HM; Marquesas HM2; Marguesas JMg 237.12 Authentic] HM,JMg\r; Anthentic JMg 237.15 Typee-truants under] [*see substantives*] 237.16 *Midsummer-Night*] HM2; ~^~ HM1 237.19 tell] [*mended for clarity*] 237.19 he^ the tourist^] HM; ~, ~ ~, JMg 237.21 years—] HM3; [*life (the earliest substantive variant here) was also at first followed by a dash, but that dash was scratched out subsequent to the cancellation of* in bloom of life *(see substantives, both entries for line 21)*] HM1,HM2

238.22,26,28 Ah/The/From] [*indent*] HM2; [*no indent*] HM1 238.23,29 Well/ Marvelling] [*no line-space precedes*] HM1,HM3; [*line-space*] HM2 238.23 advances,] HM1,HM4,JMg\HM; ~; HM?2; ~— HM?3; ~^ JMg 238.23 pace,] JMg\HM; ~: HM 238.25 we, . . . calm,] HM2; ~^ . . . ~^ HM1 238.26 Psyche's] [*in JMg, HM drew attention to the faulty registration of the* e] 238.27 And, musing,] HM2(D); ~^ ~^ HM1 238.28 over-run;] HM2; overrun, HM1; overrun; JMg 238.30 Paradise.] HM2; ~^ HM1

CROSSING THE TROPICS (p. 239)

Stanton Garner (1993, p. 53) speculates that Melville may have written such lines as 1–2 and 15–16, perhaps whole poems such as "Crossing the Tropics," in 1860, when he accompanied his captain-brother Tom around Cape Horn on board the *Meteor*. Whether or not Melville ever wrote a work called *The Saya-y-Manto* (meaning petticoat and mantilla), he refers to the alluring-concealing clothing arrangement in at least three other works. In "Benito Cereno" there is "a Lima intriguante's one sinister eye peering across the Plaza from the Indian loop-hole of her dusk *saya-y-manta*" (NN *Piazza Tales* volume, p. 47). In *Pierre*, Isabel tumbles "her unrestrained locks all over her, so that they tent-wise invested her whole kneeling form," resembling the "Saya of Limeean girl" (bk. 8, sect. ii). And in *Clarel* (4.26.97–98), the Prodigal invokes "chat of love-wile and duenna / And *saya-manto* in Peru."

DISCUSSION. 239.10 Gama's] Vasco da Gama (ca. 1469–1524), the Portuguese navigator who discovered the sea route to India around the Cape of Good Hope, in 1497–98; this first passage to India is the subject of Camoëns's *Lusiads*.

EMENDATIONS. 239.0[*subtitle*] ^The . . . Manto^] NN; "~ . . . ~" HM 239.0[*subtitle*] Manto] JMg\HM; manto HM 239.9 fanned^—] JMg\HM; ~,— HM 239.15 sleet,] JMg\HM; ~^ HM

TEXTUAL NOTES: INSCRIPTION STAGES. At least four stages of inscription-revision: A (nonextant pre-fair-copy stage); B (brown ink on thicker paper; foliated in upper middle pencil sequence); C (blue ink on thicker paper; foliated in upper middle pencil sequence); D (gray ink).

TEXTUAL NOTES: SUBSTANTIVES. 239.0 *Crossing . . . Manto*] [*leaf 1(C)* Crossing . . . manto] 239.0 *Crossing the Tropics*] HM1,HM4; [*three or four undeciphered erased words*] HM?2; The Saya-y-Manto HM?3[*HM may have considered this reading as well as the one consisting of undeciphered erased words as provisional (and partial) versions of a subtitle*] 239.0[*subtitle* From . . . Manto] HM7(D)[*see also accidentals*]; [*no subtitle present*] HM?1[*when he ink-inscribed his stage C title, HM intended no subtitle; but at the same time he earlier penciled that title, he may have penciled below and to its right* From the &c]; From the [*undeciphered erased word*] of [*three or four undeciphered erased words*] HM?2; [*at least four largely indeterminable readings, one or more beginning with* From *but consisting otherwise of undeciphered erased words, except for an* an *in one, and an* in *in another*] HM3,HM4,HM5,HM6 239.1–7 While . . . waft] [*leaf 1.clip(B)*] 239.3 love] HM1,HM3; life HM2 239.4 one] HM1,HM3; a HM2 239.4 bridal] HM2(C); [?nuptial] HM1 239.5 no rising joys] HM3,HM5; [*three undeciphered scratched-out words*] HM1; no [?dawning] joys HM2,HM?4; [*there is also an undeciphered erased word, in the right margin, along with a bracket drawing attention to the text-line*] 239.8–14 By . . . astern] [*leaf 2(B)*] 239.9 And] HM1,HM3; In HM2 239.9 chime of] HM2(D); chiming HM1 239.15–21 When . . . past] [*leaf 3(C)*] 239.16 raves the world's] HM3(D); [*three undeciphered scratched-out words*] HM1; [*undeciphered erased word*] the world's HM2 239.18 your . . . me] HM,JMg\HM2; for me your heart JMg\HM1 239.20 ²O^] HM2(D); love, HM1 239.20 oceans] HM3(D); waters HM1; [*undeciphered erased word*] HM2

TEXTUAL NOTES: ACCIDENTALS. 239.0[*subtitle*] The] HM2; the HM1 239.0[*subtitle*] Saya-y] HM2; Saya[*undeciphered scratched-out spelling and/or punctuation*] HM1 239.0[*subtitle*] Manto] JMg\HM; manto HM 239.1 Pole Star] HM2; [*underlined*] HM1 239.2,5,9,12,16,19 [*indent*] HM2; [*no indent*] HM1 239.2 Southern Cross] HM2; [*underlined*] HM1 239.2 Cross^] HM1,HM3; ~, HM2 239.5 supply.] HM2; ~[?!] HM1 239.6 Trade-Winds] HM; ~^~ JMg 239.6 abaft,] HM2; ~^ HM1 239.8 blue-and-silver] HM; ~^~^~ JMg 239.9 fanned—] JMg\HM; ~, HM1,JMg; ~,— HM2 239.11 delight^] HM; ~, JMg 239.15 When, . . . sleet,] JMg\HM2; ~, . . . ~^ HM; ~^ . . . ~^ JMg\HM1 239.20 ²O^] [*see substantives*] 239.21 past!] HM2(D); ~^ HM1

THE BERG (pp. 240–41)

EMENDATIONS. 240.1 build^] JMg\HM; ~, HM 240.8 avalanche] JMg; avalanch HM 240.13 Toppled;] JMg\HM; ~. HM 240.13 nor] JMg; Nor HM 240.15 jarred,] JMg\HM; ~^ HM 240.17 Circling] JMg\HM; Around HM 241.29 self= overcast;] JMg\HM; ~, HM 241.30 breath—] JMg\HM; ~, HM 241.37 dense stolidity] JM\HM; dead indifference HM

TEXTUAL NOTES: INSCRIPTION STAGES. At least three stages of inscription-revision: A (nonextant pre-fair-copy stage); Ba (gray ink on clips); Bb (gray ink on mounts).

TEXTUAL NOTES: SUBSTANTIVES. 240.0–6 *The . . .* fall] [*leaf 1.clip(Ba)*] 240.0[*subtitle*] *(A Dream)*] HM2[*penciled in without, but inked in with parentheses*]; [*no subtitle present*] HM1 240.2 brave] HM,JMg\HM; bare JMg 240.3 Directed as] HM2; As piloted HM1 240.4 stolid] HM1,HM3; [*undeciphered scratched-out word*] HM2 240.5 infatuate] HM1,HM3; impetuous HM2 240.6 ice-cubes] HM2; ice-splints HM1 240.7–13 Sullen *. . .* fine] [*leaf 1(Bb)*] 240.7 Sullen *. . .* crashed] HM4; In crashing tons upon HM1; Steeply [?in {?crashing} tons upon] HM?2; Crashing in tons upon HM3 240.11 Not any] HM2; Not HM1 240.11 shaft] HM2; glittering shaft HM1 240.12 A] HM2; Poised HM1 240.14–15 Nor *. . .* down] [*leaf 2(Bb)*] 240.15 stunned Ship] HM9; long decks HM1,HM3; [*undeciphered erased word*] decks HM2; crashed decks HM4,HM?6; [*undeciphered erased word {?dashed}*] [?decks] HM?5; crashed hull HM?7; [*undeciphered erased word*] ship HM8 240.16–241.26 Nor *. . .* overthrown] [*leaf 2.clip(Ba)*] 240.17 Circling] JMg\HM2; Around HM; [*?one or more undeciphered erased words*] JMg\HM?1 240.22 undermined] HM2; underwashed HM1

241.24 sliddery] HM2; slippery HM1 241.25 Slipt] HM2; Slid HM1 241.27–34 *The . . .* down] [*leaf 3.clip(Ba)*] 241.27 *The . . .* down] HM2(Bb); [*no text-line present—though an earlier version (ending* went down*) was probably inscribed on the portion of the clip now scissored away*] HM1 241.27 impetuous] HM8; [?assailing] HM1; [*two or three successive undeciphered erased words*] HM2,HM3,HM?4; [*undeciphered erased word*] HM5; infatuate HM6; [*undeciphered erased word*] HM7 241.31 bound for] HM2; doomed to HM1 241.34 rue] HM,JMg\HM; rive JMg 241.35–37 Sounding *. . .* walls] [*leaf 3(Bb)*] 241.37 dense stolidity] JM\HM; dead indiference HM; dead indiference HM\EM

TEXTUAL NOTES: ACCIDENTALS. 240.0[*subtitle*] *(A Dream)*] [*see substantives*] 240.1 Ship] HM; ship JMg 240.1–2 build^/(Her *. . .* on)] JMg\HM; ~,/^~ . . . ~, HM1; ~,—/^~ . . . ~,— HM2; ~,/(~ . . . ~) HM3 240.4 Iceberg] HM; iceberg JMg 240.5 Ship] HM2; ship HM1,JMg 240.6 made] HM1,HM3; [*underlined to query the word's appropriateness*] HM2 240.8 avalanche] JMg; avalanch HM 240.10 Along] [*line-space precedes*] HM2; [*no line-space*] HM1 240.10 pale^] HM; ~, JMg 240.13 Toppled; nor] JMg\HM; Toppled. Nor HM; Toppled, nor JMg 240.13 fine,] HM2; ~^ HM1 240.15 jarred,] HM2,JMg\HM; ~^ HM1,HM3 240.15 stunned Ship] HM2; stuned ship HM1; stunned ship JMg 240.17 snow-flanked] [*in JMg, the De Vinne reviewer indicates the* fl *for attention; in JMp, the reviewer E specifies the problem:* wrong font] 240.19 crystal] HM2; ch[*beginning of an alternate spelling*] HM→1 240.19 beaches,] HM2; ~^ HM1 240.21 base;] HM2; ~. HM1 240.22 waves—] HM1,HM3; ~, HM2

241.23 Atilt] [*in JMg, an erased* x *at the left of line 23 probably signals that some attention is to be paid, but to what exactly is not clear*] 241.24 dozing] HM,JMg\

HM; dosing JMg 241.24 ledges^] HM1,HM3; ~, HM2 241.25 edges,] HM; ~^
JMg 241.26,27 Through/The] [*in the University of Florida (Howe Collection) copy of
John Marr, HM pencils either a double check mark at the left of line 27 or overlapping
single check marks at the left of lines 26 and 27—though with what purpose is not clear*]
241.27 Ship] HM2; ship HM1,JMg 241.27 down.] HM; ~^ JM 241.28 Berg]
HM,JMg\HM; berg JMg 241.28 (methought)^] HM; (~), JMg 241.29 self-over-
cast;] HM1,JMg\HM; ~, HM2 241.30 breath—] JMg\HM; ~; HM1; ~, HM2
241.37 dense stolidity] [*see substantives*]

THE ENVIABLE ISLES (p. 242)

A piece entitled "Rammon" survives among Melville's late manuscripts: it
is a prose and verse preface that he wrote probably after, and as a narrative
introduction to, the poem that in 1888 he finally entitled "The Enviable
Isles." It will be printed in NN volume 13, *"Billy Budd, Sailor" and Other
Uncompleted Writings.*

EMENDATIONS. 242.0[*subtitle*] ^Rammon^] NN; "~" HM 242.1 ^Through]
JMg\r; "~ HM 242.1 Through] HM\EM; Thro' HM 242.2 hue,] JMg\HM; ~;
HM 242.13 dream—] JMg\HM; ~, HM

TEXTUAL NOTES: INSCRIPTION STAGES. At least three stages of inscription-revision:
A (nonextant pre-fair-copy stage); B (brown ink on thicker paper); C (gray
ink).

TEXTUAL NOTES: SUBSTANTIVES. 242.0 *The . . .* Rammon] [*leaf 1(C)*] 242.1–3
Through *. . .* sea] [*leaf 1.clip(B)*] 242.1 you reach] HM1,HM3; [*variants, if any,
scissored away*] HM?2 242.4–10 Makes *. . .* glee] [*leaf 2(C)*] 242.5–6 the sleep / . .
. sleep] [*at some indeterminate point (but see next three entries here below), penciling on
the verso of "Rammon" leaf 20 (foliated 16 in upper left corner blue pencil), then cancel-
ing with orange-red pencil, HM tried out a version of lines 5–6:* the sleep that folds
the [?tree ?true] / A deeper sleep— *and, later or earlier, on the verso of "Rammon"
leaf 19.clip I, he penciled, then canceled with blue pencil:* A deeper sleep, the <u>trance</u>
of God *the word "trance" perhaps underlined only to emphasize it as a preferred choice*]
242.5 sleep] HM1,HM3; [*undeciphered scratched-out word* {?peace}] HM2 242.6 A
. . . trance] HM?3,HM12; Another sleep, the charm HM1; A [?deeper] [?peace,],
the [?sleep] HM?2; Yet [*or* A] dreamier sleep, in [*or* the] trance HM?4,HM?5;
[?Yet {*or* A} dreamier sleep] of [?him,] HM?6; Another [?*or* A deep *or* A dream-
ier] sleep, the [*undeciphered erased word*] of [*undeciphered erased word*] HM?7,HM?8;
[*and a mass of undeciphered erased words could yield at least three more variant readings*]
HM?9,HM?10,HM?11 242.6 of God] HM1,HM3; [?of him *or some variant(s) not
readily decipherable*] HM2 242.9 pebbly] HM3; pebbly [*undeciphered scratched-out
word*] HM1; [*undeciphered erased word*] [?*plus the undeciphered scratched-out word*]

HM2 242.11–14 Sweet-fern . . . die] [*leaf 3* {*no substantive inscription*} *leaf 3.clip(C)*]
Sweet-fern . . . die] 242.12 myriads] HM2; slum[*probably the beginning of* slumber-
ers *and, though possibly an inadvertent as well as instantly corrected transposition, it could
also be that as he transcribed HM made a change from* slumberers lie *and* myriads mere
in the draft he was copying from] HM→1 242.13 Dimpling] HM2; Smiling HM1
242.14 endless] HM3; [*undeciphered scratched-out word*] HM1; unending HM2
242.14 beaches] HM,JMg\HM; benches JMg

TEXTUAL NOTES: ACCIDENTALS. 242.1 ^Through] JMg\r; "~ HM 242.1 Through]
HM\EM; Thro' HM 242.1 them^] HM2; ~, HM1 242.1 free.] HM,JMg\HM;
~, JMg 242.2,4,7,9,12,14 [*indent*] HM2; [*no indent*] HM1 242.2 hue,] JMg\HM; ~:
HM1; ~; HM2 242.3 green; and,] HM2; green. And^ HM1 242.3 marge,] HM2;
~^ HM1 242.4 dew.] HM2; ~^ HM1 242.5 But] [*line-space precedes*] HM2; [*no line-
space*] HM1 242.5 inland,] HM1,HM3; ~— HM2 242.7 hazed,] HM2; ~^ HM?1
242.7 aswoon,] HM?1,HM3; ~^ HM?2 242.13 dream—] JMg\HM; ~, HM

PEBBLES (pp. 243–49)

DISCUSSIONS. 244.2,5,7,9 Revamped/And/Shall/Truth] NN judges that these
lines are to be indented as they are in HM, even though in this "Pebble" Melville
did not reinforce his indention by inscribing next to the indented lines the red-
pencil "x"s he used in "I" and "III" to emphasize the indention of lines already
indented. (In "V" and "VI", he three times used the red-pencil "x"s to indicate
indention of lines not indented in his initial inscription.)

244.3,6 But/That] While there is a line-space in HM before each of these lines,
NN judges that Melville's omitting his paragraph-creating blue bracket (which
appears throughout these "Pebbles" and generally elsewhere) at the left of lines 3
and 6 indicates that no space should appear there; the omission of line-spaces after
lines 2 and 5 in JMg shows that the compositor made the same assumption.

245.3–4 The flattery . . . none;] "The Old Shipmaster and His Crazy Barn," a
poem Melville left in manuscript, refers to "the long hills and hollows that make
up the sea, / Hills and hollows where Echo is none" (the poem will be printed
in NN volume 13, "*Billy Budd, Sailor*" *and Other Uncompleted Writings*). The non-
echoic nature of ocean waves is also remarked in *Clarel* (4.34.49).

248.2 Dragon's] William Bysshe Stein (p. 67) suggests Revelation 12:7–11 as
the source, with its account of the "great dragon" in the war in heaven.

248.4 dove in her nest!] Hennig Cohen (*Selected Poems*, p. 223) cites Genesis
8:8–12 as a possible source of Melville's allusion here.

249.2 Angels Four] Cohen (p. 223) indicates Revelation 7:1–3 as the source.

249.4 rosmarine] The name of the herb rosemary literally means "sea-dew."
Stanton Garner (1980) points to Ben Jonson's lines in his *Masque of Blackness,* in
which the daughters of Niger are advised to steep their "bodies in that purer
brine, / And wholesome dew, call'd *Ros-marine*."

EMENDATIONS. 243.0 PEBBLES] JMg\HM [*as poem title and/or section-title; NN treats it as section-title only*]; Pebbles. [*as a poem title, with no section-title*] HM 244.4 hoar] JMg\HM; white HM 244.6 far] JMg\HM; deep HM 244.7 swerve? . . . ever?] JMp\HM; vary from sameness or sever? HM 244.9 varying . . . never] JMg\HM; one and the same forever HM 245.5 strain—] JMg\HM; ~, HM 247.1 Implacable^] JMg\HM; ~, HM 247.1 Sea:] JMg\HM; ~— HM 247.2 serene—] JMg\HM; ~, HM 248.3 mad] JMg\HM; man HM 248.3 waters^—] JMg\HM; ~,— HM 248.4 nest!] JMg\HM; ~. HM 249.1 Sea] JMg\HM; sea HM

TEXTUAL NOTES: INSCRIPTION STAGES. At least three stages of inscription-revision: A (nonextant pre-fair-copy stage); B (gray ink on superseded leaf 5 [*Billy Budd* 63 verso]); C (gray ink on unsuperseded leaves). Stage designations apply only within each "pebble." Further, for Pebble V, there must have been a revision stage between what is here designated stage B (evident on superseded leaf 5) and stage C (evident on final leaf 5).

TEXTUAL NOTES: SUBSTANTIVES. 243.0–5 PEBBLES . . . flaw] [*leaf 1.clip(?Cb)*] Pebbles . . . flaw *leaf 1(Cc)* {*no inscription*}] 243.0[*poem title and/or section-title*] PEBBLES] [*in JMg, with a pointing mark directed at the space between the end of "The Enviable Isles" and the title of the following group of short poems, HM specified* A page should come between {*then* between these P [*?beginning of* Pieces]} →*then between here bearing*] the title—Pebbles.] JMg\HM [*NN treats it as section-title only*]; Epigrams^ [*the double-underlining is not explicitly canceled*] HM1; Pebbles. HM2; PEBBLES [*on section-title page as well as at the head of the group of short poems*] JMp; [*in JMp, HM also changes the verso running head from* John Marr and Other Sailors *to* Pebbles *making it parallel to* Sea-Pieces *as a section-title*] JMp\HM; PEBBLES [*on section-title page, at the head of the group of short poems, and in the table of contents as a section-title (but not as a poem title)*] JM 243.0[*poem number or title*] I] [*the roman numeral*] HM1,HM4; Weather HM?2; The Law of the Winds HM?3 243.3 Pintado] HM2; [*undeciphered scratched-out word*] HM1 243.4 whither] HM,JMp\HM; whether JMg

244.0–9 II . . . never] [*leaf 2(?Cb)* II . . . forever] 244.4 hoar] JMg\HM; white HM 244.6 far] JMg\HM; deep HM 244.7 swerve? . . . ever?] JMp\HM; vary from sameness or sever? HM; [*six or more undeciphered erased words may constitute at least one variant reading*] JMg\HM?1; swerve? shall it deviate ever? vary from sameness or sevor JMg\HM2[*the* sevor *is JMg's misreading, but the rest presumably results from HM's not explicitly canceling the JMg passage (*vary from sameness or sevor?*) he intended his inserted words (*swerve? shall it deviate ever?*) to supplant; in JMp, either on his own or transmitting the proofreader's questioning, the De Vinne reviewer queried the result, and HM then made his revision intention clearer*] 244.9 varying . . . never] JMg\HM2; one and the same forever HM; [*six or more undeciphered erased words probably constitute at least one variant reading*] JMg\HM?1

245.0 *III*] [*leaf 3(?Cc)*] 245.1–4 In . . . none] [*leaf 3.clip I(?Ca)*] 245.1 the]
HM1,HM4; yon HM?2; these HM?3 245.5–6 Nor . . . brain] [*leaf 3.clip II(?Cb)*]
245.6 hope] HM2; throb HM1 245.6 dream] HM2; thought HM1

246.0–2 *IV* . . . there] [*leaf 3.clip III(?Cb)*] 246.0[*poem number or title*] *IV*] HM2;
III[*and/or* II] HM1

247.0–3 *V* . . . me] [*leaf 3.clip IV(?Cb)*] {*no substantive inscription*} *leaf 3.clip V(?Ca)*
V . . . me] 247.0[*poem number or title*] *V*] HM1,HM3; Sunned waters HM2

248.0–1 *VI* . . . Andean] [*leaf 4(?Cb)*] 248.0[*poem number or title*] *VI*] HM?1,HM3;
[?V] HM2 248.1 billow] HM2; [*undeciphered scratched-out word*] HM1 248.2–4 Is
. . . nest] [*leaf 4.clip(?Ca)*] 248.3 mad] JMg\HM; man HM[*transcriptional slip*]

249.0–4 *VII* . . . rosmarine] [*leaf 5(?Cb)* {*the only substantive inscription is erased*}
leaf 5.clip(?Ca) VII . . . rosmarine] 249.1–4 Healed . . . rosmarine] HM2; [*see fol-*
lowing description of superseded stage B matter] [*Superseded leaf 5(B)* {*"Billy Budd" leaf*
63 verso} Here . . . <u>Rosemarine</u> {*inscribed in ink; revised in pencil*}]

> ———"——— [*beginning device*]
> [*above beginning device, add* For Part I *and an undeciphered underlined word*
> *subsequently canceled* {*?*Weeds}—*unless that undeciphered word is to be*
> *understood as a variant for the* wayward *of line 1, below*]
> Here be waftures from the wayward [*then undeciphered erased word, then*
> no inland *then* landless *then* inhuman *then without canceling* inhuman),
> untameable *?then an undeciphered underlined word that may be a title*
> {*?*Weeds} *(as described above), then* inhuman] sea
>> Where the four winds [*then* Where angels *then* Where Angels four
>> *then* Where {*that is, the text-line is left incomplete*}] convene
> Wholesom waftures from their pitiless breath,
>> Sea-dew named <u>Rosemarine</u> [*then cancel* Sea-dew named *leaving*
>> *the text-line incomplete as* <u>Rosemarine</u> *(the spelling of which is*
>> *queried with a parenthetical* e *and question mark, then altered to*
>> <u>Rosmarine</u>)]
> ———"——— [*ending device*]

[*then cancel leaf with blue X*] HM1(B) 249.0[*poem number or title*] *VII*] HM5; [*one or*
more undeciphered erased words {*?*Rosmarine}] HM1; The [*one or two undeciphered*
erased words {*?*Rose star}] HM2; VI HM3; Rosmarine [*plus, below, the parentheti-*
cal notation To Precede] HM4 249.1 laud] HM,JMg\HM; land JMg 249.2 Yea,]
HM2; And^ HM1 249.4 wholesome] HM1,HM3; briny HM2

TEXTUAL NOTES: ACCIDENTALS. 243.0[*poem title and/or section-title*] PEBBLES]
[*see substantives*] 243.3 gannet] HM2; ganne[?k] HM1[*final letter scratched out*]

   244.1 creeds,] HM2; ~^ HM1 244.1 schools^] HM; ~, JMg *244.2,5,7,9
Revamped/And/Shall/Truth] [*indention indicated by spatial placement though not*
symbolically by inscribing a red x in the margin at the left of each line to be indented]
HM *244.3,6 But/That] [*no line-space symbolically indicated by a blue bracket added at*

the left of each line] HM2; [*line-space indicated by inscriptional placement*] HM1 244.4 Conch] HM2; conch HM1 244.7 swerve? . . . ever?] [*see substantives*]

245.1 hills^] HM,JMg\HM; ~, JMg 245.2 Blue Ridges] HM2; blue ridges HM1 245.5 strain—] JMg\HM; ~, HM

246.2 sufferance] HM,JMg\r; suffeance JMg

247.1 Implacable^] JMg\HM; ~, HM 247.1 Sea] HM,JMp\HM; sea JMg 247.1 Sea:] JMg\HM; ~— HM 247.2 Implacable] [*indent*] HM2; [*no indent*] HM1 247.2 serene—] JMg\HM; ~, HM

248.1,3 Curled/Elemental] [*no indent*] HM1,HM3; [*indent*] HM2 248.2,4 Is/ Yet] [*indent*] HM2; [*no indent*] HM1 248.3 waters—] JMg\HM; ~, HM1,JMg; ~,— HM2 248.4 nest!] JMg\HM; ~. HM

249.1 Sea] JMg\HM; sea HM 249.1 Sea—] HM2; ~, HM1 249.2 Yea,] [*see substantives*] 249.2 Angels Four] HM2; angels four HM1 249.2 convene;] HM2; ~[?,] HM1 249.3 am^ . . . breath^] HM2 ~, . . . ~, HM1 249.4 [*on leaf 5 HM inscribed* End *and a double ending device in blue pencil; subsequently, he inked in* End *at the bottom of the last galley and following the last line of Pebble VII in page proof*]

Timoleon Etc. (pp. 251–317)

NN copy-text is Melville's manuscript [HM], in Harvard MS Am 188 (387). The first and only printing in Melville's lifetime, set from Elizabeth Shaw Melville's transcript, also in Harvard MS Am 188 (387) [EM], was *Timoleon Etc.* [T] (New York: Caxton Press, 1891). In total, HM is emended at 716 points: at 462 points from EM, the printer's-copy transcript, in which most accidentals were probably first penciled by Melville before being inked in by his wife; at 168 points from Melville's revision of EM [EM\HM]; at 13 points from Elizabeth Shaw Melville's inscription in HM [HM\EM]; at 60 points from *Timoleon Etc.* [T]; at 13 points by the present edition [NN]. Substantives are emended at 216 points, accidentals at 500 points.

The HISTORICAL NOTE provides background relating to Melville's poetic development. The NOTE ON PRINTING AND PUBLISHING HISTORY, pp. 565–78 above, describes Melville's manuscript, his wife's transcript (which served as printer's copy), the six leaves of preliminaries (title, table of contents, and dedication), and the finished book; and it recounts, on the basis of these documents, the course of Melville's text through the printing process. The GENERAL NOTE ON THE TEXT supplies information on the copies used for collation and on the printer's copy for NN (pp. 580–82); comments on the sources for assessing the text, including Melville's manuscript, his wife's transcript, and the finished book (pp. 592–94); outlines Melville's methods of preparing and revising manuscripts (pp. 596–99);

sets forth the principles for emendation of the copy-text (pp. 606–17); and explains the makeup of the textual apparatus, including the system employed for recording manuscript revisions (pp. 617–20).

The only title for this book in Melville's hand, on the first of six manuscript leaves of preliminaries (see p. 576 above), is "Timoleon / And Other Ventures / in / Minor Verse." The phrase "Timoleon &c" appears in the upper right corners of the first two leaves of Melville's wife's transcript of the table of contents (the leaves listing the poems preceding the "Fruit of Travel Long Ago" section); but Melville marked it out when he prepared these leaves for the printer and added the title leaf just mentioned. The appearance of "Timoleon Etc." on the title page of the published book presumably results from a change that Melville made in proof. The two section-titles used by NN ("Fruit of Travel Long Ago" on p. 291 and "L'Envoy" on p. 317) are those in the printed table of contents and are clearly authorized by manuscript evidence; the reason for not giving "After the Pleasure Party" (p. 259) its own section-title, as it had in the first edition, is that the first-edition section-title does not mark a section parallel to the other two and is essentially a typographical device to allow the poem's epigraph (with its own title) to be segregated on the verso. NN page-breaks that coincide with stanza-breaks are listed on pp. 616–17.

[TABLE OF CONTENTS] (pp. xi–xii)

DISCUSSION. xi.13 *Monody*] This title was accidentally omitted from Melville's wife's transcript of the table of contents, but it appears in its proper place in the table of contents of the printed book. The NN table of contents is made up from the titles that appear at the heads of the poems in NN, which reflect Melville's intention as it emerges from the surviving documents. As a result, there are seven differences (besides the inclusion of "Monody" in NN) between the titles in the NN table of contents and those in the manuscript table of contents (the latter lacks the hyphen in "Night-March" and "Bye-Canal," makes one word of "Birth Night," has lowercase "Lost" and "Century" in "Fragments of a Lost Gnostic Poem of the 12th Century," and spells "Colonna" as "Collonna" and "L'Envoy" as "L'Envoi"); and there are six differences between the NN table of contents and the first-edition table of contents (the latter lacks the hyphen in "Night-March" and "Bye-Canal," makes one word of "Birth Night," capitalizes "a" in "Fragments" and the second "the" in "The Age of the Antonines," and spells "L'Envoy" as "L'Envoi"). References to the variants in these tables of contents appear in the discussions below at 259.0, 265.0, 267.0, 284.0, 286.0, 291.0, 292.0, 306.0, 309.0, and 317.0; the manuscript leaves for the preliminaries are discussed in more detail on pp. 573–75 above.

[DEDICATION] (p. 252)

DISCUSSION. 252.2 MY COUNTRYMAN] On the last of the six manuscript leaves of preliminaries (see p. 576 above), the dedication in Melville's hand is simply "To / Elihu Vedder". The additional line "MY COUNTRYMAN", which appears in the printed book, is clearly Melville's insertion, probably in proof. (In the manuscript leaves, the dedication follows the table of contents, but in the printed book it appears in a more conventional location, on the page facing the copyright page, and thus preceding the table of contents.) The dedication shows that Melville respected Elihu Vedder (1836–1923), presumably for his allegorical paintings and illustrations. Melville based "'Formerly a Slave'" in *Battle-Pieces* (p. 115 above) on a drawing by Vedder and admired the Vedder illustrations in the 1886 Houghton Mifflin edition of Edward Fitzgerald's translation of the *Rubáiyát of Omar Khayyám* (Sealts, no. 392).

TIMOLEON (pp. 253–58)

"Timoleon" re-creates in some detail the actual Timoleon, a Corinthian (ca. 411–ca. 337 B.C.) instrumental in the killing of his older brother, Timophanes, who had become a tyrant. His main source was Plutarch's life of Timoleon, perhaps in the John and William Langhorne translation of *Plutarch's Lives* (New York: Harper & Brothers, 1875). Another possible source is the account of Timoleon in Pierre Bayle's *An Historical and Critical Dictionary* (London: Harper, 1710; Sealts, no. 51, Bercaw, no. 50). Jay Leyda (*Log*, p. 829) also suggested Balzac's *The Two Brothers* (Boston: Roberts, 1887; Sealts, no. 37, Bercaw, no. 41) as an influence.

DISCUSSIONS. 253.0 (394 B.C.)] Why Melville settled on this date in his subtitle is unclear, since the poem does not focus on any particular event in Timoleon's life.

253.1 tell] NN adopts this word from EM as a replacement for "vouch" in HM. The "tell" has no extant authority in Melville's hand; but, given the routines that he and his wife followed in preparing transcriptions, the EM reading can safely be taken as representing Melville's intention (as explained more fully on p. 606 above). For other EM readings adopted in this poem on the same grounds, see the emendations in lines 12, 13, 15, 20, 26, 163, 164, 165–68, and 173.

253.3 snatched,] NN retains the copy-text comma since it seems more likely that Melville overlooked its absence in EM than that he intended to omit it.

253.6 good heart] NN emends the capitalized copy-text reading to the lowercase reading in EM. In lines 8 and 9 in EM, Melville in pencil and his wife in ink changed "Good in Weak" and "Goodness" to lowercase—revisions suggesting that he directed the change in this line also. (Cf. the discussion at 253.1 above.) For further discussion of capitalization, see p. 610 above.

253.17 ensue,] NN retains the copy-text (HM) comma; even though it was erased in EM, it appears in T, probably restored by Melville in proof.

253.19 Providence, or Chance] The Langhorne translation of Plutarch offers a distinction that may partly clarify the one Melville implies here: "When the ancients ascribed any event to *fortune,* they did not mean to deny the operations of the Deity in it, but only to exclude all human contrivance and power. And in events ascribed to *chance,* they might possibly mean to exclude the agency of all rational beings, whether human or divine" (p. 185).

254.23–24 reck . . . hem] The story of the suffering women touching the garment of Jesus is told in Mark 5:25–34.

254.25–40 When . . . foes] The tale of Timoleon's heroism rendered in these sixteen lines is described thus in the Langhorne translation of *Plutarch's Lives:*

In the battle between the Corinthians and the troops of Argos and Cle-one, Timoleon happened to serve among the infantry, when Timophanes, who was at the head of the cavalry, was brought into extreme danger; for his horse being wounded, threw him amidst the enemy. Hereupon, part of his companions were frightened, and presently dispersed; and the few that remained, having to fight with numbers, with difficulty stood their ground. Timoleon, seeing his brother in these circumstances, ran to his assistance, and covered him as he lay with his shield; and after having received abundance of darts, and many strokes of the sword upon his body and his armour, by great efforts repulsed the enemy, and saved him. (p. 174)

254.30 rash] Plutarch says Timophanes resembled Timoleon "in nothing; being rash and indiscreet of himself, and utterly corrupted besides, by the passion for sovereignty. . . . He appeared to be impetuous in war, and to court danger" (p. 174).

254.44 take. . . prolonged] NN follows EM in omitting the commas present in HM because in this passage Melville carefully went over EM to add punctuation.

254.51 looked.] NN replaces the copy-text (HM) colon with the period of EM. Although the colon in T could represent Melville's restoration of his original reading, the physical condition of EM is such that a compositor could have mistaken the period as a colon.

254.52 *he*] The underlining for italics, firmly penciled into the copy-text (HM), could not be a transcriptional querying mark since the "he" is so legible. The word is not underlined in EM, perhaps because, in looking over his wife's transcript, Melville may have thought that the expected iambic stress would be sufficient to provide the emphasis he intended. Nevertheless NN retains his earlier explicit italics in order to make his intention absolutely clear as well as to take account of the possibility that he overlooked adding the underlining to EM.

255.56 such,] NN adopts the comma from T, judging that Melville probably added it in proof, in order to avoid the ambiguity of "such a henchman".

255.60 And sooth] Here the decision and reasoning are the same as those specified in the discussion at 254.44.

255.60 grace.] NN retains the copy-text (HM) period rather than adopting the semicolon in EM because the period in T is plausibly Melville's restoration of the reading in HM.

255.72 thin.] Since in Melville's manuscript this musing by Timoleon's mother does not begin with quotation marks in line 52 but ends with them here, NN resolves the matter by adopting the EM reading at this point (without quotation marks), judging that Melville intended to omit quotation marks in his wife's transcript just as he had at first omitted them in his own (and as he normally did when characters are musing). On Melville's use of quotation marks, see pp. 612–613 above; cf. the discussion at 257.149 below.

255.74–256.112 Forsworn . . . place] Melville adds dramatized detail and analysis of motive, but subtracts almost nothing from Plutarch's account of the perjurous, disdainful Timophanes and of Timoleon's responses to him:

> Some time after [Timoleon's saving Timophanes on the battlefield], the Corinthians, apprehensive that their city might be surprised through some treachery of their allies, as it had been before, resolved to keep on foot four hundred mercenaries, [and] gave command of them to Timophanes. But he, having no regard to justice or honour, soon entered into measures to subject the city to himself, and having put to death a number of the principal inhabitants without form of trial, declared himself absolute prince of it. Timoleon, greatly concerned at this, and accounting the treacherous proceedings of his brother his own misfortune, went to expostulate with him, and endeavoured to persuade him to renounce this madness and unfortunate ambition, and to bethink himself how to make his fellow-citizens some amends for the crimes he had committed. But as he rejected his single admonition with disdain, he returned a few days after, taking with him a kinsman, named Æschylus, brother to the wife of Timophanes, and a certain soothsayer, a friend of his. . . . These three, standing round him, earnestly entreated him yet to listen to reason and change his mind. Timophanes at first laughed at them, and afterwards gave way to a violent passion; upon which, Timoleon stepped aside, and stood weeping, with his face covered, while the other two drew their swords, and despatched him in a moment. (pp. 174–75)

255.82 Old Scotia's clansman] In the "Supplement" to *Battle-Pieces,* Melville sympathetically imagines some defeated Southerners "yielding allegiance to the Union, feeling all their interests bound up in it, and yet cherishing unrebuked that kind of feeling for the memory of the soldiers of the fallen Confederacy that Burns, Scott, and the Ettrick Shepherd felt for the memory of the gallant clansmen ruined through their fidelity to the Stuarts" (p. 183 above).

256.90–92 lictors . . . Furies' rods] Vernon Shetley notes (p. 86): "Lictors accompanied high civic officials through the streets and apprehended and punished criminals, and so were responsible for enforcing the duties of citizenship, while the Furies punished those who spilled the blood of family or clan members; they avenged violations of natural relations and loyalties. Timoleon's visions thus figure concretely the conflict between political duty and natural ties."

256.94 Ate] In early Greek myth, the divinity or personification of infatuate rashness. Presumably, however, Melville has mostly in mind here what Ate became for the tragedians: an avenger of unrighteousness, a sower of discord— perhaps rather more the latter if we notice that on the superseded leaf 9 of the poem he considered "Anarch" as a variant for "Ate" (see the textual notes at 256.93–96).

256.95–96 He heeds . . . skies] Vernon Shetley (p. 88) finds an echo here of *Paradise Lost*, 1.781–84.

256.108 might";] NN retains the copy-text (and EM) semicolon (placing it after the quotation mark as in EM), though the colon in T is possibly authorial, especially given Melville's extensive reworking (in EM) of punctuation in surrounding lines.

257.130–32 Such deeps . . . nakedly] Cf. "The Conflict of Convictions" in *Battle-Pieces*: "What if the gulfs their slimed foundations bare?" (10.65 above).

257.133 falters. And] It is conceivable that "falters, and" in T is authorial, since "falters; and" was a pre-copy-text version (on the superseded leaf 12) and since Melville in general lightened the punctuation as he repointed. But NN retains the copy-text (and printer's-copy) reading since the compositor may have made the change. The *John Marr* compositors eleven times substituted commas for periods, apparently to avoid beginning a sentence with a conjunction; in six of those instances Melville restored the period, and he made further revision in two others, obviating the need to restore.

257.136 Phocion] Athenian military leader and statesman (ca. 402–317 B.C.), usually instanced (by Plutarch and others) as a type of the virtuous man. Because of his cooperation with Antipater of Macedonia, the newly triumphant Athenian democrats forced him to drink hemlock. A ship in "The Æolian Harp" in *John Marr* is named *Phocion* (226.10 above).

257.149 "To] In this poem and in "After the Pleasure Party" NN adds quotation marks at several places where the pattern of their use in HM and EM is incomplete. Those documents do not make clear whether Melville's final intention was to use quotation marks or not to use them; by adopting them, NN follows what was his intention at one time and in the process clarifies which persons are associated with which words. Accordingly, in "Timoleon" NN retains the quotation marks from HM (and EM) at this point and in lines 156 and 161 and from EM in line 172; and NN supplies quotation marks in lines 153, 165, and 169. (For the locations of quotation marks in "After the Pleasure Party" resulting from this policy, see the discussion at 260.12 below.) Melville's intention in the matter of quotation marks for characters' spoken and unspoken thoughts is discussed on p. 613 above.

257.149 second causes] In the "Supplement" to *Battle-Pieces* (p. 184 above), Melville writes that "to treat of human actions is to deal wholly with second causes."

258.157 *one*] Although it is possible that Melville's underlining in the copy-text could be meant as a restoration mark, since the word was restored in the latest reading, NN treats the underlining as a sign for italics since it is much thicker than the restoration marks below the phrase "bear with one" and was probably inscribed at the same time as "one".

258.158 Olympians] The Greek gods residing on Mount Olympus.

258.163–73 Are . . . frames] Some of the NN readings in these lines (see the emendations list below) are based only on the authority of Elizabeth Shaw Melville's hand (both in EM and as an addition to HM). Cf. the discussion at 253.1.

258.167 ye too,] The comma after "ye" in T (but not in EM) is not necessarily Melville's addition in proof, since he was inconsistent in using a comma before "too"; NN therefore does not adopt it.

258.168 sway.] NN judges that the period in T is probably Melville's restoration of his first punctuation in the lines that his wife copied into her transcript from his apparently nonextant version of them (lines 165–68, not present in HM). Once the lines were in type, he may have decided that, for clarity's sake, the period was preferable to the dash in the printer's copy.

258.176 plumes . . . phrase] Plutarch's version has it that when Timoleon, twenty years after killing his tyrant brother, accepted the Corinthian request that he go to rescue Syracuse from its tyrants, one "Teleclides, a man of the greatest power and reputation in Corinth, exhorted him in the execution of his commission: *For*, said he, *if your conduct be good, we shall consider you as the destroyer of a tyrant: if bad, as the murderer of your brother*" (p. 175).

258.177–80 On Sicily's . . . land] Because the poem focuses on the protagonist's personal dilemmas rather than his public services, it covers in only four lines the four-fifths of Plutarch's narrative that is devoted to Timoleon's delivering Syracuse and other Sicilian towns from the rule of tyrants.

258.181–88 And Corinth . . . shore] Plutarch records that Timoleon "never returned home; he took no part in the troubles of Greece, nor exposed himself to public envy"; it was the Syracusans' "joy" and "pride," he says, that Timoleon "chose to spend his days with them, and despised the splendid reception which Greece was prepared to give him, on account of his great success" (pp. 185, 186).

258.181 Absolved] For the omission of quotation marks here, see p. 613 above.

258.182 thine:] NN adopts the colon that Melville's wife inscribed in ink over the punctuation Melville penciled into her transcript. She may have misconstrued his intention, since both the upper and lower points of his penciled punctuation look like commas. But she may have erased or ink-inscribed over the evidence of his final intention to use the colon (and his earlier intention may have been to use a semicolon as in the copy-text, HM).

258.184 divine.] NN adopts the period in T as plausibly representing Melville's final decision. After trying and erasing an exclamation mark, semicolon, and colon in his wife's transcript, he left the ending unpointed, presumably deferring the decision till later.

258.185–86 Eager . . . door.] For the omission of quotation marks here, see p. 613 above.

EMENDATIONS. *253.1 tell] EM; vouch HM 253.5 stood] EM\HM; reigned HM *253.6 good heart] EM; Good Heart HM 253.8 good in weak] EM; Good in Weak HM 253.9 goodness] EM; Goodness HM 253.12 avouched] EM; declared HM 253.12 man?] EM; ~. HM 253.13 dread] EM; strange HM 253.15 strain] EM; peak HM 253.20 proved it] EM; proved HM 254.26 right,] EM; ~^ HM 254.27 well:] EM; ~, HM 254.29 place,] EM; ~^ HM 254.33 Timoleon, . . . need,] EM; ~^ . . . ~^ HM 254.37 pallor] NN; palor HM 254.39 field] T; press HM 254.41 here,] EM; ~— HM *254.44 take^ . . . prolonged^] EM; ~, . . . ~, HM *254.51 looked.] EM; ~: HM 254.53 gossips] EM\HM; babblers HM 255.55 ruled] EM\HM; urged HM 255.55 bade,] EM; ~— HM *255.56 such,] T; ~^ HM 255.57 bent,] EM; ~: HM 255.59 him, too;] EM; ~^ ~, HM *255.60 And^ sooth^] EM; ~, ~, HM 255.62 Not he,] EM; ~ ~; HM 255.63 through] HM\EM; thro' HM 255.69 brave] EM\HM; tall HM 255.72 through] EM; thro' HM *255.72 thin.^] EM; ~." HM 255.73 erred:] EM; ~. HM 255.80 do;] EM; ~. HM 255.82 clan,] EM; ~— HM 255.85 town,] EM; ~— HM 255.86 mother^—] EM; ~!: HM 256.93 But^ undeterred^] EM; ~, ~, HM 256.94 though] EM; tho' HM 256.97 mild,] EM; ~^ HM 256.102 met;] EM; ~. HM 256.103 he,] EM; ~^ HM 256.107 and^] EM; ~, HM *256.108 might";] EM; ~;" HM 256.109 pale,] EM; ~; HM 256.111 word,] EM; ~; HM 256.117 world,] EM; ~^ HM 256.119 truth,] EM; ~^ HM 257.122 atheist's] EM; Atheist's HM 257.124 deeds] T; aught HM 257.127 irrevocable] EM; irreevocable HM 257.127 doom] T; deed HM 257.128 undismayed.] EM; ~^ HM 257.130 sea^] EM; ~, HM 257.135 suffer?] EM; ~, HM 257.137 But,] EM; ~^ HM 257.138 place;] EM; ~. HM 257.139 self-outcast,] EM; ~^ HM 257.145 though] EM; tho' HM 257.145 ebb,] EM; ~. HM 257.146 bides] EM\HM; dwells HM 257.146 long;] EM; ~: HM 257.148 wrong:] EM; ~. HM 257.150 fellow-clods.] EM; ~^ HM 257.153 "Shall] NN; ^~ HM 258.156 stony,] EM; ~^ HM 258.160 brow.—] EM; ~.^ HM 258.161 recant.] EM; ~: HM *258.163 Are earnest natures] EM; Is virtue tried and HM 258.164 But fatherless shadows] EM; A fatherless shadow HM 258.165–68 Yea . . . sway] EM; [not present] HM 258.165 "Yea] [indent] EM\HM; [no indent] EM 258.165 "Yea] NN; ^~ EM 258.165 'tis] EM\HM; too EM 258.168 grievous] T; greivous EM *258.168 sway.] T; ~— EM 258.169 "But] NN; ^~ HM 258.169 given—] EM; ~, HM 258.171 reassure,] EM; ~! HM 258.172 cries."] EM; ~.^ HM\EM 258.173 Men's] EM\HM; He raved. But HM 258.173 moods, as frames,] EM; moods HM 258.173 yield] EM; yeild HM 258.177 wars,] EM; ~^ HM 258.179 isle] EM\HM; Isle HM *258.181

^Absolved] EM; "~ HM *258.182 thine:] EM; ~; HM *258.184 divine.] T; ~!
HM *258.185 ^Eager] EM; "~ HM 258.185 waits:] EM; ~; HM 258.186 Return!]
EM; ~, HM *258.186 door.^] EM; ~." HM

TEXTUAL NOTES: INSCRIPTION STAGES. At least five stages of inscription-revision:
A (nonextant pre-fair-copy stage); pre-B (pencil and dark brown ink on thicker
paper); B (gray-tan ink, narrower pen); C (tan-gray ink, wider pen; also pencil);
D (post-C pencil, including nonextant Melville inscription [see p. 606 above]).

TEXTUAL NOTES: SUBSTANTIVES. 253.0–8 *Timoleon . . .* expire] [*HM leaf 1(B)*]
253.0–12 *Timoleon . . .* man] [*EM leaf 1*] 253.0 *Timoleon /* (394 B.C.)] HM3; Timo-
leon HM1; Timoleon / ([?736] B.C.) HM2 *253.1 tell] EM[?\HM(D)]; vouch
HM 253.4 seizure] HM2; action HM1 253.4 sabre's] HM,EM2; [?saltre's] EM1
253.5 stood] EM\HM; reigned HM 253.5 stood] HM1,HM3; stood x[*the penciled*
x *is keyed to a penciled, revised, then erased note at HM leaf 1's lower left corner:* x
{*?insert* for} *a recent example /* {*?is then erase ?is and inscribe and immediately cancel*
?P} Louis Napoleon. {*?underline* Louis Napoleon.} / note {*HM's emphasis*}] HM2
253.9–20 Needs . . . Timoleon] [*HM leaf 2(Cb)*] 253.9–12 Needs . . . man] HM2;
[*see following description of superseded stage Ca inscription*] [*Superseded HM leaf 2(Ca)*
{*"Billy Budd" leaf 79.patch verso*} Needs . . . man {*foliated (upper left corner pencil)* 2;
inscribed in ink, revised in pencil}]

> Needs goodness lack the hellish [*then* the hell-born *then* the evil *then* a
> Sylla's *then* the evil] grit
> That scouts for bosh each bar and ban [*then* That scouts for bosh each
> moral ban *?then* That strikes past God to trample man *then* That
> strikes past God in scorn of man *?then (though not canceling* strikes
> *but explicitly restoring* scouts *and* bosh each*) some such reading as ?*That
> scouts {*?*God} for bosh in scorn of man *or/and ?*That scouts for bosh
> the human ban *(though* in scorn of *is not canceled, and* the human *may*
> *be part of HM's revision of the following line)*],
> As witness one, a tower of crime [*then* witness Sylla, in unconcern
> *?then ?*witness him, in unconcern *?then ?*witness him in buffoon
> crime *?then* witness him{,} the human buffoon *(though* the human *is*
> *more likely part of HM's revision of the preceding line)*],
> Sylla, fearless alike of God and man? [*then* Who died in his {*then* in}
> bed as in bed he began. *?then* Who died in bed as a babe he began.
> *?then ?*Dieing in bed fearless of God and man? *?then* Dieing in bed
> jesting at God and man? *then* Who joked in his bed at God and Man?
> *then eventually cancel all words in this line except* jesting *which was explic-*
> *itly restored by underlining after its initial cancellation—though as part of*
> *which reading is not clear—and the second* bed]

[*cancel the partial leaf (other text-lines have been scissored away) with pencil and blue pencil*] HM1(Ca) 253.12 will's] HM; will EM 253.12 avouched] EM[?\HM(D)]; declared HM 253.13–254.26 Or . . . right] [*EM leaf 2*] 253.13 dread] EM[?\HM(D)]; strange HM 253.15 strain] EM[?\HM(D)]; peak HM 253.16 such as shares] HM1,HM2; sharing even HM\EM[*an inked-in revision presumably directed by HM before he decided to restore his earlier reading*] 253.16 transgression's] HM,T; transgressions EM 253.20 proved it] EM[?\HM(D)]; proved HM; proved ed HM\EM[*a mistranscription in which EM echoes the last two letters of HM's preceding word*] 253.21–254.32 O . . . thrown] [*HM leaf 3(B)*] 253.21 crowned] HM1,HM3,HM5; wreathed HM2,HM4

254.24 dare] HM2; even dare HM1[*HM may immediately have canceled* even] 254.26 claim or] HM2; sovereign HM1 254.27–43 Two . . . on] [*EM leaf 3*] 254.30 cavalryman, alone,] HM4; cavalryman, [?for one], HM1; cavalryman lay prone HM2; trooper, spurring on, HM3 254.31 Was wrecked] HM1,HM3; Wrecked hard HM2 254.33–44 Timoleon . . . stain] [*HM leaf 4(C)*] 254.37 wrought . . . dumb] HM7,EM2; pale with passion of brotherly love HM1,HM4; pale with passion of family love HM2; pale with passion of natural love HM3; [*two or three undeciphered erased words, constituting at least one further reading*] HM?5; dumb [?with] pallor of passion intense HM6,EM1[*as she was copying, EM needed to leave a blank space in the line, since she couldn't decipher HM's penciled* pallor of passion] 254.38 Stark terrors] HM2,HM4,HM6; The terrors HM1; A terror HM3; White terrors HM5 254.39 his brother] HM3; the maimed one HM1; [*two or three undeciphered erased words, constituting at least one further reading, though perhaps a variant of* death around *in line 38*] HM2 254.39 the field] HM1,T; press HM2; the press HM3,EM 254.41 rest, in claim rest] HM2; rest^ forever HM1; rest, forever rest HM?2 254.44–54 And . . . fair] [*EM leaf 4*] 254.45–255.56 Yes . . . share] [*HM leaf 5(C)*] 254.48 Develop into] HM,EM\HM,EM2; [*words omitted (?because EM could not decipher them), though later penciled in by HM, then inked in by EM*] EM1 254.53 gossips] EM\HM; babblers HM

255.55–71 But . . . way] [*EM leaf 5*] 255.55 ruled] EM\HM; urged HM 255.57–68 When . . . man] [*HM leaf 6.patch(C)* When . . . grace *HM leaf 6(B)* When . . . loth {*superseded portion*} But . . . man {*unsuperseded portion*}] 255.57–60 When . . . grace] HM2; [*see following description of superseded stage B text*]

> When boys they were I helped the bent. [*then* bent: *then* bent.]
> Prompted by me [*then* me,] who weighed them both [*then* both,]
>   Timoleon groomed Timophones' horse [*then* colt],
> Brought in his firing [*then at least four partly undeciphered variants, including* Served him {?well ?first} *and* Tended him ever, *and* {?Forever} served him, *before settling upon* Kept tendence ever,] lovingly too [*then* too,] not loth.

[*these lines then superseded by covering with stage C patch, after further, evidently nonextant revising substantially altered lines 58–60*] HM1(B) 255.57 helped] HM1,HM3;

gave HM2 255.64 a social] HM2,HM4; her city's HM1; the social HM3 255.67 expressed] HM1,HM3; developed HM2 255.69–72 My . . . thin] [*HM leaf 7.clip(?Cb)*] 255.69 brave] EM\HM; tall HM1,HM3; strong HM2 255.72–80 Self . . . do] [*EM leaf 6*] 255.72 thin.] [*at lower right edge of HM leaf 7.clip, erased, the word mien is circled {?for insertion in text scissored away at stage Cc}*] 255.73–80 Nor . . . do] [*HM leaf 7(Cc)*] 255.74 Forsworn] HM; Foresworn EM 255.74 heart that] HM2; hart HM→1 255.77 of . . . humane] HM8; of heart benignly just HM1; [*here follow, in no certainly establishable order, at least four different readings; more readings may be hidden within two or more undeciphered erased words; and at least one decipherable erased word*— true —*may not confidently be positioned in any particular reading other than one of the three HM tried out at the bottom of leaf 7, though it may have appeared in of just heart and true as the first penciled revision he considered*] HM?2,HM?3; he was of milder mind HM?4; of true heart not malign HM?5; of just heart not malign HM?6; of nature not malign HM7 255.81–84 And . . . ran] [*HM leaf 8(?Cc)*] 255.81–256.96 And . . . skies] [*EM leaf 7*] 255.84 rescue ran] [*these words appear on both HM's later-stage leaf 8 and, erased, at the top of the earlier-stage HM leaf 8.clip*] 255.85–256.92 But . . . rods] [*HM leaf 8.clip(?Ca)*] 255.87 racks] HM1,HM3; [*undeciphered erased word {?stamps}*] HM2 255.88 loyal son] HM2; son humane HM1

256.92 fasces] HM2; faces HM1 256.93–96 But . . . skies] [*HM leaf 9(?Cc)*] 256.93–96 But . . . skies] HM2; [*see following description of superseded text that, from its revisions and final state, would seem immediately to have preceded the fair-copy that became HM leaf 9 at stage ?Cc; this superseded text is on a fragmentary leaf (measuring approximately 14.4 cm. by 5.2 cm.) now at the Harry Ransom Humanities Research Center, the University of Texas, Austin*] [*Superseded HM leaf 9(?Cb) {"The Rose" Revisions List verso}* But . . . skies {*foliated upper left corner pencil 9; inscribed by HM in gray iron-gall ink; revised by HM in pencil and gray ink*}]

> But, undeterred, he wills to act, [*then* do, *then* act, *though the soiled upper right corner of this side of the leaf may conceal a dozen or more undeciphered erased words*]
> Resolved to do [*then in pencil, then ink* Resolved thereto *then in pencil, then ink* Resolved thereon] tho' Ate [*then* Anarch *then* Ate] rise;
> He heeds the [*then* a] voice whose mandate falls [*then* calls],
> Or seems to fall [*then* call], peremptory from the skies.

[*then cancel* But . . . skies *with blue pencil*] HM1(?Cb) 256.95 the] HM2; a HM1 256.97–104 V . . . beset] [*HM leaf 9.?clip(?Cb) {?patch(?Ccb)}* V . . . heart {*unsuperseded portion*} The brother . . . beset {*superseded portion*} HM leaf 9.patch(?Ccc) The brother . . . beset] 256.97–112 V . . . place] [*EM leaf 8*] 256.97 Nor] HM2; No HM1 256.101–4 The brother . . . beset] HM2; [*see following description of superseded stage ?Cb (?Ccb) text on HM leaf 9.?clip (?patch)*]

> The brother first he seeks—alone. [*then* private seeks, *then* seeks,
> alone, *then* seeks, when alone, *then* seeks, and pleads *then* seeks,
> {*?leaving the line incomplete*}]
> And pleads [*then cancel, then restore* And pleads], but is with laughter
> met; [*then* met.]
> Returns then in accord with two [*then* Next comes he with two elders
> grave *then* Then comes he with two elders grave *then* Then comes he
> in accord with two],
> And these [*then* all *then* these] adjure the tyrant [*then* pirate *then* tyrant]
> and beset;

[*then cancel* The brother . . . beset *with orange-red penciled Xs, and replace with stage
?Ccc patch*] HM1(*?Cb ?Ccb*) 256.103 Then comes he] HM1,HM3; Returns then
HM2 256.103 in accord with two] HM1,HM5; with two [*?patriots ?patriarchs*]
[*?true ?tried*] HM2; with two [*?patriots ?patriarchs*] grave HM3; with two men
of mark HM4 256.104 these] HM1,HM3; all HM2 256.105–16 Whose . . . hurt]
[*HM leaf 10(I.B)* Whose . . . might {*unsuperseded portion preceding patch*} And
glooms . . . place {*portion superseded by stage C patch*} *HM leaf 10.patch(C)* And
glooms . . . place *HM leaf 10(...II.B)* VI . . . hurt] 256.108 testily] HM,EM2; testify
EM1[*mistranscription*] 256.109–12 And . . . place] HM2; [*see following description of
superseded stage B text on HM leaf 10*]

> And glooms upon his [upon his *scratched out and not replaced*] brother
> [*then* mute brother *then* brother] pale, [*then* pale. *then* pale,]
>> Who goes aside. [*then* Who stands aside. *then* Standing aside. *then*
>> aside. *leaving the line without a decided beginning*] With muffled face
>> [*then* Muffling his face *then* He, muffling him]
> He sobs [*then* Sobs out] the preconcerted sign [*then* sign, *then* word],
> And Right in Corinth reassumes its place.

[*then cancel with penciled and orange-red penciled Xs* And . . . place *and supersede
with latest stage C text*] HM1(B) 256.109 glooms] HM1,HM3; lours HM2 256.109
mute] HM2,HM5; just HM1; [*at least one undeciphered erased word* {*?grave*}]
HM3; panged HM4 256.110 goes] HM3; draws HM1; moves HM2 256.111 pre-
determined] HM3; authorising HM1; [*?condemnatory ?confirmatory*] HM2
256.113–257.128 VI . . . undismayed] [*EM leaf 9*] 256.113 robe, ah,] HM2; robe see
HM1 256.114 craven] HM1,HM3; vulgar HM2 256.115 ban] HM1,HM3,HM5;
curse HM2,HM4 256.117–257.128 The . . . undismayed] [*HM leaf 11(C)*] 256.118
wide] HM,EM\HM; wild EM
   257.120 Inveterate . . . fratricide] [*at the top edge of HM leaf 11.clip (see next
entry) are at least one or two undeciphered erased words that are variants of words in this
or some preceding line*] HM 257.121–24 The . . . jar] [*HM leaf 11.clip(B)* The . . . are]
257.121 time] HM1,HM3; age HM2 257.123–24 As . . . jar] [*HM leaf 11.patch(C+)*

As . . . jar *HM leaf 11.patch verso* No . . . warrant] 257.123–24 As . . . jar] [*after EM had transcribed the stage B version of these lines—* If summons or sanction Virtue heard / Lapsing it died like thunder rolled afar. *—HM inscribed many possible revisions of them on leaf 11's clip, patch, and the verso of the patch, before EM copied his final choices into both their transcripts; in the descriptions that follow here, the order and even, at times, nature of particular readings is partly problematic, because of the ways in which revisions HM considered are spread out over four writing surfaces*] 257.123 As . . . knew] HM10,EM2; If summons or sanction Virtue heard HM1,EM1; No seeming sanction Virtue heard HM?2,HM?4; No seeming sanction Virtue knew HM?3; No Revelation Virtue heard HM?5; No Revelation Virtue knew HM?6[*this reading appears on both the clip and the verso of the patch*]; The world was young, and Christ was still afar HM?7[*this reading and the one following here appear on the verso of the patch*]; No heavenly warrant [*left incomplete, perhaps to be completed by* Virtue heard/knew *though* No heavenly warrant *is closer to the beginning of a variant for line 124—* No warrant to be more than {?wildings} are] HM?8; No warrant here, and all life [*undeciphered word* {?secular}] HM9 257.124 For deeds . . . jar] T; Lapsing it died like thunder rolled afar HM1,EM1; Aloof it died like thunder rolled afar HM?2; Aloof it lapsed like thunder rolled afar HM?3; Or seemed to hear, it was like thunder rolled afar HM?4; Or seemed to hear, from thunder [?times], uncertain and afar HM?5; No warrant to be more than [?wildings] are HM6; For deeds that on the popular morals jar HM7; For acts [*or* deeds *or* aught] that on accepted morals jar HM8; For acts [*or* deeds *or* aught] that on the common morals jar HM9; For acts [*or* deeds *or* aught] that on prescriptive morals jar HM10; [?For] [?innate] acts [*this reading left incomplete, perhaps because HM could not figure out how to use the two words he put in parentheses (*[?innate] acts*) without throwing off the line scansion*] HM11; For aught that on prescriptive morals jar HM12,EM2 257.125 took] HM2; takes HM1 257.127 doom] T; deed HM1,HM3; act HM2 257.128 Herself] HM2; Itself HM1 257.128 authorised] HM1,HM3; sanctified HM2 257.129–40 Within . . . face] [*HM leaf 12(C)*] 257.129–44 Within . . . apart] [*EM leaf 10*] 257.130 sea] HM2; seas HM1 257.131 vacates its] HM2; vacate their HM1 257.132 last reserves] HM1,HM3; godlessness HM2 257.133–40 He . . . face] HM2; [*see following description of superseded stage B inscription*] [*Superseded HM leaf 12(B) {"Billy Budd" leaf 347 verso}* He . . . face {*foliated (upper left corner orange) 12; inscribed in stage B pencil; revised in pencil and stage C ink*}]

> He falters; and from Hades' hxx[→*then* glens]
> By night ambiguous tones implore:
> "Translate thee; [*then* thee!] hither come and be
> What Phocion is who feeleth man no more.
> [*line-space*]
> But, curbed in that [*then* therein *then* in that], his mood elects
> Retirement and the lonely [*then(C)* Seclusion and the lonely *then(C)*]
> Seclusion deep in loneliest *then(C)* Solitude deep in cloistral *then(C)*

Solitude and the cloistral *then(C)* Solitude and the rugged *then(C)*
Solitude and untroden *then(C—or earlier)* Solitude and the lonely *then*
Solitude and the wooded *then(C pencil)* Self exile & secluded] place;
For years a hermit, he but meets
In shade his playfellow's reproachful face

[*then cancel with orange and green pencil*] HM1(B,C) 257.137 won] HM,EM\HM;
soon EM[*misreading*] 257.141–52 Estranged . . . gods] [*HM leaf 13(B)*] 257.141
Estranged] HM1,HM3; Removed HM2 257.141 transcendent] HM3; transcend-
ing HM1; excelling HM2 257.141 deed^] HM4; act^ HM1; act, HM2; deed,
HM3(Db–d) 257.142 From common membership] HM5; Cut off from mem-
bership HM1; Estranged from membership HM2; Removed from membership
HM3; From common humanity HM4 257.145–258.160 VII . . . brow] [*EM leaf 11*]
257.146 bides] EM\HM; dwells HM 257.149 why appeal?] HM1,HM5; where-
for look, HM2,HM4; wherefor turn? HM3 257.150 Vain parleying here with]
HM2,HM4,HM6; Why parley here with HM1,HM5; Appealing here to HM3
257.151–52 To . . . gods] HM2; [*see following description of superseded matter on a
pre–stage B leaf; a clip from an even earlier stage may once have been attached to the lower
portion of this pre–stage B leaf, that clip bearing earlier versions of line 152, as well as of
two or more following lines*] [*Superseded HM leaf 13(pre–B) {"After the Pleasure Party"
leaf 6.patch verso}* My quarrel . . . quarrel]
    [*inscribed in dark brown ink:*]

    My quarrel, for this quarrel [*plus a probable three now-scissored-away
    words, the last of which is likely* gods *though only the descender of the g
    shows*] [*then revised in pencil:*] My quarrel, for [*cancel* for *and insert a
    now-scissored-away word*] this quarrel [*plus the probable three now-
    scissored-away words*]
    [*then* My quarrel, O dreaded master *then* My quarrel, O unjust {*?read-
    ing not completed*}
    then
    With you, Arch Principals, with you
    I quarrel, I quarrel but with gods{*?*}
    then cancel With . . . gods *with wavy line and start over:*
    From them, Arch Principals, to you
    I rear this quarrel

then cancel this pre–stage B text with orange pencil, as well as erase all penciled variants]
HM1(pre-B) 257.151 Principals] HM,EM2; Principal EM1[*EM evidently put down
as much as she could initially read, then later inscribed what HM told her the final letter
should be*] 257.151 rear] HM1,HM3; lift HM2 257.153–258.166 Shall . . . may] [*HM
leaf 14(C) {the last two lines on HM leaf 14 are inscribed by EM}*]
    258.155 temple] HM1,HM3; temples HM2 258.157 bear with *one*^ quite
overborne] HM5; bear with <u>one</u>, whom pangs compell HM1; tolerate <u>one</u>,

whom pangs compell HM2; bear with [*or/and* tolerate] him [*?*whose] pangs compell HM*?*3; bear with [*or/and* tolerate] earnestness quite overborne HM4 258.159 rail] HM,EM,EM\HM2; brave EM\HM1 258.160 ye set] HM,EM2; his EM1[*misreading*] 258.161–76 If . . . phrase] [*EM leaf 12*] *258.163 Are earnest natures] EM[*from nonextant stage D HM inscription*]; Is virtue tried and HM 258.164 But fatherless shadows] EM[*from nonextant stage D HM inscription*]; A fatherless shadow HM 258.165–68 Yea . . . sway] EM[*from nonextant stage D HM inscription; EM copied the lines into HM's transcript, at the bottom of HM leaf 14 and top of HM leaf 15*]; [*no text-lines present*] HM 258.165 'tis] EM\HM,HM\EM2; too EM,HM\ EM1[*EM's misreading of nonextant HM inscription that she also copied back into his transcript before he detected the error*] 258.167–76 Since . . . phrase] [*HM leaf 15(C) {first two lines on this leaf are inscribed by EM}*] 258.169 deign,] HM4; deign for once HM1; deign, ye gods, HM2; deign, ye Powers, HM3 258.169 some little] HM\ EM1,HM\EM3; some HM,HM\EM2 258.170 skies] HM2; sky HM1 258.171 Me reassure,] EM; A whisper—one! HM1; A whisper, gods! HM2; Me reassure! HM3[*Me reassure also appears as a trial phrase on the later-superseded verso ("Buddha" HM leaf 1 verso) that HM used mainly for redrafting several lines in "Venice"*] 258.171 me be] HM3; despair HM1; me [*?*learn] HM2 258.172 Like . . . cries] HM11; Proclaim that gods are not or naught, and die HM1,HM3; Proclaim that ye are not or naught, or die HM2; That god [*?*is wanting, useless for master] high HM4; That gods [*?*are wanting, useless for masters] high HM4; Virtue a dog, without a master high HM6; [*?*Is] like a dog, without a master high HM7; Even as a [*or* the] dog that for a master cries HM8,HM10; Even as with dogs that for a master cry HM9 258.173 Men's] EM\HM; He raved. But HM1[*above canceled* He raved EM *penciled, then erased* correct this]; Our EM[*from nonextant stage D HM inscription*] 258.173 moods, as frames,] EM[*from nonextant stage D HM inscription*]; moods HM 258.177–80 On . . . land] [*HM leaf 16.clip(Cd)*] 258.177–88 On . . . shore] [*EM leaf 13*] 258.180 that . . . land] HM[*that sunny ground is a possible variant that is penciled and erased at the right of the poem's title on HM leaf 1*] 258.181–88 And . . . shore] [*HM leaf 16(Cd+)*] 258.181 Absolved, and more] HM2,HM4; More than absolved HM1; Absolved, absolved HM3 258.182 Justice . . . is] HM2; Yea, long arrears of fame are HM1 258.183 thine] HM,EM,EM\HM1,EM\HM3; [*undeciphered erased word*] EM\HM*?*2 258.183 slayer] HM2; murderer HM1 258.184 man] HM1,HM3; heart HM2 258.185 Eager] HM2,HM4; Festal HM1,HM3 258.185 thy City] HM1,HM3,HM5; thy country HM*?*2; [*at least two undeciphered erased words, constituting at least one additional reading*] HM4

TEXTUAL NOTES: ACCIDENTALS. 253.0 *Timoleon* / (394 B.C.)] [*NN sets the main title in italics as a matter of design; the title is not underlined in HM; in EM,* Timoleon *is triple-underlined and* (394 B.C.) *single-underlined; in T these underlinings are translated into large and small capitals*] 253.0[*subtitle* B.C.] HM,EM; B. C. T 253.1[*part number*] I] EM2; [*underlined*] HM,EM1 253.[*indention and line-spacing*] [*five penciled horizontal marks at the top right of HM leaf 1 show HM directing EM to indent the first line of each four in her transcript, and not leave the line-space that appears after each quatrain in* *his transcript*] 253.1 If] [*indent*] HM; [*indention obscured by display capital*] T *253.3 snatched,] HM; ~^ EM 253.4 stamped] HM2; stampt HM1 253.4 seizure] HM,T; siezure EM 253.5 legalised] HM; legalized EM *253.6 good heart] EM; Good Heart HM 253.8 good in weak] EM2; Good in Weak HM,EM1 253.9–12 Needs . . . man] [*see substantives*] 253.9 goodness] EM2; Goodness HM,EM1 253.11 dumfounds] HM2; dumbfounds HM1 253.12 man?] EM; ~. HM *253.17 ensue,] HM,EM1,T; ~^ EM2 253.19 Chance] HM2; chance HM1 253.20 proved it] [*see substantives*] 253.21 thorn,] HM2; ~^ HM1 253.22 cross-tide] HM2; ~^~ HM?1 253.22 stem,] HM2; ~^ HM1

254.25[*part number*] II] HM1,HM?3; [*though HM did not explicitly (by inscribing the numeral) go through with redesignating this part as 2 his designating parts 5, 6, and 7 with arabic numerals, late in stage C, suggests his erased penciled note here—* Following No. 1 / alter throughout *—means he temporarily intended to change from roman to arabic numerals*] HM→2 254.25[*part number*] II] EM2; [*underlined*] HM,EM1 254.26 right,] EM; ~^ HM 254.27 well:] EM; ~^ HM1; ~, HM2 254.29–30 Apart . . . cavalryman] [*for some reason—possibly because she could not earlier make out HM's intentions—EM seems to have inscribed* Apart . . . cavalryman *later than the surrounding text in her transcript*] 254.29 place,] EM; ~^ HM 254.32 crippled,] HM; ~^ EM 254.33 Timoleon, . . . need,] EM; ~^ . . . ~^ HM 254.33 Timophanes'] HM,T; ~^ EM 254.41 'rest,] [*see substantives*] 254.41 here,] EM; ~— HM *254.44 take^ . . . prolonged^] EM; ~, . . . ~, HM 254.44 stain] HM,EM2; [*undeciphered scratched-out letter preceding* stain] EM1 254.49[*part number*] III] EM2; [*underlined*] HM,EM1 *254.51 looked.] EM2; ~: HM,EM1,T *254.52 he] HM2; [*not underlined*] HM1,EM 254.52 stir.] HM,EM4; ~^ EM1; ~[?:] EM2; ~[?;] EM3

255.55 ruled,] HM; ~^ EM 255.55 bade,] EM; ~— HM *255.56 such,] T; ~^ HM 255.56 share.] HM,T; ~:[*though only the bottom point is inked in*] EM 255.57 bent;] EM; ~: HM 255.59 him, too;] EM; ~^ ~, HM *255.60 And^ sooth^] EM; ~, ~, HM *255.60 grace.] HM,T; ~; EM 255.62 'he,] EM; ~; HM 255.63 through] HM2; thro' HM1 255.64 power,] HM2; ~^ HM1 255.66 translated; joyed,] HM2; translated. Joyed^ HM1[*even as he transcribed this passage, HM was not certain how he wished to punctuate it; and in making her transcription, EM had to query his intention*] 255.67 thee;] HM,T; ~: EM 255.69 Timophanes] HM2; Timophones HM1 255.72 through] EM; thro' HM *255.72 thin.^] HM1,EM; ~." HM2 255.73 erred] HM,EM2; [*undeciphered transcription error {?errect}*] EM1 255.73 erred:] EM; ~. HM 255.74 Forsworn] [*see substantives*] 255.74 heart that] [*see substantives*] 255.77[*part number*] IV] HM2; [*no part number precedes*] HM1 255.77[*part number*] IV] EM2; [*underlined*] HM,EM1 255.80 do;] EM; ~. HM 255.82 clan,] EM; ~— HM 255.83 dear,] HM; ~^ EM 255.85 terrorised] HM; terrorized EM 255.85 town,] EM; ~— HM 255.86 silent,] HM,T; ~^ EM 255.86 mother^—] HM1,EM; ~!: HM2

256.92 *fasces*] [*underlined*] HM[*see also substantives*],EM\HM; Fasces HM\EM1; fasces HM\EM2,EM 256.93 But^ undeterred^] EM2; ~, ~, HM,EM1 256.94 though] EM; tho' HM 256.97[*part number*] V] EM2; [*underlined*] HM[*a penciled V beneath the problematic clip/patch on HM leaf 9 is also underlined; moreover, HM late considered redesignating the poem's parts with arabic numerals, as is evidenced by an erased 5 on leaf 9's clip/patch*],EM1 256.97 mild,] EM; ~^ HM 256.101–4 The brother . . .

beset] [*see substantives*] 256.101 seeks] HM,EM2; [*undeciphered mistranscription*] EM1 256.102 met;] EM; ~. HM 256.103 he,] EM; ~^ HM 256.107 and^] EM; ~, HM *256.108 might";] EM; ~;" HM; ~:" T 256.109–12 And . . . place] [*see substantives*] 256.109 pale,] EM; ~; HM 256.111 word,] EM; ~; HM 256.113[*part number*] VI] EM2; [*underlined*] HM[*an erased 6 also shows HM late considering arabic numerals to designate the poem's parts*] 256.113 robe, ah,] [*see substantives*] 256.117 world,] EM; ~^ HM 256.118 wide,] HM; ~^ T 256.119 truth,] EM; ~^ HM

257.122 atheist's] EM2; Atheist's HM,EM1 257.123 As . . . knew] [*see substantives*] 257.127 irrevocable] EM; irreevocable HM 257.128 authorised] HM; authorized EM 257.128 undismayed.] EM; ~^ HM[*inadvertent omission*] 257.130 sea^] EM2; ~, HM,EM1 257.133–40 He . . . face] [*see substantives*] *257.133 falters. And] HM; falters, and T 257.135 suffer?] EM2; ~, HM,EM1 257.135 come,] HM; ~^ EM 257.137 But,] EM; ~^ HM 257.138 place;] EM; ~. HM 257.139 self-outcast,] EM2; ~^ HM,EM1 257.141 deed^] [*see substantives*] 257.145[*part number*] VII] EM2; 7 HM1; <u>VII</u> HM2,EM1 257.145 though] EM; tho' HM 257.145 ebb,] EM2; ~. HM,EM1 257.146 long;] EM; ~. HM1; ~: HM2 257.148 heaven] HM,EM\ HM; xxeaven EM[*undeciphered misreading*] 257.148 wrong:] EM; ~. HM *257.149 "To] HM2; ^~ HM1,T 257.149 why] HM,EM2; [*undeciphered misreading*] EM1 257.149 appeal?] [*see substantives*] 257.150 fellow-clods.] EM; ~-~? HM1; ~-~— HM2; ~-~^ HM3[*HM cancels all punctuation, delaying his final decision till later*]; ~^~. T 257.151 you] HM; [*not underlined*] EM 257.151 Arch Principals] HM,EM1,EM3; [*underlined*] EM2

258.156 stony,] EM; ~^ HM,T 258.156 vain?"] HM; ~?^ T 258.157 bear . . . overborne] [*see substantives*] *258.157 one] HM; [*not underlined*] EM 258.160 brow.—] EM; ~.^ HM,T 258.161 "If] HM; ^~ T 258.161 recant.] HM?1,EM2; ~: HM2,EM1 258.165–68 Yea . . . sway] [*EM copied these lines back into HM's transcript with little punctuation*] 258.165 "Yea] [*indent*] EM\HM[*HM's note directs the compositor to* Indent,—*to correspond with the rest.*]; [*no indent*] EM[*from nonextant inscription*] 258.165 "Yea] NN; ^~ HM\EM 258.165 Yea, are ye,] EM; ~^ ~ ~^ HM\EM 258.165 Then ye,] EM; ~ ~^ HM\EM 258.166 may,] EM; ~^ HM\EM *258.167 ye^] EM,HM\EM; ~, T 258.167 wrung,] EM2,EM4; ~^ EM1,EM3,T 258.168 grievous] T; greivous EM *258.168 sway.] EM?2,T; ~^ EM1,HM\EM; ~— EM3[*HM may also have considered using a period-dash here*] 258.169 deign,] HM,EM2; ~; EM1[*also see substantives*] 258.169 given—] EM4; ~, HM,EM?1; ~; EM2; ~[?:] EM?3 258.171 Me reassure,] [*see substantives*] 258.172 cries."] EM; die.^ HM[*see substantives*]; cries.^ HM\EM,T 258.173[*part number*] VIII] HM,EM2; [*underlined*] EM1 258.173 moods, as frames,] [*see substantives*] 258.173 yield] EM; yeild HM 258.174 ways:] HM,EM2; ~. EM1; ~; T 258.177 wars,] EM; ~^ HM 258.179 isle] EM\HM; Isle HM *258.181 ^Absolved] EM; "~ HM *258.182 thine:] EM; ~; HM 258.184 saviour] HM; savior EM 258.184 soldier,] HM,EM?2,T; ~^ EM1,EM3 *258.184 divine.] T; ~! HM,EM?1; ~; EM?2; ~: EM?3; ~^ EM4[*a reading in which HM is either neglecting or deciding not to decide his final punctuation here*] *258.185 ^Eager] EM; "~ HM 258.185 City] HM2; city HM1 258.185 waits:] EM; ~; HM 258.186 Return!] HM1,EM; ~, HM2 *258.186 door.^] EM3; ~." HM; ~:^ EM?1; ~;^ EM?2

AFTER THE PLEASURE PARTY (pp. 259–64)

This poem was placed after "The Weaver" in Melville's manuscript and in his wife's transcript (making it the ninth poem in the collection); and because that transcript was the printer's copy, the poem presumably appeared there in the galley proofs as well. Melville marked its move to a position after "Timoleon" on the contents list that probably went to the printer with the corrected galley proofs, where the shift was presumably also marked. (See p. 575 above.)

DISCUSSIONS. 259.0 *After . . . Party*] As a matter of design, NN does not repeat the poem title on a preceding separate page as it appears in T. That placement was probably directed by Melville in proof to facilitate the typographical treatment of the introductory poem (see the next discussion). NN also does not retain the HM hyphen in "Pleasure-Party" because Melville later inscribed the words in EM twice without a hyphen—once in pencil, once in ink. He also wrote it without the hyphen in the contents list. (Since it is not NN policy to impose consistency, the hyphenated form is allowed to stand in line 106.) At earlier stages, the poem had at least two other titles: "Urania or After the Pleasure Party" and "A Boy's Revenge or After the Pleasure Party" (see the textual notes below). The latter title was the one in the printer's copy, and Melville was still considering it at the time he marked his wife's transcript of the table of contents to show the insertion of the poem after "Timoleon": he first wrote "A Boy's Revenge" at that point and then changed it to "After the Pleasure Party," presumably at about the same time that he changed it on the proofs (see p. 575 above).

    259.0[*introductory poem*] LINES . . . *seat*] As a matter of design, NN uses extra line-spacing (and sets the title in small capitals and the poem in italic type, as in the first edition) to indicate Melville's intended setting off of "Lines Traced Under an image of Amor threatening." This introductory poem or epigraph appears on a separate leaf in Melville's manuscript (with its title underlined), and its placement on the verso of a section-title in T represents a way of carrying out Melville's original intention, probably requested by him in proof (since in EM, the printer's copy, the introductory poem—with its title double-underlined—and the beginning of the poem proper appear on the same page). NN follows EM in omitting the commas present in HM after "pride" (line 2 of the introductory poem) and after "but" and "wroth" (line 5) since Melville extensively revised the punctuation of lines 1–5 in EM, and these omissions are therefore probably intentional.

    259.1 Behind] In his manuscript, Melville penciled part numbers (1 and 2) both here, before the first line of the poem proper, and between lines 104 and 105. NN follows EM in omitting the numbers and using extra line-spacing, judging that in pointing and revising his wife's transcript he went back to his earlier plan, when he saw that spacing would accomplish his purpose just as well.

259.3 halls—] NN retains the dash that appears in both HM and EM, although the comma in T is possibly authoritative.

260.12 "Tired] On the quotation marks retained from HM at this point and in lines 18, 27, 39, 48, 54, 66, and 125, as well as those inserted by NN in lines 73, 80, 95, 104, and 141, see the discussion at 257.149 above.

260.13 urge^] NN retains the reading in HM and EM, without a comma. The comma in T is more likely to be compositorial than authorial, since it impedes the flow of lines 13–15 (cf. another likely compositorial insertion of a comma at 284.7).

260.20 Fate sprung Love's ambuscade] Cf. the poem "The Ambuscade" (unpublished by Melville) in NN volume 13, *"Billy Budd, Sailor" and Other Uncompleted Writings*.

260.23–24 'Tis Vesta . . . leap] The Roman goddess Vesta was sworn to perpetual virginity. According to Ovid (*Heriodes*, bk. 15), Sappho (fl. ca. 600 B.C.) was attracted to Phaon, a ferryman who did not return her passion, and she leapt into the sea from the Leucadian rock on the island of Lesbos. Melville visited the island in December of 1856 (*Journals*, pp. 68–69) and refers to it in *Clarel* (3.11.26–27).

260.34–35 reign; / To dote;] NN retains the semicolons in Melville's manuscript here, since their reappearance in T (in place of the colon and comma in EM) may well be authoritative. (In some copies of T—such as Harvard Copy C—the semicolon after "dote" is damaged so that it looks like a comma.)

260.41,42 O] In both interjectional and optative contexts, Melville omitted the comma after "O" seven times out of ten in his manuscript for *John Marr*; in *Timoleon* only four commas out of the ten following "O" in his own manuscript are carried over to EM, and in four other cases he did not use a comma in his own as well. NN follows EM in those six cases where a comma is omitted (in these two lines, and in 263.138, 264.151, 286.5, and 312.7), judging it probable that Melville intended the omissions.

260.41–43 Northern air . . . skies] On Nantucket Island, Massachusetts, July 7, 1852, Melville and his father-in-law, Judge Lemuel Shaw, "passed the evening with Mr. Mitchell the astronomer, & his celebrated daughter, the discoverer of comets" (Leyda, *Log*, 452). Maria Mitchell (1818–89) discovered a new comet in October 1847 and was the first professor of astronomy at Vassar College (1865–89).

260.43 chased] NN follows EM in omitting the comma present in HM (and in correcting Melville's spelling). Since Melville carried over from his own to his wife's transcript three of the four commas in lines 43–44, it seems likely that in punctuating hers he chose to alter his rhythm by not endstopping line 43.

261.45 Cassiopea in Golden Chair] In Greek myth Cassiopeia (the more common spelling today) is punished by Poseidon for her vanity in claiming that both she and her daughter Andromeda are more beautiful than the nereids. Part of the constellation Cassiopeia is conventionally figured as her Golden Chair.

261.48 ah yet,] NN retains the comma in HM, since there is not enough evidence to suggest that its omission in EM was intentional.

261.53 spleen,] NN adopts the comma from T as probably authorial, given that the revised state of both HM and EM may have kept Melville from noticing the desirability of repointing his altered line, which had no punctuation here (see the textual notes below).

261.58 her—] NN adopts the dash from T as probably authoritative. It not only throws more emphasis on "her" than the comma in HM, but it is a revision similar to nine other dashes added (or substituted for other punctuation) in T, four of which restore the latest readings in Melville's manuscript; this series of changes seems more likely to have been the work of Melville (on the proofs) than of a compositor.

262.80 me!] NN adopts the exclamation mark in T (in place of the dash in HM or the semicolon in EM). The exclamation mark presumably represents Melville's restoration of earlier punctuation in his manuscript (see the textual notes, below).

262.84–85 surge . . . thee] NN follows Melville's careful repointing of lines 84–86 in his wife's transcript (see the textual notes, below) and infers that in this process Melville deliberately omitted the commas in lines 84–85.

262.89 Selfhood] NN retains the unhyphenated form in HM, judging that Melville's failure to revise the hyphenated form in EM was an oversight.

262.91 meet and mate] Cf. line 4 of "Art" (p. 280 above): "What unlike things must meet and mate".

262.92–94 Cosmic jest . . . gate] Cf. the account in Plato's *Symposium* of how primal man came to be sexually and otherwise divided.

262.105 One] NN uses extra line-spacing before this line, as in EM, instead of the part number in HM; see the discussion at 259.1 above.

262.105 Urania] Both the muse of astronomy and Milton's muse of lofty poetry (*Paradise Lost,* 7.1–40).

263.111 spite,] NN adopts the comma in T as probably added by Melville in proof, to accompany the comma he had inserted after "boy-like" in line 112 of his wife's transcript.

263.115 Albani's porch] Melville visited the Villa Albani (now Villa Torlonia), the important gallery near Rome, on February 28 and March 14, 1857 (see *Journals,* pp. 107, 112, 468–70, 485).

263.118 Thomas a'Kempis] Thomas Hamerken von Kempen (1380–1471), German ecclesiastic, mystic, and supposed author of the *Imitatio Christi* (ca. 1417–21; Bercaw, no. 417). For NN retention of "a'Kempis" see p. 610 above.

263.119 tone;] NN adopts the semicolon from T as authorial, probably representing Melville's continuing revision of the pointing here: he had a period in his manuscript, which he changed to a comma in his wife's transcript.

263.123 Till . . . emotion] NN follows Melville's careful repointing of lines 119–24 in his wife's transcript (see the textual notes below) and presumes that he deliberately omitted the commas in line 123 (and that he directed her to make "form" lowercase in line 121).

263.129 A . . . grieve] NN follows EM, in which this musing is not under-lined for italics, as it was not initially in HM. See the discussion at 278.3 below.

263.132,134 But/Helmeted] In his manuscript Melville originally indicated neither line 132 nor line 134 as beginning new verse-paragraphs. He then pen-ciled a bracket at the left of each line, probably to set off Urania's returning to the present from her musing on the past and to set off her invocation to the "arm'd Virgin." In EM, however, Melville explicitly decided against the line-space before line 132; NN also follows EM at line 134, assuming that he intentionally omitted the bracket indicating a line-space.

263.132 arm'd Virgin!] A statue of Athena, presumably modeled on the one in the Villa Albani (pictured in Edmund Von Mach, ed., *University Prints* [Boston: University Prints, 1916], plate A102, reproduced in *Journals*, p. 470). NN adopts the exclamation mark in T as probably inserted by Melville in proof, since no Caxton Press staff member would have been likely to add it.

263.141 arm me!"] NN retains the exclamation mark in HM (which was replaced by a period in EM), since its reappearance in T plausibly represents Melville's restoration.

263.142 Fond] NN adopts the line-space from T, because it probably rep-resents Melville's restoration of an earlier line-space in his manuscript (see the textual notes below).

264.151 care.] NN retains the copy-text period, because its reappearance in T is probably Melville's own restoration; a Caxton Press staff member would not be likely to depart from copy so far as to ignore the exclamation mark in EM.

EMENDATIONS. *259.0 *Pleasure^Party*] EM\HM; ~-~ HM *259.0[*introductory poem*] *pride^*] EM; ~, HM 259.0[*introductory poem*] *me,*] EM; ~^ HM 259.0[*intro-ductory poem*] *slighted.*] EM; ~! HM 259.0[*introductory poem*] *tempt:*] EM; ~. HM 259.0[*introductory poem*] *wings,*] EM; ~; HM *259.0[*introductory poem*] *but^ wroth^*] EM; ~, ~, HM *259.1 Behind] [*no part number precedes; replace part number with double line-space*] EM\HM; 1 [*part number*] HM 259.3,4 White/Terrace] [*no indent*] EM; [*indent*] HM 259.4 and down,] EM; ~~^ HM 259.5 Mediterranean] HM\ EM; Meditteranean HM 259.8 Nor] [*no indent*] EM; [*indent*] HM 259.9 peace] EM\HM; Peace HM 260.17 so?] EM; ~! HM 260.18 tell:] EM; ~; HM 260.19 to forget!^] EM; ~~!— HM 260.20 ambuscade,] EM; ~^ HM 260.22 strife.] EM; ~! HM 260.24 leap:] EM; ~; HM 260.27 feel, . . . ween,] EM; ~ (. . . ~) HM 260.30 dear] EM\HM; warm HM 260.31 Geysers^ that] EM\HM; Gey-sers, 'twill HM 260.31 aspire—] EM\HM; ~^ HM 260.32 obstruction^] EM; ~, HM 260.32 win . . . way] EM\HM; iced delay HM 260.33,34,36,37,40,42,43 [*no indent*] EM; [*indent*] HM 260.37 control,] EM; ~^ HM *260.41 O^] EM; ~, HM 260.41 chill] EM\HM; lone HM *260.42 O^] EM; ~, HM 260.43 skies] EM\ HM; stars HM *260.43 chased^] EM; chaced, HM 261.45 Chair.] EM; ~! HM 261.46,47,49,50,55,57 [*no indent*] EM; [*indent*] HM 261.46 me,] EM; ~; HM 261.47

straw.] EM; ~^ HM 261.48 reigned,] EM; ~^ HM 261.49 Through] EM; thro'
HM 261.50 undeceived—] EM; ~^ HM 261.52 decline—] EM; ~? HM *261.53
spleen,] T; ~^ HM 261.54 demure] T; to-day HM 261.55 way,] EM; ~^ HM 261.57
May-Day—] EM; ~; HM *261.58 her—] T; ~, HM 261.59 fell!] EM; ~— HM
261.60 strung;] EM; ~, HM 261.62 so young!^] EM; ~~!— HM 261.63 strong]
EM\HM; grown HM 261.63 weak.] EM; ~! HM 261.64 remain,] EM; ~: HM
261.65 belittling] EM\HM; remembered HM 261.73 "Me] NN; ^~ HM 261.74
writ,] EM; ~^ HM 261.75 cheeks—] EM; ~? HM 262.77 How] EM; Right HM
262.77 glad,] EM; ~^ HM 262.77 lore,] EM; ~^ HM 262.78 veriest] EM\HM;
downright HM 262.80 "Could] NN; ^~ HM *262.80 me!] T; ~— HM 262.80
or set free] T; could I be HM 262.81 This . . . then] T; Pure sexless intellect, and
HM 262.83 Piercing] T; Alive into HM 262.83 paramount] T; wide HM 262.84
Nature,] EM; ~! HM *262.84–85 surge^ . . . thee^] EM; ~, . . . ~, HM 262.85
urge,] EM; ~— HM 262.86 halves—] EM; ~, HM 262.89 incomplete.] EM; ~;
HM 262.94 through] EM; thro' HM 262.95 "Ye] NN; ^~ HM 262.96 vigil,]
EM; ~— HM 262.99 Usurped] EM; Userped HM 262.100 wane:] EM; ~! HM
262.101 Light] T; Day HM 262.101 truth breaks!] T; ~~. HM 262.101 more,] EM;
~^ HM 262.102,103 But/Shivers] [no indent] EM; [indent] HM 262.102 chilled]
EM\HM; touched HM 262.103 yon] EM\HM; the HM 262.104 shore."] NN;
~.^ HM *262.105 One] [no part number precedes] EM\HM; 2 [part number] HM
262.106 forget;] EM; ~, HM *263.111 spite,] T; ~^ HM 263.112 boy-like,] EM;
~^ HM 263.115 Albani's] EM\HM; a villa's HM 263.117 carved.^] EM; ~.—
HM 263.117 No anchorite seer,] EM\HM; Aurelian clear^ HM 263.118 Not]
EM\HM; Nor HM *263.119 tone;] T; ~. HM 263.121 form] EM; Form HM
263.122 influence,] EM; ~^ HM *263.123 Till^ . . . emotion^] EM; ~, . . . ~, HM
263.124 She . . . she] T; The latent thought some utterance HM 263.124 won:^]
EM; ~:— HM 263.126 convent-shrine,] EM; ~^ HM 263.127,129,130,131,135,137
[no indent] EM; [indent] HM *263.129 A . . . grieve] [not underlined] EM; [under-
lined] HM 263.129 grieve.] EM; ~! HM 263.130 believe] EM; beleive HM 263.130
believe,] EM; ~— HM 263.131 Believe] EM; Beleive HM 263.131 submit,] EM;
~— HM *263.132 But] [no line-space, no indent] EM; [penciled bracket indicates
verse-paragraph line-space and indention] HM *263.132 Virgin!] T; ~, HM 263.133
one.] EM; ~: HM *263.134 Helmeted] [no line-space, no indent] EM; [line-space and
indent] HM 263.134 woman—] EM; ~, HM 263.136 feud] EM; fued HM 263.137
life—] EM; ~; HM 263.138 O^] EM; ~, HM 263.138 strong] EM\HM; one HM
263.139 unite,] EM; ~; HM 263.140 Transcender!] EM; ~, HM 263.140 up] EM;
up HM[the underline is in blue pencil, and may be part of HM's revising process in lines
141 and 142] *263.141 arm me!"] NN; ~~!^ HM *263.142 Fond appeal] [indented
so as to end flush with right-hand margin, and vertically line-spaced to make new verse-
paragraph] T; [indented {so as to end flush with right-hand margin,} but not line-spaced
to make new verse-paragraph] HM 263.145 Inspire] EM\HM; Inspirit HM 264.147
spare;] EM; ~: HM 264.151 O^] EM; ~, HM 264.151 too,] EM; ~^ HM

TEXTUAL NOTES: INSCRIPTION STAGES. At least five stages of inscription-revision: A (nonextant pre-fair-copy stage); pre-B (pencil); B (dark blue ink on thicker paper); C (tan-gray ink on thicker paper); D (tan-gray ink on thinner paper).

TEXTUAL NOTES: SUBSTANTIVES. 259.0–9 *After . . . peace*] [*HM leaf 1(Dc)* Lines . . . seat *HM leaf 2(Db)* After . . . peace] 259.0–9 *After . . . peace*] [*EM leaf 1* A Boys . . . seat *EM leaf 2* Behind . . . peace] *259.0 *After . . . Party*] HM5[*this is the only HM-inscribed title on HM leaf 1 that remains uncanceled or unerased; after EM had transcribed* A Boys Revenge, *or / After the Pleasure Party onto EM leaf 1, HM evidently went back to his own transcript and, with penciled parentheses and restoration underlinings, indicated his final title*],EM[*on leaf 1 of the table of contents in EM's transcript, presumably transcribed by EM from nonextant HM inscription*],EM\HM5[*on leaf 1 of the table of contents in EM's transcript*],T[*on half-title page*]; A Boy's Revenge / or / After the Pleasure-Party HM1,EM,EM\HM?3[*also appears to have been canceled and restored at some indeterminate point; EM omits the apostrophe and the hyphen*]; A Boy's Revenge HM?2,EM\HM1; Urania HM?3[*appears on HM leaf 1 as well as on HM leaf 2*],EM\HM?2,HM\EM[*not canceled*]; Urania / or / After the Pleasure Party HM?4,EM\HM4 *259.0[*introductory poem*] [*that HM intended* "Lines Traced Under an image of Amor threatening" *to be taken as a separate, introductory poem is indicated by its being added at stage D on a separate leaf, and by HM's penciled (later erased) annotation below it on EM leaf 1* Leave double space / between the above / lines & what / follows on next / page *which EM translated into the direction she inscribed at the top of EM leaf 2* Double space between this / and the preceding italicized lines *a translation she may have begun at the bottom left of EM leaf 1 in some undeciphered erased words; three or four of HM's undeciphered erased words following* threatening *in EM's transcript may constitute further directions as to placement; in T, the introductory poem is separated by positioning it on the verso of the half-title page bearing the main poem's title*] 259.0[*introductory poem*] *fury*] HM1,HM4; anger HM2; [*undeciphered erased word*] HM?3 259.0[*introductory poem*] *Downy wings*] HM4; Wings of down HM1; [*undeciphered erased word may be* downy] wings HM?2; Wings of [?downy] HM?3 259.1 upland] HM3; villa HM1; [*undeciphered erased word*] HM2 259.3 through] HM2; in HM1 259.5 Mediterranean] HM1,HM3; Tyrrhene HM2 259.8 keeps] HM,EM2; keep EM1[*mistranscription*] 259.8 bower] HM,EM2; vower EM1[*misreading*] 259.9 balsamic] HM3; <u>thy</u> balm, O HM1; the balm of HM2 259.10–260.14 From . . . reap] [*HM leaf 3.clip(Db)*] 259.10–260.23 From . . . smart] [*EM leaf 3*]

260.13–23 Look . . . smart] HM2; [*see following description of superseded stage B pencil inscription*] [*Superseded HM leaf 3/4(B pencil)* {"Billy Budd" leaf 85 verso} No . . . smart {*inscribed and revised in pencil; not foliated*}]

No, nothing moves him. Tis a verge
Whither these hurrying pulses urge

As vainly as thy [*then* Vainly as thy waste *then* Idly as thy waste] waves,
O sea,

Against yon [*then* gainst {*tacitly* 'Gainst} yon rich] banks. Waves, [*then*
Fools, *then* Fond,] do ye know

[*then cancel* No . . . know *with green and blue pencil, and probably cover over
with no longer extant revision patch*]

Tis mad to wreck the impulsion so?

No more know I, for all my wit.—

A globule [*then* Little *or* Little globule] in the infinite. [*then cancel* infi-
nite *then cancel whole line* Little . . . infinite]

Who would have dreamed [*then* What devil could dream *then* What
sprite could think][*?*,] how treacherous[*?*,][*then* crafty] laid

In nature's scheme this [*then* love's] ambuscade. [*then cancel period*]

[*then insert two lines:*

To flout me in my {*then* flout my years of} cloistral life.

And land {*then* kill *then* reef *then* rack} me in this {*then* me with *then*
without canceling* with *restore* me in this} feverous {*then* pregnant} strife]

White convert snared in Daphne's grove

Were like to me here plunged [*then* trapped] in love

Who vowed, devout, to die a maid [*then* to shun that {*then* love's}
strife *then cancel whole line* Who . . . strife]

Tis [*then* Yea *then* Tis] Vesta [*then* Vesta's] struck with Sappho's smart

[*then cancel whole leaf with blue pencil*] HM1(B pencil) 260.13 yon] HM2; the HM1
260.15–22 Passive . . . life] [*HM leaf 3(?Dc)*] 260.19 forget the] HM2; to forget the
HM1 260.22–32 And . . . way] [*HM leaf 4(D)*] 260.24–38 No . . . flame] [*EM leaf
4*] 260.24 her] HM1,HM3; that HM2 260.30 The dear desire] HM1,EM1,EM\
HM1,EM\HM6; The warm desire HM2,EM\HM2; The [*undeciphered erased
word*] desire *or* The warm [*undeciphered erased word*] EM\HM?3; [*undeciphered
erased word* {*?And ?Or*}] nature's will EM\HM4; [*?Warm*] nature's will EM\
HM5 260.31 Geysers^ that] EM\HM; Geyser, 'twill HM1; Geysers, 'twill HM2
260.32 win . . . way] EM\HM2,EM\HM4,EM\HM6; iced delay HM; melt their
[*or its*] urgent way EM\HM?1,HM\EM; urge their [*or its*] fervid way EM\HM3;
[*?rise*] their fervid [*or its*] way EM\HM?5 260.33–40 But . . . this] [*HM leaf 5 {no
substantive inscription*} HM leaf 5.clip(D) But . . . this] 260.33 here—to] HM1,HM3;
—nay HM2 260.36 blaze] HM1,HM3; fire HM2 260.39–261.52 And . . . decline]
[*EM leaf 5*] 260.40 Contemning] HM4; Foreswearing HM1,HM3; [*undeciphered
erased word*] HM2 260.41–261.50 O . . . undeceived] [*HM leaf 6(D)*] 260.41 terrace
chill] EM\HM2,EM2; turret bleak HM1,EM1; terrace [*?lone*] HM2; terrace
[*?in*] HM3; terrace lone HM4,EM\HM1 260.41 Northern] HM1,HM3; England
HM2 260.42 reaching ranging] HM2,EM1,EM\HM2; misdirected HM1;
[*?misranging*] EM\HM?1,EM?2[*a reading made plausible by the unerased* mis *of*
misreading *being apparently linked to EM's first inscription of* ranging *in her transcript*]
260.43 skies] EM\HM; stars HM

261.45 Starred] HM,EM\HM3; Queen EM\HM1; Greek EM\HM2 261.46 dream] HM,EM2; dreams EM1[*mistranscription*] 262.46–47 In . . . straw] [*perhaps related to this passage or lines 27ff. is an ink-inscribed fragment on the verso of the patch on leaf 290 of "Billy Budd"; on this former bottom quarter of a leaf, its top three-quarters now scissored away, HM inscribes in blue-gray ink:*]

I heard, I [*?*heard], [*the rest of the text-line is scissored away*]
Of jilting quick caprice within[*?.*]

[*then this fragment is canceled with pencil and blue pencil*] 261.46–49 In . . . self= sustained] HM2; [*see following description of superseded stage B inscription*] [*Superseded HM leaf 6(Bb) {"Billy Budd" leaf 88 verso} In . . . self-sustained {foliated (upper left corner pencil) 4³, inscribed in ink, revised in pencil; a stage Ba or earlier clip was once attached to the top half of this leaf}*]

In dream I throned me [*then* I throned me in my dream *then* In dream
    I throned me], nor I saw
In cell the ideot [*?then ?*In cell the mad one *?then ?*In cell the noble
    then In cell the mad one *then ?*In cell the elated mad one *then* The
    elated mad one *?then ?*The noble *then* The ideot *or (tacitly)* In cell the
    ideot] crowned with straw. [*then* straw! *then* straw,]
Long, long, too long [*?then* Long, long, {*?*too} lonely *?then* {*three unde-
    ciphered erased words} then* Long, long, too long] the ego reigned [*then
    substitute at least one whole text-line beginning with four or five undeciphered
    erased words (and probably ending* ego reigned*); then try a revision of that
    line with another undeciphered erased word or two replacing the first one or
    two undeciphered erased words of its predecessor; then try another text-line
    beginning with one or two undeciphered erased words, and continuing* and
    brag you nobly reigned *then replace all these versions with* Long, long,
    too long the ego reigned]
By self-delusion self-sustained! [*then* {*?*Was} self-delusion self=
    sustained! *?then (?as a line temporarily intended to lead into the contem-
    plated revised version of lines 48 and 49, described here below)* Go, ego go,
    and say *those contemplated revised versions of lines 48 and 49 then, if not
    earlier, inserted below lines 46 and 47, respectively (there being no other more
    convenient space remaining on the leaf for them)*
    How {*?*Now} self-delusion self sustains
        Poor {*then* Celled *then* And} captive {*then* Immured, &} mindless
            of the chains.
    *though the earlier version of line 48 has been restored (as described above), and
    the earlier form of line 49 has been rather perfunctorily canceled with a wan-
    dering mark that fails to strike out* self-sustained]

[*then cancel leaf with green pencil*] HM1(B) 261.47 the idiot crowned with]
HM1,HM7; the [*undeciphered erased word*] crowned with HM2; the moper
crowned with HM3; the loon self-crowned with HM4; the mad one crowned
with HM5; the [*?tacit, not-carried-through alteration to the possessive form of one of
the variant nouns—say, moper's*] crown of HM6 261.49 self-illusion] HM2,EM2;
self-delusion HM1,EM1 261.51–53 What . . . mine] [*HM leaf 6.patch(D+)*] 261.51
barrenly] HM2; humbled and HM1[*the erased upper portions of* humbled *and* bar-
renly *appear at the bottom edge of HM leaf 6*] 261.53–66 Envy . . . gay] [*EM leaf 6*]
261.53 Envy . . . be] HM2; Splenetic envy is that HM1 261.54–58 The . . . hell]
[*HM leaf 7(D+)*] 261.54 demure] HM1,T; to-day HM2; today HM\EM 261.56
blossoming] HM2; blossomed HM1 261.58 this] HM2; my HM1 261.59–63 His
. . . weak] [*HM leaf 7.clip(D)*] 261.59 His] [*at upper left corner of clip appears an erased and
partly-scissored-away, undeciphered letter or numeral*] 261.59 glance] HM2; eye HM1
261.62 young, so] HM2; And^so HM1 261.63 strong] EM\HM[*not copied back
into HM's transcript; on EM leaf 1, at the right of the titles, HM may also have penciled
and erased* strong man's]; grown HM1,HM3; gray HM2 261.63 weak] HM,EM2;
week EM1[*mistranscription*] 261.64–68 To . . . be] [*HM leaf 8(Db)*] 261.65 Sad . . .
pain] EM\HM; In rosary sad—remembered pain HM1; In rosary sad of [*?recol-
lected*] pain HM2; Ah, memory's rosary strung with pain! HM?3; Sad rosary of
remembered pain HM?4[*and the multiply-written-over, erased, and partly undeciphered
state of HM leaf 8 suggests the possibility of further variant text-lines*] 261.67–262.79 Like
. . . repose] [*EM leaf 7*] 261.69–72 O . . . bring] [*HM leaf 8.clip(D)*] 261.73–74 Me
. . . sung] [*HM leaf 8.patch(Dc)*] 261.73–74 Me . . . sung] HM2(Dc); [*see following
description of superseded stage Db text inscribed on HM leaf 8*]

> Me now no more high studies charm. [*then* Me now no more fair
> studies charm. *then* Me now fair studies no more charm. *?then restore*
> Me now no more fair studies charm. *and now, or earlier, cancel* charm]
> Shall all the [*then* Shall odes *and then* Shall all the] oracles said or [*then*
> *and then* or] sung. [*then* Shall great things said {*then* great [*undeciphered
> erased word*] said *then* great thoughts writ} or high themes sung]

[*then cancel whole passage and replace with HM leaf 8.patch*] HM1(Db) 261.74 or]
HM,EM\HM; on EM[*mistranscription*] 261.75–262.79 Damask . . . repose] [*HM
leaf 9(D)*] 261.76 radiant ninny] HM1,HM4; radiant ideot HM2; peony ideot
HM3

262.77 How] EM2; Right HM1,EM1,HM3; [*?no variant inscribed before rein-
scription of* Right] HM2 262.78 veriest] EM\HM[*HM also inscribed and erased
veriest in the upper right corner of EM leaf 1*]; downright HM 262.79 repose.] HM2;
[*after EM had made her transcript, but before HM had punctuated it, HM canceled the
following five lines (as revised); that in EM's transcript the first of the five was scratched out
at the bottom of EM leaf 7, as well as heavily penciled out on HM leaf 9, may indicate it
was canceled separately from the others*]

Tho' yet [*then* but *then, in EM, two undeciphered erased words (the second of which may be* though) *penciled in by HM as possible substitutes for* Tho' but] a plunderer and no more! [*then pencil-underline* more *before pencil-canceling* Tho' . . . more *in HM and scratching the text-line out in EM*] [*line-space*]
Seaward [*then indent* Seaward], a flash! Some [*then* Yon *then* Some] far ship's gun:
Hark, follows the flash the long dxxx [?dire ?dull] boom. [*then* And, hark, now comes {*then* rolls} the {*then* its *then* the} dreary boom! {*EM mistranscribed* boom *in some undeciphered way, then transcribed the word accurately*}]
Wouldst call some drowned one up from doom—
Some self-precipitated one?

[*then cancel all till-then-uncanceled text-lines in* Tho' . . . one] HM1 262.80–90 Could . . . fate] [*HM leaf 10(B)*] 262.80–91 Could . . . mate] [*EM leaf 8*] 262.80 remake] HM3(?C); [*undeciphered scratched-out word*] HM1; re-make HM2 262.80 or set free] T; could I be HM 262.81 This . . . then] T; [*one or two undeciphered scratched-out words*] intellect, and HM1; [?Unsexed ?Unsexual ?Unsound ?*perhaps not capitalized, and if not, to be preceded by the first word in the earlier reading, if there were two words, and if the first was something like* This] intellect, and HM2; Pure sexless intellect, and HM3 262.83 Piercing] T; Alive into HM 262.83 Pan's paramount] T; Pan's wide HM1,HM3; [*one under another, at upper right corner of HM leaf 10, and with a brace to their right, are three penciled and erased words HM may have considered substituting some form of here or/and in immediately following lines:* sphere / hemisphere / segment] HM2 262.86 us] HM,EM\HM; [*not present; mistranscription*] EM 262.91–94 Few . . . gate] [*HM leaf 11.clip(C)*] 262.92–104 What . . . shore] [*EM leaf 9*] 262.95–101 Ye . . . more] [*HM leaf 11(D)*] 262.95 Ye] HM2; You HM1 262.95 your] HM2; the HM1 262.100 But] HM1,HM3[*HM's reinscription of* But *in EM's transcript is a response to her penciled query; evidently, he had left the penciled variant* And *unerased*]; And HM2 262.101 Light] T; Day HM 262.102–6 But . . . forget] [*HM leaf 12(D)*] 262.102 chilled] EM\HM; touched HM 262.103 yon] EM\HM3; the poor HM1,HM3,EM\HM1; the HM2,HM4,EM,EM\HM2 262.105–263.111 One . . . spite] [*EM leaf 10*] 262.107–17 Or . . . seer] [*HM leaf 13(C)*] 262.107 lived down] HM1,HM3; down lived HM2

263.111 He long] HM1,HM3,EM,T; Long he HM2,EM\HM(D) 263.112–25 And . . . me] [*EM leaf 11*] 263.113–17 One . . . seer] [*at stage D, HM inscribes lines 113–17 on his stage C leaf 13. At some point before stage D, he seems to have removed a stage B or earlier clip from the bottom third of his leaf 13, perhaps just as he finished his stage C revisions, since, following line 112, he inscribed in evidently stage C ink, an ending device (scratched out before stage D). This ending device would usually have meant he had determined to end the poem at line 112. But his penciled (later erased) ending device, in EM's transcript, below his direction to leave a double space following line 105, suggests that the device following line 112 in his own transcript might be taken as indicating only*

an intention to double space there, an intention he changed his mind about at stage D]
263.113 late] HM2; once HM1 263.115 Albani's] EM\HM; a villa's HM 263.117
No anchorite seer,] EM\HM; Aurelian clear^ HM 263.118–31 Not . . . on] [*HM
leaf 14(D)*] 263.118 Not] EM\HM; Nor HM 263.118 monk] HM2; meek HM1
263.120 Yet far] HM,EM2; Yet for EM1[*mistranscription*] 263.121 form . . . hea-
then] HM3; supernatural Form of HM1; form august of tranquil HM2 263.122
Swayed . . . long] HM6; Tranced, yet rebuked, long time HM1; Rebuking weak-
ness, long time HM2; [*four to six undeciphered erased words, constituting at least one
variant reading, perhaps two*] HM3,HM?4; Under its influence long HM5[*and see
entry, below, for line 127*] 263.124 She . . . she] T; The emergent thought expression
HM1; Emergent thought expression HM2; The latent thought some utterance
HM3; [*four or more undeciphered erased words, constituting at least one variant reading*]
utterance HM4; [*two or three undeciphered erased words*] and utterance EM1 [*in her
initial inscribing, EM penciled in the undeciphered words, but inked in the others*]; She
rallied and this utterance EM\HM,EM2 263.126–43 To-day . . . bring] [*EM
leaf 12 Today . . . bring*] 263.127 Touched . . . moving] HM2; Moved by her
touching HM1[*six or seven undeciphered erased words, penciled in before line 127 was
ink-inscribed over them, may constitute another variant reading for line 122*] 263.130
kneel] HM?3,EM\HM; submit HM1; [*undeciphered erased word*] HM2[*EM post-
poned transcribing most of lines 130 and 131 till HM was sure of how he wanted to revise
them*] 263.132–44 But . . . long] [*HM leaf 15(D)*] 263.133 thou mightier] HM,EM2;
though EM1[*mistranscription; EM inscribed though before stopping to query HM's
intention*] 263.135 thee, far] HM1,HM3; [*?inadvertent or fleeting cancellation, since
no variants are inscribed*] HM2 263.136 makes . . . feud] HM4; late has shamed
me down HM1; [*?makes the sexual shame*] HM?2; [*and another two to four unde-
ciphered erased words may indicate a further variant reading for this line or the following
one, though they may be the penciled versions of the words later inked in*] HM?3 263.137
clogs the aspirant] HM3; checked the heavenward HM1; [*?clogged*] [*?the heav-
enward*] HM2[*and one or two more undeciphered erased words may indicate a further
variant reading for this line or the preceding one*] 263.138 strong] EM\HM; one HM
263.139 Thou . . . and] HM1,HM4; In whom such power and HM2; In whom
such power such HM3 263.140 Transcender] HM,EM\HM2; Minerva EM\
HM1 263.144–264.151 Nor . . . care] [*EM leaf 13*] 263.145–264.151 Inspire . . .
care] [*HM leaf 16(D)*] 263.145 Inspire] HM1,EM\HM; [*undeciphered erased word*]
HM2; Redeem HM3; Inspirit HM4,EM

264.151 pray] HM2; kneel HM1 264.151 have care] HM; [*EM could not make
out at least* have *and mistranscribed that word as* hew *before asking HM his intention,
then penciling in* have care *and also inking in both words, unless she had earlier also mis-
transcribed* care *as* are *and thus later had to add a* c *to transform the word*] EM

TEXTUAL NOTES: ACCIDENTALS. 259[*placement of "After the Pleasure Party"*] EM\
HM[*on leaf 1 of the table of contents in EM transcript*],T; [*poem placed after "The Weaver"*]
HM,EM,EM[*on leaf 1 of the table of contents*] 259.0 After . . . Party] [*see substantives*]
259.0[*title of introductory poem*] [*in small capitals*] T; <u>Lines Traced / Under an image</u>

of/Amor threatening HM; Lines traced/Under an image of/Amor threatening EM 259.0[*introductory poem*] *virgin^*] HM,EM1,EM3; ~, EM2 259.0[*introductory poem*] *whosoever^*] HM1,HM3,EM1,EM3; ~, HM2,EM2 *259.0[*introductory poem*] *pride^*] HM1,EM; ~, HM2 259.0[*introductory poem*] *me,*] EM2; ~^ HM,EM1 259.0[*introductory poem*] *slighted.*] HM1,EM; ~! HM2 259.0[*introductory poem*] *tempt:*] EM; ~. HM 259.0[*introductory poem*] *wings,*] EM; ~; HM *259.0[*introductory poem*] *but^ wroth^*] EM; ~, ~, HM *259.1 Behind] [*no part number precedes; replace part number with double line-space*] EM\HM[*see substantives for 259.0, above*]; [*no part number*] HM1; 1 [*part number*] HM2 259.1 Behind] [*indent*] HM; [*indention obscured by display capital*] T 259.3,4 White/Terrace] [*no indent*] EM; [*indent*] HM *259.3 halls—] HM; ~, T 259.4 and down,] EM; ~~^ HM 259.5 star-lit] HM; starlit T 259.5 Mediterranean] HM\EM; Meditteranean HM 259.8 Nor] [*no indent*] EM; [*indent*] HM 259.8 perturbed^] HM,EM2; ~, EM1 259.9 peace] EM\HM; Peace HM 259.11 discontent?] HM2; ~. HM1

*260.12 "Tired] HM2; ^~ HM1,EM 260.12 deep,] HM2; ~. HM1 *260.13 urge^] HM; ~, T 260.14 Hitherward] [*indent*] HM,EM\HM; [*no indent*] EM,T 260.17 impulsion] HM,EM2; impuxsion EM1[*undeciphered mistranscription*] 260.17 so?] EM; ~. HM1; ~! HM2 260.17,18 [*HM added x x x between these text-lines, perhaps to indicate a double line-space between stanzas, but then canceled the indication*] 260.18 An] [*indent*] HM2,EM2; [*no indent*] HM1,EM1 260.18 "An] HM2; ^~ HM1,EM,T 260.18 is,] HM,T; ~^ EM 260.18 tell:] EM; ~, HM1; ~; HM2 260.19 to forget!^] HM1,EM; ~~!— HM2[*see substantives*] 260.20 ambuscade,] EM; ~^ HM 260.21 life^] HM,EM\HM2; ~, EM1\HM1 260.22 strife.] HM1,EM; ~! HM2 260.23 'Tis] HM,T; ^~ EM 260.23 smart] HM,EM2; [?o]mart EM1[*mistranscription*] 260.24 leap:] EM; ~; HM 260.27 Now] [*indent*] HM2; [*no indent*] HM1 260.27 "Now] HM2; ^~ HM1,EM 260.27 feel, what all may ween,] EM; ~ (~ ~ ~ ~) HM 260.28 That^] HM,EM1,EM3; ~, EM2 260.31 Geysers^ that] [*see substantives*] 260.31 aspire—] EM\HM3; ~^ HM; ~, EM\HM?1; ~! EM\HM?2 260.32 obstruction^] EM; ~, HM[*see also substantives*] 260.33,34,36,37,40,42,43 [*no indent*] EM; [*indent*] HM 260.33 disdain,] HM?3,EM; ~; HM1; ~— HM2 *260.34–35 reign;/To dote;] HM,T; ~:/~~, EM 260.35 shame—] HM,EM2; ~, EM1 260.37 prairie-fires] HM; ~^~ T[*the hyphen is unclear in EM*] 260.37 control,] EM; ~^ HM 260.39 "And] HM2; ^~ HM1,EM *260.41 O^] EM; ~, HM 260.41 air,] HM,T; ~^ EM *260.42 O^] EM; ~, HM *260.43 chased^] EM; chased, HM\EM; chaced, HM

261.45 Chair.] EM; ~! HM 261.46–49 In . . . self-sustained] [*see substantives*] 261.46,47,49,50,55,57 [*no indent*] EM; [*indent*] HM 261.46 me,] EM; ~; HM 261.47 straw.] EM; ~^ HM 261.48,54,66,73 And/The/When/Me] [*indent*] HM2; [*no indent*] HM1 261.48 "And] HM; ^~ EM *261.48 ah yet,] HM; ~~^ EM 261.48 reigned,] EM; ~^ HM 261.49 Through] EM; Thro' HM 261.50 undeceived—] HM1,EM; ~^ HM2 261.51 I,] HM; ~^ EM 261.52 decline—] EM; ~? HM 261.52 Than] [*no indent*] HM,EM1,EM3; [*indent*] EM2 *261.53 spleen,] T; ~^ HM 261.54 "The] HM2; ^~ HM1,EM 261.54 peasant-girl] HM; ~^~ T[*the hyphen is faint in EM*] 261.54 demure] [*see substantives*] 261.55 way,] EM; ~^ HM 261.57 May=

Day—] EM; ~; HM *261.58 her—] T; ~, HM 261.59 fell!^] EM; ~!— HM1;
~^— HM2 261.60 briers] HM; briars EM 261.60 strung;] EM; ~, HM 261.61
meek.] HM2; ~— HM1 261.62 young, so] [*see substantives*] 261.62 so young!^]
EM; ~~:— HM1; ~~!— HM2 261.63 girls,] HM2; ~^ HM1 261.63 weak.] EM;
~! HM 261.64 To] [*HM's query, at the top of HM leaf 8 9 left out? refers to an inad-*
vertent misfoliation of leaves; because of this misfoliation, HM leaves 9–17 were at one time
each numbered one higher than finally] 261.64 remain,] EM; ~; HM1; ~: HM2 261.65
pain.] HM1,HM3; ~! HM2[*see substantives*] 261.66 "When] HM2; ^~ HM1,EM
261.74 writ,] EM; ~^ HM 261.75 cheeks—] EM; ~? HM

   262.77 glad,] EM; ~^ HM,T 262.77 lore,] EM; ~^ HM 262.79 repose.] HM2;
~[?^] HM1[*the period was both inked and, later, penciled in, presumably when the fol-*
lowing text-line was canceled] 262.79 repose.] [*see substantives*] 262.80,95,105 Could/
Ye/One] [*indent*] HM2; [*no indent*] HM1 262.80 remake] [*see substantives*] *262.80
me!] HM1,HM3,T; ~[?.] HM2; ~— HM4; ~; EM 262.84 Nature,] HM1,EM; ~!
HM2 *262.84–85 surge^ . . . thee^] EM; ~, . . . ~, HM 262.85 urge,] EM2; ~—
HM,EM1 262.86 halves—] EM; ~, HM *262.89 Selfhood] HM; Self-hood EM
262.89 incomplete.] HM1,EM; ~; HM2 262.91 mate] HM1,HM3; [*underlined*]
HM2[*?a querying underline*] 262.92 Anarch] HM2; anarch HM1 262.94 through]
EM; thro' HM 262.92 life's] HM,T; lifes EM 262.94 gate] HM1,HM3; [*underlined*]
HM2[*?a querying underline*] 262.96 vigil,] EM; ~— HM 262.99 Usurped] EM;
Userped HM 262.100 But,] HM; ~^ EM 262.100 wane:] EM; ~! HM 262.101
²breaks!] T; ~. HM 262.101 more,] EM; ~^ HM 262.102,103 But/Shivers] [*no*
indent] EM; [*indent*] HM *262.105 One] [*double line-space precedes; no part number*]
HM1,EM\HM; [*double line-space, plus part number 2*] HM2[*HM's transcript visu-*
ally indicates the double line-space he intends, though he verbally also directs wide space
and pencils in a provisional 2 preceding the poem's second section; in EM's transcript he
pencils in Leave space {*then* Leave double space} *here. and one of his ending devices*
————"——— *which direction EM translates into* Double space between this and
the foregoing.] 262.106 forget;] EM; ~, HM 262.110 hers] HM; her's T

   *263.111 spite,] T; ~^ HM 263.112 boy-like,] EM; ~^ HM 263.112 pain.^]
HM,EM\HM2; ~." EM\HM1 263.113 One] [*indent*] HM2; [*no indent*] HM1
263.117 Colossal] HM,EM2; Collosal EM1[*mistranscription*] 263.117 carved.^] EM;
~.— HM 263.117 No . . . seer,] [*see substantives*] *263.118 a'] HM; a EM *263.119
tone;] T; ~. HM; ~, EM 263.121 form] EM2; Form HM,EM1 263.122 Swayed
. . . long] [*see substantives*] 263.122 influence,] EM; ~^ HM *263.123 Till^ surged
emotion^] EM; ~, ~ ~, HM 263.124 won:^] EM; ~:— HM 263.125 "Languid]
HM2; ^~ HM1,EM 263.126 To-day] HM,T; Today EM 263.126 convent-shrine,]
EM; ~-~^ HM; ~^~, T 263.127,129,130,131,135,137 [*no indent*] EM; [*indent*] HM
263.128 mine,] HM2; ~^ HM1 *263.129 A . . . grieve] HM1,EM; [*underlined*]
HM2 263.129 grieve.] EM; ~: HM1; ~! HM2 263.130 believe] EM; beleive HM
263.130 believe,] EM; ~— HM 263.131 Believe] EM; Beleive HM 263.131 sub-
mit,] EM; ~— HM 263.131 on.] HM2; ~! HM1 *263.132 But] [*no line-space, no*
indent] HM1,EM2; [*penciled bracket indicates verse-paragraph line-space and indention*]

HM2,EM1[*an erased bracket at the left of line 131 in EM probably represents a slip of the pencil as HM considered where he might break up his long verse-paragraph*] 263.132 arm'd] HM; armed EM *263.132 Virgin!] T; ~, HM; ~^ EM 263.132 benign,] HM2; ~^ HM1 263.133 one.] EM; ~: HM *263.134 Helmeted] [*no line-space, no indent*] HM1,EM; [*line-space, indent*] HM2 263.134 woman—] HM1,EM; ~, HM2 263.135 thee,] HM?2,EM; ~^ HM?1 263.136 feud] EM2,HM\EM; feued HM→1; fued HM2,EM1 263.137 life—] EM; ~; HM 263.138 O^] EM; ~, HM 263.139 power^] HM1,HM3[*implicit*],EM; ~, HM2 263.139 peace^] HM1,HM3; ~, HM2 263.139 unite,] HM?1,EM; ~; HM2 263.140 Transcender!] HM1,EM2; ~, HM2; ~: EM1 263.140 up] HM1,EM; [*underlined in blue pencil, perhaps as part of HM's revising process in lines 141 and 142*] HM2 *263.141 arm me!"] NN; ~~!^ HM,T; ~~.^ EM1,EM3; ~~." EM2 *263.142 Fond appeal] [*indented so as to end flush with right-hand margin, and vertically line-spaced to make new verse-paragraph*] T; [*indented so as to follow the end of the preceding line, but not line-spaced to make new verse-paragraph*] HM1,HM4,EM; [*indented—or, perhaps, not intended to be indented at all—and line-spaced to make new verse-paragraph*] HM2; [*incorporated into line 141 so as to become its visual and prosodic ending*] HM3

264.146 incensed . . . wrong] [*at first, EM could not make out these words and left a blank space for them; HM then penciled them into EM's transcript, below line 149, and EM copied them into the blank space, though without the comma HM had inserted after incensed*] 264.146 wrong.] HM,T; ~, EM 264.147 spare;] EM; ~: HM 264.151 O^] EM; ~, HM 264.151 pray!^] HM1,HM3; ~!— HM2 264.151 too,] EM; ~^ HM *264.151 care.] HM,EM?1,T; ~! EM2

THE NIGHT-MARCH (p. 265)

DISCUSSIONS. 265.0 *The Night-March*] The hyphen, present in HM, EM, and T, was omitted in Melville's wife's transcript of the table of contents, as well as in the table of contents in the printed book (probably set from that transcript).

265.8 Chief] NN retains the capital letter in the copy-text (and EM), reduced to lowercase in T (see p. 610 above).

265.9 lost,] The comma before the parenthesis may be inadvertent here (a residue of the revision process), but the usage is common in Melville's manuscripts, as well as in the printing practice of his day.

265.10–11 wends . . . host] NN follows Melville's repointing of the whole poem in his wife's transcript (see the textual notes below) and presumes that he deliberately omitted the commas in lines 10–11.

EMENDATIONS. 265.1 furled,] EM; ~^ HM 265.4 bright] EM\HM; light HM 265.4 bright.] EM; ~! HM 265.5 stream,] EM; ~: HM 265.6 true;] EM; ~, HM *265.9 lost,] EM; ~^ HM *265.10–11 wends^ / And^ . . . host^] EM; ~,/~, . . . ~, HM 265.12 sends.] EM; ~! HM

TEXTUAL NOTES: INSCRIPTION STAGES. At least two stages of inscription-revision: A (nonextant pre-fair-copy stage); B (blue-green ink on thicker yellow paper).

TEXTUAL NOTES: SUBSTANTIVES. 265.0–12 The . . . sends] [*HM leaf 1(B); EM leaf 1*] 265.3 And] HM1,HM3; The HM2 265.4 bright] EM\HM; light HM[*though HM may have intended* bright *in his transcript, he wrote* light] 265.5 stream] HM2; gleam HM1 265.7 stream] HM1,HM4; gleam HM2; [*undeciphered erased word* {?chase}] HM?3 265.7 gleam] HM2; stream HM1 265.10 legends tell] HM4; rumor tells HM1; [*undeciphered erased word*] tells HM2; legend tells HM3 265.11 shining] HM1,HM3; [*undeciphered erased word*] HM2

TEXTUAL NOTES: ACCIDENTALS. 265.1 furled,] EM; ~^ HM 265.4 bright.] EM; ~! HM 265.5 stream,] EM; ~: HM 265.6 true;] EM; ~, HM *265.8 Chief] HM; chief T 265.8 view!] HM,EM2; ~: EM1 *265.9 lost,] EM; ~^ HM *265.10–11 wends^ / And^ . . . host^] EM; ~,/~, . . . ~, HM 265.12 sends.] EM,HM?1; ~! HM2

THE RAVAGED VILLA (p. 266)

In the journal of his travels through Italy in 1857, Melville mentions a number of ruined villas (see, for example, *Journals,* pp. 102, 113; also pp. 457, 487) and possibly saw others. He later owned an engraving of the one misattributed to Maecenas (see Wallace 1986). In the Middle Ages, marble statues and building blocks were routinely dumped into lime kilns on their way to becoming plaster. In Melville's time, part of the Villa of Maecenas had been converted into an iron manufactory by Lucien Bonaparte. Whether or not the limestone used there in iron production was converted from ancient materials, Melville may have made the connection, so that the "lime" of line 8 could be destined not to plaster "Mammon's tower" but to furnish it with structural or decorative iron.

DISCUSSION. 266.4 Fountain . . . Sun] NN retains the capitals in the copy-text (and EM), reduced to lowercase in T (see p. 610 above).

EMENDATIONS. 266.0 *The Ravaged Villa*] EM; [*no title*] HM 266.2 undone,] EM; ~; HM 266.6 flower:] EM; ~, HM

TEXTUAL NOTES: INSCRIPTION STAGES. At least two stages of inscription-revision: A (nonextant pre-fair-copy stage); B (blue-green ink on thicker yellow paper). A later-stage (evidently nonextant) mount, however, may once have had the undersized Melville leaf attached to it as a clip, and that possible mount may also have had inscribed on it any title(s) he had devised.

Textual Notes: Substantives. 266.0–8 The . . . tower] [*EM leaf 1*] 266.0 The *Ravaged Villa*] EM; [*no title on extant HM leaf*] HM 266.1–8 In . . . tower] [*HM leaf 1(B)*] 266.1 sylvan] HM1,HM3; [*undeciphered erased word*] HM2 266.3 wither by] HM2(C); overhang HM1 266.4 Choked] HM2(C); [*undeciphered scratched-out word*] HM1 266.7 Apollo's] HM,EM\HM2; Minerva's EM\HM1 266.8 Mammon's] HM2(C+); mill and HM1

Textual Notes: Accidentals. 266.2,4,6,8 Their/Choked/The/Makes] [*indent*] HM2[*HM inscribes* In *at left of lines 2, 4, 6, 8*]; [*no indent*] HM1 266.2 undone,] EM; ~; HM 266.3 brim,] HM,T; ~^ EM *266.4 Fountain . . . Sun] HM; fountain . . . sun T 266.6 flower:] EM; ~, HM

THE MARGRAVE'S BIRTH NIGHT (pp. 267–68)

Discussions. 267.0 Birth Night] NN retains the two separate words of the copytext; "Birthnight" appears in EM and T (and also in Melville's wife's transcript of the table of contents, and in the table of contents of T, probably set from that transcript). Although these words are hyphenated in line 15 of the poem (in HM, EM, and T), NN lets the inconsistency stand as a reflection of Melville's varying practice (see p. 608 above).

267.4 bell,] NN adopts the comma from EM; no punctuation appears in HM. The omission of the comma in T, however, may possibly represent Melville's restoration of the reading in HM.

267.8 cold,] NN adopts the comma from EM; no punctuation appears in HM. The semicolon in T, however, may possibly represent Melville's revision in proof.

268.35 cover—] NN retains the dash in the copy-text (though there is no punctuation in EM), since its reappearance in T probably represents Melville's restoration rather than an insertion by a Caxton Press staff member.

268.36 same.] NN adopts the period from T (the copy-text has a semicolon), since it probably represents Melville's restoration of the first reading in his manuscript (see the textual notes, below).

Emendations. 267.1 valley,] EM; ~— HM *267.4 bell,] EM; ~^ HM 267.7 sledging] EM; sledgeing HM *267.8 cold,] EM; ~^ HM 267.10 ledge,] EM; ~^ HM 267.13 castle,] EM; ~^ HM 267.15 birth-night, in midwinter,] EM; ~^ ~ ~^ HM 267.16 ²year.] EM; ~^ HM 267.17 holly!] EM; ~^ HM 267.18 wall;] EM; ~^ HM 267.19 plenty,] EM; ~— HM 267.20 But—] EM; ~^ HM 268.26–27 when, . . . cover,] EM; ~^ . . . ~^ HM 268.32 there;] EM; ~. HM 268.33 marvels,] EM; ~^ HM 268.34 name,] EM; ~^ HM *268.36 same.] T; ~; HM 268.38 hall;] EM; ~^ HM 268.41 Ah] [*double line-space precedes*] EM\HM; [*line-space*] HM 268.41 travail,] EM; ~^ HM 268.43 water,] EM; ~^ HM

TEXTUAL NOTES: INSCRIPTION STAGES. At least three stages of inscription-revision: A (nonextant pre-fair-copy stage); B (blue ink on thicker paper); C (tan-gray ink on thinner paper).

TEXTUAL NOTES: SUBSTANTIVES. 267.0–8 The . . . cold] [*HM leaf 1(C); EM leaf 1*] 267.0–8 *The . . . cold*] HM2(C); [*see following description of superseded text on stage B leaf*] [*Superseded HM leaf 1(B)* {"*The Return of the Sire de Nesle*" *HM leaf 1 verso*} In . . . cold {*inscribed in blue ink; revised in pencil*}]

> In ———.
> [*add below the blank underlined space (either as a possible filling of that space or as potential subtitle)* a fantasy *and also add* A Fantasy *above* In ———. *but without canceling any of these variants before final cancellation of the whole leaf*]
> ———"———— [*beginning device*]
> Up from many a [*then* Sounds from many a *then* ?Rings from many a *then* ?Rings up from the *perhaps also* Rings up many a *then* ?Rings up from each ?*then* ?Sounds up from the *then* Sounds up from each *then* ?Sounds {?up} {?from} many a] sheeted valley,
> And out of [?*then* ?From out of *then* Deep in *then* From white] woods as well,
> And down [*then* Down too {too *also indicated for restoration without having been explicitly canceled*}] from many a fleecy [?*then* from the {?whitened} ?*then* ?from each {?whitened} ?*then* ?from each {*undeciphered word*} ?*then* ?from here and there each ?*then* ?from each {*undeciphered word*} ?*then* from each fleecy] upland,
> Hark, many a [?*then* Many a *then* Hark! a *then* Hark{?,} the *then* Sounds the *then* Many {a} {the a *not explicitly restored*}] jingling bell. [*then* bell,]
> [*line-space*]
> Jovial on the saddish horses
> Hitched to sledges [*then* runners] old
> Of the hooded peasants herding [?*then* gliding *then* crouching *then* sledging]
> Under sheep-skins in the cold.

[*then cancel whole leaf with pencil and orange and green pencil*] HM1(B) 267.0 *The Margrave's Birth Night*] HM3; [*no title initially inscribed*] HM1; [*two or three undeciphered erased words*] HM2[*emphasizing that HM was undecided about the final title are his only penciling it in his transcript, and EM's also only penciling it into hers before finally inking it in*] 267.4 Jingles] HM1,HM3; Echoes HM2 267.9–20 Till . . . withal] [*HM leaf 2(C); EM leaf 2*] 267.11 There] HM1,HM3,HM5; Where HM2,HM4 267.11 brush] HM,EM[*into the blank space she initially left in her transcript, because she could not be sure which word HM intended, EM seems to have penciled* brush *before inking it in*],EM\HM2; [?shake ?shovel] EM\HM1 267.11 snow off] HM2; snow HM?1

268.21–32 May . . . there] [*HM leaf 3(C); EM leaf 3*] 268.21 May his people]
HM4; May the vassals HM1; May his vassals HM?2; How many vassals [*or* people]
HM3 268.24 the] HM1,HM3; an HM2 268.31 In his] HM1,HM3; Kind in HM2
268.33–44 No . . . white] [*HM leaf 4(C); EM leaf 4*] 268.34 None] HM,EM,EM\
HM2; Few EM\HM1 268.35 Scarce they mark void] HM4,EM,EM\HM2;
Prompted by void HM1; Prompted by HM?2[*HM may inadvertently have canceled,
then immediately restored* void]; Tho' they see void HM3; Scarce some mark void
EM\HM1 268.37 Mindless] HM2; Stolid HM1 268.43 the] HM2; flat HM1

Textual Notes: Accidentals. *267.0 *Birth Night*] HM; Birthnight EM 267.1
valley,] EM; ~^ HM1; ~— HM2 267.2 well,] HM2; ~^ HM1 *267.4 bell,] EM;
~^ HM,T 267.7 sledging] EM; sledgeing HM *267.8 cold,] EM; ~^ HM; ~; T
267.10 ledge,] EM; ~^ HM 267.12 sledge^] HM2; ~, HM1 267.13 castle,] EM;
~^ HM 267.15 birth-night, in midwinter,] EM; ~^ ~ ~^ HM 267.15 midwinter]
HM; mid-winter T[*?a misreading partly enabled by what might look like a tiny hyphen
in EM*] 267.16 after year.] EM; ~~^ HM 267.17 holly!] EM; ~^ HM 267.18 wall;]
EM; ~^ HM 267.19 plenty,] EM; ~^ HM1; ~— HM2 267.20 But—] EM; ~^
HM 267.20 withal] EM,HM2; withall HM1[*EM pencil-queried HM's second l and
at one point either HM or EM altered EM's* withal *to* withall *then restored* withal]
267.20 withal!] HM2; ~^ HM1
    268.21 contented^] HM,EM2; ~, EM1 268.24 absent] HM2; asp HM→1
[*uncompleted misinscription*] 268.26–27 when, . . . cover,] EM; ~^ . . . ~^ HM 268.29
offer;] HM2; ~^ HM1 268.30 fair,] HM2; ~^ HM1 268.31 gracious,] HM2; ~^
HM1 268.32 there;] EM; ~. HM 268.33 marvels,] EM; ~^ HM 268.34 good lord]
HM,EM,EM\HM2; Good Lord EM\HM1 268.34 name,] EM; ~^ HM *268.35
void^ . . . cover—] HM2,T; ~^ . . . ~^ HM1,EM2; ~, . . . ~, EM1 *268.36 same.]
HM1,T; ~; HM2,EM 268.38 hall;] EM; ~^ HM 268.41 Ah] [*double line-space pre-
cedes*] EM\HM; [*line-space*] HM 268.41 travail,] EM; ~^ HM 268.43 water,] EM;
~^ HM 268.44 white.] HM2; ~^ HM1

MAGIAN WINE (p. 269)

Discussions. 269.1 Miriam] Amulets could have been valuable either to the
Miriam also known as "Mary the Jew" or to the Miriam of the Bible; they could
be valuable as well to "Merlin" or for "memory," variants Melville considered
for "Miriam."
    269.2 gleam;] NN retains the copy-text semicolon (also the penultimate read-
ing Melville considered in punctuating his wife's transcript), since its appearance
in T in place of the comma in EM probably represents Melville's restoration.
    269.3 Solomon's] Among the many Solomon passages that Melville marked
in one of his Bibles (Philadelphia: Butler, 1846; Sealts, no. 62, Bercaw, no. 63), a
possibly relevant one is 1 Kings 4:27–34.

269.8 rise:] NN retains the copy-text colon (probably also the penultimate one Melville considered in punctuating his wife's transcript), since its appearance in T in place of the semicolon in EM probably represents Melville's restoration.

EMENDATIONS. 269.1 Miriam] T; Mirriam HM 269.3 appear,] EM; ~— HM 269.4 supreme.] EM; ~: HM 269.6 semblances] EM; semblences HM 269.7 through] EM; thro' HM

TEXTUAL NOTES: INSCRIPTION STAGES. At least two stages of inscription-revision: A (nonextant pre-fair-copy stage); B (tan-gray ink on thinner paper).

TEXTUAL NOTES: SUBSTANTIVES. 269.0–12 *Magian . . . hymn*] [*HM leaf 1(B); EM leaf 1*] 269.0 *Magian*] EM\HM2,EM\HM4,EM\HM6,HM2,EM2; Magic HM1,EM1,EM\HM3,EM\HM5; [*?Grxxx*] EM\HM1[*and there may be one or two other undeciphered erased variants in EM's transcript, where HM tried his differing titles both before and after inscribing* Magic *in both his own and EM's transcript*] *269.1 Miriam] HM2[*see also accidentals*],EM,EM\HM2; Merlin HM1; memory EM\HM1 269.2 gleam] HM2; glow HM1 269.3 Syrian] HM2,EM\HM2; jewelled HM1,EM; [*?one or more undeciphered erased words constitute at least one variant reading*] EM\HM?1 269.4 Opal] HM2,EM\HM1,EM\HM3; Signet HM1; [*undeciphered erased word*] EM\HM2 269.4 supreme] HM2; they show HM1 269.5 this] HM2,EM\HM; the HM1 269.5 Magian] HM2,EM\HM; Magic HM1 269.6 Thrill] HM1,HM3; Flash HM→2[*a reading considered tentatively by parenthesizing the word as well as putting a question mark after it*] 269.7 And] HM1,HM3,T; But EM\HM,HM2[But *is followed by a question mark and circled, but* And *is left uncanceled*] 269.7 wave] HM2; tide HM1 269.11 Delirious] HM,EM,EM\HM4; Comminglingly EM\HM1; In fusion EM\HM2; Bewildering EM\HM3[*not canceled*] 269.12 the] HM,EM,EM\HM2; [*what appear to be two undeciphered erased words—one above the text-line, one below—may tentatively have been intended as variants for the* the *in this or the preceding line*] EM\HM?1

TEXTUAL NOTES: ACCIDENTALS. 269.1 Miriam] T; Mirriam HM,EM\HM *269.2 gleam;] HM,EM\HM1,T; ~, EM\HM2 269.3 appear,] EM; ~— HM 269.4 supreme.] EM; ~: HM 269.6 semblances] EM; semblences HM 269.7 through] EM; thro' HM *269.8 rise:] HM,EM\HM?2,T; ~; EM\HM3; ~[?!] EM\HM1 269.9 Sybilline] HM; Sibylline EM 269.12 Ambiguous] HM,EM2; Ambxxous EM1[*undeciphered mistranscription*]

THE GARDEN OF METRODORUS (p. 270)

Melville could have found information about two figures named Metrodorus in Pierre Bayle's *An Historical and Critical Dictionary* (London: Harper, 1710; Sealts, no. 51, Bercaw, no. 50). One is Metrodorus of Chios (fourth century B.C.), notorious radical skeptic; the other is Metrodorus of Lampascus (330–277 B.C.), intimate friend of Epicurus. Melville's wife's transcript of this poem is reproduced on p. 571 above.

EMENDATIONS. 270.5 foot-path to the gate] EM\HM; foot-way thro' the grass HM 270.6 forth,] EM; ~^ HM 270.7 strange,] EM; ~^ HM

TEXTUAL NOTES: INSCRIPTION STAGES. At least two stages of inscription-revision: A (nonextant pre-fair-copy stage); B (blue ink on thicker light-yellow paper).

TEXTUAL NOTES: SUBSTANTIVES. 270.0–10 The . . . dell] [HM leaf 1(B); EM leaf 1] 270.0 The Garden] HM,EM2; Garden EM1 270.3 keeps] HM2; holds HM1 270.4 he] HM,EM2; the EM1[mistranscription] 270.5 foot-path to the gate] EM\ HM2[not copied back into HM's transcript]; foot-way thro' the grass HM; foot-way through the grass EM; foot-path to a door EM\HM1 270.6 here] HM2; and HM1 270.7 dumb] HM5; deep HM1,HM4; rapt HM2; [undeciphered erased word {?stark ?staid}] HM3

TEXTUAL NOTES: ACCIDENTALS. 270.1 The] [indent] HM; [indention obscured by display capital] T 270.5 to the gate] [see substantives] 270.6 Here] [indent] HM; [no indent] T 270.6 forth,] EM; ~^ HM 270.7 strange,] EM; ~^ HM 270.9 this] HM,EM2; thisx EM1[undeciphered mistranscription]

THE NEW ZEALOT TO THE SUN (pp. 271–72)

DISCUSSIONS. 271.0 New Zealot] Melville first named the speaker in his title "A Boy" and then "The Scientist," before he settled on "The New Zealot."

271.8 overruling] NN retains the copy-text form of this word. The hyphen in T is probably the compositor's insertion, perhaps occasioned by the slight space in EM between "over" and "ruling." De Vinne's Correct Composition, intended for printers, sanctions the hyphen with the prefix "over" when two syllables follow (p. 71).

272.23 screeds—] NN retains the copy-text dash, though the extensive revision of lines 15–23 in EM could suggest that Melville intended its omission there.

EMENDATIONS. 271.0 Zealot] EM; Zeolot HM 271.4 man, . . . abased,] EM; ~^ . . . ~^ HM 271.9 plain,] EM; ~^ HM 271.10 javelins] EM; javelins's HM 271.11 many a wild incursive] EM; more than one overwhelming HM 271.13 Mid terrors] EM\HM; In terror HM 271.15 The brood] EM\HM; Bye-blows HM 271.15 Brahma] NN; Bramha HM 271.17 Westward they rolled their] EM\HM; They rolled their bastard HM 271.18 Of . . . wove] EM; With Khans a bargain drove HM 271.20 orient] EM; burning HM 271.21 dream—] EM; ~. HM 272.22

Transmitted,] EM; ~^ HM 272.22 spread in] HM\EM; into [?fierce] HM 272.22 myths and creeds] HM\EM; [*two or three undeciphered erased words*] HM 272.22 creeds,] EM; ~— HM 272.23 delirious] HM\EM; megrims and HM 272.26 time's first] EM\HM; primal HM 272.27 clan,] EM; ~— HM 272.29 frauds] EM\HM; myths HM 272.29 fears,] EM; ~^ HM 272.32 beget,] EM; ~^ HM 272.34 quell] EM; qwell HM

TEXTUAL NOTES: INSCRIPTION STAGES. At least two stages of inscription-revision: A (nonextant pre-fair-copy stage); B (tan-gray ink on thinner paper).

TEXTUAL NOTES: SUBSTANTIVES. 271.0–12 *The . . . Cain*] [*HM leaf 1(B); EM leaf 1*] *271.0 The . . . Sun*] HM3[*see also accidentals*]; A Boy to the Sun HM1[*appears on HM leaf 1, but also as the only inscription on a superseded stage B leaf ("At the Hostelry," leaf 31.patch verso)*]; The Scientist to the Sun HM2 271.1 Persian, you rise] HM1,HM3; [*one or more undeciphered erased words may constitute a variant for the whole line or its first word*] HM?2 271.9 fling] HM3; dart HM1; launch HM2 271.11 many a wild incursive] EM,HM\EM[*from evidently nonextant HM inscription*]; more than one overwhelming HM 271.13–272.24 Mid . . . extreme] [*HM leaf 2(B); EM leaf 2*] 271.13 Mid] [*at the top of HM leaf 2 are three or four undeciphered erased words*] 271.13 Mid terrors] EM\HM,HM?2; In terror HM1,EM 271.14 came] HM,T; come EM[*mistranscription, but HM's version wavers between* come *and* came] 271.15 The brood] HM?2,HM?4,EM\HM; The cadets HM1; Bye= blows HM?3,EM[*the problem here in deciding the exact nature and order of variants arises from the facts that* The brood *seems to be the second reading in HM's transcript;* Bye-blows *is uncanceled in HM, as well as seems to be the third reading there; and not only is* Bye-blows *transcribed by EM, it is also canceled and replaced with* The brood] 271.17 Westward they rolled their] EM\HM2[*not copied back into HM*]; They rolled their crushing HM1; They pushed [*or* rolled] their cruel HM\EM1,HM\ EM3[*several revisions in lines 17–20 and 22–23 are from evidently nonextant HM inscription*]; They pushed [*or* rolled] their arrogant HM\EM2; They rolled their bastard HM2,EM1; They rolled their westward EM\HM?1,EM2 271.18 Of . . . wove] EM,HM\EM[*see also entry for 271.20*]; With Khans a bargain drove HM 271.18 night] HM\EM2; might HM\EM1[*mistranscription*] 271.20 orient] HM1,EM; burning HM2

272.22 Transmitted] HM1,HM5; [*one or two undeciphered erased words*] HM2; Transmuted HM3; [?Bedeveled ?Redivided ?Rediverted ?Redirected] HM4 272.22 spread in] HM\EM,EM; down in HM1; [*one or two undeciphered erased words*] HM2; into [?fierce] HM3[*these words originally preceded by* Transmuted *though perhaps also considered as being preceded by the conjectured* ?Bedeveled ?Redivided ?Rediverted ?Redirected *but see also entry for line 24*] 272.22 myths and creeds] HM\EM1,HM\EM5,EM; divers creeds HM1; [*two or three undeciphered erased words*] HM2; myths and mythic creeds HM\EM2,HM\EM4; rites and mythic creeds HM\EM3 272.23 delirious] HM\EM2,EM; megrims and HM;

and mythic HM\EM1 272.24 last] HM4; daft HM1; [*undeciphered erased word*] HM2; fierce HM?3[*this variant might have been considered for either the present passage or the one specified in the first entry for line 22, above*] 272.25–36 What . . . ray] [*HM leaf 3(B); EM leaf 3*] 272.26 time's] EM\HM,EM2; times EM1,HM\EM 272.26 time's first] EM\HM; primal HM 272.29 frauds] EM\HM2; fables HM1; myths HM2; [*undeciphered erased word* {?fraudful ?harmful} *or perhaps* fables *as a clarification for EM, if she had been unable to read the word in HM*] EM\HM1 272.30 these] HM,EM2; those EM1[*mistranscription*] 272.34 shades] HM1,HM5; [?shadows] HM2; [*undeciphered erased word*] HM3; [?ghosts] HM4

TEXTUAL NOTES: ACCIDENTALS. 271.0 *Zealot*] EM; Zeolot HM 271.1 Persian] [*indent*] HM; [*indention obscured by display capital*] 271.3,6,9,12,15,18,21, 272.24,27,30,33,36 [*indent; with a penciled* In *HM indicated lines 3 and 6 for indention, and inferably directed EM to indent the third and sixth lines of all following stanzas*] HM2; [*no indent*] HM1 271.4 man, . . . abased,] EM; ~^ . . . ~^ HM *271.8 overruling] HM; over^ruling EM; over-ruling T 271.9 plain,] EM; ~^ HM 271.10 javelins] HM1,EM; javelins's HM2[*the apostrophe is directly above the second* s] 271.16 scythèd] HM; scythed T 271.19 Chymist] HM; Chemist EM 271.21 energises] HM; energizes EM 271.21 dream—] HM1,EM; ~. HM2

272.22 Transmitted,] EM; ~^ HM[*see second and third entries, above, for line 22, for substantive revisions made in evidently nonextant HM inscription*] 272.22 creeds,] EM,HM1; ~— HM2 *272.23 screeds—] HM2; ~^ HM1,EM 272.27 clan,] EM; ~— HM 272.29 worse] HM2; xx worse HM→1[*undeciphered false start*] 272.29 fears,] EM; ~^ HM 272.32 beget,] EM; ~^ HM 272.33 play—] HM,T; ~:[*or, perhaps, a semicolon*] EM1; ~^ EM2 272.34 quell] EM; qwell HM 272.35 out,] HM; ~^ T[*the comma is faint in EM*]

THE WEAVER (p. 273)

DISCUSSION. 273.2,8 Arva's] Before settling on "Arva's", Melville had first written "Mecca's" in line 2 and "Allah's" in line 8; he next changed both to "Delhi's" and then to "Marva's". Arva is one of Hinduism's seers.

273.2 Shawl] NN retains the capital letter in the copy-text, reduced to lowercase in T (see p. 610 above).

EMENDATIONS. 273.3 loom,] EM; ~— HM 273.6 he^] EM; ~, HM *273.8 Arva's] EM\HM; Marva's HM

TEXTUAL NOTES: INSCRIPTION STAGES. At least two stages of inscription-revision: A (nonextant pre-fair-copy stage); B (tan-gray ink on thinner paper).

TEXTUAL NOTES: SUBSTANTIVES. 273.0–8 The . . . shrine] [*HM leaf 1(B); EM leaf 1*] 273.0 The Weaver] HM2; [*no title*] HM1 *273.2 Arva's] HM6,HM8,EM\HM2;

Mecca's HM1; Delhi's HM2; Marva's HM3,HM6,EM; [?Shushan's] HM4; [*unde-ciphered erased word*] HM?5; [?Tolo's] HM?7; [*undeciphered erased word*] EM\HM1 273.2 shrine] HM2; fane HM1 273.3 and at] HM2; and HM→1 273.7 Recluse he lives and] HM4; From every HM→1[*remainder of line not completed*]; Nor woman. He is HM2; Nor woman. He [?lives] HM3 *273.8 Arva's] HM3,EM\HM; Allah's HM1; Delhi's HM2; Marva's HM4,EM

TEXTUAL NOTES: ACCIDENTALS. 273.1,2 For] HM,EM2; [*undeciphered erased mis-transcription*] EM1 273.1 years,] HM; ~^ EM 273.1 mud-built] HM1,HM3; ~^~ HM2 *273.2 Shawl] HM; shawl T 273.3 loom,] EM; ~— HM 273.6 he^] EM2; ~, HM,EM1 273.6 wine,] HM,EM2; ~: EM1 273.7 lives^] HM,EM2; ~, EM1 273.7 abstinent^] HM,EM2; ~, EM1

LAMIA'S SONG (p. 274)

The Lamiae of classical myth, fabulous creatures female from head to breast but serpent below, were reputed to be irresistible blood-siphoners and ruiners of youth.

DISCUSSIONS. 274.5 myrtles in valleys of May] The association of the myrtle with love appears in *Mardi* (see Davis 1941).

274.6,9,11 Wend,/ah,/roam—] NN retains the punctuation in HM as more certainly authoritative than the lack of punctuation at each point in EM.

EMENDATIONS. 274.2 ^Pleasant . . . way—] EM; (~ . . . ~) HM 274.6 wend:] EM; ~! HM 274.7 descend!] EM; ~, HM 274.8 repay.] EM; ~! HM 274.9 come!] EM; ~— HM 274.10 come,] EM; ~^ HM

TEXTUAL NOTES: INSCRIPTION STAGES. At least two stages of inscription-revision: A (nonextant pre-fair-copy stage); B (blue-black ink on thicker paper).

TEXTUAL NOTES: SUBSTANTIVES. 274.0–12 *Lamia's . . . way*] [*HM leaf 1(B); EM leaf 1*] 274.0 *Lamia's Song*] HM2,EM; [*no title*] HM1; [*there are three or four undeci-phered erased words on EM leaf 1, just below where EM has inked in* Lamia's Song *and at least another two undeciphered erased words just to their left, these two probably having nothing to do with the poem's title, but rather with the wording of line 2*] EM\HM 274.2 Pleasant] HM2,EM; Mossy HM1; [*at least two undeciphered erased words on EM leaf 1 may constitute variants for this line*] EM\HM?1,EM\HM?2 274.10 the cataracts] HM5,HM7; the waterfalls HM1; [?frantic] [?falls] HM?2; [?frantic] [?waterfalls] HM?3; [*undeciphered erased word* {?falls ?waterfalls}] HM?4; [?frantic] [?torrents] HM6 274.11 hymn] HM1,HM4; foam HM2; [*undeciphered erased word, perhaps an uncompleted inscription of* foam *that HM abandoned, if he feared it might be difficult for EM to read*] HM?3

Textual Notes: Accidentals 274.1 Descend] [*indent*] HM; [*indention obscured by display capital*] T 274.1 descend!] HM,EM2; ~— EM1 274.2 ^Pleasant . . . way—] EM2; ^~ . . . ~^ HM1; (~ . . . ~) HM2,EM1[*in both HM and EM, line 2 is enclosed in penciled parentheses, perhaps to indicate it needs attending to, but just as likely indicating that HM considered parenthesizing the line; in HM, the closing parenthesis was neither canceled nor erased, though EM erased the opening parenthesis when she inked in HM's substantive revision of the line*] 274.5 May.] HM,EM2; ~! EM1 *274.6 Wend,] HM,EM1; ~^ EM2 274.6 wend:] EM2; ~! HM; ~; EM1 274.7 descend!] EM2; ~, HM,EM1 274.8 repay.] EM2; ~! HM,EM1 *274.9 ah,] HM; ~^ EM 274.9 come!] HM1,EM2; ~— HM2; ~: EM1 274.10 come,] EM; ~^ HM *274.11 roam—] HM2; ~^ HM1,EM[*HM may have neglected punctuating this line in EM, since the final descender in EM's roam looks like a short dash*] 274.12 How . . . way] HM1,HM3; [*all words here, except, perhaps,* pleasant *are underlined to distinguish them as the hymn of the cataracts*] HM2

IN A GARRET (p. 275)

The four lines of "In a Garret" were developed and expanded from two lines canceled and covered with a revision patch at the top of Melville's manuscript of "Art": "Hard to grapple and upsweep / One dripping trophy from the deep" (see the reproduction on p. 569 above). These two lines may have been an earlier beginning for the poem that became "Art" (p. 280 above). Melville may have decided to turn them into their present form when he abandoned a plan to put together a group of epigrams on art. Cf. the series of "Pebbles" in *John Marr,* pp. 243–49 above. Before Melville settled on his final title he considered "Ambition," "Schiller's Ambition," and "The spirit of Schiller." He also sidelined in pencil three stanzas in his Bulwer-Lytton translation of Schiller's "The Diver" (*Poems and Ballads* [Leipzig: Tauchnitz, 1844]; Sealts, no. 439, Bercaw, no. 606), which was his source for the underwater portion of White Jacket's account of his fall from the yardarm in chapter 92 of *White-Jacket* (1850).

Discussions. 275.1 heap—] NN adopts the dash from T, since it seems doubtful that the compositor would have substituted a dash for the comma in EM (and HM). See the discussion at 261.58 above.

275.2 Sophi] In a note to one of the translations in James Clarence Mangan's *Poems* (New York: Haverty, 1859), a book that Melville owned and annotated (Sealts, no. 347; Bercaw, no. 475), Mangan explains: "*Sophi,* a title of the Khan of Persia" (p. 227). Mangan also cites Shakespeare's "Sophi" in *The Merchant of Venice,* 2.1.

Emendations. 275.0 *Garret*] EM; garret HM *275.1 heap—] T; ~, HM

TEXTUAL NOTES: INSCRIPTION STAGES. At least four stages of inscription-revision: A (nonextant pre-fair-copy stage); B (gray ink on thinner paper); C (pencil on thinner paper); D (mount with no substantive inscription on it).

TEXTUAL NOTES: SUBSTANTIVES. 275.0–4 *In . . . trophy*] [*HM leaf 1(D)* {*unin-scribed except for foliation number 46 and penciled x at top-center*} *HM leaf 1.clip(C)* In . . . trophy *EM leaf 1* In . . . trophy] 275.0 *In a Garret*] HM5[*see also accidentals*]; Ambition HM1; Schiller's Ambition HM2; The spirit of Schiller HM3; [*HM's canceling all titles, pencil-circling the entire poem, and penciling inside the circle* Leave out *probably means that at that point he thought to pull the poem from the volume*] HM4 275.1–4 Gems . . . trophy] HM2; [*see following description of superseded stage B mat-ter*] [*Superseded HM leaf 1(B)* {*"Art" HM leaf 1, later covered by "Art" leaf 1.patch 1*} Hard . . . deep {*not foliated; inscribed in ink*}]

　　　　　　　"———— [*beginning device*]
　　　　　Hard to grapple and upsweep
　　　　　One dripping trophy from the deep.

[*cancel* Hard . . . deep *with blue pencil*] HM1(B)

TEXTUAL NOTES: ACCIDENTALS. 275.0 *In a Garret*] [*EM's pencil inscription of* In a Garret *on the superseded verso of EM leaf 1, taken together with her ink-inscribing of the poem's first line (see following entry for 275.1), is suggestive evidence that a usual transcriptional practice for her was only to pencil in HM's most recent title (if any), subject to his later changing it*] 275.0 Garret] EM; garret HM *275.1 heap—] EM1,T; ~, HM,EM2[*on the verso of EM leaf 1, EM began her transcription with* Gems and jew-els let them heap— *then canceled this beginning and started again on the present recto, probably because she had inadvertently included punctuation—punctuation which turned out to be HM's final choice in T, but which otherwise appears in neither HM's nor EM's transcript*]

MONODY (p. 276)

Before or after stipulating some "estrangement" between Melville and Nathaniel Hawthorne, nearly all the published commentaries on "Mon-ody," beginning with Lewis Mumford's 1929 biography (pp. 264–65), have uncritically assumed that the poem was a response to the death of the older writer on May 19, 1864. Harrison Hayford, after thoroughly survey-ing the issue, concluded in 1991, "Nothing in the manuscript either proves or disproves that Melville wrote the poem for Hawthorne; nor does any-thing scholars have as yet discerned show just when he wrote it" (p. 884 of "Melville's 'Monody': For Hawthorne?" in the NN *Clarel*, pp. 883–93, which includes reproductions of Melville's manuscript of the poem, his wife's transcript of it, and its first-edition printing, along with a genetic transcription of the manuscript; the relevance to *Clarel* is Walter Bezanson's 1943 suggestion that Vine in that poem is a portrait of Hawthorne, presented in revised form on pp. 593–604 of the NN *Clarel*). A longer version of Hayford's examination was originally printed as a 1990 pamphlet entitled *Melville's "Monody": Really for Hawthorne?* and was reprinted in *Melville's Prisoners* (2003, pp. 109–31, 193–200), both of which include a reproduction of Melville's manuscript of the poem. Although Arthur Stedman, who served as Melville's literary executor, reprinted "Monody" six months after Melville's death in the *Century Magazine* (45 [May 1892]: 104), there is no evidence that Melville's authority was involved in its publication.

DISCUSSION. 276.4 wrong;] NN retains the semicolon in HM (though it is a colon in EM), since its reappearance in T probably represents Melville's restoration.

EMENDATIONS. 276.10 crape:] EM; ~; HM 276.12 grape.] EM; ~^ HM

TEXTUAL NOTES: INSCRIPTION STAGES. At least three stages of inscription-revision: A (nonextant pre-fair-copy stage); B (blue-green ink on thicker yellow paper); C (gray ink on thinner cream paper).

TEXTUAL NOTES: SUBSTANTIVES. 276.0 *Monody*] [*HM leaf 1(I.C)*] 276.0–12 *Monody* . . . grape] [*EM leaf 1*] 276.1–6 To . . . song] [*HM leaf 1.clip(B)*] 276.1 him . . . him] HM1,HM3; her . . . her HM2 276.7–12 By . . . grape] [*HM leaf 1(...II.C)*] 276.7 By . . . hermit-mound] HM2; [*pencil-revising nonextant (now-scissored-away) stage B text of line 7 or 8, HM inscribed, then canceled and erased* aloof from drxx *(these words perhaps a further revision of four or five more undeciphered erased revising words, the tops of which are barely visible at the bottom edge of the clip)*] HM1 276.7 wintry] HM4; silent HM1,HM3; [*undeciphered erased word {?wintry}*] HM2 276.10 fir-tree's] HM,EM; fir-trees' T[*a misreading perhaps partly induced by the ambiguous placement of the apostrophe in EM*]

TEXTUAL NOTES: ACCIDENTALS. 276.0 *Monody*] [*the title was accidentally omitted in EM's table of contents for the volume; the leaves bearing the poem in HM's and EM's transcripts are foliated consecutively with the leaves bearing the preceding and following poems*] 276.1 loved him,] HM; ~~^ EM *276.4 wrong;] HM,EM1,T; ~: EM2[*perhaps an example of EM mistakenly inking in a colon where HM had directed a semicolon*] 276.6 Ease] [*indent*] HM2; [*indent two ems*] HM1 276.6 ease,] HM,T; ~^ EM 276.10 fir] HM,EM2; fer EM1 276.10 crape:] EM; ~; HM 276.12 grape.] EM; ~^ HM

LONE FOUNTS (p. 277)

DISCUSSIONS. 277.2 worldlings'] Melville may orally have directed his wife's use in her transcript of the singular possessive "worldling's"; but NN does not emend since the written evidence suggests that he was preocccupied with correcting her mistranscribed "worlding" to "worldlings" and overlooked how she repositioned the apostrophe when she inked in his correction.

277.7 lone founts] At one stage Melville had considered "Truth's fount" here.

EMENDATIONS. 277.0 *Lone Founts*] EM\HM[*the capital* F *supplied by EM for HM's lowercase*]; Counsels? HM 277.0 *Founts*] EM; founts EM\HM 277.5 stand;] EM; ~— HM 277.6 before,] EM; ~: HM 277.8 lore:] EM; ~— HM

TEXTUAL NOTES: INSCRIPTION STAGES. At least three stages of inscription-revision: A (nonextant pre-fair-copy stage); B (brown ink on thinner light-yellow paper); C (gray ink on thinner cream paper).

TEXTUAL NOTES: SUBSTANTIVES. 277.0 *Lone Founts*] [*HM leaf 1(I.C)* Counsels] 277.0–9 *Lone . . . evermore*] [*EM leaf 1*] 277.0 *Lone Founts*] EM\HM5[*not copied back into HM; see also accidentals*],EM2; [*no title*] HM1,EM1; Giordiano Bruno? HM2[*HM's question mark*]; Counsels? HM3[*HM's question mark*]; [*at least six or seven undeciphered erased words, constituting at least four different titles, one of which may be* Roman Admonition] EM\HM1–4 277.1–6 Though . . . before] [*HM leaf 1.clip(B)*] 277.1 Though . . . flies] HM1,HM3; [*variant reading scissored away*] HM2 277.1 glorious] HM1,HM3; [*variant reading scissored away*] HM2 277.1 flies] HM1,HM3; dies HM2 277.2 View not] HM1,HM3,EM2; Never view HM2,EM1 *277.2 worldlings'] HM2,HM4; worldling HM→1; [*undeciphered erased word* {?atheists'}] HM3; worlding EM1[*mistranscription*]; worldling's EM2[*?mistranscription*],T 277.6 Stand] HM1,HM3; Even HM→2 277.7–9 And . . . evermore] [*HM leaf 1(... II.C)*] *277.7 lone founts] HM4,HM6,EM2; the fount HM1; Truth's fount HM2; [*undeciphered erased word*] fount[?]s HM3; founts lone HM5,EM1

TEXTUAL NOTES: ACCIDENTALS. 277.0 *Founts*] EM; founts EM\HM 277.2 worldlings'] [*see substantives*] 277.5 stand;] EM; ~— HM 277.6 before,] EM; ~: HM 277.8 lore:] EM; ~— HM

THE BENCH OF BOORS (p. 278)

The variants that Melville considered for his title and first line display a number of ways of emphasizing the contrasts between his thoughtful insomniac and the "basking boors" (line 11) of David Teniers the Younger (1610–90) as seen in the insomniac's mind's eye. In his journal entry for April 10, 1857, in Turin, Melville recorded seeing "Teniers tavern scenes. The remarkable Teniers effect is produced by first dwarfing, then deforming humanity" (*Journals*, p. 122). In his "At the Hostelry," left in manuscript (see NN vol. 13, *"Billy Budd, Sailor" and Other Uncompleted Writings*), Melville imagines a symposium of old painters discussing the "picturesque" and has Adriaen Brouwer address his fellow genre painter with some of the same words and images that end up in "The Bench of Boors": " 'Hey, Teniers? Give us boors at inns, / Mud floors—dark settles—jugs—old bins, / Under rafters foul with fume that blinks / From logs too soggy much to blaze / Which yet diffuse an umberish haze / That beautifies the grime, methinks.' "

DISCUSSIONS. 278.3–4,9–10,15–16 A . . . pain / Thought's . . . found / Thought's . . . overbright] Although these couplets are underlined (for italics) in HM, there is no underlining in EM. The consistent treatment of all three couplets suggests that the omission was intentional. Melville also eliminated the underlining of "unspoken speech" in two other poems: in "After the Pleasure Party" (263.129) he did not restore the underlining that he had at an earlier stage added to his manuscript; and in "The Enthusiast" (279.18) he erased the underlining in his manuscript. (Cf. his general tendency not to use quotation marks for unspoken thoughts, discussed on p. 613 above.)

278.6 yawn,] NN adopts the comma that Melville added to his manuscript; but the absence of the comma in EM and T leaves open the possibility that he wished to restore his original reading, without the comma.

EMENDATIONS. *278.3–4,9–10,15–16 A . . . pain / Thought's . . . found / Thought's . . . overbright] [*not underlined*] EM; [*underlined*] HM 278.13 boors^] EM; ~, HM

TEXTUAL NOTES: INSCRIPTION STAGES. At least three stages of inscription-revision: A (nonextant pre-fair-copy stage); B (superseded leaf 1; black ink on a piece of white stationery with "Bath" embossed mark); C (blue-black ink on thinner cream paper).

TEXTUAL NOTES: SUBSTANTIVES. 278.0–6 *The . . . again*] [*HM leaf 1(C); EM leaf 1*] 278.0 *The Bench of Boors*] HM1,HM8; Insomnia / or / The Bench of Boors HM?2; [?Insomnia / or /] The Bench of Boors / Suggested by a Flemish painting HM?3; [?Insomnia / or /] The Bench of Boors / Suggested by a Flemish picture HM?4,HM6; [?Insomnia / or /] The Bench of Boors / Suggested by a certain picture HM5; [?Insomnia / or /] The Bench of Boors / (Suggested by a special picture) HM7 278.0–12 *The . . . ember-mound*] [*see following description of superseded stage B versions of title and lines 1–12; evidently at least one intermediate stage C version of these lines has not survived*] [*Superseded HM leaf 1(B)* {*"The Medallion"*}

HM leaf 1 verso (in Harvard MS Am 188 [369.1.5])} Tenier's' . . . ember-mound {*not foliated; inscribed in ink, revised in pencil*}]

[*title and subtitle added in pencil:*]
Tenier's [*then, without canceling first apostrophe, alter to* Tenier's'] Boors
A Revery [*cancel* A Revery]
————"———— [*beginning device*]
To night [*then (underlined)* Midnight;] I muse [*then* brood] on Teniers'
boors, [*then add dash, but without explicitly canceling comma*]
Losels blest and [*then* Losels blear and *then* Losels drunk and *then (in
the following readings* drunk *is assumed to have been tacitly canceled though
it was not explicitly lined through, whereas* and *was)* Dreamy losels *then*
Doting losels *?then* Dreamy losels *then* Dotards{,} losels *then* Sots and
losels *then* Slugs and losels] boozy [*then* drowsy] all; [*the semicolon per-
haps replaces a period*]
    Thought's tingling brain [*then* The tingling brain *then* But
    tingling brain *?then* While tingling brain *?then* While I in
    strain]
    But breedeth pain— [*then* It breeds me pain: *then* {?It ?While
    pain} calls off the hours of thought in vain: *?then* {*?tacitly* Call}
    off the hours of thought in vain:]
  Within low doors
    The drowsy [*then* boozy *then* beery *then* bench of *though, since
    beery is not canceled, another possible reading is* bench of beery]
    boors
Yawn, and drink [*then* drowse *then* quaff *then* stretch], and [*add, then
cancel dash*] doze again.
[*line-space*]
In dreams they doze [*then* doze,] the slumberous [*then* lumpish *?then*
beery *then* boozy *then* torpid *then* cozy] boors,
Their umber beer-room [*then* tavern *then* tap-room] warm and small;
  Thought's ample round
      But chill is found—
[*both the exact nature and sequence of HM's revisions of* Thought's . . .
 found *are difficult to determine; among the more likely possibilities are*
    Thought's larger round
    But chill is found—
then
    My reach and round
    But chill is found—
?then
    My reach and round but chill is found—
    {*?Saturnian*} {*?ring*} of {*?not completed*}
?or
    My {*or* Thought's} larger reach and ample round

{?Saturnian} {?ring} of chill is found
and regardless of which version of the first of these lines he was considering,
  HM seems to have tried the second as
  {?Saturnian} {?ring} of reaching thought {*?to be completed with* but
    chill is found}
and as
  {?Saturnian} {?ring} of thought sweeping {*?to be completed with*
    round}
then, leaving of *and* thought *uncanceled, he inserted, from the top of the leaf,*
  While chilled {?surround}
  The cape {?or cope} of thought's {?inclement} bound]
  Within low doors
  The cozy [*then* slugs of boozy] boors
Snugly [*then* How {s}nugly *then* Snugly] hug the ember-mound

[*then cancel leaf with blue pencil*] HM1(B) 278.1 In bed] HM2; By night HM1
278.1 Teniers' boors] HM1,HM9[*perhaps also restored once earlier*],EM[*see also
accidentals*],EM\HM2; clowns and boors HM2,HM?4; [*undeciphered erased word*]
and boors HM3; [*two or more undeciphered erased words, constituting at least two vari-
ants*] and boors HM?5,HM?6; Flemish boors HM?7; pictured boors HM?8,EM\
HM1[*the ordering of variants here is often problematic because of their great number and
positioning on the leaf*] 278.1 boors] HM1,HM3,EM\HM1,EM\HM3; boors*[*the
asterisk is keyed to another at the bottom of HM leaf 1, and HM's* <u>Note</u> {*HM's under-
lining*}. *A particular picture is here referred to.*] HM2; boors*[*HM's asterisk is
attached to a line leading to the bottom of EM leaf 1 and HM's inscription* See <u>note</u>
{*HM's underlining*} *at end of this Piece which direction refers, in turn, to his annotation
at the bottom of EM leaf 2* <u>Note</u> {*HM's underlining*} / *The reference here is to a spe-
cial canvas.*] EM\HM2 278.2 beery] HM1,HM3; Flemish HM2 278.6 Laze and
yawn] HM1,HM3; [*undeciphered erased word* {?Long}] laze and [*undeciphered erased
word* {?bask}] HM2 278.7–18 In . . . light] [*HM leaf 2(B); EM leaf 2*] 278.8 and]
HM1,HM3; as HM2 278.11 basking] HM2; slumberous HM1 278.12 Snugly]
HM1,HM4; How snugly HM2; Slumberous HM3

TEXTUAL NOTES: ACCIDENTALS. 278.1 Teniers'] HM; Tenier's EM 278.3–4,9–
10,15–16 [*deep indent*] HM; [*lines 9–10 and 15–16 indented somewhat more deeply than
lines 3–4*] EM; [*all with the same deep indent*] T *278.3–4,9–10,15–16 [*not underlined*]
HM1,EM2; [*underlined*] HM2,EM1 *278.6 yawn,] HM2; ~^ HM1,EM 278.13
boors^] EM2; ~, HM,EM1

THE ENTHUSIAST (p. 279)

DISCUSSIONS. 279.0[*epigraph*] *"Though . . . Him."*] Here Melville quotes the first
part of Job 13:15 and omits the rest: "but I will maintain mine own ways before
him." In one of his Bibles (Philadelphia: Butler, 1846; Sealts, no. 62, Bercaw, no.
63) Melville double-sidelined the whole verse and underlined "but . . . him."

279.3 hold] NN emends the copy-text "held" to the reading in EM (and T). There is little doubt that Melville's manuscript reads "held"; but the present-tense "hold" makes more sense in the context, and perhaps Melville directed the change. (The opposite situation occurs in the verse portion of "John Marr" at 199.12, where the "held" in Melville's manuscript is better than the printer's misreading, "hold", which Melville then corrected in copies of the book.)

279.13 Faith] NN retains the capital letter in the copy-text, reduced to low-ercase in T (see p. 610 above). Cf. the capitalized "Time" (line 9) and "Truth" (line 15).

279.17–18 Each . . . me] In the Langhorne translation, Plutarch reports that because Achillas (one of the assassins of Pompey) escaped, Caesar was forced to burn his own ships in the harbor at Alexandria "to prevent their falling into the enemy's hands" (p. 512).

279.18 No] NN retains the capitalized reading in HM. Although the EM reading was initially lowercase, it was changed to a capitalized one, apparently as a result of Melville's direction (see p. 610 above).

EMENDATIONS. 279.0[*epigraph*] *Him.*"] T; ~^" EM 279.2 years^—] EM; ~,— HM *279.3 hold] EM; held HM 279.5 spirits^ . . . light^] EM; ~, . . . ~, HM 279.5 that worship] T; the sons of HM 279.6 glow,] EM; glow,? HM 279.7 go,] EM; ~— HM 279.13 skies,] EM; ~? HM 279.17 Each burning boat] EM\HM; The burning fleet HM 279.19 dear,] T; ~^ HM 279.22 pall,] EM; ~; HM 279.23 Though] [*indent*] EM; [*no indent*] HM

TEXTUAL NOTES: INSCRIPTION STAGES. At least three stages of inscription-revision: A (nonextant pre-fair-copy stage); B (blue-black ink on thicker paper); C (tan-gray on thinner paper).

TEXTUAL NOTES: SUBSTANTIVES. 279.0–8 *The . . .* right] [*HM leaf 1(C); EM leaf 1*] 279.0 *The Enthusiast*] HM2; Though He slay me HM1 279.0[*epigraph*] *Though . . . Him*] HM5; [*no epigraph; the poem is titled* Though He slay me] HM1; Though He slay me HM2[*leaf position and punctuation make this reading possible as either HM's second choice of title or first of epigraph*]; Though He slay me yet will I [*at least four or five undeciphered erased words constitute at least two variant readings, one of them perhaps being* depend on him *and another* trust but {*or* but in} him HM3,HM4 *279.3 hold] EM; held HM 279.4 When interest tames] HM1,HM5; Let interest tame HM?2,HM4; [?When] [?strong] interest tames HM3 279.5 that worship] T; the sons of HM1,HM3; [*three or four undeciphered erased words constituting at least one variant reading*] HM2; that loved the EM\HM; that love the ?HM4,EM 279.7 trudge] HM?3,HM?5,HM?7,HM10; creep HM1; [*undeciphered erased word {?*slink}] HM2; [*undeciphered erased word*] HM4; tread HM6; troop HM?8; head HM?9 279.9–16 *Shall . . .* lies] [*HM leaf 2(C); EM leaf 2*] 279.9 creeping] HM2; crafty HM1 279.11 heartless] HM1,HM3,EM\HM1,EM\HM3; sordid HM2,EM\HM2 279.17–24 Each . . . light] [*HM leaf 3(B) {a patch or clip was once* *attached to the top of HM leaf 3*}; *EM leaf 3*] 279.17 Each burning boat] EM\HM; The burning fleet HM 279.18 Flames] HM4(C); [*undeciphered scratched-out word*] HM1; Reminds HM2; It flames HM3 279.18 No . . . me] HM1,HM3(C); Return is none through me HM2 279.19 So] HM1,HM4; Yet HM?2; Then HM?3 279.19 ties though] HM,EM\HM; lies how EM[*mistranscription*] 279.20 ties] HM2(C); [*undeciphered scratched-out word* {?these}] HM1 279.22 'the] HM1,HM3; thy HM2 279.23 Though] HM1,HM3; Should HM2

TEXTUAL NOTES: ACCIDENTALS. 279.0[*epigraph*] *Though . . . Him*] [*underlined for italic*] EM\HM; [*not underlined*] HM[*also see substantives*] 279.0[*epigraph*] "*Though*] HM2,EM2; ^~ HM1; (~ EM1 279.0[*epigraph*] *Him.*"] T; ~^^ HM1; ~^" HM2,EM 279.2 years—] EM; ~,— HM 279.3 it^ if discreet^] HM2,EM2; ~, ~ ~, HM1; ~, ~ ~^ EM1,T 279.5 spirits^ . . . light^] EM; ~, . . . ~, HM[*see substantives*] 279.6 glow,] HM1,EM; ~,? [*comma left uncanceled*] HM2 279.7 go,] EM; ~— HM 279.8 Conform,] HM; ~^ EM 279.10 Unnerve^] HM2; ~, HM1 279.10 the] HM,EM2; The EM1 *279.13 Faith] HM; faith T 279.13 skies,] EM; ~? HM 279.17 rear^] HM; ~, T[*the compositor mistook as a comma the top of line 18's exclamation mark in EM*] 279.18 No . . . me] HM2; [*underlined*] HM1 *279.18 No] HM,EM2; no EM1 279.19 dear,] T; ~^ HM 279.21 night:] HM2; ~. HM1 279.22 pall,] HM1,EM; ~; HM2 279.23 Though] [*indent*] EM; [*no indent*] HM[*four penciled, canceled, and erased horizontal marks at the bottom of HM leaf 2 probably have to do with some passing notion HM had as to how he might rearrange his indention pattern; exactly what that rearrangement intention might have amounted to seems inscrutable, however, unless it was to indent all odd-numbered lines*] 279.23 thee,] HM2(C),T; ~^ HM1,EM 279.24 From] HM[*a dash at the left of* From *may indicate that at some point HM considered indenting his last line*]

ART (p. 280)

What became the poem "Art" may well have been conceived as a gathering of "epigrams" about art, with a title indicating it as their common topic (see the introductory note to "In a Garret," p. 789 above). See pp. 567–69 above for reproductions of this manuscript page in its varying stages, and for a detailed description and analysis of the manuscript, see Robert C. Ryan's "Melville Revises 'Art.'"

DISCUSSION. 280.10–11 Jacob's mystic heart, . . . the angel—Art] See Genesis 32:24–32: "And Jacob was left alone; and there wrestled a man with him until the breaking of the day. And when he saw that he prevailed not against him, he touched the hollow of his thigh: and the hollow of Jacob's thigh was out of joint, as he wrestled with him. . . . Therefore the children of Israel eat not of the sinew which shrank, which is upon the hollow of the thigh, unto this day; because he touched the hollow of Jacob's thigh in the sinew that shrank." In one of his Bibles

(Philadelphia: Butler, 1846; Sealts, no. 62), Melville underlined the words Peniel and Penuel in verses 30 and 31.

EMENDATIONS. 280.1 In] [*indent*] EM; [*no indent*] HM 280.2 brave] EM\HM; bright HM 280.3 lend] EM\HM; give HM 280.4 mate:] EM; ~; HM 280.6 patience—] EM; ~,— HM 280.7 and scorn;] EM; [*pencil-underlined, probably as part of HM's considering how to revise the line*] HM 280.9 mate,] EM; ~— HM 280.10 heart,] EM\HM; ~^ HM

TEXTUAL NOTES: INSCRIPTION STAGES. At least six stages of inscription-revision: A (nonextant pre-fair-copy stage); Ba (nonextant inscription on inferred clip); Bb (gray ink on extant clip); Bc (dark gray ink on mount); Bd (gray ink on Patch 2); Be (pencil on patch 2).

A pin originally attached a stage Bb clip bearing the poem's earliest surviving inscription ("Sad patience . . . meet") to the stage Bc main leaf where "Hard to grapple . . . freeze;" is inscribed. Rather than retranscribe legible text from a previous fair copy ("Sad patience . . . meet"), Melville scissors (clips) it away from text that we may infer is so revised as to require the sort of reinscription we find on the later-stage main leaf. That is, the initial inscription on the clip is earlier (Bb) than the initial inscription on the main leaf (Bc). At the bottom of the clip, at stage Bd, Melville penciled three fair-copy lines ("Audacity . . . . With more than" plus later erased "Even Jacob"), just before stage Bd ink-inscribing (and fair-copying) the poem's last four lines on a revision patch. The stage Bd penciled lines, that is, were inscribed later than any of the inked lines on the clip or main leaf. Furthermore, the space where the stage Bd penciled lines now appear was earlier occupied by a non-surviving stage Ba (or earlier) clip attached to the bottom of the stage Bb clip ("Sad patience . . . meet") and presumably bearing an earlier, substantially different version of the poem's ending. If that ending had not been substantially different, and subsequently much revised, Melville would not have judged it necessary to make a new fair copy at stage Bd. See pp. 567–69 above for three reproductions of what became leaf 54 of the *Timoleon* manuscript.

TEXTUAL NOTES: SUBSTANTIVES. 280.0–5 *Art . . . melt*] [*HM leaf 1.patch 1(Be)*] 280.0–11 *Art . . . Art*] [*EM leaf 1*] 280.0–4 *Art . . . mate*] HM2(Be); [*see following description of superseded stage Bc matter inscribed in ink on HM leaf 1*]

> ———"——— [*beginning device*]
> Hard to grapple and upsweep
> One dripping trophy from the deep.
> [*then cancel* Hard . . . deep *with blue pencil*]
> [*after ink inscription of following stage Bc lines, insert, in pencil, the title*
> Art

and

———————"———— {*beginning device*}]
[*the following is stage Bc ink inscription*]
In him who would evoke—create,
Contraries [*then* What extremes *then* Contraries *then* What contraries]
    must meet and mate:

[*then pencil-cancel* In . . . mate *and supersede by covering over with stage Be patch*]
HMı(Bc) 280.1 well pleased we] HM2; we easy HMı 280.2 brave] EM\HM;
bright HM 280.3 form] HM,T; forms EM\HM[*not copied back into HM*] 280.3
lend] EM\HM; give HM 280.3 pulsed] HM3; a HMı; true HM2 280.5 A flame
to melt—] HM3; Flames that burn, HMı; Flame that burns, HM2 280.5 a wind
to freeze] [*HM leaf 1(Bc)* {*only uncanceled inscription*}] 280.5 a wind] HM2,EM,EM\
HM2; and winds HMı; winds EM\HMı 280.5 to] HM2; that HMı 280.6–7 Sad
. . . scorn] [*HM leaf 1.clip(Bb)*] 280.7 Humility—yet pride^] HM3; Humility—and
pride^ HMı; Humility, pride, HM2 280.8–11 Instinct . . . Art] [*HM leaf 1.patch
2(Bd)*] 280.8–10 Instinct . . . Jacob's] [*see following description of superseded stage Bb
matter on clip*]

    Reverence; love and hate twin-born;
    Instinct and culture; era meet
    [*then pencil-cancel* Reverence . . . meet *and pencil-add*]
    Audacity—reverence; love and hate
    Instinct and culture. These must mate
    With more than Even Jacob

[*then erase* Even Jacob *and pencil-cancel* Audacity . . . more than *and cover over with
stage Bd patch*] HMı(Bb) 280.8–9 Instinct and study . . . Audacity—reverence]
HM2; Audacity—reverence . . . Instinct and study HMı 280.8 study] HM2;
culture HMı 280.9 These] HMı,HM3; All HM2 280.10–11 And . . . Art] [*HM
pencil-circled these lines for attention, and only partly erased the circling*] 280.10 And . . .
mystic] HM→4,HM6; With more than even Jacob's HMı; With much of mystic
Jacob's HM2; Must fuse with Jacob's mystic HM3; [*no variant apparently inscribed
for* And] fuse with Jacob's mystic HM→5 280.11 the] HM2; that HMı

Textual Notes: Accidentals. 280.1 In] [*indent*] EM; [*no indent*] HM; [*inden-
tion obscured by display capital*] T 280.1 well^pleased] HM; ~-~ T 280.4 mate:]
HMı,EM; ~; HM2 280.5 melt—] HM,EM\HM; melt^ EM→ı[*a first mistran-
scription caused by the much-revised state of HM's transcript*]; melt—[*or a wide space
left for later insertion of a possible dash*] EM2[*a second mistranscription*][*also see substan-
tives*] 280.6 patience—] EM2; ~,— HM[*though the comma and dash may have been
inscribed at different times—the comma perhaps earlier—neither is canceled in favor of
the other*]; ~, EMı 280.7 Humility—yet pride^] [*see substantives*] 280.7 and scorn]
HMı,EM; [*pencil-underlined, probably as part of HM's considering how to revise the*

line] HM2 280.7 scorn;] HM,EM2; ~: EM1 280.8–9 study; . . . reverence.] HM2;
reverence; . . . study. HM1[*see substantives; in revising, HM transposed phrases but not
(explicitly) punctuation*] 280.9 mate,] EM; ~^ HM1[*in superseded text; see substantives
at lines 8–10*]; ~— HM2 280.10 Jacob's] HM,T; Jacobs EM 280.10 heart,] EM\
HM; ~^ HM

BUDDHA (p. 281)

DISCUSSION. 281.0[*epigraph*] *For . . . away*] When Elizabeth Shaw Melville copied
back into Melville's manuscript the epigraph that he presumably directed her to
put in her transcript, she added the source—"IV James 14." NN does not include
that citation, since its omission from both her transcript and T is probably not
inadvertent. In James 4:14, the words Melville quotes are preceded by: "Whereas
ye know not what shall be on the morrow." The phrase "life, though a vapor's
wreath" appears in "Stonewall Jackson (Ascribed to a Virginian)" (60.5 above).

EMENDATIONS. *281.0[*epigraph*] *For . . . . away*] EM; [*no epigraph*] HM 281.1 and]
EM; & HM 281.5 Nirvana!] T; ~^ HM 281.5 absorb] HM\EM; absord HM 281.5
skies,] EM; ~^ HM 281.6 Thee.] EM\HM; thee! HM

TEXTUAL NOTES: INSCRIPTION STAGES. At least two stages of inscription-revision:
A (nonextant ink fair-copy, preceded by a nonextant pre-A pencil draft); B (pen-
cil fair-copy).

TEXTUAL NOTES: SUBSTANTIVES 281.0–6 *Buddha . . . Thee*] [*HM leaf 1(B)*] Bud-
dha . . . thee *EM leaf 1* Buddha . . . Thee] 281.0 Buddha] HM1,HM3; Buddha
& the Vapor [*accompanied by additional beginning device*] HM2 *281.0[*epigraph*] *For
. . . away*] EM[*so far as the extant evidence reveals, EM inscribed the epigraph first in
her transcript, in pencil, then ink, and subsequently copied it back into HM's transcript;
since she left a wide space for inserting the epigraph into her transcript, it may safely be
inferred she had been asked to look up the quotation to verify its exact wording; none of
the epigraph's erased penciled words in EM seems determinably in HM's hand except for
his penciled and erased query following them— St. Paul? —so it would appear that EM
transcribed them directly from a Bible or/and HM's nonextant inscription of them (nonex-
tant inscription that pinhole evidence suggests could have appeared on a clip or patch once
attached to the lower half of HM); in copying them back into HM (without underlining,
quotation marks, and the period), EM indicated their source on a fourth inscription line
(a source not cited either in her transcript or in T)— IV James 14 —and penciled above
them a provisional direction not followed in either EM or T—to make 4 lines of this*]; [*no
epigraph*] HM1; [*?epigraph inscribed on nonextant clip or patch once attached to bottom
portion of HM*] HM?2 281.3 worlds,] HM,T; world^ EM[*mistranscription*]; worlds^
EM\HM[*a clear case of HM correcting the substantive mistranscription and neglecting to
add the comma from his own transcript*]

TEXTUAL NOTES: ACCIDENTALS. 281.0[*epigraph*] *For . . . away*] [*underlined*] EM2; [*not underlined*] EM1,HM\EM[*see substantives*] 281.1 Swooning] [*indent*] HM; [*indention obscured by display capital*] T 281.1 and] EM; & HM 281.1 and less,] HM; ~~^ T 281.3 Sobs] [*no indent*] HM2; [*indent*] HM→1 281.3 worlds,] [*see substantives*] 281.5 Nirvana] ?HM,T; Nervanna EM,HM\EM 281.5 Nirvana!] T; Nirvana^ HM; Nervanna^ ?HM,HM\EM,EM1; Nervanna! EM2 281.5 absorb] HM\EM; absord HM 281.5 skies,] EM; ~^ HM 281.6 Thee.] EM\HM,EM2; thee! HM; thee. EM1,T

C——'S LAMENT (p. 282)

The last name of Samuel Taylor Coleridge (1772–1834) was spelled out in earlier versions of the title. Melville is known to have owned *Biographia Literaria* (New York: Wiley & Putnam, 1847 or 1848; Sealts, no. 154, Bercaw, no. 147), though his copy has not been found, and to have borrowed, if not owned, *Notes and Lectures upon Shakespeare* (London: Pickering, 1849; Sealts, no. 155, Bercaw, no. 149).

DISCUSSION. 282.3–4 wine . . . divine] Although commas end these lines in HM, no commas appear in EM. NN assumes that the omission is deliberate, since there is a similar series of lines without line-end pointing in the third stanza.

EMENDATIONS. *282.3–4 wine^ . . . divine^] EM; ~, . . . ~, HM 282.7 earth,] EM; ~— HM 282.9 romance;] EM; ~: HM 282.11 worth,] EM; ~— HM 282.17 gone,] EM; ~^ HM

TEXTUAL NOTES: INSCRIPTION STAGES. At least two stages of inscription-revision: A (nonextant pre-fair-copy stage); B (blue-black ink on thinner paper).

TEXTUAL NOTES: SUBSTANTIVES. 282.0–10 C——'s . . . dearth] [*HM leaf 1(B)*] Coleridge's . . . dearth *EM leaf 1* Coleridge's . . . dearth] 282.0 C——'s Lament] HM6,EM\HM3[*EM reinscribed* Lament *for clarity*],T; [*no title*] HM1; Anacreon's Threnody HM2; [*?Simonides*] Threnody HM3; [*undeciphered erased word*]'s Lament HM4; Coleridge's Lament HM5,EM\HM?2,EM\HM4,EM,HM\EM; [*two undeciphered erased words, the second of which might be* Lament] EM\HM1 282.4 seemed] HM1,HM3; so HM2 282.4 divine] HM4; benign HM1,HM3; [*undeciphered erased word*] HM2 282.5 felt] HM2; knew HM[?→]1 282.8 Aladdin= land] HM2; Aladdin-clime HM1 282.11–20 And . . . stone] [*HM leaf 2(B); EM leaf 2*] 282.14 lovers'] HM2; loves' HM→1[*?inadvertent misinscription*] 282.18 me] HM1,HM3; [*undeciphered erased word*] HM2 282.18 lone] HM1,HM3; here HM2

TEXTUAL NOTES: ACCIDENTALS. 282.1 How] [*indent*] HM; [*indention obscured by display capital*] T 282.1,6,11,16 How/Ere/And/But] [*indent*] HM2; [*no indent*] HM1 *282.3–4 wine^ . . . divine^] EM; ~, . . . ~, HM 282.7 earth,] EM; ~— HM 282.8 Aladdin-land] HM; Alladin-land EM 282.9 romance;] EM; ~: HM 282.11 worth,] EM; ~— HM 282.12 Yes,] HM; [*in EM, the* Yes *is mended—perhaps by HM—to make sure its first letter is not mistakenly set in lowercase, and the comma is penciled but not inked in*] EM[?\HM] 282.17 gone,] EM[*comma penciled only*]; ~^ HM 282.18 lone,] HM; ~^ EM

SHELLEY'S VISION (p. 283)

The Shelley who speaks in Melville's poem may or may not be a representation of the historical Percy Bysshe Shelley (1792–1822), often assailed for his avowed atheism and other unconventionalities. Among the titles that Melville considered for this poem are "Shelley relates his Vision" and "H.———— relates his Vision." On February 27, 1857, Melville visited the ruins of the Baths of Caracalla in Rome and imagined that Shelley had "got his inspiration" there for *Prometheus Unbound*; later that day, by a "natural process," he visited Shelley's grave in the Protestant Cemetery a half-mile away (see *Journals,* pp. 106–7, 467, and the HISTORICAL NOTE above, p. 431). Melville owned the following Shelley titles, some volumes of which have his markings and annotations: *Essays, Letters from Abroad, Translations and Fragments* (London: Moxon, 1852; Sealts, no. 468, Bercaw, no. 638), *The Poetical Works* (Boston: Little Brown, 1857; Sealts, no. 469 [present location unknown]; Bercaw, no. 639), *Shelley Memorials* (Boston: Ticknor & Fields, 1859; Sealts, no. 466, Bercaw, no. 635), and James Thomson's *Shelley: A Poem* (London: Whittingham, 1884; Sealts, no. 520).

DISCUSSIONS. 283.3 Hate the censor] The commas after "Hate" and "censor" in HM were omitted in EM; NN assumes that this omission was deliberate, since Melville extensively revised the punctuation of lines 2–3 in his wife's transcript.

 283.10 Saint Stephen crowned] On Saint Stephen, the first Christian martyr, see Acts 6:5–7:60; cf. Luke 23:34. In Greek, Stephanos signifies "wreath" or "crown."

EMENDATIONS. 283.0 *Shelley's*] EM\HM; S————'s HM 283.1 morning] EM\ HM; sunny HM 283.2 low—] EM; ~^ HM 283.3 ^Hate . . . me—] EM; (~ . . . ~) HM *283.3 Hate^ the censor^] EM; ~, ~ ~, HM 283.6 one!] EM; ~! HM 283.7 cast] EM; flung HM 283.8 When^] EM; ~, HM 283.8 sun-lit] EM\HM; noiseless HM 283.10 crowned:] EM; ~. HM

TEXTUAL NOTES: INSCRIPTION STAGES. At least three stages of inscription-revision: A (nonextant pre-fair-copy stage); Ba (tan-gray ink on clips); Bb (tan-gray ink on mount).

TEXTUAL NOTES: SUBSTANTIVES. 283.0–4 *Shelley's . . . go*] [*HM leaf 1.clip 1(Ba)* Shelleys . . . go] 283.0–11 *Shelley's . . . awake*] [*EM leaf 1*] 283.0 *Shelley's Vision*] EM\HM4,EM; S————'s Vision HM1; S———— relates his Vision HM2; H.———— relates his Vision HM?3; S————y relates his Vision HM?4; ————'s Vision HM5; [*at least six undeciphered erased words constitute at least three variant readings*] EM\HM1–3; Shelleys Vision HM\EM 283.1 late . . . seas] EM\ HM,EM2; late by Naples' sea HM1; by a lonely sea HM2; late by sunny seas HM3,EM1 283.5–7 In . . . stone] [*HM leaf 1(Bb)*] 283.6 I too would] HM2; Let me too HM1 283.7 At] HM2; And at HM1 283.7 cast] EM2[*there appears to be no extant HM inscription of this variant, though it may have appeared on the scissored-away top portion of HM clip 2, since pinholes and the bottom portions of two or three undeciphered erased words suggest HM extensively revised one or more text-lines before scissoring away clip 2's top portion subsequent to his originally attaching the clip to the present leaf, as well as subsequent to EM's earlier inscription of the leaf in her transcript; see entry, below, for line 8*]; flung HM,EM1 283.7 a] HM2; the HM1 283.8–11 When . . . awake] [*HM leaf 1.clip 2(Ba)*] 283.8 sun-lit] EM\HM?3,EM4[*not copied back into HM; HM may earlier have inscribed* sun-lit *on the now-scissored-away top portion of clip 2*]; noiseless HM1,EM1,EM\HM?2,EM3; sunny HM?2,EM\HM?1[*there is no unmistakable HM inscription extant for this variant*],EM2 283.10 crowned] HM2; stoned HM1

TEXTUAL NOTES: ACCIDENTALS. 283.0 *Shelley's Vision*] [*see substantives*] 283.2 low—] EM; ~^ HM 283.3 ^Hate . . . me—] EM; (~ . . . ~) HM *283.3 Hate^ the censor^] EM; ~, ~ ~, HM 283.5 tone^] HM2; ~— HM1 283.6 one:] EM; ~. HM1; ~! HM2 283.8 When^] EM2; ~, HM,EM1 283.10 Saint] HM; St EM 283.10 crowned:] EM; ~. HM

FRAGMENTS OF A LOST GNOSTIC POEM OF THE 12TH CENTURY (p. 284)

DISCUSSIONS. 284.0 *Fragments . . . Century*] In Melville's various earlier titles (see textual notes below), the first word was the singular "Fragment"; his change to the plural probably came at the same time as his addition of the rows of asterisks. On his interest in series of epigraphs, see the introductory note to "In a Garret" (p. 789 above). In HM and EM, "Lost" is not capitalized in the title, nor is it capitalized in Melville's wife's transcript of the table of contents. Melville probably indicated in proof that it should be capitalized at the head of the poem, but that inferred action is concealed by the fact that all poem titles at the heads of poems are printed in full capitals in T; the table of contents in T, however, does have a capital "L". In Melville's wife's transcript of the table of contents, the word "century" is also not capitalized, though it has a capital in both HM and EM; this capital appears in the printed table of contents, which also has a capital "a", unlikely to have been Melville's intention (cf. the discussion at 286.0 for another presumably compositorial capitalization of an article). NN therefore capitalizes all the nouns and adjectives of the title but not the "a".

284.6 energy] NN adopts the lowercase reading in EM. While the first reading in that document matched the capitalized form in HM, it was then changed to lowercase, evidently a result of Melville's direction. See the discussion on p. 610 above.

284.7 clear^] NN follows the copy-text in placing no punctuation here; the comma in T is evidently the result of a misunderstanding of the meaning of "But" in line 8 on the part of a Caxton Press staff member.

EMENDATIONS. *284.0 *Fragments . . . Century*] EM\HM [*the capital L supplied by NN is obscured by the capitalization of the whole title in T;* Fragment of a lost Gnostic poem HM 284.1 state,] EM; ~^ HM 284.3 Matter] EM\HM; Apollyon HM 284.4 ancient brutal] EM\HM; old abysmal HM 284.5 Indolence] EM\HM; The do-nothing HM *284.6 energy] EM; Energy HM 284.6 hell:] EM; ~; HM 284.8 well.] EM; ~^ HM

TEXTUAL NOTES: INSCRIPTION STAGES. At least two stages of inscription-revision: A (nonextant pre-fair-copy stage); B (Melville's pencil fair-copy may imply at least one previous, much-revised draft).

TEXTUAL NOTES: SUBSTANTIVES. 284.0–8 *Fragments . . . well*] [*HM leaf 1(B); EM leaf 1*] *284.0 *Fragments . . . Century*] HM?5,EM\HM2,EM2; [*?no title*] HM?1; Fragment of a lost poem HM2; Fragment of a lost poem of the IX Century / (From the Greek) HM3[*the parenthesized* From the Greek *could have been added later, however, and thus could have created the fourth variant HM reading*]; Fragment of a lost Gnostic poem HM4,EM?1[*the erased state of EM's transcript leaves uncertain which penciled title in her hand HM revised there*]; Fragment of a lost Gnostic Poem of the 12 Century EM\HM1 284.3 Matter] HM?1,EM\HM3,EM2; [*?Satan ?Sin*] HM2,EM1; [*undeciphered erased word*] HM3; Apollyon HM4; [*undeciphered erased word*] EM\HM1; [*undeciphered erased word*] EM\HM2 284.3 in] HM?1,HM?3,HM6,EM\HM; in the HM?2,HM4,EM; [*one or more undeciphered erased words may constitute at least one other reading*] HM?5 284.4 ancient brutal] HM?1,EM[?\HM],HM?4,EM2; [*at least one undeciphered erased word*] HM2; old abysmal HM3,EM1 284.5 Indolence . . . here] HM?5,EM\HM1,EM\HM3; The [*three or four undeciphered erased words*] here HM1; Indolence is the blest one here HM2; The do-nothing is agent of heaven's [*?plan ?spleen*] here HM3; The do= nothing is heaven's ally here HM4,EM,EM\HM2 284.5 heaven's] HM,EM; heavens HM\EM 284.8 well.] HM1,HM3; [*after penciling an ending device following* *line 8, HM penciled (enclosed with braces at the right and left margins), then canceled the following quatrain:*

> Flowers are illusion[?s] and they die
> Take away the corps of the rose
> For fragrance it doth putrify,
> The [?test ?best] of a thing is its close] HM2

TEXTUAL NOTES: ACCIDENTALS. 284.0 *Fragments . . . Century*] [*see substantives*] *284.0 *Lost*] NN; lost EM\HM; LOST T[*capitalization obscured by design*] 284.0 *12th*] HM; 12TH T 284.1,15 Found/Indolence] [*a line of asterisks precedes lines 1 and 5*] HM2; [*no line of asterisks—their absence presumably coincident with the singular sense of the earlier first title word* Fragment] HM1 284.1 state,] EM; ~^ HM *284.6 energy] EM2; Energy HM,EM1 284.6 hell:] EM; ~; HM *284.7 clear^] HM; ~, T 284.8 well.] EM; ~^ HM

THE MARCHIONESS OF BRINVILLIERS (p. 285)

That this poem is Melville's response to a portrait is suggested both by the wording of the poem itself and by a rejected title, "Portrait." But whether the likeness is of Marie Madeleine Marguerite d'Aubray, Marquise de Brinvilliers (ca. 1630–76), is another matter, for the details in the poem more closely resemble the Guido Reni portrait of Beatrice Cenci than any located portrait of Brinvilliers. Melville owned an engraving of the Cenci portrait by Vincent Biondi (reproduced in Wallace 1986, and now in the collection of William Reese; also see Leyda, *Log*, p. 556, and *Journals*, p. 474). When Melville saw the original on March 3, 1857, he wrote: "Expression of suffering about the mouth — (appealing look of innocence) not caught in any copy or engraving" (*Journals*, p. 108). His use of "Marchioness" in the title rather than the French "Marquise" may suggest that he had seen a recent English book, Albert Smith's *The Marchioness of Brinvilliers* (London: Richard Bentley, 1886); but he had known her story earlier, as his references in *The Confidence-Man* (chap. 29) and *Clarel* (3.15.24) show.

EMENDATION. 285.4 weave:] EM; ~— HM

TEXTUAL NOTES: INSCRIPTION STAGES. At least three stages of inscription-revision: A (nonextant pre-fair-copy stage); B (brown ink on thicker paper); C (tan-gray ink on thinner paper).

TEXTUAL NOTES: SUBSTANTIVES. 285.0–6 *The . . . skies*] [*HM leaf 1.clip(B)*]
285.0–8 *The . . . eyes*] [*EM leaf 1*] 285.0 *The . . . Brinvilliers*] HM1,HM3[*never
canceled while HM was considering other possibilities, this reading has his penciled, circled
Right beside it*],EM\HM?1,EM\HM3,EM; The Pale [*three or four undeciphered
erased words*] HM2; The Marchioness of X [*one undeciphered erased letter; the word is
not completed*] EM\HM2; Portrait [*? / The Marchioness of Brinvilliers*] HM\EM
285.2 tender] HM2,HM4,T; pensive HM1,HM3,EM 285.4 Light] HM2; Deftly
light HM1 285.7–8 *And . . . eyes*] [*HM leaf 1(C)*] 285.7 And . . . made] HM2;
[*portions of possible revisions of an earlier version of line 7, the upper halves of two or three
scissored-away undeciphered erased words appear at the bottom edge of the clip*] HM?1
285.8 eyes.] [*at the bottom of HM leaf 1, in HM's hand, in pencil, uncanceled, unerased,
circled, and with a pointing finger inside the circle, is a version of "Herba Santa," line 34*
Gold would ease this pain *the word* ease *underlined, probably to indicate it needs to be
attended to (?to alter his earlier* eaze *to* ease*), but perhaps to indicate which word in the
line is to be changed*]

TEXTUAL NOTES: ACCIDENTALS. 285.0 *Brinvilliers*] HM,EM\HM; Brinvilliens
EM[*mistranscription*] 285.1 He] [*no indent*] HM1,HM3; [*indent*] HM2 285.2 eve,]
HM2; ~; HM1 285.4,8 Light/Her] [*indent*] HM2; [*no indent*] HM1 285.4 weave:]
EM; ~; HM1; ~;— HM?2; ~— HM?3 285.6 skies;] HM1,HM3; ~, HM2 285.7
sweetness,] HM2; ~^ HM1

THE AGE OF THE ANTONINES (pp. 286–87)

At the end of March 1877, when Melville sent his brother-in-law John C.
Hoadley (1818–86) an earlier, not very different, version of "The Age of
the Antonines" (transcribed in the textual notes below), he wrote that he
had just "found" the poem ("came across it—in a lot [batch] of papers"),
but remembered that the "lines were suggested by a passage in Gibbon
(Decline & Fall). . . . Turn to 'Antonine' &c in index." He also claimed,
"What the deuce the thing means I dont know." The first paragraph of
Edward Gibbon's *Decline and Fall of the Roman Empire* (1776–88; London:
Murray, 1846; Sealts, no. 223b) summarizes at least part of what "sug-
gested" Melville's "lines":

> In the second century of the Christian Æra, the Empire of Rome com-
> prehended the fairest part of the earth, and the most civilized portion
> of mankind. The frontiers of that extensive monarchy were guarded by
> ancient renown and disciplined valour. The gentle, but powerful, influence
> of laws and manners, had gradually cemented the union of the provinces.
> Their peaceful inhabitants enjoyed and abused the advantages of wealth
> and luxury. The image of a free constitution was preserved with decent

reverence: the Roman senate appeared to possess the sovereign authority, and devolved on the emperors all the executive powers of government. During a happy period (A.D. 98–180) of more than fourscore years, the public administration was conducted by the virtue and abilities of Nerva, Trajan, Hadrian, and the two Antonines. It is the design of this, and of the two succeeding chapters, to describe the prosperous condition of their empire; and afterwards, from the death of Marcus Antoninus, to deduce the most important circumstances of its decline and fall; a revolution which will ever be remembered, and is still felt by the nations of the earth.

The poem Melville sent Hoadley (an accomplished Latinist) may have been part of an ongoing political, philosophical, and religious dialogue between the two. (On Melville's relations with Hoadley, see Parker 2002, e.g., pp. 363–65.)

DISCUSSIONS. 286.0 *Antonines*] The two Antonine emperors were Antoninus Pius (reigned A.D. 138–61) and Marcus Aurelius (reigned A.D. 161–80). In *Clarel,* Ungar speaks feelingly about the virtue and wisdom of Marcus Aurelius in not contriving any "secular reform" (4.20.51). In the printed table of contents the second "the" of the title is capitalized; but this capital is not in HM or EM and is probably a compositor's insertion or mistake (cf. the discussion at 284.0).

286.1 Millennial years] NN follows the copy-text in not printing a hyphen between these words, since the absence of a hyphen in T probably represents Melville's restoration of the reading in his manuscript. The hyphen in EM was not, as punctuation ordinarily was, penciled in by Melville before being inked in by his wife; and there is no hyphen in the transcript he sent to John Hoadley in 1877. NN also retains the capital "M" in the copy-text, reduced to lowercase in T (see p. 610 above).

286.5 O summit] See the discussion at 260.41,42 above.

286.10 Solstice of Man] Ancient Sicilians believed that fourteen days before the winter solstice the kingfisher laid and incubated its eggs on the sea's surface, which then remained calm.

286.17 reasoned . . . feast] In his 1857–58 lecture "Statues in Rome," Melville is reported to have said of the Pompeiians: "It was not unusual for them at their feasts to talk upon the subject of death and other like mournful themes forbidden to modern ears at such scenes" (NN *Piazza Tales* volume, p. 407). (The comma after "feast" in T is not adopted here, since it seems more likely to be a compositorial insertion than a change on Melville's part from the unpointed reading in EM and the transcript sent to Hoadley in 1877.)

286.22 parvenu] NN adopts the spelling in EM, since "parvenue" in HM was probably Melville's error; it seems doubtful that he would have intended the feminine form in the context.

287.25 law . . . will] Although these words are followed by commas in the copy-text, NN adopts the EM reading, judging that in this case Melville intended the omission of the commas.

EMENDATIONS. 286.2 lines,] EM; ~^ HM *286.5 O^ summit] EM; ~, ~ HM 286.6 reigned,] EM; ~^ HM 286.11 friendly] T; various HM 286.12 fellowly] T; tolerant HM 286.12 shrines,] EM; ~^ HM 286.14 Antonines!] EM; ~. HM 286.16 sought,] EM; ~; HM 286.19 declines—] EM; ~: HM *286.22 parvenu] EM; parvenue HM 287.24 Antonines!] EM; ~. HM *287.25 law^ made will^] EM; ~, ~ ~, HM 287.27 Emperor] EM; lawgiver HM 287.28 best.] EM; ~! HM 287.29 America's] T; the future's HM

TEXTUAL NOTES: INSCRIPTION STAGES. At least three stages of inscription-revision: A (nonextant pre-fair-copy stage); B (black ink on yellow paper enclosed in Melville's March 31, 1877, letter to John C. Hoadley); C (tan-gray ink on thinner paper).

TEXTUAL NOTES: SUBSTANTIVES. 286.0–287.30 *The . . . Antonines*] HM2(C); [*see following description of superseded stage B text*] [*HM enclosed a draft of "The Age of the Antonines" in his March 31, 1877, letter to his brother-in-law John C. Hoadley (Davis and Gilman, no. 212; Correspondence, pp. 451–55). HM's letter, poem, and "P.S. to the Note" (i.e., to the letter) are inscribed in black ink, the letter on a piece of plain white unwatermarked stationery, the poem (revised in pencil and ink) on three leaves of yellow paper of the size HM habitually used for drafting his poems, and the "P.S. to the Note" on the versos of leaves 3 and 2 of the poem*]

> [*Superseded leaf 1(B)*]
> The Age of the Antonines
> ————"———— [*beginning device*]
> 1. [*the positioning of the part number suggests it may have been added after HM's inscription of the first stanza*]
> While hope awaits Millnial[*i.e.,* Millenial] years,
>   Though dim be now [*then* Though now *and one or two undeciphered erased words, perhaps constituting more than one reading, then* Though dim of late] the signs,
> Back to the past a glance be cast—
>   The Age of the Antonines!
> Oh, [*the comma added later*] summit of fate and zenith of time,
>   When a pagan gentleman reigned,
> And the olive was nailed to the inn of the world,
>   Nor the peace of the just was feigned.
>   A halcyon age—afar it shines
>   The imperial age of the Antonines!
> [*Superseded leaf 2(B)*]

2.
Hymns to the nation's federate gods
    Went up from friendly shrines;
No demagogue beat the pulpit-drum
    In the age of the Antonines!
Ere the sting was dreamed to be taken from death—
        Ere the saving of scamps [*then ?churls then an undeciphered erased*
        word, then another, then scamps] was taught,
They reasoned of fate at the flowing feast
    Nor stifled the fluent thought: [*?colon altered from period*]
        We shuffle, we sham [*then* We sham, we shuffle], while faith
        declines:
    They were <u>frank</u> in the age of the Antonines!
[*Superseded leaf 3(B)*]
<u>3.</u>
Orders and grades and due degree—
    None felt how the leveller pines;
Yea, men were better than blatantly free
    In the age of the Antonines!
Under Law, made Will, the world reposed,
    And [*then cancel, then restore* And] the Ruler's right confessed,
For the Gods elected the Emperor then—
        The foremost of men [*then* foremost *and an undeciphered erased word*
        {*?*men *?*man}, *then* foremost of men] the best!
    Ah, might we read in the Future's signs
        The Past [*then* Past Age *then* Past] revived in [*then* of *then* in] the
        Antonines!
            ————"——— [*ending device*]

[*end of superseded stage B version*] HM1(B) 286.0–10 The . . . Antonines] [*HM leaf*
1(C); EM leaf 1] 286.1 faith forecasts] HM1,HM3; [*?*fools forecast] HM2 286.5
fate, O] HM1,HM?3,HM5; [*undeciphered erased word* {*?*life}], O HM2; history
HM4 286.6 pagan] HM1,HM3; heathen HM2 286.11–20 Hymns . . . Antonines]
[*HM leaf 2(C); EM leaf 2*] 286.11 friendly] T; popular HM1; various HM2,EM\
HM,EM2,HM5; brotherly HM3; cousinly HM4,EM*?*1[*EM seems to have penciled*
in cousinly *preparatory to asking HM which word he intends*] 286.12 fellowly] T;
tolerant HM 286.13 demagogue] HM1,HM4; blatherskite HM2; fanatic HM3
286.13 the] HM1,HM3; his HM2 286.13 pulpit-drum] HM1,HM3; hollow^drum
HM2 286.16 No] HM1,HM3,EM\HM; Never HM2,EM 286.16 pledged] HM2
[*in parentheses to indicate the revision is tentative; EM at first only penciled the word*
into her transcript]; promised HM1 286.18 fluent] HM2; primitive HM1 286.21–
287.30 Orders . . . Antonines] [*HM leaf 3(C); EM leaf 3*] 286.21 they kept]
HM3,HM5,EM,EM\HM3; observed HM1,HM4;EM\HM1; [*two undeciphered*
erased words] HM2; [*undeciphered erased word*] EM\HM2 286.22–23 Few . . . fee]

HM4; [*at stage C, as represented on HM leaf 3, lines 22–23 went through three substages of revision in which there were local variants*]

> [*first substage*]
> Few [*then undeciphered erased word, then* Few *then* None *then* Few] felt
>   how the leveller [*then* parvenue *?then* leveller *?then both variants canceled*
>   *before next substage*] pines;
> Factories none, no crippled and free [*then insert three or four undeciphered*
>   *erased words above this second line before canceling all the first substage words,*
>   *now or after supplanting them with the second substage's variants*]
> [*second substage*]
> To the [*?*Proud] Man they built no shrines
> No lawmakers took the lawless one's [*then* ones'] fee
> [*then explicitly or tacitly cancel the second substage variants and supplant them*
>   *with the third substage readings*]
> [*third substage*]
> Few [*then* None] felt how the parvenue [*then add or provisionally substi-*
>   *tute* leveller] pines [*while ink inscribing, add comma*]
> No lawmakers [*alter to* lawmaker] took the lawless one's [*then* ones' *then*
>   one's] fee

HM1–3 286.22 parvenu] HM?2[*see also next entry*],EM3; parvenu leveller HM?1,EM1; leveller EM2 *286.22 parvenu] EM; parvenue HM
    287.27 Emperor] HM?2,EM[?\HM],EM[*ink-inscribed over penciled (?by HM)*
then erased Emperor *that was inserted into the blank space left when EM made her origi-*
nal transcription of the leaf]; ruler HM1; President HM3,HM?5[*?reinstated as possible*
variant after being canceled]; lawgiver HM4[*?and both* lawgiver *and* Emperor *were*
initially left uncanceled and unerased, thus causing EM to be uncertain as to HM's final
choice] 287.29 America's] HM2,HM4,EM\HM1,EM\HM3,EM2,T; the future's
HM1,HM3,HM5,EM1[*in EM, there is no apostrophe in* futures],EM\HM2,EM\
HM4,EM3 287.30 The Age restored] HM2; A return of the Age HM1

TEXTUAL NOTES: ACCIDENTALS. *286.1 Millennial^years] HM; Millenial-years
EM[*the M mended, though it seems already to have been a capital*]; millenial^years
T 286.2 lines,] EM; ~^ HM 286.3 cast—] HM2; ~^ HM1 286.4 Antonines!]
HM2,EM2; ~^ HM1; ~: EM1 *286.5 O^ summit] EM; ~, ~ HM 286.6 reigned,]
EM; ~^ HM 286.8 Nor] [*no indent*] HM1,HM3; [*indent*] HM2 286.9 A] [*indent*]
HM1,HM3; [*?no indent*] HM2[*above line 9 in his transcript, either HM queried himself*
or EM penciled the query 2 lines indent *as he decided how to handle the indention of*
lines 9 and 10 (and, by extension, that of the last two lines of each stanza)] 286.9 hal-
cyon] HM; halycon T 286.10 Solstice] [*no indent*] HM2; [*indent*] HM1 286.11
nations'] HM,T; ~^ EM 286.12 shrines,] EM; ~^ HM 286.13 pulpit-drum] [*see*
substantives] 286.14 Antonines!] EM; ~. HM 286.16 No] [*no indent*] HM1,HM3;
[*indent*] HM2 286.16 Paradise] HM2[*the s has also been mended*]; paradise HM1

286.16 sought,] EM2; ~; HM,EM1 *286.17 feast^] HM; ~, T 286.19 We] [*indent*]
HM1,HM3[*above line 19, in HM, EM queries whether 2 lines (i.e., lines 19 and 20) are
to be indented*]; [*no indent*] HM?2 286.19 We sham] [*unable to decipher* sham *EM left
space for the two words, penciled them into her transcript below line 20, then inked them
into the space she had left*] 286.19 declines—] EM; ~: HM 286.20 They] [*no indent*]
HM2[*EM pencils out above* They]; [*indent*] HM1 286.22 pines,] HM2; ~; HM1
286.23 lawmaker] HM,EM; law-maker T[*probably a misreading of EM's hand*]

    287.24 Antonines!] EM2; ~. HM; ~: EM1 *287.25 law^ made will^] EM; ~,
~ ~, HM 287.28 The] [*no indent*] HM2[*EM pencils out above* The]; [*indent*] HM1
287.28 best.] EM; ~! HM 287.29 Ah] [*indent*] HM2[*EM pencils in above* Ah]; [*no
indent*] HM1 287.29 America's] [*see substantives*]

HERBA SANTA (pp. 288–90)

Herba santa is the pharmacological name for many weeds but apparently
not for tobacco, and Melville plays on its actual and imaginable benign
potencies. In the Hendricks House *Omoo,* Harrison Hayford claims: "No
author has paid more frequent or heartfelt homage to tobacco than Mel-
ville. Scarcely a one of his books is without at least a sentence in its honor.
. . . Tobacco is an agent of 'lenitive and calm,' and the shared smoke is
Melville's repeated ritual of sociality. Ahab's pitching overboard his pipe
is a major gesture" (p. 382). Other tributes to tobacco by Melville occur in
Omoo (chap. 41), *Mardi* (chap. 121), *Redburn* (chap. 54), *White-Jacket* (chap.
91), *Moby-Dick* (chaps. 10–11, 30), the first section of "The Paradise of
Bachelors and the Tartarus of Maids," "I and My Chimney" (both in the
NN *Piazza Tales* volume, pp. 316–23, 352–77), and *The Confidence-Man*
(chap. 30).

Discussions. 288.5 autumn's Indian air] Indian summer, when tobacco is cured
("hazed" in line 4).

    288.10 Love . . . divine] The reference is both to John 3:16 ("For God so loved
the world . . . ") and to such passages as John 13:34 ("A new commandment I
give unto you, That ye love one another . . . "), as well as to the accounts of the
Last Supper in Matthew 26:26–28, Mark 14:22–24, and Luke 22:19–20, on which
differing interpretations (lines 12–13) of Christian communion ("supper divine")
are based.

    288.14 more,] NN retains the comma in HM, though its omission in EM
could possibly have been deliberate.

    289.20 hod—] NN emends the comma in HM and EM to the dash in T,
which does not seem a likely compositorial substitution (cf. the discussion at
261.58 above).

289.23 *Truce of God*] The Truce of God was the one the Church declared in 1041 in an attempt to limit local armed hostilities, at least during Lent and the more important festivals. Confirmed by the Lateran Council in 1179, agreed to by Italy, France, England, and other European countries, that Truce of God was less often honored than broken.

289.24 Calumet] The ornamented pipe of the American Indians, shared in ceremonies, often those for peace (see also line 52).

289.25 Raleigh's find] Sir Walter Raleigh (ca. 1552–1618) brought tobacco from the American Indians (line 5) back to England and Ireland in the late sixteenth century.

289.27 Gilead's] See Jeremiah 8:22 ("Is there no balm in Gilead?") and 46:11.

289.29 Insinuous, thou,] NN retains the copy-text commas, inferring that their absence in EM was Melville's oversight as he was punctuating that transcript, perhaps because he was concentrating on correcting his wife's misreading of "thou" as "now".

289.33 foredone] NN follows Melville's manuscript spelling (also in EM), judging that "fordone" in T is probably a compositorial alteration.

289.34 Gold . . . pain:] NN does not retain the quotation marks around this sentence in Melville's manuscript, since it is clear that his later intention, here and in other poems, was to render unspoken thoughts without such marks, as this phrase appears in both EM and T. See p. 613 above.

289.35 thou,] NN retains the copy-text comma, although its omission in EM (matching the first reading in Melville's manuscript) might not be an oversight.

289.38 Saint Martin's summer] Unseasonably warm weather in the Northern Hemisphere around St. Martin's Day, November 11—which also happened to be the day of the Roman Vinalia, the feast of Bacchus, so Martin came to be known as the patron saint of drunkards and innkeepers.

289.42,46–48 once^/weed^/woo,/man^] NN follows the punctuation in EM, because the fact that these four readings (three without, and one with, a comma) are the same as those in his superseded ink draft strongly suggests that they amount to Melville's restorations of his earlier readings as he was punctuating his wife's transcript. Also arguing for the deliberateness of the three omissions of commas is the fact that they occur within a seven-line stanza that Melville was otherwise carefully repunctuating.

290.52 Peace] NN adopts the capitalized word from Elizabeth Shaw Melville's transcript (she also inked this change into HM) as more likely to represent Melville's final intention than the lowercase word in his hastily penciled manuscript. See p. 610 above.

EMENDATIONS. 288.4 hazed^] EM; ~— HM 288.8[*part number*] II] EM; 2 HM 288.9 selves] EM; Selves HM 288.17 thee!] EM; ~. HM *289.20 hod—] T; ~, HM 289.21 laborers] EM; laborors HM 289.23 *Truce of God*] EM; [*not underlined*]

HM 289.27 heal,] EM; ~— HM 289.29 through] EM; thro' HM 289.31 sin,] EM;
~— HM 289.34 brooding,] EM; ~— HM *289.34 ^Gold . . . pain:^] EM; "~ . . .
~," HM 289.34 ease] T; cure HM 289.38 Saint Martin's] EM\HM; An Indian
HM 289.39 this last] EM\HM; thy mild HM 289.39 plead,] EM; ~^ HM 289.40
the first] EM\HM; another HM 289.40 first,] T; ~^ EM\HM 289.40 creed,]
EM; ~— HM 289.41 man—] EM; ~, HM *289.42 once^] EM; ~, HM *289.46
weed^] EM; ~, HM *289.47 woo,^] EM; ~,— HM *289.48 man^] EM; ~, HM
290.49 soul!] EM; ~, HM 290.49 and in] EM; within HM 290.50,52 Rehearse/
Inhaling] [*indent*] EM; [*no indent*] HM 290.50 Rehearse] EM\HM; Foredream
HM 290.50 release:] EM; ~^ HM *290.52 Peace.] EM; peace^ HM

TEXTUAL NOTES: INSCRIPTION STAGES. At least five stages of inscription-revision:
A (nonextant pre-fair-copy stage); Ba, Bb, and Bc (gray-tan ink); Bd (pencil).

TEXTUAL NOTES: SUBSTANTIVES. 288.0–7 *Herba . . .* calm] [*HM leaf 1(Bc)*] 288.0–8
Herba . . . afford] [*EM leaf 1*] 288.1[*part number precedes*] I] HM3; [*no part number*]
HM1; Part First HM2 288.3 dearer] HM,EM\HM; clearer EM[*mistranscription*]
288.4 stems] HM3; fields HM1; [*undeciphered erased word* {*?*hands}] HM2 288.5 In
autumn's] HM3; Hazed in Fall's HM1; In Fall's HM2 288.5 Indian] HM1,HM4;
Indian [*undeciphered erased word*] HM2; Indian Summer HM3 288.6 care]
HM1,HM3,HM5; pain HM2; passion HM4 288.8–13 II . . . began] [*HM leaf 2(Bc)*]
2 . . . began] 288.9–289.22 To . . . plod] [*EM leaf 2*] 288.13 Then] HM1,HM4,EM\
HM3; [*undeciphered erased word* {*?*As}] HM2,EM\HM1; [*undeciphered erased word*
{*?*What}] HM3,EM\HM2; [*EM left blank space awaiting HM's final decision*] EM
288.14–289.24 Effectual . . . come] [*HM leaf 3(?Ba ?Bb)*]
    289.20 pen] HM3; loom HM1; [*undeciphered erased word*] HM2 289.23–35 In
. . . down] [*EM leaf 3*] 289.23 the] HM2; a HM1 289.25–36 IV . . . again] [*HM leaf
4(?Ba ?Bb)*] 289.25[*part number precedes*] IV] HM2; [*no part number*] HM1 289.26
this] HM2; thy HM1 289.27 Gilead's fails] HM2,EM2; Gilead's fail HM1; Gilead
fails EM1 289.28 charm] HM2; calm HM1 289.29 Insinuous] HM2; Insinuant
HM1 289.29 thou] HM,EM\HM; now EM[*misreading*] 289.31 Some] HM1,HM3;
Many HM2 289.31 repinings] HM2,EM2; repining HM1,EM1 289.31 some
from] HM1,HM6; a few from HM2,HM4; yea, [*undeciphered erased word* {*?*even}]
[*?*from] HM3; yea, [*two undeciphered erased words* {*?*as much}] [*?*from] HM5 289.34
Gold] HM1,HM3; Pelf HM2 289.34 ease] ?Tg\HM[*this variant is from the penciled,
circled (with a pointing finger inside the circle), uncanceled, and unerased text-line HM
inscribed at an indeterminate time at the bottom of HM leaf 1 of "The Marchioness of
Brinvilliers"*: Gold would ease this pain {*ease mended, perhaps altered from eaze and
underlined, probably to indicate the word needs tending to, but perhaps to indicate this is
the only word in the line to be altered*}; *HM may well have inscribed this line when he
was revising proof, since ease appears otherwise only in "Timoleon"*],T; cure HM,EM;
help EM\HM 289.35 soothest] HM2; smoothest HM1 289.35 smoothest] HM2;
soothest HM1 289.36–48 Till . . . bleed] [*EM leaf 4*] 289.36 again.] HM2; [*following*

line 36 in HM are two canceled lines: Benignant! that canst so beguile, / And Want to Fortune all but {*then cancel, then restore, without inscribing any alternative reading,* all but} reconcile.] HM1 289.37–48 Even . . . bleed] [*HM leaf 5(Bb)*] 289.37–48 Even . . . bleed] HM2; [*see following description of superseded stage Ba leaf*] [*Superseded leaf 5* {*"Note: The Cincinnati," Version 2 (Harvard MS Am 188 [386.B.8]), leaf 2 verso*} Even . . . bleed {*foliated (upper left corner pencil) 4; inscribed in ink, revised in pencil, except where specified*}]

> Even ruffians feel thee intercede,
>> In moods are undermined [*?then ?*Though soon in moods are undermined *?then* Though soon they fling thy plea behind *?then ?*Though soon thy plea they fling behind *?then ?*Though soon lose yet thy plea behind *?then ?*An Indian-summer in the mind *?then* Feel Indian-summer in the mind *?then* At unawares {*?then ?or at the same time* St. Martin's *though neither pair of words is canceled*} summer feel {*?then* shed *though neither verb is canceled*} in mind]; [*the nature and order of variant readings here is partly problematic because of the considerable number of words present*]
> They [*then* Yes, *then* Yea,] feel thy mild [*then* blest *then* fused *then, perhaps tacitly though not explicitly, restore* mild] evangel plead
> [*then cancel* Even . . . plead *with orange pencil and by covering over with no-longer-extant stage Bab patch*]
> As did the first [*then* did the first, *then* did another] apart from creed—
>> Be peaceful, man, be kind. [*then underline* Be . . . kind *and alter period to exclamation mark*]
> [*wide line-space*]
> IV. [*then* V.]
> Rejected once O Love divine,
> To come again, can this be thine?
> [*then, ink-transcribing from a nonextant draft, HM turns two lines into three:*
> Rejected once on higher plain
> O Love Divine, to come again
>> Can this be thine?
> *then pencil-alter* O Love Divine *to read, successively,* Celestial Love *then* O Love supreme *?then* O Love Divine *then* yea Christ divine *then* O Christ divine *?then* O Love supreme *then either* O Love Divine *or* O Love Supreme *both of which readings remain largely canceled by being lined-through, though not canceled are the restoration marks below* supreme *and* Divine *and not canceled either are both instances of the penciled* O]
> Again to come, and win us too,
>> In likeness of a [*then* Yea, win us by a *then* In likeness of a] weed
> That as a god didst vainly woo,
>> As man—[*then cancel dash with pencil and ink*] didst vainly bleed?

[*then pencil-add an ending device—thereby implying, perhaps, that earlier the poem had another ending*]

[*then in blue pencil cancel the whole leaf*] HM1(Ba) 289.38 Saint Martin's] HM1,HM?3[*see accidentals*],EM\HM; An Indian HM2,HM4,HM7,EM; The Indian HM5; [*two undeciphered erased words* {?An Indian}] HM?6 289.38 summer] HM1,HM4; season HM2; Summer HM3[*coincides with HM4 reading in preceding 'entry*] 289.38 in] HM1,HM3; of HM2 289.39 this last] EM\HM; thy mild HM 289.40 As . . . creed] HM,EM\HM; [*inadvertently, EM omitted this text-line, so HM copied it into her transcript, with variants described in the two following entries*] EM 289.40 the first] EM\HM; another HM 289.40 creed] HM,EM\HM1,EM\HM3; [*undeciphered erased word*] EM\HM2 289.42[*part number precedes*] V] HM3; [*no part number*] HM1; IV HM2 289.48 more] HM2; didst HM1 289.48 bleed?] HM1,HM3; [*perhaps because he had temporarily given up on devising a satisfactory concluding section, HM penciled, then canceled and erased both End and a terminal device at the bottom of HM leaf 5*] HM2

    290.49–52 VI . . . Peace] [*HM leaf 6(Bd); EM leaf 5*] 290.49–52 VI . . . Peace] [*after provisionally deleting an earlier ending to the poem, HM redrafted in pencil the concluding stanza that appears on HM leaf 6; on HM leaf 6, EM erased, then inked in, without punctuation, HM's wording (including revisions); at the top right of HM leaf 6, HM in pencil added and circled HM copy*] 290.49[*part number precedes*] VI] HM2; [*no part number*] HM1 290.49 Forbear] HM2; But thou HM1 290.49 and in] EM[*explicit, visible HM authority for the variant does not appear on either HM leaf 6 or EM leaf 5*]; within HM 290.50 Rehearse] HM2,EM\HM1,EM,EM\HM3; Foredream HM1,HM3,EM\HM2 290.50 long] HM2; [*undeciphered erased word— perhaps only a harder-to-read* long *that HM retranscribed so EM could decipher his intent*] HM?1 290.52 passive] HM4; oblivious HM?1,HM3; tranquil HM2

TEXTUAL NOTES: ACCIDENTALS. 288.4 hazed^] EM[*see substantives at the beginning of line 5*]; ~— HM 288.5 autumn's] HM,EM; Autumn's HM\EM 288.8[*part number precedes*] II] EM; 2 HM 288.9 selves] EM2; Selves HM,EM1 288.12 wine!] HM,EM2; ~; EM1 288.13 feuds] HM,EM2; fueds EM1[*mistranscription*] *288.14 more,] HM2; ~^ HM1,EM 288.15 Herb] [*EM could not at first decipher HM's H and left a blank space for it*] 288.17 thee!] EM; ~. HM 288.18 tribal] HM2; tribxx[*undeciphered erased misspelling*] HM1 288.19 wouldst] HM; woulds't T

    *289.20 hod—] T; ~, HM 289.21 laborers] EM; laborors HM 289.21 dumb;] HM2; ~, HM1 289.22 plod,] HM,T; ~^ EM 289.23 the *Truce of God*] [*Truce of God underlined*] EM2; the truce of God [*not underlined*] HM1; the Truce of God [*not underlined*] HM2; [*EM initially left blank space for some reason, possibly because she was not sure of which wording HM intended*] EM1 289.25[*part number precedes*] IV] EM; [*underlined*] HM 289.25 Raleigh's] HM,EM2; Raliegh's EM1 289.27 heal,] EM; ~— HM *289.29 Insinuous, thou,] HM; Insinuous^ now^ EM 289.29 through] EM; thro' HM 289.31 sin,] HM1,EM; ~— [*or comma-dash*] HM2 *289.33 foredone] HM,EM\HM; fordone T; [*EM left a blank space for HM*] *to make clearer the word he intended*] EM 289.33 care,] HM; ~^ EM 289.34 brooding,] EM; ~— HM *289.34 ^Gold . . . pain:^] EM; ^~ . . . ~,^ HM1; "~ . . . ~," HM2 *289.35 thou,] HM2; ~^ HM1,EM 289.38 Saint] EM\HM; St. HM 289.38 summer] [*see substantives, the second entry for line 38*] 289.39 plead,] EM; ~^ HM 289.40 first,] EM2,T; ~^ EM\HM,EM1,EM3[*?comma inadvertently erased*] 289.40 creed,] EM; ~— HM 289.41 man—] EM2; ~, HM,EM1 289.42[*part number*] V] EM; [*underlined*] HM *289.42 once^] HM1,EM; ~, HM2 *289.46 weed^] EM; ~, HM *289.47 woo,^] HM1,EM; ~,— HM2 *289.48 man^] HM1,HM?3,EM[*the comma is half erased*]; ~, HM2[*see substantives, the second entry for line 48*]

290.49 Forbear,] HM,EM; ~^ HM\EM 290.49 soul!] EM; ~, HM 290.50,52 Rehearse/Inhaling] [*indent*] EM; [*no indent*] HM 290.50 release:] EM; ~^ HM,HM\EM 290.51 talismanic] HM,EM2; [*?talineansic*] HM\EM,EM?1[*EM seems to have mistranscribed or misunderstood HM's clarification of his intent, then copied the misapprehension into her transcript*] *290.52 Peace] EM,HM\EM; peace HM 290.52 Peace.] EM; ~^ HM,HM\EM

VENICE (p. 291)

For Melville's observations on Venice during his visit there in 1857, see his journal entries for April 1–5 (*Journals,* pp. 117–20). As in many of the other poems in *Timoleon,* Melville here tried out various titles attributing the poem to another voice—"according to" "?Shakespeare" or "?Spinoza"— before settling upon the final title.

DISCUSSION. 291.0[*section-title*] FRUIT . . . AGO] That Melville wished to have this section-title here is shown by his adding it to EM on a separate leaf and his inserting it at this point in his wife's transcript of the table of contents (see p. 573 above). Many of the poems in this section may have been intended for inclusion in the volume that Melville tried to publish in 1860 (see pp. 449–50 above).

EMENDATIONS. *291.0[*section-title*] FRUIT . . . AGO] EM\HM; [*no section-title*] HM 291.3 blue abyss,] T; gulfy main^ HM 291.4 Up-builds] T; Up-Builds HM 291.5 arcade,] EM; ~— HM 291.8 Evincing] EM\HM; Showing HM 291.9 Laborious] EM\HM; Building HM 291.10 Advanced] [*indent*] EM\HM; [*no indent*] HM 291.11 A prouder] EM\HM; Another HM

TEXTUAL NOTES: INSCRIPTION STAGES. At least four stages of inscription-revision: A (nonextant pre-fair-copy stage); B (superseded tan-gray ink draft); Ca (pencil drafts of eight of the poem's final twelve lines); Cb (pencil).

TEXTUAL NOTES: SUBSTANTIVES. *291.0[*section-title*] FRUIT . . . AGO] EM\ HM[Fruit of Travel / Long ago *on a separate leaf, triple-underlined; as a matter of design, NN does not place the section-title on a separate page*]; [*no section-title*] HM;

[*section-title in small capitals and on the recto of a separate leaf*] T 291.0–12 Venice . . .
palaces] [*HM leaf 1(Cb); Superseded HM leaf 1(B); EM leaf 1*] 291.0–12 Venice . . .
palaces] HM2(C); [*see following description of superseded HM leaf 1(B)*] [*at the end of
stage B, HM prepared an ink transcript of "Venice," complete with title, though with no
foliation number, a transcript he then proceeded to revise in pencil (as specified here, below),
until he decided to do another complete draft (in pencil), and cancel the stage B leaf, not
with his customary X-ing-out, but by pinning it behind the stage C leaf*]

Venice [*underlined; then, after the poem's first line was revised:*
Venice / (According to {*?*Shakespeare *?*Spinoza})]
[*no beginning device*]
In patience of its pigmy [*then* insect] heart [*then cancel* In . . . heart *and
replace with* With wondrous {*then* Pantheist} potency of will]
The coral [*then* zoophyte] insect [*then* creature *then* insect *then no vari-
ant left uncanceled*] of the Tropic [*then* Coral] Sea,
Slow [*then inscribe, then cancel a vertical line that would seem intended to
clarify for EM that in* Slow *he intends an* l] toiling in the gulfy deeps,
Upbuilds his beautious [*then* wondrous *?then (tacitly)* beautious *then*
won {*?beginning of* wondrous} →*then,* marvellous *then* gardened *?then
(?tacitly)* beautious *then* marvellous] gallery
And [*add horizontal line at left to indicate this text-line is to be indented*]
bright arcade,
A city [*then* A {*?*garden} *then* Sea-city *then* A city] inwrought with
richest skill
Of marble garlandry—
Showing what a worm can do.
[*line-space*]
Laboring in a shallower wave,
Though scarce with other art [*then* With self-same art developed more
{*then* full} *then* Though scarce with other art *then* With like sponta-
neous art],
A prouder worm [*followed by an undeciphered scratched-out word or begin-
ning of a word, which was replaced by* evinced his might *then by* evinced
Pan's will *then by* evinced his might *then by* evinced Pan's might]
When Venice rose in reefs of palaces.
———"——— [*ending device*]

[*this stage B leaf was not explicitly canceled, but rather supplanted after such intermediate
stage Ca draftings of whole lines and particular phrases as those described here immediately
below*] HM1(B) 291.1,2,4,5,6,9,10,11 Pantheist energy . . . Pan's might] HM2(Cb);
[*see following description of stage Ca draftings of lines and portions of lines; these stage Ca
versions are presented here in interpreted facsimile, and should be understood as temporally
preceding those in the list of substantives that follows the interpreted facsimile*] [*Superseded
HM leaf 1(Ca)* {"Buddha" HM leaf 1 verso} Advanced . . . might {*the trial lines and*

portions of lines on this superseded leaf are inscribed in pencil, as well as separated from
each other by penciled horizontal lines and circlings; with the exception of two words that
begin line 171 of "Timoleon" (a penciled Me reassure *circled with orange pencil), the trial*
wordings are from "Venice" and are canceled by lining out with blue or orange pencil before
the whole leaf is canceled with an orange penciled X}]

> Advanced in self same art
> Another agent proved m [*then immediately cancel* m] Pans might [*this ver-*
>   *sion of lines 10–11 is canceled with blue pencil*]
> [*horizontal separation line*]
> <u>Up building</u> from the / gulfy deeps [*this version of line 4 is canceled with*
>   *orange pencil*]
> Pantheist energy [*this portion of line 1 is pencil-circled, then canceled with*
>   *blue pencil*]
> [*horizontal separation line*]
> Me reassure [*this beginning of "Timoleon" line 171 is circled with orange pen-*
>   *cil and not explicitly canceled till final cancellation of this leaf*]
> The little craftsman [*this portion of line 2, pencil-circled and finally canceled*
>   *with blue pencil, is inscribed to the right and slightly above the level of* Me
>   reassure]
> [*horizontal separation line*]
> A city inwrought with many a freak [*this version of line 6 is canceled with*
>   *blue pencil*]
> [*horizontal separation line*]
> Another agent proved Pan's _____ [*this version of line 11 ends with an*
>   *underline indicating a word yet to be filled in; the line is canceled with blue*
>   *pencil*]
>   <u>long</u> arcade [*this portion of line 5 is pencil-circled, then canceled with blue*
>   *and orange pencil*]
> [*horizontal separation line*]
> Building in another wave
> Advanced in kindred art [*this version of lines 9–10 is canceled with blue*
>   *pencil*]
> [*horizontal separation line*]
> Another agent proved Pan' might [*this version of line 11 is canceled with*
>   *blue pencil*]

[*this whole leaf is canceled with an orange penciled X*] HM1(Ca)[*the following described*
variants are from stage Cb and later] 291.0 Venice] HM2; [*no title*] HM1 291.1 energy]
HM1,HM3; potency HM2 291.3 Strenuous] HM3; Up-xxxxxx HM1; Up=
building HM2 291.3 blue abyss,] T; gulfy [*undeciphered erased word* {?deeps}]^
HM1; gulfy main^ HM2,HM5[*reinscribed by EM*],EM; [*two undeciphered erased*
words {?blue profound}]^ HM3; [?depths] [?profound]^ HM4; gulfy [*undeciphered*
erased word]^ EM\HM1; blue profound^ EM\HM2 291.4 Up-builds] HM2[*see*

also accidentals]; Builds up HM1 291.4 marvellous] HM1,HM3; [*undeciphered erased word* {?great}] HM2 291.6 Erections freaked] HM2; A [*two undeciphered erased words* {?city inwrought}] HM1 291.6 fringe] HM3; freak HM1; loop HM2 291.8 Evincing] EM\HM3,EM3,HM\EM2; Showing HM,EM1; xxxxing EM\HM1; Revealing EM\HM2,EM2,HM\EM1 291.8 do.] [*line-space follows*] HM1,HM3; [*what seems to be a terminal device indicates that at one point HM considered ending the poem after line 8*] HM2 291.9 Laborious] EM\HM2,EM3; Laboring HM1; Building HM2,EM1; Industrious EM\HM1,EM2 291.9 a shallower] HM2; another HM1,EM,EM\HM2[*not copied back into HM*]; a tideless EM\HM1 291.11 A prouder] EM\HM; Another HM

TEXTUAL NOTES: ACCIDENTALS. 291.3 abyss,] [*see substantives*] 291.4 Up-builds] T; Up-Builds HM[*see substantives*]; Up^builds EM1; Upbuilds EM2 291.4 marvellous] HM; marvelous T 291.5,7 And/Of] [*indent*] HM2; [*no indent*] HM1 291.5 arcade,] HM1,EM; ~— HM2 291.10 Advanced] [*indent*] EM\HM; [*no indent*] HM

IN A BYE-CANAL (pp. 292–93)

For the first five days of April 1857, Melville explored Venice, often with Antonio, the "affable young man" he engaged as a guide for the last three days (*Journals,* p. 118). In his journal entry for April 5, he exclaimed, "Floating about philosophizing with Antonio the Merry. Ah, it was Pausillippo" (p. 120)—that is, the cessation of care that he had not found at the actual Posillipo, near Naples (p. 102; see his poem with that name, pp. 297–99 above). One hint for "In a Bye-Canal" may be found in his record of a stroll on April 5: "Walked to Rialto. Looked up and down G. Canal. Wandered further on. Numbers of beautiful women. The rich brown complexions of Titian's women drawn from nature, after all. (Titian was a Venetian) The clear, rich, golden brown. The clear cut features, like a cameo. — The vision from the window at end of long, narrow passage" (p. 119). "In a Bye-Canal" is one of the poems for which many variants survive. Melville considered several titles, among them "Don Juan" and "Joseph Andrews" (either or both followed by the words "In a Bye-Canal"), and a subtitle "(How it fared there with a reputed libertine, as told me by himself.)" He also seriously considered changing the poem's narrative point-of-view from first to third person (see the revisions in lines 8, 10, and 11). And his revisions of lines 13, 14, 15–16, and 21–22 illuminate his process of altering words, lines, and rhetorical focus.

DISCUSSIONS. 292.0 *Bye-Canal*] NN retains the hyphenated form as it stands in HM and EM, though Melville's wife did not include the hyphen in her transcript of the table of contents, nor did Melville use it when he recopied the title in that document.

292.6 Jael the wiled one] In the biblical story, Jael, the seductive wife of Heber, invited the already defeated general, Sisera, into her tent and, while he trustingly slept, clinched him to the ground with a tent peg through his temples (Judg. 4:2–21). Sisera is referred to in "The Frenzy in the Wake" (in *Battle-Pieces*, 97.11 above) and appears as a piece of allusive art in "The Bell-Tower" (NN *Piazza Tales* volume, p. 180); in *Clarel* (2.36.93), Jael is featured by Mortmain in his invoking of the names of deceptive females.

292.11 and, . . . see,] NN retains the commas in HM, judging that their omission in EM is probably not intentional.

292.16 nature . . . man] These words are capitalized in Melville's manuscript and in his wife's initial transcription; her change to lowercase was presumably directed by him (see p. 610 above).

293.26 This] The omission in EM of Melville's original quotation mark here appears to reflect Melville's intention, judging from its later deletion in his manuscript. Therefore NN leaves out the quotation mark here rather than adding one at the end of the poem. (See p. 613 above.)

EMENDATIONS. 292.3 calms far] EM\HM; dead calm HM 292.4 sight,] EM; ~: HM 292.9 Tinkles] EM\HM; Ripples HM 292.10 hark,] EM; ~! HM 292.10 response] HM\EM; responce HM 292.10 hear!] EM; ~. HM 292.13 scintillation,] EM; ~^ HM 292.14 basilisk] EM; bazalisk HM *292.16 nature] EM; Nature HM *292.16 man] EM; Man HM 292.21 noiselessly] EM; noislesly HM 292.22 lepers hand in] EM\HM; [*one or two undeciphered erased words*] in her HM 293.24 Hey! Gondolier,] T; Come, gondolier! HM 293.25 shooting] EM\HM; speeding HM 293.25 ran;] EM; ~, HM *293.26 ^This] EM; "~ HM 293.27 allow!] EM; ~. HM 293.28 sirens^] EM; ~, HM 293.30 Well,] EM; ~: HM 293.30 misses,] EM; ~^ HM 293.32 No! flee] EM\HM; No. Flee HM 293.33 wise,] EM; ~; HM

TEXTUAL NOTES: INSCRIPTION STAGES. At least four stages of inscription-revision: A (nonextant pre-fair-copy stage); B (tan-gray on thinner paper); Ca (pencil on clip); Cb (pencil on mount).

TEXTUAL NOTES: SUBSTANTIVES. 292.0–11 *In . . . see*] [*HM leaf 1(Bc)*] 292.0–12 *In . . . me*] [*EM leaf 1*] 292.0 *In a Bye-Canal*] HM2,HM9; [*no title or subtitle*] HM1; The [*undeciphered erased word*] HM?3; Don Juan HM?4; Joseph Andrews HM?5[*and either or both of* Don Juan *and* Joseph Andrews *perhaps considered at some point as being located* In a Bye-Canal]; Don Juan *or/and* Joseph Andrews *or/and* In a Bye-Canal *plus the subtitle* (How it fared there with a reputed libertine, as told to me by {*then told by then* told to me by *then* told me by} himself.) HM?6; The [*undeciphered erased word {?libertine ?boatman}*] HM?7[*see revisions HM made in lines 8, 10, and 11 before apparently deciding he would prefer not to go to the trouble of changing his rhymes in order to effect his changing of the poem's narrative point-of-*

view from first person to third]; In a Bye-Canal of Venice HM?8 292.1 swoon]
HM1,HM3,HM5; trance HM2,HM4 292.1 a trance of] HM1,HM?4,HM8; a
[*two or three undeciphered erased words {?swoon of}*] HM2; a [*two or three undeciphered
erased words {?standing ?brimming}*] HM?3; an oily HM?5; a [?mirror] HM?6;
a mirroring HM7 292.2 The] HM1,HM3; A HM2 292.3 calms far] HM1,EM\
HM,EM2; dead calm HM2,EM1; calm far HM\EM[*presumably inadvertent error
made in attempting to make HM concur with final state of EM*] 292.5 Dumb] HM2;
Even HM1 292.5 and] HM2; but HM1 292.5 night] [*HM also penciled night?
into the right margin of his transcript, possibly as a reminder to check the slaying time;
EM delayed transcribing and . . . night*] 292.6 wiled] HM1,HM4,HM6; duped
HM2; trapped HM3,HM5 292.7 A languid impulse] HM5; An impulse HM1; A
[?tranquil] impulse HM?2; An impulse languid HM?3; An impulse light HM?4
292.7 the oar] HM?3,HM6; the rythmic oar HM1,HM?4; rythmic oar HM?2;
oar HM?5 292.8 my] HM1,HM3,HM5; Carlo's HM2,HM4 292.8 indolent]
HM2; languorous HM1 292.9 Tinkles] EM\HM; Ripples HM 292.10 I hear]
HM1,HM3; is near HM2 292.11–14 A lattice . . . conjuration] HM2; [*see following
description of superseded stage Ba leaf*] [*Superseded HM leaf 1–2(Ba) {"The Parthenon"
HM leaf 4 verso} A lattice . . . leaf {inscribed in pencil}*]

> A lattice click [*then* clicks;] and, lo, I see,— [*the comma perhaps added
> after the dash and intended to replace it*]
> (Between the slats, and [*then* mute] summoning me)— [*the parentheses
> probably added after the dash*]
> What lovliest eyes of fascination [*then* conjuration *then* invitation *then*
> scintilation],
> What power [*then* terror *then* menace] of serpent [*then* basilisk]
> fascination!
> [*line-space*]
> But here [*then* But better *then* But sharper *then* But] to point the sequel
> brief,
> Best interline from another [*then* First interline from another *then*
> Insert here another ?*then* ?Let me insert another *then* Let me insert
> a private *then* Let me insert a timely *then* Let me insert a flying *then*
> Here {*then* Here ?we →*then* Here} to insert a flying *or* Here {*then*
> Here ?we →*then* Here} to insert another] leaf.

[*cancel* What menace . . . leaf *with pencil and green pencil and probably cover with stage
Bb patch; later cancel* A lattice . . . scintilation *with orange pencil*] HM1(Ba) 292.11
lo, I] HM1,HM3; [*no variant inscribed; it was probably at this point, as he looked ahead
to the difficulty of changing the rhyme word in line 12, that HM abandoned his specula-
tive altering of the poem's narrative point-of-view from first person to third*] HM→2
292.12–19 Between . . . in] [*HM leaf 2(Bc)*] 292.13–293.28 What . . . be] [*EM
leaf 2*] 292.14 What . . . of] HM3[*see also accidentals*]; What menace of bazalisk
HM1; In bazalisk glance of HM2 292.15 Fronted^] HM1,HM3; Well, [?fronted]

HM2 292.15 part] HM2; yea, and HM1 292.16 portents] HM1,HM3; perils HM2
292.16 peril] HM1,HM3; danger HM2 292.18 'Twixt] HM2; Betwixt HM1
292.18 whale's black] HM2; whale's HM1 292.18 the white] HM3; black HM1;
blue HM2 292.20–23 And . . . eye] HM2(C); [*see following description of superseded
stage Bc matter on HM leaf 2*]

> And there have I turned [*?then* And there {*?he ?have*} turned *then*
>   There turned I have *?then* {*?And* turned I have,} *then* And there have
>   turned], and silent [*then* collected *then* and silent] scanned her
> When followed me felt-footed [*then* stilettoing *then* the harpy,] Slander,
> Jaundiced [*then* Stealthiest *then* Jaundiced *then* Horrible *then* Stealthiest]
>   hag, the scorpion's kin.
> [*then add, in pencil, at top of HM leaf 2*
> But, daring more, I have withstood
> Xxxxxxx {*one or two undeciphered erased words, then* Ignorance and *then*
>   Intolerance and} the {*then cancel* Intolerance and the *and substitute* The
>   [*then add* ostracizing]} multitude
> *then erase* But, daring . . . multitude *and add, in ink, at bottom of leaf*
> And, daring more {*then* Temerarious *then* To save the Self}, I have
>   withstood]
> [*the following text-line—some version of* The ostracizing multitude *was
>   presumably inscribed on a state of HM leaf 3 that has not survived*]

[*then cancel, with pencil and orange and blue pencil, these versions of lines 20–23* And
there . . . withstood *then with a penciled brace and the word* Restore *mark at least lines
20–21* {And . . . Slander} *for restoration*] HM1(B) 292.20–23 And . . . eye] [*HM leaf
3.clip(Cb)*] 292.22 Envy and] HM2,EM\HM; Leprous HM1,EM 292.22 lepers
hand in] EM\HM; [*one or two undeciphered erased words*] in her HM 292.23 latticed]
HM?1,HM4; [*undeciphered erased word*] HM2; summoning HM3

   293.24–27 Hey . . . allow] [*HM leaf 3(Cc)* Come . . . allow] 293.24 Hey! Gon-
dolier,] T; Come, gondolier, HM1,EM; Come, gondolier! HM2 293.24 my] [*my
also appears, erased, at the bottom of the clip on HM leaf 3*] 293.25 Wake up] HM2;
[*two undeciphered erased words* {*?Awake here*}] HM1 293.25 And, shooting by, we]
EM\HM,EM2; And, speeding by, we HM1,HM3,HM5,EM1; [*?To shore then*]
we speeding HM2; And, darting by, we HM4 293.28–33 Sirens . . . son] [*HM leaf
4(B)*] 293.29–33 Sirens . . . son] [*EM leaf 3*] 293.28 true^sirens] HM3; sea-sirens
HM1; yea^sirens HM2 293.29 Sirens,] HM3; Palaced^ HM1; Sirens, palaced^
HM2 293.29 in] HM1,HM3; of HM2 293.30 Well,] EM; Well: HM1,HM3; Heart,
HM2 293.32 divine] HM2; renowned HM1 293.33 Brave, wise,] EM; Wise,
brave, HM1; Brave, wise; HM2 293.33 ^and] HM1,HM5; —[*undeciphered erased
word* {*?sea ?yea*}] HM2; [?^][*?undeciphered erased word*] HM?3; ^[?even] HM4

TEXTUAL NOTES: ACCIDENTALS. 292.0 *Bye-Canal*] HM2; bye-canal HM1 292.4
sight,] EM; ~: HM 292.9 hoar,] HM2,EM2; ~^ HM1,EM1 292.10 hark,] EM;

~! HM 292.10 response] HM\EM; responce HM 292.10 hear!] EM; ~. HM
*292.11 and, lo,] HM2; ~, ~^ HM?1,HM?3; ~^ ~, EM *292.11 see,] HM; ~^
EM 292.13 scintillation,] HM1,EM; ~^ HM2[*see substantive change* In *in line 14*]
292.14 basilisk] EM; bazalisk HM 292.15 Fronted] [*indent*] HM2; [*no indent*]
HM1 292.15 Fronted^] [*see substantives*] 292.15 part] [*see substantives*] *292.16
nature . . . man] EM2; Nature . . . Man HM,EM1 292.18 'Twixt] HM; ^~
T 292.19 in,] HM2; ~; HM1 292.21 noiselessly] EM; noislesly HM; noiselesly
HM\EM

   293.24 Hey! Gondolier,] [*see substantives*] 293.25 ran;] EM; ~, HM *293.26
^This] HM?2,EM2; "This HM1; ^this EM1 293.26 surely,] HM; ~^ EM 293.27
Naturalists] HM,EM; Naturatists HM\EM 293.27 allow!] EM; ~. HM 293.28
true^sirens] [*see substantives*] 293.28 sirens^] HM1,EM2; ~, HM2[*see substantives at
line 29*],EM1 293.29 Sirens,] [*see substantives*] 293.30 Well] [*line-space precedes*] HM2;
[*no line-space*] HM1 293.30 Well,] [*see substantives*] 293.30 misses,] EM; ~^ HM
293.31 Is] [*indent*] HM,EM; [*no indent*] T 293.32 No! flee] EM\HM; No. Flee HM
293.33 Brave, wise,] [*see substantives*] 293.33 ^and] [*see substantives*]

PISA'S LEANING TOWER (p. 294)

In Pisa on March 23, 1857, Melville recorded his impressions of the famed
tower, which was then some fourteen feet out of plumb: "Campanile like
pine poised just ere snapping. You wait to hear crash. Like Wordsworth's
moore cloud, it will move all together if it move at all, for Pillars all lean
with it. About 150 of 'em. There are houses in wake of fall" (*Journals*, p.
114; see also p. 489).

DISCUSSION. 294.3 colonades] In his manuscript, Melville first wrote "col-
lonades" and then changed the spelling to "colonades". NN retains this latter
copy-text spelling. Though "collonades" and "colonnades" are more common,
the *Oxford English Dictionary* lists "colonades" as current (Melville used it in his
1856–57 journal; see *Journals*, pp. 112, 119) and suggests a possible literary context
and usage in citing Pope's translation of the *Odyssey* (1725) with its "pompous
colonade."

EMENDATIONS. 294.0 *Pisa's*] EM\HM; The HM 294.4 master-work] T;
marvellous^work HM 294.5 tribes,] EM; ~^ HM 294.6 And,] EM; ~^ HM 294.7
plunge—] EM\HM; ~, HM 294.8 slide;] EM; ~! HM 294.9 Withholds] NN;
Witholds HM 294.10 verge,] EM; ~— HM

TEXTUAL NOTES: INSCRIPTION STAGES. At least three stages of inscription-revision:
A (nonextant pre-fair-copy stage); B (blue ink on thicker paper); C (brown
ink).

TEXTUAL NOTES: SUBSTANTIVES. 294.0–11 *Pisa's . . .* suicide] [*HM leaf 1(B); EM leaf 1*] 294.0 *Pisa's Leaning Tower*] EM\HM2; The Leaning Tower at Pisa HM2(C); The Leaning Tower HM3,EM\HM1; [*no title present*] HM1,EM 294.4 master-work] T; marvellous^work HM; dubious^work EM\HM(C)[*not copied back into HM*] 294.7 It thinks to] HM2(C); [*two or three undeciphered erased words {?fain would it}*] HM1 294.8 fain would] HM2(C); [*one or two undeciphered erased words*] HM1

TEXTUAL NOTES: ACCIDENTALS. 294.2,11 Fair/A] [*indent*] HM2; [*no indent*] HM1 294.3 trunk] [*in EM, HM mends the word for legibility*] *294.3 colonades] HM2; collonades HM1 294.4 The] [*no indent*] HM1,HM3; [*indent*] HM2 294.4 master= work] [*see substantives*] 294.5 tribes,] EM; ~^ HM 294.6 And,] EM; ~^ HM 294.7 plunge—] EM\HM(C); ~, HM 294.8 back—] HM1,HM3; ~, HM2 294.8 slide;] EM; ~! HM 294.9 'itself—] HM1,HM3(C); ~^ HM2 294.10 Hovering,] HM2(C); ~— HM1 294.10 verge,] HM2,EM; ~— HM1,HM3 294.11 suicide!] HM2(C); ~. HM1

IN A CHURCH OF PADUA (p. 295)

Visiting Padua on April 1, 1857, Melville in his journal entry noted no confessional boxes like the one in this poem, though he recorded seeing the "superb" Church of St. Anthony, the Scrovegni chapel with its frescoes by Giotto, and a "fine church," the Church of the Eremitani (*Journals*, pp. 117, 501). The image of a "diving-bell" (line 14) also appears in "In the Turret" (p. 39 above); the *Monitor*'s commander, Lieutenant Worden, is imagined "Sealed as in a diving-bell" (line 4) as he performs his dreadful duty.

DISCUSSIONS. 295.3 none.] NN follows the final reading in EM (with a period), since the punctuation in HM is superseded by Melville's later deletion of a line that had followed this one. Although the comma in T could represent Melville's restoration of the first reading in his wife's transcript, it is more likely to have been a misreading caused by the revised state of her transcript.

295.16,17 Descending/Where] In HM, "In" (in Melville's hand) is penciled at the left of line 16 and "out" (in his wife's hand) at the left of lines 15 and 17. NN follows these directions (with line 16 indented and line 17 not indented), though his wife reversed the indention of lines 16 and 17 in her transcript (which was followed in T).

EMENDATIONS. 295.1 flit,] EM; ~^ HM 295.3 fast,] EM; ~; HM 295.3 lattice] EM\HM; window HM *295.3 none.] EM; ~; HM 295.3 none.] [*line canceled following*] EM\HM; No lattice blind, nor cranny there. HM 295.4 punctured] EM\HM; lateral HM 295.4 holes^ minutely small^] EM; ~, ~ ~, HM 295.5 In lateral]

EM\HM; Punctured in HM 295.6 without,] EM; ~^ HM 295.7 an] EM\HM; the HM 295.7 if not declare] EM\HM; of all this care HM 295.9 within,] EM; ~; HM 295.10 hardly] EM\HM; never HM 295.12 yields] EM; yeilds HM 295.13 murmurer] EM; murmerer HM 295.15 hollows] EM\HM; gulfs HM 295.16 consciences^] EM; ~:— HM 295.17 Where . . . found] EM\HM; Better grope among the drowned HM

TEXTUAL NOTES: INSCRIPTION STAGES. At least two stages of inscription-revision: A (nonextant pre-fair-copy stage); B (tan-gray ink on thinner paper).

TEXTUAL NOTES: SUBSTANTIVES. 295.0–10 In . . . see] [HM leaf 1(B)] 295.0–11 In . . . sin] [EM leaf 1] 295.1 place] HM1,HM3,HM5; [?spot] HM2; space HM4 295.1 flit] HM6,EM\HM2; run HM1; [undeciphered erased word] HM2; lie HM3,EM; sleep HM?4,EM\HM1; [undeciphered erased word] HM5 295.2 box^ you see] HM1,HM5,T; box^ I see HM?2; box, behold HM?2; box^ I behold HM?4; box^ you mark EM\HM1; box^ is seen EM\HM2 295.3 lattice] EM\HM; window HM 295.3 none.] [following text-line canceled] EM\HM; [see following description of text-line canceled after EM had made her transcript] Nor [then No lattice, {then comma canceled, but restored in EM's transcript}] blind, nor cranny there. [the period becomes a comma in EM] HM,EM 295.4 punctured] EM\HM; lateral HM 295.5 In lateral] EM\HM; Punctured in HM 295.7 an] EM\HM; the HM 295.7 if not declare] EM\HM2; of all this care HM; and more declare EM\HM1 295.8 tremulous] HM2,HM5; trembling HM1,HM3; trembled HM4 295.10 hardly] EM\HM[not copied back into HM]; never HM 295.11–17 The . . . found] [HM leaf 2(B)] 295.12–17 Nor . . . found] [EM leaf 2] 295.14 Dread] HM,T; Vain EM\ HM 295.14 In thee inurned] HM2; Inurned in thee HM1 295.15 hollows] EM\ HM3,HM\EM3; gulfs HM,EM\HM2,HM\EM2; depths EM\HM?1,HM\ EM1 295.17 Where more is hid than found.] EM\HM2,HM\EM2; Better grope among the drowned. [then drowned! then drowned.] HM; And secrets of the drowned. EM,HM\EM1[there is no extant HM inscription for this variant]; Ah, grope[?s] among the drowned! EM\HM1

TEXTUAL NOTES: ACCIDENTALS. 295.1 In] [indent] HM; [indention obscured by dis-play capital] T 295.1 flit,] EM; ~^ HM[that is, no decipherable punctuation follows any of HM's variants for this passage] 295.2 box] [see substantives] 295.2 see:] HM,EM2; ~, EM1 295.3 fast,] EM2; ~; HM,EM1 *295.3 none.] EM2; ~; HM; ~, EM1,T 295.3 none.] [see substantives] 295.4 holes^ minutely small^] EM2; ~, ~ ~, HM; ~^ ~ ~, EM1 295.6 without,] EM; ~^ HM 295.8–17 Who . . . . found] [in T, lines 8–17 are set slightly to the left of the corresponding lines in the first stanza; nothing in HM or EM suggests this different positioning is authorially intended] 295.9 within,] EM; ~: HM1; ~; HM2 295.12 yields] EM; yeilds HM 295.13 murmurer] EM; mur-merer HM *295.16 Descending] [indent] HM2; [no indent] HM1,EM,T 295.16 consciences^] EM2; ~:— HM; ~— EM1 *295.17 Where] [no indent] HM,HM\ EM; [indent] EM,T 295.17 found.] [see substantives]

MILAN CATHEDRAL (p. 296)

Arriving in Milan the evening of April 6, 1857, Melville recorded that he "Walked out to see the cathedral by night." The next day he toured other local sites, saving the cathedral for last. He wrote about it in his journal: "Glorious. More satisfactory to me than St. Peters. A wonderful grandure. Effect of burning window at end of aisle. Ascended, — From below people in the turrets of open tracery look like flies caught in cobweb. — The groups of angels on points of pinacles & everywhere. Not the conception but execution. View from summit. Might write book of travel upon top of Milan Cathedral" (*Journals*, p. 121).

DISCUSSIONS. 296.1,5,8 sea/miracles/spire] NN follows EM in omitting the commas that end these lines in HM, judging these omissions to be part of Melville's systematic repointing of the passage.

296.3 The fat old plain of Lombardy] In his journal entry for April 6, 1857, Melville recorded his passage by rail "over dead level of Lombardy plain. Rich cultivation. Mulberry trees, vines. Farm houses so unlike ours. No signs of hard work as with us" (*Journals*, pp. 120–21).

EMENDATIONS. 296.1 Through] [*indent*] EM; [*no indent*] HM *296.1 sea^] EM; ~, HM 296.2 flows] EM\HM; shows HM 296.3 fat] EM\HM; rich HM 296.4 shows] EM; grows HM *296.5 miracles^] EM; ~, HM 296.7 and^] EM\HM; ~, HM 296.8 airy] EM\HM; soaring HM *296.8 spire^] EM; ~, HM 296.12 master-builder's] T; master-builders HM 296.12 here?] EM\HM; ~^ HM 296.13 given,] EM\HM; ~^ HM 296.14 Sublimely] EM; Sublimity HM 296.14 clear,] EM\HM; ~^ HM

TEXTUAL NOTES: INSCRIPTION STAGES. At least three stages of inscription-revision: A (nonextant pre-fair-copy stage); B (Melville's tan ink on thinner paper; evident in his leaf 1 now at the University of Virginia, *Barrett 6252-a); C (after Melville's stage B draft was misplaced, his wife inscribed at least the poem's last four lines in tan-gray ink on thinner paper, a draft of which four lines she labeled "HM Copy" [that label later erased]).

Foliation evidence shows that: (1) when EM first continuously foliated all the leaves in HM's transcript of *Timoleon*, "Pausilippo" was not yet included in the volume; at that time, "Milan Cathedral" was immediately followed by "The Attic Landscape"; (2) after HM inserted "Pausilippo" between "Milan Cathedral" and "The Attic Landscape," EM again continuously foliated HM's transcript from leaf 79 onward, but without noticing at first that HM's "Pausilippo" leaves had somehow been inserted between the first and second leaves of "Milan Cathedral" in his transcript; (3) when HM came to read EM's transcript of "Milan Cathedral," he had to pencil at the bottom of her first leaf of the poem, "Where[?'s] the original? / 4 *lines more*". The misplaced second leaf was then discovered, and though EM did not further refoliate it, she now (if not earlier) penciled at its top a later erased "H copy", in order to distinguish it from the copy of leaf 2 in her own transcript, since both second leaves were inscribed mostly in her hand. Also discovered was EM leaf 2, the copy of the second leaf she had probably already made from HM leaf 2 (the one identified by her as "H copy"), though it, too, had been misplaced in her transcript (at the top of EM leaf 2 is EM's erased "Milan Cathedral", an identification she would not otherwise have had to supply if that leaf had earlier been immediately preceded in her *Timoleon* transcript by a first leaf bearing the poem's title). At an undetermined time, HM leaf 1 (pencil-foliated 78 in its upper left corner) became separated from his *Timoleon* transcript, and came to rest at the University of Virginia (*Barrett 6252-a). The leaf here designated HM leaf 2 was ink-transcribed by EM (presumably from no-longer-extant HM inscription, and, as customary, without much punctuation), pencil-revised by HM, then ink-altered by EM once HM had settled upon his choices to that point, and, as just described above, twice pencil-foliated by EM into HM's complete *Timoleon* transcript—first as 79, then (mistakenly) as 86. EM's two foliation numbers, as well as corroborating textual evidence of succession, establish that HM leaf 2 was in HM's *Timoleon* transcript before he decided to put "Pausilippo" into the volume.

TEXTUAL NOTES: SUBSTANTIVES. 296.0–11 *Milan . . .* fire] [*HM leaf 1(B); EM leaf 1*] 296.0 *Milan Cathedral*] HM2; [*two or three undeciphered erased words, probably constituting an alternative title*] HM1 296.1 haze, a] HM2; haze of HM1 296.2 Over] HM2; Of HM1 296.2 flows] HM?4,EM\HM; shows HM1,HM?3,HM5,EM; glows HM?2 296.3 fat] HM2,EM\HM; rich HM1,HM3,EM[*only penciled in, probably because EM understood HM was still undecided*] 296.4 shows] HM→2,EM2[*?from HM dictation*]; grows HM1,HM3,EM1 296.6 Its tribes] HM2; The mobs HM1 296.8 airy] EM\HM; point and HM1; [*one or two undeciphered erased words*] HM2; soaring HM3,HM5,EM; [*one or two undeciphered scratched-out words*] HM4 296.11 fire.] [*below line 11 on HM leaf 1, some undeciphered erased words may indicate extensive revision that occasioned scissoring away text on the bottom fifth of the leaf*] 296.12–15 What . . . heaven] [*HM leaf 2(C){ink-inscribed by EM, pencil-revised by HM, HM's pencil revisions inked in by EM; foliated upper left corner pencil 79, then 86}; EM leaf 2*] 296.12 master-builder's] T; master-builders HM,EM 296.13 these synodic] HM2; all these heaps of HM1[*here and in following entries for lines 12–15, however, EM should be understood as the actual inscriber of the variants that occur first in HM's transcript*] 296.14 Sublimely] HM2,EM2; Sublimity HM1,HM?3[*at first, EM may have left the word space empty at the beginning of line 14 in HM's "copy," perhaps unsure as to which word HM intended in the transcript she was copying from; into that space HM may have penciled Sublimity just as he certainly penciled, above it, Sublimely ranked before settling, for a time, upon Sublimity*] 296.14 marble sessions] HM?2,HM?4,HM6; [*?at first, there is no EM inscription here in HM's "copy," since EM was awaiting either HM's clarification or further revision; in the space EM left, HM then penciled, successively, at least two undeciphered erased words, one of which is probably* sessions] HM1,HM3,HM5 296.14 clear] HM,EM\HM; ?here EM[*an eyeskip mis-transcription*] 296.15 Except] HM?1,HM3; [*at first, there is no EM inscription here in HM's "copy," since EM was awaiting either HM's clarification or further revision*] HM\EM; ?Unless HM2

TEXTUAL NOTES: ACCIDENTALS. 296.1 Through] [*indent*] HM2,EM; [*no indent*] HM1,HM3[*HM also penciled check marks at left of lines 1, 3, 4, and, possibly, 2, then erased the check marks*] 296.1 haze, a] [*see substantives*] *296.1 sea^] HM1,EM; ~, HM2 *296.5 miracles^] EM; ~, HM 296.7 and^] EM\HM2; ~, HM,EM\HM1 *296.8 spire^] EM; ~, HM 296.12 here?] EM\HM; ~^ HM 296.13 given,] EM\HM; ~^ HM 296.14 clear,] EM\HM; ~^ HM 296.15 to . . . heaven] HM\EM2; [*at first, there is no EM ink inscription here in HM's "copy"; EM may have needed to clarify only HM's final intention for line 15's first word (see entry above), but she left the whole line-space blank and/or just penciled in before she ink-inscribed the line's wording*] HM\EM1

PAUSILIPPO (pp. 297–99)

In 1857 Melville paid two visits to Posillipo, on February 20 and 23 (*Journals*, pp. 102, 104–5). Posillipo was the established name for the whole promontory along the southwest coast of the Bay of Naples, of which the city is at the northernmost point. In his journal entries for those visits Melville's spelling varied: "Posilipo," "Pausilipo," "Pausipilo, "Pausolippo," and "Pausillippo"; the Latin "Pausilypum" was the name that, in the time of Augustus, Vedius Pollio gave his nearby estate, signifying that in that place he expected to find an "end to care." Visiting the promontory and taking in the prospect on February 20, Melville recorded that he there "found not the cessation which the name expresses" (*Journals*, p. 102). Nor is it found by the "bleached" (line 16), "quelled" (line 39), "unmanned" (line 40) Silvio of the poem after his "strange immurement long" (line 16). It is not clear how much this Silvio is meant to be like the historical Silvio Pellico (1789–1854), who was condemned to death (but served ten years of a commuted prison sentence), his writings having led authorities to question his loyalty and consider him potentially a dangerous revolutionary. (Pellico is referred to in *Clarel*, 1.37.105–8.) This poem was fashioned from section 5 of "Naples," one of the poems Melville did not live to publish (see NN vol. 13, "*Billy Budd, Sailor" and Other Uncompleted Writings*). It was a late addition to Melville's manuscript for the book that became *Timoleon Etc.* Before he inserted it between "Milan Cathedral" and "The Attic Landscape," Elizabeth Shaw Melville had numbered in continuous sequence the leaves for all the other pieces then intended to appear in the volume (see the textual notes on inscription stages for "Milan Cathedral," pp. 826–27 above). Before deciding on his final subtitle for "Pausilippo," Melville had considered "1848" and, perhaps, "1846" to indicate the time of its action. At some time after stage C, Melville penciled in, but later erased, "Silvio Pellico / at Pausilippo" at the top of leaf 5 (before line 47), which shows that he considered dispensing with his narrative frame and printing only Silvio's song (lines 47–75). Some light on how to take the speaker's views at the end of the poem is cast by Melville's successive revisions of lines 77–80 (see the textual notes below).

DISCUSSIONS. 297.0 *Bomba*] Nickname of the repressive Ferdinando II (1810–59), Bourbon King of the Two Sicilies (1830–59), so called from his bombarding Sicilian cities, especially Messina, during the insurrections of 1848–49.

297.14 I . . . up] NN follows the copy-text in including this line, which does not appear in Elizabeth Shaw Melville's transcript, probably overlooked as she began a new leaf. Possibly, however, Melville directed its omission, since in many of the following lines in her transcript she was clearly following his no-longer-extant inscription or unrecorded directions (see the textual notes for lines 18, 21–29, 31–32, 34, 38, 39, 40, 46, and 76–79).

298.47 Pausilippo] NN follows EM in omitting the quotation marks that enclose Pellico's song in HM (here and in lines 51, 58, and 75; HM has no quotation mark in line 72); their systematic omission indicates that in punctuating that transcript Melville deliberately omitted them.

298.52 away] NN follows EM in omitting the comma present in HM, inferring that the omission was deliberate, part of Melville's substantial revisions.

298.54 balm] Though normally accepting the punctuation in EM, NN retains the copy-text reading here, with no punctuation after this word. The comma in EM makes no sense, and its omission in T probably results from Melville's marking of the proof.

299.77 shore.] NN adopts the period in EM as more likely to represent Melville's intention than the semicolon that appears in T (there is no punctuation at this point in HM).

299.79 down,] In adopting the revised wording of this line in EM, NN also adopts its comma, though conceivably the omission of the comma in T resulted from Melville's revision in proof.

EMENDATIONS. 297.0[*subtitle*] *(In . . . Bomba)*] EM\HM; [*not present*] HM 297.2 head] EM\HM; brow HM 297.10,15 Toward/A] [*indent*] EM; [*no indent*] HM 297.10 landau] NN; [*spelling unclear; could be the same as EM's* landau] HM 297.18 Dim trace] EM; Traces HM 297.20 girl,] EM; ~^ HM 297.20 whose filial] EM; of vestal HM 297.21–22 Toward . . . tone] EM; [*see textual notes for this complex instance*] HM 298.26 her ministering] EM; that daughter's filial HM 298.27 Anon] [*indent*] EM; [*no indent*] HM 298.27 some ramblers] EM; the saunterers HM 298.29 With . . . suppressed] EM; [*see textual notes for this complex instance*]

HM 298.30 story,] EM; ~^ HM 298.31–32 Clandestine . . . cause] EM; [*no lines present*] HM 298.34 treason;] EM (~^ HM\EM); crime^ HM 298.34 trial none] EM; against the Crown HM 298.38 blight . . . wane] T; withered antidated Eld HM 298.39 quelled enthusiast] EM; father harper HM 298.40 Unmanned . . . wrong] EM; [*no line present*] HM 298.41 Preluding, faltering;] EM; Preluding^ feebly; HM 298.45 mouth-piece] EM; mouthpiece HM 298.46 spiritless^ and spent] EM; spiritless, may-be HM *298.47 ^Pausilippo] EM; "~ HM 298.51,52 Could/Waft] [*no indent*] EM; [*indent*] HM 298.51 ^Could] EM; "~ HM *298.52 away^] EM; ~, HM 298.53 sleep,] EM; ~; HM 299.55 becharm,] T; ~^ HM 299.58 ^Did] EM; "~ HM 299.61 delight—] EM; ~, HM 299.63 fruition—] T; ~, HM 299.64 man!] EM; ~?^ HM 299.67 caravan,] EM; ~; HM 299.69 snare,] EM; ~; HM 299.73 pain:] EM; ~! HM 299.75 vain!^] EM; ~." HM 299.76 It] [*indent*] EM; [*no indent*] HM 299.76 low and languid] T; low indifferent HM 299.77 passive] EM; [*not present*] HM *299.77 shore.] EM; ~^ HM 299.78 As . . . untroubled] T; While languid looked the liquid HM 299.79 Looked . . . silent] EM; As silver doled was mutely HM

TEXTUAL NOTES: INSCRIPTION STAGES. At least six stages of inscription-revision: A (nonextant pre-fair-copy stage); Ba (blue ink on leaf foliated 32, upper left corner blue, in Harvard MS Am 188 [386.A.3]); Bb (dark blue ink on darker, thicker paper [the leaf 4 clip with upper middle pencil foliation]); Bc (blue-black ink on thicker paper); C (gray-brown ink on thinner, lighter paper); D (late pencil on thicker yellow paper, as well as on the darker, thicker paper of a superseded leaf).

TEXTUAL NOTES: SUBSTANTIVES. 297.0–9 *Pausilippo . . . Pan*] [*HM leaf 1(Dc)*] 297.0–13 *Pausilippo . . . on*] [*EM leaf 1*] 297.0[*title and subtitle*] *Pausilippo / (In . . . Bomba)*] EM\HM3; [*no title*] HM1; Pausilippo / 1848 HM2; Pausilippo HM3,EM; Pausilippo / [?1846] EM\HM?1; Pausilippo / 18[*blank space*] EM\HM→2 297.1 hill] HM1,HM3; Slope HM2 297.2 head] HM1,EM\HM[*not copied back into HM*]; brow HM2 297.4 pristine] HM,EM\HM; primitive EM[*misreading*] 297.6 pine] HM,EM\HM2; [*undeciphered erased word*] EM\HM1 297.9 find] HM,EM\ HM2; know EM\HM1 297.10–22 Toward . . . tone] [*HM leaf 2(Dc)*] 297.10 drew] HM2; [?he] drew HM1 297.13 One . . . straight] HM5; One could mark [?them and] HM→1[*uncompleted reading*]; One scarce could note them and HM→2; One scarce could mark them and HM→3; One scarce could mark and [*inscribed and erased before* straight *in the final reading was inscribed over it is an undeciphered letter or two, perhaps the beginning of an uncompleted word*] HM?→4 *297.14 I . . . up] HM; [*?line omitted inadvertently in going from leaf 1 to leaf 2 of her transcript*] EM 297.15–298.31 A . . . night] [*EM leaf 2*] 297.16 through] HM,EM\HM; with EM 297.16 strange] HM2; some HM1 297.17 by] HM2; in HM1 297.17 depressed] HM2; [?distressed] HM1[*or the final* depressed *could be a mending of an earlier one, so that EM would be able to decipher his intention*] 297.18 Dim trace] EM,HM\EM; Traces HM 297.20 whose filial] EM,HM\EM; of vestal HM 297.21–22 Toward

. . . tone] EM,HM\EM[*unpunctuated transcription from nonextant HM inscription*]; [*no equivalent text-lines present*] HM1; [*see following description of superseded stage Db predecessors of lines 21–22 inscribed, then canceled, on HM leaf 3, before HM undertook revisions on the evidently nonextant leaf EM presumably transcribed from*]

> Who, spite her sunned complexion brown,
> Not less in lineaments how grave
> His daughter seemed, xx xx [*then and in*] her air [*then and serving him*
>   *then* devote{d} *to him*]
> With something of maternal tone [*then* care].

HM2(Db) 297.22 tone] HM\EM2; air HM\EM1 297.22 tone.] HM\EM2; [*see following description of superseded versions of what became lines 27–29, lines that at stage Db immediately followed the also later superseded four lines described above as predecessors of lines 21–22*]

> Among the people hither drawn
> A murmur ran—"Tis Silvio, Silvio!"
> With inklings dim in [*line not completed*]

HM(Db) 297.23–298.29 Nor . . . suppressed] [*HM leaf 3 (Dc inscription on Db leaf)*] 297.23 question] HM2; doubt HM1 297.23 locks] HM2; long locks HM1
298.25 one's]HM,EM\HM; one EM[*mistranscription*] 298.26 Betrayed] HM,EM\HM; Evinced EM[*presumably from nonextant HM inscription; see following entries for lines 26, 27, 29, 31–32*],HM\EM 298.26 her ministering] EM,HM\EM[*presumably from nonextant HM inscription*]; that daughter's filial HM 298.27–29 Anon . . . suppressed] [*for superseded earlier versions of lines 27–29, see substantives, the second entry for line 22, above*] 298.27 some ramblers] EM,HM\EM[*presumably from nonextant HM inscription*]; the saunterers HM 298.28 rose] HM2; buzzed HM1 298.29 With . . . suppressed] EM,HM\EM[*presumably from nonextant HM inscription*]; [*for an earlier, uncompleted version of what became line 29, see substantives, the second entry for line 22, above*] HM 298.30–38 Touching . . . wane] [*HM leaf 4.clip(?Bb)* Touching . . . Eld] 298.30,33–34 Touching . . . none] HM1,HM3[*as revised, and with final lines 31–32 inserted*]; [*pencil-canceled at some indeterminable time after or before the penciled revisions described below in the entries for lines 30 and 33–34*] HM2 298.30 story] HM1,HM3; history HM2 298.30 part recalled:] HM4; and the times— HM1; and the times: HM2; now recalled: HM3 298.31–32 Clandestine . . . cause] EM,HM\EM[*presumably from nonextant HM inscription*]; [*no text-lines present*] HM 298.32–46 The . . . spent] [*EM leaf 3*] 298.34 treason] HM3,EM,HM\EM; s [*uncompleted word*] HM→1; crime HM2,HM4 298.34 trial none] EM,HM\EM[*apparently from nonextant HM inscription*]; against the king HM1,HM?4; [*probably before, but perhaps after the remaining variants described here (their order, at many points, conjectural), HM tried at least two versions of the second half of line 34, each consisting of two or three words, all of which are undeciphered erased words, except the last one in*]

the second version: urged] HM*?*2,HM*?*3; against the state HM*?*5,HM*?*7; against the crown HM*?*6; against the law HM*?*8; against the Crown HM*?*9,HM*?*11; against the King HM*?*10 298.35 profound] HM1,HM3; incurred HM2[*not explicitly canceled*] 298.36 Vain] HM2; Sad HM1 298.38 blight . . . wane] T; withered antidated eld HM1; withered antidated Eld HM2; withered antedated eld EM\HM; blight forestalling mellow time's decay EM[*presumably from nonextant HM inscription; also not copied back into HM*] 298.39–46 Hillward . . . spent] [*HM leaf 4(C)*] 298.39 quelled enthusiast] EM[*apparently from nonextant HM inscription*],HM\EM,EM\HM2,T; seated harper HM1; paternal harper HM2; father harper HM3; [*undeciphered erased word*] enthusiast EM\HM1; wrecked enthusiast EM\HM3 298.39 turned] HM1,HM5; [*undeciphered erased word*] HM2; [*undeciphered erased word*] HM3; faced HM4 298.40 Unmanned . . . wrong] EM,HM\EM[*presumably from nonextant HM inscription*]; [*no text-line present*] HM 298.41 Preluding, faltering;] EM,HM\ EM[*presumably from nonextant HM inscription; HM\EM reading lacks comma*]; Preluding^ feebly— HM1; Preluding^ feebly; HM2 298.42 wire—no more,] HM3; chord, the while^ HM1; [*?*chord—no more,] HM*?*2 298.43 constant] HM1,HM3; filial HM2 298.43 supplying] HM2; supplied HM1 298.43 voice] HM3; the voice HM1; a voice HM2 298.46 spiritless^ and spent] EM,HM\EM[*presumably from nonextant HM inscription; EM does not cancel the comma in HM*]; spiritless, may-be HM 298.47–57 Pausilippo . . . Pausilippo] [*HM leaf 5(C)*] 298.47–299.60 Pausilippo . . . serene] [*EM leaf 4*] 298.47 Pausilippo] [*no title*] HM1,HM3; Silvio Pellico / at Pausilippo HM2[*penciling in this title at the top of HM leaf 5, sometime after stage C, HM seems temporarily to have considered dispensing with the narrative frame he had created and printing only Silvio Pellico's song*] 298.50 one's] HM2; the HM1 298.51 Could light] HM3,EM\HM; Yet could HM1; Could HM*?*2,EM[*?mistranscription*] 298.53 Or] HM2; And HM1

299.58–64 Did . . . man] [*HM leaf 6.clip 1(?Bc)* {*at the top of this clip is the remainder of a penciled, then erased* Pausilippo *that HM inscribed as a revision of text now scissored away*}] 299.58 spell] HM3(D+),EM2; trance HM1; charm HM2; [*EM initially left a blank space in her transcript, since in his transcript, without canceling* trance *HM had penciled in* charm *plus a question mark*] EM1 299.59 slip] HM1,HM3; slide HM2 299.61–75 And . . . vain] [*EM leaf 5*] 299.65–70 Did . . . prove] [*HM leaf 6.clip 2(?Bc)*] 299.68 your] HM2(C); [*undeciphered scratched-out word* {*?their (the* r *in* your *seems to be in stage B ink) ?*the}] HM1 299.68 scene] HM1,HM5; charm HM2,HM4; spell HM3 299.71 Pausilippo] [*HM leaf 6(C)* {*the only inscription on HM leaf 6; the word also appears, mostly scissored away, just above, at the bottom of HM leaf 6.clip 2*}] 299.72–75 But . . . vain] [*HM leaf 7.clip(C)*] 299.76–80 It . . . ore] [*HM leaf 7(D); EM leaf 6*] 299.76 low and languid] T; low monotonous HM1; low indifferent HM2; languid listless EM,HM\EM[*presumably transcribed from nonextant HM inscription—probably from HM revision of an earlier version of EM leaf 6*] 299.77–80 The . . . ore] HM2; [*see following description of superseded stage B versions of the last four lines in Part V of HM's unpublished poem "Naples"; these text-lines appear, canceled with pencil and blue pencil, on a leaf foliated (upper left corner blue) 32* *that presently stands in Harvard MS Am 188 (386.A.3); on this leaf also appear the prose preface to Part VI of "Naples," the first text-line of Part VI canceled in blue pencil, and EM's penciled query 5 {altered to V} missing? indicating she had forgotten or never noticed HM's use of Part V for "Pausilippo"; the superseded lines read:*

> Alms, and but alms. Might these restore?
> For purse and heart alike that brim
> The <u>miserere</u> who shall hymn
> When pity's futile as the ore!]

HM1(B) 299.77 passive shore] ˙EM,HM\EM[*presumably from nonextant HM inscription*]; verge HM1; marge HM2; shore HM3 299.78 As . . . untroubled] T; While languid looked the liquid HM; As languidly the blue untroubled EM[*presumably from nonextant HM inscription*]; As languorously the blue untroubled EM\ HM,HM\EM 299.79 Looked . . . silent] EM,HM\EM[*presumably from nonextant HM inscription*]; As silver doled was mutely HM

TEXTUAL NOTES: ACCIDENTALS. 297.0[*title and subtitle*] Pausilippo / (In . . . Bomba)] [*underlined; subtitle in parentheses*] EM\HM; [*not underlined; no parentheses*] HM\ EM 297.1 A] [*indent*] HM; [*indention obscured by display capital*] T 297.1–2 A . . . head] HM2; [*the verso of EM leaf 6 of "Pausilippo" bears penciled, pencil-canceled, and erased HM inscription of lines 1 and 2, not substantively different from the text of lines 1 and 2 on HM leaf 1; HM may have begun transcribing on what later became the verso of EM leaf 6, then started over on HM leaf 1, since he judged that in the first instance he had begun too close to the top of the leaf to insert a title (with his usually-to-be-anticipated revisions); the only difference between the superseded and final HM lines is that line 1 is not indented in the earlier inscription; the superseded passage reads:* ———"——— {*beginning device*} / A hill there is that laves its feet / In Naples' bay and lifts its head] HM1 297.3 curled] HM,EM\HM; [*EM left blank space since she could not make out which word HM intended*] EM 297.4 conferred^] HM2; ~, HM1 297.7 such] HM2; f HM→1[*false start*] 297.7 shown] HM,EM[?\HM][*HM seems to have pencil-inscribed* shown *in EM (the word was later canceled and erased), in order to clarify for EM the word he intended*]; [*?blank space left*] EM 297.10 Toward] [*line-space precedes*] HM2; [*?no line-space*] HM?1[*a leaf break occurs between lines 9 and 10 in HM; in his transcript, HM pencil-added a bracket at the left of line 10, indicating "new verse-paragraph," and EM added above the line the reminder* space] 297.10,15 Toward/A] [*indent*] EM; [*no indent*] HM 297.10 Hill] HM; hill EM 297.10 landau] ?HM,NN; landeau EM[*elsewhere, HM also spells the word thus*] 297.10 drew;] HM3,EM2; ~, HM1; ~: HM2,EM1 297.13 on:] HM[*this punctuation retained along with line 14, regarding which see substantives and discussion*]; ~. EM 297.19 Seated,] HM; ~^ EM 297.20 girl,] EM; ~^ HM 297.20 mien] HM,EM\HM; mein EM[*misreading*] 297.21–22 again, . . . tone.] [*see substantives; EM did not punctuate the lines she copied back into HM*]

298.25 thread-bare] HM,T; threadbare EM 298.27 Anon] [*line-space precedes*] HM\EM; [*?no line-space; a tacit line-space may be concealed by the spatial compression of HM's pencil draft*] HM 298.27 Anon] [*indent*] EM; [*no indent*] HM 298.28 rose,] HM; ~^ EM 298.28 'Tis] HM; ^~ T 298.30 story,] EM; ~^ HM[*see substantives*] 298.30 recalled:] [*see substantives*] 298.31 night;] EM; ~^ HM\EM 298.34 treason;] EM; ~, HM[*different wording and structure influences the punctuation here; see substantives, the entries for this line*]; ~^ HM\EM 298.34 trial none] [*see substantives*] 298.36 late. All] HM2; late—all HM1 298.38 blight . . . wane] [*see substantives*] 298.39 Hillward] [*line-space precedes*] HM2; [*no line-space*] HM1 298.39 Hillward] [*indent*] HM2,EM2; [*no indent*] HM1,EM1[*false start*] 298.40 Unmanned, . . . wrong,] EM; ~^ . . . ~^ HM\EM 298.41 Preluding, faltering;] [*see substantives*] 298.42 wire—no more,] [*see substantives*] 298.43 constant] HM,EM2; cnstanx EM→1[*undeciphered mistranscription*] 298.45 mouth-piece] EM2; mouthpiece HM,EM1 298.45 mere,] HM2; ~— HM1 298.46 spiritless and spent] [*see substantives*] 298.47 Pausilippo] [*double line-space precedes*] [*the double line-space is probably tacit in both HM and EM; since the beginning of a new leaf in EM (as in HM) might mask his intentions, HM pencils and circles at the top of EM leaf 4 Leave double space here*] *298.47 ^Pausilippo] EM; "~ HM 298.47 Pausilippo, Pausilippo,] HM1,HM3; ~! ~! HM2 298.51,52 Could/ Waft] [*no indent*] EM, HM\EM; [*indent*] HM 298.51 ^Could] EM; "~ HM 298.51 Could light] [*see substantives*] *298.52 away^] EM; ~, HM 298.53 sleep,] EM; ~; HM *298.54 balm^] HM,T; ~, EM

299.55 becharm,] T; ~^ HM 297.57 Pausilippo] [*indent farther than line 55*] HM; [*indent like line 55*] T 299.58 ^Did] EM; "~ HM 299.58 invite,] HM,T; ~^ EM 299.59 between,] HM,T; ~^ EM 299.61 wake,] HM1,HM3,HM5; ~^ HM2,HM4[*perhaps not earlier intended to be superseded, the stage B comma is not explicitly canceled; HM may have "replaced" it initially (by inscribing another) because the original was concealed by the head of a pin securing the clip*] 299.61 dash,] HM1,HM3; ~^ HM2 299.61 delight—] HM1,EM2; ~, HM2,EM1 299.63 Fulfillment] HM; Fulfilment EM[*mistranscription*] 299.63 fruition—] HM2,HM4,EM1,T; ~, HM1,HM3,HM5; ~^ EM2 299.64 mine,] HM2; ~^ HM1 299.64 man!] HM2,HM4,EM; ~; HM1; ~: HM3; ~?— HM?5; ~?^ HM?6 299.67 caravan,] EM; ~; HM 299.69 snare,] HM1,EM; ~; HM2 299.71 Pausilippo] HM2; Posalipo HM1[*covered by clip*] 299.72 But] [*line-space precedes*] HM2; [*no line-space? HM may have added the penciled bracket since the leaf break otherwise conceals any intended line-space break for a new verse-paragraph*] HM?1 299.73 pain:] EM; ~, HM1; ~; HM2; ~! HM3 299.75 vain!^] EM; ~!" HM1; ~." HM2 299.76 It] [*double line-space precedes*] HM2[*in his transcript, HM directs* Leave Double space here *and in EM's he writes* Leave *though EM had probably already inscribed the rest:* Double space here]; [*no double line-space? spatial relations on HM leaf 7 offer only ambiguous evidence*] HM?1 299.76 It] [*indent*] EM; [*no indent*] HM 299.76 ceased.] HM,T; ~^ EM 299.77 tideless] HM,EM2; tidxxxx EM1[*undeciphered mistranscription*] *299.77 shore.] EM2; ~^ EM1,HM\EM; ~; T *299.79 down,] EM2; ~^ EM1,T

THE ATTIC LANDSCAPE (p. 300)

This poem registers something of a change from Melville's view in his journal entry for February 8, 1857: "Parthenon elevated like cross of Constantine. Strange contrast of rugged rock with polished temple. At Stirling [the Scottish stronghold] — art & nature correspond. Not so at Acropolis" (*Journals*, p. 99; for Melville's visit to Stirling in 1856, see *Journals*, pp. 385–86, and *Correspondence*, p. 302).

DISCUSSION. 300.2 sights] NN retains Melville's "sights" (the reading in HM and EM). The singular form in T is likely to be a compositorial error not caught by Melville.

EMENDATIONS. 300.2 see:] EM; ~; HM 300.3 "Old Romance",] EM; ^~ ~^^ HM 300.5 warm—] EM; ~: HM 300.6 Pure . . . a^] EM\HM; Outline merely, HM 300.7 face,] EM; ~— HM 300.8 their] EM\HM; this HM 300.12 The . . . here] T; We worship God here for HM

TEXTUAL NOTES: INSCRIPTION STAGES. At least two stages of inscription-revision: A (nonextant pre-fair-copy stage); B (tan-gray ink on thinner paper).

TEXTUAL NOTES: SUBSTANTIVES. 300.0–12 The . . . Greek] [*HM leaf 1(B); EM leaf 1*] *300.2 sights] HM; sight T 300.4 Or] HM,EM\HM2; No EM\HM1 300.5–12 No . . . Greek] [*left-margin pencilings in his transcript indicate that HM considered (perhaps more than once) having lines 5–6 follow 7–8, these two pairs of lines originally set out in his transcript as separate stanzas; temporarily (as finally) joining lines 5–8 into one stanza, HM may also have considered dividing lines 9–12 into two two-line stanzas; and he might also have meditated other arrangements of two-line units before reverting to his original sequencing and deciding finally to combine lines 5–8 into one stanza*] 300.5 the sense to] HM3; or gay or HM1; no gay or HM→2 300.6 Pure . . . a^] EM\ HM4[*in copying this reading back into HM, EM did not change* Outline *to lowercase*]; Outline mainly, HM1; Outline merely, HM2,EM; Outline [*one or two undeciphered erased words* {?pale, a}], EM\HM?1; Pale outline and^ EM\HM?2; [?Pale] outline [*or* Outline *plus two to four undeciphered erased words* {?among them *and* pale *and a* pale} *constituting at least one reading*]^ EM\HM?3 300.7 carved] HM2; the HM1 300.8 their sculptural] HM2,EM\HM; this linear HM1; this sculptural HM3 300.12 The . . . here] EM\HM?3[*not copied back into HM*],T; One worships God here for HM1; We [*one or two undeciphered erased words*] God here for HM2; We worship God here for HM3,EM1; That God himself here seems EM\ HM?1,EM2[*EM may have transcribed from no-longer- extant HM inscription*],HM\ EM1; The All-in-All here seems EM\HM2,HM\EM2; HE, All-in-All, seems here EM\HM4[*not copied back into HM*]

Textual Notes: Accidentals. 300.0 *Landscape*] HM2; Lanscape HM1 300.1 avid] HM,EM2; [*EM left blank space in order to query which word HM intended*] EM1 300.2 see:] EM; ~; HM 300.3 "Old Romance",] EM2; ^Old Romance^^ HM; ^old Romance^^ EM1; "Old Romance," T 300.5–12 No . . . Greek] [*see substantives*] 300.5 tint^] HM2; ~, HM1 300.5 warm—] EM; ~: HM 300.6 Pure . . . a^] [*see substantives*] 300.7 The] [*no line-space precedes*] HM2; [*line-space*] HM1 300.7 face,] EM; ~— HM 300.9 'Tis] [*in T a single opening quotation mark appears instead of an apostrophe*] 300.11 weather^] HM,EM2; ~— EM1 300.12 The . . . here] [*see substantives*]

THE SAME (p. 301)

Discussion. 301.2,4 Pellucid/Charm] NN follows EM in omitting the commas present in HM after these words, judging that the omission is part of an overall lightening of punctuation, along with the change at the end of line 2 (from a colon in HM to a comma in EM).

Emendations. *301.2 Pellucid^] EM; ~, HM 301.2 waits,] EM; ~: HM *301.4 Charm^] EM; ~, HM 301.4 authenticates.] EM; ~^ HM

Textual Notes: Inscription Stages. At least two stages of inscription-revision: A (nonextant pre-fair-copy stage); B (tan-gray ink on thinner paper).

Textual Notes: Substantives. 301.0–4 The . . . authenticates] [*HM leaf 1(B); EM leaf 1*] [*no substantive variants*]

Textual Notes: Accidentals. *301.2 Pellucid^] EM; ~, HM 301.2 waits,] EM; ~: HM *301.4 Charm^] EM; ~, HM 301.4 authenticates.] EM; ~^ HM

THE PARTHENON (pp. 302–3)

Melville saw the Parthenon "aloft" from the Piræus road, first by moonlight (February 8, 1857), and last when leaving Athens (February 11): a "Clear & beautiful day. Fine ride on box [carriage top] to Pireus. Acropolis in sight nearly whole way. . . . Fully releived against the sky" (*Journals*, p. 99). His persistent (but not only) image is "blocks of ice" for what he saw as he visited the Acropolis ruins on February 8–10, ending "Ruins of Parthenon like North River breaking up. &c" (see also the entries quoted in the introductory notes to "Greek Masonry" and "The Apparition," pp. 839 and 854 below). Incomplete evidence—consisting mainly of foliation and part-designation numbers—suggests that "The Parthenon" earlier had at least six, and then five, parts, before Melville settled on the final four. One of the deleted parts came between final parts I and II, the other between final parts III and IV. The evidence of foliation and content suggests that Melville once considered a superseded version of what became "The Apparition" (p. 313 above) both as a second Parthenon poem and as Part II of another poem on the topic (probably this poem, "The Parthenon"). The same kind of evidence also implies that at some point what became "Greek Masonry" (p. 304) and "Greek Architecture" (p. 305) may also have been considered as parts—perhaps concluding parts—of "The Parthenon."

DISCUSSIONS. 302.7 Lais] A generic term for "courtesan," presumably from two noted beauties of that name.

302.8 defined—] NN adopts the dash from T on the assumption that it is not a likely compositorial substitution for the comma in EM.

302.14–15 Spinoza . . . Dreams] For "Spinoza" Melville had "The Pantheist" at an earlier stage. In *Clarel* (2.22.110ff.; see also the NN edition, p. 777), Rolfe characterizes Spinoza (1632–77) as "a lion in brain," "Pan's Atheist," and an "erring" "visionary."

303.17 *The Frieze*] Melville here describes figures in the Panathenaic procession depicted in low relief on the 524-foot frieze of the Parthenon. Large sections of that frieze were secured by Lord Elgin in 1799–1803, purchased by the British government, and placed in the British Museum. An undated note in the second of his 1856–57 journal notebooks may indicate that Melville at some point saw the Elgin Marbles (in 1849 or 1857): "*Ruins look as much out of place in Rome as in British Museum*" (*Journals*, p. 158).

303.29,30 Ictinus/Aspasia/Pericles] Ictinus was the fifth-century B.C. chief architect of the Parthenon. Aspasia (ca. 470–410 B.C.) was the woman of beauty, wit, learning, and influence who inspired Pericles to divorce his first wife and marry her. Pericles (d. 429 B.C.) gained complete power over Athens about 460 B.C., and until his death worked to make the city architecturally the most beautiful in the world, as well as a center of art, literature, and political power.

303.29 said] In the general repointing of lines 29 and 30 in EM, either Melville or his wife erased a dash after this word (a dash follows the word in HM). While the intention may have been to replace it or substitute other punctuation, NN adopts the reading in EM as a deliberate omission; punctuation omitted before quotation marks is not unusual in Melville's manuscripts.

303.30 Art's meridian] In revising, Melville twice decided against "Art's" in favor of "Man's", but finally settled on "Art's".

EMENDATIONS. 302.1[*part title precedes*] *Seen aloft*] EM\HM; Seen HM 302.1 site,] EM; ~— HM 302.6 after-shine.] EM; ~^ HM *302.8 defined^—] T; ~,— HM 302.9 inclined,] EM; ~; HM 302.10 yet,] EM; ~^ HM 302.11 sweeping] EM\HM; total HM 302.13 true.] EM; ~! HM *302.14 Spinoza] EM\HM; The Pantheist

HM 302.14 gazes;] EM; ~, HM 303.20 —their . . . grave—] EM\HM; (~ . . . ~)
HM 303.24 after one^] EM; ~ ~, HM 303.28 glade;] EM; ~: HM 303.29 Ictinus]
[*indent*] EM\HM; [*no indent*] HM *303.29 said^] EM; ~— HM 303.30 "Hist . . .
Pericles!"] EM; ^~ . . . ~!^ HM 303.30 Hist!—] EM; ~!^ HM *303.30 Art's] EM\
HM; Man's HM

Textual Notes: Inscription Stages. At least three stages of inscription-revision:
A (nonextant pre-fair-copy stage); B (tan-gray ink on thinner paper); B+ (no
substantive inscription on mount; only penciled foliation numbers).

Textual Notes: Substantives. 302.0–6 *The* . . . after-shine] [*HM leaf 1(B);
EM leaf 1*] 302.1[*part title*] Seen aloft] EM\HM; Seen HM 302.1 Estranged] HM4;
Sublime HM1; [*two or three undeciphered erased words, constituting at least two vari-
ant readings*] HM2,HM3 302.2 Aerial] HM2; Serenely HM1 302.7–16 II . . . you]
[*HM leaf 2(B); EM leaf 2*] 302.7[*part number*] II] HM3; [*no part number*] HM1;
III HM2 302.7[*part title*] Nearer viewed] HM6; Seen nearer HM1; Seen [*?closely*]
HM2; Nearer seen HM3; Nearer scrutinized HM4; Nearer studied HM5 302.9
each] HM2,HM4; the HM1,HM3 302.11 sweeping] HM1,EM\HM; total HM2
*302.14 Spinoza] HM1,EM\HM; [*two undeciphered erased words*] HM2; The Pan-
theist HM3

303.17–25 III . . . flight] [*HM leaf 3(B); EM leaf 3*] 303.17[*part number*] III] HM2;
4 HM1 303.17[*part title*] The Frieze] HM4; The Procession[?s] on the Frieze HM1;
The Frieze, in par HM→2[*uncompleted reading*]; The Frieze (in parts) HM3 303.17
What happy] HM1,HM4; What quiet HM2; Happiest HM3 303.17 genial] HM3;
mildly HM1; happy HM2 303.21 so] HM2; too HM1 303.26–30 IV . . . Pericles]
[*HM leaf 4(B+) {no substantive inscription} HM leaf 4.clip(B)* IV . . . Pericles *EM leaf
4* IV . . . Pericles] 303.26[*part number precedes*] IV] HM4; [?V] HM?1; 5 HM?2; 4
HM3 *303.30 Art's] HM1,EM\HM1,EM\HM3; Man's HM2,EM\HM2

Textual Notes: Accidentals. 302.1 site,] EM; ~— HM 302.3 sun-cloud] HM;
suncloud EM 302.6 after-shine.] EM; ~^ HM 302.6 after-shine.] [*in HM, EM
cancels an ending mark and reminds herself to leave 2 lines of space between parts I and
II*] *302.8 defined—] T; ~, HM1,EM; ~,— HM2 302.9 inclined,] HM1,EM;
~; HM2 302.10 yet,] EM; ~^ HM 302.12 seems,] HM2; ~^ HM1 302.12 level,]
HM2,EM; ~— HM1; ~?^ HM?3 302.13 true.] HM1,EM; ~! HM2 302.14 gazes;]
EM; ~, HM 302.16 Lais] [*indent farther than line 13*] HM; [*indent like line 13*] EM
302.16 Lais—] HM2; ~^ HM1 302.16 you!] HM2; ~. HM1

303.17[*part title*] The Frieze] [*see substantives*] 303.19 frisk] HM,EM\HM;
[*undeciphered mistranscribed letter {?p}*]risk EM 303.19 curvet] HM[*to make sure the
compositor does not misread EM's inscription, HM inscribes* curvet *in her transcript*]
303.20 —their . . . grave—] EM\HM[*inscribed above line 17 in EM is HM's direc-
tion: dash*]; (~ . . . ~) HM 303.21 Contrasting] HM2; Contrating HM1 303.22
bright,] HM2; ~^ EM 303.24 after one^] HM1,EM2; ~ ~, HM2,EM1 303.26[*part

title] *Last*] HM; *last* T 303.27 died^] HM,EM2; ~— EM→1[*?inadvertent dash, and instantly corrected*] 303.28 birds,] HM,EM2,T; ~^ EM1,EM3 303.28 glade;] EM2; ~: HM,EM1 303.29 Ictinus] [*indent*] EM\HM; [*no indent*] HM 303.29 sat;] HM,EM2,T; ~^ EM1,EM3[*semicolon inadvertently not replaced after EM had erased* Ictinus sat; *in order to indent line 29*] 303.29 Aspasia] HM,EM2; Aspatia EM1[*misreading*] *303.29 said^] EM1,EM3; ~— HM,EM2 303.30 "Hist . . . Per-icles!"] EM2; ^~ . . . ~!^ HM,EM1 303.30 Hist!—] EM3; ~! HM; ~^ EM1; ~, EM2; ~— EM\HM

GREEK MASONRY (p. 304)

The evidence of foliation and content suggests that "Greek Masonry," like "Greek Architecture" (p. 305), may once have been considered as a part—perhaps a concluding part—of "The Parthenon" (pp. 302–3 above). Tacit in the terminal "congealed" of line 3 is the ice-block imagery Melville repeatedly used in his journal entries for the ruins of the Parthenon and other structures on the Acropolis when he visited there on February 8–10, 1857: "*Acropolis* — blocks of marble like blocks of Wenham ice. . . . Imperceptible seams — frozen together" and "Pavement of Parthenon — square — blocks of ice. (frozen together.) — No morter: — Delicacy of frost-work" (*Journals*, p. 99).

EMENDATION. 304.0 *Greek Masonry*] EM\HM; The masonry in Greek Temples HM

TEXTUAL NOTES: INSCRIPTION STAGES. At least three stages of inscription-revision: A (nonextant pre-fair-copy stage); B (tan-gray ink on thinner paper); B+ (no substantive inscription on mount; only penciled foliation numbers).

TEXTUAL NOTES: SUBSTANTIVES. 304.0–3 *Greek . . .* congealed] [*HM leaf 1(B+)* {*no substantive inscription*} *HM leaf 1.clip(B)* Greek . . . congealed *EM leaf 1* Greek . . . congealed] 304.0 *Greek Masonry*] EM\HM2; The masonry in Greek Temples HM1,HM4; The [*undeciphered erased word*] in Greek Temples HM2; The chrystalline in Greek Temples HM3,EM\HM1[*with spelling* Christaline]; The [*two or three undeciphered erased words* {*?Masonry in*}] Greek [*undeciphered erased word* {*?Temples*}] EM 304.1 were] HM,EM\HM1,EM\HM3,HM\EM2; [*?here*] EM1[*mistranscription*]; are EM\HM?2,EM2,HM\EM1 304.2 with] HM1,HM3; the HM2 304.3 congealed.] [*following text-lines canceled*] HM2; [*the poem earlier had two more lines:* Painstaking in their art divine / Who wrought such temples chrystalline.] HM1

TEXTUAL NOTES: ACCIDENTALS. 304.0 *Greek Masonry*] [*see substantives*]

GREEK ARCHITECTURE (p. 305)

The evidence of foliation and content suggest that "Greek Architecture," like "Greek Masonry" (p. 304 above), may once have been considered as a part—perhaps a concluding part—of "The Parthenon" (pp. 302–3 above).

EMENDATIONS. 305.0 *Greek Architecture*] EM\HM; A Hint from the Greek / As to some points going to constitute the beautiful in architecture HM 305.0 *Architecture*] EM; architecture HM 305.4 Archetype] EM\HM; Archtype HM 305.4 Archetype.] EM; ~^ HM

TEXTUAL NOTES: INSCRIPTION STAGES. At least three stages of inscription-revision: A (nonextant pre-fair-copy stage); B (tan-gray ink on thinner paper); B+ (on mount, Melville inscribes earlier title in gray-tan ink, and Mrs. Melville inscribes the final title).

TEXTUAL NOTES: SUBSTANTIVES. 305.0 *Greek Architecture*] [*HM leaf 1(B+)* {*inscribed by EM*}] 305.0–4 Greek . . . Archetype] [*EM leaf 1*] 305.0 *Greek Architecture*] EM\ HM5[*see also accidentals for capitalization*]; <u>A Hint from the Greek</u> [*double-underlined to indicate main title*] / <u>As to some points going to constitute the beautiful in arch-tecture</u> [*altered to* <u>architecture</u>] [*single-underlined to indicate subtitle*] HM1,HM3,EM; [*same title and subtitle, except that for* <u>beautiful</u> *is temporarily substituted one undeciphered erased word in HM and the first three letters of another undeciphered erased word in EM*] HM2,EM\HM1; A hint touching Architecture EM\HM2,EM\HM4; [*two to four undeciphered erased words*] EM\HM3 305.1–4 Not . . . Archetype] [*HM leaf 1.clip(B)*]

TEXTUAL NOTES: ACCIDENTALS. 305.0 *Architecture*] EM; architecture EM\ HM,HM\EM[*also see substantives*] 305.2 Form . . . Site] HM,EM\HM1,EM\ HM3; form . . . site EM\HM2 305.4 Archetype] EM\HM[*HM directs EM to check her earlier spelling*]; Archtype HM; Archttype HM\EM,EM 305.4 Archetype] HM[*see also preceding entry*],EM\HM1,EM\HM3; archetype EM\HM2 305.4 Archetype.] EM; Archtype^ HM

OFF CAPE COLONNA (p. 306)

Atop Cape Colonna (or Sounion, ancient Sunium Promontorium) are the remains of an ancient temple formerly supposed to have been dedicated to Athena but now identified as to Poseidon. The poem's speaker implies, however, that one might well consider whether they have afforded much protection to those in "many a deadlier wreck" than William Falconer (1732–69), who drew on his 1750 Cape Colonna experience aboard the

Britannia for his poem *The Shipwreck* (1762), from which Melville used lines 71 and 75–76 among the "Extracts" in *Moby-Dick* (see the NN edition, pp. xxiii, 823). Melville did not visit this part of Italy during his 1856–57 trip.

DISCUSSION. 306.0 *Colonna*] The spelling in HM, "Collonna," though changed to "Collona" in EM, was repeated in his wife's transcript of the table of contents but was corrected to "Colonna" in T, both in the table of contents and at the head of the poem.

EMENDATIONS. *306.0 *Colonna*] T; Collonna HM 306.1 Aloof] EM\HM; Silent HM 306.1 foreland lone] EM\HM; Sunium Steep HM 306.2 rise—] EM; ~, HM 306.3 columns,] EM; ~^ HM 306.5–6 They . . . blue] EM\HM; [*see textual notes for this complex instance*] HM 306.7 gods!] T; ~.— HM

TEXTUAL NOTES: INSCRIPTION STAGES. At least two stages of inscription-revision: A (nonextant pre-fair-copy stage); B (gray-tan ink on thinner paper; pinhole evidence suggests an earlier-stage clip may once have been attached to this leaf).

TEXTUAL NOTES: SUBSTANTIVES. 306.0–10 *Off . . . wreck*] [*HM leaf 1(B); EM leaf 1*] 306.1 Aloof they] EM\HM; Serene they HM1; [?At ease] they HM2; Silent they HM3,HM5; They silent HM4 306.1 foreland lone] EM\HM2[*because he fears the word will be misread as* love *HM later pencil-cancels EM's* lone *and re-pencils in and circles* lone]; Sunium Steep HM; foreland [*undeciphered erased word*] EM\ HM1 305.3 Fair] HM2; White HM1 306.5–6 They . . . blue] EM\HM2,HM\ EM2,T[*although, in revising EM, HM may have considered setting off the revised two lines as, once more, a separate middle stanza, he sent them to the printer indicated (with an inked bracket added at the left of line 5 and a penciled bracket removed from the beginning of line 7) as being attached to lines 7–10 to form a second stanza of six lines; in T, however, he reverted to his earlier plan that the lines be attached to the poem's first stanza*]; A god-like group, afar to scan—/ Synnodic and Olympian. HM1[*set off as a two-line stanza*],HM2[*joined to lines 1–4 as part of first stanza*]; [*six or more undeciphered erased words, constituting at least two readings for the first part of line 5*] [?afar to scan—]/ God-like and Olympian [*then* Look god-like and Olympian *then* A god-like group{?—} Olympian]. HM3,HM4,HM?5,HM?6; [*six or seven undeciphered erased words {?ending* to musing man}]/ A god-like group Olympian. HM7,EM; They wax, enlarged to fancy's view,/ A god-like group against the blue. EM\HM1,HM\EM1[*without the commas in line 5*] 306.10 a deadlier] HM2; another HM1; a xxxxlier EM[*mistranscription*]; deadlier HM\EM[*inadvertent omission of* a *in copying back into HM*]

TEXTUAL NOTES: ACCIDENTALS. *306.0 *Colonna*] T; Collonna HM; Collona EM 306.1 foreland lone] [*see substantives*] 306.2 rise—] EM; ~, HM 306.3 columns,]

HM1,EM; ~^ HM2 306.5 They] [*no line-space precedes*] HM2,EM1,EM3,T; [*line-space*] HM1,EM2,EM4[*and see substantives at 306.5–6*] 306.5–6 They . . . blue] [*see substantives*] 306.6 A] [*no indent*] HM,EM\HM1,EM\HM2[*with explicit verbal direction* no indent]; [*indent*] EM[*mistranscription*] 306.7 Overmuch] HM; Over much T[*EM left a slight space between* Over *and* much *as if anticipating HM might want to hyphenate the elements*] 306.7 gods!] T; ~. HM1,EM\HM1,EM\HM3; ~.— HM2,EM,EM\HM2 306.8 deck,] HM2; ~^ HM1 306.10 a deadlier] [*see substantives*]

THE ARCHIPELAGO (pp. 307–8)

In 1856–57, Melville thrice sailed through the Aegean archipelago (an earlier title for the poem was "The Isles of Greece"). Going from Constantinople to Alexandria on his second pass through the Cyclades, the island group south and east of the Greek mainland, he noted in his journal entry for December 23 and 24, 1856: "Delos, of a most barren aspect, however flowery in fable. I heard it was peculiarly sterile. Patmos, too, not remote; another disenchanting isle" (*Journals*, p. 71). In the entry for December 26 he noted, possibly for a future project: "Contrast between the Greek isles & those of the Polynesan archipelago. The former have lost their virginity. The latter are fresh as at their first creation. The former look worn, and are meagre, like life after enthusiasm is gone. The aspect of all of them is sterile & dry. Even Delos whose flowers rose by miracle in the sea, is now a barren moor, & to look upon the bleak yellow of Patmos, who would ever think that a god had been there" (p. 72). On his third pass, going from the Holy Land to Athens, he sailed at night through the Southern Sporades (the Dodecanese) off the coast of Asia Minor and recorded in his entry for February 5, 1857: "All isles rocky, naked & barren. . . . the scenery is all outline. No filling up. Seem to be sailing upon gigantic outline engravings." After daybreak, in the same entry, he "saw Samos ahead, and Patmos — quite lonely looking. . . . Was here again afflicted with the great curse of modern travel — skepticism. Could no more realize that St: John had ever had revelations here, than when off Juan Fernandez, could beleive in Robinson Crusoe according to De Foe" (p. 97).

DISCUSSIONS. 307.2 Cyclades,] NN retains the comma present in HM, even though, in punctuating EM, Melville may have decided to omit the comma because of his substantive change at the beginning of line 3, from "Most" to "They" (he often omits a comma before "they" in this construction).

307.6 Delos] Delos, in the Cyclades, is said in ancient story to be Apollo's (and his twin sister Artemis's) birthplace.

307.7 Selkirk] Alexander Selkirk (1676–1721) at his own request was set ashore on Màs Afuera, also called Mas-a-Tierra and, by Melville, "Massafuero" (see the NN *Piazza Tales* volume, p. 602), one of the Juan Fernandez islets west of Chile; he became the original of Daniel Defoe's involuntary castaway, Robinson Crusoe (see Melville's journal entry quoted above).

307.10 Theseus roved a Raleigh] Except as a conventional ravisher of brigands' daughters in some versions of the tale, the legendary Greek hero Theseus is not reputed to have ravished any but Ariadne or to have been such a rover or explorer as Sir Walter Raleigh (ca. 1552–1618), the British navigator; Theseus did touch at Delos to make a sacrifice to Apollo on his way back to Athens from slaughtering the Minotaur.

307.13 though] NN retains the copy-text reading, since "through" in EM and T (and other subsequent printings) is obviously an error.

307.14 retain, . . . true,] NN retains the commas in the copy-text, though Melville may possibly have intended their omission in EM.

308.21–24 Polynesia . . . Marquesas] Melville's Marquesan and Polynesian experiences are earlier laid out, directly and indirectly, in *Typee*, *Omoo*, and *Mardi*, as well as in "Rolfe and the Palm" (in *Clarel*, 3.29.1–81) and in "To Ned" (in *John Marr*, pp. 237–38 above).

EMENDATIONS. 307.0 *The Archipelago*] EM\HM; The Isles of Greece HM 307.3 They] EM\HM; Most HM 307.5 ray,] EM\HM; ~; HM 307.7 pray^] EM\HM; ~— HM 307.12 Unravished.] EM; ~! HM 307.14 still] EM\HM; yet HM 307.14 outline] EM\HM; contours HM 307.15 grace of form] EM\HM; graceful lines HM 307.15 earth] EM\HM; all HM 307.16 And primal] EM\HM; In nature HM 307.19 set^—] EM; ~,— HM 308.21 palms,] EM; ~; HM 308.23 Not] EM; None HM 308.24 Marquesas!] EM; ~. HM

TEXTUAL NOTES: INSCRIPTION STAGES. At least two stages of inscription-revision: A (nonextant pre-fair-copy stage); B (gray-tan ink on thinner paper).

TEXTUAL NOTES: SUBSTANTIVES. 307.0–12 The . . . Unravished] [*HM leaf 1(B); EM leaf 1*] 307.0 The Archipelago] HM1,EM\HM[*not copied back into HM*]; The Isles of Greece HM2 307.2 Sporads] HM1,HM3; Sporades HM2 307.2 and] HM2; or HM1 307.3 They] HM?2,HM?4,EM\HM[*in initially inscribing her leaf, EM left a blank space, since she could not make out which word HM intended as his final choice*]; Most HM1,HM8; Some HM3,HM5,HM7; [*undeciphered erased word {?File}*] HM6 307.3 look like isles] HM1,HM4; Isle [*uncompleted variant reading*] HM→2; isles seem isles HM3 307.4 whither] HM2; wither HM→1 307.9 bare,] HM2; gray^ HM1 307.10 roved] HM2; roamed HM1 307.11 small] HM,EM\HM?1,EM\HM?3,HM\EM2[*after leaving a blank space in her transcript (probably because she could not at first read HM's* small *EM may have penciled both* small *and* dwarfed *in her own transcript (presumably at HM's direction), as well as* dwarfed *in HM, then erased both transcripts'* dwarfed]; dwarfed EM\HM?2[*?penciled in by HM* *rather than by EM*],HM\EM1 307.12 Unravished] HM4; [*one or two undeciphered scratched-out words*] HM1; Yea, [*undeciphered erased word*] HM2; Yea, [*undeciphered erased word*] HM3 307.13–308.24 Nor . . . Marquesas] [*HM leaf 2(B); EM leaf 2*] *307.13 though] HM; through EM[*misreading*] 307.13 havoc fell] HM8,EM\ HM2; ravage fell HM1,EM\HM1; havoc [*undeciphered erased word*] HM2; shattering wars HM3; man's fell rage HM?4; wars [?or][*undeciphered erased word {?stars}*] HM5,HM7; wars and creeds HM6; havoc felt EM[*misreading*] 307.14 They still] EM\HM; They yet HM1,HM3; Still they HM2 307.14 outline] EM\HM[*not copied back into HM*]; contours HM 307.15 Their] HM1,HM3; Those HM2 307.15 grace of form] EM\HM2; graceful lines HM; [*undeciphered erased word {?firmer}*] [?lines] EM\HM1 307.15 earth] EM\HM; all HM 307.16 And primal] EM\HM; In nature HM 307.17 beauty clear] HM,EM\HM2; [?sylvan scenes] EM\HM1 307.19 picture] HM2; revel HM1 307.20 Life's revel] HM?2,HM4,HM6,HM8[*if the word is not Life's in the HM2 reading, it is an undeciphered erased word*]; The picture HM1; Thy revel HM3,HM5,HM7

308.22 breathes] HM2; sends HM1 308.23 Not] EM2[*no HM inscription survives for this variant; that the revision was a late one is suggested by EM's not copying it back into HM*]; None HM,EM1

TEXTUAL NOTES: ACCIDENTALS. *307.2 Cyclades,] HM; ~^ EM 307.5 ray,] EM\HM; ~; HM 307.6 to-day] HM; today EM 307.7 pray^] EM\HM2; ~— HM,EM\HM1 307.9 bare,] HM; ~^ EM[*initially, EM left a blank space, so she could ask HM about the word she could not decipher; also see substantives*] 307.10 Raleigh] HM,EM2; Raliegh EM1 307.12 Unravished.] EM; ~! HM 307.13 less,] HM; ~^ EM *307.14 retain, . . . true,] HM; ~^ . . . ~^ EM 307.17 the . . . yet] [*initially, EM could not make out HM's words, and so left a blank space in her transcript till she could determine his intention*] 307.19 picture, Pan,] HM,EM\HM1,EM\HM3; ~^ ~^ EM,EM\HM2 307.19 therein] HM,EM2; therin EM1 307.19 set—] EM; ~, — HM

308.21 Polynesia] HM2[*perhaps revised by EM*]; Polynisia HM1 308.21 palms,] EM; ~; HM 308.22 balms—] HM,EM\HM2; ~, EM\HM1 308.23 calms,] HM,EM\HM2; ~— EM\HM1 308.24 Marquesas!] EM1,EM3; ~. HM,EM2

SYRA (pp. 309–11)

Melville constructed the "Transmitted Reminiscence" in "Syra" largely out of impressions and speculations that he recorded in his journal on two separate visits to the Greek island in the Aegean in early and late December 1856. In his entry for December 2, he noted:

New & old Town. Animated appearance of the quay. Take all the actors of operas in a night from the theaters of London, & set them to work in their fancy dresses, weighing bales, counting codfish, sitting at tables on the dock, smoking, talking, sauntering, — sitting in boats &c — picking up rags, carrying water casks, bemired &c — will give some notion of Greek port. Picturesqueness of the whole. Variety of it. Greek trousers, sort of cross between petticoat & pantaloons. Some with white petticoats & embroidered jackets. Fine forms, noble faces. Mustache &c. — Went to Old Town. From the water looks like colossal sugarloaf. white houses. Divided from New Town by open lots. Climbed up. Complete warren of stone houses or rather huts, built without the least plan. . . . At last got to the top, a church . . . Looks very old; — probably place of defence. Poor people live here. Picturesque. Some old men looked like Pericles reduced to a chiffonier. . . . *The wharf.* . . . Carpenters & blacksmiths working in the theatrical costumes. . . . The crowds on the quays all with red caps, looking like flamingos. Long tassells — laborers wear them, & carry great bundles of codfish on their heads. — Few seem to have anything to do. All lounge. Greek signs over a pieman's. (*Journals,* pp. 53–54)

When he returned to Syra, he continued his description ("Went ashore to renew my impressions") in his entries for December 23 and 24 (pp. 71–72).

DISCUSSIONS. 309.0 *Syra . . . Reminiscence)*] This title, which appears to be the last one approved by Melville, was the outcome of a long series of revisions (see textual notes below). The title at one stage, "Syra, Long ago", was copied by Melville's wife (in the form "Syra long Ago") in her transcript of the table of contents, and the last two words were then marked out by Melville.

309.1 Scio] Scio (now Chios) was traditionally one of the seven cities claiming to be Homer's birthplace.

309.5 Here] NN adopts the reading in EM (without a comma), since the uncanceled comma in HM belongs to at least one substantive revision preceding Melville's final version (and elsewhere in lines 5 and 6 he finally adopted lighter pointing).

309.15 But,/end,/down—] NN retains the copy-text punctuation after "But" and "down" because the readings in T probably represent Melville's restoration of his earlier readings; NN also adopts the comma after "end" from T (not present in HM) since it repeats Melville's first reading as he revised EM.

309.17 forlorn—] In the final reading in HM, a dash follows the parenthetical "Multiplied . . . forlorn"; in punctuating EM, Melville, after several versions, deleted the parentheses and followed "forlorn" with a comma. NN adopts the dash with no parentheses as in T, where the punctuation probably reflects Melville's restoration of an earlier reading in both HM and EM.

309.22 earlier day] Here "earlier" means at least back to 1826 or 1830, dates Melville considered appending instead of the subtitle he finally decided on. In 1891 these years were within the memory span of the speaker indicated by another considered subtitle: "A Nonagenarian's Reminiscence." A date such as

1826 or 1830 would (as Melville presumably knew) set the time of the poem's "reminiscence" as following Syra's early nineteenth-century population increase caused by the Psara and Chios refugees fleeing the Turks—the time in which the island was beginning to prosper as a shipbuilding and transshipment center. But Melville also considered pushing the time of lines 22 and following much further back, making them a third-person "transmitted reminiscence" of Frans Hals (ca. 1580–1666), the Dutch genre painter. In line 22 Melville considered substituting first "Hals" then "Frans" for the "I" he finally kept, and in line 56 considered substituting "Hals" or "One" for the "I" there. Finally, he decided to leave the halcyon period indicated in lines 22ff. unspecified.

309.24 Homer] A fertile Syra is mentioned in the *Odyssey* (15.403).

310.27 found.] NN follows the punctuation Melville added to his wife's transcript (lines 27–28 do not appear in HM, except as copied back into HM without punctuation by his wife). Even though the semicolon in T could represent Melville's later intention (since he substantively revised the line in proof), the greater likelihood is that someone at the Caxton Press supplied it to avoid beginning the sentence that starts in line 28 with "And".

310.29 shawls,] After substantively revising line 30 in proof, Melville did not notice that a comma was now needed at the end of line 29; NN supplies one.

310.30 Eve's—] NN adopts the dash in T as probably Melville's, not a likely insertion by a Caxton Press staff member at a point where EM had no punctuation.

310.37 Anacreon] The Greek poet (ca. 572–488 B.C.) whose actual and attributed works Melville knew well in translation (Sealts, no. 147, Bercaw, no. 14) and imitated in "Anacreontics" (see p. 397 above).

310.38 Pericles] One with the same name as the fifth-century B.C. Athenian statesman (see the discussion at 303.29,30 above).

310.49 craft,] The final, copy-text, reading in HM encloses "Lighters . . . craft" in parentheses and follows "craft" with a comma; no punctuation appears in EM. NN follows the punctuation in T, where a comma is added but no parentheses, as representing Melville's final intention (since the reappearance of the comma suggests that he gave attention to this line in proof).

310.50 Phrygian cap] A close-fitting conical cap, represented in Greek art as worn by Orientals (see *Clarel*, 3.4.50).

310.53 Proserpine's] While no Greek coin would feature the Roman goddess who was raped and carried off to the underworld by Pluto, Melville often interchanges the names and fames of Greek and Roman deities. In *Clarel* (3.6.147–48), he refers to Proserpina as "Ceres' child / In Enna."

311.62 grandfather] The copy-text (and EM) reading is "grandfather's Saturn's prime"—a somewhat odd but possible reading specifying this Saturn as owned not by "these light hearts" but by their grandfather. NN adopts the reading in T, judging that Melville corrected the unintended doubling when he saw the line in proof. That the "prime" is the fabled Golden Age was more explicit in an earlier version of the line, which read "Saturn's golden prime".

311.63 toil] NN retains the unpunctuated reading in HM and EM, though the comma in T could possibly represent his later intention.

311.65 none,] Melville added this line to EM in pencil. Then his wife erased his wording and punctuation before she re-inscribed it in ink. In the process she replaced an erased period, but not this comma; NN presumes Melville did not intend the omission.

EMENDATIONS. *309.0[*subtitle*] *(A . . . Reminiscence)*] EM\HM; ^~ . . . ~^ HM 309.1 Fleeing] [*indent*] EM\HM; [*no indent*] HM 309.1–3 vines^/(Where . . . torch)] EM\HM; ~,/^~ . . . ~, HM 309.2 Where^ . . . done^] EM\HM; ~, . . . ~, HM *309.5 Here^] EM; ~, HM 309.5 isle,] EM\HM; [*when line 5 ended with* shore *it also ended with a period*] HM 309.6 here^] EM\HM; ~, HM 309.7 turbaned] EM\HM; crafty HM 309.12 fastness^] EM\HM; ~, HM 309.13 With pains] EM\HM; Forthwith HM 309.13 camp,] EM\HM; ~— HM 309.14 Stone] EM\HM; Mere HM *309.15 end,] T; ~^ HM *309.16–17 ^Multiplied . . . forlorn^—] T; (~ . . .~)— HM 309.16 now,] EM\HM; ~— HM 309.18 And^ . . . verge^] EM\HM; ~, . . . ~, HM 309.18 verge] EM\HM; edge HM 309.19 thrive;] EM\HM; ~, HM 309.23 isled resort] EM\HM; island mart HM 310.26 Sheds . . . wreck-stuff^] HM\EM; Small shops, rude shanties, HM *310.27–28 Where . . . shanty-shop] EM; [*no equivalent lines; HM added lines 27 and 28 at stage Da, after EM had already transcribed his stage C inscription*] HM 310.27 goods in transit] T; kegs, sacks, tierces EM 310.29–34 Where . . . astray] EM; [*see textual notes for this complex instance*] HM 310.29 Fez-caps . . . tobacco] EM; swords, tobacco, pistols HM *310.29 shawls,] NN; ~^ HM *310.30 Eve's—] T; ~^ EM 310.33 orderless . . . way] T; shelved promiscuous, or displayed^ HM 310.35 Above] [*line-space precedes; indent*] EM\HM; [*no line-space; no indent*] HM 310.35 Above . . . flag] EM\HM; Without. Above a tented inn HM 310.38 Dispensed] T; Retailed HM 310.38 one named "Pericles."] EM; "<u>Pericles</u>",! HM 310.40 various] EM\HM; divers HM 310.41 eyes,] EM; ~^ HM 310.42 may] EM\HM; do HM 310.43 xebecs trim] EM\HM; smallish craft HM 310.44 And some but] EM\HM; Sea-skimmers HM 310.45 strand, . . . none,] EM\HM; ~— . . . ~— HM 310.46 What . . . fry] EM; [*see textual notes for this complex instance*] 310.47 picturesquely] EM; picturesquly HM *310.49 ^Lighters . . . craft,^] T; (~ . . . ~,) HM 310.49 craft] EM\HM; brig HM 310.54 like] EM\HM; Like HM 310.55 work] EM\HM; toil HM 310.56 saw,] EM\HM; ~; HM 310.56 too.^] EM\HM; ~?— HM 310.57 Here . . . yet:] EM\HM; Commerce is but initial here. HM 310.58 Forever] EM\HM; For aye HM 310.58 this juvenile] EM\HM; will the HM 311.59 And . . . glee,] T; In these light juvenile ones whose garb^ HM 311.60 Alike profuse] T; And glee, alike HM *311.62 grandfather] T; grandfather's HM 311.62 prime] EM\HM; time HM 311.64 leisure,] EM\HM; ~^ HM 311.64 merriment, peace,] EM\HM; and Idlesse. HM *311.65 And . . . righteousness.] EM\HM; [*no line present; in HM, the poem ends with line 64*] HM

TEXTUAL NOTES: INSCRIPTION STAGES. At least four stages of inscription-revision: A (nonextant pre-fair-copy stage); B (superseded leaf 4/5 [*Billy Budd* 361 verso]); C (gray-tan ink on thinner paper); D (gray-tan ink on thinner paper).

TEXTUAL NOTES: SUBSTANTIVES. 309.0–11 *Syra . . . won*] [*HM leaf 1(C)*] 309.0–12 *Syra . . . flanks*] [*EM leaf 1*] *309.0[*title and subtitle*] Syra / . . . Reminiscence*] HM?9,EM\HM?2,EM3; Syra / In the Archipelago HM1; [?Syra /] An Egean Isle in 1830 HM2; Syra, years ago HM3; Syra, Long ago HM4,HM6,EM1[*without comma, and with* long]; Syra, 1826 HM5; Syra / A Nonagenarian's Reminiscence HM?7,EM2; Syra / [*two or more undeciphered erased words, constituting at least one variant reading*] [?Reminiscence] HM?8[*perhaps precedes reading here designated* HM?7]; Syra / A [*undeciphered erased word*] Reminiscence EM\HM1[*one or more undeciphered erased words may constitute at least one additional variant of the word preceding* Reminiscence] 309.1 Fleeing] HM,EM\HM2; [?Redeemed] EM\HM1 309.4 goods] HM,EM\HM2; all EM\HM1 309.5 an . . . isle] HM9; an isle stript long before HM→1; a far less winsome shore HM2; [*four or five undeciphered erased words*] shore HM3; [?a far less] [*undeciphered erased word*] shore HM4; an all but vacant shore HM5; an uninhabited isle HM6,HM8; this uninhabited isle HM→7 309.7 Felt safe] HM1,HM3; Secure felt HM2 309.7 turbaned] HM1,EM\HM; [?pitiless] HM2; barberous HM3; crafty HM4 309.8 Dreading] HM,EM\HM2; Fearing EM\HM1 309.11 For] HM2; They HM→1 309.11 height] HM,EM\HM2; crown EM\HM1 309.11 they] HM,EM\HM3; he EM\HM1; [?one] EM\HM2 309.11 made] HM,EM\HM2; [?ai {?*the beginning of* aimed}] EM\HM→1 309.11 prudent] HM2,EM\HM6; painful HM1; [*three or four undeciphered erased words, successive variant readings*] EM\HM1–?4; [?bravely] EM\HM5 309.11 won] HM,EM\HM2; gained EM\HM1 309.12–310.28 A . . . shop] [*HM leaf 2(C)* {Sheds . . . shop *inscribed by EM*}] 309.12 on whose flanks^] HM3,EM\HM3; not remote. HM1; nor remote. HM2; on whose top^ EM\HM1; on whose crown^ EM\HM2 309.13–310.28 With . . . shanty-shop] [*EM leaf 2*] 309.13 With pains] EM\HM3; Thereon HM1; [*one or two undeciphered erased words*] HM2; Whereon HM3; Forthwith HM4; [*one or more undeciphered erased words, constituting, perhaps, more than one variant reading, since, at some point,* Forthwith . . . their *was pencil-canceled, then restored, before HM settled upon his final reading*] EM\HM1,EM\HM?2 309.14 Stone] EM\HM; Mere HM 309.14 huts . . . clung] HM,EM\HM2; [*canceled, but no variants inscribed, unless provisional revision of* wary *(see entry below) might qualify as such*] EM\HM1 309.14 whereto] HM1,HM3; to which HM2 309.14 wary] HM,EM\HM2; cautious EM\HM1 309.15 come] HM,T; came EM[*probably not an EM misreading, but evidence of HM temporarily nodding, since EM seems to have left a space for the variant letter before querying HM as to his intention*] 309.18 building] HM,EM\HM2; campin EM\HM→1 309.18 verge] EM\HM; edge HM 309.21 mere] HM2,EM\HM4; bare HM1; there EM\HM1,EM\HM3; [*undeciphered erased word*] EM\HM2 309.22 I] HM,EM?1,EM\HM5,EM3,HM\EM2; Hals EM\HM?1,EM2,HM\EM1; [*undeciphered erased* *word*] EM\HM2; [*undeciphered erased word*] EM\HM3; Frans EM\HM4 309.23 isled resort] EM\HM,EM2; island mart HM; island [*EM could not decipher* mart *and left a blank space for the word*] EM1 309.24 known] HM2; seen HM1

310.26 Sheds . . . wreck-stuff^] EM2,HM\EM[*from nonextant HM stage Da inscription*]; Small shops and rude then^ HM1; Small shops, rude [*undeciphered erased word*], HM2; Small shops, low [*undeciphered erased word*], HM3; Small shops, rude shanties, HM4,EM1; Small shops, [*one or two undeciphered erased words, constituting one or two variant readings*] shanties, EM\HM1,EM\HM?2 310.27–28 Where . . . shanty-shop] EM[*except where later revised by HM, the authority for the wording of lines 27 and 28 is EM transcription from nonextant HM stage Da inscription*]; [*no equivalent text-lines; HM added lines 27 and 28 at stage Da, after EM had already transcribed his stage C inscription*] HM 310.27 goods in transit] T; kegs, sacks, tierces EM[*from nonextant HM stage Da inscription*],HM\EM; *following* found],HM\EM; jars, sacks, cases EM\HM(?Db+) 310.29–34 Where . . . astray] [*EM leaf 3(from nonextant HM stage Db inscription)*] *310.29–34 Where . . . astray] EM[*from nonextant HM stage Db inscription; HM added lines 30–31 at stage Dba; at stage Da, final line 32 followed line 29; further, EM did not transcribe HM's extensive stage Db revisions of final lines 29, 33, and 34 back into HM, a fact that suggests the stage Db revisions occurred just before EM's transcript was sent off to the printer; EM earlier transcribed HM's pre–stage Db revisions back into HM, then canceled her* Where swords, tobacco, pistols, shawls / Like plunder on a pirate's deck *when she realized HM's version of the first of these lines could be reinstated with restoration underlinings, and the second line had never been canceled in HM*]; [*not six lines, but four—earlier versions of final lines 29 and 32–34—revisions of which lines are described in entries here following—though it should be remarked that the much-revised condition of EM leaves 2 and 4 makes difficult or impossible even the detecting of some potential HM revisions thereon*] HM 310.29 Fez-caps . . . tobacco] EM[*from nonextant HM inscription*]; swords, tobacco, pistols HM 310.31 dimmed by] EM\HM; rueing EM[*from nonextant HM inscription*] 310.32–42 Like . . . may] [*HM leaf 3(C)*] 310.32 Like plunder] HM2; Were seen [*an uncompleted text-line*] HM→1 310.32 on] HM2; in HM1 310.33 orderless . . . way^] T; shelved promiscuous with a rout^ HM1; shelved promiscuous [*penciled comma added now or later*] or displayed^ HM2; strown, promiscuous, or displayed^ EM\ HM1,EM\HM3; strown[*?comma*] at random[*?comma*] or displayed^ EM\HM2; [*?strown, promiscuous,*] and [*undeciphered erased word*]^ EM\HM4; heaped disordered and astray. EM\HM5; orderless in such wild way^ EM[*from nonextant HM stage Db inscription*] 310.34 As . . . astray] EM[*from nonextant HM stage Dbb inscription; at stage Dbb, HM added* As . . . astray *and revised the following text-line accordingly*]; [*no exactly equivalent text-line*] HM 310.35–50 Above . . . cap] [*EM leaf 4*] 310.35 Above . . . flag] EM\HM2; Without. Above a shanty inn HM1; Without. Above a tented inn HM2; Displayed [*?above a tented inn*] EM\HM1[*one or two undeciphered erased words may be associable with the* Displayed *of this revision*] 310.36 Greek] HM,EM\HM2; [*undeciphered erased word*] EM\HM1 310.38 Dispensed] HM1,HM3,T; Retailed HM2,HM4 310.38 one named "Pericles."] EM2;

"<u>Pericles</u>", ye gods! HM1,EM1[*EM not punctuated; see also accidentals*]; "<u>Pericles</u>",! HM2[*comma not explicitly canceled*]; one named ^Pericles^^ EM\HM 310.39 for the opera's scene] HM3; for Paris stage HM→1; for the Paris stage HM→2 310.40 various] HM1,EM\HM; divers HM2 310.41 gold-shot] HM2,HM4; dangerous HM1,HM3 310.42 may] EM\HM; do HM 310.43–55 Off-shore . . . play] [*HM leaf 4(C)*] 310.43 xebecs trim] EM\HM; smallish craft HM 310.44 And some but] EM\HM2; Sea-skimmers HM; And some EM\HM?1 310.44 repute] HM2; their rig HM1 310.45–46 But . . . fry] [*presumably because HM had canceled* There did I note what busy bees, *his stage C version line 46, and because she was uncertain as to his final intention concerning line 45, EM at first left a one-line blank space in her transcript; later, she penciled, then inked line 45 into her transcript (two or three undeciphered erased words in EM may be part of an intermediate but finally rejected HM revision of the beginning of line 45 or EM's reminder to herself to query HM's intentions—or both); from HM's dictation or nonextant inscription, EM also inked* What busy bees no testy fry *into EM, and transcribed into HM (with or without HM authority for the substantive variant)* Such busy bees no testy fry *(neither version of this revised line 46 punctuated, since the understanding was that HM would look to the final pointing—which, in her transcript, he did)*] 310.46 What . . . fry;] EM[*from HM dictation or nonextant inscription; in EM, what might appear to be a penciled cancellation of* What busy bees *may be only part of EM's earlier querying of HM's intention, and this is the more likely since no substantive variants for the words seem to have been inscribed before the penciled "cancellation" line was erased*]; There did I note what busy bees, HM1,HM3; There did [*undeciphered erased word {?Cad ?uncompleted proper name}*] note what busy bees, HM→2; Such busy bees no testy fry^ HM\EM 310.49 craft] EM\HM1,EM\HM3; brig HM,EM\HM2[*the much-erased state of EM suggests HM may have considered more than these two readings*] 310.51–311.65 Blue . . . righteousness] [*EM leaf 5*] 310.51 Blue] HM2; Wide HM1 310.52 some] HM,EM\HM2; most EM\HM1 310.54–311.64 Such . . . peace] HM2; [*see following description of superseded stage B inscription*] [*Superseded HM leaf 4/5(B)* {"Billy Budd" leaf 361 verso} chatterers . . . leisure {*this partial leaf is not foliated, since its top quarter has been scissored away; it is inscribed in ink, then revised in pencil*}]

> [*pencil-added at the top of this partial leaf is a revision of a now-scissored-away text-line,* chatterers all{*?semicolon*}]
> Who make believe to work, but play.
> [*line-space*]
> What shall we think?
> Commerce [*then* Business *then neither* Commerce *nor* Business] is but beginning here:
> They laugh upon the brink^ [*then* Do they laugh upon the brink? *then* How long will the fun endure^]
> Whose costume and whose spirits both [*then* gay *then (beginning probably with the preceding line's revised state* How long will the fun endure*) turn two text-lines into three by canceling* Whose costume and whose spirits

gay *and adding* In these light-hearted ones whose cheer / And {*undeci-phered erased word* [*?*unbeseeming]} costume gay]

Alike in flowing [*then* So flowing in the] measure

Beseem would [*then* Come down from] Saturn's golden prime

When Trade was not, nor ink a blot, [*then cancel* When . . . blot,]

And [*then* When] life was Adam's leisure. [*then ?*When Trade was Adam's leisure. {*though* life *is not canceled, the second* When *is erased and* When trade *is marked for restoration; a penultimate reading (even though* was not *is not explicitly marked for restoration) might have been* When Trade was not, / When life was Adam's leisure.}]

————"———— [*ending device*]

[*cancel leaf with pencil and green pencil*] HM1(B) 310.55 work] EM\HM; toil HM 310.56–311.65 I . . . righteousness] [*HM leaf 5(C)*] 310.56 I . . . how] HM1,HM4[*succeeds EM\HM reading*],EM2; [*two or three undeciphered erased words*] [*?*one] HM2; Hals saw; and how HM3,EM1; One saw; and how EM\HM[*furthermore, such is the revised and erased state of both HM and EM that either or both may harbor further readings not readily determinable*] 310.56 musing] HM,EM2; [*?*missing] EM1 310.57 Here . . . yet:] EM\HM3[*HM\EM lacks colon*]; Commerce is but initial here. HM,EM; Here commerce is but in germ as yet: EM\HM1; Here traffic's but in germ as yet: EM\HM?2 310.58 Forever] EM\HM; For aye HM; For EM[*EM at first left a blank space in her transcript when she could not make out HM's* aye] 310.58 this juvenile] EM\HM1,EM\HM3; will the HM; [*undeciphered erased word* {*?*that *?*the}] juvenile EM\HM2

311.59 And . . . glee,] T; In these light juvenile men^ whose garb^ HM1; In these light juvenile ones^ whose garb^ HM2; In these light-hearted ones, whose garb^ EM\HM1,EM\HM3; In these light-hearted men, whose garb^ EM\ HM2 311.60 Alike profuse] T; And glee, alike HM,EM[*without comma*] *311.62 grandfather] T; grandfather's HM 311.62 prime] EM\HM2; reign HM1,EM\ HM1; time HM2 311.62,63 prime / When] [*no text-line between*] HM,EM\HM2; [*an erased penciled arrow leads from erased penciled words at the bottom of EM leaf 5 to the space between lines 62 and 63, indicating that at some juncture HM considered inserting another text-line reading* The Golden Age when gold was {*?*not} {*then* was dross}] EM\HM1 311.63 When] HM,EM\HM2; And EM\HM1[*see preceding entry*] 311.63 trade] HM1,HM3; toil HM2 311.63 not] HM,EM\HM2,EM\ HM4; none EM\HM1,EM\HM3 *311.63 toil^ nor] HM2; poverty's HM1; toil, nor T 311.64 leisure] HM,EM\HM2; [*one or more undeciphered erased words*] EM\ HM1 311.64 merriment, peace,] EM\HM[*HM\EM lacks punctuation*]; and Idlesse. HM1,HM3; [*undeciphered erased word*] Idlesse. HM2 *311.65 And . . . righteousness] EM\HM2[*HM\EM lacks punctuation*]; [*no further text-line present; in HM, the poem ends with line 64*] HM; And lucre none, [*one or more undeciphered erased words, constituting, perhaps, more than one variant reading*] was righteousness EM\HM1

TEXTUAL NOTES: ACCIDENTALS. 309.0[*title and subtitle*] Syra / . . . *Reminiscence*] [*see substantives*] *309.0[*subtitle*] (*A . . . Reminiscence*)] [*underlined*] EM\HM1,EM\HM3; [*not underlined*] EM\HM2; [*underlined; no parentheses*] HM,HM\EM 309.0[*subtitle*] *Reminiscence*] EM2,HM\EM; Reminisience EM1 309.1 Fleeing] [*indent*] EM\HM[*EM does not otherwise indicate line 1 for indention, but she re-inscribes, circles, and adds a pointing finger to HM's* Indent first line of paragraphs,],T; [*no indent*] HM,EM 309.1 Scio's] [*EM apparently only left her transcript unpunctuated, but did not (otherwise) mistranscribe; still, in EM, HM re-inscribed* Scio's *and mended EM's original* Scios] 309.1–3 vines^^ / (Where . . . torch)] EM\HM1,EM\HM5; ~,^ / ^~ . . . ~, HM1,HM3; ~,— / ^~ . . . ,— HM2; ~— / ^~ . . . — EM\HM2,EM\HM4; ~^^ / ^~ . . . ~, EM\HM?3[*perhaps EM here ink-inscribed the comma before being directed to do so*]; ~^^ / ^~ . . . ~^ ?EM 309.2 Where^ . . . done^] EM,EM\HM2; ~, . . . ~, HM,EM\HM1 *309.5 Here^] HM1,EM; ~, HM2[*in the course of substantively revising line 5, HM considered using the comma*] 309.5 isle,] EM\HM2; ~; EM\HM1; [*when line 5 ended with* shore *it also ended with a period*] HM; ~^ EM 309.6 here^] EM,EM\HM2; ~, HM,EM\HM1 309.12 fastness^] HM1,EM,EM\HM2; ~, HM2,EM\HM1 309.12 flanks^] [*see substantives*] 309.13 camp,] EM\HM1,EM\HM3; ~— HM,EM\HM2; ~^ EM *309.15 But, . . . end,] EM\HM1,T; ~, . . . ~^ HM; ~^ . . . ~^ EM,EM\HM2 *309.15 down—] HM2,EM\HM1,T; ~^ HM1,EM; ~, EM\HM2 *309.16–17 ^Multiplied . . . forlorn^—] HM2,EM\HM1,T; ^~ . . . ~, HM1,EM\HM3; (~ . . . ~)— HM3,EM\HM2; ^~ . . . ~^^ EM 309.16 now,] EM\HM; ~^ HM1,EM; ~— HM2 309.18 And^ . . . verge^] EM,EM\HM2; ~, . . . ~, HM,EM\HM1 309.19 thrive;] EM\HM; ~, HM; ~^ EM 309.19 and^ . . . more^] HM,EM,EM\HM2; ~, . . . ~, EM\HM1 309.22 I] [*indent*] HM2,EM\HM; [*no indent*] HM1,EM 309.22 I . . . day] HM,EM2; [*though her reason is not evident, EM at first only penciled in line 22*] EM1 309.23 isled resort] [*see substantives*]

310.26 Sheds . . . wreck-stuff] [*see substantives*] *310.27 found.] EM\HM; ~^ EM,HM\EM; ~; T 310.28 shanty-shop] EM; ~^~ HM\EM *310.30 Eve's—] T; ~^ EM[*see substantives at lines 29–34*] 310.33 orderless . . . way] [*see substantives*] 310.35 Above . . . flag] [*see substantives*] 310.35 Above] [*line-space precedes; indent*] EM\HM; [*no line-space; no indent*] HM 310.37 selfsame] HM; self-same T 310.38 one named "Pericles."] [*see substantives*] 310.38 Pericles] HM2,EM2; Perecles HM1,EM1 310.41 eyes,] EM; ~^ HM 310.43 Off-shore] [*line-space precedes; indent*] HM2,EM\HM,T; [*no line-space; no indent*] HM1 310.45 strand, . . . none,] HM1,EM\HM; ~— . . . ~— HM2[*the earlier commas not explicitly canceled*]; ~^ . . . ~^ ?EM 310.46 What . . . fry;] [*see substantives*] 310.47 picturesquely] EM; picturesquly HM *310.49 ^Lighters . . . craft,^] HM1[*with* brig *for* craft],HM\EM,T; (~ . . . ~,) HM2; ^~ . . . ~^^ EM 310.49 Lighters] HM,EM2; Ligtters EM1 310.50 Each] HM,EM2; Eash EM1 310.51 Eastern] HM2; eastern HM1 310.51 drawers^] HM,EM\HM2; ~, EM\HM1 310.51 vest;] HM2,EM\HM2; ~, HM1; ~: EM\HM1; ~^ EM 310.53 Proserpine's] HM,EM1,EM3; Proserpines EM2 310.54 like] EM\HM; Like HM 310.56 I] [*line-space precedes*] HM2,EM,EM\HM; [*?no *line-space (since line 56 begins HM leaf 5, the leaf division might conceal an otherwise intended line-space)*] HM1,HM?3[*in HM, the penciled bracket left of line 56 has been partially erased; though this erasure may have occurred inadvertently in the course of extensive substantive revisions, EM made her transcript with a line-space*] 310.56 I] [*indent*] HM2,EM,EM\HM; [*no indent*] HM1,HM?3 310.56 saw,] EM\HM; ~; HM; ~^ EM 310.56 too.] EM\HM2; ~: HM1,EM\HM1; ~?— HM2; ~^ EM 310.57 Here . . . yet:] [*see substantives*]

    311.59 And . . . glee,] [*see substantives*] 311.60 Alike profuse] [*see substantives*] 311.60 measure,] HM2; ~^ HM1 311.63 toil^ nor] [*see substantives*] 311.63 stress,] HM2; ~^ HM1 311.64 leisure,] EM\HM; ~^ HM,EM 311.64 merriment, peace,] [*see substantives*] *311.65 none,] EM\HM; ~^ EM,HM\EM,T

DISINTERMENT OF THE HERMES (p. 312)

It is unclear how soon Melville wrote this poem after May 1877, when German archaeologists discovered at Olympia the Hermes described by Pausanias in the second century as by Praxiteles; but it is at least one poem in the "Fruit of Travel Long Ago" section of *Timoleon* that could not have been in the volume Melville tried to publish in 1860, as many of the others may have been (see pp. 449–50 above).

DISCUSSIONS. 312.1 fair—] NN adopts the dash from T as not likely to have been supplied by anyone but Melville in place of the comma (in HM and EM).

    312.7 O] See the discussion at 260.41,42 above.

    312.9 barren,] NN retains the comma in HM, although Melville possibly intended its omission, as in EM.

EMENDATIONS. 312.0 *Disinterment . . . Hermes*] EM\HM; Suggested by the Disinterment / of the Hermes / By the German Commission HM 312.1,7 What/To] [*indent*] EM\HM; [*no indent*] HM *312.1 fair—] T; ~, HM *312.7 O^] EM; ~, HM

TEXTUAL NOTES: INSCRIPTION STAGES. At least three stages of inscription-revision: A (nonextant pre-fair-copy stage); B (blue ink on thicker, darker paper); C (tan-gray ink on thinner, lighter paper).

TEXTUAL NOTES: SUBSTANTIVES. 312.0 *Disinterment of the Hermes*] [*HM leaf 1(I.C)*] 312.0–10 *Disinterment . . . hands*] [*EM leaf 1*] 312.0 *Disinterment of the Hermes*] EM\ HM[*one or two undeciphered erased words below the title may amount to intermediate revision or directions concerning the title's final form*]; Suggested by the Disinterment / of the Hermes / By the German Commission HM 312.1–6 What . . . sift] [*HM leaf 1.clip(B)*] 312.1 forms] HM1,HM3; [*scissored-away word*] HM2 312.2 Carven demigod] HM1,HM3; demigod carved HM→2 312.7–10 To . . . hands] [*HM leaf 1(...II.C)*] 312.7 these] HM2; them HM1 312.8 arid] HM2; b [*?the beginning of* barren] HM→1 312.10 hands.] [*no further text-lines follow*] HM2; [*HM slightly revised (as indicated), then canceled the following two lines after adding a bracket at the left of the first of them to indicate their being set off as a concluding couplet-paragraph*]

> The Hermes, risen, renews its span
> In resurrection never proved by [*then* in *then both* in *and* by *left canceled*]
>   man. HM1

TEXTUAL NOTES: ACCIDENTALS. 312.1,7 What/To] [*indent*] EM\HM[*HM directs* Indent / first / lines / of the paragraphs]; [*no indent*] HM *312.1 fair—] T; ~, HM 312.4 Latium's] HM,EM\HM; Latiums EM 312.6 Alluvial^] HM,EM2; ~, EM1 *312.7 O^] EM; ~, HM 312.8 arid] HM2; [*undeciphered erased letter*] HM→1 *312.9 barren,] HM; ~^ EM 312.9 theirs^] HM,EM\HM2; ~— EM\HM1 312.10 Sterile,] HM,EM\HM1,EM\HM3; ~^ EM\HM2

THE APPARITION (p. 313)

The evidence of foliation and content suggests that Melville once considered these lines as a second poem (titled "The Same") about the Parthenon (in addition, probably, to "The Parthenon," pp. 302–3 above) and then as Part II of a poem on that topic (probably the one presently called "The Parthenon") with the part-title "Seen from the Piræus Road." Melville registered his first impression of the Parthenon on the night of February 8, 1857, as he approached Athens by the "Piræus road" (words that appear in several of the poem's earlier titles and subtitles): "Parthenon elevated like cross of Constantine" (*Journals*, p. 99). The allusion in that journal entry, as in the poem's first stanza, invokes the legend (told variously) that the Emperor Constantine (ca. A.D. 280–337), on the eve of his third and decisive battle with Maxentius in 312, was converted to Christianity when a "supernatural Cross" and the words "*in hoc signo vinces*" ("by this sign thou shalt conquer") appeared in the sky. In *Clarel*, 1.31.117–20, Rolfe shows that he has read something like chapter 20 in Edward Gibbon's *History of the Decline and Fall of the Roman Empire* (London: Murray, 1846; Sealts, no. 223b) as he notes that Constantine, "timing well the tide, / Laced not the Cross upon Rome's flag / Supreme, till Jove began to lag / Behind the new religion's stride." One source of Melville's ideas about Diogenes (lines 9–12) was his copy of Diogenes Laërtius, *The Lives and Opinions of Eminent Philosophers* (London: Bohn, 1853; Sealts, no. 183a, Bercaw, no. 216). For Melville's other journal entries regarding the "Parthenon uplifted on its rock," see the introductory notes to "The Parthenon" and "Greek Masonry" (pp. 836–37 and 839 above).

DISCUSSIONS. 313.6 Adam's] Melville's superseded draft (see the textual notes below) makes clear that by "Adam's" he here means "human's" or "humanity's."

313.7 cynic] As philosophers, the Cynics (beginning with Antisthenes in the fifth century B.C.) were concerned with the practical bases of morality and considered virtue, especially honesty (line 9), as the basis of happiness. Because "cynic" is derived from the Greek for "dog," Cynics were popularly imagined as dogs barking (as here in line 12).

EMENDATIONS. 313.0 *The Apparition . . . Athens*] HM\EM; [*see textual notes for the complex readings in HM*] 313.1 Cross,] EM; ~^ HM 313.2 air,] EM; ~^ HM 313.3 the Emperor] EM; imperial HM 313.4,8,12 And/You/In] [*no indent*] EM; [*indent*] HM 313.4 his] EM; the HM 313.6 best!] EM; ~, HM 313.7 minds] EM; moods HM 313.7 you] EM; ye HM 313.7 convert] EM; disarm HM 313.8 You try them] EM; You HM 313.8 or] EM; you HM 313.9 honest] EM\HM; noble HM 313.10 began;] EM\HM; ~: HM 313.11 seen,] EM\HM; ~^ HM 313.12 In mood nor] EM; Nor HM

TEXTUAL NOTES: INSCRIPTION STAGES. At least five stages of inscription-revision: A (nonextant pre-fair-copy stage); B (superseded leaf 1 in Harvard MS Am 188 [386.C.2]); C (nonextant stage inferable from textual gaps between stage B and stage D versions); D (tan-gray ink on thinner paper); D+ (post-D revisions in Melville's wife's hand, presumably from a nonextant Melville inscription [see p. 606 above]).

TEXTUAL NOTES: SUBSTANTIVES. 313.0–12 *The . . . Man*] [*HM leaf 1(D)*] 313.0–4 *The . . . there*] [*EM leaf 1*] 313.0–12 *The . . . Man*] HM2; [*see following descrip-tion of superseded stage B inscription*] [*Superseded HM leaf 1(B) {Draft of Preface to "At Delmonico's" and "An Afternoon in Naples" leaf 1 verso [in Harvard MS Am 188 (386.C.2)]}*] The same . . . Man {*inscribed in ink; revised and foliated in pencil; successive foliation numbers—2 then 4 then 2 again—suggest, along with title and part-number evi-dence described below, that HM at one time considered this earlier version of what became "The Apparition" as the second part of another poem on the same topic—probably "The Parthenon" (pp. 302–3)*}]

    The Same
    ————"———— [*beginning device*]
    [*then cancel* The Same *and add part number* II. *below the beginning device; then add and subsequently cancel a part title* Like the miraculous Cross *(underlined) at right of the beginning device; then insert and subsequently can-cel another part title* Seen from the Piræus Road *(not underlined); then add*

The same *(underlined) as a part title; also add, at upper left, as alternative title,* The Parthenon again *and another beginning device, a title subsequently revised to* The Parthenon seen from the Piræus road, *the evident comma either an elongated period or an indication that HM might have considered adding more words; when he added, below, at the left of his initial beginning device, a parenthesized* put it apart *the now intended to be separate poem had both a title and a part title that remained uncanceled*]
The appearing cross, abruptly bright,
   Aloft in startled air [*then* In startled air *?or/then* In startled air the th
     {*?an uncompleted reading; or the* the th *is part of an uncompleted reading in the revising of the following line*} *then* Vivid in startled air],
Pierced [*then* It pierced *then* Pierced *then* It pierced] Constantine upon
the steed [*then* the xxxx {*beginning of undeciphered word* [*?pure*]} →*then* the pagan on the steed *then* Constantine on {*or, tacitly,* upon} the steed *then* the xx {*beginning of undeciphered word—perhaps* unbeliever} →*then* the disbeliever crowned, *then* the disbeliever through]
And turned his soul's allegiance there.
[*line-space*]
With kindred [*then* other] power, appealing down,
   Miraculous human [*?then* O human {*or* O human human} *then* Divinely human *then* Ethereal {*or* Ethereal human} *then* Illustrious *then* Transcendant *then* Miraculous] Fane!
You strike with awe [*then* With awe you strike] the cynic heart [*then* one *then* heart *then* cancel whole line and substitute If cynic ones you scarce convert*]
   Convert it from [*then* Convert him from *?then* You modify *?then* {*an additional uncanceled* You *suggests the following reading might have preceded* You modify} You yet suspend *then* You lessen their] disdain.
[*line-space*]
Even Timon [*then* Through Timon *then* Even Timon *then* Through Timon *then* Timon], mad without the gate,
   When you he marked, compunction [*then* (If you he marked) compunction *then* compunction] ran; [*leaving both line 9 and line 10 incompletely revised*]
Diogenes too beheld your [*then* Diogenes *leaving the line incompletely revised*] state
   And faltered in his gibes at Man.
———"——— [*ending device*]

[*then cancel lines 9–12* Even . . . Man *with pencil before canceling whole leaf with brown pencil*] HM1(B) 313.0[*title and subtitle*] The Apparition / . . . Athens)] HM\ EM3[*possibly from nonextant HM inscription, since most of the decipherable penciled and erased words at the top of HM leaf 1 (whether in EM's or HM's hand) seem to go to make up at least one earlier title and two earlier subtitles*]; The Parthenon / (Seen from [?the Pireus road]) HM?1; The Parthenon / (The last [*then* (The *then* ?(the *then* (The first] look from the Pireus road.) HM2; [*four or more undeciphered erased words contribute to at least two more variants of title or subtitle; at different times, HM also directs that EM transcribe title and subtitle on* 4 lines *and* {?3} lines] HM3,HM4; The Parthenon / First appearing [*two or three undeciphered erased words, followed by words that may belong to a later subtitle:*] view aloft / Against [*two or three undeciphered erased words* {?the sky}] [?from the Piræus Road] HM\EM1,HM\EM?2 313.0[*subtitle*] *its*] EM\HM; [?the] EM[*perhaps a mistranscription (?caused, in part, by the extensively revised state of HM)*] 313.3 the Emperor] EM(D+)[*here and in following instances, EM transcribes from nonextant HM inscription*]; imperial HM 313.4 his soul's allegiance] EM(D+); the pagan HM1; the soul's allegiance HM2 313.5–12 With . . . Man] [*EM leaf 2*] 313.5 other] HM,EM\HM2; natural EM\HM1 313.7 minds] EM(D+); mood HM?1; moods HM2[*mended for legibility; and EM did not change moods* to minds *when she copied HM's other revisions of the line from her transcript into his*] 313.7 you] EM(D+); ye HM 313.7 convert] EM(D+); disarm HM 313.8 You try them] EM(D+); You HM 313.8 or] EM(D+); you HM 313.9 honest] EM\HM2[*not copied back into HM*]; noble HM; [?pantheist] EM\HM1 313.12 In mood nor] EM(D+); Nor HM

TEXTUAL NOTES: ACCIDENTALS. 313.0[*title and subtitle*] *The Apparition* / . . . *Athens*)] [*see substantives*] 313.0 Apparition] HM\EM2; [*undeciphered mistranscription*] HM\EM1 313.0[*subtitle*] (*The . . . Athens*)] HM\EM2; ^~ . . . ~^ HM\EM1 313.1 Cross,] EM; ~^ HM 313.2 air,] EM; ~^ HM 313.4,8,12 And/You/In] [*no indent*] EM[*from nonextant HM direction*]; [*indent*] HM[*these lines were expanded; see substantives*] 313.6 Adam's] HM,T; Adams EM 313.6 best!] EM2; ~, HM,EM1 313.10 began;] EM\HM2; ~: HM,EM\HM1; ~^ EM 313.11 seen,] EM\HM; ~^ HM 313.12 mood^] HM,EM\HM2; ~, EM\HM1

IN THE DESERT (p. 314)

After a two-day visit to Cairo and the Pyramids on December 30 and 31, 1856, and then discovering in Alexandria that he would have to wait two days for his steamer to Jaffa, Melville jotted in his journal his "impressions" on January 3, 1857, among them the one that probably more than any other led to "In the Desert": "Too much light & no defence against it" (*Journals*, p. 74). Also contributing, perhaps, was the complex of feelings expressed in "A long billow of desert forever hovers as in act of breaking, upon the verdure of Egypt. Grass near the pyramids, but will not touch them — as if in fear or awe of them. Desert more fearful to look at than ocean" (*Journals*, p. 76). (See also *Clarel*, 2.11.1–91.) Among many revealing variants in the surviving transcripts of this poem is a group showing Melville revising it to third person, titling it "Horace in Egypt" and only later substituting "Theban flamens" for "weak-eyed Horace".

DISCUSSIONS. 314.1–2 Pharoah's Night . . . croon] See Exodus 10:21–23. NN retains this copy-text spelling of "Pharoah" (changed to "Pharaoh's" in EM and then back to "Pharoah's" in T), listed in the *Oxford English Dictionary* as an eighteenth-century form.

314.3 Theban flamens] Here, generically, the priests of the god Ammon in the Thebes of ancient Egypt, rather than Boeotian celebrants in the Thebes of ancient Greece.

314.9 fierce,] NN retains the comma in HM, though its omission in EM may be part of Melville's lightening of punctuation in lines 10 and 11.

314.10 Napoleon] Napoleon invaded Egypt with forty thousand troops in July 1798, had mixed success there and in Syria, and in August 1799 turned over command to Kléber; after some wins and losses he was replaced by Menou, who in 1801 lost Egypt to the British.

314.11,17 pierce;/bright!] NN retains the copy-text punctuation after these words, since its reappearance in T (in place of the comma and period in EM) is almost certainly Melville's restoration.

314.14 Holy, holy, holy Light] An allusion to Milton's *Paradise Lost,* 3.1–6 (here quoted from Melville's copy of *The Poetical Works* [Boston: Hilliard, Gray, 1836]; Sealts, no. 358b, Bercaw, no. 499): "HAIL holy light! offspring of heav'n first-born; / Or of th' Eternal, co-eternal beam / May I express thee unblam'd? since GOD is light / And never but in unapproached light / Dwelt from eternity, dwelt then in thee, / Bright effluence of bright essence increate."

314.17 Shekinah] In Jewish theology, the radiance surrounding and manifesting the divine presence. Cf. *Clarel,* 4.9.46.

EMENDATIONS. 314.0 *In the Desert*] EM; The Egyptian Noon HM 314.1 Never] [*indent*] EM; [*no indent*] HM 314.1 Night,] EM; night^ HM 314.2 croon,] EM; ~^ HM 314.3 Did] EM; May HM 314.3 Theban flamens] EM; weak-eyed Horace HM 314.3 try] EM; affright HM 314.4 me this] EM; Egypt's HM 314.4 Noon] EM\HM; noon HM 314.5 Like . . . calm] EM; [*see textual notes*] HM 314.6 Undulates . . . frame] EM; All the circumambient frame HM 314.6 frame;] EM; ~^ HM 314.7 In one flowing] EM; Is sun-burst and in HM 314.10 won,] EM; ~— HM 314.12 bayonetted] EM; bayoneted HM 314.12 this] EM\HM; the HM 314.13 drop] EM\HM; dropped HM 314.14 Light!] EM\HM; ~, HM

TEXTUAL NOTES: INSCRIPTION STAGES. At least four stages of inscription-revision: A (nonextant pre-fair-copy stage); B (blue ink on thicker, darker paper; C (tan-gray ink on thinner, lighter paper); C+ (post-C revisions in Melville's wife's hand, presumably from a nonextant Melville inscription [see p. 606 above]).

TEXTUAL NOTES: SUBSTANTIVES. 314.0–8 *In . . . out*] [*HM leaf 1(B); EM leaf 1(C+)*] 314.0 *In the Desert*] EM(C+)[*here and in following instances, EM transcribes from evidently nonextant HM inscription*],EM\HM2; [*no title*] HM1; [*two or three* undeciphered erased words, either constituting a title in themselves, or concluding with (otherwise to be understood as added later):] in Egypt HM2,HM?3; [two undeciphered erased words {?Horace in}, perhaps to be understood as being completed by Egypt] HM?4; Noon on the Nile HM?5,HM?7; Horace in Egypt HM?6; The Egyptian Noon HM8(C); In the Egyptian Desert EM\HM1 314.2 Hebrew] HM4(C); dubious HM1,HM3; [?Talmud] HM2 314.3 Did] EM(C+)[not copied back into HM]; May HM1,HM3; Might HM2 314.3 the] HM1,HM3; a HM2 314.3 Theban flamens] EM(C+),HM\EM2; weak-eyed Horace HM; weak-eyed traveler HM\ EM1[copied back into HM from nonextant HM revision in pre–stage C+ version of EM leaf 1] 314.3 try] EM(C+),HM\EM2; affright HM; fright HM\EM1[from nonextant HM revision in pre–stage C+ version of EM leaf 1] 314.4 me this] EM(C+); Egypt's HM 314.5 Like . . . calm] EM(C+); [no exactly equivalent text-line, though line 5 was added at stage C+ as part of the revision of stanza two, in which revision, at stages B and C, HM canceled three text-lines following final line 8 (see entry, below, for 314.8)] HM(B,C) 314.6 Undulates . . . frame] EM(C+),HM\EM3; All the circumambient frame HM; All the circumambient air HM\EM1[copied back into HM from nonextant HM revision in pre–stage C+ revision of EM leaf 1]; Undulatory [two or three undeciphered scratched-out words] HM\EM2[also copied back into HM from nonextant HM revision in pre–stage C+ revision of EM leaf 1] 314.7 In one flowing] EM(C+); Is sun-burst and in HM1,HM3; Is sun-burst, and in HM2; Is sun-burst. In one HM4(C) 314.8 fiery] HM1,HM3; [undeciphered erased word {?luminous}] HM2 314.9–17 Battling . . . bright] [HM leaf 2(C); EM leaf 2] 314.8 out.] HM2(C+); [see following description of three text-lines—two from stage B, the third from stage C—canceled at stage C+ when HM added final line 5 (on which addition, see entry, above, for 314.5]

> The lucid ether with such glow
> Engirds the universe roundabout,
> The world floats as in vaccuo [alter to: vacuo]

HM1 *314.9 fierce,] HM2; vain^ HM1; fierce^ EM 314.11 Through . . . pierce] HM3; Many a Saracen was slain HM1; Through [?their] files his sword did pierce HM2 314.12 this] EM\HM2; the HM1; Egyptian EM\HM1,HM?2[one of two or three undeciphered erased words may be Egyptian though the other(s) may provisionally revise line 13] 314.13 gunners] HM,EM\HM2; [undeciphered erased word]-gunners EM\HM1[and see entry above for 314.12] 314.13 drop] EM\HM,HM[?\EM]; dropped HM1; dropt HM?2,EM[and see entry above for 314.12]

TEXTUAL NOTES: ACCIDENTALS. 314.1 Never] [indent] EM; [no indent] HM; [indention obscured by display capital] T *314.1 Pharoah's] HM,T; Pharaoh's EM 314.1 Night,] EM(C+)[mended]; night^ HM 314.2 wizards] HM2(C); wizzards HM1 314.2 croon,] EM(C+); ~^ HM 314.4 Noon] EM\HM; noon HM 314.5,9,14 Like/Battling/Holy] [no indent] HM,EM\HM2; [indent] EM\HM1 [HM penciled *in brackets to the left of lines 5 and 9 (twice); then, realizing that brackets would not serve his present purpose (for in his symbology they usually mean only "line-space," and the line-spaces between stanzas were already present and clear in both transcripts), he penciled* Indent *(perhaps at different times) opposite lines 9 and 14]* 314.6 undulates] EM2,HM\ EM; undutates EM→1[*pen slip*] 314.6 frame;] EM; ~^ HM[*see substantives, the entries for lines 5, 6, and 8 for HM revisions that led to punctuation change here*] 314.7 In one flowing] [*see substantives*] 314.7 oriflamme] HM2(C); [?ar]iflame HM1 314.8 out.] [*see substantives*] 314.9 fierce,] [*see substantives*] 314.10 won,] HM1,EM; ~— HM2 *314.11 pierce;] HM3,T; slain, HM1; slain^ HM2; pierce, EM 314.12 But, . . . sun,] HM2; ~^ . . . ~^ HM1,EM; ~, . . . ~^ EM\HM 314.12 bayonetted] EM2; bayoneted HM,EM1 314.12 sun,] HM2; ~^ HM1,EM 314.13 drop] [*see substantives*] 314.14 Light!] EM\HM2; ~, HM,EM\HM1 314.17 Shekinah] HM; [?*mistranscription* ?*only mended*] EM 314.17 Shekinah,] HM; ~^ EM 314.17 intolerably] HM,EM2; [*at first, EM left a blank space*] EM1 *314.17 bright!] HM,T; ~. EM

THE GREAT PYRAMID (pp. 315–16)

Much in this poem has a prose analogue in the extensive "impressions" in Melville's journal entries about his December 31, 1856, excursion to the Pyramids. The night of his excursion he wrote, "Never shall forget this day." Awaiting his steamer in Alexandria on January 3, 1857, he gave a full account in two long passages (*Journals*, pp. 75–76, 78), which include the following comment: "As with the ocean, you learn as much of its vastness by the first five minutes glance as you would in a month, so with the pyramid. Its simplicity confounds you." The surviving transcripts of "The Great Pyramid" provide suggestive variants (see textual notes below), such as a canceled subtitle or epigraph quoting Acts 7:22: "And Moses was learned in all the wisdom of the Egyptians."

DISCUSSIONS. 315.3 courses as in strata rise] In his journal account, Melville noted, "The lines of stone do not seem like courses of masonry, but like strata of rocks" (*Journals*, p. 78).

315.4 surmise] NN follows EM in omitting the line-end comma of HM, since Melville in punctuating his wife's transcript lightened the poem's pointing. In the process, he deleted a line-end comma in the syntactically parallel line 14. (In his manuscript he deleted another in line 29.)

315.5 Grampians] The Grampian Mountains of Scotland.

315.7 Alpine goats] In his journal Melville compared the Arab guides to "goats, or any other animal," who climb "Down one & up the other" (*Journals*, p. 76).

315.8 passes] NN adopts from EM the omission of the line-end comma, as probably a deliberate result of Melville's substantive revision (in HM) of the beginning of line 9.

315.18 sand-storms,] NN retains the copy-text comma, though possibly its omission in EM was deliberate.

315.20 You—turn the cheek] See Matthew 5:39 for Christ's saying, "whosoever shall smite thee on thy right cheek, turn to him the other also."

316.24 Past] NN retains the capital letter in the copy-text, reduced to lower-case in T (see p. 610 above).

316.33–34 Usurped . . . I AM] In Exodus 3:14, the Lord of the burning but unconsumed bush identifies himself: "I AM THAT I AM: And he said, Thus shalt thou say unto the children of Israel, I AM hath sent me unto you." Melville earlier considered titling his poem "I Am."

EMENDATIONS. 315.0 *The Great Pyramid*] EM; I Am HM 315.1 masonry—] EM\ HM; ~^ HM 315.1 and is it] EM\HM; scarce seemeth HM 315.1 man's?] EM; ~, HM 315.2 Cosmic]EM; mightier HM 315.2 artizan's.] EM\HM; ~; HM *315.4 surmise^] EM; ~, HM 315.7 rank,] EM; ~; HM *315.8 passes^] EM; ~, HM 315.9 dwarfs] EM\HM; men HM 315.12 sterile] HM\EM; arid HM 315.12 granite= knit:] EM; ~. HM 315.14 aridly . . . the] HM\EM; penetrate the vaulted HM 315.14 blue^] EM\HM; ~, HM 315.15 As lording] EM; High parching HM 315.18 on blow,] EM\HM; ~ ~^ HM 315.20 cheek.] EM\HM; ~! HM 316.21 All . . . you] EM; The elements you more than HM 316.22 Foursquare . . . suffer] EM; Userper of a place with HM 316.22 them:] EM\HM; ~; HM 316.26 Slant . . . lead] EM\HM; Deep in your bowels lurk HM 316.26 caves^] EM; ~— HM 316.27 And labyrinths rumored.] EM; Abysses—labyrinths. HM 316.27 These who] EM\HM; Whoso HM 316.28 And penetrates] EM; Your juggling voids HM 316.29 dead^] EM\HM; ~, HM 316.30 And, dying,] EM\HM; And swoons or HM 316.31 Craftsmen] [*double line-space precedes*] EM\HM; [*single line-space*] HM 316.31 Craftsmen, . . . dim,] EM\HM; ~^ . . . ~^ HM 316.32 formless into form] EM\HM; shapeless into shape HM 316.32 trim,] EM\HM; ~— HM 316.33 Usurped] HM\EM; Userped HM 316.34 start,] EM\HM; ~^ HM

TEXTUAL NOTES: INSCRIPTION STAGES. At least five stages of inscription-revision: A (nonextant pre-fair-copy stage); B (blue ink on thicker, darker paper); C (tan-gray ink on thinner, lighter paper); C+ (post-C revisions in Melville's wife's hand, in brown ink, on her leaves 1 and 3, presumably from a nonextant Melville inscription [see p. 606 above]); C++ (post-C+ revisions in Melville's wife's hand, in blue-gray ink on her pale yellow leaf 2, as well as in revisions on her leaves 1 and 3 and on Melville's leaves 1–4, presumably from a nonextant inscription [see p. 606 above]).

TEXTUAL NOTES: SUBSTANTIVES. 315.0–10 *The . . .* blank] [*HM leaf 1(C); EM leaf 1*] 315.0 *The Great Pyramid*] EM(C+)[*here and in following instances, EM transcribes from evidently nonextant HM inscription*]; Cheops HM1; I Am HM2 315.0 Pyramid] [*no epigraph*] HM,EM\HM,HM\EM2; "And Moses was learned in / all the wisdom of the Egyptians." EM(C+)[*positioned as an epigraph; the quotation marks may have been canceled earlier, separately; when EM copied the epigraph back into HM, she omitted the period, the opening but not the closing quotation marks, and added the source* Acts 7-22] 315.1 Your] HM,EM\HM,HM\EM2; Dumb EM(C+),HM\ EM1 315.1 and is it] EM(C+)[*see also accidentals*]; scarce seemeth HM 315.2 More like] HM2; Rather HM1 315.2 Cosmic] EM(C+); mightier HM1,HM3; Titan HM2 315.6 Far] HM,EM2; For EM1 315.9 Even . . . that] EM\HM2(C++),HM\ EM2; They look like men who HM1; And [*or* They] look [*or* show] like men [*or undeciphered erased word*] who HM2,HM3,HM4[*or, perhaps, more than three successive readings*]; And [*or* They] look [*or* show] like wights who HM5; And show like dwarfs who HM6; Even like the dwarfs that HM7,EM\HM1,HM\EM1; Even like to men that HM8 315.9 climb the] HM1,HM3; climbing HM2 315.11–20 Shall . . . cheek] [*HM leaf 2(B)*] 315.11–316.25 Shall . . . diadem] [*EM leaf 2(C++)*] 315.11 your] HM2; the HM1 315.12 sterile] HM\EM(C+); arid HM 315.14 aridly . . . the] HM\EM2(C+); penetrate the vaulted HM; aridly you pierce the HM\ EM1(C+) 315.15 As lording] EM(C++),HM\EM2; High parching HM; Usurping HM\EM1(C+) 315.17 pinion] HM2; pinions HM1

316.21–30 All . . . raves] [*HM leaf 3(B)*] 316.21 All . . . you] EM(C++); The elements you more than HM 316.22 Foursquare . . . suffer] EM(C++); Userper of a place with HM; Predominate not rival HM\EM(C+) 316.24 Past . . . that] HM1,HM5; [*?*long] long Past, you HM2; [*undeciphered erased word* {*?*infinite}] Past, you HM3; "dreadful Past," you HM4 316.26–35 Slant . . . Him] [*EM leaf 3(C+) Slant . . . him*] 316.26 Slant . . . lead] EM(C+),EM\HM5; Deep in your bowels lurk HM; [*?*From] [*undeciphered erased word* {*?*monstrous}] [*undeciphered erased word* {*?*bowels *?*innards}] slant EM\HM1; From inmost [*undeciphered erased word* {*?*bowels *?*innards}] slant EM\HM2; From your inmost slant EM\HM?3; From your [*undeciphered erased word* {*?*bowels *?*innards}] slant EM\HM?4 316.27 And labyrinths rumored] EM2(C+); Abysses—labrynths HM; And labyrinth rumored EM1(C+)[*mistranscription*] 316.27 These who] EM\HM; Whoso HM; Those who EM(C+) 316.28 And penetrates] EM(C+); Your juggling voids HM 316.29 dead] HM,EM\HM; dread EM(C+) 316.30 And, dying, raves] EM\HM; And swoons or raves HM; With penal graves EM(C+) 316.31–35 Craftsmen . . . Him] [*HM leaf 4(B)*] 316.32 formless into form] EM\HM(C++); shapeless into shape HM 316.33 Usurped] HM2(C++),EM\HM(C++)[*see also accidentals*]; Imposed HM1,EM 316.34 this] HM2(C++),EM\HM(C+); your HM1,EM 316.35 Imposing Him] HM3(C++),EM\HM1,EM\HM4(C++),HM\EM(C++); In awful whim HM1; [*?*An] awful whim HM2; Imposing HIM EM\HM2; Imposing him EM\HM3,EM 316.35 Him.] [*following text-lines canceled*] HM2(C+ or before*); [*see following description of lines that followed line 35 at stage B; these lines are revised in pencil, then canceled at or before stage C+*]

From fear [*then* terror *then* Fear] the dream, from power [*then* Power]
the thought [*then* From quarries of insubstantial thought]
A Form analagous [*then* A God symbolical *then* Another great <u>I Am</u>]
was wrought—
Viewless, in ages [*then* Tremendous in time] overcast.
That Form and Thou [*then* That Form and thine *then* These Twain
then The Twain *then* These two I-Ams *then* leave not lined-through only
thine] shall last and last [*then* shall last and last and last *then* shall last
and last],
Though both be naught.

[*then cancel* From . . . naught *with pencil and orange pencil, and pencil-inscribe end-
ing device following line 35, which canceling and inscribing EM reiterates at stage C+*]
HM1(B)

TEXTUAL NOTES: ACCIDENTALS. 315.0 Pyramid] [*see substantives*] 315.1 Your] [*in T,
neither "The Great Pyramid" nor "The Return of the Sire de Nesle" begins with a dis-
play capital as do all the other poems in the volume*] 315.1 masonry—] EM\HM1,EM\
HM3,EM\HM5; ~^ HM[*see substantives, both entries for line 1*]; ~, EM\HM2,EM\
HM4 315.1 and] EM\HM; And HM\EM(C+),EM 315.1 man's?] EM(C+); ~,
HM[*see substantives, both entries for line 1*] 315.2 artizan's.] EM\HM [*HM's z is
retained here, though he does not substitute it for EM's s as he punctuates her transcript*];
artizan's; HM; artisans^ EM1; artisan's. EM2 *315.4 surmise^] EM; ~— HM1;
~, HM2 315.5 Grampians.] HM2; ~! HM1 315.7 rank,] EM; ~; HM *315.8
passes^] EM[*see substantives, the entries for line 9*]; ~; HM1; ~, HM2 315.12 granite=
knit:] EM; ~. HM 315.14 blue^] EM,EM\HM2; ~, HM,EM\HM1 *315.18
sand-storms,] HM; ~^ EM 315.18 on blow,] EM\HM; ~ ~^ HM 315.20 cheek.]
HM1,EM\HM2; ~! HM2,EM\HM1; chxxx^ EM[*undeciphered mistranscription*]
     316.22 them:] EM\HM; ~; HM 316.23 infinite] HM1,HM2[*a revision of the
HM\EM reading*]; Infinite HM\EM(C+) *316.24 Past] HM; past EM(C+)[*see also
substantives*] 316.26 caves^] EM(C+); ~— HM[*see substantives, the entries for lines
26–27*] 316.27 labyrinths] [*see substantives*] 316.29 dead^] EM\HM; ~, HM[*one of
EM's restoration marks in HM seems to cancel HM's comma*] 316.30 And, dying,] [*see
substantives*] 316.31 Craftsmen] [*double line-space precedes*] EM\HM(C++)[*HM circles
his direction to* Leave double space here]; [*single line-space*] HM 316.31 Craftsmen,
. . . dim,] EM\HM; ~^ . . . ~^ HM 316.32 trim,] EM\HM; ~— HM 316.33
Usurped] EM,HM\EM; Userped EM\HM,HM[*see substantives*] 316.34 start,]
HM?2,EM\HM; ~— HM?1; ~^ HM3 316.35 Him] [*see substantives*] 316.35 Him.]
[*see substantives*]

THE RETURN OF THE SIRE DE NESLE (p. 317)

The Sire de Nesle in this concluding dramatic monologue seems not to be based on any particular person of that old French family or titular name. Arthur Stedman ("Marquesan Melville" [1891]) stated that Melville "addressed his last little poem, the touching 'Return of the Sire de Nesle,'" to his "devoted wife." Since Stedman was in personal touch with both of the Melvilles in the months before the poet's death in September 1891 and with Mrs. Melville afterward, this claim seems credible, though there is no other known evidence.

DISCUSSIONS. 317.0[*section-title*] L'ENVOY] That Melville wished to have a section-title here is shown by his adding it (in the spelling "L'Envoy") on a separate leaf in his wife's first transcript of the poem and by her placing it (in the spelling "L'Envoi") on the separate leaf in the transcript that went to the printer (who followed the "L'Envoi" spelling but placed it at the head of the poem's title, not on a separate leaf). (The "L'Envoi" spelling also appears in Melville's wife's transcript of the table of contents and in the printed table of contents.)

317.5 Kaf] The mountain in the Caucasus beneath which the Arabian hell is said to be. Melville's knowledge of Kaf could have come from William Beckford's *Vathek* (Sealts, no. 54, Bercaw, no. 54) or from Byron's *The Giaour* (in Sealts, no. 112). "Look-out Mountain" in *Battle-Pieces* refers to "Kaf the peak of Eblis" (65.5 above).

317.6 Araxes] Now called the Araks or Aras, this river flows through eastern Turkey and southern Armenia, near Ararat, the mountain upon which, in legend, Noah's ark landed.

317.7 knowledge . . . pilgrimage] NN adopts the readings in EMI and EMII, without commas, since Melville otherwise repunctuated both of these transcripts and thus probably meant to leave out the commas that had been in his manuscript.

317.10 good,] NN retains the comma that appeared in all three transcripts of the poem and was then deleted only in the one that went to the printer (EMII). Its reappearance in T therefore probably represents Melville's restoration.

EMENDATIONS. 317.2,6,10 Their/Araxes/One] [*no indent*] EM; [*indent*] HM 317.2 dearth:] EM; ~; HM 317.5 through] EM; thro' HM 317.5 fog:] EM; ~[*punctuation blotted out*] HM 317.6 span,] EM; ~: HM *317.7 knowledge^ . . . pilgrimage^] EM; ~, . . . ~, HM 317.8 man.] EM; ~^ HM 317.9 lasting] T; human HM 317.11 swarm,] EM; ~^ HM

TEXTUAL NOTES: INSCRIPTION STAGES. At least three stages of inscription-revision: A (the nonextant Melville draft upon which his wife's first transcript [EMI] is based); B (Melville's and his wife's inscription on EMI leaves 1 and 2; where inscription is in her hand only, she presumably follows his nonextant inscription [see p. 606 above]); C (Melville's post-B [i.e., post-EMI] draft in pencil; also his wife's transcription [EMII] from Melville's pencil draft).

Paper, ink, and foliation evidence suggest that before Melville had decided to include "Pausilippo" in *Timoleon,* but after he had devised a section-title, "L'Envoy," to stand alone on a section-title leaf in his wife's transcript, he undertook so much further revisions of the earlier (EMI) of her two extant transcripts of "The Return of the Sire de Nesle" that he thought it desirable to make another transcript of his own. (The earlier HM draft that lies behind and was used for making EMI has evidently not survived.) After making and revising a new pencil draft (HM), Melville copied his choices back into EMI, and from this revised EMI (which had functionally become his final version, and was later foliated to stand in his transcript) his wife made EMII, the fair copy that went to the printer.

TEXTUAL NOTES: SUBSTANTIVES. 317.0[*section-title*] L'ENVOY] [*EMI leaf 1(B)* L'Envoi] *317.0[*section-title*] L'ENVOY] EMI\HM2; L'Envoi EMI,T; The Return / Of the Sire de Nesle EMI\HM1 317.0–12 The . . . thee] [*EMI leaf 2(B); HM leaf 1(C); EMII leaf 1(C)*] 317.0[*subtitle*] A.D. 16—^] EMI\HM?4,HM; [*no subtitle*] EMI; A.D. 16—^ EMI\HM1,EMI\HM3; A.D. 15—^ EMI\HM2; 16—. EMI\HM5,EMI\HM7[*on the title line, and provisionally considered as a continuation of the title, rather than as a subtitle; however, 16— also remains uncanceled in the subtitle position below*]; XVI Century EMI\HM6; <u>A.D. 16—</u> EMII; *A. D.* 16— T 317.1 towers] HM2,EMI\HM2; vale EMI,HM1; hearth EMI\HM1 317.1 These rovings end] EMI,HM,EMI\HM5; These questings end EMI\HM1; [*two or three undeciphered erased words*] [?end] EMI\HM2; These [*one or two undeciphered erased words*] [?end] EMI\HM3; These wanderings end EMI\HM4 317.2 Their thirst is] HM2,EMI\HM4; The thirst is EMI,HM1; Deep thirst is EMI\HM1; With deep thirst EMI\HM2; Deep thirst full EMI\HM3 317.6 Araxes] EMI,EMI\ HM2,HM2,HM4[*retraced by EM, perhaps at some point when it appeared HM might be legible enough to serve as a transcript from which to make her final fair copy*],EMI\ HM4; The Indus EMI\HM1,EMI\HM3,HM1,HM3 317.6 his] EMI,HM2; its HM1 317.7 pilgrimage] EMI,HM2,EMI\HM6; travel [*then* travels] wide HM1,EMI\HM1,EMI\HM?5; travels [*undeciphered erased word*] EMI\HM2; travels long EMI\HM3; wanderings [?wide] EMI\HM4 317.9 thou, my stay] EMI,HM3[thou *reinscribed by EM*]; [*two or three undeciphered erased words*] HM1; Bxxxxx [*one or two undeciphered erased words from the previous reading*] HM2 317.9 lasting] T; cleaving EMI,HM1; human HM2,EMI\HM,EMII 317.10 lonely good] HM1,HM3,EMI\HM; only good EMI; good HM?→2[*no variant evidently inscribed to replace* lonely] 317.11 Weary] EMI,EMI\HM6,HM; [*undeciphered erased word* {?Tired}] EMI\HM1; Baleful EMI\HM2,EMI\HM4; [*undeciphered erased word*] EMI\HM3; Joyless EMI\HM5 317.11 wide world's] HM4,EMI\HM3; world's wide EMI,HM3; world's vast EMI\HM1,HM2; vain world's EMI\ HM2; world's sad HM1 317.12 blest] HM,EMI\HM2; bliss EMI\HM1

TEXTUAL NOTES: ACCIDENTALS. *317.0[*section-title*] L'ENVOY] [*see substantives*] 317.0[*subtitle*] A.D. 16—^] [*see substantives*] 317.1 My] [*in T, neither "The Great Pyramid" nor "The Return of the Sire de Nesle" begins with a display capital as do all the other poems in the volume*] 317.1 last!] EMI2,HM,EMII; ~. EMI1 317.1 end,] HM2,EMII; ~. EMI,EMI\HM2,HM1; ~; EMI\HM1 317.2,6,10 Their/Araxes/ One] [*no indent*] EMI,EMII; [*indent*] HM 317.2 dearth:] EMI,EMII; ~; HM 317.5 through] EMI,EMII; thro' HM 317.5 fog:] EMI,EMII; ~[*punctuation blotted out*] HM 317.6 span,] EMI,EMII; ~: HM *317.7 knowledge^ . . . pilgrimage^] EMI,EMII; ~, . . . ~, HM 317.8 Overflows] HM,EMI\HM; O'erflows EMI 317.8 man.] EMI,EMII; ~^ HM *317.10 good,] EMI,HM,EMII1,T; ~^ EMII2 317.10 be!] EMI,EMII,HM2; ~: HM1 317.11 swarm,] EMI,EMII; ~^ HM

Uncollected Poem (pp. 319–21)

INSCRIPTION FOR THE DEAD AT FREDERICKSBURGH (p. 321)

In early 1864 (before March 22) Lieutenant Colonel Alexander Bliss (1827–96) asked Melville to contribute some autograph example of his work to be reproduced in a volume for the benefit of the U.S. Sanitary Commission. Melville sent "Inscription For the Slain At Fredericksburgh." But on March 22, soon after sending it, he posted to Bliss a revised version entitled "Inscription for the Dead At Fredericksburgh." The differences in wording between the two versions are few but seemed so important to Melville that he urged Bliss to "*suppress*" the earlier "uncorrected draught — in fact, the *wrong sheet*" and not to include it in the volume if he could not make the substitution. Evidently all Bliss could do was to alter the title in the published table of contents to "Inscription to the dead at Fredericksburg," for on p. 189 of *Autograph Leaves of Our Country's Authors,* comp. Alexander Bliss and John Pendleton Kennedy (Baltimore: Cushings & Bailey, 1864), a facsimile of the first autograph manuscript appeared, titled "Inscription / For the Slain / At Fredericksburgh". Copies of the published book were ready to be sold at the Metropolitan Fair on April 19, Patriots' Day, for six dollars. The published version differs from Melville's preferred second one in its more distanced "Slain" for "Dead"; its citing only a "glory", not a "dreadful glory", in the first line; and its beginning the last line with "Strown" rather than "Strewn". Melville later adapted the poem to become the last stanza of "Chattanooga" in *Battle-Pieces* (pp. 67–68 above); see the introductory note to "Chattanooga" on pp. 645–46 above. For another Fredericksburg "Inscription," see p. 127 above. For background on Melville's Civil War poems, see pp. 498–512 and 530–43 above.

NN copy-text is the manuscript of Melville's intended version, "Inscription For the Dead At Fredericksburgh," now in the Bancroft-Bliss Collection at the Library of Congress. It consists of a part-sheet (9⅝ by 7¹³⁄₁₆ inches, torn along the left edge) of white wove paper embossed with the name "CONGRESS" under a three-domed building; Melville wrote in ink on one side. The variants labeled "HM2" in the following lists appear in that copy-text. The variants labeled here as "HM1" are in the manuscript of the earlier version, "Inscription For the Slain At Fredericksburgh," which is now in the Harry Ransom Humanities Research Center at the University of Texas at Austin, in a bound volume of manuscripts related to *Autograph Leaves,* including most of the holograph originals of items that appeared in that book of facsimiles. Both Melville manuscripts are signed "Herman Melville". NN makes no emendations to the revised-version copy-text.

TEXTUAL NOTES: SUBSTANTIVES. 321.0 *Dead*] HM2; Slain HM1 321.1 dreadful glory] HM2; glory HM1 321.6 Strewn] HM2; Strown HM1

TEXTUAL NOTES: ACCIDENTALS. 321.0 *Inscription*] [*"underlined" with a beginning device:* ———"———] HM2; [*underlined*] HM1 321.0 At Fredericksburgh] [*"underlined" with a beginning device:* ———"———] HM1,HM2 321.2 ascend;] HM2; ~. HM1 321.4,6 Of/Strewn] [*indent*] HM2; [*no indent*] HM1

Melville's Dated Reading in Poetry and Poetics: A Chronological Short-Title List

A selective list gleaned from Merton M. Sealts Jr., *Melville's Reading* (1988) and its supplements (including Sealts 1990 and Olsen-Smith and Sealts 2004), and Hershel Parker's biography (1996, 2002), with the Sealts number or other source at the end of each entry. The date is that on which Melville signed a book or on which he is known or suspected to have procured a book. This list does not include important undated books (see Note A) or family books, (e.g., Maria Gansevoort Melville's copy of Thomas Campbell's *The Pleasures of Hope*, no. 118), unless dated by Melville.

1846
Aug. 28   Cowper, *Poems* (no. 161)
Sept. 8   Tupper, *Proverbial Philosophy* (no. 530)

1847
Feb.   Channing, *Poems* (no. 131a)
Dec. 2   Cooke, *Froissart Ballads* (no. 158)

1848
            Macpherson, *Fingal* (no. 343)
Feb. 8   Coleridge, *Biographia Literaria* (no. 154)

Feb.	Tegnér, *Frithiof's Saga* (no. 500)
June 22	Dante, *The Vision* (no. 174; see also 1858 and 1860)

1849

	Goethe, *Autobiography* (no. 228)
	Milton, *Poetical Works* (no. 358b; see also 1860 and 1868)
	Schiller, *Poems and Ballads* (no. 439; see also 1860)
Feb. 16	*Modern British Essayists* (no. 359; see Note B)
Mar. 6	Lamb, *English Dramatic Poets* (no. 318)
Mar. 19	Harper's *Classical Library* (no. 147; see Note C)
Nov.	Butler, *Hudibras* (no. 104)
Nov. 21	Lamb, *Works* (no. 316)
Nov. 21	Lamb, *Final Memorials* (no. 317)
Dec.	Davenant, *Works* (no. 176)
Dec.	Jonson, *Works* (no. 302)
Dec.	Planche, *Lays and Legends of the Rhine* (no. 404.1)
Dec. 18	Chatterton, *Poetical Works* (no. 137)

1850

	W. Browne, *Brittania's Pastorals* (no. 91)
	E. B. Browning, *Poems* (no. 92)
	Carlyle, *On Heroes, Hero-Worship, and the Heroic* (no. 122)
	Tennyson, *In Memoriam* (no. 504)
Aug.	Wordsworth, *The Prelude* (Parker 1996, p. 742)
Nov. 27	Coleridge, *Notes and Lectures* (no. 155)

1855

Dec. 16	Schiller, *Works* (no. 437)

1857

Oct. 19 *or*	
Oct. 30	Schiller, *Works* (no. 438)

1858

	Dante, *The Vision* (no. 174; see also 1848 and 1860)
Nov.	Homer, *Batrachomyomachia* (no. 276; see also 1860)
Nov.	Homer, *Iliads* (no. 277; see also 1860)
Nov.	Homer, *Odysseys* (no. 278; see also 1860)

1859

	Emerson, *Poems* (no. 206)
	Herbert, *The Temple* (no. 270)
June 18	Willmott, *Poets of the Nineteenth Century* (no. 558a)
Sept.	Herrick, *Hesperides* (no. 271)
Sept.	Child, *English and Scottish Ballads* (no. 143)

1860
  Chalmers, *British Essayists* (no. 126)
  Fauriel, *History of Provencal Poetry* (no. 211a)
  Homer, *Batrachomyomachia* (no. 276; see also 1858)
  Homer, *Iliads* (no. 277; see also 1858)
  Homer, *Odysseys* (no. 278; see also 1858)
  Poe, *Works* (no. 404a)
  Schiller, *Poems and Ballads* (no. 439; see also 1849)
Feb.   Marvell, *Poetical Works* (no. 351)
Sept. 4   Beranger, *Songs* (no. 58)
Sept. 14   Wordsworth, *Complete Poetical Works* (no. 563a; see also Nov. 6, 1860)
Sept. 21   Milton, *Poetical Works* (no. 358b; see also 1849 and 1868)
Sept. 22   Dante, *The Vision* (no. 174; see also 1848 and 1858)
Oct. 15   Mackay, *Songs of England* (no. 342)
Nov. 6   Wordsworth, *Complete Poetical Works* (no. 563a; see also Sept. 14, 1860)

1861
April 9   Shelley, *Poetical Works* (no. 469)
April 9   Spenser, *Poetical Works* (no. 483)
July 3 *or*
July 30   Thomson, *Poetical Works* (no. 515)
Aug. 14   Tennyson, *Poetical Works* (no. 508)
Oct.   Hunt, *Rimini* (no. 290a; see also 1865)

1862
Feb. 14   Hood, *Poetical Works* (no. 279)
Feb. 15   Lockhart, *Ancient Spanish Ballads* (Parker 2002, p. 494)
Feb. 15   Mangan, *Poems* (no. 347)
Feb. 15   Moore, *Poetical Works* (no. 370; see also Oct. 25, 1862)
Feb. 17   Fergusson, *Works* (no. 215)
Feb. 26   Disraeli, *Amenities of Literature* (no. 184)
Feb. 26   Disraeli, *Curiosities of Literature* (no. 186)
Feb. 26   Disraeli, *The Literary Character* (no. 187)
Feb./Mar.   Byron, *Poetical Works* (no. 112)
Feb./Mar.   Moore, *Life of Lord Byron* (no. 369)
March   Hazlitt, *English Comic Writers* (no. 263b)
March   Hazlitt, *English Poets* (no. 263b)
March 1   Vingott, *Selections from the Best Spanish Poets* (no. 536b)
March 17   Heine, *Poems* (no. 268)
March 21   Cowley, *Works* (no. 160a)
April   Churchill, *Poetical Works* (no. 144)
April   Collins, *Poetical Works* (no. 156)
April 3   White, *Poetical Works* (no. 566)
April 6   Arnold, *Poems* (no. 21)

Oct. 25   Moore, *Poetical Works* (no. 370; see also Feb. 15, 1862)

1864
June   E. B. Browning, *Poems* (no. 93)

1865
May   Hunt, *Rimini* (no. 290a; see also 1861)

1867
Jan. 20   Stoddard, C. W., *Poems* (490b)
May 17   Camoëns, *Poems* (no. 116)
May 17   Guarini, *Il Pastor Fido* (no. 235a)
Oct. 12   Bryant, *Poems* (no. 94)

1868
          Milton, *Poetical Works* (no. 358b; see also 1849 and 1860)
Sept.   Sa'di, *The Gulistan* (no. 434)

1869
July 10   Arnold, *Essays in Criticism* (no. 17; see also 1871)
Aug. 4   Praed, *Poems* (no. 408. Inscribed to Augusta five days later)

1870
          Tennyson, *The Holy Grail, and Other Poems* (no. 503)
June 4   Gilchrist, *Life of William Blake* (no. 224)
July   Robinson, *Diary, Reminiscences, and Correspondence* (no. 428)
Sept.   Burns, *Poems* (no. 100)
Dec. 9   Habington, *Castara* (no. 236)

1871
          Crabbe, *Tales of the Hall* (no. 162a)
Jan. 20   Shakespeare, *Sonnets* (no. 465)
Jan. 27   Tennyson, *In Memoriam* (no. 505)
Feb. 13   Arnold, *New Poems* (no. 20)
Feb. 13   Arnold, *Essays in Criticism* (no. 17; see also 1869)

1873
          Bell, *Songs from the Dramatists* (no. 56)

1874
Sept. 22   Thackeray, *Ballads* (no. 511)

1875
          Tennant, *Anster Fair* (no. 500a)

Jan. 14   Fitzgerald, *Polonius* (no. 218)

1884
Oct.   Thomson, *Vane's Story* (no. 521)

1885
Jan.   Thomson, *City of Dreadful Night* (no. 517)
Oct. 7   Thomson, *Essays and Phantasies* (no. 518)

1886
Feb. 15   Omar Khayyam, *Rubaiyat* (no. 393)
Feb. 15   Thomson, *A Voice from the Nile* (no. 522)

1888
Feb.   Stedman, *Poets of America* (no. 488a)
Feb.   Thornbury, *Lays and Legends* (no. 525)
Dec. 4   Thomson, *Shelley, A Poem* (no. 520)

1889
             Salt, *Life of James Thomson* (no. 435a)

1890
Feb. 2   Salt, *Life of James Thomson* (no. 435)
April 1   Fitzgerald, *Works* (no. 217)

1891
Jan. 8   Cranch, *The Bird and the Bell* (no. 163)

Note A: Melville signed, annotated, or otherwise indicated possession of—but did not date—several important, or possibly important, books of poetry and criticism:

Arnold, Edwin, *Poems* (1879?; no. 15)
Bloomfield, *The Farmer's Boy* (1858; no. 70)
Broughton, *Selections from the Popular Poetry of the Hindoos* (1814; no. 87a)
Burns, *Poetical Works* (1856; no. 101)
Byron, *Poetical Works* (1853?; no. 112)
Chaucer, *Poetical Works* (1854–56; no. 138)
Chaucer, *The Riches of Chaucer* (1835; no. 141)
Collins, *Poetical Works* (17—; no. 464. Given away May 19, 1862)
Disraeli, *Calamities and Quarrels of Authors* (1860; no. 185. Cf. nos. 184, 186, and 187)
Gessner, *Death of Abel*, and Macgowan, *Death of Cain* (1838), Solomons, *Gospel Poems* (1843), Sanderson, *The Three Churches* (1843) (no. 223a)

Hallam, *Remains* (1863; no. 237a)

Hemans, *Poetical Works* (1859; no. 269. Given away "Xmas 1862")

Hugo, *The Literary Life and Poetical Works* (1883?; no. 290)

Keats, *Eve of St. Agnes* (ca. 1860; no. 305)

Longfellow, *Evangeline* (1848; no. 332)

Murray, *English Reader* (1819; no. 380)

Omar Khayyam, *Rubaiyat* (1878; no. 391)

Omar Khayyam, *Rubaiyat* (ca. 1886; no. 392)

Pope, *Poetical Works* (1856; no. 405)

Shakespeare, *Poetical Works* (17—; no. 464. Given away May 19, 1862)

Shenstone, *Poetical Works* (17—; no. 470. Given away May 19, 1862)

Spenser, *Poetical Works* (1788; Parker 2002, p. 578. Given away Aug. 3, 1864)

Thomson, *Poetical Works* (17—; no. 515. Given away May 19, 1862)

Waddington, *The Sonnets of Europe* (1886; no. 539)

White, *National Hymns* (1861; no. 556.1b)

Note B: Macaulay, v. 1; Alison, v. 2; Sidney Smith, v. 3; Wilson, v. 4; Carlyle, v. 5; Jeffrey, v. 6; Stephen and Talfourd, v. 7; Mackintosh, v. 8; and possibly Scott.

Note C: Virgil, v. 11–12; Horace, v. 18–19; Ovid, v. 20–21; Pindar v. 36.

Melville's Marginalia on
Poetry and Poetics

When Melville read poetry he remained alert to echoes from earlier poets and influences on later poets. He frequently jotted down cross-references and possible sources or parallels in the margins, presumably from memory, thus revealing his broad acquaintance with poets both famous and obscure. The table below reproduces such comments discovered to date, as well as some that bear on Melville's poetics. Some of the comments are from Walker Cowen, "Melville's Marginalia" (1965; repr. 1988), corroborated independently where possible; many are from Hershel Parker's or others' transcriptions of marginalia in books not known to Cowen. The list is arranged according to the date Melville acquired each book, which may or may not be the date he made his annotations. The passage that provoked Melville's remarks is quoted at the left (followed by locator information), and Melville's remarks are transcribed at the right. Editorial comments are provided in brackets; original lines that vary from Melville's annotations are supplied. All transcriptions and quotations appear literatim.

Sealts numbers refer to Merton M. Sealts Jr., *Melville's Reading* (1988), and Steven Olsen-Smith and Merton M. Sealts Jr., "A Cumulative Supplement to *Melville's Reading* (1988)" (2004). Bercaw numbers refer to Mary K Bercaw, *Melville's Sources* (1987). Wherever possible, volume and page numbers to the editions Melville owned are provided in both columns.

PASSAGES MELVILLE MARKED	MELVILLE'S ANNOTATION, WITH SOURCES AND COMMENTS

1844: Bible. New Testament (1844); Sealts, no. 65

And sounded, and found it twenty fathoms: and when they had gone a little further, they sounded again, and found it fifteen fathoms. [Acts 27:28]	Aratus [Aratus Solensis, the Stoic philosopher and poet, included in Plutarch's *Lives;* Bercaw, no. 560]

1847?: Joseph Forsyth, *Remarks on Antiquities* (1824); Sealts, no. 219

English poets cannot plead for the sonnet one successful precedent. Even the greatest of them all, Shakespeare, Milton, Spenser, split on this rock and sank into common versifiers. [vol. 1, p. 133]	[At page bottom] What pedantry is this! Yet its elegance all but redeems it. Forsyth is the most graceful of pedants.

1849: Dante Alighieri, *The Vision; or Hell, Purgatory, and Paradise,* trans. Henry Francis Cary (1847); Sealts, no. 174

[End of editor's introduction, p. xlviii]	"What execrations! What hatred against the human race! What exultation and merriment at eternal sufferings!—In this view, the 'Inferno' is the most immoral and impious book ever written." Thus savagely writes Savage Landor of the still more savage Tuscan. ["What execrations against Florence, Pistoia, Siena, Pisa, Genoa! what hatred against the whole human race! what exultation and merriment at eternal and immitigable sufferings! Seeing this, I cannot but consider the *Inferno* as the most immoral and impious book that ever was written."]

PASSAGES MELVILLE MARKED	MELVILLE'S ANNOTATION, WITH SOURCES AND COMMENTS
	Walter Savage Landor, *The Pentameron and Pentalogia* (London, 1837), p. 44; see Sealts, no. 319b. Quoted in Leigh Hunt, *Stories from the Italian Poets* (New York: Wiley & Putnam, 1846), p. 31; see Sealts, nos. 290b, 325. See also the HISTORICAL NOTE, pp. 380–81.]
[Above beginning of "Hell," p. 1]	"Thus, while he spoke, in swarms, hell's emp'ror brings / Daughters & wives of heroes and of kings; / Thick and more thick they gather round the flood, / Ghost throned on ghost, a dire assembly stood!" Odyssey, BXI. A.D. 1858 ["Thus while she spoke, in swarms hell's empress brings / Daughters and wives of heroes and of kings; / Thick and more thick they gather round the blood, / Ghost throned on ghost, a dire assembly, stood!" *Homer*, trans. Alexander Pope, bk. 11, lines 273–76; Sealts, no. 147, vol. 3, p. 109]
With hands together smote that swell'd the sounds, ["Hell," 3.26, p. 13]	"And sounds of hands among them" John Carlyle's version of the line. ["and sound of hands amongst them," *Dante's Divine Comedy: The Inferno*, trans. John A. Carlyle (1849); Sealts, no. 173a, p. 27]
No sooner to my listening ear had come / The brief assurance, than I understood / New virtue into me infused, and sight / Kindled afresh, with vigour to sustain / Excess of light however pure. ["Paradise," 30.55–59, p. 511]	Blake [Blake's rough sketch, "Dante in the Empyrean, drinking at the River of Light.——Canto XXX," illustrates lines 84–96 of this canto and is listed in the appendix to Alexander Gilchrist, *Life of William Blake, "Pictor Ignotus,"* 2 vols. (London, 1863), 2:223; Sealts, no. 224. Melville scored nearly the entire canto.]

PASSAGES MELVILLE MARKED	MELVILLE'S ANNOTATION, WITH SOURCES AND COMMENTS

1849: John Milton, *The Poetical Works of John Milton*, 2 vols. (1836); Sealts, no. 358b

[vol. 1, back flyleaf]	In Bartas [Guillaume Salluste du Bartas, French epic poet translated into English by Joshua Sylvester and mentioned frequently in the editorial notes to this volume]
Heav'n, hell, earth, chaos, all; the argument / Held me awhile misdoubting his intent, / That he would ruine (for I saw him strong) / The sacred truths to Fable and old song: / (So Sampson grop'd the temple's posts in spite) / The world o'erwhelming to revenge his sight. ["Complimentary Verses," "On Paradise Lost," by Andrew Marvell, vol. 1, p. cxxviii]	It is still "misdoubted" by some. First impressions are generally true, too, Andrew.
The Verse [vol. 1, p. [cxxxii], Milton's short preface describing his versification and defending the absence of rhyme.]	The music of the P. L. Like a fine organ—fullest & deepest tones of majesty, with the softness & elegance of the Dorian flute. Variety without end scarcely equalled by Virgil. Cowper in "Letters" ["Was there ever anything so delightful as the music of the Paradise Lost? It is like that of a fine organ; with all the softness and elegance of the Dorian flute, variety without end, and never equalled, unless, perhaps by Virgil." See Thomas Taylor, *Life of William Cowper, Esq.* (Philadelphia: Edward C. Riddle, 1841), p. 206.]

PASSAGES MELVILLE MARKED	MELVILLE'S ANNOTATION, WITH SOURCES AND COMMENTS
Above th' Aonian mount, while it pursues [*Paradise Lost,* 1.15, vol. 1, p. 2]	Tasso ["O heavenly Muse, that not with fading bays / Deckest thy brow by the Heliconian spring, / But sittest crowned with stars' immortal rays / In Heaven, where legions of bright angels sing"; Torquato Tasso, *Jerusalem Delivered,* 1.2, trans. Edward Fairfax (1600). Tasso's poem *La Gerusalemme liberata* (1580) is frequently cited in the editorial notes to this and other editions of *Paradise Lost.* "Heliconian" is a synonym for "Aonian."]
Things unattempted yet in prose or rhyme [*Paradise Lost,* 1.16, vol. 1, p. 2]	Ariosto ["In the same strain of Roland will I tell / Things unattempted yet in prose or rhyme," Ludovico Ariosto, *Orlando Furioso,* 1.2, trans. William Stewart Rose (1831)]
and there to pine / Immovable, infix'd, and frozen round, / Periods of time; thence hurried back to fire. [*Paradise Lost,* 2.601–3, vol. 1, p. 60]	Dante ["I come / To take you to the other shore across, / Into eternal darkness, there to dwell / In fierce heat and in ice," *The Vision,* trans. Henry Cary, "Hell," 3.79–82; Sealts, no. 174, p. 15. Cary's note cross-references *Paradise Lost,* 2.598–601.]
on some great charge employ'd / He seem'd, or fix'd in cogitation deep. [*Paradise Lost,* 3.628–29, vol. 1, p. 104]	Dante [See "but wore / The semblance of a man by other care / Beset, and keenly press'd, than thought of him / Who in his presence stands," *The Vision,* trans. Henry Cary, "Hell," 9.100–103; Sealts, no. 174, p. 46.]

PASSAGES MELVILLE MARKED	MELVILLE'S ANNOTATION, WITH SOURCES AND COMMENTS
Nor where Abassin kings their issue guard, / Mount Amara, though this by some suppos'd / True paradise, under the Ethiop line [*Paradise Lost*, 4.280–82; vol. 1, p. 121]	The account of the old travellers, on which Johnson fo[u]nded Rasselas. [See the description of the happy valley in chap. 1 of Samuel Johnson, *The History of Rasselas Prince of Abyssinia;* Sealts, no. 300.]
others on the grass / Couch'd, and now fill'd with pasture gazing sat [*Paradise Lost*, 4.350–51; vol. 1, p. 125]	"Full of the pasture" in "As-You-Like-It" ["Anon, a careless herd, / Full of the pasture, jumps along by him, / And never stays to greet him," Shakespeare, *As You Like It*, 2.1; Sealts, no. 460, vol. 2, p. 276.]
what glorious shape / Comes this way moving, seems another morn / Ris'n on mid-noon [*Paradise Lost,* 5.309–11, vol. 1, pp. 165–66; editor's footnote: "See Dante, Il Purgatorio, c.xii"]	Dante ["The goodly shape approach'd us, snowy white / In vesture, and with visage casting streams / Of tremulous lustre like the matin star," *The Vision,* trans. Henry Cary, "Purgatory," 12.81–83; Sealts, no. 174, p. 240.]
A dreadful interval [*Paradise Lost,* 6.105, vol. 1, p. 193]	"The deadly space between" Campbell. [Thomas Campbell, "The Battle of the Baltic," line 22, in *The Poets of the Nineteenth Century,* ed. Rev. Robert Aris Willmott (New York, 1858); Sealts, no. 558a, p. 189]
Descend from heav'n, Urania, by that name / If rightly thou art call'd, whose voice divine / Following, above th' Olympian hill I soar, / Above the flight of Pegasean wing. [*Paradise Lost,* 7.1–4, vol. 1, p. [224]]	Tasso's invocation [See "Tasso" in the entry for 1849: Milton, above.]

PASSAGES MELVILLE MARKED	MELVILLE'S ANNOTATION, WITH SOURCES AND COMMENTS
His visage drawn he felt to sharp and spare, / His arms clung to his ribs, his legs entwining / Each other, till supplanted down he fell / A monstrous serpent on his belly prone, / Reluctant, but in vain; a greater power / Now rul'd him [*Paradise Lost*, 10.511–16, vol. 1, p. 347]	Dante [*The Vision,* trans. Henry Cary, "Hell," 15.85–132, describing the transformation of a spirit into a serpent, especially "He, on the earth who lay, meanwhile extends / His sharpen'd visage," lines 120–21; Sealts, no. 174, pp. 128–29. Cary cross-references Milton's lines. Melville quotes from this canto in *Pierre,* bk. 4, sect. v, p. 85.]
With complicated monsters head and tail, / Scorpion, and asp, and amphisbaena dire, / Cerastes horn'd, hydrus, and ellops drear, / And dipsas; (not so thick swarm'd once the soil / Bedropp'd with blood of Gorgon, or the isle / Ophiusa;) but still greatest he the midst, / Now dragon, grown larger than whom the sun / Ingender'd in the Pythian vale on slime, [*Paradise Lost,* 10.523–30, vol. 1, p. 348]	Lucan ["Dread Amphisbæna with his double head / Tapering," *Pharsalia,* 9.798–99, as well as the list of monsters at 700–733. See also Dante, *The Vision,* trans. Henry Cary, "Hell," 24.77–88, which has an editorial cross-reference to the latter passage in Lucan; Sealts, no. 174, p. 122.]
Oh! why did God, / Creator wise, that peopled highest heav'n / With spirits masculine, create at last / This novelty on earth, this fair defect / Of nature, and not fill the world at once / With men as angels without feminine, / Or find some other way to generate / Mankind? [*Paradise Lost,* 10.888–95, vol. 1, pp. 362–63]	So Sir Thomas Browne—also Byron somewhere [See Browne's *Religio Medici,* which contains such antifeminist statements as "The whole world was made for man, but the twelfth part of man for woman. Man is the whole world, and the breath of God; woman the rib, and crooked piece of man" (1.9, p. 105); Sealts, no. 89. Byron's verse contains similar sentiments, such as "a rib's a thorn in a wed gallant's side," *Don Juan,* 11.46; Sealts, no. 112, vol. 10, p. 182.]

PASSAGES MELVILLE MARKED	MELVILLE'S ANNOTATION, WITH SOURCES AND COMMENTS
O visions ill foreseen! better had I / Liv'd ignorant of future, so had borne / My part of evil only, each day's lot / Enough to bear; those now, that were dispens'd [*Paradise Lost*, 11.763–66, vol. 2, p. 33]	"Seek not to know" the ghost replyed in tears / "The sorrows of thy sons in future years" Virgil [*Aeneid*, trans. John Dryden, 6.867–68; Sealts, no. 147]
Myself my sepulchre, a moving grave, [*Samson Agonistes*, line 102, vol. 2, p. 161]	My own soul's sepulchre Byron [*Manfred*, 1.2.27; Sealts, no. 112, vol. 5, p. 20.]
Not less renown'd than in Mount Ephraim / Jael, who with inhospitable guile / Smote Sisera sleeping through the temples nail'd. [*Samson Agonistes*, lines 988–90, vol. 2, p. 194]	There is basis for the doubt expressed by A. Marvel in his lines to Milton on the publication of the P. Lost. There was a <u>twist</u> in Milton. From its place, the above marked passage has an interesting significance. ["the argument / Held me awhile misdoubting his intent," Andrew Marvell, "On Paradise Lost," in this edition, vol. 1, p. cxxviii]
He knew / Himself to sing, and build the lofty rhime. ["Lycidas," lines 10–11, vol. 2, p. [271]]	Spencer ["To build with level of my lofty stile," Spenser, "Ruins of Rome," 25.13; Sealts, no. 483a, vol. 8, p. 138]
How well could I have spar'd for thee, young swain, / Enow of such as for their bellies' sake / . . . But that two-handed engine at the door / Stands ready to smite once, and smite no more. ["Lycidas," lines 113–31, vol. 2, pp. 276–77]	Mark the deforming effect of the intrusion of partizan topics & feelings of the day, however serious in import, into a poem otherwise of the first order of merit.

PASSAGES MELVILLE MARKED	MELVILLE'S ANNOTATION, WITH SOURCES AND COMMENTS
Time will run back, and fetch the age of gold; ["On the Morning of Christ's Nativity," line 135, vol. 2, p. 317]	From Jesus [Jews?] to Shakespeare
The oracles are dumb, / No voice or hideous hum / Runs thro' the arched roof in words deceiving. ["On the Morning of Christ's Nativity," lines 173–75, vol. 2, p. 319]	Plutarch on the Cessation of Oracles. [Plutarchus, *Morals,* "Why the Oracles Cease to Give Answers"; Sealts, no. 404.2. See also NN *Correspondence,* pp. 262, 639–40.]

1849: Johann Schiller, *The Poems and Ballads* (1844); Sealts, no. 439

The Alp Hunter [p. 29]	Here seems the idea of Longfellow's [erasure] fine piece—"Excelsior." [Henry Wadsworth Longfellow, "Excelsior," in *The Poets of the Nineteenth Century,* ed. Rev. Robert Aris Willmott (New York, 1858); Sealts, no. 558a, pp. 479–81]

1849 (February 24): William Shakespeare, *The Dramatic Works of William Shakspeare* (1837); Sealts, no. 460

Thy death, which is no more. [*Measure for Measure,* 3.1, vol. 1, p. 369]	[At page bottom] "Our little life is rounded by a sleep" Tempest [Shakespeare, *The Tempest,* 4.1, vol. 1, p. 62]
Abhor. Sirrah, bring Barnardine hither. / *Clo.* Master Barnardine! You must rise and be hanged, master Barnardine! / *Abhor.* What, ho, Barnardine! / *Barnar.* [*Within.*] A pox o' your throats! Who makes that noise there? What are you? / *Clo.* Your friends, sir; the hangman: you must be so good, sir, to rise and be put to death. / *Barnar.* [*Within.*] Away, you rogue, away; I am sleepy. [*Measure for Measure,* 4.3, vol. 1, p. 396]	Take this, and the other texts with the one comprehensive one in The Tempest, I think, "Our little life is rounded with a sleep." [Shakespeare, *The Tempest,* 4.1, vol. 1, p. 62]

PASSAGES MELVILLE MARKED	MELVILLE'S ANNOTATION, WITH SOURCES AND COMMENTS
To make a second fall of cursed man? [*Richard II*, 3.4, vol. 4, p. 420]	To be found in Shelley & (through him) in Byron. Also in Dryden. [Possibly P. B. Shelley's *Essay on Christianity*, Byron's *Cain*, and Dryden's *Religio Laici* or Dryden's theatrical version of *Paradise Lost, The State of Innocence, and Fall of Man*.]
Your crown's awry. [*Antony and Cleopatra*, 5.2, vol. 6, p. 210]	Shelley in the "Cenci" [See P. B. Shelley, *The Cenci*, 5.4, the scene in which Beatrice, like Shakespeare's Cleopatra, dies; Bercaw, no. 637; Sealts, no. 469, vol. 1, pp. 532–38.]
[Annotation on sixth rear flyleaf]	A seaman figures in The Canterbury Tales. With many a tempest had his beard been shook. ["With many a tempest had his beard been shake," modernized version of "The Shipman's Tale," line 408, quoted in Charles Cowden Clarke, *The Riches of Chaucer*, 2 vols. (London, 1835); Sealts, no. 141, vol. 1, p. 72. Also quoted in Leigh Hunt, *The Indicator: A Miscellany for the Fields and Fireside* (New York: Wiley & Putnam, 1845), p. 72, as "With many a tempest had his beard been shaken"; see Sealts, nos. 290b, 325.]

1849 (November 14): Francis Beaumont, *Fifty Comedies and Tragedies* (1679); Sealts, no. 53

To make his happiness if then he seize it [*The Custom of the Country*, 2.1, p. 90]	"There is a tide" &c ["There is a tide in the affairs of men / Which, taken at the flood, leads on to fortune," Shakespeare, *Julius Caesar*, 4.3; Sealts, no. 460, vol. 6, p. 74]

PASSAGES MELVILLE MARKED	MELVILLE'S ANNOTATION, WITH SOURCES AND COMMENTS
And he that will to bed go sober, / Falls with the leaf still in October. [*The Bloody Brother; or Rollo. A Tragedy*, 2.2, p. 433]	Walter Scott's Song. [See "Health to Lord Melville. Air—Carrickfergus," in John Gibson Lockhart, *Memoirs of the Life of Sir Walter Scott*, 4 vols. (Paris: Baudry's European Library, 1838), 1: 297–98.]
To be excellent in evil, is your goodness; Mighty in evil, as thou art in anger [*The Lovers Progress A Tragedy*, 2.2, p. 518]	Coincidences or ———. between B-&-F & Milton. ["Evil, be thou my good"; *Paradise Lost*, 4.110; Sealts, no. 358b, vol. 1, p. 114]
That like the wounded air, no bloud may issue [*The Lovers Progress A Tragedy*, 4.2, p. 527]	Ditto [See "But their hearts wounded, like the wounded air, / Soon close; where past the shaft, no trace is found"; Edward Young, *The Complaint; or, Night Thoughts*, 1.428–30, in *The Poetical Works of Edward Young*, ed. John Mitford (1854), vol. 1, p. 18.]
By heaven / (Methinks) it were an easie leap / To pluck bright honor from the pale-fac'd Moon, / Or dive into the bottom of the Sea, / Where never fathome line toucht any ground, / And pluck up drowned honor / From the lake of Hell. [*The Knight of the Burning Pestle*, "The Prologue," p. 47]	A hint at Shakespeare in Hotspur ["By Heaven, methinks it were an easy leap, / To pluck bright honor from the pale-faced moon; / Or dive into the bottom of the deep, / Where fathom-line could never touch the ground, / And pluck up drowned honor by the locks; / So he, that doth redeem her thence, might wear / Without corrival, all her dignities"; *King Henry IV Part I*, 1.3; Sealts, no. 460, vol. 4, p. 472]

PASSAGES MELVILLE MARKED	MELVILLE'S ANNOTATION, WITH SOURCES AND COMMENTS
Laza. Let me not fall from my self; Speak I'm bound. / *Count.* So art thou ' to revenge, when thou shalt hear the fish head is gone, and we know not whither. [*The Woman-Hater,* 2.1, p. 475]	vide Hamlet ["*Ham.* Speak; I am bound to hear. / *Ghost.* So art thou to revenge, when thou shalt hear"; 4.5, Sealts, no. 460, vol. 7, p. 278]

1849 (December): Ben Jonson, *The Works of Ben Jonson* (1692); Sealts, no. 302

An Elegy [p. 556]	This may have suggested the form & spirit of Tennyson, "In Memoriam." [*In Memoriam,* Sealts, no. 505.]

1849 (December 24): Christopher Marlowe, *The Dramatic Works of Christopher Marlowe* (n.d.); Sealts, no. 348

Shall lie at anchor in the isle Arant, / Until the Persian fleet and men of wars, / Sailing along the oriental sea, / Have fetch'd about the Indian continent [*Tamburlaine the Great, a tragedy,* 3.3]	Milton [Possibly "As when far off at sea a fleet descried / Hangs in the clouds, by equinoctial winds / Close sailing from Bengala," *Paradise Lost,* 2.636–38 (Satan's flight from Hell); Sealts, no. 358b, vol. 1, p. 61.]

1850: Sir William D'avenant, *The Works* (1673); Sealts, no. 176

Madagascar, with Other Poems. ["Epitaph on I. Walker," p. 234.]	This is Admirable, [and at bottom erased] A fine character this of I. Walker. I should like to have [sat down with] him & discussed the [one word undeciphered] of Ciciro & [four words undeciphered].
Poems, on Several Occasions, Never before Printed. ["Song," p. 320: "The Lark now leaves his watry Nest"]	[At heading] What a fine Persian tone is here. Hafiz Englished. Ah Will was a trump. [See Shams-Ed-Din Muhammad Hafiz, Bercaw, no. 312.]

PASSAGES MELVILLE MARKED	MELVILLE'S ANNOTATION, WITH SOURCES AND COMMENTS

1851: Baron Georges Cuvier, *The Animal Kingdom* (1827–43); Sealts, no. 171

[On the back flyleaf]	Music—pecus—underling [?] / Little knowledge is a dangerous thing. ["A little Learning is a dang'rous Thing," Alexander Pope, *Essay on Criticism* (1711), 2.215; Sealts, no. 405]

Edmund Spenser, *The Poetical Works* (1788), Sealts, no. 483a. [This was Melville's father's edition. Helen Melville began copying annotations of Melville's from this edition into Spenser, *The Poetical Works* (1855), Sealts, no. 483, making minor transcription errors. The marginalia below are all in Melville's hand.]

[Facing title page, vol. 1]	"Spenser to me (is dear) / whose deep conceit is such / As passing all conceit needs / no defence" / Shakspeare. ["Spenser to me, whose deep conceit is such, / As passing all conceit, needs no defence," Shakespeare, "The Passionate Pilgrim," lines 81–82; Sealts, no. 464, p. 193]
And on his brest a bloodie crosse he bore [*Faerie Queene*, 1.1.2.1, vol. 1, front flyleaf]	"And on her beauteous breast a cross she wore" / Pope. ["On her white breast a sparkling cross she wore," "The Rape of the Lock," 2.7; Sealts, no. 405]
He never meant with words, but swords, to plead his right [*Faerie Queene*, 1.4.42.9, vol. 1, p. 185]	"My voice is in my sword" / Macbeth. [5.8, Sealts, no. 460, vol. 5, p. 260]
"Yea, but," quoth she, "he beares a charmed shield [*Faerie Queene*, 1.4.50.5, vol. 1, p. 187]	"I bear a charmed life" / Macbeth. [5.8, Sealts, no. 460, vol. 5, p. 260]

PASSAGES MELVILLE MARKED	MELVILLE'S ANNOTATION, WITH SOURCES AND COMMENTS
"Thyselfe thy message do to german deare;". . . "Goe, say his foe thy shield with his doth beare." [*Faerie Queene*, 1.5.13.2–4, vol. 1, p. 193]	Down to hell & say I sent thee thither. / Macbeth. ["Down, down to hell: and say—I sent thee thither," Gloucester to King Henry in *3 King Henry VI*, 5.6; Sealts, no. 460, p. 535]
And stirrd'st up th' heroes high intents [*Faerie Queene*, 3.3.2.8, vol. 3, p. 121]	"Thence to their images it flows / And in the breasts of kings & heroes glows." ["Thence to their images on earth it flows, / And in the breasts of kings and heroes glows," Pope, "Elegy to the Memory of an Unfortunate Lady," lines 15–16]
Oft from the forrest wildings he did bring, / Whose sides empurpled were with smyling red, / And oft young birds, which he had taught to sing, / His maistresse praises sweetly caroled; / Girlonds of flowres sometimes for her faire hed / He fine would dight; sometimes the squirrel wild / He brought to her in bands, as conquered / To be her thrall, his fellow servant vild; / All of which she of him tooke with countenance meeke and mild. [*Faerie Queene*, 3.7.17, vol. 3, p. 206]	Caliban [Shakespeare, *The Tempest*; Sealts, no. 460; the previous several stanzas had reminded Melville of Caliban and his mother.]
What medicine can any leaches art / Yeeld such a sore, that doth her grievance hide, / and will to none her maladie impart? [*Faerie Queene*, 4.6.1.5–7, vol. 4, p. 148]	Macbeth to the doctor ["Canst thou not minister to a mind diseased, / Pluck from the memory a rooted sorrow, / Raze out the written troubles of the brain, / And with some sweet oblivious antidote / Cleanse the stuff'd bosom of that perilous stuff / Which weighs upon the heart?" *Macbeth*, 5.3; Sealts, no. 460, vol. 5, p. 253]

PASSAGES MELVILLE MARKED	MELVILLE'S ANNOTATION, WITH SOURCES AND COMMENTS
"She wore much like unto a Danisk hood, / Poudred with pearle and stone, and all her gowne" [*Faerie Queene*, 4.10.31.7–8, vol. 4, p. 226]	"<u>Powdered with stars</u>" / Milton ["Powder'd with stars," *Paradise Lost*, 7.581; Sealts, no. 358b, vol. 1, p. 248]
Into the great Nemæan Lion's grove [*Faerie Queene*, introductory canto 6.4; vol. 5, p. 7]	"The lair of the Lion" / E. A. Poe [Edgar Allan Poe, "Ulalume," line 49; Sealts, no. 404a]
Immoveable, resistlesse, without end [*Faerie Queene*, 5.1.12.7, vol. 5, p. 13]	Milton. ["O'er heav'n's high tow'rs to force resistless way," *Paradise Lost*, 2.62; Sealts, no. 358b, vol. 1, p. 39]
And in her necke a castle huge had made [*Faerie Queene*, 5.10.25.8, vol. 5, p. 164]	Milton—In one of his sonnets ["And on the neck of crowned fortune proud / Hast rear'd God's trophies, and his work pursued," "XVI. To the Lord General Cromwell," lines 5–6; Sealts, no. 358b, vol. 2, p. 355]
Wherefore, it now behoves us to advise / What way is best to drive her to retire; / Whether by open force, or counsell wise, / Areed ye sonnes of God! as best you can devise. [*Faerie Queene*, 7.6.21.6–9, vol. 6, p. 153]	Milton's speechs of the fallen spirits in conclave. ["and by what best way, / Whether of open war or covert guile, / We now debate; who can advise, may speak," *Paradise Lost*, 2.40–42; Sealts, no. 358b, vol. 1, p. 38]
And the dull drops that from his purpled bill / As from a limbeck did adown distill [*Faerie Queene*, 7.7.31.4–5, vol. 6, p. 175]	Keats—the monk in the chapel. [John Keats, *The Eve of St. Agnes*, illus. Edward Wehnert, illustration III; Sealts, no. 305, p. 8]

PASSAGES MELVILLE MARKED	MELVILLE'S ANNOTATION, WITH SOURCES AND COMMENTS
Now in the valleys wandring at their wills, ["Virgils Gnat," 10.4, vol. 6, p. 225]	"The river wanders at its own secret will" / Wordsworth [and] How W. W. must have delighted in this stanza. ["The river glideth at his own sweet will," "Composed Upon Westminster Bridge, Sept. 3, 1803," line 12; Sealts, no. 563a, p. 191]
To build with level of my lofty stile ["Ruins of Rome," 25.13, vol. 8, p. 138]	Build the lofty rhyme / Milton. ["Lycidas," line 11; Sealts, no. 358b, vol. 2, p. [271]]

1858 (November): Homer, *The Iliads of Homer,* trans. George Chapman (1857); Sealts, no. 277

Up from the grey sea like a cloud [1.360, vol. 1, p. 14]	Exhalation / Milton—"rose like an exhalation"—the Pandemonium palace ["Anon out of the earth a fabric huge / Rose, like an exhalation," *Paradise Lost,* 1.710–11; Sealts, no. 358b, vol. 1, p. 31]
The quarter of the Myrmidons they reach'd, and found him set / Delighted with his solemn harp, which curiously was fret / With works conceited through the verge; the bawdrick that embrac'd / His lofty neck was silver twist; this, when his hand laid waste / Aëtion's city, he did choose as his especial prise, / And, loving sacred music well, made it his exercise. / To it he sung the glorious deeds of great heroës dead, / And his true mind, that practice fail'd, sweet contemplation fed. [9.183–90, vol. 1, pp. 192–93]	"Amused at ease the god-like man they found. / Pleased with the solemn harp's harmonious sound; / With this he soothes his angry soul, and sings, / The immortal deeds of heroes and of kings." Pope's version. ["Amused at ease, the godlike man they found, / Pleased with the solemn harp's harmonious sound. / (The well-wrought harp from conquer'd Thebae came, / Of polish'd silver was its costly frame.) / With this he soothes his angry soul, and sings / The immortal deeds of heroes and of kings"; Pope, *Iliad,* 9.245–50; Sealts, no. 147, vol. 1, p. 217]

PASSAGES MELVILLE MARKED	MELVILLE'S ANNOTATION, WITH SOURCES AND COMMENTS
and should we set thee free / For offer'd ransom, for this 'scape thou still wouldst scouting be / About our ships, or do us scathe in plain opposed arms, / But, if I take thy life, no way can we repent thy harms. [10.381–84, vol. 1, p. 222]	"Once a traitor, thou betrayest no more" Pope ["No—once a traitor, thou betray'st no more," Pope, *Iliad*, 10.521; Sealts, no. 147, vol. 1, p. 247.]
See, these are right / Our kings, our rulers; these deserve to eat and drink the best; / These govern not ingloriously; these, thus exceed the rest, / Do more than they command to do. [12.320–23, vol. 1, p. 264]	"Whom those that envy, dare not imitate." Pope's version. ["Whom those that envy dare not imitate!" Pope, *Iliad*, 12.386; Sealts, no. 147, vol. 1, p. 290.]
Deiphobus, now may we think that we are evenly fam'd / That three for one have sent to Dis. [13.419–20, vol. 2, p. 15]	See, on one Greek, three Trojan ghosts attend. ["See! on one Greek three Trojan ghosts attend," Pope, *Iliad*, 13:560; Sealts, no. 147, vol. 1, p. 311]
When ag'd Priam spied / The great Greek come, spher'd round with beams [22.22–23, vol. 2, p. 208]	Milton ["Spher'd in a radiant cloud," *Paradise Lost*, 7.247; Sealts, no. 358b, vol. 1, p. 234]

1858 (November): Homer, *The Odysseys of Homer*, trans. George Chapman (1857); Sealts, no. 278

Hear me, Eumæus, and my other friends, / I'll use a speech that to my glory tends, / Since I have drunk wine past my usual guise. / Strong wine commands the fool and moves the wise [14.657–60, vol. 2, p. 44]	"Since to be talkative I now commence / Let wit cast off the <u>sullen yoke of sense</u>" Pope [Pope, *Odyssey*, 14.524–25; Sealts, no. 147, vol. 3, p. 168]

PASSAGES MELVILLE MARKED	MELVILLE'S ANNOTATION, WITH SOURCES AND COMMENTS

1859: Ralph Waldo Emerson, *Poems* (1858); Sealts, no. 206

The Humble-Bee [p. 60]	"Happy thing! Thou seem'st to me almost a little god to be!" Anacreon – 'The Grasshopper'. [*Anacreon,* trans. Thomas Bourne, ode 43, "On the Grasshopper"; Sealts, no. 147, p. 51]

1859 (October 15): Charles Mackay, ed., *Songs of England* (1857); Sealts, no. 342

This Bottle's the Sun of Our Table [p. 133; song from Richard Brinsley Sheridan's comic opera *The Duenna*]	Good for "Old Sherry" [A popular nickname for Sheridan, used by Lord Byron and others.]

1860 (February 15): James Clarence Mangan, *Poems* (1859), Sealts, no. 347

The Bride of the Dead [p. 256]	The May Queen [Poem and book by Tennyson; Sealts, no. 507]
Then saw I thrones, / And circling fires, / And a Dome rose near me, as by a spell, / Whence flowed the tones / Of silver lyres, / And many voices in wreathèd swell; / And their thrilling chime / Fell on mine ears / As the heavenly hymn of an angel-band—/ "It is now the time, / These be the years, / Of Cáhal Mór of the Wine-red Hand!" ["A Vision of Connaught in the Thirteenth Century," p. 434]	T's "Haroun al Raschid" ["The fourscore windows all alight / As with the quintessence of flame, / A million tapers flaring bright / From twisted silvers looked to shame / The hollow-vaulted dark, and streamed / Upon the mooned domes aloof / In inmost Bagdat, till there seemed / Hundreds of crescents on the roof / Of night new risen, that marvellous time, / To celebrate the golden prime / Of good Haroun Alraschid"; Tennyson, stanza 12 of "Recollections of the Arabian Nights," Sealts, no. 508, vol. 1, p. 16]

PASSAGES MELVILLE MARKED	MELVILLE'S ANNOTATION, WITH SOURCES AND COMMENTS

1860 (February 15): Thomas Moore, *The Poetical Works* (1856); Sealts, no. 369

The "Living Dog" and "The Dead Lion" [poem, vol. 3, p. 102.]	Leigh Hunt Byron [written above the title to indicate that Hunt was the "living dog" and Byron "the dead lion"]

1860 (February/March): Lord Byron, *The Poetical Works* ([1853?]); Sealts, no. 112

[On Milton:] Would *he* adore a sultan? *he* obey / The intellectual eunuch Castlereagh? [*Don Juan,* dedication, stanza 11; vol. 9, p. 105]	What an awful clincher [?] on W. C. & S. [Wordsworth, Coleridge, and Southey renounced their revolutionary politics for the reactionary views of Robert Stewart, Viscount Castlereagh, a Tory whom Byron despised.]
If *you* think 't was philosophy that this did, / I can't help thinking puberty assisted. [*Don Juan,* canto 1, stanza 93; p. 149]	This is a touch from Dean Swift. [See Bercaw, nos. 683, 684]

1860 (March): William Hazlitt, *Lectures on the English Poets* (1859; bound with *Lectures on the English Comic Writers*); Sealts, no. 263b

he is even without God in the world [Lecture 1, "On Poetry in General," p. 22]	True: no gods, I think, are mentioned in Ossian. [James Macpherson, *Fingal;* Sealts, no. 343]

PASSAGES MELVILLE MARKED	MELVILLE'S ANNOTATION, WITH SOURCES AND COMMENTS
If it were indeed possible to shew that this writer was nothing, it would only be another instance of mutability, another blank made, another void left in the heart, another confirmation of that feeling which makes him so often complain, "Roll on, ye dark brown years, ye bring no joy on your wing to Ossian!" [Lecture 1, "On Poetry in General," p. 22.]	I am rejoiced to see Hazlitt speak for Ossian. There is nothing more contemptible in that contemptible man (tho' good poet, in his department) Wordsworth, than this contempt for Ossian. And nothing that more raises my idea of Napoleon than his great admiration for him.—The loneliness of the spirit of Ossian harmonized with the loneliness of the greatness of Napoleon. [James Macpherson, *Fingal;* Sealts, no. 343]
The great fault of a modern school of poetry is that it is an experiment to reduce poetry to a mere effusion of natural sensibility . . . for their minds reject, with a convulsive effort and intolerable loathing, the very idea that there ever was, or was thought to be, anything superior to themselves. [Lecture 3, "On Shakspeare and Milton," pp. 62–63]	Wordsworth was in the writer's mind here, very likely.
but after reading the Excursion, few people will think it [*Candide*] *dull* [Lecture 6, "On Swift, Young, Gray, Etc.," p. 136.]	Wordsworth so called it. [The Solitary in *The Excursion,* bk. 2, refers to *Candide* as "this dull product of a Scoffer's pen"; Sealts, no. 563a, p. 409.]
[Passage jibing at Samuel Rogers's "Pleasures of Memory," lecture 8, "On the Living Poets," pp. 176–77]	This is pretty much all spleen. Rogers, tho' no genius, was a painstaking man of talent who has written some good things. "Italy" is an interesting book to every person of taste. In Hazlitt you have at times to allow for indigestion. [*Italy* (1822–28), Rogers's travel verses]

PASSAGES MELVILLE MARKED	MELVILLE'S ANNOTATION, WITH SOURCES AND COMMENTS

1860 (March 4): Anne Louise Germaine Staël-Holstein, *Germany* (1859); Sealts, no. 487

Events like those of the Iliad interest of themselves, and the less the author's own sentiments are brought forward, the greater is the impression made by the picture; but if we set ourselves to describe *romantic* situations with the impartial calmness of Homer, the result would not be very alluring. ["Of Romances," vol. 2, p. 58]	Admirable distinction. In the "Idylls of the King" (Tennyson) we see the Homeric, or rather Odyssean manner pervading <u>romantic</u> stories, and the result is a kind of "shocking tameness." [Melville quotes the phrase "shocking tameness" from Francis Jeffrey, review of Robert Southey, *Roderick: The Last of the Goths, Edinburgh Review* (June 1815); collected in Sealts, no. 359, *The Modern British Essayists*, vol. 6, p. 424. For "Idylls of the King" see Tennyson, *The Poetical Works;* Sealts, no. 508.]
the opinions of Goethe are much more profound, but they do not present any greater consolation to the soul. [vol. 2, p. 60]	It is delightful and wonderful to see — passim — such penetration of understanding in a woman, who at the same time possesses so feminine & emotional a nature. — who would one compare Madam De Stael too? — Mrs. Browning? — Mrs. B. was a great woman, but Madam De S. was a greater.

1861 (August 14): Alfred, Lord Tennyson, *The Poetical Works;* Sealts, no. 508

[Pasted on front flyleaf: clipping of a critic's accusation that Tennyson borrowed the meter for "The Charge of the Light Brigade" from Michael Drayton's "The Battaile of Agincourt" (1627), with eight lines from Drayton quoted.]	stuff by a Small Man [This annotation is enclosed in a drawing of a hand pointing up toward the clipping; Melville directs his sarcasm toward the critic's accusation, not toward Tennyson.]

PASSAGES MELVILLE MARKED	MELVILLE'S ANNOTATION, WITH SOURCES AND COMMENTS

1862 (March 17): Heinrich Heine, *The Poems of Heine, Complete* (1861); Sealts, no. 268

["Clarissa," p. 98]	[By title:] Swinburne's inspiration is tracable distantly in some of these things. — Especially in Queen Mary. [See Algernon Charles Swinburne's poem "Adieux à Marie Stuart," the epilogue to his dramatic trilogy *Chastelard, Bothwell,* and *Mary Stuart.* See also Swinburne, *Laus Veneris, and Other Poems and Ballads,* Sealts, no. 492a.]
["The Return Home," p. 183]	[Above title:] The poetical part of The Reisebilder [Early in his career Heine wrote a series of travel narratives, *Die Reisebilder* (or *Pictures of Travel*).]

1862 (March 21): Abraham Cowley, *The Works* (1707, 1711); Sealts, no. 160a

His *Faith* perhaps in some nice Tenets might/Be wrong; his *Life,* I'm sure, was *in the right.* ["Miscellanies," vol. 1, p. 46]	"He can't be wrong whose life is in the right." Pope. ["His can't be wrong whose life is in the right," *Essay on Man,* 3.306; Sealts, no. 405]
Nothing in *Nature's sober* found, / But an eternal *Health* goes round. / Fill up the *Bowl* then, fill it high, / Fill all the *Glasses* there, for why / Should ev'ry Creature drink but *I,* / Why, *Man* of *Morals,* tell we why? ["Drinking" from "Anacreontiques," vol. 1, p. 49]	Acme & Septimius p. 561 v. 2 [See Cowley's "Ode. Acme & Septimius out of Catullus," vol. 2, p. 561 of this edition.]

PASSAGES MELVILLE MARKED	MELVILLE'S ANNOTATION, WITH SOURCES AND COMMENTS
I'll teach him a *Receipt* to make / *Words* that *weep,* and *Tears* that *speak,* ["The Prophet," vol. 1, p. 113]	"Thoughts that breathe and words that burn" [Thomas Gray, "The Progress of Poesy: A Pindaric Ode," 3.3.4]
["The Inconstant." "I Never yet could see that Face / Which had no Dart for me," vol. 1, p. 153]	[Beneath title:] Sheridan's Song [See the air from Richard Brinsley Sheridan's *The Duenna* (1775), which begins "I ne'er could any lustre see / In eyes that would not look on me"; Sealts, no. 471.]
Since the whole *Stock* may soon exhausted be, / Bestow't not all in *Charity.* / Let *Nature,* and let *Art* do what they please, / When all's done, *Life is an Incurable Disease.* ["To Dr. Scarborough," no. 6 in "Pindarique Odes," vol. 1, p. 237]	Pope [Perhaps "The Muse but served to ease some friend, not Wife, / To help me through this long disease, my Life," "An Epistle to Dr. Arbuthnot," 131–32; Sealts, no. 405.]
He has liv'd well, who has lain well hidden. Which if it be a Truth, the World (I'll swear) is sufficiently deceiv'd: For my part, I think it is, and that the pleasantest Condition of Life is in *Incognito.* ["Several Discourses by Way of Essays, in Verse and Prose," vol. 2, p. 700]	See Addison [Perhaps "Thus I live in the world, rather as a Spectator of Mankind, than as one of the Species," Joseph Addison, *The Spectator,* no. 1, Bercaw, nos. 3a, 662.]
This humble Roof, this rustick Court (said he) / Receiv'd *Alcides* crown'd with Victory. / Scorn not (great Guest) the Steps where he has trod, / But contemn Wealth, and imitate a God. [Verse extract from the *Aeneid* in "Several Discourses by Way of Essays, in Verse and Prose," vol. 2, p. 714]	"Dare to be poor" Dryden's Æneid. [And, in another hand, "Aeneid lib: 8. v178"; Sealts, no. 147.]

PASSAGES MELVILLE MARKED	MELVILLE'S ANNOTATION, WITH SOURCES AND COMMENTS
And Business thou wouldst find, and wouldst create: / Business! the frivolous Pretence / Of human Lusts, to shake off Innocence; / Business! the grave Impertinence; / Business! the thing which I of all things hate, / Business! the Contradiction of thy Fate. ["Verses Written on Several Occasions," vol. 2, p. 586]	[Rear free endpaper, verso:] 586— Business &c
That from all which I have written I never receiv'd the least Benefit, or the least Advantage, but, on the contrary, have felt sometimes the Effects of Malice and Misfortune. ["Preface" to *Cutter of Cole-man Street. A Comedy,* vol. 2, p. [800]]	How few will credit this; nevertheless how true, one doubts not, said by a man like Cowley.
The Works of Mr. *John Milton,* containing his Paradise Lost and Paradise Regain'd; to which is added *Samson Agonistes,* and Poems on several Occasions compos'd at several Times. In 2 Vols. 8 *vo.* ["Books Printed for Jacob Tonson, at Grays-Inn Gate," vol. 2, p. [895]]	33 years after his death.

1862 (March 22): Ralph Waldo Emerson, *Essays: Second Series* (1844); Sealts, no. 205

It is a secret which every intellectual man quickly learns, that, beyond the energy of his possessed and conscious intellect, he is capable of a new energy. . . . As the traveller who has lost his way, throws his reins on his horse's neck, and trusts to the instinct of the animal to find his road, so must we do with the divine animal who carries us through this world. ["The Poet," p. 29]	Wordsworth. "One impulse from a vernal wood" &c / This is an original application of the thought. ["The Tables Turned; An Evening Scene on the Same Subject," line 21; Sealts, no. 563a, p. 337]

PASSAGES MELVILLE MARKED	MELVILLE'S ANNOTATION, WITH SOURCES AND COMMENTS
So the poet's habit of living should be set on a key so low and plain, that the common influences should delight him. His cheerfulness should be the gift of the sunlight; the air should suffice for his inspiration, and he should be tipsy with water. ["The Poet," p. 32]	This makes the Wordsworthian poet — not Shakespearian.

1862 (April): Charles Churchill, *The Poetical Works* (1854); Sealts, no. 144

When to the top the bold adventurer's got, / He reigns vain monarch o'er a barren spot, / Whilst in the vale of ignorance below / Folly and vice to rank luxuriance grow; ["The Author," vol. 2, p. 168]	Wordsworth [Perhaps "The Prelude," 8.495–97: "Ere long, the lonely mountains left, I moved, / Begirt, from day to day, with temporal shapes / Of vice and folly thrust upon my view"; *The Prelude* (New York: Appleton, 1850), p. 227; see the HISTORICAL NOTE, p. 491n.]

1862 (April 6): Matthew Arnold, *Poems* (1856); Sealts, no. 21

Sohrab and Rustum. An Episode. [poem, p. [31]]	(from the "Shah Nameh" of Firdousi) [The *Shah-nameh,* or *Book of Kings,* is the Persian national epic.]
To A Friend [poem, p. [172]]	Homer, Epictetus, Sophocles [For Homer, see Sealts, nos. 147, 277, and 278; for Epictetus, see Bercaw, no. 257; for Sophocles, see Sealts, no. 147.]
But Wordsworth's eyes avert their ken. / From half of human fate; / And Goethe's course few sons of men / May think to emulate. ["Obermann," p. 312]	True as to Wordsworth. Of Goethe it might also be said that he averted his eyes from everything except Nature, Intellect, & Beauty.

PASSAGES MELVILLE MARKED	MELVILLE'S ANNOTATION, WITH SOURCES AND COMMENTS
Whose one bond is that all have been / Unspotted by the world. ["Obermann," p. 316]	That is very noble—why? Because it is nobly true—ideally—
The Youth of Nature [p. 322]	"And oft suspend the dashing oar / To bid his gentle spirit rest" / Collins—of Thompson "Now let us, as we float along / For him suspend the dashing oar" Wordsworth—of Collins. How beautifully appropriate therefor this reminiscent prelude of Arnold concerning Wordsworth. [William Collins, "Ode on the Death of Thomson," lines 15–16; Sealts, no. 156, p. 64. Wordsworth, "Remembrance of Collins," lines 17–18, *The Complete Poetical Works,* Sealts, no. 563a, pp. 346–47.]

1862 (September): Jean de La Bruyère, *The Works of M. De La Bruyere* (1776); Sealts, no. 314

The finest and most beautiful thoughts concerning Manners have been carried away before our times, and nothing is left for us but to glean after the ancients, and the most ingenious of the Moderns. [Essay, "Of Works of Genius," vol. 1, p. 17]	Pope's Preface [See 1716 preface to Pope's *Works:* "Among the moderns, their success has been greatest who have most endeavoured to make these ancients their pattern"; Sealts, no. 405.]
There are few men so accomplished, or so necessary, but have some failings or other which will make their friends bear the loss of them with the greater patience. [Essay, "Of Personal Merit," vol. 1, p. 58]	True. Shakespeare goes further: none die but somebody spurns them into the grave. ["Who dies, that bears / Not one spurn to their graves of their friends' gift?" *Timon of Athens,* 1.2; Sealts, no. 460, vol. 5, p. 379]

PASSAGES MELVILLE MARKED	MELVILLE'S ANNOTATION, WITH SOURCES AND COMMENTS
but, as opposed to wise, able, and virtuous men, vulgar includes as well the Great as the Little. [Essay, "Of the Great," vol. 1, p. 230]	"Both the great vulgar and the small" Cowley And of the two the G.V. are the vulgarest. ["Hence, ye profane; I hate ye all;/Both the Great, Vulgar, and the Small," Abraham Cowley, "Horace. L. 3. Ode. I./Odi profanum vulgus, &c"; Sealts, no. 160a, vol. 2, p. 751. In his copy of Cowley, Melville struck the comma after "Great."]
but how shall I fix this Proteus, who changes himself into a thousand dissimilar figures? [Description of a courtier in an essay, "Of the Fashion," vol. 2, p. 54]	Pope ["Hence Bards, like Proteus long in vain ty'd down,/Escape in Monsters, and amaze the town," *Dunciad*, 1.37–38; Sealts, no. 405]
The duty of a judge consists in the administration of justice; his trade is delaying it. Some judges understand their duty, and mind their trade. [Essay, "Of Custom," vol. 2, p. 77]	Dean Swift has made more of this distinction [See *Gulliver's Travels*, 2.6, particularly the passage in which the king of Brobdingnag asks Gulliver whether "Judges had any Part in penning those Laws, which they assumed the Liberty of interpreting and glossing upon at their Pleasure"; Bercaw, no. 683.]

1863 (March): William Hazlitt, *Table Talk* (1845); Sealts, no. 266a

To die is only to be as we were before we were born [Essay 12, "On the Fear of Death," p. 124]	[At page bottom:] This is very fine— This modernizing & familiarizing of the grand thought of Lucretius. ["Nor aught imports it that he e'er was born,/When death immortal claims his mortal life," Titus Lucretius Carus, *On the Nature of Things*, trans. John Mason Good (1805), bk. 3, lines 896–97]

PASSAGES MELVILLE MARKED	MELVILLE'S ANNOTATION, WITH SOURCES AND COMMENTS

1867 (May 17): Luis de Camoëns, *Poems* (1824); Sealts, no. 116

And sweetest eyes that e'er were seen! ["Madrigal," p. 40]	[At page bottom:] Mrs. Browning's verses on this. [Elizabeth Barrett Browning, "Catarina to Camoens; dying in his absence abroad, and referring to the poem in which he recorded the sweetness of her eyes"; *The Poems . . . A New Edition* (New York, 1860); Sealts, no. 93]

1867 (October 27): Sir Henry Taylor, *Notes from Life in Seven Essays* (1853); Sealts, no. 495.1

"I would persuade you," says that very brilliant and remarkable writer, "that banter, pun, and quibble, are the properties of light men and shallow capacities; that genuine humor and true wit require a sound and capacious mind, which is always a grave one." ["The Ways of the Rich and Great," p. 186]	Landor's "Imaginary Conversations," 1st series, Vol. 2, p. 404, 2nd edition. ["Alfieri and Salomon the Florentine Jew," Vittorio Alfieri speaking to Salomon; Walter Savage Landor, *Imaginary Conversations of Literary Men and Statesmen*, 2 vols., 2d ed. (London: H. Colburn, 1826), p. 404; see also Landor, *The Works . . .* ; see also Sealts, no. 319b]

1869 (December): Sir Joshua Reynolds, *The Literary Works* (1855); Sealts, no. 423

our great Lyric Poet, when he conceived his sublime idea of the indignant Welsh bard [p. 106]	Gray [Thomas Gray, "The Bard: A Pindaric Ode"; Bercaw, no. 310]
I must resume my discourse, following my author's text, though with more brevity than I intended, because Virgil calls me. [p. 400]	And Virgil, damn him, calls. Pope. ["And Homer (damn him) calls," quoted in Thomas Moore, *Life of Lord Byron*; Sealts, no. 369, vol. 2, p. 24n.]

PASSAGES MELVILLE MARKED	MELVILLE'S ANNOTATION, WITH SOURCES AND COMMENTS

1870?: Thomas Warton, *The History of English Poetry* (undated reprint of edition of 1778 & 1781); Sealts, no. 547a

With nightes starres thick-powdred every where, [p. 770]	Milton ["Powder'd with stars," *Paradise Lost*, 7.581; Sealts, no. 358b, vol. 1, p. 248]
His dart, anon, out of the corpse he tooke, / And in his hand (a dreadful sight to see) / With great triumph eftsoons the same he shook, / That most of all my fears affrayed me. [p. 775]	"And shook a dreadful dart" Milton [*Paradise Lost*, 2.672; Sealts, no. 358b, vol. 1, p. 63. A footnote in Melville's edition of *Paradise Lost* cites Sackville's *Introduction to Mirror for Magistrates* (1610), p. 266, as the source for this parallel.]
[Scores a discussion of Shakespeare's sources for *Romeo and Juliet* that includes this quotation from George Turberville's "An Epitaph on the Death of Maister Arthur Brooke" who drowned on a passage to New Haven:] Apollo lent him lute for solace sake, / To sound his verse by touch of stately string; / And of the neuer-fading baye did make / A laurell crowne, about his browes to clinge, / In proof that he for myter did excel, / As may be iudge by Iulyet and her Mate; / For ther he shewde his cunning passing well / When he the tale to English did translate.—/ Aye mee, that time, thou crooked dolphin, where / Wast thou, Aryon's help and onely stay, / That safely him from sea to shore didst beare, / When Brooke was drownd why was thou then away? [pp. 931–32]	[Top of page 932:] Milton's dirge. [See "Lycidas," particularly "Yet once more, O ye laurels, and once more / Ye myrtles brown" (lines 1–2); "He knew / Himself to sing, and build the lofty rhime" (lines 10–11); "Where were ye, Nymphs, when the remorseless deep / Clos'd o'er the head of your lov'd Lycidas?" (lines 50–51); and "O ye dolphins, waft the hapless youth" (line 164); Sealts, no. 358b, vol. 2, pp. 271, 273, 279]

PASSAGES MELVILLE MARKED	MELVILLE'S ANNOTATION, WITH SOURCES AND COMMENTS

1870 (December): *The Works of Eminent Masters* (1854); Sealts, no. 564

["The Unknown Masterpiece," a legend about a monk who paints and chooses to remain anonymous (vol. 1, p. 190)]	"Pictor Ignotus" of Browning ["Pictor Ignotus. [Florence, 15—.]," in *Poems,* by Robert Browning, 2 vols. (Boston: Ticknor, Reed, & Fields, 1850), 2:321–23]

1871 (July 10): Matthew Arnold, *Essays in Criticism* (1865); Sealts, no. 17

Homer's manner and movement are always both noble and powerful: the ballad-manner and movement are often either jaunty and smart, so not noble; or jog-trot and humdrum, so not powerful. [p. 321]	If this be intended to apply — for example — so all the ballads in Bishop Percy's Collection [rest erased] [Bishop Thomas Percy, *Reliques of Ancient English Poetry* (1765). See also Francis James Child, *English and Scottish Ballads* (Boston, 1857–59; Sealts, no. 143), passim]

1873: Robert Bell, ed., *Songs from the Dramatists* (1854); Sealts, no. 56

[Reprints the poem "Fools" from Ben Jonson's *Volpone; or, the Fox* (1605); pp. 114–15.]	Erasmus's Folly—This seems a versifying of the first of it. [Desiderius Erasmus, *In Praise of Folly* (1509); Bercaw, no. 258a]

The Sources of Melville's
Notes (1849–1851) in a
Shakespeare Volume

The notes commented on, transcribed, and reproduced in this RELATED DOCUMENT are pencil notes Melville wrote on both sides of the last blank leaf in the last volume of his *The Dramatic Works of William Shakspeare* (7 vols., Boston: Hilliard, Gray, 1837), his set now at Houghton Library. (The Hilliard, Gray edition uses the spelling "Shakspeare" in its title and throughout.) This set bears no acquisition date, but almost surely is the edition that Melville rhapsodized about in his letter to Evert A. Duyckinck from Boston on February 24, 1849. In recognition of the significance of these notes, Harrison Hayford and Lynn Horth put into the 1988 Northwestern-Newberry edition of *Moby-Dick* a RELATED DOCUMENT headed "Melville's Notes (1849–51) in a Shakespeare Volume." This present document is prepared by Hershel Parker to acknowledge and to celebrate the current state of knowledge about these notes. It is accompanied by a clearer photographic reproduction of the notes than technology allowed in 1988. The transcription printed in 1988 is altered at one point: "?making ?almxxxx" is now printed as "making almanacks" (Jay Leyda's 1949 reading, now established as correct). Where Hayford and Horth identified the notes as inscribed on [524], first, then on [523], this note refers to them as being on the verso and, subsequently, the recto of the last blank leaf.

Melville's penciled notes in the last volume of his copy of *The Dramatic Works of William Shakspeare*, on the verso of the last blank leaf. Courtesy of Houghton Library, Harvard University: AC85.MC4977.ZZ837s v. 7.

On different occasions over a period of days, weeks, or months, between (at the earliest) late February 1849 and the end of June 1851, Melville filled the verso with notes and then began to write on the recto. (The terminal date is based on the unprovable assumptions that Melville wrote down the notes before incorporating some of the words into *Moby-Dick* and before, still later, using some of them in his letter of June 29, 1851, to Nathaniel Hawthorne.) While the notes do not obviously fall into absolutely distinct groups, they in fact come from three sources. And although he made the notes from three sources, Melville did not necessarily make them in three sittings; days or longer may have elapsed between his writing down the first and the last note of the middle stage, in particular.

In each instance Melville presumably had borrowed a book and desired to take notes on it while it was in his possession. As far as we know, in making such records he never used a notebook or blankbook or a more formal retrieval device such as the *Index Rerum* his brother Gansevoort had used. Insofar as he had a habitual way of notetaking from borrowed books, it was to make notes in books he already owned and intended to keep. When shelved properly, the last volume of Shakespeare's *Dramatic Works* would have been within easy reach for making notes and consulting them or adding to them. None of the notes obviously relate to Shakespeare. While all of the notes are of interest to scholars, those relating to *Moby-Dick* are of paramount interest.

We now know not only that the jottings are Melville's reading notes (at times combined with literary planning notes), we also know what books the notes come from. In December 2007, during the preparation of this volume of Melville's *Published Poems,* Scott Norsworthy discovered that the first set of notes Melville inscribed, those at the top of the verso, lines 1–11, were from a series of essays by Leigh Hunt first published in the early 1820s in his short-lived London journal *The Indicator* and reprinted in *Essays* (London: Edward Moxon, 1841). Melville's friend Evert Duyckinck had in his library an American edition, Leigh Hunt's *The Indicator: A Miscellany for the Fields and the Fireside* (New York: Wiley & Putnam, 1845), for it had appeared in two parts in a series Duyckinck himself edited, Wiley & Putnam's Library of Choice Reading, a series parallel to the one in which Melville had been introduced to the United States, the Library of American Books. A copy of this edition of *The Indicator* was among the books presented to the Lenox Library in 1878 from the "Duyckinck Collection," after Duyckinck's death, and that copy has been chosen for digitizing by Google Books. Although it is not among the books Duyckinck recorded as loaned to Melville, chances are high that Melville was taking notes from a copy of the Wiley & Putnam edition owned by Duyckinck. (While the

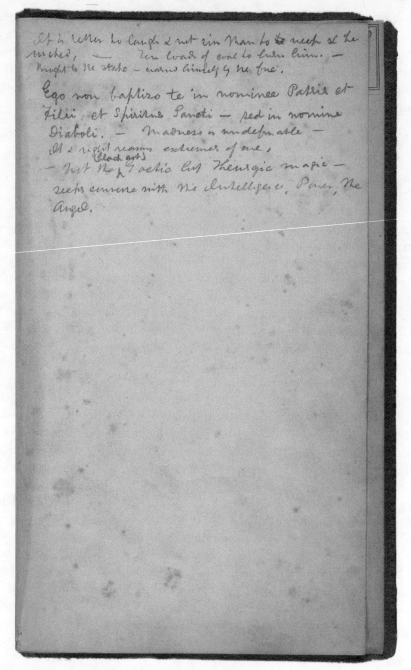

Melville's penciled notes in the last volume of his copy of *The Dramatic Works of William Shakspeare,* on the recto of the last blank leaf. Courtesy of Houghton Library, Harvard University: AC85.MC4977.ZZ837s v. 7.

present volume was at the press, Geoffrey Sanborn published his independent discovery of Melville's use of Hunt's *The Indicator*.)

In September 2007, a few months before his discovery that the *Indicator* was one of Melville's sources, Norsworthy had discovered the source of the second set of notes Melville made, the middle set beginning with the citation of Cain, Reuben, and Absalom (verso 12–30: the first volume of Thomas Roscoe's four-volume *The German Novelists* [London: Henry Colburn, 1826]). In this instance, from the start Melville was dramatizing the notes he took down from Roscoe about Doctor Faustus and Mephostophiles (Roscoe's spelling), interspersing them with his own notes for a story, apparently one set in Manhattan involving a female interlocutor and perhaps involving the Devil as a Quaker. In January 2008, gleaning after Norsworthy, Hershel Parker found the source in Roscoe for the single sentence inscribed at the top of the recto, "It is better to laugh & not sin than to weep & be wicked" (recto 1–2). The source is on 1.149, not in the section on "Doctor Faustus" but in the earlier section on "Howleglass, the Merry Jester."

The group of notes starting on the recto on the second line, after the conclusion of the sentence just quoted, are by far the most famous notes Melville ever made, much debated ever since Charles Olson, the first scholar to examine the Houghton set, used the group in his *"Lear and Moby-Dick"* (1938). What Olson focused on, and what most intrigued generations of Melville scholars, was the inverted Latin baptismal formula "in nomine diaboli" which Ahab uses in *Moby-Dick* and which Melville in the June 29, 1851, letter to Hawthorne declared to be that book's secret motto. In 1992 Geoffrey Sanborn published his discovery that those notes (lines 32–40) are from "Superstition and Knowledge" (unsigned but by Francis Palgrave) in the July 1823 London *Quarterly Review.*

Some of the earliest notes from Leigh Hunt (possibly made as early as late February or early March 1849) record material Melville had just used in finishing *Mardi,* which was already off his hands when he acquired the set of Shakespeare. Apparently he wanted to keep a few notes on material he might later use as well as a little material he had already used (perhaps incorporating it into *Mardi* after only a preliminary scan of the Hunt book). The notes on verso 5–7 relate to *Mardi* (chap. 138, pp. 440–41). Those on verso 1–3, however, relate to *White-Jacket* (chap. 86, p. 363), which was written August–September 1849.

Here, given without the fuller contexts supplied by Sanborn and Norsworthy in their articles, are the words in the sources (the most significant words given in bold) and the final form of Melville's notes. Readers will find much fuller accounts in the articles by Sanborn and Norsworthy, but the present listing will stand as a supplement to "Melville's Notes (1849–51) in a Shakespeare Volume" in the 1988 *Moby-Dick;* although that discussion is superseded by our present knowledge of the sources of Melville's notes, it is still important for its account of the often-reprinted Hilliard, Gray *Dramatic Works* and for its physical description of the relevant leaves of Melville's copy of the seventh volume of that edition.

Hunt, 1:169–70: chap. 30, "Seamen on Shore":
Chaucer, who wrote his Canterbury Tales about four hundred and thirty years ago, has among his other characters in that work a SHIP-MAN. . . .

> A shipman was there . . .
> Hardy he was, and wise, I undertake;
> **With many a tempest had his beard been shake.**

Melville:
1 A seaman figures in The Canterbury Tales
2 With many a tempest had his beard been
3 shook. —

Hunt, 1:25: chap. 7, "Advice to the Melancholy" [quoting Francis Bacon]:
"If you fly physic in health altogether, it will be too strange for your body when you need it. . . . As for the passions and studies of the mind," says he [Bacon, in "Of Regiment of Health"], "avoid envy, anxious fears, anger fretting inwards, subtle and knotty inquisitions, joys and exhilarations in excess, **sadness not communicated" (for as he says finely, somewhere else ["Of Friendship"], they who keep their griefs to themselves are "cannibals of their own hearts").**

Melville:
3   Secret grief is a
4 cannibal of its own heart — <u>Bacon.</u>

Hunt, 2:24–25: chap. 46, "Superfine Breeding":
There is an anecdote in Aulus Gellius (*Noctes Atticæ,* lib. 10, cap. Vi.) which exhibits, we think, one of the highest instances of what may be called polite blackguardism, that we remember to have read. . . .
  Claudia, the daughter of Appius Cæcus, in coming away from a public spectacle, was much pressed and pushed about by the crowd; upon which she thus vented her impatience:—

"What should I have suffered now, and how much more should I have been squeezed and knocked about, if my brother Publius Claudius had not had his ships destroyed in battle, with all that heap of men! I should have been absolutely jammed to death! **Would to heaven my brother were alive again, and could go with another fleet to Sicily, and be the death of this host of people, who plague and pester one in this horrid manner!"** . . .

Insolence and want of feeling appear to have been hereditary in this Appian family: which gives us also a strong sense of their want of capacity; otherwise a disgust at such manners must have generated in some of the children.

Melville:

5 <u>Claudia</u> of the <u>Appian</u> family, "I wish
6 some fight or pestilence would thin out
7 this crowd." <u>Arrogance</u>.

Hunt, 2:104–14: chap. 58, "A Human Animal, and the Other Extreme":
"The Honourable William Hastings, a gentleman of a very singular character," says our informant, "lived in the year 1638, and by his quality was son, brother, and uncle to the Earls of Huntingdon." . . . **He lived to be an hundred; never lost his eye-sight, but always wrote and read without spectacles.** . . . On one side of this end of the room was the door of a closet, wherein stood the strong beer and the wine. . . . On the other side was the door into an old chapel, not used for devotion. **The pulpit, as the safest place, was never wanting of a cold chine of beef, venison pasty, gammon of bacon, or great apple-pie, with thick crust extremely baked.["]** . . . In short, to be candid on all sides with the very earthly memory of the Honourable Mr. William Hastings, we take a person of his description to be **a good specimen of the animal part of the human nature**, and chiefly on this account, that the animal preserves its **health**. . . . At the age of a hundred he was able to read and write without spectacles; not better perhaps than he did at fifteen, but as well. **At a hundred, he was truly an old boy, and no more thought of putting on spectacles than an eagle.** . . . But he wanted a soul to turn his perceptions to their proper account? . . . It is remarkable, that the same ancient family . . . edified the world not long after with as complete a specimen of the other half of human nature. Mr. William Hastings' soul seems to have come too late for his body, and to have remained afterwards upon earth in the shape of his fair kinswoman, Lady Elizabeth Hastings, daughter of Theophilus, seventh Earl of Huntingdon. An account of her follows that of her animal kinsman, and is **a most extraordinary contrast**. This is the lady who is celebrated by Sir Richard Steele in the *Tatler* under the name of Aspasia. . . . It seems pretty clear from all these accounts, that this noble-hearted woman, notwithstanding her beauty and sweet temper, was as imperfect a specimen of animal humanity as her kinsman was of spiritual. . . . When cant lives as long and healthy a life as his, or as good a one as hers, it

will be worth attending to. Till then, the best thing to advise is, **neither to be canting, nor merely animal, nor over-spiritual;** but to endeavour to enjoy, with the greatest possible distribution of happiness, all the faculties we receive from nature.

Melville:

  8 <u>Roast beef in the pulpet.</u>

  9 An animal of a man — "do eagles wear
10 spectacles?" — Health. — <u>Contrast:</u> an
11 over spiritual man.

Roscoe, 1:271:

Yet so it often happens that devout parents are afflicted with **froward godless** children; as it was also in the case of Cain (Gen. iv.) in that of Reuben, (49.) and also that of Absalom, so dearly beloved by his father. [The first use of "also" refers to Faustus's parents, who died not knowing of his descent into "depravity."]

Melville:

12 "Yes, Madam, Cain was a godless froward boy, &
13 Reuben (Gen: 49) & Absalom."

Roscoe, 1:270:

Doctor Faustus was . . . born of honest **pious** parents in the year 1491. . . . Faustus, however, soon ungraciously set at nought his uncle's pious intentions.

Melville:

13   Many pious men
14 have impious children

Roscoe, 1:278:

The next time, the Doctor shewed him [the demon, as yet unnamed] the articles of the **compact** which he had drawn up, namely: **Imprimis,** That the demon should obey him in every thing he required, or chose to exact, during the whole term of the Doctor's natural life. **Secondly,** That he should be bound to answer every question, upon every subject put to him, without any quibble or demur: Thirdly, That he must there reply to all the different interrogatories that the Doctor chose to trouble him with.

Roscoe, 1:281–82:

Imprimis: Let Doctor Faustus swear, promise, and sign, that he holds the **said service** and obedience from the devil, upon a lease of years, to have and to hold.

Secondly, that the Doctor, for further assurance of the same, shall sign and witness it with his own hand and blood. Thirdly, that he shall declare all Christians to be his natural enemies. Fourthly, he must forswear the Christian faith. Fifthly, that he must watch and pray, that no one may prevail upon him to return to it. Before the signing and execution of these conditions, a certain number of years to be mentioned, at the expiration of which the demon was to return to fetch the Doctor away.

Roscoe, 1:288:

Mephostophiles . . . insisted that Faustus should preserve another copy by him, to prevent all chance of litigation or mistake.

Melville:

15 A formal compact — Imprimis — First — Second.
16 The aforesaid soul. said soul &c — Duplicates —

Roscoe, 1:298–99:

[Mephostophiles in answer to inquiries about "temptations of the devil" rehearses the biblical temptations of Adam, Eve, Cain, Saul, David, and Solomon.]

Melville:

17 "How was it about the temptation on the
18 hill?" &c — D begs the hero to form
19 one of a <u>"Society of D's"</u> — his name would be weighty
20 &c — Leaves a letter to the D — "My
21 Dear D" —

Roscoe, 1:295 [The "governments" or departments of Hell]:

1. Lucus Mortis; 2. Stagium Ignis; 3. Terra Tenebrosa; 4. Tartarus; 5. **Terra Oblivionis;** 6. Gehenna; 7. Herebus; 8. Barathrum; 9. Styx; and 10. Acheron.

Roscoe, 1:305:

"Because all we **Hellites,** or damned spirits, being once separated from grace, must remain in a state of reprobation to all eternity."

Roscoe, 1:308:

He [Faustus] next began **to make almanacks,** for he was one of the best astrologers and almanack-makers of his time; well versed in calculating nativities, and setting down prognostications, as the world well knows.

Roscoe, 1:309:

When Doctor Faustus had been for the space of two years employed in **making his almanacks,** he once more summoned his demon to inquire what might be his opinion, and proficiency in regard to astronomy and astrology.

Roscoe, 1:310:

"I could easily cast you some prognostications fit for **almanacks.**"

Roscoe, 1:391–92:
Before they set off to the **ball,** he [Faustus] sprinkled a few magical drops upon the young man's features which improved them, and his whole appearance very surprisingly.

Roscoe, 1:320:
Suddenly was heard a loud rumbling noise, and there issued two huge dragons from the dense clouds with a chariot yoked at their tails. It was attended by black footmen in flame-coloured livery, one of whom called out, "**Doctor Faustus's coach.**"

Roscoe, 1:312:
Upon hearing this [question from Doctor Faustus "respecting the creation of the world and of the first man"], Mephostophiles secretly resolved to pass off a false and profane account upon the Doctor, and he said; "**The world, my dear Faustus, to say the truth, never was created**, or without form, nor will it ever perish. And the same in regard to man, his evil generation has continued from eternity, and it is all nothing that you hear of his origin, and in fact the earth itself may very well have engendered him with the help of a hot sun."

Melville:
22 "Terra Oblivionis" "Hellites" — At the Astor find him
23 making almanacks — going to a ball takes a long
24 time making toilette. — The Doctor's coach stops
25 the way. — "Do you beleive all that stuff?
28 Receives visits from the principal d's — "Gentlemen" &c.

Roscoe, 1:321:
During his tour of "the infernal regions," Faustus encounters "the shades of many heathens, fierce and stately forms of emperors, kings, princes and their lords."

Roscoe, 1:404:
Mephostophiles to Faustus: "Why, dear Faustus, all this complaining; what avails such pusillanimity; knew you not that your life and soul were long since forfeited, and that at all events you must die once, though you had yet an age to live. Besides, the Turks and Jews, and **other unchristian kings** and heathens must all die, and be condemned everlastingly as well as you. Come, take courage, it will perhaps not be quite so bad as you imagine; and the devil has promised that you shall still keep your life and soul to be held under his lease and sway. **With such comfort** did his demon Mephostophiles strive to cheer his master; but it was false as it was hollow, and quite at variance with the holy scriptures."

Melville:
29 Arguments to persuade — "Would you not rather
30 be below with kings than above with fools?"

At some point, Melville focused belatedly on this passage:

Roscoe 1:293–94:

"Now Lucifer was one of the most beautiful angels under these ["angelic governors" or archangels]; the most beautiful of whom was Raphael: the other two were Gabriel and Michael."

In the space after "Dear D" (line 21) Melville wrote "Conversation upon Gabriel, Micheal & Raphel — gentlemanly &c" and used a caret to indicate that he wanted it to follow "temptation on the hill?' &c" (line 18).

Roscoe 1:149:

"methinke it be **better** to passe the tyme with such a mery jeste, and **laugh** thereat, and do **no synne,** than for to **wepe** and do **synne.**"

Melville:

31 It is better to laugh & not sin than to weep & be
32 wicked.—

Quarterly Review, p. 444: Palgrave quotes from a Scottish town's expenses in 1633 of £3.6s.8d. for "**ten loads of coals *to burn them***" (that is, William Coke and Alison Dick).

Melville:

32   Ten loads of coal to burn him.—

Quarterly Review, p. 446 [On the "last execution of a Scottish witch," a grandmother executed at Dornock in 1722]:

After being brought out for execution, the weather proving very severe, the poor old woman sat composedly before the pile, **warm**ing herself **by the fire** prepared to consume her.

Melville:

33 Brought to the stake — warmed himself by the fire.

Quarterly Review, p. 447:

Upwards of six hundred women were executed in the bishopric of Bamberg alone. The accusations bear the stamp of raving madness. Priests were convicted of baptising in the following form: — **Ego non baptizo te in nomine Patris et Filii et Spiritus Sancti — sed in nomine Diaboli.**

Melville:
34 Ego non baptizo te in nominee Patris et
35 Filii et Spiritus Sancti — sed in nomine
36 Diaboli. —

Quarterly Review, p. 449:
Madness is almost **undefinable**. **Right reason** and insanity are merely the
extreme terms of a series of mental action, which need not be very long.

Melville:
36   Madness is undefinable —
37 It & right reasons extremes of one.

Quarterly Review, pp. 452–53:
The doctrine delivered at Simancas, however, was **not Goetic Magic**, or that
which is vulgarly termed the **Black Art**, but the high and pure Theurgy which
repels all converse with the evil demon. Theurgical magic, the magic which **seeks**
its **converse with the Power, the Intelligence**, and **the Angel**, might have
been first diffused in Spain by the sectaries of the Gnostic doctrines, who appear
to have found numerous adherents in that country during many centuries. ·

Melville:
38 — Not the Goetic but Theurgic magic —
39 seeks converse with the Intelligence, Power, the
40 Angel

[Later Melville careted in an insertion above line 38 after "the": "(black art)."]

Melville's Notes in a Hazlitt Volume

A mong Melville's book purchases in 1862 was William Hazlitt's *Lectures on the English Comic Writers* and *Lectures on the English Poets,* the two volumes bound as one (New York: Derby & Jackson, 1859; Olsen-Smith and Sealts, no. 263b). Melville's marginalia in this volume include the notes reproduced here, on the page opposite and above the beginning of the text in *Lectures on the English Comic Writers.* (See section 10 of the HISTORICAL NOTE, pp. 464–97 above, for Melville's book-buying and note-taking during 1862.)

As Melville's *"Jeffrey on Alfieri."* indicates, the notes on the first page are from Francis Jeffrey's review, *"Memoirs of the Life and Writings of Victor Alfieri. Written by Himself.* 2 vol. 8vo. pp. 614. London, 1810," in the *Edinburgh Review* 30 (January 1810): 274–99, perhaps in a reprinting such as in Melville's Jeffrey volume in *Modern British Essayists* (Philadelphia: Carey & Hart, 1847–48; Sealts, no. 359). Melville's "(Alfieri himself)" on the second page indicates that the words copied there are from *The Autobiography of Vittorio Alfieri, The Tragic Poet,* as translated by C. Edwards Lester (New York: Paine & Burgess, 1843).

Notes Melville inscribed in his copy of Hazlitt's *Lectures on the English Comic Writers* and *Lectures on the English Poets* (2 vols. in 1; Derby & Jackson, 1859), on the page opposite the beginning of *Lectures on the English Comic Writers*. Courtesy of William S. Reese.

Discerning with a mind that has
refined from the subject the best
thoughts & rejecting the dross.
(Alfieri himself)

LECTURES

ON THE

ENGLISH COMIC WRITERS.

LECTURE I.—INTRODUCTORY.

On Wit and Humour.

MAN is the only animal that laughs and weeps; for he is the only animal that is struck with the difference between what things are, and what they ought to be. We weep at what thwarts or exceeds our desires in serious matters: we laugh at what only disappoints our expectations in trifles. We shed tears from sympathy with real and necessary distress; as we burst into laughter from want of sympathy with that which is unreasonable and unnecessary, the absurdity of which provokes our spleen or mirth, rather than any serious reflections on it.

To explain the nature of laughter and tears, is to account for the condition of human life; for it is in a manner compounded of these two! It is a tragedy or a comedy—sad or merry, as it happens. The crimes and misfortunes that are inseparable from it, shock and wound the mind when they once seize upon it, and when the pressure can no longer be borne, seek relief in tears: the follies and absurdities that men commit, or the odd accidents that befal them, afford us amusement from the very rejection of these false claims upon our sympathy, and end in laughter. If everything that went wrong, if every vanity or

2

Notes Melville inscribed in his copy of Hazlitt's *Lectures on the English Comic Writers* and *Lectures on the English Poets* (2 vols. in 1; Derby & Jackson, 1859), at the top of the page where *Lectures on the English Comic Writers* begins. Courtesy of William S. Reese.

Attain the highest result. —
A quality of Grasp. —
The habitual choice of noble subjects. —
        The Expression. —
Get in as much as you can. —
        Finish is completeness, fulness,
not polish. —
        Greatness is a matter of scale. —
        Clearness & firmness. —
The greatest number of the greatest ideas. —
Greatness is determined for a man at
his birth. There is no making oneself
great, in any act or art. But there
is such a thing as the development
of greatness — prolonged, painful, and
painstaking.

Melville's notes on the front flyleaf of his copy of Vasari's *Lives of
the Most Eminent Painters, Sculptors, and Architects,* volume 1. Courtesy of
Houghton Library, Harvard University: *AC85.M4977.Zz850v.

Melville's Notes in a Vasari Volume

As he did with his Shakespeare and Hazlitt volumes purchased in 1862, Melville also took notes in his copy of Giorgio Vasari, *Lives of the Most Eminent Painters, Sculptors, and Architects* (5 vols., London: Bohn, 1849–52; Sealts, no. 534a). See section 10 of the HISTORICAL NOTE, pp. 464–97 above. Reproduced on the facing page are his notes on the front flyleaf of volume 1. As Scott Norsworthy found, the specific source for some of Melville's notes on artistic greatness is John Ruskin's *Modern Painters*.

Works Cited

Abbott, Jacob. *The Harper Establishment*. New York: Harper & Brothers, 1855.

Alfieri, Vittorio. *The Autobiography of Vittorio Alfieri, The Tragic Poet*. Trans. C. Edwards Lester. New York: Paine & Burgess, 1843.

Arnold, Matthew. *Essays in Criticism*. Boston: Ticknor & Fields, 1865.

—————. *Poems*. Boston: Ticknor & Fields, 1856.

Barker, Nicolas. *The Future of Typographical Studies*. Chapel Hill: Hanes Foundation, Rare Book Collection, University of North Carolina, 1996.

Battenfeld, David H. "The Source for the Hymn in *Moby-Dick*." In *Moby-Dick*, ed. Hershel Parker and Harrison Hayford, pp. 574–77. New York: W. W. Norton, 2001. Originally published in *American Literature* 27 (November 1955): 393–96.

Baym, Nina. "Melville's Quarrel with Fiction." *PMLA* 94 (October 1979): 909–23.

Berthold, Dennis. "Melville and Dutch Genre Painting." In *Savage Eye: Melville and the Visual Arts,* ed. Christopher Sten, pp. 218–45. Kent, Ohio: Kent State University Press, 1991.

—————. "Melville, Garibaldi, and the Medusa of Revolution." *American Literary History* 9 (1997): 425–59.

Bezanson, Walter. "Melville's Reading of Arnold's Poetry." *PMLA* 69 (June 1954): 365–69.

Bezanson, Walter, ed. *Clarel*. New York: Hendricks House, 1960.

Blair, Hugh. *Lectures on Rhetoric and Belles Lettres*. New York: Duyckinck, 1817.

Boatner, Mark Mayo, III, Allen C. Northrop, and Lowell Miller. *The Civil War Dictionary.* New York: McKay, 1959.

Brodhead, Richard H. "All in the Family." Review of *Herman Melville: A Biography,* by Hershel Parker. *New York Times Book Review,* June 23, 2002, p. 13.

Browning, Elizabeth Barrett. *Prometheus Bound, and other Poems; including Sonnets from the Portuguese, Casa Guidi Windows, etc.* New York: Francis & Co., 1851.

Bryant, John, ed. *Tales, Poems, and Other Writings.* By Herman Melville. New York: Modern Library, 2001.

Buell, Lawrence. "Melville the Poet." In *The Cambridge Companion to Herman Melville,* ed. Robert S. Levine, pp. 135–56. New York: Cambridge University Press, 1998.

Byron, George Gordon, Lord. *The Poetical Works.* Boston: Little, Brown, 1853.

Center for Editions of American Authors. *Statement of Editorial Principles and Procedures.* Rev. ed.; New York: Modern Language Association of America, 1972.

Channing, William Ellery. *Poems.* Boston: J. Munroe, 1847.

Chapin, Henry, ed. *John Marr and Other Poems.* By Herman Melville. Princeton, N.J.: Princeton University Press, 1922.

Chapman, George, trans. *Homer's Batrachomyomachia . . . .* Ed. Richard Hooper. London: Smith, 1858.

———. *The Iliads of Homer.* Ed. Richard Hooper. 2 vols. London: Smith, 1857.

Charvat, William. "Melville." In *The Profession of Authorship in America: 1800–1870,* by William Charvat, ed. Matthew J. Bruccoli, pp. 204–61. Columbus: Ohio State University Press, 1968.

Chatterton, Thomas. *Poetical Works.* Cambridge, Eng.: Grant, 1842.

Churchill, Charles. *The Poetical Works . . . With Copious Notes and a Life of the Author.* Boston: Little, Brown, 1854.

Cody, David. " 'So, then, Solidity's a crust': Melville's Apparition and the Explosion of the Petersburg Mine." *Melville Society Extracts* 78 (September 1989): 1, 4–8.

Coffler, Gail. *Melville's Classical Allusions: A Comprehensive Index and Glossary.* Westport, Conn.: Greenwood Press, 1985.

Cohen, Hennig, ed. *The Battle-Pieces of Herman Melville.* New York: Thomas Yoseloff, 1964.

———. *Selected Poems of Herman Melville.* Garden City, N.Y.: Doubleday Anchor, 1964. Reprinted with revisions, Carbondale: Southern Illinois University Press, 1968; New York: Fordham University Press, 1991.

Cowen, Walker. "Melville's Marginalia." Ph.D. diss., Harvard University, 1965. Reprint, New York: Garland, 1988.

Cowley, Abraham. *The Works of Abraham Cowley.* 3 vols. London: Tonson, 1707, and Charles Harper, 1711.

Currie, Janette. "From Altrive to Albany: James Hogg's Transatlantic Publication." *STAR-Project Archive* (February 2004), www.star.ac.uk/Archive/Publications.httm.

Dante Alighieri. *The Vision; or Hell, Purgatory, and Paradise.* Trans. Henry Cary. London: Bohn, 1847.

Davenant, William. *Works.* London: Printed by T. N. for Henry Herringman, 1673.

Davis, Merrell R. "The Flower Symbolism in *Mardi.*" *Modern Language Quarterly* 2 (December 1941): 625–37.

—————. *Melville's "Mardi": A Chartless Voyage.* New Haven: Yale University Press, 1952. Reprint, Hamden, Conn.: Archon Books, 1967.

Davis, Merrell R., and William H. Gilman. *The Letters of Herman Melville.* New Haven: Yale University Press, 1960.

Day, Frank L. "Herman Melville's Use of *The Rebellion Record* in His Poetry." M.A. thesis, University of Tennessee, 1959. Lexington: University of Kentucky Press, 1960; Clemson, S.C.: Clemson University Digital Press, 2002.

—————. "Melville and Sherman March to the Sea." *American Notes & Queries* 2 (May 1964): 134–36.

Delbanco, Andrew. "The Great White Male." Review of *Herman Melville: A Biography,* by Hershel Parker. *New Republic,* September 30, 2002, pp. 33–37.

—————. *Herman Melville: His World and Work.* New York: Knopf, 2005.

De Vinne, Theodore Low. *Correct Composition.* New York: Century, 1901.

—————. *Manual of Printing Office Practice.* 1883. Ed. Douglas C. McMurtrie. New York: Press of Ars Typographica, 1926.

—————. *Modern Methods of Book Composition.* New York: Century Co., 1904.

Dewey, Orville. *Autobiography and Letters.* Ed. Mary A. Dewey. Boston: Roberts Brothers, 1883.

—————. *Old World and the New.* New York: Harper & Brothers, 1836.

Dickens, Charles. *The Letters of Charles Dickens.* The Pilgrim Edition. Oxford: Clarendon. Vol. 4, 1844–46, ed. Kathleen Tillotson, 1977. Vol. 5, 1847–49, ed. Graham Storey and K. J. Fielding, 1981. Vol. 6, 1850–52, ed. Graham Storey, Kathleen Tillotson, and Nina Burgis, 1988.

Dictionary of American Naval Fighting Ships. Washington: Government Printing Office, 1963.

Disraeli, Isaac. *Amenities of Literature, Consisting of Sketches and Characters of English Literature.* London: Routledge, 1859.

—————. *The Calamities and Quarrels of Authors, with Some Inquiries Respecting their Moral and Literary Characters, and Memoirs for our Literary History.* London: Routledge, 1860.

—————. *Curiosities of Literature.* London: Routledge, 1859.

—————. *The Literary Character; or, The History of Men of Genius, Drawn from Their own Feelings and Confessions.* London: Routledge, 1859.

Durham, Philip. "Prelude to the Constable Edition of Melville." *Huntington Library Quarterly* 21 (1957–58): 285–89.

Dwyer, J. H. *An Essay on Elocution; with Elucidatory Passages from Various Authors to which are added Remarks on Reading Prose and Verse, with Suggestions to Instructors of the Art.* 2d ed. New York: G. & C. Carville, & E. Bliss, 1828.

Edwards, Mary K Bercaw. "An Old Sailor's Lament: Herman Melville, the Stone Fleet, and the Judgment of History." *The Log of Mystic Seaport* 55.3/4 (2004): 57–71.

Emerson, Ralph Waldo. *Essays, Second Series.* Boston: Munroe, 1844.

Emmons, Richard. *The Fredoniad: or, Independence Preserved. An Epick Poem of the Late War of 1812.* 4 vols. Boston: Published for the Author, by William Emmons, 1827.

Emmons, William. *The Battle of Bunker Hill, or The Temple of Liberty; an Historical Poem in Four Cantos.* New York: Printed by Sackett & Sargent, 1839.

Exman, Eugene. *The House of Harper.* New York: Harper, 1967.

Faggen, Robert, ed. *Selected Poems: Herman Melville.* New York: Penguin, 2006.

Fergusson, Robert. *The Works of Robert Fergusson.* London: Fullarton, 1857.

Fiess, Edward. "Byron and Byronism in the Mind and Art of Herman Melville." Ph.D. diss., Yale University, 1951.

Freeman, Douglas Southall. *The South to Posterity.* New York: Scribner's, 1939.

Freeman, F. Barron. *Melville's "Billy Budd."* Cambridge: Harvard University Press, 1948.

Franklin, S. R. *Memories of a Rear-Admiral.* New York: Harper, 1898.

Freibert, Sister Lucy Marie. "Meditative Voice in the Poetry of Herman Melville." Ph.D. diss., University of Wisconsin–Madison, 1970.

Garner, Stanton. *The Civil War World of Herman Melville.* Lawrence: The University Press of Kansas, 1993.

————. "Melville and Sandford Gifford." *Melville Society Extracts* 48 (November 1981): 10–12.

————. "Melville and Thomas Campbell: The 'Deadly Space Between.'" *English Language Notes* 14 (1977): 289–90.

————. "Melville's Scout Toward Aldie, Part I and II." *Melville Society Extracts* 51 (September 1982): 5–16; 52 (November 1982): 21–14.

————. "Rosmarine: Melville's 'Pebbles' and Ben Jonson's *Masque of Blackness.*" *Melville Society Extracts* 41 (February 1980): 13–14.

Gilman, William H. *Melville's Early Life and "Redburn."* New York: New York University Press, 1951.

Greenwood, Grace [Sarah Jane Clarke]. *Haps and Mishaps of a Tour in Europe.* Boston: Ticknor, Reed, & Fields, 1853.

Greg, W. W. "The Rationale of Copy-Text." *Studies in Bibliography* 3 (1950–51): 19–36. Reprinted in his *Collected Papers,* ed. J. C. Maxwell, pp. 374–91. Oxford: Clarendon Press, 1966.

Grey, Robin, and Douglas Robillard with Hershel Parker. "Melville's Milton: A Transcription of Melville's Marginalia in His Copy of *The Poetical Works of John Milton.*" *Leviathan* 4 (March and October 2002): 117–204.

Haberstroh, Charles, ed. *John Marr.* Folcroft, Pa.: Folcroft Library Editions; Norwood, Pa.: Norwood Editions, 1975.

Hayford, Harrison. "Melville's 'Monody': Really for Hawthorne?" Pamphlet, Evanston: Northwestern University Press, 1990. Reprinted in *Melville's Prisoners,* pp. 109–31. Evanston: Northwestern University Press, 2003.

————. "The Significance of Melville's 'Agatha' Letters." *ELH, A Journal of English Literary History* 13 (December 1946): 299–310.

————. *The Somers Mutiny Affair*. Englewood Cliffs, N.J.: Prentice-Hall, 1959.

Hayford, Harrison, and Walter Blair, eds. *Omoo*. New York: Hendricks House, 1969.

Hayford, Harrison, and Merton M. Sealts Jr., eds. *Billy Budd, Sailor (An Inside Narrative)*. Chicago: University of Chicago Press, 1962.

Hazlitt, William. *Lectures on the English Comic Writers* and *Lectures on the English Poets*. 2 vols. in one. New York: Derby & Jackson, 1859.

Heffernan, Thomas F. "Melville and Wordsworth." *American Literature* 49 (1977): 338–51.

Heflin, Wilson. "New Light on Herman Melville's Cruise in the *Charles and Henry*." *Historic Nantucket* 22 (October 1974): 6–27.

Hemans, Felicia. *The Poetical Works*. Boston: Phillips, 1859.

Higgins, Brian, and Hershel Parker. *Herman Melville: The Contemporary Reviews*. Cambridge: Cambridge University Press, 1995.

Higgins, Brian, and Hershel Parker. *Reading Melville's "Pierre; or, The Ambiguities."* Baton Rouge: Louisiana State University Press, 2006.

Hogan, Robert E. "Melville's Examination of Heroism in 'At the Cannon's Mouth.'" *Ball State University Forum* 23 (Summer 1982): 69–72.

Hollander, John, ed. *American Poetry: The Nineteenth Century*. Vol. 2. New York: The Library of America, 1993.

Hood, Thomas. *The Poetical Works of Thomas Hood*. Boston: Little, Brown, 1860.

Hopkins, Frank. *The De Vinne and Marion Presses*. Meriden, Conn.: The Columbiad Club, 1936.

Howard, Leon. *Herman Melville: A Biography*. Berkeley: University of California Press, 1951.

————. "Historical Note." In *Pierre; or, The Ambiguities*, ed. Harrison Hayford, Hershel Parker, and G. Thomas Tanselle, pp. 365–79. Evanston and Chicago: Northwestern University Press and The Newberry Library, 1971.

Irving, Washington. *The Sketch-Book of Geoffrey Crayon, Gent*. Ed. Haskell Springer. Boston: Twayne, 1978.

Jaffe, David. "'Sympathy with the Artist': Elizabeth Melville and Elihu Vedder." *Melville Society Extracts* 81 (May 1990): 10–11.

Jarrard, Norman, ed. "Poems by Herman Melville: A Critical Edition of the Published Verse." Ph.D. diss., University of Texas, 1960.

Jones, John Bush. "Galley Proofs in America: A Historical Survey." *Proof* 4 (1975): 153–64.

Kames, Henry Home, Lord. *Elements of Criticism*. New York: Collins & Hannay, Collins & Co., and G. & C. Carvill, 1829.

Kelley, Philip, and Ronald Hudson, eds. *The Brownings' Correspondence*. Vol. 5. Winfield, Kansas: Wedgestone Press, 1987.

Kinter, Elvan, ed. *Letters of Robert Browning and Elizabeth Barrett Browning*. Cambridge: Harvard University Press, 1969.

Levine, Robert S. "Introduction." *The Cambridge Companion to Herman Melville,* ed. Levine, pp. 1–11. Cambridge: Cambridge University Press, 1998.

Levy, Leo B. "Hawthorne, Melville, and the *Monitor.*" *American Literature* 37 (1965): 33–40.

Leyda, Jay. *The Melville Log: A Documentary Life of Herman Melville, 1819–1891.* 2 vols. New York: Harcourt, Brace, 1951. Reprinted with a Supplement, New York: Gordian Press, 1969.

Life in a Man-of-War or Scenes in "Old Ironsides" During her Cruise in the Pacific. By a Fore-Top-Man. Philadelphia: Lydia R. Bailey, Printer, 1841.

Ljungquist, Kent. "'Meteor of the War': Melville, Thoreau, and Whitman Respond to John Brown." *American Literature* 61 (1989): 674–80.

Madison, R. D. "Melville's Sherman Poems: A Problem in Source Study." *Melville Society Extracts* 78 (September 1989): 8–11.

Mangan, James Clarence. *Poems of James Clarence Mangan.* New York: Haverty, 1859.

Mathieu, Bertrand. "'Plain Mechanic Power': Melville's Earliest Poems, *Battle-Pieces and Aspects of the War.*" In "Symposium: Melville the Poet," ed. Douglas Robillard, special issue, *Essays in Arts and Sciences* 5, no. 2 (July 1976): 116–21.

McAuley, David. "A Source for Melville's 'The March into Virginia.'" *Melville Society Extracts* 55 (September 1983): 12–13.

McWilliams, John P. *The American Epic: Transforming a Genre, 1770–1860.* New York: Cambridge University Press, 1989.

Mead, Joan Tyler. "Tradition and Functions of the Songs in 'Midnight, Forecastle.'" *Melville Society Extracts* 83 (November 1990): 3.

Melville, Herman. *Battle-Pieces.* Facsimile with commentary by Sidney Kaplan. Gainesville, Fla.: Scholars' Facsimiles and Reprints, 1960.

———. *Clarel.* Ed. Harrison Hayford, Alma A. MacDougall, Hershel Parker, and G. Thomas Tanselle. The Writings of Herman Melville 12. Evanston and Chicago: Northwestern University Press and The Newberry Library, 1991.

———. *The Confidence-Man: His Masquerade.* Ed. Harrison Hayford, Hershel Parker, and G. Thomas Tanselle. The Writings of Herman Melville 10. Evanston and Chicago: Northwestern University Press and The Newberry Library, 1984.

———. *Correspondence.* Ed. Lynn Horth. The Writings of Herman Melville 14. Evanston and Chicago: Northwestern University Press and The Newberry Library, 1993.

———. *Journals.* Ed. Howard C. Horsford with Lynn Horth. The Writings of Herman Melville 15. Evanston and Chicago: Northwestern University Press and The Newberry Library, 1989.

———. *Mardi and A Voyage Thither.* Ed. Harrison Hayford, Hershel Parker, and G. Thomas Tanselle. The Writings of Herman Melville 3. Evanston and Chicago: Northwestern University Press and The Newberry Library, 1970.

————. "Memoir of Thomas Melvill, Jr." In *The History of Pittsfield (Berkshire County,) Massachusetts, from the Year 1800 to the Year 1876,* by J. E. A. Smith, pp. 399–400. Springfield, Mass.: Bryan, 1876.

————. *Moby-Dick, or, The Whale.* Ed. Harrison Hayford, Hershel Parker, and G. Thomas Tanselle. The Writings of Herman Melville 6. Evanston and Chicago: Northwestern University Press and The Newberry Library, 1988.

————. *Omoo: A Narrative of Adventures in the South Seas.* Ed. Harrison Hayford, Hershel Parker, and G. Thomas Tanselle. The Writings of Herman Melville 2. Evanston and Chicago: Northwestern University Press and The Newberry Library, 1968.

————. *The Piazza Tales and Other Prose Pieces, 1839–1860.* Ed. Harrison Hayford, Alma A. MacDougall, G. Thomas Tanselle, et al. The Writings of Herman Melville 9. Evanston and Chicago: Northwestern University Press and The Newberry Library, 1987.

————. *Pierre; or, The Ambiguities.* Ed. Harrison Hayford, Hershel Parker, and G. Thomas Tanselle. The Writings of Herman Melville 7. Evanston and Chicago: Northwestern University Press and The Newberry Library, 1971.

————. *Pierre; or, The Ambiguities: The Kraken Edition.* Ed. Hershel Parker, pictures by Maurice Sendak. New York: HarperCollins, 1995.

————. *Poems.* [Ed. Raymond Weaver.] London: Constable, 1924. Reprint, New York: Russell & Russell, 1963; Tokyo: Meicho Fukyu Kai, 1983.

————. *Redburn: His First Voyage.* Ed. Harrison Hayford, Hershel Parker, and G. Thomas Tanselle. The Writings of Herman Melville 4. Evanston and Chicago: Northwestern University Press and The Newberry Library, 1969.

————. *"Weeds and Wildings Chiefly: With a Rose or Two:* Reading Text and Genetic Text." Ed. Robert C. Ryan. Ph.D. diss., Northwestern University, 1967.

————. *White-Jacket; or, The World in a Man-of-War.* Ed. Harrison Hayford, Hershel Parker, and G. Thomas Tanselle. The Writings of Herman Melville 5. Evanston and Chicago: Northwestern University Press and The Newberry Library, 1970.

Metcalf, Eleanor Melville. *Herman Melville: Cycle and Epicycle.* Cambridge, Mass.: Harvard University Press, 1953.

Milder, Robert. "Herman Melville 1819–1891: A Brief Biography." In *A Historical Guide to Herman Melville,* ed. Giles Gunn, pp. 17–58. New York: Oxford University Press, 2005.

————. "Melville's 'Intentions' in *Pierre.*" *Studies in the Novel* 6 (Summer 1974): 186–99.

Milton, John. *The Poetical Works of John Milton.* 2 vols. Boston: Hilliard, Gray, 1836.

Minnigerode, Meade. *Some Personal Letters of Herman Melville and a Bibliography.* New York: The Brick Row Bookshop, 1922.

The Modern British Essayists. 8 vols. Philadelphia: Carey & Hart, 1847–48.

Molloy, Mary. "The Old Sailor's Lament: Recontextualizing Melville's Reflections on the Sinking of 'The Stone Fleet.'" *New England Quarterly* 64 (1991): 633–42.

Moore, Thomas. *Life of Lord Byron*. Boston: Little, Brown, 1853[?].

————. *The Poetical Works of Thomas Moore*. Boston: Little, Brown, 1856 [1854?].

Moss, Sidney. *Poe's Literary Battles: The Critic in the Context of His Literary Milieu*. Durham, N.C.: Duke University Press, 1963.

Mumford, Lewis. *Herman Melville*. New York: Harcourt, Brace, 1929.

Murray, Henry A. "Introduction" and "Explanatory Notes." In *Pierre; or, The Ambiguities,* ed. Murray, pp. xiii–ciii, 429–504. New York: Hendricks House, 1949.

Norsworthy, Scott. "Melville's Notes on Thomas Roscoe's *The German Novelists*." *Leviathan* 10.3 (October 2008): 7–37. Special Issue: Melville's Sources II.

Olsen-Smith, Steven, and Dennis C. Marnon. "Melville's Marginalia in *The Works of Sir William D'Avenant:* A Transcription." *Leviathan* 6 (March 2004): 79–102.

Olsen-Smith, Steven, and Merton M. Sealts Jr. "A Cumulative Supplement to *Melville's Reading*." *Leviathan* 6 (March 2004): 55–77.

Olson, Charles. "*Lear* and *Moby-Dick*." *Twice a Year* 1 (Fall–Winter 1938): 165–89.

Parker, Hershel. *Herman Melville: A Biography, 1819–1851* and *Herman Melville: A Biography, 1851–1891*. 2 vols. Baltimore: Johns Hopkins University Press, 1996, 2002.

————. "Herman Melville's *The Isle of the Cross*." *American Literature* 62 (March 1990): 1–16.

————. "Historical Note." In *Pierre; or, The Ambiguities,* ed. Harrison Hayford, Hershel Parker, and G. Thomas Tanselle, pp. 379–401. Evanston and Chicago: Northwestern University Press and The Newberry Library, 1971.

————. "*The Isle of the Cross* and *Poems:* Lost Melville Books and the Indefinite Afterlife of Error." *Nineteenth-Century Literature* 62 (June 2007): 29–47.

————. "Melville and Politics." Ph.D. diss., Northwestern University, 1963.

Parker, Hershel, ed. *Gansevoort Melville's London Journal, and Letters from England, 1845*. New York: New York Public Library, 1966.

Plutarch. *Plutarch's Lives*. Trans. John and William Langhorne. New York: Harper & Brothers, 1875.

Pommer, Henry. *Milton and Melville*. Pittsburgh: University of Pittsburgh Press, 1950.

Poole, Gordon. "Naples in the Time of Melville: Italian Politics 1857." *Melville Society Extracts* 105 (June 1996): 8–9.

Poole, Gordon, ed. *"At the Hostelry" and "Naples in the Time of Bomba."* Naples: Istituto Universitario Orientale, 1989.

Powell, Thomas. *The Living Authors of America*. New York: Stringer & Townsend, 1850.

—————. *The Living Authors of England*. New York: D. Appleton & Co., 1849.

Puett, Amy. "Melville's Wife: A Study of Elizabeth Shaw Melville." Ph.D. diss., Northwestern University, 1969.

The Rebellion Record: A Diary of American Events. Ed. Frank Monroe. 11 vols. New York: Putnam & Van Nostrand, 1861–68.

Robillard, Douglas, ed. *John Marr and Other Sailors with Some Sea-Pieces: A Facsimile Edition*. Kent, Ohio: Kent State University Press, 2006.

—————. *Poems of Herman Melville*. New Haven, Conn.: College & University Press, 1976. Rev. ed., Kent, Ohio: Kent State University Press, 2000.

Royster, Paul, ed. *John Marr*. Electronic facsimile, Lincoln: Libraries at University of Nebraska–Lincoln, 2005.

—————. *Timoleon*. Electronic facsimile, Lincoln: Libraries at University of Nebraska–Lincoln, 2005.

Ruskin, John. *Modern Painters. Of Many Things*. New York: Wiley & Halsted, 1856.

Ryan, Robert C. "Melville Revises 'Art.'" In *Melville's Evermoving Dawn: Centennial Essays*, ed. John Bryant and Robert Milder, pp. 307–20. Kent, Ohio: Kent State University Press, 1997.

Ryan, Robert C., ed. "*Weeds and Wildings Chiefly,* with a Rose or Two, by Herman Melville: Reading Text and Genetic Text, Edited from the Manuscripts, with Introduction and Notes." Ph.D. diss., Northwestern University, 1967.

Sanborn, Geoffrey. "Lounging on the Sofa with Leigh Hunt: A New Source for the Notes in Melville's Shakespeare Volume." *Nineteenth-Century Literature* 63 (June 2008): 104–15.

—————. "The Name of the Devil: Melville's Other 'Extracts' for *Moby-Dick*." *Nineteenth-Century Literature* 47 (September 1992): 212–35.

Sandberg, Robert A. "'The Adjustment of Screens': Putative Narrators, Authors, and Editors in Melville's Unfinished *Burgundy Club* Book." *Texas Studies in Literature and Language* 31 (Fall 1989): 426–50.

—————. "Melville's Unfinished *Burgundy Club* Book." Ph.D. diss., Northwestern University, 1989.

Schultz, Elizabeth. "Melville's Agony: After the Whale." Review of *Herman Melville: A Biography,* by Hershel Parker. *Common Review* 2 (Winter 2002): 40–46.

Sealts, Merton M., Jr. *The Early Lives of Melville*. Madison: University of Wisconsin Press, 1974.

—————. "Historical Note." In *The Piazza Tales and Other Prose Pieces, 1839–1860,* ed. Harrison Hayford, Hershel Parker, and G. Thomas Tanselle, pp. 457–533. Evanston and Chicago: Northwestern University Press and The Newberry Library, 1987.

————. "Melville and Richard Henry Stoddard." *American Literature* 43, no. 3 (November 1971): 359–70.

————. *Melville's Reading: Revised and Enlarged Edition*. Columbia: University of South Carolina Press, 1988.

————. "A Supplementary Note to *Melville's Reading* (1988)." *Melville Society Extracts* 80 (February 1990): 5–10.

————. "Thomas Melvill, Jr., in *The History of Pittsfield*." *Harvard Library Bulletin* 35 (Spring 1987): 201–17.

Shetley, Vernon. "Melville's 'Timoleon.'" *Emerson Society Quarterly* 33 (1987): 83–93.

Shurr, William H. *The Mystery of Iniquity: Melville as Poet, 1857–1891*. Lexington: The University Press of Kentucky, 1972.

Smith, J. E. A. *The History of Pittsfield, (Berkshire County,) Massachusetts, From the Year 1800 to the Year 1876*. Springfield, Mass.: C. W. Bryan & Co., 1876.

Spenser, Edmund. *The Poetical Works*. 8 vols. in 4. London: J. Bell, 1787–88.

Staël, Anne Louise Germaine (Necker), Baronne de. *Germany*. New York: Derby & Jackson, 1859.

Stedman, Arthur. "Marquesan Melville" (1891). In *The Early Lives of Melville*, by Merton M. Sealts Jr., pp. 101–10. Madison: University of Wisconsin Press, 1974.

Stein, William Bysshe. *The Poetry of Melville's Late Years*. Albany: State University of New York Press, 1970.

Stoddard, Richard Henry, et al. *Poets' Homes: Pen and Pencil Sketches of American Poets and Their Homes*. Boston: D. Lothrop & Co., 1877.

Tanselle, G. Thomas. *Introduction to Scholarly Editing*. 2d ed. Charlottesville: Book Arts Press, University of Virginia, 2002. Also at www.rarebookschool.org.

————. "The Sales of Melville's Books." *Harvard Library Bulletin* 17 (1969): 195–215.

————. *Textual Criticism Since Greg: A Chronicle, 1950–2000*. Charlottesville: Bibliographical Society of the University of Virginia, 2005.

Taylor, Henry. *Notes from Life in Seven Essays*. Boston: Ticknor, Reed, & Fields, 1853.

Tennant, William. *Anster Fair*. Edinburgh: Cockburn, 1812.

Tennyson, Alfred Lord. *The Princess*. New ed. Boston: Ticknor & Fields, 1855.

Thorp, Willard, ed. *Herman Melville: Representative Selections*. New York: American Book Co., 1938.

Tichenor, Irene. *No Art Without Craft: The Life of Theodore Low De Vinne*. Jaffrey, N.H.: David R. Godine, 2005.

Tilton, Eleanor M. "Melville's 'Rammon': A Text and Commentary." *Harvard Library Bulletin* 13 (Winter 1959): 50–91.

Tuckerman, Henry T. "Giuseppe Garibaldi." Review of William Arthur, *Italy in Transition*. *North American Review* 92 (January 1861): 15–56.

————. *The Rebellion: Its Latent Causes and True Significance. In Letters to a Friend Abroad*. New York: James G. Gregory, 1861.

————. *Thoughts on the Poets.* New York: C. S. Francis & Co., 1846.

Vasari, Giorgio. *Lives of the Most Eminent Painters, Sculptors, and Architects.* 5 vols. London: Bohn, 1849–52.

Vedder, Elihu. *The Digressions of V.* Boston and New York: Houghton Mifflin, 1910.

Vincent, Howard P. *The Tailoring of Melville's "White-Jacket."* Evanston: Northwestern University Press, 1970.

Vincent, Howard P., ed. *Collected Poems of Herman Melville.* Chicago: Packard & Co., Hendricks House, 1947.

Vogel, Dan. "Note: 'The Coming Storm.'" *Melville Society Newsletter* 11 (Summer 1955): [1–2].

Wallace, Robert K. *Melville and Turner: Spheres of Love and Fright.* Athens: The University of Georgia Press, 1992.

————. "Melville's Prints and Engravings at the Berkshire Athenaeum." *Essays in Arts and Sciences* 15 (June 1986): 59–90.

Warren, Robert Penn, ed. *Selected Poems of Herman Melville.* New York: Random House, 1970. Reprint, Jaffrey, N.H.: David R. Godine, 2004.

Weaver, Raymond. *Herman Melville: Mariner and Mystic.* New York: Doran, 1921.

Weed, Thurlow. *Autobiography of Thurlow Weed.* Ed. Harriet A. Weed. 2 vols. Boston: Houghton, Mifflin, 1883.

Wert, Jeffry D. *Mosby's Rangers.* New York: Simon & Schuster, 1990.

White, Henry Kirke. *The Poetical Works and Remains.* New York: Appleton, 1857.

Wordsworth, William. *The Complete Poetical Works of William Wordsworth.* Ed. Henry Reed. Philadelphia: James Kay, Jun. & Brother, 1839.

Index of Titles and First Lines

935